WHERE *to* AND *SnoWboard*

Published in Great Britain by
NortonWood Publishing

tel 0844 9911 123
email w19@wheretoski.co.uk

Editors Chris Gill and Dave Watts
Assistant editors Mandy Crook,
Sheila Reid, Lucy Dodsworth,
David Dalton, Alison Shakspeare,
Rebecca Miles

Contributors Minty Clinch,
Alan Coulson, Nicky Holford,
James Hooke, Eric Jackson,
Tim Perry, Ian Porter, Adam Ruck,
Helena Wiesner, Fraser Wilkin

Advertising manager
Dave Ashmore

Direct advertising enquiries to
publisher@wheretoski.co.uk

Design by Val Fox
Production by Guide Editors
Contents photos generally
by Snowpix.com / Chris Gill
Production manager
Sarah Carreck
Proofreader Sally Vince
Printed and bound in Italy
by Lego SpA

Cover photo: Val Thorens, France
© P.Lebeau – OT Val Thorens

This edition published 2014
Copyright (text and illustrations)
© Chris Gill and Dave Watts 2014

The right of Chris Gill and Dave
Watts to be identified as Authors of
this Work has been asserted by
them in accordance with the
Copyright, Design and Patents Act
1988.

All rights reserved. No part of this
publication may be reproduced,
stored in a retrieval system or
transmitted, in any form or by any
means, electronic, mechanical,
recording or otherwise, in any part
of the world, without the prior
permission of the publishers. All
requests for permission should be
made to the editors at this address:
publisher@wheretoski.co.uk.

Although every care has been taken
in compiling this publication, using
the most up-to-date information
available at the time of going to
press, all details are liable to change
and cannot be guaranteed. Neither
NortonWood Publishing nor the
editors accept any liability
whatsoever arising from errors or
omissions, however caused.

10 9 8 7 6 5 4 3 2 1

ISBN-13: 978-0-9558663-6-4

A CIP catalogue entry for this book
is available from the British Library.

Book trade sales are handled by
Faber Factory Plus
Bloomsbury House
74–77 Great Russell Street
London WC1B 3DA

tel 020 7927 3800
bridgetlj@faber.co.uk

**Individual copies of the book can be
bought (for delivery anywhere in the
world) at a discount price by going to
our website:
www.wheretoskiandsnowboard.com**

WHERE *to* SKI
AND *Snowboard* 2015

The Definitive Guide
to the 1,000 Best Winter Sports Resorts in the World

Edited by
Chris Gill
and
Dave Watts

NortonWood

THE MOUNTAIN IS EVERYTHING

Make it your own

La Plagne | Pas de la Casa | Söll | Sestriere | Tignes | St Anton and loads more

Visit crystalski.co.uk or call 020 8939 0859

ATOL protected. For info
please see our booking conditions.

CRYSTAL
SKI HOLIDAYS

Contents

About this book
Why, 20 years on, it has no competition
10

The editorial
The editors have their say on matters of moment
13

What's new?
New lifts and other major resort developments
23

20 years on
We look back on the changes since our first edition in 1994
28

Piste extent update
How resorts are modifying their piste km claims
32

Cutting your costs
Results of this year's updated Resort Price Index survey
35

New gear for 2015
Cool kit for next season – skis, boots, gadgets
40

Short breaks
A quick fix of the white stuff?
43

Luxury chalets
Is there a better kind of ski holiday?
45

Smart apartments
Independence with comfort
49

Family holidays
Editor Gill offers his advice
52

Buying property
Make the process painless
57

Corporate trips
Motivate your staff and clients
61

Flying to the snow
More and ever more choice of route
63

Travelling by rail
Make tracks to the mountains
65

Drive to the Alps
And ski where you please
67

Drive to the French Alps
And make the most of them
71

CHGL TOURIST OFFICE

ROSSIGNOL

INVESTORS IN PROPERTY

EASYJET

That's the start of it – turn the page for the heart of it ...

You'll appreciate the lengths we go to to find you a dream ski holiday

Ski*line*.co.uk

The skiers' travel agent

We search the whole ski market so you don't have to

Call 020 8313 3999

ATOL 7018 PROTECTED

ABTA
ABTA No. L6436

Contents 2

Choosing your resort
Get it right first time
74

Resort ratings at a glance
All the big resorts evaluated
77

Resort shortlists
To help you spot resorts that
will suit you and your party
83

Our resort chapters
How to get the best out of them
86

RESORTS IN DETAIL
The heart of the book:
570 pages of information,
analysis and evaluation;
chapter list over the page
88

Ski businesses
Tour operators, ski travel agents
and others
659

Resort directory / index
Page references for 400 resorts,
at-a-glance summaries of around
1,000 others
665

Resort chapters

ANDORRA 88

Excellent British-oriented ski schools, but charmless villages – and no longer the bargain it once was

Arinsal	90
Soldeu	92

FRANCE 194

Unrivalled for big, high, snow-sure ski areas with convenient lodgings – but be prepared for high food and drink prices in the best-known ones

Alpe-d'Huez	198	Megève	267	Serre-Chevalier	325
Les Arcs	208	Les Menuires	274	Ste-Foy-Tarentaise	334
Avoriaz	218	Méribel	280	St-Martin-de-B'ville	337
Les Carroz	223	Montgenèvre	289	La Tania	340
Chamonix	225	Morzine	294	Three Valleys	344
Châtel	235	Paradiski	301	Tignes	346
Courchevel	240	La Plagne	303	Val Cenis Vanoise	355
Les Deux-Alpes	250	Portes du Soleil	314	Val d'Isère	358
Flaine	256	Pyrenees	315	Val Thorens	368
Les Gets	263	La Rosière	319	Vars / Risoul	375
La Grave	265	Samoëns	323		

AUSTRIA 98

Charming villages, lively après-ski, friendly locals and modest prices; but many resorts are at low altitudes – a problem in mild weather

Bad Gastein	104	Obertauern	154
Bad Kleinkirchheim	107	Saalbach-H'glemm	157
Ellmau	110	Schladming	163
Hintertux	113	Sölden	167
Ischgl	118	Söll	172
Kitzbühel	125	St Anton	179
Lech	133	Stubai valley	188
Mayrhofen	142	Zell Am See	190
Obergurgl	148		

ITALY 382

Jolly villages, up-to-the-minute lift systems and snowmaking, and modest prices – but few extensive ski areas to rival those of France

Cervinia	387	Passo Tonale	418
Cortina d'Ampezzo	393	Sauze d'Oulx	420
Courmayeur	398	Sella Ronda	425
Livigno	403	Selva	433
Madonna di C'glio	407	Sestriere	440
Monterosa Ski	412	La Thuile	442

GERMANY 378

Has a great deal in common with Austria, over the border. There is one first-division resort, and dozens of minor ones

Garmisch-Partenkirchen 380

SWITZERLAND 444

Some uniquely cute villages and spectacular scenery; at current exchange rates (CHF1.45 to £1), prices are still difficult to bear

Adelboden	451	Mürren	479
Andermatt	454	Saas-Fee	483
Champéry	456	St Moritz	488
Crans-Montana	459	Val d'Anniviers	495
Davos	461	Verbier	499
Engelberg	468	Villars	510
Grindelwald	470	Wengen	513
Klosters	474	Zermatt	518
Laax	476		

USA 528

Great service, mostly crowd-free slopes, frequent snowfalls and safe ungroomed runs; some costs are very high but food and drink are bearable at $1.64 to £1

California	**532**	**Utah**	**573**
Heavenly	533	Alta	574
Mammoth	538	Canyons	576
Squaw Valley	543	Deer Valley	578
Colorado	**545**	Park City	580
Aspen	546	Snowbird	585
Beaver Creek	553	**Rest of the West**	**587**
Breckenridge	555	Big Sky	588
Snowmass	560	Jackson Hole	593
Vail	562	**New England**	**598**
Winter Park	569		

CANADA 600

A lot in common with the USA, but with some very distinctive resorts and grand scenery – and less of a culture gap than you find in the USA

Western Canada	**602**
Banff	603
Big White	609
Fernie	611
Kicking Horse	617
Lake Louise	619
Revelstoke	624
Silver Star	627
Sun Peaks	629
Whistler	631
Eastern Canada	**640**

THE REST

SOUTHERN EUROPE		EASTERN EUROPE		UNITED KINGDOM	
Spain	**641**	**Bulgaria**	**648**	**Scotland**	**655**
SCANDINAVIA		**Romania**	**651**	FAR EAST	
Finland	**643**	**Slovenia**	**652**	**Japan**	**656**
Norway	**645**				
Sweden	**647**				

9

Dave Watts

Chris Gill

Twenty years ago, in 1994, we started this page with this:

Why Where to Ski?

This is a new guide to ski resorts. It sets out to help you pick the ideal resort – or at least the best resort – for your next holiday, whether you are a beginner or an expert skier. It is not the only such book on the market, but we are confident that it is the best.

Well, now *it is* the only such book on the market. The books that we set out to compete with in 1994 have folded their tents. Other titles have appeared, but only briefly. We have managed to survive. How have we done it? By producing the book we wanted to read.

• Every edition is the result of a thorough, painstaking process of **checking, updating and reviewing** the book's contents. We visit countless resorts every season, but even those we can't get to are reconsidered with the same care. In any one year, some chapters change hugely as a result, others hardly at all.

• The book also benefits enormously from the **hundreds of reports** that readers send us on the resorts they visit. Every year, we give a free copy of the book to the 100 readers who send in the best reports – and one of them wins a free week in a smart French resort apartment, courtesy of Lagrange Holidays. Read page 12.

• By making the most of technology we are able to publish at the right time while going to press late in the summer – so we can make the book **up to date for the season ahead**. Our earliest editions went to press in June; this year, it's 28 July.

• We work hard to make our information **reader-friendly**, with clearly structured text, comparative ratings and no-nonsense verdicts for the main aspects of each resort.

• We don't hesitate to express **critical views** – we learned our craft at Consumers' Association, where Chris became editor of *Holiday Which?* and Dave became editor of *Which?* itself.

• Our resort chapters give an **unrivalled level of detail** – including scale plans of each major resort, so that you get a clear idea of size – and all the facts you need.

• We use **colour printing** fully – we include not only piste maps for every major resort but also scores of photographs, carefully chosen so that you can see for yourself what the resorts are like.

Our ability to keep on investing in *Where to Ski and Snowboard* is largely due to the support of our advertisers, some of which have been with us since that first edition in 1994 – read our retrospective chapter on page 28. We are grateful for that support.

We are absolutely committed to helping you, our readers, to make an informed choice; and we're confident that you'll find this edition the best yet. Enjoy your skiing and riding this season.

Chris Gill and Dave Watts – Long Melford, 28 July 2014

A FREE LUNCH DOES EXIST!

Alpine Answers, the UK's leading specialist ski travel agency, are giving our readers an exclusive offer

Simply book your next ski holiday through Alpine Answers and get a 5% discount. That should be enough to finance a FREE blow-out mountain lunch?

ALPINE ANSWERS use over twenty years of ski holiday planning to offer the ultimate chalet & hotel collection across the world's best ski resorts.

To find out more and register for the discount simply go to our online form at: www.bit.ly/wtss-aa

Call: **020 7801 1080**
www.alpineanswers.co.uk

 ATOL NO. 4791

 ABTA NO. D4050

Send us reports on the resorts you visit!

Write a helpful resort report: the odds are you'll win a free book – plus the chance to win a week in France with Lagrange

There are too many resorts for us to visit them all every year, and too many hotels, bars and mountain restaurants for us to check them all out. So we are always keen to encourage readers to send in reports on their holiday experiences. Every year, we give 100 copies of the new edition to the writers of the best reports – and put their names into the hat to win a week in a smart Lagrange apartment.

LAGRANGE

Two of Lagrange's top properties – Les Fermes Emiguy in Les Gets and Les Chalets de l'Adet in St-Lary ↓

Your resort reports must be based on visits made during the 2014/15 season, and must be received by the end of April 2015. We much prefer to receive reports in digital form. Ideally, use our online form reached via www.wheretoskiandsnowboard.com; or you can send an email to reports@wheretoski.co.uk – but please give your report a clear structure, using the same headings that we use in our resort chapters. And it's vital that you give us the date of your trip, plus your postal address, to send your book to if you win one.

The first name out of our digital hat wins a free week in a Lagrange residence. The details of your options will be made clear on our website. With the exception of Christmas/New Year and the period around February half term, you'll be able to choose your travel dates (subject to availability).

SKI HOSTING: ROUND TWO

If you're on our email list (join at the website trailed on most pages) you'll know there is a battle being fought over the legality of guiding or 'hosting' of clients around ski resort slopes by tour operator employees. Back in February 2013 the British chalet operator Le Ski was found guilty of illegal guiding by a local court in Albertville; with the support of 11 other tour operators, Le Ski appealed to a higher court in Chambéry, and the appeal result is due about the time this edition is published in September 2014.

The French prosecution position is that their law requires anyone who is paid to guide others around the slopes to be a fully qualified instructor. The tour operators' position is that the French law has no legitimate basis and conflicts with European law, and that instructor qualifications are irrelevant to the service of ski hosting. The Méribel ESF is also seeking compensation for loss of earnings, although Le Ski is based in Courchevel – bizarre.

We're 100% behind Le Ski, and we'll continue to follow the case closely through our website.

MORE ON PISTES

A year ago we drew attention to the observations we had been making over many years about overstated claims of piste km, and to the excellent recent work in this area of German consultant and writer Christoph Schrahe. We have an update on page 32.

An amusing recent discovery is that the size of ski resorts can depend on how rich you are. We reckon Big Sky in Montana now has about 230km of trails, making it 10th largest in the world. But you can ski in to Big Sky from the Yellowstone Club, an exclusive private resort with another 85km or so. If you can afford to join, you therefore can ski an area of 315km – 3rd largest in the world.

MATTERHORN CHALETS

Chalet Ulysse in Zermatt is one Swiss property where you'll be able to enjoy a catered chalet holiday this coming season ↓

A SWISS CHALET HOLIDAY? YOU'LL NEED A HEFTY BUDGET

Switzerland is an expensive destination these days; with the pound at about 1.45 Swiss francs, everything is 65% more expensive in £££ than it was seven years ago. One of the best ways to have a holiday there without taking out a second mortgage has been to take a catered chalet holiday, where you are to a degree insulated from local costs. Not any more: the Swiss government has ruled that the country's minimum wage must be paid to staff employed by UK companies, just as if they were employed by a Swiss company.

The details are rather complex, but the basic Swiss minimum wage for the youngest unskilled employees is based on CHF 3,407 per month, which with 10.65% holiday pay plus the existence of a '13th month' in Switzerland for salary purposes works out at an effective cost of CHF 4,084 per month; this currently equates to a UK salary of £33,800.

This hike in costs would have a huge impact on operators in the more price-sensitive part of the market. Inghams and sister companies Ski Total and Esprit Ski have pulled out of all their chalets and chalet hotels with the exception of Inghams' chalet hotel in Verbier. It's a great shame. Andy Perrin, CEO of parent company Hotelplan, told us: 'There are no winners here. We tour operators lose, our guests who love Switzerland lose, and all the myriad Swiss suppliers in resort who have relied on this business for decades also lose.'

Operators at the top of the market with fatter margins are less seriously affected, but not immune. Scott Dunn has dropped its two chalets in Zermatt, for example. Chairman Andrew Dunn said: 'With the minimum wage and other legislation, to make our programme financially viable we needed to grow our portfolio dramatically; we decided instead to focus on other areas for now.'

But ski industry veteran Ed Mannix sees all this as an opportunity. He has launched Matterhorn Chalets, an upmarket chalet operation in Zermatt, offering the swanky 12-bed chalet Ulysse with built-in local mountain guide (or instructor). 'At our position in the market,' says Mannix, 'quality of service is the priority. Pay your staff a professional wage and they'll do a professional job.'

A SEASON OF CONTRASTS

Yet again we find ourselves editing these pages in sweltering heat – although not a prolonged heatwave of the kind we endured last summer. You might think last season in the Alps didn't match up to 2013, either; but in fact it depends on where you went. We came close to being marooned in the Dolomites in January. Below, Fraser Wilkin presents a more scientific analysis.

The Alps' 2013–14 ski season was notable for three main reasons:
- *exceptional snowfall in Italy and the southern Alps*
- *a lack of snow in the north-eastern Alps (ie Austria)*
- *high temperatures, particularly in the northern Alps.*

It was the Christmas period that really defined Italy's remarkable winter, with huge snowfalls across the board (over 2m in just 48 hours in Madesimo). This set the tone for January and February, when storm after Mediterranean storm continued to slam into the southern side of the Alps, leading to considerable disruption in Lombardy and the Dolomites.

Late-season conditions were more benign, but all Italian resorts finished with above-average snowfall, and some central and eastern regions declared it their snowiest winter for over 60 years. Cervinia clocked 8.3m at resort level, Madesimo over 9m and Passo Tonale a whopping 11.6m, making it the snowiest resort in the Alps; it averages 5m.

SNOWPIX.COM / CHRIS GILL

Corvara in the very snowy Italian Dolomites, January 2014, and a run that Harry Potter would find comfortable. Yes, you guessed: it links run 5 to run 4 ↓

Discover Tux-Finkenberg

245 km of ski runs and 365 days of the year snowfun on the Hintertux Glacier.

Rooms, Brochures, Information:
Tourist Board Tux-Finkenberg · A-6293 Tux · Lanersbach 401
Tel. +43/5287/8506 · e-mail: info@tux.at · **www.tux.at**

Zillertal.at

Except in the extreme south of the country – which basically is on the south side of the Alps – Austria had a decidedly sub-standard season. Yes, there was still some reasonable piste skiing on offer (particularly at altitude), but the lack of snow restricted any serious off-piste, and the lower valleys were often green, even in the depths of winter. The likes of Kitzbühel and Söll managed only 1.5m at resort level (average 2.5m). Even famously snowy Warth (newly connected to Lech), with the Alps' highest average snowfall of 10.6m, saw just 5.8m – its second-lowest total on record.

In France, again, the southern Alps did best – mostly above par, with a massive 10m for Isola 2000 near Nice, its second-snowiest winter on record. But the northern French Alps had a reasonable season, with the heaviest snowfalls in Haute Savoie – Avoriaz clocked an average 7.8m. Tarentaise resorts were a little below average though, with 4.4m for Val d'Isère and 5.4m for La Rosière.

In Switzerland, too, the bulk of the snow fell in the far south, close to the Italian border, with regular dumps in St Moritz, Saas-Fee and Zermatt – the last clocking 4.4m at resort level, well above par for this relatively dry corner of the Alps. Up on the glacier (on the Italian border, in other words) the figure was close to 13m. Further north, snowfall was more erratic, and warm Föhn winds kept low-lying valleys devoid of snow for much of the winter.

Across the pond, Colorado was back on form after two very forgettable seasons (Loveland led the region with 10.6m of snow, some 20% above average), but California was disastrous, with Mammoth (4.6m) seeing half of what it would normally expect. In western Canada, the usual comparisons were reversed: coastal Whistler picked up after a disappointing start, but was no match for Lake Louise in the Rockies: its 6.8m was 60% above normal.

ARLBERG BUS BLUES

We had a great week in the Arlberg at the end of last season, indulging ourselves in the fabulous food in Inghams' flagship chalet hotel in St Christoph and skiing St Anton, Lech, Zürs and Warth. Luckily we hit a late, brief recovery from the snow drought that Fraser Wilkin writes about above – snow started falling as we drove up the Arlberg pass on the Saturday night – and two days later the sun came out. Perfect. Or nearly so.

The piste map says: 'Enjoy your dream … 340km of downhill pistes … a winter sports region of freedom, of variety and of comfort.' The people who wrote this need to queue for the 0928 bus from St Christoph to Lech one sunny March morning, and see whether they get on, and how comfortable they find it if they do. Having endured this once, the next day we dug the editorial motor out of its snowdrift and drove to Zürs.

There are free and regular ski-buses, and there are post buses. But all get seriously crowded at busy times, leaving people at the roadside to use the waiting taxis. And the post buses are neither free nor frequent. It's not good

SNOWPIX.COM / CHRIS GILL

Austria did get some snow last season, in late March at least. The editorial motor outside Inghams' excellent chalet hotel in St Christoph, where we had intended to leave it for the week; but the poor bus services led us to press the VW into service for several trips to Lech ↓

SPORTHOTEL
St. Christoph

enough. A reader who also visited last season agrees: 'This is supposed to be one ski area. There should be lots of FREE buses, so we can make the most of the fantastic slopes these places offer, NOT spend our time waiting for buses.'

Other resorts manage to lay on bus services that meet the demand – Val d'Isère being a notable example.

AUSTRIA AGAIN: EARLY LIFT CLOSING

We make no apology for nagging the Austrians yet again over the business of early lift closures, a source of regular complaint.

An experienced reporter writes about Zell im Zillertal, a resort with no pistes to the valley: 'Only complaint: most lifts close at 4pm, then the lift down to the valley closes at 4:30. They start announcements nagging you at 4:20. Ridiculous. Absurd. If you get to the top of Übergangsjoch at 4pm, you can only just ski down to Wiesenalm for 4:30 – and you definitely can't stop for a beer on the way. Downlifts need to run until at least 5pm.' Indeed they do.

Tucked away in the small print of this year's SkiWelt piste map is a news item that offers a glimmer of hope that Austrian resorts might be seeing the light: 'Insanely long skiing pleasure: As of 25th January 2014 the closing time [of lifts, we presume] will be extended from 4pm to 4.30pm. From 15 to 30 March 2014 the [lifts] will open at 8am instead of 8.30am.'

'Insanely long' may be quite an appropriate description. We're not convinced of the merits of opening the SkiWelt's lifts in spring at 8am – there's a case for delaying it until 11am, when there's a chance the previous day's slush, frozen overnight, will have softened again; but the extension beyond 4pm is welcome.

SNOWPIX.COM / CHRIS GILL

No trip to the Alta Badia region of the Dolomites is complete without a descent of the famous 'hidden valley' run between Cortina and San Cassiano. At the end, where it's flat, the idea is that you are dragged along behind a horse-drawn sleigh; we feel safer in the sleigh ↓

Build your own shortlist: www.wheretoskiandsnowboard.com

HOTEL **eiger** MÜRREN
★★★★

Perfect hideaway in the Swiss Alps.

Family run Hotel in car free Mürren

www.hoteleiger.com
Tel. +41 33 856 54 54 | info@hoteleiger.com

Ski and Snowboard

Berner Oberland 🇨🇭

ADELBODEN
Frutigen

- One of the top three ski regions in Switzerland
- All kind of slopes for every level
- The world's biggest Fondue-Igloo

AWARD-WINNING

SKI
HOLIDAYS

Ski Olympic

book online at
skiolympic.com
01302 328 820

Not for the first time we point out that lifts elsewhere offer appreciably longer skiing days, of which the most inspiring example is the Diavolezza cable car outside St Moritz; this runs (to an altitude a whisker short of 3000m) until 4.30pm for most of the season, and to 5pm from the end of February.

AVOIDING HELLISH HALF-TERM HOLIDAYS

It's common knowledge that taking kids out of school to go on holiday in term time is now effectively banned. You need the head teacher's permission, and to get that there must be 'exceptional circumstances'. You can be fined 'for taking your child on holiday during term time without the school's permission', which you might say implies that it is possible to get permission, but the message is that 'exceptional circumstances' means matters of life and death, not a late-booking bargain.

It seems obvious to us that in these circumstances Britain needs to adopt the French system of zones, so that the winter half-term holidays are spread over a three- or four-week period.

And while we're on the half-term holidays theme: as usual, our introduction to France (page 194) includes the dates of the French school holidays, including the notorious Paris fortnight.

FAT SKI FRUSTRATION

Devoted reporter Tanya Booth writes to prompt us to raise the issue of the ski slots on the outside of older gondola cabins which, having been designed 40 years ago (or even 20), won't accept modern freeride or all-mountain skis. We agree it's a problem, particularly since the cabins concerned tend to be too small to take the skis inside with you. But it's not just ancient gondolas: another devoted reporter, Maureen Grenville, tells us that the new Pléney gondola at Morzine has racks that will take fat skis only one at a time, not in pairs. If ski resorts were serious businesses, they would sort this out to keep customers happy. Don't count on it.

AUSTRIA'S BIZARRE MANAGEMENT OF SKI ROUTES

We continue to campaign for a more rational approach to the management of steep, frequently used slopes in Austria that bear the label 'ski route'. The basic problems are that resorts are not obliged to patrol them, so it's not safe to ski them alone, and that it's easy to get confused about which runs are pistes and which are routes – a problem compounded by the bizarre fact that many routes are groomed. But there are other problems, too.

Ski routes are marked on the mountain less thoroughly than pistes, and there is no consistency in the way they are marked. In the Arlberg last winter we found the top Rendl ski route had the markers down the middle. The standard route from Schindlergrat

↑ On some ski routes, you're supposed to slalom round the markers; on others, stay to one side

SNOWPIX.COM / CHRIS GILL

SNOWPIX.COM / CHRIS GILL

Another Austrian speciality: mad numbering of pistes; you're in trouble if you're colour-blind ➔

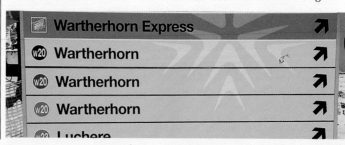

Wartherhorn Express

Wartherhorn

Wartherhorn

Wartherhorn

Luchere

↑ Family and friends of editor Gill, on the hunt for the best Kaiserschmarrn in Austria, struck pancake gold in the cosy Kriegeralpe, above Lech; it's strictly a late-afternoon treat here – served from 3pm

SNOWPIX.COM / CHRIS GILL

had them close to but not quite on the left side for most of the run, then at the traverse section they switched to the right (uphill) side. How are you meant to make sense of this in a whiteout?

What was also clear in the Arlberg was that ski routes were not closed despite obviously inadequate snow cover – rocks and bushes were protruding on some runs, and possibly lurking close to the surface on others. Having broken three ribs a few seasons back by skiing into one submerged off-piste rock and landing on another, editor Gill is very alert to these dangers.

I DON'T BELIEVE IT DEPARTMENT

We're as keen as the next man on a bit of cracking Wensleydale, but we're not fans of Alpine meals consisting of industrial quantities of industrial-grade cheese. Also, our doctors don't approve of high-fat cheese – an argument we regularly wheel out when being taken to dinner by Swiss tourist office personnel, who seem to think a kilo or two of high-fat gloop is a treat for lowlanders like us.

But we may be on shaky ground. Our man in the Valais, Bruno Huggler, claims that 'cheese from the Alps contains more of the healthy Omega 3 fatty acid than other cheeses, produced in an industrial way'. And what do you know: a bit of Googling throws up countless websites in support. Of course, you don't know whether the cheese you are offered in the Alps is actually Alpine. We'll now feel better about eating Gruyère, but we're still not convinced about raclette or fondue.

THANKS TO YOU

We are, as ever, grateful to all the hundreds of readers who sent in reports last season – reports that are crucial to our annual updating and revision process. As usual, the most useful 100 reports have earned a free copy of this edition, and the readers' names have gone into the hat for a free week in a smart Lagrange apartment in the French Alps. And the lucky winner is ... Jim Reed – congratulations, Jim. Please send in reports next season – Lagrange is again providing a prize; read page 12.

We are also indebted to the readers who make up for the inadequacy of resort picture libraries by sending in photos for publication. If we use any of your pics, you get a copy of the book – and the satisfaction of seeing your photos in print, of course. This year we have used multiple pictures provided by Tanya Booth, Rod Garvey, Simon Medley, Brian Walker and Paul Carter, and individual ones from Stuart McWilliam, Alan Liptrot, David Maxwell-Lees, Claire Paul, Kerry Lewis and Michael Marlais.

The UK's best selling winter sports magazine!

The ultimate guide to your season: Resort Reviews; Insider tips from leading professionals including Graham Bell, Martin Bell and Warren Smith; Exclusive competitions; **And much more...**

OFFER 1

Get six interactive issues direct to your iPad for just £9.99 (RRP £17.94)

OFFER 2

Get six issues of Telegraph Ski and Snowboard print edition for just £19.99*
+ Free delivery to your door

Order online now at
telegraph.co.uk/skisubs
Or call 020 8955 7002 quoting
offer code 'TSS2015'

SAVE 25%!

*This offer is valid for UK subscriptions only. This offer cannot be used in conjunction with any other subscription offer and closes on 30 September 2015. The normal cost of six issues is £27 based on the cover price of £4.50. Full T&Cs online

What's new?

In this chapter we summarize major developments in ski resorts last season and those planned for 2014/15. Most major resort chapters have a 'News' panel near the start; you'll find many more news items in those panels. To keep up to date, sign up for our email newsletters on our website at www.wheretoskiandsnowboard.com.

ANDORRA

SOLDEU
2013/14: The ski school opened a Freeride Center with 10 specialist instructors. Two snow parks were improved.

AUSTRIA

ELLMAU
2014/15: The Aualm quad chair up to Zinsberg is due to be upgraded to an eight-seater.

HINTERTUX
2013/14: On the glacier, the big Tuxer Fernerhaus restaurant and the tiny Spannagelhaus nearby were both fully renovated.

ISCHGL
2014/15: A 28-seat gondola will replace the old 4-seat Pardatschgrat gondola, which should help reduce morning queues.
2013/14: A new 150-person cable car to Piz Val Gronda opened up a big area of off-piste; there's a new 3km red piste too.

KITZBÜHEL
2014/15: A double chair is planned for neglected Bichlalm.
2013/14: At Jochberg, the old double chair and drag were replaced by a 10-seater gondola, the Wagstättbahn.

LECH
2013/14: A new 10-seat gondola linked Lech with the Warth ski area, adding 68km of pistes (covered by the Arlberg lift pass).

MAYRHOFEN
2013/14: Swanky six-packs with all mod cons replaced double chairs on Rastkogel and Ahorn. A new fun slope for terrain park novices was partly opened on Ahorn.

OBERTAUERN
2014/15: The Panoramabahn fast quad on Seekarspitz is to be replaced by a six-pack with covers and heated seats.

SAALBACH
2014/15: An eight-seat chair will replace the Polten quad. A second gondola out of the valley is being built at Leogang.
2013/14: A six-pack replaced the Rosswald T-bar on Reiterkogel.

SCHLADMING
2013/14: The Gipfelbahn 'pulse' gondola on Hochwurzen was replaced by a proper 10-seat gondola.

SOLDEN
2014/15: The Wasserkar triple chair from below the Gaislachkogl gondola mid-station is due to be replaced by a six-pack.

23

AWARD-WINNING
SKI
HOLIDAYS

Ski Olympic

book online at
skiolympic.com
01302 328 820

ST ANTON
2013/14: The Tanzböden T-bar on Galzig was replaced by a six-pack.

ZELL AM SEE
2013/14: An eight-seat chair replaced the Glocknerbahn quad and the parallel drag above Areitalm. A new fun slope opened.

FRANCE

ALPE-D'HUEZ
2014/15: Snowmaking is planned for the Sarenne black run.
2013/14: On the main beginner area a chondola replaced five draglifts and another drag was replaced by a moving carpet. Plus a new Folie Douce opened (as in Val d'Isère etc).

LES ARCS
2014/15: Immediately above 1800 a new activity zone is being built, with a new gondola replacing the Villards chair.
2013/14: A new 4-star hotel opened just above 1800, the Aiguille Grive. New mountain restaurants opened near 1600 and 1800.

AVORIAZ
2014/15: The Dromonts hotel is to be completely renovated.

LES CARROZ
2013/14: A new spa/sports centre with outdoor pool opened.

CHAMONIX
2014/15: The ancient Plan Joran chair at the base of Les Grands Montets is due to be replaced by a 10-person gondola.

CHATEL
2014/15: Two new fast chairs are planned to link the Super-Châtel and Linga areas. An aquatic centre opened in the village centre.

COURCHEVEL
2014/15: A six-pack is due to replace the adjacent Aiguille du Fruit and Gravelles chairs at Praméruel between 1650 and 1850. The ancient Forêt gondola from Le Praz is to be replaced by a six-pack.

FLAINE
2014/15: A new 'fun zone' for kids is planned for Flaine Forêt. A 5-star, ski-in/ski-out Pierre & Vacances Premium residence will open at Montsoleil. Ski Total is opening the resort's first catered chalets.
2013/14: The Diamant Noir double chair was replaced by a fast quad. The beginner area at Flaine Forêt was revamped.

MEGEVE
2014/15: There are plans to replace both Mont Joux chairs with one six-pack, with a new Folie Douce near the top (as in Val d'Isère etc).

MENUIRES
2013/14: A 1200m-long roller-coaster-style ride on rails was built.

MERIBEL
2014/15: The Loze chair to the Col de la Loze is due to be upgraded to a fast quad, for quicker access to Courchevel.
2013/14: Inuit Village is a new children's area beside the altiport.

MONTGENEVRE
2014/15: The new Durancia leisure and wellness centre will open. CGH will open their new central residence Napoléon.

MORZINE
2014/15: In the Super-Morzine area, there are plans to replace the Proclou and Seraussaix chairs with six-packs.
2013/14: The Pléney gondola was replaced by a new 10-seater.

La Plagne

2014/15: The chairlift out of Bellecôte towards Centre (Colosses) is to be replaced by an eight-pack of huge carrying capacity.

2013/14: The inadequate double chair at Les Bauches was replaced by a disused quad. The La Roche chair below Centre was upgraded to a six-pack. Two long black runs from the glacier were reopened.

La Rosiere

2014/15: A six-pack is due to replace two draglifts to Le Roc Noir.

Serre-Chevalier

2014/15: The Croix de la Nore draglift on the way to Briançon from Chantemerle is due to be replaced by a quad chair.

2013/14: The Chantemerle cable car was replaced by an eight-seat gondola. Two hotels in Villeneuve reopened as 4-stars.

Ste-Foy

2013/14: The slow Gran Plan chair out of the village was replaced by a fast quad. A new mountain restaurant, les Marquises, opened.

La Tania

2014/15: The ancient Forêt gondola from Le Praz is due to be replaced by a six-pack to a lower top station at mid-mountain.

2013/14: A long six-pack was built from below mid-mountain to the top, replacing two draglifts.

Tignes

2013/14: The first phase of the MGM/CGH Kalinda village at Tignes 1800 opened. The gondola from Tignes-le-Lac was replaced by a faster 10-seat one. The Suites du Nevada hotel became a 5-star.

Val Thorens

2014/15: The fast Portette quad and the slow Plan de l'Eau are to be

Build your own shortlist: www.wheretoskiandsnowboard.com

Specialists in tailor-made ski holidays, luxury ski hotels and flexible ski weekends

snow-wise
SKI HOLIDAY EXPERTS

020 3397 8450
www.snow-wise.com

replaced by six-packs designed to operate in high winds.
2013/14: The 3 Vallées 1 chairlift out of the village became a
chondola. In the 'fourth valley', the Peyron chair from Plan
Bouchet is now a six-pack and a 1300m zipwire has been installed.

ITALY

CORTINA
2013/14: Inghams opened a central chalet hotel.

LIVIGNO
2013/14: Off-piste skiing and heli-skiing are, we are assured, now
allowed after being banned for several years.

MADONNA DI CAMPIGLIO
2013/14: A new red piste was created in the Cinque Laghi area.

MONTEROSA SKI
2014/15: Ski Total has taken over one of our favourite hotels, the
4-star Breithorn, and will be running it as a chalet hotel.

PASSO TONALE
2014/15: If all goes to plan, a new gondola will open from Passo
Paradiso to the top of the glacier, replacing the existing lifts.

SELLA RONDA
2014/15: An eight-person gondola is to replace the queue-prone
Borest quad chairlift linking Corvara and Colfosco.
2013/14: A new six-pack was built between Arabba and Passo
Pordoi, going up to the Carpazza chair.

SELVA
2013/14: The Dantercëpies gondola was replaced, with increased
capacity, plus more parking and better services at the base.

SWITZERLAND

ADELBODEN
2014/15: A 10-person gondola is to replace the cable car out of
Lenk, going up to Metschstand and accessing Adelboden's slopes.
2013/14: A hybrid 6/8-seat chondola carrying 2,400 passengers an
hour replaced the existing Hahnenmoos gondola.

CRANS-MONTANA
2014/15: A six-pack is to replace the Cabane de Bois double chair to
Les Violettes. The Momentum Ski Festival and City Ski Champs will
be held here again – from 12 to 15 March 2015.

DAVOS
2014/15: The 50-person Jakobshorn cable car from Platz is to be
replaced by a new cable car twice the size.

MÜRREN
2014/15: Two ancient T-bars on the lower slopes are to be replaced
and a moving carpet is to be installed on the village nursery slopes.

SAAS-FEE
2014/15: The renovated Aqua Allalin leisure centre and attached
168-bed youth hostel are due to open in September 2014.

ST MORITZ
2014/15: A new sports centre in Bad should be open with indoor
and outdoor pools, wellness area, fitness centre and restaurants.

VAL D'ANNIVIERS
2013/14: A new 125-person cable car opened, linking Grimentz
village to the heart of the Zinal ski area.

New for 14/15

★★★★
La Grange aux Fées
Valmorel, France

CGH
HÔTELS · RÉSIDENCES · SPAS D'ALTITUDE

Brand new, ski in/ski out residence offering
4★ apartments with luxurious spa amenities

peak retreats

Call 0844 576 0173
peakretreats.co.uk

◈ABTA
ABTA No.W5537

VERBIER
2014/15: As we go to press in July, the 4 Vallées area pass is not expected to be offered, following a dispute between lift companies. 2013/14: A new gondola from Le Châble linked Verbier to the Bruson ski area. The chairlift from Siviez to Plan-du-Fou (for access to Nendaz) was replaced by a gondola. A cutting-edge 5-star hotel – W Verbier – opened at Médran.

ZERMATT
2013/14: The Sunnegga funicular was upgraded.

USA – CALIFORNIA

MAMMOTH
2014/15: Rhythm Ridge, a new four-acre area of bowls, berms, banks and bumps for all levels, is due to open. 2013/14: June Mountain, a scenic 30-minute drive away, reopened. Beginner terrain park areas were expanded.

USA – COLORADO

ASPEN
2014/15: A $10 million kids' centre is being built at Buttermilk.

BEAVER CREEK
2014/15: The focal Centennial chairlift is being replaced by a hybrid chondola with greatly increased capacity.

BRECKENRIDGE
2013/14: A new 500-acre Peak 6 area opened, served by a six-pack.

VAIL
2013/14: A six-pack replaced the Mountaintop quad at Mid-Vail.

USA – REST OF THE WEST

BIG SKY
2013/14: In 2013 the resort acquired the two smaller resorts right next door – Moonlight Basin and Spanish Peaks.

CANADA

SUN PEAKS
2014/15: New trails are planned, adding 500 acres of terrain and making Sun Peaks the second biggest ski area in Canada.

WHISTLER
2014/15: The Whistler Village gondola is to be replaced. 2013/14: A six-pack replaced the queue-prone Harmony chair. The slow Crystal chair on Blackcomb was replaced by a fast quad.

Build your own shortlist: www.wheretoskiandsnowboard.com

In 1994, John Major was prime minister; Tony Blair was elected leader of the Labour party; Sunday trading was legalized in England and Wales; the National Lottery was started; Switzerland announced the introduction of VAT; Nelson Mandela was elected president of South Africa. And this book was published for the first time.

It's amazing to think that New Labour has come and gone while we've been slaving away at our Mac screens, devoting our summers to production of yet another edition. As the 20th such summer comes to an end, we thought we'd indulge in a little retrospective.

BE DAMNED

We worked with big-name publishers to produce our first three editions, but our relationship ended in tears when the publisher decided to print in the Far East to save money. But the five-week extra shipping time meant editing the book in February, March and April – not a great idea, we thought.

We've published the book ourselves ever since (printing mainly in Italy, since you ask).

A BIT OF BACKGROUND

This book has its roots in another. Editor Gill was the founding editor of the original consumerist, warts-and-all ski resort guidebook, *The Good Skiing Guide*. He produced the first edition for his employer, *Which?*, in 1985. Until then, resort guides were descriptive but uncritical, and made no comparisons. *The Good Skiing Guide* was all about analysis and comparison. (Note: *The Good Ski Guide* is a different publication, completely unrelated.)

Chris left *Which?* in 1985 to go freelance, but edited the GSG for a further seven years, until he disagreed with the publishers about the future direction of the project. He then got together with fellow *Which?* alumnus Dave Watts to produce this rival book. The first edition appeared in 1994, by which time *Which?* had hired new editors. The two titles slugged it out in the marketplace until *Which?* pulled the plug in 2005 – 20 years on.

STILL IN BUSINESS

We made two key decisions when planning our first edition: to print in colour on decent paper, and (putting our *Which?* days firmly behind us) to carry advertising. Even now, book publishers don't really carry advertising on a serious scale. Back then, it was literally unheard of.

It's gratifying that most of the holiday companies that advertised in our first edition are still around, and still advertising with us. Three companies have advertised in every edition: Esprit Ski, Le Ski and Ski Independence. There are five others that were with us at the start and are with us still: Ski Amis and Stanford skipped one edition; Ski Peak, Ski Total and Skiworld missed two. And another group joined us for our second or third edition and have been with us ever since, give or take the odd missed year: Alpine Answers, Erna Low, Frontier Ski, Lagrange, Ski Famille, Ski Olympic. We're grateful to all our advertisers for their support, but particularly grateful to this eminent group, who put their trust in us in those early years, and have stayed with us, more or less, throughout.

Bladon Lines was the biggest advertiser in our first edition, and the dominant player in the

FAVOURITES

The resorts that produced the most reader reports last season:

Val d'Isère
Tignes *
Zermatt
Obergurgl
Saalbach
Méribel
Chamonix *
Courchevel
La Plagne *
La Thuile *
Serre-Chevalier *
Flaine

Stars indicate resorts new to the list since 1994. Out have gone Les Arcs, Verbier, Alpe-d'Huez, Val Thorens, Cervinia and Morzine.

chalet business back then. If memory serves, it was Inghams that bought the business and then abolished the brand. Another lost brand is Enterprise – the second-biggest operator of ski packages 20 years ago, with 17% of the market.

EDITORIAL CONCERNS

In 1994, as now, we were concerned about safety, and about how resorts fail to behave sensibly in their management of runs. We argued for the first but not the last time that the 'ski routes' or 'ski tours' that had replaced black pistes in resorts such as Verbier, Zermatt and St Anton were a shame and a scandal – read this year's editorial, and you'll see we are still banging on about it.

We were concerned, too, about ski school standards, particularly in France and in relation to children. Editor Gill, having had his offspring reduced to tears by the ESF in Val d'Isère a couple of years earlier, took a special interest in reports from readers of children being left behind on the mountain, and so on. Thanks to higher standards driven by competition between schools, and especially competition from British-run schools, such stories are now rare, but the culture gap between the British and the French is still there.

ACROSS THE POND

We noted in 1994 that 'North America is here to stay' – perceptive, no? – and that Canada in particular was attracting a lot of interest in the UK: 'One of us is deeply sceptical of the merits of travelling to the west coast of Canada to ski a single resort close to the warm Pacific Ocean and at an altitude of 650m – even if it does have North America's biggest vertical drop (1600m). The other of us has been to Whistler, and is besotted with it.' Some years on, the sceptic (Gill) went to Whistler, too, and was duly converted. It may have been the day's heli-skiing that clinched it.

20 YEARS OF GLOBAL WARMING?

Of course, it's in the last 20 years that we've all got used to the idea of global warming, and started to worry about its impact on skiing. But maybe we've been worrying unnecessarily. We reproduce here a graph published on the Kitzbühel website, showing the average temperatures on the Hahnenkamm, above the town, over the last 20 years. And, as you can see, there is a clear trend ... it has got appreciably colder. There is hope for us yet. (As you may detect, last winter bucked the trend – read Fraser Wilkin on last season in our editorial, page 13.)

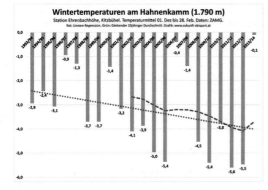

Wintertemperaturen am Hahnenkamm (1.790 m)
Station Ehrenbachhöhe, Kitzbühel. Temperaturmittel 01. Dez bis 28. Feb. Daten: ZAMG.
Rot: Lineare Regression. Grün: Gleitender 10jähriger Durchschnitt. Grafik: www.zukunft-skisport.at

THE INTERNET

Amazingly, we've been in the website business almost since the start. From 1995 to 1997 our stuff appeared on a site called SkiIn, run by a far-sighted guy from Paris. In 1997 we set up our own site, and the edition published that year included a half-page explanation of what the internet could do for you, and how to get connected. We knew it wouldn't last, though.

THE MARKET

How the market has changed in 20 years – figures drawn from the annual Crystal Ski Industry Report

Ski holidays
1994 747,000
2008 1,230,000
2014 868,000

Non-school trips
1994 600,000
2008 1,100,000
2014 754,000

Breakdown 1993
Austria 33%
France 29%
Switzerland 11%
Italy 8%
Bulgaria 8%
North America 2%

Breakdown 2004
France 36%
Austria 20%
Italy 16%
Andorra 14%
Switzerland 5%
North America 6%
Bulgaria 2%

Breakdown 2014
France 33.5%
Austria 28%
Italy 16%
Andorra 7%
Switzerland 6.5%
North America 4%
Bulgaria 2%

Over the 20 years:
France has grown its share a bit, although it may have passed its peak.
Austria suffered a disastrous decline during our first decade, but has now largely recovered.
Italy doubled its share during our first decade, and held it.
Switzerland now has only about half the share it once had.
Bulgaria has only one quarter the share it had 20 years back.
Andorra grew to a spectacular peak in the noughties, but has lost ground.
North America also peaked in the noughties.

PACKAGES STILL RULE

In 1994, the deregulation of Europe's aviation industry was only just getting under way, as was the use of the internet for commercial purposes. Ryanair was tiny; EasyJet was yet to be launched. You might think the huge growth of these airlines in the last 20 years would have resulted in a major shift away from package holidays; but it seems not. Back then, says the Crystal Ski Industry Report, 72% of holidays were packages; despite the different circumstances, the figure is still an amazing 66%.

GOOFY OR ... WHAT WAS THE OTHER ONE?

The first three editions of the book were called *Where to Ski*; no mention of snowboarding. But we were aware of this novel activity: we bought in a chapter from specialist authors, who picked out the best resorts for practitioners. And in 1997 we sent ourselves off to Vail to learn to do it, having carefully identified a course that was guaranteed to be free of teenagers brought up on skateboards. Later that year, we published *Where to Ski and Snowboard*, complete with special sections in each chapter for the amusement of boarders.

CHALETS AND APARTMENTS

In the 1997 edition we introduced a feature chapter about luxury chalets. When the editors get together with skiing chums from the 80s, there is a tendency to slip into Pythonesque reminiscences about chalets with paper-thin walls, bathrooms shared between five bedrooms and hot water that ran out at 4.30pm. By the late 90s, such things were increasingly rare, and genuinely indulgent chalets were in contrast easy to find. Our new chapter was a celebration of that development, and still is (it's on page 45). Our focus is on affordable luxury; you don't have to pay a fortune to get an outdoor hot tub, these days.

But it was a few years later that we detected another shift – the step change in the quality of French apartment developments, kick-started by the builder MGM. We first stayed in one of their properties at Arc 1800 in 2000; it wasn't perfect, but it was a whole lot better than what went before. At the end of 2003, Arc 1950 opened its doors, built by Canadian Intrawest, and by the mid-noughties there were enough 'smart apartment' developments to justify another regular feature chapter (it's on page 49).

DEAR READERS

Over the years, thousands of readers have sent us reports on their skiing trips, and we are grateful to them all. But there are some who deserve a special mention. We are simply in awe of Maureen Grenville, who has sent in 143 reports; she is one of a trio who have earned a free copy of all 19 editions – the others being Alison Biden and Sally Robson. John Hyman missed only one year. Julie Sheard is another who won books in both 1994 and 2014. Alan Shepherd missed just the first year. Jon Christian Didrichsen has won 'only' 17 free books, but comes second to Maureen with 102 reports. Others who have filed many reports are Guy Senior, Allen Joslin, and Michael Marlais, our top-scoring American reporter. We must also mention Linda Wilkins for her annual bulletin on Kitzbühel, and Keith Wild, for his exhaustive surveys of the bars in every resort he visits. Last but not least, Tanya Booth has had 30 of her photos printed in the book, over the last seven editions.

THE BIG IMPROVEMENTS: OUR ANNIVERSARY ALPINE AWARDS

In the last 20 years, some resorts have sorted out their problems, and some have not. We've picked the best and the worst.

AUSTRIA

Most improved resort: Kitzbühel We were saying in 1994 that the resort suffered from 'shockingly bad peak-season queues', and noted that the Hahnenkamm cable car out of the town had an hourly capacity of just 380 people; laughable. All sorted now.

Worst persistent problem: St Anton We said in 1994 'the blue pistes from Galzig can get very crowded' – a gently expressed view of a problem that has simply got worse and worse.

Best new link For 2013/14 a new gondola linked the Alps' snowiest areas – Lech and Warth – to form a powder-pig paradise.

FRANCE

Most improved resort: Tignes-le-Lac In those days Tignes-le-Lac was seriously inhospitable – the road up the valley to Val Claret was yet to be buried in a tunnel. Whereas Val d'Isère of course had just had the Olympic makeover that transformed it from a bit of a dump to a very pleasant resort.

Worst persistent problem: La Plagne We complained that 'the old gondola from Bellecôte via Belle Plagne to Roche de Mio is still a bad bottleneck', a complaint you will find repeated this year.

Best new link In 2003/4 the double-decker Vanoise Express cable car opened, linking Les Arcs and La Plagne to form Paradiski – an area big enough to rival the Trois Vallées.

ITALY

Most improved resort: Val Gardena Selva, Santa Cristina and Ortisei have become polished resorts with serious lift and snowmaking systems in the last 20 years.

Worst persistent problem: Cortina A minor quibble this: access to the different slope sectors is still a messy business.

Best new link For 2011/12 a long gondola linked Madonna di Campiglio to Pinzolo, adding excellent wooded slopes to Madonna's predominantly open area.

SWITZERLAND

Most improved resort: Verbier We moaned at length – in a special feature panel – about the shortcomings of Verbier: serious queues, overcrowded pistes, poor grooming, shortage of snowmaking, shortage of easy pistes, poor signposting and piste maps. The resort has come a long way since then, in most respects.

Worst persistent problem: Grindelwald We wrote of vast queues for the Männlichen gondola, which took half an hour to the top; 20 years later, nothing has changed – improvements are promised, but not for at least three more seasons.

Best new link Last season a new gondola from Le Châble gave Verbier-based skiers painless access to the excellent, spacious tree skiing of backwater Bruson.

YVES GARNEAU /
VERBIER ST-BERNARD

Two awards for Verbier, one of Switzerland's top resorts ↓

Piste extent update

Slow progress towards comparable figures

by **Chris Gill**

In our 2014 edition we brought together for the first time the concerns we had raised over many years about optimistic claims of piste km, and the excellent recent work in this area of German writer and consultant Christoph Schrahe. He measured the slopes of all the big resorts, and found most of them overstate the extent of their pistes, often by surprising amounts. In the worst cases, the claims overstated the reality by 120%, and many areas overstated by 50% or so. Here's an update on how resorts are dealing with these challenges.

IT'S MAINLY A MATTER OF TURNS

Until we came to prepare our feature article last year, it had not occurred to us that there might be more than one way of measuring the length of a piste. We assumed that you would simply measure the piste down the centre line, following the curves of the piste but not deviating from that line. This is how Christoph Schrahe measured pistes, too, and it is how the FIS measures race courses.

But one of the key things we established last year is that many of the overstated claims of resorts are based on this chain of thought: on most pistes, skiers execute turns; they therefore follow a path that is longer than the measured length of the piste; and this longer path is a more meaningful figure than the simple measured length. The problem is, some resorts do it, and some don't.

The Grand Massif area, for example, assumes that your track down the mountain is a continuous series of linked semicircles. So instead of skiing 10m down the line of the piste, for example, you ski a semicircle with a diameter of 10m; the distance travelled, as any primary school pupil could tell you, is 10 x pi/2. So the piste length is multiplied by pi/2 or 1.57 – ie adding 57%.

AUSTRIAN ACTION

Christoph Schrahe's report attracted a lot of attention in Austria, partly no doubt because major Austrian resorts dominated the very short list of areas with accurate piste km figures, while other major Austrian resorts had figures wildly different from Schrahe's. As we reported last year, the national association of lift companies was quick to issue guidelines about piste measurement, and by last summer some resorts had taken action. The Zillertal resorts cut their claim for the whole valley from 666km to 487km; Mayrhofen cut its claim from 159km to 133km; more radically, Hochzillertal cut its claim from 181km to 88km.

We didn't mention last year the area shared by Austrian Ischgl and Swiss Samnaun. The Schrahe report put the extent of the area at 154km – much less than the claimed figure of

ISCHGL FIGURES

The three ways in which Ischgl now conveys the extent of its pistes are shown in this graphic from the resort website

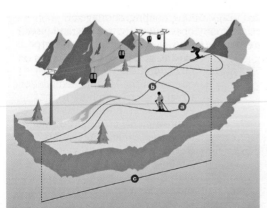

32

Claimed total /
measured total /
% by which these
top ski areas
overstate their
km, according to
Schrahe

Trois Vallées
600 / 493 / 22%
**Les Arcs-La
Plagne**
425 / 378 / 12%
Sella Ronda
360 / 309 / 17%
Portes du Soleil
(excludes Morzine
and Les Gets)
402 / 263 / 53%
Zermatt-Cervinia
313 / 252 / 24%
Milky Way
400 / 251 / 59%
**Val d'Isère-
Tignes**
300 / 232 / 29%

OUR FIGURES

You may find some
of the numbers
above don't match
the ones we quote in
our resort chapters.
This is because
Christoph Schrahe
has focused entirely
on linked areas,
whereas our figures
will often include
other local hills that
are not linked.

238km. In the wake of the report, the resort published on its website three alternative figures based on three different methods, explained with the aid of the drawing reproduced on the left:
method a – based on the track a skier might follow (ie much like the Grand Massif figure explained above): 238km
method b – the length measured directly down the slope – the approach taken by Schrahe: 172km
method c – the length as you would measure it on a map – the lowest figure, because the length measured down the slope is of course more than the length measured horizontally: 163km.

Similarly, the Stubai glacier area now offers two sets of figures on its website. It describes these as 'Fall Line – the length of the route from the start of the slope to the end of the slope – straight ahead' and 'Effective Route – the length of the route covered by skiers on average on the respective slope'. (The reference to the fall line is wrong, incidentally – many gentle stretches of piste slope from side to side, so measuring down the fall line would get you nowhere.)

The Stubai glacier totals are 62km and 104km. But the main 'Skiing' page of the site says '110km of runs (50km easy/blue, 32km intermediate/red, 6km difficult/black, 19.5km ski routes)'.

ITALIAN INDIFFERENCE

We looked at two Italian areas in particular last year – Monterosa Ski and Courmayeur, both (as it happens) in the Val d'Aosta in the north-west of the country.

Back in 2010, in our 2011 edition, we suggested that the run lengths published on the Monterosa lift company website were about double the lengths you would estimate by looking at topographical maps. Around the end of 2010, the lift company quietly revised its tables, roughly halving the lengths. We summarized all this in our 2014 edition and now the website pages listing the halved run lengths start with the following notice:

ATTENTION!
*Data shown in these charts of Lifts and Slopes are meant to provide ...
approximate information, numbers and news about our domain skiable,
for our fans. For the publication, we have reported those parameters that
can be found in the technical documents we own. Some values can be
different from the experience of the skiers because they are the result of
technical data and not of the real way on the slopes.*

In other words: 'We are now doing the proper thing and publishing the measured lengths of our slopes, but when you ski them you'll find the slopes longer than these figures suggest.' Fair enough – except that the promotion of the area and its resorts still relies on the old, way-too-big figures from 2010. In its 2013–14 press material, the lift company was still speaking of 'the 180km of runs of one of the biggest ski resorts in Italy'. The Aosta valley's UK website does the same.

Then there is the incredible and extreme case of Courmayeur. This small area has always claimed an unlikely 100km of pistes. Two years ago, the lift company came clean and explained that 64km of the 100km were off-piste runs; the piste total was a mere 36km. The total has since been upped to a magnificent 39km. But again the marketing material uses the misleading larger figure: the Aosta valley UK website refers to '100km of pistes'.

DO IT YOURSELF

Above is our plot of the run from top to bottom of the mountain at Alagna in the Monterosa Ski area, in Italy

FRENCH FOLLY

Another resort we mentioned last year was Les Deux-Alpes, in the southern French Alps. We have long felt (and have said, in many editions) that its claim of about 200km was difficult to accept, and Schrahe reckoned the claim exceeded the reality by 70%. When last year we invited them to explain, the resort's normally helpful PR people simply stopped replying to our emails.

Now, to our amazement, the resort has side-stepped the whole issue by adopting the American approach and stating an area instead of a total length. Actually, they've done something slightly different from the American approach. American resorts quote the total area of land you are allowed to ski, most of which is ungroomed, although all of it is avalanche-safe; Les Deux-Alpes quotes the area of groomed pistes. The figure is 410 hectares. We're aware of one or two other areas that are going in the same direction – the Tignes piste map now quotes 480 hectares of piste, and 3,200 hectares of off-piste.

DO IT YOURSELF

Christoph Schrahe's work revolved around digitising the route of each piste using clever software. If you want to check the length of a piste yourself, you can use a similar but less clever technique using Google Maps – these now show pistes for many ski resorts, not only in North America but also in Europe. At the same time, Google has introduced a gadget that gives you the length of any route you plot on a map; you mark the route by plotting points, which are joined by straight lines, so if you want an accurate result you have to plot a lot of points. The screen grab above shows an example – in Monterosa, as it happens.

Of course, you are using Ischgl's method c, when what you ideally want is method b. But you won't be too far out unless it's a seriously steep run. The resort now states a length for this run (from the mountaintop to Alagna) of 7.1km. Our Google Maps figure was almost exactly 7km.

SORTING OUT THIS MESS

As we said last year, we think inflating the length of runs by making arbitrary assumptions about how skiers behave is ludicrous. But in the end it doesn't matter how pistes are measured; what matters is that resorts should measure their pistes in a standard way, so that you don't get one resort adding nothing to the directly measured length, another adding 57% and a third adding 120%.

Switching to publishing the area of groomed runs doesn't help, either – it simply divides Europe's resorts into those with figures that can be compared, although at present not reliably, and those with figures that mean nothing at all.

Ski resort obsessives can get a copy of Christoph Schrahe's report from schrahe@ski-weltweit.de – 99 euros.

Cutting your costs

We name the resorts where your pound will go further

by **Chris Gill**

RPI	**120**
lift pass	£220
ski hire	£130
lessons	£135
food & drink	£170
total	**£655**

RPI	**100**
lift pass	£200
ski hire	£115
lessons	£120
food & drink	£125
total	**£560**

RPI	**90**
lift pass	£190
ski hire	£90
lessons	£80
food & drink	£120
total	**£480**

LIFT PASSES

Our lift pass figures are for the pass we reckon you're most likely to buy.

In Europe, where a resort sells a pass covering other linked resorts, we have used that pass price.

Where available, in North America we have used special passes aimed at the international market.

LESSONS

Our budget figure is half the cost of a four-hour private lesson for two people.

Generally, we have looked at the main schools. You may pay more, or less.

Where the standard offering is a lesson of 2.5 hours, say, we scaled the cost up to four hours.

Our Resort Price Index figures are now an established feature of this book – our response to the weakened pound and resulting high cost of staying in a top ski resort. We aim to make it simple to see which resorts are affordable, and which are not. Our figures cover not only food and drink (which is what we focused on at the start, five years back) but also the costs of lift passes, ski hire and lessons. Our RPI figures are now based on a total of all four costs; but, as you can see from the examples in the margin, we also show the separate costs that feed into the RPI calculation.

The food and drink element of the RPI, as in earlier years, is based partly on prices noted by our faithful readers. If you find this survey helpful, please contribute to the exercise next season, via our website.

In January 2009, when we were first inspired to embark on this price survey caper, it was possible to buy euros at a UK airport for almost a pound per euro. Parity made it easy to know what a round was costing you, but had nothing else to recommend it. Since then, the published tourist rates (a bit higher than what you end up getting if you just walk up to an airport bureau de change counter) have fluctuated mainly between 1.1 and 1.2 euros to the pound. A year ago, in July 2013, the pound was at the low end of its range, but now it is back up to 1.2. Of course, things may be different by the time the skiing season rolls around.

We have stuck to the policy, adopted last year, of basing our comparisons on the average cost in the main eurozone destination countries – Andorra, Austria, France and Italy. (In earlier years, our RPIs were based on the average costs across Europe, but with the Swiss market somewhat reduced and prices there typically higher than elsewhere, we think it's sensible to omit them.)

In margin boxes in each resort chapter we present budget figures for the four items we've considered, and a total. And at the top of the box, we give the resulting RPI. This index compares the total budget for the resort to the average across all eurozone resorts; 100 represents the average resort. Our RPI figures are colour coded, as shown in the margin on the left. Index figures of 120 up are coloured red, and figures of 90 down are green; ones in between are blue. Note that the overall RPI is only part of the picture, though; in particular, the total and RPI don't always reflect the cost of food and drink, which can be swamped by other costs.

Vaujany, a unique village resort with amazing amenities.

- Very affordable, less commercial than the Savoie resorts.
- Sharing world class skiing of Alpe d'Huez 3300m-1100m.
- Ski Peak are the exclusive specialists to Vaujany offering a comprehensive service and award winning accommodation.

Ski Peak   Tel: 01428 608070   www.skipeak.com

SKI AMIS

Catered Chalets in Superb Locations

020 3411 5439
www.skiamis.com

SKI HIRE

Our budget figures are for 'performance' skis to suit a keen intermediate or advanced skier; not a beginner or top-end demo ski. We looked at several shops.

You can get serious discounts online.

EXCHANGE RATES

We converted prices to £££ using tourist rates in July 2014:
€1.21
1.45 Swiss francs
US$1.64
CAN$1.73

The margin panels dotted around this chapter explain exactly what we have included in our 'basket' of items. One particular thing to be aware of is that many people will spend a lot more on food and drink than our modest budget figure – so beware resorts where that figure is high, because your expenditure may be two or three times our budget.

The group of resorts with roughly average blue-coded RPIs (from 95 to 115) is largely French and Austrian, with some Italian resorts and four Swiss. The green-coded low-cost group has eastern European countries at the bottom, but then includes a fair few Italian resorts, plus quite a few in Austria and France. The cheapest resorts in the main Alpine countries are Passo Tonale in Italy, a great place to learn to ski on good snow, and Val Cenis in France.

The red-coded pricey group is dominated by resorts in North America and Switzerland, with just the most fashionable resorts in France and Austria – Courchevel, Méribel and Lech – getting red RPIs. In the top slot are Aspen and Beaver Creek, closely followed by Vail and Snowmass – all in Colorado.

THE PICTURE BY COUNTRY

Swiss prices remain high. Only four Swiss resorts fall outside our red high-cost group when you look at the overall RPI. All Swiss resorts are expensive for eating and drinking, with budget figures, even for our very modest 'basket', ranging from £180 to £235 – that is, £30 to £40 a day. You could easily spend £100 a day. For lift passes, too, many resorts are pricey. For lessons and ski hire, the picture is much more mixed.

All resorts in North America fall well inside the pricey red-coded group overall, mainly because of expensive lift passes and lessons (the latter particularly in the US). Ski hire costs are generally high, though there are a few resorts that match Europe in this respect. The picture is less clear when you come to look at your daily food

WAYS TO KEEP HOLIDAY COSTS UNDER CONTROL

A good way of avoiding the full impact of high resort restaurant prices is to go on a catered chalet holiday. You get afternoon tea as part of the deal, so your lunchtime needs can be minimized; some tour ops offer 'piste picnic' packed lunches at low cost; crucially, you get wine included with dinner – and you can organize your own aperitifs, or buy beer and mixers in the chalet at modest cost. In these difficult times the demand for catered chalet holidays has soared, and operators have expanded their programmes. Inghams now operates 77 properties, sister company Ski Total over 100.

There are other ways to control costs. A few tour operators such as Ski 2 offer 'all-inclusive deal' options, quoting a price that includes half-board, vouchers for lunch at mountain restaurants, lift pass, and more. Inghams now has an all-inclusive deal covering the lift pass, kit hire, a packed lunch and evening drinks. Crystal has two deals in selected resorts, one including ski/board hire and lift pass, the other including lunch and evening drinks. And yes, you can combine the two. Club Med is a well-established operator of big hotels where everything is included.

And there is self-catering – it's now easy to find comfortable apartments with ample room to prepare meals and a dishwasher to deal with the aftermath – and with swanky spas and pools attached, in many cases.

If you're travelling solo, you'll be aware of the heavy charges that usually apply for single occupancy of a room. Check out Singles Ski Holidays, which buys up single rooms in advance so that it can offer singles accommodation at the best prices.

RPI	Resort	Country	Page	RPI	Resort	Country	Page
50	Poiana Brasov etc	Romania	651	95	Bad Gastein	Austria	104
60	Bansko etc	Bulgaria	648	95	Courmayeur	Italy	398
65	Kranjska Gora etc	Slovenia	652	95	Formigal etc	Spain	641
75	Passo Tonale	Italy	418	95	Hintertux / Tux valley	Austria	113
80	Val Cenis Vanoise	France	355	95	Obertauern	Austria	154
85	Ellmau	Austria	110	95	Saalbach-Hinterglemm	Austria	157
85	Monterosa Ski	Italy	412	95	Samoëns	France	323
85	Ste-Foy-Tarentaise	France	334	95	Schladming	Austria	163
85	Vars / Risoul	France	375	95	Sella Ronda	Italy	425
90	Arinsal	Andorra	90	95	Selva / Val Gardena	Italy	433
90	Cervinia	Italy	387	95	Serre-Chevalier	France	325
90	Garmisch-Partenkirchen	Germany	380	95	The Pyrenees	France	315
90	La Grave	France	265	100	Bad Kleinkirchheim	Austria	107
90	La Rosière	France	319	100	Châtel	France	235
90	La Thuile	Italy	442	100	Flaine	France	256
90	Livigno	Italy	403	100	Les Carroz	France	223
90	Mayrhofen	Austria	142	100	Les Deux-Alpes	France	250
90	Montgenèvre	France	289	100	Les Gets	France	263
90	Sauze d'Oulx	Italy	420	100	Megève	France	267
90	Sestriere	Italy	440	100	Morzine	France	294
90	Söll	Austria	172	100	Stubai valley	Austria	188
				100	Zell am See	Austria	190

Cutting your costs

37

Build your own shortlist: **www.wheretoskiandsnowboard.com**

Champoluc holiday prices all include lift pass and lunches

• Great value Italian resort

• Extensive range of accommodation to suit all budgets

• Book your own flights to take advantage of all the best prices

• Inclusive prices

• British ski school

• Discounts for groups

www.ski-2.com

Visit our comprehensive website,
at www.ski-2.com,
call us on 01962 713330
or email us at info@ski-2.com

ABTA The Travel Association

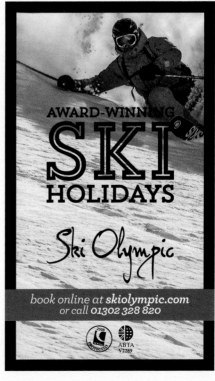

AWARD-WINNING
SKI HOLIDAYS

Ski Olympic

book online at **skiolympic.com**
or call **01302 328 820**

ABTA V2289

SINGLES SKI HOLIDAYS

* Skiing in France, Austria, Switzerland and Italy
* Eight resorts offering different levels of skiing and snowboarding
* Rooms for sole use
* Flights from a range of UK and Ireland airports
* 7 night prices from £545 including flights, half board & ski hosting
* **NEW** – learn to ski weeks in France

Call now on **0871 200 0625**
or visit **www.singlesskiholidays.com**

and drink budget. All the most expensive places are in Switzerland, but then come Canadian and American resorts mixed up with the top end of the French resorts.

Although France doesn't stand out from our overall RPI figures as expensive, compared with Austria and Italy it is way more expensive in one respect: food and drink; nearly all resorts come in with budget figures of £120 or more – £20 a day – and most of the resorts that are most popular on the UK market come in at £135 or more – and this is for very modest consumption, remember.

Both Austria and Italy have more resorts where the costs overall are below average, and have plenty of resorts with below-average food and drink costs. We have put together some food and drink comparisons below.

In Andorra, Soldeu comes in slightly above average, with Arinsal below. Spain costs less than average, and Slovenia appreciably less. But Bulgaria and Romania retain a firm grip on the real budget end of the market.

EUROZONE
In these two tables we show the lowest and highest budget figures in the resorts of Austria, France, Germany and Italy – and the figures for the most costly Swiss resorts.

FOOD & DRINK
Our budget figure is for six days' modest consumption – each day, a cheap pasta or pizza lunch and four different drinks – a quarter-litre of house wine, a small beer, a coke and a large coffee or cappuccino. This is intended to be fair to countries where one kind of drink may be more expensive than others. You may spend much more than our budget figure (we certainly do), especially where the budget figure itself is quite high.

EUROZONE EXTREMES: FOOD/DRINK		
Resort	Country	Budget
LOW		
Monterosa Ski	Italy	£100
Passo Tonale	Italy	£100
Garmisch-Partenk'n	Germany	£105
Bad Gastein	Austria	£110
Ellmau	Austria	£110
Pyrenees	France	£110
Saalbach	Austria	£110
Sauze d'Oulx	Italy	£110
Sestriere	Italy	£110
Sölden	Austria	£110
Söll	Austria	£110
HIGH		
Chamonix	France	£145
Megève	France	£145
La Plagne	France	£145
La Tania	France	£145
Avoriaz	France	£150
Flaine	France	£150
Lech	Austria	£150
Tignes	France	£155
Val d'Isère	France	£155
Val Thorens	France	£155
Méribel	France	£175
Courchevel	France	£190
And in Switzerland, the top price:		
St Moritz	Switzerland	£235

EUROZONE EXTREMES: LIFT PASSES		
Resort	Country	Budget
LOW		
Ste-Foy-Tarentaise	France	£130
Val Cenis Vanoise	France	£140
Passo Tonale	Italy	£160
Pyrenees	France	£160
La Rosière	France	£160
Sauze d'Oulx	Italy	£160
Sestriere	Italy	£160
Vars / Risoul	France	£160
HIGH		
Les Arcs	France	£210
La Plagne	France	£210
Tignes	France	£210
Val d'Isère	France	£210
Cortina d'Ampezzo	Italy	£220
Courchevel	France	£230
Les Menuires	France	£230
Méribel	France	£230
St-Martin-de-B'ville	France	£230
La Tania	France	£230
Val Thorens	France	£230
And in Switzerland, the top price:		
Zermatt	Switzerland	£260

A FREE LUNCH DOES EXIST!

Alpine Answers, the UK's leading specialist ski travel agency, are giving our readers an exclusive offer

Simply book your next ski holiday through Alpine Answers and get a 5% discount. That should be enough to finance a FREE blow-out mountain lunch?

ALPINE ANSWERS use over twenty years of ski holiday planning to offer the ultimate chalet & hotel collection across the world's best ski resorts.

To find out more and register for the discount simply go to our online form at: www.bit.ly/wtss-aa

Call: **020 7801 1080**
www.alpineanswers.co.uk

 ATOL NO. 4791

 ABTA NO. D4050

New gear for 2015

Skis, boots and other gear that have impressed us

by **Dave Watts**

There is lots of good gear out there to help you enjoy your skiing holiday more. This year we've tested next season's new skis but also some boots, goggles and an aid to help you ski better. Here we report on the stuff we liked, and plan to use.

EDITOR WATTS TRACKS DOWN THE TOP SKIS

Last March I went on a week-long test of the new skis for 2014/15 in Kühtai, at 2020m one of Austria's highest resorts. The test was organized by the trade body Snowsports Industries of Great Britain, and there were almost 800 pairs of skis available.

There were some exciting new developments – especially in the all-mountain category, aimed at people who want to ski both on- and off-piste. I'd advise anyone who fancies even a dabble in ungroomed terrain between pistes to go for an all-mountain ski because, in general, they work just as well as piste skis on groomed runs but are more versatile.

Salomon has a new range of all-mountain skis called the X-Drive, which did well in our test and replaces the Enduro range. They come in widths from 75mm to 88mm underfoot – I now feel uncomfortable

↑ Almost 800 pairs of skis from 19 different brands were available to test at the 2014 UK industry ski test in Kühtai in Austria

DAVE WATTS

skiing anything less than 80mm and loved the X-Drive 80Ti and X-Drive 8.8FS, which both work well on-piste and in the powder and crud. Rossignol has extended its Air Tip technology (which makes the ski lighter and easier to ski) to its all-mountain Experience range. It also looks great, with a glimmering honeycomb section at the tips of the skis. The Experience 84 and 88 were two of my favourite skis on the test. Dynastar has a new Powertrack range of all-mountain skis, Blizzard a new X-Power range replacing its Magnum skis, and Nordica an NRGY range varying from 80mm to 100mm underfoot – I thought the 90 was superb and excellent on- as well as off-piste, despite its width.

In the other ski categories, Rossignol has a new range of Hero race skis and Volkl has revamped its hugely successful Mantra freeride ski. Women-specific skis were on the test in abundance, and our women testers particularly liked the Volkl range across the board. Head has a complete new Joy range of women's skis covering all the ski categories and with names such as Total Joy (all-mountain) and Big Joy (big mountain). It claims the skis are super-light due to use of a crystal called graphene, which is also 'the strongest material on the planet' – it seems to work, as they did well in the test. K2 has a complete new range of Potion all-mountain skis ranging from 74mm to 84mm underfoot, which also did well.

BOOTS THAT MOULD TO YOUR FEET

In our new gear chapter last year, we featured Salomon's Max Custom Shell boots, where both the shell and inner boot are heated and moulded to your foot. Avid readers will know that I got a pair for the 2012/13 season and loved them. It had always taken me a couple of seasons to get new boots to the stage of being really comfortable. But these were amazingly so from day one – no pain or pressure points at all. And the lateral support and stability around the ankle and lower shin was extraordinarily firm. That meant that when I rolled my ankle to edge the ski the transmission felt very precise and powerful. This season they felt just the same and even during two-hour lunches that Editor Gill insists on, it doesn't occur to me to unclip them, they are so comfortable. This season Atomic is introducing a similar concept (called Memoryfit) to some of its boots, including its Hawx range, which was my boot of choice before the Salomons came along.

POLES AND GOGGLES THAT MAKE LIFE EASIER

Leki Trigger S ski poles do away with conventional straps. Instead, your hand attaches to the pole using a loop between your thumb and forefinger which clicks in to a mechanism on the ski pole. A strap with the loop on comes with the pole and you wear it on your glove. Or you can buy a special Leki ski glove with a loop built in. The most important advantage is that it releases just like a ski binding if you have an accident. With conventional straps the pole might not come off and an injury could result. And, of course, you don't have the faff of threading your hands through straps – you just click in and press a button to release.

MAXIMUM SECURITY
HIGHEST COMFORT
PURE JOY

TRIGGER S

✔ PATENDED TECHNOLOGY
✔ THE FIRST SECURITY SKI BINDING IN A SKI POLE
✔ PERFECT COMFORT
✔ GREAT POWER TRANSMISSION

LEKI UK f
WWW.LEKI.DE
PHONE NUMBER 01250 873863

I wear specs, can't see much without them and can't get on with contact lenses. I've tried everything bar laser surgery for a hassle-free way of seeing while skiing. Fine days and cold snowy days are trouble-free. It's those warmer days when it's misty or wet snow is falling that are the problem. Put the goggles over the specs and pretty soon the spec lenses fog up. The best solution I have found are Smith Turbo goggles with a battery operated fan – the fan keeps the air circulating and the lenses fog-free, except in really muggy conditions, which are fairly rare. I've tried goggles with prescription lens inserts before but they've fogged up too. So I was dubious when a company new to the ski goggle market asked me to try a pair of their goggles with inserts. Near the end of the season, I found a perfect day to test them – it was so muggy that my Turbos were misting up. So I tried the Sportviz goggle instead, fully expecting them to mist up within minutes. But two hours later they were still giving perfect visibility. The lenses I used were coated with a special anti-fog treatment that they say should last for at least 12 months; I'll let you know next year what happened after that; you cannot get them retreated but you can use standard anti-fog sprays and liquids. See www.sportviz.com.

↑ Editor Watts wearing the Sportviz goggles with prescription inserts that didn't fog up even on a muggy day

SNOWPIX.COM / CHRIS GILL

FIND YOUR SWEET SPOT

Last year at the Kühtai ski test I also tried SkiA's new Sweetspot Ski Trainer – designed to help you improve your balance. I now have a set to use at home. When you are skiing, your centre of balance should be near the centre of the arch of your foot not, as many people think, on the balls of your feet. The idea is that the trainer gets you used to balancing correctly, and you then try to replicate the same feeling whenever you are skiing.

The trainer comes with blocks that you fix under the centre of your ski boots. You then try to balance on them on a hard surface while making various movements such as bending, stretching and tilting your legs as if edging. It is surprisingly difficult at first, but when you are in balance you can certainly feel the sweet spot. There are four pairs of blocks; you start with the widest and move on to progressively narrower ones. The trainer comes with special exercises designed by Hugh Monney, founder of the British Alpine Ski School – who highly recommends it, as do other leading instructors, race coaches and competitors – including Britain's best-ever Olympic downhiller Martin Bell and current UK skicross racer Emily Sarsfield. Go to www.skia.com for more details.

(SKIA)
Get Ready, Get Set, Go Skiing
Train Anywhere, FAST

Emily Sarsfield, UK #1 Ski Cross

skia.com

Making the most of a quick snow-fix

MOMENTUM SKI

Weekend
and a la carte
ski holiday
specialists

100%
Tailor-Made

Premier
hotels and
apartments

Flexible
travel
arrangements

020 7371 9111
WWW.MOMENTUMSKI.COM

Short break trips to the Alps can give you three refreshing days on the snow and leave you with the feeling of having been away for ages. We love them and frequently take them. Whether you travel independently or as part of a package, short-stay trips are easier to arrange now; the choice of airlines, destination airports and onward transfers is wider than ever. Midweek trips can be even better than weekends: cheaper deals and, depending on the resort, perhaps quieter slopes.

With just a few days to enjoy, you'll need to plan your short break carefully; but that's all part of the fun. We sum up the options here, with a few handy tips to help you to maximize your slope time. Also see our Corporate ski trips chapter on page 61, which gives ideas for fun activities on a short break away.

WHERE SHALL WE GO?
Resorts closest to your arrival airport may seem the obvious starting point, but travelling a bit further can avoid any weekend crowds. You could also try smaller resorts that you might not normally bother with for a week's holiday.

Geneva is the classic gateway to the western Alps, with Chamonix just over an hour away, and other major French resorts such as Megève, Flaine and Morzine close by. Allow extra time for the Trois Vallées and Tarentaise resorts. You could also head into Switzerland and visit Villars or Verbier, or try the new (for 2013/14) link between Grimentz and Zinal in Val d'Anniviers.

In Italy, Turin is an underused alternative approach to the Aosta valley, with Courmayeur, Champoluc and La Thuile conveniently reached; Sauze d'Oulx and Montgenèvre in the Milky Way are even nearer.

Further east, in Switzerland, Engelberg and Andermatt are popular options easily accessible from Zürich. So is St Anton. Also in Austria, Innsbruck allows you to combine a city break with doorstep skiing. There are lots of resorts surrounding the city, and the Stubai valley with its reliable glacier is nearby. Similarly Salzburg has lots of resorts within an hour or two.

The Pyrenees offer short-break opportunities too: flights into Pau (where we flew to for two days' skiing recently) and Lourdes put you close to Cauterets, Barèges-La Mongie, Peyragudes and St-Lary-Soulan. And for a budget break, you could explore Slovenia very cheaply, with flights to Ljubljana – the nearest ski area is just 8km from the airport.

ski²

www.ski-weekends.com

• Book your own low cost flights, but all of our prices include transfers to resort

• Arrive on any day of the week and stay for any number of nights

• Short transfer times

• Choice of hotels to suit all budgets

• Friendly, personal service

• Exclusive access to the Ski 2 nursery and ski school

**Visit our comprehensive website,
call us on 01962 713330
or email us at sales@ski-2.com**

ABTA
The Travel Association

Alpine Weekends

Weekend ski trips, corporate events and flexible skiing holidays

020 8944 9762

www.alpineweekends.com

STC Ski

Specialists in Tailor-Made Short Breaks & Holidays

01483 771 222
www.stcski.co.uk
ski@stcski.co.uk

Discover the difference with SkiWeekends

#loveski

Prices from **£200**

skiweekends.com

WHERE TO STAY?

The range of short-stay accommodation is improving, but can still be limited in some major resorts – places such as Chamonix, Crans-Montana and Morzine, with big summer or conference business, are easier. From Salzburg or Innsbruck you could take the daily shuttles to different resorts. If you have a rental car, valley towns such as Chur, Sion and Interlaken in Switzerland, Aosta in Italy, Moûtiers and Bourg-St-Maurice in France and Radstadt in Austria are cheaper bases from which you can visit different resorts nearby.

PRICING THE OPTIONS

Costs vary enormously. Tour operators have special deals with hotels and can organize the essentials to save you time.

Around 50% of Ski 2's business is short breaks to Champoluc in Italy's Monterosa ski area. Three nights' B&B in a 3-star hotel, transfers from any of six airports within striking distance (meeting any flight), a three-day lift pass, first-day guiding and lunches costs from £494 (£506 for a half-board package); you book your own flights. Stanford Skiing offers three- and four-night stays in catered chalets or self-catered apartments in Megève; prices for a catered chalet are from £310 excluding flights and transfers.

Ski Weekend is the original short-break ski specialist. A four-night B&B package to Chamonix including flights and transfers costs from £400. Don't confuse them with Skiweekends.com, which offers overnight coach travel or flight options – a four-night half-board coach package (including two nights on the coach) to Brides-les-Bains (for Méribel) giving three days of skiing costs from £200. Momentum offers flights, car hire and three nights' B&B in a 3-star hotel in Courmayeur from £399. STC Ski says three nights half-board in a Kirchberg 3-star including flights and transfers costs from £345. These companies and Alpine Weekends will tailor-make short breaks to many resorts.

TIPS FOR THE TRIP

Unless booking at short notice, avoid low resorts (where snow may be unreliable) and high, treeless resorts (where slopes may close in bad weather). Go for early or late flights to get the most slope time, but note that Sunday evening traffic can be horrendous with locals going home. Book a transfer or rental car in advance and choose a different car hire company from the one your airline promotes to avoid queuing with others from your flight. Taxis are generally very expensive, and public transport is rarely convenient (though Switzerland has good rail links). Rather than take your skis/board, consider renting: most airlines charge hefty carriage fees.

Ski Weekend

the ultimate short break

we are the original short break ski specialists

over **25** years

01392 878 353
www.skiweekend.com

Stanford Skiing

Megève Specialists

huge ski area
close to Geneva
short breaks
chalets & hotels

family run - friendly knowledgeable staff

01603 477471

www.stanfordskiing.co.uk

by **Dave Watts** | The catered chalet holiday is a uniquely British idea. The deal, in case you're new to it, is that tour operators install their own cooks and housekeepers in chalets for the season and provide half-board plus teatime cake and, usually, travel from the UK. So you get the privacy and relaxed atmosphere of a temporary home in the mountains, without the hassle of self-catering or the cost of eating out in restaurants every night. In the beginning, in the 1960s and 70s, chalet holidays meant creaky old buildings with spartan furniture and paper-thin walls. My, how things have changed. When we first visited Méribel in 1974, en-suite bathrooms were unheard of. They are now the norm. Spacious and plush living rooms with log fires are common (but spacious and plush bedrooms are less so). Spa facilities such as a sauna, steam room and hot tub are common too; some chalets even have a swimming pool. And all at prices we ordinary mortals can contemplate paying. It's these chalets that this chapter is about.

↑ Spacious and comfortable living rooms are the norm in top chalets – this is Ski Olympic's Parc Alpin in Méribel

SKI OLYMPIC

Ski Expectations
01799 531888
skiexpectations.com

ski EXPECTATIONS

Europe's Top Resorts,
the USA, & Canada

Because of the huge number of chalet holidays available, choosing the right one can be difficult. Some very helpful websites have been set up by agents, allowing you to sift out chalets that suit you best; some advertise in this chapter and elsewhere in the book.

45

The greatest concentration of smart chalets is found – surprise, surprise – in **Méribel**. Ski Total has a wide range of properties here, including two with the firm's top Platinum rating; they have hot tubs, of course – and a cinema and billiard room in the case of chalet Isba. Purple Ski has five top-notch and highly individual chalets – in good positions, with lovely interiors and outdoor hot tubs. Ski Olympic runs the Parc Alpin, formerly a boutique hotel, as a very smart chalet hotel – 12 luxurious rooms with plasma TVs, dinky swimming pool and sauna. Skiworld has the swish Laetitia with hot tub, sauna and cinema room. Other companies to consider include Consensio, Meriski and VIP.

Over the hill is **Courchevel**, a resort of parts (it has recently renamed these parts but we are using the old names – see p241). 1850 is well established as the 'smartest' resort in France, with the highest prices and the swankiest hotels and chalets. Supertravel has five lovely luxurious chalets here including their flagship Montana, right on the main piste, built with reclaimed ancient timbers and with a split-level living/dining room and a mini wellness centre with steam room, hot tub and monsoon shower. Other operators such as Kaluma, Consensio and Scott Dunn also have lovely chalets here, and Ski Total has some bordering on the luxury category.

The big UK chalet centre is 1650, where Le Ski now has 18 chalets, sleeping from 2 to 22; 13 of them have sauna, steam or hot tub. And their flagship Scalottas Lodge has five apartment chalets

SKI AMIS

Catered Chalets
in Superb
Locations

020 3411 5439
www.skiamis.com

LUXURY
SKI CHALETS

www.luxury-ski-chalets.co.uk
sales@luxury-ski-chalets.co.uk
020 3080 0231

with fabulous views, leather armchairs and sofas, solid wooden floors and hi-tech lights and heating. One of Ski Olympic's flagship Gold Collection chalets is here – Monique, with TVs in the bedrooms, an outdoor hot tub and a free bar from 4.30 to 9.30pm. Skiworld has some smart-looking chalets too – the 21-bed Estrella is one of its best, with outdoor hot tub. Down in Le Praz, Mountain Heaven has three chalets, including the adjoining Emilie (with traditional exterior but cutting-edge style within) and Jardin d'Angele (cosily traditional and we had a comfortable stay there last season); they share a sauna, steam room and outdoor hot tub.

In **La Tania**, not far away off the road towards Méribel, Ski Amis has seven smart-looking places, all but one with outdoor hot tub and some with its Premium service.

In **Les Menuires** there are smart places on offer in the recently developed areas. In Reberty, Powder N Shine has three lovely looking chalets, all with indoor hot tub and sauna and one with an outdoor hot tub too – they pride themselves on the quality of their food and all three have chefs who have worked in Michelin-starred restaurants; Ski Olympic has four chalets here with saunas and hot tubs. Ski Amis has several chalets with outdoor hot tubs in Les Bruyères and others with hot tubs and saunas in Le Bettex. And in **St-Martin** the Alpine Club has two luxurious chalets in the quiet hamlet of Villarabout, one newly built in traditional style with a double-height, open-plan living room and the other a beautiful 100-year-old farmhouse with spectacular views.

Val d'Isère is the great rival to Méribel in the French chalet business. The local specialist, YSE, has several very swish places. Le Ski's chalet Angelique, in a back street of La Daille, is very different to the norm: inside it looks more like a mini stately home than a chalet (and has a steam room and gym); next door and new for 2014/15 is Vieille Maison, which dates from the 18th century and is being totally refurbished for the coming season. Skiworld's 11 chalets include two of their top properties: Tolima, with sauna, and Madeleine, with outdoor hot tub. Ski Total has 14 smart places, including two very swanky ones in their Platinum range (one with outdoor hot tub, one with a sauna). Crystal's range includes three of its Finest properties, with saunas. And Inghams has a flagship 24-bed chalet hotel with sauna, steam and hot tub in Le Fornet. Other companies to look at include Scott Dunn and Consensio.

In **Tignes** Skiworld's programme includes some chalets with sauna and hot tub, and a swanky chalet hotel with pool and sauna. Ski Total has some very smart places, lots with outdoor hot tub and sauna, some with pool and two in their top-of-the-market Platinum range. Snowchateaux's chalet Chardon used to be Robert Maxwell's private apartment and has a large living room with floor-to-ceiling windows with great views; and it has an outdoor hot tub. Crystal and Inghams have some smart chalets too.

The other great French mega-area, Paradiski, offers lots of chalets in **La Plagne** and growing numbers at **Peisey-Vallandry**, on the Les Arcs side of the cable car from La Plagne. Few chalets stand out, but Ski Amis has a Premium service chalet in each of these resorts.

There are lots of chalets in **La Rosière**, but few notable ones. Mountain Heaven has two in its Premium range here, both with outdoor hot tubs: we stayed in the splendid Penthouse last season and loved the huge living room with floor-to-ceiling windows and great views; the renovated farm-style Chez Robert is just 30m from the lifts. Ski Olympic has two chalet apartments in a building with pool, sauna, steam room and hot tub. Crystal has a couple of places in its Finest programme with access to sauna and outdoor hot tub.

Chalets are not common in **Avoriaz**, so it's good to see that Ski Total's handful includes one of its Platinum chalets, with sauna and log fire. In **Alpe-d'Huez**, Ski Total, Skiworld and Inghams all have smart places with outdoor hot tubs.

In Austria, **St Anton** is chalet central. Supertravel has eight smart-looking chalets including three apartments newly built for last season, that share an outdoor pool, sauna and steam room. Skiworld's flagship Monte Vera has huge bedrooms, sauna and infra-red room. Many of Ski Total's dozen chalets have saunas but none qualify for its top Platinum rating. Crystal has three of its Finest chalets here, including the cool 32-bed Inge, with wellness area and fabulous views. Inghams' programme includes four chalets in a stylish new building in the Gastig area, with shared spa and

Do you long for a sauna in your chalet, or perhaps your own exclusive pool?

⊕ABTA

THE CHALET SPECIALIST

Ski Total

● Catered chalets serving 4 or 5 course dinners with quality complimentary wine
● 75% of chalets with either hot-tub, sauna, steam room or swimming pool
● 18 premier resorts in Austria, France and Italy
● Flights from 9 regional airports across the UK

Tel: **01483 791933**   Book online at **skitotal.com**

Build your own shortlist: **www.wheretoskiandsnowboard.com**

↑ Is this a stately home in Berkshire? No, it's Le Ski's chalet Angelique in Val d'Isère

LE SKI

pool, and, just over the hill in St Christoph, its flagship chalet hotel – ski-in/ski-out, with a sauna, good-sized pool and fab food when we stayed last season. Ski Total has three smart chalet hotels (all with saunas, one with a pool) in nearby Lech. Others operators to look at are Flexiski, Kaluma and Scott Dunn.

Italy has never had a chalet in our luxury category, but this season Ski Total has taken over our favourite 4-star hotel in **Champoluc** and will be running it as a chalet hotel. It is full of lovely wood beams and ceilings and has sauna, steam and hot tub. We can't wait to give it a try in its new guise.

In Switzerland, most of the larger (and lower cost) companies have pulled out of running chalets because of changes in the minimum wage legislation – see the 'Editorial' on page 13. But pricier plush chalets are still available, though, for example Ski Verbier in, er, **Verbier** and Supertravel (which has a handful of smart places sharing a pool and sauna in the same building) in **Zermatt**. VIP also has a couple of places in both. In cute little **Grimentz** (see our Val d'Anniviers chapter), Mountain Heaven has some smart chalets that can be booked catered or self-catered.

There are very few catered chalets in North America but Skiworld has a couple of good ones in both **Breckenridge** and **Vail**.

Powder ☆ *Shine*
Delicious Alpine Catered Chalets

Award Winning
Owner Run Catered Chalets
Les 3 vallées

tripadvisor
2014 Winner
Certificate of Excellence

☎ 0845 163 7596
www.powdernshine.com
REBERTY VILLAGE 2000M, THREE VALLEYS

AWARD-WINNING
SKI
HOLIDAYS
Ski Olympic

book online at *skiolympic.com*
or call **01302 328 820**

ABTA
V2289

Smart apartments

Enjoy full independence in comfortable surroundings

by **Dave Watts**

Apartment holidays used to be the budget option for most people – at least on holidays to France. Shoehorn six people into a studio advertised for six and you'd have a cheap but not very comfortable time. Now things have changed, especially in France where lots of plush new apartment blocks ('residences', as the French say – sounds so much better) have been built in recent years. Most have dishwashers, and many share a pool, sauna, steam room and gym to add to the pampering. Some even have comfortable furniture to relax in, too. Sure, the budget option still exists, but now you can have a comfortable apartment holiday with all the other advantages that it brings (see below). We've looked for smart apartments to recommend throughout the Alps and have included them in the resort chapters.

I've been taking my annual ski holiday with my wife and a couple of friends in apartments for over 25 years. That's because we value the freedom an apartment gives you. You don't have to stick to meal times (and meals) dictated by the hotel or chalet staff and you can slob around in whatever clothes you want. And, crucially in our case, you are free to have a big lunch up the mountain without worrying about having to eat a huge half-board meal in the evening; if you don't want a big dinner, you can buy snacks such as oysters, smoked salmon, pâté and local cheeses along with a good bottle of wine or two from the supermarket. If you are hungry, you can go out to a restaurant to eat. Staying in an apartment doesn't mean having to cook big meals – not for us anyway.

When we started this apartment lark, we couldn't find the sort of thing we were looking for in tour operators' brochures (there were no web sites to browse in those days) – all the apartments were of the 'cram 'em in and make it cheap' variety. So we ended up booking independently. Now, at least in France – the country that used to have the smallest, most sordid apartments – a few tour operators (including those advertising in this chapter) offer some

49

SKI COLLECTION

Most smart apartment residences have pools, saunas, steam rooms and even gyms. This is Edenarc, above Arc 1800 →

★★★★
apartments
inc. Wifi,
pools & spa

0844 576 0173
peakretreats.co.uk

ABTA
ABTA No. W5537

peak retreats

Heavenly
Skiing...
at down to earth prices

mh
Mountain Heaven

· Superb catered & self catered accommodation ·
· Great ski areas in the French & Swiss Alps ·
· Snow secure resorts · We only have on/near piste locations ·
· Fantastic prices & no hidden extras ·

0151 625 1921
www.mountainheaven.co.uk

really smart places, mostly with leisure facilities such as pools, saunas and steam rooms. Some even have big reception areas and restaurants, just like hotels (though we'd prefer them to give the rooms more space and reception less).

The French smart apartment concept was kick-started by places built by MGM. They now have 26 4-star residences in the Alps, managed by their sister company CGH and are the biggest provider of smart apartments. Their newest development is Kalinda Village at Tignes 1800 and they have a residence opening in Valmorel in December 2014. Montagnettes was another pioneer of the concept. Now these two have been joined by other brands. PV Holidays launched its Pierre & Vacances Premium brand a few winters ago, and it now features 13 residences in 11 French resorts. Lagrange has 17 Alpine and six Pyrenean residences in its Prestige range.

So why the big change? Xavier Schouller of Peak Retreats, Ski Collection and Pyrenees Collection, which specialize in selling plush apartment holidays in French ski resorts, says, 'A lot of smart new residences have been built recently because of tax breaks for people buying them – you get the VAT back if you agree to rent them out for several years, and French residents can set costs against income tax too. This is good news for people wanting to rent an apartment for a holiday – we now have over 200 residences on our books.' Xavier's favourite residences are Ski Collection's Le Centaure in Flaine and Koh-i Nor in Val Thorens and Peak Retreats' Kalinda Village in Tignes 1800.

Erna Low sells a lot of apartment holidays too and their managing director Jane Bolton says, 'We have been selling self-catering holidays for over 20 years. The widest selection is still found in France, where we now have hundreds of residences to choose from, but we also have spacious, comfortable apartments available in Switzerland, Austria, Italy, the US and Canada.'

Ski Amis is best known as a catered chalet company, but it has moved into apartments in a big way. Instead of offering big residences such as the companies mentioned above do, it offers mostly privately owned apartments and chalets, mainly in the

SKI COLLECTION
We often find the rooms a little smaller than we'd like – note the sliding door on the bedroom to save space. This is Le Hameau du Kashmir in Val Thorens ↓

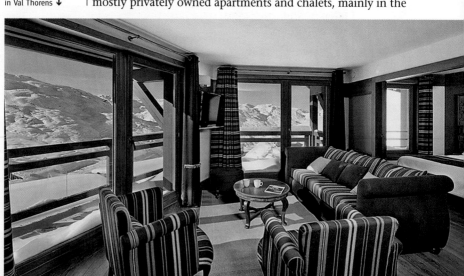

Some residences are more like hotels, with big, plush reception areas and a restaurant. This is Le Hameau du Kashmir in Val Thorens →

SKI COLLECTION

LAGRANGE Prestige

High-standard Self-catering Apartments

020 7371 6111
lagrange-holidays.co.uk

Tarentaise, which includes the Trois Vallées, Paradiski and Espace Killy resorts. Mountain Heaven, which also does catered chalets, has some smart apartments in Tarentaise resorts and in Grimentz in Switzerland. Or you can rent independently; as well as contacting local rental agencies there are some good websites to try, such as www.holidaylettings.co.uk and www.homeaway.co.uk.

WHAT TO CHECK BEFORE BOOKING

So what do you need to look for if you're booking what you hope is a smart apartment? Most importantly, you still need to check whether the space is enough to meet your expectations – and whether the number it's advertised for involves anyone sleeping in the living room, in bunk beds, on a mezzanine or in a cabin (which can mean an alcove). Also check the number of bathrooms and toilets. If the leisure facilities such as a pool, sauna, steam room and gym are important to you, check whether there is a charge for using these; sadly, there often is. And while most smart apartments come with a modern design, dishwasher and smartish furniture, we're sometimes disappointed by the lack of really comfy sofas and easy chairs (often because sofas double up as beds and are comfier to sleep in than sit on), by the size of the living rooms and, especially, the bedrooms, and by the lack of storage space – so if those are important to you, check them too.

Smart apartments

51

Tailored
SKI HOLIDAYS
TO FRANCE
★★★★
4-star apartments
with doorstep skiing
free wifi & spa

Accommodation only or self-drive packages
Call our experts on **0844 576 0175**
⊕ABTA
ABTA No.W5537
SkiCollection.co.uk

Build your own shortlist: www.wheretoskiandsnowboard.com

A contradiction in terms?

by **Chris Gill**

Thinking of taking the children skiing? You must be mad; pack them off to their granny for the week. If you take them with you, you'll immediately double the already high costs of a ski holiday, at the same time halving the amount of skiing you get. And ahead will stretch an ever-increasing financial burden, while the brats' skiing skills will rapidly put your own to shame.

If that's the kind of advice you welcome, you've probably had the sense to avoid child-rearing altogether. Having children is, after all, largely about making sacrifices that rationally are difficult to justify. If you've had kids, and you're skiers, you'll probably want to take them skiing if a way can be found to do it.

If that introduction seems curiously familiar, you must be a faithful reader with an excellent memory. In this 20th anniversary edition, I thought I would allow myself to revisit my first attempt to tackle the choices that parents face, published 15 years ago in *Where to Ski and Snowboard 2000*, starting with the original introduction reproduced above.

I'll offer some pointers, just as I did back then, to resorts to consider and tour operators you might go with. But I start by suggesting that you first of all get clear what stage(s) of childhood your offspring have reached; obviously, the help you'll need in looking after them during your trip will depend on that.

ESPRIT Ski
No.1 For Family Skiing

SAVE UP TO £920 PER FAMILY
with our Esprit Family Savers

13 TOP RESORTS in France, Austria and Italy

★ **We focus 100% on families**, guaranteeing complete dedication to family needs
★ **Dedicated Esprit Nurseries** with qualified English-speaking nannies
★ **Exclusive Children's Ski Classes** with max. 8 children to one instructor
★ **FREE evening Baby-Listening / Child Patrol Service** available
★ **Strict child care ratios** and procedures based on our 32 years' child care experience
★ **Catered chalets & Chalet Hotels**, specially for families
★ **Flights from 8 regional airports** across the UK

★ **NEW Baby And Toddler Weeks**

☻ **FREE infant places** saving £115
☻ **Half-price Nursery Places** saving £157
☻ **Half-price Skiing & Day Care for toddlers** saving £207
☻ **BAT-Weeks** run on 11, 18, 25 Jan, 1 & 22 Feb

Call **01483 791 900**
visit **espritski.com**

ABTA
The Travel Association
V4871

AWARD-WINNING

SKI
HOLIDAYS

Ski Olympic

book online at
skiolympic.com
01302 328 820

A PERSPECTIVE: THE SEVEN AGES

BABE IN ARMS You can leave babies with anyone who can attend to their immediate needs; fluent English is not necessary. So resort nurseries are well worth looking into, although it's doubtless less stressful to hand over your precious bundle to a British nanny employed by your tour operator.

TODDLER You can arrange to put your darling on skis, but what's the point unless she is going to get regular opportunities to repeat the experience? Would it be more for your gratification than hers? Entrust her to an English-speaking nursery with some outdoor on-snow play facilities.

INFANTS If she takes to it, she can have fun on skis, zooming around your resort's 'snow garden' and learning to ski in the process. I wouldn't want to put you off taking that route, but if your child lacks resilience you may take the view that skiing can be left to the next stage, and that the priority at this stage is just having fun in the company of other British kids.

JUNIORS My experience has supported the view that children who get taken to the mountains once a year are most likely to make good progress on skis once they are able to apply themselves and have the resilience to overcome hurdles – at or about the age of seven. Ski school tuition or diy parental guidance? We used both, although our kids protested at going to school while on holiday.

Snowbizz
The Family Ski Specialist

* Highly Rated Exclusive Ski School
* In House Private Nursery
* Doorstep Skiing
* Family Run for 28 Years
* Competitive Prices
* Flights from Gatwick Stansted and Manchester

01778 341 455
sales@snowbizz.co.uk · www.snowbizz.co.uk
ABTA V1411 - ATOL 2463 - AITO

Family holidays

53

Build your own shortlist: **www.wheretoskiandsnowboard.com**

Family Ski™

Perfect family skiing holidays
in high quality ski chalets with
outstanding childcare

+44 (0) 1684 540 333
www.familyski.co.uk
Designed with the family in mind

ABTOT
The Association of Bonded
Travel Organisers Trust Ltd

The catered chalet holiday is as popular as ever, especially with families. Since en-suite bathrooms and comfy sofas became the norm rather than the exception, the attractions of the chalet – more private and less formal than hotels – have increased considerably. Now, more people are discovering the merits of the chalet's bigger cousin, the chalet hotel.

Chalet operators have for years set the pace in childcare. It was a natural extension of hiring British gels as cooks and housekeepers to hire a few as nannies, too; then all the operator had to do was identify a suitable room in a suitable chalet, and bingo – a crèche was born. For British parents unable to handle the brutality of French nurseries, the chalet was the obvious solution.

Chalet hotels are a larger version of the same thing, with some additional advantages. Some are purpose-built, but usually they are based in buildings that have operated as proper hotels. As a result, bedrooms typically are more generous than in chalets. Facilities are often better – there is likely to be a bar (with prices below resort norms, if you're lucky), and there may be a swimming pool, spa or gym, for example. There may be a menu choice at dinner.

Two of the most long-established tour operator firms dominate the family chalet hotel market. Esprit Ski was the original family chalet specialist; its programme is still dominated by standard chalets – in total over 50 – but it now also includes seven chalet hotels – five in major French resorts plus one in Gressoney (Monterosa, Italy). Mark Warner specializes in chalet hotels, and has crèches in most (but not all) properties. The editorial Gill family took several successful holidays with these firms in the days when the kids were small.

Strikingly, these firms major on top resorts. They both have chalet hotels with childcare in Méribel, Val d'Isère and La Plagne. Esprit's flagship is the super-cool Deux Domaines at Belle-Plagne, which has a decent pool and spa – young children are not allowed in the latter – and a good ski-in/ski-out location on the lower edge of the village. The other Esprit resorts in France are Alpe-d'Huez and Courchevel. Mark Warner also has family-oriented properties in Tignes and Les Deux-Alpes, and in St Anton and Zell am See in Austria.

Ski Famille

EXCLUSIVE - à la carte Child Care

With 23 years experience arranging holidays "en famille" we know exactly what skiing parents and children need and want.

- Child Care (babies to 12 year olds) in the comfort of your own chalet. No snowy trudge or bus ride to a central crèche; just put on your skis and leave the rest to us
- Superb facilities and stimulating activities for children of all ages
- Fully qualified nannies
- Ski school drop off and pick up service
- High quality chalets in superb locations, many with a hot tub, sauna or steam room
- Delicious food, complimentary wines and attentive service
- Many free child places

Call to book: **01252 365 495**
www.skifamille.co.uk
ATOL 10863 ABTOT 5141

IMPROVER Once the child has found her skiing feet the theory would be that it really is time to hand her over to the professionals in the ski school. Obvious requirements: good spoken English, small class sizes, lunchtime care. Less obvious considerations: arrangements for getting the child to and from the school, and for care when lessons are over but you are still bashing the pistes. The services of tour operators can be invaluable here.

REAL SKIER Once your child can keep up, you'll be off round the Trois Vallées together, and the whole project will start to pay off. But don't drop the ski school lessons altogether.

EXPERT Find a mogul field above a restaurant terrace, where you can sit in comfort and watch her bounce down the hill.

WHERE TO GO
My own rules, developed over many years, were:
• avoid resorts where there is a lot of schlepping around from one place to another, on foot or in buses
• don't worry about finding a perfect resort – the resort is only part of the holiday mix, and other components matter just as much
• but make sure the resort suits you as well as the children
• remember that amusement after the lifts close is a key factor – whether it's sledging, skating, swimming, whatever
• an absence of traffic around your lodgings is a great help.

WHO TO GO WITH
The firms advertising in this chapter are mostly small, specialized companies going to a small range of resorts that they know inside out (only one resort, in the case of Ski 2). They are basically owner-

The family ski specialists to the fabulous Monterosa ski area

• Traditional Italian alpine resort

• Our own nursery run by fully qualified British staff

• 'Family-friendly' accommodation

• Short transfer from airport to resort

• Friendly, helpful resort staff

• British, B.A.S.I. qualified ski instructors

• Child and group discounts

www.familyskiholidays.co.uk

Visit our comprehensive website, call us on 01962 713330 or email us at sales@ski-2.com

ABTA
The Travel Association

AWARD-WINNING

SKI

HOLIDAYS

Ski Olympic

book online at skiolympic.com or call 01302 328 820

ABTA
V2289

operated, so you can expect them to be very responsive. Most operate catered chalets, where you share a house or a flat with others (you can of course take the others with you if you wish).

Esprit Ski is a bit different: a chalet operator on a much bigger scale – it's one of the biggest ski holiday operators in the UK, in fact – offering chalets in 10 French resorts plus a few others elsewhere.

These operators provide a range of childcare options, geared to the different stages of childhood I've been talking about – ideally taking care of the après-ski session and providing an early evening meal for the younger ones. Don't forget that there are mainstream operators such as Crystal that operate childcare in some of the many resorts where they sell holidays.

The list on the right shows who goes to which resorts; it covers the advertisers in this chapter and one or two others, to give you an idea of your options. Note that some of the smaller operators don't have full childcare facilities in every chalet or even every resort.

WHO GOES WHERE?

Austria Obergurgl Esprit Ski.
Niederau Crystal. **St Anton** Esprit Ski.

France Alpe-d'Huez Esprit Ski. **Les Arcs** Esprit Ski, Ski Amis. **Ardent** (Avoriaz) Family Ski. **Les Coches** (La Plagne) Family Ski. **Courchevel** Esprit Ski, Ski Amis, Ski Olympic. **Les Gets** Esprit Ski, Ski Famille. **Les Menuires** Family Ski, Ski Amis, Ski Famille, Ski Olympic. **Méribel** Esprit Ski, Ski Amis, Ski Olympic. **Peisey-Vallandry** (Les Arcs) Esprit Ski, Ski Amis, Ski Olympic. **La Plagne** Crystal, Esprit Ski, Ski Amis, Ski Famille, Ski Olympic. **Puy-St-Vincent** Snowbizz. **La Rosière** Esprit Ski, Ski Olympic. **St-Martin-de-Belleville** Ski Amis. **La Tania** Le Ski, Ski Amis. **Tignes** Crystal, Esprit Ski, Ski Amis. **Val d'Isère** Esprit Ski, Ski Amis, Ski Olympic. **Val Thorens** Ski Amis.

Italy Canazei Crystal. **Champoluc** Ski 2. **Claviere** Crystal. **Gressoney** Esprit Ski. **Val di Fassa** Crystal.

Slovenia Kranjska Gora Crystal.

Inspirational ski race training for youngsters in Champoluc, Italy

- Race training for 1 to 12 weeks for youngsters, aged 8 to 12

- Learn the very best in proven Italian race techniques

- Comprehensive and structured education programme

- Unrivalled resort infrastructure

- Flexible travel arrangements and good quality accommodation

www.ski2racing.com
Visit our comprehensive website, call us on 01962 713330 or email us at info@ski-2.com

SKI 2 RACING – COACHING FOR YOUR KIDS?

The success of Ryan, Alysha and Charlotte Brown (the children of Ski 2 director Simon Brown) in ski races across Europe is testimony to the expertise of their Italian race coaches.

Ski 2 can now offer other youngsters the chance to benefit from the same training routine, while continuing their schooling in Champoluc.

Children joining the Ski 2 Racing programme spend their mornings race training with local coaches and their afternoons furthering their education with two fully trained English teachers. 'House parents' supervise the youngsters at other times, and the Ski 2 resort team offer any other support and guidance the youngsters might need.

Accommodation is in the family-run 3-star Hotel Petit Prince, which offers doorstep skiing at the ski area of Antagnod, close to Champoluc.

Prices – including everything except flights – start at around £1,200 per week, with reductions for longer stays. Short courses are now also available for children holidaying with Ski 2.

Buying property

by **Dave Watts**

Buying a place in a ski resort is an ambition for lots of keen skiers and snowboarders. Buying in the Alps is more affordable than a year ago because the £ has risen by around 10% against the euro and a bit less against the Swiss franc. Interest rates in Europe are low as well, so getting a mortgage in euros or francs is affordable too.

Simon Malster, managing director of Investors in Property, has been selling property in the Alps for over 25 years. He says: 'We're getting a lot of interest from British buyers at the moment, especially for sale and leaseback properties in the 200,000 to 500,000 euros price range in French resorts.' With these you buy a new-build property and agree to lease it back to the developer or property management company for at least 11 years in return for rental income of, say, 3.5% to 4%, allowing for using it yourself for a couple of weeks. A big advantage of doing this is that you get back 20% VAT charged on the price of new-build properties.

'We are seeing more and more buy-to-let investors buying Alpine property to diversify their portfolio. You can get French mortgages at the moment from around 3.2% fixed for 20 years, so it makes a lot of sense. Many investors also like the idea of getting fun out of their investment by using it themselves,' says Malster. They currently have a ski-in/ski-out development of 124 4-star apartments with communal pool, sauna etc in Les Menuires in the Trois Vallées with a guaranteed rental return of up to 5.2% – prices start at 153,000 euros for a one-bedroom apartment. They also have 5-star apartments for sale right in the middle of Chamonix at the foot of the Aiguille du Midi cable car – two-bedroom apartments here cost from around 500,000 euros.

Malster also has 'some lovely apartments in the centre of Châtel in the Portes du Soleil. These have one to three bedrooms,

Buy with the French Alps specialist

0844 576 0173
peakretreats.co.uk

ABTA
ABTA No. W5537

peak retreats

INVESTORS IN PROPERTY
↓ The Châtel apartments are light and airy with lovely views

↑ The apartments at La Tzoumaz near Verbier, where you are obliged to put them on the rental market when not using them yourself

panoramic views and are light and airy thanks to large picture windows' – prices start at around 360,000 euros for two bedrooms.

Erna Low Property specializes in France and has a sales office in Arc 1950 as well as London. François Marchand, the general manager, says: 'We have some really nice resale properties in Arc 1950. We also have around 30 very high-quality apartments in the lovely old village of Tignes-les-Brévières with excellent spa facilities (the big swimming pool is the size that you would expect in a development of 150 units) – a two-bedroom apartment costs from around 300,000 euros.' At a similar price there are also apartments in the MGM-built/CGH-operated Kalinda Village development at Tignes 1800, just above Tignes-les-Brévières. And there are properties in Les Gets in the Portes du Soleil. Marchand says: 'These are really high-end properties where buyers will be able to have an input into the design and so opt for either a huge living room and two bedrooms or less living space and four bedrooms, say. Prices range from 630,000 to 1.4 million euros.'

SWISS PROPERTIES STILL AVAILABLE

In 2012, the Swiss effectively voted to stop the building of second homes in ski resorts. 'But developments that already had a building permit can still be built,' says Simon Malster of Investors in Property. 'And it seems like new developments may still be permitted, provided the owners rent these properties on a commercial basis,' he adds. They are already selling a ski-in/ski-out development in La Tzoumaz (part of the Verbier ski area) where purchasers are obliged to rent their apartments (when not using them themselves) for 15 years from the date of purchase – prices for two-bedroom apartments start at around 550,000 francs.

Malster adds: 'We are also about to start marketing a huge new development to be built next to the lift at the foot of the Piste de l'Ours (the World Cup race piste) between Les Collons and Veysonnaz. The building permit was given before 2012 so these apartments will be classed as second homes, but a full rental and professional management programme is available if required. We also have some stunning developments in Crans-Montana.'

www.investorsinproperty.com
SKI PROPERTY SPECIALISTS SINCE 1986

We've Got the Alps Covered

Investors in Property are the leading ski property specialists selling ski chalets and apartments in Austria, France and Switzerland. If you are looking to buy a chalet on the slopes, a rental investment or an apartment in a luxury hotel take a look at our website.

Switzerland
- Crans-Montana
- Engelberg
- Grimentz
- Grindelwald
- Saas Fee
- Verbier ski area
- Villars
- Wengen

Austria
- Bad Gastein
- Bramberg
- Ischgl
- Kitzbühel
- Lech
- Saalbach
- Wald
- Zell am See

France
- Chamonix
- Grand Massif
- Les Trois Vallees
- Megeve
- Paradiski
- Portes du Soleil
- Sainte-Foy-Tarentaise
- Val d'Isère and Tignes

www.investorsinproperty.com

↑ The big building on the left contains the apartments for sale in Kappl near Ischgl

INVESTORS IN PROPERTY

AUSTRIAN OPTIONS TOO

Investors in Property has been selling an increasing number of properties in Austria too. In most cases, properties are available to foreigners as long as they agree to make them available for renting when not using them – this also means that you save up to 20% VAT on the purchase price. In a few rare cases, some new properties have 'second-home status' and do not have to be rented out. Jessica Delaney says, 'We have some lovely ski-in/ski-out apartments in Kappl which has its own small ski area and there are longer-term plans to link it to St Anton's Rendl area. It is also just 8km from Ischgl's extensive ski area. The first phase sold out last year and now we have the second and final phase which will have access to full hotel facilities including a spa with swimming pool, steam rooms and saunas, a lounge and bar area, and a restaurant.' Prices for two-bedroom properties start at around 700,000 euros.

'We are also excited about some charming chalets, which are very rare to find in Austria,' says Delaney. They are close to three ski areas served by regular free buses: the local Bramberg area with 60km of pistes (five minutes), the Kitzbühel area with 170km of pistes (15 minutes) and the Zillertal Arena with 140km of pistes (20 minutes). Each chalet is stand alone and built to order so buyers can have a say in design and styling. The price for a three-bedroom, three-bathroom chalet is 390,000 euros.

CONTACTS

Investors in Property
020 8905 5511
www.investorsin property.com

Erna Low Property
020 7590 1624
www.ernalowproperty. co.uk

WHAT TO LOOK FOR WHEN BUYING A HOME IN THE SNOW

First, you need to decide whether you want somewhere just for the skiing or whether you want a place in a resort that is attractive in the summer as well. Many French resorts developed after the 1950s can be deadly dull in summer, whereas others are attractive for summer as well as winter use. Second, if you want the place primarily for skiing and snowboarding, you will want reliable snow. And with climate change likely to continue, that means going for somewhere with access to high, snow-sure slopes and with good snowmaking. Third, if you intend to use the place frequently yourself, you will probably want somewhere within a couple of hours of an easily accessible airport. Fourth, make sure you understand the legal and other aspects – buying and running costs, all types of taxes and any resale restrictions. It is highly advisable to get professional advice on these. Fifth, make sure you understand any arrangements that you may be offered for 'sale and leaseback' or 'guaranteed return' from renting it out – these can vary enormously and may enable you to save money on the purchase price in some circumstances. Sixth, if you are intending to rent the property out yourself, don't overestimate the income you will get from it.

Corporate ski trips

A great way to motivate your staff and clients

by **Dave Watts**

Corporate ski trips used to be big business. Ten years ago we had 13 advertisers in this chapter. Now we have three (two years ago we had only one). Obviously, the recession hit hospitality budgets. But the market is recovering and operators report increased business.

Amin Momen of Momentum Ski, which does a lot of corporate business, says, 'The market is up around 35% for us compared with two seasons ago. We find corporate clients are looking for something different rather than the usual day clay pigeon shooting or at Wimbledon.' Momen tries to think of different ideas to attract ordinary customers as well as corporate business. This season he is running the second Mountain Gourmet Ski Experience with Michelin-starred chefs Heston Blumenthal, Marcus Wareing and Sat Bains cooking for guests at mountain huts and in village restaurants. It is being held in Courmayeur in Italy from 9 to 12 January and includes three days' skiing. And in December he is running a trip to Innsbruck with Amy Williams, who won the gold medal in the skeleton event at the 2010 Winter Olympics in Vancouver. Guests will get the chance to go down the 1975 Olympic track as a passenger in a bobsled and then on their own on a skeleton (after technique training from Amy).

Ski Weekend will have been going 28 years this season and was pretty much the pioneer of short-break ski holidays. About 70% of their business is to Chamonix and they know it like the back of their hand, with access to a huge range of accommodation, guides and instructors. They organize their own ski courses, off-piste adventures and heli-skiing and do a lot of corporate business with a large number of regular clients. Other activities they offer include: mini-Olympics on the mountain, dinners at private locations designed by a 3-Michelin-starred chef, skijoring, husky-sledding, a private charter train trip to dinner up the mountain in Chamonix, and a skidoo safari to a mountain refuge in Courmayeur for dinner. They also take corporate trips to a wide range of other resorts, including Morzine, La Clusaz, Cortina, Gstaad, Vail, and Niseko in Japan (where they are taking two long-weekend groups this season along with Chamonix instructors and mountain guides).

Andrew Peters of STC Ski says, 'We arrange a variety of trips – from companies that simply want to invite clients for a holiday to those who want full conference facilities. We go to resorts across the Alps, such as: Zell am See, St Anton, Ischgl, Kitzbühel and Bad Gastein in Austria; Morzine, Val d'Isère and Chamonix in France.'

Roger Walker of Ski 2 (a company that specializes in Champoluc in the Monterosa area of the Italian Alps) says: 'Our corporate clients tend to be a little different from those of other companies. Their focus is more about team bonding than on entertaining clients. Most don't want us to organize meeting facilities either – the trip is more about a bunch of friends who work for the same company going on holiday together, rather than a corporate event. Companies like the fact that we will pick guests up from any of six airports within striking distance – perfect for people arriving from different parts of the world.'

Ski Weekend
the ultimate short break

we are the original
short break
ski specialists

over **25** years

01392 878 353
www.skiweekend.com

STC Ski

Specialists in Tailor-Made Short Breaks & Holidays

01483 771 222
www.stcski.co.uk
ski@stcski.co.uk

HOW TO ORGANIZE IT

Organizing a corporate trip yourself is a real hassle. People based in different areas of the country are likely to want to fly from different airports and at different times of day. And many hotels in the Alps don't want to take bookings for just a few days, or to provide the number of single rooms that you might want. Numbers are likely to change as people drop out for various reasons. Your group is likely to have skiers and boarders of widely differing abilities and maybe some beginners or non-skiers, so you need to organize ski instructors or guides to lead different groups. You need to organize equipment (and maybe clothing) rental and lift passes. You might want to organize 'jollies' such as dinner up the mountain and a torchlit descent back or a lunchtime BBQ on the piste. And you might need rooms to hold business meetings in. But that's what you use a tour operator or event organizer for – to deal with all the hassle and organize things on your behalf. And the great thing is that they don't charge you any extra for doing all that – it's part of the business to them.

Because corporate trips tend to be short, you'll want to keep the travel time to the minimum. Transfer times from airports to resorts generally range from one to four hours, and you'll probably want to operate at the lower end of that range if you can. That's why resorts such as Courmayeur and Champoluc in Italy (close to Geneva and Turin airports), Engelberg in Switzerland (close to Zürich), Kitzbühel in Austria (close to Salzburg and Innsbruck) and Garmisch in Germany (close to Munich) are popular. All these resorts have hotels that are happy to offer short-break bookings too.

THE MOMENTUM SKI FESTIVAL – CRANS-MONTANA, VALAIS, 12 TO 15 MARCH 2015

The Momentum Ski Festival incorporates the City Ski Championships (now in its 16th year) and a Business Forum run in association with the Financial Times. The Forum is chaired by the FT and the focus is dependent on the panel members – last year's was largely about teamwork and included Olympic skeleton gold medallist Amy Williams. The debate was followed by a lively Q&A session.

The festival includes a full programme of après-ski, with stand-up comedy, live bands and big-name DJs. There will be drinks parties hosted by Cavendish Ware and the Valais and dinners with entertainment at different venues, culminating in the prize-giving dinner on the Saturday with prizes and trophies presented by sponsors such as JeanRichard and Swiss International Airlines. Celebrity guests are likely to include Damon Hill, Colin Jackson, Graham Bell and Konrad Bartelski.

With the City Ski Championships, two races are held on the Friday: the Radar Trap Challenge (speed skiing) and the Accenture Dual Parallel Slalom. But the main event is the Saturday GS race on the World Cup Piste Nationale with live commentary by the BBC's Matt Chilton. This year as well as a competition for teams from City firms there will also be one for clubs such as the Lansdowne and Queens. On both days there'll be a race-side buffet and Snow+Rock will offer ski tuning, boot fitting and demo ski testing.

For more details call 020 7371 9111 or visit www. cityskichampionships.com.

MOMENTUM SKI

Flying to the snow

by **David Dalton**

There are lots of flights to the Alps and Pyrenees – including flights from quieter, queue-free regional airports. But finding your way through the minefield of routes and extra charges is hard work – and the extras can double or triple the basic cost. This brief tour of the flying business should help you navigate.

Budget airlines go to mainstream airports such as Geneva and Milan but also to smaller places, making it easier to get to many resorts in many parts of Europe, including parts of Austria, the Dolomites, the Pyrenees, Slovenia and eastern Europe. You'll find a wide choice of affordable transfers too. National carriers can be competitive, both on cost and destination, so don't ignore them when planning a trip. Note that some winter services stop operating in the spring before the ski season ends.

THE LEADING GROUP

EasyJet has a big range of flights, many to Geneva, from a broad choice of UK hubs. Other key destination airports include Zürich, Basel, Innsbruck, Salzburg, Munich, Turin, Milan and Lyon. From Stansted, Ljubljana is handy for Slovenia and eastern Austria.

Ryanair operates mainly from Stansted, with an increasing choice of flights from other UK airports. Routes and flight frequency change regularly, but a wide choice is offered – including Lourdes (for the western and central Pyrenees), Memmingen (Germany and western Austria), Linz (eastern Austria), Plovdiv (Bulgaria) – and Grenoble for the southern French Alps three times a week.

Jet2.com has flights to Geneva, Salzburg, Chambéry, Grenoble, Munich and Turin – mainly from northern England, but also from Edinburgh and Belfast – with a dedicated ski website.

Flybe serves Geneva, Zurich, Salzburg, Milan, Chambéry, Nice and, unusually, Stuttgart (handy for Germany and western Austria) – mainly from Southampton but also from Exeter, Birmingham, Newcastle and Glasgow. From airports in Scotland, Flybe serves Bergen in Norway.

British Airways goes to lots of relevant airports, including Innsbruck, from a variety of UK ones.

Swiss has lots of flights to Zürich and Geneva, some to Basel.

Monarch flies to Grenoble, Innsbruck, Friedrichshafen, Munich, Verona, Venice and Barcelona, with some flights from each of Gatwick, Luton, Manchester, Birmingham and Leeds-Bradford.

PRICING IT UP ...

Charges and rules for baggage and for equipment carriage vary and change frequently, so it's important to check the detail at the time you are considering a booking.

In July 2014, on flights to Geneva EasyJet was charging £25 return for one checked bag of up to 20kg, if booked online. With the more expensive Flexi fare, one checked bag was free. Skis and/or boots (checked in online) cost another £60 return. Ryanair was charging from £50 to £100 return for bags checked in online, depending on size; but skis/board would cost £100 return.

ONLINE BOOKING

Most budget airlines expect you to book online, and charge less if you book online such 'extras' as hold baggage and ski carriage too.

THE EXTRAS

Charges on top of basic flight costs vary between airlines. In July 2014, we looked at three (Jet2, EasyJet and Flybe) for flights to Geneva for a week in February 2014. Basic return fares varied from £85 to £100. Extra charges included:

checked-in 20kg bag return: £25-£39

skis/board/boots return: £50-£60

Reserved seat return: £4.96-£30

Credit card payment fee: Around £4-£6: 2% with EasyJet, 2.5% with Jet2, 3% with Flybe

These can add over £100 to the original cost, and the priciest of our flights worked out at over £204.

Also, you might be offered insurance for, say, £12 (which may not cover winter sports adequately – do check) and missed flight insurance for £9.50.

63

SKI AMIS

Catered Chalets in Superb Locations

020 3411 5439
www.skiamis.com

BA 'with-baggage' fares allow one checked-in bag up to 23kg free (there are other fares that don't); additional bags on European flights cost from £40 return. Your skis/boards will be considered your one piece of checked baggage as long as they're packed in a proper ski bag weighing no more than 23kg and no longer than 190cm. So you could take skis for free if you took no other checked bag.

Although their staff are ill-informed about these arrangements, Swiss and Lufthansa will carry one set of skis and boots free, in addition to your regular baggage allowance of 23kg. Note that some airlines, Lufthansa and Jet2 among them, require you to call customer services to 'register' your skis within 24 hours of making a booking.

There are other extras that inflate the price too (read the margin panel on the previous page). Airport costs such as drop-off parking fees can also add to the overall spend.

On some busy flights, EasyJet now say your carry-on bag may have to go into the hold if it exceeds dimensions of 50x40x20cm (the normal maximum for cabin bags is 56x45x25cm); they tell us you will not be charged for this.

FROM PLANE TO RESORT
Car rental can be cost-effective for a short break or a group – but, again, watch for hidden extras.

Most Swiss and Austrian airports have good public transport links to lots of resorts. Special rail passes may be cheaper than return tickets (read our intro to Switzerland on page 444 for Swiss pass information). In Italy, buses run to the Dolomites from Verona and Innsbruck, and to the Aosta valley from Turin.

Reaching French resorts is slightly trickier, but private minibus transfers are plentiful. Tour operator Ski Amis offers a public shared minibus service from Geneva and Chambéry to the Trois Vallées, La Plagne Montalbert and Peisey-Vallandry on Saturdays. Transfer companies and their relevant links are listed on our website (click on Directory).

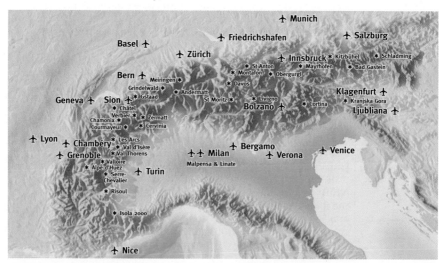

Travelling by rail

Make tracks to the snow (greener ones)

by **Lucy Dodsworth**

Whether you're a rail enthusiast or not, rail travel has its advantages for travelling to the snow. Depending on where you start and where you plan to finish your journey, it can be very relaxed; if you live in Hampstead and ski in Les Arcs, you're in luck. And fares can be competitive, once airline baggage charges are taken into account.

There are efficient high-speed trains direct from London to the French Alps, and lots of options if you are prepared to change in Paris. Some resorts have their own railway stations and others are easily reached by onward bus or taxi transfers.

The starting point of most European rail trips is likely to be the Eurostar high-speed train from London St Pancras, Ebbsfleet or Ashford stations. Except for direct services to the French Alps and high-speed to Switzerland, all details below are for last season, as those for 2014/15 had not been announced when we went to press.

DIRECT SERVICES TO THE FRENCH ALPS

Eurostar operates weekly direct services to the Tarentaise region – to Moûtiers for the Trois Vallées and to Bourg-St-Maurice (the end of the line) for Les Arcs, La Rosière, Ste-Foy, Tignes and Val d'Isère. Generally allow up to an hour or so for onward transfers. You can book bus transfers at www.altibus.com.

We can recommend the daytime service, which operates from 20 December 2014 until 4 April 2015 (returning on 11 April). You travel on Saturday, so you get the regular six days' skiing: you leave London at 9.39am and arrive in Bourg at 6.52pm. The return service leaves Bourg at 9.34am and arrives in London at 4.13pm.

The overnight service operates from 19 December 2014 to 3 April 2015 (returning on 11 April). There are no special sleeping arrangements – you doze (or not) in your seat. You travel out over Friday night and back over Saturday night, so you get eight days on the slopes: you leave London on Friday evening at 7.39pm and arrive at Bourg at 6.23am. The return service leaves Bourg on Saturday evening at 10.15pm and arrives in London at 7.16am.

A Standard adult return costs from £149 (non-flexible). A Standard Premier ticket (non-flexible) – which gets you a bigger seat pitch and meals (hot dinner and continental breakfast for overnight travel; continental breakfast and hot lunch for daytime passengers) – costs from £229.

INDIRECT SERVICES TO THE FRENCH ALPS

The French regular rail network (SNCF) can get you to lots of places such as Chambéry, Briançon and Grenoble, for onward buses to more southerly resorts. For Chamonix, an overnight train from Paris Austerlitz, with a change at St-Gervais, would put you in your resort by 10am the next day; last season prices started at £128 return. A pre-bookable taxi service to get you between the Paris stations is offered through snowcarbon.co.uk; you ring, email or book online to reserve a place, and the driver will meet your train. It costs 65 euros each way for up to eight people. SNCF has Youth and Senior saver cards. The Youth Card (for 12–27 year olds) costs

When quality
and value
matter,
do more with

zenith
·holidays·

0203 137 7678
zenithholidays.co.uk
ABTA
ABTA No.Y1542

£45 and entitles you to 25% to 60% discount, depending on times/ days and peak periods. The Senior Card (for over 60s) costs £58.50 and gets you 25% to 50% discount.

HIGH-SPEED TO SWITZERLAND

There are no longer direct Eurostar services to the Swiss Alps. Instead, for the 2014/15 season, you take the Eurostar to Lille and transfer by crossing the platform to a high-speed Lyria des Neiges TGV train to Geneva. At Geneva, you switch to normal Swiss railway services. This service to Geneva will run on Monday, Thursday, Saturday and Sunday, starting in December 2014. Further details had not yet been announced when we went to press and were expected to be available at the end of September 2014. Regular high-speed TGV trains from Paris also serve Geneva, Zürich and Basel, where you can change to connect with most Swiss resorts. Many resorts, such as Andermatt, Engelberg, Davos, Klosters, Grindelwald, Wengen and Zermatt, have convenient local railway stations. It's easy to get to others, such as Saas-Fee and Verbier, by a combination of train and post bus.

AUSTRIA AND GERMANY

Many Austrian resorts also have their own stations or are easy to reach by post bus from a nearby station. City Night Line is part of a large network of European rail services, with weekend sleeper trains departing from Paris and Amsterdam. Winter services from Paris Est include trains direct to Innsbruck or Wörgl (Fridays), arriving late morning; or via Munich (daily). Onward connections can get you to resorts such as St Anton, Zell am See, Mayrhofen and the SkiWelt. From Munich it's an easy hop to Garmisch-Partenkirchen. Typical fares from London to Munich including Eurostar start from £219 return. Check out www.citynightline.de for more details.

THE ITALIAN JOB

Most Italian resorts are hard work to reach by train, but there are exceptions. The Dolomites are close to the line through Trento and Bolzano, reachable from Munich (as an onward connection from the City Night Line – prices to both start at £66 return from Munich), from Innsbruck (prices to both from £49 return), or from Verona to the south (return prices start at £36 return to Trento and £35 return to Bolzano). Resorts of the Val di Susa are easily reached via trains from Paris Gare de Lyon to Turin and Milan. These run three times a day and stop at Bardonecchia and Oulx – 15 minutes by bus from Sauze d'Oulx and a bit further from Sestriere. Return fares from Paris start at £96 for a flexible fare or £79 for a non-flexible fare. Journeys are bookable through Voyages-sncf.com.

PLANNING AND BOOKING

Rail fares have few of the extra charges that airlines make. But the cheapest fares are best secured early. Booking is normally no more than 90 days in advance, but Eurostar's direct service can be booked from 31 July and French winter services from mid-October. Main sites include: Voyages-sncf.com, Eurostar (www.eurostar.com), Swiss railways (www.sbb.ch/en) and Austrian railways (www.oebb.at/en/). Some local lines, such as Martigny to Le Châble (for Verbier) and Bex up to Villars, may have to be organized separately. Other useful websites include www.seat61.com and www.snowcarbon.co.uk.

Drive to the Alps

And ski where you please

by **Chris Gill**

Because the Channel gets in the way, and because the British Isles are the centre of the low-cost airline business, we Brits are inclined to travel to the Alps by air whether we are buying a package holiday or travelling independently. The French, the Germans and the Dutch, in contrast, mainly go by car. But for British skiers, too, driving to the Alps can have lots of advantages.

Even for those going on a pretty standard week in the Alps, many people find driving is less hassle than taking flights. For families (especially those going self-catering), it simplifies the job of moving half the contents of your house to the Alps. If there are four or five people in your party, the cost can be low. If you fancy something a bit more adventurous than a standard week in one resort, taking a car opens up the exciting possibility of visiting several resorts in one trip – maybe even making up your plans as you go along, so that you go wherever the snow is looking best.

The experience of driving out can be a pleasant one. Crossing the Channel is slick and painless using the fast and frequent Eurotunnel Le Shuttle trains through the tunnel – read the feature panel below. And, although cross-Channel ferries can't compete with Le Shuttle in terms of crossing time, they are faster than they have ever been (as well as more comfortable).

EASY DOES IT WITH EUROTUNNEL LE SHUTTLE

We're now in the habit of using Eurotunnel Le Shuttle to cross the Channel if we're driving to the Alps. (Admittedly, both of the editors are based in what you might loosely call south-east England, and if we were further north we'd certainly be considering ferries across the North Sea.)

The terminal at Folkestone is very straightforward to reach. Junction 11A of the M20 takes you directly to the check-in gates. Check-in deadline is half an hour before departure. The check-in system recognizes your number plate, and without human intervention prints your boarding pass. After a quick visit to the shops in the terminal to pick up the stuff you've forgotten, it's into the marshalling yard for a few minutes before boarding the train.

If you're at the front of the queue, once on the train you drive the whole length of it before parking – and that will mean a quick exit at the other end. Within minutes of boarding you're gliding into the tunnel. If you want a quick nap while crossing, take earplugs.

You can be on the autoroute south of Calais 75 minutes after arrival at Folkestone. Overall, an early start from large parts of southern England can have you in a resort near Geneva in time for dinner without taking too many liberties with the speed limit.

EUROTUNNEL

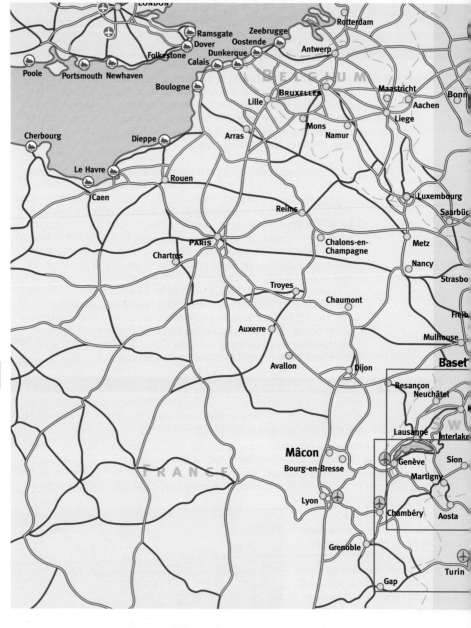

This map should help you plan your route to the Alps, at least in outline. All the main routes from the Channel and all the routes up into the mountains funnel through (or close to) three 'gateways', picked out on the map in larger type – Mâcon in France, Basel in Switzerland and Ulm in Germany.

Decide which gateway suits your destination, and pick a route to it from your planned arrival port at the Channel. Occasionally, using a different Channel port will lead you to use a different gateway.

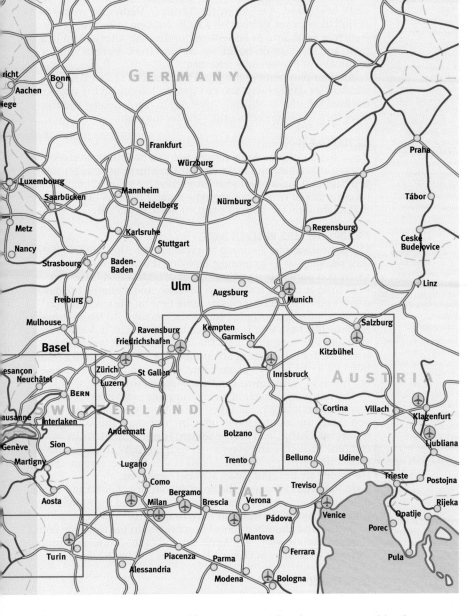

The boxes on the map correspond to the areas covered by the more detailed maps in our introductory chapters on the four main Alpine countries, starting on these pages:

Austria page 98
France page 194
Italy page 382
Switzerland page 444

ATTENTION SVP!

The UK motoring organizations say that when driving in France you must now carry:

• a warning triangle
• a reflective jacket that you can put on in the event of a breakdown or an accident, kept in the main passenger compartment – not stowed in the boot
• an unused, in-date, French-certified breathalyser – the advice is to carry two, in case you want to use one.

If you have a satnav, it must be incapable of displaying speed camera locations. They say software updates are available with this data absent. A set of spare light bulbs is recommended.

For two seasons now we have had an electronic tag on our windscreen that means we can bowl through autoroute toll barriers at 30kph; highly recommended. We got ours at an APRR desk in a service area for 10 euros. We pay about 2 euros for each calendar month in which we use the device. Tolls are charged to a credit card. You can get a tag from a special UK website set up by the SANEF toll company – www.saneftolling. co.uk – but the costs are higher. If you can handle a French site, you can sign up cheaply at APRR's website, www. telepeagepourtous.fr

What's more, the attractions of driving are not confined to the south of England. A reader writes: 'Living in Derbyshire we can be at Hull in just over an hour for a night crossing to Zeebrugge (for French or Swiss alps) or Rotterdam (for Austria). After a night in a cabin and breakfast on-board, we can start the 8–10 hour journey to the Alps at 8.30am fully refreshed'.

Another plus point of driving is that you can easily extend the standard six-day holiday. You can spend a full day on the slopes on the final Saturday (a blissfully quiet day in many resorts) and then drive for a few hours before stopping for the night.

AS YOU LIKE IT

If you fancy visiting several resorts, you can do it in three ways: use one resort as a base and make day trips to others; use a valley town as a base, and make resort visits from there; or go on a tour, moving on every day or two. There are some notable regional lift passes that might form the basis of a trip, in Austria especially.

AROUND THE ALPS IN SEVEN DAYS

The most rewarding approach to exploring the Alps – although the least relaxing – is to go touring, enjoying the freedom of going where you want, when you want. Out of high season there's no need to book accommodation in advance. And a touring holiday doesn't mean you'll be spending more time on the road than on the piste, provided you plan your route carefully. An hour's drive after the lifts have shut is all it need take, normally. It does eat into your après-ski time, of course. The major thing that you have to watch out for is the cost of accommodation. Checking into a resort hotel for a night or two doesn't come cheap, and can seem a rip-off. But hotels in valley towns can be very good value.

The following chapter has some suggestions for a trip to France. Austria offers lots of possibilities. In the west, you could take in the best skiing the country has to offer, by combining the Arlberg resorts with Ischgl, and maybe Sölden. Further east, it is easy to combine Hintertux and Mayrhofen with the SkiWelt resorts and Kitzbühel. Driving around in Austria is a doddle, because most of the resorts are low, and passes are rarely involved.

In Italy you can stay in the beautiful old city of Aosta and visit a different resort (such as Courmayeur, Cervinia and the Monterosa resorts) each day. Elsewhere in Italy, touring makes more sense.

Switzerland also offers lots of possibilities. In the west, you could combine Verbier with Val d'Anniviers and Crans-Montana. Further east, you could start in Davos/Klosters and end up in Flims.

BE PREPARED

Winter tyres make a big difference to a car's grip on ice and snow. These tyres are compulsory in Austria for the whole winter period. In other Alpine countries, we understand that they are not; but many 'experts' warn that if you go without them and have an incident, you could be in trouble. You may still need chains in really deep snow. But winter tyres will keep you going in pretty difficult conditions if your car also has traction control, to stop the wheels spinning. This usually forms part of the electronic stability systems now fitted to many new cars (sometimes as an option).

Cars hired in Austria and Switzerland should always be equipped with winter tyres. Cars hired elsewhere may not be.

Drive to the French Alps

To make the most of them

by **Chris Gill**

If you've read the preceding chapter, you'll have gathered that we are pretty keen on driving to the Alps in general. But we're particularly keen on driving to the French Alps. The drive is a relatively short one, whereas many of the transfers to major French resorts from Geneva airport are relatively long.

Of course, the route from the Channel to the French Alps is through France rather than Germany, which for Francophiles like us means it's a pleasant prospect rather than a vaguely off-putting one. Especially if you are using Eurotunnel or a short ferry crossing, rather than a ferry to one of the Normandy ports, the drive is pleasantly low-pressure. Not only because you don't have to tangle with Paris but also because you don't have to use the always-busy Paris–Lyon autoroute.

The French Alps are the number-one destination for British car-borne skiers. The journey time is surprisingly short, at least if you are starting from south-east England. From Calais, for example, you can comfortably cover the 900km/560 miles to Chamonix in about nine hours plus stops – with the exception of the final few miles, the whole journey is on motorways. And except on peak weekends, when half the population of Paris is on the move, the traffic is relatively light, if you steer clear of Paris.

With some exceptions in the southern Alps, all the resorts of the French Alps are within a day's driving range, provided you cross the Channel early in the day (or overnight). Saturday is still the main changeover day for resorts, and Saturday traffic into and out of many resorts can be heavy. This is especially true between Albertville and the Tarentaise resorts (from the Trois Vallées to Val d'Isère). Things are nothing like as bad as they were 25 years ago, before road improvements for the 1992 Olympics removed some of the main bottlenecks; but the resorts have expanded further in that time, and sadly the jams are back – on peak-season Saturdays you can encounter serious queues around Moûtiers. There are traffic lights placed well away from the town, to keep the queues and associated pollution away from Moûtiers.

DAY-TRIP BASES

As we explained in the previous chapter, a car opens up different kinds of holiday for the adventurous holidaymaker – day tripping from a base resort, for example.

In the southern French Alps, Serre-Chevalier and Montgenèvre are ideal bases for day tripping. They are within easy reach of one another, and Montgenèvre is at one end of the Milky Way lift network, which includes Sauze d'Oulx and Sestriere in Italy – you can drive on to these resorts, or reach them by lift and piste. On the French side of the border, a few miles south, Vars/Risoul is an underrated area that is well worth a visit for a day. The major resorts of Alpe-d'Huez and Les Deux-Alpes are also within range, as is the cult off-piste resort of La Grave. Getting to them involves crossing the high Col du Lautaret, but it's a major through-route and is not allowed to close for very long in normal winter conditions.

Self-drive packages inc. FREE Eurotunnel upgrade

0844 576 0173
peakretreats.co.uk

ABTA
ABTA No. W5537

peak retreats

SKI AMIS

Catered Chalets
in Superb
Locations

020 3411 5439
www.skiamis.com

The Chamonix valley is an ideal destination for day tripping. The Mont Blanc Unlimited lift pass covers all the Chamonix areas, plus Courmayeur in Italy (easily reached through the Mont Blanc tunnel) and Verbier in Switzerland (a bit of a trek, even if the intervening passes are open). Megève and Les Contamines are close by, and Flaine and its satellites are fairly accessible. You could stay in a valley town such as Cluses, to escape resort prices – but Chamonix itself is not a wildly expensive town.

In the Tarentaise region, Bourg-St-Maurice is an excellent base for visiting several resorts – Les Arcs is accessible by funicular, and La Plagne is of course linked to Les Arcs. La Rosière is only a short drive away, with a link to La Thuile. Ste-Foy is just up the valley. And at the end of the valley are Val d'Isère and Tignes. We had a great week skiing all of these resorts from a comfortable apartment based in Bourg a few seasons ago.

MOVING ON
An alternative approach in the Tarentaise region if you want to include the famous Trois Vallées area is to stay in a series of different resorts for a day or two each, moving on from one to the next in the early evening; this way, you could have the trip of a lifetime (and save a lot on après-ski beers).

GETTING THERE
There are three 'gateways' to the different regions of the French Alps. For the northern Alps – Chamonix valley, Portes du Soleil, Flaine and neighbours – you want to head for Geneva. If coming from Calais or another short-crossing port, you no longer have to tangle with the busy A6 from Paris via Beaune to Mâcon and Lyon. The relatively new A39 autoroute south from Dijon means you can head for Bourg-en-Bresse, well east of Mâcon. For the central Alps – the mega-resorts of the Tarentaise, from Valmorel to Val d'Isère, and the Maurienne valley – you want to head for Chambéry. For the southern Alps – Alpe-d'Huez, Les Deux-Alpes, Serre-Chevalier – you want to head for Grenoble. And for either of these gateways first head for Mâcon and turn left at Lyon.

If you are taking a short Channel crossing, there are plenty of characterful towns for an overnight stop between the Channel and Dijon – Arras (our favourite), St-Quentin, Laon, Troyes, Reims. All have plenty of choice of budget chain hotels, some of them in central locations where you can easily enjoy the facilities of the town (ie the brasseries).

From the more westerly Channel ports of Le Havre or Caen, your route to Geneva or Mâcon sounds dead simple: take the A13 to Paris then the A6 south. But you have to get through or around Paris in the process. The most direct way around the city is the notorious périphérique – a hectic, multi-lane urban motorway close to the centre, with exits every few hundred yards and traffic that is either worryingly fast-moving or jammed solid. If the périphérique is jammed, getting round it takes ages. The more reliable alternative is to take a series of motorways and dual carriageways through the south-west fringes of Greater Paris. The route is not well signed, so it's a great help to have a competent navigator.

Major Resorts
Expert knowledge

**Self-drive
specialist**

SkiCollection.co.uk
0844 576 0175
ABTA Bonded W5537

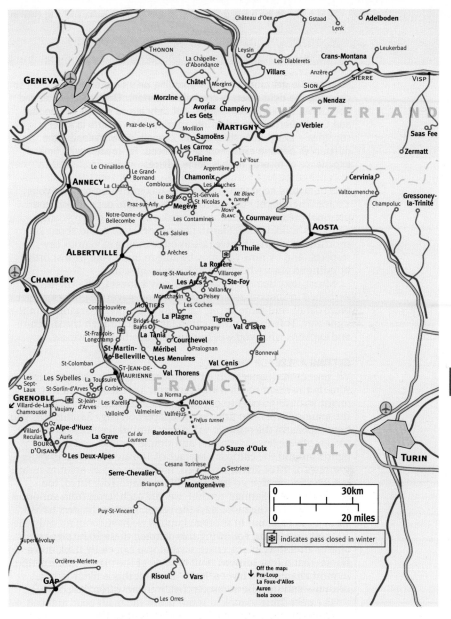

Pick the right gateway – Geneva, Chambéry or Grenoble – and you can hardly go wrong. Generally, there are no mountain passes involved. The exception is the approach to Serre-Chevalier and Montgenèvre, which involves the 2060m Col du Lautaret; the road is a major one and is ploughed frequently, but we felt the need for chains here on one occasion. Crossing the French–Swiss border between Chamonix and Verbier involves two closure-prone passes – the Montets and the Forclaz. When necessary, one-way traffic runs beside the tracks through the rail tunnel beneath the passes.

Most people get to go skiing or boarding only once or twice a year, so choosing the right resort is crucially important. Chamonix, Châtel and Courchevel are all French resorts, but they are as similar as Cheddar and Camembert. If you bring into consideration resorts in other countries – Ischgl in Austria, say, or Zermatt in Switzerland – the differences become even more pronounced. For readers with limited experience of resorts, here is some advice.

Lots of factors need to be taken into account when making your choice. The weight you attach to each of them depends on your personal preferences, and on the make-up of the group you are going on holiday with. Starting on page 83 you'll find about 20 shortlists of resorts that we rate as outstanding in various key respects. And by now you may be able to build your own shortlist by going to www.wheretoskiandsnowboard.com.

Minor resorts and regions not widely known in the UK are described in short chapters of two or three pages. Major resorts get more detail, and more pages. Each resort chapter is organized in the same way. This short introduction takes you through the structure and explains what you will find under each heading we use.

GETTING A FEEL FOR THE PLACE

We start each chapter with a two-line verdict, in which we aim to sum up the resort in a few words. If you like the sound of it, you might want to go next to our unique Resort Price Index (RPI), in the margin. Explained fully in the chapter on page 35, this tells you how expensive the resort is, taking account of the prices of lift passes, private lessons, ski hire and simple lunches and drinks; figures around the eurozone average of 100 are presented in blue, low ones of 90 or less are in green, high ones of 120 or more are in red. The figures that go into the RPI calculation are listed, too.

Then, in the 'Ratings' section, we rate each resort from various points of view – the more stars the better. Longer chapters have a set of 19 ratings, but in shorter chapters we have room for only the 10 most important. Following this chapter, these 10 ratings are set out for all resorts in one chart, so that you can easily track down resorts that might suit you. Still looking at the margin information, in most chapters we have a 'News' section; this is likely to be of most use and interest in resorts that you know from recent visits.

The next thing to look at is our list of the main good and bad points about the resort and its slopes, picked out with ✚ and ▬. This is followed by a summary in **bold type**, in which we've aimed to weigh up the pros and cons, coming off the fence and giving our view of who might like the resort. These sections should give you a good idea of whether the resort is likely to suit *you*, and whether it's worth reading our detailed analysis of it.

You'll know by now, for example, whether this is a high, hideous, convenient, purpose-built resort with superb, snow-sure, challenging slopes but absolutely no nightlife; or a pretty, traditional village with gentle wooded slopes, ideal for beginners on the rare occasions when it has some decent snow.

Stanford Skiing

Megève
Specialists

huge ski area
close to Geneva
short breaks
chalets & hotels

family run - friendly
knowledgeable staff

01603 477471

www.stanfordskiing.co.uk

74

THE RESORT

In this first section of each chapter, we try to sort out the character of the place for you. Later, in the 'Staying there' section, we tell you more about the hotels, restaurants, bars and so on. Resorts vary enormously in some key respects and we have separate sections for each of the following headings. These match our star ratings.

ski EXPECTATIONS 01799 531888

THE SKI HOLIDAY CONSULTANCY

with over 25 years experience in Europe's Top Resorts, the USA & Canada

The service is friendly, the information is accurate and the advice is free

Just one call away from your ideal holiday

01799 531888
www.skiexpectations.com

Village charm At the extremes of the range are the handful of really hideous modern apartment-block resorts thrown up in France in the 1960s, and the ancient, captivating mountain villages of which Switzerland has an unfair number. But it isn't simply a question of old versus new. Some purpose-built places can have a much friendlier feel than some long-established resorts with big blocky buildings. Some places are working towns. Some are full of bars, discos and shops; others are peaceful backwaters. Traffic may choke the streets; or the village may be traffic-free.

Convenience This means how easy it is to get around the resort once you are there (not how easy the resort is to get to from the UK). Some places can be remarkably strung out, whereas others are surprisingly compact; our village plans are drawn to a standard scale, to help you gauge this. And of course proximity of lodgings to pistes determines how much walking or bussing you do.

Scenery Mountains are of course generally scenic, but there are differences, from the routinely hilly Colorado to the incredible scenery of the Italian Dolomites and the Swiss Jungfrau region.

THE MOUNTAINS

Extent of slopes Some mountains and lift networks are vast and complex, while others are much smaller and lacking variety. As last year, we have a special feature about this aspect on page 32.

Fast lifts Gondolas and fast chairlifts travel at three times the speed of slow chairlifts – cable cars and funicular railways even faster; these lifts offer short ride times, and most also shift queues quickly. We summarize the kinds of lifts you'll spend your time on. On our piste maps, we use a chair symbol to identify only fast chairs; lifts not marked with a symbol are slow chairs or draglifts.

Queues Monster queues are largely a thing of the past, but it still pays to avoid the resorts with the worst queues, especially in high season. Crowding on the pistes is more of a worry in many resorts, and we mention problems of this kind under this heading.

Terrain parks We summarize here the specially prepared fun parks and other terrain features most resorts now arrange for those who like to do tricks on their skis or board.

Snow reliability This is a crucial factor for many people, and one that varies enormously. In some resorts you don't have to worry at all about a lack of snow, while others are notorious for treating their paying guests to ice, mud and slush. Whether a resort is likely to have decent snow on its slopes normally depends on the height, the orientation of the slopes (north-facing good, south- and west-facing bad), its snow record and how much snowmaking it has. But bear in mind that in the Alps, high resorts tend to have rocky

Choosing your resort

Build your own shortlist: www.wheretoskiandsnowboard.com

AWARD-WINNING

SKI
HOLIDAYS

Ski Olympic

book online at
skiolympic.com
01302 328 820

terrain, where the runs (and particularly the 'off-piste' terrain outside the prepared runs) will need more snow than the pasture land of lower resorts. In the 'Key facts' section we list the latest amount of snowmaking the resorts claim to have, and comment on it in the snow reliability text.

For experts, intermediates, beginners Most (though not all) resorts have something to offer beginners, but relatively few will keep an expert happy for a week's holiday. As for intermediates, whether a resort will suit you really depends on your skill and inclinations. Places such as Cervinia and Obergurgl are ideal for those who want easy cruising runs, but have little to offer intermediates looking for more challenge. Others, such as Sölden and Val d'Isère, may intimidate the less confident intermediate. Some areas linking several resorts, such as the Trois Vallées and Portes du Soleil, have vast amounts of terrain, so you can cover different ground each day. But some other well-known names, such as Mürren and Courmayeur, have surprisingly small areas.

For boarders In earlier editions we had a special panel in longer chapters but we now deal with boarders' requirements in the main text, commenting on things like flat areas (bad) and the main types of lifts – gondolas, cable cars and chairs (all good) or draglifts (bad).

For cross-country We don't pretend that this is a guide for avid cross-country skiers. But we do try to help.

Mountain restaurants Here's a subject that arouses strong views. To some, having a decent lunch served at your table in civilized surroundings – either in the sun, contemplating amazing scenery, or in a cosy hut, sheltered from the elements – makes or breaks the holiday. Others regard a long midday stop as a waste of valuable skiing time, as well as valuable spending money. We are firmly in the former camp. We get very disheartened by places with miserable restaurants and miserable food (eg many resorts in America); and there are some resorts that we go to partly because of the cosy huts and the food (eg Zermatt).

Schools and guides This is an area where we rely heavily on readers' reports of their own or their friends' experiences.

For families We sum up the merits of the resort for families, where possible evaluating the childcare arrangements. Again, to be of real help we need first-hand reports from people with children.

STAYING THERE

Chalets, hotels, apartments Some resorts have few hotels or few catered chalets. Note that we also have feature chapters on notably good chalets and apartments. If there are interesting options for staying in isolation on the slopes above the resort village, or in cheap valley towns below it, we pick them out.

Eating out The range of restaurants varies widely. Even some big resorts have little choice because most visitors dine in their apartments or hotels. Most American resorts offer lots of choice.

Après-ski Tastes and styles vary enormously. Most resorts have pleasant places in which to have an immediate post-skiing beer or hot chocolate. Some then go dead. Others have noisy bars and discos until the early hours.

Off the slopes This is largely aimed at assessing how suitable a resort is for someone who doesn't intend to use the slopes, such as a non-skiing spouse. But of course it is also of interest to anyone who wants some variety of evening entertainment.

Resort ratings at a glance

The RPI figures in the second row for each resort are our Resort Price Index figures, based on a comparison of the costs of food and drink, lift pass, ski hire and a private ski lesson. An average eurozone resort has an RPI of 100.

ANDORRA   AUSTRIA

	ARINSAL	SOLDEU		BAD GASTEIN	BAD KLEIN-KIRCHHEIM	ELLMAU	HINTERTUX / TUX VALLEY	
Page	90	92		104	107	110	113	
RPI	90	115		95	100	85	95	
Extent	*	***		***	**	****	***	
Fast lifts	**	**		***	**	****	***	
Queues	***	***		***	****	****	***	
Snow	****	***		***	***	**	*****	
Expert	*	**		***	**	*	***	
Intermediate	**	****		****	***	****	***	
Beginner	****	****		**	**	****	**	
Charm	*	*		***	**	***	***	
Convenience	***	***		**	***	***	**	
Scenery	***	***		***	***	***	***	

	ISCHGL	KITZBÜHEL	LECH	MAYRHOFEN	OBERGURGL	OBERTAUERN	SAALBACH-HINTERG'M
Page	118	125	133	142	148	154	157
RPI	105	105	125	90	110	95	95
Extent	****	***	***	***	**	**	***
Fast lifts	*****	*****	****	****	*****	****	*****
Queues	****	***	****	*	*****	****	****
Snow	****	**	****	***	*****	****	**
Expert	****	***	****	**	**	***	**
Intermediate	****	****	****	***	***	****	****
Beginner	**	**	****	**	****	***	***
Charm	***	****	****	***	****	**	****
Convenience	***	**	***	*	****	****	****
Scenery	***	***	***	***	***	***	***

	SCHLADMING	SÖLDEN	SÖLL	ST ANTON	STUBAI VALLEY	ZELL AM SEE	
Page	163	167	172	179	188	190	
RPI	95	110	90	110	100	100	
Extent	***	***	****	***	***	**	
Fast lifts	****	****	****	****	***	****	
Queues	****	***	***	***	***	***	
Snow	****	****	**	****	*****	**	
Expert	**	***	*	*****	***	**	
Intermediate	****	****	****	***	***	***	
Beginner	***	***	**	*	**	***	
Charm	***	**	***	****	****	*****	
Convenience	***	**	**	***	**	***	
Scenery	***	***	***	***	****	***	

The RPI figures

The figures in the second row for each resort are our Resort Price Index figures, based on a comparison of the costs of food and drink, lift pass, ski hire and a private ski lesson. An average eurozone resort has an RPI of 100.

FRANCE

	Alpe-d'Huez	Les Arcs	Avoriaz	Les Carroz	Chamonix	Châtel	Courchevel
Page	198	208	218	223	225	235	240
RPI	105	105	105	100	105	100	140
Extent	★★★★	★★★	★★★★★	★★★★	★★★	★★★★★	★★★★★
Fast lifts	★★★★	★★★★	★★★★	★★★	★★★	★★	★★★★
Queues	★★★★	★★★	★★★	★★★	★★	★★★	★★★★
Snow	★★★★	★★★★	★★★	★★★	★★★★	★★	★★★★
Expert	★★★★	★★★★★	★★★	★★★★	★★★★★	★★★	★★★★
Intermediate	★★★★	★★★★	★★★★	★★★★★	★★	★★★★	★★★★★
Beginner	★★★★★	★★★	★★★★	★★★★	★★	★★★	★★★★
Charm	★★	★★	★★	★★★★	★★★★	★★★	★★
Convenience	★★★	★★★★	★★★★★	★★★	★	★★	★★★★
Scenery	★★★★	★★★	★★★	★★★★	★★★★★	★★★	★★★

	Les Deux-Alpes	Flaine	Les Gets	La Grave	Megève	Les Menuires	Méribel
Page	250	256	263	265	267	274	280
RPI	100	100	100	90	100	110	125
Extent	★★★	★★★★	★★★★★	★	★★★★★	★★★★★	★★★★★
Fast lifts	★★★★	★★★	★★★		★★	★★★★	★★★★★
Queues	★★	★★★	★★★	★★★★	★★★★	★★★★	★★★★
Snow	★★★★	★★★★	★★	★★★	★★	★★★★	★★★
Expert	★★★★	★★★★	★★★	★★★★★	★★	★★★★	★★★★
Intermediate	★★	★★★★★	★★★★	★	★★★★	★★★★★	★★★★★
Beginner	★★★	★★★★★	★★★★	★	★★★	★★★	★★★★
Charm	★★	★	★★★★	★★★	★★★★	★★	★★★
Convenience	★★★	★★★★★	★★★	★★★	★★	★★★★★	★★★
Scenery	★★★★	★★★★	★★★	★★★★	★★★★★	★★★	★★★

	Mont-Genèvre	Morzine	La Plagne	La Rosière	Samoëns	Serre-Chevalier	Ste-Foy-Tarentaise
Page	289	294	303	319	323	325	334
RPI	90	100	110	90	95	95	85
Extent	★★	★★★★★	★★★★	★★★	★★★★	★★★★	★
Fast lifts	★★	★★★	★★	★★★	★★★	★★★	★★★★
Queues	★★★★	★★★	★★	★★★★	★★★★	★★★	★★★★★
Snow	★★★★	★★	★★★★	★★★	★★★	★★★	★★★★
Expert	★★★★	★★★	★★★★	★★	★★★★	★★★	★★★★
Intermediate	★★★★	★★★★	★★★★★	★★★	★★★★★	★★★★	★★★
Beginner	★★★★★	★★★	★★★★	★★★★★	★★	★★★★	★★
Charm	★★★	★★★	★★	★★★	★★★★	★★★	★★★
Convenience	★★★	★★	★★★★★	★★★	★	★★★	★★★★
Scenery	★★★	★★★	★★★	★★★★	★★★★	★★★	★★★

Want to see the full set?

Major resort chapters in the book have an additional nine ratings shown at the start of each chapter. And you can see the full set of ratings for 200+ resorts on our website.
www.wheretoskiandsnowboard.com

	St-Martin-de-B'ville	La Tania	Tignes	Val Cenis Vanoise	Val d'Isère	Val Thorens	Vars / Risoul
Page	337	340	346	355	358	368	375
RPI	110	115	115	80	110	115	85
Extent	★★★★★	★★★★★	★★★★★	★★★	★★★★★	★★★★★	★★★
Fast lifts	★★★★	★★★★	★★★	★★★	★★★★	★★★★★	★
Queues	★★★★	★★★★	★★★★	★★★★	★★★★	★★★★	★★★★
Snow	★★★	★★★	★★★★★	★★★	★★★★★	★★★★★	★★★
Expert	★★★★	★★★★	★★★★★	★★	★★★★★	★★★★	★★
Intermediate	★★★★★	★★★★★	★★★★★	★★★★	★★★★★	★★★★★	★★★★
Beginner	★★	★★★	★★	★★★★	★★★	★★★★	★★★★
Charm	★★★★	★★★	★	★★★	★★★	★★	★★
Convenience	★★★	★★★★	★★★★	★★★	★★★	★★★★★	★★★★
Scenery	★★★	★★★	★★★	★★★	★★★	★★★	★★★

GERMANY ITALY

	Garmisch-Partenk'n	Cervinia	Cortina d'Ampezzo	Courmayeur	Livigno	Madonna di Campiglio
Page	380	387	393	398	403	407
RPI	90	90	115	95	90	105
Extent	★	★★★	★★	★	★★	★★★
Fast lifts	★★★	★★★★	★★★	★★★★	★★★★	★★★★
Queues	★★★	★★★★	★★★★	★★★★	★★★★	★★★★
Snow	★★★	★★★★★	★★★	★★★★	★★★★	★★★
Expert	★★★★	★	★★	★★★	★★★	★★
Intermediate	★★★	★★★★	★★★	★★★★	★★★	★★★★
Beginner	★	★★★★★	★★★★★	★	★★★★	★★★
Charm	★★★	★★	★★★★	★★★★	★★★	★★★★
Convenience	★★	★★★	★	★	★★	★★★
Scenery	★★★★	★★★★	★★★★★	★★★★	★★★	★★★★

	Monterosa Ski	Passo Tonale	Sauze d'Oulx	Sella Ronda	Selva / Val Gardena	Sestriere	La Thuile
Page	412	418	420	425	433	440	442
RPI	85	75	90	95	95	90	90
Extent	★★	★★	★★★★	★★★★★	★★★★★	★★★★	★★★
Fast lifts	★★★★★	★★★★	★★★	★★★★	★★★★	★★★	★★★
Queues	★★★★	★★★★	★★★	★★★	★★★	★★★	★★★★★
Snow	★★★★	★★★★	★★	★★★★	★★★★	★★★★	★★★★
Expert	★★★★	★	★★	★★	★★★	★★★	★★
Intermediate	★★★★	★★★	★★★★	★★★★★	★★★★★	★★★★	★★★★
Beginner	★★	★★★★★	★	★★★★	★★★	★★★	★★★★
Charm	★★★	★★	★★	★★★	★★★	★	★★★
Convenience	★★★	★★★	★★	★★★	★★★	★★★	★★★
Scenery	★★★★	★★★	★★★	★★★★★	★★★★★	★★★	★★★

Resort ratings at a glance

Build your own shortlist: **www.wheretoskiandsnowboard.com**

The RPI figures

The figures in the second row for each resort are our Resort Price Index figures, based on a comparison of the costs of food and drink, lift pass, ski hire and a private ski lesson. An average eurozone resort has an RPI of 100.

SWITZERLAND

	ADELBODEN	ANDERMATT	CHAMPÉRY	CRANS-MONTANA	DAVOS	ENGELBERG		
Page	451	454	456	459	461	468		
RPI	120	110	125	135	130	110		
Extent	★★★	★★	★★★★★	★★★	★★★★	★★		
Fast lifts	★★★	★★	★	★★★★★	★★★★	★★★		
Queues	★★★	★★	★★★★	★★★	★★★	★★		
Snow	★★★	★★★★	★★	★★	★★★★	★★★		
Expert	★★	★★★★	★★★	★★	★★★★	★★★★		
Intermediate	★★★	★★	★★★★	★★★★	★★★★★	★★★		
Beginner	★★★★	★	★★	★★★	★★	★★		
Charm	★★★★	★★★★	★★★★	★★	★★	★★		
Convenience	★★	★★★	★	★★	★★	★		
Scenery	★★★★	★★★	★★★★	★★★★	★★★★	★★★★		

	GRINDELW'D	KLOSTERS	LAAX	MÜRREN	SAAS-FEE	ST MORITZ		
Page	470	474	476	479	483	488		
RPI	125	130	130	125	135	150		
Extent	★★★	★★★★	★★★★	★	★★	★★★★★		
Fast lifts	★★★★	★★	★★★★★	★★★★★	★★★★	★★★★		
Queues	★★	★★	★★★★	★★★	★★★★	★★★		
Snow	★★	★★★★	★★★	★★★	★★★★★	★★★★		
Expert	★★	★★★★	★★★	★★★	★★	★★★★		
Intermediate	★★★★	★★★★★	★★★★★	★★★	★★★★	★★★★		
Beginner	★★★	★★★	★★★★	★★★	★★★★	★★		
Charm	★★★★	★★★★	★★★	★★★★★	★★★★★	★★		
Convenience	★★	★★	★★★	★★★	★★	★		
Scenery	★★★★★	★★★★	★★★	★★★★★	★★★★	★★★★		

	VAL D'ANNIVIERS	VERBIER	VILLARS	WENGEN	ZERMATT			
Page	495	499	510	513	518			
RPI	115	140	115	120	140			
Extent	★★	★★★★★	★★★	★★★	★★★★			
Fast lifts	★	★★★★	★★	★★★★	★★★★★			
Queues	★★★★	★★★	★★★	★★★	★★★			
Snow	★★★★	★★★	★★	★★	★★★★			
Expert	★★★★	★★★★★	★★	★★	★★★★			
Intermediate	★★★	★★★	★★★	★★★★	★★★★			
Beginner	★★★	★★	★★★★	★★★	★★			
Charm	★★★★★	★★★	★★★	★★★★★	★★★★			
Convenience	★★	★★	★★	★★★	★★			
Scenery	★★★★	★★★★	★★★	★★★★★	★★★★★			

Resort ratings at a glance

Resort news and key links: www.wheretoskiandsnowboard.com

Want a shortlist shortcut?

Our website will build a shortlist for you: you specify your priorities, and the system will use our resort ratings to draw up a shortlist – confined to one area or country, if you like.

www.wheretoskiandsnowboard.com

USA

	CALIFORNIA HEAVENLY	MAMMOTH MOUNTAIN	SQUAW VALLEY	COLORADO ASPEN	BEAVER CREEK	BRECKENR'GE	SNOWMASS
Page	533	538	543	546	553	555	560
RPI	150	150	150	180	180	160	175
Extent	★★★	★★★	★★★	★★	★★★	★★★	★★★
Fast lifts	★★★★	★★★★	★★★	★★★★	★★★★★	★★★★	★★★★★
Queues	★★★★	★★★★	★★★★	★★★★	★★★★★	★★★★	★★★★
Snow	★★★★	★★★★	★★★★	★★★★★	★★★★★	★★★★★	★★★★★
Expert	★★★	★★★★	★★★★	★★★★★	★★★★	★★★★	★★★★★
Intermediate	★★★★	★★★★	★★	★★★★★	★★★★	★★★★	★★★★★
Beginner	★★★★	★★★★	★★★★	★★★★★	★★★★★	★★★★★	★★★★★
Charm	★	★★	★★★	★★★★	★★	★★★	★★
Convenience	★	★★	★★★★	★★	★★★★	★★★	★★★★★
Scenery	★★★★	★★★	★★★	★★★	★★★	★★★	★★★★

	VAIL	WINTER PARK	UTAH ALTA	CANYONS	DEER VALLEY	PARK CITY	SNOWBIRD
Page	562	569	574	576	578	580	585
RPI	175	135	145	165	165	160	150
Extent	★★★★	★★★	★★★	★★★	★★	★★★	★★★
Fast lifts	★★★★★	★★★★	★★★★	★★★	★★★★	★★★	★★★★★
Queues	★★	★★★★	★★★	★★★★	★★★★	★★★★	★★★
Snow	★★★★★	★★★★★	★★★★★	★★★	★★★★	★★★★	★★★★★
Expert	★★★★	★★★★	★★★★★	★★★★	★★★	★★★★	★★★★★
Intermediate	★★★★★	★★★★	★★★	★★★★	★★★★	★★★★	★★★
Beginner	★★★	★★★★★	★★★	★★	★★★★	★★★★	★★
Charm	★★★	★★	★★	★★	★★★	★★★	★
Convenience	★★★	★★★	★★★★★	★★★★	★★★★	★★	★★★★★
Scenery	★★★	★★★	★★★	★★★	★★★	★★★	★★★

	REST OF THE WEST BIG SKY	JACKSON HOLE					
Page	588	593					
RPI	150	145					
Extent	★★★★	★★★					
Fast lifts	★★	★★★★					
Queues	★★★★★	★★★					
Snow	★★★★★	★★★★					
Expert	★★★★	★★★★★					
Intermediate	★★★★	★★					
Beginner	★★★★★	★★★					
Charm	★★	★★★					
Convenience	★★★★	★★★★					
Scenery	★★★	★★★					

Resort ratings at a glance

Build your own shortlist: www.wheretoskiandsnowboard.com

Want to keep up to date?

Our website has weekly resort news throughout the year, and you can register for our monthly email newsletter – with special holiday offers, as well as resort news highlights. **www.wheretoskiandsnowboard.com**

CANADA

	Banff	Big White	Fernie	Kicking Horse	Lake Louise			
Page	603	609	611	617	619			
RPI	150	140	145	160	150			
Extent	★★★	★★★	★★★	★★★	★★★			
Fast lifts	★★★★	★★★★	★★	★★★	★★★★			
Queues	★★★★	★★★★★	★★★★	★★★★	★★★★			
Snow	★★★★	★★★★★	★★★★	★★★★	★★★			
Expert	★★★★	★★★	★★★★★	★★★★	★★★★			
Intermediate	★★★★	★★★★	★★	★★	★★★★			
Beginner	★★★	★★★★	★★★★	★★★	★★★			
Charm	★★★	★★	★★	★★	★★★			
Convenience	★	★★★★	★★★★	★★★★	★			
Scenery	★★★★	★★★	★★★	★★★	★★★★			

	Revelstoke	Silver Star	Sun Peaks	Whistler				
Page	624	627	629	631				
RPI	145	140	145	165				
Extent	★★★	★★★	★★★	★★★★				
Fast lifts	★★★★★	★★★★	★★	★★★★★				
Queues	★★★★★	★★★★★	★★★★★	★★				
Snow	★★★★	★★★★	★★★★	★★★★				
Expert	★★★★★	★★★★	★★★	★★★★★				
Intermediate	★★	★★★	★★★★	★★★★★				
Beginner	★★	★★★★	★★★★	★★★				
Charm	★★	★★★	★★★	★★★				
Convenience	★★★	★★★★★	★★★★	★★★★				
Scenery	★★★★	★★★	★★★	★★★				

www.wheretoskiandsnowboard.com

Our website is designed to complement this book. We like to think it's one of the best in the ski business. On the site you'll find lots of interest to the keen skier/boarder:

- twice-weekly news and updates on all the major resorts in Europe and North America
- full editors' ratings for 200 resorts
- interactive shortlist builder – you plug in what you want most from a resort (eg village charm, extensive slopes) and up pops a shortlist to suit you
- snow reports and resort weather forecasts
- links to thousands of useful sites such as resorts, tour operators, ski schools, airlines

- free competitions with great prizes
- special offers from leading tour operators
- blogs from the editors on their travels
- dozens of background feature articles
- forums where you can exchange views, seek advice, give vent to those grumbles
- a resort reporting system, where you can file a report and maybe win a prize
- a sign-up for monthly e-newsletters

Resort shortlists

To help you spot resorts that will suit you

To streamline the job of drawing up your own shortlist, here are some ready-made ones. Many lists we've confined to Europe, because North America has too many qualifying resorts (eg for beginners) or because they do things differently there, making comparisons between here and there invalid (eg for off-piste).

Major Resorts
Expert knowledge

**4★ apartments,
high-altitude
skiing**

SkiCollection.co.uk
0844 576 0175
ABTA Bonded W5537

SOMETHING FOR EVERYONE
Everything from good nursery slopes to challenges for experts
Alpe-d'Huez, France 198
Les Arcs, France 208
Aspen, USA 546
Courchevel, France 240
Flaine, France 256
Mammoth Mountain, USA 538
Vail, USA 562
Val d'Isère, France 358
Whistler, Canada 631
Winter Park, USA 569

INTERNATIONAL OVERSIGHTS
Resorts that get less attention than they deserve
Alta, USA 574
Andermatt, Switzerland 454
Bad Gastein, Austria 104
Big Sky, USA 588
Laax, Switzerland 476
Monterosa Ski, Italy 412
Sella Ronda, Italy 425
Sölden, Austria 167
Val d'Anniviers, Switzerland 495
Vars / Risoul, France 375

HIGH-MILEAGE PISTE-BASHING
Extensive intermediate slopes with big, slick lift networks
Alpe-d'Huez, France 198
Les Arcs, France 208
Cervinia, Italy 387
Ellmau, Austria 110
Flaine, France 256
Kitzbühel, Austria 125
Laax, Switzerland 476
La Plagne, France 303
Portes du Soleil, France 314
Sella Ronda, Italy 425
Selva / Val Gardena, Italy 433
Söll, Austria 172
Three Valleys, France 344
Tignes, France 346
Vail, USA 562
Val d'Isère, France 358
Whistler, Canada 631
Zermatt, Switzerland 518

RELIABLE SNOW IN THE ALPS
Alpine resorts where snow is rarely in short supply
Cervinia, Italy 387
Chamonix, France 225
Courchevel, France 240
Les Deux-Alpes, France 250
Hintertux / Tux valley, Austria 113
Lech, Austria 133
Obergurgl, Austria 148
Obertauern, Austria 154
Saas-Fee, Switzerland 483
Sölden, Austria 167
Val d'Isère, France 358
Val Thorens, France 368
Zermatt, Switzerland 518

OFF-PISTE WONDERS
Alpine resorts where you can have the time of your life
Alpe-d'Huez, France 198
Andermatt, Switzerland 454
Chamonix, France 225
Davos, Switzerland 461
La Grave, France 265
Klosters, Switzerland 474
Lech, Austria 133
Monterosa Ski, Italy 412
St Anton, Austria 179
Tignes, France 346
Val d'Isère, France 358
Verbier, Switzerland 499

DRAMATIC SCENERY
Mountains that are spectacularly scenic as well as snowy
Chamonix, France 225
Cortina d'Ampezzo, Italy 393
Courmayeur, Italy 398
Grindelwald, Switzerland 470
Heavenly, USA 533
Lake Louise, Canada 619
Megève, France 267
Mürren, Switzerland 479
Sella Ronda, Italy 425
Selva / Val Gardena, Italy 433
St Moritz, Switzerland 488
Wengen, Switzerland 513
Zermatt, Switzerland 518

Authentic villages in large ski areas

0844 576 0173
peakretreats.co.uk

⏚ABTA
ABTA No. W5537

peak retreats

BACK-DOOR RESORTS
Cute little Alpine villages linked to big, bold ski areas
Les Brévières (Tignes), France 346
Champagny (La Plagne), France 303
Leogang (Saalbach), Austria 157
Montchavin (La Plagne), France 303
Peisey (Les Arcs), France 208
Le Pré (Les Arcs), France 208
Samoëns (Flaine), France 323
St-Martin (Trois Vallées), France 337
Stuben (St Anton), Austria 179
Vaujany (Alpe-d'Huez), France 198

VILLAGE CHARM
Traditional character – whether villages or towns
Aspen, USA 546
Champéry, Switzerland 456
Courmayeur, Italy 398
Les Gets, France 263
Kitzbühel, Austria 125
Lech, Austria 133
Megève, France 267
Mürren, Switzerland 479
Saas-Fee, Switzerland 483
Samoëns, France 323
Val d'Anniviers, Switzerland 495
Wengen, Switzerland 513
Zermatt, Switzerland 518

BLACK RUNS
Steep, mogully, lift-served slopes, protected from avalanche
Alta, USA 574
Andermatt, Switzerland 454
Aspen, USA 546
Beaver Creek, USA 553
Chamonix, France 225
Courchevel, France 240
Jackson Hole, USA 593
Snowbird, USA 585
Whistler, Canada 631
Winter Park, USA 569
Zermatt, Switzerland 518

POWDER PARADISES
Resorts with the snow and terrain for powder perfection
Alta, USA 574
Andermatt, Switzerland 454
Big Sky, USA 588
Big White, Canada 609
Fernie, Canada 611
La Grave, France 265
Jackson Hole, USA 593
Kicking Horse, Canada 617
Lech, Austria 133
Monterosa Ski, Italy 412
Revelstoke, Canada 624
Snowbird, USA 585
Ste-Foy-Tarentaise, France 334

CHOPAHOLICS
Resorts where you can have a day riding helicopters or cats
Aspen, USA 546
Courmayeur, Italy 398
Fernie, Canada 611
Lech, Austria 133
Monterosa Ski, Italy 412
Revelstoke, Canada 624
La Thuile, Italy 442
Verbier, Switzerland 499
Whistler, Canada 631
Zermatt, Switzerland 518

TOP TERRAIN PARKS
Alpine resorts with the best parks and pipes for freestyle thrills
Les Arcs, France 208
Avoriaz, France 218
Cervinia, Italy 387
Davos, Switzerland 461
Les Deux-Alpes, France 250
Ischgl, Austria 118
Laax, Switzerland 476
Lech, Austria 133
Livigno, Italy 403
Mayrhofen, Austria 142
Méribel, France 280
La Plagne, France 303
Saalbach-Hinterglemm, Austria 157
Saas-Fee, Switzerland 483
St Moritz, Switzerland 488

WEATHERPROOF SLOPES
Fairly snow-sure slopes if the sun shines, trees in case it doesn't
Les Arcs, France 208
Courchevel, France 240
Courmayeur, Italy 398
Laax, Switzerland 476
Schladming, Austria 163
Selva / Val Gardena, Italy 433
Serre-Chevalier, France 325
Sestriere, Italy 440
La Thuile, Italy 442

MOTORWAY CRUISING
Long, gentle, super-smooth pistes to bolster frail confidence
Les Arcs, France 208
Breckenridge, USA 555
Cervinia, Italy 387
Cortina d'Ampezzo, Italy 393
Courchevel, France 240
Megève, France 267
La Plagne, France 303
Snowmass, USA 560
La Thuile, Italy 442
Vail, USA 562

RESORTS FOR BEGINNERS
Gentle, snow-sure nursery slopes and easy long runs to progress to
Alpe-d'Huez, France 198
Cervinia, Italy 387
Courchevel, France 240
Flaine, France 256
Montgenèvre, France 289
Passo Tonale, Italy 418
La Plagne, France 303
La Rosière, France 319
Saas-Fee, Switzerland 483
Soldeu, Andorra 92

SPECIALLY FOR FAMILIES
Where you can easily find lodgings surrounded by snow
Les Arcs, France 208
Avoriaz, France 218
Flaine, France 256
Lech, Austria 133
Les Menuires, France 274
Montchavin, France 303
Mürren, Switzerland 479
La Plagne, France 303
La Rosière, France 319
Saas-Fee, Switzerland 483
Ste-Foy-Tarentaise, France 334
Vars / Risoul, France 375
Wengen, Switzerland 513

SNOW-SURE BUT SIMPATICO
High-rise slopes, but low-rise, traditional-style buildings
Andermatt, Switzerland 454
Arabba, Italy 425
Argentière, France 225
Ischgl, Austria 118
Lech, Austria 133
Monterosa Ski, Italy 412
Obergurgl, Austria 148
Saas-Fee, Switzerland 483
Sella Ronda, Italy 425
Val d'Anniviers, Switzerland 495
Zermatt, Switzerland 518

SPECIAL MOUNTAIN RESTAURANTS
Where satisfying lunches can add something extra to a holiday
Alpe-d'Huez, France 198
Cortina d'Ampezzo, Italy 393
Courmayeur, Italy 398
Kitzbühel, Austria 125
Megève, France 267
La Plagne, France 303
Saalbach-Hinterglemm, Austria 157
Sella Ronda, Italy 425
Selva / Val Gardena, Italy 433
Zermatt, Switzerland 518

MODERN CONVENIENCE
Plenty of slope-side lodgings where you can ski from the door
Les Arcs, France 208
Avoriaz, France 218
Courchevel, France 240
Flaine, France 256
Les Menuires, France 274
Obertauern, Austria 154
La Plagne, France 303
La Tania, France 340
Tignes, France 346
Val Thorens, France 368

LIVELY NIGHTLIFE
Where you'll have no difficulty finding somewhere to boogie
Chamonix, France 225
Ischgl, Austria 118
Kitzbühel, Austria 125
Mayrhofen, Austria 142
Méribel, France 280
Saalbach-Hinterglemm, Austria 157
Sauze d'Oulx, Italy 420
Sölden, Austria 167
St Anton, Austria 179
Val d'Isère, France 358
Verbier, Switzerland 499
Zermatt, Switzerland 518

OTHER AMUSEMENTS
Plenty to divert those not skiing or boarding
Bad Gastein, Austria 104
Chamonix, France 225
Cortina d'Ampezzo, Italy 393
Davos, Switzerland 461
Kitzbühel, Austria 125
Megève, France 267
St Moritz, Switzerland 488

AFFORDABLE FUN
Low in our RPI league table with good, reasonably extensive slopes
Ellmau, Austria 110
Mayrhofen, Austria 142
Monterosa Ski, Italy 412
Montgenèvre, France 289
La Rosière, France 319
Sauze d'Oulx, Italy 420
Schladming, Austria 163
Serre-Chevalier, France 325
Söll, Austria 172
La Thuile, Italy 442
Val Cenis Vanoise, France 355
Vars / Risoul, France 375

Resort shortlists

Build your own shortlist: www.wheretoskiandsnowboard.com

FINDING A RESORT

The bulk of the book consists of the chapters listed on the facing page, devoted to individual major resorts, plus minor resorts that share the same lift system or pass. Sometimes we devote a chapter to an area not dominated by one resort – then we use the area name (eg Monterosa Ski in Italy, Stubai valley in Austria, Val d'Anniviers in Switzerland).

Chapters are grouped by country: first, the six major European countries (including Germany); then the US and Canada (where resorts are grouped by states or regions); then minor European countries; and finally Japan. Within each group, resorts are ordered alphabetically.

Short cuts to the resorts that might suit you are provided (on the pages preceding this one) by a table of comparative **star ratings** and a series of **shortlists** of resorts with particular merits.

At the back of the book is an **index** to the resort chapters, combined with a **directory** giving basic information on hundreds of other minor resorts. Note that if the resort you are looking up is covered in a chapter devoted to a bigger resort (eg Argentière in the Chamonix chapter), the page reference will be to the start of the chapter, not to the exact page on which the minor resort is described.

There's further guidance on using our information in the chapter 'Choosing your resort', on page 74 – designed to be helpful particularly to people with little or no experience of ski resorts, who may not appreciate how big the differences between one resort and another can be.

READING A RESORT CHAPTER

There are various standard items at the start of each resort chapter. In the left margin, **star ratings** summarize our view of the resort, including its suitability for different levels of skill. The more stars, the better. In major resort chapters we give an expanded set of 19 ratings. Then comes our **Resort Price Index** – explained in outline on the facing page and in detail in the feature chapter on page 35.

We give web addresses of the **tourist office** (in North America, the ski lift company) and phone numbers for recommended **hotels**. We give star ratings for hotels – either official ones or ones awarded by major tour operators. The UK tour operators offering **package holidays** in major resorts are listed in the chapter, along with those going to minor resorts covered in the same chapter.

Our **mountain maps** show the resorts' own classification of runs. On some maps we show black diamonds to mark expert terrain without defined runs. We do not distinguish single-diamond terrain from the steeper double diamond.

We include on the map any lifts definitely expected to be in place for the coming season.

MAJOR LIFTS

On our piste maps we use the following symbols to identify **fast lifts**. Slow chairlifts do not get a chair symbol.

   fast chairlift

   gondola

   hybrid chondola

   cable car

   railway/funicular

THE WORLD'S BEST WINTER SPORTS RESORTS

To find a minor resort, or if you are not sure which country you should be looking under, consult the index/directory at the back of the book, which lists all resorts alphabetically.

ANDORRA	**88**
Arinsal	90
Soldeu	92

AUSTRIA	**98**
Bad Gastein	104
Bad Kleinkirchheim	107
Ellmau	110
Hintertux	113
Ischgl	118
Kitzbühel	125
Lech	133
Mayrhofen	142
Obergurgl	148
Obertauern	154
Saalbach-H'glemm	157
Schladming	163
Sölden	167
Söll	172
St Anton	179
Stubai valley	188
Zell Am See	190

FRANCE	**194**
Alpe-d'Huez	198
Les Arcs	208
Avoriaz	218
Les Carroz	223
Chamonix	225
Châtel	235
Courchevel	240
Les Deux-Alpes	250
Flaine	256
Les Gets	263
La Grave	265
Megève	267
Les Menuires	274
Méribel	280
Montgenèvre	289
Morzine	294
Paradiski	301
La Plagne	303
Portes du Soleil	314
Pyrenees	315
La Rosière	319
Samoëns	323
Serre-Chevalier	325
Ste-Foy-Tarentaise	334
St-Martin-de-B'ville	337
La Tania	340
Three Valleys	344
Tignes	346
Val Cenis Vanoise	355
Val d'Isère	358
Val Thorens	368
Vars / Risoul	375

GERMANY	**378**
Garmisch-Parten'n	380

ITALY	**382**
Cervinia	387
Cortina d'Ampezzo	393
Courmayeur	398
Livigno	403
Madonna di C'glio	407
Monterosa Ski	412
Passo Tonale	418
Sauze d'Oulx	420
Sella Ronda	425
Selva	433
Sestriere	440
La Thuile	442

SWITZERLAND	**444**
Adelboden	451
Andermatt	454
Champéry	456
Crans-Montana	459
Davos	461
Engelberg	468
Grindelwald	470
Klosters	474
Laax	476
Mürren	479
Saas-Fee	483
St Moritz	488
Val d'Anniviers	495
Verbier	499
Villars	510
Wengen	513
Zermatt	518

USA	**528**
CALIFORNIA	**532**
Heavenly	533
Mammoth	538
Squaw Valley	543

COLORADO	**545**
Aspen	546
Beaver Creek	553
Breckenridge	555
Snowmass	560
Vail	562
Winter Park	569

UTAH	**573**
Alta	574
Canyons	576
Deer Valley	578
Park City	580
Snowbird	585

REST OF WEST	**587**
Big Sky	588
Jackson Hole	593

NEW ENGLAND	**598**

CANADA	**600**
WESTERN CANADA	**602**
Banff	603
Big White	609
Fernie	611
Kicking Horse	617
Lake Louise	619
Revelstoke	624
Silver Star	627
Sun Peaks	629
Whistler	631

EASTERN CANADA	**640**

THE REST	
SPAIN	**641**
FINLAND	**643**
NORWAY	**645**
SWEDEN	**647**
BULGARIA	**648**
ROMANIA	**651**
SLOVENIA	**652**
SCOTLAND	**655**
JAPAN	**656**

RESORT PRICE INDEX BOXES

Our RPI figures show how prices in each resort compare with the average eurozone resort, taking account of food and drink, lift pass, ski hire and lessons. RPIs around the average figure of 100 are in blue boxes. RPIs of 90 or less get a green box. RPIs of 120 or more get a red box. Our price survey is fully explained, and some of the results are summarized, in our chapter on 'Cutting your costs', on page 35.

RPI	90
RPI	100
RPI	120

Our resort chapters

87

Build your own shortlist: www.wheretoskiandsnowboard.com

Andorra

Andorra is a tiny, almost entirely mountainous state sandwiched between France and Spain. It built its prosperity on the twin pillars of tax-haven status and low-cost tourism – particularly winter tourism, and particularly in the UK market. Andorra used to be seen primarily as a cheap and cheerful holiday destination, attracting singles and young couples looking for a good time in the duty-free bars and clubs, as well as learning to ski or snowboard. But the place has changed radically over the last 25 years and has tried to move upmarket.

LIFT PASS

Ski Andorra
The Ski Andorra pass covers all Andorran areas and allows skiing at any single one of them each day: €205 for five non-consecutive days

Soldeu, the main resort, is no longer cheap. Our price survey shows it to be more expensive than many high-profile Alpine resorts that have much more appeal. And its popularity has fallen. According to the Crystal Ski Industry Report, a decade ago Andorra's share of the UK ski market was 14%; it is now around 7%. And a decade ago we received several reader reports a year; this year we received none.

The main resorts – **Soldeu** and **Pas de la Casa** (which share the fairly extensive Grandvalira ski area) and **Arinsal** (linked to **Pal** to form a much more modest area) – are covered in the two chapters that follow this.

The other main ski area is **Arcalis**, tucked away at the head of a long valley with no accommodation at its base. For non-beginners it makes a very worthwhile day trip, particularly from Arinsal and Pal, with which it shares a lift pass. The terrain is varied and scenic, the slopes are usually deserted except at weekends, and the snow is usually the best in Andorra. There is excellent intermediate and beginner terrain, but what marks it out is the expert terrain, including lots of off-piste between the marked runs.

The capital, **Andorra la Vella**, is choked by traffic and fumes but worth a visit for its duty-free shopping and the splendid Caldea spa at Escaldes-Engordany, just outside the centre, with a fantastic array of pools, baths and treatments.

TOURIST OFFICES

Ski Andorra
www.skiandorra.ad
Arcalis
www.vallnord.com

GRANDVALIRA

← Andorra is a good place to learn to ski but is no longer cheap and cheerful

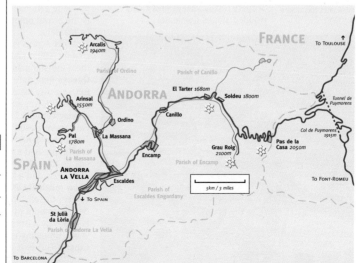

Arinsal

Lively base that suits beginners (thanks to an excellent school), with a cable car link to Pal to keep intermediates amused

TOP 10 RATINGS

Extent	★
Fast lifts	★★
Queues	★★★
Snow	★★★★
Expert	★
Intermediate	★★
Beginner	★★★★
Charm	★
Convenience	★★★
Scenery	★★★

RPI	90
lift pass	£160
ski hire	£115
lessons	£60
food & drink	£120
total	**£455**

+ Lively bars

+ Ski school geared to British needs

+ Cable car link with Pal, and lift pass shared also with Arcalis

+ Pretty, treelined slopes in Pal

− Arinsal slopes are bleak and very confined (though this does mean children can't stray far)

− Linear, dour village with no focus

− Poor bus link to Arcalis

Tour operators used to bring British beginners here in large numbers. Low prices and the Brit-oriented ski school were key factors; but prices are no longer that different from those in more attractive Austrian and Italian resorts.

VALLNORD

The accommodation, bars and restaurants are set along this road, which dominates the village ↓

THE RESORT

Arinsal sits near the head of a steep-sided valley north of Andorra la Vella. Pal has a more open setting in another valley. The two are linked by cable car.

The valley town of La Massana is linked by gondola to Pal's slopes, and makes a better base for those wanting to spend some time at Arcalis (read the Andorra introduction). The Vallnord lift pass covers all of these areas.
Village charm The resort is a long, narrow village of grey, stone-clad buildings. It's no beauty, but the atmosphere is friendly and relaxed, the people friendly and helpful.
Convenience The main gondola starts from the village centre and you have to ride it down as well as up; the alternative is a six-pack 1km away at Cota, with a piste to return. There are free buses linking the lift bases. You can leave kit at the top of the lift.
Scenery Shady valleys and nicely wooded slopes dominate.

THE MOUNTAINS

The slopes are in an open but extremely narrow bowl, facing east. Pal has the most densely wooded slopes in Andorra. Most face east; those down to the link with Arinsal face north. The piste map is very poor, covering distant Arcalis as well as Arinsal and Pal and showing the roads and local hamlets in more detail than the ski areas – nuts! There's a 'Freeride area' marked but not explained. Signposting is good though.
Slopes Arinsal's slopes consist essentially of a single, long, narrow bowl above the top gondola station at Comallempla, served by a network of chairs and drags, including a six-pack. Almost at the top is the cable car link with Pal. Pal's slopes are widely spread around the mountain, with four main lift bases, all reachable by road. The main one, La Caubella, at the opposite extreme from the Arinsal link, is the arrival point of the gondola from La Massana.
Fast lifts Access is by gondola or fast chairlift. Other fast chairs exist, but there are still many slow lifts too.
Queues Reporters note few problems. But you may meet queues to ride the gondola down, and for the nursery moving carpets. The cable car link with Pal can be closed by high winds.
Terrain parks Arinsal's big freestyle area impressed a recent reporter; it has its own lift, rails and jumps, a snowcross and a beginner zone.
Snow reliability With most runs above 1950m, the easterly orientation and a decent amount of snowmaking, snow is relatively assured even in poor snow years. Grooming is good.
Experts This isn't a great area for experts, but there is a 'freeride area'

KEY FACTS	
Resort	1475m
	4,840ft
Slopes	1550-2560m
	5,090-8,400ft
Lifts	31
Pistes	63km
	39 miles
Green	16%
Blue	36%
Red	38%
Black	10%
Snowmaking	
	296 guns

UK PACKAGES

Crystal, Inghams, Neilson, Ski Line, Skitracer, STC, Thomson

Phone numbers
From abroad use the prefix +376

TOURIST OFFICE

Arinsal and Pal
www.vallnord.com

marked on the map and some good tree skiing in Pal. Arcalis has more off-piste (and two 'freeride areas').

Intermediates Arinsal offers a fair range of difficulty, but competent intermediates will want to explore the much more interesting, varied and extensive Pal slopes, and perhaps make a day trip or two to Arcalis.

Beginners Around half the guests here are beginners. A special pass is available (15.50 euros per day), though we guess most people will book ski rental/pass/tuition packs from their tour operators. The nursery slopes are wide, gentle and set apart from the main runs and a reporter with a beginner girlfriend thought they were great. They can get crowded, though. There are longer easy runs to progress to as well.

Snowboarding It's a fine place to learn, but over half the lifts are drags and some of them are vicious. There are some flat sections in Pal.

Cross-country There isn't any.

Mountain restaurants These are mainly uninspiring self-service snackeries, and crowded. The Igloo does 'good hearty fare from a varied menu'.

Schools and guides The school is crucial to the appeal of the resort; over half the instructors are native English speakers. A recent reporter says: 'All instructors spoke good English and were helpful; rates were good and our daughter thoroughly enjoyed her sessions.'

Families There are themed ski kindergartens for four- to eight-year-olds and nurseries for children aged one to four at both Pal and Arinsal.

STAYING THERE

Hotels The Princesa Parc (736350) is a big, glossy 4-star place near the gondola – 'great value, excellent facilities'; swanky spa (open to non-residents) and a bowling alley. Rooms in the hotel Arinsal (838889) are not large, but the hotel is ideally placed and has a pleasant bar. The 3-star Crest (738020) is at the bottom of the run to Cota, handy for the fast chair up to the slopes. The Husa Xalet Verdú (737140) is a smooth little 3-star – 'great cost-effective base: good-sized room, friendly staff and decent food'. The Micolau (737707) is a characterful stone house near the centre with a jolly, beamed restaurant.

Apartments There is a reasonable choice of places.

Eating out The Sidreria Pub Herri serves traditional Basque food. Cisco's is a Tex-Mex place in a lovely wood and stone building. The Surf disco-pub has been recommended for its steaks.

Après-ski Arinsal has plenty of lively bars 'from full-on 18–30 drink fests to great family places'. The hotel Arinsal has good-value pints. The Derby Irish pub 'manages to do great live music and beer while being family-friendly'. For a wilder time try El Cau or Surf.

Off the slopes Activities include helicopter rides, dog sledding, snowmobiling, snowshoeing, tobogganing, snow bikes, ice-diving and paragliding. Andorra la Vella is half an hour away by taxi or infrequent bus: 'A shopper's paradise,' says a recent visitor.

Arinsal

91

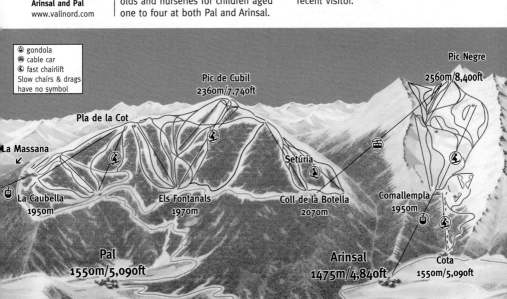

SNOWPIX.COM / CHRIS GILL

Soldeu

Our favourite place to stay in Andorra: not an attractive village, but centrally placed in the impressive Grandvalira ski area

RATINGS

The mountains

Extent	★★★
Fast lifts	★★
Queues	★★★
Terrain p'ks	★★★★
Snow	★★★
Expert	★★
Intermediate	★★★★
Beginner	★★★★
Boarder	★★★★
X-country	★
Restaurants	★★
Schools	★★★★★
Families	★★

The resort

Charm	★
Convenience	★★★
Scenery	★★★
Eating out	★★★
Après-ski	★★★★
Off-slope	★

RPI   115

lift pass	£200
ski hire	£155
lessons	£105
food & drink	£140
total	**£600**

NEWS

2013/14: The ski school opened a Freeride Center with 10 specialist instructors to teach off-piste skills. New jibs were added to Snowpark El Tarter, and new lines of kickers and rails plus a sound system were added to Snowpark Xavi at Grau Roig. Snowmaking was increased by 5%.

+ Rivals some serious Alpine resorts in terms of size

+ Excellent beginner and early intermediate terrain

+ Ski school has excellent British-run section for English-speaking visitors

− Village is spread along a busy through-road, lacking atmosphere

− Slopes can get very crowded

− Expensive lift pass, and beginners are charged the full cost

− Not much to do off the slopes

If we were planning a holiday in Andorra, it would be in Soldeu (or the isolated hotel at Grau Roig, up the road). It is best placed to explore the extensive Grandvalira area. But the village is a difficult place to like, and beginners be warned: you are forced to buy one of Europe's priciest passes.

THE RESORT

Soldeu is set on a steep hillside facing the ski area across the valley. It is on the busy road that runs down the valley from France to Andorra la Vella and on to Spain. The Grandvalira ski area is shared with several alternative bases. Chief among them is Pas de la Casa, near the French border; El Tarter, a few miles down the valley from Soldeu, also has both lifts and return pistes. Further down still, Canillo and Encamp have gondolas but no pistes. Outings to other resorts in Andorra are possible – Arcalis in particular is worth the trip, but it's easiest by car. The Ski Andorra pass covers them all.

VILLAGE CHARM ★
An urban ribbon
The village is an ever-growing ribbon of modern hotels, apartments and bars, with the occasional shop; the buildings have traditional stone cladding and mostly chalet-style roofs. Sounds OK, but it isn't; this is not a place to wander about at teatime – there is no focus or atmosphere, and traffic on the through-road can be heavy and sometimes fast.

CONVENIENCE ★★★
Over the river
A steep hillside leads down from the village to the river, and the slopes are on the opposite side. A gondola or a six-pack takes you to the heart of the slopes at Espiolets, and a wide bridge across the river forms the end of the piste home, with elevators to take you up to street level. There are ski lockers at the bottom or top of the gondola. Along the road down to El Tarter,

hotels and apartments are sold by tour operators under the Soldeu banner – so check where your proposed accommodation is if you want to avoid long walks or lots of bus rides. There is a valley bus running fairly frequently.

SCENERY ★★★
Unremarkable
Soldeu sits in a long, quite attractively wooded valley, and from the slopes there are wide mountain views, but they don't include notable drama.

THE MOUNTAINS

Soldeu's main local slopes are on open mountainsides; there are runs in the woods back to Soldeu and El Tarter, but they can be challenging, especially when conditions are not particularly good. Reporters praise signposting, but classification of the runs often overstates difficulty. The piste map is very cramped.

EXTENT OF THE SLOPES ★★★
Pleasantly varied but crowded
The resort claims 210km of pistes, but the Schrahe report (read our feature on piste extent) suggests that the total is around 50km fewer.

The village gondola rises over wooded, north-facing slopes to **Espiolets**, a broad shelf that is virtually a mini-resort – the ski school is based here, and there are extensive nursery slopes. From Espiolets, a gentle run to the east takes you to an area of long, easy runs served by a six-pack. Beyond that is an extensive area of more varied slopes that links with the Pas de la Casa area. Going west from

KEY FACTS

| Resort | 1800m |
| | 5,910ft |

Grandvalira (Soldeu/El Tarter/Pas/Grau Roig)

Slopes	1710-2560m
	5,610-8,400ft
Lifts	64
Pistes	210km
	130 miles
Green	15%
Blue	38%
Red	28%
Black	19%
Snowmaking	65%

LIFT PASSES

Prices in €

Age	1-day	6-day
under 12	32	162
12 to 17	41	216
18 to 64	44	240
65 plus	25	150

Free Under 6, 70 plus
Beginner Pass €30 per day in Canillo, El Tarter, Grau Roig and Pas de la Casa
Notes Covers all lifts in Soldeu, El Tarter, Canillo, Grau Roig and Pas de la Casa; pedestrian and half-day passes available
Alternative pass
The Ski Andorra pass covers all Andorran areas and allows skiing at any single one of them each day; €205 for five non-consecutive days

PAUL CARTER

Soldeu has fabulous beginner and early intermediate terrain
→

Espiolets takes you to the open bowl of **Riba Escorxada** and the arrival point of the gondola up from El Tarter. From here, another six-pack serves sunny slopes on Tosa dels Espiolets, and a fourth goes to the high point of Tossal de la Llosada and the link with **El Forn** above Canillo.

FAST LIFTS ★★
Fine access but ...
Most of Grandvalira's key lifts are high-speed chairs or gondolas, but there are a lot of slow lifts too.

QUEUES ★★★
Some bottlenecks
The lift system generally copes. There can be morning queues for the gondola, but the next-door chair offers an alternative. Up the mountain, the chairlifts in both directions out of Grau Roig ('pronounced Rosh') are the main bottleneck; the quad at Cubil and access to Tosa Espiolets are also awful, said a February visitor. You may find crowds on some blue slopes (including lots of school classes snaking along) – the reds and blacks are much quieter.

TERRAIN PARKS ★★★★
There are three
The main park – Snowpark El Tarter – above Riba Escorxada has a good reputation. Features normally include a triple line of kickers, huge gap jump, jib and giant airbag. There's a great selection of rails, including a big rainbow rail and wave-box and a wall

ride. For beginners there are three small jumps, a 5m medium jump and a couple of fun boxes. A half-pipe is built when conditions permit. A draglift serves the park, and a fast quad nearby takes you slightly higher up.

Snowpark Xavi at Grau Roig is for beginners and intermediates and has kickers, jibs, rails and boxes.

The Sunset Park Peretol, above Bordes d'Envalira, caters for all levels. It has an intriguing 'street' zone that resembles a village square, they say. It is floodlit in the evenings, with music. A park-only day pass is available.

SNOW RELIABILITY ★★★
Much better than people expect
Despite its name (Soldeu means Sun God) the slopes generally enjoy reliable snow. Most slopes are north-facing, with a good natural snow record; there's extensive snowmaking, and excellent grooming helps maintain good snow.

FOR EXPERTS ★★
Hope for good snow off-piste
It's a limited area for experts – on-piste, at least. The Avet black run going directly down to Soldeu deserves its grading, but most of the other blacks do not. The blacks on Tosa dels Espiolets, for example, are indistinguishable from the adjacent (and more direct) red and blue. And don't go looking for moguls – the grooming is too thorough.

But there is plenty of off-piste potential and off-piste routes are

ACTIVITIES

Indoor Spas, pools, hot tubs (in hotels), bowling (at Pas)

Outdoor Helicopter rides, paragliding snowmobiling, dog sledding, snowshoeing, snow biking (not all in Soldeu itself)

marked on the piste map in the bowl above Riba Escorxada and above El Forn – these are shown dotted on our map. And the ungroomed, liftless bowl between Riba Escorxada and El Forn is served by a snowcat tow. The off-piste remains untouched for days because most visitors are beginners and early intermediates. There's no explanation on the piste map of whether off-piste routes are avalanche controlled, marked or patrolled. Heli-skiing is available too.

FOR INTERMEDIATES ★★★★
Lots to explore
There is plenty to amuse intermediates. The area east of Espiolets is splendid for building confidence, and those already confident will be able to explore the whole mountain. Riba Escorxada is a fine section for mixed-ability groups. The Canillo/El Forn sector has an easy, little-used blue run along the ridge with excellent views all the way to Pal and Arinsal and an easy black in the valley. Many of the blues and reds have short steeper sections, preceded by a 'slow' sign and netting in the middle of the piste to slow you down.

FOR BEGINNERS ★★★★
Good, but not ideal
In some respects this is an excellent place to start, particularly because of the school. But it's not ideal: you have to go up the mountain to the nursery slopes, which is not only inconvenient but also expensive. There is no special beginner pass here (unlike other base villages in the area). If you buy a ski pack through your tour operator, you may not care, of course. Soldeu's Espiolets nursery area is vast, and there's a smaller area at Riba Escorxada, above El Tarter – each with a moving carpet. They are relatively snow-sure, and there are numerous easy pistes to move on to (though the crowds can be off-putting). The runs to resort level can be quite challenging because of crowds and snow conditions. Near-beginners are often better off riding a lift down.

FOR BOARDERS ★★★★
Pick of the Pyrenees
Soldeu has become the home of snowboarding in the Pyrenees. This is a perfect place for beginners to learn on wide, gentle slopes that are served mainly by chairs, not drags. Just be wary of the plentiful flat spots. For the

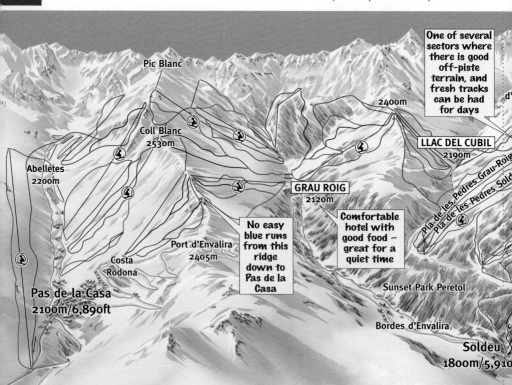

Pic Blanc

Coll Blanc
2530m

Abelletes
2200m

Costa
Rodona

Pas de la Casa
2100m/6,890ft

Port d'Envalira
2405m

No easy blue runs from this ridge down to Pas de la Casa

GRAU ROIG
2120m

Comfortable hotel with good food – great for a quiet time

One of several sectors where there is good off-piste terrain, and fresh tracks can be had for days

2400m

LLAC DEL CUBIL
2190m

Pla de les Pedres-Grau Roig
Pla de les Pedres Sol

Sunset Park Peretol

Bordes d'Envalira

Soldeu
1800m/5,910

SCHOOLS

Soldeu
t 753191

Classes
5 3hr-days: from
€129

Private lessons
From €98 for 2hr

CHILDCARE

Nurseries run by ski school
t 753191
Ages 1 to 4

Snow gardens run by ski school
t 753191
Ages 3 to 6

Ski school
Ages 6 to 11

more advanced, Soldeu offers some good off-piste and the best terrain parks in the Pyrenees. Backcountry enthusiasts should also visit Arcalis, which has the steepest terrain, and Pal, for the tree runs.

FOR CROSS-COUNTRY ★☆☆☆☆
Head for Grau Roig
The nearest loops are at Grau Roig (read the Pas de la Casa section), reachable by bus.

MOUNTAIN RESTAURANTS ★★☆☆☆
Not a highlight
Restaurants are marked but not named on the piste map. A recent reporter said bluntly: 'Poor – head to the village.' But an earlier reporter enjoyed 'really nice Catalan sausage, roast cod, beef shank and pasta' at various places. The table-service section of Arosseria Pi de Migdia at the top of the El Tarter gondola has been recommended. Not far away, the Riba Escorxada restaurant includes a trattoria-pizzeria with a neat little terrace. At Espiolets, the Gall de Bosc (steakhouse) has table-service. But the best places are over towards Pas de la Casa – read that section. There is a picnic room at Espiolets.

SCHOOLS AND GUIDES ★★★★★
One of the best for Brits
The school is well set up to deal with the huge numbers of beginner Brits, with a dedicated team of mostly native English-speaking instructors led by an Englishman. Reporters are almost all extremely positive (we have only one mildly dissenting voice in the stack of reports we have on file). Our most recent reporter said the school was 'brilliant – catered for our mixed-ability group well'.

Off-piste skills are being taught at the new Freeride Center.

FOR FAMILIES ★★☆☆☆
Unconvincing
Soldeu doesn't strike us as a great place for families, with its busy through-road and remote nursery slopes. Whether skiing or not, children are looked after at the mid-mountain stations. There are nurseries and snow gardens for children aged three to six at various points, and three kids' circuits with themed runs – at Riba Escorxada above El Tarter and two in Grau Roig.

Soldeu

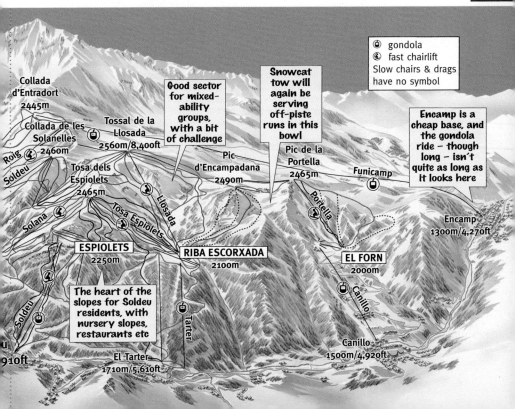

gondola
fast chairlift
Slow chairs & drags have no symbol

Collada d'Entradort
2445m

Collada de les Solanelles
2460m

Roig
Soldeu

Tossal de la Llosada
2560m/8,400ft

Good sector for mixed-ability groups, with a bit of challenge

Tosa dels Espiolets
2465m

Solana

Tosa Espiolets

Llosada

Pic d'Encampadana
2490m

Snowcat tow will again be serving off-piste runs in this bowl

Pic de la Portella
2465m

Portella

Funicamp

Encamp is a cheap base, and the gondola ride – though long – isn't quite as long as it looks here

Encamp
1300m/4,270ft

ESPIOLETS
2250m

RIBA ESCORXADA
2100m

EL FORN
2000m

The heart of the slopes for Soldeu residents, with nursery slopes, restaurants etc

Soldeu

Tarter

Canillo

Canillo
1500m/4,920ft

910ft

El Tarter
1710m/5,610ft

↑ Pas de la Casa is set in a bleak position near the top of a pass and its slopes are above the treeline – not good in poor weather
GRANDVALIRA

UK PACKAGES

Soldeu Absolutely Snow, Crystal, Crystal Finest, Elegant Resorts, Inghams, Neilson, Ski Line, Skitracer, STC, Thomson, Zenith
El Tarter Absolutely Snow, Crystal, Interactive Resorts, Neilson, Ski Club Freshtracks, Skitracer, Thomson
Canillo Absolutely Snow
Pas de la Casa Absolutely Snow, Crystal, Inghams, Lagrange, Neilson, Skitracer, Thomson, Zenith

Pierre ⓢ Vacances
Holidays made for me

Best price guarantee for ski in/out budget studios up to spacious 3 bedroom apartments

pierreetvacances.co.uk

STAYING THERE

Hotels Beware hotels sold under the Soldeu name that are actually some way out of town.
*****Sport Hotel Hermitage (870670) At the foot of the slopes; all bedrooms are suites with mountain views. A huge spa is part of the hotel.
****Euro Esquí (736666) On road to El Tarter but there is a shuttle. 'Large rooms and good buffet food.'
****Himàlaia (878515) Central, with sauna, steam and hot tub.
****Piolets Park (871787) Beside the gondola, with a pool and spa.
****Sport (870600) Over the road from the other two Sports. Spa. Lively, comfortable bar and disco-bar.
****Sport Hotel Village (870500) Right by the Hermitage. Stylish public areas – comfortable chairs and sofas, high ceilings, beams and picture windows. Spa.
**Bruxelles (851010) Recommended for its helpful staff and cleanliness; 50m from the lift.

EATING OUT ★★★☆☆
Some atmospheric places
Most of Soldeu's restaurants are hotel-based. But we've enjoyed meals in two atmospheric old restored buildings: Fat Albert's (steaks, fish, burgers) and Borda del Rector (Andorran cuisine), nearer to El Tarter than Soldeu.

APRES-SKI ★★★★☆
No shortage of live music
Lots of bars have regular or occasional live music or DJs – reader favourites include the Aspen, Fat Albert's and the Villager (with Elvis nights too).

OFF THE SLOPES ★☆☆☆☆
Head downhill
Soldeu has lots of sporting activities, including snowmobiling and dog sledding, but is otherwise not great in this respect. The Sport Hotel Hermitage (pricey) and Piolets Park (cheaper) both have excellent spas. Down in Canillo is the Palau de Gel (see below). Andorra la Vella, the capital of Andorra, has good shopping and the Caldea spa (an amazing array of pools, baths and treatments).

LINKED RESORT – 1710m
EL TARTER

El Tarter is rather sprawling, with no real centre, and is quiet at night. But it's otherwise a good base for the area. There are two blue runs to the resort, and a black that is an FIS (International Ski Federation)-approved downhill race course.

LINKED RESORT – 1500m
CANILLO

This acceptably pleasant spot has no runs to valley level, but has a gondola up to El Forn. The impressive Palau de Gel has lots of diversions – an Olympic ice rink plus pool, gym, sports hall etc.

LINKED RESORT – 1300m
ENCAMP

Encamp is a traffic-choked town with a long gondola to Cortals, one of the high points of the Soldeu slopes, where there is a beginner area, and onward pistes to Soldeu. There is no return piste.

ski racer
CHALETS, HOTELS
& APARTMENTS
Call us today
020 8600 1650
skitracer.com

Pas de la Casa 2100m

+ Some conveniently placed hotels
+ Andorra's liveliest nightlife
+ Attractive hotel at Grau Roig

− Village an eyesore and traffic-choked
− Weekend crowds from France
− Few trees for poor-weather days

Pas has the reputation as Andorra's wildest party resort, and we don't doubt it. Having driven through it and skied down to it, we are quite happy to stay over the hill in Soldeu – or, for doorstep access to the Grandvalira slopes, at secluded Grau Roig. So are you, it seems: reports are rarely sighted.

Village charm Pas is a sizeable collection of dreary concrete-box-style apartment blocks and hotels, a product of the late 1960s and early 1970s. The central area at the base of the slopes is traffic-free, but elsewhere traffic and fumes are intrusive. By contrast, the mini-resort of Grau Roig over the ridge from Pas has an isolated hotel in an attractively wooded setting.

Convenience Most accommodation is conveniently placed near the lift base and slopes. There are plenty of shops and bars, as well as a sports centre.

Scenery Pas has a bleak position near the top of a high mountain pass, but there are fine views from the ridges.

THE MOUNTAIN

Slopes The slopes above Pas are all open, and vulnerable to bad weather. But there is some attractively wooded terrain over the ridge in the Grau Roig valley. From there a single lift goes on further west to the rest of the Grandvalira ski area. In the opposite direction of Pas, a six-pack serving two runs heads towards another ridge and the French border.

Fast lifts Fast chairs exist, but they are outnumbered by slow ones and drags.

Queues Queues are rarely serious during the week, except at key bottlenecks. But at weekends and French school holidays some can develop, especially at Grau Roig.

Terrain parks There's one on the Pas side, together with a snowcross, and another at Grau Roig.

Snow reliability The combination of height and lots of snowmaking means good snow reliability, but we've generally found snow quality to be better in the Soldeu sector.

Experts There are few challenges on-piste, but there seem to be plenty of off-piste slopes inviting exploration – above Grau Roig, in particular.

Intermediates The local slopes suit confident intermediates best – especially those over the ridge, above

Grau Roig; more timid intermediates would be better off based in Soldeu.

Beginners There are beginner slopes in Pas and Grau Roig. The Pas area is a short but inconvenient bus ride out of town. Progression to longer runs is easier in the Grau Roig sector.

Snowboarding Boarding is popular with the young crowd that the resort attracts. Drags are usually avoidable.

Cross-country There are 8km of loops near Grau Roig.

Mountain restaurants The Rifugi dels Llacs de Pessons above Grau Roig at the head of the bowl is our favourite: a cosy, beamed table-service place with good local food. The Grau Roig hotel is another good option.

Schools and guides The ski school has a high reputation, but a reporter complains of big classes ('16 in one').

Families There are ski kindergartens at Pas and Grau Roig, and a non-ski one at the latter for one to four year olds.

STAYING THERE

Hotels The Himàlaia-Pas (735515) is in a good position, with a pool and sauna. But the Grau Roig hotel (755556) is in a league of its own; comfortable and smart, with a spa and 'lovely food'.

Apartments Those in the Frontera Blanca are simple, but in pole position at the foot of the slopes.

Eating out It's not a resort for gourmets – but there is a wide enough choice of places to eat. Local tips include Cal Padrí (Catalan food) and KSB (Kamikaze Surf Bar – steakhouse).

Après-ski Après-ski can be very lively, at least at peak holiday times. Popular places include Déjà Beer, a quirky pub with tapas, Paddy's Irish Bar and the Underground.

Off the slopes You can go snowmobiling, snowshoeing, take a helicopter ride, visit the leisure centre, and take a trip to Andorra la Vella for stylish shopping and the impressive Caldea spa.

GETTING THERE

Air Toulouse 175km/110 miles (2hr30)

Rail L'Hospitalet-Près-L'Andorre (20km/ 13 miles); buses and taxis to Soldeu

Central reservations phone number
Call 801074
Phone numbers
From abroad use the prefix +376

TOURIST OFFICE

www.grandvalira.com

Build your own shortlist: **www.wheretoskiandsnowboard.com**

Austria's holiday recipe is quite distinctive. It doesn't suit everybody, but for many holidaymakers nothing else will do; in particular, French resorts will not do. Austria is the land of cute little valley villages clustered around onion-domed churches – there are no monstrous modern apartment blocks here. It's the land of prettily wooded mountains, reassuring to beginners and timid intermediates in a way that bleak snowfields and craggy peaks will never be. It's the land of friendly, welcoming people who speak good English. And it's the land of jolly, alcohol-fuelled après-ski action – in many resorts starting in mid-afternoon with dancing in mountain restaurants, and going on as long as you have the legs for it.

Back in the 1980s, Austria dominated the British skiing market. But gradually the powerful allure of the high, snow-sure French mega-resorts began to exert itself. By 1995 France had taken the lead, and it has kept it ever since. The pendulum is now swinging back: the annual Crystal Ski Industry Report shows that Austria's market share has risen over the last decade or so from 20% to 28%. But for the moment France is still well ahead, at around 33%.

There are three key factors in the revival: lift systems – these days, the most efficient lift systems in Europe are not in France but in Austria; snowmaking, which is now so widespread that you can expect reliable snow-cover even at the low altitudes typical of Austrian villages; and low on-the-spot prices. As our price survey shows, Austrian resorts are generally cheaper than the big French resorts that Brits tend to flock to – especially for eating and drinking.

Being the land of cute valley villages and friendly wooded mountains does have a downside: resorts that conform to this pattern are at low altitude, and as a result don't offer reliably good natural snow. Last season was an especially bad year for snow in Austria – resorts like Kitzbühel and Söll received 40% less than their normal amount of snow (after a few bumper seasons). But it is in years like 2014 that snowmaking comes into its own. Most low resorts have radically improved their snowmaking in the last 20 years. So despite the snow drought, readers repeatedly told us they had a good time on piste (but not off): 'almost every run was open' was a typical comment about pistes in the low SkiWelt area this season. Of course, snow isn't simply a matter of covering the slopes: quality matters too, and it's still the case that low altitude tends to go hand in hand with slushy snow in the middle of the day and icy snow at the start and end of the day. But piste grooming has improved things greatly over the years too and again, this was reflected in comments from reporters such as: 'they did a brilliant job in difficult conditions,' said a Kitzbühel reporter.

SNOWPIX.COM / CHRIS GILL

← Like Kitzbühel (pictured here) most Austrian resorts have lots of mountain restaurants. And many of them go straight from lunch into après-ski mode

There are some resorts that don't conform to the Austrian pattern, of course, including some excellent high-altitude ski areas – notably Obergurgl, Ischgl and Obertauern. We had a fab morning in Ischgl on their last day of the season, 4 May 2014, when there was no shortage of snow and even some fresh powder. There are also some excellent glacier areas in Austria, including what we reckon are the world's best, at Hintertux and in the Stubai valley.

↑ Ischgl is one of the most snow-sure Austrian resorts – we had a great morning's skiing here on 4 May this year

TVB PAZNAUN-ISCHGL

Western Austria also has areas that get huge amounts of snow – the Lech/ Zürs/Warth ski area is the snowiest corner of the Alps (the three resorts were linked by a new gondola for 2013/14).

THE WORLD'S BEST LIFT SYSTEMS

The improvement in Austrian lift systems over the last decade comes as a surprise to many people. When we invented our 'fast lifts' rating a few years back, we certainly got some surprises. The European resorts with the highest proportions of fast lifts in their networks are Saalbach-Hinterglemm and Ischgl, both in Austria. Kitzbühel, Obergurgl and Obertauern also get five stars.

SKI ROUTE CONFUSION

In many resorts you have to deal with chaotic handling of the concept of 'ski routes'. If a resort's piste map explains what a ski route is (and many don't), it often says a ski route is a run that is marked and avalanche controlled but not groomed or patrolled. Officially, we are told, the rule throughout Austria is that a ski route is 'marked, protected against avalanche hazards and can be groomed and patrolled'. In practice, many routes are groomed; they may or may not be patrolled. This is madness. If such a run is groomed *and* patrolled, it is a piste, and should be identified as such so that people skiing solo can confidently go down it. If it is groomed *but not* patrolled, it opens up the insane possibility that people skiing solo might descend it by mistake.

THE PARTY STARTS EARLY

These days, one of the things that annoys us most about Austrian skiing is the strange business of opening hours or, strictly speaking, closing hours. As spring approaches, lift closing times in the rest of the Alps, even for some high-altitude cable cars, drift towards 5pm or even later. In most Austrian resorts, basically the lifts shut at around 4pm, even if there are three hours of daylight remaining. Nuts.

You're welcome to stay on the mountain drinking, and descend at leisure, and it has crossed our minds that the lift companies may be in the pay of the breweries. Instead of skiing on, people pack into mountain restaurants well before the end of the day and gyrate in their ski boots on the dance floor, on the tables, on the bar, on the roof beams. There are open-air ice bars, umbrella bars and transparent 'igloo' bars in which to shelter from bad weather. Huge quantities of beer and schnapps are drunk, often to the accompaniment of German drinking songs or loud Europop music. In many resorts the bands don't stop playing until after darkness falls, when the happy punters slide off in the general direction of the village to find another watering hole.

After dinner (for those who pause for dinner, that is) the drinking and dancing start again and carry on in town in bars and clubs until the early hours.

Of course, not all resorts conform to this image. 'Exclusive' Lech and Zürs, for example, are full of rich, cool, 'beautiful' people enjoying the comfort of 4- or 5-star hotels. And villages such as Westendorf and Obergurgl are pretty, quiet, family resorts. But lots of big-name places with the best and most extensive slopes are also big party towns – notably St Anton, Saalbach-Hinterglemm, Ischgl and Sölden.

Après-ski is not limited to drinking and dancing. There are lots of floodlit toboggan runs, and UK tour operator reps organize folklore, bowling, fondue, karaoke and other evenings.

GOOD-VALUE, HIGH-QUALITY LODGING

One thing that all Austrian resorts have in common is reliably comfortable accommodation – whether it's in 4- or 5-star hotels with pools, saunas and spas or in great-value, family-run guest houses, of which Austria has thousands. Catered chalets and self-catering apartments are in general much less widely available than in French resorts.

The Germanic aversion to credit cards causes problems for many of our reporters. Many establishments do not accept cards – even quite upmarket hotels, as well as many ski lift companies. So check well in advance, and be prepared to pay in cash. Note also that although we give phone numbers for 'Editors' choice' mountain restaurants, many will not take reservations.

BUT STILL PUTTING UP WITH SMOKING

As other parts of the Alps have cut out smoking in bars and restaurants, Austria has lagged behind, much to the displeasure of many British visitors. In theory, there is progress. In 'multiple room establishments' the 'main room' now has to be non-smoking. In places with only one room, it's only in small places where you should now have to put up with smoke. But in practice, we find annoying smoke in most bars and some restaurants wherever we go.

GETTING AROUND THE AUSTRIAN ALPS

Austria presents few problems for the car-borne visitor, because practically all the resorts are valley villages, which involve neither steep, winding approach roads nor high-altitude passes.

The motorway along the Inn valley runs from Kufstein via Innsbruck to Landeck and, with one or two breaks, extends to the Arlberg pass and on to Switzerland. This artery is relatively reliable except in exceptionally bad weather – the altitude is low, and the road is a vital link that is kept open in virtually all conditions.

The Arlberg – which divides the Tirol from Vorarlberg, but which is also the watershed between Austria and Switzerland – is one of the few areas where driving plans are likely to be seriously affected by snow. The east–west Arlberg pass itself has a long tunnel

underneath it; this isn't cheap, and you may want to take the pass road when it's clear, through Stuben, St Christoph and St Anton. The Flexen pass road to Zürs and Lech branches off northwards, just to the west of the Arlberg summit; this is often closed by avalanche risk even when the Arlberg pass is open.

All cars must display a motorway toll sticker, available at petrol stations, post offices and newsagents. There's a 10-day one for 8.50 euros and a two-month one for 24.80 euros. From 1 November to 15 April winter tyres must be fitted. Be aware that cars hired in Germany or Italy might not meet this requirement.

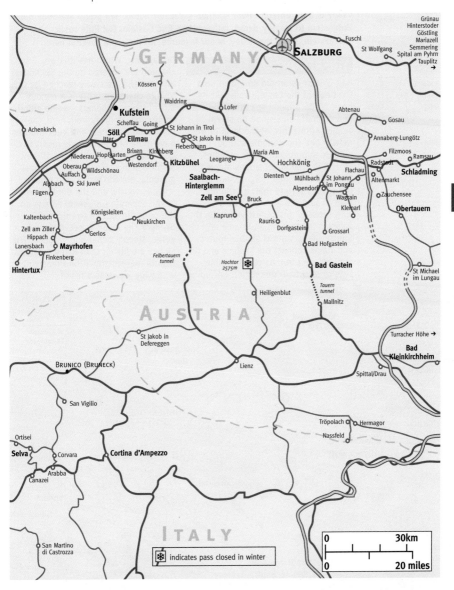

indicates pass closed in winter

0   30km

0   20 miles

Bad Gastein

*If you fancy 'taking the cure', there are few better resorts;
even if you don't, you're likely to be impressed by the slopes*

TOP 10 RATINGS

Extent	★★★
Fast lifts	★★★
Queues	★★★
Snow	★★★
Expert	★★★
Intermediate	★★★★
Beginner	★★
Charm	★★★
Convenience	★★
Scenery	★★★

RPI   95

lift pass	£190
ski hire	£80
lessons	£115
food & drink	£110
total	**£495**

➕ Excellent, testing long runs for confident intermediates

➕ Good mix of high, open slopes and lower woodland runs

➕ Good mountain restaurants

➕ Excellent thermal spas, but ...

➖ Main resorts are spa towns, lacking the usual Austrian resort ambience

➖ Valley slopes are split into five areas, and having a car helps

➖ Lacks genuinely easy long runs

With its essentially red-gradient mountains and spa-town resorts, the Gastein valley is a bit different from Austrian ski resort norms. We prefer spacious Bad Hofgastein to steeply tiered, rather urban Bad Gastein. But little rustic Dorfgastein, down the valley, is our favourite. All three are covered here.

THE RESORT

Bad Gastein is an old spa town near the head of the Gastein valley. At its heart is the original spa area, laid out in a compact horseshoe on steep slopes. Above this, at the level of the railway and the gondola station, is a modern suburb with more lodgings.

The Stubnerkogel slopes above the town link with Bad Hofgastein, down the valley. Beyond that, a separate area of slopes above Dorfgastein links with Grossarl in the next valley. Up the valley is another separate area at Sportgastein. Various ski-bus routes and trains connect the villages and lift stations, and 'run as per timetable'. Lots of resorts in this region (including

Schladming, which has its own chapter) are covered by the Ski Amadé lift pass and are easily reached by car.

Village charm The core is a curious mix of towny buildings – some grand, some modest. Away from here, the more modern hotels and guest houses have more of a normal ski resort feel.

Convenience The higher part of the resort is handy for the Stubnerkogel gondola, but the resort as a whole spreads widely, and the double chair to the separate Graukogel area is on the opposite side of town.

Scenery The resort is set in virtually a gorge, steeply tiered and wooded. The slopes are higher than many Austrian resorts (particularly at Sportgastein), with wide views as a result.

104

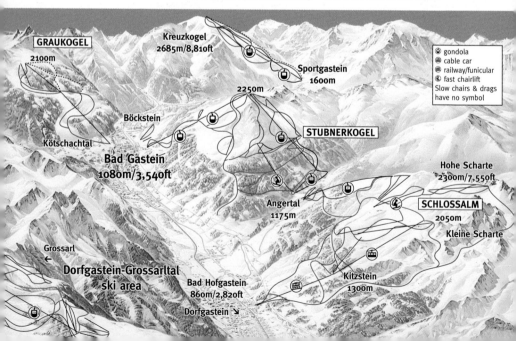

GRAUKOGEL
2100m

Kreuzkogel
2685m/8,81oft

Sportgastein
1600m

2250m

Böckstein

STUBNERKOGEL

Kötschachtal

Bad Gastein
1080m/3,54oft

Hohe Scharte
2300m/7,550ft

Angertal
1175m

SCHLOSSALM
2050m

Kleine Scharte

Grossarl

Dorfgastein-Grossarltal
ski area

Bad Hofgastein
860m/2,82oft

Kitzstein
1300m

Dorfgastein ↘

gondola
cable car
railway/funicular
fast chairlift
Slow chairs & drags
have no symbol

NEWS

2014/15: A new ski route is planned from the top station of the Kaserebenbahn (on skier's right of the Schlossalm sector) into Angertal. The Gasti children's park is being expanded.

2013/14: Snowmaking was increased by 3km for Stubnerkogel on the run back to town. The new Fun Slope Gastein opened.

KEY FACTS

Resort	1080m
	3,540ft

The Gasten valley and Grossarl areas

Slopes	840-2685m
	2,760-8,810ft
Lifts	42
Pistes	218km
	135 miles
Blue	26%
Red	60%
Black	14%
Snowmaking	60%

Bad Gastein, Bad Hofgastein, Sportgastein only

Slopes	860-2685m
	2,820-8,810ft
Lifts	25
Pistes	129km
	80 miles

THE MOUNTAINS

Most of the pistes are genuine red runs; this is not a resort for timid intermediates who prefer easy cruising blues. And many are on open slopes; this is a quite exposed region. Sportgastein is especially vulnerable. Graukogel is wooded. The piste map tries to cover all the areas in one view, and is difficult to follow.

Slopes From the Stubnerkogel gondola a long blue run goes back to base, but most runs head for Angertal, which links with Bad Hofgastein.

Fast lifts There are several gondolas, but also lots of slow chairs and T-bars.

Queues There are few major problems.

Terrain parks There is a 'quiet and well-run' park on Stubnerkogel.

Snow reliability The slopes go a bit higher than many Austrian rivals – Sportgastein much higher – and there is decent snowmaking.

Experts The few black runs are not severe, but many reds are long and satisfying. Graukogel has some of the most testing pistes. There is plenty of good off-piste – by the Jungeralm chair on the shady side of Stubnerkogel, for example. Sportgastein has a ski route from top to bottom.

Intermediates Confident intermediates, will find long, leg-sapping red runs in all sectors. The valley in general and Stubnerkogel in particular are not nearly so good for blue-run skiers. Sportgastein has a good range of runs, up to an easy black.

Beginners There are adequate nursery areas near the gondola station and at Angertal. But progression is awkward

– the mountains are essentially steep. The few easy long runs are boring paths. There are no free lifts.

Snowboarding The valley hosts snowboard events, and there is good freeriding. Draglifts are dotted around.

Cross-country There are 45km of trails in the area, but most are low down.

Mountain restaurants There are lots of pleasant huts doing decent food; but they can get crowded. Reader tips include Bellevue Alm, Waldgasthof and Hirschenhütte.

Schools and guides Past reports on the school have been favourable.

Families Facilities are quite good. Angertal has a snow adventure park.

STAYING THERE

Hotels There are lots of smart 4- and 3-star hotels with spa facilities. The Grüner Baum (25160) is a lovely retreat, but isolated (they have a shuttle). Reader tips include the quite grand Elizabeth Park (25510) and the quirky, friendly Mozart (26860).

Eating out Choice is reasonable. The traditional Jägerhäusl has been tipped for its lovely food and large portions. The Amici is a good-value Italian.

Après-ski Bars are lively at close of play, evenings more subdued. Silver Bullet and Haeggbloms are among the most popular. Bars for a quiet late drink include Bellini and Ritz. There are a couple of discos and a casino.

Off the slopes The thermal spa/pool facilities are excellent and extensive – but expensive. There's ice climbing, and there are quite a few shops. Excursions to Salzburg are possible, and worthwhile.

Bad Hofgastein 860m

➕ Sunny, spacious setting
➕ Lovely long runs

➖ Lacks ski resort ambience
➖ Funicular from base can be crowded

Bad Hofgastein is a sizeable, spacious, quiet spa town set on flat ground in the widest part of the valley, with funicular access to the slopes.

Village charm The pedestrianized centre is compact, and pleasant enough to stroll around, with lots of shops and restaurants. But it does feel like a town; there's little traditional Austrian rustic charm. There is a sizeable park next to the centre.

Convenience The resort spreads widely across the flat valley floor; the funicular is an efficient ski-bus ride from many lodgings. It's a longer ski-bus ride to Angertal.

Scenery Good valley views.

THE MOUNTAINS

Schlossalm is a broad, open bowl, with runs through patchy woods to both Bad Hofgastein and Angertal.

Slopes The funicular to Kitzstein is followed by a cable car to the Schlossalm slopes. These link to Stubnerkogel via Angertal.

Fast lifts Getting up the mountain can be slow, and a few old chairs remain.

Queues The access lifts are queue-prone at peak times – and the cable car can be closed by wind.

↑ Sportgastein is quite different from the other sectors, with essentially no trees, and high-Alpine views

GASTEINERTAL TOURISMUS

UK PACKAGES

Alpine Answers, Crystal, Crystal Finest, Erna Low, Ski Miquel, STC, Thomson, White Roc **Bad Hofgastein** Crystal, Ski Club Freshtracks, Skitracer, Solos, STC, Thomson **Grossarl** Inntravel

Phone numbers
From elsewhere in Austria add the prefix 06434 (Bad Gastein), 06432 (Bad Hofgastein), 06433 (Dorfgastein); from abroad use the prefix +43 and omit the initial '0'

TOURIST OFFICE

For all resorts in the Gastein valley: www.gastein.com

Terrain parks The new Fun Slope Gastein mixes a piste and snow park, with bridges, tunnels and jumps.
Snow reliability Snowmaking is fairly extensive, but snow-cover down to the bottom is unreliable.
Experts There are no real challenges on the local pistes, but there is ample opportunity to go off-piste.
Intermediates The Schlossalm slopes offer a good range of red runs, from easy to testing; the few blues are not all entirely easy. There are splendid long reds to the valley floor (we loved Hohe Scharte Nord – 1440m vertical).
Beginners There is a small nursery area at the funicular station. You have to catch a bus to the bigger nursery area at Angertal. And then you have few options for progression.
Snowboarding Good freeriding. Draglifts are dotted around though.
Cross-country Bad Hofgastein makes a fine base for cross-country when its lengthy valley-floor trails have snow.
Mountain restaurants A 2014 reader favourite is 'wonderfully atmospheric' self-service Aeroplanstadl for 'excellent traditional pub-type dishes'. For table-service, a repeat visitor favours the out-of-the-way Hofgasteinerhaus ('varied menu, uncrowded'), while another reporter likes the small and simple but 'surprisingly good' Kitzsteinalm ('excellent pork cutlets').
Schools and guides 'Good teaching that pushed us,' says a recent report.
Families See Bad Gastein.

STAYING THERE

Hotels We enjoyed a stay at the 4-star Bismarck (66810) – excellent food, fairly central. Reader tips include the Impuls Tirol (6394) – 'quality five-course dinners and spa' – and St Georg (61000) – 200m to the lift.
Apartments The Alpenparks resort is said to be 'excellent', and a 2014 reporter found the 'simple' Aparthaus Schmidt 'good value and spacious'.

Eating out There's plenty of choice. Reader tips include Piccola Italia, Salzburgerhof ('excellent steaks'), and Pizzeria Rudi's Klause ('pleasant traditional style stube').
Après-ski Quiet by Austrian standards. At close of play there are plenty of takers for the central Piccolo ice bar and for the Aeroplanstadl on the hill (though be aware 'the funicular closes early'). Head to Cafe Weitmoser, a historic little castle, for cakes. There are said to be a couple of disco bars.
Off the slopes The huge Alpen Therme Gastein spa has excellent pools etc. Other amenities include good shops, walking and a full-size ice rink.

DOWN-VALLEY VILLAGE – 830m

DORFGASTEIN

Dorfgastein is a quiet, rustic village. It has its own extensive slopes, shared with Grossarl in the next valley, which offer some good long runs. A two-stage gondola and alternative chairlift start a little way outside the village. There is a nursery slope here, and another at the gondola mid-station. Like the other sectors, the mountain is essentially of red gradient, and best suits confident intermediates. On the front side there is one good long blue, but it doesn't go all the way to the valley. There are pleasant huts. We and readers rate the excellent table-service Wengeralm – 'outstanding' says a 2014 visitor. Other reader tips include the Jagahütte ('great atmosphere and food') and the 'lovely rustic' Harbachhütte. The ski schools get good reviews. Off-slope amenities are limited, but there's a pool with sauna and steam. Evenings are quiet. Reporters love the 4-star hotel Römerhof (7777) – 'great food, lovely spa, good value', and a five-time visitor recommends the Gastehaus Schernthaner apartments (7232).

BAD KLEINKIRCHHEIM TOURIST OFFICE

Bad Kleinkirchheim

Large resort tucked away in Carinthia, with marvellous spa facilities and a ski area best suited to intermediates

TOP 10 RATINGS	
Extent	★★
Fast lifts	★★
Queues	★★★★
Snow	★★★
Expert	★★
Intermediate	★★★
Beginner	★★
Charm	★★
Convenience	★★★
Scenery	★★★

RPI	100
lift pass	£180
ski hire	£110
lessons	£120
food & drink	£115
total	**£525**

NEWS

2014/15: Women's World Cup Downhill and Super G races will be held here on 10 and 11 January 2015.

KEY FACTS

Resort	1090m
	3,580ft
Slopes	1090-2055m
	3,580-6,740ft
Lifts	26
Pistes	103km
	64 miles
Blue	17%
Red	75%
Black	8%
Snowmaking	97%

- ➕ Mainly red intermediate slopes
- ➕ Virtually 100% snowmaking
- ➕ Two superb thermal spas
- ➕ Cheap, even by Austrian standards
- ➖ Spread-out town
- ➖ Still a lot of slow chairs and T-bars
- ➖ Slopes limited in extent and variety
- ➖ Après-ski quiet

BKK, as the Brits call it, is downhill race hero Franz Klammer's favourite ski area – he learned to ski here, there's a World Cup downhill run named after him and he skis with guests here a few times a year (see margin panel).

Given Klammer's endorsement, it's no surprise that the resort has some serious skiing: 75% of its slopes are classified red and suit confident intermediates best. It is perhaps a surprise that there are few real challenges for experts.

THE RESORT

BKK is tucked away on the edge of the Nock Mountain National Park in Carinthia, in the far south-east of Austria, near the Italian and Slovenian borders. The nearest airports are Klagenfurt (around 50 minutes away) and Ljubljana (90 minutes). Salzburg is less than two hours away.

The lift pass covers St Oswald, a smaller village at the far end of the shared ski area, and all the resorts in Carinthia – useful for visiting other resorts if you have a car.

BKK's spa facilities are excellent with indoor and outdoor thermal pools, different types of sauna – including a tepidarium (which is a sauna with a lower temperature so you can sit there longer) – and steam rooms, solariums, hot tubs, massage and therapy rooms. There are also water slides, waterfalls and massage jets in the pools. The Thermal Römerbad reopened in 2007 after complete refurbishment and is set over three floors, with 13 different types of sauna and steam rooms. We tried it and thought it was superb; we could happily have spent days there. 'World class – we went for an hour and stayed all day,' says a 2014 reporter.

Village charm The mainly chalet-style buildings with sloping roofs are more appealing than the austere blocks of some spa resorts. But it is a sprawling place with no real centre.

Convenience The town is very spread out along the valley, and the most convenient place to stay is near one of the main lifts out. A free ski-bus links all the main lift stations, and some buses also go to St Oswald.

Scenery The scenery you gaze at from the spa pools is of gently rounded, rather than dramatic, mountains.

KAISERBURG 2055m/6,740ft — Strohsack 1905m — MAIBRUNN 1760m/5775ft — Priedröf 1965m/6,445ft — NOCKALM — Wieser Nock 1970m/6,460ft — Brunnach 1910m/6,270ft — 1370m — 1025m — 1280m — St Oswald — Bad Kleinkirchheim 1090m/3,580ft — Feldkirchen ↓

gondola
fast chairlift
Slow chairs & drags have no symbol

FRANZ KLAMMER

Klammer is one of the most famous downhill skiers of all time and, at the age of 60, is still a national hero in Austria.

He won Olympic Gold at Innsbruck in 1976 and a record 25 World Cup Downhills. He was born near Bad Kleinkirchheim, learned to ski at BKK, and it remains his favourite resort.

A few times a year he skis with anyone who signs up for the experience – last season there were three-hour early-morning sessions before the lifts opened to the public followed by brunch in the Klammerstub'n at the top of the mountain. A 2014 reporter who joined him said it was 'brilliant, he made everyone feel special and never stopped smiling'.

UK PACKAGES

Inghams, STC

THE MOUNTAINS

BKK has shady home slopes and sunnier ones shared with St Oswald. Throughout, they are mainly wooded and of intermediate standard (75% are classified red).

Slopes BKK's main home slopes are reached by lifts from two different parts of the village. A two-stage gondola goes up to the area's high point, Kaiserburg, at one end of the ski area, where a couple of T-bars serve the highest slopes. And a fast quad takes you to the other end of the mountainside at Maibrunn. Pistes go down from both peaks to the gondola mid-station, where a double chair takes you to above Maibrunn.

From the same end of the village as the Maibrunn quad, successive old double chairs and a drag take you up the other side of the valley to the Nockalm slopes, which link in with St Oswald's slopes further along the valley. This area can also be accessed by a gondola midway between BKK and St Oswald, which can be reached by ski-bus. At St Oswald a gondola goes up to Brunnach, at the far end of the shared ski area.

Three slow quads link the Nockalm and St Oswald slopes, and most of the other upper lifts are drags.

Fast lifts There are three gondolas and one fast chair but the other lifts are all slow chairs or T-bars.

Queues A 2014 reporter advises going to Nockalm in the morning to avoid any queues for the local slopes.

Terrain parks The park is at Nockalm and has jumps, rails and boxes.

Snow reliability In general, BKK's main home slopes are north-facing and keep their snow best. The Nockalm-St Oswald slopes are more sunny. Virtually all the pistes are covered by snowmaking. Grooming is of a 'very high standard,' says a 2014 visitor.

Experts BKK has little to keep experts interested for a week. The best and most challenging black is the Franz Klammer World Cup run, which goes from Strohsack to the gondola base (the short top section is very steep and often closed). Off-piste tours are popular and the resort organizes a three-hour 'taster tour' with a guide.

Intermediates Virtually all the slopes are ideal for good intermediates and many are long (up to 1000m vertical). For timid intermediates, the Nockalm and St Oswald sectors are best.

Beginners The nursery slopes at the top of the Nockalm gondola are much warmer and sunnier than the low shady BKK ones. Once off the nursery slopes, there is a long blue the length of the Nockalm gondola. But that's it – no other long, easy blues.

Snowboarding Best for experienced boarders. Beginners may struggle with the many T-bars.

Cross-country Some of the 54km of tracks are at 1900m at the top of the Nockalm; 8km have snowmaking.

Mountain restaurants There are 23 mountain restaurants and huts. We enjoyed the cosy Brentlerhütte (excellent ham) on the way down from Nockalm to the valley and Zum Poldl above St Oswald. A 2014 visitor recommends the Strohsack for its 'oompah band and friendly service'.

Schools and guides There are four schools to choose from, three based in BKK and one in St Oswald.

Families From 10 January to 6 March 2015 a child under 12 can ski for one euro a day if they are with an adult with a 6-day pass. The ski schools run a Bobo children's club.

STAYING THERE

Hotels The two 5-star hotels, the Pulverer (744) and the Thermenhotel Ronacher (282), are both near the high-speed chair and have excellent spa facilities. The 4-star Almrausch (4240) is close to the chairlift to Nockalm and, says a 2014 reporter, is 'as good as it gets'. The 4-star Kirchheimerhof (278), at the top of the nursery slopes has panoramic views and a spa. The St Oswald (5910) is near the Brunnach gondola and has a smart spa and excellent wine cellar.

Apartments There are lots of self-catering apartments to rent.

Eating out Plenty of choice. We loved the atmospheric old Loystub'n in the hotel Pulverer.

Après-ski It is quieter than most Austrian resorts. But near the main gondola base are the Almstube, Viktoria Pub, Club MC 99 and the Take Five Dancing Club.

Off the slopes You can buy lift tickets that include the use of the thermal spas. There are also some good walks (including the Spa Boulevard at the top of the gondola from St Oswald), a tennis centre, squash courts, outdoor ice rink, curling, tubing, snowshoeing, horse riding, sleigh rides and a 4km floodlit toboggan run.

Phone numbers
From elsewhere in Austria add the prefix 04240; from abroad use the prefix +43 4240

TOURIST OFFICE

www.badkleinkirchheim.at

Inghams

Austria
SKI BKK
Bad Kleinkirchheim
Carinthia

FREE Lift Passes
For adults & children
From 7 Mar to 4 Apr

Inghams and BKK have been chosen by the Austrian National Tourist Office for their 'Ski Again' campaign, encouraging you back to the slopes with inclusive ski packages.

inghams.co.uk/skiagain

SAVE £££s WITH OUR *Inghams PLUS* DEALS

CASH-BACK OFFER! SAVE £50 per couple | GROUPS – UP TO 1 IN 5 GO FREE
EARLY BOOKING DISCOUNT - SAVE UP TO £40 per couple
FREE SPA VOUCHER AT THE HOTEL ESCHENHOF | FREE EQUIPMENT OFFER FOR CHILDREN
FREE LIFT PASS IN LOW SEASON | USE YOUR LIFT PASS FOR SKI OR SPA T&Cs apply
CHOOSE FROM OUR RANGE OF 7 HOTELS | 7 NIGHTS FROM £749 per person

SKI WITH OLYMPIC CHAMPION AND SKI LEGEND, FRANZ KLAMMER from only £65 per person subject to availability

Franz Klammer – Abfahrt
Klammer Stich →

Call us on **01483 371 236**
inghams.co.uk/bkk

100% BONDED SECURITY

ABTA
The Travel Association
ABTA NO.V4871

Terms and Conditions apply to all offers.

Ellmau

A good base on the extensive SkiWelt circuit, combining charm with reasonable convenience – good value, too

TOP 10 RATINGS

Extent	★★★★
Fast lifts	★★★★
Queues	★★★★
Snow	★★
Expert	★
Intermediate	★★★★
Beginner	★★★★
Charm	★★★
Convenience	★★★
Scenery	★★★

RPI	85
lift pass	£180
ski hire	£65
lessons	£75
food & drink	£110
total	**£430**

KEY FACTS

Resort	800m
	2,620ft
Entire SkiWelt	
Slopes	620-1955m
	2,030-6,410ft
Lifts	91
Pistes	280km
	174 miles
Blue	48%
Red	46%
Black	6%
Snowmaking	82%

+ Part of the SkiWelt, Austria's largest linked ski area

+ Excellent nursery slopes

+ Quiet, charming family resort – more appealing than Söll

+ Cheap, even by Austrian standards

+ Snowmaking is now very extensive and well used; even so ...

− Low altitude can mean poor snow

− Main lift a bus or drag from village

− Runs on upper slopes mostly short

− Few challenges on-piste

− Limited range of nightlife

− The SkiWelt slopes can get crowded

− Piste map and signposting poor

If you like the sound of the large, undemanding SkiWelt circuit, Ellmau has a lot to recommend it as your base – as does Scheffau, also covered here. But also consider the several resorts covered in the Söll chapter.

THE RESORT

Ellmau sits at the north-eastern corner of the big SkiWelt – Austria's biggest network. Other parts of it are covered in our chapter on Söll. You can also progress (via Brixen) to the slopes of Kitzbühel; these and various other ski areas within reach are covered by the Kitzbüheler Alpen AllStarCard ski pass.
Village charm Although sizeable, the village remains quiet, with traditional chalet-style buildings, welcoming bars and shops, and a pretty church.
Convenience Accommodation is scattered; there is some out by the funicular to the main slopes, but we prefer to stay in the compact centre of the village. There is a bus service, but

reporters complain of overcrowding.
Scenery The village and the slopes enjoy great close-up views of the craggy Wilder Kaiser, across the valley.

THE MOUNTAINS

The piste map is hopelessly over-ambitious in trying to show the whole SkiWelt area in a single view and reporters complain of poor and confusing signposting (see Söll chapter for more on all this).

Most slopes are heavily wooded, with a mix of short runs at altitude and much longer ones to the villages.
Slopes The funicular railway on the edge of the village takes you up to Hartkaiser, from where a fine long red leads down to Blaiken (Scheffau's lift

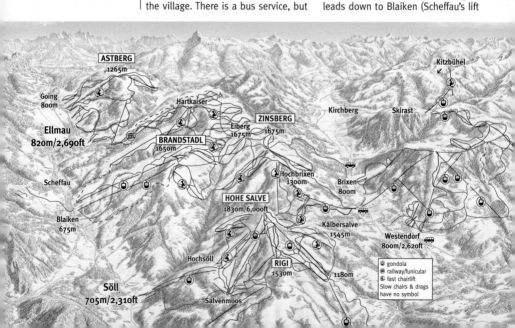

↑ A funicular takes you up from the edge of the village to Hartkaiser

SNOWPIX.COM / CHRIS GILL

NEWS

2014/15: The Aualm quad chair up to Zinsberg is due to be upgraded to an eight-seater. A new 1.2km red run with snowmaking is planned for the Brixen area. The panoramic Bergkaiser mountain restaurant is being refurbished and will have seating for 200. There are plans for yet more snowmaking.

2013/14: Snowmaking facilities were expanded with the construction of a new reservoir at Hohe Salve.

base station). Here, one of two gondolas takes you up to Brandstadl. Immediately beyond Brandstadl, the slopes become rather bitty; an array of short runs and lifts link Brandstadl to Zinsberg. From Zinsberg, long, south-facing pistes lead down to Brixen, where a gondola goes up to Choralpe in Westendorf's area. Part-way down to Brixen you can head towards Söll, and if you go up Hohe Salve, you get access to a long run to Hopfgarten.

Ellmau and Going share a pleasant little area of slopes on Astberg, slightly apart from the rest of the area, and well suited to the unadventurous and to families. One piste leads to the funicular for access to the rest of the SkiWelt. The main Astberg chair is midway between Ellmau and Going.

Fast lifts The main access lift is a fast funicular. Fast chairs are increasingly common on the upper slopes.

Queues Lift upgrades have greatly improved this once queue-prone area, and most reporters find few queues. But there are several bottlenecks at slow chairs around the mountain, and when snow is poor the links between Zinsberg and Eiberg get crowded.

Terrain parks The local Kaiserpark has beginner and expert boxes, rails and kickers, as well as a chill-out zone. There's also a snowcross.

Snow reliability With a low average height, and important links that get a lot of sun, the snowmaking that the SkiWelt has installed is essential; the Ellmau-Going sector now claims 95% of slopes are covered. Snowmaking can, of course, be used only when temperatures are low enough. The north-facing Eiberg area above

Scheffau holds its snow well. Grooming is excellent, and reports have praised the snowmaking.

Experts There is a ski route from Brandstadl down to Scheffau and a little mogul field between Brandstadl and Neualm, but the main challenges are in going off-piste.

Intermediates With good snow, the SkiWelt is a paradise for those who love easy cruising. There are lots of blue runs, and many of the reds deserve a blue classification. It is a big area, and you get a feeling of travelling around. In good snow the long red runs to the valley – down the Hartkaiser funicular, for example – are excellent. The main challenge arises when ice and slush can make even gentle lower slopes tricky. For timid intermediates Astberg is handy.

Beginners Ellmau has an array of good nursery slopes covered by snow-guns. The main ones are at the Going end, but there are some by the road to the funicular. The Astberg chair opens up a more snow-sure plateau at altitude. The Brandstadl area has a section of short easy runs.

Snowboarding Ellmau is a good place to learn as its local slopes are easy.

Cross-country The SkiWelt area has a total of 196km of trails, including long and challenging ones, but trails at altitude are lacking.

Mountain restaurants There are many small places providing good-value food in pleasant surroundings and happily marked on the piste map. The Rübezahl Alm above Ellmau is one of our favourites – a lovely old hut with good food (the ribs have been recommended) and lots of different

Ellmau

111

Build your own shortlist: **www.wheretoskiandsnowboard.com**

LIFT PASSES

SkiWelt Wilder Kaiser-Brixental

Prices in €

Age	1-day	6-day
under 16	22	110
16 to 17	35	175
18 plus	44	219

Free Under 7
Senior No deals
Beginner Points cards
Notes Ski-bus included; single ascent and part-day options
Alternative pass Kitzbüheler Alpen AllStarCard covers: Schneewinkel (St Johann), Kitzbühel, SkiWelt, Ski Juwel, Skicircus Saalbach-Hinterglemm and Zell am See-Kaprun

UK PACKAGES

Crystal, Neilson, Ski Club Freshtracks, Skitracer, STC, Thomson
Scheffau Crystal, Inghams, STC, Thomson
Going Inghams, STC

Phone numbers
From elsewhere in Austria add the prefix 05358; from abroad use the prefix +43 5358

TOURIST OFFICES

Wilder Kaiser
(Ellmau, Söll, Scheffau, Going)
www.wilderkaiser.info
SkiWelt
www.skiwelt.at

rooms and areas that make it very cosy; but it gets very busy. The Tanzbodenalm near Brandstadl above Scheffau is pleasantly woody, serving delicious deer stew; 'great service, good food and wide choice'. Other reporter tips include: the Jägerhütte (below Hartkaiser), and the jolly Hartkaiser ('toilets accessed by escalator!'). The Jochstub'n has a self-service part and a 'cute, lively' bar: 'good for an end of afternoon drink'. The panoramic Bergkaiser and the Blattlalm on Astberg both have great views. Then there's the Aualm below Zinsberg for cakes and glühwein, the Brandstadl and the pleasantly rustic Neualm above Scheffau and, a bit lower down, the 'excellent' Bavaria – which has 'great-value lunch specials'.

Schools and guides There are three schools and a specialist snowboard school in Ellmau, two in Scheffau and another in Going. The Scheffau school is praised this year: 'excellent, properly evaluated and put into proper groups'.

Families Ellmau is an attractive resort for families: 'Probably the best family resort I have visited – from ski school to alternative attractions,' says a recent visitor. Both the Ellmauer and the Top schools have their own fun parks and play areas. The leisure centre and toboggan run are popular.

STAYING THERE

Ellmau is essentially a hotel and guest house resort.

Chalets A 2014 reporter said Crystal's chalet Hartkaiser was 'well run, had good food, a bus stop outside and was good budget accommodation'.

Hotels The Bär (2395) is an elegant, relaxed luxury place. The Kaiserhof (2022) is another luxury option. The Sporthotel (3755) is 'incredible for the price', with 'huge five-course meals, gorgeous pool/spa facilities, huge lounge'. The Hochfilzer (2501) is central and well equipped (with outdoor hot tub, indoor pool, sauna, steam); the simpler Pension Claudia is under the same ownership. The Kaiserblick (2230) has good spa facilities and is right by the piste.

Apartments There is a wide variety. The Landhof apartments – with pool, sauna and steam room – have impressed a regular visitor.

Eating out The jolly Lobewein is a splendid, big, central chalet, with cheerful service in countless rooms. The Ellmauer Alm has been tipped.

Après-ski Bettina is good for coffee and cakes. Memory is the early-evening riotous party pub. Pub 66 and Ötzy Bar have regular events such as karaoke and 'erotic dancers'. The Ellmauer Alm has live entertainment. Tour operator reps organize events such as sleigh rides and tubing, and bowling and Tirolean folklore evenings in Söll. Ski night (torchlit walk, ski instructor display, glühwein, music) has a party atmosphere each week. The toboggan run from the Astberg lift is also recommended.

Off the slopes A guest card conveys various discounts, including entry to the KaiserBad leisure centre. There's a pool. The many excursions include Innsbruck, Salzburg and Vitipeno. Valley walks may be spoiled by the busy main road.

LINKED RESORT – 745m

SCHEFFAU

Little Scheffau is one of the most attractive of the region's villages and is well placed for quick access to most parts of the SkiWelt area – though the village itself is not convenient for the lifts, which are a short bus ride away. You can ski down to the gondolas at Blaiken, unless of course you opt to leave your kit at the lift station. The village spreads up quite a steep slope. Reporters recommend the 3-star Alpin (85560), the central Gasthof Weberbauer (8115) and the 'well-priced' Waldrand (8158). Après-ski is 'non-existent', says one happy reporter, but there are a couple of bars – the Sternbar is lively after the lifts close. There's bowling but little else to do off the slopes.

LINKED RESORT – 775m

GOING

Going is a tiny, attractively rustic village, ideal for families looking for a quiet time. It is well placed for the limited but quiet slopes of the Astberg and for the vast area of nursery slopes shared with Ellmau. Prices are low, but as it's at one extreme end of the SkiWelt, it's not an ideal base for covering the whole of the region on the cheap unless you have a car to speed up access to Scheffau and Söll (or you're happy to take buses). The Lanzenhof (2428) is a cosy central pension, where we have enjoyed an excellent dinner. There's an ice rink.

TVB TUX / JP FANKHAUSER

Hintertux / Tux valley

Small, unspoiled, traditional villages, high snow-sure glacier slopes and lots of other areas covered by the valley lift pass

TOP 10 RATINGS

Extent	★★★
Fast lifts	★★★
Queues	★★★
Snow	★★★★★
Expert	★★★
Intermediate	★★★
Beginner	★★
Charm	★★★
Convenience	★★
Scenery	★★★

RPI   95

lift pass	£190
ski hire	£80
lessons	£100
food & drink	£115
total	**£485**

NEWS

2013/14: The Lämmerbichl double chair on Rastkogel was replaced by a six-pack with heated seats and covers. On the glacier, the big Tuxer Fernerhaus restaurant and the tiny Spannagelhaus nearby were both fully renovated.

➕ Hintertux has one of the best year-round glaciers in the world

➕ Lanersbach's slopes form part of an extensive area, linked to Mayrhofen

➕ Wide-ranging area lift pass

➕ Some excellent off-piste

➕ Quiet, traditional villages

➖ Not the place for shops and throbbing nightlife

➖ Not ideal for beginners or timid intermediates

➖ Still some draglifts and slow chairs on the glacier slopes

➖ Glacier can be cold and bleak

For guaranteed good snow, Hintertux is simply one of the best places to go. Its glacier is not only extensive; it is one of the two most challenging and interesting lift-served Alpine glacier areas (along with Stubai). But the quieter, friendlier, non-glacial slopes down the valley, linked to the slopes of Mayrhofen, are also well worth exploring (check out the Mayrhofen chapter too).

The Tux valley, effectively the top end of the Zillertal, offers a variety of small villages. At the end of the valley, directly below the glacier, is **Hintertux**; a few km down the valley, the major resorts are **Lanersbach** and next-door **Vorderlanersbach**. Lower down still is **Finkenberg**. There is also lodging in Juns and Madseit, which are villages between Hintertux and Lanersbach.

All the major resort villages have gondolas into the local slopes: the Lanersbach one goes to Eggalm, and you can ski to Vorderlanersbach from there; the Vorderlanersbach one goes to Rastkogel, and from there you can ski into Mayrhofen's Penken-Horberg slopes; and the Finkenberg one goes up to Penken, meeting the lifts above Mayrhofen.

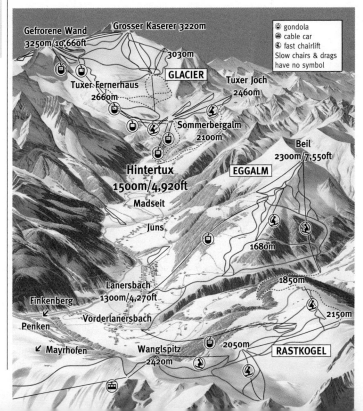

Gefrorene Wand 3250m/10,666ft

Grosser Kaserer 3220m

3030m

gondola
cable car
fast chairlift
Slow chairs & drags have no symbol

Tuxer Fernerhaus 2660m

GLACIER

Tuxer Joch 2460m

Sommerbergalm 2100m

Beil 2300m/7,550ft

Hintertux 1500m/4,920ft

EGGALM

Madseit

Juns

1680m

1850m

Lanersbach 1300m/4,270ft

Finkenberg

2150m

Vorderlanersbach

Penken

2050m

RASTKOGEL

Mayrhofen

Wanglspitz 2420m

Resort news and key links: www.wheretoskiandsnowboard.com

↑ From Tuxer Joch you get good views across to the main Hintertux glacier area
SNOWPIX.COM / CHRIS GILL

KEY FACTS

Resort	1500m
	4,920ft

Ziller valley	
Slopes	630-3250m
	2,070-10,660ft
Lifts	178
Pistes	487km
	303 miles
Blue	26%
Red	63%
Black	11%
Snowmaking	75%

Ski and Glacier World Zillertal 3000	
Slopes	630-3250m
	2,070-10,660ft
Lifts	63
Pistes	193km
	120 miles
Blue	26%
Red	58%
Black	16%
Snowmaking	86%

Hintertux only	
Slopes	1500-3250m
	4,920-10,660ft
Lifts	21
Pistes	59km
	37 miles

The higher villages are linked by frequent free ski-buses. A cheap (1.50 euros) night-bus runs until 2.30am. Finkenberg is less well served.

There are some good rustic restaurants and bars and a few places along the valley with discos or live music. But nightlife tends to be quieter than in many Austrian resorts.

The Tux valley and Mayrhofen lifts form what is called the Ski and Glacier World Zillertal 3000. The Superski lift pass also covers other Ziller valley resorts (read the Mayrhofen chapter). The SGWZ3000 piste map is very clear, and names all mountain restaurants.

Hintertux 1500m

- Departure point for the excellent high glacier slopes
- Liveliest of the villages for après-ski
- Quiet later in the evening
- Remote setting
- Not much to do off the slopes

Life in Hintertux revolves around the glacier; staying at the base gets you up the mountain early, and means you don't have far to stagger after joining in the teatime revelry. But later on, it may feel too quiet for some.

Village charm The resort is little more than a small collection of hotels and guest houses, in traditional style. Well, two collections actually – see below.
Convenience The main village is a 15-minute walk from the lifts, but there are also hotels at the lift base – the obvious place to stay in our view.
Scenery There are fabulous views from the high points of the glacier.

THE MOUNTAINS

Hintertux's slopes are fairly extensive and, for a glacier, surprisingly varied and occasionally challenging. Only the final ski route to the valley is in trees.
Slopes A series of three big twin-cable gondolas goes from the base to the top of the glacier in around 30 minutes. The second and third stages are linked by a short slope at Tuxer

Fernerhaus. A second smaller gondola also goes to Tuxer Fernerhaus, with a 10-seat gondola above it. Above Tuxer Fernerhaus there are further chairs and draglifts with links across to another 1000m-vertical chain of lifts below Grosser Kaserer. Behind Gefrorene Wand is the area's one sunny piste.

Descent to the valley involves a short six-pack ride to Sommerbergalm and then a ski route to the base. At Sommerbergalm a fast quad serves short, easy slopes below Tuxer Joch and accesses a second ski route to the base – down a deserted valley.
Fast lifts There are high-capacity gondolas all the way to the top, but the shorter lifts serving most of the slopes are T-bars and slow chairs.
Queues The gondolas make light work of any queues. But the main runs can

Super-skipass Zillertal

Prices in €

Age	1-day	6-day
under 15	21	101
15 to 18	38	179
19 plus	47	224
Free	Under 6	
Senior	No deals	
Beginner	No deals	

Notes 1-day pass covers Hintertux glacier, Eggalm, Rastkogel and Penken areas; 2-day and over passes include all Ziller valley lifts; part-day passes available

get crowded, and then it is best to go to the quieter lifts on skier's left.

Terrain parks Europe's highest World Cup half-pipe is on the glacier (a popular summer hang-out), and there is a terrain park for all levels with jumps, fun boxes and rails.

Snow reliability Snow does not come more reliable than this. Even off the glacier, the other slopes are high and face north, making for very reliable snow-cover. The runs from Tuxer Fernerhaus and Tuxer Joch down to Sommerbergalm have snowmaking, as does the longer ski route to the valley – bizarre, for a ski route.

Experts There is more to amuse experts here than on any other glacier, with a proper black run at glacier level and steep slopes beneath. A lot of the off-piste is little used.

Intermediates The area particularly suits good, confident intermediates. The long runs down from Gefrorene Wand and Kaserer are fun. And the ski routes to the valley are very satisfying. Moderate intermediates will love the slopes served by drags up on the glacier, and the Tuxer Joch area.

Beginners There is a short nursery slope at valley level, but then you're riding the gondola up to and back from Sommerbergalm, where there are blue runs served by drags and a chair. You'll need a full lift pass.

Snowboarding There are some great off-piste opportunities, but boarders complain about the number of T-bars.

Cross-country See Lanersbach.

Mountain restaurants For some time our favourite has been Gletscherhütte, at the top of the area – good shielded terraces with BBQ, and table-service in parts of the cosy, woody interior. 'Good-value, hearty meals,' says an endorsing reporter. But we haven't

visited the ancient Spannagelhaus refuge lower down since it was transformed into 'an inviting table-service restaurant' with a wide-ranging menu. There are big self-service places at the main lift junctions: newly renovated Tuxer Fernerhaus 'sets the standard for such places', according to a 2014 visitor; Tuxer Joch Haus has great glacier views.

Schools and guides The three schools serve all the resorts in Tux, but we lack reports. Tux 3000 has guiding, touring and freeriding programmes.

Families Most of the ski schools run classes for children from age four, and lunch is provided. There's a children's fun area on the glacier.

STAYING THERE

Most hotels are large and comfortable and have spa facilities, but there are also more modest pensions.

Hotels We think it makes sense to stay close to the lifts. Closest is the 4-star Neuhintertux (8580) used by our regular reporter ('food not spectacular, but spa very good'); next door is the more intimate Vierjahreszeiten (8525) ('pleasant, good food, smaller spa').

Apartments There are plenty of self-catering apartments.

Eating out Mainly hotel-based.

Après-ski There can be a lively après-ski scene both at mid-mountain (Sommerbergalm) and at the base. The Hohenhaus Tenne has several different bars; the Rindererhof is another popular place to gather, and there are a couple of local bars.

Off the slopes Lots of ice activities on the glacier – climbing, natural ice palace, etc. The hotel spa facilities are excellent, including a thermal pool at the Kirchler, but there are many more options in Mayrhofen.

Lanersbach 1300m

+ Pleasant, compact village
+ Well placed for skiing the glacier and for the Mayrhofen slopes

- Village fairly quiet by Austrian standards
- Few easy local runs for novices

Lanersbach and neighbouring Vorderlanersbach are attractive bases for accessing both the glacier and the valley resorts, with the particular attraction that you can ski home to them from the Eggalm sector.

Village charm Lanersbach is small, attractive, spacious and traditional. The quiet centre near the pretty church is delightfully unspoiled and is bypassed by the busy road up to Hintertux that passes the main lift. Vorderlanersbach is a mini version.

Convenience Lanersbach has everything you need in a resort. The centre is within walking distance of the Eggalm gondola. Vorderlanersbach has its own gondola up to Rastkogel.

Scenery These are attractive villages in a long, pretty and varied valley.

GETTING THERE

Air Innsbruck 90km/ 55 miles (1hr30); Salzburg 190km/ 120 miles (2hr30); Munich 215km/ 135 miles (3hr)

Rail Local line to Mayrhofen; regular buses from station

UK PACKAGES

Hintertux Snow-wise **Lanersbach** STC **Finkenberg** Crystal, STC, Thomson

SNOWPIX.COM / BEN RILEY

Sommerbergalm at Hintertux is a major lift junction – seen here from the main glacier area, with the Tuxer Joch slopes to the left ↓

THE MOUNTAINS

Slopes The slopes of Eggalm, accessed by the gondola from Lanersbach, offer a small network of pleasantly varied intermediate pistes, usually delightfully quiet. You can descend on red or blue runs back to the village or to Vorderlanersbach, where a gondola goes up to the higher, open Rastkogel slopes; here, two fast chairlifts serve some very enjoyable long red and blue runs, and link with Mayrhofen's slopes. The linking run has red and black variants; both can get very mogulled, and many people opt to ride the jumbo cable car down; a short rope tow cuts out the need to hike up to the top station. The lower half of the run back from Rastkogel to Eggalm is a ski route; it is narrow but not steep, and it is served by snowmaking. The alternative is to ride the gondola down to Vorderlanersbach (there are no pistes) and get a bus to Lanersbach.

Fast lifts 'Great,' was the verdict of a previous visitor. Gondolas are the access lifts, and Eggalm and Rastkogel each have two six-packs.

Queues We have no reports of any problems. Indeed, Eggalm can be delightfully quiet.

Terrain parks The nearest parks are at Mayrhofen and Hintertux.

Snow reliability Snow conditions are usually good, at least in early season; by Austrian standards these are high slopes, and snowmaking covers some runs on both Eggalm and Rastkogel. But Rastkogel is excessively sunny. The grooming is 'OK – not great'.

Experts There are no pistes to challenge experts, but there is a fine off-piste route starting a short hike from the top of the Eggalm slopes and finishing at the village.

Intermediates The local slopes suit intermediates best, with some excellent, challenging red runs – and you have Mayrhofen's slopes, too.

Beginners Lanersbach has a nursery slope (as do Madseit and Juns), but there are few ideal progression slopes on Eggalm – most of the easy runs are on the higher lifts of Rastkogel.

Snowboarding The area isn't great for novices – there are draglifts dotted around, some in key places.

Cross-country There are 28km of cross-country trails around Madseit and Vorderlanersbach.

Mountain restaurants There are quite a few rustic places doing simple food, but demand exceeds supply, and self-service is the norm. There are two table-service exceptions on Eggalm. Egger Schialm is tucked away from the main runs, so is less busy – excellent Tirolergröstl, friendly people, good prices. Lattenalm has splendid views of the Tux glacier. On Rastkogel, the self-service Heidi's Schistadl is the 'best-value hut I've visited', says a recent reporter.

Schools and guides There are three schools in the valley, but we lack recent reports on them.

Families The Playarena in Vorderlanersbach nursery takes newborn babies up to teenagers, and most of the schools take children from four upwards. There's a children's snow garden on Eggalm.

STAYING THERE

Both villages are essentially hotel-based resorts.

Hotels The better places tend to be on the main road, but complaints of noise are few. The Lanersbacherof (87256) is a good 4-star with a pool, sauna, steam room and hot tub close to the lifts. The 3-star Pinzger (87541) and Alpengruss (87293) are cheaper alternatives. In Vorderlanersbach the 3-star Kirchlerhof (8560) has been recommended in the past and has a wellness area.

Apartments Plenty available locally.

Eating out Mainly hotel-based, busy, and geared to serving dinner early.

The Forelle is noted for its trout dishes, not surprisingly.

Après-ski Nightlife is generally quiet by Austrian standards. Try the Kleine Tenne or the Bergfriedalm – an old wooden building with traditional Austrian music ('Worth staying in Lanersbach just for this bar'). Gletscherspalte is a disco ('more commercial and with a younger crowd than Bergfriedalm').

Off the slopes Facilities are fairly good, and the bus service throughout the valley is extensive. Some hotels have pools and fitness rooms open to non-residents. Innsbruck and Salzburg are possible excursions.

Finkenberg 840m

- ➕ Fast lift access to the main slopes
- ➕ Pleasant, uncrowded village that appeals to families, but ...

- ➖ Lodging sprawls along a steep and busy main road
- ➖ No pisted runs to resort level

If you want to ski Mayrhofen's extensive area but avoid the après-ski crowds, Finkenberg makes a quieter alternative – and with direct access to the slopes. But the only way home is an itinerary (not shown on some maps).

Village charm The resort is a collection of traditional-style hotels, bars, cafes and private homes. There is a central pretty area around the church.

Convenience Most of the buildings (and hotels) are spread along the busy, steep, winding main road up to Lanersbach. Beware slippery pavements. Some hotels are within walking distance of the gondola, and many of the more distant ones run their own minibuses; there is also a village minibus service.

Scenery Steep mountains rise up on both sides.

THE MOUNTAIN

Slopes A two-stage gondola gives direct access to the Penken slopes – and in good conditions you can ski back to the village on a ski route (though it is often closed).

Fast lifts See Mayrhofen.

Queues Few problems reported. The gondola to and from the Penken may have queues at peak times.

Terrain parks The Mayrhofen park is easily accessed.

Snow reliability The local slopes are not as well endowed with snowmaking as those on Mayrhofen's side.

Experts Not much challenge, except off-piste and the Harakiri piste (read the Mayrhofen chapter).

Intermediates The whole area opens up from the top of the gondola.

Beginners There are nursery areas at the top of the gondola, on Penken, but Mayrhofen is a better base.

Snowboarding See Mayrhofen.

Cross-country Cross-country skiers have to get a bus up to Lanersbach.

Mountain restaurants Read the Mayrhofen chapter.

Schools and guides The Finkenberg is the main one, but the Sunny and Skipower schools also operate here.

Families The Finkenberg school takes children from age four.

STAYING THERE

Hotels The 5-star Sporthotel Stock (6775), owned by the family of downhiller Leonard Stock, has great spa facilities. There are several 4-stars, for example, the Eberl (62667) – 'excellent food more than made up for old-fashioned room' – and the Kristall (62840), which is 150m from the gondola with good wellness/spa facilities. The 3-star B&B hotel Harpfner (62094) has been highly recommended in the past.

Eating out Mainly in hotels, notably the Eberl.

Après-ski The main après-ski spots are the lively Laterndl Pub at the foot of the gondola and Finkennest.

Off the slopes OK for the active: curling, ice skating, swimming and good local walks.

Build your own shortlist: www.wheretoskiandsnowboard.com

Phone numbers

From elsewhere in Austria use the prefix 05287 (Hintertux, Lanersbach), 05285 (Finkenberg); from abroad use the prefix +43 and omit the initial '0'

TOURIST OFFICE

www.tux.at

Ischgl

Ischgl is unique: high, snow-sure slopes, a superb lift system, and a traditional-style Tirolean village. Perfection? Well, not quite ...

ISCHGL TOURIST OFFICE

RATINGS

The mountains

Extent	★★★★
Fast lifts	★★★★★
Queues	★★★★
Terrain p'ks	★★★★★
Snow	★★★★
Expert	★★★★
Intermediate	★★★★
Beginner	★★
Boarder	★★★★★
X-country	★★★
Restaurants	★★★★
Schools	★★★
Families	★★

The resort

Charm	★★★
Convenience	★★★
Scenery	★★★
Eating out	★★★★
Après-ski	★★★★★
Off-slope	★★★

RPI	105
lift pass	£180
ski hire	£140
lessons	£110
food & drink	£125
total	**£555**

118

NEWS

2014/15: A new 28-seat gondola will replace the old 4-seat Pardatschgrat gondola, which should help reduce morning queues. Work has started on a new underground car park.

2013/14: A new 150-person cable car to Piz Val Gronda (at the top right of our piste map) has opened up a big area of off-piste; there's a new 3km red piste down too.

+ Traditional-style village with a traffic-free core

+ High slopes with reliable snow

+ Broad area of slopes linked to Samnaun in Switzerland

+ Superb modern lift system

+ Après-ski like nowhere else, with an unmatched number of exceptionally lively places

− Village is densely developed, and has a rather urban, glitzy feel

− Not ideal for beginners or timid intermediates, for various reasons

− Few seriously steep runs

− Very little wooded terrain

− Treks to the gondolas for some

− Après-ski can be a bit tacky

Ischgl's slopes are more like those of a purpose-built French resort than a typical Tirolean place – high, snow-sure and fab for intermediates. It can't compete with the big boys in terms of extent but it's plenty big enough for all but the keenest piste-basher for a week. And its lift system (with over 80 per cent of them fast, including 22 fast chairs) is far better than anything in France.

But the village and vibes are most definitely Austrian – largely built in traditional chalet style and raucous après-ski that lasts from after lunch till dawn. Last season we were there, along with 20,000 others, for the Robbie Williams end-of-season concert on the slopes, and the next day, 4 May, was one of our best ski days of the season, with wonderful fresh powder first thing.

The place has its drawbacks – see our list of minus points above. But if you fancy something different, consider giving it a try.

THE RESORT

Ischgl is a compact village tucked away south of St Anton in the long, narrow Paznaun valley on the Swiss border; the ski area is shared with Samnaun in Switzerland. The Silvretta lift pass also covers Galtür further up the valley (see the end of this chapter) and Kappl and See down the valley (covered in the resort directory, at the back). All are linked by ski-buses and worth visiting; they make cheaper, quieter bases. A car allows trips to St Anton too. But heavy snowfalls can close the valley road for days due to avalanche danger.

VILLAGE CHARM ★★★☆☆
More town than village

The buildings are predominantly in traditional chalet style, with one or two modern exceptions – this is no rustic backwater – the narrow streets have a towny feel, and the style is swanky and brash rather than tasteful. There's a selection of lively bars and a better-than-usual selection of fashion shops – 'more luxury shops than Lech', says a reporter. The narrow main street plus a couple of side streets are mostly traffic-free – the valley road up to Galtür bypasses the village.

CONVENIENCE ★★★☆☆
Beware of the bypass

Choose location with care and beware of lodgings on the wrong side of the bypass road. You can leave your kit up at Idalp, Pardatschgrat and at the base lifts. Gondolas go up to mid-mountain from two points about 500m apart. The best location, overall, is on or near the main pedestrian street between the two. The eastern gondola station is separated from the main street by a low hill but is reached by an underground moving walkway.

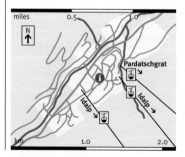

KEY FACTS

Resort	1400m
	4,590ft
Slopes	1400-2870m
	4,590-9,420ft
Lifts	44
Pistes	238km
	148 miles
Blue	20%
Red	64%
Black	16%
Snowmaking	
	1100 guns

TVB PAZNAUN-ISCHGL

Idalp is the hub of the slopes and where two of the gondolas from the village arrive; it also has the good sunny nursery slope and the terrain park just above it ↓

SCENERY ★★★☆☆
Good at the top
The wooded flanks of the valley rise steeply from the village, which gets almost no sun in January. But above the treeline, the Silvretta range is revealed in all its glory.

THE MOUNTAINS

Practically all the slopes are above the treeline, the main exception being the steep lower slopes above the village.

The piste map is OK but we found signposting inadequate: there are no big piste maps at the top of lifts and better direction markers are needed. The run numbering is confusing: a run may have multiple tributaries, or may split part-way down, with the variants having the same number. All this means trouble navigating, especially in poor visibility. There are two varieties of ski route – plain and 'extreme' – clearly stated to be 'not monitored'.

EXTENT OF THE SLOPES ★★★★☆
Extensive cross-border cruising
Ischgl claims 238km of pistes. That is more than any other Austrian ski area except the SkiWelt (Söll, Ellmau etc). But the Schrahe report (see our feature chapter on piste extent) puts it on a par with Kitzbühel and smaller than Saalbach-Hinterglemm. And the resort itself now publishes two other measurements based on methods more like Schrahe's; these give piste lengths of 163km to 172km. Whatever, it's a fair-sized area that will keep

many intermediates happy for a week.

The sunny **Idalp** plateau, reached by the 24-person Silvrettabahn or the eight-seat Fimbabahn, is the hub of the slopes. It can be very crowded around there. Pardatschgrat, reached by a new 28-seat gondola for 2014/15, is about 300m higher. From Idalp, lifts radiate to a wide variety of mainly north-west- and west-facing runs and to the Swiss border.

The red runs back down to Ischgl provoke regular complaints. Neither is easy, conditions can be tricky, and countless reckless skiers make these runs even more hazardous. Both have final stretches that probably should be black. The wide, quiet piste down the Velilltal looks better, but turns rather nasty lower down and joins the steep 'black' bottom part of run 1A. Quite a few people choose, very sensibly, to ride the gondolas down.

A short piste brings you from Idalp to the lifts serving the **Höllkar** bowl, leading to a high point at Palinkopf, from which you can go down to the new Piz Val Gronda cable car at the ski area's south-western end. Runs of 800m to 900m vertical from the top of the cable car and from Palinkopf go down to the **Fimbatal**.

On the Swiss side, the hub of activity is **Alp Trida**, surrounded by south- and east-facing runs with great views. From here a scenic red run goes down to Compatsch, for buses to Ravaisch (for the cable car back up) and Samnaun. From Palinkopf there is a lovely, long red run down a beautiful

Ski Total

ARE HERE IN

Ischgl

▶ Quality chalets
▶ Top locations
▶ Excellent value
▶ 17 more resorts

skitotal.com

01483 791 933

LIFT PASSES

VIP Skipass

Prices in €

Age	1-day	6-day
under 17	28	132
17 to 59	44	219
60 plus	44	197
Free	Under 8	
Beginner	No deals	

Notes Covers Ischgl and Samnaun and local buses; half-day pass and non-skier pass available; family reductions; 2-day-plus pass available only to those with a guest card staying in Ischgl Mathon or Samnaun

Alternative pass
Silvretta pass covers Ischgl, Samnaun, Galtür, Kappl and See

Resort news and key links: www.wheretoskiandsnowboard.com

valley to Samnaun – not difficult, but very sunny in parts and prone to closure by avalanche risk. There is a long flat stretch at the end.

FAST LIFTS ★★★★★
One of the best
Ischgl is near the top of our fast league table and over 80% of its main lifts are fast – mainly fast chairs. Not surprisingly, reporters praise the lifts – 'best resort I've been to in 20 years', 'superb', say reporters.

QUEUES ★★★★☆
Piste crowds more of a problem
We have still been getting reports of morning queues out of the valley ('get to the main gondola at 8.30-8.45am to avoid them'). But they are not the problem they once were, and for 2014/15 things should improve again because of the replacement of the

Pardatschgrat gondola (see 'News') resulting in an increase in capacity of over 1,000 people per hour. Crowds on the runs are an issue though, especially at Idalp, and on the easier runs on the Swiss side.

TERRAIN PARKS ★★★★★
One of Europe's best
Ischgl is a top place for freestylers. The huge 'excellent' PlayStation Vita park above Idalp is the big draw – 1600m long, and always well maintained.

It has beginner, public and pro lines, revamped each year. Overall, the park obstacles have an impressive creative flair. It has 20 kickers between 6 and 20 metres, 30 jib and slide elements and an airbag jump. There is another park at Velillscharte and a small park on the Swiss side.

🚡 gondola
🚠 cable car
🚡 fast chairlift
Slow chairs & drags have no symbol

Lovely long run, with a jolly restaurant at the end, on the outskirts of Samnaun – so a great way to end the morning or the day

Greitspitz
2870m/9,420ft

Lange Wandb

Salaas

Greitspitz

Samnaun
1840m/6,040ft

Alp Trida
Sattel
2490m

Viderjoch II

Idjoch
2760m

Idjo

Ravaisch

Pendelbahn

Luftseilbahn

Sattel

Viderjoch I

Flimjoc

Laret

Flimsattel

Velill

Compatsch

Alp Trida
2265m

Marmotte

Velillscharte
2555m

ALP TRIDA

Muller

Vishitz

Not a slow lift in sight in this sector – or in most other sectors, actually

Grivalea

Grivalea
2700m

2640m

SNOW RELIABILITY ★★★★
Very good

All the slopes apart from the runs back to the resort are above 1800m, and many on the Ischgl side are north-west-facing. So snow conditions are generally reliable; many reporters comment on excellent early/late season conditions and we experienced no shortage in May 2014. Snowmaking covers over half the slopes, including the descents to Ischgl and Samnaun. Reporters praise the grooming – 'outstanding' says a 2014 visitor.

FOR EXPERTS ★★★★
Plenty to do

Ischgl can't compare with St Anton for exciting slopes. But by general Tirolean standards it serves experts well. All the blacks are genuine ones and in combination with testing reds offer excellent, challenging descents.

Palinkopf, Greitspitz and Pardatschgrat all have some good steep blacks and the wooded lower slopes of the Fimbatal are delightful in a storm. There is plenty of off-piste, and powder doesn't get tracked out too quickly, particularly on the Swiss side. The new Piz Val Gronda cable car has opened up a big new area of off-piste including a fabulous big bowl. We had an excellent off-piste day a few seasons ago that included exploration of the shady side of Velilltal. There are also ski routes – number 39 from Palinkopf is a testing 1000m descent.

FOR INTERMEDIATES ★★★★
Something for everyone

Most of the slopes are wide, forgiving and ideal for intermediates – and there are plenty of them.

Our favourite runs are those from Palinkopf and Piz Val Gronda down to

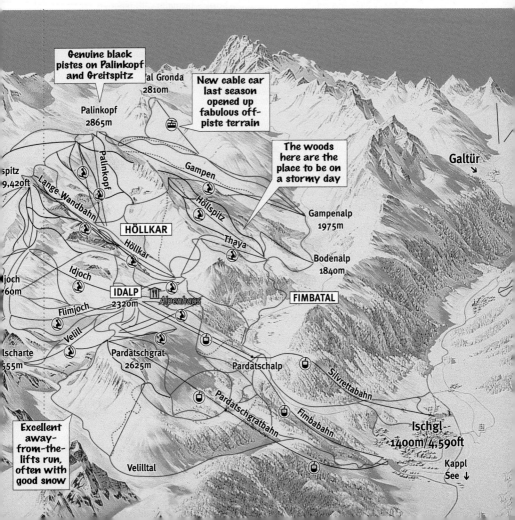

SCHOOLS

**Schneesport-
Akademie**
t 5257/5404

Classes
5 days (3hr) €185

Private lessons
€118 for 90min; each
additional person €25

CHILDCARE

**Kindergarten (ski
school)**
t 5257/5404
Non-skiing children
10am to 4pm; ski
kindergarten for ages
3 to 5

Ski school
From age 5

Gampenalp at the edge of the ski area and the beautiful isolated red run which drops 1000m from Palinkopf down to Samnaun in Switzerland. But there are lots of other options on Palinkopf, Greitspitz and Pardatschgrat. The reds down the beautiful Velilltal and the red from Greitspitz into Switzerland are great for quiet, high-speed cruising. For easier motorway cruising, there is lots of choice, including the runs down around Alp Trida on the Swiss side – but these can get crowded.

FOR BEGINNERS ★★★★★
Up the hill with the crowds
Up the mountain at Idalp there are good, sunny, snow-sure nursery slopes served by two moving carpets, drags and two fast chairs, but there are no special deals for beginners – you must buy a full lift pass to reach them. The blue runs on the east side of the bowl offer pleasant progression, and from there it's a small step to Switzerland – but these blue runs do get crowded.

FOR BOARDERS ★★★★★
Pretty much perfect
Ischgl has long been a popular spot for snowboarders, with its long, wide, well-groomed slopes served by snowboard-friendly gondolas and fast chairlifts. The off-piste terrain is above the treeline, easily accessible and makes for great riding for most ability levels. Ischgl is home to one of Austria's best terrain parks, and Silvretta Sports and Intersport Mathoy are recommended snowboard shops.

FOR CROSS-COUNTRY ★★★★★
Plenty in the valley
There are 100km of loops in the Ischgl, Galtür and Wirl area. Some trails tend to be shady, especially in early season, and are away from the main slopes, which makes meeting downhillers for lunch inconvenient.

MOUNTAIN RESTAURANTS ★★★★★
Good modern choices
Mountain restaurants generally offer good quality and choice. But they tend to be big, and despite this capacity can be stretched at peak times. They are clearly marked on the piste map. **Editors' choice** On the Austrian side at Idalp, the Alpenhaus (6840) is very much a designer place, with both table-service (upstairs) and self-service areas. We're interested only in the

former, although service is itself a bit slack. Food is good though and the relaxed ambience is great; a recent reporter confirms our view. On the Swiss side at Alp Trida the Marmotte (+41 81 868 5221) wins no prizes for interior design but does good food in calm and comfortable surroundings. **Worth knowing about** In the Fimbatal the 'lovely' Paznauner Thaya has self-service with famously good pizza, and table-service with good food upstairs; often with live bands or throbbing disco music. Bodenalp is a bit of a relic but some reporters like it ('very Austrian'). At Pardatschgrat, the glass-sided Pardorama is impressive, less crowded than lower places and has self- and table-service sections. A recent reporter liked the 'modern' refurbished self-service Höllboden.

On the Swiss side the woody Alp Bella is good value and a consistent favourite with reporters for traditional food and 'old hut' atmosphere. Recent reports on the Alp Trida are enthusiastic. The glass-sided Salaas is very stylish and spacious, but otherwise unremarkable.

SCHOOLS AND GUIDES ★★★★★
More reports please
The school meets up at Idalp. We lack recent reports but past reporters have been very happy, with instructors speaking sufficient English and giving good lessons. The school also organizes off-piste tours.

FOR FAMILIES ★★★★★
High-altitude options
Children can have lunch with their ski instructor; but small kids would be better off in Galtür or Kappl, where there are good play areas – see the end of this chapter for more on Galtür and the resort directory at the back of the book for more on Kappl.

STAYING THERE

Chalets Ski Total is the only chalet operator. They had the 58-bed chalet hotel Abendrot built for them a few years ago. We stayed there in 2014 and were impressed by the spacious, modern bedrooms and en-suite bathrooms. Central, a few minutes from the gondolas and with no noise disturbance at night. Total also has the 22-bed Zita, near the Fimbabahn and, new for 2014/15, the 30- to 40-bed Belmonte near the new Pardatschgrat

ALPINE ANSWERS
The UK's No.1 Chalet Specialist

For choice and service look no further!

alpineanswers.co.uk
call: 020 7801 1080

ABTA

GETTING THERE

Air Innsbruck 100km/ 60 miles (1hr30); Zürich 240km/ 150 miles (3hr); Munich 300km/ 185 miles (3hr30)

Rail Landeck (30km/19 miles); buses from station

UK PACKAGES

Alpine Answers, Crystal, Crystal Finest, Erna Low, Inghams, Interactive Resorts, Kaluma, Mountain Beds, Oxford Ski Co, Ski Bespoke, Ski Expectations, Ski Independence, Ski Line, Ski Total, Skitracer, Snow Finders, Snow-wise, STC, Thomson, Zenith
Galtür Crystal, Crystal Finest, Inghams, Ski Line, STC, Thomson, Zenith

ACTIVITIES

Indoor Silvretta Centre (bowling, billiards, swimming pool, tennis, sauna, solarium, massage), museums, concerts

Outdoor Ice rink, curling, sleigh rides, hiking tours, 7km floodlit toboggan run

gondola. The Belmonte and Abendrot have sauna and steam rooms.
Hotels There is a good selection from luxurious and pricey to simple B&Bs.
*****Trofana Royal (600) One of Austria's most luxurious hotels, with prices to match. A celebrity chef runs the kitchen. Sumptuous spa facilities.
****Christine (5346) The best B&B in town? Big rooms, central location, helpful owners, good spa, pool.
****Elisabeth (5411) Right by the Pardatschgrat gondola, with lively après-ski. Pool, sauna and steam.
****Goldener Adler (5217) Central, traditional ambience but designer rooms; good food. Pool, sauna, spa.
****Gramaser (5293) Near the Trofana Royal. We've enjoyed staying here; friendly staff, excellent food.
****Jägerhof (5206) Friendly staff, good food, large comfortable rooms. Sauna, steam, spa.
****Madlein (5226) Convenient, 'terribly chic', modern hotel. 'Excellent' pool, sauna, spa. Nightclub.
***Alpenglühn (5294) Central and good-value B&B.
***Arnika (5244) A few minutes' walk from the Fimba gondola. 'Beautiful, gorgeous food, great staff.'
Apartments Some attractive apartments are available. The Golfais by the Pardatschgrat gondola and the apartments in the hotel Solaria (with use of its spa) have been suggested.

EATING OUT ★★★★☆
Plenty of choice
Most restaurants are hotel-based. A 2014 reporter recommends the Yscla hotel for 'fine dining'. We enjoyed excellent, varied meals at the popular Grillalm in hotel Gramaser, which also has the Steakhouse ('very good food and service'). Reporter tips include: the Bära Falla ('great pizza and Tirolean food'), Nona ('pizza and Tirolean food, reasonable prices'), Allegra ('really good steaks and a pasta happy hour'). The Trofana Alm, which is as much a bar as a restaurant, and the Kitzloch, with its galleries over the dance floor, are good for grills and fondue.

APRES-SKI ★★★★★
Very lively
Ischgl is the liveliest resort in the Alps, we've concluded after a lot of in-depth research. The fun starts in the early afternoon – mountain restaurants such as Paznauner Thaya slide into après

mode directly after lunch – and it doesn't stop; lots of people are still in ski boots late in the evening.
The obvious ports of call in the village are the Trofana Alm near the Silvrettabahn and the Schatzi bar of the hotel Elisabeth by the Pardatschgratbahn – with scantily clad dancing girls ('At least 500 people watching,' said a 2014 reporter). Next door is Freeride, with friendly staff, ski movies and (last time we heard) no dancing girls. Across the river the Kitzloch is one of the places for dancing on the tables in ski boots. Niki's Stadl offers 'surreal madness' thanks to its lively DJs. Feuer & Eis ('great atmosphere') and the basement Kuhstahl are packed all evening – the latter is one reporter's all-time favourite après-bar. The Golden Eagle pub is popular with Brits looking for somewhere to sit. We enjoyed a quiet drink at the 'friendly' Kiwi ('weissbier on tap') and cocktails at pricey Guxa.
Later on, we enjoyed dancing to a live band in the huge Trofana Arena, which also has pole dancing, as does the Coyote Ugly. Other nightclubs include Pacha (as in Ibiza and London), Living Room and Posthörndl, with an ancient Rome theme.

OFF THE SLOPES ★★★☆☆
No sun but a nice pool
The village gets little sun in the middle of winter, and the resort is best suited to those keen to hit the slopes. But there's no shortage of off-slope activities. There are lots of maintained paths including many at altitude (the tourist office claims over 1000km in the valley), a 7km floodlit toboggan run and a splendid sports centre with swimming pool and bowling. And you can browse upmarket shops. It's easy to get around the valley by bus, and the Smuggler Card for pedestrians enables them to use certain lifts.

LINKED RESORT – 1840m

SAMNAUN

Small, quiet duty-free Samnaun is in a corner of Switzerland more easily reached from Austria. We know of no UK tour operators going here, but a recent reporter reckons more Brits are finding their way here.

There are four small components, roughly 1km apart: Samnaun-Dorf, prettily set at the head of the valley and the main focus, with some swanky hotels and duty-free shops; Ravaisch, where the cable car goes up; tiny Plan; and the hamlets of Laret and Compatsch, at the end of the main piste to the valley. We've stayed happily on the edge of Dorf in the Waldpark B&B (8602255), and a reporter recommended the Montana (8619000) for 'comfy rooms, fab pool, three great restaurants'. Other tips: 4-star Muttler (8618130) and Des Alpes (8685273). There's a smart AlpenQuell spa-pool-fitness centre.

The Schmuggler Alm at the bottom of the long run from Palinkopf is a popular lunch and après-ski spot. The Almraus (hotel Cresta) at Compatsch has been recommended for drinks. The school has a good reputation.

UP-VALLEY VILLAGE – 1585m

GALTÜR

Galtür is a charming, peaceful, traditional village clustered around a pretty little church, amid impressive mountain scenery at the head of Ischgl's Paznaun valley. Many visitors find the resort very quiet – there are just a few shops, restaurants, and a 'fantastic bakery for coffee and cakes', but a recent visitor 'loved the contrast from bustling Ischgl'.

Sunnier and cheaper than Ischgl, Galtür is a good base for families and mixed-ability groups. Galtür's own slopes rise to 2295m above a lift base at Wirl, a short bus ride from the village. The free buses to Ischgl are regular and quick but overcrowded at peak times even in January; and they stop at around 7pm. Taxis to Ischgl's nightlife are economic if shared. But a recent visitor warns that the roads to both Wirl and Ischgl were closed due to avalanche danger for two days – meaning he was unable to ski.

Galtür's Silvapark ski area has different 'sectors' to help guests make the most of the mountain; there are freeride, bumps and family sectors, for example. The slopes can be bleak in poor weather, and have only 40km of pistes, served by two fast chairs, a gondola and some long draglifts. Queues are rare. The slopes are fairly high, so pretty snow-sure; we had good snow on a warm March visit. Grooming is good.

Most runs are classified red, though some would be blue elsewhere. Run 8 is one of our favourites; a broad, long cruise with great views of the frozen dam below. The main blue piste can get crowded and has a steepish section at the top, but it is a long, pretty cruise to the valley. There are some challenges – reds and a black served by the fast Ballunspitze chair are short and steep. And there are a couple of ski routes to try. The area on the far right of the piste map, served by a slow double chair and a T-bar, is quiet, shady and has some good off-piste in a bowl and among well-spaced trees. There's a terrain park, and a fine nursery area at the base.

The school is 'excellent' and offers small classes. Kinderland has its own tow, carousel, moving carpet and cartoon characters. There are 100km of cross-country loops in the Galtür, Ischgl and Wirl area. The cosy, wooden Wieberhimml mountain hut is a lively, sunny spot for drinks. And we had good food at the Panorama Tenne, beside the gondola. The Faulbrunnalm at the top of the gondola is 'never overcrowded'. The Addis Abeba is a hip bar near the Soppalift drag.

There are good hotels. A 2014 reporter says the 4-star Büntali (8465) 'is a very comfortable and quiet, about 2 minutes walk from the village centre'; wellness area. The 4-star Almhof (8253) has 'excellent evening meals, every course a work of art'. A reporter who stayed at the Alpenhotel Tirol (8206) for the third time in 2013 says it is 'a good family hotel, with food and service second to none'. Flüchthorn (8202) has a 'charming restaurant' and Tirolean atmosphere.

Off-slope facilities are limited, apart from the impressive Alpinarium, an avalanche-protection structure and exhibition centre built after the avalanche that devastated the village in 1999. Much of the information is in German only, but it's worth a visit. There's a sports centre with pool, tennis and squash – and night skiing and tobogganing on Wednesdays.

Phone numbers
Calling long-distance
Add the prefix given below for each resort; when calling from abroad use the country code +43 and omit the initial '0'

Ischgl
05444

Galtür
05443

Samnaun
(Switzerland)
From elsewhere in Switzerland add the prefix 081; from abroad use the prefix +41 81

TOURIST OFFICES

Ischgl
www.ischgl.com

Samnaun
(Switzerland)
www.samnaun.ch

Galtür
www.galtuer.com

KITZBÜHEL TOURIST OFFICE

Kitzbühel

Despite the racy image, the slopes are mostly pretty tame; the town centre at the base, though, is something special – cute and lively

RATINGS

The mountains

Extent	★★★
Fast lifts	★★★★★
Queues	★★★
Terrain p'ks	★★★
Snow	★★
Expert	★★★
Intermediate	★★★★
Beginner	★★
Boarder	★★
X-country	★★★
Restaurants	★★★★
Schools	★★★★
Families	★

The resort

Charm	★★★★
Convenience	★★
Scenery	★★★
Eating out	★★★★
Après-ski	★★★★
Off-slope	★★★★★

RPI	105
lift pass	£190
ski hire	£115
lessons	£115
food & drink	£120
total	**£540**

NEWS

2014/15: A double chair is planned for Bichlalm to serve its area of ungroomed slopes. A new lake for snowmaking is due to be built. Several runs in the Ehrenbachhöhe area are due to be remodelled.

2013/14: At Jochberg, the old double chair and drag were replaced by a 10-seater gondola, the Wagstättbahn.

➕ Extensive, attractive, varied slopes offering a sensation of travel

➕ Beautiful medieval town centre

➕ Vibrant nightlife

➕ Lots to do off the slopes

➕ Hotels to suit every budget

➕ Excellent mountain restaurants

➖ Low altitude means snow is often poor low down (though snowmaking is fairly extensive)

➖ Surprisingly few challenges on-piste

➖ Mediocre resort-level nursery area

➖ Some crowded pistes

➖ Town sprawls widely

Kitzbühel's Hahnenkamm downhill race course is the most exciting on the World Cup circuit, and race weekend is one of the jolliest parties in the Alps. But the place has powerful attractions for the rest of the season too.

The lift system has improved hugely in the last decade and a big new gondola at Jochberg last season just squeezed the fast lift rating up to ★★★★★.

Sadly, it doesn't get the same rating for snow – for us, the great weakness of the place. It's not a matter of quantity, but of quality. Just once, we arrived in a storm and had good piste conditions to valley level. Normally we don't. The fact is, Kitzbühel needs more altitude.

The authorities are obviously alert to this, and amazingly have managed to raise the place by a few metres: although topo maps have always shown the centre at a smidge over 760m, these days the resort puts itself at 800m. Very enterprising; but it'll take more than that to do the trick.

THE RESORT

Kitzbühel is a large valley town with its major ski area on one side and a couple of minor ones on the other. The major area, spreading south-west from the famous Hahnenkamm directly above the town, is reached by gondola from just outside the town centre and shared with Kirchberg, another substantial resort and covered at the end of the chapter.

The 'still great value' Kitzbüheler Alpen AllStarCard lift pass covers seven separate ski areas in the region – read 'Lift passes'. One of those – the SkiWelt – is accessible by the Ki-West gondola, a short bus ride from Skirast.

VILLAGE CHARM ★★★★
Medieval town centre

The largely car-free medieval centre – with quaint church, cobbled streets and attractively painted buildings – is delightful and a compelling place to stay. Many visitors love the upscale, towny ambience and swanky shops and cafes. But the resort spreads widely, and busy roads surround the old town. This is no quiet little village.

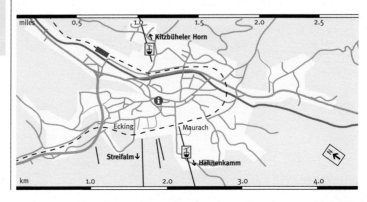

KEY FACTS	
Resort	760m
	2,490ft
Slopes	800-2000m
	2,620-6,560ft
Lifts	51
Pistes	170km
	106 miles
Blue	40%
Red	46%
Black	14%
Snowmaking	
	820 guns

CONVENIENCE ★★☆☆☆
Choose your spot carefully

A gondola from the edge of the town goes up to the Hahnenkamm, the start of the main area of slopes. Across town, close to the railway station but some way from the centre, another gondola accesses the much smaller Kitzbüheler Horn sector.

The size of Kitzbühel (compare the map below with other Austrian resorts, such as Ischgl) makes choice of location important. Many visitors prefer to be in the centre of town and close to the Hahnenkamm gondola. Beginners should bear in mind that the Hahnenkamm nursery slopes are often lacking in snow, and then novices are taken up the Horn. Views have varied on the free buses. The circular route and high-season crowding have led some recent reporters to walk instead, but a regular visitor rates them 'quick, efficient and uncrowded'. There are ski/boot depots at obvious points.

Best snow is normally here on Kitzbühel's highest slopes

A big gondola connects the two main areas of slopes at mountain-top level – great views

Big new gondola for 2013/14 squeezed the resort up to ★★★★★ for fast lifts

Start of the famous World Cup downhill run which ends in the resort

SCENERY ★★★★★
Attractive valley views

Kitzbühel is set at a junction of broad, pretty valleys, among partly wooded mountains. There are good views from Pengelstein across both valleys (the minor peak of Gr Rettenstein is prominent) and to the SkiWelt. From the Resterhöhe slopes, in particular, there are great panoramic views of the high Alps to the south, including Grossvenediger directly south and Grossglockner slightly east of south.

THE MOUNTAINS

Kitzbühel's extensive main area of slopes – shared with Kirchberg and other villages – offers some open runs higher up but they soon run into patchy forest lower down. Most slopes face north-east or north-west.

The piste map is pretty clear but readers' views on signposting vary. And many readers find that run classifications exaggerate difficulty.

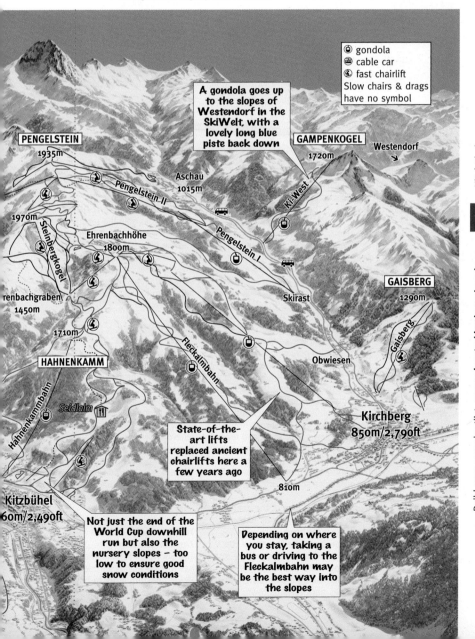

gondola
cable car
fast chairlift
Slow chairs & drags have no symbol

A gondola goes up to the slopes of **Westendorf** in the SkiWelt, with a lovely long blue piste back down

State-of-the-art lifts replaced ancient chairlifts here a few years ago

Not just the end of the World Cup downhill run but also the nursery slopes – too low to ensure good snow conditions

Depending on where you stay, taking a bus or driving to the Fleckalmbahn may be the best way into the slopes

PENGELSTEIN
1935m
1970m
Steinbergkogel
Ehrenbachhöhe
1800m
renbachgraben
1450m
1710m
HAHNENKAMM
Seidalm
Hahnenkammbahn
Kitzbühel
6om/2,490ft
Aschau
1015m
Pengelstein II
Pengelstein I
Flecklalmbahn
810m
GAMPENKOGEL
1720m
Ki-West
Westendorf
Skirast
Obwiesen
GAISBERG
1290m
Gaisberg
Kirchberg
850m/2,790ft

Kitzbühel's Hahnenkamm Downhill race, held in mid- to late January each year (23 to 25 January in 2015), is the toughest as well as one of the most famous on the World Cup circuit. On the race weekend the town is packed, and there is a real carnival atmosphere, with bands, people in traditional costumes and huge (and loud) cowbells everywhere. The race itself starts with a steep icy section before you hit the famous Mausfalle and Steilhang, where even Franz Klammer used to get worried. The course starts near the top of the Hahnenkamm gondola and drops 860m to finish amid the noise and celebrations right on the edge of town. The course is normally closed from the start of the season until the race is over, but after the race weekend ordinary mortals can try most of the course, if the snow is good enough – it's an unpisted ski route mostly. We found it steep and tricky in parts, even when going slowly – it must be terrifying at race speeds of 80mph or more.

KITZBÜHEL TOURISMUS

LIFT PASSES

Prices in €

Age	1-day	6-day
under 16	24	117
16 to 18	38	187
19 plus	47	233

Free Under 7
Senior 60+: day pass €38 on Tue & Thu; 80+: season pass €20
Beginner Reduced pass for Gaisberg and Ganslern chairs only; six free lifts (two in Kitzbühel)
Notes Covers Kitzbühel, Kirchberg, Reith, Aurach, Jochberg, Mittersill/ Hollersbach; hourly and pedestrian tickets; 50% reduction on pool entry

Alternative passes Kitzbüheler Alpen AllStarCard covers Kitzbühel, Schneewinkel (St Johann), SkiWelt, Ski Juwel, Skicircus Saalbach, Zell-Kaprun, Fieberbrunn, Waidring; Salzburg Super Ski Card covers 22 ski areas in the Salzburg province

EXTENT OF THE SLOPES ★★★★★
Big but bitty
The slopes can be divided into several identifiable areas. The **Hahnenkamm** gondola takes you to the bowl of Ehrenbachgraben, a major lift bottleneck in the past but, thanks to new lifts in the last few years, now a place you might want to do laps on the steep slopes of Steinbergkogel.

Beyond is the slightly lower peak of **Pengelstein**, with an eight-pack up to it from the Steinbergkogel area. Long west-facing runs go down to Skirast, where there is a gondola back up, or to Aschau. Ski-buses from these points will take you to the Ki-West gondola towards Westendorf and to Kirchberg.

Pengelstein is also the start of the impressive 30-person cross-valley 3S gondola to **Wurzhöhe** above Jochberg. This peak-to-peak link has fabulous views (especially if you hit the cabin with the partial glass floor).

Further lifts then take you to the **Resterhöhe** sector – well worth the excursion, for better snow and fewer crowds. There is a long, scenic, sunny red run to Breitmoos, mid-station of the gondola up from Hollersbach. Runs are otherwise short, but mostly served by fast chairs.

The second stage of the gondola on **Kitzbüheler Horn** leads to the sunny Trattalm bowl; or a cable car takes you up to the summit of the Horn, from where a fine, solitary piste leads down into the Raintal on the east side. There's a blue piste and two ski routes back towards town.

The separate **Bichlalm** area, which last season offered guided snowcat skiing is due to have a new double chair for 2014/15 to access the ski routes and off-piste.

FAST LIFTS ★★★★★
Rapid improvement but ...
Lift upgrades saw the resort move from ★★★ to ★★★★ four years ago; and the big new gondola at Jochberg last season just squeezed it into the five-star category. But it still has some slow chairs and T-bars and the trip back from Resterhöhe still involves one of each.

QUEUES ★★★★★
Much improved
Recent reporters have had few queue problems. But there can still be peak-time queues for the Hahnenkamm gondola out of the town and occasional queues up the hill, especially at the weekends. The cross-valley gondola to Wurzhöhe has relieved pressure on the slopes closer to town, by encouraging people to use the Resterhöhe slopes. But the Trattenbach chair and particularly the Gauxjoch drag you need to get back from Resterhöhe can build queues on busy afternoons.

TERRAIN PARKS ★★★★★
Double the fun
The Snowpark Hanglalm at Resterhöhe has lots for advanced riders – several kicker lines, from big to huge, as well as advanced rails, a plethora of butter

boxes and a visually pleasing wooden obstacle section. Pro riders love the park's centrepiece – a huge gap jump. But it also has an area aimed at beginners and intermediates. The park in nearby Westendorf is excellent – well worth the trip. The park on the Kitzbüheler Horn is a beginner park.

SNOW RELIABILITY ★★★★★
More snowmaking now
The problem is that Kitzbühel's slopes have one of the lowest average heights in the Alps, and the Horn is also sunny. Even in an exceptionally good snow year some reporters complain of worn patches, ice and slush on the lower slopes. In a normal year, the lower slopes can be very tricky when slushy or more especially when icy (though the snow at the top is often OK). The expansion of snowmaking has improved matters when it's cold enough to make snow – runs down to Kitzbühel, Kirchberg, Klausen and Jochberg are covered. One reporter found conditions 'better than feared' because of this. But many slopes still remain unprotected. If snow is poor, head for Resterhöhe. March 2014 visitors found grooming was 'very good in difficult conditions'.

SNOWPIX.COM / CHRIS GILL
These black runs down Steinbergkogel are fabulous when they've been groomed ↓

FOR EXPERTS ★★★★★
Plan to go off-piste
Steep slopes – pistes and off-piste terrain – are mostly concentrated in the Steinbergkogel-Ehrenbachgraben

area, equipped with three fast chairs. Direttissima is seriously steep, but sometimes groomed – fabulous. The other blacks dotted around are easier. There are plenty of long, challenging reds. When conditions allow, there is plenty of gentler off-piste to be found – some of it close to pistes, some requiring a guide. The long ski routes from Pengelstein towards Jochberg and Hechenmoos are delightful in good snow. The ski routes and off-piste at Bichlalm should be served by a new double chair this season.

FOR INTERMEDIATES ★★★★★
Lots of alternatives
The Hahnenkamm area is prime intermediate terrain but can get crowded. Good intermediates will want to do the World Cup downhill run, of course (see the feature panel opposite). And the long blues of around 1000m vertical to Klausen, Kirchberg and Skirast are satisfying. The black to Aschau is not difficult, and is a lovely way to end the day (check the bus times first).

The Wurzhöhe runs are good for mixed abilities, and the short, high runs at Resterhöhe are ideal if you are more timid. There are easy reds down to Pass Thurn and Jochberg. This area tends to be much quieter than Hahnenkamm and Pengelstein. Much of the Horn is good cruising, and the east-facing Raintal is excellent (but it has a slow double chair back).

Kitzbühel

129

MOMENTUM SKI

Weekend & a la carte
ski holiday specialists

100% Tailor-made

Premier hotels
& apartments

Flexible travel
arrangements

020 7371 9111
WWW.MOMENTUMSKI.COM

UK PACKAGES

Alpine Answers, Alpine
Weekends, Carrier,
Crystal, Crystal Finest,
Elegant Resorts, Erna
Low, Inghams, Kaluma,
Momentum, Mountain
Beds, Neilson, Oxford
Ski Co, Ski Line, Ski
Safari, Skitracer, Snow
Finders, Snow-wise,
Snowscape, STC,
Thomson
Kirchberg Crystal,
Inghams, Ski Bespoke,
Snowscape, STC,
Thomson

SNOWPIX.COM / CHRIS GILL

Despite its 5-star
rating for fast lifts,
Kitzbühel still has a
fair number of T-bars
and slow chairs ↓

AUSTRIA

FOR BEGINNERS ★★★★★
Not ideal

The Hahnenkamm nursery slopes are
no more than adequate, and prone to
poor snow conditions – but at least
they have some free lifts. There are
nursery areas with free lifts at
Jochberg, Pass Thurn and Aschau, too.
The Horn has a high, sunny, nursery-
like section, and quick learners will
soon be cruising home from there on
the long Hagstein piste. There are
some easy runs to progress to if the
snow is OK. Day lift passes just for the
Horn slopes are available. But there
are better resorts to learn in.

FOR BOARDERS ★★★★★
Gaining recognition

Kitzbühel was never known as a
snowboarders' hub, but it is growing
in popularity, year on year. There are
two decent parks and some good off-
piste runs and fun natural obstacles
on the Hahnenkamm and around
Pengelstein. All the major lifts are now
gondolas or chairlifts – so the area
suits beginners well. But a couple of
reporters have drawn attention to the
many flat linking runs, on which
boarders struggle – one versatile chap
ditched his board after a day, and
rented skis instead.

FOR CROSS-COUNTRY ★★★★★
Plentiful but low

There are around 60km of trails
scattered around. Most are at valley
level and prone to lack of snow, but a
reporter who got lots of snow highly
recommends them.

MOUNTAIN RESTAURANTS ★★★★★
A highlight

There are many attractive restaurants,
most offering table-service – one of
the highlights of this resort. No fewer
than 60 are marked and named on the
piste map and there is a useful
booklet describing them, in both
English and German.

Editors' choice Bärenbadalm (0664 855
7994), halfway to Resterhöhe, has a
cool, modern bar area with flat-screen
TVs, a roaring log fire and comfy
armchairs and sofas; you can eat there
or in various dining areas with a more
rustic feel. We've had delicious oriental
beef strip salad and crispy pork ribs
here. Endorsed by reporters. But the
terrace is spoiled by the adjacent lift
station – not a criticism you can level
at the Panoramaalm up at Resterhöhe.
This has both a beautiful, intimate
interior and a fine terrace including a
great bar (get there early to bag a
spot). Excellent food, 'efficient, friendly
staff'. Seidlalm (63135), right by the
lower part of the downhill course, is
quiet and delightfully rustic.

Worth knowing about In the
Hahnenkamm sector we had a jolly
meal at Berghaus Tyrol ('Try the woks,'
says a reporter) and a fabulous strudel
at the Sonnbühel – lovely situation,
sheltered and with a good view. One
Kitz regular lists Hahnenkammstüberl
among her favourites. Other tips are
Hochkitzbühel ('wonderfully light and
airy', 'good menu, food quality and
table-service') and Hochbrunn ('best
Gröstl mit Ei').

On Pengelstein, Usterweis is a nice
woody traditional place; Gauxerstad'l

Rote Teufel
t 62500

Element3
t 72301

Ski-Alpin
t 0664 102 0623

Spirit4Motion
t 0664 266 0527

Snowsports
t 0664 390 0090

Classes (Rote Teufel prices) 6 days (2hr am and pm) €220

Private lessons
From €85 for 1hr

CHILDCARE

There is no non-ski nursery, but babysitters and nannies can be hired

Ski school
From age 3

GETTING THERE

Air Salzburg 75km/ 45 miles (1hr30); Innsbruck 95km/ 60 miles (1hr30); Munich 175km/ 110 miles (2hr30)

Rail Mainline station in resort

---

has 'a limited menu but good, friendly service and mountainous portions'. The hotel Ehrenbachhöhe at the top of Fleckalmbahn does 'classic mountain fare with plentiful portions and efficient service,' says a 2014 visitor.

At Wurzhöhe/Resterhöhe, try Hanglalm, Sonnalm, Bruggeralm ('cheap and cheerful with a very pleasant veranda') or Berggasthaus Resterhöhe ('wonderful blutwurstgröstl and so welcoming').

On the Horn, there's the Hornköpfl-Hütte and Gipfelhaus, which has 'super views'. The Adlerhütte is 'a favourite' of a Kitzbühel regular.

On the pistes down to Kirchberg the Fleckalm 'offers better service and food than some of the smarter places'. We can recommend the meaty gulaschsuppe at the Maieralm.

SCHOOLS AND GUIDES ★★★★
Red Devils rule
The Kitzbühel Rote Teufel (Red Devils) is the largest. The other schools emphasize their small scale. Element3 is an adventure company offering ski/snowboard classes. Reports please.

FOR FAMILIES ★
Not an ideal choice
It's rather a spread-out resort for family holiday purposes. Rote Teufel takes kids from age three.

STAYING THERE

Kitzbühel is essentially a hotel resort.
Chalets Crystal has two big (30 beds or so) chalets close to the Hahnenkamm gondola.
Hotels There is an enormous choice.
★★★★★Schloss Lebenberg (6901) Modernized 'castle' with smart wellness centre; inconvenient location but free shuttle-bus. Pool.
★★★★★Tennerhof (63181) Luxurious former farmhouse, with renowned restaurant. Beautiful panelled rooms. Relais & Châteaux. Pool, spa.
★★★★Best Western Kaiserhof (75503) By the Hahnenkamm gondola. Spa, pool.
★★★★Maria Theresia (64711) Central. 'Food good, rooms well appointed and staff very helpful.' Sauna, steam.
★★★★Rasmushof (65252) Right on the slopes by the race finish area, close to centre of town.
★★★★Schwarzer Adler (6911) Central, traditional hotel turned swanky boutique hotel. Roof-top pool, spa.

STC Ski
Specialists in Tailor-Made Short Breaks & Holidays
01483 771 222
www.stcski.co.uk
ski@stcski.co.uk

★★★★Tiefenbrunner (66680) Central, traditional, family-run. Pool, spa. 'The standards set by the highly visible owners are impeccably high, the food is superb and the facilities faultless,' says a regular visitor this year.
★★★Edelweiss (75252) Close to centre. 'Most welcoming hotel we've ever stayed at; supply bags for you to take food from breakfast table for lunch.'
★★★Strasshofer (62285) Central. 'Great location, friendly, good food – hard to beat for brilliant value,' says a regular.
★★Mühlbergerhof (62835) Small, friendly pension in good position.
Apartments Many of the best are attached to hotels.

EATING OUT ★★★★
Something for everyone
There is a wide range of restaurants to suit all pockets, including pizzerias and fast-food outlets (even McDonald's) as well as gourmet dining.

The Neuwirt in the chic Schwarzer Adler hotel is regarded as the best in town, and wins awards from food guides. The Chizzo offers fine dining in one of the oldest buildings in Kitzbühel. Good, cheaper places include the traditional Huberbräu-Stüberl, Zinnkrug, Eggerwirt and, a little out of town with great views, Hagstein (traditional farm food). The Goldene Gams restaurant in the hotel Tiefenbrunner has a wide menu. Both the Centro and the Barrique are recommended for their pizzas. And the rustic Moro di Venezia serves 'simple Italian food'. For something different take a taxi to Rosi's Sonnbergstub'n. Choose the speciality lamb or duck and expect to be serenaded by Rosi herself.

Seidlalm is the place for a jolly Tirolean evening on the lower slopes. On Fridays you can dine at the top of the Hahnenkamm gondola.

Kitzbühel

131

Build your own shortlist: **www.wheretoskiandsnowboard.com**

ACTIVITIES

Indoor Aquarena centre (pools, slides, sauna, solarium, steam baths – discounted entry with lift pass); Sportpark (tennis, bowling, climbing wall), fitness studios, beauty centres, museums, casino, cinema

Outdoor Ice rink (curling and skating), tobogganing, ballooning, 65km of cleared walking paths, paragliding

Phone numbers
From elsewhere in Austria add the prefix 05356 for Kitzbühel and 05357 for Kirchberg; from abroad use the prefixes +43 5356 / +43 5357

TOURIST OFFICES

Kitzbühel
www.kitzbuehel.com
Kirchberg
www.kirchberg.at

APRES-SKI ★★★★
A main attraction

Nightlife is one of Kitz's attractions, and a recent reporter found 'plenty of lively bars for après-ski'. As the lifts close the town is jolly without being much livelier than many other Tirolean resorts. The Streifalm bar at the foot of the slopes is popular. 'The outside bar at Chizzo was great fun,' says a recent reporter whose favourite bar was the Pavillon. Praxmair and Rupprechter are among the most atmospheric cafes for teatime cakes and pastries. The Centro and the 'quaint' Ursprung have been recommended for pre-dinner drinks.

The Lichtl Pub has thousands of lights hanging from the ceiling. The Londoner is a bit of an institution, appealing particularly to young Brits, but a grown-up visiting this year enjoyed it ('packed, live band until around 7pm'). The heated terrace of the Stamperl, across the road, was doing a roaring trade when we visited a few seasons ago. La Fonda is 'worth a look' says a reporter, as 'it's frequented by locals'. Highways and Take Five are discos.

OFF THE SLOPES ★★★★★
Plenty to do

The lift pass gives a 50% reduction for the pools in the Aquarena. There's skating, ice hockey matches, bowling etc at the Sportpark and paragliding. There's an 'interesting' museum and a casino. The railway makes excursions easy (eg Salzburg, Innsbruck).

LINKED RESORT – 850m
KIRCHBERG

Kirchberg is a large, busy, spread-out town, with plentiful restaurants and shops and an unremarkable but pleasant centre. The road from Kitzbühel towards Innsbruck bypasses the centre, but traffic is still intrusive.

The slopes it shares with Kitzbühel are accessed via a choice of three gondolas, all requiring the use of 'regular and efficient' ski-buses or affordable taxis (unless you opt to stay at a lift base rather than in the town). The Maierlbahn goes from a station 1km from the centre, while the Fleckalmbahn goes up from Klausen beside the road to Kitzbühel about 1.5km out. The third is over 3km out at Skirast. Another 2km on from Skirast is a gondola into Westendorf's

slopes. These are linked to the main SkiWelt slopes via Brixen, which can also easily be reached by train or bus – read the chapter on Söll for more on these. There is a small nursery slope at the bottom of the separate Gaisberg sector, with a free lift, but it's at low altitude, and so prone to poor snow.

The village has a wide choice of lodging; the 4-star Klausen (2128) is convenient for the Klausen gondola, and a 2014 visitor enjoyed the Haus Alpenblick (2234), a five-minute walk from the centre – 'welcoming, good food, plenty of beers to try'. The 'very comfortable' Pension Hollaus (2392) 'slightly up the hill from the main road' was also recommended this year. Most restaurants are hotel-based, but there are a couple of pizzerias, a Chinese ('best crispy duck') and a steakhouse.

There is some après action, both at teatime and later on. The restaurants on the home runs do good business as the lifts close. Rohrerstadl, just above Skirast, is tipped for 'animated' après-ski – 'live group; staff very attentive'. One reporter reckons the Boomerang is 'the most lively and welcoming bar, with pool table and efficient table-service'. Several places operate as discos later.

Off the slopes there's floodlit tobogganing on Gaisberg and a leisure centre, and some hotels have pools.

LINKED RESORT – 925m
JOCHBERG

Jochberg – 10km south of Kitzbühel – is not so much a village as a straggle of accommodation along a busy road – it has nothing you could call a centre. There's a church, a bank, a post office, a ski depot, a supermarket, half a dozen restaurants and a couple of bars. But if you're after accommodation close to the lifts, it's worth considering.

Access to the slopes has been greatly improved with a 10-seater gondola replacing an old, slow double chair, and a quite long T-bar above it – a development we guess is not unrelated to the opening in 2011 of the cutting-edge 5-star Kempinski Hotel das Tirol a few metres away.

Most of the other lodgings are small pensions and apartments, but there is also the 4-star Jochbergerhof. Of the restaurants the Alpenland is recommended by a reporter: 'Good value, friendly service, superb food.'

LECH TOURIST OFFICE

Lech

Simply one of the best: a captivating village with exceptionally snowy slopes that saw some serious expansion in 2013/14

RATINGS

The mountains

Extent	★★★
Fast lifts	★★★★
Queues	★★★★
Terrain p'ks	★★★★
Snow	★★★★
Expert	★★★★
Intermediate	★★★★
Beginner	★★★★
Boarder	★★★★
X-country	★★★
Restaurants	★★★
Schools	★★★★
Families	★★★★★

The resort

Charm	★★★★
Convenience	★★★
Scenery	★★★
Eating out	★★★
Après-ski	★★★★
Off-slope	★★★

RPI	125
lift pass	£190
ski hire	£165
lessons	£145
food & drink	£150
total	**£650**

NEWS

2013/14: A new 10-seat gondola linked Lech with the Warth ski area, adding 68km of pistes (covered by the Arlberg lift pass).

+ Traditional village in a picturesque riverside setting

+ Excellent snow record

+ Sizeable area of slopes shared with Zürs – now enlarged by a link to humble little Warth

+ Access by bus to the slopes of St Anton and Stuben

+ Some very lovely hotels

+ Lively après-ski scene

– Pricey, by Austrian standards

– Surprisingly limited shopping

– Few non-hotel bars or restaurants

– Local traffic intrudes on main street

– Hardly any challenging pistes

– Nearly all slopes above treeline

– Blue runs down to Lech are rather steep for nervous novices

– Still a few slow, old lifts

Lech is a long-standing favourite of ours; its combination of charm, varied slopes and good snow is difficult to beat (though more decent mountain restaurants would be no bad thing). And now its attractions are reinforced by a gondola link to the snowiest slopes in the Alps at Warth, adding 50% more pistes and lots of off-piste. We made multiple trips to check out the Warth link and slopes in 2014, and rate the expansion highly – as did holiday skiers we talked to riding the gondola back to their humble digs in Lech.

Lech and linked Zürs are the most fashionable resorts in Austria, each able to pull in Porsche-borne Germans by the thousand. Putting aside their 5-star hotels, though, they don't feel particularly exclusive. Lech has always been the more attractive base – to compete, Zürs needs a tunnel bypass, and then a makeover – but the Warth gondola link reinforces its advantage.

THE RESORT

Lech is an old farming village set in a high valley that spent long periods of winter cut off from the outside world until the Flexen Pass road linked Zürs to Stuben at the end of the 19th century. Seriously heavy snow can close the road for days on end, marooning visitors in Lech and Zürs.

Not far from the centre is the cable car up to Oberlech: a small, traffic-free area of 4-star hotels set on the piste.

Zug is a hamlet 3km from Lech, with a lift into the Lech slopes. It's not ideal for sampling Lech's nightlife, but there is an evening bus service.

Lech is linked by lifts and runs to higher Zürs to the south, and now by gondola (but not by piste) to Warth to the north. Both resorts are described at the end of this chapter. St Anton, not linked but covered by the lift pass, gets its own chapter.

The road to Warth is closed in winter. The other resorts in this area can be reached by bus, but the service is rubbish. There are free and regular ski-buses linking Lech, Zürs and Alpe Rauz for the St Anton lifts. And there are post buses to St Anton via Alpe Rauz and St Christoph. But all get seriously crowded at busy times, leaving people at the roadside at the mercy of the waiting taxi drivers. And the post buses are neither free nor frequent. It's not good enough.

The Sonnenkopf area at Klösterle, reached by free ski-bus from Stuben, is also covered by the Arlberg pass.

VILLAGE CHARM ★★★★
Busy main street

The village is attractive, with upmarket hotels built in traditional chalet style, a gurgling river plus bridges, and a high incidence of snow on the streets. But don't expect a rustic idyll: away

SKIWORLD

Catered chalets, hotels and self catering apartments in

Europe, USA and Canada

skiworld.co.uk

08444 930 430

ABTA V2151 ATOL 2036

◢ **Inghams**

LECH

▶ **Picturesque and snow-sure skiing**
▶ **Ski the Arlberg** ▶ **Quality Hotels**

inghams.co.uk **01483 371 236** ABTA V4871 ATOL 0025

slopes. Just across the river are the chairlifts for Lech's main area of slopes. Chalets, apartments and pensions are dotted around the valley, and the village spreads for 2km. Some of the cheaper accommodation is quite a walk from the lifts.

Oberlech is a tiny place with pistes where you would expect streets, and an underground tunnel system linking the hotels and cable car station – used routinely to move baggage, and by guests in bad weather. The cable car works until 1am, allowing access to the nightlife down in Lech.

from the central area the place is fairly ordinary, and the appeal is somewhat dimmed by traffic on the main street, especially at weekends when car-borne visitors arrive and depart.

CONVENIENCE ★★★☆☆
It's a long village
The heart of the village is a short stretch of the main street beside the river, with most of the main hotels, the main shop (Strolz) and the Rüfikopf cable car, for access to the Zürs

SCENERY ★★★☆☆
In a bright spot
Lech is in a fairly sunny position at the junction of two attractive valleys, with adequately impressive scenery, largely thanks to the Omeshorn looming to the south. It is high and open, with very few trees. From the top slopes there are views to the Valluga above St Anton in one direction, and to Warth in the other.

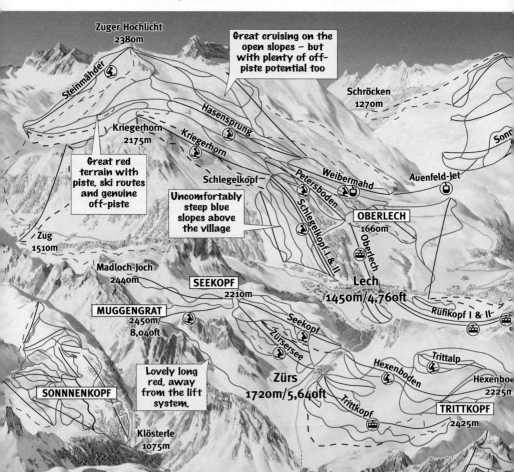

KEY FACTS

Resort	1450m
	4,760ft

Arlberg region

Slopes	1075-2650m
	3,530-8,690ft
Lifts	97
Slopes*	340km
	210 miles
Blue	42%
Red	42%
Black	16%
Snowmaking	56%

For Lech-Zürs-Warth-Schröcken only

Slopes	1450-2450m
	4,760-8,040ft
Lifts	47
Slopes*	180km
	112 miles
Blue	41%
Red	44%
Black	15%
Snowmaking	46%
* pistes and ski routes	

THE MOUNTAINS

Practically all the slopes are treeless, the main exception being the lower runs just above Lech. Most are quite sunny – very few are north-facing.

The toughest runs are called 'ski routes'. The piste map says these are marked and avalanche controlled but not groomed or patrolled. We applaud the clear explanation (lacking in many resorts), but we think many of them should be patrolled pistes. Ski routes form the only ways down to Zug and Lech as part of the popular Lech-Zürs 'White Ring' circuit and are treated like pistes, as are several other ski routes. To add to the confusion, routes are sometimes groomed – we've found the Zürs to Zug route has been groomed on all our recent visits.

The piste map also marks 'high-Alpine touring runs'. These are simply off-piste runs that would not appear on the piste map at all in most resorts. That's fair enough – but don't go without a guide.

The piste map is too ambitious in covering the whole of the Arlberg region, including Warth, in one view: it is unclear and misleading in places – particularly around Oberlech and down from Zürs to Zug and Lech. There's a smaller separate map that shows the White Ring circuit. Warth publishes its own map, covering its slopes much more clearly; let's hope they continue to do so – though really we'd like to see a booklet of several maps.

Piste marking is OK in general. But, confusingly, the same number is given to multiple pistes in places; there are three blue runs numbered 34a, for example. Piste classification sometimes understates difficulty.

EXTENT OF THE SLOPES ★★★★★
One-way traffic

The main slopes centre on **Oberlech**, 250m above Lech (just below the treeline), and can be reached by cable car or chairlifts. The wide, open pistes above here are served by a handful of chairlifts.

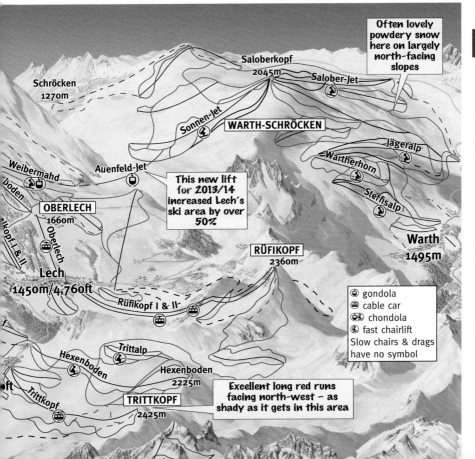

Often lovely powdery snow here on largely north-facing slopes

Saloberkopf 2045m — Salober-Jet

Schröcken 1270m

Sonnen-Jet

WARTH-SCHRÖCKEN

Jägeralp

Wartherhorn

Steffisalp

Weibermahd

...boden

Auenfeld-Jet

This new lift for 2013/14 increased Lech's ski area by over 50%

OBERLECH 1660m

Oberlech

...kopf I & II

Lech 1450m/4,760ft

RÜFIKOPF 2360m

Warth 1495m

Rüfikopf I & II

- ⊙ gondola
- ⊜ cable car
- ⊙⊖ chondola
- ⊘ fast chairlift
- Slow chairs & drags have no symbol

Trittalp

Hexenboden

Hexenboden 2225m

TRITTKOPF

Excellent long red runs facing north-west – as shady as it gets in this area

...oft

Trittkopf

2425m

↑ Tiny Warth and its neighbour Schröcken are the snowiest resorts in the Alps
SNOWPIX.COM / CHRIS GILL

Resort news and key links: www.wheretoskiandsnowboard.com

LIFT PASSES

Arlberg

Prices in €

Age	1-day	6-day
under 16	29	141
16 to 19	44	204
20 to 64	48	235
65 plus	44	204

Free No one; day pass €10 if under 8, €21 if over 75

Beginner Points ticket

Notes Covers St Anton, St Christoph, Stuben, Lech, Zürs and Warth, and bus linking Alpe Rauz, Zürs and Lech; also Sonnenkopf (9 lifts) at Klösterle, 7km west of Stuben and Pettneu (3 lifts) just east of St Anton; single ascent, part-day and pedestrian options

The new link to the slopes of **Warth** is a 10-seat gondola which has been grafted on to the Weibermahd chondola on the slopes beyond Oberlech. You ride the gondola back to Lech too – the gondola goes over flattish land. It arrives close to the bottom of red slopes on the sunny side of Saloberkopf. These red slopes can't be avoided, so the link is unattractive to blue run skiers who lack the confidence to tackle reds. Over the hill is a broad, shady mountainside laced with runs of all kinds, served by a mix of fast and slow chairlifts. (Strictly, some of these slopes belong to another village, Schröcken, but it is a bus ride from the slopes and lifts.)

The **Rüfikopf** cable car takes Lech residents to the start of the Lech-Zürs circuit, the White Ring, which can be done only in a clockwise direction, via the west-facing slopes of Zürs.

At the south end of these slopes is a cable car to the high point of **Trittkopf**. At the north end, chairs go up the west-facing slopes and up the east-facing mountainside to **Seekopf**. (You may find the piste map confusing at the north end of Zürs: the lift company has deliberately made it inaccurate in order to make it clearer – a spectacular piece of thinking.)

A six-pack goes from near here up to **Muggengrat** (the highest point of the Zürs area) and a long, scenic, lift-free red run back to Zürs.

From Seekopf you can ski down to the Madloch chair – slow, and liable to closure by wind – which leads to long, scenic and piste-like ski routes back to Lech or to Zug, where a slow chairlift goes up to the shoulder of Kriegerhorn above Oberlech.

FAST LIFTS ★★★★☆
Hot stuff

A high proportion of lifts are now fast. Seven chairlifts have the luxury bonus of heated seats. But there are still a few slow, old lifts that you can't avoid using if you want to explore the area fully (in particular, the chairs to Madloch-Joch above Zürs and from Zug to Kriegerhorn).

QUEUES ★★★★☆
Still a few bottlenecks

There have been significant lift improvements, and feedback is generally positive, but there are still one or two bottlenecks – the Schlegelkopf fast quad out of Lech and the crucial Madloch double chair mentioned under 'Fast lifts' generate peak-time queues – so can the Rüfikopf cable cars to Zürs. The resort theoretically limits numbers on its slopes to 14,000, for safety reasons – and apparently does stop day-ticket sales on some sunny weekends. The slopes certainly seem much quieter than those of St Anton.

TERRAIN PARKS ★★★★
In Lech
The park, beside the Schlegelkopf chairlift, is one of the better terrain parks in Austria. Obstacles are prepared daily; the medium and pro lines have kickers, boxes and a 9m-wide wall ride. The rails are also set in lines so you can hit several in a row. There's also a 6m down rail and a rainbow rail. The easy line has a funbox, kickers and rollers and a 4m down rail – great for practice. There's also a park on the Warth slopes.

SNOW RELIABILITY ★★★★
One of Austria's best
Lech and Zürs both get a lot of snow. Lech gets an average of almost 8m of snow each season, almost twice as much as St Anton and three times as much as Kitzbühel; Zürs gets substantially more than Lech; and Warth gets an astonishing 11m. Taken together with good grooming ('perfect' said a recent reporter) and excellent snowmaking, this normally means good snow coverage until late April. But because of the sunny exposure, the lower slopes of Lech can suffer and the snow become heavy. The main slopes of Warth, in contrast, are north-facing, so hold their exceptional amounts of snow very well.

FOR EXPERTS ★★★★
Off-piste is the main attraction
For the competent skier who prefers to stick to patrolled runs the area is very limited. There are no black pistes above Lech, and one short (although rewarding) one above Zürs. Warth has added many more, but they rarely approach true black gradient. But the two types of off-piste route explained earlier offer lots to enjoy. There is also plenty of other excellent off-piste, much of it accessed by long traverses; and in comparison with St Anton, fresh powder lasts well here.

Many of the best runs start from the top of the fast Steinmähder chair, which finishes just below Zuger Hochlicht. Some routes involve a short climb to access bowls of untracked powder. From the Kriegerhorn there are shorter off-piste runs down towards Lech and a very scenic long ski route down to Zug (followed by a slow chair and a rope tow to pull you along a flat area). Most runs, however, are south- or west-facing and can

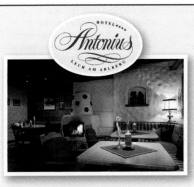

Ski right to and from the door of this centrally located, charming hotel, with only a 2 minutes walk to the center and lifts.

Enjoy comfort, traditional atmosphere and typically great Austrian hospitality of the owner Family Strolz.

Big breakfast buffet and daily après-ski snack. Relax in the front of the open log fire or in the sauna area of the hotel.

Family Strolz look forward to your visit.

Hotel Garni Antonius★★★★
A-6764 Lech/Arlberg
Tel +43 5583 2462
www.antonius.at

Tannbergerhof
The core of Lech ★★★★s

Enraptured
BY NATURE

Inspired
BY FLAIR

• 89 years of tradition
• Exclusive comfort
• Top class Haube cuisine
• Right next to the lifts

The Hot Spots
IN LECH

Tannberger Ice and Day Bar, with the best Glühwein in the world!
(acc. to Sunday Times)

Lech am Arlberg • info@tannbergerhof.com
Tel.: +43 5583 / 22 02

www.tannbergerhof.com

Build your own shortlist: www.wheretoskiandsnowboard.com

UK PACKAGES

Alpine Answers, Alpine Weekends, Bramble Ski, Crystal, Crystal Finest, Elegant Resorts, Erna Low, Flexiski, Inghams, Interactive Resorts, Jeffersons, Kaluma, Luxury Chalet Collection, Momentum, Mountain Beds, Oxford Ski Co, Powder Byrne, Scott Dunn, Ski Bespoke, Ski Club Freshtracks, Ski Expectations, Ski Independence, Ski Line, Ski Safari, Ski Total, Skitracer, Skiworld, Snow Finders, Snow-wise, STC, Supertravel, Thomson, White Roc **Oberlech** Kaluma, Oxford Ski Co, Ski Bespoke **Zug** Oxford Ski Co **Zürs** Alpine Answers, Alpine Weekends, Carrier, Crystal, Inghams, Kaluma, Momentum, Oxford Ski Co, Powder Byrne, Scott Dunn, Ski Bespoke, STC, Thomson **Warth** Alpine Answers, Momentum, Snow-wise, STC

suffer from sun. At the end of the season, when the snow is deep and settled, the off-piste off the shoulder of the Wöstertäli from the top of the Rüfikopf cable car down to Lech can be superb, as can Zuger Hochlicht. There are also good runs from the Trittkopf cable car, including a tricky one down to Stuben. And there is a lot of scope for departures from the Madloch itinerary to Zug.

The Warth link has opened up some excellent off-piste opportunities. There are routes from Zuger Hochlicht to the Warth lifts, from the Warth slopes to Schröcken (bus back to the Warth lifts) and from two or three points on the Warth slopes to points down the valley from Lech.

The steeper red runs (notably on Zuger Hochlicht and both sides of Zürs) are well worth a try, as is the lovely away-from-the-lifts Langerzug ski route to Lech on the Rüfikopf side (steep start, then a gentle cruise, flattish run-out). Heli-skiing is also available on weekdays.

FOR INTERMEDIATES ★★★★
Flattering variety for all
The pistes in the Oberlech area are nearly all immaculately groomed blue runs, the upper ones above the trees, the lower ones in wide swathes cut through them. It is ideal territory for cruisers not wanting surprises. But timid intermediates may find the final blue-run descents to Lech (as opposed to Oberlech) uncomfortably steep.

Strong intermediates will want to do the circuit to Zürs and back. Whether it's wise for less confident intermediates to tackle the red ski routes from Madloch depends on the conditions. They are not steep, and part or all of them may be groomed despite their non-piste status, but parts can be heavily mogulled and busy, and lots of people find the runs a struggle.

More adventurous intermediates will want to spend time on the fast Steinmähder chair on Zuger Hochlicht – a choice of satisfying pistes and ski routes, and from there take the scenic red run all the way to Zug (the latter part on an easy ski route rather than a piste, so not to be skied alone). They may even want to give the Langerzug ski route (see 'For experts') a go. The slopes of Lech are an excellent place to try skiing ungroomed snow for the first time.

Zürs has many more interesting red runs, on both sides of the village. We like the north-west-facing reds from Trittkopf and the excellent run from Muggengrat, away from the lifts.

Warth has excellent intermediate slopes to explore, of all colours. Carving down the top-to-bottom groomed black runs down the Salober-Jet chair was a highlight of our last visit – though they are not long (less than 400m vertical).

FOR BEGINNERS ★★★★
Easy slopes in all areas
The main nursery slopes are at Oberlech, but there is also a nice dedicated area in Lech. There are good, easy runs to progress to. You can buy a points card rather than a full lift pass.

FOR BOARDERS ★★★★
Easy riders, but mind the flats
Lech's upper-crust image has not stood in the way of its snowboarding development, and it is a popular destination for freeriders. There are few draglifts to deter novices; but beware of the many flat/uphill sections on the west-facing slopes at Zürs.

FOR CROSS-COUNTRY ★★★
Picturesque valley trail
A 21km trail starts from the centre of Lech and leads through the beautiful but shady valley, along the river to Zug and back. There are three other shorter trails. In Zürs there is a 4km track to the Flexen Pass and back.

MOUNTAIN RESTAURANTS ★★★
Still not a strong point
The hotels in Oberlech have long dominated the lunch scene here, but the options are slowly widening. Restaurants are clearly marked (and named in minute type) on the piste map – except the ones in Oberlech. **Editors' choice** Rud-Alpe (418250) is not far above Lech, but high enough to count as a mountain restaurant. It's a welcoming, rustic place, lovingly built using timbers from other old huts. We've had excellent lunches here, efficiently served – last season, veal goulash. Endorsed by several reporters. Kriegeralpe (0664 4422697), much further up, lacks views but is great on a bad day – rustic and charming, with jolly service. It's notable for the fab Kaiserschmarrn served late in the day – the main

SCHOOLS

Lech
t 2355

Oberlech
t 2007

Exklusiv
t 2719

Omeshorn Alpincenter
t 39880

Classes (Lech prices)
6 days (2hr am and
2hr pm) €270

Private lessons
€320 for 4hr; each
additional person €25

CHILDCARE

Mini-clubs
t 0664 123 9993

Kinderland Lech
From age 3

Kinderland Oberlech
From age 2

Little Zürs
From age 2

Babysitting list
Held by tourist office

Ski school
From 3½

menu is very limited in the usual Austrian way; but we had great gröstl last season, and readers also approve ribs and gulaschsuppe.

Worth knowing about Above Zürs, we had an excellent lunch last season at Seekopf – good table-service on the huge terrace; approved by readers. We and reporters have also enjoyed the modern, woody Balmalp, above Zug: cool music (loud outside, quieter inside); simple food – 'excellent gulaschsuppe', ribs, pasta, pizza, salad; good views. The Panorama restaurant at Rüfikopf is tipped for 'extremely efficient and friendly staff, and delicious, enormous burgers'.

At Oberlech there are several big sunny terraces set prettily around the piste. Quite often you'll find a live band playing outside one. Reader tips include Burgwald ('excellent chicken burgers'), Petersboden ('lovely spot, good turkey salad and strudel'), Ilga Stüble, the lovely old Alter Goldener Berg ('sheepskins on seats') and the Mohnenfluh.

For the moment, the huts at Warth are noticeably cheaper than those at Lech. Auenfelder Hütte is a pleasant chalet with table-service inside and out; 'food good', but we found service stretched. Hochalp has a small, unremarkable terrace, but inside is a 'lovely space, delicious food'. Korbersee is in a lovely spot, with 'excellent food and service'.

SCHOOLS AND GUIDES ★★★★
Excellent in Lech

We get good reports on the Lech school, few reports at all on the others. One regular visitor has been satisfied for several years and a 2013 visitor had a 'great time' on his off-piste private lesson with the Lech school, but warns: 'Take your own avalanche gear.' Omeshorn Alpincenter and Exklusiv are alternative schools, also with guiding.

FOR FAMILIES ★★★★★
Oberlech's fine, but expensive

Oberlech makes an excellent choice for families who can afford it, particularly as its hotels are so conveniently placed for the slopes. Reporters have praised the family-friendly approach, especially to children using the lifts. There are kids' clubs in Lech, Oberlech and Zürs and Goldener Berg has an in-house kindergarten.

Lech

139

Build your own shortlist: www.wheretoskiandsnowboard.com

HOTEL *Schwarzwand* ❄❄❄❄
LECH AM ARLBERG

enjoyment   harmony   freedom

Friendly service ❄ Comfortable suites and rooms ❄ Relaxing 'Oasis'

Walter Elsensohn and his team look forward to hearing from you!

A-6764 Lech am Arlberg 308
Telephone +43 5583 2469 Fax 5583 27766

www.schwarzwand.com   hotel@schwarzwand.com

Ski Total

ARE HERE IN
Lech

▶ **Quality chalets**
▶ **Top locations**
▶ **Excellent value**
▶ **17 more resorts**

skitotal.com
01483 791 933

ACTIVITIES

Indoor Sports park (fitness studios, tennis, bowling, climbing wall, sauna), hotel swimming pools, museum, galleries, library, ice rink (in hotel Monzabon)

Outdoor Cleared walking paths, ice rink, curling, snowshoeing, toboggan run (from Oberlech), paragliding, horse-drawn sleigh rides

GETTING THERE

Air Innsbruck 115km/ 70 miles (1hr30); Friedrichshafen 130km/80 miles (1hr45); Zürich 195km/120 miles (2hr15)

Rail Langen (15km/ 9 miles); regular buses from station

STAYING THERE

Chalets There are a few chalets run by UK tour ops, including three chalet hotels by Ski Total, one with pool and all three with sauna; and two chalets in Zug by Skiworld, both with sauna.

Hotels There are six 5-stars, over 40 4-stars and countless other places.

LECH

*****Arlberg (21340) Elegantly rustic central chalet, widely thought to be the best in Lech. Pool.

*****Post (22060) Lovely old Relais & Châteaux place on the main street; pool, sauna, steam. One of our favourites.

****Antonius (2462) Traditional family-run B&B hotel in a quiet spot two minutes from the centre. Lovely panelled breakfast room, bar. Spa.

****Kristiania (25610) Small luxury place on outskirts; shuttle. 'Gourmet paradise, outstanding service, but expensive.'

****Monzabon (2104) Right by the ski school meeting point. Food, staff and attractive stube have been praised. Pool, spa, indoor ice rink.

****Plattenhof (2522) A few minutes from the centre but near Hinterweiss drag and runs. A repeat visitor this year was very happy: 'Lovely suite, excellent food; really nice pool.'

****Schwarzwand (2469) By the separate nursery slope, so perfectly positioned for beginners. Sauna, steam room, solarium. Food, service and value for money are praised.

****Tannbergerhof (2202) Splendidly atmospheric inn on the main street, with ever-popular outdoor bar. 'Wonderful restaurant.' Steam, sauna.

***Lech (22890) Slightly out of centre towards Zürs. 'Charming, with superb staff, great food,' says a 2014 report.

OBERLECH

****Montana (2460) Welcoming chalet run by the family of Patrick Ortlieb. Reporters praise food and service. Smart wellness centre with pool, steam room, three types of sauna.

****Pension Sabine (2718) 'Excellent food, great service and wonderful spa,' says an American reporter who has been going here for years.

Apartments There are lots available to independent bookers.

EATING OUT ★★★☆☆
Mainly hotel-based

There are over 50 restaurants in Lech, but nearly all of them are in hotels. A conspicuous and stylish exception is Skihütte Schneggarei, a big, spacious wooden building at the foot of the slopes doing a good range of modern dishes but also great pizzas. For an 'authentic Italian meal', though, head for Lech's only Italian-run pizzeria, Don Enzo Due.

In Zug, there are two pricey places. The Rote Wand is excellent for traditional Austrian food ('beautiful old-fashioned restaurant, attentive but not fussy service'). But one regular reporter prefers the 'warm welcome' at the Klosterle, 'a lovely restored farmhouse'.

APRES-SKI ★★★★☆
Good but expensive

At Oberlech, the umbrella bar of the Burg hotel is popular at close of play, as is the champagne bar in hotel Montana. Readers also like the Ilga.

Down in Lech there are places for cakes and coffee, but the outdoor bars of hotels Krone (in a lovely, sunny setting by the river) and Tannbergerhof (where there's an afternoon as well as a late-night disco) are more popular. In midwinter at least, we prefer to head inside to the cool and lively Schneggarei (read 'Eating out') along with many ski instructors; it's non-smoking (hooray!). Later on, the K Club (Krone hotel) and Archiv Bar liven up. Readers like the Fux Jazzbar (with live music and a huge wine list) and the bar in the hotel Tannbergerhof.

After 7.30pm the free resort bus becomes a pay-for bus (five euros) called James, which runs until 3am.

OFF THE SLOPES ★★★☆☆
At ease

For a fashionable resort, the range of shops is surprisingly limited – Strolz's plush emporium (including a champagne bar) right in the centre is the main attraction. It's easy for pedestrians to get to Oberlech or Zug for lunch. The village outdoor bars are ideal for posing. There are 40km of prepared winter walking trails – the one along the river to Zug is particularly beautiful; the tourist office produces a good map. There's also snowshoeing. There's a sports centre (no pool, but spa, climbing, bowling).

The floodlit sledging run from Oberlech is popular with families and is highly recommended (but beware toboggan theft – one reporter had three stolen).

Phone numbers
From elsewhere in
Austria add the prefix
05583; from abroad
use the prefix +43
5583

TOURIST OFFICES

Lech / Zürs
www.lech-zuers.at
Warth / Schröcken
www.warth-
schroecken.com

SNOWPIX.COM / CHRIS GILL

The glorious shady
mountainside above
Zug has just the
Madloch ski route
down it – no lifts –
and a lot of good off-
piste terrain ↓

ZÜRS

Some 10 minutes' drive towards St
Anton from Lech is Zürs. Austria's first
recognizable ski lift was built here in
1937. Zürs is a rare thing: a highly
fashionable and expensive resort
where the main occupation of visitors
is skiing rather than parading. It has
some excellent hotels (mainly 4-stars
but including four 5-stars); once inside
them, all is well with the world. But
the village as a whole doesn't have
much appeal – it has no real centre,
few shops and a lot of intrusive traffic
to/from Lech on the central through-
road. We enjoyed the 5-star Zürserhof
(25130) – great service, food and spa
facilities. The family-run 4-star Guggis,
in a good position near the main lifts,
is warmly welcoming, and has a
modern spa; two family apartments as
well as rooms. Toni's Einkehr (a rustic
hut at the foot of the Trittkopf slopes)
is one of the few non-hotel restaurants
and has been recommended. Nightlife
is quiet: Vernissage is said to be the
best spot. There's a disco in the
Edelweiss hotel and a piano bar in the
Alpenhof.

Many of the Zürs instructors are
booked up for private lessons for the
entire season by regular clients.

WARTH

Warth is a tiny village at the east end
of a broad ski area; equally small
Schröcken is detached from the
slopes, at the other end. The village
spreads across the hill from the base
of its chairlift – about 1km end to end.

There are several hotels close to
the lift, including two 4-stars that get
enthusiastic reviews from reporters.
The small Lechtalerhof (5583 2677)
wins on points – 'very good
restaurant, exceptionally professional
but friendly staff, great spa/pool'. The
Sporthotel Steffisalp (5583 3699) is
right at the lift, with an après-ski hut
and an umbrella bar – 'very friendly
staff, superb spa'; food is 'excellent' in
one view, just 'good' in another.

It's a small, quiet place, but there
are bars and restaurants, mainly in
hotels, in which to make merry. There
are 20km of walking trails, 21km of
cross-country and 'brilliant'
tobogganing two evenings a week.

Lech

Build your own shortlist: www.wheretoskiandsnowboard.com

★★★★ Hotel
Guggis
ZÜRS AM ARLBERG

A winter full of
unforgettable moments

Lech ☀ ARLBERG

- Small & familiar 4 star Hotel in the
  middle of Zürs
- Ski run right in front of the Hotel
- Large sunny terrace
- À la Carte at lunchtime & gourmet
  menus in the evenings
- Elegant spa area

HOTEL GUGGIS · Family Walch · 6763 Zürs am Arlberg
Tel.: +43 5583 / 21 66 · info@guggis.at

www.guggis.at

Mayrhofen

Large, lively resort with relatively reliable snow on local slopes and access to other good areas nearby, including a glacier

RATINGS

The mountains

Extent	★★★
Fast lifts	★★★★
Queues	★
Terrain p'ks	★★★★★
Snow	★★★
Expert	★★
Intermediate	★★★
Beginner	★★
Boarder	★★★★
X-country	★★
Restaurants	★★★
Schools	★★★★
Families	★★

The resort

Charm	★★★
Convenience	★
Scenery	★★★
Eating out	★★★
Après-ski	★★★★
Off-slope	★★★★

RPI	90
lift pass	£190
ski hire	£85
lessons	£80
food & drink	£115
total	**£470**

NEWS

2014/15: The fun slope on Ahorn will be fully open. The Ahorn valley run will be changed to black classification. A single numbering system will be adopted for pistes across all local hills.

2013/14: Swanky six-packs with all mod cons replaced the Lämmerbichl double chair on Rastkogel and the Ebenwald double chair on Ahorn. A new fun slope for terrain park novices was partly opened on Ahorn.

➕ Attractive, traditional village with lively après-ski

➕ High, snow-sure slopes by local standards – plus the Hintertux glacier nearby

➕ Several other worthwhile resorts nearby and on the same lift pass

➕ Good for confident intermediates who enjoy challenges, but ...

➖ Not so good for timid intermediates and near-beginners

➖ Long queues for the main gondola

➖ Buses are a key feature, and are often oversubscribed

➖ Runs mostly short

➖ Few steep pistes, although they do include Austria's steepest (possibly)

➖ No pistes to the valley locally

Mayrhofen is easy to like – a neat, polished, animated village in a pleasant rural setting – and we always enjoy our visits. But we have the use of a car, so we don't have to mess with the Penken gondola or the complex and often crowded bus services. Without a car, we'd budget for some taxis.

If what is attracting you is the relatively snow-sure slopes, bear in mind that you can access those slopes from quieter villages further up the valley, covered in the Hintertux chapter. Lanersbach and next-door Vorderlanersbach also have the merit, rare in these parts, of pistes back to the village.

THE RESORT

Mayrhofen is a fairly large resort sitting in the flat-bottomed, steep-sided Zillertal. Most shops, bars and restaurants are on one long street, with hotels and pensions spread over a wider area.

Free buses and trains link several different areas on the Ziller valley lift pass, including the excellent glacier at Hintertux (which has its own chapter). At the end of this chapter we cover the Zillertal Arena area, which starts at Zell am Ziller, not far away, and links to Gerlos and Königsleiten. The other major area is Hochfügen/ Hochzillertal above Kaltenbach, dealt with in the directory at the back of the book; it has a low profile in the UK, but is well worth exploring. There's a good train service to Innsbruck and Salzburg.

VILLAGE CHARM ★★★
Traditional and spacious

As the village has grown, architecture has been kept traditional, and the place merges with the surrounding fields in a rather charming way. The valley road bypasses the village and the centre is almost, but not quite, traffic-free. The steep-sided valley makes an attractive setting, but also means the village doesn't get a very long day of sun in midwinter.

CONVENIENCE ★★★★★
Pick your spot

It's quite a big village, centred on a long main street. The church, the tourist office and the main traditional hotels are at the north end, with the bus/railway station on the nearby bypass; the gondola to the major

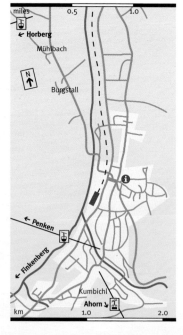

↑ This guy's got it easy – he has hit the Harakiri piste on a day when it is taking an edge
MAYRHOFNER BERGBAHN

KEY FACTS

Resort	630m
	2,070ft
Ziller valley	
Slopes	630-3250m
	2,070-10,660ft
Lifts	177
Pistes	489km
	303 miles
Blue	26%
Red	63%
Black	11%
Snowmaking	75%

Mayrhofen-Lanersbach only (ie excluding Hintertux glacier)

Slopes	630-2500m
	2,070-8,200ft
Lifts	55
Pistes	134km
	83 miles
Snowmaking	100%

Penken-Horberg sector of slopes is 700m away at the south end, with the Ahorn cable car another 200m south, over the river. You can leave kit at the lift stations (for a fee). Obvious places to stay are near the Penken gondola or near the station.

The buses serve other resorts, and alternatives to the Penkenbahn – particularly the Horbergbahn from Mühlbach, across the valley. The bus services are comprehensive and reliable, but crowded and complex. Get the vast timetable leaflet and do some homework. Note that the Finkenberg service runs hourly at best.

SCENERY ★★★☆☆
Views to the glacier
Mayrhofen is set between its two steep-sided mountains. From the top of each there are good views to the high peaks to the south, including the Hintertux glacier.

THE MOUNTAINS

Many of Mayrhofen's slopes are above the treeline, though there are more trees than the piste map suggests in the valley at the heart of the Penken-Horberg sector. Many of the pistes are challenging reds, and some reporters note that the blues are also often relatively tough.

There are two piste maps in circulation, which are easily confused because they are identical on the back

side. On the front side, one shows only the linked local slopes; the other shrinks things a bit to include distant Hintertux. Sadly, the designers have managed to make the larger-scale Mayrhofen-only map less clear, particularly in the very complex area at the top of Penken. They have done this by the simple device of plastering it with the names of lifts and restaurants – a masterly display of incompetence. The two maps mark some restaurants in different spots; all very un-Austrian.

Signposting is generally good, but less so in that tricky area on Penken. Last time we visited, we very nearly ended up descending to Finkenberg, with our car sitting in Mühlbach.

As elsewhere in Austria, there are unexplained 'ski routes', including the runs to the valley from Penken-Horberg. You may find some are groomed, but we presume all are unpatrolled. Take care.

EXTENT OF THE SLOPES ★★★☆☆
Fair-sized but inconvenient
Mayrhofen now measures its pistes in the Austrian standard fashion, and has cut in its claimed total to 134km. Read our feature on piste extent, at the front of the book.

The larger of Mayrhofen's two areas of slopes is **Penken-Horberg**, accessed by the Penkenbahn gondola from one end of town. It is also accessible via the Horbergbahn gondola at Mühlbach

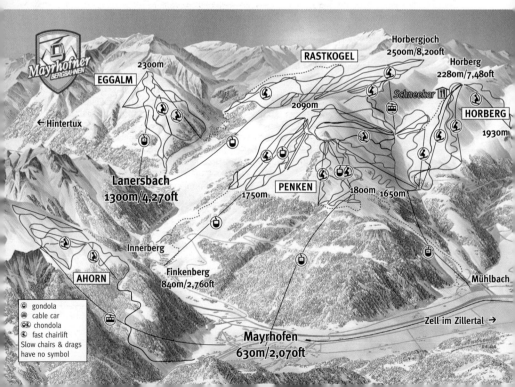

skiracer*

CHALETS, HOTELS & APARTMENTS

Call us today

020 8600 1650

skitracer.com

LIFT PASSES

Superskipass Zillertal

Prices in €

Age	1-day	6-day
under 15	21	101
15 to 18	38	179
over 19	47	224

Free Under 6

Senior No deals

Beginner No deals

Notes 1-day pass covers Mayrhofen areas only; 2-day+ passes include all Zillertal valley lifts; part-day passes

and another at Finkenberg, both a bus ride away from the village. If snow-cover is good enough (it rarely is), you can ski to Finkenberg or Mühlbach on ski routes (the Finkenberg route is not on one of the two local piste maps).

A big cable car links the Penken area with the **Rastkogel** slopes above Vorderlanersbach, which is in turn linked to **Eggalm** above Lanersbach – read the Hintertux chapter. Getting back to Penken-Horberg from Rastkogel on skis means braving a busy, steep mogul field with red and black variants, but you can avoid it by taking the cable car down.

The **Ahorn** area is pleasant but very small, and tends to be neglected – despite being accessed by Austria's largest cable car (carrying 160) with an eight-pack serving the slopes at the top. There is a lovely, long run to the valley (about 1300m vertical), being changed this year from red to black.

FAST LIFTS ★★★★
Capacity is the issue
Look at the map and you'll see that a good proportion of the lifts are fast – gondolas and high-speed chairs. Readers are impressed. But that doesn't help getting people up from town first thing or down at close of play (read 'Queues' below).

QUEUES ★
Still a problem
Previous reporters have seen waits of 15 to 30+ minutes for the Penkenbahn in the morning, and more queues to ride down in the afternoon. One way to deal with them is to stroll over to the gigantic and naturally queue-free Ahorn cable car and do a few warm-up laps of 1300m vertical on that. Another tactic used by one reporter this year was 'to get to the lift when it opens at 8am', which is a bit extreme for our taste since it involves rising about 6.30am. Or you can catch a bus to one of four alternative access gondolas, the obvious one being the Horbergbahn at Mühlbach. But this is surrounded by car parks, and gets a lot of day-trip business; here, too, there may be queues to get down as well as up the hill.

Up the mountain, queues are not unknown – even in low season. But more of a problem are overcrowded pistes. A previous reporter said, 'Never in 40 years of skiing have I skied on such dangerous, overcrowded pistes.' A 2014 visitor had safety concerns too: 'Runs crossing each other are poorly delineated and we saw a horrendous crash.' The run back from Rastkogel, down the jumbo cable car, is a nightmare at the end of the day.

Mayrhofner BERGBAHNEN

EGGALM

2300m

RASTKOGEL

Horbergjoch
2500m/8,200ft

Horberg
2280m/7,480ft

Schneekar

HORBERG

1930m

2090m

← Hintertux

Lanersbach
1300m/4,270ft

PENKEN

1750m   1800m 1650m

Innerberg

Finkenberg
840m/2,760ft

AHORN

Mühlbach

Mayrhofen
630m/2,070ft

Zell im Zillertal →

⊙ gondola
⊜ cable car
⊙⊙ chondola
⊙ fast chairlift
Slow chairs & drags have no symbol

Air Innsbruck 70km/
45 miles (1hr15);
Salzburg 170km/
105 miles (2hr);
Munich 195km/120
miles (2hr30)

Rail Local line through
to resort; regular
buses from station

TERRAIN PARKS ★★★★★
Something for everyone
One of the finest parks in the Alps (Vans Penken Park) lies beneath the Sun-Jet chairlift out of the valley between Penken and Horberg. There's a separate kids' park and intermediate, advanced, fun and pro areas, with a total of 11 kickers, two hips and 36 boxes and rails. There is no longer a half-pipe, though. Experts should bear in mind the World Cup pipe at Hintertux. Ahorn now has a novice-oriented fun slope.

SNOW RELIABILITY ★★★★★
Good by Tirolean standards
The area is better than most Tirolean resorts for snow because the slopes are relatively high – mostly above 1500m. Snowmaking covers the whole Ahorn area (including the lovely run to the valley), all the main slopes on Penken-Horberg and some on Rastkogel and Eggalm. Hintertux is one of the best glaciers in the world. Grooming is 'impressive'.

FOR EXPERTS ★★★★★
Commit to Harakiri
What is claimed to be one of Austria's steepest pistes, Harakiri, plunges down into the valley between Penken and Horberg. It is certainly steep for a European piste, and does offer a worthwhile challenge, particularly when it is rock-hard. (When we last skied it, it had a few cm of fresh on a smooth base, which was delightful.) But we don't believe the claimed average gradient of 78% (38°); it might be that steep in one or two spots. Usually, it is wonderfully quiet.

The other black runs are not steep. The long ski route to Mühlbach is quite challenging but rarely has good snow. There is, however, quite a lot of decent off-piste to be found in various parts of the area.

FOR INTERMEDIATES ★★★★★
On the tough side
Most of Mayrhofen's intermediate slopes are on the steep side of the usual range – great for confident intermediates; many of the runs in the main Penken-Horberg area are quite short, though, with verticals in the 300m/400m region. With access to the Lanersbach slopes, there is quite a bit of ground to cover, including lovely quiet runs on Eggalm – read the Lanersbach section of the Hintertux

STC Ski

Specialists in Tailor-Made
Short Breaks & Holidays

01483 771 222
www.stcski.co.uk
ski@stcski.co.uk

chapter. Don't miss Ahorn's excellent, quiet run to the valley, which doesn't merit its new black classification.

There are few really gentle blue runs, making the area less than ideal for nervous intermediates or near-beginners (and therefore for beginners, too). Some of the best are over at Rastkogel; be sure to use the linking cable car to return, rather than skiing back to Penken. The crowding on many runs can add to the intimidation factor. Ahorn offers a sanctuary.

FOR BEGINNERS ★★★★★
OK if it works for you
Despite its reputation for teaching, Mayrhofen is not ideal for beginners. You have to ride up the mountain to the nursery slopes, and there are no special lift passes so you'll need the full one. The Ahorn nursery slopes are excellent – high, extensive, sunny and crowd-free. But if you are with non-beginner mates, they will want to be on Penken. There are very few easy blues to progress to.

FOR BOARDERS ★★★★★
A popular hang-out
Mayrhofen has long been popular with snowboarders. But beginners may have a hard time getting around, as the terrain tends to be relatively steep, the nursery slopes are inconvenient, and the area still has a few draglifts. Intermediates and upwards, however, will relish the abundance of good red runs and easily accessible off-piste. The terrain park is one of the best in Europe. The Snowbombing music festival is held here each year.

FOR CROSS-COUNTRY ★★★★★
Head up the valley
There are 28km of trails in the area. Snow in the valley is not reliable but higher Vorderlanersbach has a much more snow-sure trail.

↑ Penken, seen here from Horberg, has some nice areas of off-piste glades, to use the American term
MAYRHOFNER BERGBAHN

UK PACKAGES

Alpine Weekends, Crystal, Crystal Finest, Erna Low, Inghams, Interactive Resorts, Neilson, Rude Chalets, Ski Expectations, Ski Line, Skitracer, Skiworld, STC, Thomson **Zell im Zillertal** Crystal, Thomson **Gerlos** STC

SCHOOLS

Die Roten Profis
t 63900
SMT
t 63939
Mayrhofen 3000
t 64015
Skimayrhofen.com
t 62829

Classes (3000 prices)
6 4hr-days €163
Private lessons
From €59 for 1 hour

MOUNTAIN RESTAURANTS ★★★☆☆
Plenty of them

Most of the many mountain restaurants are attractive and are clearly marked on the piste maps (though as we have noted, the two maps don't always agree). Recent visitors have been impressed with the quality and value for money.

Editors' choice Schneekar (64940) at the top of Horberg is our kind of place – beams and open fire inside, individual bookable tables on the terrace (a very rare thing in Austria), charming service, good view, excellent food. We had a good cheese, onion and bacon tart here. Readers endorse our view in all respects; notable Germknödel, apparently.

Worth knowing about The modern Panorahma by the draglifts down from the Finkenberg gondola is roundly recommended this year – 'friendly staff, wide range of tasty food, good value'. Nearby Christa's Skialm is self-service but atmospheric, with 'simple Tirolean specialities'. Also recommended in 2014 were Grillhof Alm ('the best pizza'), Bergrast ('very comfortable and atmospheric') and Horberg. For restaurants in the Rastkogel and Eggalm sectors, read the Hintertux chapter.

SCHOOLS AND GUIDES ★★★★☆
Excellent reputations

Mayrhofen's ski schools have good reputations. Mayrhofen 3000 offered 'very good value and very good instruction' for a previous visitor's group. An off-piste guide from the Skimayrhofen.com school provided 'good service and good value'.

FOR FAMILIES ★★☆☆☆
Good but inconvenient

Mayrhofen majors on childcare, and the facilities are excellent. But children have to be bussed around and ferried up and down the mountain.

STAYING THERE

Chalets There are several large chalets. Skiworld has the Stoanerhof near the Ahorn cable car. Crystal has the Haus Tirol – 'a good inexpensive base, very conveniently located' on the main street (so noise can be a problem in some rooms). In contrast, Inghams' St Lukas is set in 'a very pretty copse', a short walk from the centre.

Hotels Note that the Penken gondola is 1km from the real centre, so 'central' does not mean 'close to lifts'. There's an ice-hotel on Ahorn.

★★★★★Elisabeth (6767) The only 5-star, slightly out of the centre.

★★★★Gutshof Zillertal (8124) A reporter loved this place on the southern outskirts, with 'almost free' hire cars. 'Good meals, great deal.' Pool, spa.

★★★★Neue Post (62131) An old favourite, central: 'Spacious but old-fashioned bedrooms; excellent breakfasts.' Small pool, sauna, steam.

★★★★Neuhaus (6703) 'Well appointed, comfortable, friendly.'

★★★★Sporthotel Manni (63301) On main street, between station and gondola. 'Large comfortable rooms, good steaks, excellent beer.'

★★★★Zillertalerhof (62265) 'Excellent food and service, great pool, sauna.' Central.

Apartments There are plenty available; Landhaus Gasser is central ('modern

CHILDCARE

Wuppy's Kinderland
t 63612
Ages 3mnth to 5yr

Crèche (SMT school)
t 63939
From age 2

Babysitting list
at tourist office

Ski school
From ages 4 or 5

ACTIVITIES

Indoor Leisure pool, (pool, sauna, massage), fitness centre

Outdoor Ice rink, curling, 40km of paths, ice climbing, horse-drawn sleigh rides, snowshoeing, paragliding, tobogganing

Phone numbers
From elsewhere in Austria add the prefix 05285 (Mayrhofen), 05282 (Zell), 05284 (Gerlos), 06564 (Königsleiten); from abroad use the prefix +43 and omit the initial '0'

TOURIST OFFICES

Mayrhofen
www.mayrhofen.at

Zillertal Arena
Zell im Zillertal
www.zell.at

Gerlos
www.gerlos.at

Königsleiten
www.wald-koenigsleiten.at

and well equipped but in traditional style') and the Apart Mountain Lodge ('very modern') has rear garden access to the Ahorn lift.

EATING OUT ★★★★★
Wide choice

There's a wide range of restaurants, from local specialities to Chinese. We've had good, satisfying meals at the jolly, friendly Tiroler Stuben near the station. Wirtshaus zum Griena is a lovely rustic old building on the edge of town, serving 'hearty local food' – too much like a mountain restaurant for our taste, but popular with families. The set menu at the Gasthof Brücke was 'excellent quality and value'. A 2014 reporter rated the cafe attached to the Neue Post hotel as 'excellent', and a past reporter had the 'best wiener schnitzel ever' there.

APRES-SKI ★★★★★
Lively

Après-ski is a great selling point – 'Unpretentious and friendly, with little of the lager lout mentality that can prevail elsewhere.' At close of play, the bars at the top of the Penkenbahn and Horbergbahn gondolas do good business, while in the village the Ice Bar at the hotel Strass and Brück'n Stadl (Gasthof Brücke) get packed out. Some of the other bars in the Strass are rocking places later on, including the Speak Easy Arena, with live music and dancing until 4am. Mo's American theme bar is 'lively but not too noisy', has live music and is 'stylish', as is the Harakiri bar. Scotland Yard is popular with Brits but 'expensive and tatty', reckoned one visitor. For a quiet drink we head to the bars of the big traditional hotels – the Neuhaus or the Neue Post. Catch the big rugby matches (etc) at the Movie bar. The resort currently hosts the Altitude Comedy Festival in the spring.

OFF THE SLOPES ★★★★★
Good for all

Innsbruck and other resorts are easily reached by train or bus. There are also good walks and sports amenities, including the swimming pool complex – with saunas, steam room and solarium. Pedestrians have no trouble getting up the mountain to meet friends for lunch. 'Several cafes and an ice-cream parlour make just walking the streets a very pleasant experience,' says a previous visitor.

ZILLERTAL ARENA

The Zillertal Arena was created in 2000 by linking the slopes of Zell am Ziller, 10km down the valley from Mayrhofen, to those above the villages of Gerlos and Königsleiten. They now share an area about as big as the Mayrhofen-Lanersbach area. The slopes are quite high, as in Mayrhofen, but they also get a lot of sun, so the snow message is a mixed one.

The slopes suit intermediates best. You can really get a sense of travelling around: the trip from one end to the other is 17km and takes you over several peaks and ridges. According to a reporter, a return trip is a full day's skiing, with little time to deviate from the main route along the way. Most runs are short – the longest, down to Gerlos, is 4km.

Zell is the main town in the Zillertal, and a real working town rather than just a resort. There are some good hotels, including the 4-star Zapfenhof (2349) on the outskirts (with pool) and the Brau (2313) in the centre. The town is a bus ride from the two gondolas into the ski area. You have to ride these down as well as up. Après-ski centres around a few bars near the base of the gondolas.

Gerlos has the advantage of being centrally situated in the Zillertal Arena ski area, allowing you to explore in either direction each day. It is a bustling resort that straddles the road up to the Gerlos pass; an 'efficient' bus service takes you to the gondola into the slopes. Après-ski is lively and there are several good local hotels, including the 4-star Gaspingerhof (52160) with a very smart spa.

Königsleiten is very spread out, in a scenic wooded setting above a dam, with half a dozen hotels including the 4-star Königsleiten (82160). It has more extensive local slopes than Gerlos, on either side of the Gerlospass road, but less vertical. On the north side (reached by a gondola from the village) the runs are mostly genuine reds, radiating from the peak of Königsleitenspitze (2315m). The lower southern sector has a row of quad chairs serving easier slopes.

Both Gerlos and Königsleiten attract a strikingly large proportion of Dutch visitors.

OBERGURGL TOURIST OFFICE

Obergurgl

A combination of high altitude and traditional Tirolean atmosphere keeps regulars going back, despite the drawbacks

RATINGS

The mountains

Extent	★★
Fast lifts	★★★★★
Queues	★★★★★
Terrain p'ks	★★
Snow	★★★★★
Expert	★★
Intermediate	★★★
Beginner	★★★★
Boarder	★★
X-country	★★
Restaurants	★★★
Schools	★★★★
Families	★★★★

The resort

Charm	★★★★
Convenience	★★★★
Scenery	★★★
Eating out	★★★
Après-ski	★★★★
Off-slope	★★

RPI 110

lift pass	£200
ski hire	£135
lessons	£110
food & drink	£135
total	**£580**

NEWS

2014/15: There are plans to upgrade the Kirchenkar draglift (on the far left of our piste map) to a 10-person gondola but it may not happen until the 2015/16 season.

2013/14: The terrain park was remodelled with new jumps.

KEY FACTS

Resort	1930m
	6,330ft
Slopes	1795-3080m
	5,890-10,100ft
Lifts	24
Pistes	110km
	68 miles
Blue	32%
Red	50%
Black	18%
Snowmaking	99%

148

➕ Glaciers apart, one of the most snow-sure resorts in the Alps; good for a late-season holiday

➕ Excellent area for beginners, timid intermediates and families

➕ Queue- and crowd-free, with slick lifts in the main

➕ Quiet, chalet-style village with little traffic and good hotels

➕ Jolly Tirolean teatime après-ski

➖ Limited area of slopes, with no tough pistes

➖ Exposed setting, with very few sheltered slopes for bad weather

➖ Little to do outside the hotels

➖ Village is fragmented, and lacking a real centre

➖ For a small Austrian resort, hotels are rather expensive

There are, of course, other resorts with reliably good snow, or with uncrowded easy and intermediate pistes, or with traditional chalet-style architecture, or with little or no traffic, or with teatime raves on the slopes. But we're hard pressed to think of other resorts that match all of Obergurgl's attractions.

The resort attracts a lot of British visitors, many returning time after time, booking the same hotel a year in advance to avoid disappointment, and it's not difficult to see why. Many reporters stress what a good resort it is for families.

THE RESORT

Obergurgl has grown out of a traditional mountain village, set in a remote spot near the head of its valley – the highest parish in Austria and usually under a blanket of snow.

The village is small and has three main parts. First you come to a cluster of hotels near the Festkogl gondola. The road then passes another group of hotels set on a little hill (beware steep, sometimes icy walks here). Finally you reach the nearest thing to a centre – a little square with a church, a fountain, the hotel Edelweiss und Gurgl and an underground car park.

Even higher Hochgurgl, linked by a mid-mountain gondola, is little more than a handful of hotels at the foot of its own area of slopes.

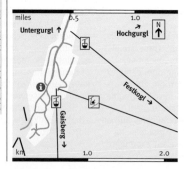

The lift pass is quite pricey, for a small resort. But for any keen skier it's worth paying an extra 10 euros (at the time of buying your main pass) for a day in Sölden, a short free bus ride down the valley (buses every hour).

VILLAGE CHARM ★★★★
On the quiet side
Obergurgl has no through-traffic and few day visitors, so the place is calm and relaxed. The village 'centre' is mainly traffic-free, and entirely so at night. It's quite jolly immediately after the slopes close, but rather subdued later; most people stay in their hotels.

CONVENIENCE ★★★★
Lifts at both ends
Obergurgl is a small place, and there are lifts at both ends. The Hohe Mut gondola station is close to the 'centre', and nowhere is a long walk from a lift. But you may need to use the free shuttle-buses (eg to get to ski school) – we're told they're every 10 minutes now. Hochgurgl looks like a convenient ski-in/ski-out resort, but nearly all the hotels are separated from the snow by roads and/or stairs.

SCENERY ★★★
Panoramic peaks
There are fabulous panoramic views from the top of the lifts.

E&G

EDELWEISS
GURGL

* * * *

DISCOVER OBERGURGL

ENDLESS SKIING UP TO 3000M

CELEBRATE WITH US

**MANY ANNIVERSARY HIGHLIGHTS
AND SPECIAL OFFERS**

Ski in and ski out at the Hotel
Edelweiss & Gurgl, your 4*-ski-resort
situated at 1930m above sea level in
the most snow-sure area of the Alps.

www.edelweiss-gurgl.com

HOTEL EDELWEISS & GURGL
HOSPITALITY & SERVICE SINCE 1889
125 YEARS

Hotel Edelweiss & Gurgl

Tel.: +43 5256 6223
info@edelweiss-gurgl.com

Ski Total

ARE HERE IN

Obergurgl

▶ Quality chalets
▶ Top locations
▶ Excellent value
▶ 17 more resorts

skitotal.com

01483 791 933

LIFT PASSES

Prices in €

Age	1-day	6-day
under 16	31	133
16 to 18	36	185
18 to 59	47	246
60 plus	41	215

Free Under 9
Beginner Limited pass covering nursery lifts
Notes Covers Obergurgl and Hochgurgl, and local ski-bus; part-day passes and non-skier tickets available

AUSTRIA

THE MOUNTAINS

Most of the slopes are very exposed. Wind and white-outs can shut the lifts, and severe cold can limit enthusiasm, especially in early season. If the weather is bad but not that bad, another problem arises: in our view, and that of many reporters, piste edge marking is dangerously slack – there are huge drop-offs that are not marked, and slopes seem to be marked either on one side only (often the uphill side) or in the middle only. Crazy. The piste map is fine – it's not a complex area – but signposting is not great. Classification of runs can overstate difficulty.

EXTENT OF THE SLOPES ★★☆☆☆
Limited cruising
The total area of slopes is quite limited. A gondola links the Obergurgl and Hochgurgl ski areas at mid-mountain level. It closes absurdly early at 4pm. There are no piste links.

Obergurgl is the smaller of the two linked areas. It is in two sections, with links at altitude in only one direction. The gondola from the village entrance and the Rosskar fast quad chair go to the higher **Festkogl** section. This is served by a short drag and a longer chair up to 3035m. From here you can head down to the gondola base or over to the **Hohe Mut** sector. This is also reached from the village via a gondola, which goes on to the sector high point at Hohe Mut. Lower down are slopes served by a slow quad and a six-pack.

As well as pistes, there are three or

four ski routes, the status of which is not explained on the piste map.

The slopes of **Hochgurgl** consist of high, gentle bowls, with fast lifts serving the main slopes above the village, but drags serving the more testing outlying slopes. From the top stations there are spectacular views to the Dolomites. A single run leads down through the woods to Untergurgl.

There's night skiing on 8km of slopes in Obergurgl once a week, and on 3km in Hochgurgl.

FAST LIFTS ★★★★★
Among the best
The system is pretty impressive. Most lifts are now high-capacity gondolas or fast chairs.

QUEUES ★★★★★
No problems
Nearly all reporters say queues are not a problem – 'fantastic'; 'not even at peak times'; 'a key reason why people return here every year'.

TERRAIN PARKS ★★☆☆☆
Park life improves
The park is on Hohe Mut. It was remodelled last year and has a six-metre long box, curved box, rails and kickers for beginners and advanced riders. 'Good little jumps, box, trees to weave in and out of,' says a 10-year-old in 2014.

SNOW RELIABILITY ★★★★★
Excellent
Obergurgl has high slopes and is about the most snow-sure of Europe's non-glacier resorts – even without its

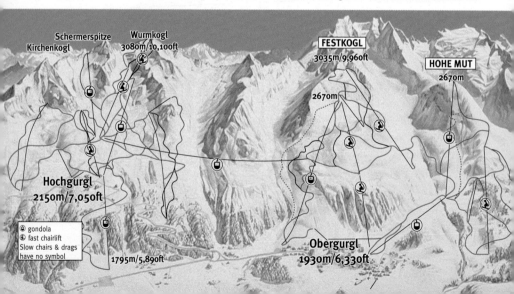

Schermerspitze
Kirchenkogl
Wurmkogl
3080m/10,100ft

FESTKOGL
3035m/9,960ft

HOHE MUT
2670m

2670m

2670m

Hochgurgl
2150m/7,050ft

◉ gondola
⬥ fast chairlift
Slow chairs & drags have no symbol

1795m/5,890ft

Obergurgl
1930m/6,330ft

↑ Obergurgl is high, snow-sure and has some very comfortable hotels – mostly 4-star and none less than 3-star

ÖTZTAL TOURISMUS

snowmaking, which is claimed to cover 99% of the pistes. The resort has a long season. Piste grooming is good, say most reporters.

FOR EXPERTS ★★✩✩✩
Not generally recommendable

There are few challenges on-piste – most of the blacks could easily be red, and where genuinely black it's only for short stretches (for example, at the very top of Wurmkogl). The ski routes are more challenging, particularly the one from Hohe Mut when mogulled. There is a lot of easy off-piste to be found – the top school groups often go off-piste when conditions are right. Slopes around the Kirchenkar lift (the far left of our piste map) are good for untracked powder. And there are more serious routes – a reporter found untracked powder in the Königstal, on skier's left from Wurmkogl. In poor visibility head for the trees above David's Hütte (on the bottom right of our piste map).

FOR INTERMEDIATES ★★★✩✩
Good but limited

There is some perfect intermediate terrain here, made even better by the normally flattering snow conditions. The problem is, there's not much of it. Keen piste-bashers will quickly be itching to catch the bus to Sölden.

Hochgurgl has the bigger area of easy runs, and these make good cruising. For more challenges, head to

the Vorderer Wurmkogl lift, on the right as you look at the mountain.

The Obergurgl area has more red than blue runs but most offer no great challenge to a confident intermediate. There is some easy cruising around mid-mountain on Festkogl. The blue run from the top of this sector to the village, via the Hohe Mut sector, is 1100m vertical. And there's another long enjoyable run down the length of the gondola, with a scenic black run and ski route variant (neither of them very steep) in the adjoining valley.

On Hohe Mut, there are very easy runs in front of Nederhütte and back towards the village. The red from Hohe Mut is narrow and in places winding.

FOR BEGINNERS ★★★★✩
You pays your money

There is one lift that is free only to ski school pupils, and three other beginner lifts (covered by a special day pass) serving adequate slopes, at each end of Obergurgl, and just above Hochgurgl – an awkward walk from most of the hotels, but otherwise satisfactory. After that you require a full lift pass. The gentle run under the gondola from the mid-station of the Hohe Mut gondola to the village is ideal to move on to (but can be crowded in the afternoon). The easy broad slopes served by the Bruggenboden chair are also suitable, as are the gentle blues above Hochgurgl (you can catch the ski-bus

ESPRiT
FOR FAMILIES IN
Obergurgl
Family Ski
Chalets
Dedicated
Nurseries
Exclusive Ski
Classes
12 More Resorts
espritski.com
01483 791 900

SCHOOLS

Obergurgl
t 6305

Hochgurgl
t 6265

Exclusiv
t 0664 182 6969

Alpinsport
t 0664 185 0333

Tyrolean
t 0664 422 8370

Classes (Obergurgl prices) 6 days (2hr am and pm) €242

Private lessons
From €140 for 2hr

OTZTAL TOURISM

The high point at Wurmkogl with fabulous views and the air traffic control tower (see 'Mountain restaurants') ↓

to the gondola and ride it down as well as up to avoid red runs).

FOR BOARDERS ★★★★★
Lacks challenge

Beginners can access most of the slopes without having to ride draglifts. There's some good off-piste potential for more advanced riders; a recent visitor singles out the area around the Steinmann chair in the Hohe Mut sector. There's also a terrain park.

FOR CROSS-COUNTRY ★★★★★
Limited but snow-sure

Three small loops, two at Obergurgl and one at Hochgurgl, amount to just 12km of trail. At Hochgurgl 1km is floodlit. All are relatively snow-sure and pleasantly situated but, like the slopes, very exposed in bad weather. Lessons are available.

MOUNTAIN RESTAURANTS ★★★★★
Not much choice

Hut choice is limited, but most reports are positive.
Editors' choice Hohe Mut Alm (639632) has table-service, fabulous glacier views from the big terrace, a woody interior and good hearty food – endorsed by reporters, though one complained of slow service. But it gets packed early and doesn't take bookings.
Worth knowing about The jolly Nederhütte, not far above village level, is hugely popular with readers and turns into the focal après-ski venue after lunch (see opposite); reporters agree that service is amazingly speedy but views on the food quality differ.

The Top Mountain Star at Wurmkogl looks like an air traffic control tower, has great 360° views, a varied menu but a modern bar ambience. Kirchenkarhütte by contrast is a simple self-service rustic hut that serves simple food and is very small and often crowded (but 'a gem', 'delicious, generous portions' say 2014 reporters).

SCHOOLS AND GUIDES ★★★★★
Excellent reports

We have received only positive reports of the Obergurgl school and guides. A 2014 reporter was 'very impressed' with her five-year-old's progress: 'The snow gardens are excellent.' Her 10-year-old son 'rated his instructor highly'; 'he had technique in the mornings and fun in the afternoons'. Past comments include: 'exceptionally good instruction', 'excellent instructors'. Demand is high and it is advisable to book ahead during all peak periods.

FOR FAMILIES ★★★★★
Highly rated by reporters

'Great for families and very child-friendly après-ski,' said a 2014 reporter. Children's ski classes start at four years and children from age three can either join Bobo Miniclub (outdoor activities) or Bobo Kindergarten (indoor). There's lunchtime supervision for ski school and kindergarten children alike. Many hotels offer childcare of one sort or another (the Alpina has been recommended), and Esprit Ski is a family-specialist UK chalet operator here.

CHILDCARE

Alpina & Hochfirst hotel kindergartens
From age 3
Bobo Miniclub & Kindergarten (Obergurgl school)
t 6305
From age 3

Ski schools
From age 4

UK PACKAGES

Alpine Answers, Crystal, Crystal Finest, Esprit, Inghams, Interactive Resorts, Momentum, Mountain Beds, Neilson, Oxford Ski Co, Ski Club Freshtracks, Ski Expectations, Ski Line, Ski Monterosa, Ski Safari, Ski Total, Skitracer, Snow Finders, Snow-wise, STC, Thomson
Hochgurgl Crystal, Crystal Finest, Inghams, Ski Expectations, Skitracer, Snow Finders, Thomson

GETTING THERE

Air Innsbruck 95km/ 60 miles (1hr30); Salzburg 275km/ 170 miles (3hr15); Munich 245km/ 150 miles (3hr30)

Rail Ötz 45km/ 28 miles; regular buses from station

ACTIVITIES

Indoor Pools, saunas, whirlpools, steam baths and massage in hotels; indoor golf, indoor horse riding

Outdoor Natural ice rink, curling, snowshoeing, winter hiking paths, tobogganing

Phone numbers
From elsewhere in Austria add the prefix 05256; from abroad use the prefix +43 5256

TOURIST OFFICE

www.obergurgl.com

STAYING THERE

Demand for rooms exceeds supply, and for once it is true that you should book early to avoid disappointment.
Chalets Ski Total has a big chalet here, and family-specialist sister company Esprit Ski has two.
Hotels Accommodation is of high quality: most hotels are 4-stars, and none is less than a 3-star.
OBERGURGL
****Alpina de Luxe** (6000) Big, smart; excellent children's facilities. 'Wonderful, well-run, traditional hotel with exceptional food and fantastic pool/sauna/spa.'
****Austria Bellevue** (6289) Family-run, outdoor pool, spa. 'Good service and atmosphere, immaculately clean, professional staff.'
****Bergwelt** (6274) 'Comfortable rooms, excellent food.' Indoor, outdoor pools and spa facilities.
****Edelweiss und Gurgl** (6223) The focal hotel; on the central square, near the main lifts. Splendid spa with indoor and outdoor pools, hot tub, saunas and steam rooms.
****Gotthard-Zeit** (62920) Convenient for skiing, but uphill from the village. 'One of the best and friendliest hotels I have stayed in,' says a recent visitor. Pool, sauna, steam and hot tub.
****Hochfirst** (63250) Five minutes from gondola. Ski-bus stop outside. Indoor/outdoor pool, spa, hot tub.
****Hohe Mühle** (6767) Slightly out of town. 'Amazing spa built into old water mill, food top-notch.'
***Pension Hohenfels** (6281) Opposite the Festkogl gondola. Basic, but 'food, location and service superb, couldn't fault it', says a 2014 visitor.
HOCHGURGL
*****Top Hotel Hochgurgl** (6265) Relais & Châteaux – the only 5-star in the area. Good position.
****Riml** (6261) Ski-in/ski-out location. 'Clean, comfortable, good food.'
***Alpenglühn** (6301) Beside Hochgurgl gondola. 'Excellent breakfast buffet and good five-course dinner. Run by a British woman and her ex-ski instructor husband.'
Apartments The Lohmann residence (6201) is modern and well placed.

EATING OUT ★★★☆☆
Wide choice, limited range
Hotel à la carte dining rooms dominate almost completely. The Romantika at the hotel Madeleine ('proper Italian

pizzas, friendly and efficient service') and the Belmonte ('has a real buzz, food top-notch, doesn't take bookings, always a queue') are popular pizzerias. For fine dining, head for the restaurant in the Edelweiss und Gurgl. Some evenings you can eat on the hill, at Hohe Mut Alm (we've had good reports of its 'gourmet fondue') or at David's Skihütte.

APRES-SKI ★★★★☆
Lively early, quiet later
Obergurgl is more animated than you might expect in the early evening. Reporters agree that it's dead later on. Nederhütte at the Hohe Mut mid-station is the place to be when the lifts close, which in practice means getting there well before then. 'The best après ever,' says a 2014 visitor. 'It rocks from the first anthem until the time you want to leave. Schnapps and dancing on your table/chair are obligatory – great fun!' The dancing is often enhanced by live music, said to be 'enjoyed by all age groups'. You ski home afterwards (or ride down on a snowmobile). All the bars at the base of the Rosskar and Hohe Mut lifts are also popular at close of play – try the Pic-Nic ('can get smoky'), or the Hexenkuchl at the Jenewein. The Eisloch (ice dome bar) outside the hotel Alpina is popular.
We hear that the Krumpn's Stadl barn (which used to be the liveliest place later in the evening) has closed and may not reopen. Reporters have enjoyed the Tuesday ski school display/mountain party/night ski on Festkogl and the 'thoroughly entertaining' night-time tobogganing. Hochgurgl is very quiet at night except for live music in Toni's Almhütte bar (Sporthotel Olymp).

OFF THE SLOPES ★★☆☆☆
Very limited
There isn't much to do during the day – hardly any shops, limited facilities of other kinds. There is an ice rink. Innsbruck is over two hours away by post bus. Sölden (20 minutes away) has a leisure centre and some shops. There are buses to Längenfeld (for the Aqua Dome thermal spa). Pedestrians can ride gondolas to some of the restaurants for lunch, or walk part-way up the Hohe Mut area; there are 12km of hiking paths. The spas at the Crystal and Bergwelt hotels are open to non-residents at a cost of 30 euros.

Obertauern

French-style convenience and snow-sure slopes meet Austrian après-ski – an unusual combination; great for a short break

TOP 10 RATINGS

Extent	★★
Fast lifts	★★★★
Queues	★★★★
Snow	★★★★
Expert	★★★
Intermediate	★★★★
Beginner	★★★
Charm	★★
Convenience	★★★★
Scenery	★★★

- ➕ Excellent snow record
- ➕ Quite a lot of ski-in/ski-out lodging
- ➕ Efficient modern lifts
- ➕ Good mountain restaurants
- ➕ Lively but not intrusive après-ski

- ➖ Village not notably charming, and spreads along the pass a long way
- ➖ Slopes limited in extent – and in vertical, in particular
- ➖ Bleak, exposed setting
- ➖ Few off-slope diversions

Obertauern's combination of attractions is unique. If you're hooked on Austrian après-ski but looking for a change from slush and ice, moving up in the world by 1000m or so could be just the ticket. But note the minus points above.

RPI	100
lift pass	£180
ski hire	£100
lessons	£115
food & drink	£125
total	**£520**

RPI	95
lift pass	£170
ski hire	£100
lessons	£105
food & drink	£125
total	**£500**

154

THE RESORT

Obertauern is different from the Austrian norm – a mainly modern development at the top of the Tauern pass. The slopes and lifts form a snow-sure circuit around the village.

Village charm Built in (high-rise) chalet style mixed with stylish modern architecture, the resort is not unattractive but is not a classic Austrian charmer. Most lodgings are set along the through-road; there is traffic, but it's not heavy. The nearest thing to a central focus is a junction with a side road that has some of the best bars and smart ski shops.

Convenience Lifts go up at various points, and with care you can find ski-in/ski-out lodgings.

Scenery The setting is satisfyingly rugged, with some long views from the high points of the area.

THE MOUNTAINS

Most of the slopes are above the treeline, and bad weather can make skiing impossible (as we found on our last visit). But there are some lightly wooded lower slopes.

Slopes Lifts radiate from the village to form a piste circuit that can be travelled either way in a couple of hours. Runs are short, and vertical is limited – most major lifts are in the 200m to 400m range. There is floodlit skiing twice a week.

Fast lifts Fast chairs dominate, and lifties reportedly manage to fill them.

Queues Crowded pistes can be more of a problem than queues. The Sonnenlift chair can have problems at ski school time; but our 2014 reporters had no major issues.

Terrain parks The Spot is a small park above the Almrausch hut, near the

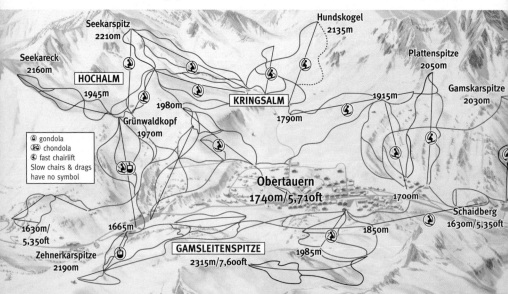

OBERTAUERN
Where snow is at home!

It's snowtime in Obertauern from late November to early May!

- Get the fantastic holiday feeling in one of the best skiing resorts of the Alps with a snow guarantee.
- Enjoy perfect winter sports conditions in a romantic atmosphere.
- Ski in – ski out: straight from your hotel onto the slope.

Obertauern at a glance:
100 km of slopes, 26 cable cars and lifts, night skiing, snowkiting school, 5 skiing and snowboarding schools, fun park for snowboarders.

Attractive package periods:
- 19.11. – 20.12.2014: Opening Weeks
- 10.01. – 31.01.2015: Powder Snow Weeks
- 14.03. – 21.03.2015: 50 years anniversary The Beatles – Help!
- 21.03. – 28.03. / 04.04. – 03.05.2015: Sun & Fun Weeks

Tourism Office Obertauern I Austria I 5541 Obertauern
+43 6456 7252 I info@obertauern.com

OBERTAUERN
WWW.OBERTAUERN.COM

KEY FACTS

Resort	1740m
	5,710ft
Slopes	1630-2315m
	5,350-7,600ft
Lifts	26
Pistes	100km
	62 miles
Blue	60%
Red	36%
Black	4%
Snowmaking	90%

UK PACKAGES

Alpine Answers, Crystal, Crystal Finest, Inghams, Snow Finders, Snow-wise, STC, Thomson

Phone numbers
From elsewhere in Austria add the prefix 06456; from abroad use the prefix +43 6456

TOURIST OFFICE

www.obertauern.com

Kehrkopfbahn quad, on the far left on our piste map.

Snow reliability Excellent because of altitude (exceptional, for Austria) and extensive snowmaking.

Experts There are genuinely steep black pistes from the top Gamsleiten chair. The icy race course under the Schaidbergbahn is a challenge. And try the black run from Seekarspitz and the ski route from Hundskogel (flat to start, steep moguls later).

Intermediates Most of the circuit is of intermediate difficulty. Stay low for easier pistes, or try the tougher runs higher up; you can't do the whole circuit without skiing reds.

Beginners There are good nursery slopes in several places, notably by the car parks at the western end of the resort. The Schaidberg chair leads to a high-altitude beginners' slope, and there are longer easy blues from there and on the lower Edelweissbahn.

Snowboarding Draglifts are optional except for beginners. Blue Tomato is a specialist school.

Cross-country 26km of trails locally.

Mountain restaurants There are lots, but they are often crowded. Readers praise the friendly staff (and the Tiroler gröstl) at the table-service Sonnhof; other tips include Flubachalm ('lovely gulaschsuppe and gröstl'), and the lively Hochalm.

Schools and guides Past reviews of both Krallinger and Koch schools have been positive.

Families The resort isn't particularly family-oriented, and nursery slopes can be inconvenient, but most ski schools do take children. The kindergarten takes babies.

STAYING THERE

Hotels Practically all accommodation is in hotels (mostly 3-star and 4-star) and guest houses. The Steiner (7306) has been praised: 'Wonderful, faultless hotel – engaging staff, first-class food, extensive spa.' Two others are regularly tipped by readers: the Latschenhof (7334) – 'amazing food, great spa', 'great spa, 50m from a run' – and the Marietta (72620) – 'friendly, well-run; lovely spa'.

Eating out The choices are mostly hotels (the Latschenhof is highly recommended) though two gourmet places opened last year. Some of the après-ski bars turn themselves into restaurants – the Almrausch does 'superb food'.

Après-ski Several restaurants above village level get lively as the lifts close – Hochalm and Edelweiss, for example. There are several cute woody chalets at the base that throb at teatime: Latsch'n Alm, Lürzer Alm ('dancing on the tables encouraged'), and Gruber Stadl. WeltcupSchirm is a 'superb' lively umbrella bar; Qu Bar is 'very loud'. The Tauernkönig hotel, hidden away off the 8a home run, has 'a cosy outdoor après area'. Later on, Monkey's Heaven and the People bar have dancing. We had a quiet beer and used the free Wi-Fi in the modern, glass-fronted Mund Werk.

Off the slopes There's an excellent, large sports centre (no pool, but some hotel pools are open to the public). There are marked walks up to Kringsalm and sleigh rides. Salzburg is an easy trip.

Saalbach-Hinterglemm

Lively, noisy, traditional-style villages and extensive, varied, prettily wooded slopes; pity they are mostly so sunny

RATINGS

The mountains

Extent	★★★
Fast lifts	★★★★★
Queues	★★★★
Terrain p'ks	★★★★
Snow	★★
Expert	★★
Intermediate	★★★★
Beginner	★★★
Boarder	★★★★★
X-country	★★
Restaurants	★★★★
Schools	★★★★
Families	★★★

The resort

Charm	★★★★
Convenience	★★★★
Scenery	★★★
Eating out	★★★
Après-ski	★★★★★
Off-slope	★★

RPI	95
lift pass	£190
ski hire	£110
lessons	£80
food & drink	£110
total	**£490**

➕ Large, well-linked, intermediate circuit, good for mixed groups

➕ Impressive lift system

➕ Saalbach is a pleasant, lively village, largely car-free in the centre

➕ Dozens of good mountain huts

➕ Extensive snowmaking, but ...

➖ Most slopes are sunny as well as low, and the snow suffers

➖ Limited steep terrain

➖ Both villages spread widely

➖ Both are noisy from 4pm and Saalbach can get rowdy at night

Saalbach-Hinterglemm gets ever closer to completing its mission to abolish the slow lift. Last season, yet another six-pack replaced a T-bar above Hinterglemm. Leaving aside baby drags and the like, only four slow lifts remain, of which only one is unavoidable (if doing the circuit anticlockwise). Amazing.

The valley has a lot going for it in other respects, too. Sadly, good snow isn't one of them. The altitudes are modest, but the bigger problem is that most of the slopes face south. The snowmaking is good enough to make a midwinter visit here a fairly safe bet, but problems can arise as spring approaches.

THE RESORT

Saalbach and Hinterglemm are separate villages, their centres 4km apart, which have expanded along the floor of their dead-end east-west valley. They haven't quite merged, but have adopted a single marketing identity. A 'ski-circus' links the two, with lifts and runs on both sides of the valley. At the eastern end is a link to Leogang, in the next valley.

Saalbach has a justified reputation as a party town – but those doing the partying seem to be a strangely mixed bunch. Big-spending BMW and Mercedes drivers staying in the smart, expensive hotels that line the main street share the bars with teenagers spending more on alcohol than on their cheap and cheerful pensions.

Hinterglemm is a more diffuse collection of hotels and holiday homes, where prices are lower and less cash is flashed.

Several resorts in Salzburgerland are reachable by road. The nearest are Hochkönig to the north and Zell am See to the south. There are two regional passes to consider – read the 'Lift passes' panel in the margin.

VILLAGE CHARM ★★★★
Very appealing
Saalbach is an attractive, characterful village, with traditional-style (although mostly modern) buildings huddled together around a classic onion-domed church. Hinterglemm is less cute, with a rather featureless centre spread along a single main street. Both villages are free of through-traffic. And both are lively from mid-afternoon until the early hours. Saalbach in particular can get rowdy, with drunken revellers still in their ski boots late in the evening.

CONVENIENCE ★★★★
Lifts near the centre
Saalbach is more convenient than most Austrian villages, with lifts into three sectors of the slopes starting

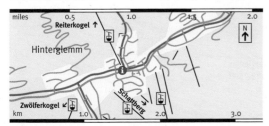

KEY FACTS

Resort	1000m
	3,280ft
Slopes	930-2095m
	3,050-6,870ft
Lifts	55
Pistes	200km
	124 miles
Blue	45%
Red	48%
Black	7%
Snowmaking	90%

close to the traffic-free village centre; the result, if staying centrally, is near to an ideal blend of Austrian charm with French convenience. Hinterglemm also has lifts and runs close to the centre, and offers quick access to some of the most interesting slopes – and, importantly, to most of the north-facing runs. A few reporters find walking through the villages from one side of the slopes to the other an irritant.

The valley bus service is fine, but not perfect: it finishes early, gets very busy at peak times and doesn't reach hotels or lifts in central Hinterglemm, or hotels set away from the main road. A Nightliner bus runs infrequently between the resorts in the evening.

SCENERY ★★★☆☆
Pleasant rather than dramatic
The villages are flanked by modest, broad mountain ridges. The high points give more dramatic views of the mountains to the north.

THE MOUNTAINS

The runs form a 'circus' almost entirely composed of broad slopes between swathes of forest, so this is quite a good area in bad weather. The signposting and piste map are good (and consistently praised by reporters). But some reporters reckon that many of the blues and reds are of much the same gradient.

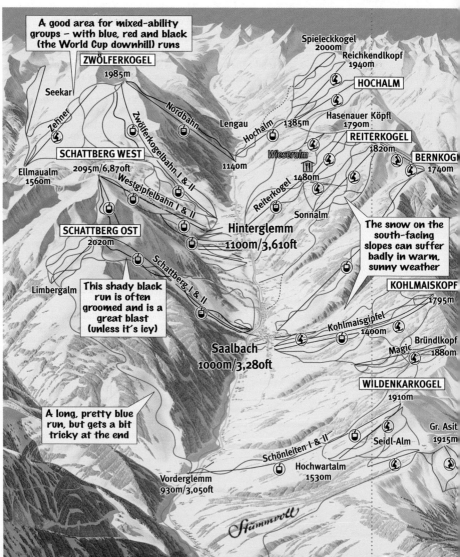

A good area for mixed-ability groups – with blue, red and black (the World Cup downhill) runs

This shady black run is often groomed and is a great blast (unless it's icy)

A long, pretty blue run, but gets a bit tricky at the end

The snow on the south-facing slopes can suffer badly in warm, sunny weather

NEWS

2014/15: An eight-seat chair with heated seats and covers will replace the Polten quad on the way to Leogang. A second gondola out of the valley is being built at Leogang, with 10-seat cabins. A matching piste is planned, but the timing of that is unclear. Snowmaking capacity is being extended over two years.

2013/14: A six-pack (heated seat, with covers) replaced the Rosswald T-bar on Reiterkogel.

EXTENT OF THE SLOPES ★★★☆☆
User-friendly circuit

Travelling anticlockwise, you can make a complete circuit of the valley on skis, crossing from one side to the other at Vorderglemm and Lengau – if you wish you can stick to blues almost the whole way. Going clockwise, you have to do a shorter circuit through Saalbach – there is no lift at Vorderglemm – and there is more red-run skiing to do.

On the south-facing side, five sectors can be identified, each served by a lift from the valley – named on our map. The links across these slopes work well: when traversing the whole hillside you need to descend to the valley floor only once – at Saalbach, where the main street separates Bernkogel from Kohlmaiskopf.

The Wildenkarkogel sector connects via Seidl-Alm to the slopes of **Leogang**; a small, high, open area served by fast lifts leads to a long, north-facing slope down to the base of an eight-seat gondola near Hütten, 3km from Leogang village. An additional 10-seat access gondola is under construction from the nursery slope about half-way between Leogang and the original gondola station.

Back in the main valley, the north-facing slopes are different in character: two widely separated and steeper mountains, one split into twin peaks. An eight-seat gondola rises from Saalbach to **Schattberg Ost**, where the high, open, sunny slopes behind the peak are served by a fast quad. The slightly higher peak of **Schattberg West** is reached by gondola from Hinterglemm. Another gondola makes the link from Schattberg Ost to Schattberg West. The second north-facing hill is **Zwölferkogel**, served by a two-stage eight-seat gondola from Hinterglemm. A six-pack and draglift serve open slopes on the sunny side of the peak, and a second gondola from the valley provides a link from the south-facing Hochalm slopes.

The Hinterglemm nursery slopes are well used, and floodlit every evening.

FAST LIFTS ★★★★★
The world's best

Saalbach-Hinterglemm has the highest proportion of fast lifts of any major resort in the world (just under 90%). There is one surprise when doing the circus: the parallel T-bars to the top of Bernkogel when going from Saalbach to Hinterglemm. The resort says a replacement is 'under discussion'.

QUEUES ★★★★☆
High season weaknesses

Given the fast lifts, it's not surprising that queues are few, but they do occur – notably last winter when Austrian and Dutch school holidays coincided. In peak season you can hit queues at the Zwölferkogelbahn out of Hinterglemm, the Schattberg X-Press and Kohlmaiskopfbahn out of Saalbach and the Schönleiten lifts at and above Vorderglemm. The Limberg quad on the back of Schattberg can be a problem, too.

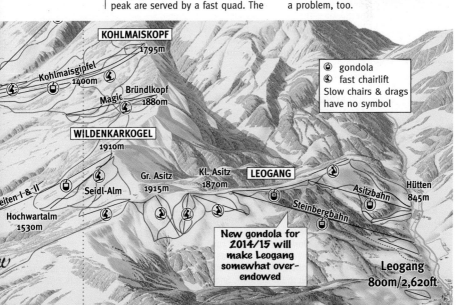

↑ Hinterglemm now pretty well fills the available space on the valley floor; on the left, Zwölferkogel

TVB SAALBACH-HINTERGLEMM

Resort news and key links: www.wheretoskiandsnowboard.com

LIFT PASSES

Prices in €

Age	1-day	6-day
under 16	23	114
16 to 18	35	171
19 plus	46	228

Free Under 6
Senior No deals
Beginner Points card

Notes Covers Saalbach-Hinterglemm and Leogang, and the ski-bus; also Reiterkogel toboggan run at night; part-day and non-skier passes

Alternative passes Salzburg SuperSkiCard covers 22 ski areas in the Salzburg province; Kitzbüheler Alpen AllStarCard covers Kitzbühel, Schneewinkel (St Johann), SkiWelt, Ski Juwel, Skicircus Saalbach, Zell-Kaprun

GETTING THERE

Air Salzburg 85km/ 55 miles (1hr30); Munich 220km/ 135 miles (3hr)

Rail Zell am See 18km/11 miles; hourly buses

TERRAIN PARKS ★★★★☆
Main one has its own gondola
The popular Nightpark just above Hinterglemm is served by its own heated gondola, is floodlit until 9.30pm (except Sundays) and includes Big Air, kickers, wall ride and rails, plus a beginner line. There are other parks below Hochalm and Kl. Asitz towards Leogang, and a snowcross and park for beginners on Bernkogel.

SNOW RELIABILITY ★★☆☆☆
A tale of two sides
Most slopes are below 1900m and the south-facing slopes are in the majority; they can suffer from the sun and we've often seen strips of machine-made snow amid green and brown fields – 'impressive' snowmaking covers 90% of the area. The north-facing slopes keep their snow better but can get icy. The long north-facing run to Leogang – a favourite of ours – often has the best snow in the area. Piste maintenance is good.

FOR EXPERTS ★★☆☆☆
Little steep stuff
There are a few challenging slopes on the north-facing side. The long (4km) Nordabfahrt run beneath the Schattberg Ost gondola is a genuine black – a fine fast bash first thing in the morning if it has been groomed and is not icy. The Zwölferkogel Nordabfahrt at Hinterglemm is less consistent, but its classification is justified by a few short, steeper pitches. The World Cup downhill run from Zwölferkogel is interesting, as is the 5km Schattberg West-Hinterglemm red (and its 'ski route' variant). Snow

conditions and forest tend to limit the off-piste potential. Given decent snow, however, you can have a good time.

FOR INTERMEDIATES ★★★★☆
Paradise for most
The sunny side of the area is ideal for both the mileage-hungry piste-basher and the more leisurely cruiser, although many of the blues can be quite testing. The otherwise delightful blue run from Bernkogel to Saalbach can get really crowded. For more of a challenge, the long red runs to the valley are good fun.

The north-facing area also has some more challenging runs, with excellent relentless reds from both Schattberg West and Zwölferkogel, and a section of relatively high, open slopes around Zwölferkogel – good for mixed-ability groups wishing to ski together. None of the black runs is beyond an adventurous intermediate, unless icy. The long, pretty blue from Schattberg to Vorderglemm gets right away from lifts – but is a bit steep and tricky towards the end, and probably should be red.

FOR BEGINNERS ★★★☆☆
Head for Hinterglemm
Saalbach's two sunny nursery slopes are right next to the village. The upper one is served by a short six-pack but gets a lot of through-traffic. There are short, easy runs to progress to at Bernkogel and Schattberg.

Hinterglemm's spacious nursery area is separate from the main slopes and faces north so lacks sun in midwinter but is more reliable for snow later on. Progression is aided by

SCHOOLS

Saalbach

Fürstauer
t 8444

Snow Academy
t 668256

Zink
t 0664 162 3655

Board.at
t 20047

EasySki
t 0699 111 80010

Hinterglemm

Snow & Fun
t 7511

Activ
t 0676 517 1325

Board.at
t 7541

Total
t 0676 560 0669

Classes (Fürstauer prices) 5 days (4.5hr) from €178

Private lessons From €143 for 3hr, for 1 or 2 people; extra person €15

CHILDCARE

Several hotels have nurseries

Ski schools From about age 4

UK PACKAGES

Alpine Answers, Alpine Weekends, Crystal, Crystal Finest, Erna Low, Inghams, Interactive Resorts, Neilson, Ski Bespoke, Ski Expectations, Ski Line, Ski Miquel, Ski Safari, Skitracer, Snow Finders, Snowscape, STC, Thomson **Leogang** Interactive Resorts, Zenith

a gondola serving the blue slope that is also used for night skiing. There are lots of other easy blue runs to move on to, especially on the south-facing side of the valley.

FOR BOARDERS ★★★★★
Good all-rounder
Saalbach is great for boarding. Slopes are extensive, lifts are mainly chairs and gondolas, and there are pistes to appeal to beginners, intermediates and experts alike – with few flats to negotiate. For experienced boarders, there's off-piste terrain between the lifts if snow conditions permit.

FOR CROSS-COUNTRY ★★★★★
Go to Zell am See
In midwinter the 10km of valley trails get very little sun, and are not very exciting. There is a high trail on the Reiterkogel. But the area beyond nearby Zell am See is better.

MOUNTAIN RESTAURANTS ★★★★★
Excellent quality and quantity
The area is liberally scattered with huts – we lost count at 55 – most of them pleasant, lively, rustic places offering 'good variety, prices and service', to quote one satisfied customer this year. All are marked and named on the piste map.
Editors' choice The Wieseralm (6939), at the heart of the Hinterglemm south-facing slopes, is a welcoming woody chalet doing table-service of satisfying dishes; fine terrace; endorsed by recent reporters ('top class').
Worth knowing about In opposite directions across the mountainside from Wieseralm, reporters this year tip Rosswaldhütte and Sonnalm – 'good range, very friendly staff'. Reporters regularly tip the Alte Schmiede above Leogang, a lovely stone-and-wood hut that is also a kind of museum. 'Attentive' table-service of 'excellent food, even vegetarian options', a big fireplace, huge terrace and DJ; gents' toilet amuses most reporters. Readers also like the huge, three-level Asitzbräu nearby, claimed to be Europe's highest brew-pub – 'delicious Austrian food'. Asteralm on Kohlmaiskopf is recommended for the first time this year – 'good selection, extremely helpful staff'. Sky Rest above the Schattberg lift station has table-service and 'great views'.
There's a picnic room at the top station of the Schattberg X-Press.

SCHOOLS AND GUIDES ★★★★★
More reports would be good ...
There's plenty of choice. A 2013 reporter says the Fürstauer school was 'highly rated' by his group: 'Friendly instructors and good value; our beginner was skiing red runs confidently by the end of the week.'

FOR FAMILIES ★★★★★
Hinterglemm tries harder
Saalbach doesn't go out of its way to sell itself to families, although it does have a ski kindergarten. Hinterglemm probably makes a better family base, with some good hotel-based nursery facilities – at the Theresia for example. And its nursery slope is better.

STAYING THERE

Chalets Inghams has a chalet hotel (with a sauna), which is right by the Reiterkogel gondola in Hinterglemm.
Hotels Both villages have lots of hotels, mainly 3-star and 4-star. Be aware that some central hotels suffer from disco noise, and front rooms from street noise into the early hours. All the hotels we list are in Saalbach; there are plenty in Hinterglemm too (including one rather gaudy 5-star, the Alpine Palace), but they don't seem to generate many reports.
★★★★Alpenhotel (6666) Central with countless bars and restaurants (a 2013 reporter especially enjoyed the Italian), nightclub; small pool, hot tub.
★★★★Herzblut (6294) Has no stars – we've awarded four. Recently built, big B&B place in a quiet but convenient location. 'Excellent breakfast, spacious rooms, extremely friendly staff.' Spa.
★★★★Neuhaus (7151-0) Central location (insist on upper rooms to escape street noise) – 'Superb gourmet food, very accommodating staff.'
★★★★Panther (6227) Central, wellness centre, outdoor pool: 'Excellent food, comfortable room, pleasant staff.'
★★★★Saalbacher Hof (7111) Major central hotel, renovated in 2010; 'fantastic food and staff' and 'lovely ambience'. Spa and 'nice pool'.
★★★Haider (6228-0) Best-positioned of the 3-stars, right next to the main lifts.

EATING OUT ★★★★★
Wide choice of hotel restaurants
This is essentially a half-board resort, with strikingly few restaurants other than those in hotels. In Saalbach, the Kohlmais Stub'n (Aparthotel Astrid) at

↑ Despite expansion and all the modern lifts, Saalbach retains a lot of charm
TVB SAALBACH-HINTERGLEMM

Resort news and key links: www.wheretoskiandsnowboard.com

ACTIVITIES

Indoor In hotels: swimming pools, sauna, massage, solarium; tennis, museum, gallery, bowling, casino

Outdoor Ice rink, curling, tobogganing, sleigh rides, snowshoeing, snowmobiling, quad bikes, ice karts, 40km of cleared paths, archery, paragliding

Phone numbers
From elsewhere in Austria add the prefix 06541 (Saalbach), 06583 (Leogang); from abroad use the prefix +43 and omit the initial '0'

TOURIST OFFICES

Saalbach
www.saalbach.com

Leogang
www.leogang-saalfelden.at

the foot of the slopes has friendly service, a warm woody ambience and creative regional food. La Trattoria at the Alpenhotel, does 'excellent, authentic pizzas and pastas'.

APRES-SKI ★★★★★
It rocks from early on
'The best après-ski in the Alps,' claims the resort website, and it is certainly among the best. The site lists over 20 venues. Saalbach, in particular, is very lively from mid-afternoon until the early hours, and can get quite wild. We are now getting reports of topless dancing in some bars.

On the hill above Saalbach, the Berger Hochalm under the Magic chair rocks from early afternoon, with a happy hour from 3pm; 'Banging!' says a 57-year-old reporter. Then it's down to the rustic Hinterhag Alm, an institution – 'Everybody meets here at 4pm' they say, and that's how it seems; live bands ensure a 'totally mental' atmosphere until people start to slide down to the already packed Bauer's Schi-Alm – an old cow shed with attached umbrella bars. Both are 'noisy, drunken places, but good fun'. There are alternatives: Bäckstättstall and the main bar of Berger's Sporthotel have dancing when the lifts close. Bobby's Pub attracts a very young crowd, is cheap, has bowling, games machines, sport on TVs and serves Guinness. Zum Turm (a converted medieval jail) and Spitzbub (a converted garage) are loud and lively. The Ötzi bar 'is always good for

a night out – good prices, friendly staff, dancing on tables'. There are late-night clubs under various central hotels, and several pole dancing dives.

We get few reports on the après-ski in Hinterglemm, but the rustic goat-themed Goasstall just above the village is 'one of the great après bars in Austria – like the Mooserwirt in St Anton, but much more lively'. Crikey!

OFF THE SLOPES ★★★★★
Surprisingly little to do
The resort is not very entertaining if you're not into winter sports. There are few shops other than supermarkets and ski shops. But there is some good walking (eg up the valley beyond Lengau) including guided walks twice weekly, and the gondolas can be used. Many good restaurants are reachable by lift. At Hinterglemm a floodlit treetop walk is open all year round. There are long, fun toboggan runs above both Saalbach and Hinterglemm. Excursions to Zell am See and Salzburg are possible, and recommended by reporters.

LINKED RESORT – 800m

LEOGANG

Leogang sits in a pretty valley beneath the impressive Birnhorn. It is quietly attractive but is set on a busy road leading to Fieberbrunn and St Johann.

It may seem to offer a good budget base for skiing the slopes of Saalbach-Hinterglemm, but in practice it suits best those who are content with the good, generally quiet local slopes plus the runs at the eastern end of the main circuit; getting to the best slopes at the far end of the circuit, beyond Hinterglemm, takes quite a time. The nursery slopes are good.

Lodging is widely scattered, but there are good hotels and apartments available. The new gondola (read our 'News' panel) is being built right next to the 4-star hotel Krallerhof (8246-0), making it the obvious place to consider first. (We note that the restaurants at the top of the gondola are in the same stable; surely not both owned by the mayor, by any chance?) Restaurants are hotel-based. The rustic old chalet Kraller Alm is the focal teatime and evening rendezvous. Activities off the slopes are very limited, but there is the mile-long Flying Fox zipwire that whistles along at 80mph.

SCHLADMING TOURIST OFFICE

Schladming

Pleasant old valley town in Styria, with a famous racing hill directly above, links to three other mountains; plus other areas nearby

RATINGS

The mountains

Extent	★★★
Fast lifts	★★★★
Queues	★★★★
Terrain p'ks	★★★
Snow	★★★★
Expert	★★
Intermediate	★★★★
Beginner	★★★
Boarder	★★★
X-country	★★★★
Restaurants	★★★★
Schools	★★★
Families	★★★★

The resort

Charm	★★★
Convenience	★★★
Scenery	★★★
Eating out	★★★
Après-ski	★★★
Off-slope	★★★

RPI	95
lift pass	£190
ski hire	£80
lessons	£100
food & drink	£115
total	£485

NEWS

2013/14: The Gipfelbahn 'pulse' gondola on Hochwurzen was replaced by a proper 10-seat gondola. There is a new panorama cable car at the Dachstein glacier. One of the cabins has a 'balcony' for up to 10 passengers to ride in the open air. At the top is a cantilevered Sky Walk with a glass bottom.

➕ Ideal for intermediate cruising		➖ Slopes lack variety
➕ Very sheltered slopes, among trees		➖ Very little to entertain experts
➕ Lots of good mountain restaurants		➖ Nursery slopes not central
➕ Appealing town with friendly people		➖ Runs to valley level are not easy
➕ Very cheap for meals and drinks		

One slope may be rather like another here, but with its four linked mountains Schladming offers the keen intermediate a real sense of travelling around on the snow. And its solid, valley-town ambience makes it a pleasant change from the Austrian rustic-village norm. The town has had a major injection of investment recently, thanks to the 2013 Alpine World Ski Championships.

THE RESORT

The old town of Schladming sits at the foot of Planai, one of four linked ski mountains. It has a long skiing tradition: the town has hosted many World Cup races and in 2013 hosted the World Championships, triggering lots of new construction.

At the foot of the next mountain to the west, Hochwurzen, is Rohrmoos – a quiet, scattered satellite village set on an elevated slope that forms a giant nursery area. To the east is the small, attractively rustic village of Haus, at the foot of the highest of the four mountains, Hauser Kaibling.

Timetabled 'efficient' free ski-buses link the villages and lift bases. A night-bus runs until 1am (5 euros); taxis can be more economic for groups.

The multi-day lift pass also covers many other resorts in the region; trips are feasible to Bad Gastein, Wagrain/ Flachau, Zauchensee and Hochkönig (and to Obertauern – not on the pass). A car is useful for these trips.

There are direct trains from Salzburg, so Schladming makes an excellent short break destination.

VILLAGE CHARM ★★★☆☆
Pleasant car-free centre

Most of Schladming's buildings are solid and traditional, and at its heart there's a pleasant, traffic-free main square, prettily lit at night, around which you'll find most of the shops, restaurants, bars and some appealing hotels. The ultra-modern Planet Planai area nearby at the base of the gondola is a complete contrast. The busy main road bypasses the town.

CONVENIENCE ★★★☆☆
Reasonably compact

Much of the accommodation is close to the town centre; the sports centre and tennis halls are five minutes' walk away, as is the gondola to Planai. There is also accommodation out by the Planai-Hochwurzen lift link, and further down the valley (eg Pichl).

SCENERY ★★★☆☆
Four points of view

All four mountains are broadly similar, pleasantly wooded and share decent views along the Ennstal and to the more dramatic Dachsteingruppe, across the valley to the north.

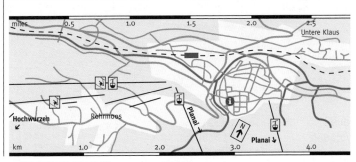

LIFT PASSES

Ski Amadé

Prices in €

Age	1-day	6-day
under 17	23	114
17 to 19	35	170
20 plus	46	227

Free Under 6

Senior No deals

Beginner No deals

Notes Day-pass price is for Schladming-Dachstein only; part-day tickets available; 2-day-plus passes cover the 860km of pistes and 270 lifts in five regions: Schladming-Dachstein; Gastein; Salzburger Sportwelt; Grossarl; Hochkönig

Alternative pass Salzburg Super Ski Card: all lifts in Salzburgerland, including Zell am See, Kaprun and Saalbach-Hinterglemm

THE MOUNTAINS

Most pistes are on the wooded north-facing slopes above the main valley, with some going into the side valleys higher up; there are a few short open slopes above the trees.

Piste maps here can be confusing. The whole four-mountain area is covered on one map, but the individual mountains also do their own maps (Planai and Hochwurzen do a combined one) which also show mountain restaurants in their own areas but not in the others.

As in many Austrian areas, you may encounter multiple pistes identified by the same number. Add to this poor signposting, and finding your way around can be tricky. A regular and experienced reporter 'made a wrong turn three times in one day' in 2014.

EXTENT OF THE SLOPES ★★★☆☆
Four linked sectors
The resort claims a total of just over 120km of pistes – a modest figure, but it's enough to scrape into our ★★★ rating. Each of the sectors has a variety of runs to play on, and you get a satisfying feeling of travelling around a lot.

Planai is the local mountain, reached directly by gondola from the edge of the town centre. It is linked to **Hauser Kaibling** at altitude via the high, wooded bowl between them. At the base of the mountain, the village of Haus has a cable car and gondola into the slopes. Links to the mountains to the west, **Hochwurzen** and **Reiteralm**, are at valley level (and

the first involves riding a gondola down from Planai). Our favourite area is Reiteralm – a hi-tech lift system and nicely varied terrain, extended down into Preuneggtal a few years ago by a new gondola and runs.

Several lower runs go across poorly signposted roads – care is needed.

There are several other separate mountains nearby covered by the local lift pass – including Fageralm (only slow chairlifts and T-bars, but lovely quiet, wide, easy cruising pistes and rustic huts – a very relaxing change of pace), Galsterbergalm, the Dachstein glacier and Stoderzinken.

FAST LIFTS ★★★★☆
Some neglected links
Each linked sector has gondola access from the car parks at the bases, and there are now lots of fast chairs. But the slow chairlift from Schladming to Hochwurzen, and the one from Pichl to Reiteralm are obvious weaknesses.

QUEUES ★★★★☆
Only at the Planai gondola
Queues for the Planai gondola at peak times are the only issue. A March 2014 reporter waited 20 minutes one day. But they can be avoided by catching a bus to another mountain's lift station.

TERRAIN PARKS ★★★☆☆
Three to try
Planai has a park above Lärchkogel, with medium and pro kicker lines, jumps, boxes and rails. Reiteralm's park is similarly well equipped; there's also a half-pipe. Hochwurzen's park is floodlit until 10.30pm.

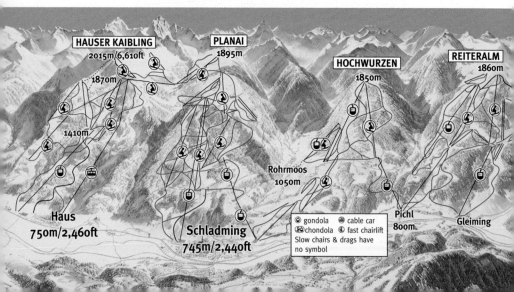

HAUSER KAIBLING 2015m/6,610ft · 1870m · 1410m · Haus 750m/2,460ft · PLANAI 1895m · Schladming 745m/2,440ft · HOCHWURZEN 1850m · Rohrmoos 1050m · Pichl 800m · REITERALM 1860m · Gleiming

gondola	cable car	
chondola	fast chairlift	

Slow chairs & drags have no symbol

KEY FACTS

Resort	745m
	2,440ft

Schladming's four linked mountains

Slopes	745-2015m
	2,440-6,610ft
Lifts	44
Pistes	122km
	76 miles
Blue	38%
Red	56%
Black	6%
Snowmaking	99%

GETTING THERE

Air Salzburg 90km/ 55 miles (1hr15); Munich 260km/ 160 miles (3hr)

Rail Main-line station in resort

SNOW RELIABILITY ★★★★☆
Excellent in cold weather
The northerly orientation of the slopes helps keep the pistes in good shape. The serious snowmaking operation makes it a good choice for early holidays; coverage is comprehensive and the system is put to good use. But at this altitude poor conditions on the lower slopes are a natural hazard. Piste grooming is good.

FOR EXPERTS ★★☆☆☆
Strictly intermediate stuff
Schladming's status as a racing venue doesn't make it macho. The steep black finish to the Men's Downhill course and the mogul runs at the top of Planai and Hauser Kaibling are the only really challenging slopes there. Reiteralm has two steep black runs (one very short) at the top and some good tree runs. Hauser Kaibling's off-piste is good, but limited; it has two itineraries, not notably steep.

FOR INTERMEDIATES ★★★★☆
Red runs rule
The area is ideal for intermediate cruising. The majority of runs are red but the gradient of many is similar to the blues. The final section of the red below Rohrmoos is steep though.

Newish lifts have improved access to more challenging slopes at the top of Planai and Hauser Kaibling, as well as a short but pretty blue from the high point. The black racing pistes in these sectors, and the red alternatives, are ideal for fast cruising but can get very icy and tricky on the lower sections.

Hauser Kaibling has a lovely blue running from top to bottom, and Reiteralm has some gentle blues.

FOR BEGINNERS ★★★☆☆
Good slopes but poorly sited
The ski schools generally take beginners to the extensive but low-altitude Rohrmoos nursery area – fine if you are based there. But for residents of central Schladming, it's a bus ride. There are lots of easy runs to progress to, though getting to them can be tricky.

FOR BOARDERS ★★★☆☆
Fine for all but experts
Schladming is popular with boarders. Most lifts on the spread-out mountains are gondolas or chairs, with some short drags around. The area is ideal for beginners and intermediates, except when the lower slopes are icy, though there are few exciting challenges for expert boarders bar the off-piste tree runs.

FOR CROSS-COUNTRY ★★★★☆
Huge network of trails
There are almost 500km of trails in the region, and the World Championships have been held at nearby Ramsau.

MOUNTAIN RESTAURANTS ★★★★☆
A real highlight
There are plenty of attractive rustic huts, mostly table-service and with good food. Some of the individual

SCHOOLS

Tritscher
t 22647
Hopl (Hochwurzen-Planai)
t 61525

Classes (Tritscher prices) 5 days €183
Private lessons From €108 for 2hr; each additional person €22

CHILDCARE

Mini club (Tritscher school)
t 22647
For ages 3 and 4
Nannies Details at tourist office

Ski school From age 4

ACTIVITIES

Indoor Swimming pool, sauna, fitness club, bowling, museum, cinema
Outdoor Ice skating, curling, tobogganing, snowshoeing, sleigh rides, 50km of cleared paths

UK PACKAGES

Alpine Answers, Crystal, Crystal Finest, Rocketski, STC, Thomson, Zenith

Phone numbers From elsewhere in Austria add the prefix 03687; from abroad use the prefix +43 and omit the initial '0'

TOURIST OFFICE

www.schladming-dachstein.at
www.skiamade.com

mountain piste maps mark them.

On Hauser Kaibling, Schoarlhütte has a real mountain-hut atmosphere and is renowned for its ribs. For a good gröstl, try Krummholzhütte.

On Planai, reporters love Onkel Willy's Hütte – 'very traditional, good service and value'. Schafalm impressed a recent visitor despite being packed on a snowy day.

On Hochwurzen, the 'picturesque, sweet little' Hochwurzenalm is tipped for big portions of gulaschsuppe. The large self-service Hochwurzenhütte at the top is good, too. Tauernalm, at Rohrmoos, offers 'very good food, cheerful service'.

On Reiteralm the Schnepf'n Alm, Gasselhöh Hütte and the Jaga Stüberl ('impeccable service' and 'delicious crispy pizzas') have been praised.

On Fageralm, we've enjoyed the tiny Zeffererhütte, and a reporter enjoyed Unterbergalm.

SCHOOLS AND GUIDES ★★★☆☆
A good report
We had a rave review last year of a private lesson with Tritscher: 'Best I've had – corrected things that have dogged me for years; brilliant.'

FOR FAMILIES ★★★★☆
Rohrmoos is the place
The extensive gentle slopes of Rohrmoos are ideal for building up confidence. There are Kinderlands on Planai, Reiteralm and Fageralm.

STAYING THERE

Packaged accommodation is in hotels and pensions, but there are plenty of apartments for independent travellers.
Hotels Most lodging is mid-range but a few upmarket places exist.
★★★★Falkensteiner Schladming (214-0) New in 2012. A few minutes from the Planai gondola. Modern wooden interior. Indoor/outdoor pool, sauna.
★★★★Sporthotel Royer (2000) Big and comfortable, a few minutes from the Planai gondola. Pool, sauna, steam. We stayed here in 2013; the food was terrific and plentiful.
★★★Aqi (23536) Cool modern place, built in 2008. Opposite Planai gondola. 'Helpful staff, spacious quiet room, good food, plentiful breakfast.'
★★★Kirchenwirt (22435) Off the main square. 'Quaint, rooms a good size, staff friendly and helpful, food was simple but good.'

★★★Planai (23429) New two years ago, big and bright, modern and functional, directly opposite the Planai gondola.
Apartments A reader tips the 'spacious, excellent' Bella Vista apartments.

EATING OUT ★★★☆☆
Some good places
An experienced reporter says that best in town is the cool Tischlerei – 'Exudes quality: very hospitable team, immensely impressive cooking.' Many of the other good places are in hotels; tips include Johann's in the Posthotel, the Kirchenwirt and Neue Post. The small, family-run Friesacher Lanstuberl does 'expertly cooked steaks'. Maria's Mexican does a roaring trade in 'spicy and delicious' Tex-Mex, amid an 'all-round feel-good ambience'. Biochi specializes in organic and vegetarian food. We liked the Lasser Cafe and the Stadttor for coffee and cakes, and the Schwalbenbräu brewery.

APRES-SKI ★★★☆☆
Hohenhaus gets lively
Some of the mountain huts have live or loud music in the afternoon. On Hochwurzen, try Tauernalm at Rohrmoos. In town, the focus is the huge Hohenhaus Tenne by the Planai gondola station, the largest après-ski bar in Europe, and 'definitely the hot spot'; fabulous main bar, dance floor and regular live music. Platzhirsch (with umbrella bar) opposite also gets busy. In the main square, the Posthotel's upmarket umbrella bar Cabalou is lively, with slick service. Many of the central bars stay open until the early hours – but this isn't Ischgl. Cult and Angels are nightclubs.

OFF THE SLOPES ★★★☆☆
A few things to do
The town has a few shops, museum, pool and an ice rink. Hochwurzen has a floodlit 7km toboggan run. Some mountain restaurants are accessible to pedestrians. Trips to Salzburg are easy.

LINKED RESORT – 750m
HAUS

Haus is a fairly self-contained village, with its own ski schools, kindergartens and railway station. Hotel prices are generally lower here. The user-friendly nursery slopes are between the centre and the gondola. Excursions are easy, but off-slope activities and nightlife are very limited.

FRANK HEUER

Sölden

The resort needs a bypass tunnel, but slopes reaching glacial heights and an impressive lift system offer compensation

RATINGS

The mountains

Extent	★★★
Fast lifts	★★★★
Queues	★★★
Terrain p'ks	★★★
Snow	★★★★
Expert	★★★
Intermediate	★★★★
Beginner	★★★
Boarder	★★★★
X-country	★
Restaurants	★★★
Schools	★★★
Families	★★

The resort

Charm	★★
Convenience	★★
Scenery	★★★
Eating out	★★★
Après-ski	★★★★★
Off-slope	★★

RPI 110

lift pass	£200
ski hire	£135
lessons	£115
food & drink	£110
total	**£560**

NEWS

2014/15: The Wasserkar triple chair from below the Gaislachkogl gondola mid-station is due to be replaced by a six-pack.

2013/14: At the top of Gaislachkogl the Ice Q restaurant, lounge and panoramic terrace opened. And the Almstube at the middle station was renovated.

KEY FACTS

Resort	1380m
	4,530ft
Slopes	1350-3250m
	4,430-10,660ft
Lifts	33
Pistes	144km
	89 miles
Blue	47%
Red	33%
Black	20%
Snowmaking	67%

+ Excellent snow reliability, with access to two glaciers

+ Fairly extensive network of slopes suited to adventurous intermediates

+ Impressive lift system

+ Wide choice of huts for its size

+ Very lively après-ski/nightlife

− Towny resort is spread along a road that is busy with through-traffic

− You may need a bus to the lifts

− Main runs are almost all above the trees; only a couple are sheltered

− English not universally spoken

− Town centre can get rowdy

'We were very surprised that we were the only people getting off the transfer coach in Sölden, while the other 50 went on to Obergurgl,' said a reporter a few years ago. Yes: the resort's low profile in the UK is curious, given the powerful appeal of its snow-sure mountains and (if you like that kind of thing) its very lively après-ski scene. We always enjoy visits here and so do the readers we hear from. And perhaps things are changing: chalet operators Ski Total and Skiworld are now well established here.

THE RESORT

Sölden is a long, towny place in the Ötz valley leading up to Obergurgl. Gondolas from opposite ends of town go up to the peak of Gaislachkogl and the lift junction of Giggijoch, with most of the shops, restaurants and hotels in between them. A road winds its way above the town through various hamlets up to Hochsölden – a group of 4-star hotels and little else.

When buying a six-day lift pass you can opt to pay 10 euros extra for a day in nearby Obergurgl (the half-hourly buses are included in the lift pass). You can also get buses down the valley to Längenfeld where there is a big thermal spa. With a car you could make trips to St Anton or Ischgl.

VILLAGE CHARM ★★
Not a strong point
Despite its traditional Tirolean buildings, a pretty church among them, Sölden is no charmer. There's a good selection of shops and bars, but the ambience is towny (prominent ads for strip clubs don't help), and it is strung along the valley road running through it, lacking a central focus. More seriously, the central strip is badly affected by traffic on the road. The place attracts a lively crowd, and the partying can spill into the street. Across the river there's a quieter area, mainly of hotels and guest houses. Hochsölden offers splendid traffic-free isolation up the mountain.

CONVENIENCE ★★
Lifts at either end
It's a long town, and the gondola stations are almost a mile apart. So you may face a good walk to the lifts, or a ride on the free shuttle-buses. Places over the river from the main street aren't necessarily remote from the lifts. Hochsölden is ski-in/ski-out.

SCENERY ★★★
Go for the Big 3
Sölden promotes its Big 3 viewing platforms with spectacular 360° views from peaks over 3000m. But lower down things are less spectacular.

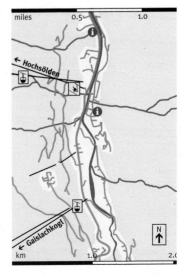

Ski Total

ARE HERE IN
Sölden

▸ **Quality chalets**
▸ **Top locations**
▸ **Excellent value**
▸ **17 more resorts**

skitotal.com

01483 791 933

LIFT PASSES

Prices in €

Age	1-day	6-day
under 15	24	123
15 to 19	36	185
20 to 63	48	246
64 plus	41	210
Free	Under 5	

Senior Min. age for senior women is 59

Beginner No deals

Notes Part-day and pedestrian options

THE MOUNTAINS

Practically all the slopes you spend your days on are above the treeline, though there are red and black runs through trees to the village.

The piste map – published in compact Z-card and a much bigger format – is adequately clear.

EXTENT OF THE SLOPES ★★★★★
Long run network

The ski area is not enormous. The resort claims 144km, but the Schrahe report (read our Piste Extent feature) puts the total at 91km, which sounds much nearer the mark to us. But it does go high. All sectors offer serious vertical and some long runs, which the piste map sets out in juicy (and only occasionally misleading) detail. It's 1880m vertical and a claimed 15km from the top of the glacier to the village; the other four runs listed, including from Gaislachkogl and Hainbachjoch are 8km to 10km with verticals of 1060m to 1690m.

There are two similar-sized sectors above the town, linked by fast six-packs out of the intervening Rettenbachtal. At the south end of town, a gondola leads up to an impressive three-cable gondola to **Gaislachkogl**. The terrain above the mid-station is served by a fast six-pack

(new to 2014/15) and a slow double. There are links south towards Gaislachalm and north towards the Rettenbachtal. Another gondola from the north end of the resort goes to **Giggijoch**. Fast lifts from here serve wide, open slopes below Rotkogljoch, from where a series of fast chairs and gondolas (one a cross-valley affair with no piste beneath it) leads to the glaciers – first the **Rettenbach**, and then the **Tiefenbach**. It may be a long journey (at least five lifts to reach the top from the village) but with luck the reward will be quiet slopes with excellent powdery winter snow. Below Giggijoch, and reached by red and black runs, is Hochsölden, served by a slow double chair back up.

FAST LIFTS ★★★★★
Well-linked system

There are still some slow lifts around – including (avoidable) T-bars on the glaciers, but most of the area is very well served by fast chairs and gondolas, and the resort hovers on the brink of ★★★★★.

QUEUES ★★★★★
Giggijoch's not so great

The Giggijoch gondola at one end of town still generates big queues in the morning peak. By contrast, the Gaislachkogl gondola seems to be

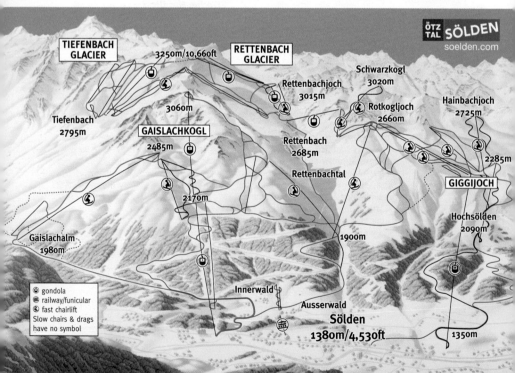

Looking up to the Rettenbach glacier; the snow there is always good but it takes an age to reach it (at least five lifts from the village) →
WENDY KING

GETTING THERE

Air Innsbruck 85km/ 50 miles (1hr15); Zürich 275km/ 170 miles (3hr15); Munich 285km/ 175 miles (3hr15)

Rail Ötz (30km/ 19 miles); buses from station

relatively queue-free. One reporter says it's worth taking the bus to the other gondola to avoid the Giggijoch queues. Key lifts to and from the glacier, such as the Einzeiger chair and Seiterkar chair, get busy. Both chairs to Rotkogljoch (gateway to the glaciers) are queue-prone but shift crowds fast. The slopes above Giggijoch get very busy. There is a weekend influx.

TERRAIN PARKS ★★★☆☆
Sufficiently equipped
The park above Giggijoch is well established and regularly upgraded. As well as beginner, intermediate and pro kickers, there are rails and various types of boxes. There's also a chill-out zone. There's a small, fun snowcross on blue run 15 and just off it a timed slalom. The Tiefenbach glacier has an early-season park.

SNOW RELIABILITY ★★★★☆
Rarely a problem
The slopes are high and roughly east-facing; and there are two extensive glaciers. Snowmaking covers 67% of the area, including all slopes on Giggijoch. Grooming is thorough, and reportedly goes on during the day, which is unusual these days. Even in a generally poor season, such as 2014, you can usually count on coverage to resort level.

FOR EXPERTS ★★★☆☆
Off-piste challenges
Few of the black pistes dotted around Sölden's map are serious, and some are silly. And one reader last year was distressed by the grooming of blacks, and consequent lack of moguls. But a 2014 visitor found the black World Cup race piste (31 at the foot of the Rettenbach glacier) 'a real blast in the morning'. There are quite a few non-trivial reds, notably on Gaislachkogl – with some steeper pitches above the mid-station – and the length and vertical of some of the runs present their own challenges. There are extensive off-piste possibilities, eg into Rettenbachtal.

FOR INTERMEDIATES ★★★★☆
Serious verticals
Most of Sölden's main slopes are genuine red runs ideal for adventurous intermediates; there are several easy blacks, too. Keen piste-bashers will love the serious verticals and long runs to be done (notably the one from Gaislachkogl) – but after a couple of days will agree that the claimed extent of 144km is optimistic.

There are two obvious targets for less confident intermediates. The long, quiet blue run above Gaislachalm is great for cruising, and below it a gentle blue through the trees offers by far the most friendly return to the resort. And the blues above Giggijoch offer gentle gradients; but crowds, too.

The glaciers are accessible to blue-

SKIWORLD

Catered chalets, hotels and self catering apartments in

Europe, USA and Canada

skiworld.co.uk

08444 930 430

ABTA V2151   ATOL 2036

SCHOOLS

Sölden-Hochsölden
t 2364

Yellow Power
t 2255

Vent
t 8123

Freeride Center
t 0650 415 3505

Vacancia Tirol
t 3100

Ötztal
t 3821

Classes (Sölden prices) 5 days (4hr per day) €201

Private lessons From €140 for 2hr for 1-2 people; each additional person €30

CHILDCARE

Kindergarten (run by Sölden school)
t 2364
Age 6mnth to 3yr

Ski school
From age 3

When quality and value matter, *do more* with

zenith ·holidays·

0203 137 7678

zenithholidays.co.uk

ABTA
ABTA No.Y1542

run skiers, and are almost entirely of blue-run gradient – the red runs down the Seiterkar chair offer a bit of a challenge. But it's best to return via the linking gondola to the Giggijoch slopes – the busy blue run down the Rettenbachtal is narrow (it's a road), and eventually turns into a tricky red (with an optional black variant).

FOR BEGINNERS ★★★★★
Crowded nursery slopes
The beginners' slopes, served by a pair of parallel draglifts, are situated just above the village at Innerwald and are reached by a free funicular. Progression to longer runs usually means the blues at Giggijoch; these are wide and gentle, but very busy in places. Hochsölden is on a steep slope – avoid at all costs.

FOR BOARDERS ★★★★★
Long, wide runs
Sölden is quite popular with boarders. The nursery slope involves drags, but after that draglifts can be avoided and you'll enjoy the wide, open blue runs above Giggijoch. Intermediates will relish the long runs and open terrain, and there's great freeriding for experienced boarders. There are some flat sections of piste in the Rettenbachtal and on the runs to the resort. There's a decent terrain park.

FOR CROSS-COUNTRY ★★★★★
Little to entertain
There are a couple of loops by the river to Hof (back end of town), another 5km trail to Rechenau and a 7km trail at Zwieselstein, between Sölden and Obergurgl.

MOUNTAIN RESTAURANTS ★★★★★
Few notable places
There are 30 huts listed, all usefully marked on the piste map and summarized in a separate leaflet. Most offer traditional food. But those in the main area can get crowded.

We like the rustic Gampe Thaya – simple food, table-service, lovely terrace, cosy interior. We've also enjoyed good käsespätzle at the peaceful Heidealm above Gaislachalm (accessed via a ski route). Both places have fabulous views up the Oetztal towards Obergurgl.

A 2014 reporter raves about the new Ice Q at the top of Gaislachkogl – 'oozes class but at reasonable prices, local meats, top-notch salads and

fantastic desserts'. Hühnersteign in the Rettenbachtal is famous for its chicken (Hühner!), and the Stabele just below it is equally famous for its gigantic burgers. At Giggijoch a 2014 reporter endorses the Wirtshaus table-service option: 'excellent food, attentive service, good value'. Below Hochsölden, the 'quaint' Eugen's Obstlerhütte was recommended for its 'beautifully presented traditional food'. The Panorama Alm, just above town, seems a good place for an afternoon sunbathe and drink, with beanbags, deckchairs and music.

SCHOOLS AND GUIDES ★★★★★
Wide choice, lacking feedback
Sölden has five schools; all restrict class sizes. We lack recent reports, though past feedback has been positive.

FOR FAMILIES ★★★★★
Few special facilities
Sölden does not go out of its way to cater for families. The intrusive main road traffic and possibly lengthy walks make it less attractive. But there are kindergartens at two schools and children aged four to seven pay a euro per day to use all the slopes.

STAYING THERE

Chalets Skiworld has two 25- to 30-bed chalets a short walk from the Giggijoch lift and the town centre: 2013 and 2014 visitors to chalet Paul Gruner praise the position and 'excellent staff and food and large rooms'. Ski Total has its chalet hotel Hermann above the village; recent reporters were very happy with the food, wine, staff and the chalet itself (consisting of a traditional and a more modern building), but one was less happy with its location.
Hotels There is one 5-star hotel but most are good 3- or 4-stars. Take care if looking at very central places – there are noisy bars.
★★★★★Central Spa (22600) Fairly central but also the biggest and best in town – the only 5-star; warmly welcoming; major spa, fitness room, pool.
★★★★Bergland (22400) Hip, recently built place next to the funicular to Innerwald, with big fifth-floor spa, outdoor hot tub and decent pool.
★★★★Erhart (2020) Across the river 500m from the Gaislachkogl gondola. 'Excellent location, superb food,' says

↑ The Giggijoch area has good easy cruising blue runs; but the pistes here do get crowded

ÖTZTAL TOURISMUS

Sölden

171

Build your own shortlist: www.wheretoskiandsnowboard.com

UK PACKAGES

Alpine Weekends, Crystal, Crystal Finest, Interactive Resorts, Momentum, Neilson, Ski Line, Ski Safari, Ski Total, Skitracer, Skiworld, Snow Finders, Snow-wise, Snowscape, STC, Thomson, Zenith

ACTIVITIES

Indoor Freizeit Arena (swimming, sauna, fitness centre, bowling, indoor tennis, climbing wall)

Outdoor Ice rink, curling, snowshoeing, 30km of walking trails, tobogganing, paragliding

Phone numbers
Except for the tourist office, from elsewhere in Austria add the prefix 05254; from abroad use the prefix +43 5254

TOURIST OFFICE

www.soelden.com

a reporter. Spa/fitness facilities.
****Grauer Bär (2564) Near the Gaislachkogl lift. Comfortable rooms, good food. Wellness area.
****Stefan (2237) By the Giggijoch gondola. We've stayed happily here – good food. Fair-sized wellness area.
****Valentin (2267) Next to the Gaislachkogl lift. 'Reasonable prices; good food, small spa, no pool.'
Apartments The Gaislachkogl apartments (2246) are close to the gondola, with wellness facilities. Guests also get free entry to the Freizeitarena leisure centre.

EATING OUT ★★★☆☆
A reasonable choice
Many of the hotels have à la carte restaurants, serving traditional Austrian food. Hotel Bergland is 'one of the few places that do fondue'. There are various pizzerias (Gusto was praised last year for its 'huge, good-quality, good-value pizzas') and a steakhouse – Joe's Höhle in hotel Castello has been recommended for grilled steaks. We usually end up in the Tavola in the hotel Rosengarten (because it doesn't take reservations) and haven't been disappointed. S'Pfandl, above the town at Ausserwald, makes a jolly outing for traditional Tirolean food.

APRES-SKI ★★★★★
Throbbing until late
Sölden's après-ski is justly famous. It starts up the mountain, notably at

Giggijoch at the cosy Eugen's Obstlerhütte, or at Bubi's Schihütte on Gaislachkogl ('men come round the tables with accordions singing Austrian songs') and progresses (possibly via Philipp's Eisbar at Innerwald) to packed bars in and around the main street.

The hotel Liebe Sonne's Schirmbar is 'the place to be': 'The best après in town,' says a seasonaire – lively and packed, usually overflowing into the road. Fire and Ice is a two-storey glass-fronted place that parties from 3pm to 3am (theoretically). There are countless other places, with live bands at, er, Live, and throbbing discos, some with table dancing and/or striptease – Katapult has go-gos dancers and guest DJs. And if you've any energy left, Kuhstall 'parties till 5–6am'. Reader tips for quieter places include Grizzly's and Die Alm.

OFF THE SLOPES ★★☆☆☆
Disappointing for its size
The Freizeit leisure centre has a swimming pool, saunas, gym, tennis and bowling. There's an ice rink and a 5km floodlit toboggan run. A reporter enjoyed the Wednesday night ski show on Gaislachkogl. Trips to Innsbruck are possible. Aqua Dome is a 'beautiful' thermal spa centre at Längenfeld, now reached by regular buses. There are sleigh rides up the valley at Vent.

Söll

The ski area is big, but the attractive village is surprisingly small and intimate; shame it is not set right by the lifts

RATINGS

The mountains

Extent	★★★★
Fast lifts	★★★★
Queues	★★★
Terrain p'ks	★★★
Snow	★★
Expert	★
Intermediate	★★★★
Beginner	★★
Boarder	★★
X-country	★★★
Restaurants	★★★
Schools	★★★
Families	★★★

The resort

Charm	★★★
Convenience	★★
Scenery	★★★
Eating out	★★
Après-ski	★★★★
Off-slope	★★

RPI   90

lift pass	£180
ski hire	£80
lessons	£100
food & drink	£110
total	**£470**

NEWS

2014/15: The Aualm quad chair up to Zinsberg is due to be upgraded to an 8-seater. A new 1.2km red run with snowmaking is planned for the Brixen area. There are plans for yet more snowmaking.

2013/14: A new reservoir for snowmaking was built at Hohe Salve.

+ Part of the SkiWelt, Austria's largest linked ski and snowboard area
+ Local slopes are north-facing, so they keep their snow relatively well
+ Lovely intermediate cruising runs
+ Pretty village with lively après-ski
+ Cheap, even by Austrian standards
+ Snowmaking is now very extensive and well used; even so ...

− Low altitude can mean poor snow
− Long walk or inadequate bus service from the village to the lifts
− Runs on upper slopes mostly short
− Few challenges except Hohe Salve
− Not ideal for beginners
− The SkiWelt slopes can get crowded
− Piste map and signposting poor

Söll has long been popular with British beginners and intermediates, attracting both youths and families looking for fun of different kinds. The resort is in fact far from ideal for beginners, but the SkiWelt can be a great area for intermediate cruising. Whether it is depends on the snow. If the weather is coming from Russia, this area can have the best snow in the Alps; but usually it isn't, and the snow may suffer from afternoon thaws and night-time frost.

Many visitors are surprised by the small size of the village (in particular, there aren't many shops) and the long trek out to the slopes. You may prefer to stay near the lifts and trek into the village in the evening. Or you may prefer, like us, to stay in one of the other SkiWelt resorts – Ellmau along the valley (which has its own chapter) or Westendorf over the hill (covered at the end of this chapter), which has quicker access to the Kitzbühel slopes.

THE RESORT

Söll is a pleasant, friendly village, bypassed by the main valley road; although its chalet-style buildings are spread quite widely, the core is compact – you can explore it on foot thoroughly in a few minutes.

The resort is part of the vast SkiWelt area – Austria's largest area, and one of the largest in the Alps. You can also progress (via Brixen) to the slopes of Kitzbühel; these and various other ski areas within easy reach, such as Waidring, Fieberbrunn and St Johann, are covered by the Kitzbüheler Alpen AllStarCard ski pass.

VILLAGE CHARM ★★★
Follows tradition

Söll is quite attractive, with chalet-style buildings and a huge church near the centre (its graveyard prettily lit by candles at night).

CONVENIENCE ★★
Not for the slopes

The slopes are well outside the village, on the other side of a busy road crossed by a pedestrian tunnel. You can leave your equipment at the bottom of the gondola for a small charge. There is some accommodation out near the lifts, but most is in or around the village centre. From there, it's the ski-bus or a 15-minute walk to the lifts. A base on the far side of the village may mean that you board the bus before it gets too crowded. But the bus does not serve every corner.

SCENERY ★★★
Head for Hohe Salve

Söll sits in a woody valley, below the distinctive dome-shaped peak of Hohe Salve. From the top, there are good views to the whole SkiWelt and the craggy Wilder Kaiser ridges.

miles   0.5   1.0   1.5

ℹ

N

🚠 ⬉ Hohe Salve

km   1.0   2.0   3.0

SÖLL TOURIST OFFICE

Söll

LIFT PASSES

SkiWelt Wilder Kaiser-Brixental

Prices in €

Age	1-day	6-day
under 16	22	110
16 to 17	35	175
18 plus	44	219

Free Under 7

Senior No deals

Beginner Points cards

Notes Ski-bus included; single ascent and part-day options

Alternative pass
Kitzbüheler Alpen AllStarCard covers: Schneewinkel (St Johann), Kitzbühel, SkiWelt, Ski Juwel, Skicircus Saalbach-Hinterglemm and Zell am See-Kaprun

KITZBUHELER ALPEN / KURT TROPPER

Brixen is a sprawling place but in a great position. Gondolas go up both sides of the valley – to the main SkiWelt circuit one way and to Westendorf's slopes the other ↓

THE MOUNTAINS

Although there are some open slopes high up, and the prominent high point of Hohe Salve is noticeably bare, most of the slopes are heavily wooded.

The piste map is better than it was, using arrows to show which way runs go where that is in doubt. We stick to the view, though, that it is hopelessly over ambitious in trying to show the whole area in a single view; the result is simply inadequate for route finding, especially on the Zinsberg side of Hohe Salve and between Eiberg and Brandstadl. What's needed are separate maps for the main sectors.

Signposting is also heavily criticized by visitors (including nearly all 2014 reporters); it helps once you realize that the signs point out the direction to the next lift you want and use the number of the lift to indicate the colour of the run. But one 2014 reporter said, 'Everyone complained about the signposting and we got lost a few times.'

EXTENT OF THE SLOPES ★★★★☆
Short run network
The SkiWelt will easily keep an average intermediate amused for a week. The peaks are not high – with the exception of Hohe Salve they are

all under 1700m. In good snow there are long red runs to be done to the valley, but most of the skiing is on the upper slopes where most runs are very short (often less than 300m vertical).

A gondola takes all but complete beginners up to the mid-mountain shelf of Hochsöll, where there are a couple of short lifts and connections in several directions. These include an eight-seat gondola to the high point of Hohe Salve. From here there are runs down to Kälbersalve, Rigi and Hopfgarten. Rigi can also be reached by chairs and runs without going to Hohe Salve – to which it is itself linked by chairs. Rigi is also the start of runs down to Itter and to Hopfgarten. From Kälbersalve you can head down south-facing runs to Brixen or up to Zinsberg and on towards Ellmau. From Brixen, a gondola goes up to Choralpe in Westendorf's area and a lovely north-facing red piste comes back down. From Choralpe you can also head off towards Kitzbühel.

FAST LIFTS ★★★★☆
Still some slow chairs
Lifts from the valley are mainly gondolas, and there are now quite a few fast chairs on the upper slopes. But there are still some slow chairs. T-bars can generally be avoided.

KEY FACTS	
Resort	700m
	2,300ft
Entire SkiWelt	
Slopes	620-1955m
	2,030-6,410ft
Lifts	91
Pistes	280km
	174 miles
Blue	48%
Red	46%
Black	6%
Snowmaking	82%

QUEUES ★★★☆☆
Some high-season waits

Lift upgrades have greatly improved this once queue-prone area. In peak season getting out of Söll at ski-school time in the mornings can be a problem, and there are still some bottlenecks on the mountain. When snow is poor, the links between Zinsberg and Eiberg get crowded.

TERRAIN PARKS ★★★☆☆
Local and floodlit

Söll has its own park below Hochsöll with beginner and expert lines; features include boxes, frames and rails. It's floodlit for night riding.

SNOW RELIABILITY ★★☆☆☆
Erratic – but has artificial help

After a series of good seasons, with several reporters experiencing good fresh powder for much of their holidays, last season was a poor one for the SkiWelt (as it was for most of Austria).

With a low average height, and important links that get a lot of sun, the snow in the SkiWelt can suffer badly in warm weather even in good seasons. So the snowmaking that has been installed is essential. At 225km and covering 82% of the area's pistes, it is Austria's biggest snowmaking installation. Reporters have been impressed by its use and by the grooming – 'excellent' say some this year.

FOR EXPERTS ★☆☆☆☆
Not a lot

The black runs from Hohe Salve are challenging pistes, the steepest of them including a short pitch that locals claim is steeper than Mayrhofen's Harakiri. The black run

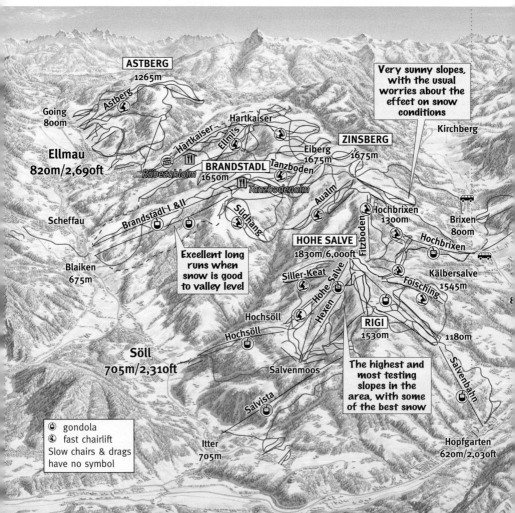

ASTBERG 1265m

Very sunny slopes, with the usual worries about the effect on snow conditions

Going 800m

Astberg

Hartkaiser

Ellmi's

Kirchberg

Eiberg 1675m

ZINSBERG 1675m

Ellmau 820m/2,690ft

Rübezahlalm

BRANDSTADL 1650m

Tanzboden

Tanzbodenalm

Aualm

Hochbrixen 1300m

Brixen 800m

Scheffau

Brandstadl I & II

Südhans

Fitzboden

Hochbrixen

Blaiken 675m

Excellent long runs when snow is good to valley level

HOHE SALVE 1830m/6,000ft

Siller-Keat

Hohe-salve

Foisching

Kälbersalve 1545m

Hochsöll

Hexen

RIGI 1530m

1180m

Hochsöll

Söll 705m/2,310ft

Salvenmoos

The highest and most testing slopes in the area, with some of the best snow

Salvenbahn

Salvista

⊙ gondola
④ fast chairlift
Slow chairs & drags have no symbol

Itter 705m

Hopfgarten 620m/2,030ft

Söll-Hochsöll
t 5454

Knolln
t 0664 594051

Classes (Söll prices)
5 4hr-days €165

Private lessons
€58 for 1hr; each
additional person €25

alongside the Brixen gondola also deserves respect, especially if the snow is in poor condition because of its south-facing aspect. Those runs apart, the main challenges are gentle off-piste routes – from Brandstadl down to Söll, for example.

FOR INTERMEDIATES ★★★★☆
Mainly easy runs

When blessed with good snow the SkiWelt is a paradise for those who love easy cruising and don't mind short runs. It is a big area, and you really get a feeling of travelling around. There are lots of blue runs and many of the reds could be blue. In general the most difficult slopes are those from the mid-stations to the valleys – to Blaiken, Brixen and Söll, for example. For more challenging reds head for Westendorf (and don't miss the excellent red down to Brixen).

FOR BEGINNERS ★★☆☆☆
Not ideal

The big area of nursery slopes between the main road and the gondola station is fine when snow is good – gentle, spacious, uncrowded and free from good skiers whizzing past. But it can get icy or slushy. In poor snow the Hochsöll area may be used. None of the lifts is free, but points cards are available. Progression to longer runs is likely to be awkward – there aren't many blue runs in this part of the SkiWelt. One is the narrow blue from Hochsöll, on which fast learners can get home.

FOR BOARDERS ★★☆☆☆
Great cruising

Söll is a good place to try out boarding: slopes are gentle and there are plenty of gondolas and chairs. And it has its own terrain park. For competent boarders it's more limited – the slopes of the SkiWelt are tame.

FOR CROSS-COUNTRY ★★★☆☆
Neighbouring villages are better

Söll has about 25km of local trails, but they are less interesting than those between Hopfgarten and Kelchsau and around and beyond Ellmau. There is a total of 196km in the SkiWelt area. Lack of snow-cover can be a problem.

MOUNTAIN RESTAURANTS ★★★☆☆
Good, but crowded

There are quite a few jolly little chalets. Our favourites in the SkiWelt are covered in the Ellmau chapter – Tanzbodenalm near Brandstadl, and Rübezahlalm above Ellmau.

At the lower corner of the Hochsöll slopes, the atmospheric converted cow shed Stöcklalm is an excellent spot. The highly rated Hohe Salve (top of the gondola) offers a large revolving terrace and good views (from the toilets as well, say reporters). Other reporter recommendations include the Stoagrub'nhütte above Hopfgarten. Read the Ellmau chapter, too.

SCHOOLS AND GUIDES ★★★☆☆
Good 2014 report

Söll-Hochsöll and Knolln are the main schools. The beginners in the party of a 2014 visitor had 'excellent teachers' from the Söll-Hochsöll school and he had a private lesson that 'pushed us and improved technique greatly – well worth it'.

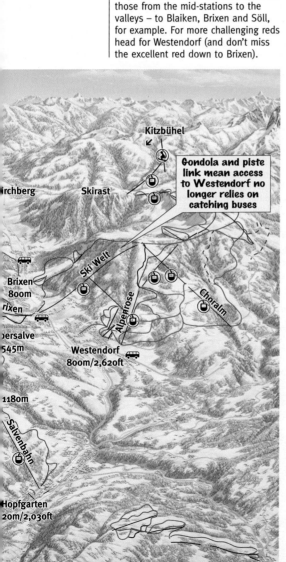

Kitzbühel

Gondola and piste link mean access to Westendorf no longer relies on catching buses

Irchberg Skirast

Brixen
800m

rixen

Ski Welt

ersalve
545m

Westendorf
800m/2,620ft

Alpenrose

Choralm

1180m

Salvenbahn

Hopfgarten
20m/2,030ft

CHILDCARE

Club 'Flocki'
t 0680 312 0010
Ages up to 30mnth

Monti's Kinderwelt (Bambinis)
t 5454
Ages 3 to 5

Ski school
From age 5

SNOWPIX.COM / CHRIS GILL

The SkiWelt's slopes are ideal for easy cruising but aren't usually this quiet. The Hohe Salve (pictured) has the steepest runs
↓

FOR FAMILIES ★★★☆☆
High and low options

At the base of the gondola, Hexenkinderland is a new supervised area for small kids based around a 'witches' theme and allows them to play while getting used to skis. Monti's Kinderwelt at the gondola mid-station takes children from age three and is well equipped with play areas and nursery slopes. Club Flocki is an option in the village.

STAYING THERE

Chalets Crystal and Inghams each have a chalet here.
Hotels There is a wide choice of simple gasthofs, pensions and B&Bs, plus better-quality hotel accommodation.
****Alpenpanorama** (5309) Far from lifts but with own bus stop; wonderful views; pleasant rooms.
****Bergland** (5454) Well placed between the village and lifts. Apartments as well as rooms. 'Lovely cooked breakfast.'
****Feldwebel** (5224) Central, recommended for food and value.
****Greil** (5289) Attractive, but out of the centre and far from the lifts. Indoor pool, five different saunas.
****Postwirt** (5081) A reader favourite – attractive, central, traditional, with stube; outdoor pool, sauna, steam.

***Eggerwirt** (5236) Between centre and main road, bus stop outside.
***Hexenalm** (5544) Close to the lifts, with a popular après-ski bar and spa.
Pension Sonnenhof (5160) 'Good-quality home cooking, spotlessly clean rooms, excellent staff.'
Apartments The central Aparthotel Schindlhaus has nice accommodation. Some of the best apartments in town are in the Bergland hotel.

EATING OUT ★★☆☆☆
A fair choice

Some of the best restaurants are in hotels – those in the Postwirt and the Feldwebel have been recommended by past reporters. The 'rustic' Dorf Stub'n offers traditional dishes and steaks – 'fantastic value meat fondue', says a 2014 visitor. Rossini is also recommended this year – 'excellent pizzeria'. Chicos is a Mexican.

APRES-SKI ★★★★☆
Still some very loud bars

Söll is not as raucous as it used to be, but it's still very lively and a lot of places have live music. At teatime bars such as Moonlight and Hexenalm, close to the gondola base, are lively. As is Salvenstadl (Cow Shed) on the edge of the village, recommended by a 2014 reporter. The Red Horse Pub is new and was also recommended this year ('great, lively, atmospheric bar').

Söll

Build your own shortlist: www.wheretoskiandsnowboard.com

UK PACKAGES

Crystal, Inghams, Neilson, Ski Line, Skitracer, STC, Thomson, Zenith **Hopfgarten** Contiki, Crystal, Erna Low, Rocketski, STC, Thomson **Westendorf** Crystal, Inghams, Interactive Resorts, STC, Thomson

ACTIVITIES

Indoor Swimming pool with sauna, solarium and massage; bowling, squash
Outdoor Natural ice rink (skating, curling), sleigh rides, 3km of floodlit toboggan runs, walks, dog sledding, snowshoeing, tubing, paragliding

GETTING THERE

Air Innsbruck 80km/ 50 miles (1hr); Salzburg 85km/ 55 miles (1hr30); Munich 145km/ 90 miles (2hr)
Rail Wörgl (13km/ 8 miles); Kufstein (13km/8 miles); bus to resort

Later on, the large, central Whisky-Mühle disco can get wild, especially after the bars close. The hotel Austria bar has been recommended by a past reporter. Rossini is good for cocktails and live music.

OFF THE SLOPES ★★☆☆☆
Toboggan runs the main attraction

There are two toboggan runs (4km and 3km) from the top of the gondola. Both are floodlit on Wednesday to Saturday, one until 10.30pm, the other until 2am. The large baroque church is worth a visit. Coach excursions go to Salzburg, Innsbruck and even Vipiteno, in Italy.

LINKED RESORT – 705m
ITTER

Itter is a tiny village half-way between Söll and Hopfgarten, with a gondola starting some way outside the village that goes up to mid-mountain. There's a hotel and half a dozen gasthofs and B&Bs. The school has a rental shop, and there are nursery slopes close to hand but few easy longer runs to progress to locally. Here, as elsewhere, the home run is red.

LINKED RESORT – 620m
HOPFGARTEN

Hopfgarten is an unspoiled, friendly, traditional resort set off the main Kitzbühel-Innsbruck road at the western extremity of the SkiWelt and with a two-stage gondola (largely queue-free, to judge by reports) from the village to the top of Hohe Salve.

When snow is good, the runs down to Hopfgarten are some of the best in the SkiWelt, but they get the damaging afternoon sun. There is a beginners' slope in the village, but it is sunny as well as low. Hopfgarten is one of the best cross-country bases in the area. There are fine trails to Kelchsau (7km) and the Itter-Bocking loop (15km) starts nearby.

Cheap and cheerful gasthofs, pensions and little private B&Bs are the norm, and most are within five minutes' walk of the gondola. Restaurants are mostly hotel-based, but there is a pizzeria. Après-ski is generally quiet. There's a reasonable range of off-slope activities, and trains run to Kitzbühel and Innsbruck (or Salzburg).

LINKED RESORT – 800m
BRIXEN IM THALE

Brixen im Thale spreads a long way along the valley running along the south side of the SkiWelt area. It is not particularly cute, but it is traditional in style and is pretty quiet now that it is bypassed by the main valley road. From the skiing point of view it has a great location, with lifts going up both sides of the valley. On the north side, a gondola goes to Hochbrixen and the main SkiWelt slopes; lifts diverge for Hohe Salve and Söll, or Astberg and Ellmau. In the opposite direction, a gondola goes up to Choralpe above Westendorf, which links to the slopes of Kitzbühel (via a short bus ride after a long blue run down). The local slopes suit confident intermediates best, on both sides of the valley. The nursery area is secluded, but a bus ride away.

There are plenty of hotels and pensions but not many restaurants – most are hotel-based. Après-ski is not a highlight though there are two or three bars by the gondola station. Brixen is on the same railway line as Hopfgarten.

Westendorf 800m

+ Pleasant, traditional village
+ Challenging local slopes
+ Good local beginner slopes but ...
- Local slopes not ideal territory for progression from the nursery slopes
- Getting to main SkiWelt takes time

Westendorf is a quiet, attractive village with good local slopes for confident intermediates; it is slightly off the main SkiWelt circuit, but has easy access to Kitzbühel's area – so it is an appealing base if you plan to spend time on both.

Village charm The village is small with traditional buildings, including an attractive onion-domed church. It has a relaxed, rustic atmosphere. The quite lively late-night scene can mean a bit of noise in the streets.
Convenience The centre is close to the nursery slopes, and a five-minute walk or free ski-bus ride from the main lift. There are also regular buses to the

Phone numbers
From elsewhere in Austria add the prefix 05358 (Wilder Kaiser), 05333 (Söll), 05332 (Hohe Salve), 05335 (Hopfgarten, Itter), 05334 (Brixen, Westendorf); from abroad use the prefix +43 and omit the initial '0'

TOURIST OFFICES

WILDER KAISER
(Söll, Scheffau, Going, Ellmau)
www.wilderkaiser.info

HOHE SALVE
(Hopfgarten, Itter)
www.hohe-salve.com

KITZBÜHELER ALPEN
(Brixen, Westendorf)
www.kitzbueheler-alpen.com

SKIWELT
www.skiwelt.at

lifts at Brixen, for quick access to the SkiWelt circuit.

Scenery The slopes here offer a bit more drama than some of the other hills nearby, and the views include the craggy Wilder Kaiser to the north.

THE MOUNTAIN

Westendorf's local slopes are separated by one valley from the main SkiWelt circuit to the north and by another valley from the Kitzbühel slopes to the east. There's a pleasant mix of open and wooded slopes.

Slopes A two-stage gondola goes to Talkaser, one of the four minor peaks that make up the local area. From there, you can head for Choralpe and Brixen (via a splendid 5.5km-long red run of over 1000m vertical), or for Fleiding and Gampenkogel. All the local peaks have short east- or west-facing runs. A longer blue run of around 800m vertical goes from Gampenkogel to the Kitzbühel connection (which involves a short shuttle-bus ride to the Pengelstein gondola at Skirast).

Fast lifts The two gondolas make for good access but once up the mountain there are still a lot of slow lifts on the local slopes.

Queues The only report of queues is '15 minutes one afternoon for the Choralm gondola'.

Terrain parks There's an excellent park with something for all levels including jumps, boxes, kickers and rails.

Snow reliability Not a strong point of the region, because of the low altitude. But snowmaking is extensive and grooming excellent.

Experts The pistes are among the most testing in the SkiWelt area (black 112 is one of the steepest around), and there is off-piste to be explored.

Intermediates Great for confident intermediates: nearly all Westendorf's terrain is genuinely red in gradient.

Beginners The village nursery slopes are extensive and excellent. There are a couple of genuine blues to progress to on the lower mountain, but further progression can be challenging.

Snowboarding Most lifts are chairs and gondolas, and the park is great. But some runs have tedious flat sections.

Cross-country There are lots of trails, but snow-cover is unreliable.

Mountain restaurants There are good table- and self-service places. On our most recent visit we particularly liked Ki-West – good location, atmosphere

and food. Alpenrosenhütte, Brechhornhaus and the Gassnerwirt are popular. Choralpe self-service is tipped by a 2014 reporter: 'Best views in SkiWelt, spacious, modern, huge portions.'

Schools and guides There are three schools: Westendorf ('Very good,' says a reporter), Top and Snow&Co.

Families Westendorf sells itself as a family resort. The ski school kindergartens take children from the age of three.

STAYING THERE

There are plentiful hotels and guest houses, both near the village centre and further afield.

Hotels 4-star places tipped by readers include the Jakobwirt (6245) – 'lovely food, great spa' – and Schermer (6268). Other past recommendations: the 3-star Post (6202) and the central Pension Elisabeth (8940). The small Glockenstuhl (6175) is a short walk away with a good spa. There are places out near the gondola.

Apartments The Schermerhof apartments are of good quality.

Eating out Most of the best restaurants are in hotels. The Wastlhof, Klinglers and Berggasthaus Stimmlach (a taxi ride out) are other possibilities.

Après-ski There are more lively spots than you might expect in a small, cute village. The Liftstüberl and Gerry's Inn are packed at close of play. The Kibo bar near the bottom of the nursery slopes is 'friendly' with 'a great atmosphere'. In's Moment (aka Campbell's Bar) in the basement of the Jakobwirt hotel is 'terrific', with Mr Campbell himself described as 'a very genial host'. The funky Moskito Cafe Bar has live music. Karat is a smart lounge bar.

Off the slopes There are excursions to Innsbruck and Salzburg, plus pretty walks and sleigh rides.

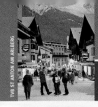

St Anton

If what you seek is dumps, bumps, boozing and bopping, there's nowhere quite like it – and with a neat Tirolean town as a bonus

RATINGS

The mountains

Extent	★★★
Fast lifts	★★★★
Queues	★★★
Terrain p'ks	★★★
Snow	★★★★
Expert	★★★★★
Intermediate	★★★
Beginner	★
Boarder	★★★★
X-country	★★
Restaurants	★★★
Schools	★★★
Families	★★★★

The resort

Charm	★★★★
Convenience	★★★
Scenery	★★★
Eating out	★★★★
Après-ski	★★★★★
Off-slope	★★

RPI   110

lift pass	£190
ski hire	£140
lessons	£115
food & drink	£135
total	**£580**

NEWS

2014/15: The three lifts at Pettneu are to reopen and will be covered by the Arlberg pass.

2013/14: The Tanzböden T-bar on Galzig was replaced by a six-pack.

Nearby Lech (covered by the lift pass) was linked by a new gondola to Warth, increasing the size of the Lech-Zürs ski area by over 50 per cent – read the Lech chapter.

+ Varied terrain for experts and adventurous intermediates

+ Heavy snowfalls, lots of snow-guns

+ Car-free village centre retains solid traditional charm

+ Very lively après-ski and nightlife

+ Improved lift system has cut queues from the base areas, but ...

− Some pistes dangerously crowded

− Slopes can be tough for near-beginners and timid intermediates

− Most tough runs are unpatrolled

− Snow quality can suffer from sun

− Resort sprawls, with long treks from some lodgings to key lifts and bars

− Centre can be noisy at night

St Anton is one of the world's best resorts for competent skiers and riders, particularly those with the energy to après-ski as hard as they ski. If you want to, you can party from 3pm to 3am. Good luck!

But the place doesn't suit everyone. If you are thinking of trying an Austrian change from a major French resort, or of going up a gear from Kitzbühel or Söll, be sure that you are not going to get thrown by blues that get heavily mogulled, reds that might be black and runs that are dangerously crowded. As we've been saying for years, the resort needs to create an alternative to the busy blue run down from its main mountain.

THE RESORT

St Anton is the western extremity of the Tirol, at the foot of the road up to the Arlberg pass. It is at one end of a lift network that spreads across to St Christoph and over the pass to Stuben. These two tiny villages are described at the end of the chapter.

The resort is a long, sprawling place, almost a town rather than a village, squeezed into a narrow valley. As it spreads east down the valley, it thins out before broadening again to form the suburb of Nasserein, and then the nominally distinct St Jakob. Development spreads west up the hill towards the Arlberg pass – first to Oberdorf, then Gastig, 10 minutes' walk from the centre.

The ski pass covers Lech, Zürs and Warth – now linked to Lech – and the Sonnenkopf area above Klösterle. The nearby resorts can be reached by bus, but the service is rubbish.

There are free and regular ski-buses linking Alpe Rauz (on the edge of St Anton's slopes) with Zürs and Lech. And there are post buses from St Anton to Lech via St Christoph and Zürs. But all get seriously crowded at busy times, leaving people at the roadside to use the waiting taxis. And the post buses are neither free nor frequent. It's not good enough.

Klösterle can be reached by free ski-buses from Stuben. Serfaus, Ischgl and Sölden are feasible outings by car.

VILLAGE CHARM ★★★★
Traditional but lively

Although it is commercialized and busy, St Anton is full of character, its traffic-free main street lined by traditional-style buildings. It is a bustling place, day and night. Its shops meet everyday needs well – a well-stocked Spar, for example, and an excellent bookshop that sells good numbers of this book every year.

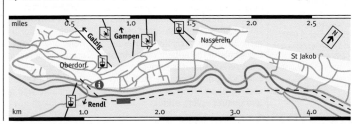

ST. ANTON & BEYOND!

TAILOR-MADE OR ACCOMMODATION ONLY SPECIALISTS

01502 471960

info@mountainbeds.com
www.mountainbeds.com

KEY FACTS

Resort	1305m
	4,280ft

Arlberg region	
Slopes	1075-2650m
	3,530-8,690ft
Lifts	97
Slopes*	340km
	211 miles
Blue	42%
Red	42%
Black	16%
Snowmaking	56%

St Anton, St Christoph and Stuben	
Slopes	1305-2650m
	4,280-8,690ft
Lifts	38
Slopes*	120km
	75 miles
Blue	45%
Red	35%
Black	20%
Snowmaking	86%
* pistes and ski routes	

LIFT PASSES

Arlberg

Prices in €

Age	1-day	6-day
under 16	29	141
16 to 19	44	204
20 to 64	48	235
65 plus	44	204
Free	No one; day pass €10 if under 8, €21 if over 75	
Beginner	Points ticket	

Notes Covers St Anton, St Christoph, Stuben, Lech, Zürs and Warth, and linking bus; also Sonnenkopf (9 lifts) at Klösterle, 7km west of Stuben and Pettneu (3 lifts) just east of St Anton; single ascent, part-day and pedestrian options

CONVENIENCE ★★★☆☆
Not bad for a large resort

The hub of the resort is at the western end of the main street, close to the base stations of the lifts to Gampen (a fast quad chair), to Galzig and to Rendl (modern gondolas). Staying on or close to this main street is ideal to keep treks to the lifts short.

Nasserein has an eight-seater gondola up to Gampen, and makes an appealing base for a quiet time. The nightlife action is a short bus ride or 15-minute walk away. Staying between the centre and Nasserein, you can use the Fang chairlift to get to other lifts.

SCENERY ★★★☆☆
Head for the Valluga

St Anton squeezes into a narrow, partly wooded valley. The scenery becomes more impressive as you ride up the lifts, either towards the dramatic Valluga, or across the valley up to Rendl, which opens up a splendid panorama.

THE MOUNTAINS

The main slopes are essentially open: only the lower Gampen runs and the run from Rendl to the valley offer much shelter from bad weather.

St Anton vies with Val d'Isère for the title of 'resort with most underclassified slopes'. Many blue and reds seem tough for their colour. Paradoxically, none of the blacks is seriously steep; this is because the toughest runs are called 'ski routes'. The piste map says these are marked and avalanche controlled but not groomed or patrolled. We applaud the clear explanation (lacking in many resorts), but many of these are popular runs that are treated just like pistes, and they should be patrolled pistes. To add to the confusion, some of the routes are groomed.

At Lech, Zürs and Warth (but no longer at St Anton) the piste map also marks 'high-Alpine touring runs'. These are simply off-piste runs that do not appear on the map at all in most resorts – don't go without a guide.

The piste map is designed more for marketing than navigation, covering the whole of the Arlberg region in one view. As a result, it is unclear and misleading in places. The local TV channel shows the state of the pistes and queues – very useful.

EXTENT OF THE SLOPES ★★★☆☆
Don't ignore Stuben and Rendl

St Anton's slopes fall into four main sectors, three of them linked. The major sector is that beneath the local high spot, the **Valluga**, accessed by the jumbo gondola to Galzig, then a cable car to Vallugagrat. The tiny top stage of the cable car to the Valluga summit is for sightseeing and people with a guide heading for the tricky off-piste run to Zürs. Vallugagrat gives access to St Anton's famous high, sunny bowls, and to the long, beautiful red/blue run to Alpe Rauz.

From here there's a six-pack, Valfagehr, to return, or you can go on to explore the rather neglected slopes of **Stuben**. The shady slow old chair from the village can be a cold ride, but blankets are available. The reward is north-facing slopes that hold powder well and some deserted off-piste. The run to Alpe Rauz and the high Valluga runs can also be accessed by riding the Schindlergrat fast triple chair, though some also involve a hike. Other runs from Galzig go to St Christoph and into the Steissbachtal.

Beyond this valley, with lift and piste links in both directions, is the **Kapall-Gampen** sector, reachable by chairlift from central St Anton or gondola from Nasserein. From Gampen at mid-mountain, pistes lead back to St Anton and Nasserein. Or you can ride a six-pack on up to Kapall to ski the treeless upper mountain.

Rendl is a separate mountain, reached by a gondola from the centre of town. A handful of lifts serve the west-facing upper runs, and there's a good north-facing piste to the valley – the place to go in bad weather.

FAST LIFTS ★★★★☆
Fast access, patchy higher up

Access from the village is by smart gondolas or fast chairs. But while the Gampen and Galzig sectors have a lot of fast chairs higher up, Rendl and Stuben still have a lot of slow ones.

QUEUES ★★★☆☆
Much improved, but ...

Queues are not the problem they once were, and reporters have had few problems in recent years. But there can be queues for key lifts, including the Valluga cable car from Galzig ('15-minute wait seemed the norm,' said a March 2013 report), the alternative Schindlergrat chair to

HOTEL MAIENSEE

FAR AWAY FROM EVERYDAY

6580 ST. CHRISTOPH AM ARLBERG · AUSTRIA
+43(0) 5446 2804 · STAY@MAIENSEE.COM

WWW.MAIENSEE.COM

Ski Total

ARE HERE IN
St Anton

▶ **Quality chalets**
▶ **Top locations**
▶ **Excellent value**
▶ **17 more resorts**

skitotal.com
01483 791 933

Schindler Spitze, the Zammermoos chair out of the Steissbachtal, and the gondola from Nasserein first thing.

But more of a worry than queues are the crowded pistes – the blues you take to get home from the upper mountain are often dangerously crowded, and the problems are compounded by recklessly fast skiers and by moguls on the lower parts.

TERRAIN PARKS ★★★★★
Small, but perfectly formed
The 320m-long Stanton park on Rendl, just below the top of the gondola, is pretty good – a jib line, intermediate and pro lines, beginner area, all including jumps, kickers, boxes and rails, plus fun-cross for the kids, chill area and daily maintenance.

SNOW RELIABILITY ★★★★★
Generally very good cover
If the weather is coming from the west or north-west (as it often is), the Arlberg region gets it first, and as a

result St Anton gets heavy falls of snow – and neighbouring Lech, Zürs and Warth get even more. These resorts often have much better conditions than other resorts of a similar height, and we've had great fresh powder here as late as mid-April. But many slopes face south or south-east, causing icy or heavy conditions at times. As spring approaches, in particular, it's vital to time descents of the steeper runs off the Valluga to get decent conditions. The lower runs are well equipped with snowmaking, which generally ensures the home runs remain open. Grooming is good.

FOR EXPERTS ★★★★★
One of the world's great areas
St Anton vies with Chamonix, Val d'Isère and a handful of other resorts for the affections of experts. There are countless opportunities for going off-piste; read the feature panel for some of them. The runs in the huge bowls below the Valluga are justifiably world-

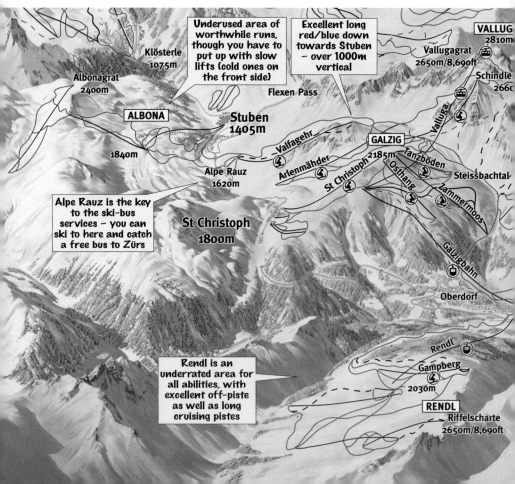

Underused area of worthwhile runs, though you have to put up with slow lifts (cold ones on the front side)

Excellent long red/blue down towards Stuben – over 1000m vertical

VALLUG 2810m

Klösterle 1075m

Vallugagrat 2650m/8,690ft

Albonagrat 2400m

Schindle 2660

Flexen Pass

ALBONA

Stuben 1405m

Valfagehr

GALZIG

Valluga

Arlenmähder 2185m

Tanzböden

Alpe Rauz 1620m

St Christoph

Osthang

Steissbachtal

Zammermoos

Alpe Rauz is the key to the ski-bus services – you can ski to here and catch a free bus to Zürs

St Christoph 1800m

Galzigbahn

Oberdorf

Rendl

Gampberg 2030m

Rendl is an underrated area for all abilities, with excellent off-piste as well as long cruising pistes

RENDL
Riffelscharte 2650m/8,690ft

GETTING THERE

Air Innsbruck 95km/ 60 miles (1hr15); Friedrichshafen 130km/80 miles (1hr45); Zürich 195km/120 miles (2hr15); Munich 225km/140 miles (3hr30)

Rail Main-line station in resort

ST ANTON
CHOOSE FROM 144 CATERED CHALETS, APARTMENTS & HOTELS

Skiline.co.uk

CALL US ON 020 8313 3999

ALPINE ANSWERS
The UK's No.1 Chalet Specialist

For choice and service look no further!

alpineanswers.co.uk
call: 020 7801 1080

ABTA

famous, and immediately after a fresh snowfall you can see tracks going all over the mountain; there are ski routes in the bowls too. Lower down, there are challenging runs in many directions from both Galzig and Kapall-Gampen. These lower runs can be seriously affected by the sun.

Don't overlook the Rendl area, which has plenty of open space served by the top lifts, and several quite challenging runs. This is a great area for a mixed group and usually quieter than the main sector. The Sonnenkopf area, down-valley from Stuben, is even quieter and has several ski routes – and more serious off-piste, including an 'excellent' route to Langen. Read the Stuben section, too.

FOR INTERMEDIATES ★★★☆☆
Some real challenges
St Anton is well suited to good, adventurous intermediates. As well as

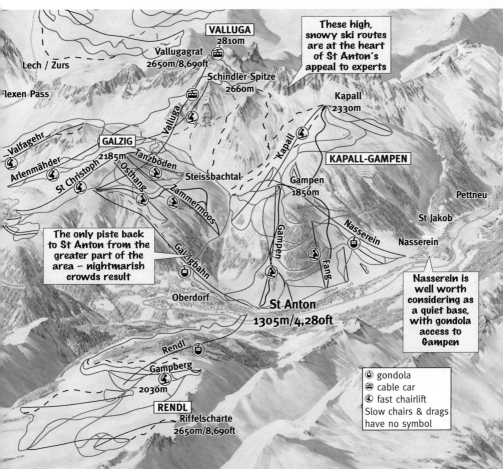

VALLUGA
2810m

Vallugagrat
2650m/8,690ft

These high, snowy ski routes are at the heart of St Anton's appeal to experts

Schindler-Spitze
2660m

Lech / Zurs

Flexen Pass

Valluga

Kapall
2330m

Valfagehr

Arlenmähder

GALZIG
2185m

St Christoph

Tanzböden

Osthang

Zammermoos

Steissbachtal

Kapall

KAPALL-GAMPEN

Gampen
1850m

Pettneu

St Jakob

Nasserein

Nasserein

The only piste back to St Anton from the greater part of the area – nightmarish crowds result

Galzigbahn

Gampen

Fang

Oberdorf

St Anton
1305m/4,28oft

Nasserein is well worth considering as a quiet base, with gondola access to Gampen

Rendl

Gampberg
2030m

RENDL
Riffelscharte
2650m/8,690ft

☉ gondola
☺ cable car
☒ fast chairlift
Slow chairs & drags have no symbol

The Arlberg region has lots of very varied off-piste. Here are just a few of the huge number of possibilities you could explore with a guide.

Runs from Rendl
An easy first venture away from the pistes is to go beyond the furthest lift to the rolling powder bowls of Rossfall. More serious routes take you well away from all lifts. The North Face, accessed from the Gampberg chair, offers challenging terrain for a confident off-piste skier. The Riffel chairlifts access the imposing Hinter Rendl – a gigantic bowl with a huge descent to St Anton, often in deep powder. A variant involves a climb to Rendl Scharte and a testing descent with sections of 35° to Pettneu.

Runs from Albona, above Stuben
Stuben's outstanding terrain is suited to the more experienced off-piste skier. The open treelines of the Langen forest, where the powder is regularly knee to waist deep, provide fabulous tree skiing. A 30-minute climb from Albonagrat to Maroikopfe opens up runs westwards down undulating open slopes to Langen, or eastwards down steep 40° slopes to Verwalltal ending at an old hunting lodge.

Runs from the Valluga
The runs from the summit cable car of the Valluga will make your pulse race as you trace a steep line between cliff bands in the breathtaking scenery of the Pazieltal, leading down to Zürs. Here, at the top of the Madloch chairlift and after a short climb, you can be roped down into the steep Valhalla Couloir, accessing 1200m vertical of open slopes ending at Zug, near Lech.

SKIWORLD

Catered chalets, hotels and self catering apartments in

Europe, USA and Canada

skiworld.co.uk

08444 930 430

ABTA V2151 ATOL 2036

MOMENTUM SKI

Weekend & a la carte ski holiday specialists

100% Tailor-made

Premier hotels & apartments

Flexible travel arrangements

020 7371 9111

WWW.MOMENTUMSKI.COM

lots of testing pistes, they will be able to try some of the ski routes in the Valluga bowls. The run from Schindler Spitze to Alpe Rauz is very long (over 1000m vertical), varied and ideal for good intermediates. Alternatively, turn off from this part-way down and take the Steissbachtal to the lifts back to Galzig or Gampen. The Kapall-Gampen section is also interesting, with sporty bumps among trees on the lower half. Good intermediates may enjoy the men's downhill run from the top of this sector to the town.

Timid intermediates will find St Anton less to their taste. There are few easy cruising pistes; most blue runs here would be red in most other resorts, and get bumpy, especially if there is fresh snow (the blue 1 home run often has testing moguls at the end of the day). The gentlest cruisers are the short blues on Galzig and the Steissbachtal – we skied the latter in the early morning last season, and enjoyed it for the first time ever – but they get extremely crowded and unpleasant in the afternoon. The blue from Kapall to Gampen is wide and cruisy.

The underrated Rendl area has a variety of trails suitable for good and moderate intermediates, including the excellent long blues served by the slow chairlifts on skier's left, Riffel 1 and Salzböden. The long wooded run to the valley (over 1000m vertical from the top) is much the best run in the St Anton area when visibility is poor.

FOR BEGINNERS ★✶✶✶✶
Far from ideal
The best bet for beginners is to start at Nasserein, where the nursery slope is less steep than the one close to the main lifts. There are further slopes up at Gampen and a short, gentle blue run at Rendl, served by an easy draglift. But there are no other easy, uncrowded runs for beginners to progress to. A mixed party including novices would be better off based in Lech or Zürs.

FOR BOARDERS ★★★★✶
Freeriding heaven
For many, St Anton is the Mecca of Austrian freeriding and expert boarders flock here. The terrain is far from ideal for beginners, but there are few T-bars to contend with.

FOR CROSS-COUNTRY ★★✶✶✶
A decent amount
There are 40km of easy/medium trails, and snow conditions are usually good.

MOUNTAIN RESTAURANTS ★★★✶✶
Adequate options
There are plenty of restaurants, and some of them are excellent. Most but not all are marked on the piste map, and named in ridiculously minute type. **Editors' choice** We often lunch at the atmospheric Hospiz Alm (3625) on the fringe of St Christoph, famed for its slide down to the toilets as well as its satisfying table-service food and amazing wine cellar. Service gets

SCHOOLS

Arlberg
t 3411

St Anton
t 3563

Alpine Faszination
t 0676 630 2136

St Anton Classic
t 3311

Classes (Arlberg prices) 6 days (2hr am and 2hr pm) €257

Private lessons
€174 for 2hr; each additional person €20

GUIDES

Piste to Powder
t 0664 174 6282

TVB ST ANTON AM ARLBERG / JOSEF MALLAUN

There's lots of easy off-piste (and some less easy) on the sunny slopes above St Christoph ↓

stretched at times, and it can be expensive. Recent visitors approve: 'unforgettable', 'open fire, friendly service, king prawns simply excellent'. Rodelalm (30188) is not marked on the piste map, but is on skier's far left of the Gampen slopes (reachable on blue run 24). It has a lovely beamed interior, and we have had good traditional food here; the rotisserie chicken is 'terrific', too.

Worth knowing about Verwallstube on Galzig is in a class of its own – an expensive table-service place with splendid views. We've had seriously good lunches here a couple of times. Up at 2650m, the 'small and cosy' Valluga View of course has great views as well as 'simple but good-value food'. On the way to Stuben, Ulmer Hütte has a 'fantastic queuing system for a small choice of quick snacks'.

At the top of Kapall the 'rustic' self-service is tipped for 'great views and tasty, piping hot gulaschsuppe'.

On Rendl, the spacious Rendl restaurant is about as good as self-service gets – we've had good stir fry cooked to order, and a 2014 visitor had 'hot and tasty food from the grill'. The terrace (aka Rendl Beach) has great views of the terrain park action. On the valley run there is good table-service food in the cosy Bifang-Alm.

At Stuben the Albona Bergrestaurant at the very top is a simple hut serving simple food. Lower down, the Albona self-service place gets packed, even on a quiet day, but serves 'good food'. Recommended options in the village are Willi's Pilsstüble (pizza, ribs) or the Post hotel ('really good Wiener schnitzl' and 'good value and service').

SCHOOLS AND GUIDES ★★★☆☆
Good reports

The St Anton and the Arlberg schools are under the same ownership but operate separately. Recent reports have been positive, and a reporter had an 'excellent private lesson with a patient and careful instructor'. Piste to Powder is a specialist off-piste outfit run by British guide Graham Austick. We get good reports – a 2013 visitor said, 'They are part of the reason I keep going back' – but also remarks on their high prices. St Anton Classic is a private instruction/guiding outfit. A 2014 visitor had a 'very good local guide' from Arlberg Alpin at Stuben.

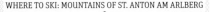

WHERE TO EAT & SLEEP WELL:

DAS SONNBICHL
GENUSSHOTEL · ST. ANTON AM ARLBERG

6580 St. Anton am Arlberg
St. Jakober Dorfstraße 11
www.sonnbichl.cc

DER STEINBOCK
DIE URIGE PENSION IN ST. ANTON AM ARLBERG

6580 St. Anton am Arlberg
St. Jakober Dorfstraße 13
www.dersteinbock.at

Build your own shortlist: www.wheretoskiandsnowboard.com

ESPRIT
FOR FAMILIES IN
St Anton

Family Ski
Chalets
Dedicated
Nurseries
Exclusive Ski
Classes
12 More Resorts

espritski.com
01483 791 900

UK PACKAGES

Alpine Answers, Alpine Elements, Alpine Weekends, Bramble Ski, Carrier, Crystal, Crystal Finest, Elegant Resorts, Erna Low, Esprit, Flexiski, Friendship Travel, Igoski, Inghams, Interactive Resorts, Kaluma, Mark Warner, Momentum, Mountain Beds, Neilson, Oxford Ski Co, Powder White, Scott Dunn, Ski Bespoke, Ski Club Freshtracks, Ski Expectations, Ski Independence, Ski Safari, Ski Total, Ski-Val, Skitracer, Skiweekends.com, Skiworld, Snow Finders, Snow-wise, Snoworks, Snowscape, STC, Supertravel, Thomson, VIP, White Roc
Stuben Alpine Answers, Kaluma, STC
St Christoph Alpine Answers, Carrier, Flexiski, Inghams, Jeffersons, Kaluma, Momentum, Powder Byrne, Scott Dunn, Ski Bespoke, Ski Line, STC

FOR FAMILIES ★★★★
Nasserein 'ideal'

The youth centre attached to the Arlberg school is excellent, and the special slopes both for toddlers (at the bottom) and bigger children (at Gampen) are well done. Children's instruction is reportedly very good. At Nasserein there is a moving carpet on the baby slope. There's also a good children's area by the Gampen fast quad. Nasserein makes a good base, and family chalet specialist Esprit has its own facilities here.

STAYING THERE

There's a wide range of places to stay, from quality hotels to cheap and cheerful pensions and apartments, and a good choice of chalets.

Chalets This is by a wide margin Austria's catered chalet capital. Ski Total has a dozen places ranging from 6 to 24 beds, including four smart custom-built places in one building in Nasserein, with wellness areas; Supertravel has eight smart-looking places, including three apartments newly built for last season that share an outdoor pool, sauna and steam room; Skiworld has 12 places including the flagship Monte Vera, with huge bedrooms, sauna and infra-red room; Crystal has half a dozen properties, including the cool 32-bed Inge; Inghams has seven, including four cool places in a stylish new building in the Gastig area, with shared spa and pool; in Nasserein family specialist Esprit has chalets of all sizes, including a big, smart place next to the gondola.

Hotels There are dozens of 4- and 3-star places, and a couple of 5-stars.
★★★★Bergschlössl (2220) Charming 10-room B&B right by lifts. 'Beautifully furnished, excellent value.'
★★★★Fahrner (22360) Up the hill. 'Unpretentious, clean rooms, friendly, first-rate food, good wine cellar.'
★★★★Pepi's Skihotel (283060) Stylish, modern B&B right by the Rendl lift.
★★★★Post (22130) Ancient place bang in the centre, with good spa and pool.
★★★★Schwarzer Adler (22440) Centuries-old inn on main street. Varying bedrooms. Nice pool.
★★★Nassereinerhof (3366) Close to the Nasserein gondola; sauna, steam.'
★★★Sonnbichl (2243) In a quiet residential area on the eastern fringe of Nasserein, right next to ski-bus stop; sauna, solarium.

★★Steffeler (2872) Central B&B. Simple but welcoming; good breakfasts.
Steinbock (2577) Simple B&B next to Sonnbichl (same owners) and similarly convenient for the ski-bus.
Apartments There are plenty available, but few package deals. Past tips include the Bachmann apartments in Nasserein and Haus Rali at the western end of St Anton.

EATING OUT ★★★★
Some excellent spots

There's a lot of half-board lodging in St Anton, so the restaurant scene is not huge. Our standard port of call for a drink or two and a relaxed meal is the cool Hazienda – a basement place in the main street, with a wide-ranging menu. For more of a blowout, it's up the hill to the village museum's restaurant – excellent, sophisticated food served in elegant panelled rooms. Reader tips: Underground on the Piste ('great steaks, great music' and 'cosy and atmospheric'), Fuhrmannstube ('lovely traditional food, friendly service; you share tables'), Skiing Buddha ('excellent Thai food, very good service'), Pomodoro ('tasty pizzas'), Fahrnerstube up the hill in Oberdorf ('pretty decor, good hearty food'), and Tenne ('good Austrian food') and Dolce Vita ('pizzas hit the spot, attentive service'), both in Nasserein

APRES-SKI ★★★★★
Throbbing till late

St Anton's bars rock from mid-afternoon until the early hours. And as our indefatigable bar specialist Keith points out this year, 'there is plenty of variety, whether you're 16 or 60'.

It all starts in a collection of bars on the lower slopes. Heustadl is the first you come to, and still the place for 'great German cover bands' on the terrace; cosy inside. Next is Sennhütte, also with 'a lovely traditional atmosphere'. A bit lower, the formerly scruffy Krazy Kanguruh has had a complete makeover; it is now quite stylish inside, and its enlarged terrace gets packed. Next door Taps has also been smartened up and extended – whereas the famous Mooserwirt, down the hill a bit, struck us last season as a bit tired. Griabli, opposite, is quieter; we enjoyed a live band there. All this is followed by a slide down the piste, possibly in the dark.

The bars in town are in full swing

CHILDCARE

Kindergartens (run by ski schools)
t 2526 / 3563
From age 30mnth;
must be toilet trained

Ski schools
From age 5

ACTIVITIES

Indoor Swimming pool, sauna, massage, fitness centre, sports centre (tennis, squash, climbing), bowling, museum, library

Outdoor Cleared walking paths, natural ice rink (skating, curling), sleigh rides, snowshoeing, tobogganing, climbing, paragliding

BOOKSHOP

Bookshop (Anton Eiter)
Dorfstrasse 28
6580 St Anton
t +43 676 5859 152
On the main street and stocks this guidebook

Phone numbers
From elsewhere in Austria add the prefix 05446 (St Anton and St Christoph), 05582 (Stuben); from abroad use the prefix +43 and omit the initial '0'

TOURIST OFFICES

St Anton
www.stantonamarlberg.com
St Christoph
www.tiscover.com/st.christoph
Stuben
www.stuben.com

by 4pm, too. The open-terrace Base Camp at the lift base can be 'a lot of fun' and 'attracts a mixed crowd and ski instructors'. Back up the piste slightly, Underground on the Piste is an institution, run by the eccentric Joan; 'quite small but very cosy and atmospheric', 'great party, live band'. Galzig Bistro, between the main lift stations, is a cool modern place we like for a drink and snack.

In the main street, the Bodega is good for pre-dinner drinks and tapas. The pubby Piccadilly is rated by Keith as 'the most animated après bar in town', with 'good entertainment, good music and efficient staff'. It gets a second wind later on, at which point Keith favours Bar Cuba ('crammed but a good atmosphere') and Alibi – 'convivial mix of locals and visitors'.

OFF THE SLOPES ★★★★★
Some entertainment
We and reporters love the excellent, but pricey Arlberg-well.com, a leisure centre with great indoor and outdoor pools and lots of spa options. A separate sports centre has an indoor climbing wall and outdoor ice climbing. It's not a place for indulgent shopping. It's easy to visit Innsbruck by train. Some of the better mountain huts are accessible by lift or bus. There are 70km of walking trails, although a 2014 reporters says signposting was patchy.

LINKED RESORT – 1800m
ST CHRISTOPH
St Christoph is a small collection of smart hotels, restaurants and bars just down from the summit of the Arlberg pass. It does not pretend to be a village – the Arlberg pass road has no pavements, and there are only sports shops. Hospiz Alm (read 'Mountain restaurants') gets some business at

après time, and is open for dinner, but is much more pricey than at lunch.

The key attractions of the place are queue-free lifts in the morning, and a crowd-free home piste with good snow at the end of the day. There are decent beginner slopes served by draglifts and a fast quad chairlift to the heart of St Anton's slopes at Galzig, but the blue back down is not an easy run to progress to. You can't miss the huge 5-star Arlberg-Hospiz (2611). More attractive to us is the warmly welcoming 4-star Maiensee (2804), right by the chairlift, with health and spa facilities and treatments. Last season we enjoyed a stay at Inghams' flagship chalet hotel here – ski-in/ski-out, with good-sized pool and sauna. The public areas were looking tired, but the bedrooms were fine and the food was superb – the best we've had in a chalet in a very long time. 'Great value,' too, a reader points out.

Post buses to and from St Anton are free unless you offer the driver money, but not free to Zürs and Lech.

LINKED RESORT – 1405m
STUBEN
Stuben is linked by lift and piste over the Arlberg pass to St Anton. It's a tiny, unspoiled village with an old church and a few hotels, bars and shops. Heavy snowfalls often add to the charm factor.

Stuben has sunny nursery slopes separate from the main slopes, but a lack of easy runs to progress to makes it unsuitable for beginners – less suitable than St Anton, even. We've had good reports of the school.

Evenings are quiet, but several places have a pleasant atmosphere. The charming old Post (761) and Albona (712) are very comfortable. The Hubertushof (7710) is 'welcoming, efficient; excellent food and facilities'.

Stubai valley

Austria's biggest glacier area, they say, and certainly one of the best; down the valley, a string of appealing village bases

TOP 10 RATINGS

Extent	★★★
Fast lifts	★★★
Queues	★★★
Snow	★★★★★
Expert	★★★
Intermediate	★★★
Beginner	★★
Charm	★★★★
Convenience	★★
Scenery	★★★★

RPI   100

lift pass	£180
ski hire	£115
lessons	£95
food & drink	£120
total	**£510**

KEY FACTS

Resorts	935-1000m
	3,070-3,280ft
Slopes	935-3210m
	3,070-10,530ft
Lifts	46
Pistes	104km
	65 miles
Blue	40%
Red	31%
Black	29%
Snowmaking	87%

➕ High, snow-sure glacier slopes plus lower bad-weather options

➕ Quiet, pretty Tirolean villages

➖ A lot of shuttling up and down the valley to and from the glacier

➖ Few challenging pistes

The Stubaier Gletscher ranks alongside Hintertux as one of the most extensive and rewarding glacier ski areas in the Alps. Neustift is the nearest major village, 20km away. But another 5km down valley, livelier Fulpmes is at the base of the Stubaital's best low-altitude area, Schlick 2000.

The 30km-long Stubai valley lies a short drive south of Innsbruck (there's also an antique tram to Fulpmes). The glacier is of course at the head of the valley. There is simple accommodation to be had in hamlets like Falbeson (10km from the glacier) or Krössbach (15km). But there are three bigger villages – Neustift, Fulpmes and Mieders – their own wooded ski areas, covered along with the glacier (and linking buses) by the Stubai Super Skipass. These resorts, described in this chapter, amount to a sizeable area of mostly intermediate terrain. All have impressive toboggan runs – the valley has 11 in total.

The glacier offers an extensive area of runs between 3200m and 2300m. In the wake of the Schrahe report (read our feature on piste extent) the lift company now publishes a realistic total of 75km of pistes plus 29km of ski routes, making our total of 104km. But note that ski routes are 'only with

ski instructor or Alpine experience' (says the piste map in German), which goes against the general rule.

Two gondolas go up from the huge car park at Mutterberg to a mid-station at Fernau, and then to the two mid-mountain stations of Eisgrat and Gamsgarten. A third gondola from Eisgrat goes to the top of the slopes. Elsewhere, there is a mix of ancient and modern chairlifts and the usual glacier drag lifts.

The slopes are broken up by rocky peaks giving more sense of variety than is normal on a glacier. There are lots of fabulous long blue and red cruising runs. The two shorter black pistes are very much at the easy end of the spectrum. The much longer Daunhill black (1.8km, 600m vertical) that opened a couple of years back is said to have a maximum gradient of 31°, so it's steeper; with its own private fast quad, it could be heavenly to do laps on. Much the toughest is the 4km Fernau-Mauer at the eastern extremity of the area – after the gentlest and widest of starts this drops steeply towards the Fernau mid-station. There is also a lovely 10km ski route (Wilde Grub'n) from Gamsgarten to the valley – start with a cruise from the top of the glacier for a total of 1450m vertical. And there's proper off-piste to be explored – there's a special map with 11 freeride runs shown (and described in German).

There are good beginner slopes at Eisgrat and Gamsgarten, where there is also a major children's area with childcare. Higher up there is a family fun slope, being extended this year.

The area is popular with snowboarders. There are lots of natural hits and kickers across the mountain, and a big terrain park at the top of the area which this year is getting an additional rope tow.

188

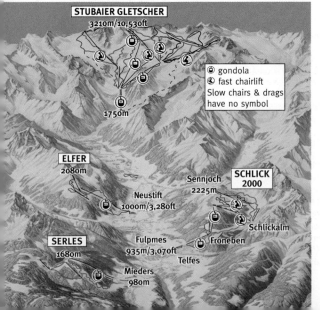

STUBAIER GLETSCHER
3210m/10,530ft

1750m

🚠 gondola
🚡 fast chairlift
Slow chairs & drags have no symbol

ELFER
2080m

SCHLICK 2000

Sennjoch
2225m

Neustift
1000m/3,28oft

SERLES
1680m

Fulpmes
935m/3,070ft

Froneben

Schlickalm

Telfes

Mieders
980m

↑ Gamsgarten is the major gathering point on the glacier, with lots of amenities
TVB STUBAI TIROL

NEWS

2014/15: An extra lift – a rope tow – is to be built to serve the easier lines of the snow park at the top of the glacier area. The family fun slope on the Eisjochferner run will be extended.

2013/14: On the glacier, the buildings at Gamsgarten were revamped, with an extended restaurant, terrace, and new sports shop. At Schlick 2000 the Zirmachbahn six-pack replaced the Zirmach draglifts to the top of Sennjoch; there are three new pistes, two blacks and a blue.

UK PACKAGES

Neustift Crystal, Crystal Finest, Momentum, Snowscape, STC, Thomson, Zenith
Fulpmes Crystal, Snowscape, Thomson

Phone numbers
From elsewhere in Austria add the prefix 05226; from abroad use the prefix +43 5226

TOURIST OFFICE

www.stubai.at

Queues are not a serious problem. The access gondolas and Eisjoch six-pack can get busy at weekends.

Gamsgarten has a huge self-service place, and excellent food in the table-service Zur Goldenen Gams. Eisgrat has a cool building including a serious table-service section, Schaufelspitz. Both areas have picnic rooms. At Jochdohle, Austria's highest restaurant (3150m) gives good views. Dresdner Hütte is a proper climbing refuge.

Après-ski starts up the mountain in the lively Gamsgarten bar and Ice Cube bar at Fernau.

935m

FULPMES

Fulpmes (with its satellite village of Telfes) sits at the foot of Schlick 2000, the most extensive of the lower ski areas. It is an attractive, sizeable working village not dominated by skiing. The glacier is 25km away.
Uphill from the village a two-stage gondola takes you to Kreuzjoch (2135m), opening up excellent views across the Stubaital and across the Schlick slopes to the dramatic Kalkkogel range. Most of the skiing is below the top gondola station – essentially a single open slope centred on a quad chair rising 580m, plus a six-pack serving shorter runs on skier's left. It is north-facing, so keeps snow well, and grooming is good. There are about five different pistes down, mostly of red difficulty (though partly labelled black) with some easier blue options. There is also a ski route – challenging at the best of times, very much so if snow is poor. And there is a fair amount of off-piste – 'relatively safe', notes a regular.

Below the main slopes is a long easy run-out to the gondola mid-station at Froneben (1365m). This is the location of the nursery slopes,

including Big Ron's Kinderland, with moving carpets and fun features, and a couple of thumping après-ski bars. The blue run winding through woods to the village from here is good fun or tricky, depending on conditions. There is a terrain park. Queues are rare but the gondola gets busy at peak times.

There are some good huts, with table-service options at the top of the gondola and at Zirmachalm ('great gulaschsuppe'). You can be towed by snowcat to Galtalm, in woods below Kreuzjoch, for 'great food and views'.

There's a good choice of 3- and 4-star hotels, most with pools and spa facilities. The 4-star Stubaierhof (62266) is central. Café Dorfkrug has 'good quality food, friendly service'.

The nearest leisure centre is in Neustift, but Fulpmes has ice skating, snowshoeing and toboganing.

1000m

NEUSTIFT

Neustift is the major village closest to the glacier, 20km away. It's an attractive, traditional Tirolean village, with limited local slopes at Elfer.
The slopes at Elfer consist of a narrow chain of runs and lifts from Elferhütte at 2080m down to the village. The pistes are all red, and it is a quiet place for intermediates to practise. This area is north-east-facing; there is a sunny nursery slope at village level and some 40km of cross-country trails.

There is a big 5-star Relais & Châteaux hotel, and lots of 4-stars and 3-stars spread around the area. In the outlying hamlet of Neder, the glacier lift company runs the family-oriented 4-star Happy Stubai (2611).

Nightlife is focused on the Dorf and Bierfassl bars and the Nachtkastl and Scala Club discos. Most restaurants are hotel-based. The big leisure centre has two pools, saunas and bowling.

Stubai valley

Build your own shortlist: www.wheretoskiandsnowboard.com

Zell am See

A real one-off, this: a summer resort town in a lovely lakeside setting, with varied local slopes and an excellent glacier nearby

TOP 10 RATINGS

Extent	★★
Fast lifts	★★★★
Queues	★★★
Snow	★★
Expert	★★
Intermediate	★★★
Beginner	★★★
Charm	★★★★
Convenience	★★★
Scenery	★★★

RPI	100
lift pass	£190
ski hire	£95
lessons	£105
food & drink	£115
total	**£505**

ZELL AM SEE-KAPRUN

Zell and the Areitalm slopes seen from across the frozen lake; the faraway pointy peak is Kaprun's Kitzsteinhorn ↓

+ Varied, wooded slopes with fine views down to the lake

+ Charming summer resort town with lots to do off the slopes

+ Excellent glacier nearby (on the lift pass) on Kaprun's Kitzsteinhorn

− Sunny, low-altitude slopes

− Limited local slopes, especially when snow low down is poor

− Some hotels are distant from the lifts; buses can be crowded

Like St Moritz, Zell is a town beside a lake (frozen if you're lucky). The similarities end there; but Zell is a towny resort that makes a refreshing change from the Austrian norm of rustic chalet-style villages. From the skiing point of view, the appeal is greatly strengthened by having Kaprun's excellent glacier just down the road.

THE RESORT

Zell is a year-round resort town set between a large lake and the unusual, horseshoe-shaped mountain. There are gondolas into the slopes from here and from the suburb of Schüttdorf, about 3km south of Zell. It's a short bus ride to the glacier slopes of Kaprun, on the lift pass and covered in this chapter. Saalbach is also easily reached by bus.

Village charm Zell has a charming, traffic-free medieval centre. The major through-road is buried in a tunnel, but it's a busy little place and there is still quite a bit of traffic passing close to the centre.

Convenience There are lodgings close to each access gondola – from the edge of town, and from Schüttdorf – and close to several lifts going up from Schmittental, in the heart of the U-shaped mountain. There are 'good bus services' serving other points.

Scenery Zell am See enjoys a pretty lakeside setting and the mountain offers good views south to the high mountains, including Kaprun's distinctive Kitzsteinhorn.

LET
THE HAPPINESS
IN!

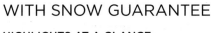

WINTER PARADISE
WITH SNOW GUARANTEE

HIGHLIGHTS AT A GLANCE:
- Glacier skiing: high altitude, 100% snow guarantee
- Great après ski (range of bars and restaurants)
- Suitable for all abilities
- Stunning lakeside views
- Range of activities
- Peakworld 3000 at Glacier Kitzsteinhorn
- Schmittenhöhe with an incredible 360-degree view

Zell am See-Kaprun Tourismus
5700 Zell am See, phone +43 (0) 6542-770
welcome@zellamsee-kaprun.com, www.zellamsee-kaprun.com

NEWS

2013/14: An eight-seat chair replaced the Glocknerbahn quad and the parallel drag above Areitalm. A new fun slope (a bit like a beginner terrain park) opened off the Hochmais lift, next to the snow park. On the Kitzsteinhorn, Black Mamba is a steep new black piste.

UK PACKAGES

Crystal, Crystal Finest, Erna Low, Inghams, Mark Warner, Mountain Beds, Neilson, Ski Club Freshtracks, Ski Line, Ski Safari, Skitracer, Skiweekends.com, Snow Finders, Snowscape, STC, Thomson, Zenith **Kaprun** Crystal, Crystal Finest, Erna Low, Inghams, Interactive Resorts, Neilson, Ski Line, Skitracer, Snow Finders, Snowscape, STC, Thomson, Zenith

THE MOUNTAINS

Zell's mountain is open at the top, mostly densely wooded lower down.

Slopes Above the lifts out of Zell and Schüttdorf a final gondola goes to Schmittenhöhe, meeting the gondola from Schmittental. The several lifts on the back of the hill and on the sunny slopes of the northern arm of the horseshoe mountain are accessed via Schmittenhöhe or by cable car from Schmittental. Black runs descend from various points to Schmittental; easier runs go down the southern arm to Zell and Schüttdorf. The slopes steepen – it's a red run to Schüttdorf, a black to Zell, or a winding blue.

Fast lifts Only the sunny Sonnkogel sector now relies on slow lifts.

Queues Away from peak season there are no problems. If snow in lower resorts is poor, the queues at the Kitzsteinhorn can be 'horrendous'.

Terrain parks Schmittenhöhe has a half-pipe by the Glocknerbahn chairlift, and this season will have a fun park by the Hochmaisbahn.

Snow reliability Many of Zell's slopes get a lot of sun and, although there is full snowmaking, at these altitudes there is still a danger of slush and ice. Piste grooming is 'fabulous'.

Experts Zell has several black runs, but they are not seriously steep and are usually groomed. Off-piste terrain is limited, but there is a nice 'glade' area on the back of the hill.

Intermediates Good intermediates have a couple of fine, long runs, but this is not a place for high mileage. The wide Sonnkogel runs are relatively quiet – great for carving. The timid can cruise the southern ridge blues.

Beginners A reporter with novice kids advises that the nursery slopes at Schüttdorf are better than those at Schmittental. There are lovely long easy runs to progress to.

Snowboarding Most lifts are chairs, gondolas or cable cars. Snowboard Academy is a specialist school.

Cross-country There's a total of 35km, some lit at night, and more at Kaprun.

Mountain restaurants Zell has quite a few welcoming huts, though some can get crowded. They are named on the piste map. A reader who got around lots of them favours Breiteckalm, Glocknerhaus and Hochzelleralm for 'friendly service and good food'. Pinzgauer Hütte ('wonderful venison') is secluded, away from the piste; you get a skidoo tow back – fun, but may involve queuing.

Schools and guides There is a choice of schools; we lack recent reports.

Families Staying in Schüttdorf means you have direct gondola access to the Areitalm snow-kindergarten.

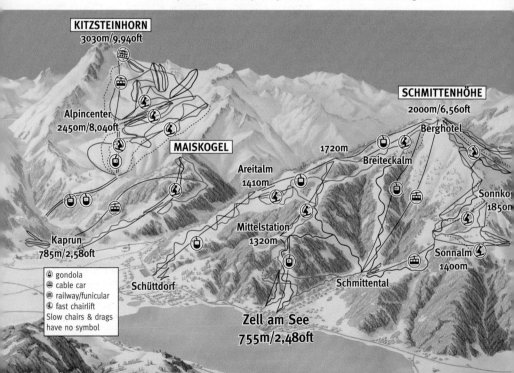

KITZSTEINHORN
3030m/9,940ft

Alpincenter
2450m/8,040ft

MAISKOGEL

Areitalm
1410m

1720m

SCHMITTENHÖHE
2000m/6,560ft

Berghotel

Breiteckalm

Sonnko
1850m

Kaprun
785m/2,580ft

Mittelstation
1320m

Schmittental

Sonnalm
1400m

gondola
cable car
railway/funicular
fast chairlift
Slow chairs & drags
have no symbol

Schüttdorf

Zell am See
755m/2,480ft

STC Ski

Specialists in Tailor-Made
Short Breaks & Holidays

01483 771 222
www.stcski.co.uk
ski@stcski.co.uk

KEY FACTS

Resort	755m
	2,480ft

Zell and Kaprun

Slopes	755-3030m
	2,480-9,940ft
Lifts	53
Pistes	138km
	86 miles
Blue	34%
Red	43%
Black	23%
Snowmaking	100%

Zell (Schmittenhöhe) only

Slopes	755-2000m
	2,480-6,560ft
Lifts	26
Pistes	77km
	48 miles
Snowmaking	100%

Kaprun only

Slopes	785-3030m
	2,580-9,940ft
Lifts	23
Pistes	61km
	38 miles
Snowmaking	100%

Phone numbers

From elsewhere in Austria add the prefix 06542 (Zell), 06547 (Kaprun); from abroad use the prefix +43 and omit the initial '0'

TOURIST OFFICE

www.zellamsee-kaprun.com

STAYING THERE

Hotels There is a broad range of hotels and guest houses. Three 4-star hotels have recently been tipped by reporters. Two this year rave about the Berner (779) – 'superb', 'lovely food, ski-in/ski-out in good conditions'; outdoor pool. The St Georg (768) is 200m from the CityXPress gondola – 'great staff', 'sumptuous food'. The 'exceptionally friendly' Heizmann (72152) is also close to the lifts.

Apartments There are lots of options bookable locally.

Eating out Zell has quite a few non-hotel options – 'all good value' says a reporter – but we get few specific reports. Kumpferkessel, Arts and Giuseppe's have all been tipped by reporters.

Après-ski There are plenty of cafes and bars. Start at the top of the slopes at the Berghotel – where the bar has a good vibe, live music and dancing. In town, there are lots of lively bars. Pinzgauer Diele club rocks. O'Flannigan's is the main sports bar, with all that that entails, though one reader prefers A Little Bit of Irish. Ginhouse is good for a quiet drink, particularly, er, gin. Villa Crazy Daisy is 'a jumping place with a great atmosphere'; live music often.

Off the slopes There is plenty to do. In midwinter you can often walk across the frozen lake; there are marked paths up at Schmittenhöhe, too. Plus there are good sports facilities, Alpine flights, and you can watch ice hockey. Trips to Salzburg and Kitzbühel are possible and rewarding – good train service, we hear.

OUTLYING RESORT – 785m

KAPRUN

Kaprun is a pleasant and quite lively village, with a pretty church, and it's bypassed by the road up to the lifts to its Kitzsteinhorn glacier. However, it sprawls over a considerable area, so it's worth picking your spot with care.

There is a small area of easy intermediate slopes on the outskirts of the village on the low hill of Maiskogel. But most people will want to spend their time on the glacier.

This is reached by a two-stage gondola to Alpincenter at 2450m, with other lifts in parallel. A cable car then goes up to the top of the area at over 3000m. The main slopes are in a big bowl above Alpincenter, served by a quad chair, two six-packs and lots of T-bars. There are also runs down to the mid-station of the gondola.

There are three 'excellent' terrain parks on the glacier including one for novices, and a super-pipe.

The high black runs present no challenge to experts (they used to be red), but a new black piste is now open lower down, going to the gondola mid-station, with a claimed gradient of 32° – a proper black. In that same area, the resort now operates a set of similarly steep itineraries – mostly with verticals of around 500m. Sadly, these runs are apparently not avalanche protected, so you still need full off-piste kit and experience to use them. This is a strange and undesirable setup.

Most pistes are mainly gentle blues and reds – great easy cruising for intermediates. One particularly entertaining red goes down to the gondola mid-station, away from the lifts. For beginners there are nursery slopes next to the village and gentle blues to progress to, both at Maiskogel and on the glacier.

The 18km of cross-country trails on the Kaprun golf course are good, and at altitude there is one short loop.

There's a decent choice of mountain restaurants on the glacier. One of the best is the Gletschermühle near the Alpincenter. The Krefelder Hütte below it is a genuine mountain refuge. Häuslalm near the gondola mid-station has a 'good atmosphere'.

Crystal has a big chalet here. There's a decent choice of hotels. The 4-star Sonnblick (8301) has been recommended, as has the 3-star Mitteregger (82070). There are of course restaurants and bars, but we lack recent reports. There's a sports centre, bowling at the Sportsbar, sleigh rides and a motor museum.

Build your own shortlist: www.wheretoskiandsnowboard.com

France

Around a third of British skiers and snowboarders choose France for their holidays – more than any other country. It's not difficult to see what attracts us: France has the biggest lift and piste networks in the world, and most are at high altitude, ensuring good snow for a long season. The best of them have state-of-the-art lift systems, too – though it's a myth that all French lift systems are wonderfully efficient. Another common myth is that French resort villages are all soulless, purpose-built service stations, thrown up without concern for appearance during the 1960s and 1970s.

Many French resorts are now distinctly lively in the evening – a great change over the last 20 years. And some even have the on-mountain après scene that is so common in Austria, mainly thanks to the Folie Douce chain that started in Val d'Isère and has expanded to Méribel, Val Thorens and Alpe-d'Huez – and now to Megève, even.

The big French resorts have a reputation for high prices, and in some respects it is well earned: the bars and restaurants of major resorts such as Courchevel, Méribel, Val d'Isère and Val Thorens are painfully pricey. But when you take other holiday costs into account, most French resorts are not expensive compared with their main Alpine rivals (as shown by our RPI figures). And UK tour operators do a great job in keeping catered chalet holidays affordable, with lots of food and wine included in the price. The euro exchange rate has improved in the last year, easing the pain, although not affecting comparisons with other eurozone countries, of course.

KEEPING COSTS DOWN

Chalet holidays are not the only way of economizing. Renting one of the new generation of genuinely comfortable and stylish apartments and catering for yourself is an attractive option that should keep your bar bills down – read our smart apartments chapter on page 49. Other ideas include staying in a relatively cheap valley town (such as Bourg-St-Maurice, below Les Arcs) and eating packed lunches – we mention picnic rooms at the end of the 'Mountain restaurants' section of resort chapters.

ANY STYLE OF RESORT YOU LIKE

The main drawback to France, hinted at above, is the nature of some of the high-altitude purpose-built resorts. It's partly that the worst of them look hideous, but it's also that they were designed to cram in the maximum number of beds and that they are holiday camps rather than real communities. But even the worst places have learned from past mistakes, and newer developments have been built in a traditional chalet style.

If you prefer, there are genuinely old mountain villages to stay in, linked directly to the big lift networks. These are not usually as convenient for the slopes, but they give you a feel of being in France rather than in a winter-holiday factory. Examples include Montchavin or Champagny for La Plagne, Vaujany for Alpe-d'Huez and St-Martin-de-Belleville for the Trois Vallées. There are also old villages with their own slopes that have developed as resorts while retaining at least some rustic ambience – such as Serre-Chevalier.

SNOWPIX.COM / CHRIS GILL
← The French invented the purpose-built resort, and Courchevel 1850 (now called Courchevel) was one of the first

Resort news and key links: www.wheretoskiandsnowboard.com

Getting around the French Alps

Pick the right gateway city as your initial Continental target – Geneva,
Chambéry or Grenoble – and you can hardly go wrong. The only high pass
you need worry about is on the approach to Serre-Chevalier and
Montgenèvre – the 2060m Col du Lauteret; but even here the road is a
major one, and kept clear of snow or reopened quickly after a fall (or you
can fly to Turin and avoid that pass). Crossing the French-Swiss border
between Chamonix and Verbier involves two closure-prone passes – the
Montets and the Forclaz. When necessary, one-way traffic runs beside the
tracks through the rail tunnel beneath the passes.

Two other resorts deserve a special mention. Megève is an exceptionally charming little town combining rustic style with sophistication. And then there is Chamonix, a big, bustling town sitting literally in the shadow of Mont Blanc, Europe's highest peak, and the centre of the most radical off-piste terrain in the Alps.

SKI AMIS
Catered Chalets in Superb Locations
020 3411 5439
www.skiamis.com

INSTRUCTION OR GUIDING?

Gone are the days when the Ecole du Ski Français was the only ski school in town. Most resorts now have lots of competing schools, and many are run and staffed by highly qualified British instructors – the prime example being New Generation, which continues to get rave reviews from our reporters, and now operates in 11 resorts.

Most experienced skiers don't want to join a school; but many do like to be shown around the slopes of an unfamiliar resort, and to be introduced to other skiers of a similar standard. So they're keen on the ski guiding/hosting services that British chalet companies have operated for many years – until last season, when a French court ruled that the practice was illegal unless the staff member held the highest ski instructor qualification. Le Ski, the tour operator being prosecuted, is appealing against the decision; the next court decision is expected in September 2014, after we go to press. Meanwhile, tour operators have suspended their hosting.

EASY PISTES

France remains unusual among European countries in rating pistes on a four-point scale. The very easiest runs are classified green; except in Val d'Isère, they are reliably gentle. This is a genuinely helpful system that ought to be used more widely. Some French resorts, sadly, don't use it – notably Les Arcs and La Plagne.

PLAT DU JOUR

Despite the prices, France has advantages for foodies. Table-service in mountain restaurants is common, and most places do food – often including a plat du jour – that is much more varied and interesting than what is served in Austria. Most resort villages have restaurants serving good, traditional French food and regional specialities. But don't expect much other than those options.

DRIVING AMBITION?

The French Alps are easy to get to by car; on page 71 there is a chapter on driving to the French Alps. Driving is still popular, despite the growth of budget airlines; for self-caterers it has the advantage that you can stock up in good-value valley supermarkets.

AVOID THE CROWDS

French school holidays mean crowded slopes, so they are worth avoiding. The country is divided into three zones, with fortnight holidays staggered between 7 February and 8 March 2015 (ie a week earlier than in 2014). Avoid 14 Feb to 1 March in particular, when Paris is on holiday.

OT ALPE-D'HUEZ / AGENCE NUTS

Alpe-d'Huez

Impressive and sunny slopes above a hotchpotch of a purpose-built village, but with attractive alternative bases

RATINGS

The mountains

Extent	★★★★
Fast lifts	★★★★
Queues	★★★★
Terrain p'ks	★★★
Snow	★★★★
Expert	★★★★
Intermediate	★★★★
Beginner	★★★★★
Boarder	★★★★
X-country	★★★
Restaurants	★★★★
Schools	★★★★
Families	★★★

The resort

Charm	★★
Convenience	★★★
Scenery	★★★★
Eating out	★★★★
Après-ski	★★★★
Off-slope	★★★★

RPI   105

lift pass	£200
ski hire	£130
lessons	£75
food & drink	£135
total	**£540**

KEY FACTS

Resort	1860m
	6,100ft
Slopes	1100-3330m
	3,610-10,920ft
Lifts	80
Pistes	250km
	155 miles
Green	31%
Blue	26%
Red	31%
Black	12%
Snowmaking	35%

198

➕ Extensive, high, sunny slopes, split interestingly into different sectors, with some very long runs

➕ Vast, gentle, sunny nursery slopes

➕ Efficient access lifts from villages

➕ Livelier than many French resorts

➕ Good, traditional alternative bases

➖ Some main intermediate runs get badly overcrowded in high season

➖ Many runs get too much sun, so slush and ice are hazards

➖ Many tough runs are high, and exposed – very few woodland runs

➖ Spread-out resort village

There are few single resorts to rival Alpe-d'Huez for extent and variety of terrain – in wintery conditions it's one of our favourites. But as the season progresses the effects of the strong southern sun become more and more of a problem.

If you don't like the look of the village, think about the smaller bases described at the end of this chapter – especially Vaujany.

THE RESORT

Alpe-d'Huez is a large, modern resort on a high, open, sunny plateau east of Grenoble. It was developed for skiing, but consists mainly of large numbers of undistinguished small buildings rather than monolithic blocks.

The resort spreads down a gentle slope in a triangular shape from the main lift station at the top corner. The main village is divided into three named 'quarters'; Vieil Alpe includes the original chalet-style part of the village, at the lower end. Outside the central triangle there are four satellite 'quarters'. The major one is Les Bergers, a second major lift base at the eastern corner of the resort; it has a chalet suburb spreading uphill.

A blue piste descends from the west side of the resort to the original (but much expanded) village of Huez, where there is lodging (and a lift to the main resort).

The lift pass gives days in some other resorts (including Les Deux-Alpes, Serre-Chevalier and Montgenèvre – see Lift passes notes in the margin on page 203). There are buses twice a week to Les Deux-Alpes, but the proper thing to do is to go by helicopter – we agree with readers that this is 'fantastic fun' (70 euros last season; three days a week). The merits of a cross-valley lift are being carefully considered.

VILLAGE CHARM ★★
Bit of a hotchpotch

The central buildings come in all styles; on the fringes there are more sizeable, modern buildings, and areas of chalets. Vieil Alpe has a trace of charm, and as a whole the resort is not unpleasant. The central Avenue des Jeux is a kind of focus, with the ice rink, indoor-outdoor swimming pool, and many of the shops, bars and restaurants.

CONVENIENCE ★★★
Choose your spot with care

Very few lodgings are ski-in/ski-out. Staying near one of the two major lift bases is the best plan – or in one of the chalets uphill of Les Bergers. The place is too big to get around on foot. There's a slow bucket-lift (with a piste beneath it) running in daytime through the centre to the main lifts. This opens a bit late (8.45am) and builds queues at peak times. There are also chairlifts across the bottom of the resort up to Les Bergers. The free ski-bus service around the resort usually

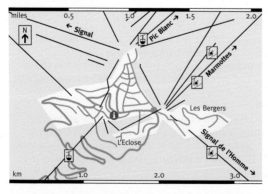

2014/15: There are plans to install 65 snow-guns on the Sarenne black run with the aim of keeping it open all season.

2013/14: On the main beginner area a chondola replaced five draglifts and another drag was replaced by a moving carpet. The Romaines chair from Les Bergers was lengthened and a new green run built off the top of it. A Folie Douce mountain restaurant, as in Val d'Isère etc, opened.

LAURENT SALINO / ALPE-D'HUEZ TOURISME

A great view of the resort, from Les Bergers in the foreground to the Signal hill on the right
↓

runs to its timetable, but reporters find the 20-minute interval between buses too long, and capacity inadequate. The satellite quarters are a bit of a trek from the centre – and a reader points out that there are no proper footways – but they have their own lifts, bars and restaurants.

SCENERY ★★★★☆
Splendid panoramic views
The resort has a fabulous high setting on a sunny plateau. There are splendid views of the Ecrins peaks.

THE MOUNTAINS

Practically all the slopes are above the treeline, and so there may be little to do when a storm socks in or the wind picks up. Piste classification is rather unreliable. There are certainly some tough blues; but readers' views seem to be complicated by snow conditions, which in such a sunny resort are naturally very variable. The piste map is OK but has very small type; some reporters find signposting less than ideal.

EXTENT OF THE SLOPES ★★★★☆
Several well-linked areas
Alpe-d'Huez is a big-league resort, with impressively extensive and varied

Mega-resort skiing from a quiet base? Check out Vaujany p207.

slopes. It offers many long runs, with big verticals. But its claim of 250km of pistes is an exaggeration. The lift company has told us that it adds around 25% to its fall-line piste lengths to allow for your turns. The Schrahe report (see our piste extent feature) put the total at 176km, which points to an addition of more like 40%.

The slopes divide into four sectors, with good connections between them.

The biggest sector is directly above the village, on the slopes of **Pic Blanc**. The huge two-stage Grandes Rousses gondola – aka the DMC (a reference to its technology) and marked on the piste map just as 'first stage' and 'second stage' – goes from the top of the village. The first stage to 2100m is now duplicated by a state-of-the-art chondola which can transport 3,900 people an hour.

Above the DMC, a cable car goes up to 3330m on Pic Blanc itself – the top of the small Sarenne glacier and start of the longest piste in the Alps (read our feature panel). The glacier is also reached via the Marmottes six-pack, then a two-stage gondola (the

Alpe-d'Huez

199

Ski Total

ARE HERE IN
Alpe d'Huez

▶ **Quality chalets**
▶ **Top locations**
▶ **Excellent value**
▶ **17 more resorts**

skitotal.com

01483 791 933

first stage of which also serves lower runs from Clocher de Macle).

The alternative from Pic Blanc is to take a 300m tunnel through the ridge to the front face, where a west-facing black mogul field awaits you.

The epic Sarenne black run ends in a gorge that separates the main resort area from **Signal de l'Homme**. It is crossed by a down-and-up fast chairlift from the Bergers part of the village. From the top you can take excellent north-facing slopes towards the gorge, or head south to Auris or west to tiny Chatelard/La Garde.

On the other side of town from Signal de l'Homme is the small **Signal** sector, which is reached by draglifts next to the main gondola or by a couple of chairs lower down. Runs go down the other side of the hill to

Villard-Reculas. One blue run back to Alpe-d'Huez is floodlit on Thursdays.

The **Vaujany-Oz** sector consists largely of north-west-facing slopes, reached from Alpe-d'Huez via red runs. (There is blue-run access too if you are prepared to do a short stretch of easy red.) At the heart of this sector is L'Alpette, the mid-station of the cable car from Vaujany; it can also be reached by a gondola from Oz. Beyond L'Alpette, the slopes around Montfrais are blue, with the notable exception of the shady black La Fare, which plunges down to L'Enversin, just below Vaujany. The descent from Pic Blanc to L'Enversin is 2230m vertical – the second biggest in the world (beaten, as it happens, by near-neighbour Les Deux-Alpes). The links back to Alpe-d'Huez are by cable car from L'Alpette,

skitracer *

CHALETS, HOTELS
& APARTMENTS
Call us today
020 8600 1650
skitracer.com

or a second gondola from Oz. You can also reach Oz from the mid-station of the DMC at 2100m, down an excellent red with blue variant most of the way.

FAST LIFTS ★★★★☆
Pretty efficient overall
Gondolas and fast chairs are the main access lifts and serve most areas adequately – and last year the new chondola going the full length of the main nursery area replaced no fewer than five old draglifts. But there are still some old chairs and draglifts.

QUEUES ★★★★☆
Mainly at village level
We considered cutting our rating to ★★★ after a couple of years of rising complaints, but two of the main troublespots were relieved last season

Mega-resort skiing from a quiet base? Check out Vaujany p207.

by the lengthening of the Romains chair from Les Bergers so that it reaches mid-mountain (relieving pressure on the Marmottes I chair) and the replacement of five drags by a state-of-the-art chondola in parallel with the DMC gondola. Even with these improvements, though, we suspect ski school start periods will need to be avoided, morning and afternoon. More reports needed please. The village bucket-lift is said to generate lengthy queues first thing. There can also be waits for the cable car up to Pic Blanc.

Over much of the area a greater problem than lift queues is that some

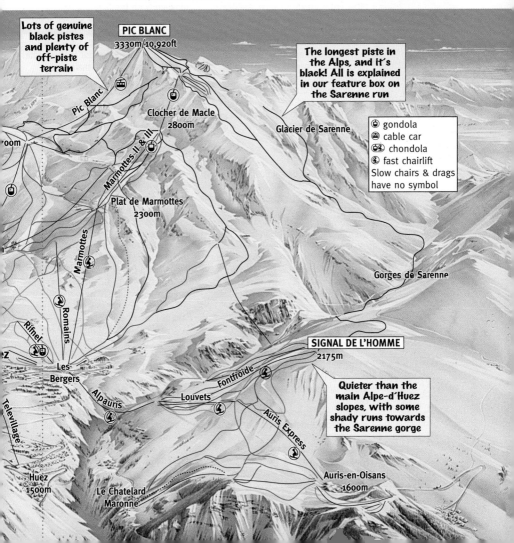

Lots of genuine black pistes and plenty of off-piste terrain

PIC BLANC
3330m/10,920ft

Pic Blanc

Clocher de Macle
2800m

Marmottes II & III

Plat de Marmottes
2300m

Marmottes

Romains

Rifnel

oom

Les Bergers

Televillage

Alpauris

Huez
1500m

Le Chatelard
Maronne

Louvets

Fontfroide

Glacier de Sarenne

The longest piste in the Alps, and it's black! All is explained in our feature box on the Sarenne run

Gorges de Sarenne

SIGNAL DE L'HOMME
2175m

Auris Express

Quieter than the main Alpe-d'Huez slopes, with some shady runs towards the Sarenne gorge

Auris-en-Oisans
1600m

○ gondola
◎ cable car
◎ chondola
④ fast chairlift
Slow chairs & drags have no symbol

It's no surprise that most ski runs that are seriously steep are also seriously short. The really long runs in the Alps tend to be classified blue, or red at the most. The Parsenn runs above Klosters, for example – typically 12km to 15km long – are manageable in your first week on skis. So you could be forgiven for being sceptical about the 'black' Sarenne run from the Pic Blanc: even with an impressive vertical of 2000m, a run 16km long has an average gradient of only 11% – typical of a blue run.

But the Sarenne is a run of two halves. The bottom half is virtually flat (boarders beware), but the top half is a genuine black if you take the direct route – a demanding and highly satisfying run (with stunning views) that any keen, competent and fit skier will enjoy. The steep mogul field near the top can be avoided by taking an easier option (or by using the Marmottes III gondola). The run gets a lot of sun, so snow conditions are highly variable; pick your time with care – there's nothing worse than a sunny run with no sun. Occasionally during the season you can ski the Sarenne by moonlight or head torch: take the last lift up, have a 'simple meal', then ski down with guides. This season the cost was 72 euros per person.

Pierre & Vacances
Holidays made for me

Best price guarantee for ski in/out budget studios up to spacious 3 bedroom apartments

pierreetvacances.co.uk

ESPRIT
FOR FAMILIES IN
Alpe d'Huez
Family Ski
Chalets
Dedicated
Nurseries
Exclusive Ski
Classes
12 More Resorts

espritski.com
01483 791 900

pistes can be unbearably crowded. The Chamois and Couloir runs from the top of the DMC gondola are among the most crowded we've seen, anywhere, despite the laudable efforts of the lift company to divert skiers coming up the Vaujany cable car on to the Belvedere and excellent Bartavelles runs. Crowds can also make life miserable on the red Rousses to Vaujany and Poutrans to Oz – 'Carnage all the way,' said one recent reporter.

In contrast, the slopes at Auris are 'lovely and quiet – excellent skiing'.

TERRAIN PARKS ★★★★★
Big and varied

A big park stretches almost all the way down the first stage of the DMC. One of our keen 'park rat' reporters says, 'It is definitely the best-placed and possibly the best-designed park I've seen. It has everything from an easy beginner line to enormous jumps and an airbag, with lots of rails too.' Other reporters praise it as well. There's also a half-pipe and a 'fast, aggressive' snowcross. And there's a beginners' park above Vaujany.

SNOW RELIABILITY ★★★★★
Affected by the sun

Alpe-d'Huez is unique among major purpose-built resorts in the Alps in having mainly south- or south-west-facing slopes. The strong southern sun can affect piste conditions even in January, and late-season conditions may alternate between slush and ice on most runs. One March 2013 visitor would have liked to have seen some runs closed, so tricky was the ice, while a January 2014 visitor complained of 'many black pistes closed all week' and another was

puzzled at 'no attempt to keep the Sarenne run open' – that might explain why they are planning to install 65 snow-guns on the Sarenne for next season. There are shady slopes above Vaujany and at Signal de l'Homme. The glacier area is small. Snowmaking is not comprehensive, but is now quite extensive, covering the main runs above Alpe-d'Huez, Vaujany and Oz.

FOR EXPERTS ★★★★★
Plenty of blacks and off-piste

There are long and challenging pistes as well as some serious off-piste.

The black slope beneath the Pic Blanc cable car will be on your agenda. Despite improvements to the tunnel exit, the start of the actual slope is often awkward. The slope is of ordinary black steepness, but can be very hard in the mornings because it gets the afternoon sun. Get information on its condition. The long Sarenne run on the back of Pic Blanc is described in the panel above. The black Fare piste to L'Enversin is good – varied, and well away from the lifts but not steep; it faces west, and relies heavily on artificial snow.

The Marmottes II gondola serves genuine black runs and a red from Clocher de Macle; Balcons is steep and quiet, often with good snow; Clocher de Macle is easier but busier; don't miss the beautiful, long, lonely Combe Charbonnière (but there's a fairly long traverse on moderately steep ground at the start). The Lièvre Blanc chairlift serves further testing slopes – Balme, looping away from the lifts, is a black, and one or two mogully reds would be classified black in many resorts. In good snow conditions, the steep La Fuma run down to Le Chatelard (open

Build your own shortlist: www.wheretoskiandsnowboard.com

LIFT PASSES

Prices in €

Age	1-day	6-day
under 13	38	191
13 to 64	47	238
65 to 71	38	191
72 plus	14	72

Free Under 5

Beginner Four free lifts; Première Glisse pass covers 19 lifts

Notes Covers Alpe-d'Huez, Auris, Oz, Vaujany and Villard-Reculas; half-day passes; discounts for families; 6-day-plus passes allow one day's skiing at each of Serre-Chevalier, Puy-St-Vincent, Montgenèvre, and the Milky Way in Italy, and two days in Les Deux-Alpes; also night skiing, night tobogganing, one entry to the ice rink, to the swimming pool and to one sports centre activity during the day

Alternative passes Alpe-d'Huez only, Auris only, Oz-Vaujany only, Villard-Reculas only; pedestrian

GETTING THERE

Air Grenoble, 105km/ 65 miles (1hr30); Chambéry, 130km/ 80 miles (1hr45); Lyon 155km/95 miles (2hr); Geneva 215km/ 135 miles (2hr45)

Rail Grenoble (63km/ 39 miles); daily buses from station

as a piste only in good snow) is worth trying. And the Col de Cluy from Signal de l'Homme is long and gets away from all the lifts.

The off-piste possibilities are immense, and some are described in our feature panel. Some of these routes away from the lifts are shady, in contrast to the main slopes.

FOR INTERMEDIATES ★★★★
Fine selection of runs
Good intermediates have a fine selection of runs all over the area. In good snow conditions the variety of runs is difficult to beat.

Every section has some challenging red runs to test the adventurous intermediate. The Canyon run is one of the most challenging. There are lovely long runs down to Oz – the Champclotury blue from the mid-station of the gondola above Oz is a lovely, gentle run and usually quiet – and to Vaujany, with space for some serious carving. The Villard-Reculas and Signal de l'Homme sectors have long challenging reds. Those at Signal de L'Homme are quieter, so they keep their snow better. The Chamois red from the top of the gondola down to the mid-station is quite narrow, and miserable when busy and icy and/or heavily mogulled. Fearless intermediates should enjoy the super-long Sarenne black run.

For less ambitious intermediates, there are usually blue alternatives, except on the upper part of the mountain. The main Couloir blue from the top of the big gondola is a lovely run, well served by snowmaking, but like the red Chamois it does get scarily crowded at times.

There are some great cruising runs above Vaujany; but the red runs between Vaujany and Alpe-d'Huez can be too much for early intermediates. You can travel via Oz on gondolas if you are that keen to get around.

Unreliable piste classification (read 'The mountains') can complicate life for early intermediates.

FOR BEGINNERS ★★★★★
Good facilities
The large networks of green runs immediately above the village and above the Les Bergers area form nursery areas as good as you will find anywhere. Sadly, these slopes carry a lot of fast through-traffic, despite being declared low-speed zones. In

> **Mega-resort skiing from a quiet base? Check out Vaujany p207.**

each area two short beginner lifts are free, and a special lift pass covers more lifts to progress to.

FOR BOARDERS ★★★★
Suits the adventurous
The resort suits experienced boarders well – the extent and variety of the mountains mean that there's a lot of good freeriding to be had; the off-piste is vast and varied and well worth checking out with a guide. The terrain park is good, too. There are quite a few flat areas to beware of though. The nursery slopes are excellent and now have fast chairlifts bottom to top. Planète Surf is the main shop.

FOR CROSS-COUNTRY ★★★
High-level and convenient
There are 50km of trails, with six loops of varying degrees of difficulty, all at around 2000m and consequently relatively snow-sure.

MOUNTAIN RESTAURANTS ★★★★
Some excellent rustic huts
There are more rustic places with table-service than is usual in high French resorts, and almost all readers are impressed – 'it's why we come here' is one emphatic view. But the restaurants in the more obvious positions get over-busy, and some charge for the toilets. The piste map does not identify restaurants. The resort's pocket guide covers 16 places, marked on a tiny piste map.

The big news last season was the opening of a branch of the ever-expanding Folie Douce franchise, complete with dairy-style restaurant La Fruitière. Reports please!

Editors' choice The cosy little Chalet du Lac Besson (0476 806537) is an oasis of calm – tucked away on the cross-country loops north of the 2100m mid-station of the DMC gondola (and reached by a special access piste, the Boulevard des Lacs). Food and service are excellent. It's repeatedly endorsed by reporters.

Worth knowing about Immediately above the resort, the best option (apart from the new Fruitière) is Plage des Neiges, at the top of the Babars chair – favourite of several reporters: 'lovely rustic bustling place', 'creamy rich tartiflette', 'very friendly'. We await

FRANCE

204

Resort news and key links: www.wheretoskiandsnowboard.com

Major Resorts
Expert knowledge

4★ ski apartments with spa

SkiCollection.co.uk
0844 576 0175
ABTA Bonded W5537

↑ The 'village' isn't a pretty sight but it's not as bad as some French purpose-built resorts

LAURENT SALINO / ALPE-D'HUEZ TOURISME

SCHOOLS

ESF
t 0476 803169

Easyski International
t 0476 804277

Masterclass
t 0679 673456

Stance
t 0680 755572

Classes (ESF prices)
6 days (3hr am and 2½hr pm) €245

Private lessons
€46 for 1hr, for 1 or 2 people

GUIDES

Mountain guide office
t 0476 804255

reports on Signal 2018, the glass-walled, pyramid-shaped place opened a few seasons ago at Signal; it includes a smooth table-service section. On the back of the hill, the cosy Bergerie above the Villard-Reculas lift base has impressed some readers.

Combe Haute, at the foot of the Chalvet chair towards the end of the Sarenne run, serves 'lovely' food in 'charming, rustic surroundings'. Up on Signal de l'Homme, L'Hermine is 'good value, with cheerful service'. Lower down in the woods on the fringe of this area, the little Forêt de Maronne hotel at Chatelard (aka La Garde) is 'excellent value' with 'charming staff'. We had a very satisfactory lunch a few seasons ago at Perce-Neige, just below the Oz-Poutran gondola mid-station. It has a wood-burning stove and a 'great snug atmosphere', and does 'terrific salads and a lovely chocolate cake'. Near the Alpette lift station, La Grange pleases readers. Down the hill slightly, Auberge de l'Alpette (aka Chez Passoud) is an unpretentious place doing good food. Further down, Airelles is a rustic hut built into the rock, with a roaring log fire; we get consistently good reports – 'excellent tartiflette', 'lovely food, friendly staff'.

SCHOOLS AND GUIDES ★★★★
Masterclass worth a try
Reports on the ESF are generally positive and one 2014 reporter said of lessons organized by Esprit Ski: 'Our children liked their instructors and made huge improvements.' But we also heard from an adult beginner who had a 'distressing experience' as the instructor 'shouted and humiliated' her group so much she couldn't return for her remaining three lessons.

Recent reports on British instructor Stuart Adamson's outfit Masterclass are universally positive. He 'did wonders for the lost confidence' of the woman who had the distressing ESF experience, and her more experienced partner 'improved immensely'.

Another recent reporter made 'good progress' in boarding lessons with ESI.

FOR FAMILIES ★★★
Plenty of choice
There's Les Intrépides day care centre for children aged three months to six years. The ESF runs the Chalets des Enfants for children aged over two and a half years: it combines ski lessons with activities in a day care centre. Family specialist Esprit operates here (read 'Chalets' in the next section) and has comprehensive childcare arrangements.

STAYING THERE

There's quite a good range of options of all kinds of lodging. There is a Club Med in the Bergers quarter – highly recommended by a repeat visitor.
Chalets Skiworld's chalets include some with hot tub and sauna and a splendid looking one in their top Signature range down in Huez. Crystal has a central 34-bed chalet hotel plus three chalets ('Basic en-suite rooms, but good food and attentive staff,' says a 2013 visitor to one of them). Ski Total has five chalets, most with sauna and two with outdoor hot tubs. Inghams has two chalets (one with outdoor hot tub, one with sauna) plus a 70-bed chalet hotel ('excellent staff, good natured, good little bar'). The VIP chalets near the main lifts are also 'excellent'. Family specialist Esprit has a 60-bed chalet hotel in the old village

CHILDCARE

Les Intrépides
t 0476 112121
Ages 3mnth to 4yr
Chalet Enfants (ESF)
t 0476 803169
From age 2½
Tonton Mayonnaise
(Easyski)
t 0476 804277
Ages 2½ to 3½

Ski schools
From 4 to 12

UK PACKAGES

Alpine Answers, Alpine Weekends, Club Med, Crystal, Crystal Finest, Erna Low, Esprit, Inghams, Interactive Resorts, La Source, Lagrange, Mountain Beds, Neilson, Oxford Ski Co, Pierre & Vacances, PowderBeds, Rocketski, Ski Club Freshtracks, Ski Collection, Ski Expectations, Ski France, Ski Independence, Ski Line, Ski Supreme, Ski Total, Skitracer, Skiworld, STC, Thomson, VIP, Zenith
Villard-Reculas La Source
Oz-en-Oisans Erna Low, Lagrange, Peak Retreats
Vaujany Erna Low, Peak Retreats, Pierre & Vacances, PowderBeds, Ski Peak

('Childcare top-notch, location perfect; staff were troopers') and two separate chalets using the child care facilities of the chalet hotel.

Hotels There are more than in most high French resorts – mainly 3-star.
****Alpenrose (0427 042804) On the fringe of Les Bergers – 'Possible to ski back, but a hike up to Marmottes I,' says a reporter. Spa.
****Au Chamois d'Or (0476 803132) Good facilities, modern rooms, one of the best restaurants in town and well placed for the main gondola. Spa.
***Pic Blanc (0476 114242) Across the car park from the lifts at Les Bergers. Comfortable; we stayed in a big ('superior') room.
***Royal Ours Blanc (0476 803550) Heart of the village; pool, sauna, steam, hot tub. 'Good food, nice staff,' said a reporter.

Apartments There are lots available, though few are notable. Among the smartest are those in CGH's residence Cristal de l'Alpe with pool, hot tubs, fitness stuff etc, and a prime central location. The Pierre & Vacances residence Ours Blanc is 'newly refurbished to a high standard', but is not ideally located. Ski Collection and Erna Low offer these properties. One of Skiworld's chalets is available on a 'flexible catering' basis and it has the Crystal de l'Alpe too. The supermarket at Les Bergers is reported to be the best in town.

EATING OUT ★★★★
Good value
Alpe-d'Huez has dozens of restaurants, some of high quality; many offer good value by ski resort standards. A pocket booklet lists over 30 of them.

Widely thought to be about the best is Au P'tit Creux, although we lack recent reports. Readers' recommendations include: Genepi (French cuisine: food generally praised but service criticized), Smithy's Tavern (Tex-Mex and grills) and Au Trappeur ('super pizza'). Other reader tips include: Alaska ('great pizzas and beer'), Edelweiss ('great Savoyard dishes, tables tight but excellent atmosphere'), Grenier (French and Savoyard) and Pinocchio pizzeria.

APRES-SKI ★★★★
Plenty going on
The idea is that you now end your afternoon dancing on the tables at the new Folie Douce. In the village there's a wide range of bars, some of which get fairly lively later on. There are several British-run bars in chalet hotels. One is the Underground under the Chamois hotel in Vieil Alpe – 'open mike nights and live music'. Smithy's Tavern is 'great fun, lots of dancing, gets very hot'. Other places tipped by reporters include O'Bar ('beer really cheap') and the Etalon ('nice chilled-out bar run by friendly staff'). Late-night places include the Sporting, Igloo and the Caves de l'Alpe.

OFF-PISTE FOR ALL STANDARDS

There are vast amounts of off-piste terrain in Alpe-d'Huez, from fairly tame to seriously adventurous. Here we pick out just a few of the many runs to be explored – always with guidance, of course.

*There are lots of off-piste variants on both sides of the Sarenne run that are good for making your first turns off-piste. The **Combe du Loup**, a beautiful south-facing bowl with views over the Meije, has a black-run gradient at the top, and you end up on long, gentle slopes leading back to the Sarenne gorge. **La Chapelle Saint Giraud**, which starts at Signal de l'Homme, includes a series of small, confidence-boosting bowls, interspersed with gentle rolling terrain.*

*For more experienced and adventurous off-piste skiers, the **Grand Sablat** is a classic that runs through a magnificently wild setting on the eastern face of the Massif des Grandes Rousses. This descent of 2000m vertical includes glacial terrain and some steep couloirs. You can either ski down to the village of Clavans, where you can take a pre-booked helicopter or taxi back, or traverse above Clavans back to the Sarenne gorge. In the **Signal** sector, there are various classic routes down towards the village of Huez or to Villard-Reculas.*

*The north-facing Vaujany sector is particularly interesting for experienced off-piste enthusiasts. Route finding can be very tricky, and huge cliffs and rock bands mean this is not a place in which to get lost. From the top of Pic Blanc, a 40-minute hike takes you to Col de la Pyramide at 3250m, the starting point for the classic route **La Pyramide** with a vertical of over 2000m. Once at the bottom of the long and wide Pyramide snowfield, you can link into the Vaujany pistes.*

Like the resort?
You'll love our handpicked accommodation
0844 576 0173
peakretreats.co.uk
ABTA
ABTA No. W5537
peak retreats

ACTIVITIES

Indoor Sports centre (tennis, gym, squash, aerobics, swimming, shooting range, climbing wall, adventure trail), sauna, cinemas, concerts, theatre, library, museum

Outdoor Ice rink, curling, cleared walking paths, tobogganing, dog sledding, snowshoeing, snowmobiling, microlight flights, sightseeing flights, ice cave, skijoring, off-road vehicle tours, paragliding, ice-driving school, snow kiting

Phone numbers
From abroad use the prefix +33 and omit the initial '0' of the phone number

TOURIST OFFICE

www.alpedhuez.com

OFF THE SLOPES ★★★★
Good by high-resort standards

There is a wide range of facilities, praised by recent non-skiers, including a big and very popular indoor-outdoor pool ('warm, with friendly staff'), an Olympic-size ice rink – plus an indoor pool and a splendid sports centre. Note that a six-day-plus lift pass gets you one free visit to each of these activities. There's also an ice-driving school and a toboggan run, and you can try paragliding and snowmobiling. A visit to the Ice Cave at the top of the DMC gondola is highly recommended by reporters. Shopping is not impressive. The helicopter excursion to Les Deux-Alpes is exciting. There are 35km of well-marked local walkers' trails (map available); the lifts 'cope well with pedestrians', and there's a special lift pass. The better mountain restaurants are widely spread, so meetings with skiing friends may not work well. There are 'good' weekly organ concerts in the 'interesting church', and there's a museum.

LINKED RESORT – 1500m
VILLARD-RECULAS

Villard-Reculas is a tiny unspoiled village just over the hill (Signal) from Alpe-d'Huez, and set on a small shelf between open snowfields above and tree-filled hillsides below. A fast quad takes you up to Signal from V-R, but the return lifts are slow.

V-R is the tiniest resort we have stayed in: one restaurant, one shop-cum-restaurant, two sports shops. If you don't like ski resorts, this is just the place. On the other hand, a reporter last year called it 'the most boring resort I have been to'.

Although the village is small, its chalets are spread widely, and practically everyone needs transport to the lifts. There is a shuttle-bus but we hear it gets crowded.

Accommodation is mainly self-catering, booked either through the tourist office or La Source – an English-run agency. We were impressed by the little apartment we stayed in a few seasons ago, owned by the community.

La Source also runs an eponymous catered chalet – a carefully converted stone building with a lovely, spacious, vaulted living room at the bottom opening on to a terrace (complete with hot tub) giving knockout views. It is warmly furnished with armchairs and sofas, and a wood-burning stove. Food is excellent, and there's a minibus to the lifts. We have had several good reports from readers, too.

The local slopes have something for everyone. For beginners, it may seem near-ideal, with several lifts serving green runs at village level. Sadly, these runs are mostly of blue gradient; a reporter last year who agreed with that assessment also pointed out that they get icy (from afternoon sun). The blue runs in both directions from Signal are also not entirely easy, especially when icy. So V-R is less than ideal for novices. For confident intermediates, it's fine. And there is challenging skiing on and off the Forêt black piste from Signal. The tiny branch of the ESF gave a recent reporter 'good' lessons.

LINKED RESORT – 1350m
OZ-EN-OISANS STATION

The small purpose-built ski station above the old village of the same name has been built in an attractive style, with much use of wood and stone, and has nursery slopes, skating rink, bars, restaurants, supermarket and two mid-range hotels. The pool in the Villages Club du Soleil is open to all. But nightlife is quiet.

The slopes above Oz are about the best in the area when snow is falling. Two gondolas whisk you out of the resort: one goes to L'Alpette, above Vaujany; the other goes in two stages to the mid-station of the DMC above Alpe-d'Huez.

The smart Chalet des Neiges apartments have a pool, sauna, fitness area, bar and restaurant. Available via Peak Retreats (who also feature detached chalets), Lagrange and Erna Low.

LINKED RESORT – 1600m
AURIS-EN-OISANS

Auris-en-Oisans is another small, purpose-built ski station – a series of wood-clad, chalet-style apartment blocks with a few shops, bars and restaurants set just above the treeline. Quite appealing to families.

Build your own shortlist: www.wheretoskiandsnowboard.com

LINKED RESORT – 1250m

VAUJANY

Vaujany is a quiet village that has expanded over the years, perched on a sunny hillside opposite its own sector of the domain. Hydroelectricity riches have financed huge investment in infrastructure.

A giant 160-person two-stage cable car whisks you up into the heart of the Alpe-d'Huez lift system. Alternatively, a two-stage gondola takes you less dramatically to the local slopes at Montfrais via a mid-station below the tiny hamlet of La Villette.

As you enter the village, you come to a couple of small, simple hotels. The Rissiou is well run by British tour operator Ski Peak: 'Comfortable and convenient, nightly fine-dining experience with a great selection of wines.' Ski Peak also has luxurious catered chalets in Vaujany and La Villette plus some 4-star apartments with two to five bedrooms. It runs a minibus service for guests. Peak Retreats (no relation) has a wide choice of apartments; Erna Low features some too.

Once past the Rissiou, you come to a recently built complex around a small pedestrian square, Place Centre Village, with spacious, mid-range apartments built in traditional style. There's a good ski shop, restaurants, food shops, a cafe/bar and a cavernous underground car park – and an escalator down to the nearby cable car and gondola stations. An elevator takes you further down the hill to the 'extraordinarily large' sports centre with a pool with a big slide, and a newish ice rink and bowling alley.

An impressive enclosed escalator goes up the hillside past chalets and farm buildings to the top of the village, where sizeable apartment buildings are grouped around the Place de la Fare – a small car-free zone with a small supermarket, a food shop, a couple of bars and a couple of restaurants. Since most of the visitor beds are up here, it is naturally the focus of evening activity.

There are no slopes leading directly to the village. But there is a 'pulse' gondola up from L'Enversin, below the village, where the Fare black run finishes (a great run and not steep – read 'For experts' earlier in this chapter), or you can take a blue to the mid-station of the Montfrais gondola and ride down the lower stage.

Beginner children are taken to a gentle roped-off area at the top of the gondola – 'suited our children' says a 2014 visitor – and adult beginners to the nursery slope at Alpette, the cable car mid-station. There's a self-service restaurant with sunny terrace right by the children's learning area. The ESF children's ski school has been praised ('small classes'), as has the nursery ('as good as it gets, good English spoken, not expensive'). The adult ESF gets the thumbs up this year too.

Phone numbers
From abroad use the prefix +33 and omit the initial '0' of the phone number

TOURIST OFFICES

Villard-Reculas
www.villard-reculas.com

Oz-en-Oisans
www.oz-en-oisans.com

Auris-en-Oisans
www.auris-en-oisans.com

Vaujany
www.vaujany.com

Selected chalets in Vaujany   ADVERTISEMENT

SKI PEAK *www.skipeak.net*   T **01428 608070** F **01428 608071**

The Vaujany (Alpe d'Huez) specialists with four catered chalets including award-winning Saskia (featured). Chalet Saskia has ten en-suite bedrooms, two generous lounges, a games room with bar-football and table tennis and a spectacular terrace with top of the range spa. The cuisine is second to none.

SNOWPIX.COM / CHRIS GILL

Les Arcs

Three first-generation purpose-built villages plus a couple of attractive alternatives set among varied and extensive slopes

RATINGS

The mountains

Extent	★★★
Fast lifts	★★★★
Queues	★★★
Terrain p'ks	★★★★
Snow	★★★★
Expert	★★★★★
Intermediate	★★★★
Beginner	★★★
Boarder	★★★★
X-country	★★
Restaurants	★★★
Schools	★★★★
Families	★★★★

The resort

Charm	★★
Convenience	★★★★
Scenery	★★★
Eating out	★★★
Après-ski	★★
Off-slope	★

RPI   105

lift pass	£210
ski hire	£125
lessons	£65
food & drink	£135
total	**£535**

NEWS

2014/15: Immediately above 1800 a new activity zone is being built, with a new gondola replacing the Villards chair and serving a short winding piste, a fun slope and a toboggan run; and a new beginner area with moving carpet and a new restaurant are to open at the top. A new kids' snow garden and an aquatic centre will open at the base. Two other new lifts are planned for the 2015/16 season.

2013/14: A smart new 4-star hotel opened just above 1800, the Aiguille Grive. New mountain restaurants opened near 1600 and 1800.

+ Varied slopes – on and off-piste

+ Lots of genuinely challenging skiing

+ Some excellent woodland runs

+ Car-free, mainly convenient villages, including cute 1950

+ Some quiet alternative bases

+ Fast cable car link to La Plagne

− Original village centres lack charm, and aren't the most convenient

− Fairly quiet nightlife

− Lots of flat linking runs

− Accommodation in high villages is nearly all in apartments

We've always liked Les Arcs' slopes: they offer long descents, plenty of steep stuff, plenty to keep intermediates happy plus woods to head to in a storm. And for those who really like to travel on skis, the link to La Plagne takes the amount of skiing into the Trois Vallées league.

We've never been keen on the functional main villages. We're aware that their various architectural styles are highly regarded by some; we're not among them, but our real objection is to their dreary mall-style shopping centres. Newer Arc 1950 is something else: a resort that's not only more pleasant to inhabit than the others, but also very conveniently arranged. There are attractive developments on the slopes above Arc 1800. And Peisey-Vallandry is a quiet, attractive and convenient base for exploring the La Plagne ski area as well – you're right next to the linking cable car.

THE RESORT

Les Arcs is made up of four modern resort units, all purpose-built, traffic-free and apartment-dominated.

Arcs 1600 and 1800 stand a couple of km apart, roughly at the treeline on a broad, steepish mountainside overlooking the town of Bourg-St-Maurice (covered at the end of this chapter). Both consist mainly of large apartment blocks sitting below their slopes, with some development beside the slopes. 1600 was the first Arc, built at the top of a funicular up from Bourg. 1800 is much the largest Arc, and recently has been expanding up the hillside.

Arc 2000 and 1950 are quite separate – on the far side of the mountain ridge, at the bottom of a high, treeless bowl. Arc 2000 consists of half a dozen huge, linked apartment blocks, plus more recently built chalet-style blocks. Just below Arc 2000 and linked to it by a short gondola, the mini-village of Arc 1950 was built from scratch by IntraWest (of Whistler fame) in traditional style, opening its doors in 2003.

The numbers in the village names relate only loosely to their altitudes. 'Arc 2000' was dreamt up in the 60s to evoke the millennium – the future; its altitude is actually over 2100m.

At the southern end of the area is Peisey-Vallandry, from where a cable

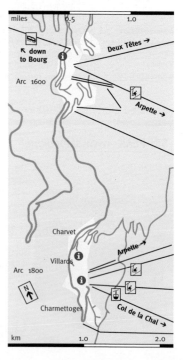

KEY FACTS

Resort	1600-2120m
	5,250-6,960ft
Slopes	1200-3225m
	3,940-10,580ft
Lifts	51
Pistes	200km
	124 miles
Green	1%
Blue	50%
Red	32%
Black	17%
Snowmaking	
	267 guns

Paradiski area	
Slopes	1200-3250m
	3,940-10,660ft
Lifts	141
Pistes	425km
	264 miles
Green	8%
Blue	53%
Red	25%
Black	14%
Snowmaking	
	626 guns

OT LES ARCS / M TEYBOZ

Arc 2000, on the right, is about on the treeline. The roofs of Arc 1950 are just visible on the left ↓

car links with La Plagne, covered by the Paradiski passes. Even from Arc 1950 you can be at the cable car in 20 minutes. At the northern end of the ski area, at much lower altitude, is the rustic hamlet of Villaroger. These outlying villages are described at the end of the chapter.

Day trips by car to Val d'Isère–Tignes are possible. La Rosière and Ste-Foy-Tarentaise are closer. If taking a car, be warned: you have to pay for parking at Arcs 1950 and 2000 – the only free parking is throughout 1600 and before the entrance to 1800. And we hear there is no longer free parking at the valley station of the funicular.

VILLAGE CHARM ★★
Head for 1950

The apartment blocks of Arcs 1600 and 1800 are low-rise, and not hugely intrusive when seen from the slopes. Arc 1600 is set in the trees and has a friendly, small-scale atmosphere. Bigger Arc 1800 has three main parts. Le Charvet and Les Villards are focused on small shopping centres, mostly open-air but still seeming claustrophobic. Big apartment blocks run across and down the mountain. Charmettoger has apartment blocks, too, but also smaller, wood-clad buildings. Le Charvet has spread up the hill in recent years, and now has

an identifiable upmarket suburb, Le Chantel.

Arc 2000 consists of futuristic large blocks with swooping roof lines, plus some large chalet-style blocks.

Arc 1950 has been designed to be cute; its smaller apartment buildings have been finished in traditional style, and they are clustered around a pleasant, traffic-free square and street – quite lively at close of play.

Reporters repeatedly comment on the friendliness of the locals.

CONVENIENCE ★★★★
Generally very good

Arcs 1600 and 1800 offer some very convenient lodgings a few yards from the lifts, but also some that are less convenient than they look – you can walk miles within the apartment buildings to get to (and from) the snow. The central area in Arc 1600 is good for families: uncrowded, compact, and set on even ground. Arc 1800 is more spread out, and some of the best lodgings are up the hill at Le Chantel. At the very top is the newish Edenarc development. These high developments are a bit isolated, but a mini-cable car up to this area is planned for 2015/16. The main lifts depart from Les Villards. A 2013 visitor found 'the 1600/1800 buses run to a pretty strict timetable, and are

Les Arcs

Ski Total

ARE HERE IN
Les Arcs 2000

▸ **Quality chalets**
▸ **Top locations**
▸ **Excellent value**
▸ **17 more resorts**

skitotal.com
01483 791 933

generally efficient, linking with the funicular etc'.

Arc 2000 and Arc 1950 are compact, ski-in/ski-out places, with lifts starting below them as well as above. But getting around Arc 2000 on foot can be quite an effort and we've had reports of antiquated elevators out of action frequently. All the bits of Arc 1950 we've stayed in or looked at are genuinely ski-in/ski-out. You park directly under the apartment buildings, which is a rare bonus at the start and end of your stay.

SCENERY ★★★☆☆
Attractively varied

Arcs 1600 and 1800, and the slopes, enjoy views across the valley to Mont Blanc. The lower villages enjoy good views along the Nancroix valley and to La Plagne's splendid north face of Bellecôte. Higher up, Arc 2000 and Arc 1950 sit beneath the Aiguille Rouge, high point of the slopes – great views from the top.

THE MOUNTAINS

Les Arcs' terrain is very varied; it has a good mixture of high, open, snow-sure slopes and lower woodland runs (notably above Peisey-Vallandry).

EXTENT OF THE SLOPES ★★★☆☆
Well planned and varied

Our ★★★ rating relates to just the Les Arcs area; the whole Paradiski area easily scores five stars.

Arc 1600 and Arc 1800 share a west-facing mountainside laced with runs down to one or other village. At the southern end is an area of woodland runs above Peisey-Vallandry.

From various points on the ridge above 1600 and 1800 you can head down into the wide Arc 2000 bowl. From there, lifts take you to the high points of the area, the Aiguille Rouge and the Grand Col. As well as a variety of steep runs back to Arc 2000, the Aiguille Rouge is the start of an epic run (over 2000m vertical and 7km

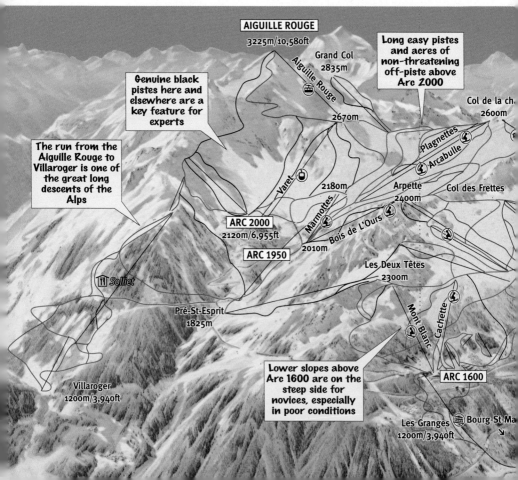

SKIWORLD

Catered chalets, hotels and self catering apartments in

Europe, USA and Canada

skiworld.co.uk
08444 930 430

ABTA V2151 ATOL 2036

LES ARCS

CHOOSE FROM 164 CATERED CHALETS, APARTMENTS & HOTELS

Skiline co.uk

CALL US ON 020 8313 3999

SKI AMIS

Catered Chalets in Superb Locations

020 3411 5439
www.skiamis.com

long) down to the tiny unspoiled village of Villaroger.

The resort identifies nine black runs and one red as Natur' (never groomed) – not popular with reporters (see 'Snow reliability'). On the lower half of the Aiguille Rouge is a speed-skiing run, sometimes open to the public.

On Thursdays outside high season the First Tracks scheme (10 euros) allows you up the mountain an hour early to ski deserted pistes.

FAST LIFTS ★★★★☆
Generally good

Each of the four main villages and Peisey-Vallandry have fast chair or gondola access to the slopes, and most of the lifts higher up are fast, too. The main irritants now are all in the same area, on the left of the map: the three successive, seriously slow chairs up from Villaroger and the two chairs up in different directions from Pré-St-Esprit.

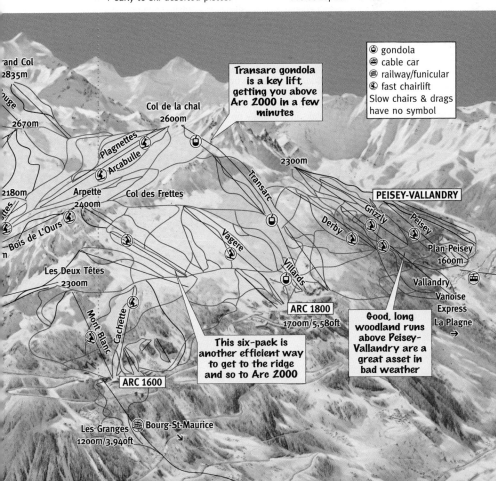

Transarc gondola is a key lift, getting you above Arc 2000 in a few minutes

ⓖ gondola
ⓒ cable car
ⓡ railway/funicular
ⓕ fast chairlift
Slow chairs & drags have no symbol

This six-pack is another efficient way to get to the ridge and so to Arc 2000

Good, long woodland runs above Peisey-Vallandry are a great asset in bad weather

ARC 1600
ARC 1800
1700m/5,580ft

PEISEY-VALLANDRY

Plan-Peisey
1600m

Vallandry

Vanoise Express
La Plagne →

Les Granges
1200m/3,940ft

Bourg-St-Maurice

Les Deux Têtes
2300m

and Col
2835m

2670m

2180m

Col de la chal
2600m

2300m

Plagnettes
Arcabulle
Arpette
2400m
Col des Frettes
Bois de L'Ours
Transarc
Vagere
Villards
Derby
Grizzly
Peisey
Mont Blanc
Cachette

Pierre & Vacances premium

Perfect spacious apartments with spas and swimming pools.

pierreetvacances.co.uk

ESPRIT
FOR FAMILIES IN
Les Arcs

Family Ski Chalets
Dedicated Nurseries
Exclusive Ski Classes
12 More Resorts

espritski.com
01483 791 900

OT LES ARCS

Arc 1950, a decade old now, successfully combines traditional style and ski-in/ski-out convenience ↓

QUEUES ★★★★★
Not without problems

Queues aren't generally an issue in low season, and peak-time queues are improving. But the lifts above Arc 2000 present problems, especially on sunny days. The busy Varet gondola to the shoulder of the Aiguille Rouge shifts its queue quickly because it has lifties pulling people out of the queue to fill the cabins – excellent. Queues for the cable car to the top can be serious in clear weather ('40 minutes at noon in March' said a 2013 report); it dates from 1981, holds only 70 people and clearly needs replacing. The Arcabulle chair has the potential for 'five-to-ten-minute waits'. At 1800 the Transarc gondola is queue prone, especially late in the day. At Plan-Peisey, morning queues for the Peisey chair (and for the Derby above it) are not unknown, partly because of arrivals on the Vanoise Express from La Plagne; and a March 2013 reporter waited 25 minutes for the Vanoise Express itself.

At peak periods dangerously crowded pistes can be a problem.

TERRAIN PARKS ★★★★★
One excellent park

The Apocalypse Parc is between Arcs 1600 and 1800, and is served by a snowboarder-friendly J-bar lift. For years, this has been one of the most advanced parks in the Alps – on a par with the main park at Avoriaz. Three kicker lines are in place for all levels.

There is a good rail and box line, a big wall ride, a spine jump and a large gap jump, plus towards the end of the season a water jump is introduced – variety and fun for all. 'All it lacks is a half-pipe,' a reporter notes.

There are snowcross runs below Col de la Chal and above Plan-Peisey.

SNOW RELIABILITY ★★★★★
Good – plenty of high runs

A high percentage of the runs are above 2000m, and when necessary you can stay high by using lifts that start around that altitude. Most of the slopes face roughly west, which is not ideal. Those from the Col de la Chal and the long runs down to Villaroger are north-facing, and the blacks on the Aiguille Rouge are shady enough to keep their snow well. Snowmaking is limited.

Grooming is generally good but most reporters think the Natur' runs should be groomed sometimes – they say they are often deserted due to their condition.

FOR EXPERTS ★★★★★
Challenges on- and off-piste

Les Arcs has a lot to offer experts – at least when the high lifts are open (the Aiguille Rouge cable car, in particular, is often shut in bad weather).

Most black runs are now Natur' runs, become huge mogul fields and are often deserted – a huge shame. The lack of many groomed blacks

Erna Low

Experts to the Alps since 1932,
build your own ski holiday
with flights and transfers at

www.ernalow.co.uk
020 7584 2841

LIFT PASSES

Les Arcs / Peisey-Vallandry

Prices in €

Age	1-day	6-day
under 14	35	177
14 to 64	46	235
65 plus	35	177

Free Under 6

Beginner Points card for one lift in each of Arcs 1600/1800/2000

Senior 72 plus: 1-15 days €7

Notes Options: half-day pass; one-day Paradiski extension; family reductions

Alternative Découverte pass with one-day Paradiski extension

Paradiski Unlimited

Prices in €

Age	1-day	6-day
under 14	39	208
14 to 64	51	277
65 plus	39	208

Free Under 6

Senior 72 plus: 1-15 days €10

Notes Covers Les Arcs and La Plagne areas; family reductions

means that the steeper groomed reds can get very busy. One of the quieter reds (and one of our favourites) is the lower part of the epic Aiguille Rouge-Villaroger run, which has remarkably varying terrain – the start is a narrow black shelf, which can be awkward (but this can be avoided by taking the Lanchettes chair from Arc 2000).

There is also a great deal of off-piste potential. There are steep pitches on the front face of the Aiguille Rouge and secluded runs on the back side, towards Villaroger. A short climb to the Grand Col accesses several routes, including a quite serious couloir and an easier option. From Col de la Chal there is an easy route down towards Nancroix. The wooded slopes above 1600 are another attractive possibility and there are open slopes beside the pistes all over the place.

FOR INTERMEDIATES ★★★★
Plenty for all abilities
One strength of the area is that most main routes have easy and more difficult alternatives, making it good for mixed-ability groups. An exception is the solitary Comborcière black from Les Deux Têtes down to Pré-St-Esprit, which has no nearby alternatives. This long mogul field justifies its classification and can be great fun for strong intermediates. Malgovert, from the same point towards Arc 1600, is a red Natur' piste and is tricky – it is narrow, as well as mogulled.

The woodland runs at either end of the domain, above Peisey-Vallandry and Villaroger, and the bumpy Cachette red down to 1600, also include some challenges. We especially like the Peisey-Vallandry area: its well-groomed, tree-lined runs have a very friendly feel and are remarkably uncrowded much of the time, allowing great fast cruising. Good intermediates can enjoy the run to Villaroger.

The lower half of the mountainside above 1600/1800 is great for mixed-ability groups, with a choice of routes through the trees. The red runs from Arpette and Col des Frettes towards 1800 are quite steep but usually well groomed (except Clair Blanc).

Cautious intermediates have plenty of blue cruising terrain. Many of the runs around 2000 are rather bland and prone to overcrowding. Edelweiss is more interesting, with a short red alternative, and takes you to Arc 1950 from Col des Frettes. The blues above 1800 are attractive but also crowded. A blue favourite of ours is Renard, high above Vallandry – usually with excellent snow.

And, of course, you have the whole of La Plagne's slopes to explore.

FOR BEGINNERS ★★★☆☆
No long greens
There are 'ski tranquille' beginner zones at each of the three main Arcs, and up the hill on the treeline above Vallandry and Plan-Peisey. Around 10 of the beginner lifts are free to use (in 1800, 2000 and Villaroger – but not 1600, strangely). A chairlift in Peisey-Vallandry is free at weekends as are additional chairs in 1600, 1800 and 2000 – you can buy a points card to use them during the week. Sadly, the resort does not use the valuable green run classification common to most other French resorts. In all sectors there are long, wide blue runs to move on to, and some are gentle enough to be green – eg Forêt down to Vallandry.

FOR BOARDERS ★★★★☆
A pioneering place
Ever since 1983 when Regis Rolland introduced the sport in the cult film Apocalypse Snow, Les Arcs has been a hot spot for snowboarders. It offers excellent freeriding, including steeps, gullies, trees, natural jibs and hits.

Build your own shortlist: **www.wheretoskiandsnowboard.com**

**High-standard
Self-catering
Apartments**

020 7371 6111
lagrange-holidays.co.uk

Best price
guarantee
for ski in/out
budget studios
up to spacious
3 bedroom
apartments

pierreetvacances.co.uk

book online at
skiolympic.com
01302 328 820

Major Resorts
Expert knowledge

**4★ ski
apartments
with spa**

SkiCollection.co.uk
0844 576 0175
ABTA Bonded W5537

And there are plenty of wide-open rolling slopes for intermediates and beginners too, especially at Vallandry and 1800. The terrain park is great and is served by a snowboarder-friendly draglift. Most other lifts are chairs and gondolas. But beware of some long flat areas – especially at Arc 2000 and some linking blue runs (you may find it easier to take the wider reds).

FOR CROSS-COUNTRY ★★★★★
Very boring locally
Short trails, mostly on roads, is all you can expect, but the pretty Nancroix valley's 40km of pleasant trails are accessible by free bus.

MOUNTAIN RESTAURANTS ★★★★★
Steadily improving
The range and quality of restaurants is gradually improving, most recently with two promising newly built places – Chalet Grillette at mid-mountain above 1800 and Le Sanglier qui Fume just above 1600. Reports, please.

Editors' choice Chalet du Solliet (0668 960407) above Villaroger is a charming woody chalet with a warm ambience, table- or self-service and great views. We've had excellent lunches here and readers agree – 'Best mountain restaurant we visited by a large margin,' says one reporter this year.

Worth knowing about Chalets de l'Arc, just above Arc 2000, is a rustic place built in wood and stone. Once a favourite, it went through a dodgy patch a few years back, but now we hear of 'friendlier service', and 'excellent plat du jour'. Just up the hill, the tiny Bulle is tipped for cheap pizza. The other good options in this sector are not very mountainous. Down at Pré-St-Esprit, the 500-year-old Belliou la Fumée is set beside a car park; but it is charmingly rustic, and we and readers have had good meals here – as we have at the Ferme at Villaroger – 'friendly people, huge portions'. Two other places worth considering at resort level are the new hotel Aiguille Grive at 1800 and Chalet de l'Arcelle at 1600.

Above 1800, the little Blanche Murée is a simple table-service chalet praised for value and dishes such as 'wild boar with gratin dauphinois'. Higher up, the Arpette pleases most reporters – 'mainly fast food but well cooked and big quantities'.

Above Plan-Peisey, the busy Cordée was endorsed again in 2013 – 'top-notch food and service' and 'good-value set menus' – and this year. The Enfants Terribles (the tarted up Poudreuse) impresses most visitors – it has a 'fabulous atmosphere' serves 'very good omelette and chips' as well as 'fantastic buckets of hot chocolate'.

SCHOOLS AND GUIDES ★★★★★
Several, including a Brit school
British school New Generation is consistently recommended: 'Worth every cent – excellent instructor who was good at analysing our skiing and suggested improvements that really made a difference'; 'Fourth year we have used them for private lessons, outstanding each time'. The ESF branch here is evidently not in the forefront of the reform movement: 'On est en France, on parle Français!' was how one instructor justified his lack of English this year. Arc Aventures (International school – ESI) and Spirit in 1950 have had better reports.

FOR FAMILIES ★★★★★
Convenient choices
Les Arcs is a good choice for families wanting convenience, with lots of slope-side lodgings. There is a children's area at 1800, complete with moving carpets, tobogganing and a climbing wall. There are also a couple of 'discovery' pistes, at 1800 and 1600, for children to find out about flora and fauna of the Alps. Arc 1950 is particularly family-friendly, with a good programme of kids' activities. Comments on kids' ski classes have been positive.

Family specialist tour op Esprit has a dozen chalet units in Arc 2000 and six in Peisey-Vallandry (see end of chapter).

STAYING THERE

Most resort beds are in apartments. There is a long-established Club Med presence in Arc 2000 and there's a smarter one at Peisey-Vallandry.

Chalets There are lots of catered chalets in the Peisey-Vallandry area, handy for the link to La Plagne – covered at the end of this chapter. There are also lots of apartments operated as catered chalets in smart residences with pools in Arc 2000 – operators include Ski Total (8 units in one residence), Inghams (7 units), Crystal (6 units) and family specialist Esprit. Skiworld operates a couple of

www.ski-i.com

ski independence
Call the Tailor-made Ski Specialists
0131 243 8097

Heavenly
Skiing...
at down to earth prices
mh**
Mountain Heaven

· Superb catered & self catered accommodation ·
· Great ski areas in the French & Swiss Alps ·
· Snow secure resorts · We only have on/near piste locations ·
· Fantastic prices & no hidden extras ·

0151 625 1921
www.mountainheaven.co.uk

SCHOOLS

ESF Arc 1600
t 0479 074309

ESF Arc 1800
t 0479 074031

ESF Arc 1950
t 0479 082419

ESF Arc 2000
t 0479 074752

Arc Aventures 1800
t 0479 076000

Evolution 2 Arc 2000
t 0479 078553

New Generation
t 0479 010318
0844 770 4733 (UK)
www.skinewgen.com

Privilège Arc 1800
t 0479 072338

Spirit 1950
t 0479 042572

Classes (ESF prices)
6 3hr-days €165

Private lessons
From €40 for 1hr

GUIDES

Bureau des Guides
t 0479 077119

CHILDCARE

La Cachette (1600)
t 0479 077050
Ages 4mnth to 12yr

Club mini (1800)
t 0479 074031
Ages 3 to 8

Le Cariboo (1950)
t 0479 070557
Ages 9mnth to 3yr

Garderie 2000
t 0479 076425
Ages 1 to 8

Ski school
Generally from age 3

units, and also has a couple of proper individual chalets above 1800.

Hotels The choice of hotels in Les Arcs is gradually widening – notably with the arrival of the Aiguille Grive – but we dropped a couple of listings last year for lack of positive reports. More reports welcome.

****Aiguille Grive** (1800) (0479 402030) Newly built, impressive wood-and-glass place just above the village, with rooms and six separate chalets.

****Mercure** (1800) (0479 076500) Previously the Grand Paradiso. 80 comfortable rooms and suites, sauna.

***Arcadien** (1600) (0479 041600) Tipped by a repeat visitor – 'solid breakfast, big rooms, good people'.

***Cachette** (1600) (0479 077050) 'Pleasant rooms, helpful staff, very good food'; but expect many kids.

Apartments There are still plenty of cramped apartments in the older resort units, but now there are lots of good, modern apartments available through the many operators and agents that advertise with us.

All the residences in 1950 are worth considering. The Manoir Savoie, one of the several residences operated by Radisson Blu, is tipped this year – 'excellent: cosy apartment, warm outdoor pool, nice hot tub'. Pierre & Vacances operate the other residences under their Premium brand. Above 1800, Alpages de Chantel is another Premium property with pool etc – very convenient for skiing and sledging, but a bit isolated. Edenarc, further up the hill, looks attractive, with indoor/outdoor pool, spa and fitness room. The Roc Belle Face development in central 1600, built in tiers down the hillside, is a Lagrange Prestige property, with a small pool.

EATING OUT ★★★☆☆
Mostly uninspiring
An ad-based (therefore not comprehensive) guide is given away locally. The choice is generally uninspiring. One of the best places is Chalet de l'Arcelle on the fringe of Arc 1600; it has a warm, quirky wood and stone interior and a mouth-watering carte; and 'you can't fault them for value for money' says our latest reporter. Also in 1600, the Cairn is 'wood-panelled, with prompt, friendly service' and serves Italian as well as Savoyard dishes.

Arc 1800 has about 15 restaurants but as a regular visitor says, 'they are pretty similar and won't excite anyone'. In Arc 2000, Chez Eux has been our reporters' favourite, but disappointed one party in 2014. Kilimanjaro, on the other hand, seems revitalized – 'Lots of atmosphere, fast service, good food.' Arc 1950 has a reasonable choice for a small place, but demand exceeds supply. Brasserie 1950 is tipped for 'good food', but service is erratic. La Vache Rouge was one reporter's favourite this year. La Table des Lys ('excellent food, super wines') and Chalet de Luigi ('good selection of pastas') have been tipped.

APRES-SKI ★★☆☆☆
Arc 1800 is the place to be
Nightlife is not lively and mainly revolves around the bars. 1800 is the liveliest; some places have regular live music. The cosy Etranger is 'the place to go' and is popular with instructors says a regular. Chez Boubou at Charvet is more British and shows Premiership football matches. The Golf hotel's jazz bar is 'the place to go for an early evening drink'. The J.O. bar is open until the early hours and has a friendly atmosphere. Reporters like the friendly Red Hot Saloon for bar games.

Although it's quieter, there are

Build your own shortlist: www.wheretoskiandsnowboard.com

Like the resort?
You'll love our handpicked accommodation

0844 576 0173
peakretreats.co.uk

ABTA
ABTA No. W5537

peak retreats

GETTING THERE

Air Chambéry 130km/80 miles (1hr45); Geneva 165km/100 miles (2hr30); Grenoble 195km/120 miles (2hr30); Lyon 205km/125 miles (2hr30)

Rail Bourg-St-Maurice; frequent buses and direct funicular to resort

ESPRIT
FOR FAMILIES IN
Peisey Les Arcs
Family Ski Chalets
Dedicated Nurseries
Exclusive Ski Classes
12 More Resorts
espritski.com
01483 791 900

several options in 1600. The Abreuvoir, with live music and pool, is one reporter's 'favourite ski resort bar' with frequent live bands and pool tables. In Arc 2000 the Whistler's Dream and Crazy Fox 'were the only busy bars but full of boozed-up Brits', says a 2013 reporter. At 1950, O'Chaud was a recent reporter's bar of choice, 'and a favourite with the Russian oligarchs, judging by champagne consumption'.

OFF THE SLOPES ★☆☆☆
Very limited

The new snow-zone on the slopes at 1800 opening in December 2014 will be open in the early evening, but also will include a new aquatic centre. Les Arcs is not really the place for an off-the-slopes holiday, but several of the newer apartment blocks have pools, and there are 'excellent' spa facilities at the Sources de Marie in Arc 1950. There's bowling at 1800 and skating at 1800 and 2000. The cinemas have English films weekly. You can visit the Beaufort cheese dairy and go shopping in Bourg-St-Maurice, and there are walks.

LINKED RESORT – 1600m
PEISEY-VALLANDRY

Plan-Peisey and Vallandry are small ski stations built in a traditional chalet style above the old village of Peisey, which has a bucket-lift up to Plan-Peisey. They sell themselves as Peisey-Vallandry, but the local cluster of villages, including one called Nancroix, is collectively known as Peisey-Nancroix. So that's clear then, eh?

Both resorts have good nursery slopes high up the hill on the treeline, reached by chairlift. Of course, this means paying to get up there.

The cable car to La Plagne starts from **Plan-Peisey** – one hotel, a few shops, bars and restaurants but no real focus other than the lift station. A six-pack takes you to the local slopes.

UK operator Ski Amis has a 'premium service' chalet here with a hot tub (and several self-catered chalets and apartments). Family specialist operator Esprit has six neat chalets, each with outdoor hot tub and sauna or steam room – 'brilliant location, very comfortable', said a 2013 reporter.

The hotel Vanoise (0479 079219) has a good location, a pool and a fitness room: 'Staff were very friendly despite our appalling French, and the food was much better than expected,' says a recent visitor. The Arollaie is a Lagrange Prestige apartment development, with a small pool, hot tub, spa.

For a meal out, we'd head down to the Ancolie at Nancroix – a fabulous traditional auberge with welcoming hosts and excellent food. (Be aware that taxi drivers may rip you off for the short journey if you're not careful.) Of the local places, reporters like the Vache ('small and friendly, English run') and Chez Felix ('super food, popular with locals'). The Solan is nicely rustic and has been recommended in the past – more reports please. Après-ski is very quiet, but a 2013 visitor liked

---

Selected chalet in Peisey-Vallandry   ADVERTISEMENT

SKI AMIS *www.skiamis.com*   T **0203 411 5439**

- Premium service chalet to sleep 14-16 people
- Outside hot-tub
- Excellent catering with full English breakfast every day, afternoon tea and four course evening meal
- Pre-dinner drinks, canapés, after dinner liqueurs
- Unlimited good quality wine
- Excellent access to Les Arcs and La Plagne

sales@skiamis.com

SKI AMIS

↑ CHALET SERMOZ

CHALET SERMOZ ↑

ACTIVITIES

Indoor Squash (1800), saunas, solaria, multi-gym (1800), museums, cinemas, bowling (1800, 2000)

Outdoor Ice rinks (1800, 2000), dog sledding, cleared paths, tobogganing, snowshoeing, paragliding, horse riding, skijoring, snowmobiling, ice grotto

UK PACKAGES

Action Outdoors, Alpine Answers, Alpine Elements, Club Med, Crystal, Erna Low, Esprit, Inghams, Interactive Resorts, Lagrange, Mountain Beds, Neilson, Pierre & Vacances, Powder White, PowderBeds, Ski Amis, Ski Beat, Ski Club Freshtracks, Ski Collection, Ski Expectations, Ski France, Ski Independence, Ski Line, Ski Olympic, Ski Total, Ski Weekend, Skitracer, Skiweekends.com, Skiworld, Snow Finders, Snow-wise, Snowchateaux, SnowCrazy, Thomson **Peisey-Vallandry** Club Med, Erna Low, Esprit, Lagrange, Mountain Heaven, Peak Retreats, PowderBeds, Ski Amis, Ski Beat, Ski Collection, Ski Hiver, Ski Independence, Ski Olympic, Snow Finders, Snowchateaux **Bourg-St-Maurice** Chill Chalet, Erna Low, Peak Retreats, Ski Collection **Villaroger** Mountainsun

Phone numbers
From abroad use the prefix +33 and omit the initial '0' of the phone number

TOURIST OFFICES

Les Arcs
www.lesarcs.com

Peisey-Vallandry
www.peisey-vallandry.com

Bourg-St-Maurice
www.bourgsaint maurice.com

L'Armoise in Peisey ('a quiet little French bar') and Au Planté du Bâton in Plan-Peisey ('a great fun quiz night and happy hour').

There is lodging down the hill in the characterful old village of **Peisey**, complete with fine baroque church. The other, mostly old, buildings include a few shops and a couple of bars and restaurants – a reader enjoyed the Ormelune. UK tour operator Mountain Heaven has a renovated old farm building run as a catered chalet with six en-suite rooms; there are three more in an annex, plus a sauna. A 2013 reader enjoyed staying at The Goat Shed, a 'simple but welcoming' catered chalet on the outskirts of Peisey run by a British couple, with minibus service to and from the slopes.

Vallandry is a few hundred metres away from Plan-Peisey and linked by shuttle-bus. A fast quad takes you into the slopes. There are lots of chalets and a small pedestrian-only square at the foot of the slopes with a small supermarket and a ski shop.

Ski Olympic has a big piste-side chalet hotel here – La Forêt. Orée des Cimes is a smart CGH apartment complex right by the Grizzly chairlift, with a pool, hot tubs and spa. Orée des Neiges is another luxury apartment development with free use of the Cimes' pool etc, 1.3km away. Both developments are available through several of our advertisers.

There are several restaurants. The Calèche does 'large portions of Savoyard classics'. The Mont Blanc bar has 'friendly staff', a 'good atmosphere' and table football, and is one of the cheaper options for lunch.

LINKED RESORT – 1200m
VILLAROGER

Villaroger is a charming, quiet, rustic little hamlet with three successive slow chairlifts going up to a point above Arc 2000; its slopes are not suitable for beginners. It has a couple of small bar-restaurants.

DOWN-VALLEY RESORT – 850m
BOURG-ST-MAURICE

With a funicular railway link to Arc 1600, Bourg-St-Maurice is marketed as part of Les Arcs, and does make a viable cheaper alternative to staying on the hill. Not surprisingly, it is very

different – it is not a ski resort, but a real valley town, with proper everyday shops and sizeable supermarkets. It is at the end of the TGV railway line, and therefore is very appealing to rail travellers.

The funicular station is a walkable distance from the TGV platforms, but a drive or bus ride from most parts of Bourg. The advertised travel time to Arc 1600 is seven minutes, but that's for non-stop services, which in our experience are rare. In practice, staying in Bourg rather than Les Arcs costs you an hour a day in extra travelling time – a non-trivial impact.

The plus side, of course, is that everything from accommodation to beer is cheaper. Depending on the time of the season and the exact comparison you make, you can rent an apartment for 30% to 60% off the cost of a similar apartment on the hill. If you plan to ski Les Arcs (and La Plagne), you simply need to balance the cost savings against that lost hour a day.

But if you fancy a bit more variety, the appeal of Bourg-St-Maurice becomes clear. We spent a week here a few years back and had a fab time skiing a different resort every day, from La Plagne to Val d'Isère. The more remote resorts are best accessed by car, though there are buses. But you can easily ski La Rosière (and linked La Thuile in Italy) by taking a bus to the chairlift above Séez, which goes up into the slopes of La Rosière (and saves you a long, winding drive up the hill).

The CGH Coeur d'Or apartments, with good pool, hot tub and spa, are close to the two major supermarkets, and a walk from the town but a drive (or free shuttle-bus ride) from the funicular. A reporter has recommended the hotel Angival (0479 072797), centrally set in a quiet back street, and the Petite Auberge (0479 070586), on the outskirts and run by an English couple.

Bourg has some good, unpretentious restaurants. The Refuge in the main street was recommended by a reliable reporter: 'Delicious, great service, always packed – reservation essential.' We've had excellent meals at the Tsablo (also in the main street) and the Arssiban (just outside the centre). Bar Martin (which doubles as a fishing tackle shop) has been tipped for a pre-dinner beer.

SNOWPIX.COM / CHRIS GILL

Avoriaz

Arguably the definitive purpose-built resort: conveniently arranged, usually snowy, uncompromisingly traffic-free

RATINGS

The mountains

Extent	★★★★★
Fast lifts	★★★★
Queues	★★★
Terrain p'ks	★★★★★
Snow	★★★
Expert	★★★
Intermediate	★★★★
Beginner	★★★★
Boarder	★★★★★
X-country	★★★
Restaurants	★★★★
Schools	★★★
Families	★★★★

The resort

Charm	★★
Convenience	★★★★★
Scenery	★★★
Eating out	★★★
Après-ski	★★★
Off-slope	★

RPI 105

lift pass	£200
ski hire	£125
lessons	£75
food & drink	£150
total	**£550**

KEY FACTS

Resort	1800m
	5,910ft

Portes du Soleil	
Slopes	950-2275m
	3,120-7,460ft
Lifts	194
Pistes	650km
	404 miles
Green	12%
Blue	43%
Red	36%
Black	9%
Snowmaking	
	1074 guns

Avoriaz only	
Slopes	1100-2275m
	3,610-7,460ft
Lifts	34
Pistes	75km
	47 miles
Green	10%
Blue	51%
Red	27%
Black	12%

➕ Good position on the Portes du Soleil circuit, and good local slopes

➕ Very successful design – car-free, with ski-in/ski-out lodgings

➕ Good children's facilities

➕ Snow generally good and sometimes superb, but ...

➖ Low altitudes and exposure to westerlies mean some risk of poor snow lower down, and rain

➖ Architecture doesn't suit everyone

➖ Lacks a slick bag-delivery system

➖ Can get very crowded at weekends

➖ Hardly any hotels

Of the many purpose-built resorts thrown up in France in the 1960s, Avoriaz is probably the best designed. From most points of view, it works. One particularly neat trick is that the resort is sunny but most of the local slopes are shady.

Avoriaz missed out on the smart apartment developments that transformed French self-catering a decade or so ago, but it has recently more than caught up, with some fabulous new places. Now, how about a few more hotels?

THE RESORT

Avoriaz is a purpose-built resort perched on a sloping shelf above a dramatic high cliff a few km from lower, long-established Morzine.

It is entirely free of wheeled traffic; cars are left in paid-for parks at the edge of the village – book a space underground to avoid a chaotic departure if it snows (14.50 euros a day).

Avoriaz is on the main lift circuit of the Portes du Soleil – for an overview, look at our separate chapter. It has links to Châtel in one direction and to Champéry in Switzerland, in the other. It is linked by gondola (but not by piste) to Morzine, which shares a separate area of slopes with Les Gets. All four of these linked resorts get their own chapters, and are covered by the Portes du Soleil pass.

The hamlets of Ardent and Les Prodains are on the fringes of the Avoriaz ski area with lifts into it. Both are described in this chapter. Car trips to Flaine and Chamonix are possible.

VILLAGE CHARM ★★★★★
One of the best modern places
The village is all angular, dark, wood-clad, high-rise buildings – almost all apartments. It's not what you would call charming, but it is at least designed coherently. What's more, the snow-covered paths and pistes give the place a friendly Alpine feel, and both we and reporters have enjoyed the ambience, both day and night.

Family-friendly events are laid on all season. A floodlit cliff behind the resort adds to its nocturnal charm. The lifties have been noted as friendly.

CONVENIENCE ★★★★★
Ready to drag that bag?
As our scale plan suggests, it's a compact place (turn to the Chamonix chapter for a stark contrast). While you are resident, it all works well. Mostly, you can ski from close to the door, and no door is more than 500m from the central shops and bars. Although the upper part of the village is set on a steep slope, escalators and elevators (not entirely reliable) inside the buildings help you get around.

But arrival day and (particularly) departure day are something else.

If you are staying in the new Amara development, you can park your car in the basement (assuming you can face the charges). And if you are staying in the Falaise quarter, near the reception building, you can drag your luggage to your apartment on a borrowed sled.

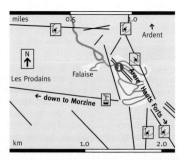

2014/15: In the Super-Morzine area there are plans to replace the Proclou and Seraussaix chairs with a six-pack each. The blue Zore and Abricotine runs are to be reshaped. And the Stash terrain park is to be enlarged. The Dromonts hotel is under new ownership and is to be entirely renovated.

LIFT PASSES

Portes du Soleil

Prices in €

Age	1-day	6-day
under 16	36	178
16 to 19	43	214
20 to 64	48	238
65 plus	43	214

Free Under 5
Beginner Special pass €25 a day; points cards
Notes Family discounts; 5hr pass
Alternative pass Avoriaz only

SNOWPIX.COM / CHRIS GILL

Avoriaz was built for convenience, but not all the buildings are as stark as these ↓

If you are staying elsewhere, it isn't so simple. Some lodgings are up to 800m from the drop-off point, which is a long way to drag your bags, especially if you hit deep, soft snow as we did a few winters ago. So you are probably going to need a ride on a snowcat or a horse-drawn sleigh, for which demand can exceed supply, particularly on departure day.

SCENERY ★★★ ☆☆
Cliff-top panorama

The village is high, and its position on a sunny balcony gives good views down across Morzine. From the high points there are great views of the Dents Blanches and the Dents du Midi.

THE MOUNTAINS

The slopes closest to Avoriaz are bleak and treeless, but fairly snow-sure.

The piste map divides the Avoriaz slopes into four sectors – beginner, family, forest and expert. We (and many reporters) think this is a nonsense – for example, the family sector includes three ungroomed runs and some tough reds. The map also marks five runs – a blue, two reds and two blacks – as 'snowcross' runs (an unfortunate name as this is what we and many resorts now call 'boardercross' and 'skiercross' courses in the interests of political correctness). These runs are marked

and patrolled but ungroomed. We think the concept of red and blue runs that are never groomed is not something that should be encouraged; OK, leave them powdery after a snowfall but don't let huge bumps form so that intermediates avoid them. The map showing the full Portes du Soleil shows these runs as ordinary pistes. On the other hand signposting is very good – a view endorsed by almost every recent reporter.

EXTENT OF THE SLOPES ★★★★★
360˚ choice

The village has lifts and pistes fanning out in all directions. Facing the village are the slopes of **Arare-Hauts Forts**, and when snow is good, there are long, steep runs to Les Prodains, way below the resort, where a big gondola brings you back. To the left, lifts go off to the **Chavanette** sector on the Swiss border – a broad, undulating bowl. At the border is the infamous Swiss Wall – now an itinéraire. It's a long, steep mogul slope with a tricky start, but not the terror it is cracked up to be unless it's icy. You can ride the chair down. At the bottom is the open, gentle terrain of Champéry.

From the ridge behind Avoriaz you can descend into the prettily wooded **Lindarets-Brocheaux** valley, from where lifts go over to Châtel's Linga sector or up to Pointe de Mossettes, another way into Switzerland.

Avoriaz

219

Tailor made, long weekend and short break French Alps ski holiday specialists.

Hanski
Ski. Explore. Relax.

web: www.hanski.co.uk
tel: 01638 596373
mob: 07833 612061

PowderBeds.com

Ski Hotels & Apartments

UK PACKAGES

Alpine Answers, Alpine Elements, Club Med, Crystal, Crystal Finest, Erna Low, Hanski, Igoski, Inghams, Interactive Resorts, Lagrange, Neilson, Pierre & Vacances, Powder White, PowderBeds, Rude Chalets, Ski Collection, Ski France, Ski Independence, Ski Line, Ski Total, Skitracer, Skiweekends.com, Snow-wise, STC, Thomson, VIP, White Roc, Zenith
Ardent Family Ski Company

FRANCE

220

FAST LIFTS ★★★★☆
Good system here and at Linga
In the Avoriaz sector the lifts are impressively modern. And on the nearby Linga slopes, on the way to Châtel, you'll again be mainly riding fast lifts. But beyond Châtel, and on the Swiss side of the Portes du Soleil, there are still lots of slow chairs and draglifts.

QUEUES ★★★☆☆
Still some problems
One long-standing problem – the queue to get up from Les Prodains, below the resort, when snow attracts crowds from Morzine – has been tackled by the replacement of the old cable car by a big gondola (and we mean big: cabins with 35 seats). But some high-season reports speak of

queues for the chairlifts from Les Lindarets (the valley between Avoriaz and Châtel) back to Avoriaz. You may also meet congestion on the runs down to Les Lindarets in the morning, especially when deep snow slows everyone down. Peak-time crowds on the pistes around the village can be hazardous, too; one reporter found the concentration of kids during French holidays 'just foul'.

TERRAIN PARKS ★★★★★
Still leading the way
Avoriaz built the first terrain park in France, in 1993. It is still leading the way, and there are five parks and a super-pipe, all 'very well' maintained. Check www.snowparkavoriaz.com for details. Park lift passes are available.

The expert park is at Arare, and the kicker and rail lines are superbly designed and shaped. It also has an airbag jump – 'The most fun I had all trip,' says a recent visitor. Beginners and intermediates should head to La Chapelle – a 500m-long park littered with jumps of all sizes and fun little boxes and rails. Parkway is great for beginners and kids. It has mini-jumps and ride-on boxes, with traffic lights for safety. The Stash, in the Lindarets valley, is a great innovation imported from California – routes cut through the forest, and wooden and natural elements bringing all-mountain riding and freestyle together; great fun and due to be enlarged for 2014/15. The fifth park is the Lil'Stash – a mini version for younger kids. Just above the village is a good super-pipe. And there's a snowcross (that they call boardercross) too.

SNOW RELIABILITY ★★★☆☆
High resort, low slopes
Although Avoriaz itself is high, its slopes don't go much higher – and some parts of the Portes du Soleil circuit are much lower. But it has a good snow record; two seasons ago it got the most in the Alps – a staggering 11.8m (that's 465in, for comparison with places like Utah). And considering their altitude, the north-west-facing slopes below Hauts Forts and Chavanette hold snow well – much better than over the border on the sunnier Swiss slopes. But when snow is sparse, the smooth, grassy slopes of lower Morzine-Les Gets can deliver better conditions than the rocky ones around Avoriaz.

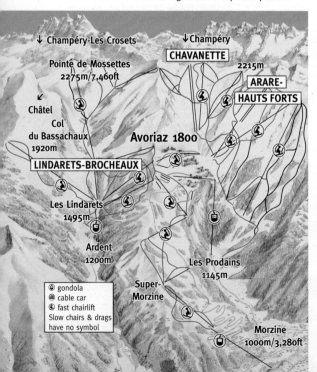

↓ Champéry-Les Crosets   ↓Champéry

CHAVANETTE

Pointe de Mossettes
2275m/7,460ft

2215m

ARARE-
HAUTS FORTS

↙
Châtel
Col
du Bassachaux
1920m

Avoriaz 1800

LINDARETS-BROCHEAUX

Les Lindarets
1495m

Ardent
1200m

Les Prodains
1145m

Super-
Morzine

gondola
cable car
fast chairlift
Slow chairs & drags
have no symbol

Morzine
1000m/3,28oft

Pierre & Vacances
Holidays made for me

Best price guarantee for ski in/out budget studios up to spacious 3 bedroom apartments

pierreetvacances.co.uk

SCHOOLS

ESF
t 0450 740565
Evolution 2
t 0450 740218
Alpine (AASS)
t 0450 383491

Classes (ESF prices)
6 (4.75hr) days €190
Private lessons
From €44 for 1hr, for
1 or 2 people

CHILDCARE

Les P'tits Loups
t 0450 740038
3mnth to 5yr
**Children's Village
Annie Famose**
t 0450 740446
From age 3

Ski schools
Ages 4 to 12

GETTING THERE

Air Geneva 85km/
55 miles (1hr45);
Lyon 220km/135
miles (3hr)

Rail Cluses (44km/
27 miles) or Thonon
(46km/28 miles); bus
and cable car to
resort

Ski Total

ARE HERE IN
Avoriaz

▸ **Quality chalets**
▸ **Top locations**
▸ **Excellent value**
▸ **17 more resorts**

skitotal.com

01483 791 933

FOR EXPERTS ★★★☆☆
Several challenging runs
Tough terrain is scattered about. The challenging runs down from Hauts Forts to Les Prodains (including a World Cup downhill) are excellent. There is a tough red and several long, truly black runs, including one of the ungroomed so-called 'snowcross' runs we've talked about. Snow conditions on the lower runs can be poor, but there is snowmaking. The Swiss Wall at Chavanette will naturally be on your agenda and there are other worthwhile blacks on the Swiss side. Châtel's Linga sector is well worth a trip. And there's plenty of good off-piste if you take a guide.

FOR INTERMEDIATES ★★★★☆
Virtually the whole area
Although some sections lack variety, the Portes du Soleil circuit through Châtel, Morgins and Champéry is excellent for all grades of intermediates, provided snow is in good supply on the lower slopes. Timid types not worried about pretty surroundings need not leave the Avoriaz sector: there are quiet and scenic blues to Les Prodains and at Super-Morzine. And the Arare and Chavanette sectors are gentle, spacious, above-the-treeline bowls. The Lindarets area is also easy, with pretty runs through the trees, but there are some long flat sections.

Further afield, Champoussin has a lot of easy runs, reached without too much difficulty via Les Crosets and Pointe de l'Au. Better intermediates have virtually the whole area at their disposal. The runs down to Pré-la-Joux and L'Essert on the way to Châtel, and those either side of Morgins, are particularly attractive – as are the long runs down to Grand-Paradis near Champéry when snow conditions allow. Pointe de Mossettes offers a less challenging route to Switzerland than the Swiss Wall itinéraire at Chavanette.

FOR BEGINNERS ★★★★☆
Convenient, but you pay
The nursery slopes seem small in relation to the size of the resort, but appear to cope. The slopes are sunny, yet good for snow, and link well to longer, easy runs. Our reservations are that the pistes can be busy, and that there are no free lifts.

FOR BOARDERS ★★★★★
Plenty to keep you busy all week
Avoriaz is great for expert riders. As well as state-of-the-art 'conventional' parks, there's The Stash. For safe freeriding after a dump, head for the 'snowcross' runs. For something more extreme, the long cliff band accessed from the Arare lift is perfect for cliff drops of all sizes. It is well worth hiring a guide to exploit the off-piste riding. There are some flat sections, especially in the Lindarets valley but very few draglifts, making this a good choice for novices too.

FOR CROSS-COUNTRY ★★★☆☆
Varied, with some blacks
There are 45km of trails, mainly between Avoriaz and Super-Morzine, plus Lindarets and Montriond.

MOUNTAIN RESTAURANTS ★★★★☆
Good choice over the hill
There are some good places, marked but not named on the piste map. **Editors' choice** The hamlet of Les Lindarets in the next valley consists of countless rustic restaurants – it is a popular tourist spot in summer. Our two favourites are the Terrasse (0450 741617) on a sunny day and the jolly Crémaillière (0450 741168) on a snowy one – both endorsed as 'excellent' by a reporter this year.
Worth knowing about A reporter raves about Les Alpages, just above Les Lindarets – 'ate there at least three times – huge and tasty steak with pepper sauce; such friendly service'. In the same area are the Barmettes with 'tasty crêpes and friendly service' and Mamo's Café ('very good soup', 'lovely Savoyard crêpe'). On the Super-Morzine slopes, the newish L'Passage is 'cosy, friendly, with great service'.

SCHOOLS AND GUIDES ★★★☆☆
Positive reports
A 2014 reporter thought the ESF 'patient, helpful – and the cheapest'. But another observed 'classes averaging 12'. We lack recent reports on the other schools.

FOR FAMILIES ★★★★☆
Very appealing
With snow everywhere and not a wheeled vehicle to be seen, Avoriaz has obvious appeal. Then there's the Village des Enfants, which takes children from age three. Its facilities are excellent. Check out Ardent.

Major Resorts
Expert knowledge

4★ ski apartments with spa

SkiCollection.co.uk
0844 576 0175
ABTA Bonded W5537

CATERED CHALETS
9-24 pers IN MORZINE

www.hostsavoie.co.uk

ACTIVITIES

Indoor Altiform fitness centre (sauna, gym, hot tub), Aquariaz fun swimming pool, squash, cinema, bowling

Outdoor Ice rink, dog sledding, mountain biking on snow, walking, snowshoeing, ski jöring, paragliding, snowmobiling, sleigh rides, helicopter flights, segway, 'yooner' tobogganing, caving

Phone numbers
From abroad use the prefix +33 and omit the initial '0' of the phone number

TOURIST OFFICE
www.avoriaz.com

Pierre & Vacances
premium

Perfect spacious apartments with spas and swimming pools.

pierreetvacances.co.uk

STAYING THERE

Alternatives to apartments are few.
Chalets Inghams has a chalet for 12. Ski Total has four neighbouring chalets including Marie in its Platinum range. All are ski-in/ski-out and have saunas. For family-oriented places, check out Ardent.
Hotels
***Dromonts Under new ownership and due to be refurbished. Reports welcome.
Apartments Pierre & Vacances' smart newish Amara development is an exciting addition, and the obvious place to stay if your budget will cope. It's almost a self-contained mini-resort, with its own shops, restaurants, spa, pool and underground parking (80 euros a week). The main lobby has a spacious lounge/bar, and a big terrace with great views. The apartments are stylish, and spacious by French standards. You can ski from the door to the Proclou fast chair. The Atria Crozats apartments are not quite in the same league, but are smartly furnished. For convenience, you might prefer the 'very comfortable' Saskia Falaise apartments, 'nicely renovated in Alpine wood style'. Agencies such as Ski Collection, Inghams, Crystal, PowderBeds and Erna Low offer some or all of these residences. Hanski specializes in short breaks here.

EATING OUT ★★★☆☆
A few interesting options
There are about 25 restaurants; but demand can exceed supply. We had an excellent dinner on our last visit at the Alpine-cool Bistro – good menu, excellent braised veal; live jazz sax when we were there. The cute, cosy old Chalet d'Avoriaz (aka Chez Lenvers) pleased one reporter last year: 'Excellent omelette, nice staff, good value.' A few bars are worth noting: Chapka does tapas, Tavaillon

('the best burgers in town') and Intrêts ('well-priced steak').

APRES-SKI ★★★☆☆
The bars are fun
A few bars have a good atmosphere, particularly in happy hour. There's DJ-fuelled action on the terrace of the Chalet d'Avoriaz at close of play. Other top tips are Tavaillon for sports TV ('very popular, spectacular cocktail of the day') and Shooters. Chapka is a hip bar with TV, live music and pool ('nice atmosphere'). For late-night dance action, the Place has bands.

OFF THE SLOPES ★☆☆☆☆
Not much at the resort
There's not a lot to keep non-skiers interested – few shops and activities. But there's a pedestrian/cross-country skiing pass which allows access to certain lifts. The smart newish Aquariaz is a big leisure pool complex with lush vegetation from Cambodia, and all sorts of features to amuse children, in particular. We've only toured it, but a reporter who got immersed rates it 'excellent'. The Altiform fitness centre has steam, saunas and hot tubs. The pool at the Amara development is open to non-residents. A recent reporter enjoyed bowling.

LINKED RESORT – 1200m
ARDENT

Ardent is a very quiet little place at the foot of the gondola up to Les Lindarets. It has the basics of life, including a bar and a ski shop. It seems ideal for families, and the Family Ski Company has eight chalets here, most with outdoor hot tub, some with sauna, none more than a short stroll from the gondola station.

LINKED RESORT – 1145m
LES PRODAINS

Les Prodains is at the foot of the cliffs on which Avoriaz sits, with a big newish gondola up them. There are some chalets and small hotels. The 3-star Lans (0450 790090) is a traditional family-run place, 300m from the lift – a regular visitor stayed twice last season and rates it highly – 'simple but cosy with wonderful food'. Host Savoie has a three-bedroom chalet here and another couple of places a bus ride away.

Les Carroz

A friendly family resort that makes a more compelling base than Flaine (or Samoëns) for the impressive Grand Massif area

SNOWPIX.COM / CHRIS GILL

TOP 10 RATINGS

Extent	★★★★☆
Fast lifts	★★★☆☆
Queues	★★★☆☆
Snow	★★★☆☆
Expert	★★★★☆
Intermediate	★★★★★
Beginner	★★★★☆
Charm	★★★★☆
Convenience	★★★☆☆
Scenery	★★★★☆

RPI   100

lift pass	£190
ski hire	£115
lessons	£85
food & drink	£135
total	**£525**

NEWS

2013/14: Aquacîme, a new spa/sports centre with outdoor pool opened. The snowcross on the Cupoire slope was extended.

PISTE MAP

Les Carroz is covered on the Flaine map

SNOWPIX.COM / CHRIS GILL

The village nursery slopes are quiet and without through-traffic
↓

+ Part of the big, varied Grand Massif

+ Pleasant, traditional village in a lovely balcony setting

+ Wooded slopes good in a storm

− Still lots of slow old chairlifts

− Village and local slopes are at modest altitudes

− Nightlife not a highlight

You pass through Les Carroz on the drive up to Flaine. You're welcome to carry on up, if you like; these days, we prefer to pull off at the lower village. Not only is it a much more pleasant place to spend time, it also makes more sense as a skiing base. In bad weather, you can ski the local slopes; when the sun comes out you can head off to more exposed slopes elsewhere in the Grand Massif.

THE RESORT

Les Carroz is a traditional village that has spread widely across a sunny, wooded shelf. It claims an altitude of 1200m, but only the top fringes of the village are that high – the centre is at about 1120m. It is linked to Morillon, Samoëns and Flaine; the latter two get their own chapters.

Village charm Les Carroz has the lived-in feel of a real village, where life revolves around the neat central square, with its small shops, cafes and restaurants. Traffic on the through-road to Flaine intrudes only at weekends.

Convenience Your lodgings may be some distance from the gondola or from the centre, or both; there are free ski-buses on five lines; you may find you need to use a timetable, though.

Scenery There are good views from the upper village, and the partly wooded valleys between here and Flaine are very scenic.

THE MOUNTAINS

The slopes directly above the village are densely wooded, but there are lots of open slopes towards Flaine. Some blue runs involved in the trip to Flaine have tricky steep sections.

Slopes Read the Flaine chapter for views on the extent of the Grand Massif pistes. The village gondola rises 600m, serving blue runs and launching you towards the other linked resorts.

Fast lifts Outside the Flaine bowl, there are lots of slow chairs – Tête des Saix has a spectacular gathering of them. More investment is needed to solve the problem.

Queues In high season the gondola may have 15-minute morning queues; and you can expect delays and crowded pistes on the way to Flaine – and very crowded runs on the way back at the end of the day.

Terrain parks There isn't one.

Snow reliability The Les Carroz runs are west-facing and low, and can suffer from strong afternoon sun; but a few runs have snowmaking. The slopes of Morillon and Samoëns, on the other hand, are north-facing, and the latter are a bit higher, too – so the snow keeps in better condition.

Experts There are some proper black pistes above Samoëns and in the next-door Molliets valley, but the main interest is the extensive off-piste in various sectors, including the Molliets and Vernant valleys between Les Carroz and Flaine. Don't miss Flaine's Combe de Gers.

Intermediates As our ★★★★★ rating suggests, this is a great area, whether you like a challenge or not. Most people can get around the whole area,

223

milk**hotel**

Contemporary decor – Ski in Ski out

route des servages 74300 les carroz
tel.: +33 (0)6 17 77 70 23
www.milkhotel.fr

KEY FACTS

Resort	1120m
	3,670ft

Grand Massif ski area (Les Carroz and all linked resorts)	
Slopes	700-2480m
	2,300-8,140ft
Lifts	68
Pistes	265km
	165 miles
Green	12%
Blue	45%
Red	33%
Black	10%
Snowmaking	
	218 guns

Phone numbers
From abroad use the prefix +33 and omit the initial '0' of the phone number

TOURIST OFFICE

www.lescarroz.com

Perfect spacious apartments with spas and swimming pools.

pierreetvacances.co.uk

although there are some tricky blues to contend with.

Beginners Pretty good: the village nursery slopes are quiet and there are also green and easy blue runs at the top of the gondola, with excellent longer blue runs to progress to.

Snowboarding Some of the linking runs at altitude are almost flat. But there are few draglifts to deal with.

Cross-country There are 25km of tracks between Morillon and Les Carroz, some quite challenging.

Mountain restaurants They are marked but not named on the resort piste map. Read the Flaine and Samoëns chapters too. The 'lovely rustic' Chalet les Molliets at the bottom of the Molliets chair is popular. Reporters liked the food (and the toilets) at the Anfionne on the Plein Soleil home run. Above Morillon, we've had an excellent plat du jour at the rustic Igloo – 'busy, but efficient and friendly', 'awesome salads'. Reporters continue to rate Chalet d'Clair – 'very friendly table-service', 'good vibe, cosy, wide menu, great burgers', 'best hot chocolate'.

Schools and guides There is regular praise for the ESF: 'The best we've encountered,' says a visitor. Others have praised the International school: 'Kids enjoyed it and progressed well.'

Families Pick lodgings near the lifts would be our advice. The ESF runs a kindergarten for infants aged 3 months to 3 years; the Loupiots club offers activities for children aged 3 to 12.

UK PACKAGES

360 Sun and Ski, Crystal, Erna Low, Hanski, Lagrange, Peak Retreats, Pierre & Vacances, PowderBeds, Ski Independence, Ski Line, Skiology.co.uk, STC, Thomson, Zenith

STAYING THERE

Hotels There are five hotels, including two at the top of the village, beside the Timalets red home run (with a link to the gondola). Servages d'Armelle (0450 900162) is a lovely little 4-star, housed in two old chalets. The nearby Milkhotel (0450 900618) has been highly recommended: 'friendly staff', 'good set menu'.

Apartments Les Chalets de Jouvence is an excellent CGH low-rise residence in an ideal location next to the Telecarroz draglift (for access to the gondola); we had a very spacious apartment here a couple of seasons ago; readers were impressed too – 'lovely pool'. Les Fermes du Soleil is a similar Pierre & Vacances Premium residence with pool, hot tubs etc, close to the centre. Both are available through Peak Retreats and Erna Low.

Eating out Best in town is Aux Petits Oignons, a cosy place run by a charming couple; we had excellent meals here in 2012 and 2013. The very appealing Bistrot Grill du Gron was booked out when we visited, but is 'a carnivore delight'. Hotel les Airelles has a cosy restaurant. Other reader tips are Spatule, Piccolo and Agora.

Après-ski On the slopes, the Anfionne is good for a quiet beer on the way home. In the village the Marlow pub has 'a bit of a buzz'; Cave 59 is a wine bar; Pointe Noire and Carpe Diem are other options.

Off the slopes Outdoors there's ice skating, snowshoeing, dog sledding and skijoring. There's a cinema. And the new Aquacîme sports/spa centre with outdoor pool opened last season.

OT CHAMONIX MONT-BLANC

Chamonix

HQ of French and arguably European mountaineering, with a magnetic attraction for tourists and off-piste thrill seekers alike

RATINGS

The mountains

Extent	★★★
Fast lifts	★★★
Queues	★★
Terrain p'ks	★★★
Snow	★★★★
Expert	★★★★★
Intermediate	★★
Beginner	★★
Boarder	★★★
X-country	★★★
Restaurants	★★
Schools	★★★★★
Families	★★

The resort

Charm	★★★★
Convenience	★
Scenery	★★★★★
Eating out	★★★★★
Après-ski	★★★★
Off-slope	★★★★★

RPI   105

lift pass	£190
ski hire	£120
lessons	£100
food & drink	£145
total	£555

NEWS

2014/15: The ancient Plan Joran chair at the base of Les Grand Montets is due to be replaced by a 10-person gondola. This should greatly reduce the queue problem there.

2013/14: Step into the Void, an enclosed glass viewing area (including a glass floor) above a '1000m precipice', opened at Aiguille du Midi. A new 4-star hotel, the Héliopic, opened at the foot of the Aiguille du Midi cable car.

➕ A lot of very tough terrain, especially off-piste

➕ Amazing cable car to the Aiguille du Midi, for the famous Vallée Blanche

➕ Stunning views wherever you are

➕ Other resorts covered on extended lift pass, notably sunny Courmayeur

➕ Town steeped in Alpine tradition

➕ Lots of affordable hotels – and many will take short bookings

➖ Several separate mountains, widely separated; bad for mixed abilities

➖ Inadequate bus services

➖ Bad weather can shut the best runs

➖ Still some old lifts, and serious queues in key spots

➖ It's a busy town, with lots of road traffic; not a relaxing place

➖ Shady and cold in midwinter

Chamonix could not be more different from the archetypal high-altitude, purpose-built French resort. It hasn't been designed to deliver the smoothest possible experience to the widest possible market. It hasn't been designed.

You don't have to be an expert to enjoy the place – Editor Gill once took his blue-run-skiing wife and novice kids for a week here, and lived to tell the tale. But it is the expert and the adventurous would-be expert who really must give Chamonix a permanent place on their shortlist, despite its serious drawbacks.

THE RESORT

Chamonix is a long-established, year-round tourist town that spreads for miles along the valley in the shadow of Mont Blanc.

On either side of the centre, just within walking distance, are base stations of the cable car to the Aiguille du Midi (for the famous Vallée Blanche glacier run) and a gondola to Le Brévent. A third high-altitude area, La Flégère, is linked to Le Brévent by cable car and reached by its own cable car from the village of Les Praz.

At the top of the valley are the villages of Argentière, beneath the Grands Montets and Le Tour (with the foot of the Balme slopes (with an alternative base at Vallorcine). These villages are described at the end of the chapter, but their slopes are taken in to the main part of the chapter.

Down the valley is Les Houches, with the most sheltered slopes in the valley. This is wholly described at the end of the chapter; its lifts are not covered by the normal Chamonix pass.

Free ski-buses link all these points but can get very crowded ('even in January') and be 'infrequent and unreliable'. Don't expect additional buses to meet varying demand (eg when everyone wants to get to Les Houches in bad weather). There are also hourly trains along the valley, free with a guest card, and usually recommended by reporters.

The Mont Blanc Unlimited lift pass covers not only Les Houches but also Verbier in Switzerland and Courmayeur in Italy. The first is a major expedition; the second is of more practical use, not least because the weather can be good in Italy when it is lousy in Chamonix. And there are buses (free

Tailor made, long weekend and short break French Alps ski holiday specialists.

Hanski
Ski. Explore. Relax.

web: www.hanski.co.uk
tel: 01638 596373
mob: 07833 612061

with the Mont Blanc lift pass) through the Mont Blanc tunnel several times daily. Having a car is useful in lots of ways, and makes that outing to Verbier a more practical proposition.

VILLAGE CHARM ★★★★☆
Lots of atmosphere

It's a bustling place, with scores of hotels and restaurants and shops selling everything from tacky souvenirs to high-tech climbing gear. The car-free centre is full of atmosphere, with cobbled streets and squares, beautiful old buildings, a fast-running river and pavement cafes. Away from the centre, there are lots of apartment blocks. There are some disused buildings, and traffic clogs the streets at times.

CONVENIENCE ★☆☆☆☆
You don't come here for that

The obvious place to stay for the full experience is close to the centre, where you can be a short walk from the gondola to Brévent. Or you adapt to life on the buses or trains.

SCENERY ★★★★★
As dramatic as it gets

The mountains above Chamonix are not just high – the mighty Mont Blanc is the highest in Western Europe – they are also truly spectacular. The ride up to the Aiguille du Midi is breathtaking in every sense (we've known of people needing to lie down for a while when they get to the top).

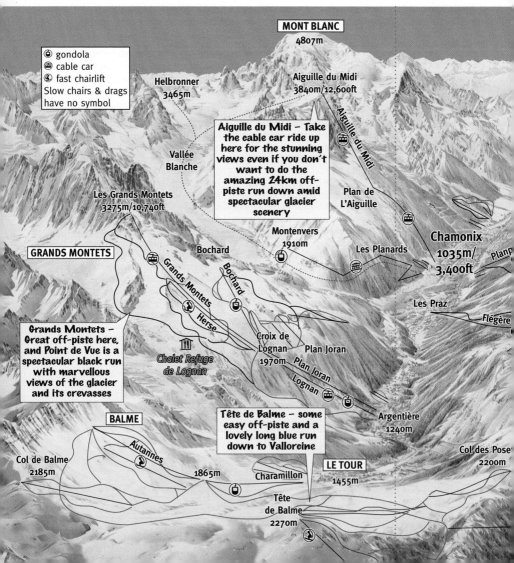

Key:
- 🚡 gondola
- 🚠 cable car
- 💺 fast chairlift
- Slow chairs & drags have no symbol

MONT BLANC 4807m

Helbronner 3465m

Aiguille du Midi 3840m/12,600ft

Aiguille du Midi – Take the cable car ride up here for the stunning views even if you don't want to do the amazing 24km off-piste run down amid spectacular glacier scenery

Vallée Blanche

Plan de L'Aiguille

Les Grands Montets 3275m/10,740ft

Chamonix 1035m/ 3,400ft

GRANDS MONTETS

Bochard

Montenvers 1910m

Les Planards

Les Praz

Planp

Flégère

Grands Montets

Bochard

Herse

Grands Montets – Great off-piste here, and Point de Vue is a spectacular black run with marvellous views of the glacier and its crevasses

Chalet Refuge de Lognan

Croix de Lognan 1970m

Plan Joran

Plan Joran

Lognan

Argentière 1240m

BALME

Autannes

Col des Pose 2200m

Tête de Balme – some easy off-piste and a lovely long blue run down to Vallorcine

Col de Balme 2185m

1865m

Charamillon

LE TOUR 1455m

Tête de Balme 2270m

KEY FACTS

Resort	1035m
	3,400ft
Slopes	1035-3840m
	3,400-12,600ft
Lifts	42
Pistes	115km
	71 miles
Green	12%
Blue	42%
Red	31%
Black	15%
Snowmaking	
	139 guns

THE MOUNTAINS

Practically all the slopes – with the notable exception of Les Houches – are above the treeline. There are some runs down through woods to the valley floor but the black ones from Brévent and Flégère, in particular, are often closed due to lack of snow or poor conditions and can be unpleasantly tricky if open.

The piste map has maps for each individual area as well as the valley as a whole. Signposting and piste marking are OK. But in sectors other than Balme, the classification of runs often understates difficulty – in particular, some of the blues would be classified as reds in other resorts.

EXTENT OF THE SLOPES ★★★★★
Very fragmented

The gondola for **Brévent** departs a short, steep walk or bus ride from the centre. There are runs on open slopes below the arrival point, and a cable car goes on to the summit. There is a lift link to **Flégère**, also accessible via an inadequate old cable car from the village of Les Praz. These sunny areas give stunning views of Mont Blanc.

Up the valley at Argentière a cable car or the new gondola takes you up to the high slopes of **Les Grands Montets**. Chairs and a gondola serve open terrain above mid-mountain, but much of the best terrain is accessed by a further cable car of relatively low capacity, not covered by the standard

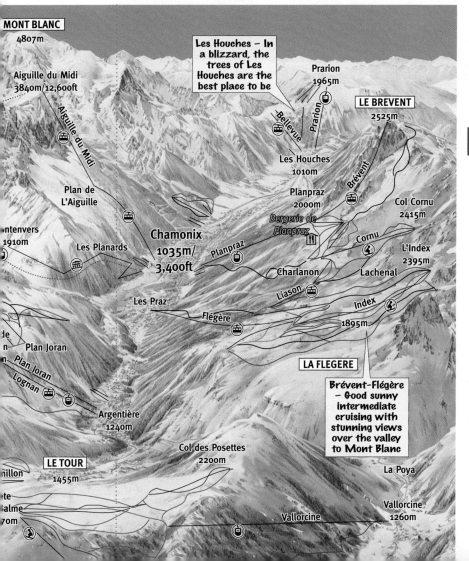

MONT BLANC
4807m

Aiguille du Midi
3840m/12,600ft

Les Houches – In a blizzard, the trees of Les Houches are the best place to be

Prarion
1965m

LE BREVENT
2525m

Bellevue

Prarion

Aiguille du Midi

Plan de L'Aiguille

ntenvers
1910m

Chamonix
1035m/
3,400ft

Les Planards

Les Houches
1010m

Planpraz
2000m

Bergerie de Planpraz

Planpraz

Col Cornu
2415m

Cornu

L'Index
2395m

Lachenal

Charlanon

Liason

Les Praz

Flégère

Index
1895m

LA FLEGERE

Brévent-Flégère – Good sunny intermediate cruising with stunning views over the valley to Mont Blanc

le
n Plan Joran

Plan Joran

Lognan

Argentière
1240m

Col des Posettes
2200m

LE TOUR

illon   1455m

te
alme
om

La Poya

Vallorcine
1226m

Vallorcine

↑ The views of Mont Blanc from Brévent and Flégère are breathtaking. This is the Panoramic restaurant at the top of Brévent

OT CHAMONIX / T HARRINGTON

MOMENTUM SKI

Weekend & a la carte ski holiday specialists

100% Tailor-made

Premier hotels & apartments

Flexible travel arrangements

020 7371 9111
WWW.MOMENTUMSKI.COM

Resort news and key links: www.wheretoskiandsnowboard.com

lift pass (read 'Lift passes'). This shady area can be very cold in early season.

A little way further up the valley, the secluded village of Le Tour sits at the foot of the broad **Balme** area. A gondola goes up to mid-mountain, with a mix of drags and chairs above. There is also a lift up from Vallorcine.

Plus there are several low beginner areas dotted along the valley.

FAST LIFTS ★★★☆☆
Not enough
Cable cars and gondolas serve each sector, but many need upgrading. The five fast chairs are widely scattered. Many reporters are scathing: 'the worst lift system I've seen', 'disgraceful' are two 2014 views.

QUEUES ★★☆☆☆
Ancient lifts, serious queues
Access to Brévent was transformed by the gondola upgrade a few years ago. And hopefully the new gondola for 2014/15 at the Grands Montets will reduce the serious waiting times at the bottom there. But at mid-mountain, the top cable car will remain a famous bottleneck. You can book slots in advance (on the spot or online), preferably the day before, or join the 'standby' queue, which we've found to be an effective alternative.

The valley has other problem lifts too. The ancient 60-person Flégère cable car can generate queues of an hour or more – to go down as well as

up. There may be queues for the lift up to Balme at La Tour, too; it can be quicker to take the train to Vallorcine.

Crowded pistes and skiers travelling too fast for the conditions can also be a problem in places – most notably on parts of the Grands Montets.

TERRAIN PARKS ★★★☆☆
A couple of options
The Summit Park on Grands Montets incorporates features for all levels and includes kickers, rails, jumps, boxes, hips, tables and a step-up feature. There's also a snowcross course. At Brévent there's an airbag jump; you can be filmed doing it to view on the internet later.

SNOW RELIABILITY ★★★★☆
Good high up; poor low down
The top runs on the north-facing Grands Montets slopes above Argentière generally have good snow, and the season normally lasts well into May. The risk of finding the top lift shut because of bad weather is more of a worry. There's snowmaking on the busy Bochard piste and the run to the valley. Balme has a snowy location, a good late-season record and snowmaking on the run down to the valley at Le Tour. The largely south-facing slopes of Brévent and Flégère suffer in warm weather, and the steep black runs to the resort are often closed. Don't be tempted to try these unless you know they are in

LIFT PASSES

Chamonix Le Pass

Prices in €

Age	1-day	6-day
under 16	39	196
16 to 64	46	230
65 plus	39	196

Free Under 4
Beginner No deals
Senior 75 plus: 50% of adult price
Notes Covers Brévent, Flégère, Balme, Grands Montets except top cable car, plus four small beginner areas; family reductions; part-day pass
Alternative pass
Mont Blanc Unlimited (MBU) covers all the above plus Les Houches, Montenvers train, Aiguille du Midi and Helbronner cable cars, Lognan-Grands Montets cable car, Courmayeur (Italy) – and (for 6-day-plus passes only) Verbier (Switzerland)

GETTING THERE

Air Geneva 90km/ 55 miles (1hr15); Lyon 220km/ 135 miles (2hr15)

Rail Station in resort, on the St Gervais-Le Fayet/Vallorcine line

good condition – they can be very tricky. Snowmaking was increased at Flégère three seasons ago to improve the link to Brévent. Some of the low beginners' areas have snowmaking. Piste grooming is generally OK.

FOR EXPERTS ★★★★★
One of the great resorts
Chamonix is renowned for its extensive steep terrain and deep snow. To get the best out of the area you really need to have a local guide. There is also lots of excellent terrain for ski touring on skins. Read the feature panel for more off-piste possibilities.

The Grands Montets cable car offers stunning views from the observation platform above the top station – if you've got the legs and lungs to climb the 121 steep metal steps. (But beware: it's 200 more slippery steel steps down from the cable car before you hit the snow.) The ungroomed black pistes from here – Point de Vue and Pylones – are long and exhilarating. The former sails right by some dramatic sections of glacier, with marvellous views of the crevasses.

The Bochard gondola serves a challenging red back to Lognan and a black to either Plan Roujon or the chairlift below. Shortly after you have made a start down the black, you can head off-piste down the Combe de la Pendant bowl.

At Brévent there's more to test experts than the piste map suggests – there are a number of variations on the runs down from the summit. Some are very steep and prone to ice. The red and black runs in Combe de la Charlanon are quiet, and there is excellent off-piste if the snow is good.

At Flégère there are further challenging slopes – in the Combe Lachenal, crossed by the linking cable car, say – and a tough run back to the village when the snow permits. The short draglift above L'Index opens up a couple of good steep runs (a red and a black) plus a good area of off-piste.

Balme boasts little tough terrain on-piste, but there are off-piste routes from the high points to Le Tour, towards Vallorcine or into Switzerland.

FOR INTERMEDIATES ★★★★★
Plenty of better resorts
Chamonix is far from ideal for intermediates unless they relish challenging slopes and trying off-piste. If what you want is mile after mile of

lift-linked cruisy pistes, you should go elsewhere. For less confident intermediates, the Balme area above Le Tour is good for cruising and usually free from crowds. There are excellent shady, steeper runs, wooded lower down, on the north side of Tête de Balme, served by a fast quad. A lovely red run goes on down to Vallorcine, but it is prone to closure.

The other areas have some blue and red runs. Even the Grands Montets has an area of blues at mid-mountain. The step up to the red terrain higher up is quite pronounced, however.

If the snow and weather are good, confident intermediates can join a guided group and do the Vallée Blanche (read our feature panel).

FOR BEGINNERS ★★★★★
Head for Balme
Chamonix is far from ideal for beginners, too – there are countless better resorts in which to learn. There are limited but adequate nursery slopes either side of the town – Savoy, at the bottom of Brévent, and Les Planards, on the opposite side (dark and cold in midwinter). Moving on to longer runs means taking a lift up to Brévent or Flégère. La Vormaine, at Le Tour, is a much better bet: extensive, relatively high, sunny and connected to the slopes of the Balme area, where there are easy long runs to progress to. But it's 12km from Chamonix itself.

FOR BOARDERS ★★★★★
Leave it to the experts
The undisputed king of freeride resorts, Chamonix is a haven for advanced snowboarders who relish the steep and wild terrain, especially on the Grands Montets. This means, however, that in peak season it's crowded, and fresh snow gets tracked out very quickly. Keen riders should check out former British champion Neil McNab's excellent extreme backcountry snowboard camps at: www. mcnabsnowboarding.com.

The rough and rugged nature of the slopes means they are not best suited for beginners but rather for more adventurous riders willing to try true all-mountain riding. The easiest terrain is at the Balme area, though there are quite a few difficult drags here (you can avoid these if you can hack the cat tracks to take you to other lifts, says a reporter). Most lifts elsewhere are cable cars, gondolas and chairs.

Chamonix is renowned as an extreme sports Mecca, with arguably some of the best off-piste skiing in the world. And while thrill-seekers and off-piste specialists are spoiled for choice, there is plenty for those looking for their first powder experience, too.

Les Houches and **Balme**, *at opposite ends of the Chamonix Valley, are ideal for a first taste off the beaten track. The forested slopes of Les Houches are easy to navigate on bad-weather days, with gentle blue runs bringing you back to the valley. Balme's open slopes are perfect for a foray into deep snow in between the pistes, with firmer ground just a few reassuring metres away.*

Snowboarders flock to **Flégère** *after a snowfall, its array of boulders and drop-offs turning it into a massive terrain park. The open bowl of Combe Lachenal is easily accessed from the top of the Index lift, and the south-facing slopes of this ski area provide excellent spring skiing.*

From the top of **Les Grands Montets** *(3275m) skiing is mostly off-piste and on glacial terrain. The vast north-facing slope of the main face offers countless ways down, satisfyingly steep without being intimidating, with snow conditions that are often among the best in the valley. Off the back, there are several rewarding ways down to the Glacier d'Argentière. In the opposite direction you have access to the steep Pas de Chèvre run. Skiing under the colossal granite spire of Le Dru, with views of the Vallée Blanche, is an unforgettable experience. The Couloir du Dru and the Rectiligne are also on this face, reserved for the adventurous – with some slopes of 40/45°.*

These are just some of the options, but the possibilities are endless. Together with heli-skiing on the Italian side of Mont Blanc and in neighbouring Switzerland, the wealth of off-piste on offer could keep you skiing for a lifetime.

This is a trip you do for the stunning scenery. The views of the glacier and the spectacular rock spires beyond are simply mind-blowing. The standard run, although exceptionally long, is not steep – mostly gliding down gentle slopes (in places a bit too flat for snowboarders) with only the occasional steeper, choppy section to deal with. In the right conditions, it is well within the capability of a confident, fit intermediate. If snow is sparse, as it often is in early season, the run can be very tricky, with patches of sheet ice and exposed rocks, and narrow snow bridges over gaping crevasses. If fresh snow is abundant, different challenges may arise. Go in a guided group and check conditions before signing up at the Maison de la Montagne or other ski school offices. The trip is popular – on a busy day 2,500 people do it. To miss the crowds, go very early on a weekday, or in the afternoon if you are a good skier and can get down quickly.

The cable car takes you to 3840m and the 3842 cafeteria (claimed to be Europe's highest restaurant) – check out the amazing view of Mont Blanc from here while you adjust to the dizzying altitude. Be prepared for extreme cold, too. A tunnel delivers you to the infamous ridge-walk down to the start of the run. Except at the start of the season, the walk is well prepared, with regular steps cut in the snow and fixed ropes to hang on to. If you have a backpack capable of carrying your skis, and crampons to give some grip, it's no problem; ask for them when you book your guide. Without those items, it can be tiring and worrying. Many parties rope up to their guides.

There are variants on the classic route, of varying difficulty and danger; on our last descent we did a mixture of the Petit Envers du Plan and the Vrai Vallée Blanche in 20cm of fresh snow under a blue sky with few other people around – it was absolutely magical, with hundreds of fresh-track turns among all that stunning scenery. Lack of snow often rules out the full 24km run down to Chamonix; a steep stairway (be warned: 311 steps) leading to a slow gondola links the glacier to the station at Montenvers, for the half-hour mountain railway ride down to the town.

SNOWPIX.COM / CHRIS GILL

Ski coaching. Chamonix.
Achieve optimum
results with
focussed and
friendly tuition.
+33(0)616871853
powderama.com

SCHOOLS

ESF
t 0450 532257

BASS
t 0845 468 1003 (UK)

Evolution 2
t 0450 555357

Ski Sensations
t 0682 105922

Classes (ESF prices)
6 half-days: €158

Private lessons
€124 for 2hr, for 1 or
2 people

GUIDES

**Compagnie des
Guides**
t 0450 530088

Chamonix Experience
t 0977 485869

CHILDCARE

**Panda Club
(Evolution 2)**
t 0450 555357
From age 3

Piou Piou (ESF)
t 0450 532257
From age 3

Babysitter list
At tourist office

Ski schools
Ages 3 to 12

If you do the Vallée Blanche, be warned: the usual route is very flat in places, so be prepared to scoot.

FOR CROSS-COUNTRY ★★★✰✰
A decent network of trails
Most of the 53km of prepared trails lie at valley level – and were highly rated by a recent visitor. But the trails are shady and often icy in midwinter, and they fade fast in the spring sun. Catch the bus rather than ski between the Chamonix and Argentière areas, suggests a reporter, as the link is by 'steep and difficult trails'.

MOUNTAIN RESTAURANTS ★★✰✰✰
Mainly dull, lacking choice
Editors' choice On Brévent the Bergerie de Planpraz (0450 530542) is a wood and stone building with self- and table-service sections and good food; but it gets very busy. On the Grands Montets the tiny, rustic Chalet-Refuge de Lognan (0688 560354), off the Variante Hôtel run to the valley, has marvellous views and satisfying, simple food. Recent reporters agree.
Worth knowing about On the Grands Montets, one regular visitor rates Plan Joran 'probably the best in the valley'; it has table- and self-service, and a big terrace. There is a picnic room at Lognan. Tucked away in the woods to skier's right of the home run, the Crémerie du Glacier is a cosy spot for a croûte.

On Brévent the little Panoramic at the top enjoys amazing views over to Mont Blanc, and the food is fine. On Flégère the recently renovated table-service Adret is 'not outstanding, but definitely pretty good'. The Chavanne is one reader's favourite despite the 'small choice' of food – 'amazing view'. At Balme, at the top of the gondola from Le Tour, there's an adequate self-service and a picnic area. Ecuries de Charamillon is in a renovated farmhouse.

SCHOOLS AND GUIDES ★★★★★
The place to try something new
The schools here are particularly strong in specialist fields – off-piste, glacier and couloir skiing, ski touring, snowboarding and cross-country. English-speaking instructors and mountain guides are plentiful.

At the Maison de la Montagne are the main ESF office and the HQ of the Compagnie des Guides, which is highly rated and has taken visitors to the

---

mountains for 150 years (we and reporters have had very good guides from here and a 2014 reporter who did the Vallée Blanche said their guide 'gave our 12-year-old lots of confidence'). Both organizations offer week-long 'tours' taking clients to a different mountain or resort each day.

A 2014 reporter's wife went back for the second year running to Evolution 2 and found her instructor 'excellent, giving her renewed confidence to tackle steeper slopes'.

Powderama is run by British instructor Simon Halliwell and offers five-day and weekend courses plus specialized one-day clinics (off-piste, piste, moguls).

FOR FAMILIES ★★✰✰✰
Very limited
Childcare is available from some of the ski schools. Evolution 2's Panda Club is used by quite a few British visitors; reports have been enthusiastic but the Argentière base can be inconvenient. Les Houches has better facilities, with a day care centre and children's club.

STAYING THERE

There is all sorts of accommodation, and lots of it. Several weekend specialists operate here including Ski Weekend, who started up in Chamonix way back in 1987 and offer chalets, hotels, apartments and optional on- and off-piste courses. Other short-break specialists include Momentum, Hanski and Ski Weekends (not to be confused with their singular rival).
Chalets Many chalets are run by small specialist operators such as Collineige. Inghams runs the 60-bed Sapinière – overlooking the nursery slope at the bottom of Brévent and not far from the centre – as a chalet hotel: 'Comfortable, well placed, run to a very high standard,' said a reporter. They also have two central chalet apartments for six that can be combined to sleep 12.
Hotels There's a wide choice, many modestly priced, the majority with no more than 30 rooms or so. Bookings for short stays are no problem – the peak season is summer. Club Med has three linked buildings near the centre. Out at Le Lavancher is the 'hameau hôtelier' Les Chalets de Philippe (0607 231726) – a secluded cluster of lovingly furnished wooden chalets, most sleeping no more than three or

Ski Weekend
the ultimate short break

we are the original
short break
ski specialists

over *25* years

01392 878 353
www.skiweekend.com

UK PACKAGES

Action Outdoors, Adventure Base, Alpine Answers, Alpine Elements, Alpine Weekends, Bigfoot Chamonix, Carrier, Chalet la Forêt, Chamonix.uk.com, Club Med, Collineige, Cru Chalets, Crystal, Crystal Finest, Elegant Resorts, Erna Low, Flexiski, Hanski, High Mountain, Huski, Igoski, Inghams, Inspired to Ski, Interactive Resorts, Jeffersons, Kaluma, Lagrange, Luxury Chalet Collection, Momentum, Mountain Beds, Mountain Tracks, Neilson, Oxford Ski Co, Peak Retreats, Pierre & Vacances, PowderBeds, Rude Chalets, Ski Bespoke, Ski Club Freshtracks, Ski Collection, Ski Expectations, Ski France, Ski Independence, Ski Line, Ski Weekend, Skitracer, Skiweekends.com, Snow Finders, Snow-wise, STC, Thomson, Tracks European Adventures, White Roc, Zenith

four, with meals taken either in your own chalet or in a small central dining room.

*****Auberge du Bois Prin (0450 533351) A small modern chalet with a big reputation; great views; bit of a hike into town (closer to Brévent).

*****Hameau Albert 1er (0450 530509) Smart, 100-year-old chalet-style Relais & Châteaux hotel with farmhouse annexe. Restaurant with two Michelin stars. Pool.

*****Mont-Blanc (0450 530564) Grand 19th-century place in a central location. Refurbished and reopened in 2013 with spa and pool.

****Jeu de Paume (Lavancher) (0450 540376) Alpine satellite of a chic Parisian hotel: a beautifully furnished modern chalet halfway to Argentière.

****Morgane (0450 535715) Cool modern style; excellent restaurant, Michelin-starred; good location near Aiguille de Midi cable car; pool, sauna.

***Alpina (0450 534777) Striking modern place just north of centre. Much the biggest in town – 138 rooms, most with balconies and mountain views. Sauna, hot tub.

***Croix-Blanche (0450 530011) Small, simple hotel and brasserie in centre.

***Lanchers (0450 534719) Near Flégère. Tipped repeatedly by reporters for accommodation, food and friendly service.

***Mercure (0450 530756) Next to the station. Comfortable rooms, friendly service. Has its own ski hire facilities.

***Oustalet (0450 555499) In Chamonix Sud. 'Well situated, really helpful staff, good breakfast, spacious room, spotless.'

***Prieuré (0450 532072) Mega-chalet on northern ring-road – handy for drivers, quite close to centre. Sauna, hot tub. 'Friendly, comfortable, good food, excellent dessert buffet.'

Le Vert (0450 531358) In Le Gailland, a mile from Chamonix, with en-suite rooms for one to six people. Lively bar, top DJs, pool table, Sunday roast.

Apartments Many properties in UK package brochures are in convenient blocks in Chamonix Sud but are rather cramped if you fill them to capacity. The Ginabelle is different – a Pierre & Vacances Premium residence near the station, with pool, spa and fitness facilities, also available through Peak Retreats, Erna Low and Skitracer. Zenith has a wide range of self-catered chalets, sleeping from six to 18.

EATING OUT ★★★★★
Plenty of quality places
Chamonix offers more variety than is normal in French resorts. The top hotels all have excellent restaurants, and there are many other good places. One or two advertising-based guides are distributed locally.

It's some years since we ate at the hotel Morgane's Bistrot; it was excellent then, and it has had a Michelin star since 2007. The Impossible is a favourite with us and with readers – a rustic chalet a short walk out of the centre with a varied menu. And we always enjoy the intimate Atmosphère, by the river, despite its two-sitting system – endorsed by a 2014 reporter. Alan Peru gets the thumbs up this year: 'good food and relatively reasonable prices'. Café de l'Arve at the hotel de l'Arve, offers a modern, creative menu ('haute-cuisine without the haute-prices'). According to a regular reporter the Panier des 4 Saisons is 'very possibly the best restaurant in Chamonix' with its inventive modern regional French cuisine. The 'cosy' Monchu does good Savoyard food and service at reasonable prices. The Calèche gets booked up well ahead and is short on space but does 'excellent' traditional and more adventurous dishes. Munchie offers a mix of French and Scandinavian cooking that makes a refreshing change.

Value-oriented reader tips include Pitz and Neopolis (both pizza), La Flambée ('good pizza, pasta, steak and local dishes') and the Poèle.

APRES-SKI ★★★★☆
You have to know where to go
Chamonix attracts a lot of young Brits and Scandis – blokes, mainly – wanting to après-ski hard after skiing hard. But it is not Austria, or even Méribel, and it does not have one of the rapidly expanding Folie Douce on-mountain party places. It's a big town, and you have to know where to go. One exception is an obvious place at Flégère – the Rhododendrons, which has live music.

In the town, the teatime après zone that we hear most about is beside the train station. The Swedish-run Chambre Neuf has 'good cover bands, pitchers of beer and even dancing on the tables – great fun'. Elevation 1904, opposite, is a bit quieter.

ACTIVITIES

Indoor Sports complex (swimming pool, sauna, steam room, tennis, squash, ice rink, fitness room, climbing wall), museums, library, cinemas

Outdoor Ice rink, snowshoeing, walking paths, tobogganing, dog sledding, paragliding

OT CHAMONIX / M DALMASSO

Nearly all the photos the Chamonix tourist office sends us feature Mont Blanc and its glaciers – not surprising really ↓

Towards the river in Rue Whymper, the Lapin Agile is a relaxed wine bar doing Italian-style appetizers. Over the river is the central square with La Terrasse ('really characterful old high-ceilinged place'). To the left is Rue du Dr Paccard. The Pub gets packed with Brits. Or turn right for the key Rue des Moulins. Bar'dUp is a small, relaxed place with live music and DJs. Mix is a 'wicked' cool DJ bar. Top tips for grown-ups are Privilege, a relaxed, woody, rustic-chic place with table-service and live acoustic music and the Quartz Bar, next to the Albert 1er hotel which is 'swanky and chic, smart dress only'. Soul Food is 'cool, French'. In Chamonix Sud, Monkey Bar is frequented by 'those in the know'.

Just outside the centre, MBC is a Canadian-run microbrewery, often with live bands – 'good ambience, great beer and apparently reasonable food'.

There's a variety of nightclubs and discos. Amnesia (formerly The Garage) claims to be the biggest. The White Hub is allegedly open from 11pm to 7am; just the times we are tucked up in bed. Real action enthusiasts may want to look at getting out of town to Le Vert ('hippest nightspot in town').

OFF THE SLOPES ★★★★★
An excellent choice
There's more off-slope activity here than in many resorts. Everyone other than those with medical issues should ride the Aiguille du Midi cable car. Excursion possibilities are endless. The Alpine Museum is 'very interesting but all in French', the library has some English language books and there's a good sports centre with a pool, ice skating and ice hockey matches.

OUTLYING VILLAGE – 1240m
ARGENTIERE

This old village is in an impressive setting towards the head of the valley, 9km from Chamonix. There's a fair bit of modern development, and the road through to Le Tour, Vallorcine and Switzerland gets uncomfortably busy, but it still has a rustic appeal.

The lifts to the Grands Montets are about 600m from the slightly elevated centre of the village. It's a fair hike, but there are buses. Readers like two central hotels: the 3-star Couronne (0450 540002) – recommended by three separate 2014 reporters and 'cheap, comfortable, charming; friendly staff but rooms at front can be noisy' – and the 2-star Dahu (0450 540155) – 'good room, excellent breakfast'. Out near the lifts are the 4-star Grands-Montets (0450 540666), with pool – excellent rooms and service said a 2014 report – and the 3-star Montana (0450 541499).

Le Cristal d'Argentière is a smart Lagrange Prestige residence, between the centre and the lifts, with a decent pool (available through Peak Retreats and Erna Low).

There's a reasonable choice of inexpensive, unpretentious restaurants and bars in the central area. An old favourite is the Office, offering a traditional Brit-pub atmosphere and menu; 'good burgers, pie and chips'; 'live music'; 'part of the reason I return to Argentière every year'. The two central hotels mentioned above both have attractive restaurants. Reader recommendations include the P'tite Verte ('excellent value three-course dinner') and the Stone ('excellent pizzas, pasta and steak'). Other tipped

Chamonix

Build your own shortlist: **www.wheretoskiandsnowboard.com**

Like the resort?

You'll love our handpicked accommodation

0844 576 0173
peakretreats.co.uk

⊕ABTA
ABTA No.W5537

peak retreats

UK PACKAGES

Argentière Action Outdoors, Adventure Base, Alpine Answers, Bigfoot Chamonix, Collineige, Erna Low, Lagrange, Marmotte Mountain Adventure, Mountain Beds, Peak Retreats, PowderBeds, Ski Club Freshtracks, Ski Weekend, White Roc
Les Houches Adventure Base, Alpine Answers, Erna Low, Lagrange, Peak Retreats, PowderBeds, Ski Expectations, Zenith
Vallorcine Erna Low, Peak Retreats, PowderBeds

Phone numbers
From abroad use the prefix +33 and omit the initial '0' of the phone number

TOURIST OFFICES

Chamonix/Argentière
www.chamonix.com
Les Houches
www.leshouches.com

bars are the Savoy ('unpretentious, wonderful pizzas') and the Slalom for 'tapas and good wine'.

OUTLYING VILLAGE – 1455m

LE TOUR

Le Tour is a charming, unspoiled little village 12km from Chamonix at the foot of the Balme area. The valley's best nursery slopes are next to the village, at La Vormaine. A gondola from the edge of the village serves the Balme slopes, an area of mainly easy runs also reachable from Vallorcine.

OUTLYING VILLAGE – 1260m

VALLORCINE

Vallorcine is a small, but developing, traditional mountain village over the Col des Montets, near the Swiss border and 16km from Chamonix. The village shares with Le Tour the main valley's Balme area.

A gondola and a chairlift take you to Tête de Balme. A gentle red run leads back to the village, but it is prone to closure. There's a separate small area of local slopes at La Poya.

Accommodation is mainly in apartments. The 4-star L'Ours Bleu, with pool and spa facilities, is featured by Peak Retreats and Erna Low. There's a limited choice of restaurants and bars. The Café Comptoir at the foot of the Forêt Verte run is 'stylish, rustic and upscale – book ahead'. The Arret Bougnete in the station specializes in local dishes and has a wide selection of drinks – 'worth a visit waiting for the train back to Chamonix' says a regular visitor (it takes 20 minutes).

OUTLYING VILLAGE – 1010m

LES HOUCHES

Les Houches is 6km down the valley from Chamonix. The wooded slopes are popular when bad weather closes other areas, but are not covered by the standard Chamonix pass. It has great views of the Mont Blanc massif.

It's a pleasant village, with an old core around a pretty church, but modern developments in chalet style have spread along the road at the foot of the slopes (to an extent a visitor returning after some years' absence found 'incredible'). Some developments are quite a way from the widely separated lifts going to opposite ends of the slopes – a

gondola and a queue-prone cable car. On the mountain, all the lifts are slow though there are plans to replace a couple of drags with a fast quad but we're told this will not take place until 2015/16. There are some awkward links in the network. Snow-cover on the lower slopes is not reliable, but there is a fair amount of snowmaking.

There are nursery slopes and open, gentle runs at the top of the main lifts, with long, worthwhile runs back towards the village – blue, red and a token black that is Chamonix's World Cup Downhill course – a fine intermediate run. There is a decent terrain park. But there are lots of draglifts and flat areas for boarders to avoid. The ESF gets good reports for children's classes – 'helpful, sensitive to needs', 'flexible'.

Beyond the summit ridge is a very gentle area with cross-country loops and below that some sunny woodland runs with views across to Megève.

In good weather the slopes are quiet, and the views superb from the several attractive restaurants. The 250-year-old Vieilles Luges has a 'creative menu: leek and cheese crumble, Reblochon cheesecake'.

The village is quiet – 'bring the board games' says a 2014 visitor, but there are some pleasant bars and restaurants – Piccolina serves 'great pizzas'. The 2-star Campanules (0450 544071) is recommended this year: 'Brilliant staff, basic but spotless rooms, cosy, shuttle-bus to slopes.' Granges d'En Haut (0450 546536) consists of luxury chalets where you could self-cater but there are also two restaurants including the new gourmet Crystal; spa, small pool.

There are some good apartments with pools, including the 4-star CGH Hameau de Pierre Blanche and Hauts de Chavants (both available through Peak Retreats and Erna Low).

OT CHATEL / JEAN-FRANÇOIS VUARAND

Châtel

A distinctively French base in the huge Portes du Soleil circuit which spans the French–Swiss border; extensive local slopes too

RATINGS

The mountains

Extent	★★★★★
Fast lifts	★★
Queues	★★★
Terrain p'ks	★★★
Snow	★★
Expert	★★★
Intermediate	★★★★
Beginner	★★★
Boarder	★★
X-country	★★★
Restaurants	★★★
Schools	★★★
Families	★★★

The resort

Charm	★★★
Convenience	★★
Scenery	★★★
Eating out	★★★
Après-ski	★★★
Off-slope	★★

RPI	100
lift pass	£200
ski hire	£115
lessons	£65
food & drink	£130
total	**£510**

NEWS

2014/15: The big news is that two new fast chairs are planned to link the Super Châtel and Linga ski areas. A new slope is planned for 2015/16 from Super Châtel to Vonnes where the two chairs will meet. An aquatic centre, the Forme d'O, opened in the summer in the village centre. It has several indoor pools, an outdoor pool, saunas and steam rooms.

- ✚ Very extensive, pretty, intermediate terrain on Portes du Soleil circuit, with good local slopes
- ✚ Wide range of cheap and cheerful, good-value accommodation
- ✚ Pleasant, lively, French-dominated village, still quite rustic in parts

- ▬ Traffic congestion can be a problem at weekends and in peak season
- ▬ Low altitude and exposure to westerlies means some risk of rain and poor snow
- ▬ Still mainly slow lifts on Super-Châtel and over the Swiss border

Châtel offers an attractive blend of qualities much like that of Morzine – another valley village in the Portes du Soleil. But Châtel (with a claimed 30 working farms) is a bit more rustic and down to earth. It is also right on the Portes du Soleil circuit and very close to the Swiss border. This season, at long last, its two local sectors of slopes are due to be linked by lifts (rather than just a bus) – a fast quad and a six-pack. On busy days it's worth trying the uncrowded slopes of nearby La Chapelle-d'Abondance and Torgon.

THE RESORT

Châtel is a much expanded village near the head of the wooded Dranse valley, at the north-eastern limit of the huge French-Swiss Portes du Soleil ski circuit. It has two separate sectors of slopes, one linked to its French neighbour – high, purpose-built Avoriaz – and the other linked to two resorts in Switzerland: Morgins (which is on the Portes du Soleil circuit) and Torgon (which is not on the circuit).

A few kilometres down the valley is rustic La Chapelle-d'Abondance, with lifts into the Torgon slopes – covered at the end of this chapter.

VILLAGE CHARM ★★★
Rustic style, urban traffic
Châtel is still an attractive village, despite the inevitable expansion, and reporters remark on the friendly locals. Modern, unpretentious chalet-style hotels and apartments rub shoulders with old farms where cattle still live in winter. But it is no rustic idyll: life revolves around two streets that are far from traffic-free and lots of visitors take cars, which can clog the centre – especially at weekends.

CONVENIENCE ★★
No perfect position
Although there is a definite centre, the village sprawls along and up the hillside from the road in from Lake Geneva. The road diverges up towards Morgins and along the valley towards the Linga and Pré-la-Joux lifts. There is

a free bus service linking the sectors. Staying centrally simplifies après-ski outings – the bus finishes at 8pm most days – and has in the past helped with catching the ski-bus to the outlying lifts before it gets very crowded. The planned chairlift link will make the bus less vital now and it will make the suburb of Vonnes, where the two chairs will meet, a convenient place to stay. There is accommodation out near the Linga lift, too.

SCENERY ★★★
Lots of variety
Châtel's broad valley setting is very scenic, with Linga providing a splendid

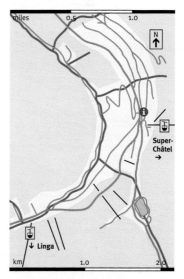

KEY FACTS

| Resort | 1200m |
| | 3,940ft |

Portes du Soleil	
Slopes	950-2275m
	3,120-7,460ft
Lifts	194
Pistes	650km
	404 miles
Green	12%
Blue	43%
Red	36%
Black	9%
Snowmaking	
	1074 guns

Châtel only	
Slopes	1100-2205m
	3,610-7,230ft
Lifts	43
Pistes	83km
	52 miles
Green	21%
Blue	36%
Red	30%
Black	13%

backdrop and pleasantly woody slopes curving in both directions. The lifts above Torgon give great views over Lake Geneva. As you travel around the Swiss side of the Portes du Soleil circuit the dramatic Dents du Midi are constantly coming into view.

THE MOUNTAINS

Châtel sits between two sectors of the main Portes du Soleil circuit, each offering a mix of open and wooded slopes. For notes on the circuit read our special chapter on it. The local piste map is clear, not least because it doesn't try to show everything in a single view. Other resorts please take note. Signposting is good too.

EXTENT OF THE SLOPES ★★★★★
Two sectors to choose between
Châtel has a worthwhile amount of local skiing, in two separate sectors which are due to be lift-linked for 2014/15.

Directly above the village is **Super-Châtel** – an area of easy, open and lightly wooded slopes that is accessed by a gondola or a two-stage chair. From here you can embark on a clockwise Portes du Soleil circuit by heading to the Swiss resort of Morgins. Or you can head north for the slopes straddling a different bit of the Swiss border, above **Torgon** (with fab views of Lake Geneva). From this season you should also be able to take a chair down to Vonnes (there should be a piste by 2015/16) and then another up to the **Linga** sector, where you can start an anticlockwise

tour of the Portes du Soleil circuit. This sector can also be reached by bus from Châtel; if you stay on the bus it takes you to the Pré-la-Joux/Plaine Dranse area, closer to the link with Avoriaz. There is night skiing at Linga on Thursdays.

FAST LIFTS ★★★★★
Luxurious Linga
Linga and the Plaine Dranse area are well served for fast lifts but in the Super-Châtel sector the lifts beyond the access gondola are almost entirely slow chairs and drags, whether you head for Morgins or for Torgon. Hence our rating.

QUEUES ★★★★★
Bottlenecks have been eased
In recent years queues have been eased throughout the Portes du Soleil by the installation of several fast new chairlifts. Locally Linga is no problem but Super-Châtel is: queues form for the gondola when school parties gather (and you can also face queues to get down again if the sunny home slope is shut because of poor snow), and reporters have also found lengthy queues for the slow Morclan chair and the Tour de Don, Chermeu and Chalet Neuf draglifts at certain times of the day.

TERRAIN PARKS ★★★★★
One size suits all
The Smoothpark at Super-Châtel has lines to suit both beginners and experienced freestylers, and they include rails, kickers and boxes; there's a snowcross too.

↑ There's great red and blue run cruising in the Linga-Pré-la-Joux sector. This is Les Combes, right in the centre of it

OT CHATEL / JEAN-FRANÇOIS VUARAND

LIFT PASSES

Portes du Soleil

Prices in €

Age	1-day	6-day
under 16	36	178
16 to 19	43	214
20 to 64	48	238
65 plus	43	214

Free Under 5
Beginner Points card
Notes Family discounts; 5hr pass
Alternative pass Châtel only

GETTING THERE

Air Geneva 80km/ 50 miles (1hr30)

Rail Thonon les Bains (40km/25 miles)

SNOW RELIABILITY ★★☆☆☆
The main drawback

The main drawback of the Portes du Soleil as a whole is that it is low, and exposed to mild weather from the west, so snow quality can suffer when it's warm. But a lot of snowmaking has been installed at Super-Châtel and on runs down to resort level. Linga and Plaine Dranse are mainly north-facing and generally have the best local snow. The pistes to Morgins and towards Avoriaz get full sun. Grooming is 'very good' say 2014 reporters.

FOR EXPERTS ★★★☆☆
Some challenges

The best steep runs – on- and off-piste – are in the Linga and Pré-la-Joux area. Beneath the Linga gondola and chair there's a pleasant mix of open and wooded ground, which follows the fall line fairly directly. And there's a serious mogul field between Cornebois and Plaine Dranse. Two pistes from the Rochassons ridge are steep and kept well groomed. On the way to Torgon from Super-Châtel, the Barbossine black run is long, steep and quite narrow and tricky at the top. There's plenty of good lift-served off-piste to be explored with a guide: we did a great run from Tête du Linga over into the next (deserted) valley of La Leiche – read the special off-piste feature panel in our Morzine chapter.

FOR INTERMEDIATES ★★★★☆
Some great local terrain

When conditions are right the Portes du Soleil is an intermediate's paradise. Good intermediates need not go far from Châtel to find amusement: Linga

and Plaine Dranse have some of the best red runs on the circuit. The moderately skilled can do the Portes du Soleil circuit without problem, and will particularly enjoy runs around Les Lindarets and Morgins. Even timid types can do the circuit, provided they take one or two short cuts and ride chairs down the trickier bits. But some blues are difficult when conditions are poor – in particular, one reporter witnessed skiers 'in tears' on the way down to Morgins from Châtel.

Visits to Avoriaz for the Hauts Forts runs are worthwhile for competent and adventurous intermediates. And note that the runs back to Plaine Dranse are real reds, and the Rochassons piste, especially, can get extremely busy at the end of the day.

Don't overlook the Torgon sector, which has some excellent slopes, including challenging ones.

FOR BEGINNERS ★★★☆☆
Three possible options

There are good beginners' areas at Pré-la-Joux (a bus ride away) and at Super-Châtel (a gondola ride above the village). And there are nursery slopes at village level if there is snow there. Reporters have praised the Super-Châtel slopes and lifts, which 'allow the beginner to progress' and 'safely practise' on gentle gradients away from the main runs. Getting up to them is a bit of an effort, though. The home run from Super-Châtel can be tricky – narrow, busy, steep at the end and often icy at the end of the day – but you can ride the gondola down. The Pré-la-Joux slopes are less varied, with some steeper draglifts.

Build your own shortlist: www.wheretoskiandsnowboard.com

Like the resort?
You'll love our handpicked accommodation

0844 576 0173
peakretreats.co.uk

◆ABTA
ABTA No. W5537

peak retreats

CHILDCARE

Mouflets Garderie
t 0450 813819
Ages 4mnth to 4yr

Piou Piou (ESF)
t 0450 732264
Ages 3 to 6

Les Pitchounes
t 0450 813251
Ages 3 to 5

Ski schools
Generally from age 5

OT CHATEL / JEAN-FRANÇOIS VUARAND

The village sprawls along and up from the road in from Lake Geneva. The Super-Châtel sector is in the distance on the left of this pic ↓

FOR BOARDERS ★★☆☆☆
Best for beginners – beware drags
Avoriaz is the hard-core destination for boarders in the Portes du Soleil and has a great selection of terrain parks plus a super-pipe – see that chapter. Châtel is not a bad place to learn or to go to as a budget option. But many lifts in the Super-Châtel sector are drags, and reporters warn that they can be a 'painful experience'. The Linga area has good, varied slopes and off-piste possibilities and more boarder-friendly chairlifts.

FOR CROSS-COUNTRY ★★★☆☆
Pretty, if low, trails
There are pretty trails (12km) along the river, around Lake Vonnes and through the woods on the lower slopes of Linga, but snow-cover can be a problem. When combined with La Chapelle-d'Abondance's trails, the total is 40km. The tourist office produces good maps.

MOUNTAIN RESTAURANTS ★★★☆☆
Some quite good local huts
Restaurants are marked but not named on the piste map.
   A cluster of cosy huts can be found at Plaine Dranse. We get regular reports from a devotee of the 'camp and cosy' Vieux Chalet, aka Chez Babeth: 'The food is excellent but it has become increasingly pricey;

Babeth the owner is absolutely barking.'
   In the Linga area the Ferme des Pistes is a lovely cosy old barn (complete with stable-door) that pleased a 2013 reporter with 'a huge plateful of spud, ham and cheese'. The chapter on Avoriaz has some tips at Les Lindarets, in the valley between the resorts.
   There are picnic rooms at Plaine Dranse and at the tops of the gondolas in the Super-Châtel and Linga sectors.

SCHOOLS AND GUIDES ★★★☆☆
Plenty of choice
There are several schools in Châtel, including a branch of BASS (British Alpine Ski & Snowboard School) as well as the usual ESF and International schools.
   A 2014 reporter says: 'I learned with ESF at Super-Châtel and the instructors were generally very good but their standard of English varied.'

FOR FAMILIES ★★★☆☆
Some good facilities
The ESF-run Piou Piou nursery offers indoor and outdoor activities plus getting a taste for skiing. Châtel Ski Sensations has its own nursery area with a draglift and chalet at Linga.

SCHOOLS

ESF
t 0450 732264
ESI Pro Skiing
t 0450 733192
Henri Gonon
t 0450 732304
Châtel Sensations
t 0450 813251
BASS
t 0450 739375
Ecole Ski Academy
t 0681 665280

Classes (ESF prices)
6 half-days (2.25hr
am) €136
Private lessons
€40 for 1hr for 1 or 2
people

UK PACKAGES

Absolute Alps, Connick, Erna Low, Hanski, Interactive Resorts, Lagrange, Mountain Beds, Oxford Ski Co, Peak Retreats, PowderBeds, Ski Addiction, Skialot, Snow Finders, Snowfocus, Susie Ward **La Chapelle-d'Abondance** Chalet Le Dragon, Ski Addiction, Ski La Cote

ACTIVITIES

Indoor Spas in hotels, cinemas, library, bowling
Outdoor Ice rink, walks, cheese factory visits, ice diving, ice fishing, snowshoeing, 'snake-glisse', 'yooner' tobogganing, horse sleigh rides and dog sledding in La Chapelle

Phone numbers
From abroad use the
prefix +33 and omit
the initial '0' of the
phone number

TOURIST OFFICES

Châtel
www.chatel.com
La Chapelle-d'Abondance
www.lachapelle74.
com

STAYING THERE

This is emphatically a French resort. No big tour operators feature it.
Hotels Practically all the hotels are 2-stars, mostly friendly chalets, wooden or at least partly wood-clad. But there are some smarter places.
****Macchi (0450 732412) Smart, modern chalet, spacious comfortable rooms, central, good food; small pool, spa; central.
***Belalp (0450 732439) Simple chalet, small rooms.
***Fleur de Neige (0450 732010) Woody chalet near centre, good food; spa, pool.
***Kandahar (0450 733060) One for peace lovers: a logis by the river, a walkable distance from the centre.
**Choucas (0450 732257) Central location.
**Roitelet (0450 732479) Basic, near the centre.
Apartments Peak Retreats offers three recently built properties that set a new standard for Châtel, all with pools and various spa facilities – CGH's Chalets d'Angèle, Grand Lodge and Grand Ermitage. Erna Low has Chalets d'Angele too. Châtel's village supermarkets are reported to be small and overcrowded, but there is a large supermarket out in the direction of Chapelle-d'Abondance.

EATING OUT ★★★☆☆
Fair selection
There is an adequate number and range of restaurants. The Macchi and Fleur de Neige hotels both have ambitious restaurants. We've also enjoyed the Table d'Antoine restaurant of the hotel Chalet d'Alizée, though that was a few years ago. The rustic Vieux Four does ambitious dishes alongside Savoyard specialities. The Poya does 'a blend of traditional and contemporary cuisine'. The Pierrier and the Fiacre ('mains/pizzas good value') are more modest, everyday restaurants, good for families.
It's worth a trip to the eccentric hotel Cornettes in La Chapelle-d'Abondance (described on the right).

APRES-SKI ★★★☆☆
All down to bars
The Tunnel bar is very popular with the British and has a DJ or live music every night. The Avalanche is a very popular English-style pub. The Godille – close to the Super-Châtel gondola

and crowded when everyone descends at close of play – has a more French feel. The Isba is the locals' choice, and shows extreme-sports videos. The bowling alley has a good bar.

OFF THE SLOPES ★★☆☆☆
Bad for meeting up
There's the new Forme d'O aqua centre. Those with a car can easily visit places such as Geneva, Thonon and Evian. There are pleasant walks and ice skating; you can visit the cheese factory or the two cinemas, or join in daily events organized by the tourist office.
The Portes du Soleil as a whole is less than ideal for non-skiers who like to meet their more active friends for lunch: they are likely to be at some distant resort – maybe in another country – at lunchtime, and even if they are not, very few lifts are accessible to pedestrians.

DOWN-VALLEY VILLAGE – 1010m

LA CHAPELLE-D'ABONDANCE

This unspoiled, rustic farming community, complete with old church and friendly locals, is 5km down the valley from Châtel. It has its own quiet little north-facing area of easy wooded runs, and a gondola starting on the outskirts links it to slopes between Torgon in Switzerland and Super-Châtel, and so to the Portes du Soleil circuit.
Chalet le Dragon is a British-run catered chalet opposite the gondola.
The hotel Cornettes (0450 735024) is an amazing 3-star with 4-star facilities, including an indoor pool, a sauna, a steam room and hot tubs. It has an atmospheric bar and an excellent restaurant with good-value menus. The hotel has been run by the Trincaz family since 1894. Look out for the showcases displaying their collections of puppets and dolls and for other eccentric touches, such as ancient doors that unexpectedly slide open automatically.
And L'Echo de la Corne apartments were recommended this year ('reasonably priced, convenient for the gondola or driving to Châtel').
Nightlife is virtually non-existent – just a few quiet bars, a cinema and torchlit descents. The Fer Rouge is a popular microbrewery, with live music.

Châtel

Build your own shortlist: www.wheretoskiandsnowboard.com

SNOWPIX.COM · CHRIS GILL

Courchevel

Arguably the best of the half-dozen resorts that make up the famous Trois Vallées – with a choice of four different villages

240

RATINGS

The mountains

Extent	★★★★★
Fast lifts	★★★★
Queues	★★★★
Terrain p'ks	★★
Snow	★★★★
Expert	★★★★
Intermediate	★★★★★
Beginner	★★★★
Boarder	★★★★
X-country	★★★★
Restaurants	★★★
Schools	★★★★
Families	★★★★

The resort

Charm	★★
Convenience	★★★★
Scenery	★★★
Eating out	★★★★★
Après-ski	★★★★
Off-slope	★★★

RPI   140

lift pass	£230
ski hire	£155
lessons	£140
food & drink	£190
total	**£715**

KEY FACTS

Resort	1260-1850m
	4,130-6,070ft

Trois Vallées	
Slopes	1260-3230m
	4,130-10,600ft
Lifts	180
Pistes	600km
	373 miles
Green	13%
Blue	39%
Red	38%
Black	10%
Snowmaking	33%

Courchevel/ La Tania only	
Slopes	1260-2740m
	4,130-8,990ft
Lifts	58
Pistes	150km
	93 miles
Green	20%
Blue	36%
Red	35%
Black	9%

➕ Extensive, varied slopes

➕ Impressive snowmaking and piste grooming, and a decent lift system

➕ Partly wooded setting

➕ Choice of four very different villages

➕ Some great restaurants and top-notch hotels

➖ Unremarkable villages – downtown 1850 is particularly disappointing, for an upmarket resort

➖ Very high prices in 1850, and in mountain restaurants generally

➖ The French feel has been lost, with huge numbers of foreign visitors

➖ Not great for the indolent non-skier unless glitzy shops are your thing

Courchevel's ski area is the most compelling sector of the famous Trois Vallées, the biggest linked ski area in the world; if we're heading for the 3V, more often than not we'll head for Courchevel.

But it's not one destination, it's four. Swanky 1850 catches the headlines, with its airstrip, ritzy hotels and six two-Michelin-star restaurants. The other villages have none of 1850's pretensions and high prices. There are plenty of affordable catered chalet holidays on sale here, even (thanks to the miracles worked by UK tour ops) in 1850. Sadly, there are few affordable lunches.

You may have noticed that we're not going along with the recent rebranding of the component villages; more on this in the box on the facing page.

THE RESORT

The numbers in the village names used until 2011 implied altitudes, and although they were seriously inaccurate they did give clues to altitude: 1850 is higher than 1650, etc.

What we persist in calling Courchevel 1850 was one of the first French resorts to be purpose-built after World War 2. The other villages were developed later, although they already existed as old hamlets.

1850 is big enough to have several distinguishable quarters. The main lift base and the central area around it is La Croisette; the resort spreads a long way up the hillside on the left through the chalet-filled suburbs of Cospillot and Nogentil to the altiport, the resort's famously hazardous little airstrip. Part of these suburbs is the Jardin Alpin, a forested area with some of the swankiest hotels (and more modest chalets and apartments), served by its own gondola. On the opposite, right-hand side of La Croisette is another little 'downtown' area, with the suburbs of Chenus above it and Plantret below.

The other resort villages are smaller and simpler. The main part of 1650 has grown up along the road that links

the resorts (though traffic is not very intrusive on weekdays); and the centre, below the lift base area, has been attractively developed and is lined with good local shops, restaurants and bars. Opposite the

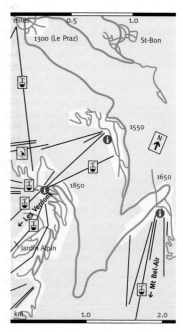

2014/15: A six-pack is due to replace the adjacent Aiguille du Fruit and Gravelles chairs at Praméruel between 1650 and 1850. The ancient Forêt gondola from Le Praz is due to be replaced by a six-pack taking a different line to a lower top station at mid-mountain, near the Bouc Blanc restaurant. On the Park City red run snowmaking is to be improved to ensure a reliable link between 1850 and 1650.

2013/14: There were major changes above La Tania: a long six-pack was built from below mid-mountain to the top, replacing two draglifts, one of which was moved down the hill to become the Stade drag; the Col de la Loze and Crêtes chairs were removed.

A new mountain restaurant, the Cave des Creux, opened above the altiport. A new 5-star hotel, the Apogée, opened in the Jardin Alpin. Various runs were re-classified – notably, Creux and Lac Creux from red to blue.

main gondola (reached by an escalator) individual chalets spread down the hill. Then there is another area of chalet development spreading up the slopes to an area known as Belvedère. 1650 has its own distinct sector of slopes, connected to 1850. It also has a great Intersport rental shop right opposite the main gondola that has excellent demo skis.

1550 is a bit of a backwater, with a few blocks and many more individual properties, directly below 1850. Le Praz is an old village on a plateau at the bottom of wooded slopes.

With a car, Champagny (linked to La Plagne's slopes) is easily reached.

VILLAGE CHARM ★★☆☆☆
Not a strong point
Courchevel 1850 has most of the smart hotels and shops, and you would expect it to be a pretty smooth place in general. The reality is a let-down; when compared with other smart resorts, 1850 does not impress.

The approach has been smartened up somewhat but is still rather dreary, and at the hub of the resort, La Croisette, you are confronted by the back side of the main lift station building, complete with garage entrances. Past this point, things improve again: the streets are lined by smart shops and jolly restaurants. But the nearest thing to a central focus is where a hairpin bend on the busy road through the resort to the affluent suburbs touches the slopes. The areas above the centre are more pleasant – in places, peacefully rustic – and of course if you are going to be closeted in a 5-star hotel in the Jardin Alpin you may not care much about village ambience.

Central 1650 is more attractive, and has a friendly traditional feel once you get away from the through-road up to 1850. 1550 is a pleasantly quiet, spacious mini-resort, bypassed by the road to 1850. Le Praz suffers from the

through-traffic, but away from the road is a low-key rustic place, with a friendly atmosphere, relatively unspoiled despite expansion for the 1992 Olympics – the ski jump is a prominent legacy.

CONVENIENCE ★★★★☆
Varies – research your location
The villages all have lifts into the slopes, with much of the lodging close by, but in all cases you need to be careful about location if you want to avoid walks. Frequent free buses link the villages.

1850 has several pistes running through it, and a high proportion of ski-in/ski-out lodgings. Central 1650 lodgings are a short walk from the lifts; those down the hill below the centre are served by a long, three-stage covered escalator. There are slope-side lodgings at the lift base, and on skier's right as you descend to the village. 1550 is arranged along the bottom of the slopes, with lifts immediately above most of the lodgings. In Le Praz the lifts start a short walk outside the village.

SCENERY ★★★☆☆
Some good views
Most of the villages enjoy a pretty woodland setting, and from parts of them and from the slopes above there are good views to Mont Blanc and over the valley to Champagny and Bellecôte (in the La Plagne ski area).

THE MOUNTAINS

Although there are plenty of trees around the villages, most of the slopes are essentially open, with the notable exception of the runs down to 1550 and to Le Praz, and the valley between 1850 and 1650.

We have few complaints about the piste map or general signposting. They have stopped handing out maps of which pistes have been groomed but

NAME CHANGES FOR THE COURCHEVEL VILLAGES

In 2011, the villages that make up Courchevel were given new names. Courchevel 1850 is now called just Courchevel; 1650 revived the name of the old village it is based on and is now Courchevel Moriond; 1550 became Courchevel Village. Le Praz (sometimes called 1300) is Courchevel Le Praz. Most signs on the mountain still use the old names, and for the moment, we're doing the same.

The old names were implicitly related to altitude. We revealed many years ago that the names exaggerated the altitudes – central 1850 is at about 1750m, and you have to go way up the hill to the Biollay and Coqs lifts to reach 1850m – so we should perhaps welcome the changes. But the piste map now explicitly states altitudes based on the old names, which is outrageously dishonest.

Le Ski
the chalet specialists

COURCHEVEL
VAL D'ISÈRE & LA TANIA

❄ 17 chalets to suit all budgets
❄ Post-ski pampering
❄ Civilised Sunday flights included
❄ Delicious food & drink

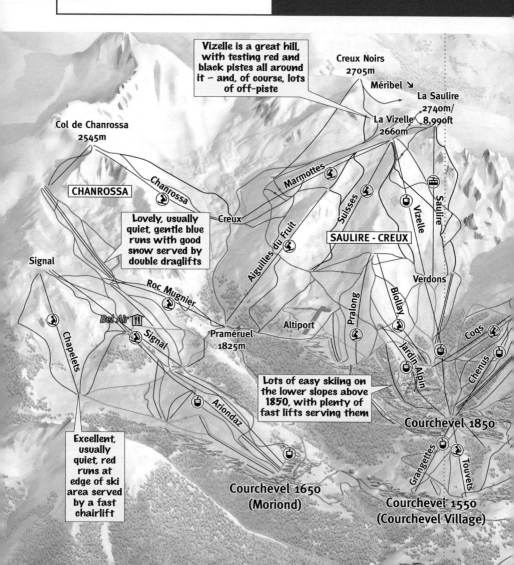

Vizelle is a great hill, with testing red and black pistes all around it – and, of course, lots of off-piste

Creux Noirs
2705m

Méribel ↘

La Saulire
2740m/
8,990ft

La Vizelle
2660m

Col de Chanrossa
2545m

CHANROSSA

Chanrossa

Creux

Marmottes

Suisses

Vizelle

Saulire

Lovely, usually quiet, gentle blue runs with good snow served by double draglifts

Aiguilles du Fruit

SAULIRE - CREUX

Signal

Roc Mugnier

Verdons

Biollay

Pralong

Bel Air

Signal

Praméruel
1825m

Altiport

Chapelets

Jardin Alpin

Cogs

Chenus

Lots of easy skiing on the lower slopes above 1850, with plenty of fast lifts serving them

Courchevel 1850

Ariondaz

Excellent, usually quiet, red runs at edge of ski area served by a fast chairlift

Grangettes

Touvets

Courchevel 1650
(Moriond)

Courchevel 1550
(Courchevel Village)

**32 years
of catered chalet
holidays**

**BOOK
ONLINE**
100% FINANCIAL
PROTECTION

Any questions?
01484 954397
www.leski.com

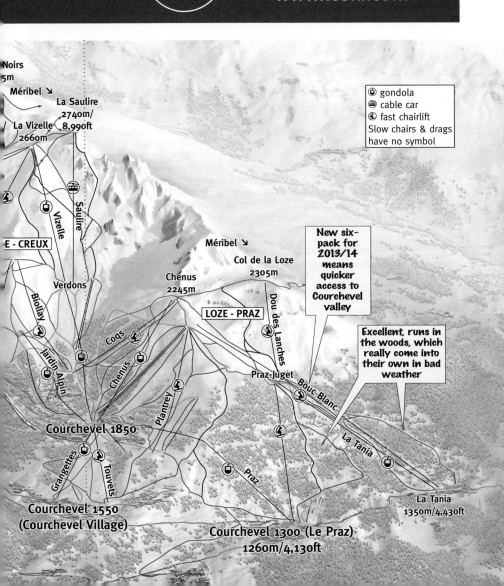

Noirs
5m

Méribel ↘

La Saulire
2740m/
8,990ft

La Vizelle
2660m

E - CREUX

Saulire

Vizelle

Verdons

Biollay

Jardin Alpin

Coqs

Chenus

Méribel ↘

Col de la Loze
2305m

Chenus
2245m

Dou des Lanches

LOZE - PRAZ

New six-
pack for
2013/14
means
quicker
access to
Courchevel
valley

Excellent runs in
the woods, which
really come into
their own in bad
weather

gondola
cable car
fast chairlift
Slow chairs & drags
have no symbol

Plantrey

Praz-Juget

Bouc Blanc

Courchevel 1850

La Tania

Grangettes

Touvets

Praz

**Courchevel 1550
(Courchevel Village)**

La Tania
1350m/4,430ft

Courchevel 1300 (Le Praz)
1260m/4,130ft

↑ La Croisette, the focus of what is now called Courchevel, but we are still calling it Courchevel 1850; altitude 1750m

SNOWPIX.COM / CHRIS GILL

Resort news and key links: www.wheretoskiandsnowboard.com

AWARD-WINNING
SKI
HOLIDAYS

Ski Olympic

book online at
skiolympic.com
01302 328 820

you can now get this information on the Trois Vallées smartphone app and it appears in notices posted in lift stations. They also list recommended 'pistes du jour' – a really good idea.

We were surprised last season to find that the long Creux piste from La Saulire had been changed from red to blue classification; skiing it again confirmed our impression that the top part is too steep for a blue, and several readers agree.

EXTENT OF THE SLOPES ★★★★★
Huge variety to suit everyone
A network of lifts and pistes spreads out from 1850. The main axis is the **Verdons** gondola, leading to a second gondola to La Vizelle and a nearly parallel cable car up to La Saulire. These high points of the **Saulire-Creux** sector give access to a wide range of terrain above Courchevel and to Méribel and thus the whole of the Trois Vallées. Next to the Verdons gondola is the Jardin Alpin gondola, which serves the hotels until 8pm and also links to lifts and pistes beyond.

To the right looking up, the Chenus gondola goes towards the **Loze-Praz** sector, which forms a second link with Méribel – these days you have to descend to Bouc Blanc, at mid-mountain above La Tania, to make the link. Runs also go back from here to 1850, and through the woods to La Tania, Le Praz and 1550.

The main gondola from 1650 goes

to Bel Air and further lifts on into the **Chanrossa** sector. This sector has links to Saulire-Creux at two points – Praméruel and Creux.

FAST LIFTS ★★★★★
Plenty of them
You will occasionally find yourself on a slow chair, but there are only a couple of places where slow lifts are not avoidable. The piste map makes the distinction between slow and fast chairs, which helps. Many of the chairs are now equipped with a 'Magnestick' system where the safety bar is held down automatically until very near the top – this can be quite scary when you first encounter it.

QUEUES ★★★★★
Not a problem
The lift system is impressive, and even in peak season queues are minimal. But there can be a build-up at 1850 as the ski school gets going. The Biollay chair is very popular with the ski school; it was upgraded to a six-pack a few seasons ago, but can still build queues – two March reporters had to wait '10 to 15 minutes'. At 1650, the lifts at the base can have queues. Upgrades are in the pipeline.

TERRAIN PARKS ★★★★★
Freestyle for all the family
The Family Park below Verdons is now the main park and has lines to suit different levels, with a variety of

Pierre & Vacances premium

Perfect spacious apartments with spas and swimming pools.

pierreetvacances.co.uk

COURCHEVEL
CHOOSE FROM 204 CATERED CHALETS, APARTMENTS & HOTELS

Skiline.co.uk

CALL US ON 020 8313 3999

SUPERTRAVEL**SKI**
020·7204·4691

Book a full chalet and receive a **FREE case of 6 bottles of Champagne** delivered to your chalet or home when you quote 'ski/snow2015'

Luxury chalet holidays

COURCHEVEL·ST ANTON·ZERMATT

LIFT PASSES

Trois Vallées

Prices in €

Age	1-day	6-day
under 13	46	222
13 to 64	57	277
65 plus	51	249
Free Under 5, 75 plus		
Beginner Limited pass		

Notes Covers Courchevel, La Tania, Méribel, Val Thorens, Les Menuires and St-Martin; reductions for families and other groups. Options: pedestrian and half-day passes

Alternative passes Courchevel/La Tania + 3V extension; Courchevel 1650 only

jumps, rails, tables and obstacles including, at certain times, an airbag jump; there's also a snowcross. There are two smaller 'fun zones' above 1650: Snake Park has a snowcross and Fun Park has large bumps. The Wood Park above 1550 has, er, wooden rails and tables.

SNOW RELIABILITY ★★★★
Very good

The combination of Courchevel's northerly orientation, its height, an abundance of snowmaking and excellent grooming usually guarantees good snow down to at least 1850 and 1650. The snow is usually much better than in Méribel, where the slopes (particularly the slopes you ski from the Courchevel ridge) get more sun. The runs to Le Praz are prone to closure in warm weather.

FOR EXPERTS ★★★★
Entertaining pistes, and ...

There is plenty to interest experts, even without considering the rest of the Trois Vallées. The most obvious expert runs are the shady couloirs you

can see on the right as you near the top of the Saulire cable car. All three main couloirs were once black pistes (some of the steepest in Europe), but only the Grand Couloir remains a piste – the widest and easiest of the three, but reached by a narrow, bumpy, precipitous access ridge.

The shady slopes of La Vizelle and Creux Noirs are not seriously steep, but all the runs – tough reds and not-tough blacks – offer a worthwhile challenge. If you like groomed blacks in the early morning, keep an eye on the grooming notices at lift bases/ ticket offices to see when Suisses, Combe Pylones or M is groomed. Chanrossa often has the most serious bumps. The blacks above Le Praz can be great fun, too – again, they are not seriously steep, but offer a vertical of almost 1000m.

There is a huge amount of off-piste terrain, including lots next to the pistes. The runs off Dou des Lanches through the trees down to La Tania and off the top of Creux Noir (via a little walk) down to join up with the Creux piste are recommended. The

---

ONE OF THE BEST FOR OFF-PISTE SKIING

Courchevel's image is of upmarket luxury and pampered piste skiing. But it is a great resort for off-piste too (always go with a guide). Manu Gaidet is a Courchevel mountain guide and a ski instructor with the Courchevel ESF. He is also one of the world's top freeriders, and won the Freeride World Championship three years running. We asked him to pick out a few of the best runs.

For a first experience off-piste, the Tour du Rocher de l'Ombre is great. Access is easy from the left of the Combe de la Saulire piste, and you are never far from it. It is very quiet, the slope is very broad and easy and you get a real sense of adventure as you plan your way between the rocks. And the view of the Croix des Verdons is impressive. Keep to the left for the best snow.

The Chanrossa chairlift opens up several routes. Les Avals is one of my favourites, involving a short climb to the ridge to the south. This run is not technically difficult and is particularly beautiful in spring conditions. Another possibility is to traverse towards the Aiguille du Fruit, and pick your spot to start skiing down to Creux. And there is Plan Mugnier, a shady run with normally very good snow, but more difficult. It's for experienced off-piste skiers only and starts with a 20-minute hike.

Le Curé is in the Saulire area: this narrow gully starts under a towering rock and offers a steady 35° slope; it is only for expert skiers who don't mind climbing to the Doigt du Curé starting point.

SKIWORLD

Catered chalets, hotels and self catering apartments in

Europe, USA and Canada

skiworld.co.uk

08444 930 430

ABTA V2151 ATOL 2036

SCHOOLS

ESF in 1850
t 0479 080772

ESF in 1650
t 0479 082608

ESF in 1550
t 0479 082107

Supreme
t 0479 082787
(UK: 01479 810800)

New Generation
t 0479 010318
0844 770 4733 (UK)
www.skinewgen.com

Magic
t 0479 010181

Oxygène
t 0479 419958

BASS
t 0679 512405
(UK: 07092 206321)

RTM
t 0615 485904

Classes
(ESF 1850 prices)
6 5hr-days €346

Private lessons
From €105 for 1½hr

wooded areas in general are great for bad weather.

In good snow conditions you can ski all the way down (around 2000m vertical) from La Saulire to Bozel.

There is plenty of other off-piste terrain in this valley to try with a guide – read the feature panel.

FOR INTERMEDIATES ★★★★★
Paradise for red-run skiers

For confident intermediates, Courchevel's local slopes are simply fabulous. Every sector has long, testing red runs and easy blacks, and there is abundant easy off-piste to experiment in. There are too many excellent runs to list; every high point – Signal, Chanrossa, Vizelle, Creux Noirs, Saulire, Chenus, Loze – offers one, two, three, four notable descents.

For timid intermediates, we're not so enthusiastic. The red runs from Vizelle and Saulire can be quite testing, especially late in the day. But there are some excellent sectors to focus on. The long, narrow sector of blue slopes above 1650 is superb, and there is an array of excellent blue slopes above and below 1850 – the Biollay and Pralong fast chairs are the ones to head for here. The runs down to La Tania are long, rolling cruises, but how easy they are depends crucially on snow conditions.

FOR BEGINNERS ★★★★
Great graduation runs

There are excellent nursery slopes above both 1650 and 1850. At 1650, there are short drags right above the village. At 1850 there is a small but good beginner area in the Jardin Alpin, reachable by the gondola, and an excellent bigger one at Pralong, near the altiport. Absolute beginners have to get to this by road. There are nine free beginner lifts – at least one in each village, five in 1850. 1550 and Le Praz have small nursery areas; but the 1550 one is quite steep. There are excellent long runs to progress to.

FOR BOARDERS ★★★★
Upmarket all-rounder

Despite being an upmarket resort, Courchevel has always been popular with snowboarders. There are miles of well-groomed pistes, good freeride terrain and the lifts are in general very modern and quick, with few drags. The resort's freestyle facilities are not what you would call hard-core, though.

FOR CROSS-COUNTRY ★★★★
Long wooded trails

Courchevel has around 60km of trails. Le Praz is the best village, with trails through the woods towards 1550, 1850 and Méribel. Given enough snow, there are also loops around the village.

MOUNTAIN RESTAURANTS ★★★
Fine if you can afford them

Mountain restaurants are plentiful and pleasant, but uncomfortably pricey. Fortunately, the local lift pass permits lunch above La Tania; and the 3V pass gets you to Les Menuires, St-Martin and Val Thorens, where there are some excellent spots; read those chapters. The piste map does not name restaurants.

Editors' choice The Bel Air (0479 080093), above 1650, has long stood out for its warm welcome, efficient service, good food, splendid tiered terrace, nice woody interior and (by local standards) reasonable drinks prices. But even here the food is unpleasantly pricey (25 euros for the plat du jour including a big salad).

Worth knowing about We've enjoyed Pilatus, just below the altiport: good service and huge portions ('good tartiflette', says a 2013 reporter). The Courcheneige on the Bellecôte slope is a long-standing reader favourite and was tipped again this year by a regular for 'the unbeatable range of nice food'. The Soucoupe at Loze is a traditional place and has 'a wonderful grill with a real fire in its centre' – very expensive though. We've had mixed experiences at Verdons at the top of the gondola – head for the atmospheric woody upstairs room tucked away off the first room you come to, and hope for more enthusiastic service than we had in 2014. When we called in for a pastry last February, entry to the famously pricey Chalet de Pierres, between Verdons and 1850, was policed by an unsmiling Amazonian who directed us to a shabby cafe area; we won't be going back (except to check on the price of a spag bol – 32 euro in 2014).

SCHOOLS AND GUIDES ★★★★
Plenty of choice

We've had many positive reports on New Generation (run by top British instructors) – for example, 'Really good, excellent English from a French instructor who was really patient with our little terrorist.' Reporters also

Bureau des Guides
t 0623 924612

Village des Enfants (1850)
t 0479 080847
Ages 18mnth to 3yr

Les P'tits Pralins de Moriond (1650)
t 0479 063472
Ages 6mnth to 6yr

Maison des Enfants (1550)
t 0479 082107
Ages from 18mnth

Ski schools
Most offer lessons from age 3 or 4

SNOWPIX.COM / CHRIS GILL

Creux Noirs is a good little hill, on- and off-piste; seen here from La Saulire, where Courchevel meets Méribel ↓

praise another Brit-based outfit, RTM Snowboarding: 'Great backcountry coaching. Provided split boards and skins for free, extended the four-hour session to all day for free, did a lot of serious backcountry hiking.' A 2013 visitor recommends Magic: 'Our learner had two private lessons and went from beginner to a black run; her confidence was sky high.' BASS and Supreme are other Brit-run schools.

We get positive reports on the ESF, particularly on its handling of children. The Méribel ESF is taking part in the legal action against chalet operator Le Ski that put an end to tour operator ski guiding throughout France last season, but we understand that the Courchevel branch is not involved.

The Bureau des Guides runs all-day off-piste excursions.

FOR FAMILIES ★★★★☆
Lots of suitable options
Courchevel is a good choice for families; there is lots of convenient lodging and gentle slopes. A variation of the 'Magnestick' system (see 'Fast lifts'), using a magnet in the back of a special bib to hold children securely on chairlifts, has been fitted to many

fast lifts. The ESF Club des Piou Piou at 1650, for kids aged three to five, is reportedly 'very well run'. Several UK chalet operators run nurseries. Family specialist Esprit Ski operates in 1850 – read 'Chalets', under 'Staying there'. The Indiens blue above 1650 with an 'exciting natural half-pipe and Indian village' was a hit with a 2013 reporter and family.

STAYING THERE

Chalets There are lots available – specialist agents list dozens of them. 1650 is UK chalet central. Le Ski, which celebrated its 30th year there in 2013, now has an impressive 18 chalets in 1650, sleeping from 2 to 22; 13 of them have sauna, steam or hot tub. Its flagship Scalottas Lodge has five apartment-chalets and we've stayed in two of them, both with fabulous views, leather armchairs and sofas, solid wooden floors, a jacuzzi bath and hi-tech lights and heating. Ski Olympic is also a 1650 specialist, with the central Avals chalet hotel (complete with Rocky's bar) plus two large chalets. Skiworld has four chalets in 1650, including the traditional but

Courchevel

AWARD-WINNING
SKI HOLIDAYS
Ski Olympic
book online at *skiolympic.com*
or call **01302 328 820**
ABTA V2289

Build your own shortlist: **www.wheretoskiandsnowboard.com**

Ski Total

ARE HERE IN
Courchevel

▶ Quality chalets
▶ Top locations
▶ Excellent value
▶ 17 more resorts

skitotal.com
01483 791 933

ACTIVITIES

Indoor Bowling, ice rink, cinemas, cookery courses, library; in hotels: health and fitness centres (swimming pools, saunas, steam room, hot tub, water therapy, weight training, massage)

Outdoor Hang-gliding, helicopter flights, paragliding, microlighting, flying lessons, snowshoeing, snowmobile rides, ballooning, walking on cleared paths, tobogganing, ice climbing, segway

smooth Estrella, with hot tub, and two in 1550. Crystal also has two eight-person units in one building in 1650. Inghams has five chalets and the very central 30-bedroomed chalet hotel les Anémones in 1850, and two chalets with hot tub and sauna in 1650.

Ski Total has a huge chalet bang in the centre of 1650, and in 1850 five chalets and a central 60-bed chalet hotel, the Coq de Bruyeres – 'fantastic: friendly staff, amazing food, short walk to the lifts'. Also in 1850, family specialist Esprit Ski has two standalone chalets, and a chalet hotel with a good pool, sauna and hot tub right next to the lifts at Pralong. We get glowing reports on its childcare and service – three in 2013 ('our kids had a terrific time') and three in 2012.

Down in Le Praz, Mountain Heaven has three chalets. We enjoyed a very comfortable stay in the cosily traditional Jardin d'Angele last season. This shares an excellent little spa area (and outdoor hot tub) with the quite different Emilie – traditional exterior, but cutting-edge style within. The third chalet is a converted farmhouse in the core of the old village.

Supertravel has five very luxurious chalets in 1850 – liberally endowed with saunas, hot tubs and steam rooms. Other luxury operators in 1850 include Consensio, Kaluma and Scott Dunn.

Hotels There are more than 40 hotels, mostly at 1850 and many of them very swanky. Two were awarded the new 'Palace' rating three years ago – the Cheval Blanc and the Airelles – to distinguish them from the 5-star standard invented only a few years back; amazingly, 15 hotels now hold 5-star status. The prices of the top places give new meaning to the word 'exorbitant' – it is possible to pay £1,000 per person per night without too much difficulty.

COURCHEVEL 1850
*****Lana (0479 080110) Bottom of the Bellecôte piste. Pool, sauna, steam, hot tub, spa. 'Good restaurant, excellent wine list, very good service, rooms are quite small though comfortable,' says a 2013 visitor.
*****Sivolière (0479 080833) Set among pines on the western edge of the village, with a reputation for friendly service despite the stars.
****Chabichou (0479 080055) Distinctive white building, right on the slopes; family-run, friendly and rustic, with very good food plus the option of a restaurant with two Michelin stars.
***Courcheneige (0479 080259) Ski-in/ski-out location on the Bellecôte piste, with a rustic restaurant. 'Friendly staff, comfortable rooms, excellent food with good choices every night.'
COURCHEVEL 1650
*****Manali (0479 080707) Smart and welcoming; slope-side, just above the gondola, with terrace; spa and pool.
****Portetta (0479 080147) Neat place at foot of slopes, with steam, sauna, spa, good restaurant.
***Seizena (0479 082636) Stylish and central (over road from the gondola).
COURCHEVEL LE PRAZ
***Peupliers (0479 084147) Traditional, smart, good restaurant.

Selected chalets in Courchevel

ADVERTISEMENT

MOUNTAIN HEAVEN *www.mountainheaven.co.uk*   T **0151 625 1921**

Mountain Heaven has three wonderful catered chalets in the resort of Courchevel Le Praz, a true Savoyard village and the prettiest of the four Courchevel villages with great access to the whole of the Three Valleys. Chalet Jardin d'Angele is one of our Flagship Chalets, with eight bedrooms, and Chalet Emilie, with its architect-designed luxury interior and four bedrooms, has been nominated as one of the best new chalets in the world. Chalet Louis is our great value chalet located right in the heart of the village.

Email: info@mountainheaven.co.uk

HIGH QUALITY ACCOMMODATION ↑

Alpine Answers, Alpine Elements, Alpine Weekends, Carrier, Consensio, Crystal, Crystal Finest, Elegant Resorts, Erna Low, Esprit, Flexiski, Friendship Travel, Inghams, Inspired to Ski, Interactive Resorts, Jeffersons, Kaluma, Lagrange, Le Ski, Luxury Chalet Collection, Mark Warner, Momentum, Mountain Beds, Neilson, Oxford Ski Co, Pierre & Vacances, Powder White, PowderBeds, Scott Dunn, Silver Ski, Ski Amis, Ski Bespoke, Ski Bluebird, Ski Collection, Ski Expectations, Ski France, Ski Independence, Ski Olympic, Ski Total, Ski Weekend, Skitracer, Skiweekends.com, Skiworld, Snow Finders, Snow-wise, Snoworks, STC, Supertravel, Thomson, White Roc **Le Praz** Mountain Heaven, Ski Deep

Air Chambéry 110km/ 70 miles (1hr30); Geneva 150km/ 95 miles (2hr15); Grenoble 175km/ 110 miles (2hr15); Lyon 190km/ 120 miles (2hr15)

Rail Moûtiers (23km/ 14 miles); transfer by bus or taxi

Phone numbers
From abroad use the prefix +33 and omit the initial '0' of the phone number

www.courchevel.com

Apartments If you want to self-cater in real style, take a look at the chalets in the resort literature. Returning to Earth ... Ski Amis has privately owned apartments in several parts of the resort. Mountain Heaven has apartments in Le Praz. The best big residences are the Montagnettes Chalets de la Mouria in 1650 (we stayed there happily in 2013) with spa; and the Chalets du Forum in central 1850 – a Pierre & Vacances Premium residence; these and various other properties are available through Erna Low and other agencies.

EATING OUT ★★★★★
Pick your price
You can eat very well here, but you have more choice if you have a fat wallet. A non-comprehensive pocket guide is distributed. In 1850 there are no fewer than six places with two Michelin stars.

Leaving those aside ... a regular visitor recommends Chabotté ('very good food, not that expensive') – owned by, next to and much cheaper than the starred Chabichou. Le Génepi is reported to be 'wonderful – cosy, charming, with good food'. For the budget conscious, the Passage serves 'yummy pizzas' at 'affordable prices'. La Luge also does 'decent burgers and salads'. More reports on affordable places, please.

In 1650 two places that do pizza, pasta and Savoyard dishes have been tipped by reporters – the Petit Savoyard ('good food, friendly and professional staff') and La Table de Marie ('reasonably priced, varied menu, service with a smile'). The Arc en Ciel (formerly the Eterlou) is another source of pizza, with a 'warm, friendly atmosphere'.

At 1550 the Oeil de Boeuf at the foot of the slopes is 'excellent, great steaks cooked on an open fire'.

In Le Praz, the small and unpretentious Michelin-starred Azimut is much more affordable than equivalent places in 1850 (three-course menus from 28 euros), and we had a delicious meal there in 2012. The Table de Mon Grand-Père has superb food and atmosphere but prices approaching 1850 levels. Bistrot du Praz is also expensive but worth it, say reporters. Cave de Lys is an atmospheric vaulted wine bar that is a lovely spot for a quiet drink, and serves tapas-style snacks.

ALPINE ANSWERS
The UK's No.1 Chalet Specialist

For choice and service look no further!

alpineanswers.co.uk
call: 020 7801 1080
ABTA

APRES-SKI ★★★★☆
The choice is yours
At close of play there are bars around the Croisette that are good for a relaxing drink; we like the Tremplin (but not its prices). Kudeta is 'good value at happy hour' and later its disco pumps until 4am, as does the Grange – a Moroccan-style place. There are some exclusive nightclubs, such as Caves. The Mangeoire piano bar gets going late, with live music. Tremplin has karaoke. P'tit Drink specializes in wine and tapas. The bar of hotel Olympic has 'pints for 3 euros'.

In 1650 there are several lively bars within a few yards of each other. The Bubble and Rocky's are Brit-run, and the Bubble and the Boulotte fill up with chalet staff letting their hair down. We like the Schuss for a quiet drink. The lively Funky Fox has pool, live music or DJs, and the Clinik disco stays open late.

In 1550 there are a handful of bars that can develop a lively atmosphere – the Caterail has DJs and live music.

OFF THE SLOPES ★★★☆☆
Not ideal
There is quite a bit to do, but the emphasis is very much on physical activities. A guide to walks is available from the tourist office. A pedestrian lift pass for the gondolas and buses in Courchevel and Méribel makes it easy for non-skiers to get up the mountain to meet others for lunch. There is no public pool (there is one in the pipeline). Cinemas in 1850 and 1650 show English-speaking films. Snowshoeing among the trees and 'seriously awesome' tobogganing from 1850 to 1550 are popular. And you can take joyrides from the altiport. There is a guide listing fashion and jewellery shops in 1850 – the prices in these shops are stratospheric and the customers mostly rich Russians.

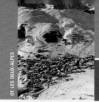

Les Deux-Alpes

Sprawling resort with a high, narrow ski area that will disappoint many intermediates; popular for summer skiing and boarding

250

RATINGS

The mountains

Extent	★★★
Fast lifts	★★★★
Queues	★★
Terrain p'ks	★★★★★
Snow	★★★★
Expert	★★★★
Intermediate	★★
Beginner	★★★
Boarder	★★★★
X-country	★★
Restaurants	★★★
Schools	★★★
Families	★★★★

The resort

Charm	★★
Convenience	★★★
Scenery	★★★★
Eating out	★★★★
Après-ski	★★★★
Off-slope	★★

RPI 100

lift pass	£190
ski hire	£110
lessons	£75
food & drink	£135
total	**£510**

NEWS

2014/15: Work has begun on the promised new blue run to the village but it won't be ready until the 2015/16 season at the earliest.

2013/14: New slow zones have been marked on the slopes and map. The terrain park on Toura, now called Freestyle Land, has been improved and split into different zones.

- ➕ High, snow-sure, varied slopes, including an extensive glacier
- ➕ Lots of good off-piste terrain
- ➕ Stunning views of the Ecrins peaks
- ➕ Wide choice of affordable hotels

- ➖ Piste network modest by big resort standards, and congested in places
- ➖ Home runs are either steep and icy or dangerously overcrowded
- ➖ Virtually no woodland runs

Les Deux-Alpes is a big resort, with a tall mountain. But it doesn't come from the standard major resort mould: it is not at all swanky, and good-value hotels are not hard to find. Its mountain is unusual, too: tall and narrow, offering a splendid Alpine feel, some long runs, but with pistes limited in total extent.

We've been complaining since 1994 about the dangerous home runs here. We were told three years ago that the resort was planning a blue alternative to the icy blacks and hideously crowded green. We're told work has begun on it but it won't be ready until the 2015/16 season at the earliest. However, there's now a new red run back to the village; we look forward to trying it.

THE RESORT

Les Deux-Alpes is a long, narrow village sitting on a high col. It is modern, but gives the impression that its development has been unplanned.

Four sectors can be identified. As you enter from the north you pass through an area centred on the tourist office; from here, roads go off left up to Les 2 Alpes 1800; go straight on instead, and you come to the effective centre, with the major gondola stations, outdoor ice rink and lots of shops and restaurants; at this point you enter a long one-way system, and finally come to Alpe de Venosc.

The six-day pass covers La Grave and gives two days in Alpe-d'Huez and days in Serre-Chevalier (an hour away) and other resorts. A car would be handy to make the most of these options. There are day-trip buses twice a week to Alpe-d'Huez, but a better plan is to splash out 70 euros on the splendid helicopter day trip (available three days a week).

VILLAGE CHARM ★★
Lively, but that's all

The village is a long, sprawling collection of apartments, hotels, bars and shops, most lining the two streets that form the one-way traffic system. There is a wide range of building styles, from old chalets through 1960s blocks to more sympathetic recent buildings. Alpe de Venosc has the most character and the best shops. The resort's buildings look better as you leave than when you arrive – all the balconies face south. The place has quite a buzz in the early evening.

CONVENIENCE ★★★
Fine if you pick your spot

It's a long village – well over 2km end to end – but lifts are dotted fairly evenly along it, and it's not difficult to find lodgings within walking distance of one of the major ones. We'd go for Alpe de Venosc and the newish Diable chair. Les 2 Alpes 1800 is inconvenient for shopping and nightlife. A free shuttle-bus links all parts of the resort every 15 minutes. A digital system at the stop lets you know how long you've got to wait.

(map)

miles 0.5 1.0

N ↑ Mont-de-Lans

Village →

ⓘ

Jandri Express →

down to Venosc

Diable →

km 1.0 2.0

KEY FACTS

Resort	1650m
	5,410ft
Slopes	1300-3570m
	4,270-11,710ft
Lifts	48
Pistes	203km
	126 miles
Green	21%
Blue	47%
Red	21%
Black	11%
Snowmaking	
	226 guns

OT LES DEUX ALPES / B LONGO

The centre is made of two main streets and traffic is limited by a one-way system ↓

SCENERY ★★★★☆
High southern peaks
The resort sits high among the southern Alps, with great views from the upper slopes of the Ecrins peaks.

THE MOUNTAINS

The main slopes are all above the treeline, though there are trees directly above the village.

The piste map is very unusual for the Alps in breaking the slopes down into several separate maps. It's a good idea, but poorly executed – the map is still unclear around mid-mountain. Views vary about the logical but boring scheme of naming runs after the lift they lead to and distinguishing them by numbers (eg Fée 1, Fée 2, ... Fée 6, Fée 7).

A few blue runs have short steep sections and some readers complain that some should be classified red. And some runs are different colours on the map and the mountain. Reporters find the signposting OK.

EXTENT OF THE SLOPES ★★★☆☆
Surprisingly small
For a big resort, Les Deux-Alpes has a disappointingly small area of pistes. The main area goes high and stretches a long way – almost 8km from top to bottom – but it is very narrow.

Since our 2000 edition we have been querying the claimed extent. They used to claim 225km on the piste map; last year it was reduced to 220km; but these figures apparently include cross-country loops. The Schrahe report discussed in our piste extent feature put the total of downhill pistes at 134km. Perhaps because of that, the resort now tells us it is not using km any longer. Instead it says it is talking about hectares (of marked and groomed pistes) – bonkers and not comparable with any other resort as far as we are aware.

To us, even Schrahe's figure feels too high. One reason is that the slopes just above the village don't usually figure in your day – one side is too sunny to offer reliable conditions, and the other side is not well connected.

The morning-sun side of Les Deux-Alpes, now branded **Vallée Blanche**, is served by lifts at either end of town. It is relatively low (the top is 2100m) so has only short pistes back to town.

On the broad, gentle slope east of the resort are about 10 beginner lifts, and above them a steep slope rising to the ridge of **Les Crêtes**. Lifts go up to the ridge from four points spread along the village. To get back to base you have a choice of a long, winding, narrow green run, often very crowded (and sometimes closed), a newish red run that we haven't skied yet and three short black runs. The blacks are usually mogulled, and often icy at the end of the day (they get the afternoon sun). Many visitors ride down.

At long last the alternative blue run to the village is going to materialize.

skiracer

CHALETS, HOTELS
& APARTMENTS
Call us today
020 8600 1650
skiracer.com

Ski Total

ARE HERE IN
Les 2 Alpes

▷ Quality chalets
▷ Top locations
▷ Excellent value
▷ 17 more resorts

skitotal.com
01483 791 933

Work began in summer 2014 but it won't be ready until at least the 2015/16 season.

The Crêtes ridge has lifts and gentle runs along it, and behind it lies the deep, steep Combe de Thuit. Lifts span the combe to the mid-mountain station at **Toura**, at the heart of the slopes. We seem to spend a lot of time on three key fast chairlifts in this area – Bellecombes, at the top of the Combe; Glaciers, carrying on towards the glacier; and Fée, on its own slightly separate hill. The section of the mountain around and below Toura is very narrow – there is one main way down, and it gets crowded in the afternoon; but there are now three ways to avoid the worst of the crowds, so they are much less problematic than they once were.

The top **Glacier du Mont de Lans** section has long, easy runs with great views, served by an underground funicular and draglifts. There are steeper slopes off to the north, served by chairs. From the top you can descend all the way to Mont-de-Lans – a descent of 2270m that we believe is the world's biggest on-piste vertical. In the opposite direction, a walk (or snowcat tow) takes you to the famously challenging slopes of La Grave (read our separate chapter).

FAST LIFTS ★★★★
Main lifts OK, but ...
Les Deux-Alpes has some impressive lifts, with fast chair alternatives to the gondolas. But there are still a few draglifts and slow chairs around.

QUEUES ★★
Problems remain
The village is large, and queues for the gondolas in the morning can be serious. The newish Diable chair has improved the total lift capacity out of the village, and we have no reports of huge queues there. But the big Jandri gondola still attracts crowds – it offers a more direct way to the high slopes than the Diable, and is more convenient if you are not staying at the south end of the village. The lifts at the junction of the two sectors, at the north end of the village, are also reported to build queues.

Up the mountain there may be queues in late season for the lifts to the glacier, and the Crêtes area gets busy in peak season. The top lifts are prone to closure if it's windy, putting pressure on the lower lifts. There may be queues for the gondolas back to the village when snow is poor. Some 2014 reporters were concerned about crowding on the slopes even outside peak holiday periods.

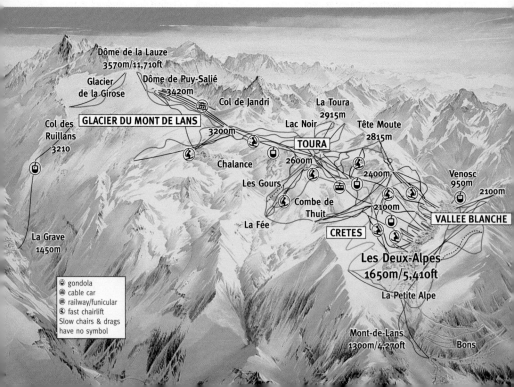

Dôme de la Lauze
3570m/11,710ft

Glacier de la Girose

Dôme de Puy-Salié
3420m

Col de Jandri

La Toura
2915m

Col des Ruillans
3210

GLACIER DU MONT DE LANS

3200m

Lac Noir

Tête Moute
2815m

Chalance

TOURA
2600m

Les Gours

2400m

Venosc
959m

2100m

Combe de Thuit

2100m

VALLEE BLANCHE

La Fée

CRETES

Les Deux-Alpes
1650m/5,410ft

La Grave
1450m

La Petite Alpe

Mont-de-Lans
1300m/4,270ft

Bons

○ gondola
▣ cable car
▣ railway/funicular
▣ fast chairlift
Slow chairs & drags
have no symbol

The off-piste routes in Les Deux-Alpes are numerous, and varied in difficulty. But never try them without the right equipment and a qualified guide.

*Both sides off the **Bellecombes** piste offer a wide range of varying terrain; it's important to take care here – there are several small cliff faces. For those keen to tackle couloirs, this descent offers small ones that are ideal for your first attempts; they can be avoided, though.*

*Traversing across the top of the black Grand Couloir piste leads to the **North Rachas** area, with off-piste faces that normally offer good snow conditions all winter. The first large valley leads to three couloirs – one fairly broad and easy, the others much narrower and steeper. Traversing further leads to a much wider descent that avoids the three couloirs.*

*Strong skiers will enjoy the famous **Chalance** run (our favourite), which starts just below the glacier and descends 1000m to join the Fée 1 piste; there are several variations, mixing wide-open slopes and rocky pitches. These faces are at times subject to quite a high avalanche risk.*

*Traversing above the north face of the Chalance leads to the couloir **Pylone Electrique** – a steep, narrow 200m-long couloir with the reward below it of an excellent wide powder field of moderate gradient. A rest on the Thuit chairlift is a must after this adrenaline-charged descent.*

*As well as these routes within the local lift network, there is a renowned descent to **St-Christophe** (you get a taxi back), and the famous **La Grave** terrain (see separate chapter) is easily accessed.*

LIFT PASSES

Prices in €

Age	1-day	6-day
under 13	36	180
13 to 64	45	225
65 plus	36	180

Free Under 5, 72 plus
Beginner Five free lifts
Notes Family rates; half-day and pedestrian passes; 6-day pass includes entry to swimming pool and ice rink, and two days in Alpe-d'Huez and one day in Serre-Chevalier, Puy-St-Vincent, Montgenèvre and Sestriere (in Italy)
Alternative pass Discovery Ski – covers 21 lifts

GETTING THERE

Air Grenoble 110km/ 70 miles (1hr45); Chambéry 130km/ 80 miles (2hr); Lyon 160km/100 miles (2hr); Geneva 220km/ 135 miles (2hr45)

Rail Grenoble (70km/43 miles); buses from station

TERRAIN PARKS ★★★★★
One of the best

The winter terrain park, Freestyle Land, is located above Toura. For 2013/14 it was re-styled and split into several areas: Easy Park for beginners with a mini pipe, rails and tables; Park Avenue for jibbing; Zone Slide for beginners and families; Slopestyle with four tables; a Wall which is 10m long and 6m high; a big air; a half-pipe; a snowcross. The Kid Park is at Les Crêtes. In summer the park moves up to the glacier and is even bigger.

SNOW RELIABILITY ★★★★☆
Excellent on higher slopes

The snow on the higher slopes is normally very good, even in a poor winter. On a tour in March 2012 that involved skiing crud in most resorts, we enjoyed packed powder most of the day here. Above 2200m most of the runs are north-facing, and the top glacier section guarantees good snow. But the runs just above the village from Les Crêtes face west, so they get afternoon sun and are often icy. Snowmaking covers some of the lower slopes – apparently including the home green run.

When we visited in 2012, some runs were kept closed in the morning because they were dangerously hard, and opened only once they had softened. This is an excellent scheme.

FOR EXPERTS ★★★★☆
Off-piste is the main attraction

The area offers excellent off-piste – read the panel above. In the past, five routes (including Chalance, described above) were identified as itinéraires, but they are no longer on the map.

There are a few black pistes. The run down the Bellecombes chair is a genuine black, with the best chance of good snow. Fée 6 from above Toura has one steep pitch at the end. Fée 5 isn't much more testing than the adjacent red. The runs down to the resort often have poor snow. The short black higher up served by the Super Diable chairlift is among the steepest.

FOR INTERMEDIATES ★★☆☆☆
Limited cruising

Less confident intermediates will love the quality of the snow and the gentle runs on the upper mountain. But Les Deux-Alpes can disappoint keen intermediates because of the limited extent of the pistes. Avid piste-bashers will cover them all in a couple of days. A lot are either rather tough – some of the blues could be reds – or boringly bland. The runs higher up generally have good snow, and there is some great fast cruising, especially from the glacier to Toura and on the mainly north-facing pistes served by the chairlifts off to the sides. The chairlifts at the glacier serve great carving pistes. The Vallée Blanche area has quite testing red runs; but the snow there is often in poor condition.

Like the resort?

You'll love our handpicked accommodation

0844 576 0173
peakretreats.co.uk

ABTA
ABTA No. W5537

peak retreats

↑ It's certainly a long, sprawling, narrow village. The Vallée Blanche ski area is on the far side and Les 2 Alpes 1800 is on the right

OT LES DEUX ALPES / B LONGO

UK PACKAGES

Action Outdoors, Alpine Answers, Club Med, Crystal, Crystal Finest, Erna Low, Friendship Travel, Inghams, Interactive Resorts, Lagrange, Mark Warner, Neilson, Peak Retreats, Pierre & Vacances, PowderBeds, Rocketski, Ski Club Freshtracks, Ski Collection, Ski Expectations, Ski France, Ski Line, Ski Supreme, Ski Total, Skitracer, Skiworld, STC, Thomson, Zenith

Resort news and key links: www.wheretoskiandsnowboard.com

FOR BEGINNERS ★★★
Good slopes
The nursery slopes beside the village are spacious and gentle, and five lifts are free. The runs along the ridge above them are excellent, too, except when crowded at the end of the day. The glacier also has a fine array of long, very easy slopes.

FOR BOARDERS ★★★★
Big appeal
Les Deux-Alpes has become a snowboard Mecca in summer when the pros descend en masse. In the winter, the limited pisted slopes aren't as off-putting to boarders as to skiers. Although the focus is on the terrain park, the freeriding is not to be underestimated, with plenty of steep challenging terrain. Beginners will find the narrow, flat crowded areas mid-mountain and the routes down to the village intimidating. Most of the lifts on the higher slopes are chairs (and so boarder-friendly). In town there is a huge airbag to get a feeling of what air-time is all about.

FOR CROSS-COUNTRY ★★
Needs very low-altitude snow
There are small, widely dispersed areas. Given good snow, Venosc, reached by a gondola down, has the only worthwhile picturesque ones. Total trail length is 25km.

MOUNTAIN RESTAURANTS ★★★
A few good places
The restaurants at the major lift junctions are generally unremarkable. Happily there are exceptions.
Editors' choice Diable au Coeur (0476

799950) at the top of the Diable lift has excellent food (delicious confit de canard on our last visit) and service. Readers agree ('we ate there 3 times in a week it was so good'). The terrace gives good views, but sit as far as you can from the noisy adjacent chairlift machinery. The bigger Chalet la Toura (0671 667461), in a fine position with a big terrace at Toura in the middle of the slopes, is pleasantly woody, and serves good food; endorsed by a 2014 reporter.
Worth knowing about The Pano, also at Toura, has 'a wide range of daily specials' but is notable mainly for its (brief) après session. There is a small table-service restaurant attached to the big self-service at the bottom of the glacier at 3200m. The Fee was rated as 'superb' by a 2014 reporter. The Bergerie on the Vallée Blanche slopes has been recommended in the past.

There are picnic rooms at the Toura lift junction, and at the glacier near the top of the cable car.

SCHOOLS AND GUIDES ★★★
Fair selection to choose from
A recent reporter was pleased with his son's progress with the ESF. There are plenty of other schools to choose from and a 2014 visitor had 'excellent private lessons with Easiski'. Freeride Attitude is a free off-piste safety course that sounds well organized.

FOR FAMILIES ★★★★
Fine facilities
The village nursery takes kids from six months to two years, the kindergarten from two to six years, and there are

Les Deux-Alpes

Build your own shortlist: www.wheretoskiandsnowboard.com

SCHOOLS

ESF
t 0476 792121

International St-Christophe
t 0476 790421

European
t 0476 797455

First Trax
t 0476 113941

Evolution 2
t 0695 978220

Easiski
t 0682 795734

Classes (ESF prices)
6 days €250

Private lessons
From €45 for 1hr for 1 or 2 people

GUIDES

Bureau des guides
t 0476 113629

CHILDCARE

Crèche du Bonhomme de Neige
t 0476 790262
Ages 6mnth to 2yr

Garderie le Bonhomme de Neige
t 0476 790677
Ages 2 to 6

Ski schools
Snow gardens for ages 3 to 6; classes for ages 6 to 12

ACTIVITIES

Indoor Swimming pool, hot tub, sauna, sports centres (Acqua Center, Espace 1800 Forme), squash, cinemas, games rooms, bowling, museums, library

Outdoor Ice rink, snowmobiling, paragliding, snowshoeing, ice climbing, tobogganing, ice gliding, sleigh rides

Phone numbers
From abroad use the prefix +33 and omit the initial '0' of the phone number

TOURIST OFFICE

www.les2alpes.com

chalet-based alternatives run by UK tour operators. A 2014 reporter who went with Club Med said 'their childcare was second to none'.

STAYING THERE

The resort has that rarity in high French resorts, an abundance of affordable hotels. There is a Club Med.

Chalets Ski Total, new to the resort last year, has two newly built chalets well placed at the Venosc end of the resort, with the unusual facility of a mini pool (5m long) on the terrace. Skiworld has five varied chalets including a fab looking one in its top 'signature' range with an outdoor hot tub. Crystal has five, one in its 'finest' range with a hot tub. Inghams has three chalets and Zenith has several that can be rented catered or self-catered. Mark Warner runs a chalet hotel with pool up near 1800.

Hotels There are about 30 hotels, of which the majority are 2-star or below.
****Chalet Mounier (0476 805690) Smartly modernized. Good reputation for food. Pool, steam, sauna, hot tub. At the Venosc end of the resort.
***Côte Brune (0476 805489) Transformed in recent years, now a charming woody chalet. On the snow, near Jandri Express. We stayed here in 2012: comfortable rooms, good food.
**Lutins (0476 792152) Central, basic, convenient, clean and friendly.
Turan (0476 792760) Ski-in/ski-out beside lifts. 'Good value. Hearty buffet.'

Apartments There are plenty of large apartment blocks, but most are notable chiefly for the value they offer. Pierre & Vacances, for example, has two of its value-oriented Maeva residences. Peak Retreats offers lots of options including three luxury residences and some cute four-bedroom chalets. Erna Low has lots of apartments and individual chalets.
Out of resort Close to the final ascent to Les Deux-Alpes are two small hotels, near-ideal for anyone planning to visit Alpe-d'Huez, La Grave and Serre-Chevalier as well as Les Deux-Alpes – the Cassini (0476 800410) at Le Freney, and Panoramique (0476 800625) at Mizoën. An alternative is to stay in the Venosc valley, in a hamlet close to the gondola; Peak Retreats has cute-looking, large chalets there with private pools and saunas.

EATING OUT ★★★★★
Plenty of choice
There are about 50 restaurants, including lots of simple places such as crêperies. The P'tit Polyte restaurant in the hotel Chalet Mounier has a high reputation. Reader tips include La Grange, Alisier, Patate, Cloche, Crêpes à Gogo ('sounds dreadful but actually a lovely Alpine bar with nice snack food'), Eli's ('good steak, duck etc'), Smokey Joes (Tex-Mex) and Etable. You can get a relatively cheap meal at Bleuets bar, and the Vetrata.

APRES-SKI ★★★★★
Not as lively as before?
Les Deux-Alpes has traditionally been one of the liveliest of French resorts, but reports seem to suggest that it has become quieter in recent years.

On the mountain, an attempt is made to deliver Austrian-style post-lunch après action at the Pano at Toura ('very lively') and Diable au Coeur. There are plenty of places to try in the village – the resort website lists about 25. Smokey Joes is a popular central sports bar and the Secret has live music and a wide choice of beers. The Red Frog has a big-screen TV and shows sports. Smithy's Tavern and Mini Bar 'attract the younger crowd and the seasonaires'. The main bar at 1800 is O'Brians. Bars favoured by reporters are the Polar Bear pub ('the pick for the 30s English crowd, with just enough space for a dance later on') and Pub le Windsor (a smaller, quieter place popular with locals). The Avalanche is a popular nightclub ('crushingly busy').

OFF THE SLOPES ★★★★★
Limited options
The pretty valley village of Venosc is worth a visit by gondola, and you can take a scenic helicopter flight to Alpe-d'Huez. There are lots of walks, a big outdoor pool (free with a 6-day lift pass) and the Acqua Center has a sauna, steam room and hot tub. There's an outdoor artificial ice rink, and three toboggan runs. Several mountain restaurants are accessible to pedestrians. The White Cruise is a snowcat ride across the glacier, providing wonderful views. There is now an ice cave in the glacier, complete with ice sculptures. The resort has a simulator that lets you experience what it's like to be caught in an avalanche.

OT FLAINE / PHOTOZOOM

Flaine

Still expanding, high-altitude, purpose-built resort sharing a big, broad area of varied slopes with more rustic alternatives

RATINGS

The mountains

Extent	****
Fast lifts	***
Queues	***
Terrain p'ks	*
Snow	****
Expert	****
Intermediate	*****
Beginner	*****
Boarder	***
X-country	**
Restaurants	**
Schools	***
Families	****

The resort

Charm	*
Convenience	*****
Scenery	****
Eating out	**
Après-ski	*
Off-slope	*

RPI 100

lift pass	£190
ski hire	£115
lessons	£70
food & drink	£150
total	**£525**

NEWS

2014/15: A new 'fun zone' for kids is planned for the beginner area at Flaine Forêt. A new 5-star, ski-in/ski-out Pierre & Vacances Premium residence will open at Montsoleil. Ski Total is opening the resort's first catered chalets.

2013/14: The Diamant Noir double chair on the upper slopes was replaced by a fast quad. The beginner area at Flaine Forêt was revamped, and a draglift specially designed to make life easy for novices was installed. The pool and spa at the smart new Centaure residence opened for everyone to use.

+ Part of the big, varied Grand Massif

+ Reliable snow in the main bowl

+ Compact, convenient, mainly car-free village, plus traditional villages on the lower fringes of the area

+ Excellent facilities for children

– Still some slow old chairlifts

– Original 1960s buildings block-like and austere (though newer chalet-style developments very attractive)

– Bad weather can close most runs

– Nightlife very quiet

Flaine is best known as a convenient resort catering particularly well for families, but it has a much broader appeal than that. The Grand Massif is an excellent and extensive area, with plenty to amuse anyone.

Apartments rule here. There are some very good ones, though; and this season Ski Total is running some as catered chalets. There are wider lodging options in the outlying traditional villages – Samoëns and Les Carroz (which have their own chapters) and Morillon (covered here).

THE RESORT

Flaine was built from scratch in the 1960s at the foot of a big snowy bowl. It's high, but not super-high (it is set among trees); the road in from Les Carroz actually involves a final descent from a col some 250m higher. The architecture of the main village is distinctive and uncompromising; it has its admirers, not including us.

The road in passes two satellite mini-resorts: Hameau de Flaine – lots of small chalets and the residence Refuge du Golf – and Montsoleil, developed by Intrawest. The main resort is tiny, as our plan shows. There are two parts: Forum, centred on a square blending with the slopes, and bigger Forêt – up the hillside, linked by two lifts (vulnerable to snow, we hear), with its own bars and shops.

A car gives you the option of visiting the Portes du Soleil, Megève or Chamonix.

VILLAGE CHARM ★
Not to our taste
The concrete Bauhaus-style blocks that form the core of Flaine were supposed to exhibit 'the principle of shadow and light'. They look shocking from the approach road; from the slopes they are somewhat less obtrusive, blending into the rocky grey hillside a little.

As a place to inhabit, Flaine has an austere feel, and some buildings are now looking tatty. In contrast, the Hameau de Flaine is built in an attractive traditional chalet style, as is

Montsoleil. The main resort is largely traffic-free, and the heart of Forum is completely, but roads do penetrate the village for access to the residences.

CONVENIENCE ★★★★★
A fine example
The main resort is compact and convenient. Hameau de Flaine is about 1km from the main village, and has one shop, one bar, one restaurant. Montsoleil is much nearer to the mother ship (a few hundred metres' walk) and it has linking pistes. There's a 'very good' free bus service; in the evening, we are told it is replaced by a free bookable taxi service.

SCENERY ★★★★
Good all around the Massif
The scenery within the area is quite varied, with rocky ridges and partly wooded hillsides – the views from the dividing ridges across the Vernant and Molliets valleys are particularly lovely. To the south-west, the Aravis chain looks dramatic, while there are great views of the Mont Blanc massif from the high points.

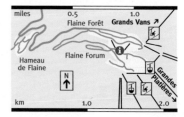

KEY FACTS

Resort	1600m
	5,250ft
Grand Massif (Flaine, Les Carroz, Morillon, Samoëns, Sixt)	
Slopes	700-2480m
	2,300-8,140ft
Lifts	68
Pistes	265km
	165 miles
Green	12%
Blue	45%
Red	33%
Black	10%
Snowmaking	
	218 guns
For Flaine only	
Slopes	1600-2480m
	5,250-8,140ft
Lifts	22
Pistes	140km
	87 miles

SNOWPIX.COM / CHRIS GILL

They say the concrete blocks blend into the hillside. Judge for yourself ↓

THE MOUNTAINS

The slopes in the Flaine bowl are mainly open, but the lowest slopes are wooded. Outside the bowl, above the other villages (Les Carroz, Morillon, Samoëns), it's the opposite – most of the runs are below the treeline.

The latest piste map is a vast improvement on the previous version, with a better attempt to define the individual bowls; but it is still difficult to read, and sometimes misleading. Piste classification is generally accurate, but the blue Tourmaline back to Flaine under the Grands Vans chair is an exception – distinctly tough (and crowded at the end of the day). Reporters find signposting very good.

EXTENT OF THE SLOPES ★★★★☆
A big white playground

Grand Massif is an impressive area; but its claimed 265km of pistes is an exaggeration – measured down the fall line the total is only 170km. Read our feature on piste extent at the front of the book. A large part of the domain lies outside the main Flaine bowl; the links are vulnerable to bad weather.

The **Grandes Platières** jumbo gondola speeds you in a single stage up the north-west-facing Flaine bowl to the high point of the Grand Massif. Both the Aup de Veran gondola and the Tête des Verds fast chair offer

alternatives, linking to other fast chairs on the upper mountain. There are essentially four or five main ways down the largely treeless, rolling terrain back to Flaine. On skier's right, the Cascades blue run leads away from the lift system behind the Tête Pelouse down to the outskirts of Sixt, dropping over 1700m in its exceptional 14km length. The gentle/flat top half is hard work, especially for boarders, and the run is scenic rather than exciting. At the end you can get a bus (often crowded) to the lifts at Samoëns.

On the near side of the Tête Pelouse, a broad catwalk leads to the experts-only **Gers** bowl.

Back at Platières, an alternative is to head left down the lovely long red Méphisto to a quieter area of slopes beneath Tête des Lindars.

The eight-seat Grands Vans chair gives access to the extensive slopes of **Les Carroz**, **Morillon** and **Samoëns** via the wide Vernant bowl. This and the adjacent Molliets bowl have lift bases with car parks on the road between Les Carroz and Flaine.

FAST LIFTS ★★★☆☆
Gradual progress

Replacement of the Diamant Noir double chair for last season was very welcome, and effectively opened up an additional fast route to the top. But there are still some frustrating lifts

Pierre & Vacances
premium

Perfect
spacious
apartments
with spas and
swimming
pools.

pierreetvacances.co.uk

inside and (especially) outside the Flaine bowl. Read the chapters on Les Carroz and Samoëns.

QUEUES ★★★☆☆
New lifts have eased problems
Hefty investment in new lifts over the last few years has paid dividends and most recent reporters have had few problems except at peak season. The exception is that short queues build for the main gondola to Platières; but it has a singles line and there are alternative ways up. In French school holidays all the major lifts can build queues at peak times – especially unavoidable link lifts between Flaine and the other villages such as Grands Vans, Vernants and Corralanche.

As much of a problem as queues is that some of the blue runs forming links between the resorts get seriously crowded, especially at the beginning and end of the day – Silice and Tourmaline on the way from Samoëns to Flaine, and Perce-Neige at Tête des Saix on the way to Morillon and Les Carroz.

TERRAIN PARKS ★☆☆☆☆
No real park now
The only real park in the Grand Massif has been scrapped for this season, we are told. There will be a new Ze Forest 'fun space' with 'slaloms, banks and a trail in the forest'.

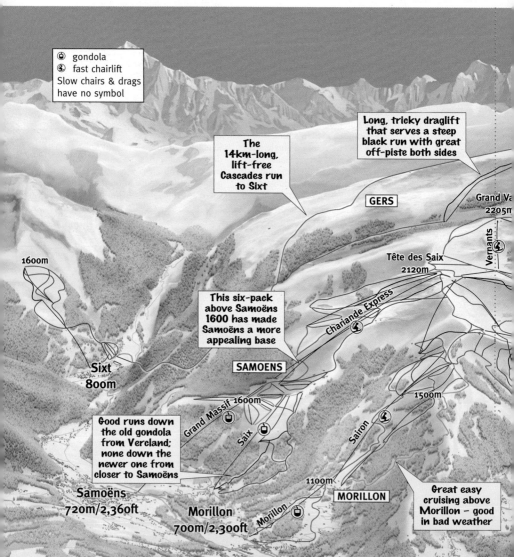

ⓖ gondola
ⓕ fast chairlift
Slow chairs & drags
have no symbol

Long, tricky draglift that serves a steep black run with great off-piste both sides

The 14km-long, lift-free Cascades run to Sixt

GERS

Grand Va
2205m

Vernants

1600m

Tête des Saix
2120m

This six-pack above Samoëns 1600 has made Samoëns a more appealing base

Chariande Express

SAMOENS

Sixt
800m

Grand Massif 1600m

Saix

1500m

Sairon

Good runs down the old gondola from Vercland; none down the newer one from closer to Samoëns

Samoëns
720m/2,360ft

1100m

Morillon
700m/2,300ft

Morillon

MORILLON

Great easy cruising above Morillon – good in bad weather

LIFT PASSES

Grand Massif

Prices in €

Age	1-day	6-day
under 16	33	171
16 to 64	44	225
65 plus	42	217

Free Under 5, 75 plus
Beginner Three free lifts
Note Family discounts
Alternative pass Flaine area only

SNOW RELIABILITY ★★★★☆
Usually keeps its whiteness

Most of the main bowl faces north-west, and keeps snow well. There is snowmaking on many of the lower runs. The slopes outside the bowl are lower. Grooming is excellent.

FOR EXPERTS ★★★★☆
Great fun with guidance

Flaine has some seriously challenging terrain. But much of it is off-piste, and although some looks temptingly safe this impression is mistaken. The Flaine bowl is riddled with rock crevasses and potholes, and should be treated with glacier-style caution.

All the black pistes are genuine. The Diamant Noir, close to the line of the main gondola, is tricky because of moguls, narrowness and other people, rather than great steepness; the first pitch is the steepest. To skier's left of Diamant Noir are several short, steep off-piste routes through the crags.

The Lindars Nord chair serves a worthwhile slope that often has the best snow in the area.

The Gers draglift, outside the main bowl, serves great on- and off-piste expert terrain in a north-facing bowl (of about 550m vertical) that normally has good snow top to bottom. The Onyx piste is a proper black and nearby off-piste slopes reach 45°. There are more adventurous ways in from the Grand Vans and Véret lifts. Further serious black pistes go down

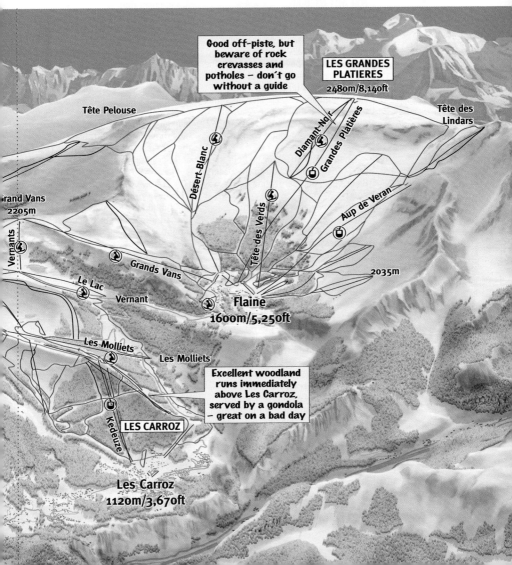

Good off-piste, but beware of rock crevasses and potholes – don't go without a guide

LES GRANDES PLATIERES
2480m/8,140ft

Tête Pelouse

Diamant-Noir

Grandes Platières

Tête des Lindars

Grand Vans
2205m

Désert-Blanc

Aup de Veran

Vernants

Tête-des-Verds

Grands Vans

Le Lac

2035m

Vernant

Flaine
1600m/5,250ft

Les Molliets

Les Molliets

Excellent woodland runs immediately above Les Carroz, served by a gondola – great on a bad day

LES CARROZ

Kedeuze

Les Carroz
1120m/3,670ft

Tailor made, long weekend and short break French Alps ski holiday specialists.

Hanski
Ski. Explore. Relax.

web: www.hanski.co.uk
tel: 01638 596373
mob: 07833 612061

4-star self-catering apartments in France
Major resorts, expert knowledge

4-star luxury residence
Le Centaure in Flaine:
Ski in/ski out, well suited to families.
Highest resort in the Grand Massif, close to Geneva.

Ski Collection

Accommodation only or self-drive package deals
call us on 0844 576 0175 SkiCollection.co.uk

ABTA
ABTA No.W5537

SCHOOLS

ESF
t 0450 908100

Internationale
t 0450 908441

Moniteurs Indépendants
t 0450 937978

Master Class
t 0450 908716

Ski Clinic
t 0666 139281

Freecimes
t 0664 118329

François Simond
t 0450 908097

Bruno Uyttenhove
t 0610 183082

Flaine Mountain
t 0603 294486

Classes (ESF prices)
6 3hr-days €153

Private lessons
From €44 for 1hr

CHILDCARE

Les Petits Loups
t 0450 908782
6mnth to 3yr

Rabbit Club (ESF)
t 0450 908100
From 3yr

La Souris Verte (ESI)
t 0450 908441
3yr to 5yr

Hotel MMV Le Flaine
t 0492 126262
18mnth to 14yr

Ski school
Ages 30mnth to 11yr;
English-speaking
tuition: Catherine
Pouppeville (0609
266008)

from Tête des Saix towards Samoëns. A reader recommends the Corbalanche piste and the off-piste bowl to skier's right, above the little Airon lake.

FOR INTERMEDIATES ★★★★★
Something for everyone
Flaine is ideal for confident intermediates, with a great variety of pistes (and usually the bonus of good snow, at least above Flaine itself). The diabolically named reds that dominate the Flaine bowl tend to gain their status from short steep sections rather than overall difficulty. The relatively direct Faust is great carving territory and Méphisto is popular with lots of reporters.

There are gentler cruises from the top – Cristal, taking you to the Désert Blanc chair, and Serpentine all the way home.

The connection with the slopes outside the main bowl is a blue run that can be tricky because of crowds, narrowness or poor snow. Once the connection has been made, however, all intermediates will enjoy the long tree-lined runs down to Les Carroz, as long as the snow is good. (The Perce-Neige run along the ridge to get to them is a bit narrow and exposed, though.) The long runs down to Morillon 1100 slopes are also excellent easy-intermediate terrain.

FOR BEGINNERS ★★★★★
Two good nursery areas
There are excellent nursery slopes below Forum and across the hill from Forêt, served by free lifts, which make a pass unnecessary until you are ready to go higher up the mountain. The major Forêt area was revamped last season, with a new Balacha draglift specially designed to make life easy for novices and a remodelling of the green run.

There are some gentle blues to

progress to on skier's right of the main bowl, beneath Tête Pelouse. An alternative is to get the bus over the hill to the Vernant valley where a fast chair serves the long, gentle, quiet Arolle green run.

FOR BOARDERS ★★★☆☆
Beware the draglifts
Flaine suits boarders quite well – there's lots of varied terrain and plenty of off-piste with interesting nooks and crannies, including woods outside the main bowl. The key lifts are now chairs or gondolas (but beware the draglifts marked as difficult on the piste map plus the Aujon draglift). Black Side is the local specialist shop, with a cafe and bar in the central Forum.

FOR CROSS-COUNTRY ★★☆☆☆
Very fragmented
The Grand Massif claims 64km of tracks but only about 13km of that is around Flaine itself.

MOUNTAIN RESTAURANTS ★★☆☆☆
Few options in the bowl
The piste map marks restaurants but does not name them.

Editors' choice We had an excellent lunch a couple of seasons ago (fine burger, good salad, giant tartiflette) at the Pente à Jules, a new chalet in a fine position where the Faust and Almandine red runs meet, near the bottom of the woods. Even in January and in its first season, it was packed.

Worth knowing about We've also eaten well at the rustic Blanchot (table-service section, naturally) just above the treeline on skier's right. There is a self-service place at the top of the main gondola. At the upper nursery slopes, the Bissac was tipped last year. At Forum level, across the piste from the gondola, are two attractive, woody chalets – the Michet and the fast-food-oriented Eloge ('good food,

UK PACKAGES

Action Outdoors, Alpine Answers, Classic Ski, Crystal, Erna Low, Hanski, Inghams, Lagrange, Neilson, Pierre & Vacances, PowderBeds, Ski Club Freshtracks, Ski Collection, Ski France, Ski Independence, Ski Line, Ski Total, Ski Weekend, Skitracer, Snow-wise, Thomson, Zenith **Morillon** Alps Accommodation, Erna Low, Hanski, Lagrange, Peak Retreats, PowderBeds, STC **Sixt** Peak Retreats

GETTING THERE

Air Geneva 80km/ 50 miles (1hr30)

Rail Cluses (30km/ 19 miles); regular bus service

staff pleasant' says a 2014 visitor). You can of course eat in the village, at places very close to the gondola.

Outside the Flaine bowl, we have always liked the remote and cosy Gîte du Lac de Gers (0450 912076) – book in advance and use the piste-side phone to ring for a snowcat to tow you up from the Cascades run. But it is under new management, so please send us reports. Be aware that you have to ski on down to Sixt, and then ski back to Flaine via the Samoëns lift system. Other places outside the bowl are covered in the Samoëns and Les Carroz chapters.

There are picnic rooms dotted around the Grand Massif, clearly marked on the piste map.

SCHOOLS AND GUIDES ★★★☆☆
Mixed reports

A 2014 reporter who has used the ESF for five years for his children says 'the instructors have always been good and go out of their way to ensure the children enjoy themselves'. Another had private lessons with the International school that 'really helped me'. We received good feedback on the Moniteurs Indépendants last year.

FOR FAMILIES ★★★★☆
Parents' paradise?

Flaine prides itself on being a family resort, and the number of English-speaking children around is a bonus. The schools offer classes for children from the age of three.

STAYING THERE

Accommodation is overwhelmingly in self-catering apartments.
Chalets Ski Total is running three chalets here for 2014/15. Two are in the Refuge du Golf and have access to a pool and a spa area with sauna, steam, hot tub. The other is a proper little chalet in the Hameau de Flaine. Total will be running a minibus service to and from the lifts and there's a piste nearby that goes past Montsoleil to Flaine Forêt.
Hotels B&B is available at the Cascade restaurant (0450 908766), up the hill.
Apartments For a combination of comfort and convenience, the CGH 4-star residence Centaure, a few metres from the gondola, takes some beating – and last season its spa, gym and 25m pool opened. The apartments are cleverly designed so that all have

Flaine

NEW THIS YEAR
Chalets Marmot, Bouquetin & Ibex

ABTA
The Travel Association

THE CHALET SPECIALIST

Ski Total

Now offers three comfortable and well-appointed catered chalets in this high-altitude snow-sure resort.

Ski Total Savers incl. cash-back, ski pack offers & free group places | 4-course dinners with complimentary wine
Cooked breakfast | Free Wifi | Flights from Southampton, Gatwick, Heathrow, Manchester & Edinburgh

Tel: **01483 791933** Book online at **skitotal.com**

Build your own shortlist: **www.wheretoskiandsnowboard.com**

Like the resort?

You'll love our handpicked accommodation

0844 576 0173
peakretreats.co.uk

◆ABTA
ABTA No. W5537

peak retreats

ACTIVITIES

Indoor Climbing wall, gym, bowling, cinema, cultural centre with art gallery and library

Outdoor Ice rink, snowshoeing, dog sledding, walking, snowmobiling, paragliding, helicopter rides, quad bikes, ice driving, snow kiting

Phone numbers
From abroad use the prefix +33 and omit the initial '0' of the phone number

TOURIST OFFICES

Flaine
www.flaine.com

Morillon
www.ot-morillon.fr

a south view. But you may prefer the 5-star Terrasses d'Eos or next door, and new for this season, Terrasses d'Hélios residences – both Pierre & Vacances Premium properties, in ski-in/ski-out positions slightly outside the village at Montsoleil; both are comfortable, with pool, sauna, steam, hot tub. In Flaine Forêt, P&V also has the Forêt. Lagrange has several properties, including attractive chalets out at Hameau – also the location of the Refuge du Golf, with pool. Most of these are available through Ski Collection and Erna Low.

EATING OUT ★★☆☆☆
Limited choice

The choice is adequate, no more. We get most reports on the Brasserie les Cîmes in Forum: 'Simple but well-cooked food, good portions, caters very well for families'; 'lots of atmosphere'; 'extensive menu, reasonable prices'. The tiny Grain de Sel is 'friendly, excellent value'. The Sucré Salé at Forêt does 'excellent, filling and healthy food at good prices' and 'is well known for its pitta bread wraps'. Other 2004 reader tips: Michet across the piste from the gondola ('huge roaring fire, extensive gourmet style menu'), Cascade ('will pick you up in a snowmobile, huge portions of fondue'). The Ancolie in Hameau has a reputation for fine dining and will pick you up and drop you off.

APRES-SKI ★☆☆☆☆
Take your Kindle

'Don't go to Flaine for nightlife,' says a reporter who spent two months there. You don't have much choice of venue: 'Only two main bars really get going,' says a recent reporter: the Dutch-run Flying Dutchman in Forêt ('lively venue full of students singing Dutch songs; good-value drinks') and the White Pub, which has a big-screen TV, rock music and a happy hour; live music some nights; 'in need of refurbishment and fresh air' said a 2014 reporter. The Perdrix Noire also has an English pub atmosphere. The bar at the bowling alley is popular with families (and stays open until 3am). The Caves is a nightclub.

OFF THE SLOPES ★☆☆☆☆
Curse of the purpose-built

Flaine is not great for people who don't want to hit the slopes. But there is a fine ice-driving circuit where you can take a spin in your car or in theirs. Snowmobiling and dog sledding are popular, and there's a cinema. The pool, gym and spa at the Centaure residence are open to the public. Some weeks there are concerts – classical, jazz, rock and pop. Shopping is extremely limited.

LINKED RESORT – 700m

MORILLON

Morillon is a small, quiet, traditional old village, with a few cafes, restaurants, bars, supermarket and shops spread out along the road through. Newer buildings are in chalet style and are quite attractive. There's a 3-star hotel, the Morillon (0450 901032). A gondola goes up to the mid-mountain mini-resort of Morillon 1100 (aka Les Esserts), with slope-side apartments at the foot of wide, gentle and tree-lined slopes. A choice of red and blue runs go to the valley but snow on them is not reliable, although the area as a whole is north-facing.

Morillon 1100 has the essentials of life – two ski schools, three ski shops, a bakery, a supermarket, a couple of restaurants, and the Madison pub with live music.

SNOWPIX.COM / CHRIS GILL

← Flaine is a great resort for families; and no, not all the pistes are this narrow

Les Gets

Traditional-style village with a very French feel, providing serious competition for its more established linked neighbour, Morzine

TOP 10 RATINGS

Extent	★★★★★
Fast lifts	★★★
Queues	★★★
Snow	★★
Expert	★★★
Intermediate	★★★★
Beginner	★★★★
Charm	★★★★
Convenience	★★★
Scenery	★★★

RPI   100

lift pass	£200
ski hire	£120
lessons	£70
food & drink	£135
total	£525

NEWS

2013/14: A mini-snowcross for kids and families opened on Chevannes.

Extent rating
This is for the whole Portes du Soleil area

Piste map
Refer to the map in the Morzine chapter

ARE HERE IN
Les Gets

▶ Quality chalets
▶ Top locations
▶ Excellent value
▶ 17 more resorts

skitotal.com
01483 791 933

LAGRANGE
Prestige

High-standard
Self-catering
Apartments

020 7371 6111
lagrange-holidays.co.uk

➕ Good-sized, varied and lightly wooded slopes shared with Morzine

➕ Attractive chalet-style village

➕ Usually few queues or crowds locally unless good weekend weather attracts a weekend influx

➕ Part of the vast Portes du Soleil ski pass region, but …

➖ It's quite a long way to the main Portes du Soleil circuit at Avoriaz

➖ Low altitude and exposure to westerlies means risk of rain and poor snow

➖ Few challenging pistes

➖ Slow, old chairs in some sectors

➖ Weekend crowds

Les Gets is an attractive, small, family-friendly resort with a very French feel to it, partly because of appetizing food and wine shops lining the main street. The area of slopes that it shares with slightly lower Morzine offers the most extensive local network in the region, and in some respects Les Gets is the better base for that shared area.

Think about whether you intend to visit the main Portes du Soleil circuit repeatedly. If you have a car, you could quite easily access it by driving to the gondola at Ardent. If you don't, the circuit is much more easily accessed from Morzine, with its quicker access to Avoriaz.

THE RESORT

Les Gets is an attractive, sunny village of traditional chalet-style buildings, on the low pass leading to Morzine. The main road over the pass bypasses the village centre.

The local pass saves a fair bit on a Portes du Soleil pass, and makes a lot of sense for many visitors.
Village charm The village has a quiet ambience that appeals to families, though it does liven up at weekends. The main street is lined with attractive food shops, other shops and restaurants. The centre is fairly pedestrian-friendly, too, and a popular outdoor ice rink adds to the charm.
Convenience Although the village has a scattered appearance, most facilities are close to the main lift station. Depending on where you stay, you may have long walks, but there is a road-train shuttle that appeals mainly to families, and also free conventional buses around the village. Buses to Morzine cost 1.50 euros per journey. You can store skis and boots at the Perrières ski shop. And there are now ski lockers at Chavannes.
Scenery There are good views from the high points: from Mont Chéry, in particular, you get a great panorama of the village and slopes, with Mont Blanc beyond.

THE MOUNTAINS

Slopes The main local slopes – accessed by a gondola and a fast chairlift from the nursery slopes beside the village – are shared with Morzine, and are mainly described in that chapter. On the opposite side of Les Gets is Mont Chéry, accessed by a gondola followed by a chair or drag. The slopes here include some of the most challenging in the area, and are usually very quiet. Both sectors offer wooded and open slopes. Signage is considered 'very good'.
Fast lifts The village lifts are gondolas, but there are a lot of slow chairs both on Mont Chéry and in some sectors of the slopes shared with Morzine. A Christmas 2013 visitor found a lot of lifts kept stopping or breaking down.
Queues Read the Morzine chapter. Mont Chéry is usually crowd-free.
Snow reliability The nursery slopes benefit from a slightly higher elevation than Morzine, but otherwise our general reservations about the lack of altitude apply. You may get rain. The runs to the resort have snowmaking. The front slopes of Mont Chéry face south-east – bad news at this altitude (and in poor snow years they can be closed for much of the time); but the other two flanks are shadier. Grooming is good ('Pisteurs worked wonders;

Like the resort?
You'll love our handpicked accommodation
0844 576 0173
peakretreats.co.uk

⊕ABTA
ABTA No.W5517

peak retreats

ESPRIT
FOR FAMILIES IN
Les Gets
Family Ski Chalets
Dedicated Nurseries
Exclusive Ski Classes
12 More Resorts
espritski.com
01483 791 900

KEY FACTS

Resort	1170m
	3,840ft

Portes du Soleil	
Slopes	950-2275m
	3,120-7,460ft
Lifts	194
Pistes	650km
	404 miles
Green	12%
Blue	43%
Red	36%
Black	9%
Snowmaking	
	1074 guns

Morzine-Les Gets only	
Slopes	1000-2010m
	3,280-6,590ft
Lifts	49
Pistes	120km
	75 miles
Snowmaking	
	130 guns

Phone numbers
From abroad use the prefix +33 and omit the initial '0' of the phone number

TOURIST OFFICE

www.lesgets.com

could ski back to resort in March in a poor snow year and warm temperatures'). The grassy slopes don't need much snow-cover, and in a sparse snow year you may do better here than in higher, rockier resorts such as Avoriaz.

Terrain parks The park on Mont Chéry has kickers, rails and boxes for all ability levels. There's a snowcross on Chavannes plus a new mini-snowcross for kids and families.

Experts Black runs on the flank and back of Mont Chéry are quite steep and often bumped. In good snow there's plenty to do off-piste, including some excellent wooded areas.

Intermediates High-mileage piste-bashers might prefer direct access to the main Portes du Soleil circuit, but the local slopes have a lot to offer, with excellent reds on Mont Chéry.

Beginners The village nursery slopes are convenient. At Chavannes there is a bigger and more snow-sure Mappy's area with four free lifts (you pay for a return gondola trip to reach it). There are lots of easy runs to progress to – including the Bleuets on Chavannes.

Snowboarding The local slopes are good for beginners and intermediates.

Cross-country There are 12km of good, varied loops locally.

Mountain restaurants Read the Morzine chapter for places on the shared slopes. There are two restaurants on Mont Chéry giving great views. At the top is the Grande Ourse, run by an English family, offering snacks and table-service lunches ('very friendly and fun, with good atmosphere'). At mid-mountain there's the Belvedère – and a picnic room. Over the back near the foot of the Chéry Nord lift the 'friendly' Chanterelles is recommended for its 'tasty, traditional French food'.

Schools and guides There's a choice of schools, including at least two that are British-run. We had a good 2014 report on BASS: 'Our son thoroughly enjoyed himself with endlessly patient instructors'. And Les Gets Snowsports has been praised in the past.

Families This is a good resort for families. There are comprehensive facilities, including an American Indian-themed trail area on Chavannes with teepees and various activities – called the Grand Cry Territory. Major British family specialist tour operators Esprit Ski and Ski Famille offer catered chalet holidays here.

STAYING THERE

There is a good selection of chalets and mid-range hotels.

Chalets Families have a wide choice: Ski Famille has eight chalets, including the 'very comfortable' Chalet Marjorie, and Esprit Ski has five, four in one building with its own crèche. Ski Total has four, most with outdoor hot tub and sauna. VIP's plush Altitude Lodge, on the piste up at Les Chevannes, is highly praised by a regular visitor; hot tub and sauna. Private catered Chalet le Frene has also been praised.

Hotels The Ferme de Montagne (0450 753679) is small, plush and luxurious but on the edge of town. Of the 3-stars, the Crychar (0450 758050), at the foot of the slopes, is one of the best. The similarly convenient 4-star Marmotte (0450 758033) was renovated for last season. In 2012 we stayed happily in the pleasant 2-star Stella (0450 758040).

Apartments Lagrange has two prestige properties – the central Sabaudia apartments and Les Fermes Emiguy (both with pool, hot tub, sauna etc). Peak Retreats offers the latter plus other apartments and several self-catered chalets (some luxurious). Erna Low also has Les Fermes Emiguy.

Eating out The Ferme de Montagne (see 'Hotels') serves delicious food in lovely surroundings. The Tourbillon, Choucas and Outa have been recommended, as has the Fruitière for fondue and raclette. Try the Tyrol for pizza and the rustic Vieux Chêne for Savoyard specialities.

Après-ski Après-ski is quiet, especially on weekdays. But there are half a dozen bars; the obvious first target is the Irish Pub and the Black Bear above it. The Igloo disco is popular. The George bar in the Regina hotel is new.

Off the slopes There's an outdoor ice rink and bowling, quite a few shops, a cinema and the intriguing Mechanical Music Museum. Husky sleigh rides, snowshoeing, parapenting and micro-brewery visits are possible; also visits to Geneva, Lausanne and Montreux.

UK PACKAGES

Alpine Answers, Alpine Elements, Alpine Inspirations, Consensio, Crystal, Esprit, Ferme de Montagne, Flexiski, Hanski, Hugski, Igoski, Lagrange, Luxury Chalet Collection, Mountain Beds, Oxford Ski Co, Peak Retreats, PowderBeds, Reach4theAlps, Ski Expectations, Ski Famille, Ski Independence, Ski Line, Ski Total, Ski Weekend, Skitracer, Skiweekends.com, Snow Finders, STC, Thomson, VIP, Zenith

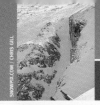

SNOWPIX.COM / CHRIS GILL

La Grave

A world apart: an unspoiled mountain village beneath high, untamed off-piste slopes, some of them extreme and hazardous

TOP 10 RATINGS

Extent	★
Fast lifts	
Queues	★★★★
Snow	★★★
Expert	★★★★★
Intermediate	★
Beginner	★
Charm	★★★
Convenience	★★★
Scenery	★★★★

RPI   90

lift pass	£190
ski hire	£100
lessons	£55
food & drink	£130
total	**£475**

NEWS

La Grave does not change much, and that is half the charm of the place.

➕ Legendary off-piste mountain

➕ Usually crowd-free

➕ Usually good snow conditions

➕ Link to Les Deux-Alpes

➕ Easy access by car to other resorts

➖ Poor weather means closure

➖ As a holiday base, suitable for experts only

➖ Through-traffic detracts from Alpine village atmosphere

➖ Little to do off the slopes

La Grave enjoys cult status among experts. It has around 500 visitor beds and just one serious lift serving a high, wild and almost entirely off-piste mountainside. The result: an exciting, usually crowd-free area. Strictly, you ought to have a guide, but in good weather many people go it alone.

THE RESORT

La Grave is a small, unspoiled village built along the road up to the Col du Lautaret. A car is useful for access to Les Deux-Alpes down the valley and Serre-Chevalier over the pass.

Village charm The centre has a rustic feel, some welcoming hotels and friendly inhabitants. But it is a bit plain, and traffic on the through-road can be intrusive.

Convenience The single serious lift starts a short walk below the centre.

Scenery La Grave is set on a steep hillside facing the impressive glaciers of majestic La Meije. Great views.

THE MOUNTAINS

A slow two-stage 'pulse' gondola (with an extra station at a pylon (P1) half-way up the lower stage) ascends into the slopes and finishes at 3200m. Above that, you are towed by a piste machine to access a drag serving a blue run on a glacier slope of about 350m vertical. From the top (after a walk) you can ski to Les Deux-Alpes. But the reason that people come here is to explore the legendary slopes back towards La Grave.

The slopes can be closed by bad weather or avalanche danger. If they are, a reader recommends going to the tiny resort of Le Chazelet, which has short pistes and easy off-piste served by several lifts. Assuming the Col du Lautaret was open, we would head for the lovely woods of Serre-Chevalier.

Slopes The main slopes offer no defined, patrolled, avalanche-protected pistes – but there are two marked itinéraires (with several variations). Neither is particularly steep. The Chancel route passes the eponymous refuge, and descends 1400m to the P1 station; it involves a long traverse through trees, which may consist of 'energy-sapping icy moguls'. The Vallons de la Meije offers several variants, one going the full 1750m vertical to the valley, another ending at the bottom of the upper gondola. People do take these routes without a guide or avalanche equipment, but we couldn't possibly recommend it.

There are many more demanding routes, including couloirs that range from straightforward to seriously hazardous, and long descents from the glacier to the valley road below the

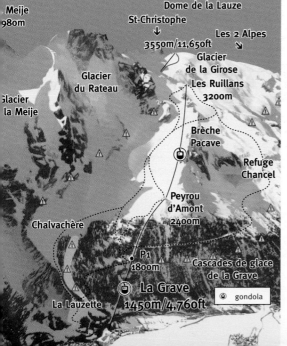

Meije 980m

Glacier la Meije

Glacier du Rateau

Chalvachère

La Lauzette

Dome de la Lauze

St-Christophe ↓ 3550m/11,650ft

Les 2 Alpes ↘

Glacier de la Girose

Les Ruillans 3200m

Brèche Pacave

Refuge Chancel

Peyrou d'Amont 2400m

P1 1800m

Cascades de glace de la Grave

La Grave 1450m/4,760ft

🚡 gondola

Hello La Grave

Self Catered
Apartments
Ski Coaching
+ Ski Touring
Snowshoe
Adventures
Winter Skills

eurekaski
MORE FROM YOUR MOUNTAIN HOLIDAY

eurekaski.com/lagrave

KEY FACTS

Resort	1450m
	4,760ft
Slopes	1450-3550m
	4,760-11,650ft
Lifts	4
Pistes	5km
	3 miles
Green/Blue	100%

The figures relate
only to pistes;
practically all the
skiing – at least 90%
– is off-piste

| Snowmaking | none |

UK PACKAGES

Alpine Answers,
EurekaSki, Mountain
Tracks, Ski Club
Freshtracks, Ski
Weekend

Phone numbers
From abroad use the
prefix +33 and omit
the initial '0' of the
phone number

TOURIST OFFICE

www.lagrave-lameije.
com

OT LA GRAVE LA MEIJE

Dream on: untouched
powder like this won't
last long, even in La
Grave →

village, with return by taxi, bus, or
strategically parked car. You can also
descend a 'spectacular' valley to
St-Christophe, returning by taxi or bus
and the lifts of Les Deux-Alpes.

The dangers are considerable
(people die here every year), and good
guidance is essential. Blindly following
tracks is dangerous; they may lead to
a big cliff that people have been roped
down or jumped off.

Fast lifts There aren't any, and there's
no need for any.

Queues The lift can build queues if
conditions are very good, especially
on March weekends. If there's a queue
at the bottom, don't ski down to P1.

Terrain parks There aren't any.

Snow reliability The chances of powder
snow on the high, north-facing slopes
are good.

Experts La Grave's uncrowded off-piste
slopes have earned it cult status
among hard-core skiers. Only experts
should contemplate a stay here.

Intermediates The itinéraires get
tracked into a piste-like state, and
adventurous intermediates could
tackle them.

Beginners Novices tricked into coming
here can go up the sunny side of the
valley to the easy slopes at Le
Chazelet, which has a fast quad and
two snow-guns.

Snowboarding There are no special
facilities for boarders, but advanced
freeriders will be in their element on
the open off-piste powder.

Cross-country There is a total of 20km
of loops in the area.

Mountain restaurants Surprisingly,
there are three. The excellent, tiny

Refuge Chancel, where supplies and
waste are backpacked in and out, is
the pucka La Grave experience: paper
plates, communal tables, good food,
table-service. Les Ruillans at the top
'does a good plat du jour'.

Schools and guides There are claimed
to be 30 or so guides, working
through a bureau. 'Excellent' is the
verdict of one of our most reliable
reporters. Serre-Chevalier-based New
Generation ski school is again offering
two-day ProXplore off-piste guiding for
2014/15.

Families Not really a family resort, but
nearby Le Chazelet is more geared up.
The tourist office knows of babysitters.

STAYING THERE

Hotels There are several simple
options. The Brit-run 3-star Edelweiss
(0476 799093) has quite basic rooms
but they're 'comfortable', 'the food is a
good standard' and there's a 'great
wine list'. The Skiers Lodge/Hotel des
Alpes (0476 110318) offers all-inclusive
week-long packages including guiding;
a past reporter had an excellent week.

Apartments Bookable through the
tourist office. EurekaSki offers a
selection.

Eating out Most people eat in hotels.
The Vieux Guide serves the 'best food'
in the resort, says a local.

Après-ski The Castillan and Pierre
Farabo are the standard teatime
venues. Later on, the bars of the
Skiers Lodge and Bois des Fees may
have live music.

Off the slopes This isn't a resort for
non-skiers, unless you are keen on ice
climbing.

Megève

One of the traditional old winter holiday towns; best for those who enjoy relaxed cruising and spectacular views

OT MEGÈVE

267

RATINGS

The mountains

Extent	*****
Fast lifts	**
Queues	****
Terrain p'ks	***
Snow	**
Expert	**
Intermediate	****
Beginner	***
Boarder	**
X-country	****
Restaurants	****
Schools	***
Families	***

The resort

Charm	****
Convenience	**
Scenery	*****
Eating out	****
Après-ski	**
Off-slope	****

RPI 100

lift pass	£170
ski hire	£125
lessons	£70
food & drink	£145
total	**£510**

NEWS

2014/15: There are plans to replace both Mont Joux chairs with one fast six-pack, which will start lower down. A new Folie Douce (as in Val d'Isère etc) is due to open at the top of Mont Joux near the new chair. More snowmaking is planned for the red run from Le Bettex to St-Gervais.

2013/14: More snowmaking was installed. Two new restaurants opened and the Manège hotel has been revamped to become the M de Megève and is now a 5-star, one of seven.

- ➕ Extensive easy, scenic slopes
- ➕ Charming old town centre
- ➕ Some very smart hotels and shops
- ➕ Some special mountain restaurants
- ➕ Good for weekend trips
- ➕ Great when it snows – woodland runs with no one on them
- ➕ Plenty to do off the slopes

- ➖ Low altitude of slopes means a risk of poor snow, though the grassy terrain does not need deep cover
- ➖ Lots of slow, old lifts remain
- ➖ Three separate mountains
- ➖ Few challenging pistes
- ➖ Very muted après-ski (though a new Folie Douce is set to change that)
- ➖ Meals and drinks pricey

Megève has a medieval heart but it was, in a way, the original purpose-built French ski resort – developed in the 1920s as a response to Switzerland's irritatingly swanky St Moritz. Although Courchevel long ago took over as France's top resort, Megève's smart hotels still attract the old money. Happily, the rest of us can enjoy it, too. And just look at that list of plus points above.

This is one of our favourite places to be in falling snow, when Megève regulars take one look and retreat to their duvets. But when the sun is out and we want to zip around the pistes, we get very frustrated by the number of slow lifts. The resort still has a lot to learn from St Moritz (never mind Saalbach).

THE RESORT

Megève is in a lovely sunny setting and has a beautifully preserved, partly medieval centre. Visitors are mainly well-heeled French people, who come here for an all-round holiday.

The skiing divides into three sectors. One is directly accessible by lifts from close to the centre and from the southern edge of town, another from an elevated suburb or from an out-of-town lift base; these two are linked by cable car. The third involves a bus or free horse-drawn sleigh, for most people.

There are several alternative bases (which offer some good-value lodging) on the fringes of the area. St-Gervais and Le Bettex above it (described at the end of this chapter) have gondola access to the main sector. But beware slow access lifts from otherwise attractive spots. The slopes also link with La Giettaz; this has interesting local terrain, but is out on a limb and is not a sensible base.

The Evasion Mont Blanc lift pass also covers Les Contamines. Plans to create a link with this resort have existed for ages, and now the Megève piste map has been redrawn to include it. Don't hold your breath.

A car is handy for outings like that,

and for using the Princesse gondola, slightly out of town.

VILLAGE CHARM ****
Old France at its best

Megève's charming old centre is car-free and comes complete with open-air ice rink, horse-drawn sleighs, cobbled streets and a fine church. Lots of smart clothing, jewellery, antique, gift and food shops add to the chic atmosphere. The main Albertville road bypasses the centre, and there are expensive underground car parks. But people arrive here mainly by car, and the resulting traffic can be a problem

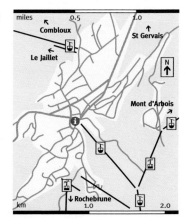

MOMENTUM SKI

Weekend & a la carte
ski holiday specialists

100% Tailor-made

Premier hotels
& apartments

Flexible travel
arrangements

020 7371 9111
WWW.MOMENTUMSKI.COM

at times, particularly if you are based
outside the very centre. 'Seems to get
worse every year,' notes a reporter.

CONVENIENCE ★★✩✩✩
Stay close to a lift
Unless you have a car, staying close to
one of the main lifts makes a lot of
sense. Some of the best hotels are
above the centre, close to the Mont
d'Arbois gondola. But many lodgings
depend on the free ski-buses, which
are not super-frequent.

SCENERY ★★★★★
Beautiful town, beautiful views
The slopes are prettily wooded, but
what earns Megève its five stars is the
view of Mont Blanc from many of the
runs – especially the red Epaule along
a ridge above St-Nicolas-de-Véroce.

THE MOUNTAINS

The slopes are largely below the
treeline – this is a great resort in poor
weather – though there are extensive
open areas, particularly higher up in
the Mont d'Arbois sector.

Piste classification frequently
exaggerates difficulty. The piste map
could be improved, particularly in the
Mont d'Arbois sector.

EXTENT OF THE SLOPES ★★★★★
More than enough for a week
Each of the three mountains has a
worthwhile amount of terrain, and
they add up to a great deal of skiing.

The town is most directly linked
with the **Rochebrune** sector – a
gondola goes up from the centre of
town, and a cable car from the

Stanford Skiing - The Megève Specialist

chalets - hotels - apartments - short breaks - ski guiding
flexible travel - family run - friendly knowledgeable staff

01603 447471   **www.stanfordskiing.co.uk**

KEY FACTS	
Resort	1100m
	3,610ft
Slopes	850-2355m
	2,790-7,730ft
Lifts	88
Pistes	325km
	202 miles
Green	19%
Blue	29%
Red	39%
Black	13%
Snowmaking	
	552 guns

southern edge. A network of gentle, wooded, north-east-facing slopes, served by drags and mainly slow chairlifts, leads to the high point of Côte 2000, which often has the best snow but is now often used for racing, reducing the pistes available to recreational skiers.

At just above resort level the Rocharbois cable car goes across the valley to link Rochebrune to the gondola for the bigger **Mont d'Arbois** sector, starting from an elevated suburb of the resort. The Princesse

gondola starting a couple of miles north of the town (with extensive free car parking) offers another way up. A two-stage gondola comes up from St-Gervais via Le Bettex. You can work your way over to Mont Joux and up to the small Mont Joly area – Megève's highest slopes. And from there you can go to the backwater village of St-Nicolas-de-Véroce (preferably via the splendid Epaule ridge run, with wonderful views of Mont Blanc).

The third area is **Le Jaillet**, accessed by gondola from just outside the

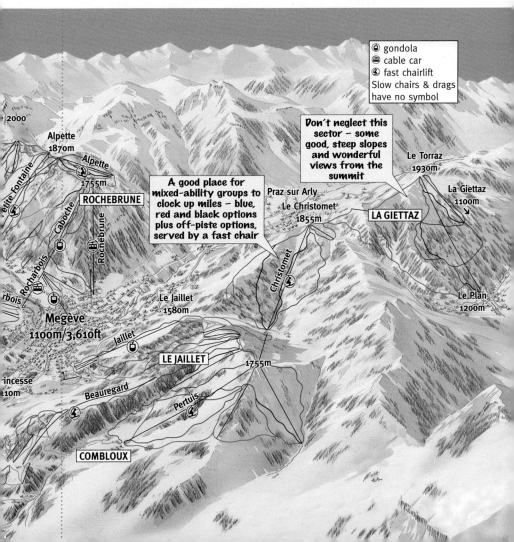

- 🚠 gondola
- 🚡 cable car
- ⛷ fast chairlift
- Slow chairs & drags have no symbol

Don't neglect this sector – some good, steep slopes and wonderful views from the summit

A good place for mixed-ability groups to clock up miles – blue, red and black options plus off-piste options, served by a fast chair

2000
Alpette 1870m
Alpette 1755m
ROCHEBRUNE
Petite Fontaine
Caboche
Rochebrune
Rocharbois
rbois
Megève 1100m/3,610ft
Jaillet
Le Jaillet 1580m
LE JAILLET
1755m
incesse 10m
Beauregard
Pertuis
COMBLOUX
Praz sur Arly
Le Christomet 1855m
Christomet
LA GIETTAZ
Le Torraz 1930m
La Giettaz 1100m
Le Plan 1200m

Tailor made, long weekend and short break French Alps ski holiday specialists.

Hanski
Ski. Explore. Relax.

web: www.hanski.co.uk
tel: 01638 596373
mob: 07833 612061

SNOWPIX.COM / CHRIS GILL

The views of Mont Blanc from the Epaule red run along a ridge above St-Nicolas-de-Véroce are simply stunning ↓

north-west edge of town, or from the separate village of Combloux. The high point of Le Christomet is linked to the slopes of tiny **La Giettaz** – worth the trip, not least for spectacular views.

FAST LIFTS ★★☆☆☆
Still far too many slow ones
Megève continues to lag way behind its rivals in the uplift business. Gondolas and cable cars provide the main access, and fast chairs are dotted around – but overall three out of four lifts are slow. The new six-pack on Mont Joux for 2014/15 is the first new fast chair for three seasons.

QUEUES ★★★★☆
Few weekday problems
Megève is relatively queue-free during the week, mostly. But sunny weekends (when day-trippers from Geneva appear) and school holidays can mean some delays. The long, steep Lanchettes and Roche Fort drags between Côte 2000 and the rest of the Rochebrune slopes can have long queues – as can the cable car that links the two mountains. A recent reporter found long queues at the Epaule chair on a sunny Saturday. Crowded pistes at Mont Joux and Mont d'Arbois can also be a problem. On a snowy day the slopes can be delightfully quiet as the Parisians choose to stay in bed, leaving the powder to you and us.

TERRAIN PARKS ★★★☆☆
Four, surprisingly
The park near the bottom of Rochebrune was designed particularly for beginners. There is a 500m-long snowcross course and an airbag jump nearby. There is also a park on Mont d'Arbois, with a good line of jumps for all ability levels. Plus a host of rails and a snowcross. Combloux also has a park and La Giettaz a smaller park, albeit with a real multitude of jump sizes and a few rails. Both have snowcross courses – 'great fun' says a 2014 visitor.

SNOW RELIABILITY ★★☆☆☆
The area's main weakness
The slopes are low, with very few runs above 2000m, and quite sunny – the Megève side of Mont d'Arbois gets the afternoon sun. So in a poor snow year, or in a warm spell, snow on the lower slopes can suffer badly. Fortunately, the grassy slopes don't need much depth of snow. There is extensive snowmaking, but that can't work in warm weather. Grooming is very good but read 'For experts', below.

FOR EXPERTS ★★☆☆☆
Off-piste is the main attraction
One of Megève's great advantages for expert skiers is that there is not much competition for the powder – many days after a fresh dump you can often make first tracks on good slopes. The

Evasion Mont Blanc

Prices in €

Age	1-day	6-day
under 15	35	165
15 to 64	43	205
65 plus	40	185

Free Under 5, over 80
Beginner Three free lifts; Rochebrune pass covers 6 lifts; three other limited passes, each covering one or two lifts
Notes Megève, La Giettaz, Combloux, St-Gervais, St-Nicolas, plus Les Contamines; family discounts; pedestrian pass

Alpine Answers, Alpine Weekends, Carrier, Erna Low, Flexiski, Hanski, Inghams, Kaluma, Lagrange, Luxury Chalet Collection, Momentum, Mountain Beds, Oxford Ski Co, Peak Retreats, Pierre & Vacances, PowderBeds, Scott Dunn, Simon Butler Skiing, Ski Bespoke, Ski Collection, Ski Expectations, Ski Independence, Ski Weekend, Skiweekends. com, Snow Finders, Snow-wise, Stanford Skiing, STC, White Roc
St Gervais Erna Low, Hanski, Holiday in Alps, Inghams, Lagrange, Mountain Beds, Peak Retreats, PowderBeds, Ski Club Freshtracks, Ski France, Ski Weekend, Ski Weekender, Snowcoach, Zenith
Combloux Erna Low, Peak Retreats
La Giettaz Erna Low

Stanford Skiing - The Megève Specialist
chalets - hotels - apartments - short breaks - ski guiding
flexible travel - family run - friendly knowledgeable staff
01603 447471   www.stanfordskiing.co.uk

resort now leaves several runs ungroomed after a snowfall, so you get to enjoy the powder for a bit.

The Mont Joly and Mont Joux sections offer the steepest slopes. The top chair here serves a genuinely black run, with some serious off-piste off the back of the hill; and the slightly lower Epaule chair has some steep runs back down and also accesses some good off-piste, as well as pistes, down to St-Nicolas. The steep area beneath the second stage of the Princesse gondola can be a play area of powder runs among the trees. Côte 2000 has a small section of steep runs, including good off-piste.

The terrain under the Christomet chair on Le Jaillet can be a good spot to develop off-piste technique, given decent snow – and a reporter recommends the extensive woods at La Giettaz.

FOR INTERMEDIATES ★★★★
Superb if the snow is good
Good intermediates will enjoy the whole area – there is so much choice it's difficult to single out any particular sectors. Keen skiers are likely to want to focus on the fast lifts, and happily several of these serve excellent terrain: the Princesse and Bettex gondolas on Mont d'Arbois, the Fontaine and Alpette chairs on Rochebrune and the Christomet chair in the Le Jaillet sector. But don't confine yourself to those – there are lots of other interesting areas, including the shady north-east-facing slopes on the back of Mont d'Arbois and Mont Joux and the front of Rochebrune, and the genuinely red/black slopes of La Giettaz. The slopes above Combloux are well worth exploring, particularly the quiet reds and black served by the Jouty chairlift. For those who want to try out powder, some reds and blues are left ungroomed after a snowfall.

Megève is also a great area for the less confident. There are long, easy blue runs in all sectors. A number of gentle runs lead down to Le Bettex and La Princesse from Mont d'Arbois, while nearby Mont Joux accesses long, easy runs to St-Nicolas. Alpette and

Côte 2000 are also suitable. As is most of Le Jaillet, especially the long easy runs down to Combloux.

FOR BEGINNERS ★★★
Good choice of nursery areas
There are beginner slopes at valley level, and more snow-sure ones at altitude on each of the main mountains. There are also plenty of very easy green runs to progress to.

FOR BOARDERS ★★
Beginner friendly
Boarding doesn't really fit with Megève's rather staid, upmarket image – there are no specialist schools – and there are quite a few flat linking runs to deal with. But freeriders will love it after snowfalls. It's a good place to try snowboarding for the first time, with plenty of fairly wide, quiet, gentle runs and a lot of chairlifts and gondolas. The draglifts are generally avoidable (except between Alpette and Côte 2000, unless you take the bus).

FOR CROSS-COUNTRY ★★★★
An excellent area
There are 38km of varied trails spread throughout the area. Some are at altitude, making meeting with Alpine skiers for lunch simple.

MOUNTAIN RESTAURANTS ★★★★
Something for all budgets
Megève has some chic, expensive, gourmet places, but plenty of cheaper options too. Stanford Skiing's website has an absolutely essential guide to download. The piste map marks restaurants but does not name them. The tourist office restaurant guide includes huts; it is not comprehensive. Sadly, our favourite Auberge du Christomet on Le Jaillet is rumoured to have been bought by Russians and became very glitzy and pricey last season. The new table-service Fruitière in the Folie Douce due to open for 2014/15 should be up to the usual high standard. Reports please!
Editors' choice On Mont d'Arbois, La Ravière (0450 931571), tucked away in the woods near the Croix chair, is a tiny rustic hut that serves good food

Megève

271

Build your own shortlist: **www.wheretoskiandsnowboard.com**

Ski coaching. Chamonix.
Achieve optimum results with focussed and friendly tuition.
+33(0)616871853
powderama.com

SCHOOLS

ESF
t 0450 210097

Evolution 2
t 0450 555357

International
t 0450 587888

Freeride
t 0680 306898

Summits
t 0450 933521

Agence de Ski
t 0699 185200

BASS
t 0845 468 1003 (UK)

Revolution Glisse
t 0667 608964

Ski Pros
t 0681 610615

Powderama
t 0616 871853

Ski Technique
t 0616 766948

Classes (ESF prices)
5 2.5hr-days €155

Private lessons
€43 for 1hr

GUIDES

Bureau des Guides
t 0450 215511

CHILDCARE

P'tites Frimousses
t 0450 211869
Ages 1 to 3

Club Piou Piou
t 0450 589765
Ages 3 to 4

Ski schools
From age 5

but has a limited choice (around four main courses); booking is essential and you must have at least two courses.
Worth knowing about Mont d'Arbois is well endowed. The famously expensive Idéal 1850 is said to be excellent. There are several modest, small places worth seeking out. We liked Sous les Freddy's, near the Arbois chair; very good meat platter and home-made desserts. Gouet, on the Gouet piste, offers 'friendly family service with great mountain fare'. The tiny Refuge de Porcherey above St-Nicolas offers 'lovely food and ambience' and a 'delicious white vin chaud spiced with red peppercorns'; but beware – the kitchen closes early (1.30pm when we failed to get lunch there a couple of seasons ago).

On Rochebrune/Côte 2000 the Alpette is the prestige place – 'good for a blowout'. We had a satisfying lunch in 2012 at Javen d'en Haut. Babotch near there is tipped by two visitors this year for its 'extremely good food'. Radaz serves 'well-presented generous portions of food' in several small rooms. Super Megève at the top of the cable car is 'pricey but good', with 'great atmosphere and attentive service'. On the back of the hill, Chalet le Forestier is an atmospheric hut with 'reliable plat du jour'. For those who need to watch the budget, Petite Fontaine is a '4-star good-value snack bar'.

On Le Jaillet, Face au Mont Blanc does a great fixed-price buffet. Reporters rate the Auberge Bonjournal towards La Giettaz – 'good menu, fair value, great views', 'friendly staff, nice ambience'. The tiny self-service Balcons de Lydie has 'fair prices' and the 'best view in Megève'. Picnic rooms are marked on the piste map.

SCHOOLS AND GUIDES ★★★★★
Plenty of choice
The ESF is of course the major school. A regular visitor sees huge class sizes every season ('up to 20; though most are only just into double figures and most people we speak to seem content'). Happily, it has lots of competition here, not only from the International school but also from smaller French schools and some British-run outfits. A 2014 reporter and her friend – 'two nervous ladies from Wiltshire' – revelled in the 'idiosyncratic technique' of Megève

Mike at Ski Pros. Powderama, based in Chamonix, offers private lessons here.

Heli-skiing (in Italy) and expeditions to the Vallée Blanche (in Chamonix) can be arranged, and mountain guides are available (we've had a great morning powder skiing in the trees with Alex Périnet: 0685 428339).

FOR FAMILIES ★★★★★
Language problems
The kindergartens offer a wide range of activities. But lack of English-speaking staff could be a drawback. The slopes are family-friendly and the schools rated by reporters. There are snow gardens in the main sectors.

STAYING THERE
There is an impressive range of accommodation. Stanford is the Megève specialist. Hanski does short breaks here.
Chalets Stanford has three central chalets. We've happily stayed at the cheap and cheerful Sylvana – a creaky old hotel, between the Rochebrune cable car and the centre, endorsed by recent reporters – 'great position: quiet but five minutes' walk from centre', 'good food'. Right in the centre, the Rond-Point is another old hotel. The smarter 10-bed Les Clochettes is next to the Sylvana.
Hotels Megève offers a range of exceptionally stylish hotels, mainly quite small and built in chalet style. Seven lovely but very pricey places have now been elevated to 5 stars.
★★★★★Fer à Cheval (0450 213039) It's rustic-chic at its best, with a lovely wood interior. Spa and pool.
★★★★★Flocons de Sel (0450 214999) Food-oriented eight-room place in a cluster of chalets secluded a few km out. Three Michelin stars. Spa.
★★★★Chalet St Georges (0450 930715) Central, close to the gondola. Warmly welcoming, with 24 rooms and suites. Read 'Eating out', below.
★★★Coin du Feu (0450 210494) Mid-sized chalet between Rochebrune and Chamois lifts.
★★Gai Soleil (0450 210070) Simple Logis de France place. 'Good location, excellent breakfast, wonderful staff', says a discriminating reporter.
Apartments Loges Blanches is central and smart, with restaurant and outdoor pool; bookable via Ski Collection and Erna Low. Stanford also has a couple of apartments.

Like the resort?

You'll love our handpicked accommodation

0844 576 0173
peakretreats.co.uk

ABTA
ABTA No. W5537

peak retreats

Stanford Skiing - The Megève Specialist

chalets - hotels - apartments - short breaks - ski guiding
flexible travel - family run - friendly knowledgeable staff

01603 447471   www.stanfordskiing.co.uk

ACTIVITIES

Indoor Sports centre (tennis, ice rink, curling, climbing wall, swimming pool, sauna, solarium, gym), beauty treatments, health and fitness centres, museum, cinemas, casino, language courses, concerts and exhibitions, bridge, painting courses

Outdoor Cleared paths, snowshoeing, tobogganing, ice rink, horse-drawn carriage rides, ice climbing, adventure park, dog sledding, sightseeing flights, paragliding, ballooning

GETTING THERE

Air Geneva 90km/ 55 miles (1hr15); Chambéry 95km/ 60 miles (1hr15); Lyon 170km/ 110 miles (2hr15)

Rail Sallanches (12km/7 miles); regular buses from station

Phone numbers
From abroad use the prefix +33 and omit the initial '0' of the phone number

TOURIST OFFICES

Megève
www.megeve.com
St-Gervais
www.st-gervais.net

EATING OUT ★★★★☆
Very French

The tourist office produces a pocket guide with photos. There are lots of upmarket restaurants, many of them in the better hotels and the Flocons de Sel (read 'Hotels') has the top place in town – but it also has a more modest branch, Flocons Villages, that is popular with locals and got two rave reports from readers in recent years – 'beautifully presented, outstanding value', 'miraculous lamb and veal, wonderful desserts, exceptional bread'.

Meat, 'beautifully cooked', is a speciality at the 'superb' Table du Trappeur in the Chalet St Georges hotel. The Brasserie Centrale does precisely what brasseries were invented to do – 'good entrecôte-frites and crème brûlée'. The Vieux Megève is the place for cheesy specialities. The Café 2 la Poste is on a roundabout by the main road and 'looks like it should have plastic tablecloths but is charming, friendly, half the price of most other places'.

APRES-SKI ★★☆☆☆
Strolling and jazz

Megève's sedate image is set to change for 2014/15 with the opening of a new Folie Douce (of Val d'Isère etc fame) at the top of Mont Joux; doubtless there will be loud and lively parties there every afternoon. That will be a bizarre contrast with life in town, which we expect will remain sedate. It is a pleasant place to stroll around after the lifts close but if there are lively bars for a post-piste beer, they have so far eluded us. And those looking for loud disco-bars later may be disappointed, too. The 5 Rues is our choice – a very popular jazz club-cum-cocktail bar, open all evening, that gets some big-name musicians. It's pricey, but cocktail measures are large, so 'one per hour is enough', a reporter notes. The Cocoon is a Brit favourite, with live music and British sports TV. The casino is more slot machines than blackjack tables. Palo Alto has two discos.

OFF THE SLOPES ★★★★☆
Lots to do

There is a 'fantastic' sports centre with a spa, fitness room, pool, indoor and outdoor ice rinks and cinemas. Shopping is a serious business and trips to Annecy and Chamonix are possible. Walks are excellent, with 50km of marked paths. Meeting friends on the slopes for lunch is easy.

LINKED RESORT – 850m
ST-GERVAIS

St-Gervais is a handsome 19th-century spa town set in a narrow river gorge, with access to the slopes shared with Megève by a gondola from the fringes. It's a pleasant place, with interesting food shops, cosy and sophisticated bars (we liked the trendy Pur bar for cocktails and posh nibbles), thermal baths and an Olympic ice rink. Prices are noticeably lower than in Megève. The resort has a train station and there are efficient bus services.

The lodgings are mostly modest. Two hotels convenient for the gondola are the Liberty Mont Blanc (0450 934521), a pleasantly traditional place with pool and sauna, and the 3-star Carlina (0450 934110), with a small pool and sauna. The Féline Blanche (0450 965870) is a hip boutique place with just 10 rooms done out in black and white. The basic 2-star Val d'Este (0450 936591) has one of the best restaurants in town (Le Sérac).

Fermes de St Gervais is a smart Lagrange Prestige residence with a pool, a mile out of town; available through Peak Retreats.

The gondola from the edge of town goes to the satellite of Le Bettex. The good nursery slope here and green run above it, make it an attractive base for beginners. We enjoyed dining at the lovely rustic Chalet Rémy.

On the opposite side of St-Gervais is a rack-and-pinion railway, which in 1904 was intended to go all the way to the top of Mont Blanc. It was never completed, and terminates at the top of the ski area of Les Houches (see the Chamonix chapter); but sadly there are no lift pass sharing arrangements.

Les Menuires

The bargain base for the Trois Vallées – with increasing amounts of stylish accommodation as well as the original dreary blocks

AGENCE NUTS

RATINGS

The mountains

Extent	★★★★★
Fast lifts	★★★★
Queues	★★★★
Terrain p'ks	★★★
Snow	★★★★
Expert	★★★★
Intermediate	★★★★★
Beginner	★★★
Boarder	★★★★
X-country	★★★
Restaurants	★★★
Schools	★★★
Families	★★★★

The resort

Charm	★★
Convenience	★★★★★
Scenery	★★★
Eating out	★★★
Après-ski	★★★
Off-slope	★

RPI 110

lift pass	£230
ski hire	£125
lessons	£85
food & drink	£135
total	**£575**

+ Speedy, mostly queue-free access to the huge Trois Vallées area

+ Lots of slope-side accommodation, with traffic well separated

+ Low prices by local standards

+ Distinct French atmosphere

− Big, plain blocks and gloomy indoor shopping malls in the centre

− Main intermediate and beginner slopes get a lot of sun

− Some slopes can get very crowded

Les Menuires arguably has the best position in the Trois Vallées, and we've warmed to it as better (and better-looking) lodgings have continued to be built. As our RPI shows, it is much more affordable than more upmarket Courchevel and Méribel and we now view Les Menuires as a very attractive proposition – especially the traditional-style bits we've christened 'Belles-Menuires'.

THE RESORT

Les Menuires is a purpose-built resort, dominated by large apartment blocks, with about 60% of the visitors French. It has excellent links to Val Thorens in the same valley and to the Méribel valley. The core of the resort is La Croisette, a horseshoe of 1960s- and 1970s-built apartment blocks plus a claustrophobic underground shopping mall with a gondola and fast chairlift into the heart of the Trois Vallées slopes. Recent development has added various suburbs to the original core, and a second lift base across the mountainside at Les Bruyères.

VILLAGE CHARM ★★★★★
Much improved

The original buildings that surround the main lift base are among the most brutal examples of the monolithic architecture of the 1960s and 1970s. They still dominate the centre of the resort; but more recent developments in the suburbs have been built in much more attractive chalet style in stone and wood, and many UK tour operators have their accommodation there. Read our Belles-Menuires feature later in the chapter.

A couple of the original buildings have been demolished (as we advised way back in the 1990s), and they have

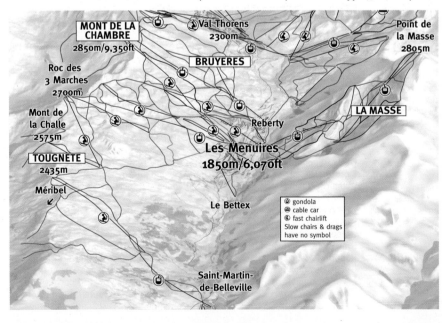

MONT DE LA CHAMBRE
2850m/9,350ft

Val Thorens
2300m

Point de la Masse
2805m

Roc des 3 Marches
2700m

BRUYERES

Mont de la Challe
2575m

LA MASSE

Reberty

TOUGNETE
2435m

Les Menuires
1850m/6,070ft

Méribel

Le Bettex

gondola
cable car
fast chairlift
Slow chairs & drags have no symbol

Saint-Martin-de-Belleville

↑ We're not fans of the central buildings, although it's the indoor shopping mall that we really dislike

OT LES MENUIRES / G LANSARD

NEWS

2014/15: A new blue run is planned for the La Masse sector.

2013/14: Two new Liberty Ride areas were created – marked, patrolled and avalanche protected but not groomed – one near the Masse 2 chair and one near the Pylones black. A 1200m long rollercoaster-style ride on rails was built.

been replaced by attractive chalet-style blocks. And the 'front de neige' has been smartened up.

CONVENIENCE ★★★★★
Easy to get around on skis
For most visitors, the resort is very conveniently arranged for skiing – a great deal of the accommodation is ski-in, and much of it ski-out.

If you stay in the central area, nothing is more than a short stroll away. If you stay in some of the outposts, it may be different. They have their own shops and bars, but if you want more choice, you are reliant on buses that are scheduled to run every 20 minutes until 8pm, then every 40 minutes until 11pm. In the mornings, too, you may have some hiking to do if you want to start from a lift other than the nearest one.

SCENERY ★★★☆☆
Go up high
The scenery can be rather bleak, but there are grand views from the peaks of the ski area on both sides, especially from La Masse.

THE MOUNTAINS

Les Menuires is set just about on the treeline, with almost all the slopes above it. Piste map and signposting are good, and piste classification is reliable.

EXTENT OF THE SLOPES ★★★★★
Part of the huge Trois Vallées
Les Menuires is well positioned for exploring the whole Trois Vallées. The major part of the local area spreads across the west-facing mountainside between Les Menuires and St-Martin, with links to the Méribel valley at four points, and at the southern end links to Val Thorens at the head of the valley. A gondola and fast chair go up from La Croisette, and the same from Les Bruyères. A gondola to the separate and unjustly neglected sector of La Masse, across the valley, starts below the village.

FAST LIFTS ★★★★☆
Good all over
The major lifts up to the peaks are now powerful gondolas or fast chairs. The main slow ones left affect Le Bettex residents and beginners only.

QUEUES ★★★★☆
Very slight
Queues are not usually a problem; most reporters comment that there are few. But the Bruyères gondola (for access to Val Thorens) is consistently mentioned by reporters ('15-minute queues at opening time'), and the Mont de la Chambre chair can also get very busy at peak times. Crowded slopes are more of a problem in general, particularly those leading down to the resort centre.

Build your own shortlist: www.wheretoskiandsnowboard.com

Les Belles-Menuires

La Plagne has its Belle-Plagne – why shouldn't Les Menuires have its Belles-Menuires? Or should it be Beaux-Menuires? Whatever ... We've made up this name to represent the attractive, chalet-style suburbs of Les Menuires – places where Méribel habitués might be happy.

These suburbs aren't simply built in chalet style – they also contain actual chalets. Most of them are operated by British tour operators who advertise on

DOWN THE HILL

Below the main resort centre in Le Bettex, Ski Amis has a cluster of smart chalets with outdoor hot tubs and saunas, 150m from the piste and the Bettex chairlift. Also in Le Bettex is the Hameaux des Airelles residence, available from Ski Collection. Le Bettex is very quiet at night, and a taxi ride from the centre of Les Menuires.

this spread, and are marked, approximately, on our map. They are concentrated up the slope in Reberty 2000, or down in Les Bruyères, a micro-resort complete with ice rink and swimming pool – and a major lift, the Bruyères gondola. The area shown also has the resort's best hotels, some smart apartment residences (read the margin panel), and an excellent slope-side restaurant, the Ferme.

Down the valley, on the opposite side of the resort centre, are further traditional-style, small-scale, relatively upmarket developments (read the left margin panel).

Ski Famille

EXCLUSIVE - à la carte Child Care

With 23 years experience we know exactly what parents and children need and want. Our chalets in Reberty 2000 offer....

○ *Child Care (babies to 12 year olds) in the comfort of your own chalet. No trudge to a central crèche* ○ *Fully qualified nannies*
○ *High quality chalets in great locations*
○ *Many free child places on selected weeks*
○ *Delicious food and complimentary wines*

Call: **01252 365 495** www.skifamille.co.uk
ATOL 10863 ABTOT 5141

Selected chalets in Les Menuires

ADVERTISEMENT

SKI AMIS *www.skiamis.com*   T **0203 411 5439**

- Chalets de Bruyeres – 5 chalets for 12-16 people – ski-in/ski-out
- Chalets de Bettaix – 4 chalets for 8-10 people
- Hot-tubs, free WIFI, satellite TV
- Excellent catering with full English breakfast every day, afternoon tea and three course evening meal
- Unlimited good quality wine

sales@skiamis.com

↑ CHALETS DE BETTAIX   **SKI AMIS**   CHALETS DE BRUYERES ↑

APARTMENTS

In Reberty 2000, Chalets du Soleil and Chalet Julietta are offshoots of the next-door 4-star hotel Kaya, with access to the Kaya's facilities, such as spa and restaurant.

Slightly lower down, Alpages de Reberty is a Pierre & Vacances Premium residence with pool, sauna etc.

La Sapinière includes the Montagnettes residence Hameau de la Sapinière, with sauna, steam room and hot tub, and a restaurant – and a local supermarket will deliver free of charge.

Down in Les Bruyères, Le Chalet du Mont Vallon Spa Resort has a pool, gym, sauna, steam and a serious restaurant.

Several agencies including apartment specialists Ski Collection offer these and other residences.

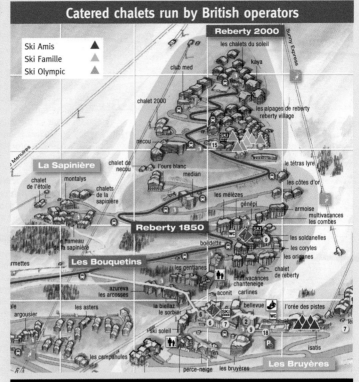

Catered chalets run by British operators

Ski Amis ▲
Ski Famille ▲
Ski Olympic ▲

Ski Olympic

book online at **skiolympic.com**
or call **01302 328 820**

LIFT PASSES

Trois Vallées

Prices in €

Age	1-day	6-day
under 13	46	222
13 to 64	57	277
65 plus	51	249

Free Under 5, 75 plus
Beginner Limited pass

Notes Covers Courchevel, La Tania, Méribel, Val Thorens, Les Menuires and St-Martin; reductions for families and other groups. Options: pedestrian and half-day passes

Alternative passes
Les Menuires/ St-Martin only; Vallée de Belleville only

TERRAIN PARKS ★★★☆☆
Family-friendly
The BK park near the top of the Becca chair has blue and red lines of jumps and rails plus two snowcross courses. On La Masse there's the Walibi Gliss slalom and snowcross area. There's a big airbag jump at the foot of the Slalom area.

SNOW RELIABILITY ★★★★☆
Coverage good, quality variable
The main west-facing slopes obviously get lots of strong afternoon sun. They have lots of snowmaking, but the snow lower down is often icy in the morning and slushy later on. La Masse's height and more shady orientation ensure good snow for a long season. Grooming is 'fantastic', says a 2014 visitor.

FOR EXPERTS ★★★★☆
Head for La Masse
The upper slopes of La Masse, served by the second stage of a fast jumbo gondola, are virtually all of stiff red or easy black steepness – great fast cruises when groomed, of almost 660m vertical, and with some of the best snow in the Trois Vallées. They are also usually very quiet compared with the rest of the slopes near here because La Masse is set off the busy Trois Vallées 'circuit', and most people doing the circuit from Méribel, Courchevel and Val Thorens don't make the detour.

There is also a huge amount of off-piste, including the wide, sweeping, not-too-steep Vallon du Lou off the back of La Masse towards Val Thorens (this used to be a marked itinéraire

Ski Collection

Major Resorts
Expert knowledge

4★ ski apartments with spa

SkiCollection.co.uk
0844 576 0175
ABTA Bonded W5537

SKI AMIS

Catered Chalets in Superb Locations

020 3411 5439
www.skiamis.com

KEY FACTS

Resort	1800m
	5,910ft

Trois Vallées	
Slopes	1260-3230m
	4,130-10,600ft
Lifts	180
Pistes	600km
	373 miles
Green	13%
Blue	39%
Red	38%
Black	10%
Snowmaking	33%

Les Menuires / St-Martin only	
Slopes	1400-2850m
	4,590-9,350ft
Lifts	34
Pistes	160km
	99 miles
Green	15%
Blue	47%
Red	30%
Black	8%

FRANCE

278

and was one of our favourite runs in the whole Trois Vallées). Or you could try the new Liberty Rides.

Read the other Trois Vallées resort chapters too.

FOR INTERMEDIATES ★★★★★
600km of pistes to choose from

With good snow, the slopes above the village on the west-facing side, virtually all blue and red, have a lot to offer. Don't miss La Masse as well – read 'For experts' above.

But the real attraction is the easy access to the rest of the Trois Vallées and its 600km of pistes, most of which are ideal intermediate terrain. There are lifts to four different points from which you can drop into the Méribel valley, and you can be at the far end of the Courchevel ski area in 1650 in around 90 minutes if you don't get distracted on the way. To get to Val Thorens, there's an easy blue run from the top of the Montaulever draglift that is quieter than the main

runs down from the top of the Bruyères gondola.

Read the other Trois Vallées resort chapters too.

FOR BEGINNERS ★★★★★
Snow quality a concern

The resort's nursery areas are pretty good, with five moving carpets that are free – but snow quality here remains a concern because of the sunny aspect. A special lift pass is available for beginners, and there is a green run to the village from the Roc des 3 Marches gondola, and lots of easy blues to progress to, but they are prone to crowds.

FOR BOARDERS ★★★★★
Beware flat parts

Slushy afternoon snow on the west-facing slopes won't worry boarders as it does skiers, but the early-morning ice might. You'll still want to escape and explore the vast amount of terrain elsewhere in the Trois Vallées. The local terrain park is far from hard core, but Méribel's two great parks are easy to reach. Locally, there are few draglifts but beware some flattish sections of piste.

FOR CROSS-COUNTRY ★★★★★
Limited and low

The 28km of trails are along the valley between St-Martin and Les Menuires.

BRIAN WALKER

Les Belles-Menuires, as explained on the previous spread ↓

SCHOOLS

ESF
t 0479 006143
Ski School
t 0667 586777
Prosneige
t 0479 041835
Snowbow
t 0684 890411

Classes (ESF prices)
6 5hr-days €198
Private lessons
€50 for 1hr for 1 or 2
people

CHILDCARE

Les Piou Piou (ESF)
t 0479 006379
Ages 3mnth to
30mnth
Mini club (ESF)
t 0479 006379
Ages 31mnth to 5yr

Ski school
From age 3 or 4 to 12

GETTING THERE

Air Chambéry 115km/
70 miles (1hr30);
Geneva 150km/
95 miles (2hr15);
Grenoble 180km/
110 miles (2hr15);
Lyon 190km/
120 miles (2hr15)
Rail Moûtiers
(25km/15 miles)

ACTIVITIES

Indoor Centre Sportif
(swimming pool,
sauna, steam, fitness,
squash), library
Outdoor Tobogganing,
outdoor pool (hotel
Bruyères), cleared
paths, snowshoeing,
paragliding,
snowmobiling,
mountain biking on
snow

Phone numbers
From abroad use the
prefix +33 and omit
the initial '0' of the
phone number

TOURIST OFFICE

www.lesmenuires.com

MOUNTAIN RESTAURANTS ★★★★★
Affordable fare
There are some good places here
charging affordable prices.
Editors' choice The Grand Lac (0479
082578) is a big chalet in a fine spot
at the bottom of the Granges chair
where we've always had very good
service and food – endorsed by a 2014
visitor who rates the hot choc 'the
best outside Italy'. Way across the hill,
the Alpage (0479 007516) is also
consistently praised; we had a good
meal there in 2013, and we hear the
dining area was successfully expanded
for last season.
Worth knowing about The Sonnailles,
off the valley-bottom Cumin run, is
another favourite. On the La Masse
side, Roches Blanches at the top of
the first gondola has 'impressive food
and service' and 'good, fresh pizzas'.
In the almost-a-mountain-restaurant
category, the Ferme, piste-side at
Reberty 2000, is excellent ('I'd stay in
a cardboard box in the middle of a
piste just to eat here every day'),
while 'traditional' Maison de Savoy,
down in Reberty 1850, is singled out
this year: 'Our favourite – good food
and prices, friendly service.' Consider
the slope-side hotel terraces in
Reberty, too, such as the Ours Blanc.

SCHOOLS AND GUIDES ★★★★★
Try the Ski'School
The ESF gets mixed reviews; it seems
to do a lot of off-piste stuff. A group of
instructors operating here and in
St-Martin under the startling name of
Ski'School offer only private lessons
and are said to be 'really good'.

FOR FAMILIES ★★★★★
Lots of options
Good facilities. There are kids'
'villages' with indoor and outdoor
facilities at both La Croisette and Les
Bruyères. Ski Famille is a family
specialist with three chalets in Reberty
and its own childcare arrangements.

STAYING THERE

La Croisette consists mainly of large
apartment blocks. Reberty/Les
Bruyères has hotels and chalets too.
Chalets See our Belles-Menuires
feature earlier in the chapter.
Hotels There are good places on the
slopes at Reberty/Les Bruyères.
★★★★Kaya (0479 414200) Smart and
modern with good spa and restaurant.

★★★★Ours Blanc (0479 006166) Chalet
style, sauna, steam, tub, good food.
★★★Isatis (0479 004545) In chalet
style, right at the Bruyères gondola –
17 suites, all with hot tubs.
★★★Neige et Ciel (0479 007516) Slope-
side family 'club' hotel with nursery
and kids' club – 'great place, very
good buffet meals'.
Apartments There are lots of new
developments in chalet style, most of
them covered by our Belles-Menuires
feature. In Preyerand, just below the
main resort centre, is the chalet-style
4-star residence Les Clarines, with spa
and pool, run by CGH and featured by
Ski Collection. Ski Amis has units in all
parts of the resort. Erna Low has a
good range of properties.

EATING OUT ★★★★★
Mix of gourmet and Savoyard
We had very good traditional and
gourmet meals at the Cocon des
Neiges (hotel Isatis). Up the slope in
Reberty, the K (hotel Kaya) is a good
gourmet option. Consider some of the
places mentioned in 'Mountain
restaurants' too – the Ferme, Maison
de Savoy and Ours Blanc. Other recent
tips include the Chouette ('efficient,
jolly', 'great crêpes'), and the Vieux
Grenier ('great atmosphere').

APRES-SKI ★★★★★
Not a lot of choice
It's pretty quiet in the evening. A
reporter favourite for close-of-play
beers is the Chouette at Les Bruyères.
There is no shortage of bars in La
Croisette, but we're not tempted by
those in the claustrophobic mall. There
are discos at Croisette and Bruyères.

OFF THE SLOPES ★★★★★
Great sports centre
There is an impressive sports/spa/pool/
fitness centre, the newish roller-
coaster, a 4km-long toboggan run,
mountain biking on snow,
snowmobiling, snowshoe outings,
snowscooters and paragliding. But this
is basically a destination for skiers
and boarders, and not very appealing
for others.

UK PACKAGES
Absolutely Snow, Crystal, Crystal Finest, Erna Low,
Family Ski Company, Lagrange, Neilson, Pierre &
Vacances, Powder N Shine, Powder White,
PowderBeds, Richmond Holidays, Ski Amis, Ski
Collection, Ski Famille, Ski France, Ski
Independence, Ski Line, Ski Olympic, Ski Supreme,
Skibug, Skitracer, Skiweekends.com, Thomson

Les Menuires

Build your own shortlist: www.wheretoskiandsnowboard.com

Méribel

A sprawling but comfortable, upmarket chalet-style resort in the centre of the incomparable Trois Vallées

SNOWPIX.COM / CHRIS GILL

RATINGS

The mountains

Extent	★★★★★
Fast lifts	★★★★★
Queues	★★★★
Terrain p'ks	★★★★
Snow	★★★
Expert	★★★★
Intermediate	★★★★★
Beginner	★★★★
Boarder	★★★★
X-country	★★★
Restaurants	★★★
Schools	★★★★
Families	★★★

The resort

Charm	★★★
Convenience	★★★
Scenery	★★★
Eating out	★★★
Après-ski	★★★★★
Off-slope	★★★

RPI   125

lift pass	£230
ski hire	£130
lessons	£110
food & drink	£175
total	**£645**

KEY FACTS

Resort	1400-1700m
	4,590-5,580ft

Trois Vallées	
Slopes	1260-3230m
	4,130-10,600ft
Lifts	180
Pistes	600km
	373 miles
Green	13%
Blue	39%
Red	38%
Black	10%
Snowmaking	33%

Méribel only	
Slopes	1400-2950m
	4,590-9,680ft
Lifts	41
Pistes	150km
	93 miles
Green	9%
Blue	44%
Red	37%
Black	10%

➕ Central to the Trois Vallées, the biggest lift network in the world

➕ Pleasant chalet-style architecture

➕ Impressive lift system

➕ Very lively après-ski scene

➕ Excellent piste maintenance and snowmaking; nevertheless ...

➖ Snow on the west-facing side suffers from afternoon sun

➖ Sprawling main village

➖ Expensive, particularly for food and drink

➖ Full of Brits

➖ Some pistes can get crowded

A loyal band of regular visitors just love Méribel, and it's not difficult to see why. For keen piste-bashers who like to rack up the miles but dislike tacky post-war resorts, it's difficult to beat: unlike other modern purpose-built resorts, Méribel has always insisted on chalet-style architecture.

Other 3V resorts have the edge in some respects. For better snow opt for Courchevel or Val Thorens; for lower prices, Les Menuires or St-Martin.

THE RESORT

Méribel was founded in 1938 by a Brit, Peter Lindsay, and has retained a strong British presence and influence ever since. It consists of two main resort villages.

The original resort is built on a steepish west-facing hillside with the home piste running down beside it to the main lift stations in the valley bottom, slightly below the village centre. The resort now spreads widely away from the centre and the piste; various quarters can be identified – among them Mussillon, beside the road in to the resort, where many individual chalets are located.

A road winds up from the centre to the top of the main village. Then one road goes on through woods to the altiport (a snow-covered airstrip) while another goes under the home piste to the suburb of Belvedere.

The satellite resort of Méribel-Mottaret, a mile or two up the valley, is centrally placed in the Trois Vallées ski area. The hamlet of Méribel-Village, on the road to Courchevel, has grown into a pleasant, quiet micro-resort.

You can stay in the valley below Méribel, in the spa town of Brides-les-Bains – linked by gondola and described at the end of this chapter – or in the village of Les Allues at a mid-station of the gondola.

A car is useful for outings to other resorts such as Les Arcs, Val d'Isère, Tignes and La Rosière; you can access La Plagne via Champagny.

VILLAGE CHARM ★★★★★
Built with style

Méribel is one of the most tastefully designed of French purpose-built resorts. The buildings are wood-clad, chalet-style and mainly low-rise, and they include a lot of individual chalets as well as big chalet-shaped blocks of apartments. Mottaret lacks these smaller chalets, and looks more block-

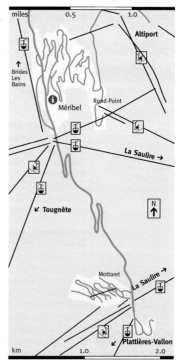

Méribel

NEWS

2014/15: The Loze chair to the Col de la Loze is due to be upgraded to a fast quad, making this route to Courchevel much more attractive. The Inuit Village is due to have two new trails built in the woods.

2013/14: A couple of disused rooms at the Chaudanne lift base were turned into a picnic room and lounge area. Inuit Village is a new children's area beside the altiport. It has whoops, banked turns and slalom. The Moon Park now has features made from foam rubber for beginner riders to practise on, and the snowcross has been enlarged. The Roc de Fer run has been improved. And the Doron blue back to Chaudanne has been widened.

like as a result, despite wood cladding. Even so, it's more attractive than many other resorts built for slope-side convenience, but has nothing like the feel of a village.

CONVENIENCE ★★★☆☆
Shuttle to the slopes, usually
Although some lodgings are right on the piste beside the village, many depend on using free (and now 'excellent') public buses which run until midnight or private minibuses to and from the slopes. There are collections of shops and restaurants at a couple of points on the road through the resort – Altitude 1600 and Plateau de Morel.

Méribel-Village is a small place; it has some luxury chalets and apartments, but very limited amenities – a good bread shop, a small supermarket, a bar, a pizzeria and a couple of restaurants.

Mottaret has spread up both steep sides of the valley, though most of the blocks are on the east-facing side. Many lodgings are ski-in/ski-out, but not all. Both sides are served by lifts for pedestrians – but the gondola up the east-facing slope stops at 7.30.

SCENERY ★★★☆☆
Head for Vallon
The village is attractively set in woodland, below long craggy ridges – a satisfying although unspectacular scene. But there are wonderful glacial views from Mont du Vallon at the head of the valley.

THE MOUNTAINS

Most of the slopes are above the treeline, but there are some sheltered runs for bad-weather days. Piste classification is not always reliable – a problem compounded by exposure of many slopes to the sun. Signposting is excellent. The piste map is adequate; but it could be so much better if it covered the two sides of the valley separately. They have stopped handing out maps of which pistes have been groomed but you can now get this information on the Trois Vallées smartphone app or on the Méribel website and it appears on small notices posted at various places.

EXTENT OF THE SLOPES ★★★★★
Centre of a huge area
Leaving aside the rest of the Trois Vallées, this is a big area. Lifts go up to nine high points on the ridges above the resort: two entry points to the Courchevel valley, no fewer than six entry points to the Belleville valley (shared by St-Martin, Les Menuires and Val Thorens) and one to Mont du Vallon, a very worthwhile cul-de-sac.

On the morning-sun side, chairs go up to the first two links with St-Martin, and some relatively quiet slopes back towards Méribel. To the left, a gondola and then a six-pack go from Méribel to **Tougnète**, for both Les Menuires and St-Martin. You can also head down to **Mottaret** from here. From there, a fast chair then a drag take you to Belleville entry point number four.

BRIAN WALKER

The satellite resort of Méribel-Mottaret: the resort spreads up the far slope on the right, and the near slope on the left →

Pierre & Vacances
premium

Perfect spacious apartments with spas and swimming pools.

pierreetvacances.co.uk

South of Mottaret are some of the best slopes in the valley, in the **Plattières-Vallon** sector at the head of the valley. The top stage of the old Plattières gondola (the first two stages were replaced by a 10-seater for 2012/13) ends at the fifth entry point to the Belleville valley. To the east of this is the big stand-up gondola to the top of Mont du Vallon. The Côte Brune fast quad from near this area goes up to Mont de la Chambre, the sixth link with the next valley, and the only one giving direct access to Val Thorens.

On the afternoon-sun side, gondolas leave both Méribel and Mottaret for **Saulire**, the main link to Courchevel. The other is from the altiport – a much more attractive route now that it goes via a new fast quad to Col de la Loze, replacing a very slow old chair.

FAST LIFTS ★★★★★
Highly efficient system
Modern chairs and gondolas serve both sides of the valley, with good links into the rest of the Trois Vallées.

QUEUES ★★★★☆
3V traffic a persistent problem
The area is generally queue-free most of the time but there are a few bottlenecks. More singles lines are appearing – but the lift company could achieve a lot by employing lifties to

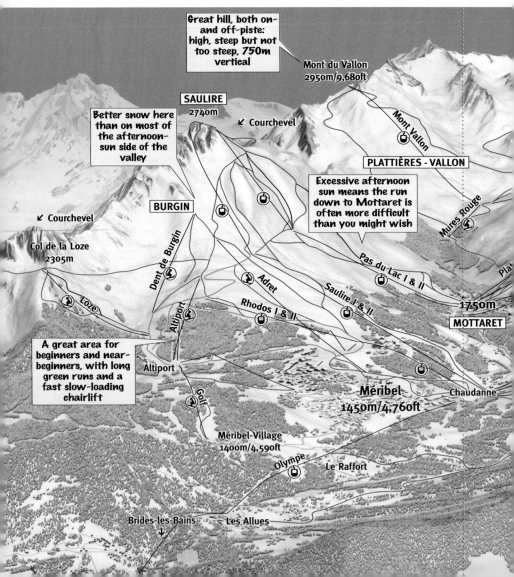

Great hill, both on- and off-piste: high, steep but not too steep, 750m vertical

Mont du Vallon
2950m/9,680ft

SAULIRE
2740m

↙ Courchevel

Mont Vallon

PLATTIÈRES - VALLON

Better snow here than on most of the afternoon-sun side of the valley

Excessive afternoon sun means the run down to Mottaret is often more difficult than you might wish

BURGIN

↙ Courchevel

Col de la Loze
2305m

Dent de Burgin

Adret

Rhodos I & II

Loze

Altiport

Pas du Lac I & II

Saulire I & II

Mures Rouge

Pla

1750m

MOTTARET

A great area for beginners and near-beginners, with long green runs and a fast slow-loading chairlift

Altiport

Golf

Méribel
1450m/4,760ft

Chaudanne

Méribel-Village
1400m/4,590ft

Olympe

Le Raffort

Brides-les-Bains

Les Allues

AWARD-WINNING
SKI
HOLIDAYS

Ski Olympic

book online at
skiolympic.com
01302 328 820

usher people into half-empty cabins and on to chairs, North American style.

We and reporters alike have found that the six-pack above the Tougnète gondola is a serious bottleneck – it comes nowhere near coping with the combination of people coming up the gondola and people descending the four good pistes above – and in spring the problem is made worse by pedestrians bringing it to a stop. A major upgrade is needed.

The new Plattières gondola has cut queues at Mottaret but put more pressure on the old gondola third stage (which remains in place above the new lift) and the Côte Brune chair used by people heading onward to Mont de la Chambre and Val Thorens. The newish gondola from Méribel to La Saulire shifts a lot of people quickly.

In this central valley the most serious problems result from the tidal flows of people passing through in the morning (when the tide coincides with the start of ski school) and in the late afternoon, when crowds on the runs to Mottaret can also be a problem.

Most people returning from Val Thorens form a queue for the Plan des Mains chair so as to avoid the flat start of the 'blue' Ours valley run. Confident skiers can by-pass Plan des Mains by traversing above it, off-piste; with a guide, of course.

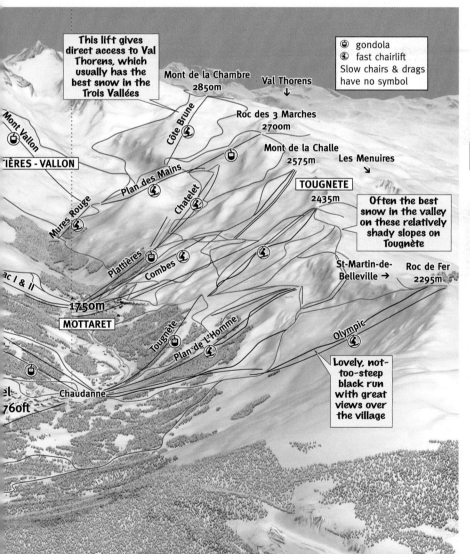

This lift gives direct access to Val Thorens, which usually has the best snow in the Trois Vallées

gondola
fast chairlift
Slow chairs & drags have no symbol

Mont de la Chambre 2850m

Val Thorens ↓

Côte Brune

Roc des 3 Marches 2700m

Mont de la Challe 2575m

Les Menuires ↓

Mont Vallon

IÈRES - VALLON

Plan des Mains

Mures Rouge

Chatelet

TOUGNETE 2435m

Often the best snow in the valley on these relatively shady slopes on Tougnète

Plattières

Combes

St-Martin-de-Belleville →

Roc de Fer 2295m

ac I & II

1750m

MOTTARET

Tougnète

Plan de L'Homme

Olympic

Lovely, not-too-steep black run with great views over the village

el

Chaudanne

76oft

SKIWORLD

Catered chalets, hotels and self catering apartments in

Europe, USA and Canada

skiworld.co.uk
08444 930 430

ABTA V2151 ATOL 2036

LIFT PASSES

Trois Vallées

Prices in €

Age	1-day	6-day
under 13	46	222
13 to 64	57	277
65 plus	51	249

Free Under 5, 75 plus
Beginner Mini pass
Notes Covers Courchevel, La Tania, Méribel, Val Thorens, Les Menuires and St-Martin; reductions for families and other groups. Options: pedestrian and half-day passes

Alternative passes
Méribel and Méribel-Mottaret only + 3V extension

TERRAIN PARKS ★★★★☆
Two great areas

Méribel has two big parks. Moonpark – at mid-mountain on Tougnète and served by the Arpasson draglift – covers over 25 acres. In charge are the respected Ho5 crew. There are kickers, tables, rails and boxes all made of wood, with beginner, intermediate and expert lines, a snowcross and a 'chill and grill' BBQ zone. You can be filmed and watch the results on a big screen.

Under the new Plattières gondola, the Area 43 park was massively expanded a couple of seasons ago to be 1200m long with lots of features, lines for different abilities, 220m of rails, a half-pipe, snowcross and air bag jump. You can have your run recorded and play it back online.

Kids get their own mini-snowcross courses, P'tit Moon, plus Moon Wild, an animal-themed piste in the forest – all on the west-facing slopes.

SNOW RELIABILITY ★★★☆☆
Not the best in the Trois Vallées

Méribel's slopes aren't the highest in the Trois Vallées, and they mainly face roughly east or west; the latter (the runs down from Courchevel) get the full force of the afternoon sun. In late season you soon get into the habit of avoiding this side in the morning, when it is still rock-hard having frozen overnight. Skiers coming over from Courchevel can get a real shock. The run down from Saulire to Mottaret is a particular problem – often like concrete for its whole 1000m vertical; in our countless visits over many years, we've only once found this run enjoyable. The slopes above Altiport get less direct sun and generally have decent snow. And the morning-sun side (the Tougnète side of the valley) can be excellent. At the southern end of the valley, a lot of runs are north-facing and keep their snow well, as do the runs on Mont du Vallon.

Snowmaking has been increased to the point where the lower runs have substantial cover. Lack of snow is rarely a problem. Grooming is good.

FOR EXPERTS ★★★★☆
Exciting choices

The size of the Trois Vallées means experts are well catered for. In the Méribel valley, Mont du Vallon has lots to offer. The long, steep Combe Vallon run here is classified red; it's a wonderful, long, fast cruise when groomed (which it normally is), but presents plenty of challenge when mogulled. And there's a beautiful off-piste run away from the pistes, leading back to the bottom of the gondola.

A good mogul run is down the side of the double Roc de Tougne draglift

---

MERIBEL'S BEST OFF-PISTE RUNS

Méribel has a lot of very good off-piste to discover. Here, we pick out some of the best runs for skiers with at least some off-piste experience. Don't tackle them without guidance.

The run from near Roc de Fer to Le Raffort, a mid-station on the gondola from Brides-les-Bains, is an adventure with exceptional views. You ride the Olympic chairlift, go along the ridge, then ski a gentle bowl to finish among the trees.

The wide, west-facing slope above Altiport is enjoyable when the snow is fresh – varied terrain, from average to steep, some open some wooded, reached from the Tétras black run.

There are lots of runs suitable for more accomplished off-piste skiers. One is the Cairn, from the Mouflon piste at the top of the Plattières 3 gondola; it starts in a fairly steep couloir and becomes wider, with a consistent pitch, until you reach the Sittelle piste.

The Roc de Tougne draglift accesses some challenging runs. To the right of the Lagopède red piste is an area guides call the Spot – a rather technical and steep descent to the Sittelle piste. Alternatively, a 15-minute hike brings you to the Couloir du Serail, leading to the Mouflon red piste – a favourite because of the vertical, the constant pitch and the quality of snow.

Some of the best routes in the Méribel valley are accessed from the other valleys. The Col du Fruit is a classic, far away from the lifts and resorts. You ride the Creux Noirs chairlift in Courchevel, then walk along the ridge for 15 minutes before descending through the national park to Lac de Tueda and the cross-country tracks ... 800m of flat ground from the Mottaret lifts. Some of the best snow is accessed from the 3 Vallées chairlift at Val Thorens. Ducking the rope at the top takes you into varied terrain mixing couloirs and gentle slopes, with exposures from north-east to north-west. Eventually you join the red Lac de la Chambre piste down to Plan des Mains.

Ski Total
ARE HERE IN
Méribel

▶ Quality chalets
▶ Top locations
▶ Excellent value
▶ 17 more resorts

skitotal.com
01483 791 933

ALPINE ANSWERS
The UK's No.1 Chalet Specialist

For choice and service look no further!

alpineanswers.co.uk
call: 020 7801 1080   ABTA

Discover the difference
with SkiWeekends
#loveski

Prices from
£200

skiweekends.com

UK PACKAGES

Adventure Base, Alpine Action, Alpine Answers, Alpine Elements, Alpine Weekends, Avery Crest, Belvedere Travel, Club Med, Consensio, Crystal, Crystal Finest, Delicious Mountain, Elegant Resorts, Erna Low, Esprit, Flexiski, Friendship Travel, Inghams, Interactive Resorts, Lagrange, Luxury Chalet Collection, Mark Warner, Meriski, Momentum, Mountain Beds, Neilson, Oxford Ski Co, Pierre & Vacances, Powder White, PowderBeds, Purple Ski, Scott Dunn, Silver Ski, Ski Amis, Ski Basics, Ski Beat, Ski Bespoke, Ski Blanc, Ski Club Freshtracks, Ski Collection, Ski Cuisine, Ski Expectations, Ski France, Ski Hame, Ski Independence, Ski Line, Ski Olympic, Ski Supreme, Ski Total, Ski Weekend, Skitracer, Skiweekends.com, Skiworld, Snow Finders, Snow-wise, SnowCrazy, STC, Supertravel, Thomson, VIP, White Roc
Mottaret Alpine Answers, Crystal, Neilson, Pierre & Vacances, Scott Dunn, Ski France, Ski Independence, Thomson
Brides-les-Bains Crystal, Erna Low, Lagrange, Peak Retreats, PowderBeds, Skiweekends.com, Thomson

which leads up to Mont de la Challe. And there are steep, unrelenting runs from Tougnète back to Méribel – the upper Ecureuil piste is a black and the adjacent Combe Tougnète is a red. At the north end of the valley the Face run was created for the women's downhill race in the 1992 Olympics; served by a fast quad, it's a splendid cruise when freshly groomed.

Nothing on the Saulire side is as steep as on the other side of the valley. The Mauduit red run is quite challenging, though – it used to be classified black. Throughout the area there are good off-piste opportunities – read our feature panel, and the other Trois Vallées resort chapters.

FOR INTERMEDIATES ★★★★★
Paradise found
Méribel and the rest of the Trois Vallées form something close to paradise for intermediate skiers and riders; there are few other resorts where a keen piste-basher can cover so many miles so easily and with such satisfaction. Virtually every slope in the region has a good intermediate run down it.

For less adventurous intermediates, the Sittelle blue run from the top of the new Plattières gondola back down towards Mottaret is an ideal cruise – gentle and generally in good condition because of its aspect. But it can get very crowded and the lower part can get bumpy and slushy later in the day.

Even early intermediates should find the runs into the other valleys well within their capabilities, opening up vast amounts of intermediate terrain, often with better snow.

Virtually all the pistes on both sides of the Méribel valley will suit more advanced intermediates. Few of the reds are easy.

FOR BEGINNERS ★★★★★
Strengths and weaknesses
Méribel continues to improve its appeal to beginners. At the core of this appeal is an excellent long green slope – gentle, wide, tree-lined – at Altiport, where Editor Watts learned to ski [cough] years ago. This is a lift or bus ride above the resort, which is not ideal. But the slope is served by a free draglift (and by a fast chair going higher, not free). And there are green runs from the top and bottom of the drag back to Rond-Point, at the top of the village, where there is another free drag; beginners should take a lift or bus down from there as the blue run lower down is not easy (although widened last season). And a green run goes from the mid-station of the Saulire gondola so that novices are able to ski from that point. The Mini lift pass gives access to a limited number of gentler slopes.

There is a small nursery slope at Rond-Point which is mainly used by the children's ski school.

At Mottaret, facilities are less impressive. There is an enclosed beginner area beside the village with a covered moving carpet; you can graduate from there to an almost flat green along the valley to the main Méribel lifts (though it gets busy).

FOR BOARDERS ★★★★★
Good all round
The terrain is good and varied, with a worthwhile number of tree runs. Mont du Vallon has some very good steep freeriding that stays relatively untracked. There are lots of red runs here for intermediates and gentle blues and greens for beginners. The two terrain parks are top-notch too. Most lifts are chairs or gondolas, but beware of flat sections on the main routes to and from Val Thorens – and avoid the Ours blue run down to

ESPRIT
FOR FAMILIES IN
Méribel

Family Ski
Chalets
Dedicated
Nurseries
Exclusive Ski
Classes
12 More Resorts

espritski.com
01483 791 900

CHILDCARE

Les Saturnins
t 0479 086031
Ages 18mnth to 3yr

Les Piou Piou
t 0479 086031
Ages 3 to 5

Childminder list
Available from the
tourist office

Ski school
Ages 5 to 13

OT MERIBEL / JM GOUEDARD

Chalet Central: you
have a wider choice
of chalet holidays
here than anywhere
else ↓

Mottaret from Mont du Vallon, which is very hard work. Specialist shops include Avalon Rider (which is in central Méribel).

FOR CROSS-COUNTRY ★★★★★
Scenic routes
There are about 33km in the Méribel valley. The main area is in the forest near Altiport and is great for trying cross-country for the first time. There's also a loop around Lake Tueda, in the nature reserve at Mottaret, and for the more experienced an 8km itinéraire from Altiport to Courchevel.

MOUNTAIN RESTAURANTS ★★★★★
A disappointing choice
There are few places in this valley worth singling out, and there aren't enough restaurants to meet the demand, so many places get crowded. Sadly, we still have no reports on the major new arrival of recent years, the Fruitière; looks like we'll have to check it out ourselves. Restaurants are not named on the piste map.

We've had a good lunch in the table-service part of Plan des Mains, and a 2014 visitor had 'a very nice lunch from the extensive menu'. The Chardonnet, mid-station of the Pas du Lac gondola, is said to be popular for its steak tartare prepared at the table; reports, please. The Crêtes, on the Tougnète ridge, has a fine position

and rustic interior; a regular visitor says the 'menu is limited but the food is divine'. The Rhododendrons, at the top of the Altiport drag and Rhodos gondola, is a popular self-service – 'very good, and decent value', says a 2014 reporter. The Coeur de Cristal, low down beside the Adret chair, does 'excellent food, generous portions', 'lovely with nice washrooms'.

This is one of the few resorts where we are easily persuaded to descend to resort level for lunch, on one of four excellent slope-side hotel terraces – in the main village either the Adray Télébar or the Allodis, at the altiport the, er, Altiport ('fabulous – best ever Savoyard meat platter'), or at Mottaret the Arolles ('good food at reasonable prices').

SCHOOLS AND GUIDES ★★★★★
Some excellent British schools
There are several British-run schools. New Generation, which operates in many French resorts including Méribel, gets excellent reports – 'the perfect amount of jokes, drills, talks and brilliant skiing' – and is endorsed again this year.

BASS is also Brit-run and a 2013 visitor is full of praise for the 'friendly instructor – we all improved massively'. Parallel Lines has been tipped, too. Magic in Motion is run by an Anglo-French team and has a number of native English-speaking instructors.

We've had mixed reports on this branch of the ESF, the most recent of them encouraging.

FOR FAMILIES ★★★★★
A popular chalet choice
Méribel is a sensible choice for families wanting a chalet holiday. What it lacks in convenience it gains in an impressive area, with gentle beginner slopes and a couple of fun family areas (the new Inuit Village with whoops, a tunnel, banked turns and slaloms, and Moon Wild nature trail through the woods – both above Altiport).

Magnestick child safety systems have now been fitted to fast chairlifts in the area to prevent them opening until near the end of the ride. But we rarely get reports on childcare facilities – no doubt many readers use the facilities of chalet operators. Family specialist Esprit operates chalets here – read the next section.

Major Resorts
Expert knowledge

4★ ski apartments with spa

SkiCollection.co.uk
0844 576 0175
ABTA Bonded W5537

SCHOOLS

ESF Méribel
t 0479 086031

Magic
t 0479 085336

New Generation
t 0479 010318
0844 770 4733 (UK)
www.skinewgen.com

Parallel Lines
t 0844 811 2779 (UK)

Snow Systems
t 0479 004022

BASS
t 0679 512405

Snow D'Light
t 0479 550773

Classes (ESF prices)
5 half-days (2.5hr per day): from €200

Private lessons
From €100 for 1.5hr for up to 4 people

GUIDES

Mountain guide office
t 0479 003038

STAYING THERE

Chalets Méribel has more catered chalets than any other resort. Many of them are recently built luxury places with spas, hot tubs and more. Many rely on minibus services.

The widest choice is from Ski Total, with 12 properties in the mid-to-large size range. Two deservedly get Total's top Platinum rating. Hot tubs, of course, and cinema and billiard room in the case of chalet Isba. Skiworld has 9 chalets of various sizes, including one swanky place with sauna, hot tub and cinema room.

Purple Ski has five top-notch and highly individual chalets – in good positions, with lovely interiors and hot tubs, plus another chalet. Ski Olympic has two properties at 1600: the smooth Parc Alpin with 12 luxurious rooms (all with plasma screen TVs), dinky swimming pool and sauna; and Charlotte with eight rooms (and no children allowed). Inghams has six chalets including one new to their programme this season, plus a 60-bed chalet hotel in a prime spot near the lifts at Chaudanne. Crystal has four chalets, one new for 2014/15 with sauna and hot tub.

Family specialist Esprit has a 60-bed chalet hotel in a good slope-side position, up at Rond-Point – 'excellent; childcare beyond exemplary', says a recent guest – and two mid-sized standalone chalets.

Hotels Méribel doesn't compete with Courchevel in the fancy hotel stakes, although it does have one 5-star.

www.interactiveresorts.co.uk
sales@interactiveresorts.co.uk
020 3080 0200

MERIBEL
****Allodis (0479 005600) Out of town at Belvedere, but ski-in/ski-out and excellent in every other way. Seriously good restaurant, superb service, pool, sauna, nice terrace.
****Altiport (0479 005232) Smart and luxurious hotel, isolated at the foot of the Altiport lifts.
****Grand Coeur (0479 086003) Our favourite almost-affordable hotel in Méribel. Just above the village centre. Welcoming, mature building with plush lounge. Huge hot tub, sauna etc.
***Adray Télébar (0479 086026) Welcoming piste-side chalet with pretty rooms and restaurant with good food and popular lunch terrace.
***Merilys (0479 086900) At Rond-Point. B&B hotel plus apartments. Recommended by a regular reporter: 'Very nice room, excellent breakfast.'
MOTTARET
****Alpen Ruitor (0479 004848) Central, with spa, hot tub. 'Very comfortable, good lounge, well worth the expense.'

Build your own shortlist: www.wheretoskiandsnowboard.com

Selected chalets in Méribel

ADVERTISEMENT

PURPLE SKI *www.purpleski.com*   T **01885 488799**

Purple Ski are known for the extraordinary level of service, cuisine and wines we offer in our luxury chalets in Méribel. With one member of staff to every two guests, we will ensure that you have the most memorable ski holiday you have ever had.

* Professional chefs
* Personal service
* On tap Veuve Clicquot
* Domain bottled wines
* En-suite bedrooms
* Private minibus service and transfers
* Hot tubs, saunas, Sky TV and wi-fi internet access

email: michael@purpleski.com

Pierre & Vacances
Holidays made for me

Best price
guarantee
for ski in/out
budget studios
up to spacious
3 bedroom
apartments

pierreetvacances.co.uk

ACTIVITIES

Indoor Parc Olympique (ice rink, swimming pool, climbing wall), fitness centres, bowling, library, cinemas, museum, heritage tours

Outdoor Flying lessons, snowmobiles, snowshoeing, ice climbing, sleigh rides, cleared paths, paragliding

GETTING THERE

Air Chambéry 100km/60 miles (1hr15); Geneva 140km/90 miles (2hr); Grenoble 170km/ 105 miles (2hr); Lyon 180km/ 110 miles (2hr)

Rail Moûtiers (18km/11 miles); regular buses

Phone numbers
From abroad use the prefix +33 and omit the initial '0' of the phone number

TOURIST OFFICE

www.meribel.net

***Arolles** (0479 004040) On the piste near Table Verte lift, with the 'best ever staff, food from good to superb, lovely lounge'. Pool and sauna.

Apartments The two most impressive larger residences are Pierre & Vacances Premium properties: Les Fermes de Méribel is a classic tasteful MGM-built development of six large chalets with the usual good pool, gym, sauna, steam in Méribel-Village (available through various agents, including Ski Collection and Skiworld); Les Crêts is a big residence up at Mottaret. Chalet Apsara is a very swanky chalet for eight in Les Allues, available through Erna Low and Ski Collection. Ski Amis has a good range of apartments.

EATING OUT ★★★★☆
Some good places to try
There is a reasonable selection of restaurants, from pizza and pasta to ambitious French cuisine – though no Michelin stars, strangely. For the best food, in plush surroundings, you won't beat the top hotels. The Zinc brasserie and Escale gourmet restaurant are at the highly regarded Altiport hotel. We've also enjoyed the Kouisena, with its very rustic, intimate interior and open-fire grills. For 'all French' fine food, the Orée du Bois has been recommended. The Galette is tipped this year for its 'great atmosphere, service and authentic raclette'. The Taverne does 'flavoursome sea bass'. In Mottaret, Table du Ruitor is 'expensive but good quality'.

In Méribel-Village, the simple Brit-run Lodge du Village (pasta, Tuscan specials) is a favourite of one regular.

APRES-SKI ★★★★★
Méribel rocks – loudly
We checked out the newish Folie Douce by the mid-station of the Saulire gondola and it was packed and rocking at 4pm on a sunny March afternoon. It makes a welcome rival to the long-standing teatime hot spot of Rond-Point at the top of the village – 'great for music and atmosphere'. We're told the Arpasson hut (Tougnète) now has 'blaring music' too.

In town, try Jack's, not far from the main lift stations ('superb live music'). The ring of bars on the main square do good business at teatime. The Doron attracts a younger crowd for videos, pool and live bands. The Poste injects a bit of French cool into the scene ('good drinks, nice young

crowd'). The popular Dick's Tea Bar has had a revamp and is now called O'Sullivan's. It has a gastro-pub (The Den) next door. But they're away from the centre and slopes. Aviatic is a bar/ club at the Altiport hotel.

In Mottaret the bars at the foot of the pistes get packed at teatime.

In Méribel-Village, the bar at Lodge du Village has live music at teatime a couple of nights a week.

OFF THE SLOPES ★★★☆☆
Quite a bit to do
The Olympic Centre has the ice rink where the Olympic events were held in 1992 and where you can watch regular hockey matches. It also has bowling, a climbing wall, a gym, a good public pool and a spa – these last two irritatingly separate, a reporter points out. You can take joyrides in the little planes that operate from the altiport. There are 25km of pleasant marked walks in several areas – eg between Méribel and the altiport area; down through hamlets to Les Allues (return by bus or gondola); and at Plan de Tueda, beyond Mottaret – 'gorgeous'. There's a good map of them, says a reporter. There is a pedestrian's lift pass, and accessible restaurants to meet friends for lunch. Mottaret has a cinema. Shopping is very limited.

BRIDES-LES-BAINS

Brides-les-Bains is an old spa town way down in the valley, with a gondola built to ferry athletes up to Méribel events in the 1992 Olympics. It offers a quieter, cheaper alternative base, with some simple hotels, good-value apartments, and adequate shops and restaurants. Skiweekends.com runs a neat-looking chalet hotel here – the Verseau – with shuttle to the Méribel gondola. There is a casino and cinema, but evenings are distinctly quiet. We have reports of one lively bar. The gondola ride is supposed to take 25 minutes, but may take 40. It arrives in Méribel at a point irritatingly short of the main lifts and closes irritatingly early, at 5pm. In good conditions you can ski off-piste to one of the mid-stations, in exceptional conditions all the way to the bottom.

Given a car, Brides makes a viable base for visiting other resorts. An obvious target is La Plagne, reached via Champagny.

SNOWPIX.COM / CHRIS GILL

Montgenèvre

Once a bit of a backwater, this famously snowy resort is developing nicely, but urgently needs to find the cash for more new lifts

RATINGS

The mountains

Extent	★★
Fast lifts	★★
Queues	★★★★
Terrain p'ks	★★★
Snow	★★★★
Expert	★★★★
Intermediate	★★★★
Beginner	★★★★★
Boarder	★★★
X-country	★★★
Restaurants	★★
Schools	★★★
Families	★★★★

The resort

Charm	★★★
Convenience	★★★
Scenery	★★★
Eating out	★★
Après-ski	★★
Off-slope	★

RPI 90

lift pass	£170
ski hire	£95
lessons	£85
food & drink	£115
total	**£465**

NEWS

2014/15: The new Durancia leisure and wellness centre will open at the west end of the village. CGH will open their new residence Napoléon, in a prime central position. There are plans to improve the slopes on the Italian side of Colletto Verde.

2013/14: An area for novice boarders was created in the beginner area. Three runs – two blacks and a red – were designated as mogul runs, and are never groomed.

- ➕ Varied local slopes, plus access to Italian Milky Way resorts, notably Sauze d'Oulx and Sestriere
- ➕ Good local snow record
- ➕ All bases covered: excellent nursery slopes, plenty of cruising and good off-piste terrain that is underused
- ➕ A lot of accommodation close to the slopes, some right on them

- ➖ Sauze and Sestriere take time to reach without road transport
- ➖ Lots of slow lifts throughout the Montgenèvre slopes, seriously undermining its appeal for some
- ➖ Little to challenge experts on-piste
- ➖ Limited range of restaurants and après-ski places

Montgenèvre is right on the Italian border, at one end of the big cross-border Milky Way network, and gets much better snow than its Italian neighbours – it is set on a minor pass, a position that delivers snow whichever way the wind is blowing, but most importantly when it's blowing from the west.

The resort has made big strides in recent years, banishing through-traffic and developing modern upscale lodgings. But it now needs to prioritize investment in fast lifts – getting around the pistes can be a painfully slow-motion affair. If you're focused on the under-exploited off-piste, the slow lifts matter less.

THE RESORT

Montgenèvre is a small village sitting on a high east-west pass only 2km from the Italian border. The village is set on the sunny slope above the main street (the through-road is now buried in a tunnel) looking over the nursery slopes at the foot of the north-facing slopes of Les Gondrans. Behind the village are the south-facing slopes of Le Chalvet. Both sectors have piste links with Claviere, just over the Italian border and gateway to the other Italian resorts of the Milky Way – Sansicario, Sestriere and Sauze d'Oulx. But it takes time to get to those resorts on skis.

There are lift pass sharing arrangements with Serre-Chevalier and Puy-St-Vincent, easily reached by car, and with rather less easily reached Les Deux-Alpes and Alpe-d'Huez, which involve going over the Col du Lautaret – high, but not usually a problem.

VILLAGE CHARM ★★★
Rustic and quiet

Cheap and cheerful cafes, bars and restaurants line the street running along the bottom of the nursery slopes, now carrying only local traffic. A couple of narrow parallel streets with a few bars and restaurants and a church lie behind it. The old buildings give it a rustic and lived-in feel. Friendly natives and generally good snow add to the charm factor. The Hameau de l'Obélisque development at the eastern end of the village is wood-clad in chalet style.

CONVENIENCE ★★★
Never far from a lift

It's a compact village – most of the lodgings are less than five minutes from a lift – but the main gondolas are at opposite ends, and getting from one end to the other on skis can take ages. The free bus service worked well for us. Some of the newer lodgings in Hameau de l'Obélisque are right on the slopes and a little draglift makes them ski-out as well as ski-in.

SCENERY ★★★
Look north or south

The area is broken up by rocky outcrops and woods, with good views from the higher slopes on both sides of the pass.

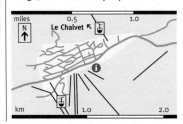

miles · 0.5 · 1.0 · N · Le Chalvet · km · 1.0 · 2.0

When quality and value matter, *do more* with

zenith ·holidays·

0203 137 7678
zenithholidays.co.uk

ABTA
ABTA No.Y1542

KEY FACTS

Resort	1850m
	6,070ft

Montgenèvre-Monts de la Lune (Claviere)

Slopes	1760-2630m
	5,770-8,630ft
Lifts	32
Pistes	110km
	68 miles
Green	10%
Blue	27%
Red	45%
Black	18%
Snowmaking	55%

Milky Way
Slopes	1390-2825m
	4,560-9,270ft
Lifts	75
Pistes	400km
	249 miles
Blue	25%
Red	56%
Black	19%
Snowmaking	60%

THE MOUNTAINS

The slopes offer lots of variety – some high and open, some wooded lower down. Run classification on the local map, the Milky Way map and on the mountain are not reliably consistent. And many of the run classifications exaggerate difficulty; the black runs are not steep. Signposting is mainly adequate. The local piste map is admirably clear.

EXTENT OF THE SLOPES ★★☆☆☆
Nicely varied

Our stars are based on the local slopes; the Milky Way as a whole easily gets a ★★★★ rating, although the Schrahe report discussed in our piste extent feature makes it clear that it is not quite as big as we thought.

The north-facing slopes above Montgenèvre and Claviere divide into three sectors. The high, open slopes of **Les Gondrans** are reached by the Chalmettes chondola from the west end of the village; a green run brings you back. From the same gondola or by riding a chairlift to the lower, steeper wooded peak of Le Prarial you can access the sector of **l'Aigle**, which has links at valley level and at altitude via Colletto Verde to the **Monti della Luna** slopes of Claviere.

The sunny sector behind the village of Montgenèvre – **Le Chalvet** – has long been accessed by a gondola from the east end of the village. A more recently added alternative access is the Serre Thibaud chondola, starting halfway between Montgenèvre and Claviere. This chondola has opened up new blue and black runs into the main Chalvet bowl and into the valley beyond the Col de l'Alpet. The Chalvet runs are mainly on open slopes above the gondola; there are blue and green runs back to Montgenèvre, and a blue run to Claviere – though it has a flat part that is hard work. There is also a blue run down a lift-free valley from Col de l'Alpet towards Claviere, but it doesn't reach the village.

FAST LIFTS ★★☆☆☆
A persistent weakness

The main lifts out of the village are a chondola and a gondola. But slow chairs and drags predominate on the upper slopes; this is a real weakness of the resort, and a regular cause of complaints from reporters. Investment is needed urgently, and there is little sign of it at present: for example, the upgrade of the chairlift on Le Chalvet, announced two years ago has not happened, and it's not clear when it will. We are told the resort is concentrating investment in the Durancia wellness centre. The piste map appears to identify fast chairlifts, but actually fails to do so reliably.

QUEUES ★★★★☆
Not a problem

Recent reporters have found the area pretty queue-free, even in peak season – a February half term 2014 visitor found 'not a single queue', and we had much the same experience. Crowds aren't a problem, 'even on a weekend' says a 2014 visitor.

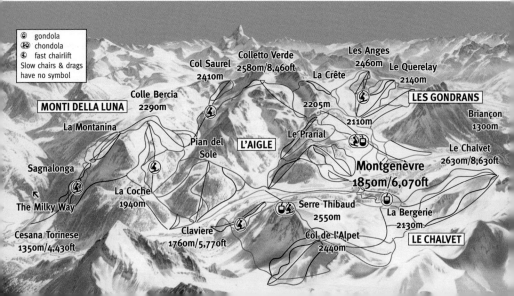

gondola
chondola
fast chairlift
Slow chairs & drags have no symbol

MONTI DELLA LUNA
La Montanina
Colle Bercia 2290m
Sagnalonga
The Milky Way
Cesana Torinese 1350m/4,430ft
La Coche 1940m
Pian del Sole
Col Saurel 2410m
Colletto Verde 2580m/8,460ft
Claviere 1760m/5,770ft
L'AIGLE
Le Prarial
2205m
Serre Thibaud 2550m
Col de l'Alpet 2440m
La Crête
2110m
Les Anges 2460m
Le Querelay 2140m
LES GONDRANS
Briançon 1300m
Le Chalvet 2630m/8,630ft
Montgenèvre 1850m/6,070ft
La Bergerie 2130m
LE CHALVET

LIFT PASSES

Montgenèvre + Monts de la Lune

Prices in €

Age	1-day	6-day
under 15	25	166
15 to 64	37	208
65 plus	28	188

Free Under 6; 75 plus
Beginner Free lift in beginner area; lesson and lift deals
Notes Montgenèvre and Claviere (1-day pass is for Montgenèvre plus 10 Italian slopes only); 6-day-plus pass allows one day in the Milky Way, Alpe-d'Huez, Serre-Che, Puy-St-Vincent, Deux-Alpes; pedestrian pass
Alternative passes Via Lattea (Milky Way) International

GETTING THERE

Air Turin 110km/ 70 miles (1hr30); Grenoble 170km/ 105 miles (2hr45); Lyon 235km/ 145 miles (2hr45); Marseille 265km/ 165 miles (3hr15)

Rail Briançon (12km/ 7 miles) or Oulx (18km/11 miles); buses available from both

TERRAIN PARKS ★★★☆☆
Various facilities

There's a jump with an airbag to cushion landings on the lower slopes of the Gondrans sector and snowcross runs in both main sectors – 'great fun', says a reporter. There's a beginner snow park at the base area, and a regular park at Claviere with five boxes and jumps that are suitable for beginners – 'well maintained', but 'really needs its own short lift'.

SNOW RELIABILITY ★★★★☆
Excellent locally

Montgenèvre has a generally excellent snow record, receiving dumps from storms funnelling up the valleys to the east and west. The high north-facing slopes naturally keep their snow better than the south-facing area. Snow-guns now cover 55% of the area, including most lower slopes. 'Snow management is excellent,' says a 2013 reporter.

FOR EXPERTS ★★★★☆
Some excellent off-piste

The local pistes offer few challenges – the Tetras piste on Le Chalvet is steep, but the other blacks are not. There is, however, ample off-piste terrain and it is wonderfully neglected. On the Gondrans side, there's a small 'freeride zone' of ungroomed slopes that are avalanche controlled, but the real interest lies elsewhere.

We had a great day with a guide here in February 2013, getting fresh tracks down the lovely, lightly wooded east face of Serre Thibaud from the eponymous chondola, then more down Combe de Grand Charvia, accessed by a short hike from the long, slow Rocher d'Aigle chair. After lunch, a run of 1000m vertical off the back of Les Gondrans took us down the Vallon de la Vachette to the bottom of the Montgenèvre pass. We skied all of these runs without seeing any other skiers or boarders.

The Rocher de l'Aigle chair offers lots of other options, too. In addition to off-piste variants on the red runs it serves on both sides of Colletto Verde, it accesses the classic off-piste run that everybody does, with and without guidance – the Vallon de la Douare, leading down towards the Brousset chair. If you're prepared to hike, there are further slopes on La Plane, overlooking Claviere, and on Le Chenaillet, next to Les Gondrans. There are further good powder areas

MONTGENÈVRE
Ski-in ski-out
4★ apartments with pool
peakretreats.co.uk/Montgenevre

ABTA
ABTA No. W5537

peak retreats

accessed from the top lifts on the Italian side.

Back on the Chalvet side, the remote north-east-facing bowl beyond the Col de l'Alpet is superb in good snow and has black pistes, too. Heli-skiing can be arranged in Italy.

FOR INTERMEDIATES ★★★★☆
Plenty of cruising terrain

The overclassified blacks (mainly concentrated in the Chalvet sector) are just right for adventurous intermediates, and there are some excellent reds – such as the pleasantly narrow tree-lined runs to Claviere from Pian del Sole, and both the runs from Colletto Verde. Average intermediates can confidently explore the whole area – few of the reds are particularly challenging. Timid intermediates have some lovely long runs on which to build confidence on both the Gondrans and Chalvet sectors – the Phare is a particularly fine long blue on the latter. Getting around the area as a whole would be easier if the easiest reds were classified blue – key runs from Colle Bercia and from Pian del Sole, for example. The runs down to the village are easy cruises.

The only real drawback of the area is the slow lifts noted above.

FOR BEGINNERS ★★★★★
One of the best

'One of the best' was the verdict of one reporter this year, and he is not far off target. There is a near-perfect nursery slope area at the foot of the Gondrans sector – large, gentle, with a moving carpet and draglift, fenced off so that you don't get speeding skiers going through it. Progression to longer runs could not be easier, with long, very easy green runs 'that are proper pistes' just up the hill at Les Gondrans. Le Chalvet also has the long, easy Phare blue run.

Build your own shortlist: www.wheretoskiandsnowboard.com

↑ The west end of the village and the Gondrans slopes, seen from the sunny Chalvet sector
SNOWPIX.COM / CHRIS GILL

SCHOOLS

ESF
t 0492 219046
A-Peak
t 0492 244997

Classes (ESF prices)
6 2.5hr days €155
Private lessons
From €42 for 1hr

CHILDCARE

Mini-club (ESF)
t 0492 219046
Ages 6mnth to 5
Piou Piou (ESF)
t 0492 219046
Ages 3 to 5

Ski school
For ages 5 to 14

FOR BOARDERS ★★★☆☆
Something for everyone
There's plenty to attract boarders to Montgenèvre. There are good local beginner slopes and long runs on varied terrain for intermediates. The only real drawback is that a fair number of the lifts are drags and there are some flat sections (especially getting to and from Sestriere). There are some excellent off-piste areas with a few natural hits for more advanced boarders and a dedicated freeride area in the Gondrans sector. Snowbox is a specialist shop.

FOR CROSS-COUNTRY ★★★☆☆
Travel to the best of it
The 17km of local trails offer ample variety. But the best area is the 60km of trails in the unspoiled Clarée valley, starting an 8km drive away in Les Alberts, at the bottom of the pass road's winding descent towards Briançon.

MOUNTAIN RESTAURANTS ★★☆☆☆
Head for Italy
A distinct weakness, particularly on the French side of the border. Restaurants in the Montgenèvre and Claviere sectors are marked but not named on the local piste map but not even marked on the Via Lattea map. In the Chalvet sector the table-service Bergerie gets mixed reports. At les Gondrans, les Anges is a pretty standard self-service but does 'good lasagne'. Most people eat in the

village; we head over the border where there are some pleasant simple huts. All agree that Baita La Coche is the best. It is essentially self-service, but if it's not too busy the cheerful family that run it will serve you at your table. Two seasons ago we enjoyed good pasta and, to our enduring amazement, a good Barbera d'Asti for 10 euros. The nearby Montsoleil is a smoother operation, liked by recent reporters. Col Saurel, on the Gimont chair, is fine for drinks and snacks.

SCHOOLS AND GUIDES ★★★☆☆
Encouraging reports
Reports on both A-Peak and the ESF are generally positive. One regular has put his two sons through the ESF – 'The most efficient school I have come across; tuition good, firm and friendly' – though the adults in his party had a mixed experience last season. A reporter this year had a 'helpful and informative' A-Peak instructor.

FOR FAMILIES ★★★★☆
Hugely improved
With the intrusive main road traffic banished to a tunnel, Montgenèvre is now a fine family resort – 'perfect', in the view of one reporter last year, thanks largely to the family-oriented activities available off the slopes. The excellent beginner area has the Mini-club Les Marmottes and a snow garden for young children. There is also a childcare centre. Le Chalvet has a play area up the gondola.

UK PACKAGES

Carrier, Crystal, Crystal Finest, Erna Low, Go Montgenevre, Lagrange, Neilson, Peak Retreats, PowderBeds, Rocketski, Ski Etoile, Ski Independence, Ski Miquel, Skitracer, Snow-wise, Thomson, Zenith
Claviere Crystal, Interactive Resorts, Rocketski, Skitracer, Thomson

ACTIVITIES

Indoor Cinema; spas in hotels

Outdoor Natural ice rink, snowshoeing, snowmobiling, walking, Monty Express toboggan run, ballooning

Phone numbers
From abroad use the prefix +33 and omit the initial '0' of the phone number

TOURIST OFFICES

Montgenèvre
www.montgenevre. com

Claviere
www.claviere.it

STAYING THERE

Development of Hameau de l'Obélisque, at the east end of the resort, close to the Chalvet gondola, introduced a bit of class into what was a pretty plain resort. This year the place takes another step upmarket with the opening of the new CGH apartment complex le Napoléon.
Chalets Zenith has three catered chalets here, one right by the Chalmettes lift. Crystal's chalet Ourson (one of two chalets here) is approved by a reader ('quiet, well located, very good friendly staff'), as is Ski Miquel's chalet hotel Ours Blanc ('fairly basic, but excellent food and friendly staff'). Pot de Miel is a B&B run on chalet lines (with optional dinners) by an Australian and her ski instructor husband.
Hotels There are now two smart places in Hameau de l'Obélisque – the first two entries below.
****Chalet Blanc (0492 442702) Very comfortable, lovely soft duvets and pillows, smart bathrooms. Spa. We enjoyed our 2011 stay here.
***Anova (0492 544804) Cool, relaxed, comfortable, good food. Pool, spa. We stayed here happily in 2012.
**Alpis Cottia (0492 215000) Budget B&B place over the Graal cafe and in the same ownership. Discouraging back-street entrance, up steep steps, but that apart we stayed here happily in 2013, in spacious rooms (although with weirdly tiny showers).
Apartments The big news this year is the opening by CGH of their 4-star residence le Napoléon, with the usual pool and spa facilities, in an absolutely central position opposite the nursery slopes. There are other smart 4-star residences with pool and spa at Hameau de l'Obélisque – the CGH-operated residence Chalet des Dolines and the Hameau des Airelles ('ski-in/ski-out, nice public areas, poor ski room set-up, pool not very warm'). All these properties are available through Peak Retreats.

EATING OUT ★★☆☆☆
Mainly no-frills
With about 10 no-frills places in the village, the choice is no more than adequate. La Cloche, reputedly the gourmet place, has changed hands. Jamy gets the thumbs up this year as a 'high-quality dining experience'. We've had excellent pizzas at the

Capitaine, which aims to corner the Italian market – a 2014 visitor agrees ('good quality and value'). We and readers have also enjoyed the Estable, a locals' favourite. Reader tips: Graal ('good basic food'), Caesar ('friendly; one of the best pizzas ever'), Rafale ('nice food, great fire, really friendly') and Refuge ('atmospheric and friendly').

APRES-SKI ★★☆☆☆
A few bars
The range is limited – it is a quiet village. The Refuge and the Jamy are popular cafe-bars at teatime. The Graal is a friendly, 'buzzing' place with 'a good range of beers', live music and big TVs (and free Wi-Fi); the Ca del Sol is a cosy place with an open fire ('best chocolate'). The Chaberton has pool tables, and is 'lively later on'.

OFF THE SLOPES ★☆☆☆☆
Limited
The village has little to offer the non-skier. The Monty Express 1400m-long two-seater monorail 'toboggan' run is said to be France's longest: 'Good fun, not for the faint-hearted.' A bus trip down the pass road to the beautiful old town of Briançon is possible.

LINKED RESORT – 1760m

CLAVIERE

Claviere is a small, traditional village just down the road from Montgenèvre, and a metre or two over the Italian border. It is not chocolate-box pretty but, even more than Montgenèvre, it has been transformed by removal of through-traffic. Its single main street, lined by a few shops, restaurants and hotels, is now a positively charming place to wander about.

The two main lifts – both slow quads – are conveniently close. Getting to the new Montquitaine chair is a slight uphill hike. The nursery slope is right next to the village, with a moving carpet. We've had glowing reports on the ski school's handling of kids: 'Wonderful – could not have wished for a better start.'

Readers tip several restaurants: the Kilt ('excellent pizzas, sensible prices, very friendly'), and Gran Bouc ('good food and service, but a bit pricey'). Après-ski is very quiet. The bar at the Roma hotel 'has good prices and Sky Sports'. Pub Gallo can be lively later on, they say.

Build your own shortlist: **www.wheretoskiandsnowboard.com**

OT MORZINE / P JACQUES, FOC

Morzine

A large, lively, year-round resort with its own attractive slopes and linked by lift to the main Portes du Soleil circuit

RATINGS

The mountains

Extent	★★★★★
Fast lifts	★★★
Queues	★★★
Terrain p'ks	★★
Snow	★★
Expert	★★★
Intermediate	★★★★
Beginner	★★★
Boarder	★★★★
X-country	★★★★
Restaurants	★★★★
Schools	★★★
Families	★★★★

The resort

Charm	★★★
Convenience	★★
Scenery	★★★
Eating out	★★★
Après-ski	★★★★
Off-slope	★★★

RPI   100

lift pass	£200
ski hire	£100
lessons	£70
food & drink	£135
total	**£505**

NEWS

2014/15: In the Super-Morzine area (on the way to and from Avoriaz and the Portes du Soleil circuit), there are plans to replace the Proclou and Seraussaix chairs with a six-pack each.

2013/14: The Pléney gondola has been replaced by a new 10-seater with double the hourly capacity of the old one.

Extent rating
This relates to the whole Portes du Soleil area

➕ Good-sized, varied, lightly wooded slopes shared with Les Gets

➕ Good nightlife by French standards

➕ Quite attractive chalet-style town, popular in summer

➕ Few crowds on weekdays, but ...

➖ Sunshine brings weekend crowds

➖ Just off the Portes du Soleil circuit

➖ Some lodgings remote from lifts

➖ Low altitude and exposure to westerlies means risk of rain and poor snow

➖ Few tough pistes

Morzine is quite a large, spread out, long-established year-round resort that feels more like a town than a village. It shares with Les Gets a fairly extensive local network of gentle wooded slopes, so is a good place to be in a snowstorm (but be warned: it can, and does, rain rather than snow not infrequently). For keen piste-bashers wanting to do multiple tours of the Portes du Soleil circuit it is better positioned than Les Gets but is not ideal. But that doesn't seem to deter readers: we get reports every year from satisfied customers.

THE RESORT

Morzine is as popular in summer as in winter and sprawls along both sides of a river gorge – though with the centre emphatically on the west side, at the foot of the local slopes. These are shared with slightly higher Les Gets (covered in a separate chapter). Across town is a gondola forming the link with a chain of lifts leading to Avoriaz on the Portes du Soleil circuit.

Our view that the resort suits car drivers is widely shared. But the roads are busy and the one-way system takes some getting used to. Car trips to Flaine and Chamonix are feasible.

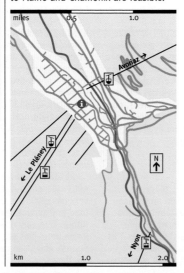

VILLAGE CHARM ★★★☆☆
Quietly attractive
The resort consists of chalet-style buildings, mostly small or mid-sized; they look cute under snow, and as that snow disappears towards spring, the village quickly takes on a spruce appearance.

Morzine is a family resort, and the village ambience tends to be fairly subdued as a result; but there are plenty of bars that get busy as the lifts close.

CONVENIENCE ★★☆☆☆
It's a big resort ...
Morzine is a town where getting from A to B can be tricky. The best plan is to stay in or near the centre of town, a short walk from one or both of the gondolas. Restaurants and bars line the streets up to the lifts to Le Pléney, where a busy one-way street runs along the foot of the slopes.

Accommodation is widely scattered; a multi-route bus service (including two electric buses) links all parts of the town to the lifts, including those for Avoriaz; there is a circular route, but only one way, which doesn't always suit your purposes. A 2014 reporter found them 'haphazard, not remotely running to timetable'. There are also buses to Les Gets, and to Ardent, which has a gondola into the Portes du Soleil circuit, missing out busy Avoriaz.

KEY FACTS

| Resort | 1000m |
| | 3,280ft |

Portes du Soleil

Slopes	950-2275m
	3,120-7,460ft
Lifts	194
Pistes	650km
	404 miles
Green	12%
Blue	43%
Red	36%
Black	9%
Snowmaking	
	1074 guns

Morzine-Les Gets only

Slopes	1000-2010m
	3,280-6,590ft
Lifts	49
Pistes	120km
	75 miles
Snowmaking	
	130 guns

LIFT PASSES

Portes du Soleil

Prices in €

Age	1-day	6-day
under 16	36	178
16 to 19	43	214
20 to 64	48	238
65 plus	43	214

Free Under 5
Beginner Lessons and lift pass packages
Notes Family discounts; 5hr pass
Alternative pass Morzine-Les Gets only

GETTING THERE

Air Geneva 90km/ 55 miles (1hr30); Lyon 210km/ 130 miles (2hr30)

Rail Cluses or Thonon (30km/19 miles); regular bus connections to resort

ALPINE ANSWERS
The UK's No.1 Chalet Specialist

For choice and service look no further!

alpineanswers.co.uk
call: 020 7801 1080   ABTA

Discover the difference with SkiWeekends
#loveski

Prices from
£200

skiweekends.com

SCENERY ★★★
Quite good from the tops
Despite their modest top heights, the local peaks of Pointe de Nyon and Chamossière are not without drama (or impressive views, including of Mont Blanc).

THE MOUNTAINS

The local slopes are mainly wooded, with some open areas higher up. The piste map is fine, and signposting and classification are both 'good'.

EXTENT OF THE SLOPES ★★★★★
Good local area, plus the PdS
Our rating is for the whole Portes du Soleil linked area, the bulk of which is reached via Avoriaz. The local area – shared with Les Gets – is a fair size.

A gondola (upgraded for 2013/14) rises from the edge of central Morzine to **Le Pléney**. Several routes return to the valley, including a run down to Les Fys – a quiet lift junction at the foot of the **Nyon-Chamossière** sector where the area's most challenging slopes are;

Chamossière is served by a six-pack, but Nyon still has a slow chair. This sector can also be accessed by a cable car starting a bus ride from Morzine. A slow chair from Les Fys along with a fast one from Le Grand Pré (further up the valley) connect with the sector of **Les Chavannes**, above Les Gets. At the far end of this sector, the bowl beneath Le Ranfoilly has no fewer than five radiating chairlifts together.

Beyond Les Gets, **Mont Chéry** is notably quiet, and well worth a visit.

Across town from the Le Pléney sector is a gondola leading (via another couple of lifts and runs) to Avoriaz and the main Portes du Soleil circuit. You take the gondola down too – there's no piste. Alternatives are a bus ride or a short drive to either Les Prodains – for a gondola to Avoriaz or a chair into the **Hauts Forts** slopes above it – or to Ardent for a gondola to Les Lindarets, from where you can head for Châtel, Avoriaz or Champéry. There's floodlit skiing on Thursdays and a torchlit descent on Tuesdays. There are lockers at the new Pléney base.

OT LES GETS / N JOLY

When the area has this much snow, it's delightful; and the trees mean it's good when it is snowing too →

Tailor made, long weekend and short break French Alps ski holiday specialists.

Hanski
Ski. Explore. Relax.

web: www.hanski.co.uk
tel: 01638 596373
mob: 07833 612061

FAST LIFTS ★★★☆☆
More fast chairs needed

The main access lifts are gondolas, cable cars or fast chairs, but higher up things are not so good: some areas are equipped with fast chairs, but others rely on slow chairs and drags.

QUEUES ★★★☆☆
Still peak-time issues, it seems

The Pléney gondola was replaced for last season by a much more powerful lift with 10-seater cabins and double the capacity of the old one. But a reporter who visited in December and March this year found there were still peak-time queues and gondolas were being allowed to go up 'half empty'. Another found it was best to catch the lift before 9.15am. More reports, please. Recent lift replacements seem to have solved most other problems.

TERRAIN PARKS ★★☆☆☆
Lots to choose from

There is a park below Pointe de Nyon, and another park and a snowcross in Les Gets. Or you can try one of the five excellent terrain parks in Avoriaz (and the super-pipe there).

SNOW RELIABILITY ★★☆☆☆
A weakness at resort level

Morzine has a very low average height, and it can rain here when it is snowing higher up (almost every year some reporters mention days of rain). But the grassy slopes don't need much snow-cover and in a sparse snow year you may do better here than in higher, rockier resorts such as Avoriaz. Snowmaking has been increased, most noticeably on the home runs and most recent reporters think grooming is good.

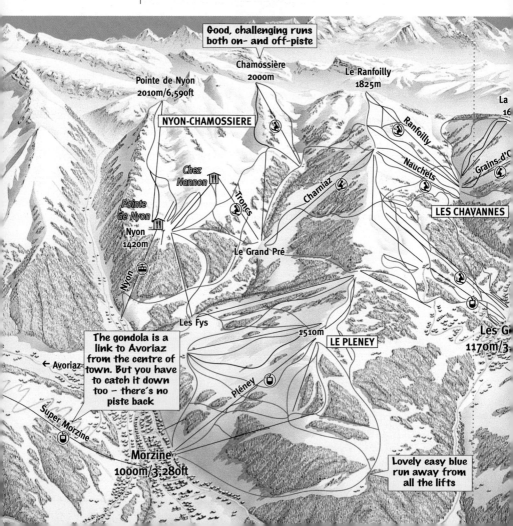

Good, challenging runs both on- and off-piste

Chamossière 2000m

Le Ranfoilly 1825m

Pointe de Nyon 2010m/6,590ft

La 16

NYON-CHAMOSSIERE

Ranfoilly

Chez Nannon

Nauchets

Grains-d'O

Troncs

Charniaz

Pointe de Nyon
Nyon 1420m

Le Grand Pré

LES CHAVANNES

Les Fys

1510m

Les Ge

The gondola is a link to Avoriaz from the centre of town. But you have to catch it down too – there's no piste back

← Avoriaz

LE PLENEY

1170m/3.

Pléney

Super Morzine

Morzine
1000m/3,280ft

Lovely easy blue run away from all the lifts

MOMENTUM SKI

Weekend & a la carte
ski holiday specialists

100% Tailor-made

Premier hotels
& apartments

Flexible travel
arrangements

020 7371 9111
WWW.MOMENTUMSKI.COM

Heavenly
Skiing...
at down to earth prices

mh* Mountain Heaven

· Superb catered & self catered accommodation ·
· Great ski areas in the French & Swiss Alps ·
· Snow secure resorts · We only have on/near piste locations ·
· Fantastic prices & no hidden extras ·

0151 625 1921
www.mountainheaven.co.uk

STC Ski

Specialists in Tailor-Made
Short Breaks & Holidays

01483 771 222
www.stcski.co.uk
ski@stcski.co.uk

FOR EXPERTS ★★★★★
A few possibilities
The runs from Pointe de Nyon and
Chamossière are quite challenging, as
are the black runs down the back of
Mont Chéry and the Hauts Forts blacks
at Avoriaz. In bad weather the
medium-altitude, lightly wooded
Ranfoilly bowl is a good place to head

for. Plus there is plenty of serious off-
piste to try with a guide – see the
feature panel overleaf.

FOR INTERMEDIATES ★★★★★
Something for everyone
Good intermediates will enjoy the fine,
challenging red and black down from
Chamossière. Aigle Rouge on Pointe de

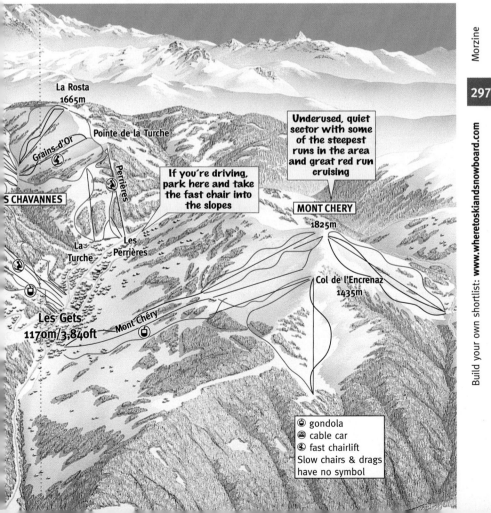

La Rosta
1665m

Pointe de la Turche

S CHAVANNES

Grains-d'Or

Perrières

La
Turche

Les
Perrières

Les Gets
1170m/3,840ft

Mont Chéry

**If you're driving,
park here and take
the fast chair into
the slopes**

**Underused, quiet
sector with some
of the steepest
runs in the area
and great red run
cruising**

MONT CHERY
1825m

Col de l'Encrenaz
1435m

⚫ gondola
⚫ cable car
⚫ fast chairlift
Slow chairs & drags
have no symbol

skiracer*

CHALETS, HOTELS
& APARTMENTS
Call us today
020 8600 1650
skitracer.com

ost
avoie
CATERED CHALETS
9-24 pers IN MORZINE

www.hostsavoie.co.uk

Inghams

MORZINE
▶ Traditional character and a massive ski area
▶ 2-FOR-1 ski/snowboard hire offer
▶ Apartments, chalets, hotels

inghams.co.uk 01483 371 236 ABTA V4871 ATOL 0025

ACTIVITIES

Indoor Swimming pool, ice rink, fitness centre (sauna, hot tub), library, cinemas

Outdoor Ice rink, snowshoeing, helicopter flights, snowmobiles, horse-drawn carriages, tobogganing, ice diving, paragliding, skijoring, 'yooner' tobogganing, segway riding

Nyon is not steep but is quite narrow, with great views. Mont Chéry, on the other side of Les Gets, has some fine steepish runs that are usually very quiet.

Those looking for something less challenging have a great choice. Le Pléney has a compact network of pistes that are ideal for groups with mixed abilities: there are blue and red options from every lift. One of the easiest cruises on Le Pléney is a great away-from-it-all blue (Piste B) from the top to the valley. Heading from Le Ranfoilly to Le Grand Pré on the blue is also a nice cruise.

The slopes down to Les Gets from Le Pléney are easy when conditions are right (the slopes face south). The Ranfoilly and Rosta sectors have cruisy reds and a couple of easy blacks served by fast chairs. And, of course, there is the whole of the Portes du Soleil circuit to explore via Avoriaz.

FOR BEGINNERS ★★★★★
Good for novices and improvers

The wide village nursery slopes are convenient, and benefit from snow-guns, though crowds are reported to be a problem. There are excellent progression runs on Le Pléney, at Nyon, and at Super-Morzine.

FOR BOARDERS ★★★★★
Great for park and ride

Morzine is very popular with boarding seasonaires because of the extensive slopes, proximity to the excellent terrain parks in Avoriaz and the lower prices here. The slopes in Morzine are great for all abilities and have very few draglifts. But a reporter complained of irritating flat areas. Plenty of tree-lined runs make for scenic and interesting snowboarding, and the more adventurous should hire a guide to explore off-piste.

OFF-PISTE RUNS IN THE PORTES DU SOLEIL AREA

The Portes du Soleil offers a lot of great lift-served off-piste. Here is a small selection. Like all serious off-piste runs, these should not be undertaken without a guide.

Morzine – Nyon/Chamossière area

From the Chamossière chairlift, heading north brings you to two runs – one on the same north-west slope as the pistes (now marked on the piste map as a 'Zone Freeride'), the other via a col down the north-east slope to the Nyon cable car – a wild area, with a great view of Mont Blanc at first.

Avoriaz area – two suggestions

From the Fornet chairlift on the Swiss border, you head west to descend a beautiful, unspoiled bowl leading down to the village of L'Erigné. In powder snow you descend the west-facing slopes of the bowl; when there is spring snow, you traverse right to descend the south-facing slopes. Medium-pitch slopes, for skiers and snowboarders.

From the top of the Machon chairlift you traverse west, beneath the peaks of Les Hauts Forts, across Les Crozats de la Chaux – a steep, north-facing slope. You then turn north to descend through the forest to the cable car station at Les Prodains. Testing terrain, for very good skiers. And be aware that the traverse can be dangerous following a snowfall.

Châtel area

From the top of the Linga chair, head north-west to cross the ridge on your right at a col and then head down the La Leiche slope to the draglift of the same name. It's a north-facing slope, starting in a white wilderness, taking you through trees back to civilization. Steep slopes – for good skiers only.

SCHOOLS

Adrénaline
t 0686 004189

BASS
t 0450 747859

Easy2Ride (E2SA)
t 0450 790516

ESF
t 0450 791313

Mint Snowboard
t 0450 841388

New Generation
t 0479 010318
0844 770 4733 (UK)
www.skinewgen.com

Synergie
t 0687 390014

Classes (ESF prices)
6 half-days €144

Private lessons
From €42 for 1hr for
1 to 2 people

GUIDES

Bureau des Guides
t 0450 759665

OT MORZINE / GILLES LANSARD

Morzine's buildings
are mainly chalet-style
and look pretty under
a blanket of snow ↓

FOR CROSS-COUNTRY ★★★★☆
Good variety
There are around 70km of varied
cross-country trails, not all at valley
level. The best section is in the pretty
Vallée de la Manche beside the Nyon
mountain up to the Lac de Mines d'Or,
where there is a good restaurant. The
Pléney-Chavannes loop is pleasant
and relatively snow-sure.

MOUNTAIN RESTAURANTS ★★★★☆
Some excellent huts
There is no shortage of good places,
offering table-service in welcoming
surroundings; restaurants are marked
but not named or described on the
piste map.
Editors' choice We have had several
very enjoyable Savoyard lunches at
the rustic Chez Nannon (0450 792115),
between Nyon and Chamossière – cosy
inside and a nice terrace. A regular
visitor endorsed this again last year: 'A
little nugget of delights.' The nearby
Pointe de Nyon (0450 044564) is a
lovely spacious place where we have
had excellent duck salad and ribs.
Worth knowing about La Païka, near
the top of La Rosta, is a 'rustic gem'
doing wood-fired grills; serious wine

list. Nearby Café la Rosta is 'really
good value'. The Wetzet at Ranfoilly 'is
very welcoming' for a mid-morning
chocolate. The Vaffieu above the
Folliets chair 'can have slow service
but the food is worth the wait'. A past
reporter raved about Lhottys at the
top of the Nauchets chairlift for its
'peasant-style mountain soup – to die
for'. Les Mouilles, at the top of the
Crusaz chair on Pléney, does 'a fine
carbonara', and has a 'cracking view'.

SCHOOLS AND GUIDES ★★★☆☆
Good reports of most
The big news for this year is that New
Generation – a highly rated British-run
school with branches in nine other
French and two Swiss resorts is
opening a Morzine branch. BASS,
another British-run school, is already
well established here.
    Last year (as in most other years)
we had a positive report on the local
ESF: 'We were thoroughly happy; they
did a first-class job with my five-year-
old, and she came on in leaps and
bounds.' We have had two very
positive comments on Easy2Ride
including a 2014 reporter who was
'very impressed that they moved

Build your own shortlist: www.wheretoskiandsnowboard.com

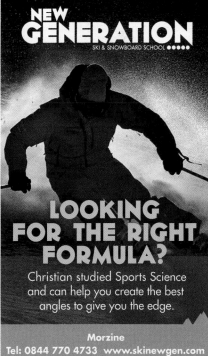

NEW GENERATION
SKI & SNOWBOARD SCHOOL ●●●●●

LOOKING
FOR THE RIGHT
FORMULA?

Christian studied Sports Science
and can help you create the best
angles to give you the edge.

Morzine
Tel: 0844 770 4733 www.skinewgen.com

CHILDCARE

L'Outa nursery
t 0450 792600
Ages 3mnth to 5yr

Piou Piou (ESF)
t 0450 791313
From age 3

Cheeky Monkeys
t 0616 122880
From 3mnth

Jack Frost's
t 07817 138678 (UK)
From 3mnth

Ski school
From age 4

UK PACKAGES

Absolutely Snow, Adventure Base, Aiglon de Morzine, Alpine Answers, Alpine Elements, Alpine Encounters, Alpine Weekends, Boutique Chalet Company, Chalet Chocolat, Chalet Entre Deux Eaux, Crystal, Erna Low, Flexiski, Hanski, Host Savoie, Igoski, Inghams, Inspired to Ski, Interactive Resorts, Lagrange, Momentum, Mountain Beds, Mountain Heaven, Neilson, Oxford Ski Co, Peak Retreats, PowderBeds, Reach4theAlps, Ride&Slide, Rude Chalets, Ski Expectations, Ski Independence, Ski Line, Ski Morzine, Ski Weekend, Skiology.co.uk, Skitracer, Skiweekends.com, Snow Finders, Snow-wise, Star Ski Chalets, STC, Thomson, VIP, White Roc, Zenith

Phone numbers
From abroad use the prefix +33 and omit the initial '0' of the phone number

TOURIST OFFICE

www.morzine-avoriaz.com

people between groups after 30 mins to match ability levels better; small groups too'.

FOR FAMILIES ★★★★✫
A fine family choice
Morzine caters well for families. On the mountain there are gentle, sheltered slopes and play areas. And there are plenty of other activities. Club des Piou Piou is run by the ESF school and takes children from three years old.

STAYING THERE

You can arrange affordable short breaks here through Ski Weekends. Hanski is a short-break specialist too.
Chalets There's a wide choice, widely spread. Mountain Heaven has a premium chalet with outdoor hot tub close to the Nyon cable car. Inghams has three good-looking chalets, two with hot tubs and all with sauna or steam. Its 12-bed Nomis is reportedly 'a lovely place'. Host Savoie has four 'comfortable and unpretentious' places all out of the town centre and near bus stops. Its Chery des Meuniers 'had good food, friendly and efficient staff and was good value' says a reporter. Ski Weekends runs the 'no-frills' chalet hotel Gourmets. A reader strongly tips the chalet hotel Dents Blanches, operated by Alpine Encounters.
Hotels Part of a general drift in France, many hotels have moved up the stars scale in the past few years. There are now six 4-stars; 3-stars dominate.
★★★★Airelles (0450 747121) Central, close to Pléney lifts. Good pool, 'great food', sauna, steam.
★★★★Bergerie (0450 791369) Rustic B&B chalet, in centre. 'Good breakfast buffet, friendly service.' Outdoor pool, massage.
★★★Alpenroc (0450 757 543) 'Friendly, convenient, comfortable.'
★★★Equipe (0450 791143) Next to the Pléney lift with decent food and 'tiny' pool, sauna, steam, hot tub. Takes short-stay bookings.
★★★Tremplin (0450 791231) At the foot of Pléney slopes. 'Rooms basic but comfortable, friendly staff, no restaurant.'
Apartments Aiglon de Morzine has 12 luxury units and is central; sauna and steam room. The Lodge is 1km from the centre and a former hotel; sauna, hot tub, gym. Both are featured by Erna Low, The Lodge also by Peak Retreats.

EATING OUT ★★★✫✫
A reasonable choice
There is a fair choice, including some fine hotel restaurants. Best in town is probably the Atelier in the hotel Samoyède, which offers traditional and modern dishes ('gourmet cuisine, stick to the set menu to keep costs under control'). A recent reporter liked the 'stylish' Chamade for its 'tasty and beautifully presented meal', but warns that service can be slow. Le Coup de Coeur is a crowded wine bar in the same ownership doing good tapas, pizza etc. For value you will not beat the unpretentious Etale with its 'huge' pizzas and equally generous Savoyard dishes. The Flamme has been highly rated in the past. The Tyrolien 'serves hearty portions to groups of British skiers'. The Combe à Zorre does 'excellent lamb', but can get over-busy at weekends. The Grillon was praised for 'a mean tartiflette, good service'.

APRES-SKI ★★★★✫
One of the livelier French resorts
Morzine's après-ski is good by French resort standards. Several places around the base area get busy as the slopes empty – the Tremplin apparently has a DJ and a 'good party atmosphere'. The Crépu is a sports bar, pleasantly quiet early on but livening up later. Other options include the long-established Bar Robinson and the Dixie ('good atmosphere, popular with seasonaires'), with sport on TV, a cellar bar and some live music. Between the slopes and the centre, and all in the same building are several spots: the Cavern, which is popular with seasonaires; the Coyote for arcade games and DJ; and the 'lively' Tibetan, with Asian decor and 'often a band'. The Opéra and Laury's are late-night haunts.

OFF THE SLOPES ★★★✫✫
Quite good; excursions possible
There's a cinema, an excellent ice rink, an indoor pool, lots of pretty walks ('booklet available from tourist office, but some walks are difficult to find and some cross pistes, which can be dangerous') and tobogganing. Visitors have enjoyed trips to the cheese factory and watching ice hockey. Morzine has a reasonable range of shops, relatively glitz-free. Buses run to Thonon for more shopping, and those with cars can drive to Geneva, Annecy or Montreux.

Paradiski

*Les Arcs and La Plagne are pretty impressive resorts individually;
the ability to explore both is the icing on the cake*

KEY FACTS

Paradiski area	
Slopes	1200-3250m
	3,940-10,660ft
Lifts	141
Pistes	425km
	264 miles
Green	8%
Blue	53%
Red	25%
Black	14%

Pierre & Vacances
Holidays made for me

Best price
guarantee
for ski in/out
budget studios
up to spacious
3 bedroom
apartments

pierreetvacances.co.uk

A decade after its opening, the 200-person double-decker Vanoise Express cable car – which crosses a wooded valley to link Les Arcs and La Plagne, and thus form Paradiski – remains the world's biggest, as far as we know. When it opened, we were a bit sceptical. Sure, it was one of the biggest ski areas in the Alps, but weren't the two resorts quite big enough individually? Well, no. We're now quite used to staying in Arc 1950 and having lunch above Champagny. We might do it only once or twice in a week, but we always do it.

The Vanoise Express cable car spans the 2km-wide valley between Plan-Peisey (on the edge of the Les Arcs area) and a point 300m above Montchavin (on the edge of the La Plagne area).

The linking of these two major resorts is A Good Thing for the great British piste-basher who likes to cover as much ground as possible. For those who like a bit of a challenge, getting from your home base to both far-flung outposts of the area – Villaroger in Les Arcs and Champagny in La Plagne – would make quite a full day.

The link is also good for experts. Those based in either resort can more easily tackle the north face of La Plagne's Bellecôte, finishing the run in Nancroix. Those based in La Plagne who are finding the piste skiing a bit tame can easily get across to Les Arcs' excellent Aiguille Rouge.

If you want to make the most of the link it's sensible to stay near one of the cable car stations. But it's easily accessible from many other bases too.

On the Les Arcs side, **Plan-Peisey** and nearby **Vallandry** are in pole position. They are basically small, low-rise, modern developments, built in a much more sympathetic style than the original Les Arcs resorts. They are quiet but expanding and quite a few UK operators have chalets and apartments in them. You can also stay in the unspoiled old village of **Peisey**, 300m below and linked by bucket-lift to Plan-Peisey. These places are covered at the end of the Les Arcs chapter.

It's easy to get to the cable car station at Plan-Peisey from the main resort parts of Les Arcs. One lift and one run is all it takes to get there from **Arc 1800**, which is the biggest of the main resort units. From quieter **Arc 1600**, along the mountainside from 1800, it takes two lifts. **Arc 2000** and the stylish **Arc 1950** development seem further away, over the ridge that separates them from 1600 and 1800; but all it takes is one fast chair to the ridge and one long run down the other side. In the valley bottom beyond Arc

AWARD-WINNING SKI HOLIDAYS

Ski Olympic

book online at
skiolympic.com
01302 328 820

mh* Mountain Heaven

Heavenly
Skiing...
at down to earth prices

· Superb catered & self catered accommodation ·
· Great ski areas in the French & Swiss Alps ·
· Snow secure resorts · We only have on/near piste locations ·
· Fantastic prices & no hidden extras ·

0151 625 1921
www.mountainheaven.co.uk

Resort news and key links: www.wheretoskiandsnowboard.com

LIFT PASSES

Paradiski
Covers lifts in whole
Paradiski area.
6-day pass €277
(65 plus and under 14
€208)

Paradiski Découverte
Covers lifts in Les
Arcs area or La Plagne
area plus one-day
Paradiski extension.
6-day pass €257
(65 plus and under 14
€193)

SkiCollection
Major Resorts
Expert knowledge

**4★ ski
apartments
with spa**

SkiCollection.co.uk
0844 576 0175
ABTA Bonded W5537

SNOWPIX.COM / CHRIS GILL

The lovely woody
slopes of Peisey-
Vallandry, seen from
the top of the Bijolin
chair high above
Montchavin and Les
Coches ➔

2000, the hamlet of Villaroger is not an ideal starting point.

On the La Plagne side, the obvious place to stay is **Montchavin**, which is below the Vanoise Express station. Montchavin is a carefully developed old village with modern additions built in traditional style. **Les Coches**, across the mountain from the station, is most easily reached with the help of a lift. It is entirely modern, but built in a traditional style. From either village, one lift brings you to the Vanoise Express cable car.

The other parts of La Plagne are some way from the cable car. But one long lift is all it takes to get from monolithic **Plagne-Bellecôte** up to L'Arpette, from which point it's a single long descent. The most attractive of the resort villages, **Belle-Plagne**, is only a short run above Plagne-Bellecôte. From the villages further across the bowl – **Plagne-Villages**, **Plagne-Soleil**, dreary **Plagne-Centre**, futuristic **Aime-la-Plagne** – you have to ride a lift to get to Plagne-Bellecôte. From **Plagne 1800**, below the bowl, add another lift. From the villages beyond the bowl – rustic, sunny **Champagny-en-Vanoise** and expanding **Montalbert** – it's going to be pretty hard work, but it's certainly possible.

RIDING THE VANOISE EXPRESS

The cable car ride from one resort to the other takes less than four minutes. The system is designed to be able to operate in high winds, so the risk of getting stranded miles from home is low. It can shift 2,000 people an hour, and although end-of-the-day crowds could be a snag in theory, they don't seem to be a problem in practice.

The lift company offers a six-day pass covering the whole Paradiski region, perhaps most likely to appeal to people based in the villages close to the lift. It's not cheap. But there is also a pass (Paradiski Découverte) that includes just one day in the other resort during the validity of the pass. Alternatively, you can buy a one-day extension to a Les Arcs or a La Plagne six-day lift pass, as and when you fancy the outing.

La Plagne

Villages from the rustic to the futuristic, spread over a vast area of intermediate terrain – mainly high and snow-sure

SNOWPIX.COM / CHRIS GILL

RATINGS

The mountains

Extent	★★★★
Fast lifts	★★
Queues	★★
Terrain p'ks	★★★★
Snow	★★★★
Expert	★★★★
Intermediate	★★★★★
Beginner	★★★★
Boarder	★★★
X-country	★★★★
Restaurants	★★★★
Schools	★★★
Families	★★★★

The resort

Charm	★★
Convenience	★★★★★
Scenery	★★★
Eating out	★★★
Après-ski	★★★
Off-slope	★

RPI — 110

lift pass	£210
ski hire	£120
lessons	£85
food & drink	£145
total	**£560**

KEY FACTS

Resort	1800-2100m	
	5,900-6,890ft	

La Plagne only

Slopes	1250-3250m	
	4,100-10,660ft	
Lifts		90
Pistes		225km
		140 miles
Green		8%
Blue		53%
Red		25%
Black		14%
Snowmaking		
		359 guns

Paradiski area

Slopes	1200-3250m	
	3,940-10,660ft	
Lifts		141
Pistes		425km
		264 miles
Green		8%
Blue		53%
Red		25%
Black		14%
Snowmaking		
		626 guns

➕ Extensive and varied intermediate pistes, plus excellent off-piste

➕ Good nursery slopes

➕ High and fairly snow-sure

➕ Wide choice of resort villages: high or low, convenient or cute

➕ Wooded runs of lower satellite resorts are great in poor weather

➕ Cable car link to Les Arcs

➖ Lift system still needs investment – serious high-season queues

➖ Pistes get very crowded in places

➖ Few challenging pistes

➖ Lower villages can have poor snow, especially sunny Champagny

➖ Brutal architecture in some villages

➖ No long green runs

➖ Upscale accommodation still rare

La Plagne is an intermediate's paradise, even if you don't use the link to Les Arcs. For experts, it has huge areas of off-piste that doesn't get skied out too quickly. We are pleased to note that this season they are reinstating the two rewarding blacks dropping 800m vertical from the glacier, wiped from the map a few seasons ago, but this is still an area where advanced intermediates and experts need to look off-piste for challenges.

Plagne-Bellecôte, effectively the hub of the lift and piste network, has had serious lift queues as long as we can remember. One of the three key lifts here is getting a major upgrade this season. Our natural tendency is to whinge about the fact that the Roche de Mio gondola needs a similar boost. But then we think about the dreadful crowding on the blue piste it serves – reached by two chairlifts as well. What this place needs is some mountain planning.

THE RESORT

La Plagne consists of no fewer than 11 separate 'villages'. Each is a self-sufficient mini-resort, though they vary widely in character. They divide basically into two groups: seven units purpose-built at altitude in a broad bowl, on or above the treeline; and four real villages, adapted and expanded for skiing, at lower altitude on the fringes of the area.

At the heart of the high-altitude area, Plagne-Centre is aptly named: it is the focal point for shops and après-ski. Directly below Centre is the chalet-filled suburb of Plagne 1800, spread across a steep hillside. A short lift ride away from Centre are the slightly higher units of Aime-la-Plagne, Plagne-Soleil and Plagne-Villages. Over a low ridge, beyond the last two, are Plagne-Bellecôte and Belle-Plagne above it.

Outside the main bowl, at the northern edge of the area, are Les Coches and Montchavin. At the southern edge is rustic Champagny. Beyond Aime-la-Plagne, at the western edge, is growing Montalbert. These outlying resorts are described later in the chapter.

A cable car from Montchavin links to Les Arcs via Peisey-Vallandry. Day trips by car to Val d'Isère-Tignes or the

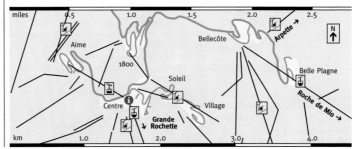

NEWS

2014/15: The chairlift out of Bellecôte towards Centre (Colosses) is to be replaced by an eight-pack of huge carrying capacity. The Arnica run down the Colorado chair at Centre is being adapted to suit novices (but will stay blue). The cable car between Centre and Aime is being renovated. Several minor lifts are being moved, replaced or removed.

2013/14: The inadequate double chair at Les Bauches was replaced using the hardware of the Coqs quad chair that linked Montalbert to Plagne-Centre. You now get to Centre via the lower La Roche chair, which has been upgraded to a six-pack. The two long black runs from the glacier, closed some years back, have been reopened. A long new toboggan run was created at Bellecôte, down the Arpette chairlift.

SKI AMIS

Catered Chalets in Superb Locations

020 3411 5439
www.skiamis.com

Trois Vallées resorts are possible. Staying in Champagny means quick access by car or taxi to Courchevel.

VILLAGE CHARM ★★☆☆☆
Take your pick

The high-altitude villages vary quite a lot in character; our rating relates to Belle-Plagne and Plagne 1800, where most Brits go.

The first unit to be built, in the 1960s, was Plagne-Centre. Typical of its time, it has ugly square blocks and dreary indoor 'malls' that house shops, bars and restaurants. A three-year project to improve these malls is now finished, so it's time we paid another visit to see if they are less claustrophobic as a result.

More recent developments are more stylish, but they can't compete with Centre in terms of facilities. Plagne 1800 is all in chalet style, so is visually inoffensive. Aime-la-Plagne, in stark contrast, is a group of monolithic blocks given a bold chalet-roof shape. Plagne-Soleil and Plagne-Villages mainly consist of small-scale apartment buildings finished in chalet style. The apartment buildings of Plagne-Bellecôte form a gigantic wall at the foot of the slopes leading down to it. By contrast, Belle-Plagne just above it is built in a pleasant chalet style, and has a mini-resort centre, though few shops.

CONVENIENCE ★★★★★
No worries at altitude

The high-altitude villages are mostly ski-in/ski-out – but much of Plagne 1800 presents challenges because of its steep setting, which has to be negotiated on foot. At Plagne-Bellecôte you'll walk further inside your apartment building than outside. Belle-Plagne is now quite large, and spread over a steepish hillside that provokes the odd complaint from our easily tired readers. Readers find Plagne-Soleil convenient.

A free bus system between the core villages within the bowl runs until 1am, and readers seem happy with it.

SCENERY ★★★☆☆
Look to the horizon

The scenery makes an attractive and varied backdrop to the less attractive core villages. Mont Blanc looms big on the horizon, especially from Montchavin and Les Coches. And there are good views over to Courchevel from the Champagny sector.

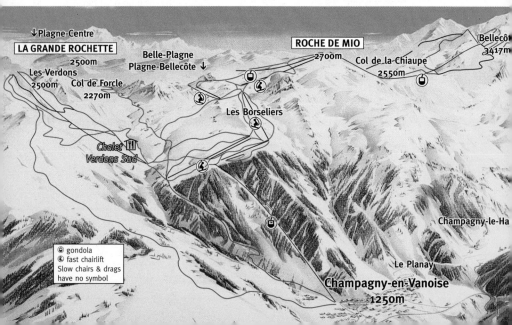

↓Plagne-Centre
LA GRANDE ROCHETTE
2500m
Les Verdons
2500m
Col de Forcle
2270m
Belle-Plagne
Plagne-Bellecôte ↓
Les Borseliers
ROCHE DE MIO
2700m
Col de la-Chiaupe
2550m
Bellecô
3417m
Chalet Verdons Sud
Champagny-le-Ha
Le Planay
Champagny-en-Vanoise
1250m

⊙ gondola
④ fast chairlift
Slow chairs & drags
have no symbol

Bellecôte doesn't have much to recommend it – apart from low prices, we guess ➜

OT LA PLAGNE / ELINA SIRPARANTA

La Plagne

305

www.wheretoskiandsnowboard.com

Build your own shortlist:

LIFT PASSES

La Plagne

Prices in €

Age	1-day	6-day
under 14	36	177
14 to 64	48	235
65 plus	36	177

Free Under 6
Beginner 10 free lifts
Senior 72 plus: 1-15 days €7
Notes La Plagne area; half-day passes; Paradiski extension

Alternative passes
Champagny only, Montchavin only, Montalbert only, Coolski for beginners; Découverte pass with one-day Paradiski extension

Paradiski Unlimited

Prices in €

Age	1-day	6-day
under 14	39	208
14 to 64	51	277
65 plus	39	208

Free Under 6
Senior 72 plus: 1-15 days €10
Notes Covers Les Arcs areas and La Plagne areas; family reductions

THE MOUNTAINS

The majority of the slopes in the main bowl are above the treeline, though there are trees scattered around most of the resort centres. The slopes outside the bowl are open at the top but descend into woodland – the best place to be in bad weather. So there is something to be said for choosing a base outside the bowl.

Some runs are more difficult than their classification suggests, while others are easier – note our warning in 'For intermediates'. Piste names and classification seem to alter regularly. Signposting is fine though piste marking can be a bit vague. The piste map is tricky to follow in places.

EXTENT OF THE SLOPES ★★★★
Multi-centred; can be confusing
Our ★★★★ rating relates to just the La Plagne area; the whole Paradiski area easily scores five stars.

La Plagne's pistes are spread over a wide area that can be broken down into seven sectors. From Plagne-Centre you can take a lift up to **Le Biolley**, from where you can head back to Centre, to Aime-la-Plagne or progress to **Montalbert**. The arrangements for getting back to Centre from Montalbert have changed – you must now descend to the upgraded La Roche chairlift, via an improved blue run. The main lift out of Plagne-Centre leads up to **La Grande Rochette**. From here

there are good sweeping runs back down and an easier one over to Plagne-Bellecôte, or you can drop over into the sunny **Champagny** sector, for excellent long runs and great views across the valley to Courchevel.

From Plagne-Bellecôte and Belle-Plagne, you can head up to **Roche de Mio**, and have the choice of a gondola or two successive fast chairs (the first of which also accesses Champagny). From Roche de Mio, runs spread out in all directions – towards La Plagne, Champagny or **Montchavin/Les Coches**. This sector can also be reached by taking an eight seat chair from Plagne-Bellecôte to L'Arpette. From Roche de Mio you can also take a gondola down then up to the **Bellecôte glacier**. It is prone to closure by high winds or poor weather. The top chair is often shut in winter – but if open, it offers excellent snow and stunning views.

The black piste below Col de la Chiaupe means that you can descend from the glacier on-piste to the Les Bauches chairlift without riding the gondola back up to Roche de Mio. Or you can go all the way to Montchavin (be warned: it gets very flat); it's 2000m vertical.

This black piste is one of a handful now marked on the piste map as Natur' (never groomed) – not popular with reporters (see 'Snow reliability'). The map also marks three draglifts (in the Montalbert/Biolley sectors) as 'difficult', and they are.

AWARD-WINNING
SKI
HOLIDAYS

Ski Olympic

book online at
skiolympic.com
01302 328 820

FAST LIFTS ★★☆☆☆
Slow progress

Many key lifts are fast, and the Montchavin/Les Coches sector is pretty much sorted, but once you start to really explore other sectors of the slopes you still find old chairs and draglifts – Inversens at Roche de Mio, all three lifts above Les Bauches and the lifts above Montalbert and out of 1800, for example. The Montalbert lifts are due to be replaced by a slick gondola, but not just yet.

QUEUES ★★☆☆☆
Serious bottlenecks remain

La Plagne's lift and piste network has some fundamental flaws. In particular, moving across the area often involves passing through Plagne-Bellecôte. This is now one of the worst bottlenecks in the Alps – long queues ('horrendous', 'worst in years') build in high season. The Roche de Mio gondola is especially bad ('it looked like half an hour – we took a different route' and '20 minutes is a standard wait most

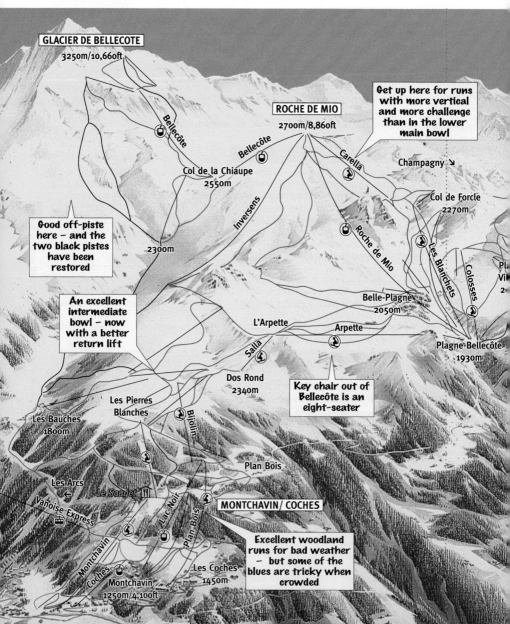

GLACIER DE BELLECOTE
3250m/10,66oft

ROCHE DE MIO
2700m/8,86oft

Bellecôte

Bellecôte

Col de la Chiaupe
2550m

Carella

Champagny ↘

Col de Forcle
2270m

Inversens

Roche de Mio

Les Blanchets

Colosses

Pl
Vi
2

Get up here for runs with more vertical and more challenge than in the lower main bowl

2300m

Good off-piste here – and the two black pistes have been restored

Belle-Plagne
2050m

An excellent intermediate bowl – now with a better return lift

L'Arpette

Arpette

Plagne-Bellecôte
1930m

Salla

Dos Rond
2340m

Key chair out of Bellecôte is an eight-seater

Les Pierres
Blanches

Bijolin

Les Bauches
1800m

Plan Bois

Les Arcs

Le Sauget

Lac Noir

Plan Bois

MONTCHAVIN / COCHES

Vanoise Express

Montchavin

Coches

Montchavin
1250m/4,10oft

Les Coches
1450m

Excellent woodland runs for bad weather – but some of the blues are tricky when crowded

ICE AND FIRE

FULLY CATERED CHALETS
PRE ARRIVAL SERVICE
COMPLIMENTARY BARS
WIFI, SAUNAS, UK TV
IN CHALET SKI FITTING

WWW.ICE-FIRE.CO.UK
0044 (0) 7855717997

A six-pack gives speedy access to the serious black runs and good off-piste off the back of the Biolley sector

gondola
cable car
fast chairlift
Slow chairs & drags
have no symbol

LA GRANDE ROCHETTE
2500m

Les Verdons
2500m

2350m

Champagny ↘

Col de Forcle
2270m

Grande Rochette

Colorado

LE BIOLLEY

Mio

Les Blanchets

Colosses

Plagne-Villages
2050m

Plagne-Centre
1970m/
6,460ft

Telemetro

Aime-la-Plagne
2100m

Plagne
50m

Plagne-Soleil
2050m

Plagne-Bellecôte
1930m

Plagne 1800

La Roche

Le Fornelet
1970m

The main bowl offers mainly easy runs of limited vertical

MONTALBERT

Montalbert

Le Forperet

Plagne-Montalbert
1350m

Longefoy
1170m

If the thrills of a day on the slopes aren't enough, you can round it off by having a go on the bobsleigh run built for the 1992 Olympic Winter Games, based in Albertville. The floodlit 1.5km run has 19 bends, generating forces as high as 3g.

You can go in a driverless bob-raft (40 euros) reaching 50mph, which most people find quite exciting

enough. Then there's the solo mono-bob (107 euros), which reaches 55mph; we found this a great thrill – we had to close our eyes on the sharper bends. Fastest of all is the racing-bob (295 euros), where three of you are wedged in a real four-man bob behind the driver – at speeds of up to 74mph. Be sure your physical state is up to the ride; there are minimum age limits. The run is open on certain days only, three days a week – book ahead. Additional insurance is available. One visitor loved the ride, but thought the staff rude: 'They rushed us through, despite the fact that we were early.'

OT LA PLAGNE / J FAVRE

LAGRANGE
Prestige

High-standard
Self-catering
Apartments

020 7371 6111
lagrange-holidays.co.uk

mornings' said 2013 reporters). The upgrade of the Colosses chair to a very powerful eight-pack this season will presumably deal with the serious queues to get to Centre.

The gondola to the glacier is queue-prone when snow is poor lower down – to get back to Roche de Mio as well as to the glacier (we found huge queues to get back at the end of the day on our most recent visit).

Plagne-Centre also has problems; the Bergerie six-pack builds queues and the Grand Rochette gondola can be 'a classic bun fight'.

The lift at the bottom of Les Bauches is now a quad, which should help with the traditional queues there.

Crowds on the pistes are now as much of a problem as lift queues. The worst-affected area is from Roche de Mio where a single blue piste takes all the traffic from several lifts. Some pistes to Bellecôte and Centre get badly crowded too.

TERRAIN PARKS ★★★★
Lots of choices

With no fewer than four terrain zones, freestylers are well catered for. There is a 90m long, 3m high half-pipe at Plagne-Bellecôte. Belle-Plagne is home to the big park, split into two, one area for everybody and the other for professionals. There is a mix of jumps, boxes, rails, tables and other obstacles, plus an airbag. There's also a small park with beginner and progression obstacles above Montalbert. Then there are three snowcross courses dotted around.

SNOW RELIABILITY ★★★★
Generally good except low down

Most of La Plagne's runs are snow-sure, being at altitudes between 2000m and 2700m on the largely north-facing open slopes above the purpose-built centres. The two sunny runs to Champagny are something else – one is often closed, the other (Les Bois) is kept open as much as possible with lots of artificial snow. Snowmaking on runs to all the villages is being improved. Grooming is good but most reporters think the Natur' runs should be groomed sometimes – unless refreshed by new snow, they can become unpleasant to ski, and then are left largely unused.

FOR EXPERTS ★★★★
Few steep pistes; good off-piste

Good news: the two long black runs from Bellecôte to the Chalet chairlift below Col de la Chiaupe, closed for some years, have been reinstated. Let's hope they can be kept open more reliably than they were before the closure. The piste linking this area to Les Bauches doesn't really deserve its black status; the Crozats black that meets it is a bit steeper, and can be tricky if snow is less than ideal.

Up on the glacier, Chiaupe merits its black status for a short stretch, but really the tough piste skiing is now confined to the Biolley sector. On the back of the hill, the Coqs and Morbleu blacks are seriously steep, Palsembleu less so. From the very top of this sector, Etroits owes its black status to a quite short pitch that is both steep

GETTING THERE

Air Chambéry 120km/
75 miles (1hr45);
Grenoble 190km/
120 miles (2hr30);
Lyon 195km/
120 miles (2hr30);
Geneva 200km/
125 miles (2hr30)

Rail Aime (18km/
11 miles) and Bourg-
St-Maurice (35km/
22 miles) (Eurostar
service available);
frequent buses from
stations

EXCLUSIVE - à la carte Child Care

Ski Famille

With 23 years experience we know exactly
what parents and children need and want.
Our chalets in Plagne 1800 offer....

- Child Care (babies to 12 year olds) in the
comfort of your own chalet. No trudge to a
central crèche ○ Fully qualified nannies
- High quality chalets in great locations
- Many free child places on selected weeks
- Delicious food and complimentary wines

Call: **01252 365 495** www.skifamille.co.uk
ATOL 10863 ABTOT 5141

SNOWPIX.COM / CHRIS GILL

Champagny is an
attractive sunny
village, but not ideal
as a base for the
Paradiski area ↓

and narrow, but is otherwise harmless.
The long Emile Allais red down to the
La Roche chair is north-facing, often
quiet and great fun in good snow.

But experts will get the best out of
La Plagne if they hire a guide and
explore the vast off-piste potential –
which takes longer to get tracked out
than in more 'macho' resorts. The
glacier and Biolley sectors have some
excellent terrain and there are good
runs from the glacier to Les Bauches
(a drop of over 1400m). For the more
experienced, the north face of
Bellecôte presents a splendid
challenge with usually excellent snow
at the top. You can descend to Peisey-

Nancroix (a drop of 2000m), enjoy a
good lunch at the charming, rustic
Ancolie (a favourite of ours) and then
catch a taxi or free bus to the Vanoise
Express cable car. Another beautiful
and out-of-the-way run starts with a
climb and goes over the Cul du Nant
glacier to Champagny-le-Haut.

FOR INTERMEDIATES ★★★★★
Great variety

Virtually the whole of La Plagne's area
is a paradise for intermediates, with
blue and red runs wherever you look.
The main drawback is that many of
them get overcrowded at times,
seriously interfering with the pleasure
and safety of skiing.

For early intermediates there are
plenty of gentle blue motorway pistes
in the main La Plagne bowl, and a
long, interesting (but often very
crowded) run from Roche de Mio to
Belle-Plagne called Tunnel (going
through, er, a tunnel). The blue runs
either side of Arpette, on the
Montchavin side of the main bowl, are
glorious cruises – but beware, the
blues further down towards
Montchavin are quite challenging. The
easiest way to and from Champagny is
from the Roche de Mio-Col de Forcle
area. Warning: the Mira piste from
Grande Rochette and the Lanche
Ronde up at Roche de Mio have steep
pitches that will upset many blue-run
skiers, although Mira has been
widened at the top and you can avoid
the moguls on the steepest section
says a reporter. Verdons, nearby, is a
great cruise, too.

Better intermediates have lots of
delightful long red runs to try. There
are challenging red mogul pitches
down from Roche de Mio to Les
Bauches (a drop of 900m) – the first
half is a fabulous varied run with lots
of off-piste diversions possible; the
second half, Crozats, is classified black

Pierre ⑤ Vacances
Holidays made for me

Best price
guarantee
for ski in/out
budget studios
up to spacious
3 bedroom
apartments

pierreetvacances.co.uk

– read 'For experts'. The Sources red to Belle-Plagne is a good run, too.

The sunny Champagny sector has a couple of tough reds – Kamikaze and Hara-Kiri. And the long blue cruise Bozelet has one steep section. The long Mont de la Guerre red, 1250m vertical from Les Verdons, is often closed; but when open, it's a fine away-from-all-lifts run with a decent red-gradient stretch halfway down, but long flattish tracks at the start and finish. There are further excellent red slopes in the other outlying areas.

FOR BEGINNERS ★★★★☆
Comprehensive facilities
La Plagne is a good place to learn, with 18 free lifts in the whole area; each village has at least one. There are good facilities for beginners, provided you go to the right bits, and generally good snow. There are beginner areas in Centre, 1800, Soleil, Aime and Bellecôte; and in (and above) Montchavin, Les Coches and Montalbert. But here, as in Les Arcs, the usual French system of green runs is not used. Although a lot of the blue slopes are easy, you can't count on that; some, as we note above, are quite testing. The resort is 'adapting' the Arnica blue run from the Colorado chair for beginners, and there is a new 'Coolski' pass for beginners.

FOR BOARDERS ★★★☆☆
Something for everyone
With such a huge amount of terrain, there is something for everyone: 'One

---

Selected chalets in La Plagne

ADVERTISEMENT

MOUNTAIN HEAVEN *www.mountainheaven.co.uk*   T **0151 625 1921**

Catered – Plagne 1800
* 4 catered chalets all in superb position, seconds from the piste
* Great value for money
* Fantastic food and wine

Self-catered – Plagne Montalbert
* High quality, spacious chalet apartments
* Ski in/out or within seconds of the piste
* No hidden extras
* Great value for money
* Unrivalled in resort services even for self-catered

↑ SELF-CATERED APARTMENTS – LA BERGERIE IN PLAGNE MONTALBERT

Email: info@mountainheaven.co.uk

SKI AMIS *www.skiamis.com*   T **0203 411 5439**

Ski Amis offer two chalets in different villages of La Plagne with excellent catering – full English breakfast, afternoon tea and a 3 or 4 course evening meal with good quality wine.

Chalet Anniek – Montalbert – premium service chalet sleeping 14-16 people in 7 en-suite bedrooms – close to the piste, lift and village centre, indoor hot-tub and sauna

Chalet Dolomites – Montchavin – budget chalet overlooking the piste and gondola lift for easy access to the Vanoise Express to Les Arcs – sleeps 8-11 people in 4 bedrooms, hot-tub on balcony

sales@skiamis.com

SKI AMIS

CHALET ANNIEK ↑

SKIWORLD

Catered chalets, hotels and self catering apartments in

Europe, USA and Canada

skiworld.co.uk
08444 930 430

ABTA V2151 ATOL 2036

PowderBeds.com

Ski Hotels & Apartments

snowchateaux
the catered chalet experience

"top 5 places to stay"
The Daily Telegraph

✳ France's top resorts
✳ Ski in / Ski out catered chalets
✳ Hot tubs, saunas, games rooms...

SCHOOLS

ESF (Belle)
t 0479 090668
Schools in all centres
Oxygène
t 0479 090399
El Pro (Belle)
t 0479 091162
Reflex (1800)
t 0613 808056
Evolution 2
(Montchavin-Coches)
t 0479 078185

Classes (ESF prices)
6 days from €222
Private lessons
From €125 for 2.5hr
for 1 or 2 people

CHILDCARE

P'tits Bonnets (Centre)
t 0479 090083
Marie-Christine
(Centre)
t 0615 215194
18mnth to 6yr
ESF nurseries (from
18 mnth or 2yr):
Aime 0479 090475
Belle 0479 090668
Snow gardens run by
ESF: ages from 3 to 5

Ski schools
3yr to 13yr or 16yr
depending on village

of the best for boarding,' says a recent visitor. Expert freeriders should hire a guide to explore the off-piste. Although this is a great place for beginners and intermediates, with huge wide-open rolling pistes, there are one or two flattish areas – for example getting across Plagne-Centre, the middle of the Tunnel run and the blue run linking Les Bauches to Montchavin. Most draglifts have been replaced, and others can be avoided; the more difficult ones are marked on the piste map. The park caters for all levels and there are three snowcross runs – read 'Terrain parks'.

FOR CROSS-COUNTRY ★★★★
Open and wooded trails
There are 8okm of prepared cross-country trails scattered around. The most beautiful of these are the 22km of winding track set out in the sunny valley around Champagny-le-Haut, accessible to those staying in Champagny. The north facing parts of the main ski area have more wooded trails that link the various centres.

MOUNTAIN RESTAURANTS ★★★★
A wide range of options
Mountain restaurants are an attraction of the area: numerous and varied – and crowded only at peak times. Many people lunch in the satellite villages. **Editors' choice** We've had excellent meals at Chalet des Verdons Sud (0621 543924) above Champagny; reporters agree – appetizing food and 'friendly and efficient' service, on a fine terrace or in the woody interior with a big fire. Above Montalbert, the Forperet (0479 555127) is quite different – a simple old farm building, doing super home-made dishes (excellent tartiflette) at good prices. The rustic Sauget (0479 078351), above Montchavin, is a great place to hole up in poor weather for some highly traditional dishes.

Worth knowing about Most readers' tips are in the Montchavin sector. They include the 'lovely' Plein Soleil at Plan Bois ('a bit cramped inside, but excellent food', 'best omelette and chips on the mountain, good crozets'); Plan Bois ('excellent food with an Austrian influence'); Pierres Blanches ('friendly, nice plat du jour and lovely wood-burning stove'). In a lovely spot at Les Bauches, Chalet du Friolin pleases visitors who opt for its 'smart, cosy' table-service section.

Above Champagny, tips include Roc des Blanchets ('great views, extensive menu'), and Borseliers ('a long-standing favourite, suitable for good or bad weather'; 'huge, varied menu'). Also tipped is the Bergerie above Villages ('wonderful atmosphere, smiling staff, varied menu'). There's a picnic room in Plagne-Centre.

SCHOOLS AND GUIDES ★★★
Reports are mixed
We had a positive report in 2014 of the ESF branch in Les Coches: 'good private lessons'. In 2013, an 11-year-old boy in 1800 got 'the usual follow-the-leader and poor communication'. We've had good reports from Champagny. Most reporters have used Oxygène in Plagne-Centre and have been well satisfied, though one reporter last year found '14 people in the group despite the website claiming they had a maximum of 8 to 10'. Antenne Handicap offers private lessons for skiers with disabilities.

FOR FAMILIES ★★★★
Good facilities
Several UK chalet operators run childcare services. In particular, several specialist family holiday companies have chalets – Esprit in Belle-Plagne, Ski Famille in 1800 and Family Ski Company in Les Coches. There are nurseries in most of the villages.

La Plagne

311

Build your own shortlist: **www.wheretoskiandsnowboard.com**

SkiCollection

Major Resorts
Expert knowledge

4★ ski apartments with spa

SkiCollection.co.uk
0844 576 0175
ABTA Bonded W5537

Action Outdoors, Alpine Answers, Alpine Elements, Club Med, Crystal, Crystal Finest, Erna Low, Esprit, Ice and Fire, Independent Ski Links, Inghams, Interactive Resorts, Lagrange, Mark Warner, Mountain Beds, Mountain Heaven, Neilson, Oxford Ski Co, Pierre & Vacances, Powder White, PowderBeds, Silver Ski, Simon Swaffer, Ski Amis, Ski Beat, Skibug, Ski Club Freshtracks, Ski Collection, Ski Expectations, Ski Famille, Ski France, Ski Hiver, Ski Independence, Ski Line, Ski Olympic, Ski Solutions, Ski Supreme, Skitracer, Ski Weekend, Skiworld, Snow Finders, Snowchateaux, STC, Thomson, VIP
Montchavin Lagrange, Peak Retreats, PowderBeds, Ski Hiver, Ski Soleil, Snowchateaux
Les Coches Erna Low, Family Ski Company, Ice and Fire, Lagrange, Mountainsun, Peak Retreats, Pierre & Vacances, PowderBeds, Ski France, Ski Independence, Ski Line, Snowchateaux
Montalbert Lagrange, Mountain Heaven, Ski Amis
Champagny Erna Low, Lagrange, Peak Retreats, PowderBeds, Ski France, Ski Independence

STAYING THERE

Chalets There are lots of catered chalets. Many are in apartments, but there are lots of proper little chalets in 1800. Crystal has about a dozen, mostly in 1800 but also three units in Belle-Plagne with a shared pool and spa, one of which approached 'food heaven' for a reporter last year. Inghams has four chalets in 1800. Mountain Heaven's mid-sized places in 1800 have had good reports ('comfortable, decent food') and they are adding a fourth brand-new chalet this season. Skiworld has over a dozen chalets dotted around several parts of the resort. Ice and Fire has a ski-in/ski-out place at Plagne-Villages, and two places with a sauna at 1800 – one new for this season. Ski Olympic has a chalet hotel on the piste at Plagne-Centre ('good value and wonderful views, a bit tatty in places'). Snowchateaux have six chalets in various parts of the area.

Family specialist Esprit has its flagship chalet hotel at Belle-Plagne, the exceptionally cool Deux Domaines – in a great position, with good pool and spa ('top quality, well run, excellent childcare', said a 2013 reporter). Rival Ski Famille now has three properties down in 1800.

Hotels There are very few.
****Carlina** (0479 097846) 'Ideal location' beside the piste below Belle-Plagne. Pleasant rooms, good restaurant, pool and spa centre. Family-friendly. 'Especially friendly staff.' We've enjoyed our stays here.
***Araucaria** (0479 092020) At Plagne-Centre; upgraded to 4-star in 2014 with a revamped wellness centre.
***Balcons** (0479 557655) 3-star at Belle-Plagne. Pool.
Apartments There is a wide choice of smart new properties, most with pools, available through the operators and agents who advertise with us. In Belle-Plagne there are two good Montagnettes residences, Le Vallon and Les Cîmes. In Plagne-Soleil the CGH-operated Granges du Soleil is very comfortable, with pool, spa and excellent views. Up at Aime is the Pierre & Vacances Premium residence Les Hauts Bois ('spacious apartments, hotel-standard spa facilities'). Lagrange has two Prestige residences: Aspen in Plagne-Villages and Chalets Edelweiss (seven chalet-style buildings sharing a pool) – right by the lift out of 1800.

EATING OUT ★★★★★
A reasonable choice
There is a decent range of casual restaurants including pizzerias and traditional Savoyard places.

In Belle-Plagne, we and readers have enjoyed meals at the hotel Carlina and the Matafan. The Face Nord is recommended for 'excellent pierrade', among other things. La Cloche does an 'excellent côte de boeuf' as well as 'really good pizzas'.

Reader recommendations in Plagne-Centre include the Métairie and Le Chaudron for traditional food. The Refuge is one of the oldest restaurants in La Plagne ('good food and value, space-age toilets'). In Plagne-Villages, the Casa de l'Ours does pizzas and steaks. In Plagne-Soleil, Monica's is 'excellent and good value'.

In Plagne 1800, we had a good evening at Petit Chaperon Rouge – friendly, cosy atmosphere in a wooden chalet with reasonable prices.

At Aime-la-Plagne, the rustic old chalet Au Bon Vieux Temps on the slopes is open in the evening and is highly praised ('excellent mushroom ravioli and tarte tatin'). The 'casual, family-friendly' Montana does pizza and the 'usual Savoyard suspects'.

APRES-SKI ★★★★★
Bars, bars, bars
Though fairly quiet during low season, La Plagne has plenty of bars, catering particularly for the younger crowd.

In Belle-Plagne, the Tête Inn and the Cheyenne are the main bars. In Plagne-Centre, the Igloo has 'icy white decor' but 'is horribly expensive'. The PlanJA is popular and has English cider, apparently. Scotty's has been known to be 'lively' (but a March 2013 visitor found it often closed early) and Mouth is also tipped. La Mine is the focal point in Plagne 1800, often with live music – plus old train and mining artefacts. Mama Mia's is a fun spot, and the Bobsleigh Bar's happy hour is recommended. Plagne-Soleil has Monica's pub. Aime-la-Plagne is quiet. There are discos at Plagne-Centre, Belle-Plagne and at Plagne-Bellecôte.

OFF THE SLOPES ★★★★★
OK for the active
As well as the sports and fitness facilities, there are plenty of winter walks along marked trails. You can ride gondolas to reach restaurants at the top. There's an ice grotto on the

ACTIVITIES

Indoor Sauna and solarium in most centres, squash (1800), fitness centres (Belle-Plagne, 1800, Centre, Bellecôte), library (Centre), climbing wall, bowling, cinemas

Outdoor Heated swimming pool (Bellecôte), bobsleigh, marked walks, tobogganing, paragliding, helicopter rides, snowmobiles, ice climbing, ice rink, ice karting, snow quad bikes, snowshoeing, dog sledding, air boarding, zip slide

Phone numbers
From abroad use the prefix +33 and omit the initial '0' of the phone number

TOURIST OFFICES

La Plagne
www.la-plagne.com

Montchavin-Les Coches
www.montchavin-lescoches.com

Champagny
www.champagny.com

glacier. Plagne 1800 has bowling and tubing, and both Plagne-Centre and Bellecôte have toboggan runs. The Olympic bobsleigh run is a popular evening activity (see feature box). There are cinemas at Aime, Bellecôte and Plagne-Centre.

LINKED RESORT – 1250m
MONTCHAVIN

Montchavin is an old farming hamlet with an attractive traffic-free centre. There are adequate shops, a kindergarten and a ski school. The local slopes have quite a bit to offer – pretty, sheltered runs, well endowed with snowmaking, with nursery slopes at village level, attractively surrounded by chalets and restaurants.

The main blue home runs from Dos Rond can be quite tricky. Après-ski is quiet, but the village doesn't lack atmosphere and has a couple of nice bars (a 2013 reporter recommends the Dos Rond bar-restaurant), a nightclub, cinema, night skiing, ice rink, and a new swimming pool and the Espace Paradisio spa complex. Ski Amis has a four-bedroom chalet new this season, with outdoor hot tub. Lagrange has a Prestige property here – Les 3 Glaciers – 'lovely rooms, great pool'. Restaurant tips include La Ferme de César ('amazing steaks') and Le Moulin à Poivre ('classic dishes').

LINKED RESORT – 1450m
LES COCHES

Les Coches is a little way above Montchavin, and shares the same slopes. It is a sympathetically designed, quiet, modern mini-resort with a traffic-free centre. The hillside setting makes for some steep walks. There are nursery slopes across the mountainside, linked by bucket-lift. It has a kindergarten, but Family Ski Company may be a better bet, with two piste-side chalets close to the village centre; chalet David is reported to be 'basic, but good cooking and excellent childcare'. Ice and Fire has a smart-looking 24-bed chalet on the piste with a sauna. Chalets de Wengen is a Lagrange Prestige property – chalet-style apartment buildings sharing a pool and spa. In 2014 'the best restaurant in town' was La Poya; previous recommendations include the Poze (pizza), the Savoy'art, and Taverne du Monchu.

LINKED RESORT – 1350m
MONTALBERT

Montalbert is a traditional but much expanded village with a nice little 'front de neige' area, with a choice of restaurant terraces. The lift out of the village is a fast one but the one after that is slow, and your progress to the main bowl depends on two further slow ones, so it takes quite a time to get to Centre. The local slopes are easy and wooded.

Restaurant choice is adequate: Abreuvoir has 'reasonable prices in happy hour', Fiftys Legend has 'prompt service', Tourmente is a popular pub with a pool table, and the Code is a 'racy but rocking' nightclub.

Ski Amis has a central seven-room chalet with all the trimmings here, and various self-catering options.

Mountain Heaven has self-catering apartments in several modern developments; the best of the apartments are notably spacious by French standards, and well furnished.

LINKED RESORT – 1250m
CHAMPAGNY

Champagny is a small, charming village in a pretty, wooded, sunny setting, with its modern expansion done sensitively; but it has drawbacks. It is remote from the link to Les Arcs – a reader based here this year seemed pleased to have got to the link in 'not much more than 90 minutes, in good conditions'. Its local slopes are exposed to full sun, and the red run to the village that is most reliably open is rather steep and narrow for nervous intermediates (though you can ride the gondola down). It is well placed for an outing by taxi or car to Courchevel.

There is a beginner area with free lifts at the top of the gondola, and a snowcross higher up beside the Rossa chairlift.

The Glières (0479 550552) is a rustic old hotel with varied rooms, a friendly welcome and good food ('good set menus and classic dishes, always brilliant'). The Ancolie (0479 550500) is smarter, with modern facilities. The Alpages de Champagny is a Lagrange Prestige property with pool and spa. The Club Alpina apartments next to the gondola have also been recommended.

The village is quiet in the evenings, but there is a cinema.

La Plagne

Build your own shortlist: **www.wheretoskiandsnowboard.com**

Portes du Soleil

Low-altitude, largely intermediate circuit of slopes straddling the French-Swiss border, with a choice of contrasting resort-

SHOWPIX.COM / CHRIS GILL

KEY FACTS

Slopes	950-2275m
	3,120-7,460ft
Lifts	194
Pistes	650km
	404 miles
Green	12%
Blue	43%
Red	36%
Black	9%
Snowmaking	
	1074 guns

Pierre @ Vacances
Holidays made for me

Best price guarantee for ski in/out budget studios up to spacious 3 bedroom apartments

pierreetvacances.co.uk

The Portes du Soleil vies with the Trois Vallées for the title 'World's Largest Ski Area', but its slopes are very different from those of Méribel, Courchevel, Val Thorens and neighbours. The central attraction is an extensive circular tour, straddling the French-Swiss border, taking you through one or two French resorts and several small Swiss ones – great for keen intermediates who like a sensation of travel. You can travel the circuit in either direction, and longer or shorter variations are possible.

We have separate chapters on the five major Portes du Soleil resorts. On the French side, high, purpose-built **Avoriaz** usually has the best snow around, and it is well placed to make the most of the slopes of Châtel and Champéry, as well as its own. Until now you had to take a bus at the lower, traditional village of **Châtel** to bridge a gap in the circuit; from 2014/15 there is due to be a chairlift link.

On the Swiss side, **Champéry** is a classic, charming mountain village; its slopes spread across the mountainside above the tiny, purpose-built satellite stations of Champoussin and Les Crosets and lead to the traditional village of Morgins in a separate valley.

Back in France are two further traditional resorts, off the main circuit but linked by lift to Avoriaz – **Morzine** and **Les Gets**. They share the biggest area of local slopes in the region.

The lifts you ride doing the circuit vary widely. In the Avoriaz sector and in the Linga sector of Châtel the lifts are mainly modern and fast. On the far side of Châtel and on the Swiss side of the network, drags and old chairlifts dominate, and progress is slow.

The slopes are low by French standards, with top heights in the range 2000m to 2275m, and low points where snow may be particularly poor in Morgins and Châtel (1200m). In general, you can expect better snow on the north-facing French side of the circuit than on the sunnier Swiss side, particularly around Avoriaz/Champéry.

In the distant past there was a booklet-style map covering the whole of the Portes du Soleil. But now each resort has a map showing local lifts and pistes – you have to pick these up as you go. There's an overview map of the circuit on the back of each one.

The Pyrenees

An underrated region with decent skiing and boarding at lower prices than the Alps, and villages that remain distinctly French

OT ST-LARY-SOULAN

RPI	95
lift pass	£160
ski hire	£125
lessons	£90
food & drink	£110
total	**£485**

It is certainly true that ski areas in the French Pyrenees can't compete in terms of extent with the mega-resorts of the Alps. But don't dismiss them: they have considerable attractions, including price – hotels and apartments can cost half as much as in the French Alps, and meals and drinks are cheaper. Provided the snow is good and you're not in search of steep mogul fields and wild après-ski, there is a surprising amount of variety packed into some of these smaller areas.

UK PACKAGES

Les Angles Lagrange, Pyrenees Collection
Ax-les-Thermes Pyrenees Collection, Zenith
Barèges Borderline
Cauterets Lagrange, Pyrenees Collection
Font-Romeu Lagrange, Pierre & Vacances, Pyrenees Collection, Zenith
La Mongie Lagrange, Pierre & Vacances, Pyrenees Collection, Zenith
Peyragudes Lagrange, Pyrenees Collection, Ski France
St-Lary-Soulan Lagrange, Pierre & Vacances, Pyrenees Collection, Zenith

The Pyrenees are serious mountains, with dramatic, picturesque scenery, and are worth considering for beginners, intermediates and quiet family holidays at a lower cost. The resorts are attractively French, and many are old mountain villages that double up as spa towns. You'll also find charmless purpose-built satellites.

Access has improved in the last few years, with low-cost airlines now using Toulouse, Pau and Lourdes airports.

The locals (including lots of Spanish) like to visit at weekends, so the slopes can get busy then. Queues are rare outside peak holidays though, and a lot of locals do cross-country rather than downhill. British visitors are still relatively few, and English is less widely spoken than in the Alps.

Cauterets

➕ Charming, old spa town
➕ Serious cross-country trails

➖ Downhill slopes very limited
➖ Long gondola ride to/from slopes

Cauterets is good for a short break; it's a relaxing old town, easy to reach, and its small downhill ski area suits a couple of days – try the cross-country too.

Many of Cauterets' buildings are well-preserved examples from the 19th century, and the thermal spas are a popular attraction for visitors.

There is a wide choice of hotels. The town's position at the head of a wide, sunny valley means traffic is rarely a problem, despite its appeal as a large year-round tourist destination.

The skiing takes place in a high, open and treeless bowl, the Cirque du Lys, reached by a long gondola from town; you have to ride it down as well as up. There is parking up at Le Courbet (1360m), from where a short gondola departs for the slopes.

The 36km of varied slopes radiate around the bowl, between 1730m and 2415m. The area just above the gondola top station is ideal for children and beginners; there are some gentle blue runs for progression too. But the area does get busy at weekends, as does the main restaurant – a self-service. The Oakley terrain park has an O-Rail and Stairset, unique in Europe.

Cauterets' jewel, though, is its 36.5km of cross-country, a short bus ride from town at Pont d'Espagne near the Spanish border. It's one of the best areas we've seen, set amid beautiful scenery and waterfalls. There are also 6km of snowshoe and walking trails.

KEY FACTS

Resort	935m
	3,070ft
Slopes	1730-2415m
	5,680-7,920ft
Lifts	11
Pistes	36km
Snow-guns	Some

TOURIST OFFICE

www.cauterets.com

315

KEY FACTS

La Mongie-Barèges	
Resort	1250-1800m
	4,100-5,910ft
Slopes	1400-2500m
	4,590-8,200ft
Lifts	34
Pistes	100km
Snow-guns	25%

TOURIST OFFICE

Domaine Tourmalet
uk.n-py.com
www.grand-tourmalet.
com

La Mongie / Barèges

☑ One of the biggest Pyrenean areas
☑ Contrasting villages but ...

☒ Purpose-built La Mongie lacks charm
☒ Lots of slow chairs and drags

Nicely varied slopes and good off-piste shared by two hugely contrasting resorts – one purpose-built, the other a centuries-old spa town.

La Mongie is a purpose-built, modern resort on one side of the high Col du Tourmalet pass (closed in winter). On the other side is Barèges, with which it shares the Grand Tourmalet ski area.

The slopes span four valleys and are nicely varied with open bowls above La Mongie and a friendly tree-lined area above Barèges – all suitable for intermediates. The black runs are considered some of the toughest in the French Pyrenees and there is a lot of excellent off-piste including from the Pic du Midi Observatory (where you can stay the night), reached by cable car from La Mongie. There are few huts but we loved the tiny wood-panelled Etape du Berger above La Mongie – where most food comes from

the owner's farm and you choose your own meat – and the rustic Chez Louisette above Barèges.

La Mongie has little charm but is convenient, with lifts and pistes on its doorstep and good restaurant terraces from which to gaze at the scenery. As well as restaurants serving traditional French and fondues etc the Bocadillo Cafe serves Spanish tapas in the evenings, along with live music.

On our 2012 visit we enjoyed our stay at a catered chalet in Barèges run by an English couple (see www.mountainbug.com). Barèges is a small, atmospheric old spa village (with a great modern addition to its traditional old spa building) with a narrow main street a free bus ride from the slopes.

KEY FACTS

Resort	830m
	2,720ft
Slopes	1700-2515m
	5,580-8,250ft
Lifts	30
Pistes	100km
Snow-guns	275

TOURIST OFFICE

www.saintlary.com

St-Lary-Soulan

☑ One of the biggest Pyrenean areas
☑ Attractive, traditional village

☒ Few challenges on-piste
☒ No runs back to the valley village

St-Lary combines an attractive, traditional village with one of the largest ski areas in the French Pyrenees – fine for intermediates wanting a sense of travel.

If you stay in the village, you ride a cable car or gondola both ways. Or you can stay up at purpose-built St-Lary 1700 (Pla-d'Adet).
Village charm St-Lary is pleasant with a narrow main street lined with wood and stone buildings.
Convenience Accommodation spreads from the centre along a river towards the hamlet of Soulan. Staying close to one of the two lifts is best.
Scenery The rocky ridges and open slopes give fine views including the Pyrenees National Park.

THE MOUNTAIN

The slopes cover three main sectors and most runs are above the treeline.
Slopes A cable car and gondola go up to an area of short slopes at St-Lary 1700. From there you can head for 1900 and a gondola towards a more extensive area of intermediate slopes.
Fast lifts Apart from the three above, there are three fast chairs; all other lifts are slow chairs and drags.
Queues 'No problem outside school holidays,' says a recent visitor, but another noted a 45-minute queue for

the lifts down in school holidays.
Terrain parks There's a park and a snowcross.
Snow reliability Reasonable; many slopes are north-east facing and almost half have snowmaking.
Experts The few black runs are not very challenging but there's off-piste at Courne Blanque and Soum de Matte.
Intermediates Most runs are gentle cruises, with a few more challenging red runs. Best for early intermediates.
Beginners Good nursery slopes, with two covered moving carpets at 1700 and a special lift pass for 1700 only.
Snowboarding There are good cruising runs, though still some old draglifts.
Cross-country Not the best choice.
Mountain restaurants L'Oule, by a lake, is an old refuge with decent self-service food. Rustic Les 3 Guides above 1900 ('excellent charcuterie, local wine by the pichet') and tiny La Cabane on the edge of 1700 do friendly table-service.
Schools and guides The four schools offer the usual options, though good spoken English cannot be guaranteed.
Families St-Lary is a good family

Pierre ⓢ Vacances
Holidays made for me

Best price
guarantee
for ski in/out
budget studios
up to spacious
3 bedroom
apartments

pierreetvacances.co.uk

PYRENEES COLLECTION /
PEYRAGUDES

Peyragudes is family-friendly and good for beginners and early intermediates ➔

LAGRANGE Prestige

High-standard
Self-catering
Apartments

020 7371 6111
lagrange-holidays.co.uk

resort, with special kids' and family areas. The day care centre at 1700 takes children from 18 months.

STAYING THERE

Hotels We enjoyed staying at the 4-star Mercure, linked to the spa and near the gondola. The 3-star Pergola is charming with a good restaurant.
Apartments 4-stars with pool, sauna, steam and hot tub include l'Ardoisière (800m from the gondola) and Cami Real (central). Pierre & Vacances has the 3-star Rives de l'Aure (near the cable car). Lagrange has the 3-star Chalets de l'Adet on the slopes.

Pyrenees Collection and Zenith have a good selection of places.
Eating out There's a fair choice, from pizzerias to grills. Our favourite is the Grange (local gourmet dishes). Other tips: the Gros Minet, Maison du Cassoule, Pergola (in old village); Myrtilles, La Cabane (at 1700).
Après-ski Nightlife is quiet, but there are a few bars. Try the Fitzroy (Irish pub), Balthazar (modern wine bar) or, at 1700, Top Ski (music and tapas).
Off the slopes There's a big spa (with pools, sauna, steam and treatments), snowmobiling, snowshoeing, dog sledding and ice skating.

KEY FACTS

Resort	1600m
	5,250ft
Slopes	1600-2400m
	5,250-7,870ft
Lifts	17
Pistes	60km
Snow-guns	60%

TOURIST OFFICE

www.peyragudes.com

Peyragudes

- ☐ Good for families
- ☐ Excellent spa nearby

- ☐ Few on-piste challenges for experts
- ☐ Snow can suffer from sun

Convenient purpose-built bases give easy access to a varied ski area which suits mixed-ability family groups well.

The resort has two purpose-built bases at the foot of its slopes. The largest is Peyresourde, which has lovely views over the Louron valley. A five-minute walk away, at the entrance to the village is the hamlet of Balestas and the majority of the resort's

accommodation. The smaller base is Les Agudes in the next valley.

Both bases have high-speed chairs which meet at the top of the ridge that separates them. The Agudes side gets the morning sun and the Peyresourde side the afternoon sun.

The Pyrenees

Be Ha-Py
Hautes-Pyrénées

Discover something different
Ski the French Pyrenees

- Charming Pyrenean mountain villages
- Ski & Spa • Unspoilt, snowsure pistes
- Prices from only £85pp*

• Saint Lary • La Mongie/Grand Tourmalet
• Cauterets • Peyragudes
Fly with Ryanair- Stansted/Lourdes (Tarbes)

Self-catering ski apartments
at exceptional value

PyreneesCollection.co.uk

Call us on **0844 576 0176**

Accommodation-only or self-drive deals
*T&Cs apply   Book now with a UK specialist tour-operator

Build your own shortlist: **www.wheretoskiandsnowboard.com**

Both bases have fine beginner areas and there are easy blue runs to progress to. There is good intermediate cruising (80% of the runs are blues and reds) including a couple of long top-to-bottom runs of up to 800m vertical – one on each side. For experts there are only four black runs but there's a lot of worthwhile off-piste.

There's one proper mountain restaurant, which was rebuilt last year following a fire; there are fine panoramic views from its terrace. It's also open on Thursday evenings, when you can get a ride up by snowmobile and enjoy a tartiflette dinner.

For après-ski, don't miss the Balnea spa down in the valley. It has themed spa areas: American Indian (with totem poles and geysers), Japanese (onsen-like with a zen garden) and Greco-Roman (with saunas, steam rooms, hot tubs and 'musical bath').

KEY FACTS

Resort	1775m
	5,820ft
Slopes	1715-2215m
	5,630-7,270ft
Lifts	23
Pistes	43km
Snow-guns	83%

TOURIST OFFICE

www.font-romeu.fr

Font-Romeu

+ High, fairly snow-sure slopes
+ Popular family resort

− Limited in extent, with shortish runs
− Weekend crowds

With Font-Romeu you can choose from a delightful old village or a purpose-built station at the foot of the woody, cruisy slopes. Beginners are well catered for.

The old village, complete with 12th-century church and contrasting modern National Scientific Research Centre, is linked to the slopes by a gondola that you ride both ways. You can also stay at Pyrenees 2000 – a purpose-built development at the foot of the lifts, and a short bus ride away.

The slopes span three partly wooded hills, with a good mix of runs, a terrain park and a snowcross. There are a couple of free beginner lifts and good progression to gentle greens. There is a local lift pass, but the Neiges Catalan pass also covers Les Angles (see below) and six other resorts in the region. There are 114km of cross-country tracks.

KEY FACTS

Resort	1650m
	5,410ft
Slopes	1650-2375m
	5,410-7,790ft
Lifts	19
Pistes	55km
Snow-guns	70%

TOURIST OFFICE

www.lesangles.com

Les Angles

+ Sheltered, tree-lined slopes
+ Good, gentle beginner terrain but ...

− English less widely spoken here
− Shortish runs that lack challenge

Les Angles is a small but charming stone village, complete with old church. The slopes are limited but relatively snow-sure and family-friendly.

Les Angles offers high but mainly wooded slopes that cover a broad hillside. Most runs are short and intermediate; over half are classified red, but there is a good proportion of gentler terrain. There are nursery slopes at village level and at 1800m – reached by free ski-bus. There is a decent terrain park and 36km of cross-country trails. Font-Romeu is 16km away. Off-slope diversions are few, but dog sledding is possible.

KEY FACTS

Resort	700-1400m
	2,300-4,600ft
Slopes	1400-2300m
	4,600-7,550ft
Lifts	17
Pistes	80km
Snow-guns	215 guns

TOURIST OFFICE

www.vallees-ax.com

Ax-les-Thermes

+ Varied terrain
+ Choice of ancient or modern base

− No run back to Ax-les-Thermes itself
− Still a lot of T-bars

Ax-les-Thermes is an attractive old spa town linked by a long gondola to its ski area and modern purpose-built resort.

A 16-person gondola links the old town to its ski area 8km away, rising 700m in altitude on the way. If you stay in town you ride the gondola both ways. Or you can stay in the purpose-built resort of Ax 3 Domaines at the foot of the slopes. The resort's name derives from the three sectors of its ski area: Bonsacre just above village level, leading to Saquet and then Campels. Together they have 80km of mainly beginner and intermediate pistes. There are a few black runs and some worthwhile off-piste. But the resort really suits families and intermediates looking for a relaxing time best.

There is a short cross-country loop at the resort but much more extensive tracks 10km away from Ax-les-Thermes. In town itself is an excellent thermal spa, the Bains du Couloubret, with 3000 sq m of indoor and outdoor pools, saunas and steam rooms.

SKIMPIX.COM / CHRIS GILL

La Rosière

A friendly, family-oriented little resort in a panoramic setting; the link to La Thuile in Italy adds much-needed interest to the skiing

TOP 10 RATINGS

Extent	★★★
Fast lifts	★★★
Queues	★★★★
Snow	★★★
Expert	★★
Intermediate	★★★
Beginner	★★★★★
Charm	★★★
Convenience	★★★
Scenery	★★★★

RPI   90

lift pass	£160
ski hire	£105
lessons	£65
food & drink	£125
total	£455

NEWS

2014/15: A six-pack is due to replace two successive draglifts up to Le Roc Noir.

KEY FACTS

Resort	1850m
	6,070ft
Espace San Bernardo (La Rosière and La Thuile)	
Slopes	1175-2610m
	3,850-8,560ft
Lifts	38
Pistes	160km
	99 miles
Green	10%
Blue	31%
Red	41%
Black	18%
Snowmaking	25%

- ➕ Pleasant, friendly resort in a sunny setting: good for families
- ➕ Fair-sized area of slopes if you include linked La Thuile in Italy
- ➕ Good beginner slopes
- ➕ Exceptionally good branch of ESF
- ➕ Heli-skiing from over in Italy
- ➕ Fine panoramic views
- ➕ Big dumps of snow when storms sock in from the west, but ...

- ➖ When storms do sock in, both local slopes and the Italian link can be bleak or closed – few trees
- ➖ Sunny slopes are affected by sun as the season progresses
- ➖ Still some slow old lifts (though recent improvements have helped)
- ➖ Local pistes rather limited and lacking variety
- ➖ Limited village diversions

La Rosière is very different from its famous neighbours such as Val d'Isère–Tignes and Les Arcs – much smaller, quieter and sunnier. Many reporters are more impressed than we are by the skiing, which mainly consists of several runs down a single (admittedly very wide) open slope. But the link with La Thuile over the border in Italy adds another dimension.

THE RESORT

La Rosière has been developed in traditional chalet style high up on the road that climbs from Bourg-St-Maurice towards the Petit St Bernard pass to Italy. In winter the road ends at a car park at the top of La Rosière, just below the main lifts. The resort has several identifiable parts, but the key distinction is between the main village and the newer satellite of Les Eucherts, a short bus ride – or a floodlit forest walk – to the east. This is more or less self-sufficient, but offers less choice of everything than the main village.

Village charm The resort is attractively built in chalet style; it is quiet, with a few shops and friendly locals; don't expect much lively nightlife. It is centred on the road to the lift station car park; so although there is no real through-traffic, the centre is far from traffic-free (Les Eucherts is a bit quieter but still centred on a road).

Convenience It's a small place, where you may have only a short stroll to a lift, but there's an 'efficient' free ski-bus. Les Eucherts has its own fast chair into the slopes.

Scenery La Rosière's sunny home slopes offer panoramic views over the Isère valley to Les Arcs and beyond.

ⓐ fast chairlift
Slow chairs & drags have no symbol

La Thuile ↘

Col du Petit
Saint Bernard
2190m

Belvedere
2610m/
8,56oft

Le Roc Noir
2330m

Col de la
Traversette
2385m

Le Gollet

La Rosière Les Eucherts
1850m/6,070ft

1500m

ESPRIT
FOR FAMILIES IN
La Rosière

Family Ski
Chalets
Dedicated
Nurseries
Exclusive Ski
Classes
12 More Resorts

espritski.com
01483 791 900

SKIWORLD

Catered chalets,
hotels and
self catering
apartments in

Europe, USA
and Canada

skiworld.co.uk
08444 930 430

ABTA V2151 ATOL 2036

SNOWPIX.COM / CHRIS GILL

There are wonderful
panoramic views –
this was taken from
Mountain Heaven's
Penthouse chalet ↓

THE MOUNTAINS

La Rosière and La Thuile in Italy share
a big area of slopes called Espace San
Bernardo. The link with Italy's slopes is
a bit prone to closure because of high
winds or heavy snow. There are few
tree-lined runs. Amazingly, the two
resorts produce separate maps
showing the whole area; and yes,
naturally, they differ. La Rosière's is
bigger, has the names of runs on and
is easier to follow.

Slopes Two fast chairs, one at the
main village and one at Les Eucherts,
take you into the slopes; then you can
progress across the mountain to Col
de la Traversette, departure point for
Italy. West of the village is a separate
sector with red and black runs through
woods to the slow Ecudets chair – and
a blue on down to the village of Seez
when snow is good.

Fast lifts The new six-pack for 2014/15
(see 'News') and another to Col de la
Traversette for 2012/13 have moved
the resort from ★ to ★★★ for fast lifts
in just two seasons. But there are still
a couple of slow chairs serving slopes
below village level.

Queues Reporters stress the lack of
queues, even at peak times. In good
weather, expect some afternoon
queues on the way back from Italy.

Terrain parks The main Poletta park
has green, blue, red and expert lines,
including a fun box, bumps, rails and
a big airbag. There's a snowcross
course under the Fort chairlift.

Snow reliability The slopes get a lot of
snow from storms coming up the
valley from the south-west, but
conditions can be badly affected by
sun or wind. On our March 2014 visit
the weather was hot and the slopes
slushy by midday – but the snow over
on the north-facing slopes in Italy was
excellent. Reporters generally agree
that the grooming is good but one
thought that standards had slipped in
2014 – more reports please.

Experts There are a couple of short,
easy but worthwhile black runs – we
particularly like Ecudets, down the
eponymous chairlift. And there is an
ungroomed, avalanche-controlled
freeride zone (called, confusingly,
'Snowcross des Zittieux'). There is
more serious, easily accessed off-piste
terrain just outside the lift network –
such as a run of almost 900m vertical
on skier's left from Col de la
Traversette down to the chairlift below
Les Eucherts. And there's heli-skiing
over the Italian border.

Intermediates The main area is a
broad open mountainside offering
straightforward red pistes, mostly at
the easy end of the spectrum and
mostly short, with verticals in the
300m to 450m range. The exception is
the Marmotte red, dropping over 800m
to the chairlift below Les Eucherts.
More interesting than anything on the
main slope is the lovely wooded
Fontaine Froide red, dropping 750m to
the Ecudets chair – but it lacks
snowmaking. Keen intermediates will
want to make multiple trips to the
more varied terrain of La Thuile.

Blue-run skiers are effectively
confined to the pistes near the village.
Not surprisingly, they get quite busy.
The longer blues running diagonally
across the main slope are just tracks
from A to B, so not of much interest.

The outing to Italy involves a red
run at the start, but it is not especially
tricky. The two draglifts that follow are
almost 3km in length – miserable in a
north or east wind.

Beginners There are good nursery
slopes and short lifts at both the main
village and Les Eucherts; four lifts are
free to use. The blue runs above are
pretty good for progression, although

Like the resort?

You'll love our handpicked accommodation

0844 576 0173
peakretreats.co.uk

⊕**ABTA**
ABTA No.W5537

peak retreats

UK PACKAGES

Alpine Answers, Crystal, Erna Low, Esprit, Green Rides, Interactive Resorts, Lagrange, Mountain Beds, Mountain Heaven, Peak Retreats, Pierre & Vacances, PowderBeds, Ski Beat, Ski Collection, Ski Expectations, Ski Independence, Ski Line, Ski Olympic, Skitracer, Skiworld, Snow Finders, SnowCrazy, Thomson

some people find them a bit on the steep side.

Snowboarding Most lifts are chairs, making the place good for novices. And the sunny slopes are good for gentle freeriding in soft snow.

Cross-country There are 5km of trails.

Mountain restaurants Options are limited, so the Antigel at the foot of the Stade de Slalom, which opened in 2013, is a welcome addition: table-service, good food, varied menu, in a light and spacious new building with lots of wood, high ceilings, red carpet, great views from the terrace – we ate here in 2014 as did two satisfied reporters. The self-service Plan du Repos in the heart of the slopes is the other main option – great views from the terrace. A 2014 visitor recommends the Relais du Petit St Bernard at the foot of the slopes for lunch.

Schools and guides We have had consistently good reports over many years of the ESF (which is run, amazingly, by a Brit, with a special English-language section). 'My friends loved their instructors and progressed really well,' says a 2014 reporter. A regular visitor has 'always been very happy' with Evolution 2. Elite Ski is a

British school offering clinics and private lessons.

Families The resort caters well for children: 'A great family resort,' says a reporter. Family specialist Esprit has its own childcare facilities here and Crystal has its own private nanny service. There is a lift pass that offers big savings to families with teenagers.

STAYING THERE

Chalets This is now a major chalet resort. Many chalets are located in Les Eucherts. The biggest operator is family specialist Esprit Ski, with 13 chalets ranging from 5 to 31 beds, plus its usual comprehensive childcare ('staff were brilliant'). Mountain Heaven has five chalets, most for 8 or 10 people; in 2014 we stayed in the Penthouse on the top two floors of an apartment building with a lovely big living room with floor-to-ceiling windows giving great views up the valley and over Ste-Foy. The bedrooms are comfortable with lots of storage space and Room 2 is huge; outdoor hot tub. Ski Olympic has three chalets (including two with access to a pool, sauna, steam and hot tub) with from 5 to 8 rooms: 'A wonderful holiday

La Rosière

321

Build your own shortlist: www.wheretoskiandsnowboard.com

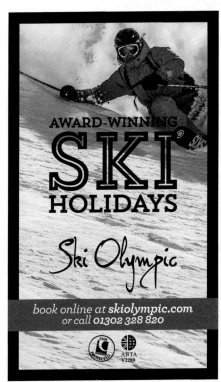

AWARD-WINNING

SKI

HOLIDAYS

Ski Olympic

book online at **skiolympic.com**
or call **01302 328 820**

ABTA
V2289

la Rosière
ESPACE SAN BERNARDO

PERFECT FOR FAMILIES
Friendly village in the heart of the Tarentaise

• 160KM INTERNATIONAL SKI AREA WITH VARIED TERRAIN
FIRST-CLASS FAMILY FACILITIES

4★ holiday packages
from **£164**pp

Book with the La Rosière specialist
Call us on **0844 576 0175**

SkiCollection.co.uk ⊕ABTA
ABTA No.W5537

©propaganda73.com

Resort news and key links: www.wheretoskiandsnowboard.com

AWARD-WINNING

SKI
HOLIDAYS

Ski Olympic

book online at
skiolympic.com
01302 328 820

Phone numbers
From abroad use the
prefix +33 and omit
the initial '0' of the
phone number

TOURIST OFFICE

www.larosiere.net

← The resort is great for families and the ESF
has an excellent reputation and is run by a Brit

OT LA ROSIERE

Lodge Hemera residences are both very smart, with pool, hot tub, sauna and steam room – featured (along with other properties) by Peak Retreats, Ski Collection, Erna Low and Crystal. For those who don't take self-catering literally, Montagne Saveurs will deliver gourmet food.

Eating out 'Not one bad meal,' says a reporter, who tried several of the dozen or so restaurants. The best in town is probably the Genépi, where we had excellent steak in 2014 – and which reporters recommend too. Other tips: McKinley ('charming with Savoie favourites and a log fire'), Marmottes ('huge portions, good Savoyarde food'), , and, in Les Eucherts, the Kitzbühel ('excellent burgers').

Après-ski Confined to a few bars. In the main village, Comptoir and Bar 1850 have a 'nice atmosphere' and sometimes live bands. At Les Eucherts, the Kitzbühel is the place to go for a post-slope beer and the Moo bar for late-night dancing (a reporter says there's an early-evening kids disco too – 'our girls wanted to go every night!').

Off the slopes It's improving, but there's not a huge amount to amuse the non-skier – cleared walks, snowshoeing and paragliding, with ten-pin bowling and ice skating at Les Eucherts. There is a cinema. Meeting skiing friends for lunch in the village is easy. But when keen skiers go off to La Thuile, they won't be coming back for lunch.

experience,' said a reporter. Skiworld has five smart mid-sized chalet apartments in the same building (with access to sauna, steam, hot tub in a neighbouring building). Crystal has five chalets and a 2013 visitor rated one of its 'Finest' properties, Cervinia, 'good value; good service'. Ski Beat has several chalets. Green Rides' chalet Jeode was praised this year ('great views, brilliant food, hot tub'.

Hotels There are a couple of 2-star hotels in the village, and more lower down the hill. Chalet Matsuzaka (0479 075313) is a Japanese-influenced 10-room 4-star at Les Eucherts.

Apartments Many of the best places are in Les Eucherts. Mountain Heaven has a couple of good looking places with three and five bedrooms and great views. The Cîmes Blanches and

---

Selected chalets in La Rosière

ADVERTISEMENT

MOUNTAIN HEAVEN www.mountainheaven.co.uk   T **0151 625 1921**

We have the best selection of catered chalets and self-catered apartments in La Rosière
* Best price guarantee
* All chalets close to the piste, ski school and the village centre with ice skating rink, shops, restaurants etc.
* Amazing panoramic views
* Superb food and wine in all catered chalets
* Your money is safe as we are a fully bonded company

info@mountainheaven.co.uk

↑ THE LOUNGE/DINING AREA

THE PENTHOUSE OFFERS STUNNING VIEWS ↑

SNOWPIX.COM / CHRIS GILL

Samoëns

Characterful and charming base for the extensive and varied Grand Massif area, with its own excellent shady slopes

TOP 10 RATINGS

Extent	★★★★
Fast lifts	★★★
Queues	★★★★
Snow	★★★
Expert	★★★★
Intermediate	★★★★★
Beginner	★★
Charm	★★★★
Convenience	★
Scenery	★★★★

RPI 95

lift pass	£190
ski hire	£105
lessons	£70
food & drink	£135
total	**£500**

PISTE MAP

Samoëns is covered on the Flaine map

Tailor made, long weekend and short break French Alps ski holiday specialists.

Hanski
Ski. Explore. Relax.

web: www.hanski.co.uk
tel: 01638 596373
mob: 07833 612061

+ Lovely historic village, with traffic-free centre and weekly market

+ Part of the big, varied Grand Massif

+ Glorious views from top heights

− Main access lift is way outside the village, and has no return piste

− Not the best base for beginners

− Limited nightlife

The impressive Grand Massif area is chiefly associated in Britain with high, purpose-built Flaine; but there are also lower, traditional village bases. And the cutest of these, if not the most convenient for skiing, is Samoëns.

THE RESORT

Samoëns is an attractive village – once a thriving centre for stonemasons, with their work much in evidence.
Village charm The resort has a small traffic-free centre of narrow streets lined by appealing food shops, and a pretty square (sadly not traffic-free) with a stone fountain, an ancient linden tree, a fine church and other medieval buildings. Also nearby is a nominally car-free area of modern development. The place as a whole retains the feel of 'real' rural France and makes a compelling base for families. There is a Wednesday market for your cheese supplies.
Convenience The village itself is compact, but as a skiing base it is not convenient. There are two gondolas into the slopes, both a drive or 'reliable and frequent' ski-bus ride from the village: an old one way across the valley at Vercland and a newer and nearer one. You can ski down to Vercland, but only on red and black runs that can be tricky or closed; there are no runs to the new one. So at the end of the day it's a gondola

then a bus; or ski to Sixt or Morillon, for a longer bus ride from there.
Scenery The village has a pretty valley setting, with attractively woody ridges and glorious views from the tops.

THE MOUNTAINS

Most of the skiing directly above Samoëns is on shady open slopes beneath the peak of Tête des Saix.
Slopes Read the Flaine chapter for views on the extent of the Grand Massif pistes. The two gondolas from the valley arrive at separate points on the hilly balcony of Samoëns 1600 (also reachable by road). A six-pack whisks you up to Tête des Saix, from which point you can proceed towards Flaine via a narrow, crowded piste followed by a fast chair in the Vernant bowl. Or you can turn right to the slopes around Morillon or Les Carroz.
Fast lifts Mountain access is now respectably quick, but the area as a whole has many slow lifts still.
Queues In general, the local lifts don't seem to present problems, though in high season you can expect delays and crowded pistes on the way to Flaine and back; a reporter found serious problems last New Year and wrote to the lift company to complain.
Terrain parks There isn't one.
Snow reliability The slopes above Samoëns face due north, so above 1600 snow is fairly reliable. There is snowmaking around 1600, and grooming is 'very good'.
Experts The upper pistes on Tête des Saix are among the most testing in the Grand Massif, and there is lots of good off-piste in the region. Don't miss Flaine's Combe de Gers.

OT SAMOËNS

← It feels like a real rural French village rather than a glitzy ski resort but it's a shame the gondola is a bus ride away

LAGRANGE Prestige

High-standard
Self-catering
Apartments

020 7371 6111
lagrange-holidays.co.uk

SAMOËNS
Wide selection of
3&4-star accommodation
handpicked by experts.
peakretreats.co.uk/Samoens

ABTA
ABTA No. W5537

peak retreats

KEY FACTS

| Resort | 720-1600m |
| | 2,360-5,250ft |

Grand Massif ski area
(Samoëns and all
linked resorts)

Slopes	700-2480m
	2,300-8,140ft
Lifts	68
Pistes	265km
	165 miles
Green	12%
Blue	45%
Red	33%
Black	10%
Snowmaking	
	218 guns

Massif ski area
(excluding Flaine)

Slopes	700-2120m
	2,300-6,700ft
Lifts	46
Pistes	125km
	78 miles

UK PACKAGES

Alps Accommodation,
Chalet Bezière, Chez
Michelle, Crystal,
Crystal Finest, Erna
Low, Hanski, Lagrange,
Peak Retreats,
PowderBeds, Ski
Expectations, Ski
Independence, Ski Line,
Ski Weekender, STC,
Thomson, Zenith

Phone numbers
From abroad use the
prefix +33 and omit
the initial '0' of the
phone number

TOURIST OFFICE

www.samoens.com

Intermediates Samoëns normally makes a satisfactory base for all but the most timid intermediates, who might be better off in Morillon. From Tête des Saix you have a choice of good long runs in various directions. In good snow the valley runs down to Vercland are highly enjoyable – the black is little steeper than the red, and is used less so it can be easier.

Beginners Beginners can buy a special pass and go up to 1600, where they will find gentle, snow-sure slopes – excellent when not crowded – but no long green runs to progress to. Morillon is a better bet in this respect, with its long winding green run. And the nursery slopes at Sixt are quiet.

Snowboarding Not a big boarding resort, partly perhaps because there are quite a few flat linking runs.

Cross-country There are 75km of trails on the valley floor around Samoëns, and tougher ones up the valley beyond Sixt and up at Col de Joux Plane.

Mountain restaurants There are several options at Samoëns 1600. We enjoyed friendly service and good food at Lou Caboëns, a small, woody place endorsed by a recent reporter. Mimy's is tipped for its 'massive burger in a lovely crusty roll'. There are some excellent spots covered in the chapters on Les Carroz and Flaine. There's a picnic room at the bottom of the Marmotte piste at 1600, and several others in the Grand Massif, marked on the piste map.

Schools and guides We've had good reports of all three alternatives to the ESF – ZigZag ('good private lessons'), 360 International and Skisession.

Families The Loupiots nursery takes kids from three months to six years old, and ski lessons are available. ZigZag has Tiny Tots one-to-one lessons for kids from three to six years.

STAYING THERE

Alps Accommodation is a British-run Samoëns specialist. And Hanski specialises in short breaks.

Chalets Owner-run chalets dominate here. We have glowing reports of chalet Bezière: 'light and airy', 'good restaurant-standard food'. And a 2014 reporter tips chalet Teresa: 'Very cosy and comfortable, five minutes from the centre, owners drive you to/from lifts.'

Hotels There are several 2-star and 3-star places. We and readers have enjoyed the 3-star Neige et Roc (0450 344072), a walk from the centre. The Glaciers (0450 344006) is 'basic' but offers 'a great location, friendly staff'.

Apartments Self-catering is mostly in small-scale developments, and quite a lot of it in individual chalets. Among many attractive options available through Peak Retreats are the Fermes de Samoëns, a smart Lagrange Prestige residence (with pool), the CGH residence La Reine des Prés and the Ferme des Fontany. Erna Low has a couple of these too.

Eating out A good selection of places. Table de Fifine, a short drive out, is a fine spot, with a beautiful wooden interior – 'welcoming and comfortable'. Monde à l'Envers offers 'great atmosphere, food and service'. Bois de Lune has 'friendly service, great food'. The Louisiane has 'great' pizzas.

Après-ski Pré d'Oscar up at 1600 is a handy spot for a drink at the end of the day. Nightlife is quiet and there is little choice of bars; Irish pub Covey's ('the liveliest') and the Savoie ('more sophisticated and laid back') are the reader favourites.

Off the slopes Samoëns offers quite a range of activities. There's dog sledding, and a reader recommends snowshoeing at Sixt. There is a sports and cultural centre and a new ice rink is due for 2015.

SNOWPIX.COM / CHRIS GILL

Serre-Chevalier

One on its own, this – more character and less swank than you expect in a big French resort, and more woodland runs

325

RATINGS

The mountains

Extent	★★★★
Fast lifts	★★★
Queues	★★★
Terrain p'ks	★★★
Snow	★★★
Expert	★★★
Intermediate	★★★★
Beginner	★★★★
Boarder	★★★★
X-country	★★★
Restaurants	★★★★
Schools	★★★★
Families	★★★

The resort

Charm	★★★
Convenience	★★★
Scenery	★★★
Eating out	★★★★
Après-ski	★★
Off-slope	★★★

RPI   95

lift pass	£190
ski hire	£105
lessons	£75
food & drink	£130
total	**£500**

NEWS

2014/15: The Croix de la Nore draglift on the way to Briançon from Chantemerle is due to be replaced by a quad chair.

2013/14: The old Chantemerle cable car was replaced by an eight-seat gondola. Two hotels in Villeneuve got makeovers and reopened as 4-stars – Grand Aigle near the Pontillas gondola and the cutting-edge Rock Noir near the Aravets gondola. A 4km bobsleigh run with 26 turns has been built at Villeneuve. Villeneuve has a new wine bar, 1420.

➕ Big, varied mountain offering a sense of travel as you ski

➕ Lots of good woodland runs

➕ Based on old villages with character

➕ Good-value and atmospheric old hotels, restaurants and chalets

➕ Very friendly and welcoming locals

➖ Busy road through the resorts, and through the heart of Le Monêtier

➖ A lot of indiscriminate new building took place in the 1960s and 70s

➖ Still too many drags and slow chairlifts at altitude

➖ Limited nightlife

This is one of our favourite places. The modern buildings of the main resort areas are off-putting, but get into the original villages and you find the kind of ambience you might look for on a summer holiday – a sort of Provence in the snow, with small family-run hotels and restaurants in old stone buildings.

And the slopes are equally distinctive, with the trees reaching appreciably higher altitudes than the Alpine norm. This is a great place to be in falling snow, as we confirmed during a quick visit in February 2013.

THE RESORT

Serre-Chevalier is made up of a string of villages set on a valley floor, linked by a busy road.

The valley runs roughly north-west to south-east, below the north-east-facing slopes of the mountain range that gives the resort its name. From the north-west – coming over the Col du Lautaret from Grenoble – the three main villages are spread over a distance of 8km – Le Monêtier (or Serre-Che 1500), Villeneuve (1400) and Chantemerle (1350). Finally, at the extreme south-eastern end of the valley, is Briançon (1200) – not a village but a town (the highest in France). As well as the main villages there are nine smaller villages, some of which give their names to the communes: Villeneuve, for example, is in the commune of little old La Salle les Alpes. Confusing? Sure is.

The resort is not at all fashionable, and is only now developing 4-star hotels. But Serre-Che has more hotels here in the modestly priced Logis de France 'club' than any other ski resort.

This is a family resort, and it gets especially busy in the February/March French school holidays.

A six-day area pass (or rather your receipt) covers a day in each of Les Deux-Alpes, Alpe-d'Huez, Puy-St-Vincent, Montgenèvre/the Milky Way, and a 25% discount on a La Grave day pass. All of these outings are possible by bus, but are easier by car. Driving via Grenoble you use the Col du Lautaret, which can be closed.

VILLAGE CHARM ★★★★★
Some quaint old parts
Each of the parts of Serre-Chevalier is based on a simple old village, with narrow cobbled streets lined by small shops, cosy bars, hotels and traditional restaurants that give each village a very French feel. Around these older parts there is a lot more modern development ranging in style from brutal to sympathetic. It is not a smart resort in any sense; even the older parts are roughly rustic rather than chocolate-box pretty. But when blanketed by snow the older villages do have an unpretentious charm.

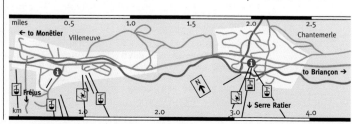

Pierre & Vacances
Holidays made for me

Best price guarantee for ski in/out budget studios up to spacious 3 bedroom apartments

pierreetvacances.co.uk

Le Monêtier is the smallest, quietest and most unspoiled of the main villages, with new building mostly in sympathetic style. But the heart of the old village is bisected by the road to Grenoble. We find the traffic intrusive, but reporters don't seem to mind it.

Because the resort as a whole is so spread out, the impact of cars and buses is difficult to escape, even if you manage without them yourself.

Briançon's 17th-century fortified old town is a delight, with its traditional auberges, pâtisseries and restaurants; it is a World Heritage Site.

Every year reporters stress how friendly and welcoming the locals are.

CONVENIENCE ★★★☆☆
Good access but expect a walk

All four main resort villages have lift access, by gondola, cable car or fast chairs, to different parts of the ski area. Briançon has a gondola from the bottom of the town; your hotel could be next to it, or not. In Chantemerle the old village is quite close to the lifts, as is a lot of accommodation; but there is still a lot further away across the busy main road. Villeneuve has quite a few lodgings close to its multiple access lifts, but the old village is across the valley; to combine character with convenience, consider the nearby hamlet of Le Bez – set between two gondolas. At the top of the valley, Le Monêtier has one main access lift, reached from the centre by bus or a 10-minute walk (hilly, and tricky when ice is around). You can leave your gear at the lift base.

Local ski-buses circulate around the villages, and there are valley buses that link all the villages (running until 11.30pm). But a reporter points out that these valley buses do not visit the lift bases of Chantemerle or Villeneuve, though they stop nearby.

SCENERY ★★★☆☆
Great views from the tops

The Serre-Chevalier range is not notably dramatic seen from the valley, though there are great views from Briançon's old town. From the area's high points there are fine views of the rugged 4000m-high Ecrins massif.

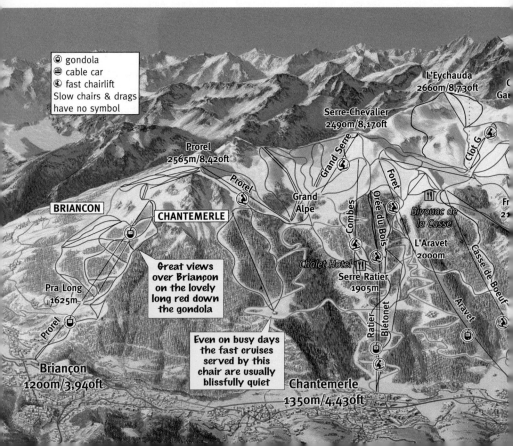

◉ gondola
⬛ cable car
⚡ fast chairlift
Slow chairs & drags have no symbol

L'Eychauda
2660m/8,730ft

Serre-Chevalier
2490m/8,170ft

Prorel
2565m/8,420ft

Grand Serre

Foret

Clot G

BRIANCON

CHANTEMERLE

Grand Alpe

Combes

Orée du Bois

Bivouac de la Casse

L'Aravet
2000m

Casse de Boeuf

Pra Long
1625m

Great views over Briançon on the lovely long red down the gondola

Chalet Hotel

Serre Ratier
1905m

Ratier

Blétonet

Aravet

Prorel

Briançon
1200m/3,940ft

Even on busy days the fast cruises served by this chair are usually blissfully quiet

Chantemerle
1350m/4,430ft

KEY FACTS

Resort	1200-1500m
	3,940-4,920ft
Slopes	1200-2735m
	3,940-8,970ft
Lifts	61
Pistes	250km
	155 miles
Green	23%
Blue	29%
Red	35%
Black	13%
Snowmaking	
	154 hectares

THE MOUNTAINS

There are trees here up to 2200m or more, and they cover almost two-thirds of the mountain, providing some of France's best bad-weather terrain (we once had a great day here when all the upper lifts were closed by high winds).

Reporters are very impressed by the improved piste signposting – 'much clearer than most resorts', said a 2013 reporter. The map is not ideal, but it is reasonably clear. Piste classification tends to exaggerate difficulty, most reporters agree.

EXTENT OF THE SLOPES ★★★★☆
Interestingly varied and pretty
Serre-Chevalier claims to have 250km of pistes; but the Schrahe report, discussed in our piste extent feature, reveals that the total when measured down the fall line is only 156km. The lift company, which is part of the dominant Compagnie des Alpes, has reviewed how it calculates its piste extent; but hasn't yet published the result. Watch this space.

The slopes are spread across four main sectors above the four main villages, and you get a real feeling of travel as you move around.

The sector above **Villeneuve** is the most extensive, reaching back a good way into the mountains and spreading over four or five identifiable bowls. The main mid-station is Fréjus. This sector is linked at altitude and mid-mountain to the slightly smaller **Chantemerle** sector. The onward link from Chantemerle to **Briançon** is over a high, exposed col via a six-pack. In the opposite direction, the link between Villeneuve and **Le Monêtier** starts with the Vallons six-pack up the Cucumelle valley. Skiing from Le Monêtier to Villeneuve involves the red run down this valley, so timid skiers may prefer to use the bus service.

FAST LIFTS ★★★☆☆
Improvements, but slowly
A range of big lifts gets you out of the valley, including a new gondola which replaced the ancient cable car from Chantemerle in 2013, and progress has been made in upgrading some of the

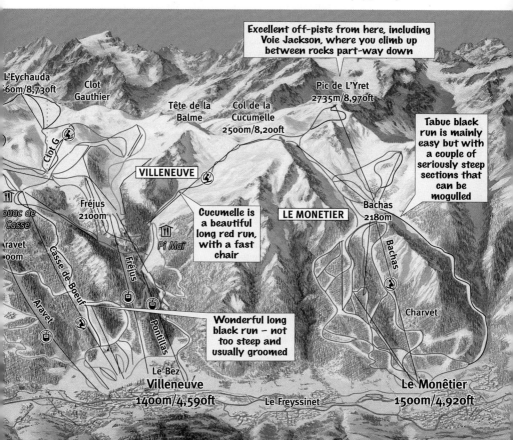

LIFT PASSES

Prices in €

Age	1-day	6-day
under 12	38	182
12 to 64	47	227
65 plus	42	204

Free Under 6, over 75

Beginner Limited pass in each area: eg Villeneuve €18

Notes Briançon, Villeneuve, Chantemerle and Le Monêtier; 6+ days give one day in Les Deux-Alpes, Alpe-d'Huez, Puy-St-Vincent, Sestriere and Montgenèvre; reductions for families

Alternative passes Individual areas of Serre-Chevalier

higher lifts. But there are still many old, slow lifts at altitude that hinder progress. In particular, the trio of slow chairs from Bachas at mid-mountain above Le Monêtier lead to complaints, though one view is that they keep the Villeneuve crowds away.

QUEUES ★★★☆☆
Still some bottlenecks

We have one report of a New Year holiday last season 'really spoiled' by queues of 'at least 20 minutes at most big lifts'. Normally there are few problems these days (we hear that the economic hard times have hit this resort more than most, which may have helped). It has to be said that we get few reports on the February peak, and we believe the lift system still has bottlenecks. When the resort gets busy in the French school holidays, head for the slow Aiguillette chair at Chantemerle (see 'For intermediates'). And consider riding the gondolas down to avoid busy home runs.

TERRAIN PARKS ★★★☆☆
Fully featured

The main parks are easily reached from both Chantemerle and Villeneuve. Legendary ripper Guillaume Chastagnol and the Serre-Che Brigade have been improving the parks for several years. The Serre-Che snow park is under the Forêt chair (but has a dedicated draglift). It incorporates about 23 different features (plus chill-out and BBQ area) – clearly marked out in three zones for all levels, including 12 tables, wall ride, rails, boxes and hip jumps. A major focus has been placed on the fabulous beginner area – 'My kids had a great time,' said a recent reporter. There's a video zone where your riding is filmed, you watch it on a screen and can download it later. A snowcross accessible by the Grande Serre or Combes lifts is 'good, fast and flowing', says a reporter. The innovative Mélèzone, beside the Champcella draglift features various fun jibs built from larch wood in a wooded setting. There's also a small, fun snowcross near the Rocher Blanc chair.

SNOW RELIABILITY ★★★☆☆
Good – especially upper slopes

Most slopes face north or north-east and so hold the snow well, especially high up (there are lots of lifts starting at altitudes above 2000m). The slopes

above Le Monêtier are high and shady, and often have the best snow. The weather is different from that of the northern Alps, and even that of Les Deux-Alpes or Alpe-d'Huez, over the col to the west. Some upper lifts may be prone to closure by high winds. Snowmaking covers 75% of the pistes, including long runs to each village. Piste grooming is generally excellent.

FOR EXPERTS ★★★☆☆
Deep, not notably steep

There is plenty to amuse experts – except those wanting extreme steeps. Seven slopes – basically, black runs left ungroomed – are identified as 'brut de neige' areas.

The broad black runs down to Villeneuve (Casse du Boeuf – our favourite) and Chantemerle (Luc Alphand) are only just black in steepness. They are regularly groomed, and are great fun for a fast blast, with their gradient sustained over an impressive vertical of around 800m. In 2013 we had a fab run on Luc Alphand in largely untracked shin-deep powder. But one or the other may be closed for days on end for racing or training. The rather neglected Tabuc run, sweeping around the mountain away from the lifts to Le Monêtier, has a couple of genuinely steep pitches (which may be heavily mogulled) but is mainly a cruise; great in falling snow, when it is even quieter than usual. For other steepish runs, look higher up the mountain to slopes served by the two top lifts above Le Monêtier and the two above Villeneuve. The runs beside these lifts – on- and off-piste – form a great playground in good snow.

There are huge amounts of off-piste terrain throughout the area – both high up and in the trees above Villeneuve and Chantemerle. We've enjoyed the Voie Jackson run accessed from the Yret chair above Le Monêtier, which includes a short climb between rocks to a deserted open bowl. The Cucumelle valley at the western side of the Villeneuve sector offers a huge area of gentle off-piste.

There are plenty of more serious off-piste expeditions, including: Tête de Grand Pré to Villeneuve or Le Monêtier, and Couloir de Roche Corneille to Le Monêtier (both a climb from Cucumelle); off the back of L'Eychauda to Puy-St-André (isolated, beautiful, taxi ride home); l'Yret

FOLLOW US f ✗

Photo accreditation: Agence Zoom

♥ Serre Chevalier Vallée ♥

FRENCH ALPS

90% of visitors can't be wrong*

7-nights from **€207**** pp including your lift pass

"This resort represents great value for Brits compared with many of the other big French resorts and it has an excellent ski area and unique ambience," says Dave Watts, travel writer and Editor of Where to Ski and Snowboard

Call our English speaking Reservations' desk for this season's special offers on **0033 (0)4 92 24 9898** or book online: **www.serre-chevalier.com**

- Tree-lined pistes from 1200-2735m • Easy access: travel by road or rail • Airports Turin 1.45hrs, Grenoble 2.45 hrs

"We will return and will definitely recom... and th...

"It's a gem of a place."

"Very friendly."

"Serre Chevalier Vallee is a great all round resort."

"Suits all leve...

"Great ski area – you have to ski hard and fast."

"Quiet slopes."

*Based on survey of British skiers December 2013.
**s/c accommodation inc. 6 day lift pass. Selected dates apply.

High-standard Self-catering Apartments

020 7371 6111
lagrange-holidays.co.uk

SCHOOLS

ESF In all centres
t 0492 241741
ESI Generation
(Chantemerle)
t 0492 242151
ESI Evasion
(Chantemerle)
t 0492 240241
ESI Monêtier
t 0683 670642
ESI Buissonnière
(Villeneuve)
t 0492 247866
New Generation
t 0479 010318
0844 770 4733 (UK)
www.skinewgen.com
Insight
t 0679 068683
Ski Connections
(Villeneuve)
t 0492 462832

Classes (ESF prices)
6 2.5hr days €157
Private lessons
From €46 for 1hr

GUIDES

Montagne Aventure
(Villeneuve)
t 0492 247440
Bureau des Guides
t 0492 247590
Office des Guides
(Villeneuve)
t 0492 247320
Montagne et Ski
(Le Monêtier)
t 0492 205335

to Le Monêtier via Vallons de la Montagnolle; Tabuc also to Le Monêtier (steep at the start in a big bowl, very beautiful).

FOR INTERMEDIATES ★★★★
Ski wherever you like
Serre-Chevalier's slopes ideally suit intermediates, who can buzz around without worrying about nasty surprises on the way. On the trail map red runs far outnumber blues – but most reds are at the easy end of the scale. The broad, open bowls above Grande Alpe and Fréjus offer lots of options. The runs on skier's right on the lower slopes of Le Monêtier are gentle, quiet and wind prettily through the woods.

There's plenty for more adventurous intermediates, though. Cucumelle on the edge of the Villeneuve sector is a beautiful long red served by the Vallons fast chairlift, with opportunities to experiment off-piste on easy slopes beside it. The red runs off the little-used slow Aiguillette chair in the Chantemerle sector are worth seeking out – quiet, enjoyable fast cruises. Other favourites include Myrtilles off the Prorel chair ('beautiful cruise'), Le Monêtier's Aya and Clos Gaillard, and the wonderful long run from the top to the bottom of the gondola at Briançon (with great views of the town).

If the reds are starting to seem a bit tame, there is plenty more to progress to. Unless ice towards the bottom is a problem, the usually well-groomed blacks on the lower mountain should be on the agenda; try them early in the day when they are uncrowded and freshly groomed.

FOR BEGINNERS ★★★★
All four areas OK
All four sectors have their own nursery areas, and cheap daily lift passes covering a handful of lifts, including access to mid-mountain where appropriate. At Chantemerle you generally go up to Serre Ratier – rated as good by a beginner reporter. At Villeneuve there are several slopes at valley level – all 'lovely' according to a skier having a first go at boarding recently – but also slopes up the Aravet gondola. At Le Monêtier the slopes are at the lift base – tipped by past reporters for 'better snow and fewer people' than elsewhere. There are also easy high runs to progress to in each sector – the best are probably the green runs above the Fréjus

gondola from Villeneuve. There are green paths from mid-mountain to Chantemerle and Villeneuve, though these may not be enjoyable late in the day when the runs become hard and others are speeding past.

FOR BOARDERS ★★★★
Plenty of scope for experts
The resort attracts a lot of boarders. The term 'natural playground' could quite easily have been coined in Serre-Chevalier. The slopes are littered with natural obstacles that seem made for confident snowboarders. Try the Cucumelle slope and the areas around the Rocher Blanc lift at Prorel for such terrain. For less expert boarders, the many draglifts can be a problem, as can the flat areas. There's a good terrain park for all abilities and ESI Generation in Chantemerle is a school that offers everything from beginners' lessons to freestyle courses.

FOR CROSS-COUNTRY ★★★
Excellent if the snow is good
There are 35km of tracks along the valley floor, mainly following the gurgling river between Le Monêtier and Villeneuve ('some nice trails') and going up towards the Col du Lautaret.

MOUNTAIN RESTAURANTS ★★★★
Some good places
Mountain restaurants are quite well distributed; they are marked on the piste map, but not named.
Editors' choice At Serre Ratier, Chalet Hotel de Serre Ratier (0492 205288) has a delightful large terrace and pretty dining room, good service and delicious food. Two other options are more expensive. Just above the Casse du Boeuf quad from Villeneuve, the Bivouac de la Casse (0492 248772) is an attractive chalet where we have repeatedly been impressed by both the food and service; reporters endorse our view, and recommend the self-service section too. Pi Maï (0492 248363) in the hamlet of Fréjus is cosy on a bad day and charming on a sunny day, and it offers excellent food such as steaks and tartiflette, and 'wholesome soup'.
Worth knowing about In the Briançon sector, the Chalet de Pra Long is a 'stunning building' at the gondola mid-station table- and self-service sections separated by a massive fireplace; 'great views and excellent food'. The little Chalet de Serre Blanc, just down

GETTING THERE

Air Turin 125km/
80 miles (2hr);
Grenoble 165km/
100 miles (2hr45);
Lyon 215km/
135 miles (3hr15)

Rail Briançon (6km/
4 miles); regular
buses from station

UK PACKAGES

Action Outdoors, Alpine
Answers, Alpsholiday,
Chalet Chez Bear, Chez
Serre Chevalier, Club
Med, Crystal, Crystal
Finest, Erna Low,
EurekaSki, Inghams,
Interactive Resorts,
Lagrange, Neilson, Peak
Retreats, Pierre &
Vacances, PowderBeds,
Rocketski, Ski
Expectations, Ski
France, Ski Line, Ski
Miquel, Ski-in.co.uk,
Skitracer, Snow Finders,
Snowed Inn Chalets,
Thomson, Zenith
Briançon Peak Retreats

from the top of Prorel, has superb views; it gets mixed reports – but 'it's cheap and you get a coffee thrown in'.

Above Chantemerle, we and a 2012 visitor loved the small table-service Troll – great, good-value food and very jolly service. Cafe du Soleil became one reader's regular haunt a few seasons ago. Grand Alpe self-service is spacious, and a bit cheaper than most.

Above Villeneuve, we and readers have enjoyed the Echaillon, a few metres off-piste from the blue run from Casse du Boeuf to Clot Gauthier – a lofty chalet with open fire and a table-service section: 'Delicious salads.' The Bercail, near the top of the Aravet lift, has impressed one discerning reporter ('best of the week') despite using the Italian system of taking orders at the bar for delivery to your table – try the veggie noodles, says a 2014 visitor. The Aravet in the same area does 'deliciously thin and crispy pizzas – very, very good'.

Above Le Monêtier the enlarged but still tiny Peyra Juana near the bottom was a 'winner' with a 2013 visitor: 'Fantastic, hearty, generous, good food. We went there every day.' The self-service Chapka at mid-mountain

'serves snacks, with lovely wood burner, super service and nice staff'. Both get packed on bad-weather days. There's plenty of room at the Flocon, near the Chapka. We had an excellent table-service lunch on the terrace here a couple of seasons ago, but we've since had mixed reports.

SCHOOLS AND GUIDES ★★★★
Choice of good outfits

You are spoiled for choice here: we get positive reports on virtually all the schools. The Serre-Che branch of New Generation, run by Gavin Crosby (formerly of EurekaSki) gets unstinting praise – 'very good private tuition, set us up for the week', 'superb', 'good teachers and competitively priced', 'our Italian teacher Simone really helped us progress'. Classes have a maximum size of six. We've skied with Gavin a couple of times, and been greatly impressed. In 2013/14 Gavin started offering off-piste coaching from first-time to expert levels.

Another British-run school is Ski Connections: 'Was very happy – small groups.' Private lessons with Brit Darren Turner of Insight changed one reader's skiing 'dramatically – well

Serre-Chevalier

Build your own shortlist: www.wheretoskiandsnowboard.com

NEW **GENERATION**
SKI & SNOWBOARD SCHOOL ●●●●●

MAKE HEADWAY
THIS WINTER

Head Coach Gavin spends summer
on his boat. In winter he'll help
you float through the powder in
Serre Chevalier and La Grave.

Serre Chevalier
Tel: 0844 770 4733   www.skinewgen.com

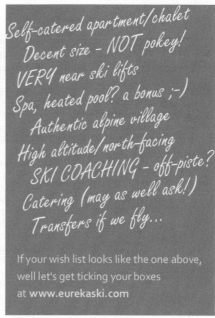

Self-catered apartment/chalet
Decent size - NOT pokey!
VERY near ski lifts
Spa, heated pool? a bonus ;-)
Authentic alpine village
High altitude/north-facing
SKI COACHING - off-piste?
Catering (may as well ask!)
Transfers if we fly...

If your wish list looks like the one above,
well let's get ticking your boxes
at www.eurekaski.com

eurekaski
MORE FROM YOUR MOUNTAIN HOLIDAY

↑ The lovely shady bowl beneath Pic de l'Yret, with multiple slow chairlifts, and trees reaching as high as 2200m
TANYA BOOTH

Like the resort?

You'll love our handpicked accommodation

0844 576 0173
peakretreats.co.uk

ABTA
ABTA No.W5537

peak retreats

worth the money.' Ecole de Ski Buissonnière are 'very good'. Even the ESF gets good feedback.

FOR FAMILIES ★★★☆☆
Facilities at each village
Serre-Chevalier is popular with French families and there are good family-friendly events and activities. For childcare, Les Schtroumpfs in Villeneuve (nine months to five years old) has been praised in the past. There is a micro-crèche (Les P'tits Loup) in Villeneuve too, taking children from three months to six years. EurekaSki can arrange childcare and private nannies.

STAYING THERE

There is a wide choice of lodging but very little of it has any claim to luxury.

EurekaSki is a local British-run operation that can fix more or less any aspect of a holiday in Serre-Che – not only accommodation of various kinds but also such things as transfers, catering, childcare, equipment, coaching and discounted lift passes.
Chalets Several operators offer catered chalets. In Villeneuve, Zenith has two chalets, including the ski-in/ski-out Ridon, and Crystal has four including a converted farmhouse in Chantemerle new to the programme for 2014/15. Inghams has introduced two mid-sized places in good positions in Villeneuve. EurekaSki has chalets with and without catering for 8 to 16 guests.

Hotels A feature of the resort is the range of simple family-run hotels – many members of the generally reliable Logis de France consortium. There are lots of 2-star as well as 3-star places, but now there are also a few 4-stars – read the 'News' panel.
LE MONETIER
****Auberge de Choucas (0492 244273) Smart but small wood-clad rooms; serious restaurant. We have enjoyed a stay there.
***Alliey (0492 244002) Charming place with well-regarded restaurant – 'Excellent food and service.'
**Europe (0492 244003) Simple well-run Logis in heart of old village.
VILLENEUVE
***Christiania (0492 247633) Civilized, family-run hotel on main road.
*Chatelas (0492 247474) Prettily decorated simple chalet by river.
Maison du Bez (0492 248696) Ski-in/ski-out, 'quirky, with cosy lounge'.
CHANTEMERLE
***Boule de Neige (0492 240016) In the old centre. Good past reports.
Marmottes (0492 241117) 'Extremely welcoming' renovated old house where Anglo-French couple offer B&B with the option of 'wonderful' dinners.
Apartments EurekaSki makes something of a speciality of self-catering chalets and apartments with pools and saunas. Chez Serre Chevalier has a wide range of properties in the resorts, too.
There is an increasing supply of high-quality residences. By the slopes

Build your own shortlist: www.wheretoskiandsnowboard.com

CHILDCARE

Les Schtroumpfs
t 0492 247095
3mnth to 6yr

Les P'tits Loup
t 0492 490086
3mnth to 6yr

Les Poussins
t 0492 240343
From 8mnth

Les Eterlous
t 0492 554246
6mnth to 6yr

EurekaSki
t 0679 462484
from 3mnth, private
nannies

Ski school
From age 5

ACTIVITIES

Indoor Swimming
pools, sauna, fitness
centres, thermal
baths, bowling,
museums, cinemas,
casino, libraries

Outdoor Ice rinks,
cleared paths, dog
sledding,
snowshoeing,
skijoring, ice driving,
snowmobiling, snow
kites, paragliding

Phone numbers
From abroad use the
prefix +33 and omit
the initial '0' of the
phone number

TOURIST OFFICE

www.serre-chevalier.
com

in Chantemerle is the 'comfortable and very well-equipped' Hameau du Rocher Blanc, in the Lagrange Prestige range (pool, gym, sauna, steam); bookable through Peak Retreats. In Villeneuve, Pierre & Vacances' well-placed residence Alpaga has been approved by reporters. So has the Hameau du Bez. In Le Monêtier the Arts et Vie is modern, right on the slopes and good value. The hotel Alliey has apartments too. Catering company Zeste (www. zesteserrechevalier.com) will deliver homemade three-course meals to your apartment ('delicious and huge portions').
At altitude Two mountain restaurants have rooms: Pi Maï (0492 248363) and the Chalet Hotel de Serre Ratier (0492 205288).

EATING OUT ★★★★
Unpretentious and traditional
In Le Monêtier, there are several good hotel-based options. At the upper end, the Maison Alliey (hotel Alliey) has a good reputation, and a reporter last year rated it 'excellent'. We've had an excellent dinner at the Auberge du Choucas. The hotel Europe has reliable cooking at more modest prices. Reporter tips include the popular Aquisana and the 'very friendly' Kawa ('excellent confit de canard; we ate there four times'). Up the valley at Le Casset, Chez Finette offers trips in a horse-drawn sleigh before dinner – 'An excellent find,' says a reporter.

In Villeneuve, two 2011 reporters recommended the 'atmospheric little' Refuge where the Alps Bell (cooking meat on a hot cast-iron bell) is popular. And two recent visitors have raved about Eau Petit Pont – 'best French meal in 40 years'. Mojo is a small, welcoming Brit-run bar-restaurant doing a good range of satisfying food at good prices.

In Chantemerle, we had an excellent dinner a few seasons ago at 34 – a cool spot with a short but wide-ranging menu. We've also enjoyed the Loup Blanc – 'Good food well presented,' says a reporter. Reporters also like the 'cool' Triptyque (traditional French dishes, 'fabulous burgers and crumble to die for').

In Briançon, there are several highly regarded places in the charming old town. A 2014 visitor recommends the Gavroche for its 'lovely ambience, great value, generous helpings and very good service'. A local tips Plaisir

d'Ambré for a 'special night out', and Pied de la Gargouille for open-fire grills. A reporter recommends Valentin ('four good courses for 26 euros'). Just outside the old town, Italian-run Mamma Mia has 'a fantastic menu and superb prices'.

APRES-SKI ★★
Quiet streets and few bars
Nightlife seems to revolve around bars, scattered through the various villages, and some reporters complain that the resort is too quiet.

In Le Monêtier the British-run Bar de l'Alpen is 'about the only place to go', say two separate reports; it has live music, sports TV, free nibbles and welcoming staff. In Villeneuve, head for the Grotte at the foot of the slopes (live music, happy hour and 'good bar food' – later on it 'doubles up as a nightclub'). The new 1420 wine bar is worth a try. The Frog is popular with Brits, while the Cocoon has 'a good local atmosphere'. In Chantemerle the Brit-run Station at the foot of the pistes is popular with Brits and 'seems to have the après all sewn up' – Sky Sports and 'sells bottled real ale'; 'live entertainment' every evening; 'pub food is good'. In Chantemerle the 'smart' VSB bar on the main road gets a mention and the Triptyque serves 'great cocktails – pricey though'. In Briançon, there's a lively teatime scene (assisted by a happy hour) at the bar next to the gondola.

OFF THE SLOPES ★★★
Try the hot baths
The old town of Briançon is well worth a visit – there are guided tours. The Parc 1326 leisure complex has pools (25m and fun options), sauna, hot tub and steam room. There is a full-size ice rink, and Briançon has a champion ice hockey team – their games make 'a good night out'. In Le Monêtier reporters enjoy the large thermal spa complex, Les Grands Bains ('superb tonic for tired limbs'), with indoor and outdoor pools, saunas, steam rooms, a 'chill-out' music grotto and a waterfall (some areas only for the over-18s). The hotel Alliey has a pool and spa. There is a public swimming pool in Villeneuve and bowling in Chantemerle. Each of the villages has a cinema and an ice rink, and there is good walking on 25km of 'well-prepared trails'. You can learn to drive a piste-basher. Paragliding is available.

Ste-Foy-Tarentaise

Tasteful, modern mini-resort appealing to families and experts – and to motorists as a base for visiting nearby mega-resorts

TOP 10 RATINGS

Extent	★
Fast lifts	★★★★
Queues	★★★★★
Snow	★★★
Expert	★★★★
Intermediate	★★★
Beginner	★★
Charm	★★★
Convenience	★★★★
Scenery	★★★

RPI	85
lift pass	£130
ski hire	£105
lessons	£85
food & drink	£125
total	**£445**

Col de l'Aiguille is the high point of the area, about 900m vertical above the village ↓

334

➕ Safe untracked powder within the lift system, and epic runs outside it

➕ Good base for visits to Val d'Isère/ Tignes, Les Arcs

➕ Great value (with the lowest lift pass price in this book)

➕ Quiet, even in peak periods, but ...

➖ Too quiet for some visitors; very little après-ski action and very few restaurants

➖ Very limited piste network

➖ Still two (out of four) slow chairlifts

➖ Now more British than French

Ste-Foy is a small, attractive, unpretentious resort developed since 1990, at the foot of what started life as a cult off-piste mountain. It remains excellent for experts but now attracts many others, including families. Keen piste-bashers will want to travel to big resorts nearby – easily done by car.

THE RESORT

Ste-Foy itself is a village straddling the busy road up from Bourg-St-Maurice to Val d'Isère. Its slopes start at Ste-Foy-Station (aka Bonconseil), which is set 4km off the main road. With a car you can visit some excellent restaurants close by and explore nearby resorts – Val d'Isère, Tignes, Les Arcs, La Plagne and La Rosière. Some tour ops organize excursions too. With a Ste-

Foy lift pass for five days or more you can buy day passes for these resorts at 25 euros a day.
Village charm Ste-Foy-Station is a complete resort in miniature, with a limited choice of bars and restaurants and a small supermarket; and these are surrounded by a cluster of chalets and chalet-style apartment blocks, all built in the traditional Savoyard style of wood and stone but without a real central focus. Lots of properties have been bought by Brits and Dutch, and some visitors find the British dominance of the place off-putting.
Convenience No accommodation is far from the lifts or nursery slopes.
Scenery The Tarentaise mountains give a dramatic backdrop to Ste-Foy's pleasant setting among the trees.

THE MOUNTAINS

There is an attractive mix of wooded slopes above the village and open slopes higher up.
Slopes The new fast quad chair out of the village ('a massive improvement') goes to Plan Bois at mid-mountain and is followed by two successive slow quad chairs. The first goes to the treeline and the second to the area high point of Col de l'Aiguille at 2620m. From here there are slopes of over 1000m vertical, almost 600m of it above the treeline. The two marked ungroomed black runs here form the basis of two special off-piste zones that are marked but not explained on the piste map; we're told they are avalanche controlled and closed when conditions aren't right. Slightly further down the hill is a less steep off-piste

KEY FACTS

Resort	1550m
	5,090ft
Slopes	1550-2620m
	5,090-8,600ft
Lifts	6
Pistes	40km
	25 miles
Green	5%
Blue	25%
Red	60%
Black	10%
Snowmaking	10 guns

NEWS

2013/14: The slow Gran Plan chair out of the village was replaced by a fast quad. A new mountain restaurant, les Marquises, opened on the Grand Solliet blue run (far left of our map).

SAINTE-FOY TARENTAISE

Ski-in ski-out 4★ self-catering apartments with pool

peakretreats.co.uk/Sainte_Foy

◆ABTA
ABTA No. W5537

peak retreats

zone, Shaper's Paradise (it has natural terrain features, and you can build your own too), again centred on a black run.

The two lower chairs serve a few pleasant runs through trees and back to the base station. The Marquise six-pack (on the left of our piste map) serves a blue run that goes into a forested area, three reds and a black.

The red and blue pistes are 'immaculately groomed', say reporters.

Fast lifts Two out of the four chairlifts on the mountain are now fast.

Queues Despite all the new building, reporters rarely find queues at Ste-Foy ('Hardly any, even in half-term week,' says a recent reporter).

Terrain parks There isn't one. But in the Shaper's Paradise area you are encouraged to build kickers and other features.

Snow reliability The slopes face roughly north-west. Snow reliability can suffer on the sunnier bits, but the resort has 10 snow-guns that it uses on the blue and red runs down to the resort.

Experts Experts can have great fun on and between Ste-Foy's black and red runs, exploring lots of easily accessible off-piste and trees, including the special zones mentioned earlier. The lack of crowds means you can still make fresh tracks days after a storm.

There's more serious off-piste on offer too, for which you need a guide. There are wonderful runs from the top of the lifts down through deserted old villages, either to the road up to Val d'Isère (you can get a bus back) or back to the base (via the deserted hamlet of Le Monal). And there's a splendid route down the north face of Foglietta in the next valley to the tiny village of Le Crot. The ski schools run group off-piste trips, with transport back to base and perhaps with lunch in the village of Le Miroir (see 'Eating out'). Heli-skiing in Italy can be arranged, including a route that also brings you back to near Le Miroir.

Intermediates The piste skiing is limited in extent and keen piste-bashers will want to visit nearby resorts too. But you can enjoy 900m vertical of uncrowded reds and blues on the upper slopes above the top of the first chairlift. The red from the Col de l'Aiguille is a superb test for confident intermediates, who would also be up to some of the off-piste routes, especially the one back to base via Le Monal.

Beginners There are good fenced-off nursery slopes with free moving carpets in the village. You can progress to a long, easy blue run (that

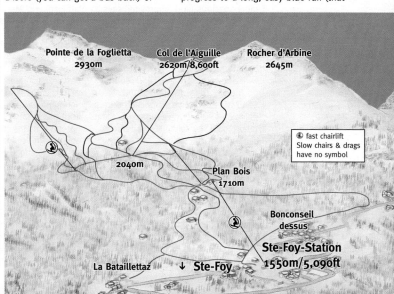

Pointe de la Foglietta
2930m

Col de l'Aiguille
2620m/8,600ft

Rocher d'Arbine
2645m

2040m

④ fast chairlift
Slow chairs & drags
have no symbol

Plan Bois
1710m

Bonconseil
dessus

Ste-Foy-Station
1550m/5,090ft

La Bataillettaz   ↓ Ste-Foy

↑ La Maison à Colonnes is a popular spot for lunch, but now has a high-altitude rival

OT STE-FOY-TARENTAISE / M JUNAK

UK PACKAGES

Alpine Answers, Alpine Weekends, Chalet One, Crystal, Erna Low, Inspired to Ski, Lagrange, Mountain Tracks, Oxford Ski Co, Peak Retreats, PowderBeds, Première Neige, Ski Bespoke, Ski Club Freshtracks, Ski Collection, Ski Independence, Ski Weekend, Thomson

Phone numbers
From abroad use the prefix +33 and omit the initial '0' of the phone number

TOURIST OFFICE

www.saintefoy.net

was classified green until 2012/13) off the new high-speed quad, then to steeper blues higher up.

Snowboarding It's a great freeriding area, with lots of trees and powder between the pistes to play in, plus the Shaper's Paradise area for building kickers and other features.

Cross-country Go elsewhere. There are no prepared trails here.

Mountain restaurants The new restaurant, les Marquises, is a welcome development – a 'small but wonderful' restored building with a big terrace; 'good but limited menu' in its first season. There are two 'rustic and charming' restaurants near the top of the first chair. Tiny Les Brevettes is cramped but cosy, with good food ('great omelettes and ravioli; new toilets') – while Chez Léon is much more spacious (and 'improving' says a Ste-Foy regular). At village level, but ski-in/ski-out, la Maison à Colonnes gets good reports.

Schools and guides A 2014 visitor is full of praise for her off-piste course with Snoworks. We get good reports on the ESF too. Evolution 2 and K Spirit are alternative schools. The local guides are 'totally great', says a recent reporter. All the schools and guides can arrange heli-skiing.

Families Les P'tits Trappeurs takes children from age 3 to 11. UK tour operator Première Neige also runs a nursery.

STAYING THERE

Chalets Auberge sur la Montagne (0479 069583) is an eight-room chalet in La Thuile at the bottom of the 4km access road to Ste-Foy station, with

minibus shuttles; it gets a rave review from a reporter this year – 'very welcoming, fantastic food, superb views (especially from hot tub)'. Skis for hire on the spot. Premiere Neige's chalet The Peak is also lavishly praised – 'amazing food'.

Hotels The smartly modernized Monal (0479 069007) down in Ste-Foy village has been tipped in the past.

Apartments Peak Retreats has apartments in the smart Etoile des Cîmes and the CGH complex Fermes de Ste-Foy (both with pool, hot tub, sauna, steam, fitness). Ski Collection also has La Ruitor apartments, quietly set at the edge of the resort 400m from the centre (with shuttle); pool and spa.

Eating out In Ste-Foy-Station the Bergerie does excellent food, the 'atmospheric' Maison à Colonnes is highly rated ('one of the best pierrades I can recall') and L'à Coeur does 'a fantastic côte de boeuf, dinosaur size', says a 2013 visitor. In the village of Le Miroir, Chez Mérie is excellent – 'the best in the Tarentaise', says a frequent visitor. In Ste-Foy village, the Monal hotel and La Grange next door are both highly rated.

Après-ski Pretty quiet. Reporters have enjoyed the Iceberg piano bar. The popular Pitchouli bar has changed hands and become l'Aprés. The bar of the hotel Monal in Ste-Foy village can get busy, too; tastings are held in the cellar wine bar there.

Off the slopes There's little to do off the slopes, but snowshoeing and dog sledding are available. Forget shopping ('I have rarely spent so little on a ski holiday').

SNOWPIX.COM / CHRIS GILL

St-Martin-de-Belleville

Explore the Trois Vallées from a traditional old village – and so avoid the Méribel crowds who descend on it for lunch

TOP 10 RATINGS

Extent	★★★★★
Fast lifts	★★★★
Queues	★★★★
Snow	★★★
Expert	★★★★
Intermediate	★★★★★
Beginner	★★
Charm	★★★★
Convenience	★★★
Scenery	★★★

RPI   110

lift pass	£230
ski hire	£125
lessons	£85
food & drink	£140
total	**£580**

NEWS

2013/14: Liberty Ride is a new off-piste area that's marked, patrolled, avalanche protected but not groomed.

KEY FACTS

Resort	1400m
	4,590ft

Trois Vallées	
Slopes	1260-3230m
	4,130-10,600ft
Lifts	180
Pistes	600km
	373 miles
Green	13%
Blue	39%
Red	38%
Black	10%
Snowmaking	33%

Les Menuires / St-Martin only	
Slopes	1400-2850m
	4,590-9,350ft
Lifts	34
Pistes	160km
	99 miles
Green	15%
Blue	47%
Red	30%
Black	8%

+ Attractively developed traditional village with pretty church

+ Access to the whole Trois Vallées

+ Long, easy intermediate runs on rolling local slopes

+ Extensive snowmaking keeps runs open in poor conditions, but ...

− Snow on runs to the resort suffers from afternoon sun, and altitude

− Only one run to ski if bad weather closes the top lifts

− No green runs for novices

− Some lodging a long trek from the lifts – transport needed

− Limited village facilities

St-Martin is a lived-in, unspoiled village with an old church (prettily lit at night), small square and buildings of wood and stone, a few miles down the valley from Les Menuires. As a quiet, relatively inexpensive, attractive base for exploration of the Trois Vallées it's unbeatable. But it is quiet.

THE RESORT

St-Martin was a backwater farming village until the 1980s, when chairlifts linked it to the slopes of Méribel and Les Menuires.

Village charm St-Martin is a pleasant old village, set on a steep slope, with its extensive modern developments all in traditional style. The main feature remains the lovely 16th-century church – prettily floodlit at night.

Convenience The village core is small, but some lodgings are quite a way from the lifts. The main lift is above the centre, but a draglift from the

village square accesses it. There are some good local shops and a few 'touristy' ones.

Scenery St-Martin has one of the more attractive locations in the valley, set among quiet, lightly wooded slopes.

THE MOUNTAINS

The whole of the Trois Vallées can easily be explored from here.

Slopes A gondola followed by a very long fast quad (a cold ride in the mornings) take you to a ridge from which you can access Méribel on one side and Les Menuires on the other. But if this lift is closed, you're stuck.

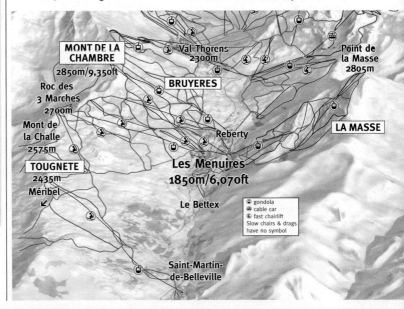

MONT DE LA CHAMBRE
2850m/9,350ft

Roc des 3 Marches
2700m

Mont de la Challe
2575m

TOUGNETE
2435m

Méribel

Val Thorens
2300m

BRUYERES

Point de la Masse
2805m

Reberty

LA MASSE

Les Menuires
1850m/6,070ft

Le Bettex

Saint-Martin-de-Belleville

gondola
cable car
fast chairlift
Slow chairs & drags have no symbol

Like the resort?

You'll love our handpicked accommodation

0844 576 0173
peakretreats.co.uk

◆ABTA
ABTA No. W5537

peak retreats

OT LES MENUIRES / G LANSARD

Day or night,
St-Martin is the most
attractive village in
the Trois Vallées ↓

Fast lifts The main local lifts are both fast – as are most key lifts in the Trois Vallées.

Queues Queues at the village gondola are not unknown, but the chair above it is a bigger problem at busy times – pistes from four points on the ridge meet around here. Upgrade needed.

Terrain parks None locally, but you can get to those above Les Menuires and Méribel relatively easily.

Snow reliability The local slopes get the full force of the afternoon sun, and the village is quite low. The home run is kept open by snowmaking to the bottom, but conditions are often poor.

Experts Locally there are large areas of gentle and often deserted off-piste. The descent from Roc de Fer to the village of Béranger is recommended. Or try the new Liberty Ride area. Head to La Masse for steep slopes.

Intermediates The local slopes are pleasant blues and reds, mainly of interest to intermediates. One of our favourite runs in the Trois Vallées is the rolling, wide, usually quiet Jerusalem red down to the top of the gondola from the ridge shared with Méribel. The Verdet blue from Roc de Fer is a lovely easy cruise and also

usually quiet. Then, of course, there's the whole of the Trois Vallées to explore.

Beginners Not ideal – there's a small nursery slope but no long green runs to progress to. The blue run down the gondola is fairly gentle, though.

Snowboarding There is some great local off-piste freeriding available.

Cross-country There are 28km of trails in the Belleville valley.

Mountain restaurants Reporters love the Grand Lac between here and Les Menuires (read the Les Menuires chapter). There are three atmospheric old places to try lower on the home run: the reliable Loy ('lovely lamb casserole, great service'), Chardon Bleu ('excellent plat du jour') and the small, woody Corbeleys – 'as good as the Grand Lac', says a 2014 visitor. Not surprisingly, many people based in Méribel and Courchevel like to ski down to St-Martin for lunch – read 'Eating out' if that's your plan.

Schools and guides A regular reporter's husband was 'very satisfied' with his lesson with British-run New Generation, which recently opened a branch here. Reports on the ESF are generally positive. A potential problem

UK PACKAGES

Alpine Answers, Alpine Club, Crystal, Crystal Finest, Erna Low, Kaluma, Mountain Beds, Mountain Lodge Adventures, Oxford Ski Co, Peak Pursuits, Peak Retreats, PowderBeds, Ski Amis, Ski Bespoke, Ski Expectations, Ski Independence, Ski Line, Skitracer, Snow Finders, STC, Thomson

Phone numbers
From abroad use the prefix +33 and omit the initial '0' of the phone number

TOURIST OFFICE

www.st-martin-belleville.com

is that when demand is low you may have to go to Les Menuires to find a class of the right level. Instructors operating here and in Les Menuires under the startling name of Ski'School offer private lessons only in English, and are reported to be 'really good'.

Families One of our regular reporters on St-Martin has five children and seems to find it near-ideal, not least because it is so small and safe. Piou Piou club at the ESF takes children from 18 months to five years old. The tourist office has a list of babysitters.

STAYING THERE

For a small village there's a good variety of accommodation.

Chalets The Brit-run Alpine Club (not really a club) has two luxurious chalets in the quiet hamlet of Villarabout, one newly built in traditional style with a double-height, open-plan living room and the other a beautifully converted, 100-year-old farmhouse with spectacular views. They get rave reviews ('delicious food', 'fabulous service') and there's a minibus service until 10pm daily.

Hotels There are several 3-stars, on which we lack recent reports. The Alp hotel (0479 089282) is in pole position by the gondola.

Apartments There are two stylish residences in piste-side locations above the village run by CGH: Chalets du Gypse follows the standard pattern – smart pool, hot tubs etc, and is available through Peak Retreats; Chalet Adèle has no fancy amenities, and is booked through CGH or owners' websites. Ski Amis has an appetizing range of properties, mostly central.

Erna Low has a couple of appealing places in Villarabout.

Eating out There is a good choice for a small village, no doubt due in part to the healthy lunchtime trade. The Voûte is the reader favourite, for pizza and more serious dishes – 'buzzy atmosphere', 'food seems to get better each year – excellent fish dishes'. The Montagnard, just about on the snow, is an atmospheric converted barn doing a good range of dishes – but regulars complain of escalating prices. The 'friendly, traditional' Lachenal, a simple hotel that suffers from changing hands quite frequently, did 'excellent food' for a reporter this year. The Eterlou does 'great grills'. The Billig is a crêperie that also does 'very good value and tasty food'. The Ferme de la Choumette, slightly out of the village, is a working farm and cheesery and is often recommended. The Ferme Auberge Chantacoucou in Le Chatelard is similar. La Bouitte, up the road in St-Marcel, has two Michelin stars; we and a reporter had splendid meals there a couple of years back; yes, it is very expensive.

Après-ski Choice is limited. The Dahlia, at the bottom of the gondola, is popular for après-ski drinks. Pourquoi Pas? 'is a favourite' of a regular visitor and has some live music sessions. Or try Bar Joker or Billig.

Off the slopes Options are limited. The village has an 'excellent' museum with 'comprehensive audio guide in English' and free concerts ('high standard') in the church. And there's dog sledding, snowshoe trips, pleasant walks and a torchlit tour of the village. Pedestrians can ride lifts to and from Méribel.

St-Martin-de-Belleville

339

THE ALPINE CLUB www.thealpineclub.co.uk   helen@thealpineclub.co.uk

Sumptuous food, exceptional service, boutique chalets
Individual rooms or exclusive chalet bookings

the alpineclub
les trois vallées

La Tania

A well-placed budget base for the Courchevel and Méribel pistes – and a pleasant place, with a good choice of catered chalets

TOP 10 RATINGS

Extent	★★★★★
Fast lifts	★★★★
Queues	★★★★
Snow	★★★
Expert	★★★★
Intermediate	★★★★★
Beginner	★★★
Charm	★★★
Convenience	★★★★
Scenery	★★★

RPI 115

lift pass	£230
ski hire	£130
lessons	£100
food & drink	£145
total	**£605**

NEWS

2014/15: The ancient Forêt gondola from Le Praz is due to be replaced by a six-pack taking a different line to a lower top station at mid-mountain, near the Bouc Blanc restaurant.

2013/14: There were major changes above La Tania: a long six-pack was built from below mid-mountain to the top, replacing two draglifts, one of which was moved down the hill to become the Stade drag; the Col de la Loze and Crêtes chairs were removed.

- ➕ Part of the Trois Vallées, with good access to Courchevel and Méribel
- ➕ Long runs through woods to the village: a great place in a storm
- ➕ Attractive, small, traffic-free village
- ➕ Much improved snowmaking, but ...

- ➖ At this altitude, snowmaking is vital in most seasons
- ➖ Limited village facilities
- ➖ Village nursery slope gets through-traffic (but higher one does not)
- ➖ The one long green run is not genuinely easy
- ➖ No proper hotels

La Tania is a good-value, family-friendly base from which to explore the slopes of its swanky neighbours, Courchevel and Méribel. The resort was built for the 1992 Winter Olympics, and at 1350m is about the lowest purpose-built French resort you'll find; its wood-clad buildings sit comfortably in a pretty woodland setting – quite a contrast to the bleakness of most French ski stations.

THE RESORT

La Tania is set just off the minor road linking Le Praz to Méribel. Free buses go to Courchevel and there's a service to Méribel during the French school holidays.

Village charm The village has grown into a quiet, attractive, car-free collection of mainly ski-in/ski-out chalets and apartments. (It did have hotels, but they no longer operate as such.) There are a few lively bars and restaurants, but nightlife is still relatively low-key.

Convenience It's a small place – you can walk around the village in five minutes – but big enough to have all the basic amenities (except a pharmacy). A gondola from one end of the village leads up into the slopes, and you should be able to ski back to a point close to your doorstep. And the lower nursery slope is central.

Scenery The resort is prettily set among the trees.

THE MOUNTAINS

The slopes immediately above both La Tania and nearby Le Praz are wooded, and about the best place in the whole Trois Vallées to be in bad weather. Above mid-mountain, the slopes are open.

Slopes The gondola out of the village goes to Praz-Juget. From below here a six-pack (which replaced a draglift for 2013/14) goes on up to the slopes above Courchevel 1850, and a fast quad goes to the link with Méribel via Col de la Loze. From all these points, varied, interesting intermediate runs can take you back into the La Tania sector.

Fast lifts Our rating is for the whole Courchevel area lift system. The lifts above La Tania have improved greatly in recent years, most recently by installation of the new six-pack on the upper slopes. But the gondola out of the village is not super-quick.

Queues The slopes above La Tania are relatively crowd-free, partly because they are not on the main Trois Vallées 'circuit'. But there may be morning queues for the gondola out of the village in peak season. The problem seems to be that it opens just in time for the ski school to pour on to it through their priority couloir, leaving everyone else waiting.

Terrain parks There is no local terrain park or half-pipe, but you can get to Courchevel's 'Family Park' fairly easily.

Snow reliability Good snow-cover down to Praz-Juget is usual all season.

SKI AMIS

Catered Chalets in Superb Locations

020 3411 5439
www.skiamis.com

Snowmaking covers the green run and the whole of the blue run back to the village; if, despite this, the runs are icy in the afternoon, you have the option of riding the gondola down.

Experts The mountainside above La Tania is steep enough to be interesting without being scary. The Dou des Lanches chairlift serves a lot of good off-piste terrain as well as an easy black piste. The Jean Blanc and Jockeys blacks from Loze to Le Praz are challenging more because of length than gradient.

Intermediates There are three lovely, long, undulating intermediate runs back through the trees to La Tania. There's little difference in gradient between the blue and the red and even the green Plan Fontaine is great

fun and popular. The red Murettes run to Le Praz is of genuine red steepness, winding and interesting. On the higher slopes both the red Lanches and the black Dou des Lanches pistes are excellent and challenging (the latter is often groomed and makes a great fast cruise when it is).

Beginners There is a good beginner area and lift right in the village, and children are well catered for. But there's a lot of through-traffic on the main slope. There's now a more snow-sure area at the top of the gondola (Praz-Juget). But the Plan Fontaine green run to the village is not an ideal progression run – fairly narrow, not all that gentle, winding and popular with better skiers whizzing down it as if it were a race course. And the step up to

LA TANIA
COURCHEVEL & VAL D'ISÈRE

❄ Our own friendly crèche
❄ Twin, triple or family rooms
❄ Fully qualified UK nannies
❄ Sunday flights & short transfers

BOOK ONLINE
100% FINANCIAL PROTECTION

32 years of catered chalet holidays

Any questions?

LeSki
the chalet specialists

01484 954397
www.leski.com

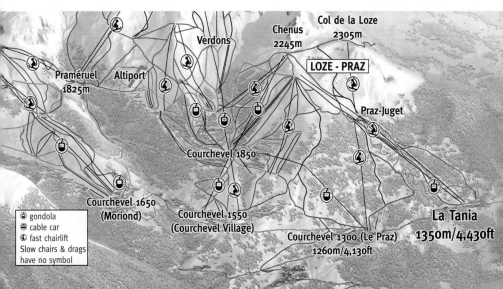

Pierre ⓢ Vacances
Holidays made for me

Best price
guarantee
for ski in/out
budget studios
up to spacious
3 bedroom
apartments

pierreetvacances.co.uk

mh✳ Mountain Heaven

Heavenly
Skiing...
at down to earth prices

· Superb catered & self catered accommodation ·
· Great ski areas in the French & Swiss Alps ·
· Snow secure resorts · We only have on/near piste locations ·
· Fantastic prices & no hidden extras ·

0151 625 1921
www.mountainheaven.co.uk

KEY FACTS

Resort	1350m
	4,430ft

Trois Vallées	
Slopes	1260-3230m
	4,130-10,600ft
Lifts	180
Pistes	600km
	373 miles
Green	13%
Blue	39%
Red	38%
Black	10%
Snowmaking	33%

Courchevel/ La Tania only	
Slopes	1260-2740m
	4,130-8,990ft
Lifts	58
Pistes	150km
	93 miles
Green	20%
Blue	36%
Red	35%
Black	9%

the blue run back to the village is quite a big one.

Snowboarding It's easy to get around on boarder-friendly gondolas and chairlifts, avoiding drags.

Cross-country There are 67km of trails in the Courchevel/La Tania area, many of them through the woods.

Mountain restaurants Bouc Blanc (0479 088026), near the top of the gondola out of La Tania, is one of our favourites in the whole Trois Vallées – and much cheaper than Courchevel alternatives. It has friendly table-service in two wood-clad dining rooms, good food (reliable plat du jour) and wine (good-value pichets) and a big terrace. We had three very satisfactory meals here in 2014. Multiple reporters endorse our view, but occasionally find service stretched.

Schools and guides Highly regarded British school New Generation gets consistently good reports – 'the best I have come across', 'absolutely fabulous,' 'brilliant' – and this year 'James gave me drills that produced a

marked increase in confidence and speed'. A 2013 reporter had a 'very good' instructor from Ski Excel (private lessons only). Past reports on Magic Snowsports have been good, those on the ESF a bit patchy.'

Families La Tania is popular with families looking for a quiet and convenient base, and a child-friendly atmosphere – 'excellent for our three-family group of 14, which included all ability levels'. La Tanière des Croës (formerly Chez Nounours) kindergarten takes both skiing and non-skiing children from four months to five years old. The chalets of UK tour operator Le Ski are open to family bookings, and it runs its own nursery in the resort. A list of babysitters is available from the tourist office. New Generation ski school takes children from the age of four.

STAYING THERE

Chalets There are lots of catered chalets here, mostly dotted around in the woods above the resort centre. Ski Amis has seven chalets sleeping from 8 to 28, and all except one with outdoor hot tubs – we have enjoyed very comfortable stays in their premium service chalets Elliot and (last winter) Balkiss. Major Courchevel operator Le Ski has three chalets here; a small one in a great piste-side location, and two largish ones that are particularly child-friendly, with family rooms. Mountain Heaven has a 10-bed chalet, new to its programme this season, with sauna and a TV room separate from the living room. Crystal

BRIAN WALKER

You get a good view of the Dou des Lanches black run and the off-piste beside it from the excellent Bouc Blanc ➔

↑ Not all of La Tania is quite as cute as the chalet quarter, immersed in the woods

SNOWPIX.COM / CHRIS GILL

Phone numbers
From abroad use the prefix +33 and omit the initial '0' of the phone number

TOURIST OFFICE
www.latania.com

has a 15-bed chalet. Alpine Elements now runs the central 165-bed hotel Montana as a chalet hotel; pool, sauna, steam, gym and hot tub.
Apartments There are no major 'smart apartment' developments. Ski Amis offers a broad range of properties, including self-catering chalets as well as regular apartments. Pierre & Vacances has the recently refurbished residences Christiania and Britania. These and other options are available from the major French specialist agencies – Peak Retreats, Erna Low and Lagrange – and from mainstream

operators such as Crystal. There is a deli, bakery and small supermarket.
Eating out In recent years the favourite restaurant among our reporters has been the Taïga, over the road from the main village: 'wonderful food'; 'popular, busy, very good'; 'fish soup outstanding'; 'reasonably priced'. This year we have a striking lack of reports, and we hear that the place may have hit a bad patch early in the season; more reports, please. We've had excellent meals at the Michelin-starred Farçon, but in the evening the prices are of course quite high. In very sharp contrast, the Ski Lodge does good-value fast food.
Après-ski It's quite lively at close of play, but again the choice is limited. The Ski Lodge has long been the focal après-ski place and has live bands – 'lively', 'friendly'. The Chrome bar has regular live music.
Off the slopes The place is very small and limited. However, tobogganing, snowshoeing, dog sledding, snowmobiling and paragliding are possibilities. There are some cleared paths and snowshoe routes. Non-skiers can go up the gondola or take the bus to Courchevel to meet skiing friends for lunch.

UK PACKAGES
Alpine Action, Alpine Answers, Alpine Elements, Crystal, Erna Low, Family Friendly Skiing, Igoski, Interactive Resorts, Le Ski, Mountain Beds, Mountain Heaven, Nick Ski, Oxford Ski Co, Peak Retreats, Pierre & Vacances, PowderBeds, Silver Ski, Ski Amis, Ski Beat, Ski Dazzle, Ski Deep, Ski Expectations, Ski France, Ski Hame, Ski Independence, Ski Line, Ski Magic, Ski Weekend, Skitracer, Snoworks, Thomson

La Tania

Build your own shortlist: www.wheretoskiandsnowboard.com

Selected chalets in La Tania

ADVERTISEMENT

SKI AMIS *www.skiamis.com*   T **0203 411 5439**

- 7 chalets to sleep from 8 to 28 people – room bookings also possible
- Hot-tubs, free WIFI and satellite TV
- Excellent catering with full English breakfast every day, afternoon tea and 3 or 4 course evening meal
- Unlimited good quality wine

sales@skiamis.com

SKI AMIS

↑ CHALET ELLIOT

CHALET TITANIA ↑

The Three Valleys

With the swankiest resort in the Alps at one end, and the highest at the other: the biggest lift-linked ski area in the world

Despite competing claims, notably from the Portes du Soleil, in practical terms the Trois Vallées cannot be beaten for sheer quantity of lift-linked terrain. There is nowhere like it for a mileage-hungry intermediate – but it has a lot to offer beginners and experts too. What's more, the area undersells itself: it expanded many years ago into a fourth valley, the Maurienne south of Val Thorens.

The Trois Vallées area is dealt with in six chapters on the four major resorts – Courchevel, Méribel, Les Menuires and Val Thorens – plus St-Martin-de-Belleville and La Tania.

None of the resorts is cheap, but of the major resorts **Les Menuires** is cheapest. The centre of the resort is an eyesore, but new developments have been built in chalet style. Les Menuires has an excellent position for exploration of the Trois Vallées.

Down the valley from Les Menuires is **St-Martin-de-Belleville**, a charming traditional village that has been expanded sympathetically. It has good-value accommodation and lift links towards Les Menuires and Méribel.

Up rather than down the Belleville valley from Les Menuires, at 2300m **Val Thorens** is the highest resort in the Alps – and at 3230m the top of its slopes is the high point of the Trois Vallées. The snow in this area is almost always good, and it includes two glaciers where good snow is guaranteed. But the setting is bleak, and the lifts are vulnerable to closure in bad weather. It's a purpose-built resort and very convenient – and better looking than Les Menuires.

Méribel is a multi-part resort. The highest component, **Méribel-Mottaret**, is perfectly placed for access to any part of the Trois Vallées. **Méribel** itself, 200m lower, is a British favourite – the most attractive of the main resorts, built in chalet style on a steep hillside.

Pierre & Vacances
Holidays made for me

Best price guarantee for ski in/out budget studios up to spacious 3 bedroom apartments

pierreetvacances.co.uk

Kaliblue

One of two points where the slopes of Méribel meet those of Courchevel – La Saulire; Méribel meets Les Menuires at five or six points →

SNOWPIX.COM / CHRIS GILL

Ski Collection

Major Resorts
Expert knowledge

4★ ski apartments with spa

SkiCollection.co.uk
0844 576 0175
ABTA Bonded W5537

Parts of the resort are very convenient for the slopes and the village centre; parts are not. The growing hamlet of **Méribel-Village** has its own chairlift into the system. You can also stay in the valley town of **Brides-les-Bains**.

Courchevel has four parts, which have recently been rebranded. Courchevel (formerly Courchevel 1850) is among the most fashionable and expensive resorts in the Alps. The other parts – Le Praz, Courchevel-Village (formerly 1550) and Courchevel-Moriond (formerly 1650) – are much less expensive. Many people rate the slopes in the Courchevel valley the best in the Trois Vallées.

La Tania was built for the 1992 Olympics, just off the minor road linking Courchevel to Méribel. It has now grown into an attractive, car-free collection of chalets and apartment blocks set among the trees, and is popular with families. It has good nursery slopes and good intermediate runs in the woods above.

The Three Valleys

345

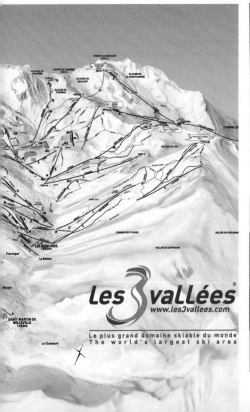

Les 3 vallées®
www.les3vallees.com

Le plus grand domaine skiable du monde
The world's largest ski area

NEW GENERATION
SKI & SNOWBOARD SCHOOL ●●●●●

LITTLE PEOPLE WITH A LOT OF SPEED?
Marco spends his summers working at Formula 1. And winters keeping your speed demons safe on the slopes of the Three Valleys.

Courchevel ● La Tania ● Méribel
Tel: 0844 770 4733 www.skinewgen.com

Build your own shortlist: **www.wheretoskiandsnowboard.com**

SNOWPIX.COM / CHRIS GILL

Tignes

Stark apartment blocks and a bleak, treeless setting are the prices you pay for the high, snow-sure slopes and varied terrain

RATINGS

The mountains

Extent	★★★★★
Fast lifts	★★★
Queues	★★★★
Terrain p'ks	★★★
Snow	★★★★★
Expert	★★★★★
Intermediate	★★★★★
Beginner	★★
Boarder	★★★★★
X-country	★★★
Restaurants	★★★
Schools	★★★★
Families	★★★

The resort

Charm	★
Convenience	★★★★
Scenery	★★★
Eating out	★★★★
Après-ski	★★★
Off-slope	★★

RPI 115

lift pass	£210
ski hire	£120
lessons	£100
food & drink	£155
total	**£585**

NEWS

2013/14: The first phase of the MGM/CGH Kalinda village at Tignes 1800 opened in December 2013. The rest of the development will open for 2015/16.

The gondola from Tignes-le-Lac has been replaced by a faster 10-seat one with easier access from the slope.

Tignespace, a sports hall/conference centre/concert hall in Le Lac, reopened after a revamp.

The Suites du Nevada hotel was upgraded to a 5-star.

+ Good snow guaranteed for a long season; about the best Alpine bet

+ One of the best areas in the world for lift-served off-piste runs

+ Huge amount of varied terrain

+ Lots of lodgings near the slopes

+ Efforts to make the resort villages more welcoming are paying off

– Resort architecture not to everyone's taste (including ours)

– Bleak, treeless setting with lifts prone to closure in bad weather

– Still a few long, slow chairlifts

– Beginners need an area pass to get to long green runs

The appeal of Tignes is simple: good snow, spread over a wide area of varied terrain shared with Val d'Isère. The altitude of Tignes is crucial: a forecast of 'rain up to 2000m' means 'fresh snow down to village level in Tignes' (or at least to Tignes 2100, as they are now trying to rebrand the main resort).

We prefer to stay in Val, which is a more human place. But in many ways Tignes 2100 makes the better base: appreciably higher, more convenient, surrounded by intermediate terrain, and with quick access to the Grande Motte glacier. And the case gets stronger as the resort tries to make the place more attractive and as more traditional chalet-style buildings appear.

The lift system has improved, too, with a burst of fast chairs on the western side of the Tignes bowl a few years ago. But investment has stalled since then, and there are still a few key links that need upgrading.

THE RESORT

Tignes was created before the French discovered the benefits of making purpose-built resorts look acceptable. But things are improving, and the villages are gradually acquiring a more traditional look and feel.

Tignes-le-Lac is the hub of the resort and is itself split into two sub-resorts: Le Rosset and Le Bec-Rouge. It's at the point where these two meet – a snowy pedestrian area, with valley traffic passing through a tunnel beneath – that the lifts are concentrated: a powerful new gondola towards Tovière and Val d'Isère, and a fast six-pack up the western slopes. There is also a suburb built on the lower slopes known as Les Almes. A nursery slope separates Le Rosset from the fourth component part, the group of apartment blocks called Le Lavachet, below which there are good fast lifts up both sides.

Val Claret is 2km up the valley, beyond the lake. From there, fast chairs head up towards Val d'Isère, up the western slopes opposite and to the Grande Motte. An underground funicular also serves the Grande Motte.

Beside the road along the valley to

the lifts is a ribbon of development in traditional style, named Grande Motte (after the peak). Val Claret is built on two levels, which are linked by a couple of (unreliable) indoor elevators, stairs and hazardous paths.

Down the valley from the main villages (which are becoming known as Tignes 2100) are two smaller places. Tignes 1800 (which used to be called Tignes-les-Boisses) – set in the trees beside the road up – is in the

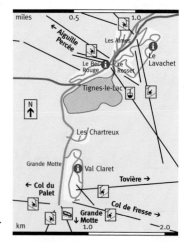

KEY FACTS

Resort	2100m
	6,890ft

Espace Killy

Slopes	1550-3455m
	5,090-11,340ft
Lifts	91
Pistes	300km
	186 miles
Green	14%
Blue	44%
Red	25%
Black	17%
Snowmaking	
	974 guns

Tignes only

Slopes	1550-3455m
	5,090-11,340ft
Lifts	45
Pistes	150km
	93 miles

LIFT PASSES

Espace Killy

Prices in €

Age	1-day	6-day
under 14	41	202
14 to 64	51	253
65 plus	41	202

Free Under 5, over 75
Beginner Six free lifts
Notes Covers Tignes and Val d'Isère; half-day and pedestrian passes; family discounts; 5-day+ passes valid for a day in the Three Valleys and a day in Paradiski (La Plagne-Les Arcs); 2-day+ pass gives free access to pool and ice rink
Alternative pass Tignes only

OT TIGNES / MONICA DALMASSO

It isn't pretty but it is snowy. The hideous blocks of Le Bec Rouge are in the foreground and Val Claret is in the distance →

midst of a 150-million-euro redevelopment, with the new MGM-built Kalinda Village being built. The first stage opened in December 2013, and the second stage is due to be ready for the 2015/16 season. Tignes-les-Brévières is a renovated old village at the lowest point of the slopes – a favourite lunch spot, and a friendly place to stay (but there's no bus service to the other Tignes 'villages'). Big gondolas from both these places arrive at the same point on the slopes.

VILLAGE CHARM ★☆☆☆☆
Functional, not fancy
Some of Tignes-le-Lac's smaller original eyesore buildings in the central part have been successfully revamped in chalet style. And some attractive new buildings have been added, both in the centre and on the fringes. But the blocks overlooking the lake from Le Bec-Rouge will remain monstrous until they are demolished. The buildings in the main part of Val Claret (Centre) are uncompromisingly 1960s style and set on a shelf above the valley floor.

So, if it's more charm you seek, stay in Les Brévières or 1800.

CONVENIENCE ★★★★☆
Good all rounder
Location isn't crucial, as a regular, free, 24-hour bus service (praised by reporters) connects all the villages except Les Brévières – but during the day the route runs along the bottom

of Val Claret, leaving Val Claret Centre residents with a climb.

A lift or ski run is never more than a few minutes' walk away in Le Lac. 'Convenience was the main reason we chose to go to Tignes for our holiday this year, and we were not disappointed,' said a recent reporter.

SCENERY ★★★☆☆
Great from the glacier
Tignes is in a high, bleak, treeless bowl; when the sun shines, the rugged mountain terrain is splendid, especially from the glacial heights of the Grande Motte.

THE MOUNTAINS

The area's great weakness is that it can become unusable in bad weather. There are no woodland runs except immediately above Tignes 1800 and Tignes-les-Brévières. Heavy snow produces widespread avalanche risk, and wind closes the higher chairs.

Piste classification here isn't perfect, but it is more reliable than in Val d'Isère, and signposting is clear. But we've had complaints that lift and piste closing time information is unreliable (and that sometimes information at the lift doesn't match the piste map).

We also had a complaint this year from someone who boarded a lift to ski a blue run only to find that it was closed due to avalanche danger. The

Ski Total

ARE HERE IN
Tignes

▷ **Quality chalets**
▷ **Top locations**
▷ **Excellent value**
▷ **17 more resorts**

skitotal.com
01483 791 933

only option was a mogulled red: 'There should have been a warning sign at the bottom.'

EXTENT OF THE SLOPES ★★★★★
High, snow-sure and varied
Tignes and Val d'Isère share a huge area of slopes known as L'Espace Killy. Locally, Tignes' biggest asset is the **Grande Motte** – and the runs from, as well as on, the glacier. An underground funicular from Val Claret whizzes you up to over 3000m in seven minutes. There are blue, red and black runs to play on up here, as well as beautiful long runs back to the resort.

The main lifts towards Val d'Isère are efficient: a high-capacity gondola from Le Lac to **Tovière**, and a fast chair from Val Claret to **Col de Fresse**. You can head back to Tignes from either lift: the return from Tovière to Tignes-le-Lac is via a steep black run, but there is an easier (though often crowded) blue run to Val Claret.

Going up the opposite side of the valley takes you to a quieter area of predominantly east-facing slopes split into two main sectors, linked in both directions – **Col du Palet** and the **Aiguille Percée**. Several years ago, this whole mountainside was at last given

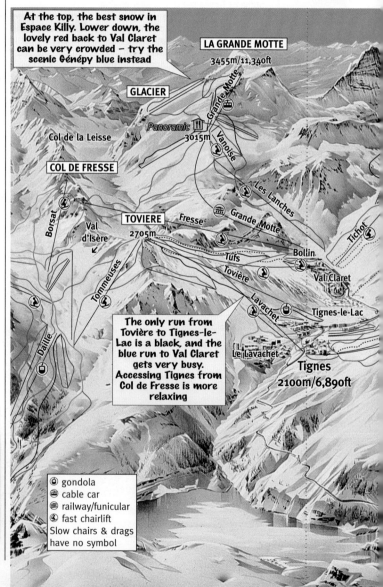

At the top, the best snow in Espace Killy. Lower down, the lovely red back to Val Claret can be very crowded – try the scenic Génépy blue instead

LA GRANDE MOTTE
3455m/11,340ft

GLACIER

Grande Motte

Panoramic 3015m

Vanoise

Col de la Leisse

COL DE FRESSE

Les Lanches

Borsat

Val d'Isère

TOVIERE
2705m

Fresse

Grande Motte

Tichot

Tommeuses

Tufs

Bollin

Tovière

Val Claret

Lavachet

Tignes-le-Lac

Daille

The only run from Tovière to Tignes-le-Lac is a black, and the blue run to Val Claret gets very busy. Accessing Tignes from Col de Fresse is more relaxing

Le Lavachet

Tignes
2100m/6,890ft

🚠 gondola
🚡 cable car
🚞 railway/funicular
🚣 fast chairlift
Slow chairs & drags have no symbol

Pierre & Vacances
premium

Perfect spacious apartments with spas and swimming pools.

pierreetvacances.co.uk

some of the fast lifts it had needed for years – but investment has stalled and some chairs still need modernizing. You can descend from the Aiguille Percée to Tignes-les-Brévières or Tignes 1800 on blue, red or black runs. There are efficient gondolas back.

FAST LIFTS ★★★☆☆
Improved but not good enough
Fast chairs and gondolas get you up the mountain from most parts of the resort. And there are some fast chairs higher up, too. But a few key slow ones remain that could do with being upgraded, including the Col des Ves

chair at the south end of the Col du Palet sector and the Aiguille Percée chair above Tignes-le-Lac. The chairs above Tignes-les-Brévières and Tignes 1800 are also old and slow, and much in need of upgrading.

QUEUES ★★★★☆
Very few
Recent reporters have experienced very few queues, even in February half-term. But if snow low down is poor, the Grande Motte funicular can generate queues; the fast chairs in parallel with it are often quicker, despite the longer ride time. These

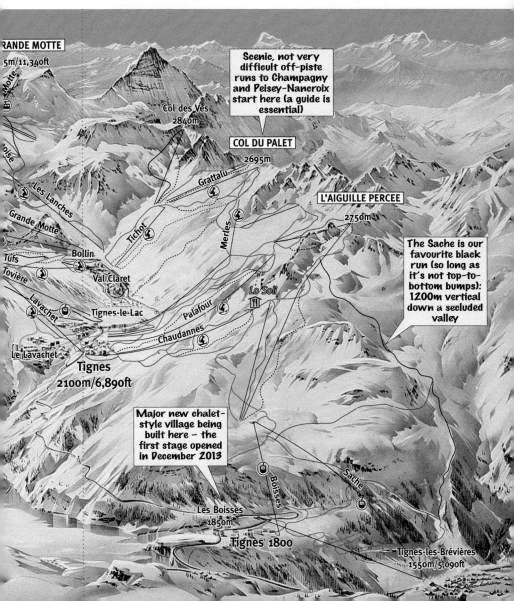

GRANDE MOTTE
5m/11,340ft

Scenic, not very difficult off-piste runs to Champagny and Peisey-Nancroix start here (a guide is essential)

Col des Ves
2840m

COL DU PALET
2695m

Grattalu

L'AIGUILLE PERCEE
2750m

The Sache is our favourite black run (so long as it's not top-to-bottom bumps): 1200m vertical down a secluded valley

Les Lanches

Grande Motte

Tichot

Merles

Bollin

Tufs

Toviere

Val Claret

Lo Soli

Lavachet

Tignes-le-Lac

Palafour

Le Lavachet

Chaudannes

Tignes
2100m/6,890ft

Major new chalet-style village being built here – the first stage opened in December 2013

Boisses

Sache

Les Boisses
1850m

Tignes 1800

Tignes-les-Brévières
1550m/5,090ft

SKIWORLD

Catered chalets, hotels and self catering apartments in

Europe, USA and Canada

skiworld.co.uk

08444 930 430

ABTA V2151 ATOL 2036

SNOWPIX.COM / CHRIS GILL

The upper part of Val Claret is very convenient for the slopes, and there are fast chairs to whisk you in three directions from here ↓

lifts jointly shift a lot of people, with the result that the red Double M run down to Val Claret can be unpleasantly crowded (the roundabout Génépy blue is a much quieter option). The worst queues now are for the cable car on the glacier – half-hour waits are common. Of course, if higher lifts are closed by heavy snow or high winds, the lifts on the lower slopes have big queues. Otherwise there are usually very few problems; crowded pistes can be more of an issue, and the blue Henri piste from Tovière to Val Claret and red Double M mentioned above are often unpleasantly crowded.

TERRAIN PARKS ★★★☆☆
Summer and winter options
Tignes was one of the first French resorts to build a terrain park, and it hosted four successive European Winter X Games until ESPN decided they were not financially viable. The park is beneath the Grattalu chair on Col du Palet and has rails and kickers split into green, blue, red and black levels ('Terrific – I thoroughly enjoyed the range of obstacles,' says a 2014

visitor), a snowcross course ('great fun') and an airbag jump. In the summer the park doubles in size and moves up to the Grande Motte for freestyle camps. The 120m-long winter super-pipe is right at the bottom of the mountain in Val Claret, which means if it's open and you have the energy to hike, you can ride it for free. There is also the Gliss park at town level in Le Lac with airbag and mini-snowcross, so a day's freestyle for free is definitely an option.

SNOW RELIABILITY ★★★★★
Difficult to beat
Tignes has summer as well as winter skiing on its glacier area. And the resort height of 2100m generally means good snow-cover right back to base for most of the long winter season – November to May. The west-facing runs down from Col de Fresse and Tovière to Val Claret suffer from the afternoon sun, although they have serious snowmaking. Some of the lower east-facing and south-east-facing slopes on the other side of the valley can suffer late in the season, too. Grooming is good – 'They push the snow around so it lasts forever,' says a 2014 visitor. But we had a couple of complaints this year: of moguls appearing on blue runs by lunchtime but not being bashed; and of black runs that were not 'naturides' being allowed to develop big moguls.

FOR EXPERTS ★★★★★
An excellent choice
Tignes has converted many of its black runs into 'naturides', which means they are never groomed (a neat way of saving money!), but they are marked, patrolled and avalanche protected. Many of them are not especially steep (eg the Ves run – promoted from red status and now renamed after the local freeride hero Guerlain Chicherit). Perhaps the most serious challenge is the long black run from Tovière to Tignes-le-Lac, with steep, usually heavily mogulled sections (the top part, Pâquerettes, is now a naturide, but the bottom part, Trolles, is a normal black). Parts of this run get a lot of afternoon sun. Our favourite black run (still a 'normal' black) is the Sache, from the Aiguille Percée down a secluded valley to Tignes-les-Brévières. It can become very heavily mogulled, especially at the bottom – you can avoid this section by taking the red

skitracer*

CHALETS, HOTELS
& APARTMENTS
Call us today
020 8600 1650
skitracer.com

TIGNES
CHOOSE FROM 153 CATERED CHALETS, APARTMENTS & HOTELS

Skiline.co.uk

CALL US ON 020 8313 3999

snowchateaux*
the catered chalet experience

"top 5 places to stay"
The Daily Telegraph

* France's top resorts
* Ski in / Ski out
  catered chalets
* Hot tubs, saunas,
  games rooms...

GETTING THERE

Air Chambéry 145km/ 90 miles (2hr); Geneva 225km/140 miles (2hr45); Lyon 220km/ 135 miles (2hr45); Grenoble 210km/130 miles (2hr45)

Rail Bourg-St-Maurice (30km/19 miles); regular buses or taxi from station

UK PACKAGES

Absolutely Snow, Action Outdoors, Alpine Answers, Alpine Elements, Carrier, Club Med, Crystal, Crystal Finest, Erna Low, Esprit, Flexiski, Inghams, Inspired to Ski, Interactive Resorts, Lagrange, Mark Warner, Mountain Beds, Mountainsun, Neilson, Oxford Ski Co, Peak Retreats, Pierre & Vacances, Powder White, PowderBeds, Ski Amis, Ski Bespoke, Ski Club Freshtracks, Ski Collection, Ski Expectations, Ski France, Ski Independence, Ski Supreme, Ski Total, Ski Weekend, Skibug, Skitracer, Skiweekends. com, Skiworld, Snow Finders, Snow-wise, Snowchateaux, Snoworks, Snowpod, STC, Thomson

Arcosses piste option part-way down.

But it is the off-piste possibilities that make Tignes such a draw for experts, and the schools organize off-piste groups. See the feature panel overleaf for a few of the off-piste runs. The bizarre French form of heli-skiing is available here: mountaintop drops are forbidden, but from Tovière you can ski down towards the Lac du Chevril to be retrieved by chopper.

FOR INTERMEDIATES ★★★★★
One of the best

For keen intermediate piste-bashers who like varied terrain and lots of it, the Espace Killy is one of the world's best areas.

Tignes' local slopes are ideal intermediate terrain. The runs on the Grande Motte glacier nearly always have superb snow. The runs from the top of the cable car are bizarrely classified red and black, but they are wide and mostly easy on usually fabulous snow, and could easily be blues. The Leisse run down to the chairlift of the same name is classified black and can get very mogulled, but usually has good snow. The red run all the way back to town is a delightful long cruise – though often crowded. The roundabout blue (Génépy) is much gentler and quieter.

From Tovière, the blue Henri run to Val Claret is an enjoyable cruise and generally well groomed. But, again, it can get very crowded.

There's lots to do on the other side of the valley, too, and the runs down from the Aiguille Percée to Tignes 1800 and Les Brévières are both scenic and fun. There are red and blue options, and adventurous intermediates shouldn't miss the beautiful Sache black run. The runs from the Aiguille Percée to Tignes-le-Lac are gentle, wide blues.

FOR BEGINNERS ★★★★★
Good nursery slopes, but ...

The nursery slopes of Tignes-le-Lac and Le Lavachet (which meet at the top) are excellent – convenient, snow-sure, gentle, free of through-traffic and served by a slow chair and a drag. The ones at Val Claret are less appealing: an unpleasantly steep slope within the village served by a drag, and a less convenient slope served by the fast Bollin chair. All of these lifts are free.

Although there are some fairly easy blues on the west side of Tignes, for long green runs you have to go over to the Val d'Isère sector. You need an Espace Killy pass to use them, and to get back to Tignes you have a choice between the blue run from Col de Fresse (which has a tricky start) or riding the gondola down from Tovière. And in poor weather, the high Tignes valley is an intimidatingly bleak place – enough to make any wavering beginner retreat to a bar with a book.

FOR BOARDERS ★★★★★
One of the best

Tignes has always been a popular destination for snowboarders. Lots of easily accessible off-piste and lower prices than Val d'Isère are the main attractions, and quite a few top UK snowboarders make this their winter home. There are a few flat areas (avoid Génépy and Myrtilles), but the lift system relies more on chairs and gondolas than drags. There are long, wide pistes to blast down, such as Grattalu, Carline and Henri, with acres of powder between them to play in. And the backside of Col de Fresse in Val d'Isère is a natural playground. There are two specialist snowboard schools (Snocool and Alliance) and a Welsh-run snowboarder chalet (www. dragonlodge.com). Go to the Snowpark shop in Tignes-le-Lac for all your equipment needs.

Tignes

351

Build your own shortlist: www.wheretoskiandsnowboard.com

TIGNES 1800 LES BOISSES

NEW 4★ luxury apartments ideal for families

peakretreats.co.uk/tignes_les_boisses

⚓ABTA
ABTA No. W5537

peak retreats

FOR CROSS-COUNTRY ★★★☆☆
Interesting variety
The Espace Killy has 44km of cross-country trails, including 20km of tracks on the frozen Lac de Tignes, along the valley between Val Claret and Tignes-le-Lac, at Tignes 1800 and Les Brévières and up on the Grande Motte.

MOUNTAIN RESTAURANTS ★★★☆☆
A couple of good places
The mountain restaurants are not a highlight. And reporters complain about charges for the toilet: 'I have never been anywhere so bad.'
Editors' choice Lo Soli (0479 069863) at the top of the Chaudannes chair is a clear favourite. From its terrace there's a superb view (shared with the adjacent self-service Alpage) of the Grande Motte. A couple of 2014 reporters were disappointed with it but another thought it excellent – more reports please. The table-service bit of the Panoramic (0479 064721) at the top of the funicular competes: wonderful views, gourmet food with a wide-ranging menu including Savoyard dishes, pasta and grills.
Worth knowing about On the nursery slope above Val Claret, the Chalet du Bollin has been recommended. So have the pizzas at the self-service at the top of Tovière ('big enough to share'); there's a good-looking table-service section too. The big Panoramic self-service at the top of the funicular gets crowded, but has great views from its huge terrace.

There are lots of easily accessible places for lunch in the resorts. One ski-to-the-door favourite of ours in Le Lac is the hotel Montana, on the left as you descend from the Aiguille Percée. Others are the Ferme des 3 Capucines, a short walk down from the bottom of the Chaudannes and Paquis chairs, and the Arbina; a 2014 reporter recommends Lo Terrachu; see 'Eating out' for more on these three.

In Val Claret past recommendations include: the Pignatta for quality and

A MECCA FOR OFF-PISTE SKIERS

Tignes is renowned for offering some of the best lift-served off-piste skiing in the world. There is a tremendous choice, with runs to suit all levels, from intermediate skiers to fearless freeriders and off-piste experts. Here's just a small selection. Don't go without a guide.

*For a first experience of off-piste, **Lognan** is ideal. These slopes – down the mountainside between the pistes to Le Lac and the pistes to Val Claret – are broad and not very difficult.*

*One of our favourite routes is the **Tour de Pramecou**. After a few minutes' walking at the bottom of the Grande Motte glacier, you pass around a big rock called Pramecou. There is then a multitude of possibilities, varying in difficulty – so routes can be found for skiers of different abilities.*

***Petite Balme** is a run for good skiers only – access is easy but it leads to quite challenging north-facing slopes in real high-mountain terrain, far from the pistes.*

*To ski **Oreilles de Mickey** (Mickey's Ears) you start from Tovière and walk north along the ridge to the peak of Lavachet, where you get a great view of Tignes. The descent involves three long couloirs, narrow and pretty steep, that bring you back to Le Lavachet.*

*The best place to find good snow is the **Chardonnet** couloirs – they never get the sun. The route involves a 20-minute walk from the top of the Merles chairlift.*

*The **Vallons de la Sache** is one of the most famous routes – a descent of 1200m vertical down a breathtaking valley in the heart of the National Park, overlooked by the magnificent Sache glacier. Starting from the Aiguille Percée you enter a different world, high up in the mountains, far away from the ski lifts. You arrive down in Les Brévières, below the Tignes dam.*

*One of the big adventures is to go away from the Tignes ski area and all signs of civilization, starting from the Col du Palet. From there you can head for **Champagny** (linked to La Plagne's area) or **Peisey-Nancroix** (linked to Les Arcs' area) – both very beautiful runs, and not too difficult.*

SCHOOLS

ESF
t 0479 063028

Evolution 2
t 0479 083529

Snocool
t 0479 243094

333
t 0479 062088

Alliance
t 0645 120824
07753 219719 (UK)

New Generation
t 0479 010318
0844 770 4733 (UK)
www.skinewgen.com

BASS
t 0679 512405

Ultimate Snowsports
t 0624 714401

Ali Ross Skiing Clinics
t 01997 421909 (UK)

Classes (ESF prices)
6 days: €273

Private lessons
From €48 for 1hr

GUIDES

Bureau des Guides
t 0479 064276

CHILDCARE

Les Marmottons
t 0479 065167
From 30mnth

Piou Piou
t 0479 063028
Ages 3 to 5

Ski schools
From age 4

4-star self-catering apartments in France
Major resorts, expert knowledge

4-star luxury residence Le Telemark in Tignes Le Lac:

First-class facilities, great for families.
Doorstep skiing with direct access to Espace Killy.

Accommodation only or self-drive package deals
call us on 0844 576 0175 SkiCollection.co.uk

ABTA No.W5537

value, the Aspen Cafe for big portions and reasonable prices and Carline for convenience and speed.

At the extremity of the lift system, Les Brévières makes an obvious lunch stop. A short walk round the corner into the village brings you to places much cheaper than the two by the piste. Sachette, for example, is crammed with artefacts from mountain life. The Armailly is recommended for its 'fantastic food' and 'varied menu that didn't break the bank'.

SCHOOLS AND GUIDES ★★★★☆
Plenty of choice

There are over half-a-dozen schools, including two specialist snowboard schools, plus various independent instructors. Reporters advise that at busy times pre-booking is essential.

Worryingly, both the latest reports we've had on the ESF involved children being taught mainly in French even though the instructors spoke good English; two children did not attend for their last day as a result.

Another 2014 reporter's group thought New Generation – a British-run school with branches in several other resorts – was 'fantastic', with 'patient instructors'. We have had glowing past reports of a British-run snowboarding school, Alliance: 'Tuition appropriate to our requirements, improved our confidence and skills greatly.'.

333 got a glowing report a couple of years back: 'Best we've ever had, all gaining in confidence after a couple of hours.' Ultimate Snowsports was also praised for 'making the lessons fun and challenging for the children in our group'. Reports on Evolution 2 have been consistently positive: 'Had a fantastic instructor – we all advanced our technique and she had us on reds by day three, blacks on day four.' Ali Ross Skiing Clinics has been praised (5-day courses; pre-booking required).

FOR FAMILIES ★★★☆☆
Good facilities

Family specialist tour operator Esprit Ski runs chalets and comprehensive childcare here. We have had good reports in the past on the Marmottons kindergarten and British-run t4Nanny (www.t4nanny.com).

STAYING THERE

There's plenty to choose from, and more luxury options are appearing.
Chalets Catered chalets run by UK tour operators are mainly in Le Lac. Skiworld has eight chalets (some with sauna/steam room/hot tub) and the swanky 42-bed Ski Lodge Aigle with pool and sauna. Ski Total has a chalet hotel and 14 chalets, including some very smart places, lots with sauna and outdoor hot tub, some with pool, and two in their top-of-the-market Platinum range. Its Chalet Anne-Marie was 'strongly recommended' by a reporter. Family specialist Esprit has 10 chalets here, including the smart, 24-person Corniche, with sauna, steam room, hot tub and lifts to all floors.

Crystal has seven places from smart to budget, including two in its 'Finest' range. Inghams has four chalets (all with hot tub and sauna) and a 30-bed chalet hotel.

Snowchateaux has three chalets, including Chardon, which has been recommended by a regular reporter: 'Used to be Robert Maxwell's private apartment; lovely large lounge with floor-to-ceiling windows and a great view of the lake'; outdoor hot tub. And Mountainsun's chalet hotel Melezes in Tignes 1800 has been recommended for 'good food and big groups'.
Hotels The few hotels are small and concentrated in Le Lac.
★★★★Campanules (0479 063436) Smartly rustic chalet in upper Le Lac, with good restaurant.

ACTIVITIES

Indoor Wellness and fitness centres (pools, saunas, Turkish baths, hot tub, spa and beauty treatments, weight training), multi-sports hall, yoga, climbing wall, cinema, library, bowling, multimedia centre

Outdoor Dog sledding, mountaineering, ice climbing, ice driving, ice diving, ice rink, paragliding, snowmobiling, snowshoeing, biking on snow, helicopter flights, snow kiting

Phone numbers
From abroad use the prefix +33 and omit the initial '0' of the phone number

TOURIST OFFICE

www.tignes.net

****Village Montana** (0479 400144) Stylishly woody, on the east-facing slopes above Le Lac. Outdoor pool, sauna, steam, hot tub.
***Arbina** (0479 063478) Well-run place close to the lifts in Le Lac, with lunchtime terrace, crowded après-ski bar and one of the best restaurants.
***Diva** (0479 067000) Biggest in town. On lower level of Val Claret. Comfortable rooms. Sauna, steam.
***Gentiana** (0479 065246) In Le Lac. Friendly, pool, sauna, steam, hot tub. We stayed here happily last season.
***Lévanna** (0479 063294) Piste side in Le Lac. Comfortable; big hot tub.
***Marais** (0479 064006) Prettily furnished, simple hotel in Tignes 1800.
***Refuge** (0479 063664) Oldest hotel in Tignes (Le Lac).
Génépy (0479 065711) Simple, Dutch-run; in Les Brévières.
Apartments There are lots of apartments in all price ranges. Ski Collection, Ski Amis, Erna Low and Skitracer have a range of options. The growing number of smart places include Jhana, Ferme du Val Claret, Nevada and Pierre & Vacances' Ecrin des Neiges in Val Claret, and Télèmark and Residence Village Montana in Le Lac. In Les Brévières, the Belvédère has very smart large apartments and chalets with three to six bedrooms. And in Tignes 1800 the new MGM-built Kalinda Village apartments operated by CGH opened last season. All the above have access to pool, sauna etc, but at extra cost in some cases. Skiworld has 'flexible catered chalets' where you can choose what catering (if any) you want.

The supermarket at Le Lac is reported to be 'comprehensive but very expensive' – 'stock up in Bourg'.

EATING OUT ★★★★☆
Good places scattered about
The options in Le Lavachet are rather limited. Our favourite there is Ferme des 3 Capucines where we had a great dinner last season: lovely food, reasonably priced, good service, nice rustic surroundings – endorsed again by a 2014 visitor ('one to return to again and again'). And we have very positive reports of the good-value, British-run Brasero. Finding anywhere with some atmosphere is difficult in Le Lac, though the food in some of the better hotels is good, particularly the Chaumière in the Village Montana. The upstairs restaurant at the Arbina is

regularly recommended: 'very good service and excellent food'; 'the three-course fixed menu is good value'. We had an enjoyable dinner a couple of seasons ago in the simpler ground-floor brasserie. British-run Lo Terrachu was highly recommended in 2014: 'Right on the lake, ridiculously good value, excellent wild boar.' The 'atmospheric' Escale Blanche is popular, with good food, but reporters disagree over its value.

In Val Claret the Caveau is tipped for a special treat. Pepe 2000 has 'friendly staff' and 'lovely pizzas'.

APRES-SKI ★★★☆☆
Hidden away
Reporters agree that there is plenty going on if you know where to find it. Val Claret has some early-evening atmosphere and popular happy hours. The Drop Zone has live music, a good atmosphere and a dance floor. Grizzly's is cool but pricey. The Couloir has a whisky lounge. A recent reporter always ended the night in the 'decidedly nice' Melting Pot.

Le Lac is a natural focus for après-ski drinks. The lively Loop has a 'fun, relaxed atmosphere', 'good' live bands and a happy hour from 4pm to 6pm, while the Embuscade has 'good beer and music and attracts a slightly older crowd', said a happy 46-year-old. The bar of the hotel Arbina is our kind of spot – cosy with friendly service. It's a great place to sit outside and people-watch. The Alpaka Lodge bar is popular with Brits and a pleasant spot, especially if you manage to grab one of the sofas by the fire. Bagus Bar has been recommended. Jack's is a popular late haunt.

Vincents in Les Brévières has been tipped by a past reporter.

OFF THE SLOPES ★★☆☆☆
Good leisure centre
Tignes is not a resort for those who do not want to use the slopes. And some activities get booked up quickly – a reporter said it was impossible to find a free dog sledding slot in April. The ice skating on the lake includes a 500m circuit as well as a conventional rink. This and the pools of the Lagon leisure centre (various pools, slides, wellness and fitness facilities, and praised by reporters) are free to use with a lift pass for two days or more. A reporter's kids 'really enjoyed' the bowling at Tignes-le-Lac.

Val Cenis Vanoise

A fair-sized mountain above an unspoiled valley, with a row of unpretentious base villages offering attractively low prices

355

TOP 10 RATINGS

Extent	★★★
Fast lifts	★★★
Queues	★★★★
Snow	★★★
Expert	★★
Intermediate	★★★★
Beginner	★★★★
Charm	★★★
Convenience	★★★
Scenery	★★★

RPI	80
lift pass	£140
ski hire	£95
lessons	£60
food & drink	£120
total	**£415**

OT VAL CENIS / L COLLINET

Handsome stone houses in the village of Lanslebourg, one of the three main places to stay ↓

- ➕ Prices well below the French norm
- ➕ Varied slopes with fairly reliable snow – most slopes face north
- ➕ Some high-quality apartments at attractive rates

- ➖ Still some slow old lifts
- ➖ Little to amuse experts on piste
- ➖ Widely separated sectors of slopes
- ➖ Quiet at night

Val Cenis Vanoise is the ski area shared by three quiet, traditional villages in the remote and unspoiled Haute Maurienne valley. It's a modest-sized area, but packs in a lot of variety. Lots of comfortable apartments at attractive prices.

THE RESORT

South of the Massif de la Vanoise, which contains so many big-name resorts, is the Haute Maurienne – the high eastern end of the great curving valley of the Arc. Its villages are marketed under the name Haute Maurienne Vanoise. Two of those villages work under the name Val Cenis. And the ski area they share with Termignon is called Val Cenis Vanoise. Confused? You will be ...

There are six main lift bases: the first resort you come to is Termignon; 6km on is Lanslebourg; then there's Les Champs, a cluster of new residences with a lift and the other necessities of life; then Lanslevillard, which has one main lift base on the outskirts and another nearer the centre; and finally its suburb, Le Haut, which has the sixth lift.

If you fancy taking a peek at the other side of the French skiing coin, 40km down the road at Orelle is a gondola into the slopes of Val Thorens and the Trois Vallées.

Outstanding value French Alpine resort

VAL CENIS VANOISE

A FAMILY FAVOURITE

Holiday packages from **£165**pp

- 125km snow sure slopes
- Perfect for beginners and intermediates

0844 576 0173

⊕ABTA
ABTA No W5537

peak retreats
co.uk

KEY FACTS

Resort	1300-1460m
	4,270-4,790ft
Slopes	1300-2800m
	4,270-9,190ft
Lifts	27
Pistes	125km
	78 miles
Green	16%
Blue	33%
Red	42%
Black	9%
Snowmaking	
	200 guns

UK PACKAGES

Crystal, Crystal Finest, Erna Low, Lagrange, MGS, Peak Retreats, Ski Line, Thomson **Termignon** Erna Low, Lagrange, Peak Retreats

Village charm The villages are not chocolate-box pretty but solidly traditional. Lanslebourg is spread along the RN6 road, with no real focus. Lanslevillard is more captivating – less regularly arranged and with more character. The valley doesn't get a lot of sun in midwinter.

Convenience It's not difficult to find lodgings that are more-or-less ski-in, even if they are plod-out. From Les Champs you can walk to the villages either side, but it's along the road.

Scenery The slopes are attractively wooded, and the Haute Maurienne gives a sense of unspoiled wilderness.

THE MOUNTAINS

There are half a dozen descents on the prettily wooded lower slopes, but most pistes are on the open upper slopes. Some blues are tough in parts.

Slopes From each of the lift bases there are fast lifts up to the treeline at mid-mountain. There are three identifiable sectors. The main network of runs on the upper slopes is above Lanslevillard. There are high-altitude links between this sector and the slopes around Col du Mont Cenis, above Lanslebourg. A long fast chair then links this sector to the slopes above Termignon. There is a winding blue piste back, but it is a pretty tedious affair, and downloading on the same chair is more attractive.

Fast lifts Not a strong point: most of the lifts out of the valley are fast, but many upper ones are not.

Queues We lack recent high-season reports, but visitors in January, March and April had few problems.

Terrain parks There is a snow park and a snowcross. Reports welcome.

Snow reliability Most of the runs are north-facing, and there is snowmaking on the runs to each of the lift bases.

Experts There are few challenges on-piste. From the top station there is a good black. But there is a lot to do off-piste – routes from virtually all the upper lifts, some staying within the lift system, some ending up outside it. But we hear the forests on the lower slopes are out of bounds.

Intermediates There are intermediate runs all over the mountain, allowing for some top-to-bottom cruises of up to 1400m vertical. To get the best out of the area you have to be prepared to handle some long draglifts.

Beginners Termignon and Lanslevillard have good nursery slopes next to the villages – and the latter has green runs down the length of the gondola from Le Haut. Then there's the splendid green from the Col du Mont Cenis to the valley, down the hairpins of the summer road to Italy.

Snowboarding Beginners should stay in Lanslevillard to avoid some long drags on the upper slopes.

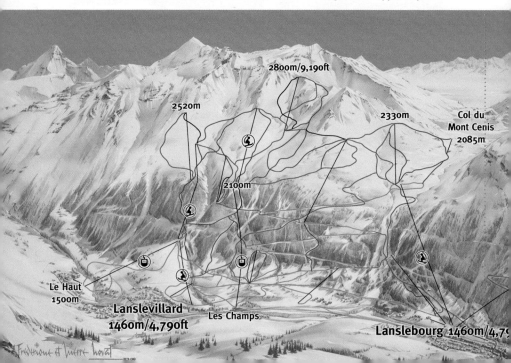

2800m/9,190ft
2520m
2330m
Col du Mont Cenis 2085m
2100m
Le Haut 1500m
Lanslevillard 1460m/4,790ft
Les Champs
Lanslebourg 1460m/4,79

Cross-country There are around 27km of trails locally, but enthusiasts will want to head 10km up the valley for the fab 130km of trails at Bessans.

Mountain restaurants There are just enough places, mostly at the mid-mountain lift junctions, marked but not named on the resort piste map. 'More friendly and hospitable than in most French resorts,' says one reporter whose favourite was the Arolle, above Termignon. Other reporters favour the Relais du Col at Col du Mont Cenis – 'delicious lunch' – and La Fema at the top of the Vieux Moulin gondola.

Schools and guides We have generally good reports on the local branch of the ESF, though there are dissenting voices. Not surprisingly in a French-oriented resort, lack of good spoken English is an occasional problem.

Families 'A good resort,' says a reporter whose children particularly enjoyed the bowling in Lanslevillard.

STAYING THERE

Hotels The best in principle is the 3-star Moulin de Marie in Lanslebourg (0479 059410). It shares its restaurant with the next-door sister hotel, the 2-star Clé des Champs (0479 059410), apparently housed in a converted sheep barn – 'friendly, good service, plain but good food'. The pair are a 'not too bad' 250m from the lift in the morning. There are half a dozen other 2-stars to choose from. A 2014 visitor chose the Hôtel Club MMV Val Cenis (0489 066630) for its 'excellent situation' and proximity to the pistes.

Apartments There is an excellent range of self-catering lodgings. Top of that range is the CGH residence Les Chalets de Flambeau, built by MGM three years ago at Les Champs, midway between the main villages, and stylishly furnished. It is highly recommended by a reporter who has stayed twice: 'very comfortable, lovely view from the balconies, friendly staff'; 'fantastic' pool, paddling pool, hot tubs, sauna and fitness. Another reader rates the Balcons du Village, within walking distance of Lanslevillard and the Le Haut gondola: 'Great location at the base of the slopes; comfortable, spacious and great value.' Peak Retreats offers these and three other attractive residences.

Eating out There is a limited but adequate range of options. A repeat visitor tips L'Arcelle in Lanslevillard – 'Good range of delicious food, from fondue to duck with bilberry sauce.'

Après-ski Après-ski is quiet, but there are 'some nice bars'.

Off the slopes Lanslevillard has all the key facilities – a pool/spa complex, an artificial outdoor ice rink, a popular bowling alley with a lively bar, and a 900m toboggan run down the length of the gondola at Le Haut.

Phone numbers
From abroad use the prefix +33 and omit the initial '0' of the phone number

TOURIST OFFICE
www.valcenis.com

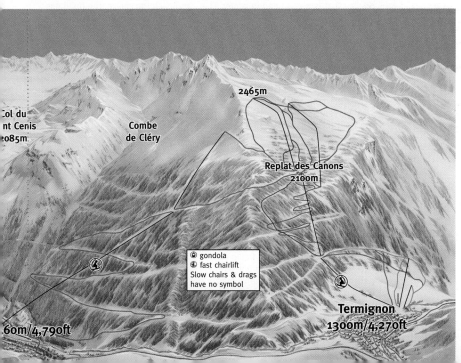

Col du
nt Cenis
.085m

Combe
de Cléry

2465m

Replat des Canons
2100m

⊚ gondola
⊛ fast chairlift
Slow chairs & drags
have no symbol

Termignon
1300m/4,270ft

.60m/4,790ft

Val d'Isère

One of the great high mega-resorts, particularly (though not only) for experts – with an attractive town at the base

OT VAL D'ISERE / AGENCE NUTS

RATINGS

The mountains

Extent	★★★★★
Fast lifts	★★★★
Queues	★★★★
Terrain p'ks	★★★
Snow	★★★★★
Expert	★★★★★
Intermediate	★★★★★
Beginner	★★★
Boarder	★★★★
X-country	★
Restaurants	★★★
Schools	★★★★★
Families	★★★★

The resort

Charm	★★★
Convenience	★★★
Scenery	★★★
Eating out	★★★★★
Après-ski	★★★★
Off-slope	★★

RPI   110

lift pass	£210
ski hire	£125
lessons	£75
food & drink	£155
total	£565

KEY FACTS

Resort	1850m
	6,070ft

Espace Killy

Slopes	1550-3455m
	5,090-11,340ft
Lifts	88
Pistes	300km
	186 miles
Green	15%
Blue	42%
Red	26%
Black	17%
Snowmaking	
	974 guns

Val d'Isère only

Slopes	1785-3300m
	5,860-10,830ft
Lifts	43
Pistes	150km
	93 miles

+ Huge area shared with Tignes, with lots of runs for all abilities

+ One of the great resorts for lift-served off-piste runs

+ Once the snow has fallen, high altitude of slopes keeps it good

+ Wide choice of schools, especially for off-piste lessons and guiding

+ For a high Alpine resort, the town is attractive, is lively at night, and offers a good range of restaurants

+ Wide range of package holidays, including some comfortable chalets

– Some green and blue runs are too challenging, and all runs back to the village are tricky

– You're quite likely to need buses at the start and end of the day (but they are very frequent and efficient)

– Many lifts and slopes are liable to close when the weather is bad

– At times it seems more British than French, especially in low season

– Expensive eating and drinking; it's one of the priciest resorts in France for this – and readers complain

Val d'Isère is one of the world's best resorts for experts – who are attracted by the extent of lift-served off-piste – and for confident, mileage-hungry intermediates. You don't have to be particularly adventurous to enjoy the resort; but it would be much better for novices and timid intermediates if the piste classifications were more reliable.

The drawbacks listed above are not crucial for most people, whereas most of the plus-points weigh heavily in the balance. For a combination of seriously impressive skiing and pleasant village ambience, it is difficult to beat.

THE RESORT

Val d'Isère spreads along a remote valley that is a dead end in winter. The road in from Bourg-St-Maurice brings you dramatically through a rocky defile to La Daille – a convenient but hideous slope-side apartment complex and the base of lifts into the major Bellevarde sector of the slopes.

Carry on into the centre of town and turn right, and you drive under the nursery slopes and major lifts up to both the Bellevarde and Solaise sectors to a lot of new development. Continue up the main valley instead, and you come first to Le Laisinant, a peaceful little outpost with a fast lift into the slopes, and then to Le Fornet, the fourth major lift station.

The developments up the side valley beyond the main lift station – in Le Châtelard and La Legettaz – are mainly attractive, and some offer ski-in/ski-out convenience. La Daille and Le Fornet have their (quite different) attractions for those less concerned about nightlife. A car is of no great value around the resort.

VILLAGE CHARM ★★★★★
Developing nicely

The outskirts are dreary, but as you approach the centre, the buildings become much more attractive (chalet-style, clad in wood and stone) and the central Val Village complex is traffic-free. Many first-time visitors find the resort much nicer than they expected: 'Val has a lovely atmosphere and charm that surprised me,' said one.

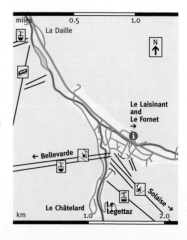

NEWS

2014/15: The resort's sixth 5-star hotel is due to open – the Yule, right on the front de neige where the Grand Paradis used to be. The Chalets du Jardin Alpin apartments are due to be refurbished.

2013/14: More snowmaking was installed on the red Joseray run back to town on Bellevarde.

OT VAL D'ISERE

These two narrow runs through the woods get very crowded and bumpy but are the easiest ways from Solaise to the village ↓

CONVENIENCE ★★★★★
Mostly fine
There is a lot of traffic around, but the resort has worked hard to get cars under control and has made the centre more pedestrian-friendly. The location of your accommodation isn't crucial, unless you want to ski from the door or be close to a nursery slope. The main lift stations are served by very efficient and amazingly frequent free shuttle-buses; but in peak periods you may have to let a few full ones pass before there's space to board. After 8pm they run every 20 minutes until 2.45am.

SCENERY ★★★★★
Valley deep, mountain high
The resort sprawls along a steep-sided river valley, beneath a series of high and partly wooded mountain ridges. There are splendid views from the Pissaillas glacier.

THE MOUNTAINS

Although there are wooded slopes above the village on all sectors, in practice most of the runs here are on open slopes above the treeline, and a lot of lifts can close in bad weather. Signposting is good. But Val d'Isère vies with St Anton for the title of 'resort with most under-classified slopes'. Many blue and some green runs (including runs to the valley) are simply too steep, narrow and even bumpy; in other resorts they would be reds, or even blacks; we have a hefty file of complaints from readers who agree with our judgement. The piste map has 'quiet skiing' zones marked on it. The local radio (96.1 FM) carries weather reports in English as well as in French.

EXTENT OF THE SLOPES ★★★★★
Vast and varied
Val d'Isère's slopes divide into three main sectors, two reachable from the village. **Bellevarde** is the mountain that is home to Val d'Isère's two famous downhill courses: the OK piste that has been used for the World Cup every December and the Face piste that was used for the 1992 Winter Olympics and the 2009 World Championships. You can reach Bellevarde quickly by underground funicular from La Daille or the powerful Olympique gondola from near the centre of town. From the top you can descend to the valley, play on a variety of drags and chairs at altitude or take a choice of lifts to Tignes' slopes (see separate chapter).

Solaise is the other mountain accessible directly from the village. The Solaise fast quad takes you a few metres higher than the parallel cable car. Once up, a short drag or rope tow takes you over a plateau and down to a variety of chairs that serve this very sunny area of predominantly gentle pistes. From near the top of this area

LeSki
the chalet specialists

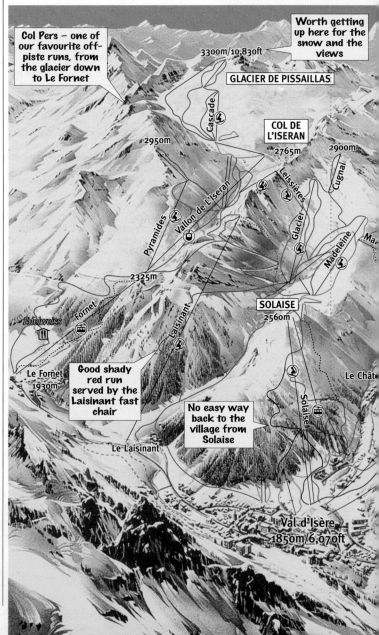

Col Pers – one of our favourite off-piste runs, from the glacier down to Le Fornet

Worth getting up here for the snow and the views

3300m/10,830ft

GLACIER DE PISSAILLAS

COL DE L'ISERAN
2765m

2900m

2950m

Cascade

Leissières

Cugnai

Vallon de L'Iseran

Glacier

Pyramides

Madeleine

Mar

2325m

Laisinant

SOLAISE
2560m

Edelweiss

Fornet

Le Fornet
1930m

Good shady red run served by the Laisinant fast chair

Le Châte

Solaise

No easy way back to the village from Solaise

Le Laisinant

Val d'Isère
1850m/6,070ft

VAL D'ISÈRE
COURCHEVEL & LA TANIA

❄ 9 chalets for 6 to 16 guests
❄ Delicious food & wine
❄ Civilised Sunday flight
❄ Short, direct transfers

Any questions?
01484 954397
www.leski.com

32 years
of catered chalet
holidays

BOOK ONLINE
100% FINANCIAL
PROTECTION

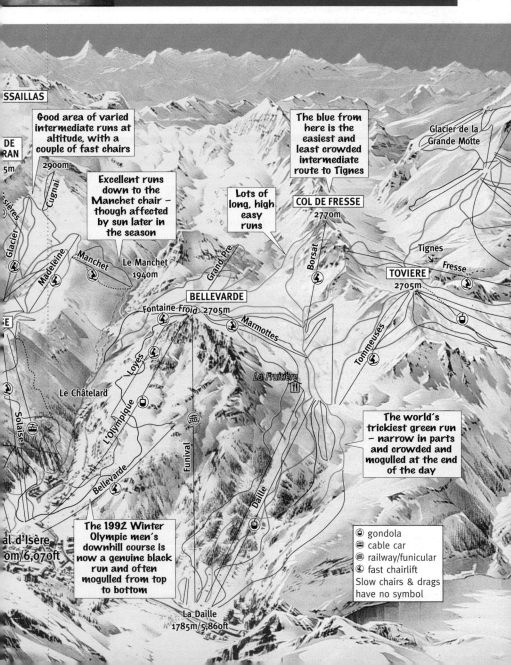

SSAILLAS

Good area of varied intermediate runs at altitude, with a couple of fast chairs

The blue from here is the easiest and least crowded intermediate route to Tignes

Glacier de la Grande Motte

DE RAN
5m

2900m

Cugnai

Excellent runs down to the Manchet chair – though affected by sun later in the season

Lots of long, high easy runs

COL DE FRESSE
2770m

Tignes

Fresse

Glacier

sères

Madeleine

Manchet

Le Manchet
1940m

Grand-Pre

Borsat

TOVIERE
2705m

E

Fontaine Froid

BELLEVARDE
2705m

Marmottes

Tommeuses

Loyes

La Fruitière

Le Châtelard

L'Olympique

The world's trickiest green run – narrow in parts and crowded and mogulled at the end of the day

Solaise

Bellevarde

Funival

Daille

al. d'Isère
0m/6,07oft

The 1992 Winter Olympic men's downhill course is now a genuine black run and often mogulled from top to bottom

☺ gondola
🚠 cable car
🚃 railway/funicular
🚡 fast chairlift
Slow chairs & drags have no symbol

La Daille
1785m/5,86oft

ESPRIT

FOR FAMILIES IN

Val d'Isère

Family Ski
Chalets
Dedicated
Nurseries
Exclusive Ski
Classes
12 More Resorts

espritski.com
01483 791 900

you can catch the fast Leissières chair (which climbs over a ridge and down the other side) to the third main area, in the valley running up to the **Col de l'Iseran**. This area can also be reached by the fast chair from Le Laisinant or by cable car from Le Fornet. At the top here is the **Glacier de Pissaillas**.

FAST LIFTS ★★★★☆
Access all areas
High-capacity lifts provide good access from the valley, and there are lots of fast chairs higher up. But there are still a few slow chairs and draglifts around.

QUEUES ★★★★☆
Few problems
Queues to get out of the resort have been kept in check by lift upgrades and additions – but there can be a short wait at the Olympique gondola up Bellevarde. On Solaise the slow Lac chair back up to the Tête Solaise can generate queues. Crowded pistes in high season is a more common complaint than queues.

TERRAIN PARKS ★★★☆☆
Beginners and experts welcome
The park is above the La Daille gondola and served by the Mont Blanc chairlift. There are lines to suit every level from beginner to expert freestylers. There are lots of table

jumps, boxes and rails of all shapes and sizes plus a large hip, a wall ride and four kicker lines from easy to pro (see www.valdisere-snowpark.com). There's also a cool zone in the middle of the park, where you can just sit back and enjoy the show. Nearby is a mini-snowcross course aimed especially at kids. 'Lots of fun jumps and mini-snowcross for the kids and me,' confirms a 2014 reporter. There was a new full-fledged, 800m long snowcross for last season in the Grand-Pré area. But head to Tignes for a super-pipe.

SNOW RELIABILITY ★★★★★
One of the best
In years when lower resorts have suffered, Val d'Isère has rarely been short of snow. In our experience of many late-April visits, even in poor snow years, decent skiing is still available. Once a big dump of snow has fallen, the resort's height means you can almost always get back to the village. But what's even more important is that in each sector there are lots of lifts and runs above mid-mountain, between about 2300m and 2900m. Many of the slopes face roughly north. And there is access to glaciers at Pissaillas or over in Tignes. There's substantial snowmaking too.

THE BEST LIFT-SERVED OFF-PISTE IN THE WORLD?

Few resorts can rival the extent of lift-served off-piste skiing in Val d'Isère. Here is a selection of what's on offer. But don't try any of it without a guide and essential safety equipment.

Some runs are ideal for adventurous intermediates looking to try off-piste for the first time. The **Tour du Charvet** *was Editor Watts' first-ever off-piste run; it goes through glorious scenery from the top of the Grand Pré chairlift on the back of Bellevarde. For most of the way it is very gentle, with only a few steeper pitches. It ends up at the bottom of the Manchet chair up to the Solaise area. The* **Pays Désert** *is an easy run with superb views on the Pissaillas glacier, high above Le Fornet and reached by traversing from the top of the lift system. You end up at the Pays Désert draglift.*

For more experienced off-piste skiers, **Col Pers** *is one of our favourite runs. Again, it starts with a traverse from the Pissaillas glacier. You go over a pass into a big, fairly gentle bowl with glorious views and endless ways down. If there is enough snow, you drop down into the Gorges de Malpasset and ski over the frozen Isère river back to the Fornet cable car. If not, you can take a higher route.*

Cugnai *is a wide, secluded bowl reached from the chair of the same name at the top of the Solaise sector. A steep (37 degree) slope at the far end descends beneath a sheer black rock wall and then narrows into a gully to the valley floor, leading to the Manchet chair.*

Banane *is reached via the Face de Bellevarde piste and is a long and impressive run (37 to 40 degrees) with spectacular views over the Manchet valley. For a real challenge intrepid experts should try the* **Couloir des Pisteurs,** *which requires a 20-minute climb from the Tour de Charvet. The view from the top is simply stunning. A very narrow steep couloir (44 degrees) bounded by rock faces brings you out on a wide open slope above Le Grand Pré, right opposite Bellevarde.*

Then there's the whole of Tignes' extensive off-piste to explore, of course.

skitracer

CHALETS, HOTELS & APARTMENTS
Call us today
020 8600 1650
skitracer.com

interactiveresorts
The **Ski Holiday** Specialists

www.interactiveresorts.co.uk
sales@interactiveresorts.co.uk
020 3080 0200

Val d'Isère
A LA CARTE

Personalised skiing holidays in Val d'Isere from the resort specialists.

Insider knowledge of Val d'Isere.
Centrally located apartments, chalets and hotels. Flexible dates available.
0033 629 89 44 57
info@skivaldisere.co.uk
www.skivaldisere.co.uk

LIFT PASSES

Espace Killy

Prices in €

Age	1-day	6-day
under 14	41	202
14 to 64	51	253
65 plus	41	202

Free under 5, over 75
Beginner Five free lifts on nursery slopes
Notes Covers Tignes and Val d'Isère; half-day and pedestrian passes; family discounts; 5-day-plus passes valid for a day in the Three Valleys and a day in Paradiski (La Plagne-Les Arcs); 2+ day pass gives one free entry to pool at Aqua Sports Centre

Alternative pass
Val d'Isère only

FOR EXPERTS ★★★★★
One of the world's best

Val d'Isère is one of the top resorts in the world for experts. The main attraction is the huge range of beautiful off-piste possibilities – see the feature panel opposite.

There may be better resorts for really steep pistes – there are certainly lots in North America – but there is plenty of on-piste action to amuse most experts, despite the small number of blacks on the piste map. And some of these have been converted to 'naturides', which means they are never groomed (a neat way of saving money!) but they are marked, patrolled and avalanche protected. Many reds and blues are also steep enough to get mogulled.

On Bellevarde the famous Face run is the main attraction – often mogulled from top to bottom, but not worryingly steep and it's a wonderful blast if it's been groomed. Epaule is the sector's other black run; where the moguls are hit by long exposure to sun, it can be slushy or rock hard (it is prone to closure for these reasons too). Most of the blacks on Solaise and above Le Fornet are now naturides (and the proper black from Solaise to the valley is no steeper than the alternative red).

Wayne Watson of off-piste school Alpine Experience puts a daily diary of off-piste snow conditions and runs on the web at www.alpineexperience.com.

FOR INTERMEDIATES ★★★★★
Quantity and quality

Val d'Isère has just as much to offer intermediates as experts. There's enough here to keep you interested for several visits – though pistes can be crowded in high season, and the less experienced should be aware that many runs are underclassified.

The Solaise sector has a network of gentle blue runs, ideal for building confidence. And there are a couple of beautiful runs from here through the woods to Le Laisinant – ideal in bad weather, though prone to closure in times of avalanche danger.

Most of the runs in the Col de l'Iseran sector are even easier – ideal for early and hesitant intermediates. Those marked blue at the top of the glacier could really be classified green.

Bellevarde has a huge variety of runs ideally suited to intermediates of all levels. From Bellevarde itself there is a choice of green, blue and red runs of varying pitch. The World Cup downhill OK piste is a wonderful rolling cruise when groomed. The wide runs from Tovière normally offer the choice of groomed piste or moguls.

A snag for early intermediates is that runs back to the valley can be challenging. The easiest way is down to La Daille on a green run that would be classified blue or red in most resorts. It gets very crowded and mogulled by the end of the day. None of the runs from Bellevarde and Solaise back to Val itself is easy. Many early intermediates ride the lifts down.

FOR BEGINNERS ★★★★★
OK if you know where to go

The nursery slope right by the centre of town is 95% perfect; it's just a pity that the very top is unpleasantly steep. The lifts serving it are free.

Once off the nursery slopes, you have to know where to find easy runs; some of the greens should be blue, or even red (see the warning in the last paragraph of 'For intermediates' above). One local instructor admits: 'We have to have green runs on the map, even if we don't have so many green slopes – otherwise beginners wouldn't come to Val d'Isère.'

A good place for your first real runs off the nursery slopes is the Madeleine green run on Solaise (a 'quiet skiing'

SKIWORLD

Catered chalets, hotels and self catering apartments in

Europe, USA and Canada

skiworld.co.uk
08444 930 430
ABTA V2151 ATOL 2036

SCHOOLS

Alpine Experience
t 0479 062881

Alp Ski Diamond
t 0621 652944

BASS
t 0679 512405

ESF
t 0479 060234

Evolution 2
t 0479 007729

iSki
t 0646 186413

Misty Fly
t 0479 073267

Mountain Masters
t 0479 060514

New Generation
t 0479 010318
0844 770 4733 (UK)
www.skinewgen.com

Oxygène
t 0479 419958

Progression
t 0621 939380

Ski Concept
t 0688 672563

Ski-lesson.com
t 0615 207108

Snow Fun
t 0479 061979

Stages Mattis
t 0479 060072

TDC
t 0615 553156

Top Ski
t 0479 061480

Classes (ESF prices)
6 days (3hr am, 2½hr pm) from €409

Private lessons
From €47 for 1hr

GUIDES

Bureau des guides
t 0687 528503

Tetra
t 0631 499275

zone served by a six-pack). The Col de l'Iseran runs are also gentle and wide, and not overcrowded. There is good progression terrain (and a big 'quiet skiing' zone) on Bellevarde, too – though getting to it can be tricky. From all sectors, it's best to take a lift back down to the valley.

FOR BOARDERS ★★★★
Watch out for flats
Val d'Isère's more upmarket profile attracts a different kind of holiday boarder from Tignes; the resort is, perhaps, seen as Tignes' less hard-core cousin. But the terrain here is great for freeriders. The easier slopes are suitable for beginners, and there are very few draglifts. But there are quite a few flat areas where you'll end up scooting or walking. Specialist snowboard shops are Orage by Misty Fly and Quiksilver.

FOR CROSS-COUNTRY ★
Limited
There are a couple of loops in each of three areas – towards La Daille, on Solaise and out past Le Laisinant – totalling 20km. More picturesque is the loop going from Le Châtelard (on the road past the main cable car station) to the Manchet chair. But keen cross-country enthusiasts should go elsewhere.

MOUNTAIN RESTAURANTS ★★★
Acceptable – but expensive
For such an upmarket resort, there are surprisingly few enjoyable places to eat on the mountain. The major places are self-service and at the top of lifts. Everywhere gets busy and high-season service can be poor. And in nearly every report we get there are remarks on how 'hideously' expensive they are. Reporters' other major gripe is that in many mountain restaurants, even if you are eating there, you have to pay to use the toilets.
Editors' choice The wood-and-stone Edelweiss (0610 287064), above Le Fornet, is our favourite for the best food and ambience. We've eaten there several times and had delicious lamb, duck and fish; reporters regularly send us rave reviews too, and 2014 saw another batch ('delicious food and atmosphere', 'superb lunch'). It's a bit cramped inside, and if it's a nice day, we prefer the sunny terrace. On Bellevarde, we had a superb lunch on the terrace of the Fruitière at the top

of the La Daille gondola in 2014 (delicious beef stew and lamb shepherds pie, attentive service). Inside is kitted out with stuff from a dairy, but tables are very crammed in.
Worth knowing about On Bellevarde, the busy table-service Trifollet halfway down the OK run always has a good plat du jour that is 'very reasonable compared to others'. The Marmottes, near the base of the chair of the same name, is one of the cheapest places to eat – an efficient self-service with a big sunny terrace, helpful staff and good food. The Peau de Vache, set between the two chairs going up Face de Bellevarde, serves 'burgers that knock anything Soho can offer into a cocked hat – they are truly wonderful'.

On Solaise, the Bar de L'Ouillette, at the base of the Madeleine chairlift, has a fun terrace with artificial palm trees and deck chairs, but the queue at its tiny self-service counter may be slow-moving.

Above Le Fornet, the Signal at the top of the cable car is our favourite; it has self- and table-service sections and a takeaway snack bar – and recent reporters recommend all three. The Cascade self-service by the foot of the chairlift with the same name is newish, light and airy with good food.

Of course, there are lots of places in the resort villages. Arolay at Le Fornet does 'a sizzling tartiflette, a lovely place for a relaxed late lunch', and the Michelin-starred Atelier d'Edmond (decorated like a carpenter's workshop and opposite the Fornet cable car) is 'serious (expensive) dining with impeccable service, good for a treat'. The terrace of hotel Brussel's in Val d'Isère, right by the nursery slopes, is 'very good and has good service'. The Sun Bar at the base of the Olympique cable car is 'reasonable quality', as is the Tartine, used by many ski instructors. In town, the Perdrix Blanche is 'very reasonable, with excellent lunch menu', and the coffee shop in the Quiksilver store serves fresh smoothies and '17 different types of burger' – and gets packed on bad-weather days.

SCHOOLS AND GUIDES ★★★★★
A very wide choice
There is a huge choice of schools, guides and private instructors – just look at the list in the margin opposite. But as they all get busy, at peak periods it's best to book in advance.

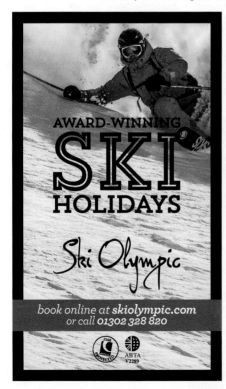

Pierre @ Vacances
Holidays made for me

Best price
guarantee
for ski in/out
budget studios
up to spacious
3 bedroom
apartments

pierreetvacances.co.uk

CHILDCARE

Le Village des Enfants
t 0479 400981
Ages 18mnth to 13yr

Le Petit Poucet
t 0479 061397
Ages from 3

Babysitter list
Contact tourist office

Ski schools
Most offer classes for ages 5 up

Practically all the schools run off-piste groups as well as on-piste lessons.

New Generation, a British-run school that operates in several resorts, has a branch here that is consistently highly praised: 'Excellent progress made with my nervous beginner, er, intermediate wife. A week of group lessons with only five in the group – can't praise them enough!' said a recent reporter. The Development Centre (TDC) is a group of British instructors that offers intensive clinics for all levels and has been recommended: 'Excellent, Steve Angus was brilliant with my son, inventive, fun, engaging, made his holiday!' says a 2014 reporter.

We also heard last year from satisfied clients of Evolution 2 ('kids' lessons good') and Pro Snowboarding ('good mix of instruction and off-piste adventure').

Alpine Experience specializes in guided off-piste groups – an excellent way to get off-piste safely without the cost of hiring a guide as an individual. We have had great mornings out with them, and reporters recommend them too: 'Had a great time, would definitely use them again,' said a 2014 visitor. Another off-piste guiding specialist is iSki. Long-standing off-piste favourites Top Ski changed ownership a few years ago, and we hear they have lost a lot of their top guides. Heli-skiing trips can be arranged.

Henry's Avalanche Talks are now on demand at various venues – see www.henrysavalanchetalk.com for details – and are 'very engaging and interesting', says a reporter.

FOR FAMILIES ★★★★
Good tour op possibilities
Many people prefer to use the facilities of UK tour operators such as family specialist Esprit Ski. But there's a 'children's village' for children from 18 months to 13 years, with supervised indoor and outdoor activities on the village nursery slopes. And Petit Poucet takes children from age three and will pick them up and take them home at any time during the day. However, a reporter who is a policeman says families need to be aware that the resort exudes a 'lager lout' feel at times.

Val d'Isère

Build your own shortlist: www.wheretoskiandsnowboard.com

NEW GENERATION
SKI & SNOWBOARD SCHOOL ●●●●●

RISE TO THE CHALLENGE

Ant spends his summers battling the elements on oil rigs. In winter he'll help you master the steeps of Espace Killy.

Val d'Isère ● Tignes
Tel: 0844 770 4733 www.skinewgen.com

Ski Total

ARE HERE IN
Val d'Isère

▷ Quality chalets
▷ Top locations
▷ Excellent value
▷ 17 more resorts

skitotal.com
01483 791 933

ALPINE ANSWERS
The UK's No.1 Chalet Specialist

For choice and service look no further!

alpineanswers.co.uk
call: 020 7801 1080   ABTA

VAL D'ISERE
CHOOSE FROM 219 CATERED CHALETS,
APARTMENTS & HOTELS

Skiline.co.uk

CALL US ON 020 8313 3999

FRANCE

366

ACTIVITIES

Indoor Sports centre (with pools, climbing wall, fitness, gym, sauna, steam, squash, climbing wall), fitness and health clubs, cinema

Outdoor Ice rink, walking, snowshoeing, ice climbing, dog sledding, ice driving, paragliding, microlight flights, helicopter flights, snowmobiling

OT VAL D'ISERE / ANDY PARANT

This must be a special occasion. There is normally traffic where these people are walking – but it's not intrusive ↓

STAYING THERE

More British tour operators go to Val (and Méribel) than anywhere else. Val d'Isère à la Carte specializes in arranging tailor-made holidays there. Club Med was recommended this year by a regular reporter after her third visit: 'Excellent food and facilities.'
Chalets This is Planet Chalet, with properties at every level of the market. YSE is a Val d'Isère specialist, with 20 varied chalets – from swanky apartments for four or six to proper big chalets. Le Ski has nine chalets, including their luxury Chalet Angelique for 12 in a back street of La Daille; inside it looks more like a mini-stately home than a chalet (and has a steam room and gym). Next door and new for 2014/15 is Vieille Maison (for eight), which dates from the 18th century and is being totally refurbished for the coming season. Le Ski also has six splendid places grouped together just up from the main street with a big outdoor hot tub. Skiworld has 11

varied chalets from the very plush chalet Madeleine with outdoor hot tub to more modest places, plus a smart 33-bedroomed chalet hotel with sauna, steam, hot tub. Ski Total has 14 smart places, including two very swanky ones in their Platinum range (one with outdoor hot tub, one with a sauna) plus a chalet hotel sleeping 80 at La Daille. Crystal has six chalets, including three smart central ones with saunas in their Finest range. Inghams has four chalets (one right on the nursery slope) and their flagship 24-bed chalet hotel with sauna, steam and hot tub in Le Fornet. Ski Olympic has an six-bed place near the centre. Esprit, the family specialist, has two chalets and a central chalet hotel with 31 bedrooms. There are some very luxurious chalets from operators like Consensio and Scott Dunn.
Hotels There are over 30, with increasing numbers at the luxury end: six 5-stars and four 4-stars.
*****Avenue Lodge** (0479 006767) Central and fairly new. Very modern decor, comfortable rooms.
*****Barmes de L'Ours** (0479 413700) Close to slopes and centre. Rooms are in a different style on each floor. Excellent pool.
*****Blizzard** (0479 060207) Central. Comfortable. Indoor-outdoor pool and sauna. Good food and lively bar.
*****Christiania** (0479 060825) Big chalet. Chic but friendly. Pool, sauna.
****Aigle des Neiges** (0479 061888) Highly rated refurbished version of former Latitudes. Central. Sauna. 'Good rooms and breakfast.'
****Auberge St Hubert** (0479 060645) On main street. Family-run, friendly.
****Tsanteleina** (0479 061213) Central on main street. Pool, hot tub, two steam rooms, sauna.
***Kandahar** (0479 060239) Smart building above Taverne d'Alsace on main street.

UK PACKAGES

Action Outdoors, Alpine Answers, Alpine Elements, Alpine Weekends, Carrier, Chardon Mountain Lodges, Club Med, Consensio, Crystal, Crystal Finest, Elegant Resorts, Erna Low, Esprit, Flexiski, Friendship Travel, Green Rides, Inghams, Inspired to Ski, Interactive Resorts, Jeffersons, Kaluma, Lagrange, Le Ski, Luxury Chalet Collection, Mark Warner, Momentum, Mountain Beds, Neilson, Oxford Ski Co, Pierre & Vacances, Powder White, PowderBeds, Scott Dunn, Ski Amis, Ski Beat, Ski Bespoke, Ski Club Freshtracks, Ski Collection, Ski Expectations, Ski France, Ski Independence, Ski Olympic, Ski Supreme, Ski Total, Ski Weekend, Ski-Val, Skitracer, Skiweekends.com, Skiworld, Snow Finders, Snow-wise, Snoworks, STC, Supertravel, Thomson, Val d'Isère A La Carte, VIP, White Roc, YSE, Zenith

GETTING THERE

Air Chambéry 145km/ 90 miles (2hr); Geneva 225km/ 140 miles (2hr45); Lyon 220km/ 135 miles (2hr45); Grenoble 210km/ 130 miles (2hr45)

Rail Bourg-St-Maurice (30km/19 miles); regular buses from station

Phone numbers
From abroad use the prefix +33 and omit the initial '0' of the phone number

TOURIST OFFICE

www.valdisere.com

***Samovar** (0479 061351) In La Daille. Traditional, with good food.
***Sorbiers** (0479 062377) Modern but cosy chalet, not far out.
Danival (0479 060065) B&B, piste-side location.
Galise (0479 060504) Central, family-run B&B.
Forêt (0479 060040) Central, recently refurbished. 'Basic rooms, very friendly staff, outstanding food.'
Apartments There are thousands of apartments available. Among the best are Chalets du Jardin Alpin at the foot of Solaise (due to be refurbished for 2014/15), Chalets du Laisinant (at Le Laisinant) and Pierre & Vacances' Balcons de Bellevarde at La Daille and Chalets de Solaise (with outdoor pool) close to the centre. Ski Collection, Ski Amis, Ski Independence, Erna Low, Skitracer and local agency Val d'Isère Agence (0479 067350) have good selections. Skiworld has a central, flexible catered chalet, where you can choose what catering (if any) you want, and also apartments. The supermarkets have been praised for 'enticing pre-cooked food'.

EATING OUT ★★★★★
Plenty of good places
The 70-odd restaurants offer a wide variety of cuisines; there's a free booklet covering some, but many worthwhile places are missing.

At the top end, two places have a Michelin star: L'Atelier d'Edmond at Le Fornet (see 'Mountain restaurants') and La Table de l'Ours, in the Barmes de l'Ours hotel, but the latter got the thumbs down this year from a regular reporter ('pretentious, expensive, slow service'). The Grande Ourse, by the nursery slope, also serves top-notch meals, and we had a delicious dinner there in 2014. The rustic Vieille Maison ('excellent, good value') behind the main road at La Daille and Arolay at Le Fornet (see 'Mountain restaurants') are rated highly by locals.

There are plenty of pleasant mid-priced places. Bar Jacques is regularly recommended for its excellent food and set menu ('Good rib of beef,' says a 2014 visitor). Casserole and Pré d'Aval have both been recommended for their good-value set menus. Corniche has a lovely traditional ambience and is regularly tipped. A local likes the Perdix Blanche: 'Good food and service and very reasonable.' Other 2014 reporter tips: Etable

d'Alain ('an old barn with farm animals on view, 15 mins walk down the Manchet valley'); Table d'Yvonne ('simple place above 5 Frères hotel'); Casa Scara (Italian); Bar 1789 ('a classic cote de boeuf, nice wine list').

APRES-SKI ★★★★☆
Plenty of choice
There are lots of bars, many with happy hours and then music and dancing later on.

The Folie Douce, at the top of the La Daille gondola, has become an institution: live bands, DJs, cabarets, packed crowds and dancing on tables on the terrace every afternoon; you can ride the gondola down. It has now been replicated in four other resorts.

At La Daille the bar at the Samovar hotel is a good spot for a quiet beer after skiing. In downtown Val, the 'friendly' Blue Note (opposite the ESF) has a 'great low-key atmosphere'. Café Face is popular, with loud music. The Moris pub (live music at teatime and later) and Saloon (under hotel Brussel's) fill up as the slopes close; Boubou and Bar Jacques are popular with locals. The Pacific Bar has sport on big-screen TVs. Barique is a 'very trendy' new wine bar with 'a great vibe, live music, with good food'. The basement Taverne d'Alsace is quiet and relaxing, as are Bar XV, the first-floor bar of the hotel Blizzard, and Wine Not (er, a wine bar). The coffee shop in the Quiksilver store serves fresh smoothies and attracts a 'cool young crowd'. The 'great fun' Grand Marnier serves 'tempting cocktails'.

Later on, Dick's Tea Bar is the main disco (go early evening for Val's 'best-value drinking', says a reporter). Doudoune is 'more expensive but nicer'. Graal is 'usually good'.

OFF THE SLOPES ★★☆☆☆
A reasonable amount to do
The sports centre (with two pools, sauna, steam, gym, climbing wall) is consistently praised by reporters; a lift pass for two days or more gets you one free swim. There's an outdoor ice rink and ice driving, and the range of shops is better than in most high French resorts. There are a few mountain restaurants that are easy for pedestrians to get to. A reporter says the nature walk from Le Fornet to Pont St Charles in late season is 'fascinating'; others enjoyed the January 'polo on snow' tournament.

Build your own shortlist: www.wheretoskiandsnowboard.com

SNOWPIX.COM / CHRIS GILL

Val Thorens

Europe's highest resort, with guaranteed good snow – and other attractions, stylish lodgings and good restaurants among them

RATINGS

The mountains

Extent	★★★★★
Fast lifts	★★★★★
Queues	★★★★
Terrain p'ks	★★★★
Snow	★★★★★
Expert	★★★★
Intermediate	★★★★★
Beginner	★★★★
Boarder	★★★★
X-country	★
Restaurants	★★★★
Schools	★★★
Families	★★★

The resort

Charm	★★
Convenience	★★★★★
Scenery	★★★
Eating out	★★★★
Après-ski	★★★★
Off-slope	★★

RPI 115

lift pass	£230
ski hire	£125
lessons	£75
food & drink	£155
total	**£585**

KEY FACTS

Resort	2300m
	7,550ft

Trois Vallées

Slopes	1260-3230m
	4,130-10,600ft
Lifts	180
Pistes	600km
	373 miles
Green	13%
Blue	39%
Red	38%
Black	10%
Snowmaking	33%

Val Thorens-Orelle only

Slopes	1800-3230m
	5,900-10,600ft
Lifts	32
Pistes	150km
	93 miles
Green	14%
Blue	37%
Red	37%
Black	12%

+ Extensive slopes for all abilities

+ One of the most snow-sure resorts

+ Fastest lift system in France

+ Compact, with ski-in/out lodgings

+ Convenient, gentle nursery slopes

+ Decent range of hotels and some very smart apartments

− Not a tree in sight

− Away from the 'front de neige', not an attractive place to walk around

− Not ideal for non-skiers

− Some very crowded pistes and dangerous intersections

− Queues for the justifiably popular Cime Caron cable car

Val Thorens continues its gradual drift upmarket, with a third 5-star hotel now open. But it remains a top place for the enthusiast looking for the best snow available and fast lifts to whizz you around. For a late trip, in particular, it's the best base in the wonderful Trois Vallées. But we normally prefer a cosier base lower down. That way, if a storm socks in, we can play in the woods; if the sun is scorching, we have the option of setting off for Val Thorens.

THE RESORT

Val Thorens is a classic purpose-built resort, high above the treeline at the head of the valley it shares with Les Menuires and St-Martin. Buses to/from Les Menuires are supposed to carry just pedestrians and cross-country skiers, not downhillers – crazy!

VILLAGE CHARM ★★
Functional but pleasantly so

Seen from the slopes, the resort is not as ugly as many of its rivals, and it has quite a lively ski resort buzz. Buildings are mainly medium-rise and wood-clad; some are distinctly stylish. But many are designed with their smart 'fronts' facing the slopes, and look very dreary from behind – the walk up the road to the centre from plush lodgings in the lower part of the village is very dull. The streets are supposedly traffic-free except for loading. But workers' cars generate traffic and Saturdays can be mayhem. You're advised to book parking in advance; we prefer lodgings with an underground garage.

CONVENIENCE ★★★★★
Ski through the centre

It's a compact village with lots of ski-in/ski-out lodging. At its heart is the snowy Place de Caron, on the slope side rather than the street side of the central buildings, where pedestrians mix with skiers and boarders. Many of the shops and restaurants are here, along with some nice hotels; the sports and leisure centres are nearby.

The resort is divided in two by a little slope (with a moving carpet lift) that leads down from here to the broad nursery slope running the length of the village (also served by moving carpets). The upper half of the village is centred on the Place de Péclet, where there is one of two shopping malls. A road runs across the hillside from here to the chalet-style Plein Sud area, where many of the catered chalets run by UK tour operators are located. You can ski to and from some of these places, but it's often very tricky – walking can be too (we've had complaints of icy, uncleared paths). The lower end of the village has some of the plushest lodgings, including 5-star places.

A free ski-bus runs every 20 minutes on two separate routes.

SCENERY ★★★
Panoramas on high

The resort sits on a sunny, west-facing slope. The views are good from the village, fabulous from the high point at Cime de Caron.

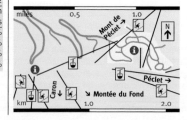

NEWS

2014/15: The fast Portette quad is to be replaced by a six-pack starting at a lower point, and the slow Plan de l'Eau by a six-pack finishing higher up – both designed to operate in high winds.

2013/14: The 3 Vallées 1 chairlift out of the village is now a chondola, called Pionniers. Both the lifts above it are now called 3 Vallées. (No, we don't know why.)

The Peyron chair from Plan Bouchet in the 'fourth valley' is now a six-pack. And the 2 Lacs fast quad from just below the village was rebuilt to increase capacity.

The hotel Fitzroy was elevated to 5-star status, and a new 5-star opened, the Koh-I Nor. A 1300m zipwire was installed from the top of the Bouchet chair in the 'fourth valley' to the top of the Thorens gondola.

THE MOUNTAINS

The main disadvantage of Val Thorens is the lack of trees. Heavy snowfalls or high wind can shut practically all the lifts and slopes, and even if they don't close, poor visibility can make skiing extremely unpleasant. Some blue runs are pretty tough.

EXTENT OF THE SLOPES ★★★★★
High and snow-sure
The resort has a wide piste going right down the front of it, leading to a number of different lifts. The big **Péclet** gondola heads more or less east from the resort and rises 700m to the Péclet glacier, with a choice of red runs or a blue down. Two of these link across to a wide area of runs beneath the ridge directly south of the resort, the high point of which is the **Pointe de Thorens**. Lifts go up to three other points on the ridge. You can take very sunny red or blue runs into the 'fourth valley', the Maurienne, from the Col de Rosaël on the ridge, served by the Grand Fond jumbo gondola.

Above **Orelle** in the Maurienne valley a six-pack (new for 2013/14) followed by a slow quad go up to 3230m on the flanks of Pointe du Bouchet, the highest lift-served point in the Trois Vallées – stunning views. The 150-person cable car to **Cime de Caron** is one of the great lifts of the Alps, rising 900m in no time at all. It can be reached by skiing across from mid-mountain, or via the Caron gondola that starts below the village. From the top there is a choice of red and black pistes down the front, or a black into the Maurienne. Nearby, the relatively low **Boismint** sector is underused, but it is a very respectable hill with a total vertical of 860m. It gets a new fast chair this season.

Chairlifts heading north from the resort serve sunny slopes above the village and also lead to the link to the Méribel valley. Les Menuires can be reached via these lifts; the alternative Boulevard Cumin along the valley is nearly flat, and can be hard work.

FAST LIFTS ★★★★★
France's fastest lift system
Recent investment means the lift system is impressive, with many gondolas and fast chairs in most of the key places. The lift upgrades last season and this mean that more than 80% of all major lifts are fast – many more than any other French resort.

QUEUES ★★★★☆
Mainly for the Cime Caron
Serious peak-time queues for the Cime Caron cable car are a continuing problem, although some reporters this year were pleased to find only short queues. You may encounter crowds elsewhere; when we visited a day last March we took to the Boismint sector to escape. Crowded pistes, especially around the village, are a bigger problem than queues – made worse by people going too fast. We agree with a recent reporter who suggests that it is time the resort imposed slow skiing zones around the village – and policed them.

OT VAL THORENS / C CATTIN

The Cime Caron cable car is one of the great lifts of the Alps, which is why its queue is one of the great queues of the Alps →

Pierre & Vacances
Holidays made for me

Best price
guarantee
for ski in/out
budget studios
up to spacious
3 bedroom
apartments

pierreetvacances.co.uk

TERRAIN PARKS ★★★★☆
Well designed

The terrain park on the 'Plateau' has been improving year-on-year. It is accessible via various chairlifts, is served by a dedicated draglift and has a nice open layout. There are different areas that range from beginner to pro, with all sorts of tables, rails and box combinations, plus an airbag jump. The hip/corner jump is excellent. The whole park is well maintained, and new obstacles are often built for local competitions. Riders can be filmed and then see their exploits on a big screen. A separate boardercross lower down has some great banked turns.

SNOW RELIABILITY ★★★★★
One of the best

Few resorts can rival Val Thorens for reliably good snow-cover, thanks to its altitude and generally north-facing slopes. Snowmaking covers a lot of the key pistes, including the crowded south- and west-facing runs on the way from the Méribel valley and in the Orelle sector. But the terrain is rocky and needs a lot of snow – we have found the higher runs patchy in early season when snow throughout the Alps has been slow to arrive, and at times like that the off-piste terrain is hazardous. 'Grooming is satisfactory,' say reporters this year.

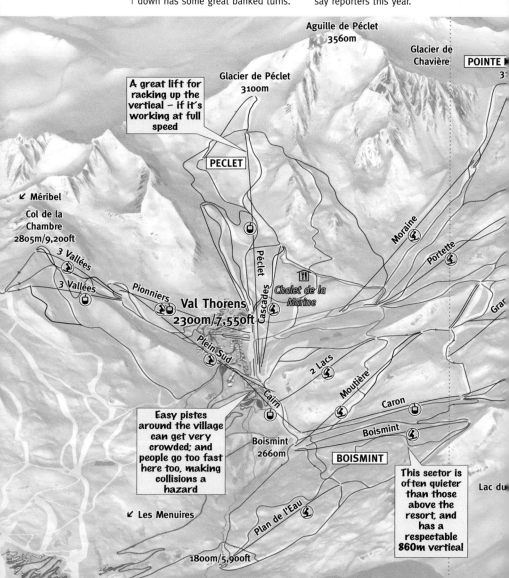

Aguille de Péclet
3560m

Glacier de Chavière

POINTE ▸

Glacier de Péclet
3100m

A great lift for racking up the vertical – if it's working at full speed

PECLET

Méribel ↙

Col de la Chambre
2805m/9,200ft

3 Vallées

3 Vallées

Pionniers

Péclet

Cascades

Péclet

Chalet de la Marine

Moraine

Portette

Gran

Val Thorens
2300m/7,550ft

Plein Sud

2 Lacs

Moutière

Caron

Cairn

Easy pistes around the village can get very crowded; and people go too fast here too, making collisions a hazard

Boismint
2660m

Boismint

BOISMINT

This sector is often quieter than those above the resort, and has a respectable 860m vertical

Lac du

Les Menuires ↙

Plan de l'Eau

1800m/5,900ft

Ski Total
ARE HERE IN
Val Thorens

▸ **Quality chalets**
▸ **Top locations**
▸ **Excellent value**
▸ **17 more resorts**

skitotal.com

01483 791 933

FOR EXPERTS ★★★★☆
Lots to do off-piste

Val Thorens' local pistes are primarily intermediate terrain; many of the blacks could easily be classified red instead. The fast Cascades chair serves a short but steep black run that quickly gets mogulled. The pistes down from the Cime Caron cable car are challenging, but not seriously steep, and there's a good, sunny black run off the back into the fourth valley.

The Falaise and Variante runs from the Grand Fond gondola can get heavily mogulled and be challenging. The sunny Goitshel run, one of the routes from the Méribel valley, is one of the easiest blacks we've seen, but it can be icy in the morning and slushy in the afternoon.

There is a huge amount of very good off-piste terrain to explore with a guide; read our feature panel overleaf. But it does require good snowfall – note our remarks in 'Snow reliability'.

FOR INTERMEDIATES ★★★★★
Great in good weather

The scope for intermediates in the Trois Vallées is enormous. A keen intermediate can get to Courchevel 1650 at the far end of the network in only 90 minutes or so, if not distracted on the way.

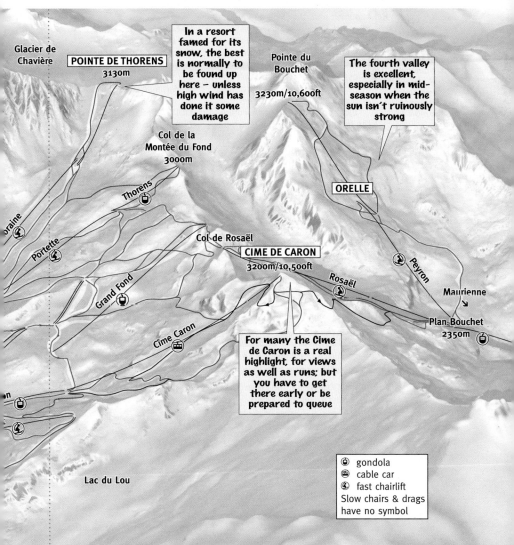

Glacier de Chavière

POINTE DE THORENS
3130m

Pointe du Bouchet
3230m/10,600ft

In a resort famed for its snow, the best is normally to be found up here – unless high wind has done it some damage

The fourth valley is excellent, especially in mid-season when the sun isn't ruinously strong

Col de la Montée du Fond
3000m

Thorens

Portette

ORELLE

Col de Rosaël

CIME DE CARON
3200m/10,500ft

Grand Fond

Rosaël

Peyron

Maurienne

Plan Bouchet
2350m

Cime Caron

For many the Cime de Caron is a real highlight, for views as well as runs; but you have to get there early or be prepared to queue

Lac du Lou

⊚ gondola
⊜ cable car
⊛ fast chairlift
Slow chairs & drags
have no symbol

SKIWORLD

Catered chalets, hotels and self catering apartments in

Europe, USA and Canada

skiworld.co.uk
08444 930 430
ABTA V2151 ATOL 2036

LIFT PASSES

Trois Vallées

Prices in €

Age	1-day	6-day
under 13	46	222
13 to 64	57	277
65 plus	51	249

Free Under 5, 75 plus
Beginner Access to Cairn, 2 Lacs and Caron lifts for 50% of Val Thorens rate; free access to one draglift and four moving carpets
Notes Covers Courchevel, La Tania, Méribel, Val Thorens, Les Menuires and St-Martin; reductions for families and other groups. Options: pedestrian and half-day passes
Alternative passes Val Thorens-Orelle only; Vallée de Belleville only

The local slopes in Val Thorens are some of the best intermediate terrain in the region. Most of the pistes are easy reds and blues (steeper on the top half of the mountain than the bottom) and made even more enjoyable by the excellent snow.

The snow on the red Col run is normally some of the best around. The blue Moraine below it is gentle and popular with the schools. The Grand Fond gondola serves a good variety of blue and red runs. The red and blue runs from the Péclet gondola are excellent. The Pluviomètre from the Trois Vallées chair is a glorious varied run, away from the lifts.

Adventurous intermediates shouldn't miss the Cime de Caron runs: the black here is very wide, usually has good snow, and is a wonderful fast cruise when freshly groomed (though reports suggest this is less likely than it was). Don't neglect the excellent, quiet Boismint area next door to Caron, either.

Blue-run skiers can now venture to the fourth valley, with the return run improved a few years back to become a blue (though not an easy one).

FOR BEGINNERS ★★★★
Good late-season choice
The slopes at the foot of the resort are very gentle and provide convenient, snow-sure nursery slopes, with four moving carpet lifts, one draglift and green runs. These are free, and there is a 50% reduction on the main lift pass for four serious lifts on the lower slopes – an excellent package. There are no long green runs to progress to, but the blues immediately above the village are easy. The resort's height

and bleakness make it cold in midwinter, and intimidating in bad weather.

FOR BOARDERS ★★★★
Reliable all season
Val Thorens has always been popular with snowboarders; it is the highest and most snow-sure of the Trois Vallées resorts, and has a younger feel compared with Courchevel and Méribel – though it's almost as pricey. Being far above the treeline, the slopes are rather bleak; however, there are great steep runs, gullies and groomed pistes for all levels. The terrain park is worth a visit. The lifts are mainly chairs and gondolas.

FOR CROSS-COUNTRY ★
Go to Les Menuires
There are no cross-country trails in Val Thorens. Your best bet is the 28km link between Les Menuires and St-Martin-de-Belleville.

MOUNTAIN RESTAURANTS ★★★★
Lots of choice
For a high modern resort, the choice of restaurants is good, and improving. The piste map names the restaurants – unlike the maps of the other valleys. It's such a simple thing ...
Editors' choice We've had several good lunches in the rustic table-service section of the Chalet de la Marine (0479 000186). It has a big terrace with 'funky' music. More reports, please. The self-service section below is also good and has a wide choice – but a regular visitor has been put off by chilly draughts. The toilets are 'the best on the piste'. The self-service Folie Douce and table-service Fruitière

FABULOUS OFF-PISTE IN VAL THORENS

Val Thorens offers a huge choice of off-piste to be explored with a guide. And because of the high altitude, the snow stays powdery longer here than in lower parts of the Trois Vallées.

For those with little off-piste experience, the Pierre Lory Pass run is ideal. It is a wide and gentle slope, reached by an easy traverse on the Chavière glacier from the top of the Col chairlift and with breathtaking views of the Aiguilles d'Arves in the Maurienne valley from the top. You then ski down the glacier du Bouchet, rejoining the lift system at Plan Bouchet.

For those with more off-piste experience, the Lac du Lou is a famous off-piste run of 1400m vertical that is easily accessible via various routes from the Cime de Caron. Because many of the slopes face north or north-west it is not unusual to find good powder most of the ski season, even in late April. The views are stunning and you'll notice the quietness and vastness of the whole valley. La Combe sans Nom in the fourth valley is also accessible from the Cime de Caron and is excellent for late season spring skiing conditions.

For the more adventurous there are many options, including hiking up from the Col chairlift to a long run over the Gébroulaz glacier down to Méribel-Mottaret.

SCHOOLS
ESF
t 0479 000286
Ski Cool
t 0479 000492
Prosneige
t 0479 010700
Attitude
t 0663 498976

Classes (ESF prices)
6 days €221
Private lessons
from €44 for 1hr for
1-2 people

CHILDCARE
Nursery (ESF)
t 0479 000286
From 3mnth to 3yr
Piou Piou (ESF)
t 0479 000286
From 3yr

Ski school
Ages 4 and over

GETTING THERE
Air Chambéry 120km/
75 miles (1hr45);
Geneva 160km/
100 miles (2hr30);
Grenoble 190km/
120 miles (2hr30);
Lyon 200km/
125 miles (2hr30)

Rail Moûtiers
(35km/22 miles);
regular buses from
station

UK PACKAGES
Action Outdoors, Alpine
Answers, Club Med,
Crystal, Crystal Finest,
Erna Low, Flexiski,
Inghams, Interactive
Resorts, Kaluma,
Lagrange, Momentum,
Neilson, Oxford Ski Co,
Pierre & Vacances,
Powder White,
PowderBeds, Scott
Dunn, Ski Amis, Ski
Bespoke, Ski Club
Freshtracks, Ski
Collection, Ski
Expectations, Ski
France, Ski
Independence, Ski Line,
Ski Supreme, Ski Total,
Ski Weekend, Skitracer,
Skiweekends.com,
Skiworld, Snow-wise,
STC, Thomson, Zenith

4-star self-catering apartments in France
Major resorts, expert knowledge

New 4-star luxury residence Koh-i Nor in Val Thorens:

Doorstep skiing in a quiet setting suited to families. Based in the heart of the Three Valleys.

Accommodation only or self-drive package deals
call us on 0844 576 0175 SkiCollection.co.uk

ABTA No.W5537

are modelled on the Val d'Isère originals, the latter with an interesting menu, well executed when we lunched there in 2013 and 2014.
Worth knowing about The rustic Chalet des 2 Lacs is a reader favourite, and we had a good lunch here a few seasons ago – warm, welcoming, log fire, good food. The Chalet des 2 Ours is repeatedly recommended for food ('delicious tartiflette'), service and views; we recently had a good tarte tatin. The Aiguilles de Péclet 'serves massive portions' but 'service is slow'. After some years in the wilderness, the Caribou has had good reports this year, including one rave: 'Warm and very cosy with large log fire, home-made, tasty food, excellent spicy vin chaud, welcoming owner.' The piste map shows picnic areas.

SCHOOLS AND GUIDES ★★★★★
Good reports
Prosneige is a small school that limits class sizes to 10 and gets very good reports. A recent reporter used them two years running and 'could not praise them enough – they really brought the children's skiing on across a wide range of ability'. The ESF offers a wide choice of private and group classes, including freestyle and freeride courses. One reporter who was very pleased with their Club Med ESF teacher one year had a bad experience the next when put into an 'English-speaking ghetto' group where 'the instructor didn't do any teaching'. There are several guiding outfits.

FOR FAMILIES ★★★★★
Some facilities
There is a children's area, Espace Junior, beside the 2 Lacs chairlift, and a good family toboggan run. The tourist office produces a handy family guide to weekly activities. We lack reports on the ESF nursery.

STAYING THERE
Accommodation is of a higher standard than in many purpose-built resorts – more comfortable and stylish. A couple of smart recent developments blur the line between hotels and apartment residences; following the tourist office, we treat them as hotels.
Chalets Most catered chalets are apartments in quite big developments – mainly relatively new ones above the resort centre. This has the advantage that you often have the use of a pool, sauna, etc in the residence. There are no notably swanky places. Skiworld has 16 units, including one with sauna and access to a pool, Crystal 11, Inghams six. Ski Total has five units that are more like actual chalets – two units in one, three in another, all with shared saunas. And it has a stand-alone chalet for 24 with use of the pool and sauna at a nearby residence.
Hotels Unusually for a high, purpose-built resort, there are plenty of hotels, including three 5-stars. There's a Club Med, too.
★★★★★Altapura (0457 747474) A reporter liked the 'unfussy atmosphere' of this stylish 5-star, with 'tip-top food and service', but found it 'ferociously expensive'. Indoor/outdoor pool etc.
★★★★★Koh-I Nor (0479 310000) New last season; rooms and suites, right at the top of the resort. Top chef. Pools, fitness, spa etc. Apartment residence next door.
★★★★Hameau de Kashmir (0479 104915) Offers suites and apartments, at the entrance to the resort. We've stayed here, and found it comfortable, but a bit cramped. Pool, spa etc.
★★★Sherpa (0479 000070) Highly recommended by a reporter this year. Cosy, lots of wood, 'friendly, great rooms, very good food, small spa – loved it'. Ski-in/ski-out.
★★★Val Chavière (0479 000033) 'Friendly, fab position, good set menu.'

↑ It's the highest resort in Europe, and it looks like it, with no trees in sight

OT VAL THORENS / B LONGO

ACTIVITIES

Indoor Sports centre (spa, sauna, fitness room, hot tub, tennis, squash, swimming pool, volleyball, table tennis, badminton, football), cinema, bowling, concerts, library

Outdoor Paragliding, snowmobiling, snowshoeing, walks, tobogganing, ice driving, bikes on snow

Phone numbers
From abroad use the prefix +33 and omit the initial '0' of the phone number

TOURIST OFFICE

www.valthorens.com

Apartments Val Thorens now has lots of smart chalet-style developments. These and many other residences are offered by the UK operators and agents who advertise with us.

Note that the swanky Koh-I Nor and Hameau de Kashmir hotels listed above also offer apartments.

In the Plein Sud area, above the main village, there are several chalet-style residences. Among the best are Chalet Altitude and Chalet Val 2400, sharing a pool. The Balcons de Val Thorens has a 'fantastic' spa with pool. Many properties up here claim to be ski-in and possibly ski-out, but a couple of reporters have confirmed our own suspicion that access can be tricky. Down near the entrance to the resort are more very smart places, all with pool, sauna etc, including the Montana Plein Sud and Oxalys.

EATING OUT ★★★★☆
Star quality
Top of the range is the Jean Suplice restaurant in the Oxalys residence, with two Michelin stars. We had a delicious and very inventive meal here; expensive, but worth it. The top hotels also have serious restaurants.

There are plenty of more modest places. A 2013 reader tips the Chamois d'Or ('superb, varied menu, became a regular'). Others liked the Petite Ferme ('decent food and prices, good pizzas'). For Savoyard stuff there's the Fondue, Auberge des Balcons, Chaumière and Cabane. The Vieux Chalet has a varied menu, including seafood and duck. The Steak Club found favour with a reporter who

'went three times – excellent pasta, steaks, burgers'. The Blanchot is a wine bar with a simple carte. An old favourite, the Galoubet, has become La Maison Blanche; reports, please.

APRES-SKI ★★★★☆
Livelier than you might expect
Val Thorens is more lively than most high-altitude ski stations. The action starts up the hill at the Folie Douce, with its compulsory table dancing. The Red Fox up at Balcons is crowded at close of play, with karaoke. The Frog and Roastbeef at the top of the village is a long-established British ghetto. The Downunder and the Saloon are lively. Quieter bars include the cosy Rhum Box Cafe (aka Mitch's). Later on, the Malaysia cellar bar rocks from 11pm until the early hours with 'top quality' live bands and dancing.

OFF THE SLOPES ★★☆☆☆
Could be worse
Val Thorens is not ideal for non-skiers. But there's a sports centre with two small pools, sauna, steam, hot tubs, gym etc and a leisure centre with bowling (pricey) and pool tables. Free weekly concerts are held in the church (recommended by a reporter), and there are twice-weekly street markets, a small cinema and an ice-driving course. The toboggan run (the longest in France) is 'great fun'. There are four walking trails marked on the reverse of the piste map. A pedestrian lift pass covers 11 lifts, allowing access to some mountain restaurants and the Cime de Caron. You can try the new 'fantastic' zipwire at 100km per hour and 50 euros a 'flight'. Buses to St-Martin and Les Menuires run five times a day except Saturdays.

OUTLYING RESORT – 900m

ORELLE

Set at the foot of the gondola from the fourth valley (there's no piste down), Orelle isn't a recognizable resort, but offers good accommodation at a bargain price. A couple of hairpins up the hill from the lift base (there's a frequent ski-bus) is Hameau des Eaux, a smart complex of 200 apartments in eight chalet-style buildings, sharing a spa with a decent pool – available through Peak Retreats and Zenith. It includes a small convenience store and a restaurant.

SNOWPIX.COM / CHRIS GILL

Vars / Risoul

Two high, purpose-built resorts in an attractive setting, with a traditional French atmosphere and a shared area of slopes

TOP 10 RATINGS

Extent	★★★
Fast lifts	★
Queues	★★★★
Snow	★★★
Expert	★★
Intermediate	★★★★
Beginner	★★★★
Charm	★★
Convenience	★★★★
Scenery	★★★

RPI 85

lift pass	£160
ski hire	£95
lessons	£75
food & drink	£120
total	**£450**

NEWS

2014/15: The Nevalhaia, a new 4-star boutique hotel, is due to open in Vars in January 2015.

+ Attractive, family-friendly resorts

+ Reasonably snow-sure and with lots of tree-lined runs

+ Among the cheapest resorts in the French Alps

− Still mainly draglifts and slow old chairs, though a few fast ones

− Few on-piste challenges for experts

− Little to do off the slopes

− Fairly remote location

Were they nearer Geneva, Vars and its linked neighbour Risoul would be better known internationally; as it is, they retain a very French atmosphere. The slopes of their shared Forêt Blanche area are, as the name implies, attractively wooded; but they aren't as extensive as you might imagine from their claimed 185km of pistes. We went back a few seasons ago for a couple of days and loved it; a week might be too much for a keen skier or boarder though.

Vars and Risoul are the most southerly French resorts to get a chapter in this book. Their shared lift system is probably the most antiquated in these pages – hence the ★ for fast lifts. And the claimed 185km of pistes is way more than was measured for the Schrahe report discussed in our piste extent feature. Schrahe put the total at a much more modest 73km.

Vars 1850m

Vars includes several small, old villages on or near the approach road, chief among them Vars-Ste-Marie. There are lifts on the fringe of this village, but the focus for most visitors is higher, purpose-built Vars-les-Claux.

Village charm Vars-les-Claux has a lot of flat-roofed apartment blocks that look much worse from up the mountain than from within the village. Reporters like the pleasant, relaxed atmosphere: 'A little gem,' said a reporter last year. Consider 'cosy' Ste-Marie, too.
Convenience It's a small place, but spread along a winding, quite steep road, with two main clusters of shops, bars, restaurants and lodgings: the original focus, at the base of the main gondola, and Point Show, 10 minutes' walk up the hill. Each of these has nursery slopes and fast lifts into the slopes. Buildings spread beyond these points, varying in convenience.
Scenery Pretty wooded slopes surround the village, and there are fine views from the high point of Pic de Chabrières at 2750m.

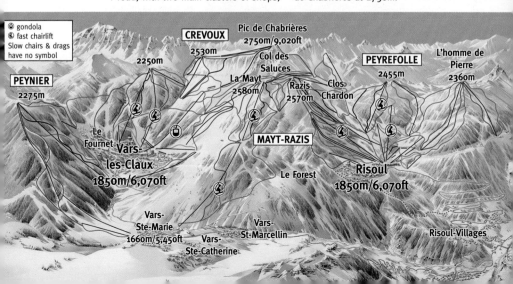

gondola
fast chairlift
Slow chairs & drags have no symbol

PEYNIER 2275m

CREVOUX 2530m

Pic de Chabrières 2750m/9,020ft

Col des Saluces
La Mayt 2580m

Razis 2570m

Clos Chardon

PEYREFOLLE 2455m

L'homme de Pierre 2360m

Le Fournet

Vars-les-Claux 1850m/6,070ft

MAYT-RAZIS

Le Forest

Risoul 1850m/6,070ft

Vars-Ste-Marie 1660m/5,450ft

Vars-Ste-Catherine

Vars-St-Marcellin

Risoul-Villages

Pierre & Vacances
Holidays made for me

**Best price
guarantee
for ski in/out
budget studios
up to spacious
3 bedroom
apartments**

pierreefvacances.co.uk

OT RISOUL

Risoul and Vars are
both pleasantly set
beneath gentle
wooded slopes ↓

THE MOUNTAINS

There are slopes on both sides of the
valley, linked by pistes and by slow
double chairlifts at the lower end of
Vars-les-Claux.

Some reporters have found piste
classification variable and the map
unclear on the links between resorts.
Slopes The wooded, west-facing
Peynier area is the smaller sector, and
reaches only 2275m. The main slopes
are in an east-facing bowl with links
to the Risoul slopes at three points.
There's also a speed-skiing course.
Beneath it are easy runs, open at the
top but dropping into trees.
Fast lifts After the three fast lifts out
of the village it's draglifts and slow
chairs unless you head down to Vars-
Ste-Marie or over to Risoul.
Queues Queues are rare outside the
French holidays, and even then Vars is
not as busy as most family resorts.
One January visitor was worried about
crowding on the slopes, with lots of
east Europeans and Russians about.

Terrain parks There are six freestyle
areas, including two newish ones – the
Girly and Kid parks. Your riding can be
filmed at the Eyssina park.
Snow reliability Not bad: the altitudes
are quite high, the orientation mostly
easterly, and snowmaking is plentiful.
Experts There is little to challenge
experts on-piste, but there is plenty of
off-piste terrain (and great off-piste
tree skiing in Risoul, too).
Intermediates These are fine
intermediate slopes, with a good mix
of decent reds and easy blues. Jas du
Boeuf from La Mayt is a gentle cruise.
The Olympique red run from the top of
La Mayt to Ste-Marie delights most
reporters and is a very respectable
920m vertical. If you can face the slow
chairlifts and tricky drags, there are
good tree-lined runs in the separate
Peynier sector, including an easy black.
Beginners There are three free lifts on
good slopes in central Vars, with lots
of progression runs throughout the
area. Quick learners will be able to get
over to Risoul by the end of the week.
Snowboarding There is good
freeriding, but beginners might find
the number of draglifts a problem.
Cross-country There are 10km of trails.
Mountain restaurants Most places are
self-service. But the Chal Heureux
table-service place is 'good, with
acceptable food and prices'.
Schools and guides A recent reporter
had 'great' private lessons with ESF.
Families The ski school runs a nursery
for children from two-and-a-half years
old, and a ski kindergarten from four.

STAYING THERE

Hotels The Ecureuil (0492 465072) is
an attractive, modern B&B chalet.
Ste-Marie has a Logis de France – the
Vallon (0492 465472).
Apartments Erna Low features five
apartment complexes, Ski Collection
four, and Pierre & Vacances has three,
including the 4-star Albane – liked by
a reporter.
Eating out There is a choice of simple,
good-value places. The Après Ski at
Point Show is worth a look, as is the
Chaudron in Ste-Marie.
Après-ski Animated at teatime; later it
revolves around one or two bars.
Off the slopes There's tobogganing,
ice skating, 34km of walking paths,
cinema, snowmobiling, snowshoeing,
dog sledding and helicopter tours.

Resort	1850m
	6,070ft

The entire Forêt
Blanche ski area

Slopes	1660-2750m
	5,450-9,020ft
Lifts	51
Pistes	185km
	115 miles
Green	18%
Blue	39%
Red	34%
Black	9%
Snowmaking	
	116 guns

UK PACKAGES

Vars Crystal, Erna Low, Lagrange, Pierre & Vacances, PowderBeds, Ski Collection, Thomson
Risoul Crystal, Erna Low, Lagrange, PowderBeds, Rocketski, Thomson, Zenith

Phone numbers
From abroad use the prefix +33 and omit the initial '0' of the phone number

TOURIST OFFICES

Vars
www.vars-ski.com
Risoul
www.risoul.com

Risoul 1850m

Risoul 1850 is a modern ski station, purpose-built from the late 1970s onwards at the top of a winding road up from the original village of Risoul. It is a quiet, apartment-based resort, popular with families – but not exclusively so.

Village charm Many of the original resort buildings are bulky eight- or nine-storey buildings, but wood-clad with some traditional style. Newer developments are attractive and chalet-style, made of wood and stone. The busy little main street, with a small range of shops, bars and restaurants, is far from traffic-free. But the locals offer a friendly welcome.
Convenience The village meets the mountain in classic French purpose-built style, with sunny restaurant terraces facing the slopes and a compact centre. Some lodgings are a short but 'knackering' uphill walk away if you miss the last lift.
Scenery Risoul has a pleasantly woody setting beneath its slopes; reporters often comment on great views.

THE MOUNTAINS
The upper slopes are open, but those back to Risoul are prettily wooded, and good for bad-weather days.
Slopes The slopes, mainly north-facing, spread over several minor peaks and bowls, and connect with neighbouring Vars at two points.
Fast lifts There are three fast chairs accessing a good number of runs, but still lots of tricky 'difficile' draglifts.
Queues Queues are rare. But see the comment under Vars about crowds.
Terrain parks La Zing is aimed at beginner freestylers, with easy jumps and rails and a snowcross.
Snow reliability Snow reliability is reasonably good; the slopes are all above 1850m and mostly north-facing. Snowmaking is fairly extensive.
Experts Risoul's main top stations access a couple of steepish descents. And there's some good off-piste terrain – including excellent, widely spaced tree skiing on not very steep slopes and areas accessed through gates that are closed when there's an avalanche risk (though these are not marked or explained on the piste map).
Intermediates There are decent reds and blues in all sectors. Almost all Risoul's runs return to the village, making it difficult to get lost.
Beginners Three free lifts serve good, convenient nursery slopes. There are lots of easy pistes to move on to.

Snowboarding There is a lot of good freeriding to be done throughout the area, although beginners might not like the large proportion of draglifts.
Cross-country There are 17km of trails.
Mountain restaurants Choice is limited. The Homme de Pierre 'brings you decent dishes cooked to order'. And the self-service Tetras is a small, attractive hut.
Schools and guides Reports on the ESF have been positive, and we had an excellent ESF guide on our visit.
Families Risoul is very much a family resort. The ESF operates a ski kindergarten slightly above the village and reached by a child-friendly lift.

STAYING THERE
Most visitors stay in apartments.
Hotels The Chardon Bleu (0492 460727) is right on the slopes. You can also stay overnight up at the Tetras mountain refuge (0492 460983).
Apartments We enjoyed the 4-star Balcons de Sirius units – good pool, hot tub and sauna; Antarés is similar. Erna Low features these.
Eating out There's a decent choice offering fairly good value. Readers' tips: Chérine (pizza, pasta), Marmite and Entre Pot. We tried L'Extrad, which served huge portions of hearty food.
Après-ski Nightlife is livelier than most people are expecting. There are several bars and the Reflex nightclub. Try the Babao and the Chalet or Eterlou for a quieter drink.
Off the slopes Limited. We enjoyed the guided night-time snowmobiling on adventurous and varied terrain. There's also toboganing, snowshoeing, skating and a cinema. Excursions to Briançon are possible.

Build your own shortlist: **www.wheretoskiandsnowboard.com**

Germany

Germany isn't a big destination for UK-based skiers. Over the page is a chapter on Garmisch-Partenkirchen, by far the most important downhill resort in Germany – famously the venue for the 1936 Olympics, when downhill racing was introduced, and Adolf Hitler got the facilities built on time. Seventy-five years later it hosted the 2011 World Championships. On this page is a non-comprehensive tour of the country's main skiing regions.

WEBSITES

Allgäu
www.allgaeu.info
www.das-hoechste.de
Bavarian Alps
www.karwendelbahn.de
www.laber-bergbahn.de
www.brauneck-bergbahn.de
Black Forest
www.blackforest-tourism.com
Harz
www.harzinfo.de
Sauerland
www.wintersport-arena.de
Saxony
www.oberwiesenthal.com
www.fichtelberg-ski.de
Thüringer Wald
www.oberhof.de

THE ALPS

Allgäu This region claims 300km of downhill runs and an amazing 800km of cross-country trails. The main lift systems operate under the regional name Das Hoechste. Highest of all is Nebelhorn (2225m) reached from the nice little town of **Oberstdorf** by a two-stage cable car to the main slopes (served by two chairs), with a third stage to the top for Germany's longest on-piste descent (7.5km). Oberstdorf is probably best known as the resort that kicks off the annual Four Hills ski jumping tournament held over each New Year period. The Post hotel has been praised for 'good, substantial, reasonably priced' meals. South of Oberstdorf you enter **Kleinwalsertal**, which belongs to Austria, strangely. The Kanzelwand slopes link with Fellhorn to form Germany's biggest area, with three six-packs, two gondolas and nine other lifts. Ifen and Walmendingerhorn are smaller areas in the valley, and the Allgäu has lots of other resorts such as Oberjoch and Pfronten.

Bavarian Alps Garmisch-Partenkirchen is covered over the page. **Mittenwald** (915m) is a cute town in a spectacular setting. The cable car to Karwendel accesses an epic ski route dropping 1300m in 6km. Across the valley, Kranzbergy has seven lifts serving wooded slopes up to 1350m.

Other resorts These are on the fringes of the Alps, with less dramatic scenery. **Oberammergau** (835m and famous for its once-a-decade Passion Play) is another cute town, with a gondola to Laber (1685m) that accesses a long ski route and a direct black piste; across town a chairlift serves Kolbensattel (1270m). There are more extensive slopes on Brauneck above **Lenggries** (680m) – a top height of 1710m, and 18 lifts including a gondola.

There are other small resorts, some near the infamous Berchtesgaden.

THE REST

Black Forest In the south-west corner: a lot of cross-country, but downhill too. Feldberg reaches 1500m with 31 lifts and 55km of pistes.

Harz A low mountain range, south of Hanover. A handful of small resorts, the biggest being Braunlage.

Sauerland Low mountains east of Düsseldorf. Some 500km of cross-country. Winterberg has 24 lifts, Willingen a gondola and seven drags.

Saxony On the border with the Czech Republic: a handful of low, small resorts, the most compelling at Fichtelberg above Oberwiesenthal.

Thüringer Wald North-east of Frankfurt: extensive cross-country, and a bit of easy downhill. The best-known resort is Oberhof.

379

GARMISCH-PARTENKIRCHEN
TOURISMUS

← Germany has
proper Alps, as here
in Garmisch-
Partenkirchen

MARKT GARMISCH-PARTENKIRCHEN

Garmisch-Partenkirchen

Twin resort towns sprawling at the foot of Germany's highest mountain, reaching glacial heights on the Austrian border

TOP 10 RATINGS

Extent	★
Fast lifts	★★★
Queues	★★★
Snow	★★★
Expert	★★★★
Intermediate	★★★
Beginner	★
Charm	★★★
Convenience	★★
Scenery	★★★★

RPI   90

lift pass	£180
ski hire	£95
lessons	£80
food & drink	£105
total	**£460**

NEWS

2014/15: Three new toboggan runs totalling 2km are to open on the Zugspitze.

2013/14: A mid-size terrain park opened near the Hexenkessel twin chair in the Classic area.

➕ Weather-proof combination of a fair-sized glacier area and wooded slopes lower down

➕ Some spectacular views

➕ Some excellent, challenging runs

➕ Good-value hotels, cheap for eating and drinking, good for short breaks

➖ Except on the glacier, very few long easy runs; beginners and timid intermediates beware

➖ Many of the best runs descend to low altitude, where conditions are rarely good

➖ Glacier access takes time

Garmisch is Germany's leading ski resort. It has two separate ski areas: one at low altitude with mainly tough runs, the other on a glacier with gentler terrain. It has plenty to amuse confident skiers for a couple of days, and with short transfers from Munich it makes a good short-break destination. We're getting few reports from readers; if you go, do let us know what you think.

THE RESORT

Garmisch and Partenkirchen are separate towns that have merged as they have spread to fill the broad, flat valley bottom beneath the Zugspitze, while keeping their centres distinct.

There are smaller resorts on the Austrian side of the Zugspitze. These and the Garmisch ski areas are covered by the Top Snow Card.

Village charm Each half of the resort is a sizeable town – spacious and pleasant but not notably captivating.

Convenience You'll need to use trains, buses or cars at both ends of the day. The Zugspitze railway starts next to the main station, more or less between the two town centres; it goes to the glacier via the other lift bases.

Scenery The Wetterstein massif, of which the Zugspitze is the peak, is impressive, and there are great panoramic views from the top.

THE MOUNTAINS

The glacier is quite separate from the lower slopes, which the resort calls the 'Classic' area. In fact, that area also divides into two parts, awkwardly linked – a higher, almost treeless part (Alpspitz) and a lower, heavily wooded part (Hausberg-Kreuzeck).

Slopes The **Hausberg-Kreuzeck** sector directly above the resort is accessed by two gondolas; these start a few km out of town and are served by the railway. These lower lifts have decent verticals and serve long runs; the lifts higher up are all much shorter. An inconspicuous narrow path and a rope

tow form the link between this sector and the base of the higher **Alpspitz** sector, more directly reached via the Alpspitz cable car. Although the altitude is modest, this sector feels like high-mountain terrain, with dramatic scenery – Dolomite-like on the isolated Osterfelder and Bernadein runs, on skier's right.

There are two routes to the glacier: there's the railway from town that serves the Classic area lift bases, which goes on to tunnel slowly through the mountain, emerging at the glacier; or there's the cable car from Eibsee that climbs an impressive 1950m to the Zugspitze – from there you have to ride another cable car down to the slopes.

Above the main lift junction are typical blue glacier slopes served by multiple drags. Below it and spreading across the bowl is a range of good red runs and some good off-piste terrain served by two six-packs and two drags. None of these lifts rises more than 400m vertical, but in other respects it's a good area.

Fast lifts Access lifts are fast, but after that it's mainly drags and slow chairs.

Queues Fine weekends attract crowds from Munich; but at other times we don't expect problems.

Terrain parks There's now a 4,000 sqm terrain park at the Classic area. It has rails, tubes and boxes.

Snow reliability The glacier area is small and remote, so conditions lower down are important. The lower main area is shady, but some of the best runs descend to valley level – ie to

MOMENTUM SKI

Weekend & a la carte ski holiday specialists

100% Tailor-made

Premier hotels & apartments

The No.1 Specialist in Garmisch

020 7371 9111
WWW.MOMENTUMSKI.COM

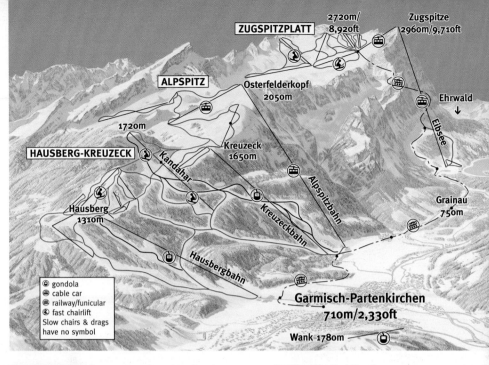

Map labels:
- ZUGSPITZPLATT 2720m/8,920ft
- Zugspitze 2960m/9,710ft
- ALPSPITZ
- Osterfelderkopf 2050m
- Ehrwald
- Elbsee
- 1720m
- Kreuzeck 1650m
- HAUSBERG-KREUZECK
- Kandahar
- Alpspitzbahn
- Grainau 750m
- Hausberg 1310m
- Kreuzeckbahn
- Hausbergbahn
- gondola
- cable car
- railway/funicular
- fast chairlift
- Slow chairs & drags have no symbol
- Garmisch-Partenkirchen 710m/2,330ft
- Wank 1780m

Build your own shortlist: www.wheretoskiandsnowboard.com

KEY FACTS

Resort	710m	
	2,330ft	
Slopes	720-2720m	
	2,360-8,920ft	
Lifts	27	
Pistes	62km	
	39 miles	
Blue	25%	
Red	70%	
Black	5%	
Snowmaking	47%	

UK PACKAGES

Momentum, STC

Phone numbers
From elsewhere in Germany add the prefix 08821. From abroad use the prefix +49 and delete the initial '0'

TOURIST OFFICE

www.gapa.de

720m. Despite comprehensive snowmaking, conditions at these altitudes can be poor even when there's great snow higher up, as we confirmed on one January visit.
Experts The long runs to the valley are challenging enough to amuse most experts, particularly the excellent Kandahar downhill race course. The final pitch of this takes real bottle when icy at the end of the day. Higher up, there are off-piste opportunities in the Alpspitz sector and on the glacier.
Intermediates For confident skiers it's fine, but this is not a hill where timid intermediates can build confidence.
Beginners Learn elsewhere. The nursery slopes are fine, but they're up the mountain and there is no beginner pass. And the only easy runs to move on to are busy links between Kreuzeck and Hausberg (or on the glacier).
Snowboarding There are drags in all sectors, though many can be avoided.
Cross-country There are 28km of trails along the valleys, of varying difficulty.
Mountain restaurants The glass-sided Gletschergarten on the glacier has a roof that can open on sunny days. Hochalm below Alpspitz in the Classic area does Bavarian fare. The Bayernhaus is worth a stop on the gentle blue run 6 from Hausberg.
Schools and guides There are several schools, but we lack reports.

Families The Kinderland centre at Hausberg looks good, with magic carpet and snow sculptures. There are family discounts on the lift pass.

STAYING THERE

Hotels There is one 5-star – Reindl's Partenkirchner Hof (943870), well placed for the rail stations – and lots of 4-stars and 3-stars. Tips are the 3-star Garmischer Hof (9110) and Atlas Post (7090), and the 4-star Zugspitze (9010). Rates are low in Alpine terms.
Apartments Can be booked via the tourist office.
Eating out There's plenty of choice – these towns have a big summer trade. Gasthof Fraundorfer and the upscale Alpenhof do hearty Bavarian food.
Après-ski There are bars at the lift bases where you can enjoy waiting for the next train home, and in town there are lots of cosy bars such as Zirbel Stube, which has live music. Peaches is a lively bar with sports on TV.
Off the slopes There's lots to do, both outdoors and indoors. Walks include one through the Partnachklamm gorge and paths on the lift-served hill that is across town from the slopes – called Wank. There's an ice rink and toboggan runs – including a 5km run at Mount Hausberg that is floodlit twice a week – and three new runs on the Zugspitze.

Italy

Italy has a lot going for it as a destination: it offers great value for money (over half the Italian resorts we cover have price index figures in our green category – the cheapest); the atmosphere is jolly; it offers reliably good food and wine; the scenery, especially in the Dolomites and Val d'Aosta, is simply stunning; the lift systems include some of the most modern in Europe; the snowmaking is state of the art (and they use it well); and the grooming is top-notch.

Italian resorts vary as widely in their characteristics as they do in location – and they are spread along the full length of the Italian border, from Sauze d'Oulx in the west to the Dolomites. There are quaint backwater villages, fashionable towns, bleak ski stations – the choice is yours.

WEEKDAY PEACE, WEEKEND CROWDS

Many Italians based in the northern cities go skiing at weekends, and it's very noticeable that many resorts are busy only then, and become peaceful once the weekend invaders retreat. It's a great advantage for those of us who are there for the whole week, and probably skiing only one day at the weekend.

This pattern is especially noticeable at chic resorts such as Cortina, Courmayeur and Madonna, and resorts that have not yet found international fame such as those in the Monterosa region. The clearest example is La Thuile, in the Aosta valley. Even at February half-term the pistes here can be semi-deserted on weekdays. In parts of the Dolomites (such as Val Gardena) that are dominated by German visitors, the Sunday evening exodus doesn't happen – like Brits, the Germans tend to go for a week.

We may be wrong, but we also think we have detected, over the last season or two, an appreciable drop in the numbers of Italian skiers – perhaps related to the economic difficulties. On our February 2013 visit, Cortina offered delightfully empty pistes.

THE LONG LUNCH LIVES

Many Italians don't take their skiing or boarding too seriously. A late start, a long lunch and an early finish are common – leaving the slopes delightfully quiet for the rest of us. Mountain restaurants are reasonably priced, and there are welcoming places almost everywhere, encouraging leisurely lunching. A persistent drag, though, is the ludicrous system in many self-service places where you have to queue to pay at the cash desk and then queue again at the counter to collect your food or drink. Italy is also the home of the hybrid-service restaurant, where you order at the bar but are served at your table. Rather like most British pubs.

AND THE LONG EVENING

We've spent a lot of time in Italy in the last couple of years, and we've started to get the hang of après-ski in resorts where Italians are the major group of guests. In its pure form après here revolves around the aperitivo – the cocktail or Prosecco taken in a cool bar immediately before dinner – normally accompanied by some

SNOWPIX.COM / CHRIS GILL
← Sestriere was the first purpose-built resort in the Alps, created in the 1930s; like many Italian resorts it is busy on sunny weekends but much quieter during the week

delicious antipasti to nibble. You need to be in your evening finery by then, of course, and with a visit to the spa to fit in as well, there isn't much time for a protracted Austrian-style drinking session at close of play.

But there are exceptions, usually where British or German guests form a big part of the clientele, such as Sauze d'Oulx and some resorts in the Sella Ronda region – here you get quite a big early-après trade both on the mountain and in the villages.

WHO NEEDS REAL SNOW?

One thing that Italian resorts do have to contend with is erratic snowfall. While the snow in the northern Alps tends to come from the west, Italy's snow tends to come from storms arriving from the south. So Italy can have great conditions when other countries are suffering (last season was a spectacular example of that); or vice versa. But vice versa tends to apply a lot of the time. As a result, Italian resorts got into snowmaking early, and have learned how to do it well – and our observation is that they tend to use it more effectively than other Alpine countries.

A lot of Italian runs seem flatteringly easy. This is partly because grooming is immaculate and partly because piste classification often seems to overstate difficulty. Nowhere is this clearer than in the linked slopes of La Thuile (in Italy) and La Rosière (in France), where a couple of lift rides take you from Italian motorways classified red to French mogul fields classified blue.

The classification of easy runs as reds creates a real problem. In

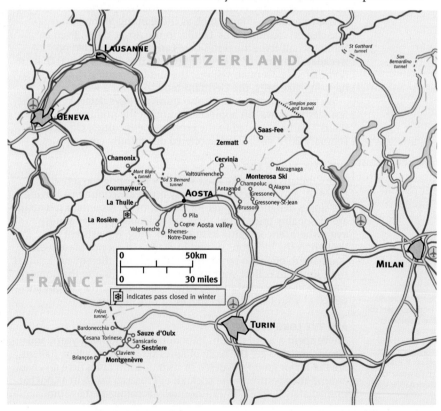

many areas – Monterosa springs to mind – the red category also includes runs that actually are a bit challenging, and precious few runs are classed as blue. For a nervous intermediate, this is bad news – you can't know which runs you'll be comfortable on, and which ones to avoid.

OFF-PISTE CONFUSION

Many Italian areas declare it illegal to go off-piste near their pistes, or to go off-piste at all, or to go off-piste outside defined routes or without a guide or without transceiver, shovel and probe. We've tried to get to the bottom of these developments; but a prompt, clear, accurate response to a slightly technical question such as this is not a speciality of Italian tourist bodies.

Some resorts tell us there are national laws; others, that it's a regional matter; others, that it's a local matter. Of course, there is then the issue of whether the law is applied and how it is policed. Where we have a clear view of the situation in a given resort, we include that in the relevant chapter. Thankfully, we have no evidence of any interference in off-piste skiing in the Aosta valley, which is Italy's off-piste/heli-skiing HQ.

Three editions ago we were told by Livigno that off-piste without a guide was officially banned. The following season they designated half a dozen slopes in one sector as freeride routes – marking them on the piste map and guarding them with entry gates equipped with gadgets to check that your avalanche bleepers are working. Excellent, we thought. Then it turned out that you were not

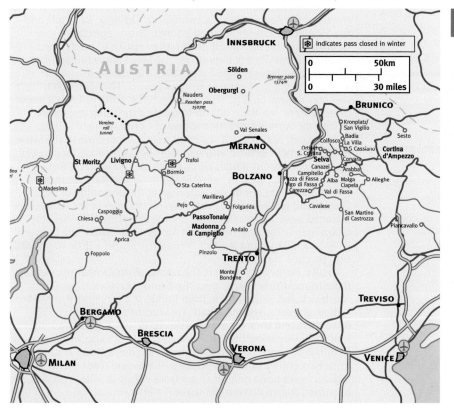

supposed to ski these routes without a guide. Now we are told that off-piste skiing is allowed everywhere with or without a guide (including on those routes that were taken off last year's piste map but will be on this year's). And heli-skiing is now promoted. And back in 2011 we were told it was a national law that banned off-piste skiing. Now we are told it is down to the local mayor to make up the rules. Bonkers!

SOME SIGHTSEEING IN VENICE?
Next time we go to the Dolomites we'll fly to Venice and get a return flight late in the day. With an early start from the resort, that will give us time to ride the water-bus to and from the city. The 'orange' line goes all the way along the Canale Grande to Santa Maria del Giglio, near San Marco. Round trip 2hr30. That would make a lovely end to a skiing trip. We had this all planned this year, but excessive snow blocking key roads out of Corvara scuppered it.

DRIVING IN THE ITALIAN ALPS
There are four main geographical groupings of Italian resorts, widely separated. Getting to some of these resorts is a very long haul, and moving from one area to another can involve very long drives (though the extensive motorway network is a great help).

The handful of resorts to the west of Turin – Bardonecchia, Sauze d'Oulx, Sestriere and neighbours in the Milky Way region – are easily reached from France via the Fréjus tunnel, or via the good road over the pass that the French resort of Montgenèvre sits on.

Further north, and somewhat nearer to Turin than Milan, are the resorts of the Aosta valley – Courmayeur, Cervinia, La Thuile and the Monterosa area are the best known. These (especially Courmayeur) are the easiest of all Italian resorts to reach from Britain or from Geneva airport (via the Mont Blanc tunnel from Chamonix in France). The Aosta valley can also be reached from Switzerland via the Grand St Bernard tunnel. The approach is high and may require chains. The road down the Aosta valley is a major thoroughfare, but the roads up to some of the other resorts are quite long, winding and (in the case of Cervinia) high.

To the east is a string of scattered resorts, most close to the Swiss border, many in isolated and remote valleys involving long drives up from the nearest Italian cities, or high-altitude drives from Switzerland. The links between Switzerland and Italy are more clearly shown on our larger-scale map at the beginning of the Switzerland section of the book than on the map of the Italian Alps included here. The major routes are the St Gotthard tunnel between Göschenen (near Andermatt) and Airolo – the main route between Basel and Milan – and the San Bernardino tunnel a little way to the east, reached via Chur.

Finally, further east still are the resorts of the Dolomites. Getting there from Austria is easy, over the Brenner motorway pass from Innsbruck. But getting there from Britain is a very long drive indeed – allow at least a day and a half. We wouldn't lightly choose to drive there and back for a week's skiing, except as part of a longer tour including some time in Austrian resorts. It's also worth bearing in mind that once you arrive in the Dolomites, getting around the intricate network of valleys on narrow, winding roads can be a slow business – it's often quicker to get from village to village on skis. Impatient Italian driving can make it a bit stressful, too.

SNOWPIX.COM / CHRIS GILL

Cervinia

One of a kind, this: for extensive, snow-sure, sunny, easy skiing,
there is nowhere to match Cervinia. Good for late season holidays

RATINGS

The mountains

Extent	★★★
Fast lifts	★★★★
Queues	★★★★
Terrain p'ks	★★★★
Snow	★★★★★
Expert	★
Intermediate	★★★★
Beginner	★★★★★
Boarder	★★★★
X-country	★
Restaurants	★★★
Schools	★★★★
Families	★★

The resort

Charm	★★
Convenience	★★★
Scenery	★★★★
Eating out	★★★★
Après-ski	★★
Off-slope	★

RPI 90

lift pass	£170
ski hire	£105
lessons	£80
food & drink	£120
total	**£475**

KEY FACTS

Resort	2050m
	6,730ft

Cervinia/Valt'nenche
Slopes	1525-3480m	
	5,000-11,420ft	
Lifts	19	
Pistes	160km	
	100 miles	
Blue	30%	
Red	59%	
Black	11%	
Snowmaking	50%	

Cervinia/ Valt'nenche/
Zermatt combined
Slopes	1525-3820m	
	5,000-12,530ft	
Lifts	54	
Pistes	360km	
	224 miles	
Blue	21%	
Red	61%	
Black	18%	
Snowmaking	61%	

➕ Miles of long, consistently gentle runs; ideal for intermediates wary of steep slopes or bumps

➕ Slopes are sunny, but high and pretty snow-sure

➕ Spectacular setting beneath the towering Matterhorn

➕ Excellent village nursery slope

➕ Valuable link with Zermatt in Switzerland, but ...

➖ Bad weather (especially high winds) can close most of the higher lifts, severely limiting your options

➖ Very little to interest those looking for challenges

➖ Not a notably attractive village

➖ Few off-slope amenities

➖ Steep climb to the main gondola, although there is a more convenient chairlift alternative

If there is a better resort than Cervinia for those who like easy cruising in spring sunshine, we have yet to find it. And then there's more easy cruising on the gentlest of Zermatt's slopes just over the Swiss border.

And for the rest of us? Well, to be frank, the rest of us are better off elsewhere. In particular, those with an eye on bumps or powder over in Zermatt should stay there, not here – access to its best slopes is still time-consuming.

The village was branded Cervinia when it was developed for skiing, but these days harks back to its mountaineering roots by prefixing that with its original name, Breuil. Ever heard of that? No, quite. So we'll stick with Cervinia.

THE RESORT

Cervinia is on the Italian side of the Matterhorn (or Monte Cervino), at the head of a long valley off the Aosta valley. The resort gets a lot of Italian weekend business, and quite a lot of Russian January business. We get a good flow of reports from mainly satisfied British visitors.

The slopes link to Valtournenche further down the valley (covered by the lift pass) and at high altitude to Zermatt in Switzerland (covered by a daily supplement, or a more expensive weekly pass). Lifts at Valtournenche may be open when Cervinia's are closed by wind – but a reporter warns that the bus service is infrequent.

Day trips by car to Courmayeur, La Thuile, Pila and the Monterosa Ski resorts of Champoluc and Gressoney are not easy, but possible (and some tour operators offer excursions). A six-day lift pass covers two days in these other resorts. Or you can buy an Aosta Valley pass for the week and optionally add two days in Zermatt.

VILLAGE CHARM ★★★★★
Getting smarter?
The old climbing village grew into a ski resort in a haphazard way, and subsequent development has been no better. The result is neither pleasing to the eye nor hideous. We sense a gradual smartening up of the centre, with wood and stone taking over from concrete. The cobbled main street is traffic-free, and the place is pleasant enough to walk around in the evening. The river separating the main strip from the nursery slopes adds some charm. But ugly apartment blocks and hotels spoil the views from the slopes.

CONVENIENCE ★★★★★
Up or down
As our plan makes clear, this is not a big place, but location is still worth considering carefully. What used to be the main lift from the village, a gondola to Plan Maison, starts a hike

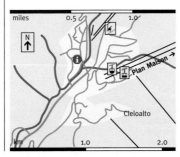

MOMENTUM SKI

Weekend & a la carte
ski holiday specialists

100% Tailor-made

Premier hotels
& apartments

Flexible travel
arrangements

020 7371 9111
WWW.MOMENTUMSKI.COM

up from the south end of the village – irritating for some, 'truly awful' for others. The alternative of successive six-packs from the nursery slopes, next to the village centre, makes this the obvious place to stay.

There are also developments above the main village, some of them closer to the gondola. Some hotels run shuttles, and an efficient public bus serves the Cieloalto complex, high up to the south of the main village.

Footpaths can be icy and tricky.

SCENERY ★★★★☆
Monte Cervino rules
The Matterhorn is less special seen from the Italian rather than from the Swiss side, but Cervinia's setting close to the mountain is very impressive by normal standards, with the peak towering above the village. Driving up in the late afternoon on our last visit, we were forced to stop and stare. There are fine views from the slopes.

THE MOUNTAINS

Cervinia's main slopes are high, open, sunny and mostly west-facing. It's an unpleasant place when the weather is bad, and the link with Zermatt is often closed by wind (sometimes for days), especially early in the season.

The piste map – which also covers Zermatt – and piste marking are up to scratch, and piste grooming is generally good. The high number of red runs on the map is misleading: most of them could be classified blue.

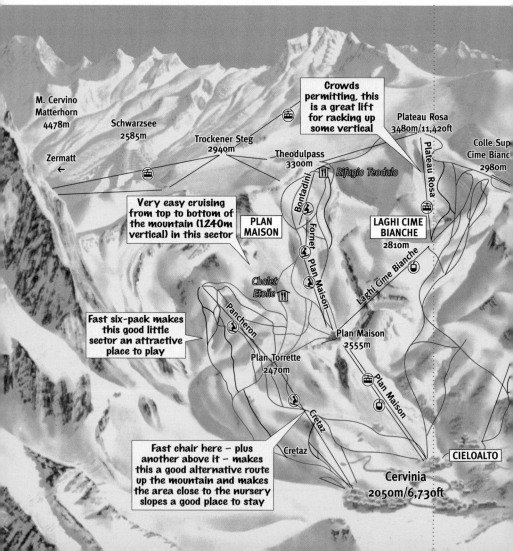

M. Cervino
Matterhorn
4478m

Schwarzsee
2585m

Zermatt
←

Trockener Steg
2940m

Theodulpass
3300m

Rifugio Teodulo

Plateau Rosa
348om/11,420ft

Colle Sup
Cime Bianc
2980m

Plateau Rosa

Bontadini

Fornet Plan Maison

PLAN MAISON

LAGHI CIME BIANCHE
2810m

Laghi Cime Bianche

Chalet Etoile

Pancheron

Plan Maison

Plan Maison
2555m

Plan Torrette
2470m

Plan Maison

Cretaz

Cretaz

CIELOALTO

Cervinia
2050m/6,730ft

Crowds permitting, this is a great lift for racking up some vertical

Very easy cruising from top to bottom of the mountain (1240m vertical) in this sector

Fast six-pack makes this good little sector an attractive place to play

Fast chair here – plus another above it – makes this a good alternative route up the mountain and makes the area close to the nursery slopes a good place to stay

Air Turin 120km/
75 miles (1hr45);
Milan Malpensa
185km/115 miles
(2hr15); Milan Linate
205km/125 miles
(2hr30); Geneva
205km/125 miles
(2hr45)

Rail Châtillon
(27km/17 miles);
regular buses from
station

EXTENT OF THE SLOPES ★★★☆☆
High, wide and easy

Cervinia has the biggest, highest, most snow-sure area of easy, well-groomed pistes we've come across. The area has Italy's highest pistes and some of its longest. At the top you are 6km as well as 1400m vertical from the village.

A deep gorge splits the slopes into two main sectors. Looking up the hill, the lifts from the village take you into the bigger left-hand sector at first.

A gondola takes you to the mid-mountain base of **Plan Maison**. We've rarely seen the parallel cable car working. A more convenient alternative for many is the six-pack from the village nursery slopes to Plan Torrette, where another six-pack serves the good slopes under the Matterhorn –

and gives quick access to Plan Maison.

Above Plan Maison, a chain of three fast quads goes on up to Theodulpass, slightly the lower of two links with the slopes of Zermatt. From Plan Maison you can instead take a gondola across to **Laghi Cime Bianche**, and the right-hand sector. From there a big cable car goes up to Plateau Rosa, the other link with Zermatt. This is also the start of the splendid, wide Ventina run back to the cable car station (or on down to the village).

Part-way down you can branch off left for **Valtournenche**. The slopes here are served by three chairlifts above a modern gondola from the village – but the final lift towards Cervinia is still a long draglift with some tricky steep sections. From top to bottom the run

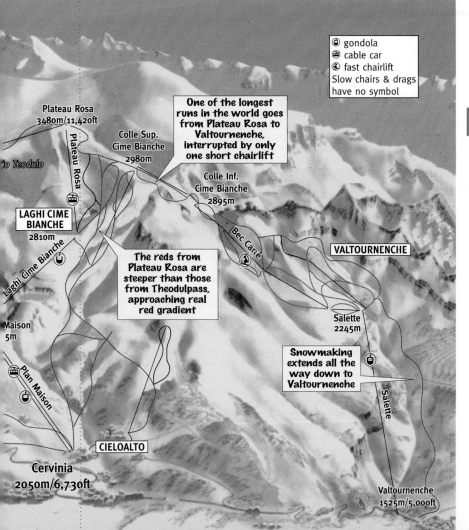

Plateau Rosa
3480m/11,420ft

Plateau Rosa

'o Teodulo

Colle Sup. Cime Bianche
2980m

One of the longest runs in the world goes from Plateau Rosa to Valtournenche, interrupted by only one short chairlift

Colle Inf. Cime Bianche
2895m

LAGHI CIME BIANCHE
2810m

Laghi Cime Bianche

The reds from Plateau Rosa are steeper than those from Theodulpass, approaching real red gradient

Bec Carré

VALTOURNENCHE

Maison
5m

Plan Maison

Salette
2245m

Snowmaking extends all the way down to Valtournenche

Salette

CIELOALTO

Cervinia
2050m/6,730ft

Valtournenche
1525m/5,000ft

🚠 gondola
🚡 cable car
🚠 fast chairlift
Slow chairs & drags
have no symbol

Resort news and key links: www.wheretoskiandsnowboard.com

↑ Staying here, close to the village centre and to the Cretaz six-pack, is convenient

ROD GARVEY

LIFT PASSES

Prices in €

Age	1-day	6-day
under 13	28	126
13 to 64	40	210
65 plus	32	168

Free Under 8 and 80+
Beginner Limited day pass €17
Notes Covers all lifts on the Italian side, including Valtournenche; half-day passes; includes Aosta Valley extension from 3 days
Alternative passes Valtournenche only; International (includes Zermatt); Aosta Valley

to the valley is almost 2000m vertical and 13km long, interrupted only by a very short quad chairlift part-way.

There is also the very small, little-used **Cieloalto** area at the bottom of the Ventina run, served by a slow old chair to the south of the village. This has some of Cervinia's steeper pistes, and the only trees in the area.

FAST LIFTS ★★★★
Few slow lifts left
Most of Cervinia's main lifts are fast. The few slow ones left are in the Valtournenche and Cieloalto sectors.

QUEUES ★★★★
Very few problems
In general, neither we nor readers have complaints about queues in the main area of slopes, though the chair above Plan Maison does still get busy. Of course, the lower lifts may be busy when upper lifts are shut by wind. The gondola station at Valtournenche has a big car park that fills up at weekends, and the lifts above the gondola can then be busy.

TERRAIN PARKS ★★★★
One of Italy's best
The 'Indian' terrain park by the fast Fornet chair is one of the best parks in Italy. Run by *Snowboard Italy*'s former editor, it is said to be over 400m long and 100m wide. There are three jump courses of different difficulties. There are various kickers, rails and walls.

Helmets are compulsory. There is no half-pipe, but Zermatt's pipe is only just over the border.

There is also a small park near the village that some of our readers have enjoyed, especially with their children.

SNOW RELIABILITY ★★★★★
A question of altitude
This is not a notably snowy corner of the Alps, and the slopes get the afternoon sun. But snow is usually good from early to late season thanks to the altitude (these slopes are among the highest in the Alps) and to good grooming and snowmaking on most key runs from top to bottom – down to Valtournenche as well as Cervinia.

FOR EXPERTS ★
Forget it
This is not a resort for experts. There are a few black runs scattered here and there, but they are not reliably open and most of them would be classified red elsewhere; we have only one sighting of moguls – on the black above Plan Torrette. Accessible off-piste terrain is limited, and high winds can play havoc with fresh snow. But of course there is some off-piste – above Plan Torrette for example – and of course conditions can be brilliant, and you then have the advantage that the snow can remain untracked for ages. Heli-skiing can be arranged.

You can head over to Zermatt for

Getting to Zermatt's classic Rothorn and Stockhorn sectors is much quicker than it once was, thanks to the Furi-Riffelberg gondola. But don't expect to spend very long on those Triftji moguls. On the way back you may meet long queues. Allow plenty of time – and beware closure of the top lifts by wind.

ACTIVITIES

Indoor Swimming pool, sauna, fitness centre, climbing wall (all at Valtournenche), museum (at Plateau Rosà)

Outdoor Natural ice rink, hiking, snowmobiling, airboarding, mountaineering, snowshoeing, ice karting, ice climbing, paragliding

more challenging slopes – look at the 'Zermatt connection' box in the margin.

FOR INTERMEDIATES ★★★★☆
Miles of long, flattering runs
Virtually the whole area can be covered comfortably by early intermediates. From top to bottom there are wide, gentle, smooth runs. Strong intermediates can find amusement at the extreme left and right of the area. The Ventina red is a particularly good fast cruise. You can use the cable car to do the top part repeatedly. The runs served by the Pancheron chair at Plan Torrette tend to be attractively quiet. But adventurous intermediates will soon be itching to be off to Zermatt.

The runs towards Valtournenche are great cruises and very popular with reporters. The 13km run all the way down is very satisfying, through splendid rocky scenery.

A reader notes that access to Zermatt via Theodulpass involves a tricky start – so early intermediates might want to go via Plateau Rosa.

FOR BEGINNERS ★★★★★
Gentle progress
A limited day pass covers the good village nursery slope, with its long moving carpet, and the adjacent chairlift. Complete beginners start there and graduate to the fine flat area around Plan Maison and the gentle blue runs above. Fast learners will be going from top to bottom of the mountain in a few days. But one reporter found many blues 'quite crowded', especially at weekends.

FOR BOARDERS ★★★★☆
Easy cruising
The wide, gentle and well-groomed slopes, generally good snow and lack of many draglifts make Cervinia pretty much ideal for beginner and early intermediate boarders. But there are some long, flat parts to beware of (notably around Plan Maison). Serious boarders will enjoy the terrain park, and there's a special pass (27 euros a day last season) that covers two chairlifts that access the park plus return trips on the Plan Maison gondola; there's also heli-boarding.

FOR CROSS-COUNTRY ★☆☆☆☆
Hardly any
There are only two short trails (both 3km or so).

Inghams

7 NIGHTS
FROM ONLY
£599

CERVINIA

INGHAMS
1934 **80** 2014
ANNIVERSARY

► An Italian superstar resort
► Ski Dec to Apr

inghams.co.uk 01483 371 236 ABTA V4871 ATOL 0025

MOUNTAIN RESTAURANTS ★★★☆☆
OK if you know where to go
There are some good places if you know where to go. They are marked but not identified on the resort piste map. Toilet facilities are a traditional cause of complaints, but several have now been improved.

Editors' choice Chalet Etoile (0166 940220), amid the blue runs above Plan Maison, is an old favourite. It's best on a sunny day; on a bad day it gets ridiculously crowded inside – though the atmosphere is all the jollier as a result. The food is excellent – we had fab fish soup on our last visit. There's a self-service section too. The much simpler Rifugio Teodulo (0166 949400) on the border at Theodulpass is another good option – excellent pasta.

Worth knowing about Reporters have tipped Plan Torrette (good food, old skiing artefacts on the wall), with self- and table-service sections. The small, cosy Rifugio Guide del Cervino at Plateau Rosa is tipped for 'desserts to die for' as well as the best view from a toilet you will ever see. The Gran Sometta on run 39 has a 'nice atmosphere, good service, excellent food'. New entrants this year are Rocce Nere at Plan Maison ('huge portions of everything from burgers to pork knuckles; cheap and cheerful'); Bardoney, at the bottom of the run down from Plan Maison ('fast table-service and fantastic goulash'); and Bontadini, down from Theodulpass ('very good value').

The restaurants are cheaper and less crowded in the Valtournenche sector. The Foyer des Guides on the red run to the valley is 'brilliant – lovely friendly service and excellent value'. Tips above Salette include Motta and Lo Baracon dou Tene.

There's a picnic room at the Plan Maison cable car station.

Cervinia

391

Build your own shortlist: www.wheretoskiandsnowboard.com

SCHOOLS

Cervino
t 0166 948744

Breuil
t 0166 940960

Classes (Cervino prices)
6 days (2hr 45min per day) €195

Private lessons
From €40 for 1hr for 1 person

GUIDES

Guide del Cervino
t 0166 948169

CHILDCARE

Club Biancaneve
t 0166 940201
Ages from 0 to 10

Ski school
From age 5

UK PACKAGES

Alpine Answers, Carrier, Club Med, Crystal, Crystal Finest, Elegant Resorts, Erna Low, Inghams, Interactive Resorts, Momentum, Mountain Beds, Ski Bespoke, Ski Club Freshtracks, Ski Line, Ski Weekend, Skitracer, Snow-wise, STC, Thomson, Zenith

Phone numbers
From abroad use the prefix +39 (and do **not** omit the initial '0' of the phone number)

TOURIST OFFICE

www.cervinia.it

SCHOOLS AND GUIDES ★★★★☆
Generally positive reports
Cervinia has three main schools. Most reports are on the Cervino school, and are positive: 'Seemed organized. Instructors spoke decent English and worked hard on technique; my friend came on in leaps and bounds.'

FOR FAMILIES ★★☆☆☆
No recent reports
The Cervino ski school runs a mini club. And there's a kindergarten area at Plan Maison.

STAYING THERE

Chalets Inghams has the 12-room chalet hotel Dragon in a great position close to the nursery slopes.
Hotels There are almost 50 hotels. Choose location with care, or look for a place with its own shuttle-bus. The Club Med has been highly praised.
★★★★★Hermitage (0166 948998) Small, luxurious Relais & Châteaux place just out of the village on the road to Cieloalto. Pool. Minibus to the lifts. Excellent staff and 'top food'.
★★★★Europa (0166 948660) Near chair out, with good past reports. Pool.
★★★★Saint Hubertus (0166 545916) Lovely, stylish apart-hotel next to the Hermitage and in related management. Dinner served in your apartment except at weekends when the restaurant is open. We stayed here in 2013 and were very impressed – excellent food, impeccable service.
★★★Breuil (0166 949537) Central, modern. 'Comfortable, friendly and spotlessly clean,' says a 2014 reporter.
★★★Edelweiss (0166 949078) At south end of village. Quirky and creaky but 'couldn't have better hosts'.
★★★Miravidi (0166 948097) Central and recently updated hotel. 'Looked after us superbly,' says a recent visitor.
★★★Serenella (0166 949041) Very 'pleasant' Italian feel (and food), good location, friendly, good value.
Apartments There are many, but few are available via UK tour ops.

EATING OUT ★★★★☆
Plenty to choose from
Cervinia's 50 or so restaurants offer plenty of choice. A long-standing reader favourite has been the Copa Pan bar's basement restaurant ('imaginative food perfectly cooked, impeccable service') but we lack recent reports. Another favourite is the

Falcone ('fine place with good pizza', 'cosy, welcoming, informal'). Other tips: Lino's at the ice rink ('particularly good' for pizza and pasta), La Grotta ('friendly, extensive menu, delicious food') and Jour et Nuit (restricted menu, good steaks). Dinner at Baita Cretaz, just above the village, makes a change ('pleasant service, good food').

APRES-SKI ★★☆☆☆
Some jolly bars
It's not a particularly lively village. 'Take a good book,' said one reporter. At teatime you can do worse than to try the cakes at the Samovar. The hotel Grivola's bars are attractively woody, friendly and lively, with free nibbles. The 'cosy' Copa Pan is lively (starting with a happy hour), with music. Lino's is rated for its happy hour and getting the last of the sun. The Yeti also has a happy hour, is popular and serves 'great free nibbles with drinks'. The bar in Inghams' chalet hotel Dragon is also popular 'but very British'. As usual in Italy, discos liven up at weekends.

OFF THE SLOPES ★☆☆☆☆
Little attraction
There is little to do for those who don't plan to hit the slopes. Amenities include hotel pools, a fitness centre and a natural ice rink. There are few diverting shops. The walks are not great. Only a few mountain restaurants are reachable by gondola or cable car, and most of these are not special.

LINKED RESORT – 1525m

VALTOURNENCHE

Some 9km down the access road and 500m below Cervinia, Valtournenche offers lower prices and a rather more traditional style, and is worth considering as an alternative base. The village spreads along the busy, steep road up to Cervinia; traffic intrudes, particularly at weekends. The resort is reported to be 'not so much quiet as dead' in the evening.

A gondola leaves from a station below the village (with a big car park). The epic run back from Plateau Rosa on the Swiss border is a great way to end the day – and has snowmaking right to the bottom.

There's a fair selection of simple hotels; some have shuttles to the lift. The 3-star Bijou (0166 92109) has been recommended in the past.

CORTINA TURISMO / DG BANDION

Cortina d'Ampezzo

A captivating town in a truly spectacular setting; do long lunches and side trips, and you won't worry about the rather limited slopes

RATINGS

The mountains

Extent	★★
Fast lifts	★★★
Queues	★★★★
Terrain p'ks	★★
Snow	★★★
Expert	★★
Intermediate	★★★
Beginner	★★★★★
Boarder	★★★
X-country	★★★★★
Restaurants	★★★★
Schools	★★★
Families	★★

The resort

Charm	★★★★
Convenience	★
Scenery	★★★★★
Eating out	★★★★★
Après-ski	★★★
Off-slope	★★★★★

RPI   115

lift pass	£220
ski hire	£120
lessons	£115
food & drink	£130
total	**£585**

NEWS

2013/14: Inghams began running the central Parc Hotel Victoria as a chalet hotel.

KEY FACTS

Resort	1225m
	4,020ft
Slopes	1225-2930m
	4,020-9,610ft
Lifts	34
Pistes	115km
	71 miles
Blue	50%
Red	35%
Black	15%
Snowmaking	95%

- ➕ Magnificent Dolomite setting
- ➕ Marvellous for novices
- ➕ Sella Ronda area within reach, just
- ➕ Attractive, very Italian town
- ➕ Lots of off-slope diversions
- ➕ No crowds or queues

- ➖ Modest area of slopes, split into several separate areas
- ➖ Erratic snow record
- ➖ Expensive by Italian standards
- ➖ Still quite a few slow lifts
- ➖ Few tough runs

There is nowhere quite like Cortina. A famous racing town and host of the 1956 Olympics, it certainly has some serious skiing. But it is Italy's most fashionable resort, and many visitors take their lunching and early-evening parading/shopping more seriously than their skiing. The result is that pressure on the slopes is low. No queues, no crowds, few pistes reduced to boilerplate by heavy traffic. We have had some of our most enjoyable piste skiing here.

The scenery is just jaw-droppingly wonderful. The town is ringed by dramatic limestone spires and cliffs tinged pink at dawn and dusk. Every time we go back the memory has faded, and our jaws drop once again.

Like all such swanky resorts, Cortina actually attracts few skiers driving Ferraris and many driving Fords (although not many Cortinas). We and our readers find it a friendly place; as a change from standard high-pressure ski resorts, we love it. With Inghams now running a good chalet hotel right on the focal Corso Italia, it sounds like a return visit is overdue.

THE RESORT

Cortina is a sizeable town spread across a wide, impossibly scenic bowl. Although it runs World Cup races, it is not a hard-core ski resort – 70% of all Italian visitors don't step on to the slopes. By 5pm everybody is cruising the Corso Italia in smart gear and laden with big bags containing additional supplies of smart gear.

Cortina is pure Italy. The Veneto region has none of the Germanic culture that you'll find in parts of Südtirol, only a few miles away.

San Cassiano in the Alta Badia area is within reach to the west, with links into the Sella Ronda – all on the extensive Superski pass. But a reporter who tried it found that doing the Sella Ronda circuit from here is hard work unless you use taxis.

VILLAGE CHARM ★★★★
Bella Italia
The heart of Cortina is the cobbled Corso Italia – traffic-free thanks to the one-way ring-road system (often busy, choked at weekends). The Corso is lined by chic shops selling designer clothes, jewellery, antiques, art and

furs. There is also an excellent co-op department store, but proper ski shops are to be found on the nearby

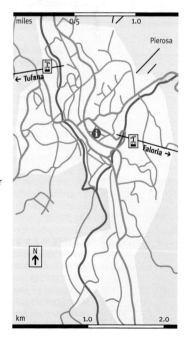

↑ There are fab views everywhere. This is from Faloria, looking across the town to Tofana

SNOWPIX.COM / CHRIS GILL

MOMENTUM SKI

Weekend & a la carte
ski holiday specialists

100% Tailor-made

Premier hotels
& apartments

Flexible travel
arrangements

020 7371 9111
WWW.MOMENTUMSKI.COM

ring road, or the streets leading to it. The picturesque church campanile adds to the atmosphere.

CONVENIENCE ★★★★★
Widely scattered
Cortina is the antithesis of the modern ski-in/ski-out resort. Walks, buses and taxis are just part of life here. Relax, and you'll get used to it. It's probably best to stay close to the Corso and the Faloria cable car, so that some days, at least, you won't need the efficient free ski-bus. Or stay in one of the swanky hotels in the suburbs that operate shuttles. A car can be useful, for getting to other areas on the Dolomiti Superski pass, such as Alta Badia.

SCENERY ★★★★★
Stand and admire
Cortina is surrounded by some of the most stunning mountain scenery in the skiing world – the Dolomite mountains are magnificent, with cliffs and peaks rising up from pretty wooded valleys, and tinged pink at dawn and dusk.

THE MOUNTAINS

There is a good mixture of slopes above and below the treeline. The three major unlinked areas are operated by different companies. More than once we have been led astray by the chaotic signing in one sector, Pomedes.

EXTENT OF THE SLOPES ★★★★★
They add up …
With 115km of pistes (including various outlying areas) Cortina's skiing is modest in extent. When planning the day we find it helpful to identify several small sectors.

A two-stage cable car from the east side of town – about 200m from the Corso – goes up to the shady, partly wooded **Faloria** area. From here you can head down to Rio Gere, and plod across the Passo Tre Croci road to reach chairlifts leading up into the limited but dramatic, sunny runs beneath **Cristallo**. Rio Gere is also reachable by bus from the town.

The town's other access lift – another cable car – starts well to the north of the centre, near the Olympic ice rink. This goes up to **Col Drusciè**, where a second stage goes on to Ra Valles and a sector of very high, shady slopes beneath **Tofana**. There is a third stage, but not for skiing purposes.

A blue piste from Col Drusciè and a panoramic black one from Ra Valles lead to the largest but least clearly identified sector. We've always called it **Pomedes**, the name of the top station (and restaurant). Resort literature may call it Pocol, after a hamlet on the edge of the sector, or Socrepes or Lacedel, at the lift base. It is a sector of two halves – serious reds and blacks at the top that get the morning sun, glorious super-easy blues at the bottom, sunny most of the day.

On the north-east fringes of the town is the tiny and rather neglected **Mietres** area.

From a point near Son del Prade, on skier's right of the Pomedes area, a bus service takes you up the road west towards Passo Falzarego and delivers you to the small but scenic **Cinque Torri** area. (There is a long-term plan for a lift link.) This area has slopes on both sunny and shady sides of a ridge. On the sunny side, a short double chair accesses a run linking to the tiny, shady **Col Gallina** area. (After a red start, this is mostly a schuss or

LIFT PASSES

Dolomiti Superski

Prices in €

Age	1-day	6-day
under 16	36	183
16 to 64	52	262
65 plus	47	236

Free Under 8

Senior Must be 65 before season starts

Beginner Points cards

Notes Covers 450 lifts and 1220km of pistes in the Dolomites, incl. all Cortina areas

Alternative pass Cortina d'Ampezzo (Cortina, San Vito di Cadore, Auronzo-Misurina)

GETTING THERE

Air Venice Marco-Polo 150km/95 miles (2hr); Treviso 140km/ 85 miles (2hr); 35-minute heli-transfers from Venice

Rail Calalzo (35km/ 22 miles) or Dobbiaco (32km/20 miles); frequent buses from station

a walk – boarders be warned.) From here you can take a blue back to Cinque Torri or a cable car from Passo Falzarego up to **Lagazuoi** – the start of a good red run back to the base station and of the famous 'hidden valley' run (more on this in the Sella Ronda chapter).

FAST LIFTS ★★★☆☆
Some in each sector
The main access lifts are cable cars and there are fast chairs scattered throughout each sector, but a lot of slow old lifts remain.

QUEUES ★★★★☆
No problem
Generally there are few lift queues or crowds on the pistes. Queues can form for the cable car to Lagazuoi, which attracts as much business from the Alta Badia resorts as from Cortina.

TERRAIN PARKS ★★☆☆☆
Challenges for all
Socrepes has a 500m-long park for both beginners and intermediates, which has kickers, boxes, rails, and a wall ride. Helmets are compulsory.

SNOW RELIABILITY ★★★☆☆
Lots of artificial help
The snowfall record is erratic, depending on storms from the Adriatic to the south. But 95% of the pistes are covered by 'excellent' snowmaking, so cover is good if it is cold enough to make snow. As so often, it's the black runs that are most vulnerable when natural snow is short – several are south-facing, and liable to closure. Grooming is 'simply excellent'.

Inghams

7 NIGHTS CATERED FROM ONLY **£599**

1934 80 2014 ANNIVERSARY

CORTINA

► **Unique and exclusive Chalet Hotel**
► **The most fashionable ski resort in Italy**

inghams.co.uk **01483 371 236** ABTA V4871 ATOL 0025

FOR EXPERTS ★★☆☆☆
Normally rather limited
A decent amount of natural snow is the key factor. Given that, you can find fresh tracks for days on end off-piste and good conditions on the few black pistes (some of which get rather too much sun).

There are short but genuinely black runs close to the lift line at the top of the Pomedes sector. The excellent Forcella Rossa from Tofana to Pomedes only just deserves to be black; but it faces south, so timing can be crucial. It goes through a gap in the rocks, and opens up to give wonderful views of Cortina way down in the valley below. Cortina's most serious piste challenge is Forcella Staunies at the top of the Cristallo area – a south-facing couloir that we have never found fully open (tougher than it looks from below, warns a reporter). This is also the launching point for some serious off-piste runs behind the hill, to the north. Locals speak highly of the ski touring possibilities, too.

There are some excellent red runs too, notably at Pomedes and Faloria.

Cortina d'Ampezzo

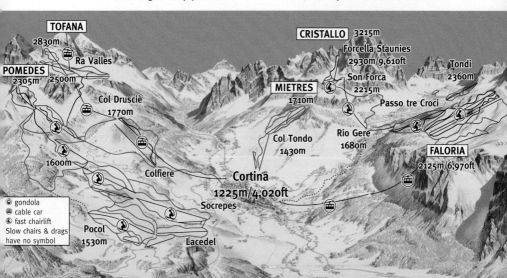

gondola
cable car
fast chairlift
Slow chairs & drags have no symbol

SNOWPIX.COM / CHRIS GILL

UK PACKAGES

Alpine Answers, Carrier, Inghams, Momentum, Oxford Ski Co, Ski Bespoke, Ski Club Freshtracks, Ski Safari, Ski Weekend, Ski Yogi, Snow Finders, STC, White Roc, Zenith

Another day, another view. This is from Tofana, looking across the town to Faloria ↓

FOR INTERMEDIATES ★★★☆☆
Fragmented and not extensive
Cortina is not a place for the avid mileage-hungry piste-basher. But its slopes are varied and interesting.

The high, shady runs at the top of Tofana are short but worthwhile, and normally have good snow. If tempted to descend via the easy black Forcella Rossa, check out the snow conditions first. The reds at the top of the linked Pomedes area offer good cruising and some challenges. Again, be aware that the blacks can be hard or icy – in this case, late in the day in particular.

Faloria has a string of excellent although fairly short north-facing runs – we loved the Vitelli red run, round the back away from the lifts. And Cristallo has a long, easy red served by a fast quad. The lower half of Staunies is a lovely easy black.

It is well worth making the trip to Cinque Torri for fast cruising – usually with excellent snow on the front, shady side. The blue and red through the woods here are indistinguishable. Do not miss the great 'hidden valley' red run from the Lagazuoi cable car.

FOR BEGINNERS ★★★★★
Wonderful nursery slopes
There are points cards for the lifts, and the slopes, although a bus ride from the town, are near-perfect. The lower part of the Pomedes area, has some of the biggest and best nursery slopes and progression runs we have seen. Be aware that some isolated blue runs elsewhere in the area may be much less friendly.

FOR BOARDERS ★★★☆☆
Wide slopes and plenty of chairs
Despite its upmarket chic, Cortina is a good resort for learning to board. The Socrepes nursery slopes are wide, gentle, served by a fast chairlift, and there are few drag-lifts. Boarderline is a specialist snowboard shop that also organizes instruction. There are some nice trees and hits under the top chairlift at Cinque Torri.

FOR CROSS-COUNTRY ★★★★★
One of the best
Cortina has around 70km of trails suitable for all standards, mainly in the Fiames area, where there's a cross-country centre and a school. Trails include a 30km itinerary following an old railway from Fiames to Dobbiaco, and there is a beginner area equipped with snowmaking. Passo Tre Croci offers more challenging trails, covering 10km. A Nordic area pass is available.

MOUNTAIN RESTAURANTS ★★★★☆
Good, but get in early
There are some excellent spots. Many can be reached by road or lift, and in some places skiers are in the minority. Prices are high in the swishest places. The piste map doesn't identify all restaurants, but the topo map on the reverse is more helpful.

SCHOOLS

Azzurra Cortina
t 0436 2694

Cristallo
t 0436 870073

Cortina
t 0436 2911

Dolomiti
t 0436 862264

Boarderline
t 0436 878261

Snowdreamers
t 0348 484 5100

Classes (Azzurra prices)
6 mornings (3hr)
€425

Private lessons
€55 for 1hr; each additional person €18

GUIDES

Gruppo Guide Alpine
t 0436 868505

CHILDCARE

Snow play areas at Socrepes, Mietres and Pierosa

Ski school
From age 4

ACTIVITIES

Indoor Saunas, health spa, fitness centre, ice stadium, curling, museums, art gallery, cinema, concerts, observatory, planetarium

Outdoor Snowshoe tours, walking paths, ice climbing and trekking, snow kiting, snowmobiling, helicopter rides, snow biking, ice driving

Phone numbers
From abroad use the prefix +39 (and do **not** omit the initial '0' of the phone number)

TOURIST OFFICE

www.cortina.dolomiti.org

Editors' choice Close to the top of Faloria, Capanna Tondi (0436 5775) does excellent food from a wide-ranging menu, with table-service in a series of small, cosy rooms and on a terrace with a great view.

Worth knowing about Baita Son dei Prade above Pocol in the Pomedes sector has been previously recommended, but we lack recent reports. Piè Tofana does ambitious food, but we weren't wowed by the results on our last visit.

There are good restaurants at Cinque Torri. Rifugio Averau has had a makeover and looked inviting when we visited. Rifugio Lagazuoi, at the top of the cable car, has great views.

SCHOOLS AND GUIDES ★★★★★
Mixed reports

There are a number of schools but we have no recent reports – previous reviews were mixed. The Guide Alpine offers off-piste and touring.

FOR FAMILIES ★★★★★
Some good lift pass deals

Described by a 2014 reporter as being 'very safe and friendly'. There's a wide choice of lift pass deals for children and there are three snow gardens plus hotel-run nurseries. But don't count on good spoken English.

STAYING THERE

Make sure you pick up a copy of *Cortina Pocket* – a very useful guide to restaurants, bars, shops and the rest.

Hotels dominate the lodgings market but there are alternatives.

Chalets Inghams took over the ideally located 4-star Parc Hotel Victoria (0436 3246) as a chalet hotel last year, and it is roundly praised by a reporter this year for its 'friendly and efficient staff, excellent food and clean, spacious rooms'.

Hotels There's a big choice, from simple pensions to 5-star palaces (which we don't bother with).

★★★★Park Faloria (0436 2959) Near ski jump, splendid pool, good food.

★★★★Poste (0436 4271) Central, on the Corso Italia. Large rooms, some with spa baths.

★★★Columbia (0436 3607) B&B hotel approved by a reader, not far from Tofana lift but a hike from town.

★★★Des Alpes (0436 862021) Way out of town. Simple but well run. Hot tub, sauna, steam.

★★★Menardi (0436 2400) Welcoming roadside inn, just out of the town.

★★★Olimpia (0436 3256) Comfortable B&B hotel in centre, near Faloria lift.

★★Montana (0436 862126) Good value, central B&B.

At altitude Rooms are available at several refuges – notably at Pomedes, at the renovated Averau at Cinque Torri and at Lagazuoi, where you can have breakfast watching the sunrise.

EATING OUT ★★★★★
Huge choice

There are lots of restaurants, with some variation on local traditional cuisine. Sadly, most of the better ones are a taxi ride out of town. The word is that the very smart El Toulà, in a beautiful old barn just on the edge of town, is now overpriced. Also on the edge, Da Beppe Sello is 'a little gem', with extraordinary salad entrées and a good meat choice'. Even further out: the resort's one Michelin-starred place – Tivoli, Meloncino al Camineto, Leone e Anna (Sardinian specialities), Rio Gere (game dishes) and Baita Fraina (pasta and meats).

In the centre there are plenty of modest places, including pizzerias – Croda Cafe claims to be the town's original, with wood-fired oven; Birreria Vienna serves until midnight.

APRES-SKI ★★★★★
Lively in high season

Cortina is a lively social whirl in high season, with lots of well-heeled Italians staying up very late – but at other times it can be quiet, or 'very dull', to quote a January visitor.

Pasticceria Lovat is one of several high-calorie teatime spots. There are some good wine bars, often doing excellent cheese and meats too: Enoteca, La Suite and LP26 have been tipped. Bar Sport is the place for grappa. Jambo is a 'nice spot for late drinks and a dance – loud but chic'.

OFF THE SLOPES ★★★★★
A classic resort

There's lots to do. There are popular walks in several sectors. There are lots of upmarket shops. Activities include swimming and skating. There is a planetarium, and an observatory at Col Drusciè. There are regular ice hockey matches. The Country Club spa is tipped for its 'real Scan feel'. Trips to Venice are easy. You can visit First World War tunnels at Lagazuoi.

SNOWPIX.COM / CHRIS GILL

Courmayeur

A seductive old village on the sunny side of spectacular Mont Blanc, but with a flawed and very limited area of pistes

RATINGS

The mountains

Extent	★
Fast lifts	★★★★
Queues	★★★★
Terrain p'ks	★★
Snow	★★★★
Expert	★★★
Intermediate	★★★★
Beginner	★
Boarder	★★★
X-country	★★★
Restaurants	★★★★
Schools	★★★★
Families	★★

The resort

Charm	★★★★
Convenience	★
Scenery	★★★★
Eating out	★★★★
Après-ski	★★★★
Off-slope	★★★

RPI   95

lift pass	£189
ski hire	£100
lessons	£100
food & drink	£115
total	**£504**

398

NEWS

2014/15: Sadly, the opening of the new two-stage cable car to Punta Helbronner on Mont Blanc has been delayed until after the 2014/15 season. A new 5-star hotel, the Grand Hotel Courmayeur Mont Blanc, is being built.

2013/14: The resort hosted the inaugural Mountain Gourmet Ski Experience featuring Michelin-starred chefs and arranged by Momentum Ski and Heston Blumenthal. The 2015 event will be held from 9 to 12 January.

➕ Charming old village; car-free centre with stylish shops and bars

➕ Stunning views of Mont Blanc

➕ Some good off-piste and heli-skiing

➕ Comprehensive snowmaking

➕ Some great mountain restaurants

➖ Very small area of pistes; and lift-served off-piste reduced while new cable car up Mont Blanc being built

➖ Lots of drawbacks for beginners

➖ No really tough pistes

➖ No runs back to the village

Courmayeur is a great place for a short midweek break or for a day trip to escape bad weather in Megève and Chamonix – we have used it for this several times. Excellent restaurants both on and off the mountain plus village bars among the most civilized in the skiing world are important factors for us too.

The piste skiing is tricky to recommend for more than a day or two, though, because it best suits competent intermediates, who are likely to have an appetite for mileage that Courmayeur will arouse but not satisfy.

THE RESORT

Courmayeur is a traditional old mountaineering village that has retained much of its character.

La Thuile is an easy drive or bus ride away; Aosta/Pila and Chamonix are not far, and Cervinia and Monterosa are reachable; all are covered by various lift passes.

VILLAGE CHARM ★★★★
Attractive and sophisticated
The village has a charming traffic-free core of cobbled streets and well-preserved old buildings. As the lifts close, the central Via Roma comes alive: people pile into the many bars, or browse the tempting delis and smart clothes shops – some now have doormen to stop celebrity-spotters, and some are appointment-only at peak times, we're told; there's also a good bookshop. An Alpine museum and a statue of a long-dead mountain rescue hero add to the historical feel of the place.

Away from the centre, there are pleasant woody suburbs but also a lot of conspicuous apartment blocks.

CONVENIENCE ★★★★
Buses to the lifts
A huge cable car on the southern edge of the village takes you to and from Plan Checrouit, at the heart of the slopes. (The cable car is now open in the evening too, to serve the bars and restaurants up there.) You cannot ski back to the village, but you can ski to

the base of the alternative gondola from Dolonne (across the valley); parking is much easier there, too. You can leave your gear up at Plan Checrouit. Buses serve both lift stations, but readers have found services 'inadequate'. Many hotels run shuttles that are welcomed by reporters.

Drivers can also go to Entrèves, up the valley, where there is a large car park at the cable car. Infrequent but timetabled buses go to La Palud, just beyond Entrèves, for the Mont Blanc cable car.

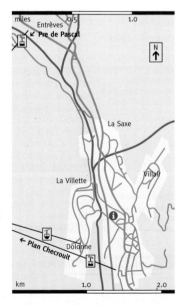

KEY FACTS

Resort	1225m
	4,020ft
Slopes	1210-2755m
	3,970-9,040ft
Lifts	18
Pistes	39km
	24 miles
Blue	27%
Red	59%
Black	14%
Snowmaking	70%

LIFT PASSES

Prices in €

Age	1-day	6-day
under 14	32	136
14 to 64	45	227
65 plus	36	182

Free Under 8 if with adult

Beginner Three free nursery lifts (but you have to pay for the access lifts to reach them)

Notes Covers Courmayeur and the Mont Blanc cable cars; 3- or 4-hour passes; weekly passes allow two days in another Aosta valley resort

Alternative passes Non-skier; Mont Blanc Unlimited (includes Chamonix valley and Verbier); Valle d'Aosta (covers Aosta Valley ski areas)

SCENERY ★★★★☆
Mont Blanc rules
The high glacial slopes of the Mont Blanc (Monte Bianco in Italian) massif overlook Courmayeur's slopes. The views from the high points at Cresta d'Arp and Cresta Youla, especially, are stunning.

THE MOUNTAINS
The slopes above the focal point of Plan Checrouit are mainly wide open, but there are also wooded areas, particularly on the back side of the hill. The piste map now shows lift names and direction, but some reporters criticize piste signposting and marking.

EXTENT OF THE SLOPES ★☆☆☆☆
Small and variable
From the time this book started 20 years ago, we were sceptical of the resort's claimed 100km of pistes. Three seasons ago, at last, it revealed that the true extent was 36km of pistes plus 64km of off-piste runs (whatever that means). It has now adjusted the 36km figure to 39km but that is still even less than we would have guessed, and less than any other major resort in this book.

There are two distinct sectors, separated by a rocky ridge. The links between the two can be a bit confusing. Above Plan Checrouit, the east-facing **Checrouit** area, accessed mainly by the Checrouit gondola, catches the morning sun. The

20-person Youla cable car goes to the top of the pistes. A further tiny cable car to Cresta d'Arp serves only long off-piste runs.

Most people follow the sun over to the north-west-facing slopes of **Val Veny** in the afternoon. These offer a mix of open and wooded slopes, with great views of Mont Blanc and its glaciers. The Val Veny slopes are also accessible by cable car from Entrèves, a few miles outside Courmayeur.

A little way beyond Entrèves a new cable car to Punta Helbronner, at the shoulder of **Mont Blanc**, is being built (completion scheduled for May/June 2015 when we went to press). The top stage of the old cable car has closed but from the second stage you can reach the famous Vallée Blanche run to Chamonix by climbing 120 steps (your skis are transported for you). Access to the Toula glacier run on the Italian side involves a bit of a climb on snow.

FAST LIFTS ★★★★☆
A decent network
The main access lifts are cable cars or a gondola. On the hill, there are fast lifts in all the key spots.

QUEUES ★★★★☆
Much improved
These days, queues are generally not a problem unless conditions trigger a weekend influx. Queues to descend at the end of the day have been a problem, especially if the run to Dolonne is closed, but evening opening of the cable car seems to

WENDY KING

The main slope above Plan Checrouit is wide and open, with good views down to town
→

MOMENTUM SKI

Weekend & a la carte
ski holiday specialists

100% Tailor-made

Premier hotels
& apartments

The No.1 Specialist
in Courmayeur

020 7371 9111
WWW.MOMENTUMSKI.COM

have put paid to that. On the back of the hill, Zerotta is a real bottleneck – we've waited 15 minutes here in March. It's worth waiting until late afternoon to ride the Youla cable car.

TERRAIN PARKS ★★☆☆☆
New and improved
A park is served by the Aretù chairlift. It has a line of rails for beginners and children, another for intermediates and a line of kickers. There is also an airbag serving two jumps.

SNOW RELIABILITY ★★★★☆
Good for most of the season
Courmayeur's slopes are not high – mostly between 1700m and 2250m. Those above Val Veny face north or north-west, so they keep their snow well, but the Plan Checrouit side is too sunny for comfort in late season. There is snowmaking on most main runs, including the red run to the valley. So good coverage in early and mid-season is virtually assured – we've been there in a snow drought and enjoyed decent skiing entirely on man-made snow. Grooming is good – 'when it snowed eight inches overnight they sensibly concentrated on the blues

first'. On the other hand, it is quite unusual for an Italian resort to leave any pistes ungroomed.

FOR EXPERTS ★★★☆☆
Off-piste is the challenge
Courmayeur has few challenging pistes. The black runs on the Val Veny side are not severe, but moguls are allowed to develop. If you're lucky enough to find fresh powder, you can have fantastic fun among the trees.

Classic off-piste runs go from Cresta d'Arp, at the top of the lift network, in three directions: a clockwise loop via Arp Vieille to Val Veny, with close-up views of the Miage glacier; east down a deserted valley to Dolonne or Pré-St-Didier; or south through the Youla gorge to La Balme, near La Thuile.

A day trip to Chamonix is appealing, especially as some classic runs on Mont Blanc start from the French side.

There are also heli-drops, including a wonderful 20km run from the Ruitor glacier that ends near Ste-Foy in France – you take a taxi from there to La Rosière, ride the lifts back up from there and descend to La Thuile (then take another taxi back).

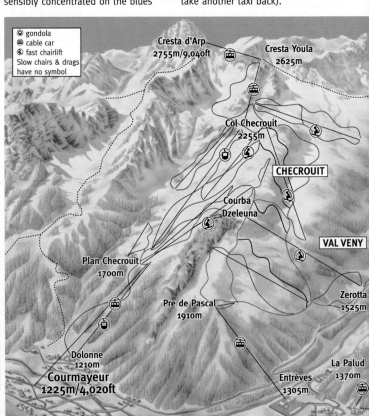

ⓖ gondola
ⓒ cable car
ⓕ fast chairlift
Slow chairs & drags have no symbol

Cresta d'Arp
2755m/9,040ft

Cresta Youla
2625m

Col Checrouit
2255m

CHECROUIT

Courba
Dzeleuna

VAL VENY

Plan Checrouit
1700m

Zerotta
1525m

Pre de Pascal
1910m

Dolonne
1210m

La Palud
1370m

Courmayeur
1225m/4,020ft

Entrèves
1305m

GETTING THERE

Air Geneva 110km/
70 miles (1hr30);
Turin 150km/95 miles
(1hr45)

Rail Pré-St-Didier
(5km/3 miles); regular
buses from station

SCHOOLS

Montebianco
t 0165 842477

Courmayeur
t 0165 848254

Classes (Montebianco
prices)
5 days (2hr per day)
€190

Private lessons
€47 for 1hr;
additional person €13

GUIDES

Guides Courmayeur
t 0165 842064

ACTIVITIES

Indoor Hotel
swimming pools,
sports centre (ice rink,
climbing wall, fitness
centre, sauna, steam
room), tennis,
museums, library

Outdoor Walking,
climbing,
snowshoeing, snow
biking

FOR INTERMEDIATES ★★★★☆
Good reds, but limited extent

It's an intermediate's mountain, for sure, laced with interestingly varied, genuine red runs. But it is small; the avid piste-basher will ski it in a day. There are a few good long runs – it's 700m vertical from Col Checrouit to Zerotta, and an impressive 1400m vertical from Cresta Youla to Dolonne. On the steeper Val Veny side of the ridge there are challenges to be found – while the reds and blues cut across the mountain, a row of easy blacks go down more directly.

For the timid intermediate, on the other hand, the area is short of confidence-building blue runs. There is basically one long blue on each side of the ridge; the one on the Val Veny side is better for the challenge-averse. Many of the reds – particularly up around Col Checrouit and down to Plan Checrouit – do have the merit that they are generally wide, which helps a lot.

FOR BEGINNERS ★☆☆☆☆
Lots of drawbacks

Of course, you can learn to ski here, but you face obstacles. To get to the free beginner lifts (at Plan Checrouit, on the ridge above that and at the top of the Entrèves cable car) you have the hassle and cost of getting up the mountain. The best starting point is the Entrèves cable car, which takes you to a moving carpet, and easy longer runs on the Peindeint top. There is a clear lack of other genuinely easy longer runs to progress to.

FOR BOARDERS ★★★☆☆
Mainly intermediate fun

Courmayeur's pistes suit intermediates well, and most areas are accessible by cable cars, chairs and gondolas (though the beginner slopes have drags). For the more adventurous, there are off-piste routes. A terrain park opened two seasons ago.

FOR CROSS-COUNTRY ★★★☆☆
Beautiful trails

There are 30km of trails. The best are the five covering 20km at Val Ferret, served by bus.

MOUNTAIN RESTAURANTS ★★★★☆
A very good choice

The area is well endowed with establishments ranging from rustic little huts that do table-service of delicious pizza, pasta and other dishes, to snack bars and a large self-service place – but strangely they are not marked on the piste map.

Editors' choice We and readers have had excellent meals at Chiecco (338 7003035) by the draglift starting below Plan Checrouit – a small hut run by the very welcoming Anna; very varied menu, including fantastic chicken curry and wild boar stew; superb tiramisu. An old favourite of ours is Maison Vieille (337 230979), a cosy, rustic place with jolly service; but we and readers have been underwhelmed on recent visits – more reports please.

Worth knowing about Another favourite at Plan Checrouit is the Christiania (book a table downstairs to escape the crowds). Nearby, the Chaumière is family-run, serving 'very good meals, especially the cheese board starter' in a new dining room and on a 'sunny terrace with superb views'. Also nearby and recommended by a Courmayeur regular is the rustic Chateau Branlant ('Fantastic – excellent mixed grill and wines'). Reporters also like Bar du Soleil, not least for the views from the terrace. Up at Col Checrouit, Chez Croux is the place to go for cakes and hot drinks. There is another clutch of worthwhile places in Val Veny: we enjoyed the smartly rustic Grolla for steaks and salads. The Petit Mont Blanc is also popular ('the roast suckling pig was fantastic').

SCHOOLS AND GUIDES ★★★★☆
Good private lessons

Past reports on private lessons with the Monte Bianco school have been fairly enthusiastic, though you can't count on good spoken English. The Courmayeur school has 'a more snowboardy and young funky image'. There is a thriving guides' association ready to help you explore the area's off-piste; it has produced a helpful booklet showing the main possibilities. We had a couple of great days with solo guide Gianni Carbone (www.giannicarbone.com), who is patient and reassuring. A recent visitor's Vallée Blanche guides were 'excellent'.

FOR FAMILIES ★★☆☆☆
Some facilities

There are children's playgrounds at Dolonne, Plan Checrouit and Val Veny, and a nursery at Plan Checrouit for children up to 10 years.

CHILDCARE

Fun park Dolonne
t 348 591 6217
9am-4.30

**Mini club Biancaneve
(Monte Bianco school)**
t 349 300 3132
Ages 0 to 10

**Ski-tots (Mammolo)
(Monte Bianco school)**
For 3 and 4 year olds

Ski schools
From age 5

UK PACKAGES

Alpine Answers, Alpine Weekends, Crystal, Erna Low, Flexiski, Friendship Travel, Inghams, Inspired to Ski, Interactive Resorts, Interski, Just Skiing, Mark Warner, Momentum, Mountain Beds, Ski Bespoke, Ski Club Freshtracks, Ski Expectations, Ski Line, Ski Weekend, Ski Yogi, Skitracer, Skiweekends.com, Snow-wise, Snoworks, STC, Thomson, Tracks European Adventures, White Roc

Phone numbers
From abroad use the prefix +39 (and do **not** omit the initial '0' of the phone number)

TOURIST OFFICE

www.courmayeur.it
www.lovevda.it

STAYING THERE

There's a wide range of packages (including some excellent weekend deals), mainly in hotels. Momentum Ski is an agent specializing in Courmayeur and can fix pretty much whatever you want here.

Chalets Mark Warner runs the central Cristallo as a chalet hotel.

Hotels There are over 50 hotels, spanning the star ratings.

*****Royal e Golf (0165 831611) Large, grand, 200-years-old, in centre. Outdoor pool, spa.

****Auberge de la Maison (0165 869811) Small, atmospheric hotel in Entrèves; owned by the same family as Maison de Filippo (see 'Eating out').

****Cresta et Duc (0165 842585) In the centre. Praised by a past reporter. Steam, sauna, hot tub.

****Villa Novecento (0165 843000) A short walk from the centre. Elegant lobby, good food and breakfasts. Sauna, steam, hot tub.

***Bouton d'Or (0165 846729) Small, friendly B&B hotel near main square, repeatedly recommended by a regular visitor: '3-star with friendly 5-star service; impossible to fault.'

***Camosci (0165 842338) 800m from centre, minibus. '5-star welcome, charming, traditional, plentiful food.'

***Courmayeur (0165 846732) Near cable car. 'Very friendly; small rooms.'

***Pilier d'Angle (0165 869760) Friendly, cosy hotel in Entrèves; rooms and self-contained chalets. Good restaurant and wellness centre.

Apartments The 3-star Grand Chalet (0165 841448) is central with spacious apartments. Hot tub, steam and sauna are also available for non-residents.

At altitude At Plan Checrouit, the 1-star Christiania (0165 843572) has simple rooms; the 3-star Super G (0165 842660) is smarter and has a lively après scene.

EATING OUT ★★★★☆
Jolly Italian evenings

There is a great choice of places. A handy promotional booklet describes many of them (in English). We've been impressed by the traditional Italian cuisine of the smart Cadran Solaire. La Terrazza serves classic and local cuisine plus pizzas and is highly recommended, both by a local and a recent visitor ('superb – owners very accommodating, excellent set meal for 20 euros'). Reporters regularly

recommend the Piazzetta ('very good and inexpensive', 'extremely friendly'). The little Pizzeria du Tunnel is a bit of an institution, and is happily endorsed by reporters – 'super food, attentive service' despite being over-busy at times. Other recommendations include Ancien Casinò ('best pizza ever, and inexpensive'), Le Vieux Pommier ('great atmosphere, serves a mixture of Italian and Savoyard fare') and Aria ('very friendly, an amazing wine list'). In Entrèves, the touristy but very jolly Maison de Filippo is rightly famous for its fixed-price, 36-dish feast. For a gourmet treat take a taxi to the Clotze in Val Ferret (same management as Chiecco – read 'Mountain restaurants'). The cable car to Plan Checrouit now works in the evening so you can catch that up to use the restaurants there.

APRES-SKI ★★★★☆
Stylish bar-hopping

You can now stay up the mountain for après (eg at the Super G) and catch the cable car down. Down in the village there's a lively evening scene – at weekends, at least – centred on stylish bars with comfy armchairs or sofas, often serving free canapés in the early evening. We like the Privé ('great cocktails', 'reasonable prices and good service') and the back room of the Caffè della Posta ('the people-watching is superb', 'laden plates of goodies arrive with each round'). Bar Roma is an old favourite and its free antipasto buffet is back, we're told. A recent reporter enjoyed the 'great service and very good food' at Petit Bistro. The American Bar has good live music. There are three nightclubs – Courmaclub, Jset and Shatush. Or try the branch of Shatush in Entrèves (free shuttle-bus service).

OFF THE SLOPES ★★★☆☆
Lots for non-slope users

The resort attracts many non-skiing weekenders, who focus on showing off their togs and buying more of them – so there are some tempting shops. You can go by bus to Aosta, or up to Plan Checrouit where there are countless spots to meet friends for lunch. The huge sports centre is good (but has no pool). Don't miss a visit to the thermal baths at Pré-St-Didier – with over 40 spa 'experiences' including saunas and outdoor pools. The Parco Avventura (10km from town) has a 'great' ropes course.

Livigno

Lowish prices and highish altitude – a tempting combination, especially when you add in a pleasant Alpine ambience

RATINGS

The mountains

Extent	★★
Fast lifts	★★★★
Queues	★★★★
Terrain p'ks	★★★★
Snow	★★★★
Expert	★★★
Intermediate	★★★
Beginner	★★★★
Boarder	★★★★
X-country	★★★★
Restaurants	★★★
Schools	★★★
Families	★★

The resort

Charm	★★★
Convenience	★★
Scenery	★★★
Eating out	★★★
Après-ski	★★★
Off-slope	★★

RPI 90

lift pass	£180
ski hire	£80
lessons	£80
food & drink	£115
total	**£455**

NEWS

2013/14: A new Freeride Project was launched (see 'For Experts'). And off-piste skiing and heli-skiing are, we are assured, now allowed after being banned for several years.

KEY FACTS

Resort	1815m
	5,950ft
Slopes	1815-2795m
	5,950-9,170ft
Lifts	31
Pistes	115km
	71 miles
Blue	38%
Red	47%
Black	15%
Snowmaking	70%

+ Reliable snow

+ Large choice of beginners' slopes

+ Impressive modern lift system

+ Cheap by the standards of high, snow-sure resorts

+ Lively, friendly, quite smart village with a good Alpine atmosphere

+ Long, snow-sure cross-country trails

– Few tough pistes (but off-piste is now allowed, we are assured)

– Bleak setting, susceptible to white-outs and lift closures

– Long transfers from some Italian airports (Innsbruck is quicker)

– Village is very long and straggling, with no buses later in the evening

– Nightlife can disappoint

Livigno's recipe of a fair-sized mountain, high altitude and fairly low prices is uncommon, and obviously attractive, and may be enough to get it on to your shortlist, especially if you are a beginner or unadventurous intermediate. But don't overlook the non-trivial drawbacks we list above.

After banning off-piste for several years up to 2012/13 the resort apparently now allows it and has heli-skiing as well. But the off-piste policy has varied so much we'd welcome reports on what it's like in 2014/15.

THE RESORT

Livigno is set in a wide, remote valley near the Swiss border; the airport transfers are long and winding. The Alta Valtellina lift pass covers Bormio (about an hour's bus ride – free with the lift pass) and Santa Caterina (another 20 minutes). The Livigno pass gets you half-price on one day in St Moritz – an excursion not easily done from any other major resort.

VILLAGE CHARM ★★★
Pleasant enough
At the core of the resort is a single, mainly pedestrian street that is just over 1km long and is lined by hotels, bars, specialist shops and supermarkets, with side streets linking to the parallel by-pass road. The buildings are small in scale and traditional in style, creating a pleasant atmosphere. Away from the central area, traffic can be intrusive.

CONVENIENCE ★★
Where you gonna stay?
It's a long, spread-out place – over 4km from one end to the other. The pedestrian core is the most attractive all-round location, but the three major lifts are out at the extremities. Unless you opt to stay near one of these, you will make heavy use of the free bus services. The main routes run every 15 minutes, but they get overcrowded at peak times, and they stop at around 8pm. The complex route map requires serious study, but reporters find the services 'regular' and 'efficient'. Taxis (including minibuses for groups) are affordable.

SCENERY ★★★
High and probably white
Livigno's high position and long ridges provide attractive views from both sides of the valley – but it can feel bleak and isolated.

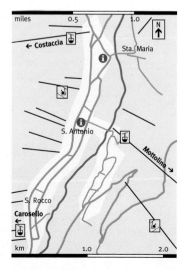

ITALY

404

Resort news and key links: www.wheretoskiandsnowboard.com

LIFT PASSES

Prices in €

Age	1-day	6-day
under 15	35	148
15 to 64	44	215
65 plus	35	148

Free Under 8

Beginner Points card

Notes Half-day passes and reduced Saturday passes; family reductions; 50% discount on day pass at St Moritz with a 3-day-plus pass

Alternative pass
Alta Valtellina pass covers Livigno, Bormio and Santa Caterina

GETTING THERE

Air Bolzano 135km/ 85 miles (2hr15); Innsbruck 180km/ 110 miles (2hr45); Zürich 205km/ 125 miles (3hr15); Friedrichshafen 200km/125 miles (3hr15); Bergamo 190km/120 miles (3hr30); Verona 280km/175 miles (3hr30)

Rail Tirano (73km/ 45 miles); Zernez (Switzerland, 28km/ 17 miles); regular buses from station

THE MOUNTAINS

The slopes are on either side of the valley and are mainly above the treeline. It's not a good place in bad weather. Signposting is adequate, but the piste map does not name or number runs. Night skiing is available on Thursdays.

EXTENT OF THE SLOPES ★★★★★
Widely spread
The slopes are more extensive than in many other budget destinations, but it's not a huge area and lots of the runs are very similar to one another.

At the north end of the village is the narrow **Costaccia** sector, reached by the two-stage Tagliede gondola (with the Cassana gondola and an adjacent six-pack offering alternative ways to the mid-station). From Costaccia, a long fast quad chairlift goes along the ridge towards the Carosello sector. The blue linking run back from Carosello to the top of Costaccia is flat in places and may involve energetic poling. **Carosello** is more usually accessed by the optimistically named Carosello 3000 gondola at the southern end of the village, which goes up, in two stages, to almost 2800m. Most runs return towards the village, but the Federia six-pack serves west-facing slopes on the back of the mountain.

The ridge of **Mottolino** is reached by a gondola or fast quad from Teola, across the valley from central Livigno. From the top, you can descend to fast quads on either side of the ridge, or take a very slow antique chair along it.

We don't show on our map a link from the nursery drags at the bottom of Carosello to those below Costaccia; it's more of a walk than a run.

FAST LIFTS ★★★★★
A positive attraction
The lift system is impressively modern, with fast chairs and gondolas covering both sectors – though draglifts still serve the valley nursery slopes.

QUEUES ★★★★★
Few problems these days
Queues are generally not a problem. Delays can occur at the main gondolas at peak times, such as the Carosello 3000. A bigger problem is that winds can close the upper lifts, causing crowds lower down.

TERRAIN PARKS ★★★★★
Serious facilities
The main park behind Mottolino is an impressive freestyle zone for all levels. It also hosts the World Rookie fest, which is on the Ticket to Ride calendar. It has kicker lines for all levels and is bordered by a big super-pipe, often used as a training ground by pros, and there are advanced rails in and around the jumps as well. There's also a huge airbag jump – perfect for trying out backflips and other advanced tricks.

Livigno's second park is at Carosello 3000. It also caters for all standards and includes another huge airbag jump. The three other parks, all near lifts with the same names and aimed at novices and juniors are the Amerikan and the San Rocco near the

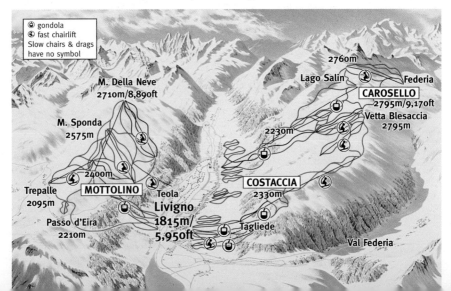

↑ This pic of the Carosello sector illustrates one of Livigno's drawbacks – most of the skiing is above the treeline, not a good place to be in bad weather

SNOWPIX.COM / CHRIS GILL

ACTIVITIES

Indoor Aquagranda wellness park (swimming pool, sauna, fitness rooms), badminton, billiards
Outdoor Cleared paths, ice rink, snowshoeing, horse riding, tobogganing, dog sledding, go-karts on ice, snowmobiling, ice climbing, paragliding

Carosello gondola and the Del Sole near the centre of town.

SNOW RELIABILITY ★★★★☆
Very good, given precipitation
Livigno's slopes are high (you can spend most of your time around 2500m) and, with snow-guns on the lower slopes of Mottolino and Costaccia, the season is long. Piste grooming is 'immaculate' – 'Never saw a mogul,' says a 2014 visitor.

FOR EXPERTS ★★★☆☆
An end to off-piste confusion?
There are several black runs on Mottolino, but they are of black steepness only in places, and they are regularly groomed. The rules about off-piste have changed year by year for the last few years (before 2012/13 it was banned completely). We are assured that in 2014/15 it will be allowed, with or without a mountain guide or instructor. There are some 'freeride itineraries' on Mottolino that can be accessed through a gate which

also has a machine to check transceivers. These are part of a Freeride Project that includes a free avalanche awareness and equipment briefing on Sunday evening plus daily avalanche bulletins in English posted on the resort's website. Heli-skiing is now available too.

FOR INTERMEDIATES ★★★☆☆
Flattering slopes
There's nothing too demanding but good intermediates will enjoy the groomed blacks on Mottolino, as well as the wide choice of reds. The woodland black run from Carosello past Tea da Borch is narrow in places and can get moguled and icy in the afternoon. Moderate intermediates have virtually the whole area at their disposal. The long run beneath the Mottolino gondola is one of the best, and there is also a long, varied, under-used blue going less directly to the valley. Leisurely types have several long cruises available; the blue beneath the fast chair at the top of Costaccia is a splendid slope.

FOR BEGINNERS ★★★★☆
Excellent scattered slopes
There's a vast array of gentle, sunny, low-traffic nursery slopes rising from the village, with lifts concentrated in three areas: north, centre, south. For progression, there are longer blue runs at the top of Costaccia and Mottolino.

FOR BOARDERS ★★★★☆
Fun of all kinds
The pistes are in general big, wide, open and rolling motorways. The new off-piste policy and the two big parks are obvious attractions for competent boarders. Beginners be warned: practically all the smaller lower slopes are serviced by drags. But the resort still attracts good numbers of beginners. Madness is a specialist school.

FOR CROSS-COUNTRY ★★★★☆
Good snow, bleak setting
Long snow-sure trails (30km in total) follow the valley floor, making Livigno a good choice, provided you don't mind the bleak scenery. There is a specialist school, Livigno 2000.

MOUNTAIN RESTAURANTS ★★★☆☆
No more than adequate
Our favourite, though not quite up to Editors' choice standard, is the

SCHOOLS

Centrale
t 0342 996276
Azzurra
t 0342 997683
Livigno Italy
t 0342 996739
Livigno Galli Fedele
t 0342 970300
Madness Snowboard
t 0342 997792
New
t 0342 997801

Classes (Centrale prices)
6 2hr-days €115
Private lessons
€38 for 1hr; each additional person €10

CHILDCARE

Kinder Club Lupigno (Centrale)
t 0342 996276
From age 3
M'eating Point
t 0342 997408
From age 3
Pollicino
t 0342 700085
From age 3mnth

Ski school
From age 4

UK PACKAGES

Crystal, Erna Low, Inghams, Livigno Snow, Neilson, Skitracer, Thomson

Phone numbers
From abroad use the prefix +39 (and do **not** omit the initial '0' of the phone number)

TOURIST OFFICE

www.livigno.eu

Berghütte, in a fine position close to the bottom of Costaccia; the food is simple but satisfying, the service efficient and friendly. Up the hill at Costaccia the upstairs restaurant 'has friendly table-service and great pasta'. Carosello has a popular self-service place and a table-service wine bar and restaurant below doing 'outstanding' pasta. Tea da Borch, in the trees lower down, has a Tirolean-style atmosphere. On Mottolino, the huge M'eating Point at the top of the gondola has a self-service section that can be excessively busy but also a small, peaceful table-service section. Lower down there are rustic restaurants at Passo d'Eira and at Trepalle, on the back of the hill.

SCHOOLS AND GUIDES ★★★☆☆
Short but sweet classes
Past reports on the schools have generally been good, praising instruction and English. Classes are rated great value for money, but are mornings only (as is usual in Italy).

FOR FAMILIES ★★☆☆☆
Not bad for Italy
The schools run classes for children from the age of four, and the Centrale school offers all-day non-skiing care for children from the age of three; the staff speak English. Beware the long, winding airport transfers.

STAYING THERE

Livigno has an enormous range of hotels and a number of apartments.
Hotels There is a wide choice.
****Bivio** (0342 996137) Welcoming chalet in centre with popular cellar bar. Good food à la carte. Pool and wellness area.
****Camana Veglia** (0342 996310) Charming old wooden chalet. Popular restaurant doing five-course gastro dinners, well placed in Santa Maria.
****Intermonti** (0342 972100) Modern with pool and other mod cons; on the Mottolino side of the valley.
****Lac Salin** (0342 996166) 'Modern, stylish, with an impressive spa,' says a 2013 report.
****Larice** (0342 996184) Stylish little B&B well placed for Costaccia lifts.
***Champagne** (0342 996437) Pleasant B&B close to centre.
***Loredana** (0342 996330) Modern chalet on the Mottolino side.
***Montanina** (0342 996060) Very central, family-run.

***Steinbock** (0342 970520) Nice little place, far from major lifts.
Silvestri (0342 996255) Comfortable place in the San Rocco area.
Apartments Available locally and from tour operators.

EATING OUT ★★★☆☆
Value for money
Livigno's restaurants are mainly traditional, unpretentious places, many hotel-based. Over the years we've had countless recommendations for where to eat. These include Cantina, in the hotel Bivio ('excellent, with a fine choice of wines'), Paprika ('good flavour, good value') and Scala ('fish a speciality; flavour, service and ambience excellent').

APRES-SKI ★★★☆☆
Adequately lively
The scene is quieter than some people expect – and the best places are scattered about; but we haven't found it lacking life. At teatime, Tea del Vidal, at the bottom of Mottolino, is 'a great lively bar with good music' – and things also get lively at the Stalet bar at the base of the Carosello gondola and at the central umbrella bar. Nightlife gets going after 10pm. The Kuhstall under the Bivio hotel is an excellent cellar bar with live music, as is the Helvetia, over the road. At the southern end of the village, Daphne's is 'one of the few lively bars in Livigno', Marco's is popular and Miky's has been recommended. Cielo is the main disco.

OFF THE SLOPES ★★☆☆☆
Some distractions
The smart, modern thermal spa/wellness centre Aquagranda has indoor and outdoor pools, saunas, steam rooms and a wide variety of massage and beauty treatments. Some visitors have enjoyed the dog sledding, and tobogganing is also popular. Walks are uninspiring. There's duty-free shopping, of course – and trips to Bormio and St Moritz.

MADONNA TOURIST OFFICE

Madonna di Campiglio

A fashionable resort amid stunning scenery – a bit like Cortina, in other words, but with a more conveniently linked ski area

RATINGS

The mountains

Extent	★★★
Fast lifts	★★★★
Queues	★★★★
Terrain p'ks	★★★
Snow	★★★
Expert	★★
Intermediate	★★★★
Beginner	★★★
Boarder	★★★
X-country	★★★
Restaurants	★★★
Schools	★★★
Families	★★★

The resort

Charm	★★★★
Convenience	★★★
Scenery	★★★★
Eating out	★★★
Après-ski	★★★
Off-slope	★★

RPI · 105

lift pass	£200
ski hire	£105
lessons	£100
food & drink	£130
total	**£535**

NEWS

2013/14: A new red piste, Nambino, was created in the Cinque Laghi area.

➕ Splendid wooded setting in the dramatic Brenta Dolomites

➕ Pleasant, stylish village, with car-free centre and a tunnel bypass

➕ Extensive, varied slopes, including the linked areas of Folgarida, Marilleva and now Pinzolo

➕ Lots of long, easy runs

➖ Although it has a compact core, the resort spreads widely along the valley, away from the lifts

➖ Tough pistes are few, and widely separated around a big area, and off-piste is formally banned

➖ Quiet from dinner time onwards

Madonna di Campiglio has worked its way into our affections gradually, over many years; we now count it as one of our favourite Italian resorts. The scenery is a key factor, as is the village ambience: it may come second to Cortina d'Ampezzo for smart shops and bars – and for scenic drama – but it is nevertheless a very attractive place.

The slopes offer plenty of variety, and a satisfying sense of travel across considerable distances – particularly since Pinzolo was linked by gondola in 2011. The lift bases of Folgarida and Pinzolo are about 17km apart.

THE RESORT

Campiglio is a well-established, quite fashionable resort, set near the head of a heavily wooded valley. Although the clientele is mainly Italian, the resort is now attracting Russian visitors in considerable numbers. The Skirama regional lift pass covers not only the several linked resorts but also others in the Val di Sole to the north, including Pejo and Passo Tonale (which gets its own chapter).

VILLAGE CHARM ★★★★
Smoothly traditional
Campiglio is mainly built in traditional Alpine style and has a towny, polished air, at least around the central, car-free Piazza Righi and nearby streets, where there are quite a few diverting shops. The village is bypassed by through-traffic. Near the centre is a small park and a lake, used for skating. The place doesn't go to sleep in the day, and is quite lively in the early evening.

CONVENIENCE ★★★
Good links between sectors
The centre is fairly compact: the main lifts bracket many of the main hotels, and are a 5/10-minute walk apart. Skiing links between the main slope sectors work well. But the resort sprawls about 3km down the valley, and some hotels are quite a way out; up the valley is the outlying suburb of

Campo Carlo Magno, where there are further major lifts and a sizeable car park as well as more hotels. The ski-bus service has not impressed reporters, and now costs a non-trivial 10 euros a week. We'd stay near a main lift, or at a hotel that runs a shuttle (many do).

SCENERY ★★★★
Splendid Dolomites
The resort has a splendid setting, with the dramatic cliffs of the Brenta group to the south-east.

THE MOUNTAINS

The upper slopes are open, the lower slopes attractively wooded; most major lifts go well above the treeline, so there are few entirely sheltered runs at Madonna – Folgarida is better in this respect. Many run classifications exaggerate difficulty.

EXTENT OF THE SLOPES ★★★
Plenty of variety
The extent of the pistes is not huge, but the slopes span large distances and give a great sense of travel.

Gondolas from close to the centre go west up to the **Pradalago** sector – which is linked via Monte Vigo to the distant slopes of **Folgarida** and **Marilleva** – and to **Cinque Laghi**, where at mid-mountain the gondola link with **Pinzolo** starts. A bit further

MOMENTUM SKI

Weekend & a la carte
ski holiday specialists

100% Tailor-made

Premier hotels
& apartments

Flexible travel
arrangements

020 7371 9111
WWW.MOMENTUMSKI.COM

from the centre, another gondola goes
east up to **Spinale**. The high **Grostè**
sector can be reached from there or by
yet another access gondola from the
outlying Campo Carlo Magno, where
there is also a fast chairlift up to
Pradalago.

FAST LIFTS ★★★★☆
Some weaknesses

Most of the key lifts are fast chairs
and gondolas, but moving around the
area you will still meet some slow lifts.
Examples include several lifts around
Monte Spolverino and Monte Vigo, on
Dos de la Pesa, on Monte Spinale and
at Pinzolo. But at least the piste map
helpfully distinguishes fast chairs.

QUEUES ★★★★☆
Not a big issue

Around Campiglio itself queues are
rarely a problem except at ski school
time in high season. You may meet
queues on the slow lifts around Monte
Vigo and Monte Spolverino.

TERRAIN PARKS ★★★☆☆
Serious efforts

The Ursus park, at Grostè, including
snowcross and quarter-pipe, is claimed
to be among the top five in the Alps
and impressed one observer this year
– 'extensive and beautifully prepared'.
There's a special boarders' pass for the
area. There is also a beginner park in
the Pradalago sector.

Madonna di Campiglio

Build your own shortlist: www.wheretoskiandsnowboard.com

KEY FACTS

Resort	1520m
	4,990ft

Madonna, Folgarida, Marilleva, Pinzolo combined area	
Slopes	800-2505m
	2,620-8,220ft
Lifts	61
Pistes	150km
	93 miles
Blue	46%
Red	38%
Black	16%
Snowmaking	95%

LIFT PASSES

Prices in €

Age	1-day	6-day
under 8	23	126
8 to 15	33	176
16 to 64	47	252
65 plus	42	227

Free Under 8 if with family-paying adult

Notes Covers, Madonna, Pinzolo, Folgarida and Marilleva

Alternative passes Madonna only, Pinzolo only; Skirama Dolomiti Adamello Brenta covers Madonna, Pinzolo, Marilleva-Folgarida, Passo Tonale, Ponte di Legno, Andalo, Pejo, Monte Bondone and Folgaria-Lavarone

SCHOOLS

Nazionale
t 0465 442850

Rainalter
t 0465 443300

Adamello Brenta
t 0465 443412

Italian Ski Academy
t 377 946 5010

Zebra
t 0465 442080

Cinque Laghi
t 0465 441650

Classes (Nazionale prices)
6 3hr-mornings from €170

Private lessons
From €42 for 1hr

SNOW RELIABILITY ★★★☆☆
Good snowmaking

Although many of the runs are sunny, they are at a fair altitude, and snowmaking is now claimed to cover 95% of the runs. As a result, snow reliability is reasonable, despite an erratic snowfall record. Reporters stress the immaculate grooming.

FOR EXPERTS ★★☆☆☆
Relax and enjoy the view

There are black pistes dotted around – basically, one per sector – but they only just merit the classification. The lower part of Spinale Direttissima on the front of Monte Spinale is claimed to be 35°, which is a proper black. Few of the local reds present much challenge; it's worth checking out Pinzolo and Marilleva. As in many resorts in Italy, off-piste is formally banned, but the ban is often ignored, and this year we have a report from a reader who 'had a great morning off-piste on Spinale with an instructor'. This is not an area famed for reliable powder, though. The lift company says that it leaves Spinale Direttissima and Pancugolo (on Cinque Laghi) ungroomed for a day after a snowfall.

FOR INTERMEDIATES ★★★★☆
A great area

Grostè and Pradalago have long, wide easy runs, and timid intermediates will love them, while confident skiers will need to seek out challenges. The long blue Pradalago Facile is a fabulous wide, scenic cruise. The nearby reds aren't a lot steeper, but the lovely, scenic black Amazzonia is quite testing. Grostè is both high and gentle, so has the feel of a glacier – but is entirely rock. All four runs at the very top are of blue gradient, although two are marked red. Lower down, Lame is a decent red. Next-door Monte Spinale has easy slopes on the back, linking to Grostè, but much tougher stuff on the front (read 'For experts'). Spinale Diretta (not to be confused with Spinale Direttissima) is an excellent genuine red. Cinque Laghi, Campiglio's racing mountain, has something for everyone. The long 5 Laghi is tricky at the top, but is then a lovely genuine blue run ending prettily in woods; the famous Fis 3-Tre is a good, varied red, quite steep towards the bottom.

Keen intermediates should not fail to explore the runs at Folgarida,

Marilleva and Pinzolo. The Malghette red run on the way back from Monte Vigo is a favourite, with fabulous views across the valley; pity it's served by a slow lift.

FOR BEGINNERS ★★★☆☆
Get out of town

There are short drags near the village, but better nursery slopes up at Campo Carlo Magno, a bus ride out. Most people seem to start on the good slopes at the top of Pradalago, and up here you are perfectly placed for progression to longer easy runs.

FOR BOARDERS ★★★☆☆
Freeriders look elsewhere

The resort is popular with freestylers, and some major events have been held here.

FOR CROSS-COUNTRY ★★★☆☆
Respectable

There are 22km of pretty trails through the woods in a scenic setting up at Campo Carlo Magno.

MOUNTAIN RESTAURANTS ★★★☆☆
A fair selection

There are plenty of restaurants, all named on the piste map. Standards vary: there are plenty of routine cafeterias, but also table-service places with character (including mountaineering refuges) doing good food – and 'toilets to die for'.

One of the most promising table-service places is the little back room at Chalet Fiat at Spinale; the stylish self-service bit has decent food, but finding a table can be a bunfight. Reader tips on Grostè: Stoppanl ('gourmet-style but modest prices, very good service and atmosphere', 'wonderful views') and Graffer ('lovely position, very reasonable prices, efficient service'); we lack recent reports on the charming Malga Montagnoli; on Pradalago: Viviani Pradalago ('superb – perfect service', 'traditional food, reasonable prices') and Cascina Zeledria ('excellent wine list', 'delightful terrace, good service', 'cook your own on a hot rock'); at Folgarida: Rosa Alpina ('super food and local wine').

SCHOOLS AND GUIDES ★★★☆☆
Insist on English

There are several schools. Nazionale is the main one; beginner and intermediate reporters this year taking

Resort news and key links: www.wheretoskiandsnowboard.com

↑ The resort has a lovely wooded setting, and the views are even better from the sector shown in this shot – Pradalago

APT MADONNA DI CAMPIGLIO, PINZOLO, VAL RENDENA

CHILDCARE

Baita del Bimbo (Rainalter school)
t 0465 443300
From age 2

Babysitter list
at tourist office

Ski schools
From age 4

When quality and value matter, *do more* with

zenith holidays

0203 137 7678
zenithholidays.co.uk

◆ABTA
ABTA No.Y1542

private lessons enjoyed 'the best instruction we have ever had'. Some schools have minibuses; apparently some will bus you to the excellent nursery slopes above Folgarida.

FOR FAMILIES ★★★☆☆
Do your own thing
The ski schools take children from four. The Rainalter Ski School offers non-ski activities for children between two and eight years. But we wonder if English is reliably spoken. The central park is an attractive feature.

STAYING THERE

There is a wide choice of hotels – dozens of 4-star and 3-star places, and two 5-stars.
Hotels
****Chalet del Brenta** (0465 443159) Stylish place well south of the centre but strongly tipped by readers in 2013 – efficient shuttle, excellent food, 'very friendly staff, surprisingly good spa'.
****Lorenzetti** (0465 441404) At southern extremity not far from the gondola for Cinque Laghi and Pinzolo, and with timetabled shuttles. Reporters agree the food is top-notch, but rooms vary. 'Glorious views.'
****Oberosler** (0465 441136) 'Design' hotel (which in this case means bold

modern decor) right next to the Spinale gondola and return piste – 'excellent food and spa', helpful staff.
***Ariston** (0465 441070) On the town square, tastefully decorated and well run by an English-speaking Italian couple. 'Highly recommended.'
***Italo** (0465 441392) Simple, quiet place 300m from Spinale lift: 'Friendly, good food,' says a 2012 reporter.
***Montana** (0465 442335) 'Faultless' B&B hotel next to the 5 Laghi piste, with 'charm and atmosphere', run by a 'lovely' family. Cheap bar where you can scoff your own takeaway meals.

EATING OUT ★★★☆☆
Some good options
There are around 20 restaurants in the resort, including three with Michelin stars. More modest reader recommendations include Antico Focolare ('spectacular ravioli in creamy nut sauce') and Le Roi ('good location, cosy, excellent service, good food at reasonable prices') – both endorsed by a reporter this year, along with Belvedere, which slipped off our list a few years back. For a gourmet treat, try the 'amazing' Da Alfiero in Piazza Palu at the south end of the park ('luxury, good service and food, reasonable prices'). Bear in mind that some of the bars also offer food.

GETTING THERE

Air Verona 150km/
95 miles (2hr30);
Bergamo 180km/
110 miles (2hr45);
Milan Linate
220km/125 miles
(3hr); Milan Malpensa
260km/160 miles
(3hr30)

Rail Trento (75km/
45 miles)

ACTIVITIES

Indoor Pools and spas
in hotels; museums

Outdoor Ice skating,
snowshoeing, ice
climbing, dog
sledding, paragliding

UK PACKAGES

Alpine Answers, Crystal,
Crystal Finest, Erna
Low, Flexiski,
Momentum, Scott
Dunn, Ski Club
Freshtracks, Ski
Expectations, Ski
Safari, Ski Yogi,
Snow-wise, Solos, STC,
Thomson, Zenith
Folgarida Alpine
Answers, Crystal, Erna
Low, Rocketski, STC,
Thomson
Marilleva Erna Low,
STC, Zenith
Pinzolo Zenith

Phone numbers
From abroad use the
prefix +39 (and do **not**
omit the initial '0' of
the phone number)

TOURIST OFFICE

www.
campigliodolomiti.it

APRES-SKI ★★★☆☆
Jolly enough at teatime
As the slopes close, people pile in to
several central places – Caffé
Campiglio and Bar Suisse, a very
welcoming cafe-bar on the main
square. Ober One at the bottom of
Spinale is 'conveniently placed but not
so popular', maybe because of the
music it pumps out. As dinner time
approaches, everyone disappears. If
some of them reappear later, it's to
head for Des Alpes, Cliffhanger or
Zangola (out of town). Cantina del
Suisse (underneath Bar Suisse) has
live music some evenings. A reporter
this year rates the little back-street
Dolomiti the best bar in town – 'used
by locals, good food, lovely staff'.

OFF THE SLOPES ★★☆☆☆
Take your Kindle
There's not a huge amount to do.
Skating on the lake and snowshoeing
are popular.

LINKED RESORT – 1400m
MARILLEVA
Marilleva is a modern resort consisting
of several 1960s-style, ugly but
functional, low-rise concrete buildings
(most of them well screened by trees,
thankfully) built on a mid-mountain
shelf at 1400m and reached by road or
gondola from the lower part of the
resort at 900m, on the valley floor.

The slopes above Marilleva are
excellent, genuine reds served by a
gondola and a six-pack (with a few
blues higher up the mountain), much
better for adventurous intermediates
than Campiglio's main Pradalago
slopes. And they are shady, so the
snow is usually the best in the area.
There's also a genuine black run on
Dos de la Pesa served by a slow two-
stage chairlift. The Orti mountain
restaurant offers 'good food, fantastic
views, reasonable prices'.

LINKED RESORT – 1400m
FOLGARIDA
Folgarida is also purpose-built, but it
is beside the road over to Campiglio,
and is much more traditional in style
than Marilleva. The resort spreads
across the mountainside between two
gondola stations, one right on the
roadside nominally at 1400m and the
other some way off the road in a much
more village-like area at 1300m. This

part in particular feels more upmarket
than Marilleva, with smart hotels and
a few shops, but there are few other
amenities. In January you may
encounter some fur-clad patrons from
Eastern Europe. The busy 4-star Park
Hotel (0463 986618) enthused one
reader with its 'lavish food, good pool
and gym' and the Benny Hill-style acts
from the enthusiastic staff.

The slopes down to Folgarida are
gentler than those above Marilleva,
though they include an easy black. Up
at Malghet Aut, where both gondolas
arrive, is a beginner area that two
observers this year rate highly.

Midway between Marilleva and
Folgarida, an eight-person gondola
runs from the valley village of Daolasa
up to Val Mastellina, below Monte
Vigo, the top section serving a long,
sweeping red with lovely views of the
Val di Sole below.

LINKED RESORT – 770m
PINZOLO
Pinzolo is the main town of the Val
Rendena, south-west of Campiglio,
and 750m lower, linked by gondola to
Campiglio. It sells itself as a family
resort, with good childcare facilities at
mid-mountain but it is little known in
the UK.

From Pinzolo, a gondola followed
by a fast chair take you via a lively
mid-mountain congregation area with
nursery slopes to the area's high point
of Doss del Sabion (2100m), where
there are great close-up views of the
Brenta massif.

It's quite a challenging area, with
genuine blacks (groomed when we
have visited) and genuine reds, some
at the steep end of the spectrum.
Most of the runs are quite short, the
conspicuous exception being the
excellent black/red run of almost 900m
vertical to the valley station of a
second gondola at Tulot, just outside
the town. Start at Doss del Sabion and
you can extend this to 1300m. Many of
the slopes are quiet and shady, so
keep snow well.

The Rifugio Doss del Sabion at the
top has a calm little table-service
restaurant as an alternative to the
often hectic terrace and self-service.
The 'very picturesque' Malga Cioca is
also strongly recommended.

There are plenty of guest houses
and hotels, mainly 3-star but with
some other options.

Monterosa Ski

At last, becoming better-known: three unspoiled and uncrowded valleys linked by pistes and with fab off-piste terrain

TOP 10 RATINGS

Extent	★★
Fast lifts	★★★★★
Queues	★★★★
Snow	★★★★
Expert	★★★★
Intermediate	★★★★
Beginner	★★
Charm	★★★
Convenience	★★★
Scenery	★★★★

RPI   85

lift pass	£170
ski hire	£95
lessons	£70
food & drink	£100
total	**£435**

NEWS

2014/15: UK tour op Ski Total has taken over one of our favourite hotels (the 4-star Breithorn) and will be running it as a chalet hotel.

+ Fabulous off-piste and heli-skiing, for both intermediates and experts
+ Slopes quiet on weekdays
+ Comprehensive snowmaking
+ Unspoiled valleys and villages
+ Panoramic views at altitude
+ Wide variety of mountain restaurants
+ Lovely long runs and a sensation of travel from place to place, but ...

– Virtually no choice of route when touring the three valleys on-piste, and a modest total extent
– Few challenges (or moguls) on-piste
– Unhelpful piste classification
– High winds can close links
– Few off-slope diversions
– Can be very busy at weekends
– Limited après-ski

Monterosa Ski's resorts – Champoluc, Gressoney and Alagna – have long been among our favourites and are popular with Italian weekenders and experts going off-piste. Until recently they have not made much impact on the international ski market but now things are changing. Champoluc was put on the UK map on a small scale by single-resort operator Ski 2, which has been operating there for 15 years and has built a great reputation; this season Ski Total is moving in with an upmarket chalet hotel – see 'News'. And last season, family specialist Esprit Ski started up in Gressoney in the next valley.

The resorts retain a friendly, small-scale, unspoiled ambience that we (and a growing band of readers) like a lot. They share a network of pistes that is modest in size but suits intermediates well and areas of off-piste that suit everyone from adventurous intermediates to experts (but guidance is needed).

There is one main village in each of three adjacent valleys: Champoluc in the western Val d'Ayas, Gressoney in the central valley and Alagna to the east. Champoluc and Gressoney are both reached from the Aosta valley, to the south. Alagna is more remote and isolated, and approached by a quite different route from the east.

Day trips to other resorts are hard work, but Cervinia, Courmayeur, La Thuile and Pila are reachable by car from Champoluc and Gressoney and are covered by the Aosta Valley pass.

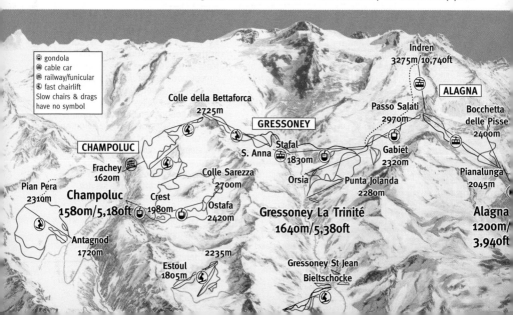

KEY FACTS

Slopes	1200-3275m
	3,940-10,740ft
Lifts	25
Pistes	73km
	45 miles
Blue	17%
Red	72%
Black	11%
Snowmaking	97%

SNOWPIX.COM / CHRIS GILL

The high nursery slopes at Crest above Champoluc are excellent; but for easy progression runs you have to catch a bus to Frachey ↓

All three villages are small-scale and pleasantly rustic, without being picture-postcard pretty. Like most Italian resorts, the villages really come to life only at weekends.

Monterosa Ski is surrounded by a string of peaks over 4000m, and some over 4500m; the panoramic views from restaurant terraces are fabulous.

THE MOUNTAINS

Open slopes dominate, but there are woodland runs lower down. The piste map and signposting are adequate. It's a shame that many runs that could be classified blue are red, leading to uncertainty for timid intermediates.

The attraction for experts and confident intermediates is the off-piste, with great runs from the high points of the lift system and some excellent heli-skiing. The Indren cable car accesses a lovely itinerary as well as more serious routes to Alagna (a guide is essential). There are few black pistes and most are not steep.

There is excellent intermediate piste skiing, with some notably long runs from the ridges to the villages. The run down to Alagna is 1760m vertical and 7km long, for example.

Although the slopes span vast distances, and give a great sense of travel, they don't add up to a huge amount of skiing. The lift company has now quietly accepted our view that its claimed run lengths needed, more or less, to be halved. The total for the linked area is now only 73km.

The main three-valley network is very simple: there is basically one main way down each mountainside. Champoluc and Gressoney have worthwhile local areas of pistes in addition to this three-valley system, but Alagna does not. The main lift system is vulnerable to bad weather, but both Champoluc and Gressoney have sheltered alternatives.

This is not a notably snowy area, but altitude helps, as does extensive snowmaking. Grooming is thorough – bumps on the pistes don't last long.

The important lifts are mainly fast chairs and gondolas. But sunny weekends bring crowds, and one or two queuing problems in the Champoluc and Alagna valleys.

Mountain restaurants are listed on the piste map. They are generally simple, friendly and good value, but there are some notably good ones too.

ski²

The ski holiday specialists to the acclaimed Monterosa Ski area, including the three resorts of Champoluc, Gressoney and Alagna.

- Holidays of any duration for families, groups and individuals
- Ski weekends and short breaks
- Our own British ski school and nursery
- Choice of departure and arrival airports
- Quality hotels and apartments
- Swift minibus transfers

Visit our comprehensive website, at www.ski-2.com, call us on 01962 713330 or email us at sales@ski-2.com

ABTA
The Travel Association

Build your own shortlist: www.wheretoskiandsnowboard.com

Champoluc 1580m

- ➕ Relaxed, traditional-style village
- ➕ Excellent beginner area at mid-mountain, but ...
- ➖ Progress to longer runs tricky
- ➖ Some tricky red runs
- ➖ Not notably convenient

Champoluc is at the western end of the three-valley network. Although it has drawbacks, it's an attractive all-round base. But what keeps many people going back is the warm welcome and the service provided by UK tour operator Ski 2. Ski Total will join them this season with a plush chalet hotel.

Champoluc is strung out along the street running from the centre past various hotels to the gondola base station, where a cluster of shops and bars forms a kind of distinct micro-resort. About 3km up the valley, a short funicular goes up from Frachey (with parking right at the base).

Down-valley from Champoluc are Antagnod and Brusson. Antagnod is a good alternative for bad-weather days, and has some decent off-piste.

Village charm There is a group of bars and restaurants at the lift base but the village lacks a real focus. But we and readers like the low-key ambience.

Convenience The village is not compact, but everything is walkable. Some hotels are a 10-minute walk from the gondola base station. You can leave kit there. There are free buses to and from Frachey, Brusson and Antagnod. And Ski 2 ferries its guests around town.

THE MOUNTAINS

Slopes The gondola from Champoluc goes up to Crest, a mid-mountain nursery area with a further gondola followed by a slow quad chairlift going on to Colle Sarezza. This area is linked to the runs above Frachey via a steep, narrow, bumpy red run, known by all and sundry as the Goat, because of the fine statue at the top; timid intermediates are better off starting at Frachey. From there, you ride lifts to Colle Bettaforca, for the descent to the Gressoney valley.

Fast lifts Most lifts are fast chairs and gondolas, but the link with Frachey involves slow chairs. You can avoid these by using the Frachey funicular.

Queues Mostly blissfully queue-free. But there are two problems at Frachey. The Alpe Mandria chair above the funicular is an unavoidable bottleneck. And the old double chair that links to the home slopes of Champoluc cannot cope with afternoon demand.

Terrain parks No real park – just a couple of jumps and a rail last season.

Experts Off-piste is the main attraction. There are few tough on-piste runs. In bad weather, head for the excellent Mandria forest area above Frachey for powder.

Intermediates There is a good mix of varied pistes that suit confident intermediates. But Champoluc has drawbacks for timid intermediates – as well as the Goat run, the red descent to Champoluc (excellent if you can hack it) can be too much for many. Some people find it worth going to the separate Antagnod area.

Beginners The high nursery slopes at Crest above Champoluc, served by two moving carpets, are excellent. For longer gentle runs, though, you need to go up the valley to Frachey. Or down the valley to Antagnod.

Snowboarding Great off-piste for experts but not ideal for intermediates or beginners (see above). No drag lifts to worry about though.

Cross-country There are 17km of trails in Champoluc; but Brusson, down-valley, has the best loops (30km).

Mountain restaurants There are three small, notably charming places serving excellent food in beautifully renovated old buildings. Our favourites are l'Aroula and Rascard Frantze, above and below the Champoluc mid-station, and endorsed by readers ('About as far a cry from French on-piste canteens as is possible to imagine,' says a 2014 reporter). Stadel Soussun above Frachey is possibly the most polished, but we've found service rather cool; close by is the 'friendly' Taconet with 'simple but hearty food'. Most popular this year is the Campo Base at the top of the Mandria chair ('welcoming, superb views, weekly Tibetan lunch'; traditional food too), while La Tana del Lupo is highly praised for the warm welcome and 'good menu'. Other reader tips include: Baita Stella Alpina, the 'atmospheric' Belvedere, Ostafa ('good value, big portions') and Lo Retsignon ('charming rustic hut, smiling family, good prices').

Schools and guides We lack recent reports on the Italian ski schools but have good reports of the Ski 2 ski school ('good, friendly instructors'). **Families** Tour operator Ski 2 has all kinds of schemes to keep children happy. And it runs Ski 2 Racing courses for would-be Olympians (see our 'Family holidays' chapter).

STAYING THERE
We've had good reports of Champoluc specialists Ski 2 ('great from pick-up to drop-off').
Chalets Ski Total is now running the lovely former 4-star hotel Breithorn as a plush chalet hotel.
Hotels For a small place, Champoluc has a good range of attractive hotels. We've enjoyed the friendly, woody 4-star La Rouja (0125 308767). The 3-star Champoluc (0125 308088) has a perfect location next to the gondola and is praised by reporters. Others have enjoyed the comfortable but rather formal 4-star Relais des Glaciers (0125 308182). The central 3-star Castor (0125 307117) has 'monumental breakfasts and charming service'.

Comfortable lodgings up the hill are a local speciality. The Hôtellerie de Mascognaz (0125 308734) is a lovingly restored group of stone chalets in a

ALPINE ANSWERS
The UK's No.1 Chalet Specialist

For choice and service look no further!
alpineanswers.co.uk
call: 020 7801 1080   ABTA

very isolated spot reached by skidoo. Three mountain restaurants have charming rooms – Stadel Soussun (348 6527222), Rascard Frantze (0125 941065) – 'Simply the best place I've stayed when skiing,' said a 2014 reporter – and l'Aroula (347 0188095), where we had a wonderfully peaceful and comfortable stay a couple of years ago and which 2014 visitors endorse.
Eating out Most restaurants are in hotels, but there are a few stand-alone places. Osteria Il Balivo is repeatedly tipped ('outstanding rillettes-filled ravioli and desserts'). But it is just topped by the Grange up at Frachey ('Just brilliant; exceptional atmosphere,

Monterosa Ski

Build your own shortlist: www.wheretoskiandsnowboard.com

NEW THIS YEAR
Chalet Hotel Breithorn

THE CHALET SPECIALIST
Ski Total

Chalet Hotel Breithorn, full of character and traditional Italian charm, is ideally situated in the charming Monterosa resort of Champoluc.

Ski Total Savers incl. cash-back, ski pack offers & free group places | 5-course dinners with complimentary wine
Free Ski Hosting 3 days a week | Whirlpool, steam-room and sauna | Flights from Gatwick, Birmingham or Manchester

Tel: **01483 791933**   Book online at **skitotal.com**

MOMENTUM SKI

Weekend & a la carte
ski holiday specialists

100% Tailor-made

Premier hotels
& apartments

Flexible travel
arrangements

020 7371 9111
WWW.MOMENTUMSKI.COM

UK PACKAGES

Champoluc Alpine
Answers, Crystal,
Crystal Finest, Erna
Low, Interski,
Momentum, Ski 2, Ski
Expectations, Ski Total,
Ski Yogi, Snow Finders,
Snow-wise, Thomson
Gressoney la Trinité
Alpine Answers, Crystal,
Crystal Finest, Erna
Low, Esprit, Inghams,
Momentum, Mountain
Tracks, Ski Club
Freshtracks, Ski Line,
Ski Yogi, Snoworks,
STC, Thomson
Alagna Alpine Answers,
James Orr Heliski, Ski
Club Freshtracks, Ski
Monterosa, Ski
Weekend

exemplary food, faultless service.'
Après-ski Near the gondola base,
readers tip the 'cosy and rustic' Atelier
Gourmand and the Bistrot – free
antipasti at both. Hotel des Glaciers'
patisserie is 'well worth the walk'.
Golosone is a small, atmospheric,
distinctly Italian wine bar; and the
West Road pub in the hotel California
has karaoke some nights. Tuesday is
music night in the hotel Castor's bar.
Later on, try Pachamama.
Off the slopes There are lovely walks
up the valley. And an outdoor ice rink.

Gressoney la Trinité 1640m

➕ Centrally placed in the three valleys	➖ Access to long easy runs involves
➕ Some convenient lodging	lifts up and then down the hill
➕ Some good mountain restaurants	➖ Slow lifts on lower local slopes

If you are planning daily excursions to Passo Salati to ski Alagna or to ride the Punta Indren cable car, Gressoney is the place to start. The big news last year was the opening of a chalet hotel by family specialist tour operator Esprit Ski.

Gressoney la Trinité is at the head of the long and beautiful Lys valley – a 40-minute drive from the Val d'Aosta. This is a resort of parts. The heart of the village is slightly away from the skiing, but there are skiers' satellites that have grown up at the lift bases: 500m away across the valley is the base station of a slow chairlift into the local slopes; there is a mini-resort conveniently clustered around the lift base, now almost as big as the village proper. The lifts for the other valleys go from a second mini-resort of Stafal, 5km away at the head of the valley (linked by a free but infrequent bus).
Village charm Gressoney la Trinité is a quiet, neat little village, cobbled in the centre, with an old church and wooden buildings – but many are closed up, in the winter at least. The satellites don't amount to much – a dense collection of hotels at the local lift base, a more spread-out one at Stafal.
Convenience The local lift base area is compact and convenient. Up at Stafal, walks to the lifts are a bit longer, but bearable from most lodgings.

THE MOUNTAINS
Slopes From Stafal, a cable car goes in one direction towards Colle Bettaforca and Champoluc, and a gondola goes in the other towards Passo Salati and Alagna. Down the valley at Gressoney, an old double chairlift accesses an area of wooded runs, with piste links (via another slow double chairlift) across the mountainside to the lifts from Stafal to Passo Salati.
Down the valley beyond Gressoney St Jean, at Bieltschocke, is a small but worthwhile (700m vertical) area of slopes served by a fast double chair.
Fast lifts The slow chairs in the woods at Gressoney are the main exceptions

to a picture dominated by fast lifts.
Queues The queue-prone gondola from Stafal to Gabiet was upgraded three seasons ago, but the one above it gets busy at times.
Terrain parks There's an 'excellent' park at Gabiet (Dream Park).
Experts Gressoney is well placed for access to Passo Salati and the cable car to Punta Indren, for off-piste runs. The only serious black run in the area is the short one from Punta Jolanda.
Intermediates On both sides of the valley there are fine, none-too-difficult reds above mid-mountain, with trickier runs lower down. The Moos run to Stafal on the Passo Salati side is a black, but it is not seriously steep.
Beginners There are nursery slopes with moving carpets at valley level at Gressoney itself and at Stafal. Then it's up the gondola to the short blue run at mid-mountain; or on up to the top for the much longer blue runs to the mid-station of the cable car from Alagna (a 2014 reporter warns these can close at busy times – presumably to avoid queues at the cable car mid-station; watch for the 'closed' signs).
Snowboarding Great off-piste for experts, easy pistes for intermediates, no drag lifts to worry about.
Cross-country There are decent trails: 23km around Gressoney St Jean.
Mountain restaurants On the local slopes, off the main system, there are two places we are itching to try. The welcoming, woody, table-service Punta Jolanda does 'great pasta' but also more serious dishes; lively bar, too. Lower down, Morgenrot is a reader favourite – 'good for a serious lunch'. Nearby, simple self-service Bedemie is 'great value'; the spag bol at 5 euros must be the cheapest in the Alps. At mid-mountain on the main slope from

ESPRIT Ski

No.1 For Family Skiing

SAVE UP TO £716 PER FAMILY in Gressoney

PLUS 12 OTHER TOP RESORTS in Austria and France

★ **We focus 100% on families**, guaranteeing complete dedication to family needs
★ **Dedicated Esprit Nurseries** with qualified English-speaking nannies
★ **Exclusive Children's Ski Classes** with max. 8 children to one instructor
★ **FREE evening Baby-Listening / Child Patrol Service** available
★ **Strict child care ratios** and procedures based on our 32 years' child care experience
★ **Catered chalets & Chalet Hotels**, specially for families
★ **Flights from 8 regional airports** across the UK

★ **NEW Baby And Toddler Weeks**

🦇 **FREE infant places** saving £115
🦇 **Half-price Nursery Places** saving £157
🦇 **Half-price Skiing & Day Care for toddlers** saving £207
🦇 **BAT-Weeks** run on 11, 18, 25 Jan, 1 & 22 Feb

Call **01483 791 900**
visit **espritski.com**

ABTA The Travel Association V6871

P Salati, Rif Gabiet serves 'excellent, good-value pasta, polenta and cakes'.
Schools and guides The school at Stafal is said to be short of English-speaking instructors. The guides of Guide Monterosa have consistently got good reports – 'very professional'.
Families Family specialist Esprit has a chalet hotel here ('childcare, location, food and wine all excellent').

STAYING THERE

Chalets We know of no small chalets, but see 'Families' above.
Hotels In the village, the Jolanda Sport (0125 366140) has had good reports. At the village lift base, the 3-star Dufour (0125 366139) has earned glowing reports; at Stafal, the modern, stylish little Nordend (0125 366807) is in the same ownership and we enjoyed our stay here in 2013. The Ellex (0125 366637) is a chalet-style eco place with 'a lovely lounge, smart bathrooms and a great spa'. The modern Chalet du Lys (0125 366806) offers good rooms and 'excellent' food.
Eating out At Stafal the bar-restaurant underneath the hotel Nordend, known as the Core or Giovanni's, does excellent food, charmingly served.

Après-ski Gressoney is pretty quiet. At Stafal, head for the bar under the Nordend ('great for a teatime beer').
Off the slopes There's an ice rink, a sports hall and a big pool.

LINKED RESORT – 1200m
ALAGNA

Alagna is a small, remote village with a solid church and some lovely old wooden farmhouses built in the distinctive Walser style. But its local skiing is very limited; in bad weather there may be little or nothing to do. So it is difficult to recommend for a holiday booked well in advance.

The mountains above Alagna offer some of the most exciting off-piste in the area, including very steep couloirs.

In good weather, the splendid 7km (1760m vertical) descent from Passo Salati to Alagna is a highlight. At the top, the black Olen piste (once rightly classified red) is a great blast and there is good, shady, off-piste beside it. The tough red Alagna piste below it is equally rewarding – though snow on the lower sections can be poor.

The gondola and (particularly) the cable car above it can build queues.

Phone numbers
From abroad use the prefix +39 (and do **not** omit the initial '0' of the phone number)

Build your own shortlist: **www.wheretoskiandsnowboard.com**

Passo Tonale

An unusual and attractive combination of high, snow-sure slopes (linked to lower Ponte di Legno) and the lowest prices in the Alps

418

TOP 10 RATINGS

Extent	★★
Fast lifts	★★★★
Queues	★★★★
Snow	★★★★
Expert	★
Intermediate	★★★
Beginner	★★★★★
Charm	★★
Convenience	★★★
Scenery	★★★

RPI 75

lift pass	£160
ski hire	£70
lessons	£70
food & drink	£100
total	**£400**

NEWS

2014/15: If all goes to plan, a new gondola will open from Passo Paradiso to the top of the glacier, replacing the existing T-bars and chairlift.

KEY FACTS

Resort	1885m
	6,180ft
Passo Tonale and Ponte di Legno combined area	
Slopes	1120-3015m
	3,670-9,890ft
Lifts	30
Pistes	100km
	62 miles
Blue	24%
Red	61%
Black	15%
Snowmaking	100%

+ Good-value mid-market lodgings

+ Sunny but snow-sure slopes

+ A row of uncrowded, easy runs

+ Link to Ponte di Legno adds attractive, steeper, treelined runs

– Not much locally for experts or keen intermediates

– Local slopes are above the treeline and are unpleasant in bad weather

– Linear village, strung along the pass road, is no beauty

Passo Tonale is a great place if you are on a tight budget, particularly for beginners and timid intermediates, with the link to Ponte di Legno, over the pass to the west, offering added interest for the more adventurous.

THE RESORT

Village charm A resort dedicated to skiing, built along a road over a high pass; many of the buildings are in chalet style, but it lacks a focus, and lacks pavements – pedestrians must compete with the traffic.
Convenience Tonale is fairly compact, with its hotels spread along the bottom of the main slope area – so all pretty convenient for the lifts.
Scenery The main slopes offer grand views of Presena, and Ponte di Legno's slopes also offer good views.

THE MOUNTAINS

The Tonale slopes are entirely above the treeline (not good in bad weather) but the linked slopes of Ponte di Legno are almost entirely wooded – a great combination. Thirty minutes east is Marilleva (free bus daily, except Saturday), linked to Madonna di Campiglio. Buy the right pass and you get a day there included, or more.

Slopes Tonale's home slopes are limited in extent. The broad, gentle, sunny area north of the pass road, served by a row of chairs and drags, is much the larger of the two sectors, but runs are short. An eight-seat gondola accesses the steeper, narrower and taller north-facing sector. A new gondola is planned to open this season above that, going to the top of the small Presena glacier.
A blue/red run through the trees (mostly easy but with a short steeper section) descends almost 600m to a slow chair into the Ponte di Legno slopes; this is followed by an easy black run – you can avoid this by riding the gondola down to PdL.
Fast lifts The system is impressive; the eight fast chairs on the Tonale slopes almost merit a ★★★★★ rating.
Queues In peak season, some lifts get busy at ski school time; the gondola back from Ponte di Legno can be busy. But generally there are no problems. At village level the pistes can get busy.

↑ There are lots of easy runs, as well as the main terrain park, on the sunny slopes immediately above the village

ADAMELLO SKI

UK PACKAGES
Crystal, Neilson, Ski Line, Skitracer, STC, Thomson, Zenith

of trails at Passo Tonale and 44km at Vermiglio (10km east).

Mountain restaurants Readers have generally been happy, particularly with the modest prices. Current reader favourite is Il Faita, on the run down to Ponte di Legno – 'food better and more varied than elsewhere, efficient service'. At Ponte di Legno, the rustic Valbione does excellent food in the upstairs table-service part ('goulash recommended', 'best pasta'). Other tips back at Passo Tonale include the village-level La Baracca and the 'convenient' Malga Valbiolo.

Schools and guides Mixed reports over the years and in 2014 from 'very good – enthusiastic and helpful' to complaints of large classes containing a wide range of abilities. English-speaking skills are improving.

Families The ski school takes kids from four, and it looks a good resort for skiing children. But there isn't much to do other than skiing.

STAYING THERE

Hotels There are around 30, most of them 3-stars, including the Sporting (0364 903781), where we had a pleasant short stay in 2012. Reporters this year enjoyed the Sport Hotel Vittoria (0364 91348) ('well located, interesting food, pleasant spa') and the Hotel delle Alpe (0364 903919), despite its poor location. We have good reports on two Crystal exclusive hotels – the Cielo Blu ('great staff, good food, spacious room' says a 2014 report) and the big, modern Paradiso (with pool, spa). Two other places in great locations have been tipped recently: the 'great, friendly' Torretta (0364 903978) and the 'excellent' 4-star Miramonti (0364 900501) with pool and spa.

Apartments There are 1,400 beds in apartments, a few on the UK market.

Eating out Reporters seem content. Mainly simple hotel restaurants, with the Torretta and Miramonti both doing excellent pizza.

Après-ski It's not wild, but there are a few spots to try. Reader tips include the 'relaxed ambience and friendly staff' at El Bait – here and at La Botte you get free après snacks. Heaven in Sport Hotel Vittoria and the Up Fun Park & Disco Pub in the Miramonti may or may not be lively later.

Off the slopes There's not a lot to do off the slopes – snowmobiling, snowshoeing, skating, dog sledding.

Terrain parks The main park close to the village, with a beginners' area, can get busy. Late in the season there is a park up on the glacier.

Snow reliability In a normal season, the altitude and setting ensure good conditions. The sunny main slopes can suffer in late season, while the glacial south side fares better. Strong wind can be a problem, but the wooded slopes of Ponte di Legno offer shelter. The snowmaking is impressive.

Experts There isn't much for experts within the lift system. But in good conditions there are epic off-piste runs from the glacier, including the impressive 16km Pisgana run towards Ponte di Legno (a vertical of 1650m).

Intermediates The gentle south-facing slopes – many labelled red but of blue gradient – are great for building confidence. Adventurous intermediates will enjoy the 4.5km Alpino piste down a deserted valley to the village, and the Presena area. The glacier runs are short and not steep. The black run beneath the gondola is easy but rewarding. The red runs at Ponte di Legno are excellent, and correctly classified. The blacks are not steep.

Beginners 'Excellent': the sunny slopes right by the village are ideal, with plenty of easy, wide blue runs to move on to, a couple of them quite long.

Snowboarding The gentle slopes and many chairlifts mean the area is good for beginners and intermediates.

Cross-country Not ideal. There are 8km

Phone numbers
From abroad use the prefix +39 (and do **not** omit the initial '0' of the phone number)

TOURIST OFFICE
www.passotonale.it
www.adamelloski.com
www.valdisole.net

Sauze d'Oulx

A lively village beneath an attractive area of slopes forming part of the extensive Milky Way; but non-trivial drawbacks persist

RATINGS

The mountains

Extent	★★★★
Fast lifts	★★★
Queues	★★★
Terrain p'ks	★
Snow	★★
Expert	★★
Intermediate	★★★★
Beginner	★
Boarder	★★
X-country	★
Restaurants	★★★
Schools	★★
Families	★★

The resort

Charm	★★
Convenience	★★
Scenery	★★★
Eating out	★★★
Après-ski	★★★★
Off-slope	★

RPI 90

lift pass	£160
ski hire	£105
lessons	£80
food & drink	£110
total	**£455**

NEWS

2014/15: A new triple chair is planned going from Capanna Mollino at Punta Rocca to Col Basset, allowing access to the Rio Nero bowl and thus to M Fraiteve without going through Sportinia.

420

- Extensive slopes, generally uncrowded – great cruising
- Mix of open and woodland runs is good for all weather conditions
- Entertaining nightlife
- Part of the Milky Way network, spreading across the border to Montgenèvre in France, but ...

- Getting to France is time-consuming without using a car or taxis
- Erratic snow record and far from comprehensive snowmaking
- Lift system needs improvement
- Not great for experts, and a poor choice for beginners
- Steep walks around the village
- Crowds on sunny weekends

Skiers with long memories are inclined to dismiss Sauze as lager-lout territory. In the 1980s and maybe 1990s the tabloid newspapers mined a rich vein of young Brits behaving badly here. There are still lots of lively bars and shops festooned in English signs, and young Brits working in them, but it is a much more civilized place now, with grown-up Brits and Italian weekenders more in evidence (this is Turin's closest major ski area). When we visit, we always seem to like the place more than we expect to.

But Sauze still has a problem: investment, lack of. It needs comprehensive snowmaking, and it needs new lifts. What the resort seems to be doing of late is reshuffling the lifts it already has, which doesn't quite do the trick.

THE RESORT

Sauze d'Oulx sits on a sloping mountain shelf facing north-west to the mountains bordering France. It is a mid-sized resort – a big village rather than a town – but it spreads quite widely. Out of the bustle of the centre, there are secluded apartment blocks in quiet, wooded areas and a number of good restaurants also tucked away.

The Via Lattea (Milky Way) lift pass covers not only next-door Sestriere and Sansicario, easily reached by lift and piste, but also the more remote slopes of Claviere and Montgenèvre – more easily reached by road, but certainly possible on skis/board.

houses roofed with huge stone slabs. But most of the resort is modern and undistinguished, made up of block-like hotels and the occasional chalet, spreading down the steep hillside from the slopes. Smart, woody hotels and apartments are lacking.

There is a central car-free zone, but at both ends of the day the rest of the village can be congested. The roads have few pavements and can be icy.

Despite the decline in lager sales, the centre is still lively at night; the late bars are usually quite full. Noise can be a problem in the early hours. An early-season visitor this year found resort staff 'without exception smiling and welcoming'.

VILLAGE CHARM ★★★★★
Falling behind?

The village has an attractive old core, with narrow, cobbled streets and

CONVENIENCE ★★★★★
Uphill struggles

The village slopes steeply. The slow Clotes chair, for the left-hand side of the network, is at the top of the village, a short climb from the centre. Some hotels are above this lift, and in good snow offer ski-in/ski-out convenience – but most are not. There is a moving carpet that cuts out part of the climb. The Sportinia fast chair, the most direct way to the heart of the slopes, is a strenuous and hazardous walk (often on slippery roads) further

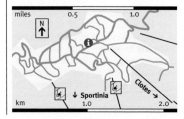

KEY FACTS

Resort	1510m
	4,950ft

Milky Way	
Slopes	1390-2825m
	4,560-9,270ft
Lifts	75
Pistes	400km
	249 miles
Blue	25%
Red	56%
Black	19%
Snowmaking	60%

Sauze d'Oulx-Sestriere-Sansicario	
Slopes	1390-2825m
	4,560-9,270ft
Lifts	41
Pistes	300km
	186 miles
Snowmaking	38%

out. There is a free ski-bus, but even in January it can be over-crowded. Consider leaving skis and boots at a ski shop near the lift base.

The smaller, lower village of Jouvenceaux is worth considering as a base, with a fast lift into the slopes and a good red run back down.

SCENERY ★★★★★
Plenty of trees
The scenery is attractively woody, especially low down and along the Val di Susa. The sunny, open slopes higher up give wide panoramic views of the mountains bordering France.

THE MOUNTAINS

The higher slopes are open, the lower ones pleasantly wooded. All in all, the piste system is a bit of a shambles. Piste classifications change from year to year, and the signs on the ground don't always match the piste map. Pistes tend to be overclassified, with reds that should be blue and blacks that should be red – and one reader this year judged some red stretches steeper than the blacks. Piste edge marking may be dangerously absent. And signposting isn't great, especially high up. Despite improvements, the Via Lattea piste map is still difficult to follow – a marketing device rather than a skiing aid. Mad.

EXTENT OF THE SLOPES ★★★★★
Big and varied enough for most
Sauze's local slopes are spread across a broad wooded mountainside above the resort, ranging from west- to north-facing. This is split by woods and ravines, and gives some sensation of travel as a result.

The heart of the skiing is **Sportinia**, a sunny mid-mountain clearing in the woods, with a ring of restaurants and hotels, and a small nursery area. This is reached directly by the fast chair outside the village mentioned above, less directly by the slow **Clotes** chair, which also accesses a rather neglected area of runs served by drags off to the left, on M Moncrons; this may or may not be open on weekdays.

A fast quad chair from Sportinia and a new triple chair from Punta Rocca above Clotes access the high, open bowl that separates Sauze from Sansicario. From here you can take a steep draglift or a slow double chairlift to the high point of the system – the major junction of **Monte Fraiteve**. From the peak you can go south to **Sestriere**. There are red and blue pistes all the way down, but the slope faces south and the bottom sections are rarely open – expect to ride the gondola. Or you can go west on splendid broad, long runs to **Sansicario** – and on to a two-stage gondola near **Cesana Torinese** that

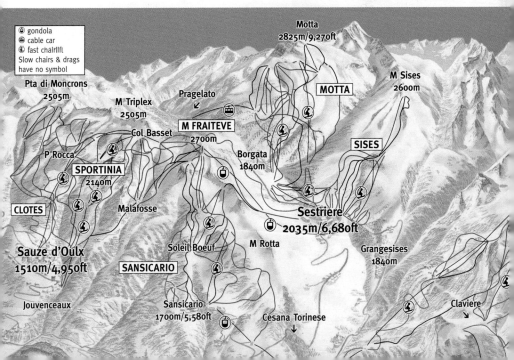

Sauze d'Oulx

LIFT PASSES

Via Lattea

Prices in €

Age	1-day	6-day
under 8	5	30
8 to 74	34	190
75+	17	102

Free No deals

Beginner Restricted day pass (€25)

Notes Covers lifts in Sauze d'Oulx, Sestriere, Sansicario, Cesana and Claviere

Alternative pass International (covers all the above plus Montgenèvre)

SNOWPIX.COM / CHRIS GILL

Sportinia is at the heart of the Sauze slopes, with several restaurants ↓

links with **Claviere** and then **Montgenèvre**, in France.

FAST LIFTS ★★★☆☆
Few and far between
Fast lifts are in a minority. There are still a lot of drags and old, slow chairlifts; to reach M Fraiteve you must choose one or the other. Things are improving, but slowly; serious investment is needed to update the lift system in various places.

QUEUES ★★★☆☆
Beware sunny weekends
There can be queues on sunny weekends and holidays, when the hordes from Turin flock in – crowds on the piste can be a problem then too. But during the week the slopes are usually quiet. All of our 2014 reporters were happy, high-season ones included. There is now serious congestion on the very confined peak M Fraiteve at busy times.

TERRAIN PARKS ★☆☆☆☆
Now established?
The previously unpredictable park now seems to have settled in a spot above Sportinia. A 2014 reader says it was 'small but pleasantly quiet'. It apparently took several days to reopen after a dump. There is a park at Sansicario too.

SNOW RELIABILITY ★★☆☆☆
Can be poor, affecting the links
The area is notorious for erratic snowfalls, suffering droughts with worrying frequency – though recent seasons have been pretty good, and Sauze got its share of Italy's generally abundant snowfall in 2013/14. The runs above Sansicario are affected by the afternoon sun. Snowmaking has been increased throughout the area (including the Sportinia nursery slopes); coverage is still far from complete, but great efforts are made to keep runs open. Grooming is in general 'immaculate'.

FOR EXPERTS ★★☆☆☆
Head off-piste
There are black runs, but most of them do not deserve their classification. We're told the black Malafosse run is not fiercely steep, but is narrow and isolated. There are quite a few off-piste opportunities between the pistes and down lift lines.

FOR INTERMEDIATES ★★★★☆
Splendid cruising terrain
The whole area is ideal for confident intermediates who want to clock up the kilometres. The less confident are not helped by the silly classification of many easy runs as red.

The Moncrons sector at the east of the area is served only by drags but offers some wonderful, uncrowded cruising, some of it above the treeline. There are some good long descents: red 11 is about 1000m vertical – a reader favourite.

At the higher levels, where the slopes are above the treeline, the terrain often allows a choice of route. Lower down are pretty runs through the woods, where the main complication can be route-finding.

The long runs down to Jouvenceaux are splendid, flattering intermediate terrain, as are those below Sportinia.

The slopes above Sansicario are also excellent, including the amiable Olympic Women's Downhill and the particularly fine red 71, away from the lifts, down to Pariol, the mid-station on the Cesana-Sansicario gondola.

FOR BEGINNERS ★☆☆☆☆
Not a good choice
Sauze presents various problems. The main nursery area up at Sportinia has only a short moving carpet, and is reached by a chairlift. There is a day

The slopes are attractively wooded, so if you are lucky enough to get a storm you can still ski enjoyably →

SNOWPIX.COM / CHRIS GILL

GETTING THERE

Air Turin 95km/ 60 miles (1hr30)

Rail Oulx (5km/ 3 miles); frequent buses

ACTIVITIES

Indoor Sauna, solarium, massage

Outdoor Ice rink, snowshoeing, walking

SCHOOLS

Sauze Sportinia t 0122 850218

Sauze d'Oulx t 0122 858084

Sauze Project t 0122 850654

Classes (Sauze Sportinia prices) 6 3hr-days €180

Private lessons €37 for 1hr

CHILDCARE

Ski school From age 4

pass covering these plus two other lifts, but there is no suitable longer slope to progress to. There is a slope at village level with a free moving carpet, but the slope is too steep for complete beginners. The mornings-only classes (normal in Italy, of course) don't suit everyone. Once off the nursery slopes, the main problem is erratic piste classification.

FOR BOARDERS ★★★★★
Too many drags
There are inescapable draglifts in a couple of areas – notably on the way back to M Fraiteve from Sansicario; but a group of snowboarders reporting this year were happy to put up with that in exchange for wide, well-groomed pistes and plentiful off-piste.

FOR CROSS-COUNTRY ★★★★★
You're on your own
There are no prepared loops in Sauze.

MOUNTAIN RESTAURANTS ★★★★★
Some pleasant possibilities
There are about 15 restaurants locally. They are generally pleasant, but can get very busy. Irritatingly, only some are marked on the piste map. There are several routine self-service places at Sportinia, plus two doing table-service. There is continuing praise from our regular reporter for the Rocce Nere ('still good food and service'); and this year, as last, we have reader approval for Monte Triplex ('very reasonable prices and unusually quiet'). In the Clotes sector there are several good bets. Clos Bourget specializes in 'large, excellent pizzas', with 'friendly table-service at reasonable prices'. And there are two

hotels with good restaurants. The 'cosy, rustic' Ciao Pais is repeatedly recommended, whether for its 'generous, very tasty' speciality of porcini pasta or its 'picturesque out-of-the-way location in the trees, excellent for a final stop'. The Capricorno lower down is the place for a serious table-service lunch; it is not cheap (a reader this year reports a £5 cover charge), and midweek in low season it can be deserted. Bar Basset below M Fraiteve offers 'friendly service' and 'excellent views on a sunny day'. Readers recommend a couple of spots on the slopes of Sansicario. Soleil Boeuf is a 'busy self-service' at mid-mountain offering 'great value'. Mavie is tipped for 'wholesome Italian food', 'excellent views and sunbathing'. Lamadia near the bottom of blue run 21 does 'good, inexpensive self-service pasta' and 'the best hot chocolate ever'.

SCHOOLS AND GUIDES ★★★★★
More reports, please
Recent reports are confined to private lessons. This year two readers endorse David Solomone of the Sportinia school, while a 2011 visitor highly recommended Roger Goodfellow of the Sauze d'Oulx school, who has been in Sauze for 30 years: 'We were of slightly different abilities but the lesson improved us all markedly.'

FOR FAMILIES ★★★★★
Yes and no
All the schools take children from four years, and spoken English should be OK. But note our reservations about the resort for beginners. The moving carpet just above the village is a great aid to sledging.

Sauze d'Oulx

423

Build your own shortlist: www.wheretoskiandsnowboard.com

skitracer*

CHALETS, HOTELS & APARTMENTS

Call us today

020 8600 1650

skitracer.com

UK PACKAGES

Alpine Weekends, Crystal, Inghams, Interactive Resorts, Neilson, Ski Club Freshtracks, Ski Line, Skitracer, STC, Thomson, Zenith **Sansicario** Crystal, Thomson

Phone numbers From abroad use the prefix +39 (and do **not** omit the initial '0' of the phone number)

TOURIST OFFICE

Sauze d'Oulx, Cesana Torinese (Sansicario) www.turismotorino. org www.vialattea.it www.comune. sauzedoulx.to.it

STAYING THERE

All the major mainstream operators offer hotel packages here.

Chalets Neilson has the catered chalet Le Valentin.

Hotels Simple 2-star and 3-star hotels form the core, with a couple of 4-stars and some more basic places.

****Relais des Alpes (0122 858585) 'Large rooms, food excellent with friendly restaurant staff.'

****Torre (0122 859812) Cylindrical landmark 200m below the centre. Two reporters this year are happy with 'spacious rooms' and 'good, generous food' but one had various reservations, including hot water problems and the 'terrible' ski room. Pool, spa (not free, generally).

***Gran Baita (0122 850183) Central place approved by a reader last year: 'Location quiet but convenient, decor a bit dated but superior rooms huge, excellent lounge, friendly staff, decent dinners, great value.'

***Miravalle (0122 858585) Simple place ('tired', says one report) chiefly notable for the value for money it offers – including free evening drinks and packed lunch.

***Stella Alpina (0122 858731) Between main lifts. Well run by Anglo-Italian family: 'friendly'; 'quiet at night'; 'good Italian food'.

**Martin (0122 858246) In Jouvenceaux. Basic, comfortable, with shuttle to the resort. 'Excellent value, helpful staff, good breakfast.'

**Villa Cary (0122 850191) Praised for an eighth year by an annual visitor: 'Still good for people on a budget.'

Apartments Plenty are available, some through UK operators.

At altitude The 4-star Capricorno (0122 850273), up at Clotes, is the most attractive and expensive hotel in Sauze – a charming little chalet beside the piste, with only 10 bedrooms. Higher up, the more modest Ciao Pais has a high reputation too. And there are places to stay at Sportinia.

EATING OUT ★★★☆☆
Caters for all tastes and pockets

Sauze has over 30 restaurants. Typical Italian banquets of five or six courses can be had in places such as the Cantun. In the old town there are several cutely rustic places. Del Falco 'is not cheap but worth it' – 'fabulous wines and blissful food'; we like the look of L'Ortiché, too – reports, please.

Paddy McGinty's steaks 'did us proud', says a reporter. Sugo's is a great place for pasta; Pizza House is 'excellent, with such a wide selection'.

APRES-SKI ★★★★☆
Suzy does it with more dignity

If cake and coffee is the order of the day, Pasticceria Gally is 'really good value' and 'a nice treat'. In most respects Sauze's bars now impress reporters, young and old – 'Classier than expected,' said one last year. Choice is wide, with many happy hours, and free antipasti in some places. Our regular reporter picks out the Grotta for the cheapest beer (well below UK prices); Max's Cafe ('busy for après and later') for its four-hour happy hour and live football; Mira ('probably the busiest') for sports TV – also tipped by another reporter for its friendly staff and happy-hour antipasti spread; Scatto Matto for its 'popular sun terrace and big cocktail menu'; and the Scotch Bar in the hotel Stella Alpina, at the foot of the Clotes home run, for 'relaxed atmosphere and friendly welcome'. Other tips include the popular Assietta, with 'generous glasses of Prosecco, and entertainment later on'; Il Lampione in the old town for a 'chilled-out atmosphere'; Osteria dei Vagabondi for late-night live music; the intimate bar Moncrons, the Club (formerly Schuss Bar); and the Cotton Club, a late-night bar with live bands.

OFF THE SLOPES ★☆☆☆☆
Go elsewhere

Shopping is limited, there are no gondolas or cable cars for pedestrians and there are few off-slope activities. Turin and Briançon are worth visiting.

LINKED RESORT – 1700m

SANSICARIO

Sansicario is ideally placed for exploration of the whole Milky Way. It is a modern, purpose-built, self-contained but rather soulless little resort, mainly consisting of apartments grouped around the small shopping precinct – but also spreading down the steep slope. The 46-room Rio Envers (0122 811937) is a comfortable, expensive 3-star hotel. The 4-star Majestic (085 8369777) has a pool. Apartments to rent are 'hard to find but cheap'. Very little happens in the evening, but the Enoteca (wine bar) is 'excellent in all respects'.

APT VAL DI FASSA / STEFANO ZARDINI

Sella Ronda

Endless intermediate slopes amid spectacular scenery, and a choice of attractive valley villages with a distinctive local culture

TOP 10 RATINGS

Extent	★★★★★
Fast lifts	★★★★
Queues	★★★
Snow	★★★★
Expert	★★
Intermediate	★★★★★
Beginner	★★★★
Charm	★★★
Convenience	★★★
Scenery	★★★★★

RPI 95

lift pass	£180
ski hire	£90
lessons	£85
food & drink	£125
total	**£480**

NEWS

2014/15: Lift capacity will be increased at Corvara with a six-pack replacing the Pralongià triple chairlift and an eight-person gondola replacing the queue-prone Borest quad chairlift to/from Colfosco.

2013/14: A new six-pack was built between Arabba and Passo Pordoi, going up to the Carpazza chair – creating a new way to the lifts towards Marmolada. The kids' fun slope above San Cassiano was expanded.

Phone numbers
From abroad use the prefix +39 (and do **not** omit the initial '0' of the phone number)

TOURIST OFFICE

www.dolomitisuperski.com
www.sella-ronda.info

PAUL CARTER

Lovely gentle run from Passo Sella, with the Gruppo del Sella dominating →

+ Vast network of connected slopes – suits intermediates particularly well

+ Stunning, unique Dolomite scenery

+ Lots of mountain huts with good food as well as fab views

+ Relatively low prices

+ Extensive snowmaking – one of Europe's best systems – but ...

− They need it: natural snowfall is erratic in this southerly region

− Few tough pistes, and off-piste is very limited – in general, banned

− Mostly short runs with limited vertical (with notable exceptions)

− Crowds on the Sella Ronda circuit

− Some old draglifts and slow chairs

A few days in Corvara last January confirmed yet again that this is one of our absolute favourite destinations. The scenery is the thing: the spectacular Dolomite scenery is like something Disney might have conjured up for a movie or a theme park.

The Sella Ronda is an amazing circular network of lifts and pistes around the Gruppo del Sella – a mighty limestone massif. Sheer cliffs rise out of gentle pasture land, which is where you ski mostly. The skiing is relaxing; the excitement comes from the views. This is one of the few destinations where we pray for sun; snowfalls would interfere with our scenery-gazing without bringing any real benefit – off-piste is off the agenda, and the snowmaking normally ensures reliably good piste skiing.

The scale of the area is some compensation for the lack of challenge; the distances you cover on skis are huge – in overall dimensions, the network beats even the famed Trois Vallées in France. There are three main resorts, each with its own slopes branching off from the main circuit: Selva gets its own chapter; this one covers Corvara and Arabba, plus nearby alternatives.

LIFT PASSES

Dolomiti Superski

Prices in €

Age	1-day	6-day
under 16	36	183
16 to 64	52	262
65 plus	47	236

Free Under 8
Beginner No deals
Note Includes all Sella Ronda resorts

KEY FACTS

Resort	1600m
	5,250ft
Slopes	1600-3270m
	5,250-10,730ft
Lifts	27
Pistes	89km

UK PACKAGES

Alpine Answers, Collett's, Inghams, Interactive Resorts, Momentum, Neilson, Ski Expectations, Ski Line, Ski Yogi, Skitracer, Snow-wise, STC

TOURIST OFFICE

www.arabba.it

CHOOSING A BASE

For good skiers wanting challenges on hand, probably the best base is Selva – covered in the next chapter along with Santa Cristina and Ortisei, slightly further down the Val Gardena. Arabba is the other obvious option.

Corvara is the best all-round bet – well placed for access to Selva, Arabba, the Sella Ronda circuit, the Alta Badia area and Cortina (and the 'hidden valley' run). Colfosco is just next door. La Villa and San Cassiano are slightly off the Sella Ronda circuit.

The Dolomiti Superski pass covers dozens of resorts around this amazing region. The lift system logs your lift rides – so you can go online to check your distance and vertical.

There are countless piste maps – a dozen Superski ones in all, plus locally produced ones for some resorts. The Alta Badia one, covering Corvara and neighbours, has the advantage that mountain restaurants are more clearly identified.

Arabba

+ Some of the best steep pistes in the Sella Ronda area – shady too
+ Quick access to Marmolada glacier

- Not a good base for novices, with more blacks than blues locally
- Off-slope activities are limited

Arabba is a small, quiet but fast-growing village appealing particularly to people looking for more challenging terrain than this region normally offers – but also immediate access to the Sella Ronda and Alta Badia sectors.

Village charm The village is small and traditional in style, but not notably picturesque. There are a few shops, bars and restaurants, but this is not a place for lively nightlife.
Convenience It's a small place, but staying in the older part can involve an uphill walk to reach the two lifts, which are a short walk apart. A newer area of hotels and chalets has developed higher up, well placed for the lifts and slopes, though perhaps not for bars.
Scenery Arabba is beautifully positioned between the stunning Gruppo del Sella and the glacial Marmolada massif, with great views at altitude in both directions.

THE MOUNTAIN

Arabba has a good mix of open and woodland slopes.
Slopes The two-stage double-cable gondola and the cable car beside it rise from the village almost 900m vertical to the high point at Porta Vescovo (2478m). From here a choice of runs return to the village or you can head off around the Sella Ronda circuit. The Porta Vescovo slopes west of Arabba (that is, on skier's left) are getting major investment – with new six-packs on both the upper and lower slopes in the last two years. These are good slopes, so new lifts are welcome, but they also create a new access to the lifts towards Marmolada. From the mid-station of the gondola, chairs take you to Passo Padon and onwards to the Marmolada glacier. This is an

excellent outing. The views from the top at 3270m are spectacular, and the 1500m vertical red run to Capanna Bill is splendid, with great snow on the top sections.

From the other side of the village, a fast quad gets you on the way to Burz, Passo di Campolongo and Corvara.
Fast lifts Key local lifts are fast, but there are slow lifts on the way to Marmolada.
Queues The outing to Marmolada can be troublesome on a busy day, with a bottleneck at the Sass de la Vegla double chair. There may be long waits for the Marmolada cable cars, especially late in the season.
Terrain park There's a park above Plan Boè, on the way to Passo di Campolongo – catering best for novices, in one reporter's view.
Snow reliability Good snow is far from assured, but snowmaking is extensive and the main runs are high and shady.
Experts Arabba has steep slopes to rival those of Selva/Val Gardena. The north-facing blacks and reds from Porta Vescovo offer genuine challenges and there is some tempting off-piste terrain too – but read the off-piste feature panel in the margin.
Intermediates The local slopes suit adventurous intermediates best – most are quite challenging. But the easy Alta Badia area is nearby.
Beginners It is not a great choice for beginners. There is a nursery slope near the Burz chair, but beyond the Arabba local slopes things get tricky.
Snowboarding The slopes of Porta

You can ski around the huge Sella massif in either direction by following very clear coloured signs; it's easily managed in a day by even an early intermediate. The clockwise route is slightly quicker and offers more interesting slopes, but is much busier – so many reporters prefer the anticlockwise route, despite a tedious series of five lifts from Corvara. Some resort piste maps include a Sella Ronda map; most take something close to a bird's eye topographical view. (Bizarrely, at least one puts south at the top.) A very detailed topo map is available from the tourist offices (and some lift stations).

The runs total around 23km and the lifts around 14km. There is one bit where no skiing is possible: at Corvara you ride a lift both ways – a queue-prone chair, which theoretically is being replaced this year by a gondola. The lifts take a total of about two hours (plus any queuing). We've done the circuit in just three and a half hours excluding hut stops; five or six hours is a realistic time when things are busy.

If you set out early and make good time, you can divert from the circuit, notably at Selva and Arabba. Less confident intermediates could explore the Alta Badia area, east of Corvara.

Not everyone likes it. You may find that 'it's a bit of a slog', or it is 'too busy and crowded', and 'not a relaxing business when it's busy'. And boarders should be aware that there are quite a few flat bits.

If you pick your time – low season or a Saturday, in good weather – and start early, we reckon it's well worth doing.

427

Sella Ronda

Build your own shortlist: www.wheretoskiandsnowboard.com

KEY FACTS

Sella Ronda
Linked network of Val Gardena, Alta Badia, Arabba, and of Canazei and Campitello in Val di Fassa

Slopes	1005-3270m
	3,300-10,730ft
Lifts	179
Pistes	433km
	269 miles
Blue	38%
Red	53%
Black	9%
Snowmaking	90%

Vescovo offer some decent challenges but there are some flat areas. The nursery slope has a draglift.

Cross-country There are no trails here.

Mountain restaurants There's lots of choice, from rustic huts to larger places. Most are lively and welcoming, and many have great views, of course. One lift-ride from the village, Rif Burz has been beautifully rebuilt in a modern but woody style. The lively Rif Plan Boè, nearby, has 'good food and service'. Rifugio Fodom just below Passo Pordoi has a 'good atmosphere' and 'excellent pizza and pasta', but watch out for the 'dire Europop'. The smart self-service Cesa da Fuoch at the mid-station of the Porta Vescovo gondola has 'excellent and reasonable fresh-cooked pasta'; Rif Luigi Gorza at the top has 'good food' as well as views. Below Marmolada, a visitor had a 'good-value' meal at Passo Fedaia, and Capanna Bill lower down is a cosy spot.

Schools The local Arabba school offers group and private classes. We have no recent reports.

Families The ski school takes quite young children.

STAYING THERE
New accommodation has been built at the top end of the village, convenient for the lifts. We know of no catered chalets here.

Hotels There are about a dozen hotels. The favourite of one regular visitor is the 4-star Grifone (0436 780034) out at Passo di Campolongo – 'remote, but food and service superb; excellent bar and health club/pool'. In the village, a 2014 visitor recommends the 'brilliant' 4-star Sporthotel (0436 79321) for its 'exceptional food' and 'traditional Tyrolean style' with 'probably the best access to both lifts'.

Apartments Self-catering accommodation is available.

Eating out Restaurant choice is limited. The central hotels all have busy restaurants. Recent reporters praised the hotel Pordoi restaurant for its 'good pizzas'. Also rated are Miky's Grill in the hotel Mesdì ('good value', 'very good quality steaks and meat; mixed grill a speciality') and Al Table ('friendly and good value', serving everything from 'simple pasta and great pizzas to well-cooked steak'). The Stube Ladina in the Alpenrose hotel has been recommended in the past. For something a bit different, you can be ferried by snowmobile up the mountain to Rif Plan Boè for dinner and dancing. Or you might just arrive at 5pm and stay for the evening.

Après-ski The après-ski is fairly limited. The atmospheric Rif Plan Boè up the mountain is good for a last drink on the way back from Corvara. According to recent reports, the central Bar Peter seems to be the focus later on – 'Loud music and always

crowded,' says a 2014 visitor. Reporters also mention Bar Heidi ('a bit more sophisticated'), the Stube in the Portavescovo hotel ('the closest thing in Arabba to a focal village bar, although it clears out at 8pm') and the Treina. Cosy hotel bars are other options in the village.

Off the slopes Off-slope diversions are few. There are some shops and cafes, and there's a small ice rink. Snowmobiling and snowshoeing are available.

KEY FACTS

Resort	1570m
	5,150ft
Slopes	1330-2530m
	4,360-8,300ft
Lifts	53
Pistes	130km
Snow-guns	392 guns

UK PACKAGES

Erna Low, Inghams, Momentum, Neilson, Ski Line, Ski Yogi, Snow-wise, STC

TOURIST BOARD ALTA BADIA / FREDDY PLANINSCHEK

The slopes above Badia, beneath Santa Croce, are a quiet backwater well worth a visit (including lunch at Rif Lee) ↓

Corvara

- ➕ One of the best locations, where Alta Badia meets the Sella Ronda
- ➕ Pleasant, relaxed village
- ➕ Local slopes suit novices, but ...

- ➖ Few challenges locally
- ➖ Some walking may be involved
- ➖ Alta Badia still has plenty of drags and slow chairlifts

Corvara rivals Selva as a base from most points of view, the exception being that of experts, who have to travel in search of challenges; for families and novices it takes some beating – though Colfosco merits consideration too.

Village charm Although it's not notably cute, the place is lively and family-friendly, with a pleasant traditional centre. There is some through-traffic, but it does not intrude hugely.

Convenience The main shops and some hotels cluster around a small piazza at the top end of the village, close to the Col Alto gondola; but the nursery slopes are quite a walk away, across the river; so are the Sella Ronda lifts but you can ski to them by riding the Col Alto gondola. The rest of Corvara sprawls quite a way along the valley; choose your spot with care.

Scenery The setting is superb: there are impressive rock faces and spires

all around the village, notably the distinctive, towering Sassongher.

THE MOUNTAIN

Corvara is well positioned, with village lifts heading off to reasonably equidistant Selva, Arabba and San Cassiano. The local slopes are gentle and confidence-boosting.

Slopes Lifts go off in three directions. A long gondola heads south towards Boè and Arabba for the clockwise Sella Ronda circuit. A new gondola will hopefully replace the chair heading west towards Colfosco and the anticlockwise route around the circuit. The area around both lifts can get

congested at peak times. Another gondola from the top of the village takes you to the slopes shared with San Cassiano and La Villa.

Fast lifts New fast lifts are gradually improving the area.

Queues There are few problems apart from long waits for the inescapable Borest chair between Corvara and Colfosco – this is due to be replaced by a gondola, which should improve things for 2014/15.

Terrain park There is a terrain park above San Cassiano, easily reached from Corvara.

Snow reliability As in the rest of the Sella Ronda area, natural snowfall is erratic, but snowmaking and grooming are excellent.

Experts Very few of Corvara's slopes offer any real challenges. The short black above Boè is really no more than a red in gradient. The much longer wooded runs down to La Villa include a just-about-genuine black, adequately tricky when icy. Otherwise, you're off to Selva or Arabba. Look at the feature panel in the margin for off-piste info.

Intermediates There's a vast network of slopes ideal for cruising and confidence-boosting. On one side is the network of rolling hills shared with San Cassiano; on the other, above Colfosco, is the more dramatically set Val Stella Alpina, off the Sella Ronda circuit, plus the long, gentle runs from Passo Gardena – essentially one long nursery slope. The red back to the village underneath the Boè cable car that goes off towards Arabba is excellent – usually uncrowded and retains good snow. The adventurous can head for the steeper, wooded pistes going down to La Villa.

Beginners There's a decent nursery area and lots of easy runs to progress to on both sides of the village, making this one of the best bases in the Sella Ronda area for beginners.

ALPINE ANSWERS
The UK's No.1 Chalet Specialist

For choice and service look no further!

alpineanswers.co.uk
call: 020 7801 1080   ABTA

Sella Ronda

Build your own shortlist: www.wheretoskiandsnowboard.com

GOURMET SKIING

The Alta Badia – the area around La Villa, including Badia, San Cassiano, Corvara and Colfosco – has over recent years built up a gourmet culture. For many years, its top hotels have run excellent restaurants, but more recently the tourist office has been involving mountain restaurants, too.

In recent seasons, a dozen mountain restaurants have served special dishes conceived by 'starred' chefs from resort restaurants in the area, plus their chums from around Europe. Both we and readers have enjoyed the results. A couple of years ago at I Tablà, for example, we had a superb dish – knuckle of pork in honey with thyme-scented polenta and chanterelles. Last winter, things changed: the emphasis was switched to a new idea, 'Slope Food'. This means appetizers or 'finger-food' rather than the main dishes of the old scheme.

At the heart of the scheme, as before, are the chefs from the three seriously good 'starred' restaurants in the Alta Badia area, all of which are in top hotels – the Rosa Alpina in San Cassiano, the Ciasa Salares in nearby Armentarola and hotel La Perla in Corvara.

The tourist office sponsors other foodie schemes too – for example, a series of mountain restaurants between La Villa and Santa Croce, above Badia, form a 'gourmet skitour' focusing on the local Ladin cuisine, detailed in a little brochure.

These schemes encourage variety and quality in mountain nosh; we approve. Whether fancy appetizers is the right way to develop the scheme, we're not so sure.

TOURIST BOARD ALTA BADIA

Off-piste skiing is generally prohibited in the Sella Ronda – as in many Italian areas. This doesn't stop people doing it altogether. And it doesn't rule out some spectacular routes, away from the pistes, where you can safely go with guidance.

There are well-known routes on the Sella massif, reached via the cable car from Passo Pordoi. Fairly direct descents go back to the pass (the very sunny Forcella) or down Val Lasties towards Canazei. But the classic run is Val Mesdì, a long, shady couloir down to Colfosco, reached by hiking across the massif. Marmolada, the highest peak of the Dolomites, offers some big descents.

There is a mountain guides office in the centre of Corvara (www.altabadiaguides.com).

Snowboarding Novices can make rapid progress on gentle slopes. A few awkward draglifts remain, but most can be avoided.

Cross-country This is one of the better bases in the area. The Alta Badia area offers 38km of trails, including a 10km valley loop on the way to Colfosco.

Mountain restaurants A highlight. In the area between here and San Cassiano there are lots of good mountain restaurants marked and named clearly on the Alta Badia local piste map. Most are woody and cosy, but Las Vegas is a wild exception – cool and minimalist; the food is excellent. Our favourite for a proper lunch is La Veranda, the very popular table-service restaurant downstairs at Col Alt. The room is nothing special, but the food is superb. Others include Bamby ('simply divine pasta'); I Tablà ('outstanding value'), Piz Arlara ('great views, friendly, amazing food'); Punta Trieste ('signature pasta puttanesca'); Capanna Nera ('cosy, great food, great service'); and Utia Bioch.

On the Passo Gardena side of Corvara, the regular reader favourite is Rif Jimmy, in a fabulous position above Passo Gardena; despite hideous crowds, we had a good lunch there in 2013. The Edelweiss above Colfosco has an 'intimate, top-notch' table-service section.

Schools There's a local branch of the Alta Badia school – reports welcome.

Families 'Plenty of activities for everyone,' said a 2014 visitor. School instructors are 'very good' with children – the ski school's Kinderland takes children from the age of three.

STAYING THERE
The best location is near the main square at the top end of the village. We know of no catered chalets here.

Hotels There are some excellent 4-star hotels. La Perla (0471 831000) is one of our all-time favourite ski hotels, offering superb food and service in a relaxed atmosphere, lovely, individual, welcoming rooms and a perfect position at the top of the village – ski down a few yards to the Col Alto gondola. Ski back to the door. Spa and small pool. The Posta Zirm (0471 836175) a few yards away is reportedly 'one of the best', with 'very friendly staff, fantastic food'. Pool. Down at the other end of the village, Col Alto (0471 831100) is also praised from all points of view – rooms, service, food. We recently stayed in a very comfortable, stylish room in the new extension. Rooms in the annexe over the road are said to be huge. 'Superb' spa and 'huge' pool. Efficient shuttles to lifts, ski to the door (snow permitting).

Eating out There's a reasonable choice. The Stüa de Michil restaurant in hotel La Perla has a Michelin star, and greatly impressed us – superb food and a warm atmosphere – though we're equally happy with the hotel's en pension food. Reader tips: La Fornella ('good food, great value'), the Stube at La Tambra hotel, Pizzeria Caterina. The Edelweiss mountain restaurant, high above Colfosco, is open in the evenings, with a snowcat to ferry you up and down.

Après-ski The fashionable place to go at close of play these days seems to

WENDY KING

Restaurants and bars on the mountain are a real highlight →

If you like runs in spectacular scenery well away from all signs of civilization, don't miss the easy red run from Lagazuoi, reached by cable car from Passo Falzarego. The pass is easily accessible from Armentarola, close to San Cassiano – shared taxis run a shuttle service (5 euros each) to the pass from here. There's also a bus from San Cassiano (but it is reported to be crowded and slow).

The run is one of the most beautiful we've come across, and delights most reporters. Views from the top of the cable car are splendid, and the run passes beneath sheer Dolomite cliffs and frozen waterfalls. The cable car has low capacity, so the run is never crowded. Make time to stop near the end at the atmospheric Rifugio Scotoni (chargrills a speciality).

At the bottom, it's a long skate to a horse-drawn sled with ropes attached, which tows you back to Armentarola (for a couple of euros). This is more of a challenge than the run, and when the snow gets rutted there is some risk of falls and pile-ups. We take the minibus alternative (there's a phone to summon it) or ride in the sled. At Armentarola there is a draglift to the run back to San Cassiano.

ALAN LIPTROT

be L'Murin, a rustic outbuilding of hotel La Perla right on the home piste. The Iceberg Lounge Bar at the hotel Col Alto is 'very cool'. Other tips: the 'tiny, cosy' L'Got for a 'classic aperitivo'; the cellar of the hotel Posta Zirm ('lively later'); Toccami.

Off the slopes There's a covered ice rink, indoor tennis courts, an outdoor climbing wall and snowshoeing. The Posta Zirm pool and spa is open to the public by reservation. There is a toboggan run up the road towards Arabba, at Cherz.

Other resorts

LINKED RESORT – 1540m
SAN CASSIANO

San Cassiano is a pleasant, quiet village, but it is off the Sella Ronda circuit, and its main lift is well outside the village. If you prefer San Cassiano to Corvara, it's probably because you particularly like one of its smart and comfortable hotels.

The local slopes, shared with Corvara, are mainly ideal for easy cruising on flattering, well-groomed runs and there's relatively quick access to the famous 'hidden valley' run (described in our feature panel). Read Corvara for mountain restaurants in general; but note that Mailga Saraghes on the home run to San Cassiano does 'the best Kaiserschmarrn in the area'. The nursery slopes are up the valley at Armentarola.

Of the hotels the Rosa Alpina (0471 849500) is stylish and deeply comfortable. Its three restaurants include the St Hubertus, which has two Michelin stars. The hotel Ciasa Salares, out at Armentarola, also has an excellent Michelin star restaurant,

La Siriola, with perhaps the youngest starred chef in Italy. Après-ski starts up the mountain with loud music at Las Vegas, but village nightlife is very limited. There is a toboggan run from Piz Sorega to the village.

LINKED RESORT – 1645m
COLFOSCO

Colfosco (aka Kolfuschg – the German influence gets stronger as you move west towards Selva/Wolkenstein) is a smaller, quieter satellite of Corvara, 2km away. It has a fairly compact centre with a group of large hotels spread along the road from Corvara towards Passo Gardena and Selva, enjoying splendid views of the Gruppa del Sella.

On the snow Colfosco is connected to Corvara and the clockwise Sella Ronda circuit by the gondola replacing the queue-prone two-way Borest chairlift. In the opposite direction, a gondola goes towards Passo Gardena. There are excellent nursery slopes, and the runs back from Passo Gardena, after a red start, are easy, long cruises,

UK PACKAGES

San Cassiano Alpine Answers, Carrier, Inghams, Momentum, Mountainsun, Powder Byrne, Scott Dunn, Snow-wise, STC **Colfosco** Inghams, Ski Club Freshtracks **La Villa** Ski Line **Canazei** Crystal, Interactive Resorts, Rocketski, Ski Line, STC, Thomson **Campitello** Crystal, Thomson

making this a great base for novices.

The Kolfuschgerhof hotel (0471 836188) is 200m from the slopes (efficient shuttles) but a 'really nice family-run hotel with fantastic food, attentive staff'. But a regular visitor to this area trumps this report with a rave about the Cappella for the second year in a row (0471 836183): 'Still absolutely superb, the half-board food is quite outstanding.' Excellent ski-in/ski-out location, too.

Although it's a small place, there are some restaurants. Black Hill is a popular place for 'excellent wood-fired pizza'. Mathiaskeller is tipped for après beers and 'excellent risotto'. Otherwise it's 'a sleepy village'.

LINKED RESORT – 1435m

LA VILLA

Like San Cassiano, La Villa is a bit detached from the Sella Ronda circuit. It's a much busier place, with the road from Brunico running through it; but it is much more conveniently arranged, with lifts and pistes on both sides of the village, and nursery slopes dotted around. We've had repeated glowing reports on the hotel Antines (0471 844234) – 'an outstanding restaurant'; 'very friendly staff'. There is said to be a public swimming pool. Inghams also run the Al Pigher chalet hotel with 'spacious public areas, superb spa facilities, stunning views'.

LINKED RESORT – 1325m

BADIA

This small roadside village (formerly known as Pedraces) is out on a limb beyond La Villa, so it's not a great base. But some will find it more interesting because there is a free bus link with Piccolino (20 minutes), where a gondola goes into the Plan de Corones/Kronplatz ski area.

The village has its own one-run ski area with a fast quad and a slow double chair to Santa Croce (2045m) where there is a famous old rifugio with fabulous views (and a tiny church). At the mid-mountain lift station is one of our favourite restaurants in Alta Badia, Rif Lee – sheltered terrace, excellent food, friendly service. 2014 visitors also rated Rif Nagler nearby and Rif Sponata on the slopes shared with La Villa ('warm welcome, excellent carbonara and rösti').

LINKED RESORT – 1465m

CANAZEI

Canazei is a sizeable, bustling, pretty, roadside village of narrow streets, rustic buildings and traditional hotels.

The village itself is slightly off the main Sella Ronda circuit, but its main slopes form part of it. A 12-person gondola (powerful, but queue-prone) rises 465m to Pecol, at the foot of the slopes of Belvedere. These are linked in one direction to the slopes of Passo Pordoi and Arabba, and in the other to Passo Sella and Col Rodella (above Campitello), and then on to Selva. A red run returns to Canazei, but it gets the afternoon sun and is often closed.

The Belvedere slopes are open and sunny, with modest verticals of about 450m. Almost all are graded red. This rules out the resort for timid intermediates and beginners, even if it does exaggerate difficulty. There is a nursery slope in the valley.

The grand 4-star Schloss Hotel Dolomiti (0462 601106) in the centre is 'Very Italian, stylish and historic,' according to a 2012 visitor. The 4-star Perla (0462 602453), also central, offers 'great food, value, amazing spa'.

There are numerous restaurants, and the après-ski is surprisingly animated. The Giardino delle Rose, Osteria and Paradis (a converted barn – 'great fun') are popular at close of play. The 'friendly' International bar and ice cream parlour is quieter. La Stua di Ladins serves local wines.

Off-slope entertainment consists of beautiful walks and shopping. There's also a pool, sauna and Turkish baths.

LINKED RESORT – 1445m

CAMPITELLO

Neighbouring Campitello is a pleasant, unremarkable village, smaller, quieter and cheaper than Canazei, and still unspoiled. A cable car starting just outside the village rises 1000m up to Col Rodella and the slopes above Passo Sella. At the start of the day this lift can build queues from the village, 'massive' ones in high season – get the bus up to Canazei's gondola. There are no pistes to the resort.

A reporter last year enjoyed the 4-star hotel Stella Montis (0462 750310), up a steep hill outside the village (has a shuttle): 'Excellent, good food, first-class spa.' Après-ski these days is reported to be rather quiet.

TOURIST OFFICES

San Cassiano, Colfosco, La Villa, Badia
www.altabadia.org
Canazei, Campitello
www.fassa.com

Selva / Val Gardena

Pleasant village amid spectacular Dolomite scenery, well placed for skiing on and off the vast Sella Ronda lift network

RATINGS

The mountains

Extent	★★★★★
Fast lifts	★★★★
Queues	★★★
Terrain p'ks	★★★
Snow	★★★★
Expert	★★★
Intermediate	★★★★★
Beginner	★★★
Boarder	★★★
X-country	★★★★★
Restaurants	★★★★★
Schools	★★★
Families	★★

The resort

Charm	★★★
Convenience	★★★
Scenery	★★★★★
Eating out	★★★
Après-ski	★★★
Off-slope	★★★

RPI 95

lift pass	£180
ski hire	£95
lessons	£85
food & drink	£125
total	**£485**

NEWS

2013/14: The Dantercëpies gondola was replaced, with increased capacity, plus more parking and better services at the base.

+ A key resort of the Sella Ronda region, so good for snowmaking, extent, scenery, mountain huts

+ Spectacular, dramatic setting

+ Excellent local slopes, with big verticals by Sella Ronda standards

+ Mix of open and wooded slopes

+ Excellent nursery slopes

– Some of the minus points of the Sella Ronda region too, notably: erratic natural snowfall, crowds on the main Sella Ronda circuit

– Buses or taxis are needed for access to easy long runs to suit near-beginners, at Plan de Gralba

– Busy road through the village

Selva is one of three sizeable resorts near the head of Val Gardena (a name well known to ski racing fans) and one of the main bases for exploration of the unique Sella Ronda region described in the chapter before this one. Selva remains one of our favourite bases in the area, essentially because of its challenging local slopes, including two race courses through woods to the valley. Beginners and timid intermediates, though, are probably better off staying in Corvara or Colfosco, described in the Sella Ronda chapter.

THE RESORT

Selva is a long roadside village in a spectacular setting in Val Gardena.

For many years this area was part of Austria, and it retains a Tirolean charm. German is more widely spoken than Italian, and many visitors are German, too. Most places have two names: Selva is also known as Wolkenstein and the Gardena valley as Gröden. We do our bit for Italian unity by using the Italian place names here. The local language, Ladin, also survives – so some places have a third name. The valley is famed for wood carvings, which are widely sold.

At the end of this chapter we describe two other bases. Santa Cristina is the next village down the valley, and almost merges with Selva; lifts from both villages meet on the steep racing hill of Ciampinoi. Further down the valley is Ortisei, the main town of Val Gardena, set beneath the distinct Alpe di Siusi area. Both bases have lifts to another distinct area, Seceda. Another possible base is the much lower village of Siusi (1005m), with a gondola up to Alpe di Siusi.

The Dolomiti Superski pass covers not only Selva and the Sella Ronda resorts but dozens of others. With a car you can reach Cortina.

VILLAGE CHARM ★★★☆☆
Pity about the traffic
The village has traditional Tirolean-style architecture and an attractive church, but is rather strung out along the main road and suffers a bit from through-traffic (and a lack of parking) as well as a lack of central focus. Selva is a civilized, low-key resort – relaxed and family-friendly, once you get away from the through-road.

CONVENIENCE ★★★☆☆
Choose your spot with care
From the village, gondolas rise in two directions. The Ciampinoi gondola goes south from near the centre of the

433

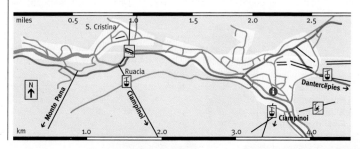

Ski Total

ARE HERE IN
Selva Val Gardena

▶ Quality chalets
▶ Top locations
▶ Excellent value
▶ 17 more resorts

skitotal.com
01483 791 933

village to start the anticlockwise Sella Ronda route. The Dantercëpies gondola, for the clockwise Sella Ronda route, starts on the opposite side of the village and slightly above it, at the top of the nursery slopes (but is also accessible via a central chairlift and a short run down). The most convenient position to stay is near this chair or one of the gondolas. At various points there are lodgings on the snow, including places on the nursery slopes.

There are local buses until early evening – 9 euros for a weekly card (or free to guests at hotels in the local Tourist Association). They generate all sorts of complaints from reporters: lack of buses; not running to time; confusion between the public and the skiers' buses. There's a night bus between Selva and Ortisei. All the 4-star hotels run their own shuttles.

SCENERY ★★★★★
Pretty in pink

The village enjoys a fabulous setting under the impressive walls of Sassolungo, immediately above the slopes of Ciampinoi, and the Gruppo del Sella – a fortress-like massif 6km across that lies at the hub of the Sella Ronda circuit (described in a separate chapter). There are knockout views as you descend from Dantercëpies, for example, and from Alpe di Siusi. A Swedish reporter this year who has visited 62 countries rates the views here 'the most beautiful I have seen'.

Marmolada
3340m

Sassolungo/
Langkofel
3180m

Canazei
1465m

Gruppo del Sella
Sella Gruppe
3150m

PASSO SELLA
2245m

Sella Ronda

Piz Sella

Sole

Sotsaslong

Comici I

Piz Seteur

Good, long blue runs for beginners to progress to – but you have to catch a bus from Selva to avoid a tricky red from Ciampinoi

↖ Sella Ronda

Piz Sella

2255m

PLAN DE GRALBA

Cir

DANTERCËPIES

2300m

Plan de Gralba
1800m

CIAMPINOI

Ciampinoi

Sochers

Saslong

Dantercëpies

Lovely long reds: the one on skier's right of the gondola used to be the Women's Downhill run

Efficient underground train links the gondolas for the Ciampinoi and Seceda sectors

Selva/Wolkenstein
1565m/5,130ft

Col Raiser

Vallunga

Col Raiser

🎠 chondola
🚡 gondola
🚠 cable car
🚟 railway/funicular
🚡 fast chairlift
Slow chairs & drags have no symbol

SEC

THE MOUNTAINS

Selva's own slopes cover both sides of the valley. The lower slopes are wooded, with open slopes higher up.

The local piste map exists in several confusing variations. The maps show neither names nor numbers for the runs, which strikes us as insane. Piste signing provokes some criticism.

EXTENT OF THE SLOPES ★★★★★
High-mileage excursions
The **Dantercëpies** gondola goes off eastwards to start the clockwise Sella Ronda circuit and serves lovely red runs back to Selva. On the other side of the valley, the **Ciampinoi** gondola goes south for the anticlockwise circuit via **Plan de Gralba** and accesses several shady pistes, leading back down to Selva and Santa Cristina, including the famous Downhill run.

In Santa Cristina, another gondola accesses Ciampinoi, and an underground train links the lift base to a gondola on the outskirts for the sunny **Seceda** area. In this sector, runs descend to Santa Cristina or to Ortisei – a red run of about 7km. And from Ortisei a gondola on the other side of the valley takes you to and from **Alpe di Siusi** – a gentle elevated area of quiet, easy runs, cross-country tracks and walks. You can proceed from here to the backwater **Monte Pana** (which is connected to Ciampinoi) by bus, but it's a slow affair.

ssolungo/
angkofel
3180m

Punta d'Oro/Goldknopf
2210m

Paradiso

Ideal area for early intermediates – very gentle pistes (almost flat in places), quiet, with superb scenery

1940m

Fiè/
Völs
880m

Mont de Seura
2115m

2000m

ALPE DI SIUSI

Siusi/
Seis
1005m

Sochers

Mont Seura

2100m

Castel Rotto/
Kastel Ruth
1060m

Saslong

1665m

MONTE PANA

Alpe di Siusi

S Cristina/
St Christina
1430m

Ortisei/
St Ulrich
1235m/4,050ft

Funicular built in 2010 offers a worthwhile alternative way to reach the Seceda cable car

The Saslong World Cup Downhill piste is a wonderful, fast, rolling cruise that's especially good in January when it's not too crowded

Beautiful long run with a vertical drop of 1300m; not steep but quite narrow in places; wonderful views over the valley and through a very picturesque canyon

Furnes

Rasciesa
2280m

SECEDA

Seceda
2520m

↑ Gentle Alpe di Siusi has a spectacular backdrop
ALAN LIPTROT

Resort news and key links: www.wheretoskiandsnowboard.com

LIFT PASSES

Dolomiti Superski

Prices in €

Age	1-day	6-day
under 16	36	183
16 to 64	52	262
65 plus	47	236

Free Under 8
Beginner Points card
Senior Must be 65 before season starts
Notes Covers 1220km of piste and 450 lifts in the Dolomites, including all Sella Ronda resorts
Alternative pass Val Gardena-Alpe di Siusi

FAST LIFTS ★★★★★
Getting better

The main access lifts are gondolas, and there are lots of fast chairs above them, so progress can be quick. But there are still a few slow chairs and drags – an irritant on Alpe di Siusi.

QUEUES ★★★★★
Still some problems

The new gondola seems to have dealt with the traditional morning queues at Dantercëpies, though the drags up to the gondola may hold you up. Other problems may arise on lifts that are part of the Sella Ronda circuit – Piz Seteur for example. Doing the circuit anticlockwise from Selva has the clear drawback that everyone ends up on the chain of lifts from Corvara at the end of the day, and facing 'hideous' queues in high season. The gondola out of Ortisei that takes you halfway to Seceda ensures that the cable car above it is over-busy in the mornings.

TERRAIN PARKS ★★★★★
Facilities spread around

There are parks, pipes and snowcross courses in various spots. There is a mile-long park on Alpe di Siusi, with lines to suit all standards. Readers and their kids have loved the family-oriented fun park at Piz Sella, with 'plenty of easy obstacles', plus an amusing jump over a car, and other challenges for the more advanced.

SNOW RELIABILITY ★★★★★
Excellent when it's cold

The slopes are not high – most are between 1500m and 2000m. Natural snowfalls are erratic, but the snowmaking is exceptionally good. During severe droughts we and readers have enjoyed excellent pistes here. The grooming is very good too – 'morning cruising is fantastic'. Problems arise only if it is too warm to make snow.

FOR EXPERTS ★★★★★
A few good runs

There are few challenges, essentially no moguls and a low likelihood of powder. There are few major off-piste routes because of the nature of the terrain, and off-piste is prohibited in places; read the off-piste panel in the Sella Ronda chapter.

The Val Gardena World Cup piste, the Saslong, is one of several steepish runs from Ciampinoi. It is open to the public much of the time – it's one of our favourite runs. There are also good reds down the same hills. The long red runs from Dantercëpies are good.

FOR INTERMEDIATES ★★★★★
Fast cruising on easy slopes

There is a huge amount of skiing to do, in several areas.

Competent intermediates will love the red and black descents from Dantercëpies and Ciampinoi to Selva

Resort	1565m	
	5,130ft	

Sella Ronda linked network: Val Gardena, Alta Badia, Arabba, and Canazei and Campitello in Val di Fassa		
Slopes	1005-3270m	
	3,300-10,730ft	
Lifts	179	
Pistes	433km	
	269 miles	
Blue	38%	
Red	53%	
Black	9%	
Snowmaking	90%	

Val Gardena-Alpe di Siusi only		
Slopes	1005-2520m	
	3,300-8,270ft	
Lifts	79	
Pistes	175km	
	109 miles	
Blue	30%	
Red	60%	
Black	10%	
Snowmaking	95%	

SCHOOLS

Selva Gardena
t 0471 795156

2000
t 0471 773125

Top School Val Gardena
t 0471 794099

Classes (Selva prices)
6 half days €206
Private lessons
From €40 for 1hr

GUIDES

Val Gardena Mountain Guide Association
t 0471 794133

(but more timid intermediates may find them too steep and/or crowded).

The blue runs in the Plan de Gralba area are gentle – great for building confidence; the red run to get there from Ciampinoi is a real obstacle – it's steep and crowded and can be icy – so you might want to go by road.

The quiet red and black runs at Mont de Seura, above Monte Pana, are worth exploring.

The gentle Alpe di Siusi above Ortisei is ideal for confidence-building. The red runs that dominate the map are mostly of blue gradient, and quiet.

The Seceda sector has good red and blue runs at altitude, and splendid runs to the valley – an easy blue/red to Santa Cristina and the beautiful red Cucasattel, passing through a natural gorge to Ortisei.

FOR BEGINNERS ★★★★★
Great slopes, but ...
The village nursery slopes below the Dantercëpies gondola are excellent – spacious and convenient. There are lots of gentle, long runs to progress to, but they are at Plan de Gralba and Alpe di Siusi, and reached by road.

FOR BOARDERS ★★★★★
Limited options
Selva attracts few boarders. There's little to challenge experts, and off-piste opportunities are limited, but the nursery slopes are good and there are lots of gentle runs to progress to. The main valley lifts are all gondolas or chairs. There are three terrain parks and a couple of half-pipes.

FOR CROSS-COUNTRY ★★★★★
Beautiful trails
There are 115km of trails, all enjoying wonderful scenery. The 12km trail up the Vallunga valley is particularly attractive, with neck-craning views all around and has 'really good tracks for skate and classic styles', says our Swedish reporter. Almost half the trails have the advantage of being at altitude, running between Monte Pana and across Alpe di Siusi.

MOUNTAIN RESTAURANTS ★★★★★
A real highlight
There are countless huts, and many of them are lively and characterful, with helpful staff, good food and modest prices. They are not identified on the main resort piste map, but they are on the Sella Ronda map on the reverse.

In the Dantercëpies sector, readers have tipped the Panorama – a cosy, rustic suntrap at the foot of the drag near the top – and the Pastura.

In the Ciampinoi area the Rif Emilio Comici, set beneath the massive Sassolungo (arrive early if you want the sun), is repeatedly tipped, notably for 'great fresh fish'. Nearby Piz Sella is recommended for pizza. Down towards Plan de Gralba, Vallongia has a cool ice bar. Piz Seteur is a lively spot with an outdoor DJ. Baita Sole is a cute but simple place with good-value food. Recently revamped Gran Sas now has a 'cool atmosphere' and 'even better food' than in the past. On the way to Selva, Valentini makes a good last stop – 'always friendly'.

Up at Passo Sella, Rif Friedrich August has Highland cattle strolling around outside, and closely related steaks on sale inside. Sella Alm is a tiny hut doing 'simple, good-value food' with 'friendly service'.

In the Seceda sector there are countless huts. Rif Odles is one reader's current favourite and a 2014 reporter recommends Sofie ('superb jumbo prawn platter'). On the run back to S Cristina, a regular visitor tips Baita Pramulin. Near the top of the long Cucasattel run, the tiny Curona is a favourite of several visitors ('friendly; best strudel'); nearer the bottom, Val d'Anna is another favourite – 'good hot chocolate, very best pastries', 'friendly staff'.

Alpe di Siusi is said to have over 40 places to choose from. We have had enthusiastic reports on Floralpina – 'Now super trendy, big windows, excellent pasta.' Our specialist reporter picks out Laurinhütte ('welcoming, excellent food, great views'), Zallinger Hütte ('charming – a great find'), Sanon Hütte ('fantastic views, cheerful service') and Mont Seuc, at the top of the gondola – 'Perfect for watching the cliffs turn red over a last drink.'

SCHOOLS AND GUIDES ★★★★★
No worries
The main Selva Gardena school has been recommended by several readers, most recently this year: 'Younger girl made good progress, elder took part in extremely good race training.' One visitor recommends the ski safari ('took us to places we would never have dreamed of getting to') but was unhappy with the large group size and range of ability on some days.

skiracer*

CHALETS, HOTELS & APARTMENTS

Call us today

020 8600 1650

skitracer.com

CHILDCARE

Selvi mini club
0471 795156
Ages 1 to 4

Casa Bimbo (at S Cristina)
0471 793013
From 0 to 3

Ski school
From age 4

ROD GARVEY

Plan de Gralba, at 1800m on the road to Passo Sella, is a viable base if you like a quiet time (with lovely easy pistes on your doorstep) ↓

FOR FAMILIES ★★☆☆☆
It's all down to the detail
At first sight, in general, the village does not seem ideal for families. But make the right arrangements, and you can have very successful family holidays here. A 2014 visitor's children praised the 'fun parks, long runs and especially the food'.

STAYING THERE

Chalets A limited choice – Crystal has one 14-bed catered chalet, and Total has the large 26-bed Soldanella.
Hotels There are about 20 4-star hotels in Selva, about 40 3-stars and numerous lesser hotels. It is not a small place. Few of the best are well positioned – though they generally operate shuttle-buses.
★★★★Aaritz (0471 795011) Best-placed 4-star, opposite the gondola.
★★★★Gran Baita (0471 795210) Large, luxurious sporthotel, with 'wonderful' facilities including pool. A walk from centre and lifts. 'Superb – huge rooms, far too much food, pleasant waiters.'
★★★★Mignon (0471 795092) Good value, close to lifts.
★★★★Oswald (0471 795151) One Californian reader's Alpine favourite. 'Good rooms, fantastic food, very helpful staff.' Has its own shuttle.
★★★★Savoy (0471 795343) Next to the 'slow but quiet' Ciampinoi chairlift.

Approved yet again by our regular devotee – 'Very welcoming, great rooms, great food, lovely indoor/outdoor pool.'
★★★Medzi (0471 795265) B&B hotel in good ski-in/ski-out position. 'Good breakfast, very helpful owners.'
★★★Miara (0471 794627) Next to the Ciampinoi gondola. 'Modern, quiet, with friendly helpful owners.'
Villa Seceda (0471 795297) A regular visitor says the recent renovation of this 'friendly' B&B near the nursery slopes has been a great success.
Apartments They are available, but we have no recent reader reports.
At altitude We had a report in 2012 of a 'fabulous' stay at the hotel Sochers (0471 792101), on Ciampinoi. Plan de Gralba on the road to Passo Sella has lodgings that are mostly ski-in/ski-out. The family-run 3-star hotel Sella (0471 795182) is strongly tipped – 'attentive, friendly staff and excellent food'.

EATING OUT ★★★☆☆
Adequate choice
The better restaurants are mainly based in hotels or, ironically, B&B guest houses. Current reader favourite – and 'popular with locals' – is La Bula ('went back three times', 'great service, very friendly and good food'). Other reader tips include: the slope-side hotel Freina ('superb seafood', 'good value and service'), the woody stube

Air Bolzano 50km/
30 miles (1hr);
Innsbruck 120km/
75 miles (1hr45);
Verona 195km/
120 miles (2hr15);
Munich 320km/
200 miles (3hr15);
Milan Linate 320km/
200 miles (3hr30)
Rail Chiusa (27km/
17 miles); Bressanone
(35km/22 miles);
Bolzano (40km/
25 miles); frequent
buses from stations

Alpine Answers, Crystal,
Crystal Finest,
Interactive Resorts,
Momentum, Neilson,
Ski Line, Ski Total, Ski
Yogi, Skitracer, Snow
Finders, Snow-wise,
STC, Thomson
Ortisei Crystal, Crystal
Finest, Inghams, Ski
Expectations, Thomson

In Val Gardena:

Indoor Swimming
pool, sauna, bowling,
ice rink, climbing wall,
fitness centre, tennis,
museum

Outdoor Sleigh rides,
snowshoeing,
tobogganing, ice rink,
paragliding, extensive
cleared paths

Phone numbers
From abroad use the
prefix +39 (and do **not**
omit the initial '0' of
the phone number)

www.valgardena.it

---

of the hotel des Alpes, for Tyrolean specialities, Rino ('huge and tasty pizza and carpaccio', 'great bruschetta'), the pizzeria of the hotel Sun Valley ('amazing'), Armin's Grillstube ('inexpensive and cosy cellar'), the Sal Fëur in the Garni Broi ('relaxed feel, generous portions').

APRES-SKI ★★★☆☆
Not without action

At close of play some of the mountain restaurants offer diversions. Piz Seteur, with its outdoor DJ, was as lively and fun as ever when we last visited. At the base, the Stua is a popular last stop – 'great place with delightful staff, great atmosphere and good prices' – and if you settle in for the evening, live music may arrive. The Kronestube has been tipped ('good atmosphere'). Café Mozart is 'a convivial place for a relaxed coffee'. Later on, the village streets are fairly quiet, but there are places to go. Goalies' Irish pub is 'good for a quiet drink' – it suits grown-ups with its classic rock music. The place to let your hair down is Luislkeller – 'the beer seems to come in one size – huge', 'hopping, with great craic', 'really lively, difficult to get in'. Yello's is a competitor. The serious nightclub is Dali, open until 3am, with dance music for 'a younger clientele'.

OFF THE SLOPES ★★★☆☆
Good variety

There are many spectacular walks, on Alpe di Siusi and Rasciesa, especially. There's a sports centre, snowshoeing, tobogganing and sleigh rides. 'Great night at the ice hockey,' says a repeat visitor. There are buses to Ortisei (if you don't fancy the lovely two-hour walk) and more distant Bolzano, with an excellent museum devoted to 5,000-year-old Oetzi the Ice Man, among many attractions. And there are coach excursions to Cortina and Verona. A group of hotels has formed Val Gardena Active, offering free excursions. Pedestrians can reach many good mountain restaurants.

SANTA CRISTINA

A few km down-valley from Selva, at the bottom of the race course from Ciampinoi, Santa Cristina is a pleasant village well worth considering as an alternative base. It has gondolas

---

towards Ciampinoi and Seceda (their base stations linked by an underground railway), and a slow chairlift up to a ring of nursery slopes at Monte Pana (but no piste back). There is accommodation up here, too. There's a good range of hotels in the village from 5-star down, and countless B&Bs.

ORTISEI

Ortisei is an attractive, prosperous market town with a life of its own apart from tourism. It's full of lovely buildings, pretty churches, smart shops and tempting cafes, and has an interesting museum, a large hot-spring swimming pool and an ice rink. The valley road follows the river, bypassing the centre. The local slopes offer an astonishing six toboggan runs – one from Rasciesa 6km long and accessed by funicular – as well as vast amounts of easy skiing. If you intend to spend time on the Sella Ronda circuit beyond Selva, plan on using the ski-buses.

The gondola to the Seceda slopes is easily reached from the centre by a 300m-long series of moving walkways and escalators. Alternatively, you can reach the top of that gondola, and the start of the Seceda cable car, by riding the Rasciesa funicular and descending a red piste. The gondola for Alpe di Siusi is a similar distance out, across the river – a footbridge from the centre is the best approach, going over the valley road too. Note that to move from one area to another involves quite a walk.

The nursery area, school and kindergarten are also over the river, along with a fair range of accommodation. The fine public indoor pool and ice rink are also here.

There are hotels and self-catering accommodation to suit all tastes and pockets, and many good restaurants, mainly specializing in local dishes. The 5-star Gardena (0471 796315) is tipped this year for its 'spacious rooms, great cuisine and friendly, helpful staff' and 'the best ski guide we have ever had'. The 5-star Adler (0471 775001) is also rated for its 'excellent food and outstanding staff'. The 'delightfully named' 4-star hotel Hell (0471 796785) also gets a mention for its excellent minibus service. Après-ski is quite jolly, and many of the bars keep going till late.

Selva / Val Gardena

Build your own shortlist: **www.wheretoskiandsnowboard.com**

SESTRIERE TOURIST OFFICE

Sestriere

Altitude is the main attraction of this, Europe's first purpose-built resort; some would say it's the only attraction

TOP 10 RATINGS

Extent	★★★★
Fast lifts	★★★
Queues	★★★
Snow	★★★★
Expert	★★★
Intermediate	★★★★
Beginner	★★★
Charm	★
Convenience	★★★
Scenery	★★★

RPI 90

lift pass	£160
ski hire	£105
lessons	£95
food & drink	£110
total	**£470**

KERRY LEWIS

There are good beginner slopes facing the sunny but not at all pretty village ↓

+ Part of the extensive Franco-Italian Milky Way area, with Sauze d'Oulx and Sansicario only one lift away

+ Local slopes suitable for most levels – some tougher runs than in Sauze and Sansicario

+ Snowmaking covers all but one or two marginal slopes, but ...

– Snowmaking is crucial, given the erratic local snowfall

– Village is a bit of an eyesore

– For a purpose-built resort, not conveniently arranged

– Weekend and peak-period queues

– Little après action during the week

Sestriere was built for snow – high, with north-west-facing slopes. Sadly, the snowfalls in this corner of Italy are notoriously erratic; but extensive snowmaking means you should be fairly safe. The place makes a great weekend away for the residents of Turin. As a holiday destination for residents of Tunbridge Wells, it doesn't have such a strong case.

THE RESORT

Sestriere was the first purpose-built resort in the Alps, developed by Fiat's Giovanni Agnelli in the 1930s.
Village charm The resort sits on a broad, sunny and windy col. Neither the site nor the village, with its rows of apartment blocks, looks very hospitable. The satellite of Borgata, a gentle blue run to the east and 100m lower, is quiet and traditional in style.
Convenience The village is not huge, and some lodgings are very close to the snow; but some are quite distant from the lifts, or the bars. There are non-free buses. Borgata is a linear place with its lifts at one end.

Scenery The slopes give extensive views across the part-wooded Milky Way to the peaks of the French border.

THE MOUNTAINS

The local skiing is on shady slopes, mainly open with some woodland, facing the village. Montgenèvre, at the far French end of the Milky Way, is more easily reached from here than from Sauze.

The piste map and piste signing combine to form a small nightmare, especially on M Motta; good luck! Piste classification is erratic, and tends to exaggerate difficulty.
Slopes The local slopes, served by drags and chairs, are in two main

440

skitracer

CHALETS, HOTELS & APARTMENTS
Call us today
020 8600 1650
skitracer.com

KEY FACTS

Resort	2035m
	6,680ft

Milky Way	
Slopes	1390-2825m
	4,560-9,270ft
Lifts	66
Pistes	400km
	249 miles
Blue	25%
Red	56%
Black	19%
Snowmaking	60%

Sestriere-Sauze d'Oulx-Sansicario	
Slopes	1390-2825m
	4,560-9,270ft
Lifts	41
Pistes	300km
	186 miles
Snowmaking	38%

UK PACKAGES

Alpine Answers, Alpine Weekends, Club Med, Crystal, Erna Low, Inghams, Momentum, Neilson, Ski Line, Skitracer, STC, Thomson, Zenith

PISTE MAP

Sestriere is covered on the Sauze d'Oulx map

Phone numbers
From abroad use the prefix +39 (and do **not** omit the initial '0' of the phone number)

TOURIST OFFICE

www.turismotorino. org
www.vialattea.it
www.comune. sestriere.to.it

sectors: Sises, directly in front of the village, and Motta, above Borgata; Motta is more varied and bigger, with more vertical. From a car park west of the village a gondola goes up over the opposite mountainside to M Fraiteve, for access to Sauze d'Oulx, Sansicario and the rest of the Milky Way. There are red and blue runs back from M Fraiteve – sunny, and not reliably open to the bottom. You may face a long walk from the end of the piste to the lifts or your lodgings.

Fast lifts The main lifts are modern fast ones, but there are still too many slow, old ones – both here and over in Sansicario and Sauze.

Queues The main lifts can have queues on sunny weekends. We lack high-season reports, but would expect the double chair back from Sauze to be a regular problem. At M Fraiteve the confined summit area can get seriously congested. There may be long queues for the gondola down.

Terrain parks The terrain park is by the parallel baby lifts on the village nursery slopes.

Snow reliability The Italian part of the Milky Way gets notoriously unreliable snowfalls, but Sestriere has extensive snowmaking. Add in altitude and orientation, and you can count on good cover on the pistes. Grooming is 'comprehensive', and 'excellent'.

Experts There are things to do – steep pistes served by the drags at the top of both sectors, three designated as mogul fields. Given good snow, there is some decent off-piste, but don't count on it; outings to snowy Montgenèvre may be more rewarding.

Intermediates Both sectors offer something for confident intermediates – Motta especially – but they don't add up to a lot, so plan on multiple visits to other linked resorts.

Beginners There are good nursery slopes directly in front of the village served by draglifts, but you need a lift pass (a special day pass covers five lifts). There are easy longer runs to progress to locally, and over in Sauze.

Snowboarding The draglifts are largely avoidable except above Sansicario. There's a specialist snowboard school.

Cross-country There are three loops covering about 10km.

Mountain restaurants Not all the huts are marked on the resort piste map. We haven't made it to the place, but the woody Raggio di Sole, on skier's right at Motta, sounds like the best

bet ('tasty, filling local dishes; happy, helpful staff'). Alpette, directly above the village, is tipped for 'simple lunches, or bombardinos as the lifts close and the sun goes down'.

Schools and guides There are four schools: the main ones are the Nazionale and Vialattea.

Families The two main schools have mini clubs for children aged three and four and offer lessons for children from the age of five.

STAYING THERE

Most accommodation is in apartments.
Hotels There are a dozen hotels, mostly 3-star or 4-star. The 3-star Biancaneve (0122 755177) has 'great food, good service'. The ideally positioned hotel du Col ('very friendly, lovely food') is exclusive to Crystal; go for rooms on the snow not the road side. Just out of the village is the swanky Ròseo (0122 7941), with swimming pool and spa. Out at Borgata, we found a warm welcome at the Banchetta (0122 70307), a traditional, family-run hotel with old photos on the walls and very good food in the dining room. Down in Pragelato there is a Club Med.
Apartments The Villagio Olimpico apartments built for the 2006 Olympics are reasonably central.
Eating out There are plenty of options. A reader favourite ('so impressed we went a second night') is Last Tango – 'fab wild boar carpaccio, pork in mustard, and violet sorbet'. We can recommend the pizzas at the popular Pinky, and a reader tips Kandahar for its cheese-burgers. Down in Borgata, the rustic Antica Spelonca has been tipped; it's in a cute vaulted cellar.
Après-ski The quietness of the place during the week disappoints some visitors. Pinky has a cafe-style bar that was packed with Brits at close of play last time we visited. The bar in the hotel du Col is popular too. Readers also tip Black Pepper – 'very lively, lovely cocktails'. One reporter says reps will organize a pub crawl for a charge. Tabata is the main club, with a cool bar upstairs and big disco below.
Off the slopes There's more to do than most visitors realize. There are some smart shops, a fitness centre, an ice rink, a sports centre and pool; the dog sledding looked good to our untrained eye. Outings are possible to nearby Pragelato and also to Turin – only 100km away by road.

Build your own shortlist: www.wheretoskiandsnowboard.com

La Thuile

A spread-out resort with a mix of ancient and modern parts and extensive, easy, snow-sure slopes linked with La Rosière in France

TOP 10 RATINGS

Extent	★★★
Fast lifts	★★★
Queues	★★★★★
Snow	★★★★
Expert	★★
Intermediate	★★★★
Beginner	★★★★
Charm	★★★
Convenience	★★★
Scenery	★★★

RPI	90
lift pass	£170
ski hire	£95
lessons	£85
food & drink	£115
total	**£465**

NEWS

2014/15: Nira Montana, a new 55-room boutique hotel with a smart spa, is due to open.

2013/14: A new B&B, Il Ciliegio, and a new restaurant, Lo Tatà (see 'Eating out'), opened.

442

+ Fair-sized area linked to La Rosière in France

+ Strikingly crowd-free slopes

+ Excellent beginner and easy intermediate slopes

− The tough runs are low down, and most low, woodland runs are tough

− The French link is exposed to bad weather, and the return is slow

− Not the place for lively après-ski

La Thuile has a lot going for it. And if you are limited to school holidays and have had enough of the peak-season crowds over the hill in France, it could be just the job – provided a quiet village appeals to you as much as quiet slopes.

THE RESORT

La Thuile is based on an old mining village that has been expanded and restored. The attractive centre, with shops, bars and restaurants, is at the entrance, with newer developments fairly widely spread. The modern Planibel complex, at the base of the lifts, looks a bit like a French purpose-built resort. The pass includes two days in other Val d'Aosta resorts, and free buses run to nearby Courmayeur, making this an easy outing which reporters recommend.

Village charm The village centre is attractive, but many people find the Planibel complex rather soulless.

Convenience The main village is a little way from the lift base and is served by a regular free bus. The Planibel complex is right by the main lift, with a few other hotels nearby.

Scenery The scenery is varied, with open bowls and lower wooded slopes overlooked by the nearby Mont Blanc massif. Good views into France.

THE MOUNTAINS

La Thuile has quite extensive slopes linked to those of La Rosière via slopes above the Petit St Bernard pass – a good area, but poorly represented on the stupidly over-ambitious piste map. Many runs marked red deserve no more than a blue rating. Strong winds can close high lifts, including the link. The only way back from La Rosière involves a long T-bar.

Slopes A gondola out of the village takes you to Les Suches and an alternative chair to 100m below it. Shady black and red runs go back down directly to the village through the trees. Chairs take you up to Chaz Dura for access to a variety of gentle bowls and slightly more testing slopes on the back of the ridge. From there two chairs go up to the link with La Rosière. Immediately above the lift base is the small Maison Blanche area.

Fast lifts Most key lifts are fast chairs.

Queues Short queues may form at the gondola first thing, but not at the chair. There are no problems once you are up the hill. Reporters regularly comment on the lack of queues: 'Non-existent, even on an Italian holiday.'

Terrain parks The Wazimu ('madness') park with kickers, boxes and a rainbow is in the Les Suches area.

Snow reliability Most of La Thuile's slopes are north- or east-facing and above 2000m, so the snow keeps well. There's also a decent amount of snowmaking; grooming is excellent. The snow was in fine condition when we were there in March 2014, when La Rosière's pistes were mostly slushy.

Experts Black pistes 2 and 3 down through the trees from Les Suches are seriously steep, usually groomed and great fun when they are. The black

Chaz Dura 2580m
Col de Fourclaz
2610m / 8,560ft
Arnouvaz
← La Rosière
Les Suches 2200m
Maison Blanche
La Thuile 1440m/4,720ft

⊚ gondola
⬧ fast chairlift
Slow chairs & drags have no symbol

KEY FACTS

Resort	1440m
	4,720ft

Espace San Bernardo (La Rosière and La Thuile)

Slopes	1175-2610m
	3,850-8,560ft
Lifts	38
Pistes	160km
	99 miles
Green	10%
Blue	31%
Red	41%
Black	18%
Snowmaking	25%

UK PACKAGES

Alpine Answers, Crystal, Crystal Finest, Inghams, Interski, Just Skiing, Momentum, Neilson, Ski Club Freshtracks, Skitracer, Snow-wise, STC, Thomson

Phone numbers
From abroad use the prefix +39 (and do **not** omit the initial '0' of the phone number)

TOURIST OFFICE

www.lathuile.net

CLAIRE PAUL

The red runs down to the left of this top ridge go down to the Petit St Bernard pass and are steeper than most of those on the front face of La Thuile's ski area ↓

slopes at the top down to the pass are easier – but there is also plenty of good off-piste here. Heli-skiing options include a 20km run from the Ruitor glacier to Ste-Foy in France, a short taxi ride from La Rosière for lifts back.

Intermediates The slopes above Les Suches are gentle blues and reds, ideal for cruising. There are also good long reds through the trees back to the resort. The red runs on the back of the top ridge, down towards the Petit St Bernard pass, are less steep. The pass road forms a very gentle red run to the village, dropping a mere 600m in 11km; avoid in fresh snow.

The skiing in La Rosière is more testing – mostly genuine red runs, sometimes with moguls, and with snow more affected by sun. The route back starts with a genuine red, and involves at least one long draglift.

Beginners There are no free lifts, but a day pass (6 euros) allows use of the moving carpet on the village nursery slope. There is also a nursery area up at Les Suches and long, easy blues to progress to. Ride the gondola down.

Snowboarding These are great slopes for learning. There are no draglifts, unless you go to La Rosière. For the more experienced there are great tree runs and good freeriding and carving runs. But there are flat sections too.

Cross-country There are 17km of loops of varying difficulty on the valley floor.

Mountain restaurants Generally not great by Italian standards, but marked on the piste map. For a good lunch, we would head for the village and eat at Lo Tatà (see 'Eating out' below) just off the piste on skier's left – look for the sign to the path to it. Higher up, we like the ambience of the Off Shore, a small hut with an eclectic mix of 1960s/70s memorabilia and music and nautical/Asian/African themes – simple food that you order at the bar. Tiny

and newish Chalet de Cantamont gets glowing 2014 reviews. Readers have also tipped the remote Riondet.

Schools and guides A 2014 visitor was impressed – her two sons' instructor 'spoke good English and they had fun'.

Families There is a mini club and snow garden. The village kindergarten and Planibel hotel club take 4- to 12-year-olds. Over fives can join ski school.

STAYING THERE

Hotels The 4-star Planibel (0165 884541) has a prime location at the lift base plus pools etc; but it is very impersonal. In sharp contrast, we were very impressed by the 4-star Miramonti (0165 883084), in the old village – smartly renovated, free shuttle, excellent food and service, swanky spa (costs extra). Chalet Eden (0165 885050), a short walk from the lifts, is a 4-star eco-hotel with a big spa, strongly tipped a couple of years back. The 3-star B&B hotel du Glacier (0165 884137), a short walk above the lifts, continues to get rave reviews, mainly thanks to its energetic owner Susanna. The 3-star B&B Boton D'Or (0165 883174) was recommended by a 2014 reporter ('close to the lifts, superb service, comfortable rooms').

Apartments The Planibel apartments are 'noisy and ugly', but they are spacious and good value.

Eating out We had a great lunch at Lo Tatà just off the slopes at the top of the village – lovely rustic building with stone walls, wood ceilings and beams. Packed but a warm welcome and free hot wine while we waited; good food and good value; a 2014 reporter who dined there endorses it too. Other reader tips include the Grotta ('friendly, good pizza, pasta, fondue'), Maison Laurent ('huge portions, charmingly chaotic'), Coppapan ('lovely pistachio-encrusted lamb cutlets') and Pepita Café ('good food, friendly service').

Après-ski 'La Cage aux Folles in the Planibel complex is the place to go at teatime and Angela's bar in town is popular with locals,' says a 2014 reporter. Nightlife is quiet. The Konver is open until late and has a regular DJ.

Off the slopes Not great. There are few shops; the Planibel has a pool; there are walks and dog sledding. Non-skiers can ride the gondola, but can't reach the best lunch spots. The thermal baths 10km away at Pré-St-Didier has over 40 spa 'experiences' including saunas and outdoor pools.

Switzerland

SWISS FRANC

Back in the winter of 2007 we were getting 2.4 Swiss francs for £1. When we went to press for this edition the rate was 1.45 francs – about 7% more than a year ago, but still low enough to make everything around 65% more pricey in terms of £££ than seven years ago. Things were even worse in 2011, when the rate hit around 1.3 francs; the Swiss authorities then decided to peg the Swiss franc to the euro, so that it would not continue to rise.

Switzerland is home to some of our favourite resorts. Only two resorts in this book are awarded ★★★★★ for both resort charm and spectacular scenery – the essentially traffic-free Swiss villages of Mürren and Wengen. Many other Swiss resorts are not far behind in the charm and scenery stakes. Many resorts have impressive slopes, too – including some of the biggest, highest and toughest runs in the Alps – as well as a lot of good intermediate terrain. For fast, queue-free lift networks, Swiss resorts are not known as pacesetters – too many historic cable cars and mountain railways for that. But the real bottlenecks are steadily disappearing. And there are compensations – the world's best mountain restaurants, for one, and pretty reliable accommodation, too.

There's no doubt that Switzerland is expensive. Our price survey shows that food and drink now costs way more than in any other skiing country. Overall holiday costs (when you add in the cost of lifts, ski hire and lessons) are less than in most North American resorts, but way above the European norm. The main problem is the strength of the Swiss franc. As our margin panel explains, the pound buys more francs than it did a year ago, but the rate against the euro has improved by slightly more – so Switzerland looks just as pricey (in comparison to France for example) as it did in 2013. Until the exchange rate improves, most people will simply go elsewhere.

A new and regrettable development this year is that the Swiss have decided to apply their minimum wage legislation to employees of foreign firms operating in Switzerland. This has had a huge and immediate impact on operators of catered chalets, particularly what you might call 'affordable' chalets. Basically, such chalets will be very rare this season. More on this below.

445

Many Swiss resorts have a special relationship with the British, who invented downhill skiing in its modern form in Wengen and Mürren by persuading the locals to run their mountain railways in winter, to act as ski lifts, and by organizing the first downhill races. An indication of the continuing strength of the British presence in these resorts is that Wengen has an English church.

TRADITIONAL YEAR-ROUND RESORTS

While France is the home of the purpose-built resort, Switzerland is the home of the mountain village that has transformed itself from traditional farming community (or health retreat) into year-round holiday resort. Many of Switzerland's most famous mountain resorts are as popular in the summer as in the winter, or more so. This creates places with a more lived-in feel to them and a much more stable local community.

Not that stable local communities are entirely a good thing. Many villages are still dominated by a handful of families lucky or shrewd enough to get involved in the early development of the area, and this has its downside as well as advantages. The ruling families have been able to stifle competition and bar newcomers from taking a slice of their action. For example, alternative ski schools – to compete with the traditional, nationally organized

JUNGFRAU REGIONAL MARKETING AG

← Chalet-style buildings and dramatic mountains are the essence of the Swiss Alps; this is Grindelwald, and the Wetterhorn

These are the main options – there are others. On any of the passes listed, children under 16 accompanied by at least one parent travel free. For updates, go to www.swiss-pass.ch.

Swiss Pass *Covers unrestricted travel by train, bus or boat on most of the Swiss travel network during the period of validity – 4, 8, 15 or 22 days; or one month. Prices: 4 days from £178; 8 days from £257*

* Includes panoramic rail routes as well as trams and buses in 41 towns

* 50% discount on the price of using most of the mountain railways

* Free entrance to about 470 museums

* 10% discount for two and more adults travelling together

Swiss Transfer Ticket *Permits travel between the Swiss border or airport and your destination, out and back, by the most direct route. Valid for one month. You can use two different airports. Prices: from £91*

SWISS-IMAGE.CH / CHRISTOF SONDEREGGER

Swiss Flexi Pass *Permits unrestricted travel across Switzerland, like the Swiss Pass, on 3, 4, 5 or 6 days of your choice during a one-month period of validity. On days when you choose to use the card, you just write the date on the card. On days when you choose not to use up one of the 3, 4, 5 or 6 days, the pass gets you a discount of 50%. There's 10% discount for two and more adults travelling together. Prices: 3 days from £170; 6 days from £271*

Swiss Card *An extension of the Transfer Ticket. As well as travel to and from your destination, you get a 50% discount on all rail, bus and boat fares during the one-month period of validity – and on some cable car fares. Prices: from £130*

school, ensuring continuing pressure to raise standards – were slower to appear here than in other Alpine countries. But this grip has been weakened over recent years, and ski school standards have risen as a result.

The quality of service throughout Switzerland is generally high. The food is almost universally of good quality, and much more varied than in neighbouring Austria. Even the standard rustic dish of rösti – potatoes grated then fried – is haute cuisine compared to Austrian sausages; crucially, it comes in countless variations, which Tiroler gröstl does not. And in Switzerland you get what you pay for: the cheapest wine, for example, is not cheap, but it is reliable.

NOT ENTIRELY TRADITIONAL
Perhaps surprisingly for such a traditional, rather staid skiing nation, Switzerland has gone out of its way to attract snowboarders. Davos, for example, may hit the headlines mainly when it hosts huge economic conferences, but yards from the conference hall there are dudes getting big air on the Bolgen slope's training kickers. Little-known Laax claims one of Europe's best terrain parks and firmly targets its marketing at the youth and freestyle markets as well as families.

Switzerland, like Italy, doesn't have much time for tree-huggers who object to the impact of helicopters on wildlife. Heli-skiing is not unrestricted, but it is available – indeed, the Zermatt helipad is like a bus station at peak times, with choppers taking off every few minutes (you can even get a heli-lift to the top of the pistes, if you find conventional lifts just too ordinary). In Austria heli-skiing is confined to Lech-Zürs and in France it is largely confined to the retrieval of clients from remote spots in valleys – you can't be deposited on a peak.

THE CHALET BUSINESS UNDER PRESSURE
One way to minimize your exposure to high Swiss prices is to stay in a catered chalet. They offer very competitive package prices, and the package usually includes wine with dinner and may include other extras. So it's very regrettable that the Swiss government has decided to apply its minimum wage legislation to the staff of these chalets, even if they are employed in the UK. The minimum wage works out at an astonishing £34,000 a year, and to cut a long story short the result is that value-conscious operators like Inghams, Ski Total and Skiworld will be operating very few chalets in Swiss resorts this season. There's more on this in our editorial, page 13.

But, as you can see from the ad below, not everyone is deterred by these high costs. Zermatt is a high-cost resort in any case, and the proprietor of Matterhorn Chalets, Ed Mannix, is a seasoned industry veteran who will have done his sums. 'Zermatt will always have its devotees,' says Mannix, 'and I believe that providing a mountain guide will allow guests to get something really special out of their stay with us.'

GETTING THERE BY TRAIN
The Swiss market in Britain picked up a bit last season (up from 5.5% of the market to 6.5%, according to the Crystal Ski Industry Report), and this is said to be partly attributable to improved access by rail – notably a high-speed service from Lille to Aigle, Martigny, Visp and Brig, with a connecting service from London. There's more information in our 'Travelling by rail' feature at the front of the book (page 65).

GETTING AROUND BY TRAIN
The Swiss railway network is famously extensive and reliable. The trains run like clockwork to the advertised timetable – if you think a Swiss train is late, make sure your watch is right before you complain. (There is, however, some truth in the cynical view that

www.wheretoskiandsnowboard.com

Build your own shortlist:

Selected chalet in Zermatt   ADVERTISEMENT

MATTERHORN CHALETS *www.matterhornchalets.com*   T **0041 (0)79 247 15 88**

We are a small and personal organization dedicated to providing our guests with some of the best that Zermatt has to offer. High class accommodation in our charming, comfortable and ideally located chalet; excellent food and wine; the services of seasoned professionals who know their resort and love what they do – plus your own local mountain guide or instructor.

book@matterhornchalets.ch

Matterhorn Chalets

the trains are able to run on time because the timetables incorporate long stops at stations.)

The rail network is a perfectly viable means of reaching many resorts. There are often linking services that run to the top of the mountain, doubling as ski lifts, too. And if a resort is not on the rail network, there will usually be efficient bus services to take you from the nearest station.

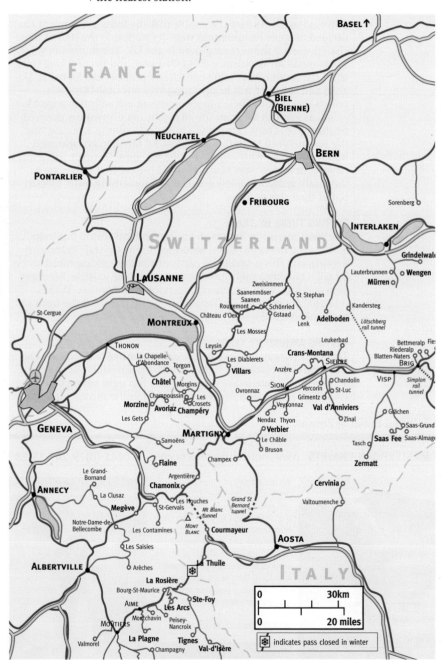

GETTING AROUND BY CAR

Access to practically all Swiss resorts is fairly straightforward when approaching from the north – just pick your motorway. But many of the high passes that are perfectly sensible ways to get around the country in summer are closed throughout the winter, which can be inconvenient if you are planning to move around from one area to another.

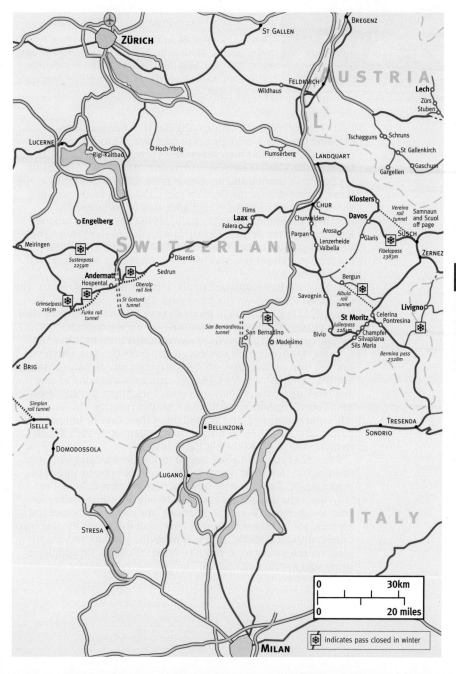

The Austrians might dispute it, but Switzerland seems to do tobogganing on an unmatched scale. It isn't just the famous Cresta run at St Moritz (check out that chapter for more information); it's that so many resorts have epic runs. The longest in the world, they say, is at Grindelwald – 15km from the Faulhorn via Bussalp to the resort; it's fantastically scenic, being surrounded by famous peaks, but it does involve a 2hr30 hike from the top of the First gondola.

There are plenty of other extraordinary runs, without the hiking penalty. Fiesch in the little-known Aletsch Arena area has a 13km run, Saas-Grund below Saas-Fee has one of 11km. Even macho Verbier has a 10km run from Savoleyres, dropping 850m.

SWISS-IMAGE.CH / CHRISTIAN PERRET

There are very useful car-carrying trains in various places, crawling over impassable passes or burrowing through the mountains to cut out huge amounts of driving. One key link is between the Valais (Crans-Montana, Zermatt etc) and Andermatt via the Furka tunnel, and another is from Andermatt to the Grisons (Laax, Davos etc) via the Oberalp pass – closed to road traffic in winter but open to trains except after very heavy snowfalls. Another rail tunnel that's very handy is the Lötschberg, linking Kandersteg in the Bernese Oberland with Brig in the Valais. (The Lötschberg Base Tunnel, opened in 2007, is lower, longer and faster, but it's not relevant to travel by car – it takes only passenger and freight trains.)

St Moritz is more awkward to get to than other major resorts. The main road route is over the Julier pass. This is normally kept open, but at 2285m it is naturally prone to heavy snowfalls that can shut it for a time. The alternatives are car-carrying rail tunnels – the Albula tunnel nearby and the Vereina tunnel from near Klosters.

These car-carrying rail services are generally painless. Often you can just turn up and drive on. But carrying capacities are obviously limited. Some services (eg Oberalp) carry only a handful of cars, and booking is vital. Others (eg Furka, Lötschberg, Vereina) are much bigger operations with much greater capacity – but that's a reflection of demand, and at peak times there may be long queues – particularly for the Furka tunnel from Andermatt, which Zürich residents use to get to the big Valais resorts.

There is a car-carrying rail tunnel linking Switzerland with Italy – the Simplon. But most routes to Italy are kept open by means of road tunnels. Read the Italy introduction for more information.

To use Swiss motorways you have to buy an annual sticker for your windscreen. These cost 40 francs, are sold at the border and are valid for 14 months – from 1 December to 31 January. If you are caught without a sticker, or if you have one but have not stuck it in place on the windscreen, you'll be fined 200 francs (in addition to being sold a sticker, of course).

Adelboden

*Traditional village with plenty to do off the snow – and with
extensive, varied and scenic slopes, some also accessible from Lenk*

TOP 10 RATINGS

Extent	★★★
Fast lifts	★★★
Queues	★★★
Snow	★★★
Expert	★★
Intermediate	★★★
Beginner	★★★★
Charm	★★★★
Convenience	★★
Scenery	★★★★

RPI   120

lift pass	£190
ski hire	£135
lessons	£110
food & drink	£190
total	**£625**

NEWS

2014/15: A 10-person gondola is to replace the cable car out of Lenk, with a second stage going on up to Metschstand, where the Lenk and Adelboden slopes meet. This will make Lenk a much more attractive base for the whole area.

2013/14: A hybrid 6/8-seat chondola carrying 2,400 passengers an hour replaced the existing Hahnenmoos gondola.

KEY FACTS

Resort	1355m
	4,450ft
Slopes	1070-2360m
	3,510-7,740ft
Lifts	57
Pistes	185km
	115 miles
Blue	44%
Red	45%
Black	11%
Snowmaking	60%

ADELBODEN TOURIST OFFICE

The scenery is both pretty and dramatic – this is the main Geils bowl →

➕ Chalet-style mountain village in a splendid setting

➕ Good off-slope leisure facilities

➕ Some pleasantly uncrowded slopes linked to Lenk, but ...

➖ Slopes are fragmented and widely spread; access can be slow

➖ Not a place for bumps but plenty of off-piste opportunities

➖ Quiet, limited nightlife

Adelboden is not quite your classic postcard-pretty village, but it comes close, and offers a good blend of attractions. We have found our primitive German brought into play here more than is usual in Switzerland, but the resort is keen to reclaim the place it once held in the affections of British skiers, and it merits serious consideration.

THE RESORT

Adelboden is a traditional village tucked away on a sunny mountainside at the head of a long valley. Its major sector of slopes is linked to the slopes in the village of Lenk, to the west. The Jungfrau resorts (Wengen, Mürren etc) to the east are within day-trip range.
Village charm The village is built more or less entirely in chalet style, and the long main street (not entirely car-free, but nearly so) is lined by chalets housing shops.
Convenience The village is fairly compact, but getting to and from the slopes usually involves a bit of hassle, or at least time. Buses to the satellite ski area of Engstligenalp are included with the lift pass; those to Elsigen-Metsch are not.
Scenery There are fine panoramas from the village and from the slopes.

THE MOUNTAINS

Adelboden's slopes are split into five varied sectors, widely spread. The main sector stretches across to Lenk, where a sixth area is reached by bus.
Slopes Village lifts access three of the sectors. A small cable car/gondola hybrid goes up to Tschentenalp, with an itinerary back to the village. An even smaller lift goes down to Oey, where a proper gondola goes up to Chuenisbärgli and then, with a quick change, on to the major sector at Sillerenbühl (taking 15 minutes in total). Sillerenbühl has three sub-sectors – Geils, Aebi and Metsch (above Lenk). There is a pretty run home to Oey.
 Engstligenalp, a flat-bottomed high-altitude bowl, is reached by a cable

car from Unter dem Birg, 4km south of the resort; Elsigen-Metsch is 5km away to the north-east.
Fast lifts The main lifts are fast, but there are still a fair few slow ones.
Queues The main access gondolas get busy at peak times; Adelboden is a popular weekend destination for residents of the capital, Bern. The new Hahnenmoos chondola, opened in December 2013, should help reduce non-trivial queues at Geils. The Bühlberg chair at Metsch can have queues. The little lift linking Oey to the centre is a real bottleneck; public and hotel buses offer a way round it.
Terrain parks The Gran Masta Park at Brenggen, near Hahnenmoos, has jumps, big air, rails, snack bar and chill-out zone. There are snowcross courses above Aebi, and at Elsigen.
Snow reliability Most slopes are above 1500m, so reliability is reasonable, especially at north-facing Tschentenalp and Luegli. Snowmaking is extensive, and grooming is good.

The snow-covered churchyard adds to the charm of the chalet-lined main street →

SNOWPIX.COM / CHRIS GILL

UK PACKAGES

Powder Byrne, PowderBeds, Ski Club Freshtracks, Solos, STC Switzerland Travel Centre

SWITZERLAND

452

Resort news and key links: www.wheretoskiandsnowboard.com

Phone numbers
From elsewhere in Switzerland add the prefix 033; from abroad use the prefix +41 33

TOURIST OFFICE

www.adelboden.ch

Experts The black pistes generally merit the rating, at least in parts, and are great fun unless you crave bumps – they are groomed regularly. Off-piste possibilities are good and don't get tracked out quickly; the Lavey and Luegli chairs in the Geils bowl access routes to Adelboden and Lenk. Engstligenalp has off-piste potential.
Intermediates All five areas deserve exploration. There is a lot of ground to be covered in the main sector; at Geils and Aebi the runs are mainly excellent wide reds, but on the sunny Metsch side there is great blue cruising. Quiet Tschentenalp is worth a visit.
Beginners There are good nursery slopes in the village and at the foot of nearby sectors. But progress to longer runs requires a bit of planning to avoid stressful stretches.
Snowboarding There are still lots of draglifts. Two specialist schools.
Cross-country There are trails along the valley to Engstligenalp where there is a high-altitude, snow-sure circuit. There are shorter trails (2km) through forest at Elsigbach.
Mountain restaurants There are plenty of pleasant spots. The self-service Hahnenmoos has cold and hot buffets.
Schools and guides A 2013 visitor thought the Swiss school 'great'.
Families Several hotels offer childcare. There are a number of 'kids paradise'

ski areas, including one at Geils. A 2013 visitor said: 'There are many flat areas where you have to push the kids.'

STAYING THERE

There is locally bookable self-catering, and some 30 pensions and hotels.
Hotels The central 4-star Beau-Site (673 2222) offers 'excellent breakfast and helpful staff'. The 3-star Bären Huldi (673 2151) is an attractive central chalet with a restaurant recommended by readers (see below). The Cambrian (673 8383), with spa and outdoor pool (even in winter), has also had good reports.
Eating out The hotel Bären has 'good prices, excellent food'; the Kreuz does 'delicious pizza and meringue'.
Après-ski There are several tea rooms and bars to head for at close of play, including some in central hotels. The village seems pretty quiet later on. More reports please.
Off the slopes There's a leisure centre that has ice skating, curling, climbing and bowling, and some hotel pools are open to the public. There are several toboggan runs of up to 5km. Some mountain restaurants are reachable on foot for lunchtime meetings, and there are well-marked paths. Lift passes are available for walkers.

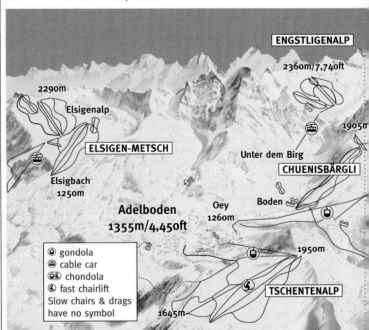

ENGSTLIGENALP
2360m/7,740ft
2290m
Elsigenalp
1905m
ELSIGEN-METSCH
Unter dem Birg
CHUENISBÄRGLI
Elsigbach
1250m
Oey
1260m
Boden
Adelboden
1355m/4,450ft
1950m
◉ gondola
🚠 cable car
◔ chondola
④ fast chairlift
Slow chairs & drags
have no symbol
TSCHENTENALP
1645m

ħotel

Beau Site
Adelboden

ħotel
Restaurant
Fitness
Spa

Boutique Hotel
Beau-Site Fitness & Spa
Familie Markus Luder
Dorfstrasse 5, CH-3715 Adelboden
Tel. +41 (0)33 673 82 82
www.hotelbeausite.ch

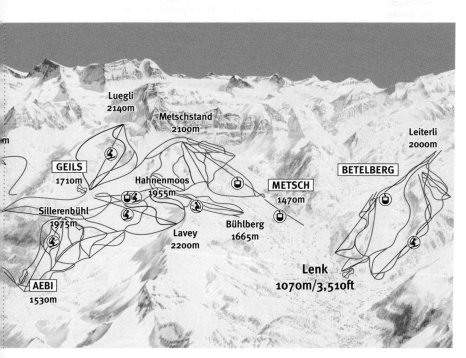

Luegli 2140m

Metschstand 2100m

Leiterli 2000m

GEILS 1710m

Hahnenmoos 1955m

BETELBERG

METSCH 1470m

Sillerenbühl 1975m

Bühlberg 1665m

Lavey 2200m

Lenk 1070m/3,510ft

AEBI 1530m

ANDERMATT TOURIST OFFICE

Andermatt

A slow-paced, old-fashioned resort with great steep, high, snowy terrain on- and off-piste – but with major changes under way

454

TOP 10 RATINGS

Extent	★★
Fast lifts	★★
Queues	★★
Snow	★★★★
Expert	★★★★
Intermediate	★★
Beginner	★
Charm	★★★★
Convenience	★★★
Scenery	★★★

RPI 110

lift pass	£180
ski hire	£95
lessons	£120
food & drink	£180
total	**£575**

NEWS

2014/15: New and faster lifts are coming, possibly for 2015, but no date is confirmed.

2013/14: The first hotel in the resort's big development, the Chedi Andermatt, opened in December 2013. Four moving carpets began operation, improving access to some lifts and restaurants.

+ Attractive, traditional village

+ Excellent snow record

+ Some serious blacks, off-piste terrain and ski-touring opportunities

− Not great for beginners, or mileage-hungry intermediates

− Limited off-slope diversions

− Busy at weekends

Little old Andermatt is virtually doubling in size with the construction of what amounts to a new village next to the original; the first of countless luxury hotels and apartments opened last season. For the moment, at least, the appeal of the tall, steep, snowy, largely off-piste Gemsstock is undiminished, but for how long? To enjoy the place in its traditional form, don't delay.

THE RESORT

Andermatt gets a lot of weekend business, but at other times can seem deserted. In winter, east–west links rely on car-carrying trains. The lift pass also covers Sedrun – 20 minutes to the east and a popular excursion (see the Directory) – and linking trains.
Village charm The town is quietly attractive. Charming wooden houses line the main street that runs from the central river bridge to the Gemsstock cable car. The new development is on the outskirts, past the station.
Convenience The centre is compact, but the lifts are on opposite sides of the town. A minibus shuttle runs half-hourly in high season, but in low season may run at weekends only.
Scenery The Gemsstock peak is well defined and higher than its neighbours, with rugged steep terrain.

THE MOUNTAINS

Andermatt's local skiing is split over two unlinked mountains, both limited in extent. Most slopes are above the trees; piste marking is slack.
Slopes A two-stage cable car from the edge of the village serves the open, steep, north-facing Gemsstock. The separate, sunny Nätschen area will soon be linked to Sedrun, raising the piste total to the 120km plus already claimed by the tourist office.
Fast lifts The Gemsstock cable car and the chair at the top of the Nätschen sector are the only fast lifts at present.
Queues The Gemsstock cable car can generate queues, even in low season.
Terrain parks At Gemsstock and above Sedrun, where there's a half-pipe.
Snow reliability The area has a justified reputation for reliable snow. Nätschen gets a lot of sun.

GEMSSTOCK
2965m/9,730ft

Sedrun ↓

Gütsch
2345m

Oberalppass
2045m

2400m

Guspis

WINTERHORN
246om

This area currently closed

Gurschen
2210m

Felsental

Lückli
2000m

NÄTSCHEN
184om

Gurschenalp
2015m

Realp →

Hospental
1455m

Andermatt
1445m/4,740ft

⬛ cable car
④ fast chairlift
Slow chairs & drags have no symbol

KEY FACTS

Resort	1445m
	4,740ft
Slopes	1445-2965m
	4,740-9,730ft
Lifts	20
Pistes	86km
	54 miles
Blue	22%
Red	46%
Black	32%
Snowmaking	36%

UK PACKAGES

Alpine Answers, Carrier, PowderBeds, Ski Club Freshtracks, Ski Safari, Ski Weekend, Snow-wise

Phone numbers
From elsewhere in Switzerland add the prefix 041; from abroad use the prefix +41 41

TOURIST OFFICE

www.andermatt.ch

SIMON MEDLEY

Gemsstock is a bit of a beast, and gets a lot of lovely snow ↓

Experts It is most definitely a resort for experts. The north-facing bowl beneath the top Gemsstock cable car is a glorious, long, steep slope (900m vertical), usually with excellent snow, down which there are off-piste routes, a ski-route and a piste. Outside the bowl, Sonnenpiste is a fine, open red run away from the lifts, with more off-piste opportunities. From Gurschen to the village there is a black run, not steep but often tricky. Routes outside the bowl go down the Felsental or Guspis valleys towards Hospental, or steeply into the deserted Untertal, to the east (ending in a bit of a walk). Nätschen has black pistes, and off-piste terrain, including ski routes.

Intermediates Intermediates needn't be put off Gemsstock: the Sonnenpiste can be tackled, and at mid-mountain there are some short blues and an easy but longer black (served by a tricky draglift). Nätschen is well worth a visit, as are the red runs of Sedrun.

Beginners Not ideal; but there is one lovely blue from Gütsch to the village.

Snowboarding The cable car accesses some great freeride terrain.

Cross-country There are trails in the valley, and at Realp to the south-west.

Mountain restaurants Inadequate. The over-busy Gurschen hut has a table-service section. You can picnic at Gurschen and at Nätschen.

Schools and guides The Swiss ski school, Andermatt Xperience and Bergschule Uri/Mountain Reality are

the options, and Snowlimit is a specialist snowboard school.

Families Family passes are available.

STAYING THERE

Andermatt's accommodation is mostly in cosy 2-star and 3-star hotels. The swanky 5-star Chedi opened in 2013.

Hotels River House (887 0025) is a stylish, upmarket boutique B&B in a 250-year-old building. Gasthaus Sternen (887 1130) is an attractive central chalet. The 3-star Sonne (887 1226), towards the Gemsstock lift, is a lovely old place. A reporter rates the Schweizerhof (887 1189) 'good value'.

Apartments The hotel Monopol-Metropol (887 1575) has apartments.

Eating out The restaurant at the River House has been well supported (meat and fish dishes with a 'modern twist'). Café Toutoune (cafe, restaurant and lounge bar) is smart, with a veggie/ Mediterranean bias. Gasthaus Sonne is a more traditional alternative.

Après-ski We like the cosy bar Alt Apothek at River House for tea and cake (live music later on). Other possibilities include the Curva at the hotel Monopol-Metropol and the Spycher. The Piccadilly pub and Dancing Gotthard liven up at weekends.

Off the slopes Toboggan run at Nätschen, snowshoeing at Gütsch and snow tubing run at Sedrun. The fitness centre at the hotel Drei König is open to the public. 20km of footpaths.

Andermatt

455

CHAMPÉRY TOURIST OFFICE

Champéry

Picture-postcard village that few UK tour operators feature these days, with access to the Portes du Soleil circuit

TOP 10 RATINGS

Extent	★★★★★
Fast lifts	★
Queues	★★★★
Snow	★★
Expert	★★★
Intermediate	★★★★
Beginner	★★
Charm	★★★★
Convenience	★
Scenery	★★★★

RPI	125
lift pass	£200
ski hire	£135
lessons	£110
food & drink	£190
total	**£635**

- + Charmingly rustic mountain village
- + Access to Portes du Soleil circuit
- + Quiet, relaxed – yet plenty to do off the slopes
- − Lift system is antiquated
- − Local slopes suffer from the sun
- − No runs back to the village
- − Not good for beginners

Champéry is great for intermediate skiers looking for a quiet time in a lovely place if you can live with the cost and the negatives. Access to Avoriaz is fairly easy – and there may be good snow in France when the Swiss side is suffering.

THE RESORT

Champéry is on the Swiss side of the Portes du Soleil region, with fairly quick links to Avoriaz in France, and to the valley between Avoriaz and Châtel.
Village charm The village is friendly and relaxed, with classic old wooden chalets and some more substantial buildings; a charming spot.
Convenience Champéry's slopes are mainly high above the village, reached by a cable car that starts at the railway station, down a steepish hill, away from the main street. The village spreads over quite an area, but there is a free shuttle-bus.
Scenery The resort sits beneath the dramatic ridge of the Dents du Midi – impressive both from the village and the slopes.

THE MOUNTAINS

Champéry's slopes are open and sunny with the exception of two partly wooded long runs to the valley.
Slopes You reach the edge of the bowl of Planachaux via the village cable car or a fast six-seat chairlift from Grand Paradis, a short, free bus ride away. With two or three further lift rides you can get up to the French border. If snow is good, there are a couple of pistes back to Grand Paradis – one curling well away from the lift system – but no pistes back to Champéry.
Fast lifts There are a few fast chairlifts but most lifts on the Swiss slopes are ancient draglifts and chairs.
Queues If snow is poor, expect end-of-day queues for the cable car down to the village. Few other problems.
Terrain parks The Superpark is a good

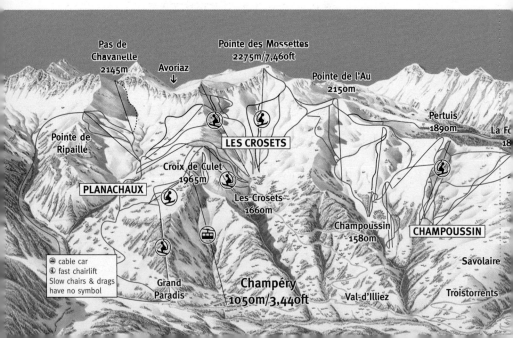

cable car
fast chairlift
Slow chairs & drags have no symbol

Pas de Chavanelle 2145m
Avoriaz
Pointe des Mossettes 2275m/7,46oft
Pointe de l'Au 2150m
Pertuis 1890m
La Fo 18
Pointe de Ripaille
LES CROSETS
Croix de Culet 1965m
PLANACHAUX
Les Crosets 1660m
Champoussin 158om
CHAMPOUSSIN
Savolaire
Grand Paradis
Champéry 1050m/3,44oft
Val-d'Illiez
Troistorrents

Build your own shortlist: www.wheretoskiandsnowboard.com

NEWS

2014/15: The Hotel du Parc has been renovated and will reopen as Champéry's first 4-star, Le White.

2013/14: The Point de l'Au double has been upgraded to a (fixed-grip) quad. There's now a special pass for the lifts to and from the Superpark at Les Crosets. A new snowcross course was built at Morgins.

UK PACKAGES

Alpine Answers, Erna Low, Momentum, Mountain Beds, PowderBeds, Scott Dunn, Ski Freedom, Ski Weekend, White Roc **Les Crosets** Mountain Lodge **Morgins** Ski Morgins

terrain park at Les Crosets. It has everything you could want. There are also three beginners' parks: the micro park at the Grand Conche chair, the Village Kids at the base, and another at the Planachaux chair. There are other (excellent) parks in Avoriaz.

Snow reliability The Swiss side of the mountain roughly faces south-east and so snow quality can suffer. More snowmaking would be good.

Experts The Swiss Wall, on the Champéry side of Pas de Chavanette, has a reputation for great steepness, which is not justified. It used to be classified black but is now an itinéraire and is long and bumpy, and provides great amusement to those riding the chairlift over it. The proper blacks in the area are worthwhile, too.

There's plenty of off-piste terrain. And at four points on the ridge the piste map has arrows indicating 'unmarked freeride itinéraires'. We don't get this variation on the usual itinerary concept. It is basically saying 'There are some popular off-piste routes starting somewhere around here', and there would be less scope for confusion if they said just that.

Intermediates Confident intermediates have the whole Portes du Soleil at their disposal. Locally, the runs home to Grand Paradis are good when the snow conditions allow. Les Crosets is a junction of several fine runs. There are slightly tougher pistes from Mossettes and Pointe de l'Au, leisurely cruising

above Champoussin, and delightful tree-lined meanders from La Foilleuse to Morgins. From Col des Portes du Soleil a long blue run goes down a quiet, wooded valley to Morgins; but after a good descent to the rustic Tovassière restaurant the run is a path, dropping a mere 200m in 4km.

Beginners Far from ideal. The Planachaux runs, where lessons are held, are steepish and small (as well as remote from the village), and some of the local blue runs could be red.

Snowboarding Not ideal for beginners (see above), and there are several draglifts (some quite steep). There are good terrain parks in Les Crosets and Avoriaz for intermediates and experts, though, and some good powder areas.

Cross-country It's advertised as 7km – not a lot – with 4km floodlit every night, and the snow is unreliable.

Mountain restaurants There are about 15 mountain restaurants between Champéry and Morgins, marked but not named on the piste map. A regular visitor reckons they are all table-service. Chez Coquoz near the Planachaux chair offers a warm welcome, a 'modern Swiss menu' and a knockout Valais wine list. The tiny Lapisa on the way to Grand Paradis is delightfully rustic – they make cheese and smoke meat on the spot.

Schools and guides The children in a 2014 visitor's party used the Swiss school – 'All made good progress and enjoyed their lessons.' It faces healthy competition from the Freeride Co and Redcarpet Snowsport School.

Families Champéry wouldn't be high on our shortlist for a family trip, given the lack of slopes at village level.

STAYING THERE

Hotels Champéry gets its first 4-star for 2014, Le White (479 0404). The 2-star des Alpes (479 1222) was recommended by a 2014 reporter as 'good value, with spacious rooms and friendly staff'. A regular visitor says the 3-star Beau Séjour (479 5858) is the best in town; other past tips are the National (479 1130) and the rustic Auberge du Grand Paradis (479 1167), which is out at, er, Grand Paradis.

Apartments The Lodge is a newish development below the village. It has smart, modern, spacious apartments with good views.

Eating out Mitchell's is stylish and modern, and we had a good meal there on our last visit. You can 'have

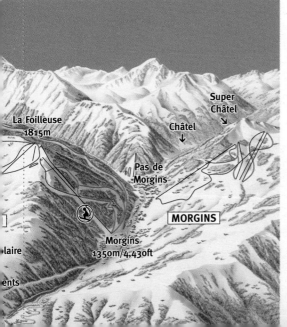

KEY FACTS

Resort	1050m
	3,440ft

Portes du Soleil	
Slopes	950-2275m
	3,120-7,460ft
Lifts	194
Pistes	650km
	404 miles
Green	12%
Blue	43%
Red	36%
Black	9%
Snowmaking	
	1074 guns

Swiss side only	
Slopes	1050-2275m
	3,440-7,460ft
Lifts	37
Pistes	100km
	62 miles

Phone numbers
From elsewhere in
Switzerland add the
prefix 024; from
abroad use the prefix
+41 24

TOURIST OFFICES

Champéry
www.champery.ch

**Les Crosets /
Champoussin / Val-
d'Illiez**
www.valdilliez.ch

Morgins
www.morgins.ch

CHAMPERY TOURISME

The Swiss side of the
Portes du Soleil gets
a lot of sun: these are
the slopes above Les
Crosets and France is
just over the ridge →

---

your steak cooked on an open fire' at the 'atmospheric' Vieux Chalet. Other reader tips are the bar of the hotel National ('hearty food'), the Farinet, Le Pub and the 'great bistro' Le Nord, beneath the 'more sophisticated' Atelier Gourmand. Café du Centre has changed hands – reports welcome.

Après-ski The yurt at the foot of the Grand Paradis chair is popular. Mitchell's, with a fireplace and big sofas, is 'fun and lively' at teatime. The Bar des Guides in the hotel Suisse is good for a quiet drink. The Crevasse and Farinet are nightclubs.

Off the slopes Walks are pleasant, and the railway allows lots of excursions. There's ice climbing on a frozen waterfall and snowshoeing. The Palladium is a big ice sports centre with various other facilities, including a pool, tennis and climbing wall.

LINKED RESORT – 1660m
LES CROSETS

A good base for a quiet time and slopes on the doorstep. The 3-star Télécabine hotel (479 0300) has 'basic rooms but extremely helpful staff, and the five-course dinner is delicious'. Mountain Lodge (UK: 0845 127 1750) is a smart chalet-style hotel that impressed a visitor last year.

LINKED RESORT – 1580m
CHAMPOUSSIN

A good family choice – no through traffic, on the slopes – is the 3-star Alpadze Lou Kra (pool, sauna, steam, gym – 476 8300). Chez Gaby is tipped for 'Valais specialities'.

LINKED RESORT – 1350m
MORGINS

Over the hill and close to Châtel in France, Morgins is a fairly scattered, but attractive, quiet resort with a gentle nursery slope right in the village. The modern hotel Helvetia (565 1875) with spa is recommended this year. The 'cosy' Buvette des Sports restaurant does 'excellent' spaghetti carbonara. Black Chili was highly recommended in 2014 ('best restaurant in the whole of the Portes du Soleil').

DOWN-VALLEY VILLAGE – 950m
VAL-D'ILLIEZ

About 4km down the valley from Champéry, Val-d'Illiez has no lifts or slopes, but there are buses and trains up to Champéry. Down in the valley bottom is the Thermes Parc thermal spa. The hotel du Repos (477 1414) is comfortable, woody and British-run.

SNOWPIX.COM / CHRIS GILL

Crans-Montana

An increasingly stylish big-town base with a fabulous panoramic view and sun-soaked slopes

TOP 10 RATINGS

Extent	★★★
Fast lifts	★★★★★
Queues	★★★
Snow	★★
Expert	★★
Intermediate	★★★★
Beginner	★★★
Charm	★★
Convenience	★★
Scenery	★★★★

RPI 135

lift pass	£220
ski hire	£150
lessons	£110
food & drink	£215
total	**£695**

NEWS

2014/15: A six-pack is to replace the Cabane de Bois double chair to Les Violettes; the Barmaz quad will also be removed. The Momentum Ski Festival and City Ski Champs will be held here again – from 12 to 15 March 2015.

2013/14: The Mont Lachaux competition run was remodelled and snowmaking was installed. The 5-star Crans Ambassador hotel reopened after refurbishment, with 60 extra bedrooms.

KEY FACTS

Resort	1500m	
	4,920ft	
Slopes	1500-2925m	
	4,920-9,600ft	
Lifts	28	
Pistes	140km	
	87 miles	
Blue	39%	
Red	50%	
Black	11%	
Snowmaking	21%	

➕ Large, varied piste area

➕ Splendid setting and views

➕ Excellent, gentle nursery slopes

➕ Very sunny slopes, but ...

➖ Snow is badly affected by the sun

➖ Large, busy, urban resort

➖ You may need a car or buses

➖ Few challenges except off-piste

We love Crans-Montana's wide views, its local scenery and some of its mountain restaurants and smart lodgings. It's just a shame that the place is more like a city than a rustic village and that the slopes face south – the strong sunshine that's so welcome in dark December can spoil the snow from mid-season on.

THE RESORT

Set on a broad shelf facing south across the Rhône valley, Crans and Montana are two towns, their centres a mile apart and their fringes merging. The resort can be reached by funicular railway from Sierre. There are also lodgings a mile east at the lift base of Les Barzettes (aka Les Violettes, the name of the hill) and further out at Aminona. Outings are possible – to Saas-Fee and Verbier, for example.

Village charm Both Crans and Montana are emphatically towns rather than villages, with little traditional Alpine character and a lot of traffic. But the wooded setting softens the urban feel a bit. Crans is the more upmarket part, with fancy shops, several 5-star hotels and a pedestrian-friendly centre.

Convenience The towns spread widely away from their respective gondola stations, and many visitors need to use cars or the free shuttle-bus.

Scenery The panoramic views over the Rhône valley to the peaks bordering Italy are breathtaking.

THE MOUNTAINS

There's a pleasant mix of open and wooded runs with few challenges. Runs are at last numbered on the piste map. Virtually all the runs are red, but many are gentle and wide enough to be blue.

Slopes The slopes are spread over a broad mountainside, with lifts from four valley bases. Gondolas from Crans and Montana meet at Cry d'Er – an open bowl descending into patchy forest. A third gondola accesses the next sector, Les Violettes. A six-pack from the mid-station here links with Cry d'Er. Above Les Violettes, a jumbo gondola goes up to the Plaine Morte

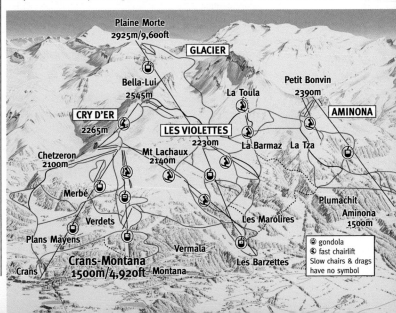

Plaine Morte 2925m/9,600ft

GLACIER

Bella-Lui 2545m

Petit Bonvin 2390m

La Toula

CRY D'ER 2265m

AMINONA

LES VIOLETTES 2230m

Chetzeron 2100m

Mt Lachaux 2140m

La Barmaz   La Tza

Merbé

Plumachit

Verdets

Les Marolires

Aminona 1500m

Plans Mayens

Vermala

Les Barzettes

Crans

Crans-Montana 1500m/4,920ft   Montana

◎	gondola
◉	fast chairlift
	Slow chairs & drags have no symbol

MOMENTUM SKI

Weekend & a la carte
ski holiday specialists

100% Tailor-made

Premier hotels
& apartments

Flexible travel
arrangements

020 7371 9111
WWW.MOMENTUMSKI.COM

UK PACKAGES

Alpine Answers, Carrier, Erna Low, Inghams, Momentum, Mountain Beds, Oxford Ski Co, PowderBeds, Ski Club Freshtracks, Skitracer, Ski Weekend, Skiworld

Phone numbers
From elsewhere in Switzerland add the prefix 027; from abroad use the prefix +41 27

TOURIST OFFICE

www.crans-montana.ch

SNOWPIX.COM / CHRIS GILL

The twin towns enjoy the definitive balcony setting above the Rhône valley →

glacier. The fourth sector is served by a gondola from Aminona. Some runs down to the valley are narrow paths.
Fast lifts With a new six-pack this season, the resort now gets ★★★★★.
Queues We know of no problems, but we lack high-season reports.
Terrain parks At Cry d'Er there's a park with features for all levels, plus a beginner park, half-pipe, airbag and snowcross.
Snow reliability The runs on the Plaine Morte glacier are very limited, and nearly all the other slopes get a lot of direct sun, with obvious effects on the snow. You may get spring snow even in January. There is snowmaking on the main runs but some runs to resort level have often been closed on our visits. Grooming is efficient.
Experts There are few steep pistes, and the only decent moguls are on the short slopes at La Toula. There's plenty of off-piste, particularly beneath La Toula, La Tza and Chetzeron – the best place to go in a storm. There are more adventurous routes outside the lift network – Les Faverges is a beautiful, easy valley bringing you to Aminona.
Intermediates There's a lot to do, including some notably long runs. The 12km run from Plaine Morte to Les Barzettes starts with top-of-the-world views and powder, and finishes among pretty woods. The Piste Nationale downhill course is a good fast cruise.
Beginners There are excellent nursery areas at resort level (on the golf course) and at mid-mountain but no special beginner passes.
Snowboarding Despite the resort's mature image, boarding is popular. Avalanche Pro is a specialist shop and school. There are few draglifts.
Cross-country There are around 20km of trails, plus a glacier trail (with limited opening).

Mountain restaurants A separate map on the back of the piste map – not a user-friendly idea – marks 23 huts. The traditional Merbé is recommended again this year, and we like the smart, cool Chetzeron too – all steel, glass, wood and stone. 2014 visitors praise the Cabane des Violettes ('generous helpings, very pleasant staff') and the self-service Cry d'Err ('lovely plat du jour; helpful and friendly staff').
Schools and guides A 2014 reporter who had group and private lessons with the Swiss school made good progress: 'Fantastic instructor.'
Families This doesn't strike us as a natural family resort.

STAYING THERE

Hotels and apartments are plentiful.
Hotels There are some very swanky lodgings. We love two dinky little places – 5-star LeCrans (486 6060), way above the town, with chalet-style suites, and Pas de l'Ours (485 9333) – chic but welcoming, on the edge of town. The 4-star Alpina & Savoy (485 0900) is 'faultless; delightful staff, the best food'. Pool, sauna.
Eating out There is a big variety of places, from French to Lebanese to Thai. Molino is a busy Italian that is 'full of character': 'excellent food, delightful staff'.
Après-ski At close of play, Dutch-run bar/restaurant Zérodix at the Crans lift base is 'the cool place to finish the day', with 'comfy sofas'. After that, Monk'is (also a club) has been recommended, and Amadeus (at the hotel Olympic) is 'nice for a drink'.
Off the slopes There are swimming pools in hotels, two ice rinks, dog sledding, tubing, tobogganing, snowshoeing, 65km of walks, a cinema, casino and model train museum. Sierre and Sion are close.

Davos

*A grey urban sprawl at the centre of a glorious Alpine playground
(for skaters and langlaufers as well as downhillers)*

RATINGS

The mountains

Extent	★★★★
Fast lifts	★★★★
Queues	★★★
Terrain p'ks	★★★★
Snow	★★★★
Expert	★★★★
Intermediate	★★★★★
Beginner	★★
Boarder	★★★★★
X-country	★★★★★
Restaurants	★★★
Schools	★★★
Families	★★

The resort

Charm	★★
Convenience	★★
Scenery	★★★★
Eating out	★★★
Après-ski	★★★
Off-slope	★★★★★

RPI   130

lift pass	£230
ski hire	£120
lessons	£121
food & drink	£210
total	**£681**

➕ Very extensive slopes

➕ Some superb, long, and mostly easy pistes away from the lifts, with trains to bring you back to base

➕ Lots of accessible off-piste terrain, with several marked itineraries

➕ Good cross-country trails

➕ Plenty to do off the slopes

➖ Davos is a huge, busy place with dreary block-style buildings, lacking ski-resort atmosphere

➖ Five separate areas of slopes

➖ Lots of T-bars on outlying mountains

➖ The only piste back to town from the main Parsenn area is a black

One of your editors learned to ski in Davos, so it has a special place in our affections. Many return visits have confirmed the appeal of its slopes, which are both distinctive and extensive, and have revealed its considerable off-piste potential. But the town/city (it could never be called a village) does not get any easier to like. Davos may be the more convenient base for access to most of the mountains it shares with Klosters, but Klosters has the welcoming, intimate feel of a ski resort, and Davos does not.

THE RESORT

Davos is set in a high, broad, flat-bottomed valley, with its lifts and slopes either side. Arguably it was the very first place in the Alps to develop its slopes. The railway up the Parsenn was one of the first built for skiers (in 1931), and the first draglift was built on the Bolgen nursery slopes in 1934. You can reach the resort by train, but the trip from Zürich airport involves two changes. The Davos Express coach transfer service is a recommended alternative.

Davos shares its slopes with the famously royal resort of Klosters,

which has its own chapter. Trips are possible by car or rail to St Moritz (via the Vereina rail tunnel) and Arosa, and by road to Laax and Lenzerheide.

VILLAGE CHARM ★★★★★
City in the mountains
The resort is more like a city than a village, and is plagued by traffic. It started life as a health resort and many of its massive luxury hotels were built as sanatoriums. Sadly, that's just what they look like, and ski resort ambience is notably lacking. It is now well known for its conference and sporting facilities too.

CONVENIENCE ★★★★★
Take the train
The resort has two main centres, Dorf and Platz, about 2km apart. Transport is good, with an 'excellent' bus service around the town as well as the railway linking Dorf and Platz to Klosters and other villages. It's a good idea to arm yourself with timetables. Easiest access to the main Parsenn area is from Dorf, via the funicular railway; Platz is better placed for Jakobshorn, the sports facilities, smarter shopping and the evening action.

SCENERY ★★★★★
Pick your viewpoint
It's an area of grand, wide views across the broad, deep, wooded valleys from one sector of the slopes to another, and to high peaks beyond.

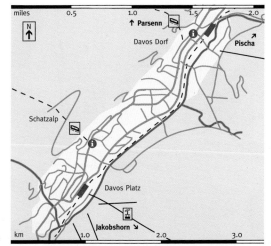

NEWS

2014/15: After 31 years of service the 50-person Jakobshorn cable car from Platz is to be replaced by a new cable car twice the size.

2013/14: A big new hotel opened – the InterContinental – and three long-standing hotels were refurbished: the Steigenberger Belvédère, the Seehof and the Rixos (formerly the Flüela).

THE MOUNTAINS

Most of the pistes are above the treeline – there are few in the woods and most are genuine blacks. Piste classification is questionable; many blue and red runs are of similar pitch. The piste map generally looks clear, but tries to cover too much ground in a small space – at some points it is simply misleading, and distances are unclear. Signposting is generally fine.

EXTENT OF THE SLOPES ★★★★☆
Vast and varied

You could hit a different mountain around Davos nearly every day for a week. The out-of-town areas tend to be much quieter than the ones directly accessible from the resort.

The Parsennbahn funicular from Davos Dorf takes you to mid-mountain, where a choice of a six-pack or a further funicular takes you on up to the major lift junction of Weissfluhjoch, at one end of the **Parsenn**. The only run back to town is a sunny black that can have poor snow (the alternative runs to Klosters are shadier). At the other end of the wide, open Parsenn bowl is Gotschnagrat, reached by cable car from the centre of Klosters. There are exceptionally long intermediate runs down to Klosters and other villages (see feature panel later in chapter).

Across the valley, **Jakobshorn** is reached by cable car (see 'News') or chairlift from Davos Platz; this is popular with snowboarders but good

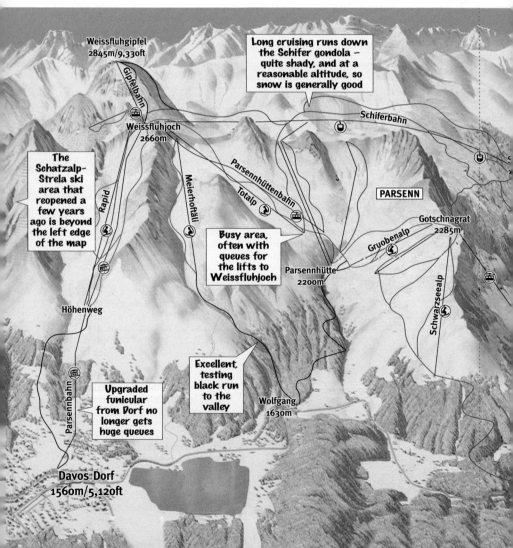

Weissfluhgipfel
2845m/9,330ft

Gipfelbahn

Long cruising runs down the Schifer gondola – quite shady, and at a reasonable altitude, so snow is generally good

Schiferbahn

Weissfluhjoch
2660m

The Schatzalp-Strela ski area that reopened a few years ago is beyond the left edge of the map

Rapid

Meierhoftäli

Parsennhüttenbahn

Totalp

PARSENN

Gotschnagrat
2285m

Gruobenalp

Busy area, often with queues for the lifts to Weissfluhjoch

Parsennhütte
2200m

Schwarzseealp

Höhenweg

Parsennbahn

Upgraded funicular from Dorf no longer gets huge queues

Excellent, testing black run to the valley

Wolfgang
1630m

Davos-Dorf
1560m/5,120ft

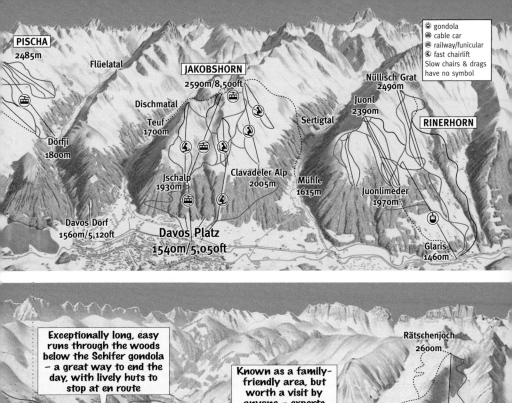
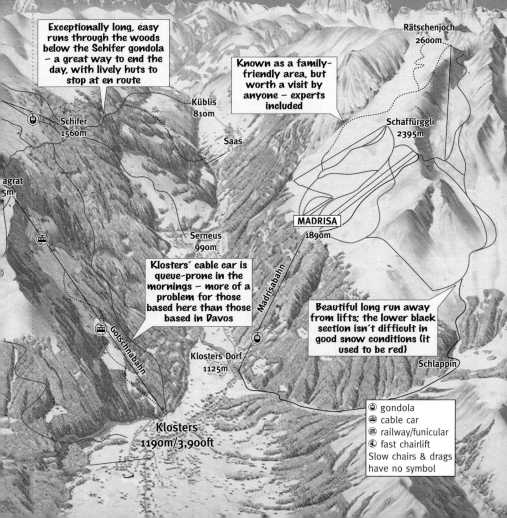

MOMENTUM SKI

Weekend & a la carte
ski holiday specialists

100% Tailor-made

Premier hotels
& apartments

Flexible travel
arrangements

020 7371 9111
WWW.MOMENTUMSKI.COM

KEY FACTS

Resort	1550m
	5,090ft
Slopes	810-2845m
	2,660-9,330ft
Lifts	56
Pistes	320km
	199 miles
Blue	23%
Red	42%
Black	35%
Snowmaking	40%

GETTING THERE

Air Zürich 160km/
100 miles (2hr);
Friedrichshafen
155km/95 miles (2hr)

Rail Stations in Davos
Dorf and Platz

for skiers too. **Rinerhorn** and **Pischa** are reached by bus or (in the case of Rinerhorn) train.

The little **Schatzalp-Strela** area above Platz – which was closed for several years – is open again, but is not covered by the main lift pass.

Beyond the main part of Klosters, a gondola goes up from Klosters Dorf to the sunny, scenic **Madrisa** area.

FAST LIFTS ★★★★
Key ones are fine but ...

The main lifts from the valley are mostly gondolas or cable cars. Higher up, Jakobshorn is very well served for fast chairs and Parsenn reasonably so (hence the 4-star rating). But the upper lifts on Madrisa, Rinerhorn and Pischa are entirely T-bars except for one slow double chair on Madrisa.

QUEUES ★★★
Few problems

Davos has improved its key lifts and generates relatively few complaints. But at peak times and weekends there can still be lengthy queues at the cable car out of Klosters and the Totalp chair on the Parsenn. Crowded pistes have raised concern – in the Parsenn sector around Weissfluhjoch especially. In contrast, the Jakobshorn is said to be quiet.

TERRAIN PARKS ★★★★
Head for Jakobshorn

The focus of the action is the big Jatz Park on Jakobshorn. At 2300m, with snowmaking to be sure, it's open from mid-November to the very end of the season, and is looked after by a small dedicated team. Four lines (including kickers from 4m to 18m, rainbow rail, down rails and a spine feature with wall ride and tyre bonk) provide something for everyone, although it's clear the better features are geared towards higher-end riders. Jakobshorn is also home to a super-pipe – one of Europe's largest; it is floodlit three evenings a week. There's also a small fun park on Rinerhorn (at the Trainer lift) and a kicker at Pischa (next to the Mitteltäli lift). There are snowcross courses on Parsenn and Madrisa.

SNOW RELIABILITY ★★★★
Good, but not the best

Davos is high by Swiss standards. Its mountains go respectably high, too. Not many of the slopes face directly south, but Pischa does suffer from excessive sun. Snow reliability is generally good higher up. Snow-guns cover several of the upper runs on the Parsenn, most on the Jakobshorn, and the home runs from the Parsenn to Davos Dorf and Klosters. Piste grooming is generally good; but the super-long runs to the valley can become a bit neglected.

FOR EXPERTS ★★★★
Plenty to do, given snow

The appeal of this area for experts depends to a considerable degree on the snow conditions. Although there are challenges to be found at altitude, most of the rewarding runs descend through the woods to valley level, and are not reliable for snow. The black pistes include some distinctive, satisfying descents. The Meierhoftäli run to Wolfgang is a favourite – quite steep and narrow. The run from Parsennhütte to Wolfgang is less challenging; it probably owes its black status to one short tricky section.

There are also some off-piste itineraries – runs that are supposedly marked but not patrolled. At one time, these runs were a key attraction for adventurous skiers not wanting to pay for guidance, but over the decade to 2005 no fewer than 10 of them disappeared from the map, including the infamous Gotschnawang run down the top stage of the Klosters cable car and its less fearsome neighbours, Drostobel and Chalbersäss. Many of these abandoned runs have had piste status at some time in the past, and are not difficult to follow if you know what you are doing. Two of the most satisfying itineraries that remain are long ones from the top of Jakobshorn, both with decent restaurants at the end. The start of the run to Mühle is not obvious, which has led more than one reporter into difficulty; once found, the run is reportedly nowhere steeper than a tough red. The run to Teufi is more often closed: it goes first down a steep 200m gully, but thereafter is easier.

There is also excellent 'proper' off-piste terrain, for which guidance is more clearly needed. Reporters have enjoyed heading away from the pistes above Serneus and Küblis. The long descent from Madrisa to St Antönien, north of Küblis, is popular, not least for the views along the way. And there are some short tours to be done. Arosa can be reached with a bit of

LIFT PASSES		
Davos/Klosters		
Prices in francs		
Age	1-day	6-day
under 13	27	133
13-17	48	232
18 plus	68	332
Free Under 6		
Senior If 65+ (women 64+), 10% reduction on passes of 3+ days		
Beginner No deals		
Notes Does not cover Schatzalp; day pass is for Parsenn only		
Alternative passes Individual areas; pedestrian single tickets		

help from a train or taxi, and was linked to Lenzerheide for 2013/14. From Madrisa you can make easy circular tours to Gargellen in Austria.

FOR INTERMEDIATES ★★★★★
A splendid variety of runs

For intermediates this is a great area. There are good cruising runs on all five mountains, so you would never get bored in a week. This variety of different slopes, taken together with the wonderful long runs to the Klosters valley, makes it a compelling area with a unique character.

As well as the epic runs described in the feature panel there is a beautiful away-from-the-lifts run to the valley from the top of Madrisa back to Klosters Dorf via the Schlappin valley (it starts off red and becomes an easy black).

The Jakobshorn has some genuine challenges, notably by the Brämabüel chairlift. Rinerhorn and Pischa have more gentle terrain.

FOR BEGINNERS ★★★★★
Platz is the more convenient

There are no free lifts but each sector offers day or half-day passes. The Bolgen nursery slope beneath the Jakobshorn is adequately spacious and gentle, and a bearable walk from the centre of Platz. Dorf-based beginners face more of a trek out to Bünda though – unless staying at the hotel of the same name. There are easy runs to progress to, spread around all the sectors. The Parsenn sector probably has the edge, with long, easy intermediate runs in the main Parsenn

bowl, as well as in the valleys down from Weissfluhjoch.

FOR BOARDERS ★★★★★
Epic

Davos is a Mecca for keen snowboarders. And Jakobshorn is the favoured mountain for many of them, with its top-notch park and super-pipe. It's also a great area to learn on. Rinerhorn has trees galore and pistes like roller-coaster rides – but be aware that all except the access lifts here and at Pischa are T-bars.

Parsenn has a snowcross and night riding, and is host to international freeride competitions on the face beneath the Weissfluhgipfel, but watch out for the flats on the runs down to the Schifer gondola. And if you have a family in tow, the kids can stay out of trouble in the small terrain park at Rinerhorn.

Synergy Snowsports is a specialist school. There are several cheap hotels geared to boarders, notably the Bolgenhof near the Jakobshorn, the Snowboardhotel Bolgenschanze and the Snowboarder's Palace.

FOR CROSS-COUNTRY ★★★★★
Long, scenic valley trails

Davos is a popular spot for langlauf, and it's not difficult to see why. It has a total of 122km of trails – classic and skating – running along the flat main valley and reaching well up into the side valleys of Sertigtal, Dischmatal and Flüelatal that lead away south-east. There is a cross-country ski centre on the outskirts of the town. Trails are free.

Davos

465

DESTINATION DAVOS KLOSTERS

Davos has multiple big ice rinks, indoor and outdoor →

SCHOOLS

Swiss Davos
t 416 2454

Top Secret
t 413 4043

Pat. Skilehrer Rageth
t 416 3901

Snow & You
t 079 636 7030

Snow Doc Davos
t 078 716 1417

Swissfreeride
t 079 429 2684

Synergy Snowsports
t UK 0141 416 3525

Classes (Swiss prices)
6 4hr-days 375 francs

Private lessons
From 90 francs for 1hr
for 1-2 people

CHILDCARE

Kinderland Pischa
t 079 660 3168
Age from 3

Topsi kindergarten
t 413 4043
Age from 30mnth

Babysitter list
At tourist office

Ski school
From age 4

MOUNTAIN RESTAURANTS ★★★☆☆
Stay high or go low

Most high-altitude restaurants are dreary self-service affairs – but there are good table-service exceptions.

Weissfluhgipfel is a long-standing favourite where we hear the cooking is still 'at the same excellent level'. The prices remain high, too. The Totalp bar is recommended 'for a marginally cheaper meal'. Gotschnagrat is 'friendly, with decent mountain fare'. Below it in the main Parsenn bowl, the Gruobenalp is a reader favourite offering 'efficient table service' and a 'good atmosphere' as well as good food. Readers enjoy the Höhenweg at the Parsennbahn mid-station. A 2013 reporter says the Berghaus Schifer is 'worthy of a mention for the staff, who are particularly friendly'. There are several rustic 'schwendis' in the woods on the way down to the Klosters valley: the Serneuser warmed us on a cold day in January 2013. Some stay open until after sunset – and sell wax torches to light your way home.

On Jakobshorn the Jatzhütte is unusual, with changing decor such as mock palm trees, parrots and pirates – and serves 'delicious soups'. Châlet Güggel is also tipped: 'excellent', 'rustic charm and efficient service'.

On Pischa, the Mäderbeiz at Flüelamäder is recommended. And on Rinerhorn, try the Hubelhütte.

There are two picnic rooms: at the Weissfluhjoch on Parsenn and at the Jatzmeder on Rinerhorn.

SCHOOLS AND GUIDES ★★★☆☆
Decent choice

There are several options but we lack recent reports. Top Secret limits groups to a maximum of eight. Guiding outfit Swissfreeride specializes in all-inclusive off-piste weeks. Synergy Snowsports provides enthusiastic guiding and instruction by Brits. Snow Doc Davos opened a couple of years ago, mainly offering guiding.

FOR FAMILIES ★★☆☆☆
Not ideal

There are plenty of amusements, but Davos is a rather spread-out place in which to handle a family. The kids' ski schools operate a themed slope at Bolgen. The Top Secret school runs the Topsi ski kindergarten. Kinderland Pischa offers childcare, and there is a snow garden on Rinerhorn. But Madrisa Land at Klosters is a more comprehensive facility.

STAYING THERE

Although most beds are in apartments, hotels dominate the UK market.

Hotels A dozen 4-stars and about 30 3-stars form the core. The tourist office runs a central booking service.

★★★★Meierhof (417 1414) In Dorf, near Parsenn funicular. 'Spacious rooms; good pool and steam room.'

★★★★Sheraton Waldhuus (417 9333) Convenient for langlaufers. Quiet, modern, tasteful. 'Spacious rooms; great pool and spa facilities.'

THE PARSENN'S SUPER-RUNS

The runs from Weissfluhjoch that head north, on the back of the mountain, make this area special for many visitors. The pistes that go down to Schifer and then on to Küblis and Serneus, and the one that curls around to Klosters, are a fabulous way to end the day, given good conditions.

The run to Saas used to be a red piste but is now marked as an ungroomed and unpatrolled route. The other runs are classified red. They are not steep, but the latter parts can be challenging because of the snow conditions – they get heavily skied, they are not reliably groomed, and by the end you are at low altitudes. Signposting is not always good, either. What marks these runs out is their sheer length (10-12km) and the resulting sensation of travel – plus a choice of huts in the woods at Schifer and lower down on the way to Klosters. You can descend the 1100m vertical to Schifer and take the gondola back up. Once past there, you're committed to finishing the descent.

If you are based in Davos, the return journey is by train (included in the lift pass).

ALAN SHEPHERD

↑ Jakobshorn is the place for park action

DESTINATION DAVOS KLOSTERS

ACTIVITIES

Indoor Swimming pools, solarium, climbing wall, tennis, squash, badminton, wellness centre, sauna, massage, ice rink, horse-riding school, golf driving range, cinema, casino, galleries, museums, libraries

Outdoor Over 150km of cleared paths, ice climbing, ice rinks, curling, snowshoeing, tobogganing, hang-gliding, paragliding

UK PACKAGES

Alpine Answers, Alpine Weekends, Carrier, Erna Low, Headwater, Inghams, Luxury Chalet Collection, Momentum, Neilson, Oxford Ski Co, PowderBeds, Ski Bespoke, Ski Club Freshtracks, Ski Safari, Ski Weekend, STC Switzerland Travel Centre, White Roc

Phone numbers
From elsewhere in Switzerland add the prefix 081; from abroad use the prefix +41 81

TOURIST OFFICE

www.davos.ch

****Waldhotel** (415 1515) In Platz. 'Looked after really well; beautiful pool,' says a recent visitor.
***Davoserhof** (417 6777) Our favourite. Small, old, beautifully furnished, excellent food; in Platz.
Alte Post (417 6777) Traditional place in central Platz.
Ochsen (417 6777) Near the train station in Platz.
Fiftyone Designer hotel. Room only; internet bookings only.

EATING OUT ★★★☆☆
Wide choice, mostly in hotels
In a town this size, you need to know where to go. For a start, get the tourist office's pocket guidebook. The more ambitious restaurants are mostly in hotels. The hotel Seehof has an executive chef who had a Michelin star when at the Walserhof Klosters. There are two good Chinese places in hotels: the Zauberberg in the Europe and the Golden Dragon in the Grischa. The Carretta in Platz is an Italian offering a wide-ranging menu, and the small and cosy Gentiana is a bistro whose speciality is fondue. Höhenweg (at the mid-station of the Parsenn funicular) is open when there is night skiing or tobogganing (Wednesday and Friday last season), but you pay to ride the funicular.

APRES-SKI ★★★☆☆
Generally quiet
At teatime, mega-calories are consumed at the Weber and Schneider's. The Scala (hotel Europe) has a popular outside terrace. Nightlife is generally quiet. The rustic little

Chämi bar is lively and popular with locals. The smart Ex Bar attracts a mixed age group. Nightclubs tend to be sophisticated, expensive and, during the week, lacking atmosphere. The pick are Cabanna, Cava Davos and Rotliechtli. Bolgenschanze and Bolgen-Plaza attract lots of boarders. There's a casino.

OFF THE SLOPES ★★★★★
Great, apart from the buildings
Looks aside, Davos has lots to offer the non-skier. The towny resort has shops and other diversions, and transport along the valley and up on to the slopes is good – though the best of the mountain restaurants are well out of range.

The sports facilities are excellent. Europe's biggest natural ice rink is supplemented by indoor and outdoor artificial rinks. Spectator events include speed skating as well as ice hockey. The Eau-là-là leisure centre incorporates pools and wellness facilities. There's a Bowling-Bar-Bistro in Platz, and a climbing wall in the Färbi sports hall.

There are lots of walks on the slopes, around the lake and along the valleys (special map available). There's tobogganing on Rinerhorn and Schatzalp (both floodlit) and from the mid-station of the cable car back to Klosters, but the best in the area is the 8.5km run from Madrisa to Saas.

A reporter recommends the local museums and galleries, and there are day trips by train to St Moritz, Scuol (for the spa) and Preda-Bergün for the 6km toboggan run.

Davos

467

Build your own shortlist: www.wheretoskiandsnowboard.com

Engelberg

A high, distinctive mountain with some classic off-piste runs, above a solid valley town dominated by an ancient monastery

TOP 10 RATINGS

Extent	★★
Fast lifts	★★★
Queues	★★
Snow	★★★
Expert	★★★★
Intermediate	★★★
Beginner	★★
Charm	★★
Convenience	★
Scenery	★★★★

RPI   110

lift pass	£190
ski hire	£95
lessons	£100
food & drink	£180
total	**£565**

NEWS

2014/15: The Rotair rotating cable car to Klein Titlis is due to be replaced by one that gives better views. Renovation work is due to be completed on the ski-in/ski-out Trübsee hotel.

2013/14: The first stage of a development of new apartments (Titlis Resort) opened near the foot of the gondola. It is due to be completed for 2014/15.

+ Reliable snow on high, shady slopes

+ Some classic off-piste runs

+ Big vertical of almost 2000m

– Fragmented slopes, some poor links

– Ski-bus needed from most lodgings

– Limited pistes, mostly above trees

Quick access from Zürich airport and abundant lodgings make Engelberg great for short breaks (for which we find the towny nature of the resort is worth putting up with). And Titlis is a compelling mountain, particularly for experts.

THE RESORT

The resort was named after the 12th-century Benedictine monastery (Engelberg means the mountain of the angel) that dominates the town as you look down from the lifts.

Village charm The place is more of a town than a village. Its grand Victorian hotels have been joined by chalet-style buildings, concrete blocks and new apartment buildings right next to the gondola. There is one traffic-free cobbled street in the old part.

Convenience It's a free shuttle-bus, sometimes over-busy, or longish walks to the lifts from most hotels.

Scenery There's lots of visual drama from the high, glacial slopes.

THE MOUNTAINS

The mainly treeless, shady slopes of Titlis rise almost 2000m above the town. The separate slopes of Brunni are sunnier and gently wooded. The slopes are numbered on the mountain and, after a blip in 2012/13, are again numbered on the piste map.

Slopes The pistes in the main area are

limited and fragmented by the glaciers and rugged terrain. There are two main sectors: Titlis-Stand and Jochpass. A gondola (plus an old funicular, which rarely runs) goes up to Gerschnialp, from where a gondola and cable car both go to Trübsee. From there two successive cable cars go up to Stand and then Klein Titlis – the latter rotating 360° on the way. From Trübsee, you can also head for Jochpass via a two-way chairlift to Alpstübli. At Jochpass the top is served by a fast six-pack. The much smaller Brunni area is served by a cable car on the other side of town.

Fast lifts High-capacity cable cars and gondolas provide the main access.

Queues Big queues form for the gondola from town at weekends and in peak season (half-hour waits are reported; quicker to use the funicular if it's running, says a regular visitor). The old Engstlenalp double chair below Jochpass can have queues too. Pistes can also get busy.

Terrain parks The park is at Jochpass and is smaller than it used to be.

Snow reliability The high, north-facing

468

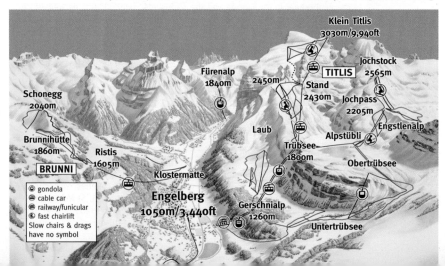

Klein Titlis
3030m/9,940ft

Jochstock
2565m

Fürenalp
1840m

2450m

TITLIS

Stand
2430m

Jochpass
2205m

Schonegg
2040m

Laub

Engstlenalp

Brunnihütte
1860m

Ristis
1605m

Trübsee
1800m

Alpstübli

Obertrübsee

BRUNNI

Klostermatte

Engelberg
1050m/3,440ft

Gerschnialp
1260m

Untertrübsee

⊙ gondola
🚡 cable car
🚃 railway/funicular
🚠 fast chairlift
Slow chairs & drags
have no symbol

KEY FACTS

Resort	1050m
	3,440ft
Slopes	1050-3030m
	3,440-9,940ft
Lifts	25
Pistes	82km
	51 miles
Blue	33%
Red	57%
Black	10%
Snowmaking	70%

UK PACKAGES

Alpine Answers, Chalet Espen, Flexiski, Inntravel, Momentum, Mountain Beds, PowderBeds, Ski Club Freshtracks, Ski Monterosa, Ski Safari, Ski Weekend, Skitracer, Snow-wise, STC, White Roc

Phone numbers
From elsewhere in Switzerland add the prefix 041; from abroad use the prefix +41 41

TOURIST OFFICE

www.engelberg.ch

MOMENTUM SKI

Weekend & a la carte ski holiday specialists

100% Tailor-made

Premier hotels & apartments

The No.1 Specialist in Engelberg

020 7371 9111
WWW.MOMENTUMSKI.COM

slopes of Titlis and Jochpass keep their snow well and have a long season. Piste grooming is 'very good'.

Experts There is lots of superb off-piste. The classic Laub run is 1000m vertical down a hugely wide, consistently steep face with great views of town. We enjoyed even more the less popular 2000m vertical Galtiberg run from the top, which ends among streams and trees, with a bus back to town – a guide is essential. The off-piste from the top of the Jochpass area to Engstlenalp has been recommended and the terrain at the top of Titlis looks great but is not without danger. There are few black pistes; the itinerary from Titlis to Stand is steep and often mogulled.

Intermediates Most runs are steep reds, and there are few easy cruises. The Jochpass area is often quieter than Titlis, with enjoyable blue and red runs, including lovely long ones down to the valley station (especially nice in the mornings when they are quiet).

Beginners There's a good isolated beginner area at Gerschnialp, smaller areas at Trübsee and Untertrübsee. You have to use lifts to and from these slopes (limited passes are available); and there are few longer easy runs to progress to – all far from ideal. Some beginners go to Brunni.

Snowboarding The beginner area is served by draglifts, so it's not ideal. But there is excellent freeriding if you hire a guide. Beware of the flat start to the runs down from Jochpass.

Cross-country One reporter's friend was 'very impressed' with the 35km trails and loops (some at altitude).

Mountain restaurants An impressive choice. Our favourite, and that of reporters, is Skihütte Stand, a woody table-service place beside the cable

car to Titlis: 'super atmosphere', 'decent coffee', 'good main courses'. Jochpass serves 'good alpen macaroni'. Try Untertrübsee for rösti with bacon and eggs. The Trübsee hotel 'is a good place to meet non-skiers'.

There are picnic rooms at Stand and Toporama at Titlis.

Schools and guides There is a choice of four schools. The guide office offers heli-skiing and ski touring.

Families Globi's Winterland at Brunni is best for families, with play areas and lifts. The Swiss ski school takes kids from age three, the kindergarten from two. Some hotels offer childcare; the tourist office has details of babysitters.

STAYING THERE

Hotels The 3-star Edelweiss (639 7878) is 'excellent for families with young children' and the 3-star Schweizerhof (637 1105) is centrally located. The Ski Lodge (637 3500) is popular – but avoid rooms above the bar. The Banlialp (639 7373) is 'basic, comfortable and serves good food', the Alpenclub (637 1243) is a central guest house and the Ramada Regina (639 5858) is 'gorgeously furnished and the spa is quite something'.

Eating out There is a huge variety of restaurants – more than 50 – from traditional Swiss to Tex-Mex (at the Yucatan) and Chinese (Moonrise). We had splendid chicken/veal dishes at the hotel Central; large portions, very well presented. The Ski Lodge serves gourmet duck and salmon. The Schweizer Haus 'is worth the 15-minute stroll from town'.

Après-ski The liveliest venue is the Chalet (bottom of the gondola) which has a popular happy hour. A 2013 visitor found the previously lively Yucatan (main square) 'quiet, even at happy hour'. The Ski Lodge bar is 'pleasant'. For dancing, try the Eden or the Spindle nightclub.

Off the slopes The 12th-century monastery and its cheese-making factory and shop are worth a visit. It's worth going up the cable cars for the views, the suspension bridge and the ice grotto. There are many walking and snowshoeing trails, tubing, sledging and a sports centre. Up the valley, a gondola goes up to Fürenalp for walking, tobogganing, snowshoeing. Lucerne is a possible train trip.

Engelberg

469

Build your own shortlist: www.wheretoskiandsnowboard.com

GRINDELWALD TOURIST OFFICE

Grindelwald

Traditional mountain village set beneath the towering Eiger and with an old cog railway still the main way up to the slopes

470

RATINGS

The mountains

Extent	★★★
Fast lifts	★★★★
Queues	★★
Terrain p'ks	★★★
Snow	★★
Expert	★★
Intermediate	★★★★
Beginner	★★★
Boarder	★★★
X-country	★★
Restaurants	★★★
Schools	★★★
Families	★★

The resort

Charm	★★★★
Convenience	★★
Scenery	★★★★★
Eating out	★★★
Après-ski	★★★
Off-slope	★★★★

RPI 125

lift pass	£220
ski hire	£110
lessons	£125
food & drink	£185
total	**£640**

NEWS

2014/15: Nothing for this season but there's a plan for fast new gondolas from Grund to Männlichen (an eight-seater) and to Eigergletscher (a 28-seater). They are currently due to be ready for the 2016/17 season.

2013/14: The Snowpark on First was redesigned to suit all levels of rider.

+ Dramatically set, beneath the north face of the Eiger

+ Lots of long intermediate runs

+ Pleasant old village with long mountaineering history

+ Fair amount to do off the slopes, including splendid walks

− Slow, queue-prone trains and gondola to access the main slopes

− Few challenging pistes for experts

− A long trek to visit Mürren

− Natural snow-cover unreliable (but substantial snowmaking now)

− Village gets little midwinter sun

For stunning views from the resort and the slopes, there are few places to rival Grindelwald. The village is nowhere near as special as Mürren or Wengen, just over the hill, but it does provide direct access to Grindelwald's own First slopes.

The main access lifts are appalling, taking half an hour to ride even if you don't have to queue (for the gondola) or wait (for the train). Grindelwald regulars accept all this as part of the scene – though they won't have to when the planned new gondolas are in place (see 'News').

THE RESORT

Grindelwald is a long village set along a road that faces the towering north wall of the Eiger, which means that the resort gets very little sun in January. Its main slopes are shared with Wengen; and there is a separate area of sunny slopes on First. Getting to the tougher, higher slopes of Mürren on snow and lifts is a lengthy business (around three hours to the top). Trips to other resorts are not very easy.

VILLAGE CHARM ★★★★
Not in the Wengen league
The central buildings are mainly in traditional chalet style, in keeping with its long mountaineering history. And the station and cog railway add to the olde-worlde charm. The village can feel very jolly at times (eg during the snow-carving festival in January, when huge sculptures are created). Although the road through goes nowhere, traffic on it can be intrusive.

CONVENIENCE ★★
Not a strong point
The most convenient places to stay are in the centre near the main station or at Grund, departure point of the main access lifts and arrival point of the main home piste, about 80m vertical lower. If you stay in the centre, you can also take the train up, but you need to catch it back up from Grund on the way home too. Staying near the centre means the gondola up to the First area is a walkable distance. At the foot of First are nursery slopes, ski school and kindergarten. Buses link the lift stations – 'Astoundingly punctual even in worst weather,' says a 2014 visitor.

SCENERY ★★★★★
Unrivalled
The mountains in these parts are legendary among climbers – from all over the slopes there are superb views, not only of the Eiger but also of the Wetterhorn and other peaks.

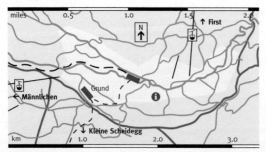

THE MOUNTAINS

The major area of slopes is shared with Wengen and offers a mix of a few wooded runs and much more extensive open slopes. The smaller First area is mainly open. Several areas are designated as wildlife reserves, where you may well spot chamois. Piste marking and the piste map are poor; the Männlichen slopes, in particular, can be confusing.

KEY FACTS

Resort	1035m
	3,400ft
Jungfrau region	
Slopes	945-2970m
	3,100-9,740ft
Lifts	45
Pistes	213km
	132 miles
Blue	33%
Red	49%
Black	18%
Snowmaking	50%

First-Männlichen-
Kleine Scheidegg

Slopes	945-2500m
	3,100-8,200ft
Lifts	28
Pistes	170km
	106 miles

GETTING THERE

Air Bern 70km/
45 miles (1hr); Zürich
155km/95 miles (2hr);
Basel 175km/
110 miles (2hr)

Rail Station in resort

EXTENT OF THE SLOPES ★★★★★
Broad and mainly gentle
The area shared with Wengen spreads broadly beneath the Eiger. From Grund, near the western end of town, you can get to **Männlichen** by an appallingly slow two-stage gondola, or to **Kleine Scheidegg** by an equally slow cog railway (with some trains starting in the centre of town). The slopes of the separate south-facing **First** area are reached by a long, slow gondola starting a walk or short bus ride east of the centre.

FAST LIFTS ★★★★★
Better high up
Getting up into the main area from the village is seriously slow (the planned new gondolas will speed things up but not till 2016/17 at the earliest – see 'News'). Fast new chairlifts have improved the area higher up – most recently, the Eigergletscher and Wixi six-packs.

QUEUES ★★★★★
Can be dreadful at the bottom
These days visitors generally find few problems once they are on the mountain, but the train and the Männlichen gondola at Grund can be crowded at peak periods. Queues for the gondola can be very bad in high season, especially on Saturdays – this is the obvious entry point for residents of Bern attracted by the special family pass deals on Saturdays. And the gondola goes very slowly, too.

TERRAIN PARKS ★★★★★
First has it all
The White Elements Snowpark on First next to the Bärgelegg lift was redesigned this year and has 650m of rails, boxes, kickers and jumps, with lines for different abilities. There is also a newish snowcross near the top of the Schilt lift – 'Best fun all week,' says a 2014 visitor.

SNOW RELIABILITY ★★★★★
Improved snowmaking helps
Grindelwald's low altitude means that natural snow is often in short supply or in poor condition. First is a bit higher than the Männlichen area, and may have better snow in midwinter; but it is sunny, and less snow-sure as spring approaches. Snowmaking has been increased recently and the resort claims that some 60% of its slopes are now covered. The last couple of times we have visited were not in bumper snow periods, but most slopes were in good condition.

FOR EXPERTS ★★★★★
Few on-piste challenges
The area is quite limited for experts, but there is some fine off-piste if the snow is good. Heli-trips are organized. We and readers have enjoyed the splendid Bort Direct black run on First. This turns into a downhill route between Bort and town and is quite tough, especially when the snow has suffered from the sun.

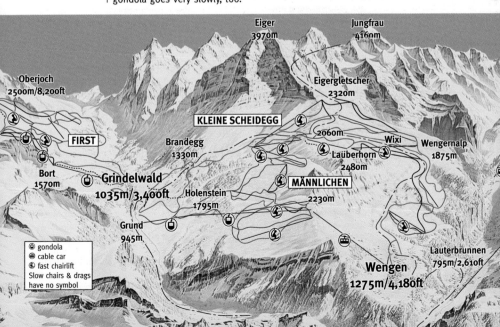

gondola
cable car
fast chairlift
Slow chairs & drags
have no symbol

A classic view of the sheer north face of the Eiger at sunset. Kleine Scheidegg is in the shade at the centre right of the photo →

JUNGFRAU REGION MARKETING AG

LIFT PASSES

Jungfrau

Prices in francs

Age	1-day	6-day
under 16	32	162
16 to 19	50	258
20 to 61	63	323
62 plus	57	291

Free Under 6 (if with parent)

Beginner Points card

Notes Covers trains between villages and Grindelwald ski-bus; day pass is First-Kleine Scheidegg-Männlichen area only; 5-day plus pass allows 50% reduction in Meiringen

Alternative passes Grindelwald and Wengen only; Mürren only; non-skier pass

SCHOOLS

Swiss
t 854 1280

Buri Sport
t 853 3353

Swiss Kleine Scheidegg
t 079 179 9090

Felix Ski Paradies
t 853 1288

Privat-ski.ch
t 079 555 6699

Classes (Swiss prices)
3 4hr-days 294 francs

Private lessons
From 85 francs for 1hr for 1 or 2 people

CHILDCARE

Snowli Club Sunshine
t 854 1280
From 6mnth

Snowli Club Bodmi
t 854 1280
From age 3

Felix Ski Paradies
t 853 1288
From age 3

Ski schools
From age 3 or 4

SWITZERLAND

472

Resort news and key links: www.wheretoskiandsnowboard.com

FOR INTERMEDIATES ★★★★
Ideal intermediate terrain
In good snow, First makes a splendid intermediate playground, though the general lack of trees makes the area less friendly than the larger Kleine Scheidegg-Männlichen area. Nearly all the runs from Kleine Scheidegg are long blues or gentle reds – great cruising terrain. On the Männlichen there's a choice of gentle but not very varied runs down to the mid-station of the gondola – and in good snow, down to the bottom. For tougher pistes, head for the top of the Lauberhorn lift and the runs to Kleine Scheidegg, or to Wixi (following the World Cup downhill course). The north-facing run from Eigergletscher served by the Eigernordwand six-pack often has the best snow late in the season.

FOR BEGINNERS ★★★
Depends where you go
The Bodmi nursery slope at the bottom of First is scenic but not particularly convenient. Snow quality can also suffer from the sun and the low altitude, and fast skiers and tobogganers racing through are off-putting. Kleine Scheidegg has a better, higher beginner area and splendid long runs to progress to, served by the railway. There are no free lifts, but a points card is available.

FOR BOARDERS ★★★
Best for intermediates
Intermediates will enjoy the area most, while experts will hanker for Mürren's steep, off-piste slopes. First is the main boarders' mountain and has the terrain park and snowcross, plus open freeride terrain near the top. There are still a few draglifts but most are avoidable.

FOR CROSS-COUNTRY ★★
OK but shady
There are around 10km of prepared classic trails and another 10km of skating tracks. Almost all are on the valley floor, so it's shady in midwinter and may have poor snow later on.

MOUNTAIN RESTAURANTS ★★★
Wide choice
There are lots, most clearly marked on the piste map. Read the Wengen chapter for additional options. Brandegg, on the railway, is regularly recommended (especially for its apple fritters and doughnuts). Other reader tips include: the Genepi on First ('tasty kebabs') and Berghaus Aspen just above Grund. On First we enjoyed Bort (as did a 2014 visitor), where the old building houses a restaurant built in contemporary style. A reader loved the tiny Alpweg not just for the food but for the welcoming, local atmosphere.
There is a picnic room at the middle-station Schreckfeld on First.

SCHOOLS AND GUIDES ★★★
Good reports
A regular visitor recommends the 'friendly, patient and knowledgeable Paul Ashton' at the Swiss School and says, 'I've always had good experiences with this school and its various instructors at all levels.' The Privat school offers off-piste guiding.

FOR FAMILIES ★★
Lacks convenience
It's not a convenient place for families because of its spread-out nature. Snowli Children's Club based at Bodmi (First) takes kids from three years old and operates a bus from the village. Snowli Club Sunshine is a nursery and play area at the top of Männlichen.

ACTIVITIES

Indoor Sports centre (sauna, steam, fitness), ice rink, curling, rope park, museum

Outdoor 100km of cleared paths, ice climbing, tobogganing, snowshoeing, 'First flyer' zip rider, paragliding

UK PACKAGES

Alpine Answers, Crystal, Crystal Finest, Elegant Resorts, Erna Low, Inghams, Momentum, Mountain Beds, Neilson, Powder Byrne, PowderBeds, Ski Weekend, Skitracer, STC, Switzerland Travel Centre, Thomson, White Roc

Phone numbers
From elsewhere in Switzerland add 033; from abroad use the prefix +41 33

TOURIST OFFICE

www.grindelwald.com

STAYING THERE

Hotels There's a 5-star, eight 4-stars and plenty of more modest places.
*****Grand Regina (854 8600) Big and imposing; right next to the station. Pool and spa.
****Belvedere (888 9999) Over 100 years old, comfortable, family-run, friendly, close to the station. Pool, steam, sauna, hot tub.
****Eiger (854 3131) 'Spacious rooms, superb service, great wellness area.'
****Schweizerhof (854 5858) Close to the station. Pool.
****Sunstar (854 7777) Near First gondola. Comfortable rooms, big wellness complex, conference facilities.
***Derby (854 5461) Modern; next to station.
***Gletschergarten (853 1721) Out past First gondola. Friendly, good English spoken, four-course meals.
***Hirschen (854 8484) Family-run; by nursery slopes. Good food.
***Wetterhorn (853 1218) Cosy, simple chalet way beyond the village, with great views of the glacier.
Apartments The Eiger hotel has apartments.
At altitude Berghaus Bort (853 1762), at the First gondola mid-station, has proper rooms and dormitories.

EATING OUT ★★★★★
Hotel-based
There's a wide choice of good hotel restaurants such as the Hirschen, Challistübli in the Kreuz & Post, Schmitte in the Schweizerhof, and the Alte Post. Hotel Spinne has the candlelit Rôtisserie, and Onkel Tom's Hütte is an Italian. A reporter recommends the Steinbock ('good food, reasonable prices, pizza cooked in wood oven, busiest place in town').

APRES-SKI ★★★★★
Getting livelier
Tipirama – a wigwam at Kleine Scheidegg, sometimes with DJs and live bands – is a fun place immediately after skiing 'if not too cold'; you can catch the train down. There are various (mainly open air) bars to stop in on the way down to Grund. The liveliest are the Rancher (on run 22), attracting a young crowd, Holzerbar (on run 21) and the Aspen hotel (just below). In town, there's the terrace of the C&M Café und Mehr is good for coffee and cake. Later on, there's live music in several bars and hotels, such as the Challibar (hotel Kreuz & Post), but it isn't a place for bopping until dawn. The Espresso bar in the Spinne hotel seems to be the liveliest and the Gepsi Bar in the Eiger hotel is a favourite of a regular visitor. The Mescalero (in the Spinne) and Plaza (in the Sunstar) are popular clubs.

OFF THE SLOPES ★★★★★
Plenty to do, easy to get around
There are many cleared paths with magnificent views and a special (but pricey) pedestrian lift pass. Many of the mountain huts are accessible to pedestrians. A trip to Jungfraujoch is spectacular (see the feature panel), and train trips are easy to Interlaken and Bern. Tobogganing is big here; the 69km of runs include what is claimed to be Switzerland's longest (15km) but it starts a 2hr30 walk from the top of the First gondola. First also has the First Flyer – a zip-wire affair – free if you have a ski pass. There's ice hockey and curling to watch, an indoor rope park and an excellent sports centre with pool. Scenic flights around the spectacular peaks from Männlichen are popular.

Grindelwald

Build your own shortlist: www.wheretoskiandsnowboard.com

THE JOURNEY TO THE TOP OF EUROPE

From Kleine Scheidegg you can take a train through a tunnel in the Eiger to the highest railway station in Europe – Jungfraujoch at 3450m. You stop twice on the way up to look out at magnificent views from galleries carved into the sheer north face of the Eiger. At the top is a big restaurant complex, an 'ice palace' carved out of the glacier and fabulous views of the Aletsch glacier (a UNESCO World Heritage Site). But it gets crowded with organized groups and feels rather touristy. The cost in 2013/14 was 58 francs with a Jungfrau lift pass for three days or more.

JUNGFRAU REGION MARKETING AG

KLOSTERS TOURIST OFFICE

Klosters

Ski the extensive slopes of Davos from a traditional village base – with Davos traffic happily banished to a bypass some years ago

TOP 10 RATINGS

Extent	★★★★
Fast lifts	★★
Queues	★★
Snow	★★★★
Expert	★★★★
Intermediate	★★★★★
Beginner	★★★
Charm	★★★★
Convenience	★★
Scenery	★★★★

RPI   130

lift pass	£230
ski hire	£100
lessons	£130
food & drink	£210
total	**£670**

NEWS

2013/14: The lovely old Wynegg hotel reopened after refurbishment by new young owners. The Piz Buin has also been refurbished.

474

+ Extensive slopes shared with Davos
+ Some lovely long intermediate runs
+ Lots of accessible off-piste terrain
+ Some cute mountain restaurants
+ Pleasant traditional village bypassed by the valley traffic

− The slopes are spread over six widely separated areas
− Preponderance of T-bars is a problem for some visitors
− Queue-prone cable car
− May be too quiet for some visitors

In a word association game, 'Klosters' might trigger 'Prince of Wales'. The resort has even named its queue-prone cable car after him. Don't be put off: Klosters is not particularly exclusive, and makes an attractive alternative to towny Davos, with which it shares its slopes.

THE RESORT

Klosters is a sizeable village with a relaxed, affluent Alpine atmosphere.
Village charm Klosters Platz is the main focus – a collection of upmarket, traditional-style hotels around the railway station. Traffic for Davos and the Vereina rail tunnel traffic takes a bypass – an improvement still much appreciated by old hands like us.
Convenience The cable car up the wooded slopes of Gotschna starts in the heart of Platz. The village spreads along the valley road, fading into the countryside; then you come to the even quieter village of Klosters Dorf, and the gondola to Madrisa. Train and bus services are good (and free).
Scenery The contrast between steeply wooded valleys and high, craggy peaks is impressive.

THE MOUNTAINS

Most of the runs are on open slopes above steeper woodland.
Slopes A cable car from the railway station in Platz takes you to the Gotschnagrat end of the Parsenn area shared with Davos. These slopes are dealt with in the Davos chapter. A gondola from Dorf takes you up to the scenic Madrisa area, which we deal with here. There's also a little slope at Selfranga (floodlit some evenings), a suburb of Platz. Be aware that Madrisa closes in spring a bit earlier than the area as a whole.
Fast lifts Apart from the gondola, it's T-bars and one slow chair on Madrisa.
Queues Queues for the Gotschna cable car can be a problem at weekends and peak times, but visitors report that they found no queues elsewhere.

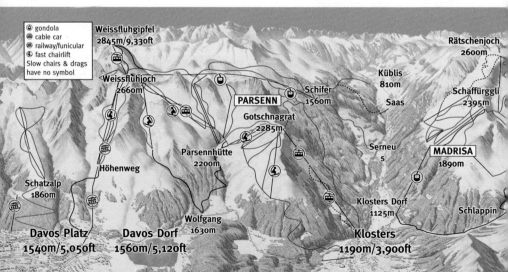

Like all the other mountains around Davos and Klosters, Madrisa is high enough to be mainly above the trees →
MICHAEL MARLAIS

KEY FACTS

Resort	1190m
	3,900ft
Slopes	810-2845m
	2,660-9,330ft
Lifts	56
Pistes	320km
	199 miles
Blue	23%
Red	42%
Black	35%
Snowmaking	40%

UK PACKAGES

Alpine Answers, Carrier, Elysian Collection, Flexiski, Inghams, Kaluma, Luxury Chalet Collection, Momentum, Neilson, Oxford Ski Co, PowderBeds, Powder Byrne, PT Ski, Ski Bespoke, Ski Expectations, Ski Independence, Ski Safari, Skitracer, Ski Weekend, Snow Finders, Snow-wise, STC, Switzerland Travel Centre, Supertravel, White Roc

Phone numbers
From elsewhere in Switzerland add 081; from abroad use the prefix +41 81

TOURIST OFFICE

www.klosters.ch

Terrain parks Madrisa has a snowcross course.
Snow reliability It's usually good higher up. A 2013 reporter thought the grooming on the Parsenn was better than that on Madrisa.
Experts The lift-served off-piste possibilities are the main appeal, on Madrisa as elsewhere in the region – and on 'family-friendly' Madrisa it doesn't get skied out so quickly.
Intermediates Madrisa is not huge, but it is all excellent intermediate terrain. The black run to the valley is not difficult unless conditions make it so.
Beginners There is a slope between Dorf and Platz, plus Selfranga; but Madrisa's higher slopes are more appealing. There are no special lift-pass deals.
Snowboarding Local slopes are good, but most boarders stay in Davos.
Cross-country There are 46km of free trails – classic and skating – and lots more up at Davos. The Swiss ski school offers lessons.
Mountain restaurants For the Parsenn/ Gotschna sector, read the Davos chapter. On Madrisa, the woody Erika at Schlappin offers 'excellent atmosphere and food'.
Schools and guides Swiss and Saas are well regarded: 'Helpful, perceptive and encouraging,' says a recent visitor of Saas. Adventure Skiing has been praised for private guiding: 'Knew the area well and was safety conscious.'
Families Madrisa Land adventure park has lots to offer children, and access is free to kids under six years old. The kindergarten there takes children from birth to six years. There is also an indoor playroom. The ski schools offer classes to children from age four.

STAYING THERE

Hotels For most people, central Platz is the best location. There's the smart Chesa Grischuna (422 2222), but the readers' favourite is the 4-star Alpina (410 2424) – recommended for 'good food and location', although one report speaks of 'arrogant' service in the restaurant. Other possibilities are the traditional British favourite, the Wynegg (422 1340) – refurbished under new management – the 3-star Rustico (410 2288) and the 4-star Silvretta Park Hotel (423 3435). For the 2014/15 season the 4-star Piz Buin has been completely refurbished – with some of the upper rooms done out in 'modern Alpine chic' style.
Apartments Apartments are available through local agencies.
Eating out Good restaurants abound, but there are few cheap and cheerful places. Top of the range is the Walserhof. Other possibilities are the restaurants of the hotels Casanna (at Platz) and Chesa Grischuna. Al Berto and Fellini are pizzerias.
Après-ski Gaudy's umbrella bar at the foot of the slopes is the focal point at the end of the day. In the village, the Chesa Grischuna has a pianist. Bär's at Piz Buin is popular all day long. The Casa Antica is a small disco.
Off the slopes Klosters is an attractive base for walking (there's a special map available) and cross-country skiing. Tobogganing is popular – there is an exceptional 8.5km run from Madrisa to Saas. There is an ice rink, and some hotel pools are open to the public. A gramophone and radio museum opened in 2012. Read the Davos chapter for ideas for train outings.

Build your own shortlist: www.wheretoskiandsnowboard.com

SWISS-IMAGE / MOUNTAIN MARKETING AG

Laax

Contrasting villages beneath high, wide, sunny slopes shared by well-heeled families and trendy young freestylers

TOP 10 RATINGS

Extent	★★★★
Fast lifts	★★★★★
Queues	★★★★
Snow	★★★
Expert	★★★
Intermediate	★★★★★
Beginner	★★★★
Charm	★★★
Convenience	★★★
Scenery	★★★

RPI   130

lift pass	£240
ski hire	£100
lessons	£130
food & drink	£190
total	**£660**

NEWS

2014/15: The super-pipe will be extended to the full 200m Olympic length.

➕ Extensive, varied slopes ideal for intermediates, shared with Flims

➕ Generally efficient lift system, although with some long ride times

➕ Some of Europe's best terrain parks, now with an Olympic super-pipe

➖ Sunny orientation means the snow conditions can be tricky in late season

➖ Bus rides or long walks from some lodgings to the lifts

➖ Most convenient lodgings are in bases we find difficult to like

Laax and neighbouring Flims share a ski area that is one of Switzerland's biggest, whether you look at overall dimensions or piste km. The mountain has other powerful attractions too, including altitude, but the sunny orientation is a bit of a liability when competing in the premier league. Which may be why, some years back, the resort decided to appeal to different markets by investing heavily in terrain parks, half-pipes, indoor freestyle facilities and high-profile events – and by adopting a new brand. The resort used to be marketed as Flims, and still is in the summer, when it continues to appeal to its traditional market of well-heeled Swiss and Germans.

THE RESORT

The resort has three separate main bases a few km apart by road: Laax, Flims and Falera. Laax and Flims are themselves resorts of parts. Laax Dorf is the original rustic village, a couple of km from a much newer big, busy lift base/hotel/parking complex, now called Laax. Flims Dorf is a traditional resort at the foot of the slopes; Flims Waldhaus is a leafy suburb.

Village charm Laax Dorf is pleasantly rustic, with quiet suburbs set around a lake. The lift base area called Laax is a sharp contrast – sharp, modern, deliberately charm-free. Flims Dorf is traditional in style but unremarkable,

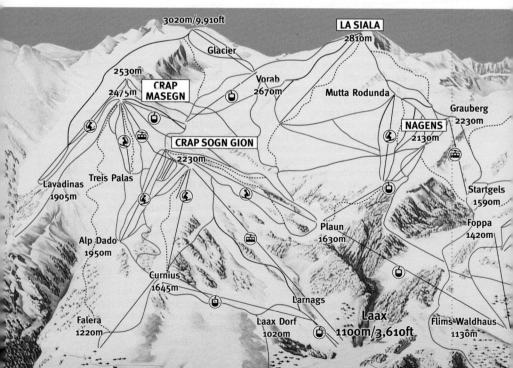

KEY FACTS

Resort	1100m
	3,610ft
Altitude	1100-3020m
	3,610-9,910ft
Lifts	29
Pistes	235km
	146 miles
Blue	29%
Red	32%
Black	39%
Snowmaking	16%

spread along the road through it (though a tunnel takes the through-traffic). Flims Waldhaus is wooded and more appealing, with upscale secluded hotels. Falera, once a quiet backwater hamlet, has been much expanded in traditional style.

Convenience It depends where you stay. The smart hotels in Waldhaus run shuttles, and there are 'quick and efficient' free ski-buses.

Scenery There are great panoramic views from the top of the glacier but lower down the views are less spectacular.

THE MOUNTAINS

The slopes are mostly open but there are also some quite long woodland runs. The piste map marks 'freeride runs' (dotted on our map), which are avalanche-controlled and patrolled – so they are effectively ungroomed pistes. Many of the black runs could really be classified red. A reporter who encountered thick mist this year speaks highly of the clear 'left' and 'right' piste edge marking.

Slopes There are long gondolas into the slopes from both Flims Dorf and Laax (plus a cable car of exceptional length from Laax) and a slow quad chair from Falera. Above mid-mountain, there is a complex web of lifts and runs. The glacier is limited; but it

accesses a superb long run to Lavadinas (an easy black).

Fast lifts The system is impressive, with enough fast chairlifts, gondolas and cable cars to scrape into our ★★★★★ category.

Queues There may be queues for the village lifts at peak times and for the glacier drags. High winds can close the upper lifts and put pressure on the lower ones.

Terrain parks Laax is one of the top resorts in Europe for freestylers and has four parks in the Crap Sogn Gion area, catering for every standard from beginner to pro-rider. Many high-profile competitions are held here. Between them, the parks have 56 obstacles, 15 kickers, an airbag and two pipes (super- and mini-) plus an 'excellent' freestyle slope to Curnius. The glacier has an early-season park, too. An indoor Freestyle Academy at the base in Laax offers tuition.

Snow reliability Upper runs are fairly snow-sure. The lower ones can suffer from sun, even early in the season, and some can close (the runs from Cassons and the glacier are also prone to closure); key ones have snowmaking but more is needed.

Experts The black pistes present few challenges, but the freeride runs add a lot of excellent terrain. The sunny aspect means that timing your descents can be crucial, though, to avoid rock-hard moguls. There is a huge amount of good off-piste terrain, notably from La Siala and Cassons.

Intermediates A superb area. Reporters are often surprised by the extent, length and variety of the slopes. The bowl below La Siala is huge and gentle. For the more confident, there are plenty of reds and some easy blacks. The sheltered Grauberg valley is a good area for long and fast runs. The long black run from the glacier is one of our favourites; it is steep only at the top. The Downhill course from Crap Sogn Gion is also excellent. Some of the freeride runs are great for trying off-piste, but others are steep.

Beginners There are beginner areas at village level (which can suffer from the sun) and at Crap Sogn Gion, and good easy runs to progress to. A beginner day pass is available on certain lifts in all three base areas.

Snowboarding Hugely popular. Apart from the top terrain parks, there's good freeriding. Many linking pistes have flat/uphill stretches though.

Laax

Build your own shortlist: www.wheretoskiandsnowboard.com

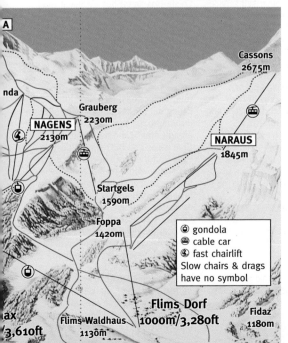

A

Cassons
2675m

nda

Grauberg
2230m

NAGENS
2130m

NARAUS
1845m

Startgels
1590m

Foppa
1420m

ⓖ gondola
ⓒ cable car
ⓕ fast chairlift
Slow chairs & drags have no symbol

Flims Dorf
1000m/3,280ft

Fidaz
1180m

ax
3,610ft

Flims Waldhaus
1130m

Resort news and key links: www.wheretoskiandsnowboard.com

MOMENTUM SKI

Weekend & a la carte
ski holiday specialists

100% Tailor-made

Premier hotels
& apartments

Flexible travel
arrangements

020 7371 9111
WWW.MOMENTUMSKI.COM

UK PACKAGES
Alpine Answers, Erna
Low, Momentum,
Powder Byrne,
PowderBeds, Ski Club
Freshtracks, Ski
Expectations, Ski
Safari, Ski Weekend,
Skitracer, Snow Finders,
Snow-wise, STC
Switzerland Travel
Centre, Zenith
Flims Alpine Answers,
Erna Low, Momentum,
Powder Byrne,
PowderBeds, Ski
Weekend, Skitracer,
Snow-wise, STC
Switzerland Travel
Centre, White Roc

Phone numbers
From elsewhere in
Switzerland add the
prefix 081; from
abroad use the prefix
+41 81

TOURIST OFFICE

Flims, Laax and Falera
www.laax.com

Cross-country There are 55km of trails.
Mountain restaurants Huts are taken
seriously here. They are described and
identified on a special Gastro Guide
piste map – an excellent idea – and
classified as Easy (self-service), Cosy
(the majority) or Exquisite (five top
spots). The two 'Exquisites' we hear
most about are Ustria Startgels (aka
Alpenrose) – 'by far the best,
outstanding game, excellent open fire
grills' – and Tegia Larnags, a 'charming'
farmhouse with typically Swiss dishes.
Tegia Curnius is a popular self-service
('excellent rösti'). Also tipped: Tegia
Miez ('simple, rustic, excellent local
meats'), Foppa ('very helpful staff and
great views'), Runca Höhe (large
heated marquee, 'good staff, fast
service') – all table-service – and self-
service Nagens ('fantastic pasta').

There are picnic rooms at Crap
Sogn Gion and at Vorab (excellent and
underused, says a reporter).
Schools and guides The school is run
by the lift company, USA-style. Past
reports on both adult and child
instruction have been positive.
Families There are 'Wonderlands' at all
three resort bases.

STAYING THERE

Hotels At Laax the 4-star 'design hotel'
Signina (927 9999) is part of
Rocksresort (see 'Apartments') and has
'excellent staff, good breakfasts, pool,
wonderful indoor tennis courts'. The
4-star Laaxerhof (920 8200) is almost
ski in/ski out and has good-sized
rooms, pool and sauna; its stubli has
been praised. Laax Dorf offers the

↑ Crap Sogn Gion has multiple bars, multiple
restaurants and multiple terrain parks – and
long views across the Rhine valley
WEISSE ARENA GRUPPE, LAAX

charming little Posta Veglia (921 4466).
In Flims Dorf the cheap and
cheerful Arena (911 2400) – with 'cool
rooms, friendly and helpful staff, good
restaurant and the best bar in town –
suits boys' trips' (see 'Après-ski').
In Flims Waldhaus the Sunstar (928
1800) is over 100 years old and has
been praised for its food and staff.
Cresta (911 3535) has 'excellent food,
service and top spa facilities'. The
Adula (928 2828) is similarly praised
by a regular visitor.
Apartments At Laax, Rocksresort is
uber-cool but the architecture is not to
everyone's taste; you can use the
facilities of the Signina hotel. The
tourist office has a list of apartments.
Eating out In Laax, Rocksresort places
include Nooba ('excellent Asian food,
friendly staff'), and the smart Grandis
(fine wines and BBQ specialities). In
Laax Dorf the Posta Veglia has a lovely
old stube, with a plainer room behind.
In Flims, a regular recommends both à
la carte restaurants of the hotel Adula.
Après-ski There are busy bars at the
lift bases at close of play. Later on,
clubs at the hotel Arena and the
Riders Palace at Laax throb until late.
Off the slopes There's a big sports
centre on the edge of Flims, with ice
rink (including ice hockey), and 100km
of 'really excellent' marked walks
reaching high up into the slopes.
Shopping is limited. Outings to historic
Chur are easy.

SNOWPIX.COM / CHRIS GILL

Mürren

The dinky, car-free mountain village where the British invented downhill ski racing; stupendous views add to the charm

RATINGS

The mountains

Extent	★
Fast lifts	★★★★★
Queues	★★★
Terrain p'ks	★★
Snow	★★★
Expert	★★★
Intermediate	★★★
Beginner	★★★
Boarder	★★
X-country	★
Restaurants	★★
Schools	★★★
Families	★★★

The resort

Charm	★★★★★
Convenience	★★★
Scenery	★★★★★
Eating out	★★
Après-ski	★★
Off-slope	★★★

RPI 125

lift pass	£220
ski hire	£125
lessons	£105
food & drink	£185
total	**£635**

NEWS

2014/15: Two ancient T-bars on the lower slopes are due to be replaced by new ones and a moving carpet is to be installed on the village nursery slopes. At Birg a new Skyline Walk viewing platform is planned.

2013/14: A new Bond World 007 exhibition opened at the top of the Schilthorn.

miles 0.5
↖ ↑down to Lauterbrunnen
Allmendhubel
ⓘ
Schilthorn
N ↑
↓ down to Stechelberg
km 0.5 1.

➕ Tiny, charming, traditional village, with 'traffic-free' snowy paths

➕ Magnificent scenery, best enjoyed descending from the Schilthorn

➕ Good sports centre

➕ Good snow high up, even when the rest of the region is suffering

➖ Extent of local pistes very limited, no matter what your level of expertise

➖ Lower slopes can be in poor condition

➖ Quiet, limited nightlife

Mürren is one of our favourite resorts. There may be other mountain villages that are equally pretty, but none of them enjoys views like those from Mürren across the deep valley to the rock faces and glaciers of the Eiger, Mönch and Jungfrau: simply breathtaking. Then there's the Schilthorn run – 1300m vertical with an unrivalled combination of varied terrain and glorious views.

But our visits are normally one-day affairs; those staying for a week are likely to want to explore the extensive intermediate slopes of Wengen and Grindelwald, across the valley. And that takes time.

It was in Mürren that the British more or less invented modern skiing. Sir Arnold Lunn organized the first ever slalom race here in 1922. Some 12 years earlier his father, Sir Henry, had persuaded the locals to open the railway in winter so that he could bring the first winter package tour here. Sir Arnold's son Peter was a regular visitor for 95 years, until his death in 2011.

THE RESORT

Mürren is one of a trio of resorts set amid the fabulous scenery of the Jungfrau group. It has an amazing position, set on a shelf high above the valley floor, across from Wengen, and can be reached only by cable car from Stechelberg or from Lauterbrunnen (via Grütschalp, where you catch a train). To get to Wengen takes around an hour: you go down to Lauterbrunnen by lift or piste, and catch a cog railway up. You can then ski to Grindelwald, but getting to the First area on the far side of Grindelwald is a very long trek.

VILLAGE CHARM ★★★★★
Picturesque and peaceful
You can't fail to be struck by Mürren's beauty and tranquillity. Paths and narrow lanes weave between little wooden chalets and a handful of bigger hotel buildings – all normally blanketed by snow.

Mürren's traffic-free status has been somewhat eroded; there are now a few delivery vehicles. But it still isn't plagued by electric carts and taxis in the way that many other traditional 'traffic-free' resorts are. Even Wengen seems busy by comparison.

CONVENIENCE ★★★
Small enough not to matter
The village is tiny by general resort standards. But it's 1km from end to end, and there is no transport, so it pays to plan your end-of-day return to the village with a bit of care.

SCENERY ★★★★★
Glorious panoramas
The views from the village and the slopes of the Eiger, Mönch and Jungfrau across the valley are magnificent. So are the 360° views from the top of the Schilthorn.

THE MOUNTAINS

Despite its small size, Mürren's ski area is interestingly varied. The lower slopes are below the treeline, but in practice it is an inhospitable area when the weather is bad.

EXTENT OF THE SLOPES ★
Small but interesting
Mürren's slopes aren't extensive. But there is something for everyone, including a vertical of some 1300m to the village. There are three connected areas. On the lower slopes, **Schiltgrat** is served by a fast quad chair at the

KEY FACTS

Resort	1650m
	5,410ft

Jungfrau region	
Altitude	945-2970m
	3,100-9,740ft
Lifts	45
Pistes	213km
	132 miles
Blue	33%
Red	49%
Black	18%
Snowmaking	40%

Mürren-Schilthorn only	
Slopes	1650-2970m
	5,410-9,740ft
Lifts	17
Pistes	54km
	34 miles

GETTING THERE

Air Bern 65km/ 40 miles (1hr); Zürich 150km/95 miles (2hr); Basel 170km/ 105 miles (2hr)

Rail Lauterbrunnen; transfer by mountain railway and cable car

south end of the village. A short funicular goes from the middle of the village to the nursery slope at **Allmendhubel** – linked by a red run and then chairlift to the slightly higher **Maulerhubel**. Runs go down from here to Winteregg and a fast quad.

Then there are the higher slopes reached by cable car to **Birg**. Below Birg, the fast Riggli chair serves a shady slope, and lower down two more chairs serve sunnier slopes. A further cable car goes up to the Schilthorn and its revolving restaurant and James Bond exhibition – check out the feature panel. In good snow you can ski from here (via a short chairlift) right down to Lauterbrunnen – almost 16km and 2175m vertical; below Winteregg, it's mostly narrow paths. Every January the Inferno race for amateurs is run over this route (without using the chairlift).

FAST LIFTS ★★★★★
Mostly OK

There's a draglift and a few slow chairs but most lifts are fast chairs and cable cars – plus a funicular.

QUEUES ★★★☆☆
Generally not a problem

Mürren doesn't get as crowded as Wengen and Grindelwald, except on sunny Sundays. But there can be queues for the cable cars to Birg and Schilthorn; the top stage has only one cabin, so if you don't get on you have to wait for it to go up and back.

TERRAIN PARKS ★★☆☆☆
One on the lower slopes

There is a terrain park on the lower slopes of Schiltgrat, with jumps, rails, boxes and a half-pipe.

SNOW RELIABILITY ★★★☆☆
Good on the upper slopes

The Jungfrau region does not have a good snow record – but we've always found Mürren has the best snow in the area. When Wengen-Grindelwald (and Mürren's lower slopes) have problems, the slopes up at Birg often have packed powder snow. The runs from below Engetal to Allmendhubel and parts of the lower slopes have snowmaking, as does the woodland path on down to Lauterbrunnen.

FOR EXPERTS ★★★☆☆
An attractive cocktail

The black run from the top of the Schilthorn starts with a steep but not terrifying pitch, in the past generally mogulled but now more often

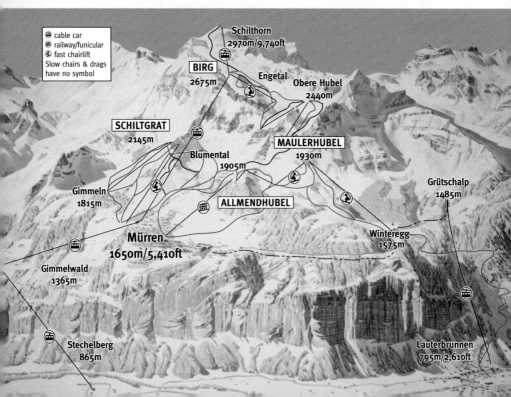

cable car
railway/funicular
fast chairlift
Slow chairs & drags have no symbol

Schilthorn 2970m/9,740ft

BIRG 2675m

Engetal

Obere Hubel 2440m

SCHILTGRAT 2145m

MAULERHUBEL 1930m

Blumental 1905m

Grütschalp 1485m

Gimmeln 1815m

ALLMENDHUBEL

Mürren 1650m/5,410ft

Winteregg 1575m

Gimmelwald 1365m

Stechelberg 865m

Lauterbrunnen 795m/2,610ft

↑ The stunning views are one of Mürren's key attractions

SNOWPIX.COM / CHRIS GILL

LIFT PASSES

Jungfrau

Prices in francs

Age	1-day	6-day
under 16	32	162
16 to 19	50	258
20 to 61	63	323
over 62	57	291

Free Under 6 (if with parent)

Beginner Points card

Notes Covers trains between villages and Grindelwald ski-bus; day pass is for Mürren Schilthorn area only; 5-day plus pass allows 50% reduction in Meiringen

Alternative passes Grindelwald and Wengen only; Mürren only; non-skier pass

ACTIVITIES

Indoor Alpine Sports Centre: swimming pool, sauna, solarium, steam bath, massage, fitness room

Outdoor Ice rink, curling, tobogganing, cleared paths, snowshoeing, paragliding

groomed. It flattens into a schuss to Engetal, below Birg. Then there's a wonderful, wide run with stunning views over the valley. Below the Engetal lifts you hit the Kanonenrohr (gun barrel). This is a shelf with solid rock on one side and a steep drop on the other – protected by nets; it is wider than it once was, and is now not seriously scary. After an open slope and scrappy zigzag path, you arrive at the 'hog's back' and can descend towards the village on either side of Allmendhubel.

There are steep mogul runs at Birg and Schiltgrat and quite a lot of off-piste potential, notably runs into the Blumental – from Schiltgrat (the north-facing Blumenlucke) and from Birg (sunnier Tschingelchrachen). And there are more adventurous runs from the Schilthorn top station.

FOR INTERMEDIATES ★★★☆☆
Limited, but Wengen nearby
Keen piste-bashers will want to make a few trips to the long cruising runs of Wengen-Grindelwald. The blue runs up at Engetal, below Birg and served by the Riggli chair, are good easy cruises and normally have good snow. The best easy cruising run on the lower slopes is the north-facing blue down to Winteregg. The reds on the other low slopes can get mogulled, and snow conditions can be poor.

Competent, confident intermediates can consider tackling the Schilthorn.

FOR BEGINNERS ★★★☆☆
Not ideal, but adequate
The main nursery slopes at Allmendhubel, up the funicular, are a

little on the steep side, but secluded and quiet. You pay via points cards. From there, you have easy blue runs to graduate to in each of the sectors; since construction of the chairlift link from Maulerhubel to Allmendhubel, getting back from Maulerhubel to the village poses no difficulty.

FOR BOARDERS ★★☆☆☆
Tough going for intermediates
The major lifts are snowboard-friendly cable cars and chairlifts. The terrain above Mürren is suitable mainly for good freeriders – it's steep, with a lot of off-piste. Intermediates will find the area tough and limited; nearby Wengen is gentler and larger.

FOR CROSS-COUNTRY ★☆☆☆☆
Forget it
There's a 12km loop along the Lauterbrunnen valley, but snow is unreliable.

MOUNTAIN RESTAURANTS ★★☆☆☆
Nothing outstanding
You'll want to visit the Schilthorn even if it's only for a drink – see the feature panel. Other reader tips include the cosy Schilthornhütte, at Obere Hubel, and the rustic, secluded Suppenalp lower down in the Blumental – but it gets no sun in January. Gimmelen is famous for its apple cake, and is self-service. The Schiltgrathüsi, near blue run 23, is 'good value' and 'a lovely coffee stop', say reporters. Winteregg is 'good and not expensive'. We normally lunch in the village on the rear terrace of the Bellevue hotel opposite the nursery slope – stunning views and wonderfully peaceful.

Mürren

481

Build your own shortlist: www.wheretoskiandsnowboard.com

SCHILTHORN – SPECTACULAR REVOLVING RESTAURANT AND AN EPIC DESCENT

Piz Gloria revolves once an hour, displaying a fabulous 360° panorama of peaks and lakes. The ambience has improved since it was renovated and reporters have enjoyed the food. As well as admiring the views from the terrace, you can visit Bond World 007, a free exhibition based on the On Her Majesty's Secret Service movie that was filmed here 45 years ago. This includes memorabilia (eg the bobsled and helicopter used in chases) and clips from the film. To get you in the mood the cable cars up occasionally play Bond theme music.

JUNGFRAU MARKETING AG

SWITCHERLAND

482

Resort news and key links: www.wheretoskiandsnowboard.com

SCHOOLS
Swiss
t 855 1247

Classes
5 half-days (2hr) 180 francs
Private lessons
From 140 francs for 2hr for 1-2 people

CHILDCARE
Kinder Paradis
t 856 8686
Ages 2 to 8
Babysitter list
Available from tourist office

Ski school
From age 3

UK PACKAGES
Inghams, Momentum, Mountain Beds, Neilson, PowderBeds, Snow-wise, SIC, Switzerland Travel Centre
Lauterbrunnen Ski Club Freshtracks, Ski Miquel

Phone numbers
From elsewhere in Switzerland add the prefix 033; from abroad use the prefix +41 33

TOURIST OFFICE
www.mymuerren.ch
www.muerren.ch

SCHOOLS AND GUIDES ★★★☆☆
No recent reports
We lack recent reports. But the school has a long tradition of teaching Brits.

FOR FAMILIES ★★★☆☆
Attractive
Mürren is attractive for a quiet family holiday, not least because of the relaxed, safe and snowy village, and the free facilities (read 'Off the slopes'). There is a nursery slope in the village which is due to have a new moving carpet for 2014/15. Children as young as three can have lessons.

STAYING THERE

Hotels There are fewer than a dozen.
****Eiger (856 5454) Chalet style; next to station. Widely recommended for good blend of efficiency and charm. Good food; pool and sauna.
***Alpenruh (856 8800) Attractively renovated chalet next to the cable car.
***Jungfrau (856 6464) Perfectly placed for families, in front of the baby slope and close to the funicular.
**Alpenblick (855 1327) Simple, small, modern chalet near the station.
Apartments There are plenty of chalets and apartments in the village for independent travellers to rent.
At altitude We have a good report of a stay at Suppenalp (855 1726): 'Good atmosphere, friendly host, excellent dinner, basic facilities, incredibly creaky – they issue earplugs.'

EATING OUT ★★☆☆☆
Mainly in hotels
The main alternative to hotels is the rustic Stägerstübli – a bar as well as a restaurant, and popular with locals, serving regional dishes. The Jägerstübli in the hotel Bellevue, the Edelweiss,

and the Alpenruh have been recommended by past reporters.

APRES-SKI ★★☆☆☆
Not entirely devoid of life
The tiny Stägerstübli is cosy, and the place to meet locals. The Bliemlichäller disco in the Blumental hotel caters for kids, the bar in the Eiger for a more mixed crowd.

OFF THE SLOPES ★★★☆☆
Tranquillity plus diversions
There is a very good sports centre, which was renovated a couple of years ago with new spa facilities. The pool and ice rink are free to those staying in Mürren with a guest card. The toboggan run from Allmendhubel to the village is popular. There are lots of prepared walking trails. Parapenting is very popular. Excursions to Bern and Interlaken are easy. Skiers can easily return to the village to meet non-skiers for lunch, and non-skiers can ascend the cable cars to the Schilthorn – though at a price.

DOWN-VALLEY VILLAGE – 795m

LAUTERBRUNNEN

This is a good budget base, with a bit of resort atmosphere and access to both Wengen (until late) and Mürren. We've happily stayed at two hotels – the 3-star Schützen (855 5050) and 2-star Oberland (855 1241), also praised for its food; the 3-star Silberhorn (856 2210) is again highly recommended by a 2013 visitor for its 'convenience right by the lifts for both Mürren and Wengen and very good, price-competitive' four-course dinners. There are bars in the hotels Horner, Steinbock and Silberhorn. Ski Miquel's chalet hotel Rosa is said to be good.

SNOWPIX.COM / CHRIS GILL

Saas-Fee

Some of the highest skiing in the Alps, plus a cute old village at the base; great for an early/late break

483

RATINGS

The mountains

Extent	★★
Fast lifts	★★★★
Queues	★★★★
Terrain p'ks	★★★★
Snow	★★★★★
Expert	★★
Intermediate	★★★★
Beginner	★★★★
Boarder	★★★★
X-country	★★★
Restaurants	★★★
Schools	★★★★
Families	★★★★

The resort

Charm	★★★★★
Convenience	★★
Scenery	★★★★
Eating out	★★★★
Après-ski	★★★★
Off-slope	★★★★

RPI 135

lift pass	£260
ski hire	£100
lessons	£125
food & drink	£205
total	**£690**

NEWS

The plan to build a new eight-person gondola from the car park at the edge of the village via the nursery slope area and Spielboden to Längfluh, and on to the top of the mountain, has been abandoned.

2014/15: The renovated Aqua Allalin leisure centre and attached 168-bed youth hostel are due to open in September 2014.

- Most runs are at exceptionally high altitude, and are snow-sure
- Great for early intermediates
- Traditional, car-free village, with clear attractions for families
- Dramatic setting amid high peaks and glaciers
- Good off-slope leisure facilities

- Small area of slopes
- Mainly easy runs, with little to amuse experts (glacier limits off-piste exploration)
- Many visitors face some long walks around the village
- Shady and cold for much of winter
- Bad weather can shut the slopes

Saas-Fee is one of our favourite places – a sort of miniature Zermatt without the conspicuous consumption. As well as the charm factor there's the super-reliable snow: you spend most of your days here at an altitude – between 2500m and 3500m – that is unrivalled in the Alps. It's a compelling combination.

But we tend to drop in here for a day or two at a time, so the limited extent and challenge of the slopes is not a worry; if we were here for a week, we'd soon be taking trips to Saas-Grund and even Zermatt.

THE RESORT

Saas-Fee is a traditional mountain village of narrow streets lined by old chalets and free of cars, which made a recent visitor feel 'safe allowing the children to wander the streets'. It's not entirely free of traffic, though: electric minibuses, taxis and vans provoke complaints, although they're not the nuisance they are in Zermatt.

The standard lift pass also covers Saas-Almagell and Saas-Grund not far away in the valley, and the latter in particular is well worth a visit – one trusted reporter this year preferred It to Saas-Fee. Trips to Zermatt are time-consuming but possible, and with a six-day pass the day pass for Zermatt costs just 30 francs.

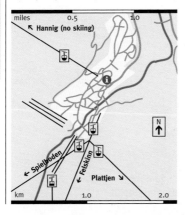

miles	0.5	1.0

↖ Hannig (no skiing)

N ↑

← Spielboden

← Felskinn

← Plattjen ↘

km	1.0	2.0

VILLAGE CHARM ★★★★★
Unpretentious rural idyll
Despite expansion, Saas-Fee still feels like a village, with cow sheds still in evidence. It doesn't have much of a central focus, but we'll forgive that; it's a charming place just to stroll around and relax in – at least when the spring sun is beating down. But it loses the sun early in the afternoon, and gets very little in midwinter.

CONVENIENCE ★★
A hike maybe
Although it's a small village, it's about 2km long, and the main slopes and most of the lifts are at one end. The bigger hotels run their own taxis. There are free but limited public minibuses and a road-train, but they are of little use – 'Very infrequent, and often full,' says a 2014 report. Most people, most of the time, just walk everywhere. The biggest lift – the Alpin Express gondola – starts from a more central location (that you can ski back to). And you can store your gear near the lifts, which helps.

SCENERY ★★★★
The Pearl of the Alps
Simply stunning, with views up to a ring of 4000-metre peaks – on a sunny day the restaurant terraces by the nursery slopes at the south end of the village are a magnet. Higher up, the views are even better.

When quality and value matter, do more with
zenith holidays
0203 137 7678
zenithholidays.co.uk
ABTA
ABTA No.Y1542

KEY FACTS

Resort	1800m 5,910ft
Slopes	1800-3500m 5,910-11,480ft
Lifts	21
Pistes	100km 62 miles
Blue	25%
Red	50%
Black	25%
Snowmaking	70%

THE MOUNTAINS

The upper slopes are largely gentle, while the lower mountain, below the glacier, is steeper and rockier, needing good snow-cover. There is very little shelter in bad weather: during and after heavy snowfalls you may find yourself limited to the nursery area.

Take it easy when climbing out of the top lift station at 3500m: some people can't handle the thin air.

Some of the red runs on the glacier should be classified blue, but some of the lower reds are pretty tough.

EXTENT OF THE SLOPES ★★
A glacier runs through it

There are two routes up to the main **Felskinn** area. The 30-person Alpin Express gondola, starting across the river from the centre of the village, takes you there via a mid-station at Morenia. The alternative is a short drag across the nursery slope at the south end of the village, and then the Felskinn cable car.

From Felskinn, the Metro Alpin underground funicular hurtles up to **Allalin**. From below here, two draglifts access the high point of the area.

Also from the south end of the village, a gondola leaves for Spielboden. This is met by a cable car that takes you up to **Längfluh**.

Between Felskinn and Längfluh is an off-limits glacier area with huge crevasses. A very long draglift from Längfluh takes you to a point where you can get down to the Felskinn area.

You can descend to the village from both the Allalin and Längfluh sectors.

Another gondola from the south end of the village goes up to the small area of slopes on **Plattjen**.

FAST LIFTS ★★★★
Too many T-bars

The area is a strange mixture of powerful fast lifts and a lot of 'ghastly long and cold T-bars', as a recent reporter put it; there are only two chairlifts. Blame the glaciers, on which it's tricky to build chairlifts. Our rating may look mysterious, but over half the lifts are fast, which puts Saas-Fee comfortably into the 4-star range.

QUEUES ★★★★
No recent problems to report

We had no problems with queues on February and March visits. Crowds on the home run from Morenia can be a problem at the end of the day.

TERRAIN PARKS ★★★★
Well developed

The big Morenia park has a plethora of kickers, rails and boxes and lines for different ability levels. Shapers are constantly changing the rail and box lines to keep the park fresh. Note that

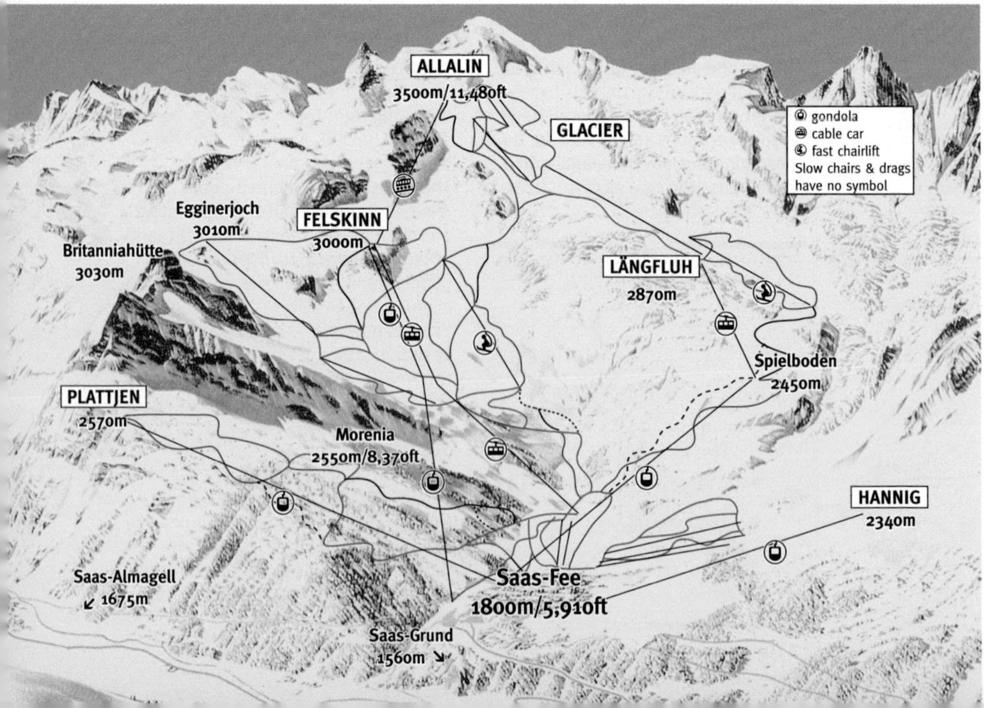
ALLALIN
3500m/11,480ft
GLACIER
gondola
cable car
fast chairlift
Slow chairs & drags have no symbol
Egginerjoch
3010m
FELSKINN
3000m
Britanniahütte
3030m
LÄNGFLUH
2870m
Spielboden
2450m
PLATTJEN
2570m
Morenia
2550m/8,370ft
HANNIG
2340m
Saas-Almagell
1675m
Saas-Fee
1800m/5,910ft
Saas-Grund
1560m

The Plattjen sector is worth a visit or two and has one of the two best mountain restaurants, the Berghaus →

SNOWPIX.COM / CHRIS GILL

LIFT PASSES

Saas-Fee

Prices in francs

Age	1-day	6-day
under 16	37	190
17 to 19	63	319
20 plus	70	370

Free Under 7
Seniors No deals
Beginner Pass for village lifts only
Notes Covers whole valley (Saas-Fee, Saas-Grund, Saas-Almagell and Saas-Balen); with 6+ day pass, day in Zermatt for additional 30 francs

Alternative passes
Passes for each of the Saastal ski areas; single and return tickets on main lifts; also afternoon passes

GETTING THERE

Air Sion 75km/ 45 miles (1hr15); Geneva 225km/ 140 miles (2hr45); Milan Malpensa 180km/110 miles (3hr); Zürich 225km/ 140 miles (3hr30)

Rail Brig (38km/ 24 miles) or Visp (27km/17 miles); regular buses from station

---

there is no longer a half-pipe. There's a park for beginner freestylers near the nursery slopes.

SNOW RELIABILITY ★★★★★
A question of altitudes
Most of Saas-Fee's slopes face north and many are above 2500m, making this one of the most reliable resorts for snow in the Alps. The glacier is open most of the year. Lower down, on the runs back to the resort, snow quality and cover can be more patchy, but snowmaking seems adequate. Grooming is done 'very well', but takes time after a dump we hear.

FOR EXPERTS ★★★★★
Not a lot to keep your interest
There is not much steep stuff – the handful of short, sharp pitches dotted around the area just about merit their black classification. The slopes around the top of Längfluh can provide good powder, and there are usually moguls above Spielboden. There is excellent tree skiing on Plattjen but it requires serious depths of snow to cover the very rocky terrain. On the main sector, crevasse danger on the glacier puts limits on off-piste even with a guide.
Saas-Fee is a leading resort for ski touring: the extended Haute Route from Chamonix ends here.

FOR INTERMEDIATES ★★★★★
Great for gentle cruising
For early intermediates and those not looking for much of a challenge or a lot of variety, Saas-Fee is ideal. For long cruises and usually excellent

snow, head for Allalin – from here down as far as Längfluh in one direction and Morenia in the other, you get gentle red runs leading to even gentler blues.
The reds from mid-mountain down to the village are a bit more challenging, notably from Längfluh and Spielboden. They have steepish, tricky sections and can have poor snow, and the blues here are mainly narrow paths – timid intermediates might prefer to take a lift down from mid-mountain. The descents all the way from Allalin to the village offer a leg-testing 1700m vertical.
Don't ignore the rather neglected Plattjen area, which is basically of red-run gradient.

FOR BEGINNERS ★★★★★
Clear attractions
There's a superb, large, out-of-the-way nursery area at the edge of the village, as snow-sure as any you will find, and covered by a special cheap pass. But one reporter judges the walk to it 'a bit of a slog'. Those ready to progress can head for the gentle blues between Felskinn and Morenia and then the easy red runs (some of which are of only blue gradient really) higher up on the glacier. But beware the linking red 10b from here to the Morenia sector, says the same reporter.

FOR BOARDERS ★★★★★
Year-round fun
Saas-Fee has backed snowboarding from its inception and provides year-round riding. The terrain suits

UK PACKAGES

Alpine Answers, Alpine Life, Crystal, Crystal Finest, Erna Low, Inghams, Interactive Resorts, Momentum, Mountain Exposure, Neilson, Oxford Ski Co, PowderBeds, Ski Bespoke, Ski Expectations, Ski Independence, Ski Line, Ski Safari, Skitracer, Skiweekends.com, Snow Finders, Snow-wise, STC Switzerland Travel Centre, Thomson, Zenith

SCHOOLS

Swiss
t 957 2348

Eskimos
t 957 4904

Optimum Snowsports
t 957 2039

Classes
5 3hr-days 229 francs
(no full-day lessons)

Private lessons
From 80 francs for 1hr

CHILDCARE

GoSulino (Hotel Alphubel)
t 079 283 3674
From age 2

Wallo (Hotel Ferienart)
t 958 1900
From age 6mnth

Swiss
t 957 2348
Ages 3 to 6

Ski school
From age 7

WORLD'S HIGHEST REVOLVING LUNCH?

If you fancy 360° views during lunch, head up to Threes!xty, the world's highest revolving restaurant at Allalin, which was refurbished a couple of seasons ago and where you can get a different vista with starters, mains and pud. Only the bit of floor with the tables on it revolves; the stairs stay put (along with the windows – watch your gloves). The other two revolving cafes in the Alps are also in Switzerland – at Mürren and Leysin – and we rate the views there better. But it's an amusing novelty that most visitors enjoy. To reserve a table next to the windows phone 957 1771.

SAAS-FEE TOURISM / SWISS-IMAGE.CH

intermediates and beginners best; there's little to satisfy experts and the glacier limits freeriding, but carvers will find wide, well-groomed pistes to shred down. The main access lifts are gondolas, cable cars and a funicular, but nearly all the rest are T-bars. The high altitude and the glacier mean the resort is a favourite for early-season and summer riding.

FOR CROSS-COUNTRY ★★★★★
Good local trail and lots nearby
There is a nice short (6km) trail on the Hannig side of the village and 26km down in the Saas valley.

MOUNTAIN RESTAURANTS ★★★★★
Huge improvements
Saas-Fee's mountain restaurants used to be mediocre at best. But in the past few years two huts have been taken over by the resort's two top hotels and improved beyond recognition. The piste map gives details and phone numbers for these and several others.
Editors' choice The Vernissage Berghaus Plattjen (just down from the top of Plattjen), in the Ferienart hotel stable, has great Alpine atmosphere, delicious hearty food, excellent service and wonderful glacier views from a tiny terrace. We look forward to trying the Spielboden hut, which was taken over and refurbished a couple of seasons ago by the Fletschorn hotel (where the food has a Michelin star). Locals rate it the best on the hill, and a reporter this year agrees – 'Amazing food, outstanding service and not too bad price-wise.'
Worth knowing about Before the two above appeared, our favourite was the cosy Gletschergrotte, slightly off the

run from Spielboden (watch for signs on the left) – 'amazing views and food' and 'good cake in the afternoon' says a 2013 reporter; beware charges for water, though. Of the self-service restaurants, the one at Längfluh has a great view of the glacier and its crevasses from its large terrace while the one at Morenia consistently impresses reporters – 'Good choice and able to cope with the numbers,' says this year's report.

For something different, a 15-minute trek from the pistes at Felskinn brings you to Britanniahütte, a real climbing refuge with great views; understandably, food is simple. There's a room in the Morenia where you can eat your packed lunch.

SCHOOLS AND GUIDES ★★★★★
Good reports
We have had consistently good reports in the last few seasons on all the schools – the Swiss school, Eskimos ('Excellent, with young and friendly instructors,' says a 2013 reporter) and British-run Optimum Snowsports ('Private lessons highly recommended' was a 2013 comment).

FOR FAMILIES ★★★★★
Safely suitable
The village and its gentle nursery slopes form a good environment for families, and the kids' fun park proved a 'great introduction' for one toddler. Several hotels have an in-house kindergarten. But make sure you read the 'Convenience' section. Two hotels offer day care and there's also a babysitting service at the Ferienart hotel. Family specialist operator Esprit has pulled out (read our Editorial).

Indoor Aqua Allalin leisure centre (new for 2014/15): swimming pool, hot tub, sauna; library, museums

Outdoor Cleared paths, ice rink (skating, curling, snow bowling), ice climbing, tubing, tobogganing, snowshoeing

Phone numbers
From elsewhere in Switzerland add the prefix 027; from abroad use the prefix +41 27

TOURIST OFFICE

www.saas-fee.ch

SNOWPIX.COM / CHRIS GILL

The close-up glacier views at Längfluh should be enough to deter you from venturing off-piste ↓

STAYING THERE

Chalets Sister companies Total and Esprit have pulled out – read our Editorial about this regrettable business.

Hotels There are over 50.

*****Ferienart (958 1900) Central top hotel. Superb blend of comfort, service and relaxed style with a great wellness area. Half-board food about the best we've had anywhere. 'Still lovely, outstanding breakfasts,' says our 2014 reporter, a regular guest. Beware of rooms with a bath in the bedroom if that's not your thing.

****Allalin (958 1000) 'Large rooms, outstanding food, fantastic staff.'

****Saaserhof (958 9898) Near lifts. Reputation for good service and food.

****Sunstar Hotel Beau-Site (958 1560) On main street. 120 years old, individually designed rooms/suites, small but stylish spa, cosy restaurant.

***Bristol (958 1212) Good location right by the nursery slopes.

***Europa (958 9600) Near the Hannig gondola. 'Clean, comfortable'; 'good food'; 'gorgeous wellness facilities'.

***Waldesruh (958 6464) Close to the Alpin Express and 'family-friendly'.

Fletschhorn (957 2131) Upmarket, elegant (Relais & Châteaux) chalet in the woods. A trek from the village and lifts, but they'll drive you; great food.

Apartments Two 2012 reporters recommended Chalet Feekatz, which has six bedrooms ('beautiful, a 10-minute walk from the centre').

EATING OUT ★★★★
Good variety
Gastronomes will want to head for the Michelin-starred and expensive Fletschhorn – endorsed by a 2012 reporter. We like the woody Bodmen, which has great food and a varied menu. As well as its main Cäsar Ritz restaurant, the hotel Ferienart has the Mandarin (Asian) and Del Ponte – 'Good Italian food in a relaxed atmosphere – we ate there twice,' says our Ferienart regular. Don Ciccio's 'serves authentic Italian food'. The Vieux Chalet (for fondue and raclette), hotel Tenne (good rösti) and the Dom Bar ('great-value burger and chicken and chips') have been recommended.

APRES-SKI ★★★★
Lively bars and clubs
At close of play, the Snowpoint umbrella bar at the foot of the slopes and the terraces of Zur Mühle and the Black Bull ('busy from 4pm onwards') in the main street are always buzzing. Later on, Nesti's ('Small but the best place,' says a 2013 reporter) and the Fee Pub are lively. The Dom Bar has live music every night. Popcorn ('real party place with international DJs'), Metropol, Poison and NightLife are other popular clubs. A 2013 visitor warns that if your revelries are too noisy between 10pm and 8am, you're at risk of a fine.

OFF THE SLOPES ★★★★
A mountain for pedestrians
The Hannig mountain is dedicated to walking, snowshoeing, paragliding and 'really good fun' tobogganing. The leisure centre, which has a 25m pool, indoor tennis and a sunbed area, is being renovated and is scheduled to reopen with a new name, Aqua Allalin, in September 2014. The Feeblitz 'roller-coaster-style' ride is good fun. The museums are interesting and if you like ice caves, don't miss the world's largest. The tourist office organizes walks every week. There are tours and tastings at a local brewery.

Build your own shortlist: www.wheretoskiandsnowboard.com

St Moritz

One of a kind: a panoramic high-altitude playground with as much happening off the slopes as on them

RATINGS

The mountains

Extent	★★★★★
Fast lifts	★★★★
Queues	★★★
Terrain p'ks	★★★★
Snow	★★★★
Expert	★★★★
Intermediate	★★★★
Beginner	★★
Boarder	★★★★
X-country	★★★★★
Restaurants	★★★
Schools	★★★
Families	★★

The resort

Charm	★★
Convenience	★
Scenery	★★★★
Eating out	★★★★
Après-ski	★★★
Off-slope	★★★★★

RPI 150

lift pass	£250
ski hire	£135
lessons	£145
food & drink	£235
total	**£765**

NEWS

2014/15: A new sports centre in Bad should be open in time for the season, offering indoor and outdoor pools, wellness area, fitness centre and restaurants.

Once again visitors will be able to buy discounted lift passes (at 35 francs a day) if they stay at least two nights in one of the 100 hotels in St Moritz that are participating in the scheme.

2013/14: The Corvatsch snow-park was revamped and extended and St Moritz's first super-pipe was built.

➕ Wonderful panoramic scenery

➕ Extensive intermediate slopes

➕ High, and fairly snow-sure

➕ Off-slope activities second to none (and a whole mountain dedicated to non-skiing activities)

➕ Some good mountain restaurants, some with magnificent views

➖ A sizeable town, with little traditional Alpine character and some big block buildings

➖ Several unlinked mountains

➖ Runs on home mountain mostly fairly easy and lacking variety

➖ Can be pricey, as you'd expect from such a fashionable resort

St Moritz is Switzerland's definitive 'exclusive' winter resort: glitzy, fashionable and, above all, the place to be seen – a place for an all-round winter holiday, with an unrivalled array of wacky diversions such as cricket on snow, and countless festivals. It has long been popular with upper-crust Brits, who come for the sledging. Well, OK: for the world-famous Cresta Run, which isn't quite the same thing. But, like all such smart resorts, it makes a perfectly good destination for anyone – and the slopes have lots to offer.

The town of St Moritz is a bit of a blot on the landscape; but that landscape is truly spectacular. Our skiing here is regularly interrupted by the need to stand and gaze, and once installed on a terrace we take some shifting.

THE RESORT

St Moritz is at the heart of the upper Engadin – the remote, high valley of the river En, which becomes the Austrian river Inn (as in Innsbruck). The valley bottom is filled by a chain of lakes, one of which separates the two parts of St Moritz. On a steep hillside above the lake, Dorf is the fashionable main town. Beside the lake is the more ordinary spa resort, St Moritz Bad. The skiing is in several separate sectors; only one, Corviglia, is reachable directly from the resort.

In winter the lake is used for eccentric activities including horse and greyhound racing, show jumping, polo, golf and even cricket. And there's a whole mountain (Muottas Muragl) set aside for not skiing – see 'Off the slopes'. The upper Engadin is superb for walking and cross-country skiing, which is very big here; the Engadin Ski Marathon attracts over 11,000 entries.

The home slopes are shared with Celerina, down the valley (see the end of the chapter). And there are other possible bases along the valleys.

There is a fabulously scenic railway from Zürich, but it's quicker to drive. A car is handy around the resort, too: the bus service is covered by the lift pass but it gets crowded at peak times

and a car greatly speeds up visits to the more distant mountains. Trips are possible to Davos and other places; you get a half-price pass in Livigno, Samnaun/Ischgl and other resorts. There is a strong Italian flavour to the area – lots of Italian visitors, workers, food and wine.

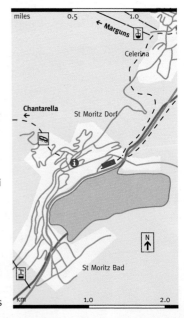

KEY FACTS

Resort	1770m
	5,810ft
Slopes	1730-3305m
	5,680-10,840ft
Lifts	56
Pistes	350km
	217 miles
Blue	20%
Red	70%
Black	10%
Snowmaking	30%

For Corviglia only

Slopes	1730-3055m
	5,680-10,020ft
Lifts	22
Pistes	100km
	62 miles

SNOWPIX.COM / CHRIS GILL

The terrace of El Paradiso is one of two spots we head for at lunchtime ↓

VILLAGE CHARM ★★★★★
Urban glitz instead
In the main resort towns there is little traditional Alpine character; St Moritz is very much a glitzy town rather than a cute village. Dorf has two main streets – lined with boutiques selling Rolex, Cartier, Hermes etc – a few side lanes and a small main square. Bad is less urban, and less prestigious. Many buildings in both parts are block-like.

CONVENIENCE ★★★★★
Bad is good – or better, at least
It's a perfectly convenient resort if you are content to ski Corviglia, stay in central Dorf and ride the funicular, or stay on the edge of Bad and use the Signal cable car. But both parts of the resort spread widely away from these lifts, and to ski other mountains transport is needed. For keen skiers, Bad is the better base – you can ski back to it from both local sectors.

SCENERY ★★★★★
Fabulous panoramas
The lake-filled valley, with 4000m peaks on the Italian border, provides mesmerizing views from Corviglia, and the close-up views of Piz Bernina from Corvatsch are stunning.

THE MOUNTAINS

There are three separate areas of slopes, covered on three very clear piste maps; our maps show only the two main areas (Corviglia and Corvatsch) close to St Moritz. The terrain is varied, with lots of long, wide, well-groomed runs – practically all on open slopes above the trees. Every Friday, from 7pm to 2am, the 4.2km piste down from the middle station on Corvatsch is floodlit.

EXTENT OF THE SLOPES ★★★★★
Three separate areas
The claimed 350km of slopes can safely be considered an exaggeration.

From St Moritz Dorf a two-stage railway goes up to **Corviglia**, a lift junction at the eastern end of a sunny and rather monotonous area of slopes facing east and south over the main valley. The peak of Piz Nair, reached from here by cable car, separates these slopes from the less sunny and more varied ones in the wide bowl above **Marguns** – and gives fabulous views across the valley to Piz Bernina. From Corviglia you can (snow permitting) head down easy paths to Dorf and Bad; at Salastrains, just above Dorf, are nursery slopes, restaurants and two hotels. There is a red run from Marguns to Celerina.

From Surlej, a few miles from St Moritz, a two-stage cable car takes you to the north-facing slopes of **Corvatsch**, which reach glacial heights. From the mid-station at Murtèl you have a choice of reds to Stüvetta Giand'Alva and Alp Margun. From the latter you can work your way to **Furtschellas**, also reached by cable car from Sils Maria. If you're lucky with the snow, you can end the day with the splendid Hahnensee run, from the northern limit of the Corvatsch lift system at Giand'Alva down to St

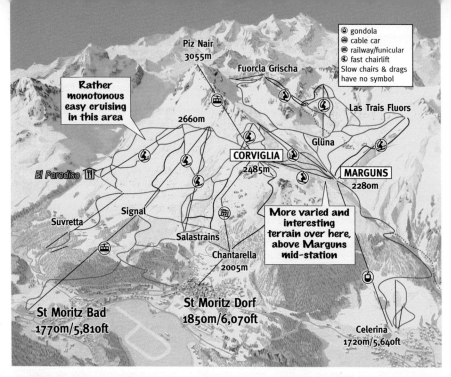

Piz Nair
3055m

Fuorcla Grischa

Las Trais Fluors

Rather monotonous easy cruising in this area

2660m

Glüna

CORVIGLIA
2485m

MARGUNS
2280m

El Paradiso

Signal

Suvretta

Salastrains

More varied and interesting terrain over here, above Marguns mid-station

Chantarella
2005m

St Moritz Bad
1770m/5,810ft

St Moritz Dorf
1850m/6,070ft

Celerina
1720m/5,640ft

gondola
cable car
railway/funicular
fast chairlift
Slow chairs & drags have no symbol

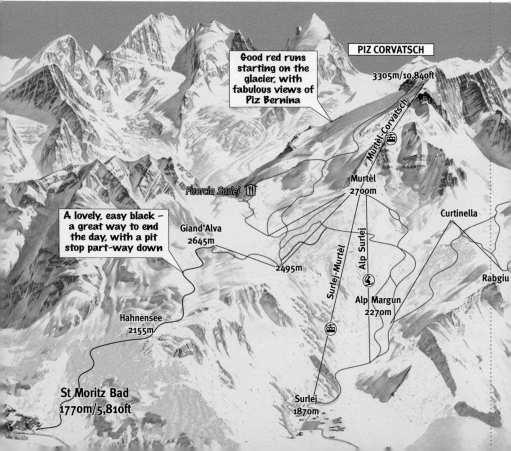

PIZ CORVATSCH
3305m/10,840ft

Good red runs starting on the glacier, with fabulous views of Piz Bernina

Murtèl-Corvatsch

Fuorcla Surlej

Murtèl
2700m

Curtinella

A lovely, easy black – a great way to end the day, with a pit stop part-way down

Giand'Alva
2645m

2495m

Surlej-Murtèl

Alp Surlej

Rabgiu

Hahnensee
2155m

Alp Margun
2270m

St Moritz Bad
1770m/5,810ft

Surlej
1870m

LIFT PASSES

Upper Engadin

Prices in francs

Age	1-day	6-day
under 13	24	122
13 to 17	49	243
18 plus	73	365

Free Under 6
Senior No deals
Beginner No deals
Notes Covers Corviglia, Corvatsch, Diavolezza-Lagalb and Zuoz, the Engadin bus services and stretches of the Rhätische Bahn railway; family discounts; 1-day price is for Corviglia only
Alternative passes Half-day and day passes for individual areas

Moritz Bad – a black-classified run that is of red difficulty for 95% of its 6km length. It often opens around noon, when the snow softens. It's a five-minute walk from the end of the run to the cable car to Corviglia.

The third area is about 20km from St Moritz (50 minutes by bus) and consists of two peaks reached by cable cars starting from car parks on opposite sides of the Bernina pass road to Italy. **Diavolezza** (2980m) has excellent north-facing pistes of 900m vertical. **Lagalb** (2895m) is a smaller area with quite challenging slopes – west-facing, 850m vertical. From the beginning of March the Diavolezza cable car runs until 5pm.

FAST LIFTS ★★★★
Plenty of options
St Moritz has invested heavily in upgrading lifts, especially on Corviglia and Marguns, where there are fast chairs all over the place. Corvatsch still has some T-bars, though. The area as a whole has a lot of modest-sized cable cars.

⊕ cable car
④ fast chairlift
Slow chairs & drags have no symbol

Interesting, varied intermediate terrain on this side of the sector

Furtschellas 2800m

la

Val Fex

Rabgiusa

FURTSCHELLAS 2310m

Excellent winding run to the valley – best done early in the day on good snow with no crowds

Sils-Furtschellas

Sils Maria 1795m ↘

QUEUES ★★★☆☆
Not much of a problem
Queues for the cable cars are not unknown – a 2014 visitor reports short queues for the Piz Nair cable car – but most reporters have had no problems.

TERRAIN PARKS ★★★★☆
World-class facilities
The park on Corviglia has three lines, the hardest including a big 12m tabletop jump, plus a brilliant 400m easy line. There are many rails and boxes of all sizes, and a new 400m family fun slope integrating easy obstacles in a snowcross course. The Freestyle Park on Corvatsch was extended last season and includes a 7m half-pipe (St Moritz's first) as well as big jumps, an air bag, rails and a snowcross.

SNOW RELIABILITY ★★★★☆
Improved by good snowmaking
This corner of the Alps has a rather dry climate, but the altitude means that any precipitation is likely to be snowy. The top runs at Corvatsch are glacial and require good snow depths to be safe. There is snowmaking in each sector, and grooming is 'magnificent – the best I've seen outside North America'.

FOR EXPERTS ★★★★☆
Dispersed challenges
Few of the black runs are genuinely steep; those at Lagalb and Diavolezza are the most challenging. But there is good off-piste terrain, and it doesn't get tracked out. There is an excellent north-facing slope immediately above Marguns, for example, and tough routes from Piz Nair and the Corvatsch summit. More serious expeditions can be undertaken – eg the Roseg valley from Corvatsch.

Out at Diavolezza, a very popular and spectacular off-piste glacier route goes off the back beneath Piz Bernina to Morteratsch. There's a 30-minute plod at first, then it's downhill, with splendid views. It is not difficult, but may take you close to crevasses; we wouldn't do it without a guide. On the front of the mountain, the Gletscher chair accesses an excellent shady run down Val d'Arlas. At Lagalb, there's off-piste down the back towards La Rosa (again, a guide is needed).

There are a few firms offering heli-drops on Fuorcla Chamuotsch, for runs back to the Engadin valley.

THE CRESTA RUN

No trip to St Moritz is really complete without a visit to the Cresta Run. It's the last bastion of Britishness (not long ago, payment had to be made in sterling) and male chauvinism (women need an invitation from a club member). Any adult male can pay 600 Swiss francs (around £400) for five rides (helmet, boots, pads etc included). You lie on a toboggan (called a 'skeleton') and hurtle head-first down a sheet ice gully from St Moritz to Celerina. Watch out for Shuttlecock corner – that's where most of the accidents happen.

ENGADIN ST MORITZ / SWISS-IMAGE.CH / JR LARRAMAN

UK PACKAGES

Alpine Answers, Alpine Weekends, Carrier, Club Med, Elegant Resorts, Erna Low, Inghams, Jeffersons, Luxury Chalet Collection, Momentum, Neilson, Oxford Ski Co, Powder Byrne, PowderBeds, Scott Dunn, Ski Bespoke, Ski Independence, Ski Line, Ski Safari, Ski Weekend, Skitracer, Snow-wise, STC, STC Switzerland Travel Centre, Supertravel

FOR INTERMEDIATES ★★★★
Good but flattering
St Moritz is great for intermediates. Most pistes on Corviglia are very well groomed, easyish reds that could well have been classified blue – ideal cruising terrain, or monotonous, depending on your view. The Marguns bowl is more interesting, including some easy blacks and the pleasant Val Schattain run away from the lifts.

The Corvatsch-Furtschellas area is altogether more varied, interesting and challenging, as well as higher and wider. There are excellent red runs in both parts of the area, including the runs from the Corvatsch glacier, which give fabulous views, and descents to the two valley stations – particularly the Furtschellas one. Do these in the morning, and at the end of the day return to St Moritz Bad via the lovely Hahnensee run – an easy black. There isn't much easy skiing at Corvatsch; some of the blues (eg the lower bit of 19) should be red.

Diavolezza is mostly intermediate stuff, too. There is an easy open slope at the top, served by the Gletscher chair, and a splendid long intermediate run back down under the lift. The link to Lagalb requires use of parts of a black run, but it is of red gradient. (Plans to improve this link seem to have stalled.) Lagalb has more challenging pistes – two reds and a genuine black.

FOR BEGINNERS ★★
Not ideal
Beginners start up at Salastrains or Corviglia, or slightly out of town at Suvretta. Celerina has good, broad nursery slopes at village level and a child-friendly lift. But progression from the nursery slopes to longer runs is

rather awkward – there are few blue runs without a difficult section. Nor are there any free lifts, or particularly helpful special passes.

FOR BOARDERS ★★★★
Very welcoming
The terrain in St Moritz is boarder-friendly. Freeride tours are available through the ski schools, and the best freeride terrain is on Diavolezza and Corvatsch, but there are several draglifts on Corvatsch. Apart from those, most of St Moritz's lifts are chairs, gondolas, cable cars and trains; beginners will enjoy the rolling blue runs, and intermediates will relish the red runs. The great thing for freeriders is that terrain can stay untracked for days. There are good parks on both Corviglia and Corvatsch. Playground in Paradise is a specialist board shop.

FOR CROSS-COUNTRY ★★★★★
Excellent
This is one of the premier regions in the Alps, with 200km of trails, some floodlit, amid splendid scenery and with fairly reliable snow. 'Fantastic,' says a 2013 visitor. But the best bases are away from St Moritz.

MOUNTAIN RESTAURANTS ★★★
Some special places
Mountain restaurants are plentiful, and include some of the most glamorous in Europe. Not surprisingly, prices can be high. The piste maps have pictures and phone numbers of the restaurants. **Editors' choice** El Paradiso (833 4002), secluded at the extreme southern end of Corviglia, has it all: breathtaking views from the big terrace ('Worth it for these alone,' says a 2014 visitor), tastefully renovated, slightly trendy interior, great service and top-notch

CHILDCARE

Schweizerhof Hotel
t 837 0707
From age 3

Palazzino – in Badrutt's Palace Hotel
t 837 1000
Ages 3 to 12

Kempinski Hotel
t 838 3838

Salastrains kids' park
t 830 0101
Run by Swiss school

Ski school
Ages from 5

SCHOOLS

Swiss
t 830 0101

Suvretta
t 836 6161

Classes (Swiss prices)
3 3hr-days 280 francs

Private lessons
From 100 francs for 1hr

ENGADIN ST MORITZ / SWISS-IMAGE.CH

St Moritz Dorf doesn't enhance the glorious Engadin landscape; Bad is out of sight to the right ↓

---

food. Fuorcla Surlej (842 6303, though we doubt they'll take a reservation), on the Fuorcla run from the Corvatsch glacier, could not be more different: a remote refuge serving basic food, sometimes very slowly. But the view of Piz Bernina and Piz Roseg from the snowy ramshackle 'terrace' is stunning. **Worth knowing about** On Corviglia, the top lift station houses several restaurants run under the umbrella title of Mathis Food Affairs, including the famously swanky Marmite. Not our cup of tea, but a trusted reporter recorded his 'best ever skiing lunch' here. The more atmospheric Chasellas is also recommended. Lej da la Pêsch, behind Piz Nair, is a cosy spot, better for a snowy day than a sunny one. On the Corvatsch side, the cosy, rustic Alpetta has been tipped in the past, and the varied menu looked good to us on a recent visit. Hahnensee, on the run of that name to Bad, is a splendid place to pause in the sun.

There are two picnic rooms: at the Lagalb cable-car base and in the Marguns restaurant building.

SCHOOLS AND GUIDES ★★★☆☆
Internal competition
There are two main schools, Swiss and Suvretta. Past reports on both have been positive, but a 2013 visitor said the Swiss instructor provided by Club Med should have demoted some in her group to a lower class. Other hotels have private instructors, too.

FOR FAMILIES ★★☆☆☆
Choose a hotel with a nursery
There's a kindergarten and children's restaurant at Salastrains, and we'd be inclined to stay up there if you can afford it – much more child-friendly than the towns. Some hotel nurseries are open to non-residents.

STAYING THERE

There is a 'very comfortable' Club Med with 'excellent food', which has its own restaurants on the main slope sectors. The tourist office can provide a list of apartments.

Hotels From Switzerland's highest concentration of 5-stars, we allow ourselves one.

★★★★★Kempinski (838 3838) Unfashionable but spacious location in Bad. 'The only 5-star where I felt vaguely relaxed,' says a young but widely experienced reporter.

★★★★Crystal (836 2626) Austere-looking central place with contrasting traditional rooms. Wellness facilities.

★★★★Monopol (837 0404) In centre of Dorf. Spa facilities.

★★★★Nira Alpina (838 6969) Fairly new 'design' hotel right by the Corvatsch cable-car station in Surlej. 'Great food, fab bar; faultless.'

★★★★Steffani (836 9696) 'Slightly old-fashioned', family owned hotel in centre of Dorf. 'Plain rooms (some with views of the lake) but lovely modern spa/pool complex.'

St Moritz

GETTING THERE

Air Zürich 220km/
135 miles (3hr15);
Friedrichshafen
210km/130 miles
(3hr15); Upper
Engadin airport 5km/
3 miles

Rail Mainline station
in resort

ACTIVITIES

Indoor Tennis,
squash, health spa,
casino, cinema,
museums, galleries

Outdoor 150km of
cleared paths, ice
rink, curling, ice
climbing, snow-
shoeing, sleigh rides,
tobogganing, para-
gliding, bobsleigh
rides, Cresta Run,
snow kiting, horse
riding

Phone numbers
From elsewhere in
Switzerland add the
prefix 081; from
abroad use the prefix
+41 81

TOURIST OFFICES

St Moritz
www.stmoritz.ch

Celerina
www.engadin.
stmoritz.ch/celerina/

****Schweizerhof** (837 0707) In central Dorf, five minutes from the Corviglia lift. Après-ski hub.

****Margna** (836 6600) Near railway and bus stations: 'Staff could not have been more helpful.'

***Laudinella** (836 0000) In Bad. Cool decor; six varied restaurants. Fitness room.

***Nolda** (833 0575) One of the few chalet-style buildings, close to the cable car in Bad.

***Sonne** (838 5959) In Bad, not far from the lake.

Landhotel Meierei (838 7000) Relaxing, traditional country hotel in a quiet setting across the lake.

At altitude The 3-star Salastrains (830 0707) is on the lower slopes of Corviglia and has great views. Muottas Muragl (842 8232), at over 2500m on the non-skiing mountain, was fully renovated a few years ago and has even better views.

EATING OUT ★★★★★
Mostly chic and expensive
A lot of restaurants here are very pricey. We liked the three smooth, expensive restaurants in the Chesa Veglia (an outpost of Badrutt's hotel): 'Nice to go somewhere with Alpine atmosphere,' says a 2014 visitor. A top, world-class restaurant is Bumanns Chesa Pirani, a fine old house out of town in La Punt. We had an excellent dinner in 2012 at the charming, polished hotel Bellavista in Surlej. Of course, you can eat more cheaply, and that often means eating basic Italian. The hotels Laudinella and Sonne, in Bad, both have wood-fired pizza ovens. The Laudinella has five other restaurants too. For something completely different, La Baracca is a big shed in the car park of the Signal cable car doing simple but thoroughly good food in a canteen-like setting.

An evening up at Muottas Muragl, between Celerina and Pontresina, offers spectacular views, a splendid sunset and dinner.

APRES-SKI ★★★★★
Caters for all ages
There's a big variety of après-skiing age groups here. The fur coat count is high – people come to St Moritz to be seen. For tea and good cakes head for Hanselmann's. The Roo bar terrace outside the hotel Hauser is a popular après drinking spot.

Bobby's Pub attracts a young crowd, as does the loud music of the Stübli, one of the bars in the hotel Schweizerhof: the others are the Muli, with dancing, and the chic Piano Bar. At the Steffani a 2014 visitor found the Cresta Bar 'lively but very smoky', while the Cava below it is louder and younger. We don't get many reports on the late-night scene. The jazz night at the Kulm is 'great for people-watching', says a 2013 reporter. Two popular discos are Vivai and King's at Badrutt's Palace (jackets and ties required). If you need to splash even more cash, try the casino.

OFF THE SLOPES ★★★★★
Excellent variety of pastimes
Even if you lack the bravado for the Cresta Run, there is lots to do. In midwinter the snow-covered lake provides a playground for events such as polo, horse racing and cricket, but then activities are limited as the lake starts to thaw. There's an annual 'gourmet festival', with chefs from all over the world. Of course, the shops are fantastic, for those with flexible plastic. There are 150km of well-marked walking trails (a map is available). Muottas Muragl is a mountain set aside for not skiing – with funicular access to snowshoeing and tobogganing – with stunning panoramic views.

Other options are paragliding, indoor tennis and curling. A new swimming pool complex with spa and wellness facilities was due to open in July 2014. Reporters rave about the views from the Bernina Express train to Italy and recommend a train trip to Scuol.

LINKED RESORT – 1730m

CELERINA

At the bottom end of the famous Cresta Run, Celerina is an appealing base if you want a quiet time – it is unpretentious and villagey, but lacks a central focus (and has very few shops). It has good access to the Corviglia-Marguns sector – a gondola to Marguns. It spreads quite widely, with a lot of second homes, many owned by Italians (the upper part is known as Piccolo Milano). There are some appealing small hotels – like the 4-star Chesa Rosatsch (837 0101). The modern Inn Lodge (834 4795) has rooms and dormitories. The Freestyle School focuses on park practice.

Val d'Anniviers

Exceptionally cute, unspoiled villages beneath high, snow-sure slopes. Sounds perfect? Well, there are some drawbacks ...

495

TOP 10 RATINGS

Extent	★★
Fast lifts	★
Queues	★★★★
Snow	★★★★
Expert	★★★★
Intermediate	★★★
Beginner	★★★
Charm	★★★★★
Convenience	★★
Scenery	★★★★

RPI   115

lift pass	£190
ski hire	£100
lessons	£120
food & drink	£185
total	**£595**

NEWS

There are medium-term plans to replace the Tzarmettaz draglift at Zinal with a chairlift accessing the top station of the Grimentz cable car, and to replace the Crêts chairlift at Grimentz along with the two draglifts above it. Don't hold your breath.

2013/14: A new 125-person cable car opened, linking Grimentz village to the heart of the Zinal ski area.

KEY FACTS

Resorts	1340-2000m
	4,400-6,560ft
Slopes	1340-3000m
	4,400-9,840ft
Lifts	43
Pistes	220km
	137 miles
Blue	36%
Red	52%
Black	12%
Snowmaking	14%

+ Charming, unspoiled villages

+ Four varied ski areas, linked in two pairs, plus a tiny fifth

+ Excellent, extensive off-piste

+ Reliable snow-cover

+ No crowds or queues

− Most lifts are T-bars; few fast chairs

− Very quiet villages; dead, even

− Almost entirely open slopes

− Travelling between the two main areas is a slow business

In some ways, Val d'Anniviers is in a bit of a time warp. There is plenty of modern accommodation and some modern lifts in key spots, including the new cable car that last season linked two of the four ski areas for the first time. But most of the villages have unspoiled rustic cores with old wooden houses and narrow lanes; and on the slopes you spend a lot of your time riding draglifts and not much time riding fast chairs (there are only four in the whole valley). Some people will find the slow pace of things here irritating. But approach the area with the right attitude and you'll probably find it all quite a refreshing change from big-name resorts with high-speed everything.

The Val d'Anniviers runs almost due south from the Rhône valley at Sierre and the narrow road up to the resorts has in places been carved out of sheer rock faces.

There are five charming main villages with lots of old wooden houses and barns, narrow paths and lanes and few shops. Some more modern development has taken place around them, but it is generally tasteful and low-rise.

On the morning-sun side of the valley, the slopes of Zinal have long been linked to those of Grimentz by a long, isolated black run, but the two resorts are now also linked by a big new cable car – forming a fair-sized linked ski area, with 110km of pistes. On the afternoon-sun side, the slopes of Chandolin and St Luc are linked at high and low altitude, and offer 75km of pistes. Although these two main areas are not far apart and are served by free bus, the trip involves a change in the little town of Vissoie, and takes about an hour.

Vercorin is a smaller separate area with just 35km of pistes, and for most visitors is irrelevant – you get there via Sierre, down in the Rhône valley. Except at Vercorin, nearly all the slopes are above the treeline and there's a lot of skiing above 2400m, which usually means good snow. All of the individual areas are small, but they add up to a decent amount.

1650m / 2000m

ST LUC / CHANDOLIN

These are the sunniest of the main ski resort villages, a few km apart, and they share a well-linked area of slopes. St Luc also has the attraction of a fabulous, characterful old hotel. A funicular goes up from the edge of St Luc and a fast chair from the edge of Chandolin. Both are served by the free ski-buses. The slopes face west to south-west, so the snow suffers from the sun. Apart from Chandolin's fast quad, there is only one other chair – the other 10 lifts are all drags.

The pistes suit beginners and intermediates best; though there are two black runs, five short itinerary routes (including one that we reckon is the steepest marked run in the Alps) and a gnarly freeride area where competitions are held. There are some testing reds, but in general the slopes are gentle, easy cruising territory. A highlight is the long, easy red run of 1230m vertical from Bella Tola at 3000m, away from all the lifts down to a bar and ski-bus stop – a great way to end the day. There's a good beginner area and a terrain park near the top of the St Luc funicular.

There are some good mountain restaurants with fine views. Above Chandolin the tiny Illhorn has a limited menu but a cosy panelled room (and fab pear tart); the Tsapé is a smart,

Combe Durand

Corne de Sorebois
2895m

Sorebois
2440m

ZINAL

Zinal
1670m/5,480ft

Piste du Chamois

Mottec

Bendolla
2130m

GRIMENTZ

Grimentz
1570m/5,150ft

Roc d'Orzi
2855m

St-Jean

Bella Tola
3000m/
9,840ft

2770m

Tignousa
2180m

St-Luc
1650m/5,410ft

Vissoie

2470m

ST LUC-CHANDOLIN

Illhorn
2600m

Chandolin
2000m/6,560ft

Mt Major
2375m

VERCORIN

Vercorin
1340m/4,400ft

Chalais

288

gondola
cable car
railway/funicular
fast chairlift
Slow chairs & drags
have no symbol

Sierre
560m/1,840ft

To
Geneva
→

UK PACKAGES

St Luc Alpine Answers, Inntravel, Mountain Beds, Ski Bespoke **Zinal** Alpine Answers, Mountain Beds, Mountain Tracks, Ski Weekend, SkiZinal **Grimentz** Alpine Answers, Erna Low, Mountain Beds, Mountain Heaven, Ski Club Freshtracks, Ski Safari, Ski Weekend

stark place, high-up, with good local cuisine; above St Luc, the Bella Tola is a traditional, basic table-service hut.

Both Chandolin and St Luc are fairly spread out with a limited choice of places to eat. But St Luc has a cute, compact old centre with a small outdoor après-ski bar. The 4-star hotel Bella Tola (475 1444) is just a few strides from here. Built in 1859, it has been beautifully renovated by its current owners, with a fine spa, sunny terrace, and good restaurant. We enjoyed staying there hugely.

1670m
ZINAL

The locals 'are a highlight, with their warmth and charm', in this small and rather plain village near the head of the valley. Its local slopes have stunning views of high peaks including the Matterhorn.
A modern cable car goes to Sorebois at 2440m, the hub of the ski area. Most of the slopes face roughly east and keep their snow well.

The runs are mainly short (some only 200m or 300m vertical) but include some good reds – our favourites are those from Combe Durand at the edge of the ski area, served by a steepish draglift that also accesses a freeride area. The one fast chairlift serves wide and gentle blue runs, ideal for novices. The two short black runs are really of red steepness. There is a longer red run (with a black variant on the lower part) back to the village. And there's great off-piste in

bowls between the pistes (and, with a guide, off the back of the ski area to the Moiry dam and on to Grimentz).

From the top of the area, Piste du Chamois is a real highlight – a long, mainly easy black run of almost 1300m vertical down a shady deserted bowl with lots of accessible off-piste, ending with a woodland path to Grimentz to catch the new cable car back.

Zinal is popular with families and there's a good beginner area and children's snow garden.

On weekends and holidays the Sorebois self-service ('decent, reasonable-value food') offers an 'all you can eat' buffet downstairs. The Bar e Vox winebar opened in 2014, 'appreciated by a more mature market than Le Pub attracts along the street'.

Zinal has a handful of hotels. The central 2-star Pointe de Zinal (475 1164) does excellent food and the 2-star Le Trift (475 1466) is 'comfortable, with adequate but small rooms and good food'. There are also a couple of catered chalets.

1570m
GRIMENTZ

Grimentz has a richly deserved reputation for its extensive off-piste. Above its very cute old village is a small area of varied pistes.
The village is spread out on quite a steep slope with a lot of new building. There is a marked separation between the cute old centre – lots of tiny old barns and narrow paths – and the skiers' accommodation. Much of this is

Selected chalets in Val d'Anniviers

ADVERTISEMENT

MOUNTAIN HEAVEN www.mountainheaven.co.uk

T 0151 625 1921

Mountain Heaven has a wonderful selection of self-catered chalets and apartments in Grimentz, all with WIFI and ranging from two to five bedrooms. We are financially bonded and offer all-inclusive prices with no hidden extras. Included in our portfolio are Le Lievre, a stunning apartment right by the piste, Chalet Mélèze, a detached chalet with a commanding position, Les Vieux Chalets no 2 & 7, which are right in the village centre, and Sur Les Pistes, an apartment situated on the piste itself.

Email: info@mountainheaven.co.uk

STUNNING BALCONY VIEWS ↑

↑ There are grand views from the slopes in all the main sectors

SIERRE-ANNIVIERS TO / PHOTO-GENIC.CH

Phone numbers
From elsewhere in Switzerland add the prefix 027; from abroad use the prefix +41 and omit the initial '0'

TOURIST OFFICES

Val d'Anniviers
www.valdanniviers.ch
Grimentz
www.grimentz.ch
St Luc
www.saint-luc.ch
Vercorin
www.vercorin.ch
Zinal
www.zinal.ch
Chandolin
www.chandolin.ch

conveniently close to the gondola up to Bendolla at 2130m – but some is less conveniently placed on the opposite side of the old village.

Bendolla has a good, roped-off beginner area and snow garden for kids, and above it are two main sectors. On the right as you look up are easy blue and red runs. On the left are steeper and quieter runs, including the long Piste Lona, which goes from the top to almost the bottom of the mountain (1300m vertical), right at the edge of the ski area; it deserves its black classification and is interestingly varied. The main run to the village is quite steep too, but you can ride the gondola down.

The real attraction for experts is the extensive off-piste. There are lots of options, including over 1500m vertical down to Vercorin, returning from there to the village of St Jean, a bus ride from Grimentz. 'The tour from the top of the system at Orzival, down the back side all the way to the Rhône valley, is one of the most fun rides I have had,' says a 2014 reporter. 'It is quite steep with some perfect tree skiing.' We had a great day skiing off-piste in the trees with a guide from the International ski school in poor visibility on our 2013 visit.

We have had positive reports on this school in the past, endorsed by a 2013 visitor – 'Our daughters enjoyed themselves and for the first time our youngest was keen to do more.'

Our favourite mountain restaurant is the rustic Etable du Marais below Grands Plans where we had good rösti and pasta dishes. We've also had good pasta at the self-service Orzival.

The functional main Bendolla restaurant is mainly self-service but it also has a small table-service section where we have had an enjoyable meal.

As the lifts close, Chez Florioz on the piste just above the village is the place for a drink. The best restaurants are probably those in the main hotels. But we have also enjoyed an excellent meal at Arlequin (a pizzeria). Bar le Country is a lively sports bar.

We have had comfortable stays and good food at the two 3-star hotels – the Alpina (476 1616), almost opposite the gondola, and the less convenient Cristal (475 3291). The 'comfortable' and 'good value' 2-star Becs de Bosson is run by a mountain guide.

UK tour operator Mountain Heaven has some smart chalets and apartments, which can be rented on a catered or self-catered basis. A satisfied 2013 reporter who stayed in their Sur Les Pistes apartment said: 'Perfect location, very good accommodation, well priced.'

1340m
VERCORIN

The smallest area of slopes in the region (we skied virtually all the pistes in 90 minutes), and isolated from other resorts.
The pretty village of Vercorin, perched on a shelf overlooking the Rhône valley, is reached by a winding road or by a cable car from Chalais, just outside Sierre. This is followed by a free ski-bus to a revamped two-stage gondola. The slopes suit intermediates best and were deserted when we were there in January 2013.

VERBIER TOURIST OFFICE

Verbier

Big, chalet-style resort that attracts powder hounds from all over the world – and big-spending night owls from Geneva

RATINGS

The mountains

Extent	★★★★★
Fast lifts	★★★★
Queues	★★★
Terrain p'ks	★★★
Snow	★★★
Expert	★★★★★
Intermediate	★★★
Beginner	★★
Boarder	★★★
X-country	★
Restaurants	★★★
Schools	★★★★★
Families	★★★

The resort

Charm	★★★
Convenience	★★
Scenery	★★★★
Eating out	★★★★
Après-ski	★★★★★
Off-slope	★★★

RPI | 140

lift pass	£240
ski hire	£135
lessons	£135
food & drink	£215
total	**£725**

NEWS

2014/15: As this chapter goes to press in early July, the 4 Vallées area pass is not expected to be offered, following a dispute between the lift companies.

2013/14: A new gondola from Le Châble linked Verbier to the heart of the Bruson ski area.

An old chairlift at Les Masses, beyond Thyon, was replaced by a quad. The chairlift from Siviez to Plan-du-Fou (for access to Nendaz) was replaced by a gondola.

A cutting-edge 5-star hotel – W Verbier – opened in December, as part of a new development at Médran.

- ➕ Extensive, challenging slopes with a lot of off-piste and long bump runs
- ➕ Upper slopes offer a real high-mountain feel, plus great views
- ➕ Sizeable, animated village in a sunny, panoramic setting
- ➕ Lively, varied nightlife
- ➕ Much improved lift system, piste grooming and signposting, but ...

- ➖ Piste map and piste naming still have some way to go
- ➖ Some overcrowded areas
- ➖ Sunny lower slopes will always be a problem, even with snowmaking
- ➖ Some long walks/rides to lifts
- ➖ Expensive bars and restaurants
- ➖ The 4 Valleys network is much less wonderful than it sounds – and may not operate this season

For serious off-piste routes and for mogul fields, Verbier is one of the world's cult resorts. It has other attractions, too: for vibrant après/nightlife it is difficult to beat, and it has some lovely swanky chalets and hotels. But what if those are not the things that float your boat? In particular, what if you're basically a mileage-hungry piste skier who maybe dabbles in powder, like so many Brits? Well, Verbier doesn't measure up well against other big-name resorts.

The slopes above Verbier plus those across the valley at Bruson (as of last season reachable by gondolas via Le Châble) are claimed to amount to a respectable 195km, but we've always felt this was an overstatement – a view supported by the work of Christoph Schrahe, discussed in our feature article on piste extent. Leaving aside the many itineraries (normally gigantic mogul fields), an energetic skier could cover the local Verbier pistes in a day.

Ah, but Verbier is part of the 4 Valleys network, we hear you say – with a claimed extent of over 400km. Well, it was, but as we go to press in late July it isn't. The Verbier lift company has fallen out with next-door Veysonnaz, and at present there is no pass-sharing agreement for the coming season. We'd guess they'll make up before the winter; but in any case the 4 Valleys is nothing to get excited about – it's an inconveniently sprawling affair, with lots of tedious links, and again the piste extent seems to be seriously overstated.

THE RESORT

Verbier enjoys an impressive setting on a wide, sunny balcony facing spectacular peaks. It's a fashionable, informal, very lively place that teems with cosmopolitan visitors. Most are younger than visitors to other big Swiss resorts.

The resort is at one end of a long, strung-out series of interconnected slopes, optimistically branded the 4 Valleys and linking Verbier to Nendaz, Veysonnaz, Thyon and other small resorts. As we explain above, this partnership may not operate during 2014/15, so bear that in mind as you read about the ski area.

These other resorts have their own pros and cons. All are much less lively in the evening than Verbier, and are appreciably cheaper places to stay. Some are more sensible bases for those who plan to stick to pistes rather than venture off-piste – the Veysonnaz-Thyon sector, in particular, is much more intermediate-friendly than Verbier. As bases for exploration

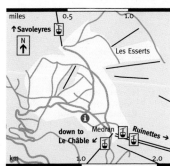

ALPINE ANSWERS
The UK's No.1 Chalet Specialist

For choice and service look no further!

alpineanswers.co.uk
call: 020 7801 1080
ABTA

of the whole 4 Valleys, only tiny Siviez is much of an advance on Verbier.

You can also stay down in the valley village of Le Châble, which has gondolas up to Verbier and the small resort of Bruson, and makes an excellent base. There's more on all these places at the end of the chapter.

Chamonix and Champéry are within reach by car. So are a few small resorts near Orsières, about 45 minutes away – Champex-Lac, La Fouly and Vichères-Liddes (covered in our

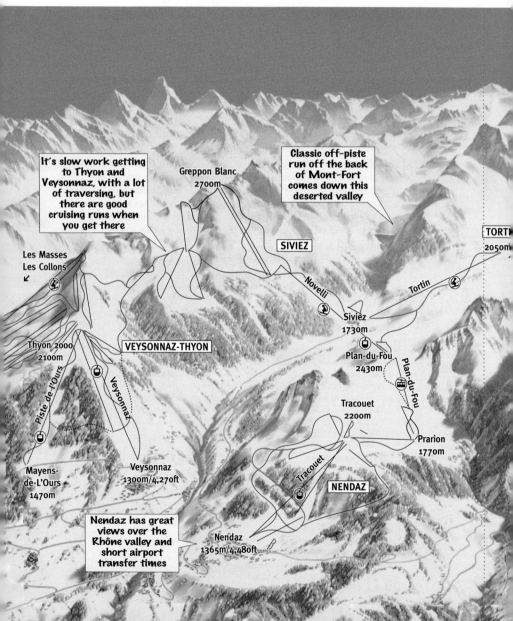

It's slow work getting to Thyon and Veysonnaz, with a lot of traversing, but there are good cruising runs when you get there

Classic off-piste run off the back of Mont-Fort comes down this deserted valley

Greppon Blanc
2700m

SIVIEZ

TORTI
2050m

Les Masses
Les Collons

Novelli

Tortin

Siviez
1730m

Thyon 2000
2100m

VEYSONNAZ-THYON

Plan-du-Fou
2430m

Plan-du-Fou

Piste de l'Ours

Veysonnaz

Tracouet
2200m

Mayens-
dè-L'Ours
1470m

Veysonnaz
1300m/4,270ft

Tracouet

Prarion
1770m

NENDAZ

Nendaz has great views over the Rhône valley and short airport transfer times

Nendaz
1365m/4,480ft

resort directory at the back of the book). But a car can be a bit of a nuisance in Verbier itself. Parking is very tightly controlled; your lodging may not have enough space for all guests' cars, which means a hike from the free parking at the sports centre or paying for parking.

Danni Sports was praised by a recent reporter: 'Extremely helpful and friendly, good choice of equipment for hire, and they do a half-price ski-service happy hour mid-week.'

VILLAGE CHARM ★★★☆☆
Busy upmarket chalet town
The resort is an amorphous sprawl of chalet-style buildings. Most of the shops and hotels (but not chalets) are set around the Place Centrale and along the sloping streets stretching both down the hill and up to the main lift station at Médran, 500m away. At close of play this street, in particular, is buzzing with après-ski activity. These central areas get unpleasantly packed with cars at weekends.

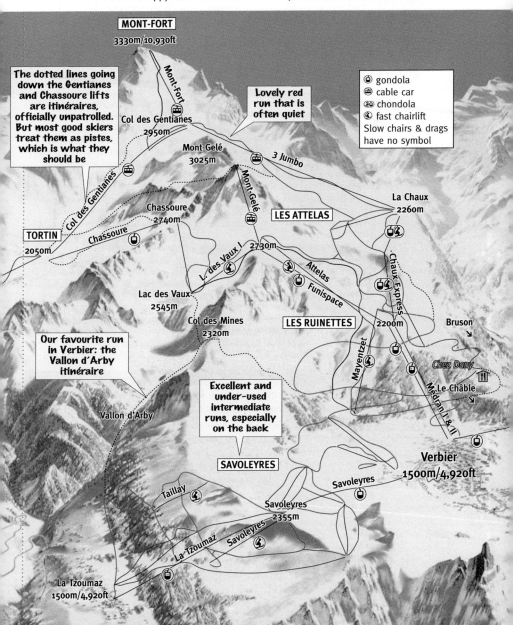

MONT-FORT
3330m/10,930ft

The dotted lines going down the Gentianes and Chassoure lifts are itinéraires, officially unpatrolled. But most good skiers treat them as pistes, which is what they should be

Col des Gentianes
2950m

Mont-Fort

Lovely red run that is often quiet

Mont-Gelé
3025m

3 Jumbo

gondola
cable car
chondola
fast chairlift
Slow chairs & drags have no symbol

Chassoure
2740m

Mont-Gelé

LES ATTELAS

La Chaux
2260m

TORTIN
2050m

Chassoure

L. des Vaux I

2730m

Attelas

Chaux Express

Lac des Vaux
2545m

Funispace

LES RUINETTES

Bruson

Col des Mines
2320m

2200m

Chez Dany

Maventzet

Médran I & II

Le Châble

Our favourite run in Verbier: the Vallon d'Arby itinéraire

Excellent and under-used intermediate runs, especially on the back

Verbier
1500m/4,920ft

Vallon d'Arby

SAVOLEYRES

Savoleyres

Taillay

Savoleyres
2355m

La Tzoumaz

Savoleyres

La Tzoumaz
1500m/4,920ft

KEY FACTS

Resort	1500m
	4,920ft

4 Valleys area	
Slopes	1500-3330m
	4,920-10,930ft
Lifts	92
Pistes	412km
	256 miles
Blue	39%
Red	44%
Black	17%
Snowmaking	13%

Verbier, Bruson and Tzoumaz/Savoleyres sectors only (covered by Verbier pass)

Slopes	1500-3025m
	4,920-9,920ft
Lifts	34
Pistes	195km
	121 miles
Blue	43%
Red	29%
Black	28%
Snowmaking	
	114 guns

CONVENIENCE ★★★★★
Pick your spot

It's a sprawling resort where most people suffer some inconvenience – alleviated by the free buses, which run on several routes until 8pm. They're generally efficient, but get overcrowded at times, and some areas have quite an infrequent service. You can store gear at Médran, which helps you cope with the overcrowding.

The Médran lift station is a walkable distance from the Place Centrale, so staying between the two has attractions. If nightlife is not a priority, staying somewhere near the upper fringes of the village may mean that you can almost ski to your door, though skiing from it is less likely. More chalets are built each year, with many newer properties inconveniently situated along the road to the lift base for the secondary Savoleyres area, about 1.5km from Médran.

SCENERY ★★★★★
A circle of Alpine peaks

Verbier is surrounded by stunning Alpine scenery; from the top of Mont-Fort there are impressive views in all directions, including Mont Blanc to the west and the Matterhorn to the east.

THE MOUNTAINS

Essentially this is high-mountain terrain. There are wooded slopes directly above the village, but the runs here are basically just a way home at the end of the day. There is more sheltered woodland skiing in other sectors of the 4 Valleys – particularly above Veysonnaz.

Signposting to the villages on the pistes has improved, and the piste map names some runs, though in very small type. However, piste names are still not posted on the mountain, and readers still complain about this 'poor state of affairs'.

EXTENT OF THE SLOPES ★★★★★
Smaller than claimed

Since the first edition of this book 20 years ago we have been saying that the 4 Valleys exaggerates the extent of its pistes. Last year the Schrahe report confirmed it (read our piste extent feature at the front of the book).

The 4 Valleys has been claiming 412km, of which about 50km are at Bruson, which leaves 362km for the linked Verbier-Nendaz-Veysonnaz slopes. Schrahe puts the total for these slopes at 164km, or 45% of the claimed figure. Verbier's local slopes amount to a claimed 195km; 45% of that is a very modest 88km, which seems to us about right. About half the size of Kitzbühel in Austria, for example.

In the local Verbier sector, **Savoleyres** is a small area effectively isolated from the major network, reached by a gondola from the north-west end of the village. This area is underrated and generally underused. It has open, sunny slopes on the front side, and long, pleasantly wooded, shadier runs on the back. You can take a catwalk across from Savoleyres to the foot of Verbier's main slopes.

The main slopes are served by lifts from Médran, at the opposite end of the village. Two gondolas rise to Les Ruinettes and then a gondola and

OFF-PISTE FOR ALL

Verbier has some of the best off-piste in the world. Here, we pick out just a few of the runs on offer. See 'For experts' for the status of itinéraires; for the other runs here you should hire a guide.

The Col des Mines and Vallon d'Arby itinéraires, accessible from Lac des Vaux, are relatively easy, though there may be some unnerving moments on the traverse to the point where they split. The first is a long, open slope back to Verbier and the latter a very beautiful run in a steep-sided valley down to La Tzoumaz. The Eteygeon itinéraire from Greppon Blanc above Siviez is 'wonderfully varied and should not be missed', says a reporter; it ends up on a road and you catch a bus back to Les Masses.

Stairway to Heaven starts with a steep climb from near Col des Gentianes. Then you drop over the ridge into a deserted valley, and it's a long, relatively easy ski down to Tortin. The Mont-Gelé cable car offers some of the most amazing terrain accessible anywhere by lift, with long runs down to Tortin on steep but open slopes. Or go down the opposite side of the mountain through the steep rock face towards Lac des Vaux (not a route for the faint hearted). The many couloirs from Attelas can also be fantastic. We love the runs off the back of Mont-Fort (except for the long walk out past Lac de Cleuson); it's a vast bowl and you can find fresh powder long after a snowfall; you end up at Siviez. And try the tree skiing in Bruson (see the end of the chapter).

↑ The chalets of Verbier spread across a wide, sunny bowl. On the left, Col des Mines; on the right, Les Ruinettes

VERBIER ST-BERNARD / YVES GARNEAU

LIFT PASSES

Verbier Grand Ski

Prices in francs

Age	1-day	6-day
under 14	36	178
14 to 24	60	302
25 to 64	71	355
65 plus	60	302

Free Under 6; over 77
Beginner Limited pass 24 francs

Notes Covers Verbier, Mont-Fort, Bruson, La Tzoumaz, including ski-buses; part-day passes; family reductions

Alternative passes
It is possible that the 4 Valleys pass covering Siviez, Nendaz, Veysonnaz and Thyon will be brought back to life

chairlift continue to **Attelas**. From Attelas a small cable car goes up to Mont-Gelé, for steep off-piste runs only. If you head back down instead, you can go west to Les Ruinettes, south to La Chaux or north to Lac des Vaux. From Lac des Vaux chairs go to Attelas and Chassoure, the top of a wide, steep and shady off-piste mogul field going down to **Tortin**, with a gondola back.

You can also ride a chondola from Les Ruinettes to the sunny, easy slopes of La Chaux. At the bottom of these slopes a jumbo cable car goes up to **Col des Gentianes** and the glacier area. The lovely, often quiet, red run back down to La Chaux is one of our favourites. A second, much smaller cable car goes up from Gentianes to the **Mont-Fort** glacier. From the top, there's only a long, steep black run back down. From Gentianes you can head down on another off-piste route to Tortin; the whole north-facing run from the top to Tortin is almost 1300m vertical, which can be moguls top to bottom. A cable car returns to Col des Gentianes.

Tortin is the limit of the Verbier lifts, so if the 4 Valleys pass is not operating you will need an extension to go any further. (Off-piste skiers planning to end up in Siviez and ride lifts back to Verbier, please note.) Below Tortin is the gateway to the rest

of the 4 Valleys, **Siviez**. From here, a new gondola takes you up to Plan-du-Fou for the long, thin **Nendaz** sector. A fast quad heads the other way towards **Veysonnaz-Thyon**, via a couple of drags and a lot of catwalks. Allow plenty of time to get to and from these remote corners.

The slopes of **Bruson**, across the valley from Verbier, are now very easy to reach thanks to the new gondola from Le Châble and are described briefly at the end of this chapter.

FAST LIFTS ★★★★☆
Locally fine
The main access lifts are gondolas and chairs. Further afield, more upgrades are needed to improve links throughout the 4 Valleys (especially between Siviez and Veysonnaz-Thyon).

QUEUES ★★★☆☆
Not the problem they were
Queues have been greatly eased by investment in powerful new lifts and have barely been a problem for reporters over the past few years. There may be queues at Médran if Sunday visitors fill the gondola from Le Châble, but they shift quickly.

Queues still occur for old lifts in the other 4 Valleys resorts, and the quad at Siviez gets busy at peak times and if the weather is poor. Bruson may have queues at its old lifts if the

Build your own shortlist: www.wheretoskiandsnowboard.com

VERBIER & BEYOND!

TAILOR-MADE OR ACCOMMODATION ONLY SPECIALISTS

01502 471960
info@mountainbeds.com
www.mountainbeds.com

skitracer

CHALETS, HOTELS & APARTMENTS

Call us today

020 8600 1650

skitracer.com

gondola from Le Châble becomes popular. Our one reporter on Bruson this year was more concerned about the poor reliability of those lifts, which sound like they are in terminal decline.

TERRAIN PARKS ★★★★★
Expert and beginner options
The Swatch Snowpark, Verbier's main freestyle area, is at La Chaux. It has separate lines for varying levels: blue, red and black. Features are varied, with kickers, boxes and rails of all types and a giant airbag. Freestyle coaching is available (check www.snowschoolverbier.ch).

SNOW RELIABILITY ★★★★★
Improved snowmaking
The slopes of the Mont-Fort glacier always have good snow, naturally. The runs to Tortin are normally snow-sure, too. But nearly all of this terrain is steep and mogulled, and much of it is formally off-piste. Most of Verbier's main local slopes face south or west and are below 2500m – so they can be in poor condition at times. Snowmaking covers the whole main run down from Attelas to Médran at the top of the village. The slopes of La Chaux, the nursery slopes and some of the Savoleyres sector are also well served. At Veysonnaz-Thyon snowmaking now covers 80% of the area. We have been very impressed with its use on the runs down to Mayens-de-L'Ours and to Veysonnaz. Piste grooming is good.

FOR EXPERTS ★★★★★
The main attraction
Verbier has some superb tough slopes, many of them off-piste and needing a guide – see feature panel. There are few black pistes; most steep runs are instead classified as itinéraires and 'marked, not maintained, not controlled'. They are said to be closed if unsafe, but this is not the formal position. Since they are not patrolled, you should not ski them alone. All very unsatisfactory. The black pistes that do exist are mostly like nearby reds. The front face of Mont-Fort is an exception: a long mogul field, with a choice of gradient from steep to intimidatingly steep. The World Cup run (Piste de l'Ours) at Veysonnaz is a steepish, often icy red, ideal for really speeding down when in good nick. The two most popular itinéraires to Tortin are both excellent in their

different ways. The one from Chassoure starts with a rocky traverse at the top and is then normally one huge, steep, wide mogul field. The north-facing one from Gentianes is longer, less steep, but feels much more of an adventure (keep left for shallower slopes and better snow).

The improved accessibility of the Bruson slopes will encourage experts to try the great tree skiing there.

FOR INTERMEDIATES ★★★★★
Be willing to travel
Many mileage-hungry intermediates find Verbier disappointing. The intermediate slopes in the main area are concentrated between Attelas and the village, above and below Les Ruinettes, plus the little bowl at Lac des Vaux and the sunny slopes at La Chaux. This is all excellent and varied intermediate territory, but there isn't much of it; and it is used by the bulk of the visitors staying in one of Switzerland's largest resorts. So it is often crowded, especially the lovely sweeping red from Attelas to Les Ruinettes. There is excellent easy blue run skiing at La Chaux, including a 'slow skiing' piste.

The under-used Savoleyres area has good intermediate slopes, usually better snow and fewer people. It is also a good hill for mixed abilities, with variations of many runs. There is a blue run linking this sector to the Médran lift base, but the way down to that link from the top is not easy.

The easier access to Bruson makes the area worth a visit. The Veysonnaz-Thyon and Nendaz sectors are also worth exploring (those not up to the itinéraires can ride the lifts down).

FOR BEGINNERS ★★★★★
OK but not ideal
There are sunny nursery slopes close to the middle of the village and at the top in Les Esserts. These are fine provided they have snow, and they are well equipped with snowmaking. Day passes covering these two areas are available. For progression, a local Verbier pass is available. Progression to longer runs is not straightforward, but there are easy blues at La Chaux and on the back of Savoleyres.

FOR BOARDERS ★★★★★
Extreme freeride heaven
Verbier has become synonymous with extreme snowboarding and is generally

seen as a freeriders' resort, with powder, cliffs, natural hits and trees all easily accessible. The final event of the Freeride world tour (see www.freerideworldtour.com) is held here every March on the Bec des Rosses. There is a lot of steep and challenging terrain to be explored with a guide, but the pistes and itinéraires will provide most riders with plenty to think about.

Chairlifts and gondolas serve the main area, with no drags. The area is far from ideal for beginners and timid intermediates, who should stick to the lower blue runs and Savoleyres. The terrain park is good.

FOR CROSS-COUNTRY ★☆☆☆☆
Little on offer

There's a 4km loop in Verbier, 10km at Les Ruinettes-La Chaux and 8km down the valley in Champsec and Lourtier.

MOUNTAIN RESTAURANTS ★★★☆☆
Improving, at last

Most restaurants are surprisingly uninspiring for such an upmarket resort. But a few new openings have improved things recently.

Editors' choice In the main area, the rustic Chez Dany (771 2524) is an old favourite – a classic chalet in the forest, on the itinéraire on skier's left of the area; we have had many good lunches here over many years, the last in 2013.

Worth knowing about At Attelas, La Vache – recently opened by the team that runs the Farinet in town – makes a great alternative to the dreary self-service places, offering pizzas, pastas, soups and salads at prices below the Verbier norm; 'exceptional', said one reporter. Service can be slow, though. The men's toilets are worth a visit (check out the Lawrence Dallaglio cubicle). We lack reports on the same team's Cuckoo's Nest, also at Attelas.

Mayen, below Ruinettes and accessible from the Col des Mines itinéraire, has 'great views' and 'very good table-service'. Carrefour, down near the nursery slopes, is 'cosy in bad conditions and excellent in good weather'.

In the Mont-Fort sector, the shacks at Col des Gentianes were replaced two years back by a giant igloo with an aluminium exterior; it's self-service and 'gets extremely busy', but it's an advance on the shacks, and offers 'a good range of food'. Down the hill, Cabane Mont-Fort is a proper mountain refuge off the run to La Chaux. The setting and the views are the highlights, but the food is good too – goulash soup, brownies, crepes all recommended; gets busy though. Further down at La Chaux, the 'excellent' table-service Dahu does 'fantastic pizza' among other things (there is also a more limited self-service section).

There are some nice places on Savoleyres, though we rarely get reports. The Croix de Coeur has great views from the terrace and 'very pleasant' table-service of good food. Don't overlook places lower down, sharing great views – the rustic Marmotte and the Namasté, and on the fringe of the village the Sonalon – 'perfect food and friendly service'.

There are two picnic rooms: at Les Ruinettes and at Savoleyres.

Verbier

505

Build your own shortlist: www.wheretoskiandsnowboard.com

danni sports
Verbier / Switzerland

SKI RENTAL · SKI TOURING · SNOW SHOES · SKI REPAIR

Professional and experienced staff · security and quality are our priority

www.danni-sports.ch

CHILDCARE

Schtroumpfs
t 771 6585
Ages 3mnth to 3yr

Kids Club
t 775 3363
Age 3 to 6

Babysitter list
At tourist office

Ski school (Swiss)
From age 4

VERBIER ST-BERNARD / ALAIN
BOUVET

There are fabulous
views in several
directions from the
top of Mont-Fort ⬎

SCHOOLS AND GUIDES ★★★★★
Good reports

There's no shortage of schools to
choose between. New Generation, well
established and a reader favourite in
several top French resorts, has its first
Swiss branch in Verbier (now joined by
another in Villars). Reports welcome.
We were very impressed with our
mountain guide from Adrenaline.
European Snowsport has been praised
for competitive pricing of private
lessons. British instructor Warren
Smith runs his Ski Academy here (five-
day courses that you have to book in
advance) – judged 'excellent' by a
reporter this year – and Powder
Extreme specializes in off-piste. We
have skied with both of these outfits
and thought them good.

FOR FAMILIES ★★★★★
Good for childcare

The nursery slopes are central, and the
Swiss school's facilities are good.
There are considerable reductions on
the lift pass price for families. The
possibility of leaving very young
babies at the Schtroumpfs nursery is
valuable. Nanny services are offered by
Chalet Services Verbier.

STAYING THERE

There are surprisingly few apartments
and B&Bs, though there are
inexpensive B&Bs in Le Châble. Hotels
are pricey for their classifications.
Chalets Of course, the lunatic Swiss
minimum wage policy (see Swiss
introduction) has had an impact in
Verbier, the chalet holiday capital of
Switzerland. But Inghams continues to
run the chalet hotel de Verbier, and
there are still plenty of upmarket
places available, eg from Ski Verbier.
Hotels Two 5-stars, five 4-stars, ten
3-stars and a few simpler places.
★★★★★Chalet d'Adrien (771 6200) Relais
& Châteaux. A beautifully furnished
29-room chalet, with top-notch food.
In a peaceful setting next to the
Savoleyres lift, with great views. 'Very
much worth its high prices,' says a
reporter this year; 'superb – attentive
service, good restaurant'.
★★★★★W Verbier (079 173 6541) Newly
opened, right by the slope and
gondola at Médran – the only ski
resort hotel in the worldwide chain of
self-consciously edgy W hotels. Take a
look at the Leicester Square one to
get a feel. Spa, gym and pool.

NEW
GENERATION
SKI & SNOWBOARD SCHOOL ●●●●●

KEEN TO RAISE
THE BAR?
Jon used to practise law in Sweden.
Now he helps clients battle the
bumps in Verbier.

Verbier
Tel: 0844 770 4733 www.skinewgen.com

SCHOOLS

Swiss
t 775 3363

Fantastique
t 771 4141

Adrenaline
t 771 7459

Altitude
t 771 6006

New Generation
t +33 479 010318
0844 770 4733 (UK)
www.skinewgen.com

European Snowsport
t 771 6222

Powder Extreme
t 076 479 8771
020 8123 9483 (UK)

Fresh Tracks
t 079 388 3729

Warren Smith Ski Academy
t 01525 374757 (UK)

Classes (Swiss prices)
5 half-days 290 francs
Private lessons
From 195 francs for
2hr for 1 or 2 people

GUIDES

Guides de Verbier
t 775 3370

GETTING THERE

Air Sion 55km/
35 miles (1hr);
Geneva 160km/
100 miles (2hr);
Zürich 280km/
175 miles (3hr)

Rail Le Châble (7km/
4 miles); regular
buses to resort or
gondola

ACTIVITIES

Indoor Sports centre
(swimming pool, ice
rink, curling, squash,
sauna, solarium,
steam bath, hot tub),
museums, galleries

Outdoor Cleared
walking paths, ice
climbing, paragliding,
snowshoeing,
tobogganing

****Nevaï** (775 4000) Modern,
minimalist, trendy, next to Farm Club
(same ownership). Après-ski bar.

****Vanessa** (775 2800) Central, with
spacious apartments as well as rooms.

***Farinet** (771 6626) Central, British-
owned, with a focal après-ski bar.

***Poste** (771 6681) Midway between
centre and Médran; pool. Some rooms
small. 'Pleasant, good food.'

***Rotonde** (771 6525) Much cheaper;
well positioned between centre and
Médran; some budget rooms.

Apartments There are surprisingly few
on the UK market. Ski Expectations
has a conveniently located four-
bedroom chalet and studio apartment.

EATING OUT ★★★★
Plenty of choice
There is a wide range of restaurants;
many are listed in a free pocket guide.

The 5-star Chalet d'Adrien is one of
the best gourmet places in town (one
Michelin star). We've had good (but
pricey) meals in the Nevaï and Cordée
des Alpes hotels, and in the Rouge
Restaurant and Club, and enjoyed
sushi at the Nomad. We've also had
good meals in the stylish, quiet
Millénium, which is 'the place to go for
top-quality venison and steaks'.

An assiduous reporter this year
identifies three 'very good' traditional
places where you can expect 'a cosy
Alpine atmosphere, open fires, good
food and service': the Ecurie, Grange
and Vieux Verbier. The ever-popular Fer
à Cheval is known for its pizzas, but
other dishes are also very good
('superb steak tartare').

You can be ferried by snowcat or
snowmobile to various restaurants on
the lower slopes, notably Chez Dany
or la Marlenaz.

APRES-SKI ★★★★★
Throbbing but expensive
On the slopes, popular stops include
the Rocks bar at Ruinettes, Chalet
Carlsberg and the yurts of Bar 1936. In
town, the Offshore Coffee Bar at
Médran is ever popular for people-
watching, milk shakes and cakes. The
Apres Ski Bar at the Farinet (with
happy hour from 4pm to 5pm and live
bands daily) and the Big Ben pub are
lively. The Nevaï hotel has live music
on its terraces, and the Rouge at the
bottom of the golf course is packed,
thanks to its popular sun deck and
resident DJs.

The Pub Mont-Fort is as popular as

ever with 'saisonnaires and would-be
saisonnaires'. The Fer à Cheval has a
'great atmosphere from après through
to the small hours'. You can party for
12 hours in the award-winning Farinet,
from happy hour at 4pm in the Apres
Ski Bar with live bands, until 4am
when the Casbah nightclub closes. It
rocks to live bands and DJs shipped in
from Ibiza regularly ('packed with
people dancing on the tables and bar
– an iconic après-ski place').

Crock No Name is a cool cocktail
bar often with a blues band or a DJ.
T-Bar is 'packed' for live rugby and
football, 'best on live music nights'.

The famous Farm Club is seriously
pricey – and in the eight years we've
been keeping records has generated
not one reader report, unsurprisingly.

OFF THE SLOPES ★★★
A few things to do
Verbier has an excellent sports centre
(with pool, saunas, hot tubs), an ice
rink with curling, dog sledding
between Les Ruinettes and La Chaux
and some nice walks. Montreux is an
enjoyable train excursion from Le
Châble, and Martigny is worth a visit
for the Roman remains and art gallery.
Reporters have recommended the spa
complex at Lavey-les-Bains. Various
mountain restaurants are accessible to
pedestrians – a walkers' pass covers
most of the local lifts. There is a
popular long toboggan run on
Savoleyres.

LINKED RESORT – 1365m
NENDAZ
Nendaz is little known in Britain but is
a major resort, with over 17,000 beds
(practically all in apartments). Most of
the resort is modern, built in
traditional chalet style. It enjoys great
views across the Rhône valley.

It's a sizeable and sprawling place,
and the centre is busy with traffic. The
local bus services are reliable, but get
oversubscribed at peak times. There
are 100km of walks, an ice rink, fitness
centre, climbing wall, and squash
courts. Neige Aventure provides 'top-
class mountain guides'.

Nendaz has its own slopes, but lots
of people staying here use it as a back
door to Verbier. If that's your plan,
check out the latest position on lift
pass sharing before you book. If the 4
Valleys pass is not operating, you
won't even be able to access Verbier

Verbier

Build your own shortlist: www.wheretoskiandsnowboard.com

UK PACKAGES

Alpine Answers, Alpine Weekends, Belvedere Travel, Bramble Ski, Carrier, Crystal, Crystal Finest, Elegant Resorts, Erna Low, Flexiski, Friendship Travel, Inghams, Interactive Resorts, Jeffersons, Kaluma, Luxury Chalet Collection, Momentum, Mountain Beds, Oxford Ski Co, Peak Ski, Powder White, PowderBeds, Scott Dunn, Ski Bespoke, Ski Expectations, Ski Freedom, Ski Independence, Ski Line, Ski Safari, Ski Verbier, Ski Weekend, Skitracer, Skiweekends.com, Skiworld, Snow Finders, Snow-wise, STC, Supertravel, Thomson, VIP, White Roc
Nendaz Alpine Answers, Erna Low, Lagrange, Mountain Beds, Peak Ski, Ski Club Freshtracks, Skiworld, STC, Ted Bentley
Veysonnaz Luxury Chalet Collection, Oxford Ski Co, Peak Ski

by driving or taking a bus to Siviez, and starting/finishing skiing there. The Verbier pass doesn't cover Siviez.

A 12-person gondola takes you to the top of the local slopes at Tracouet. This is a splendid, sunny little shelf with gentle slopes and long, shady red and blue runs back down to Nendaz. Getting back from Siviez is speeded up by a new gondola from Siviez to Plan-du-Fou, replacing the old chairlift. But skiing home still involves taking an itinéraire (or riding a cable car down) followed by a black run – too tricky for many intermediates.

Two small 3-star hotels, both about five minutes' walk from the lift, have been tipped by readers. The 'basic but pleasant' Mont-Fort (288 2616) is 'friendly' with a 'cool urban' bar. The Déserteur (288 2455) has 'excellent staff and owner' in 'nice surroundings'. There's also a plentiful supply of apartments. Christiana 2 is right opposite the gondola station, with spacious apartments.

There's quite a wide choice of restaurants, offering Tex-Mex, pizzas, Thai and sushi, as well as steaks and local mountain food. Chez Edith, a tiny restaurant on the way to Siviez, has been recommended. The Cactus Saloon is 'lively'.

LINKED RESORT – 1730m
SIVIEZ

Siviez, a small huddle of buildings in an isolated spot, is effectively a junction of the slopes of Verbier, Nendaz and Veysonnaz-Thyon. Lift pass arrangements permitting, it is the best base from which to explore the whole 4 Valleys lift network, though lodging is limited almost entirely to apartments. There are daytime buses to/from Nendaz. The long and gentle blue run through the sheltered valley from Tortin is super beginner progression territory. It is also an excellent base for doing the tough skiing of Verbier – you can end the day with a descent of 1600m vertical from Mont-Fort; no noise in the evenings; perfect.

LINKED RESORT – 1300m
VEYSONNAZ

Veysonnaz is a small, family resort, sunny in the afternoon, at the foot of an excellent, long red slope from the ridge above Thyon. A second excellent

(though often icy) red, regularly used for major races, descends to the isolated lift base of Mayens-de-L'Ours.

The resort is spread widely across and down the hillside, with extensive views across the Rhône valley. The original attractive old village, complete with church, is two hairpin bends below Veysonnaz Station, the lift base and the main focus of the place for the visitor. The link up to Thyon is an eight-seat gondola, but progress from there towards Verbier is a slow business. Taking a car means you can drive to Siviez for much quicker access to the Verbier slopes. Shuttle-buses serve the lifts, but they are not super-frequent and do not run on Saturdays.

Veysonnaz Station has the essential facilities – half a dozen bars and cafes, four restaurants, a disco or two and a wellness centre with swimming pool and spa facilities (closed Saturdays). There are adequate shops, including a butcher and baker.

Accommodation is mainly in apartments – substantial chalet-style buildings dotted along the road the lift base is on. There are plenty of smaller chalets, too. There are two 3-star hotels next to the gondola station: the Chalet Royal (208 5644) has 'stunning views', though not from all rooms, and 'generally good' food. The Magrappé (208 5700) has 'a bit of atmosphere' and is more the focus of lively après-ski. There are some B&Bs.

There are two schools: Swiss and Neige Aventure. And there is a children's day care centre on the mountain. A 5km cross-country trail has great views.

LINKED RESORT – 2100m
THYON 2000

Thyon 2000 is a purpose-built collection of plain, medium-rise apartment blocks just above the treeline at the hub of the Veysonnaz-Thyon sector of the 4 Valleys. The apartments are a bit of a blot on the landscape. It has the basics of resort life – supermarket, newsagent, a couple of restaurants (the Luge pizzeria was rated 'excellent, with friendly atmosphere and reasonable prices'), an indoor pool and a disco. A free shuttle-bus runs to Les Collons. There's a fair-sized terrain park and snowcross, children's snow garden and a kindergarten, as well as a ski school. The slopes are ideal for families and beginners, with two nursery lifts close to the accommodation. The elderly lift network shared with Les Collons and Les Masses gained one new chair last season. Snowmaking is extensive.

LINKED RESORT – 1800m
LES COLLONS

Some 300m below Thyon, at the foot of a broad, east-facing slope, Les Collons is nothing more than a couple of strings of chalet-style buildings spread along two roads following the hillside, 50m vertical apart; a lot of building has been going on recently.

Three draglifts go up towards Thyon from the upper level of the resort, and a chairlift from the lower level takes you above Thyon. There's 6km of cross-country. A free shuttle-bus runs to Thyon.

Most accommodation is in apartments, but there are also a couple of modest hotels – including the 3-star Cambuse (281 1883), just below one of the lift bases. There are a few bars and restaurants, plus a 1km toboggan run through the woods above the village. Prepared walking trails add up to a modest 8km.

LINKED RESORT – 1515m
LES MASSES

Half-a-dozen hairpins down the mountainside from Les Collons, Les Masses is no more than a hamlet at the base of the chairlifts that form the southern limit of the Veysonnaz-Thyon slopes. The chair out of the village was upgraded to a fast quad last season. Beware: the home run is a red. Accommodation is in apartments. There is a grocery and a bar/restaurant.

LINKED RESORT – 1500m
LA TZOUMAZ

This tiny hamlet sits in a quiet valley on the shady, wooded side of Verbier's Savoleyres slope sector. There are a handful of small hotels, shops and restaurants, forming a very quiet place to stay and ski this underrated sector. A free bus serves the lifts. A gondola and a couple of fast chairs serve most of the slopes here. The 10km toboggan run back to the base area is one of the longest in the region; we're told by the tourist office that it is a professional run and not suitable for

children under seven; helmets are recommended.

LINKED RESORT – 820m
LE CHÂBLE

Le Châble is a village in the valley below Verbier, set off the main road to Italy at the bottom of the hairpin road up to Verbier. Beside the main road is a huge car park and a queue-free gondola that takes 9 minutes to Verbier and goes on (without changing cabins) to Les Ruinettes – access to the slopes can be just as quick from here as from Verbier. The gondola runs till 7.30pm; buses run later. A second gondola now takes you to the heart of the slopes of Bruson. Le Châble is on the rail network (the station is near the gondolas).

There are several modest hotels; the 2-star Giétroz (776 1184) is tipped – 'comfortable, frequented by locals, good food and range of beer and wine'. Other places to eat include La Ruinette ('really good food at fairly reasonable prices and interesting wine list') and the Chat Bleu in the older part of Châble – 'pleasant, friendly place serving good food'. La Ruinette has apartments to let. The hotel de la Poste has a bar/nightclub, Manhattan.

LINKED RESORT – 1100m
BRUSON

Bruson is a small village on a shelf just above Le Châble, across the valley from Verbier. It's now reachable by a new gondola from Le Châble. The slopes above the new gondola are served by a triple chair up to a ridge, on the far side of which is a short draglift serving a tight little bowl. In addition to the intermediate pistes served by these lifts there are large areas of off-piste terrain – including tremendous skiing in well-spaced trees that is reminiscent of Canadian heli-skiing – quite steep in places. The front side of the mountain is mainly north-east facing, so it keeps its snow well. The off-piste down the back towards Orsières is good; you return by train. Bruson can be delightfully quiet and a great contrast with Verbier; whether it will remain that way with the new access gondola remains to be seen (reports, please). It would be a good place to go in white-out conditions.

Phone numbers
From elsewhere in Switzerland add the prefix 027; from abroad use the prefix +41 27

TOURIST OFFICES

Verbier / Le Châble (Bruson) / La Tzoumaz
en.verbier.ch

Nendaz / Siviez
www.nendaz.ch

Veysonnaz
www.veysonnaz.ch

Thyon 2000 / Les Collons / Les Masses
www.thyon-region.ch

SNOWPIX.COM / CHRIS GILL

Villars

Traditional year-round resort with local low-altitude slopes, a cog railway and a much-needed but far-flung glacier

TOP 10 RATINGS

Extent	★★★
Fast lifts	★★
Queues	★★★
Snow	★★
Expert	★★
Intermediate	★★★
Beginner	★★★★
Charm	★★★
Convenience	★★
Scenery	★★★

RPI 115

lift pass	£200
ski hire	£100
lessons	£110
food & drink	£190
total	**£600**

NEWS

2014/15: The snowmaking system is to be substantially extended so that all main runs and links between the resorts will be covered.

- ➕ Pleasant, traditional resort with a life outside skiing
- ➕ Fairly extensive intermediate slopes, linked by chairlift to Les Diablerets
- ➕ Distant access to glacier slopes beyond Les Diablerets
- ➕ Mountain railway is one way into the heart of the slopes

- ➖ Sunny slopes and modest altitudes mean unreliable local snow-cover – though the limited snowmaking is being improved
- ➖ Short runs on the upper slopes – verticals of 200m–300m
- ➖ Little to amuse experts on piste

Villars is popular with second-home owners because of its closeness to Geneva airport (a short drive down the hill puts you on the motorway for the airport). For many keen skiers, its low altitude and far from snow-sure slopes will make it a risky option when booking far in advance. But for a varied family holiday it has its attractions – not least the mountain railway.

THE RESORT

Villars sits on a sunny hillside looking across the Rhône valley to the Portes du Soleil. Its home slopes link to those of Les Chaux, above the delightfully rustic village of Gryon. You can get a whole area pass covering Les Diablerets (linked by a two-way lift) plus Leysin and Les Mosses (easy outings by rail or road). It also covers Glacier 3000, the small glacier area on Les Diablerets (the mountain) beyond Les Diablerets (the village). The SuperPass – introduced in 2012/13 –

includes Gstaad too. Getting to and from the glacier is a long, slow business – from Les Diablerets (the village) you need to catch a bus to the glacier lift or walk 10 mins to the Isenau area to ski down to it. Outings to Verbier are possible.

Village charm Villars is more a town than a village, with sprawling suburbs of chalets and several international schools. The focus is a longish, traffic-filled but pleasant street.

Convenience A slow cog railway goes from the main street up to the slopes around Bretaye. A gondola to Roc

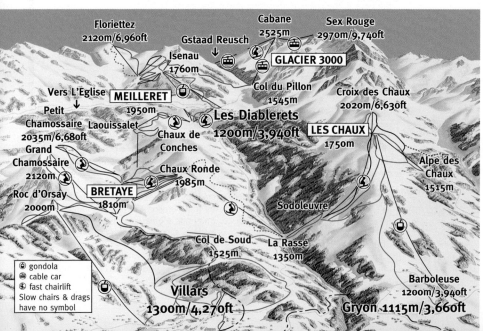

↑ The resort is a sprawl of chalets on a west-facing shelf, with dramatic views to the south
VILLARS TOURISM

KEY FACTS

| Resort | 1300m |
| | 4,270ft |

Villars, Gryon and Les Diablerets (excludes Glacier 3000)	
Slopes	1115-2120m
	3,660-6,960ft
Lifts	34
Pistes	100km
	62 miles
Blue	37%
Red	53%
Black	10%
Snowmaking	20%

d'Orsay at the other end of town is quicker. It's best to stay near one of these lifts or at a hotel with a shuttle, but there are ski-buses.

Scenery Although the slopes themselves may lack visual drama, you can't say that of the views of glacial peaks to the east and south, and across the Rhône valley to the Dents du Midi.

THE MOUNTAINS

There's a good mix of wooded and open slopes.

Slopes The cog railway goes up to the col of Bretaye, which has intermediate slopes on either side. To the east, open slopes go to La Rasse and the link to Les Chaux. There used to be another piste to La Rasse down from Chaux Ronde, but this is now an itinerary; it has a tricky section at the top that is often closed. There's an alternative blue run from Bretaye. From Les Chaux there are runs to Barboleuse above Gryon, with a gondola back up. The gondola from Villars takes you to Roc d'Orsay, from where you can head for Bretaye or back to Villars.

A long, painfully slow, two-way chairlift links via the peak of Meilleret to Les Diablerets, where there are further intermediate slopes on both sides of the village, and a long red run

from one sector to Col du Pillon for the cable car to Glacier 3000. The glacier area has very gentle slopes at the top, but there is a splendid run down the Combe d'Audon (classified black but of red gradient) with a dramatic cliff face rising up on the right. Part-way down at Oldenegg you can catch a fast chair which serves a splendid red run before going on to the valley.

Fast lifts Fast lifts exist, but so do old chairs and drags.

Queues The lifts at Bretaye get busy mainly at peak times. The buses and train can get overcrowded.

Terrain parks There's one at Chaux Ronde and another at Diablerets.

Snow reliability Low altitude and sunny slopes mean snow reliability isn't good – though on such gentle, grassy terrain, deep snow-cover isn't needed. Recent snowmaking on the runs back to town and at La Rasse are welcome improvements; and there are plans for more.

Experts Little on-piste challenge but some good off-piste with a guide.

Intermediates The local slopes offer a good variety. Les Chaux has some steeper slopes and a lovely long cruisey blue to Barboleuse. The run from Meilleret to Les Diablerets is a delightful long cruise that can be deserted first thing in the morning.

Build your own shortlist: www.wheretoskiandsnowboard.com

MOMENTUM SKI

Weekend & a la carte
ski holiday specialists

100% Tailor-made

Premier hotels
& apartments

Flexible travel
arrangements

020 7371 9111
WWW.MOMENTUMSKI.COM

Phone numbers
From elsewhere in
Switzerland add the
prefix 024; from
abroad use the prefix
+41 24

TOURIST OFFICE

www.villars.ch

VILLARS TOURISM

Bretaye is at the heart
of the local slopes –
at the top of the cog
railway ↘

Beginners The nursery slope behind the station is free to use. There is another at Gryon. There are gentle but often crowded runs at Bretaye.
Snowboarding There are a few tricky draglifts but good intermediate slopes.
Cross-country There are 50km of trails; those up the valley past La Rasse are long and pretty.
Mountain restaurants They are often oversubscribed. We like Lac des Chavonnes (a short walk below Petit Chamossaire); the Col de Soud is tipped: 'Very good food, a real sun trap.' The Golf Club does 'delicious tartiflette' and is a firm favourite of a 2014 visitor: 'It's just a lovely place to sit.' Above Gryon, we like the relatively quiet Restaurant 1882 at Les Chaux and Refuge Frience. There are picnic rooms at the top of the Roc d'Orsay gondola and at Les Chaux.
Schools and guides The two well-established schools here are joined this year by a new branch of New Generation, the school run by British instructors that gets so many glowing reports in the 10 other resorts where they operate (mainly in France).
Families La Trottinette non-ski nursery takes children up to six.

STAYING THERE

Hotels We've enjoyed staying at the 4-star central Golf (496 3838) – big rooms, spa facilities: 'Get a room with a balcony facing across the valley,' says a 2014 visitor. Nearby is the 3-star Alpe Fleurie (496 3070). The 4-star Eurotel Victoria (495 3131) is near the gondola and 'almost ski-in'.
Eating out The Sporting serves traditional dishes/grills, and the pizzas at the Pizzeria 'take some beating'.
Après-ski The rustic Buvette d'Arrivée on the home run above the top of town is popular at close of play, as is the Sporting. Try the 'very trendy' Moon Boot Lounge for cocktails.
Off the slopes Activities include paragliding, snowshoeing, skating, tobogganing, swimming and walking (there are 30km of prepared paths). Rail excursions are another option.

UK PACKAGES

Alpine Answers, Alpine Weekends, Bramble Ski, Carrier, Club Med, Erna Low, Momentum, Neilson, PowderBeds, Ski Bespoke, Ski Expectations, Ski Independence, Ski Safari, Ski Weekend, Skitracer, STC Switzerland Travel Centre, Tracks European Adventures, Zenith

NEW GENERATION
SKI & SNOWBOARD SCHOOL ●●●●●

#WINNING

Ale is an ex-professional athlete.
This winter, when he's not training
our instructor team, he'll help you
overcome your hurdles.

Villars
Tel: 0844 770 4733 www.skinewgen.com

Wengen

A charming old village, stunning scenery, an old cog railway and gentle intermediate slopes make for a relaxing and leisurely holiday

RATINGS

The mountains

Extent	★★★
Fast lifts	★★★★
Queues	★★★
Terrain p'ks	★
Snow	★★
Expert	★★
Intermediate	★★★★
Beginner	★★★
Boarder	★★
X-country	★
Restaurants	★★★
Schools	★★★
Families	★★★★

The resort

Charm	★★★★★
Convenience	★★★
Scenery	★★★★★
Eating out	★★
Après-ski	★★
Off-slope	★★★★

RPI 120

lift pass	£220
ski hire	£110
lessons	£115
food & drink	£185
total	**£630**

NEWS

Investment in lifts is on the back burner until the proposed new gondolas from Grindelwald to Männlichen and Eigergletscher are built – see 'News' in Grindelwald chapter. They will make coming back from Grindelwald much quicker.

- ➕ Some of the most spectacular scenery in the Alps
- ➕ Small, traditional, nearly traffic-free Alpine village
- ➕ Lots of long, gentle runs, ideal for leisurely intermediates
- ➕ Nursery slopes in heart of village
- ➕ Calm, unhurried atmosphere
- ➕ Good resort for families and groups that include non-skiers. It's easy to get around on mountain railways

- ➖ Limited terrain for experts and adventurous intermediates
- ➖ Natural snow unreliable (but substantial snowmaking now)
- ➖ Trains to slopes are slow and there are still a few old lifts
- ➖ Getting to/from Mürren and Grindelwald's First area are both a bit of a slog
- ➖ Subdued in the evening, with little variety of nightlife

Given the charm of the village, the friendliness of the locals and the drama of the scenery, it's easy to see why many people love Wengen – including large numbers of Brits who have been going for decades. It's great for a relaxing time, for those who don't take their skiing too seriously, for families and for mixed groups of intermediates and non-skiers.

Keen piste-bashers should not underestimate the drawbacks. If you're used to modern mega-resorts, you'll find Wengen a huge contrast, and may have difficulty adjusting. But the spectacularly scenic Jungfrau region is one that every keen skier should experience; and to experience all of it, Wengen – centrally placed between Mürren and Grindelwald – is the best base.

THE RESORT

Wengen is one of three resorts close together in the Jungfrau region. It is set on a sloping shelf above the Lauterbrunnen valley, opposite Mürren, and reached only by a cog railway, which carries on up to Kleine Scheidegg and the slopes shared with Grindelwald. Access to Mürren involves a train down to Lauterbrunnen, a cable car up and then another train (or a bus from Lauterbrunnen to a different two-stage cable car to Mürren). Access to the First area of Grindelwald is an even longer process, including skiing down to Grindelwald and crossing town – the planned new gondolas (see 'News') will speed up the return journey but not until 2016/17 at the earliest. The Jungfrau lift pass covers all three resorts. Outings further afield aren't really worth the effort.

VILLAGE CHARM ★★★★★
Almost traffic-free
The village was a farming community long before skiing arrived; it is still tiny, but dominated by sizeable hotels, mostly of Victorian origin. So it is not exactly chocolate-box pretty, but it is charming and relaxed, and almost traffic-free. There are electric hotel taxi-trucks and a few scruffy, engine-driven taxis. (Why not electric and smart taxis like Zermatt, we wonder?) The short main street is the hub. Lined with chalet-style shops and hotels, it also has the ice rink and village nursery slopes right next to it.

CONVENIENCE ★★★
Compact, but hilly in parts
Wengen is small, so location isn't as crucial as in many resorts. But those who don't fancy a steepish morning climb should avoid places down the hill, below the station (unless their hotel runs a shuttle service). The ridge where the slopes of Wengen meet those of Grindelwald is reached either by train or – much quicker (unless there's a long queue) – by cable car. Both stations are central. There are hotels on the home piste, convenient for the slopes. You can leave skis and boots at the station (we left our rental skis at Central Sport, which has a big storeroom and very friendly and helpful staff).

513

KEY FACTS

Resort	1275m
	4,180ft

Jungfrau region	
Slopes	945-2970m
	3,100-9,740ft
Lifts	45
Pistes	213km
	132 miles
Blue	33%
Red	49%
Black	18%
Snowmaking	40%

First-Männlichen-Kleine Scheidegg only	
Slopes	945-2500m
	3,100-8,200ft
Lifts	28
Pistes	170km
	106 miles

SCENERY ★★★★★
Simply the best

The views across the valley are stunning. They get even better higher up, when the famous trio of peaks comes fully into view – the Mönch (Monk) in the centre protecting the Jungfrau (Maiden) on the right from the Eiger (Ogre) on the left.

THE MOUNTAINS

Although Wengen is famous for the fearsome Lauberhorn Downhill course – the longest and one of the toughest on the World Cup circuit – its slopes are best suited to early intermediates. Most of the Downhill course is now open to the public and has excellent signs on the way explaining it. Most of Wengen's runs are gentle blues and reds, ideal for cruising.

Piste marking and piste map are poor; the Männlichen slopes, in particular, can be confusing.

EXTENT OF THE SLOPES ★★★★★
Picturesque playground

Most of the slopes are on the Grindelwald side of the mountain. From the railway station at Kleine Scheidegg you can head straight down to Grindelwald or work your way across to the top of the Männlichen. This area is served by a drag and several chairlifts, and can be reached directly from Wengen by the cable car. There are a few runs back down towards Wengen from the top of the Lauberhorn, but there's really only one below Wengernalp.

FAST LIFTS ★★★★★
OK except for the train

The fast cable car and slow train are the main access lifts; new fast chairs replacing old lifts have improved things higher up; the most recent was the Eigernordwand six-pack from below Kleine Scheidegg (on the Grindelwald side) to Eigergletscher, and the Wixi six-pack, which replaced an old double chair in 2012/13.

QUEUES ★★★★★
Village crowds, better higher up

Both the train and the cable car can be crowded at peak periods. And queues for the cable car can be lengthy ('40 minutes to an hour queue at the cable car at 9.30am,' said a February 2013 reporter; and we waited 20 minutes in low season March 2014). It is best to avoid travelling up at the same time as the ski school. Queues up the mountain have been alleviated a lot in the past few years by the installation of fast chairs, and we and reporters have experienced few problems in midweek. But weekends can be busy, especially on the Grindelwald side of the hill – the obvious entry point for residents of Bern attracted by the special family pass deals on Saturdays.

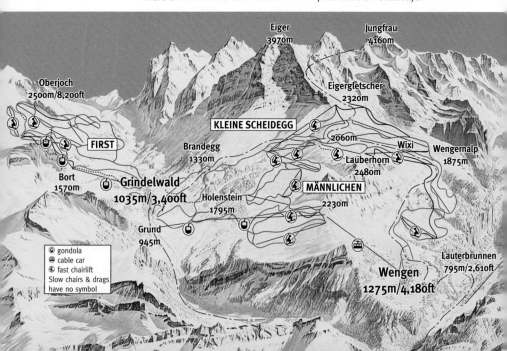

LIFT PASSES

Jungfrau

Prices in francs

Age	1-day	6-day
under 16	32	162
16 to 19	50	258
20 to 61	63	323
over 62	57	291

Free Under 6 (if with parent)

Beginner Points ticket

Notes Covers trains between villages and ski-bus; day pass is for First-Kleine Scheidegg-Männlichen area only; 5-day plus passes allow 50% reduction in Meiringen

Alternative passes Grindelwald and Wengen only; Mürren only; non-skier pass

THE BRITISH IN WENGEN

There's a very strong British presence in Wengen. Many Brits have been returning for years to the same rooms in the same hotels in the same week, and treat the resort as a sort of second home. There is an English church with weekly services, and a British-run ski club, the DHO (Downhill Only) – so named when the Brits who colonized the resort persuaded the locals to keep the summer railway running up the mountain in winter, so that they would no longer have to climb up in order to ski down again. That greatly amused the locals, who until then had regarded skiing in winter as a way to get around on snow rather than a pastime to be done for fun. The DHO is still going strong

TERRAIN PARKS ★☆☆☆☆
A fair trek

There isn't one. The nearest parks are at First and Mürren – each a fair trek.

SNOW RELIABILITY ★★☆☆☆
Improved snowmaking helps

Most slopes are below 2000m, and the few runs on the Wengen side of the ridge are sunny; the long blue run back to the village is particularly vulnerable. But a lot of snowmaking has been added recently, and some 60% of the slopes in the Kleine Scheidegg-Männlichen area are now covered. On our March 2014 visit during exceptionally hot, sunny weather, snow-cover was not a problem and most slopes were in good condition until lunchtime, when they went slushy. Several reporters also found the slopes in 'excellent' condition when they visited late in the season.

FOR EXPERTS ★★☆☆☆
Few challenges

Wengen is quite limited for experts. The only genuine black runs in the area are parts of the Lauberhorn World Cup Downhill and a couple of pistes from Eigergletscher towards Wixi. There are some decent off-piste runs from under the north face of the Eiger and the Eigernordwand lift helps with access to these. For more challenges it's well worth going to nearby Mürren, around an hour away. Heli-trips are organized if there are enough takers.

FOR INTERMEDIATES ★★★★☆
Wonderful if the snow is good

Wengen and Grindelwald share superb easy-intermediate slopes. Nearly all are long blue or gentle red runs (though there are genuine reds too); read the Grindelwald chapter. The run back to Wengen is a relaxing end to the day, although it can be crowded and the snow can be patchy.

For tougher pistes, head for the top of the Lauberhorn chair and then the runs to Kleine Scheidegg, or to Wixi (following the start of the Downhill course). You could also try the shady run from Eigergletscher, which often has the best snow late in the season. Or head for Mürren – well worth doing for adventurous intermediates for a day or two during a week's stay.

FOR BEGINNERS ★★★☆☆
Not ideal

There's a nursery slope in the centre of the village – convenient and gentle, but it gets afternoon sun and at this modest altitude the snow can suffer. There's a beginners' area at Wengernalp and some short beginner lifts up at Kleine Scheidegg, but of course to use these you have to take the train down as well as up, or tackle the blue run down to the village, which can be tricky and has some flat sections. None of these areas offers free lifts, but there are alternatives to buying a full lift pass (there is a points card). There are plenty of good, long, gentle runs to progress to on the slopes above Grindelwald, reached either by train to Kleine Scheidegg or cable car to Männlichen.

FOR BOARDERS ★★☆☆☆
Best for beginners

Wengen is not a bad place for gentle boarding – the nursery area is not ideal, but beginners have plenty of slopes to progress to, with lots of long blue and red runs served by the train and chairlifts. Getting from Kleine Scheidegg to Männlichen means an unavoidable draglift, though. And the slope back to Wengen is narrow and almost flat in places, so you may have to scoot. For the steepest slopes and best freeriding, experts will want to head for Mürren.

FOR CROSS-COUNTRY ★☆☆☆☆
There is none

There's no cross-country in Wengen itself, which seems a shame given the nature of the resort. There are 12km of tracks down in the Lauterbrunnen valley, where the snow is unreliable.

MOUNTAIN RESTAURANTS ★★★☆☆
Plenty of variety

Editors' choice The Jungfrau hotel at Wengernalp (855 1622) is an old favourite of ours and a repeat visit in 2014 reinforced our view: the menu is limited, but includes possibly the best rösti in the Alps (with Gorgonzola and egg), and the view from the terrace is breathtaking. It's pricey, operates a two-sitting booking policy and doesn't take credit cards (so take plenty of cash), but we still love it.

Worth knowing about You also get magnificent views from the narrow balcony of Wengen's highest restaurant, Eigergletscher (which we

SCHOOLS

Swiss
t 855 2022

Swiss Kleine Scheidegg
t 079 179 9090

Privat
t 855 5005

Altitude
t 853 0040

Classes (Swiss prices)
6 3hr-days 289 francs

Private lessons
From 90 francs for 1hr

CHILDCARE

Playhouse
t 076 258 5425
From 1mnth to 8yr

Snowli Club Sunshine
t 854 1280
From 6mnth

Ski school
From age 3

GETTING THERE

Air Bern 65km/
40 miles (1hr); Zürich
150km/95 miles (2hr);
Basel 165km/100
miles (2hr)

Rail Station in resort

UK PACKAGES

Alpine Answers, Club
Med, Crystal, Crystal
Finest, Inghams,
Momentum, Neilson,
PowderBeds, Ski Club
Freshtracks, Ski Line,
Ski Safari, Skitracer,
Snow-wise, STC,
Switzerland Travel
Centre, Thomson

ACTIVITIES

Indoor Swimming
pools (in hotels),
sauna, solarium,
whirlpool, massage
(in hotels)

Outdoor Ice rink,
curling, 100km of
cleared paths,
tobogganing,
paragliding,
snowshoeing

are told has changed hands and now does excellent food – reports please). The Bellevue hotel at Kleine Scheidegg is pricey and has a limited menu, but magnificent views from the terrace and a wonderfully old-fashioned wood-panelled dining room for bad weather days. 'Super service; expensive but worth it,' says a 2014 reporter. The table-service section of the restaurant at the Männlichen top station offers a 'decent range of dishes – the star being a generous plate of dried meats and cheese'. Recent reporters have enjoyed the busy Eigernordwand restaurant ('great goulash soup in a bread bowl') which has self- and table-service sections. Two 2014 reporters endorse previous recommendations for Mary's Cafe at the bottom of the Lauberhorn ('hearty, tasty mountain food', 'excellent cake'). There is a picnic room at the Männlichen top station. For restaurants above Grindelwald, read that chapter.

SCHOOLS AND GUIDES ★★★☆☆
Reports please
We have no recent reports. Guides are available for heli-trips and off-piste.

FOR FAMILIES ★★★★☆
A family favourite
It is an attractive and reassuring village for families. The nursery slope is in the centre and the Playground kindergarten in the tourist office nearby. There is a list of babysitters available at the tourist office. The train gives easy access to higher slopes.

STAYING THERE

Most accommodation is in hotels. Catered chalets and self-catering apartments are few.
Staying down in Lauterbrunnen will halve your accommodation costs and give faster access to Mürren.
Hotels There are about two dozen hotels, mostly 4-star and 3-star, with a handful of simpler places.
★★★★Beausite Park (856 5161) The best in town reputedly: 'Very well run with charming staff, good food.' Good pool, steam, sauna, massage. Situated at the top of the nursery slopes.
★★★★Caprice (856 0606) Small, smartly furnished, chalet style, just above the station. Sauna and massage.
★★★★Regina (856 5858) Grand Victorian hotel with piano bar, sun terrace, spa and fitness room just up the hill from

the station – 'Tremendous food and service, though drinks are expensive.'
★★★★Silberhorn (856 5131) Comfortable, modern, central. 'Good food, very helpful, friendly staff.'
★★★★Sunstar (856 5200) Family-friendly, modern, on main street right opposite the cable car. 'Extremely welcoming, good rooms, pool a bit cool.'
★★★★Victoria Lauberhorn (856 2929) On main street. 'Friendly, lovely spa and pool, good food.'
★★★★Wengener Hof (856 6969) No prizes for style or convenience, but recommended in the past for good food, peace, helpful staff and spacious rooms with good views.
★★★Alpenrose (855 3216) 130-year-old family-run hotel with a reputation for friendliness, service and good food; long-standing British favourite; morning shuttle service up to station.
★★★Belvédère (856 6868) Some way out, buffet-style meals, family-friendly, spacious rooms and grand art nouveau public rooms.
★★★Falken (856 5121) A long-standing British favourite next door to the Regina. 'Refined elegance from a bygone era.'
Apartments The hotel Bernerhof's decent Résidence apartments are well positioned just off the main street, and the hotel facilities are available for guests to use. Apartments are available to book independently too – we took one for our 2014 visit.
At altitude You can stay at two points up the mountain reached by the railway: the Jungfrau hotel (855 1622) at Wengernalp – with fabulous views – and at Kleine Scheidegg, where there are rooms in the grand and traditional Bellevue des Alpes (855 1212), and dormitory space above the Grindelwaldblick restaurant (855 1374) and the station buffet.

EATING OUT ★★☆☆☆
Mainly hotel-based
Most restaurants are in hotels and offer good food and service. The Silberhorn offers varied and 'excellent' meals. The Bernerhof has good-value traditional dishes. The little hotel Hirschen offers speciality steaks. The hotel Regina's food is 'excellent but they won't serve tap water'. There's no shortage of fondues in the village, and several bars do casual food. Da Sina is a steakhouse and pizzeria. Café Gruebi is the place for cakes.

Phone numbers
From elsewhere in
Switzerland add the
prefix 033; from
abroad use the prefix
+41 33

TOURIST OFFICE
www.wengen.ch

JUNGFRAU REGION MARKETING AG

There's a nice little
area in the village
centre where families
can play; and the
gentle nursery slopes
are just off to the left
of this pic ↓

APRES-SKI ★★☆☆☆
It depends on what you want
People's reactions to Wengen's après-
ski scene vary widely, according to
their expectations and their appetites.

If you're used to raving in Kitzbühel
or Les Deux-Alpes, you'll rate Wengen
dead, especially for young people. If
you've heard it's dead, you may be
pleasantly surprised to find that there
is a handful of small bars that do
good business both early and late in
the evening.

On the mountain, the outdoor
Läger Bar, next to the Männlichen
chair, is good for 'sitting in a deckchair
in the sun'. Tipirama (a wigwam at
Kleine Scheidegg) is a fun place
immediately after skiing 'if not too
cold', sometimes with DJs and live
bands; you can catch the train down.
The Start Bar on the Lauberhorn does
'tasty pancakes'. The Wäsch bar at the
Bumps section of the home run is a
popular final-run stop-off.

In the village the tiny Pickel Bar is
popular at the end of the day. The
'cosy' bar of the Silberhorn hotel gets
the thumbs up this year. The small,
traditional Tanne is also tipped. Sina's,
a little way out of the centre, next to

the Club Med, 'is probably the best
night-time bar with DJ and karaoke'.
The 'lively' Rocks Bar, with its plasma
screens showing Sky Sports, has 'the
best Guinness'. There are discos and
live music in some hotels.

OFF THE SLOPES ★★★★☆
Good for a relaxing time
With its unbeatable scenery and
pedestrian-friendly trains and cable car
(there's a special – but pricey – pass
for pedestrians), Wengen is a superb
resort for those who want a relaxing
holiday. It's easy for mixed parties of
skiers and non-skiers to meet up for
lunch on the mountain. There are
some lovely walks ('paths are superbly
signposted'), and ice skating,
tobogganing ('well worth doing') and
curling ('great fun') are popular.
Several hotels have health spas. The
cinema often shows films in English.

Excursions to Interlaken and Bern
are possible by train, as is the trip up
to the Jungfraujoch (see the
Grindelwald chapter). From Männlichen
there are scenic flights giving splendid
close-up views of the mountains and
glaciers, either by helicopter or much
cheaper small plane.

Wengen - Switzerland

HOTEL ★★★
Alpenrose
WENGEN

Perfect Package Offers
including skipass!

www.alpenrose.ch

Build your own shortlist: www.wheretoskiandsnowboard.com

SNOWPIX.COM / CHRIS GILL

Zermatt

A magical combination of just about everything you could hope to find in a ski resort, both on and off the slopes

RATINGS

The mountains

Extent	★★★★
Fast lifts	★★★★★
Queues	★★★
Terrain p'ks	★★★
Snow	★★★★
Expert	★★★★
Intermediate	★★★★
Beginner	★★
Boarder	★★★
X-country	★
Restaurants	★★★★★
Schools	★★★
Families	★★

The resort

Charm	★★★★
Convenience	★★
Scenery	★★★★★
Eating out	★★★★★
Après-ski	★★★★★
Off-slope	★★★★

RPI   140

lift pass	£260
ski hire	£135
lessons	£125
food & drink	£210
total	**£730**

NEWS

2013/14: The Sunnegga funicular was upgraded, with bigger carriages and more of them. Snowmaking capacity was increased.

- ✚ Wonderful, high, extensive slopes
- ✚ Spectacular high mountain scenery
- ✚ Charming although rather sprawling old village, largely traffic-free
- ✚ Reliable snow at altitude
- ✚ World's best mountain restaurants (but not for quick pit stops)
- ✚ Nightlife to suit most tastes
- ✚ Lots to do off the slopes
- ✚ Linked to sunny Cervinia in Italy
- ✚ Extensive helicopter operation

- ➖ You may face long walks, crowded buses or pricey taxi rides
- ➖ Far from ideal for novices
- ➖ High prices for everything, including lift pass (one of Europe's priciest)
- ➖ Slow train up to Gornergrat
- ➖ Some lift queues at peak periods
- ➖ Annoying electric taxis in 'car-free' streets detract from ambience
- ➖ Few options to ski in bad weather; can be really windy or cold too

Our verdict is short and simple: you must try Zermatt before you die. There is nowhere else to match it. Its drawbacks are non-trivial but, for us and for virtually all our reporters, these pale into insignificance compared with its attractions. Editor Watts has taken countless holidays here. Enough said.

THE RESORT

Zermatt started life as a simple farming village, developed as a mountaineering centre in the 19th century, then became a winter resort. Summer is still as big as winter here.

The village is car-free, but not traffic-free – electric buggies operating either as hotel shuttles or as public taxis zip around the streets. Residents can drive up to Zermatt, but the rest of us must park at Täsch (or more distant Visp) and arrive by train. At Täsch there's a big car park (14.50 francs a day), and you can wheel luggage trolleys on and off the trains.

Zermatt mainly attracts a well-heeled international clientele; the clientele is also relatively, er, mature for what is quite a sporty resort.

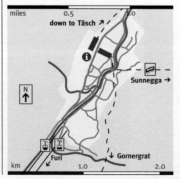

miles 0.5 / 1.0
down to Täsch ↗ /
N ↑
ⓘ
Sunnegga →
Furi
Gornergrat ↓
km 1.0 2.0

VILLAGE CHARM ★★★★
Old and new in harmony

The resort is a mixture of ancient chalets and barns, grand 19th-century hotels and modern buildings, most in traditional style but some decidedly funky. The oldest, most charming part of the village has narrow lanes and old wooden barns with slate roofs, many of them supported on stone 'legs'. But the resort now sprawls along both sides of the river with a lot of new building at both ends and up the steep mountainsides.

Arriving at the station, it all seems very towny, especially if there is no snow on the ground. The centre doesn't have the relaxed, rustic feel of other car-free Swiss resorts, such as Wengen and Saas-Fee. The main street running away from the station is lined with luxury hotels, restaurants, banks and glitzy shops. The electric taxis are intrusive, especially at busy times.

CONVENIENCE ★★★★★
Lifts at opposite ends

The village is small enough to get around on foot in the evenings, but not in ski boots and carrying skis. There is a free ski-bus service; but it is inadequate at peak times, especially from the Matterhorn area at the end of the day. Electric taxis are pricey.

You arrive at a fair-sized square at the north end of the resort, where you

KEY FACTS

KEY FACTS		
Resort	1620m	
	5,310ft	
Zermatt only		
Slopes	1620-3820m	
	5,310-12,530ft	
Lifts		35
Pistes		200km
		124 miles
Blue		16%
Red		61%
Black		23%
Snowmaking		70%
Zermatt-Cervinia-Valtournenche combined		
Slopes	1525-3820m	
	5,000-12,530ft	
Lifts		54
Pistes		360km
		224 miles
Blue		21%
Red		61%
Black		18%
Snowmaking		61%

SNOWPIX.COM / CHRIS GILL

It's worth queuing for the spectacular ride to the Klein Matterhorn; the piste you emerge on is the highest in Europe ↓

find ranks of electric taxis and hotel shuttles and horse-drawn sleighs.

The cog railway to the Gornergrat sector starts from near the main station. The Sunnegga underground funicular for the Rothorn sector is a few minutes' walk away, but the lifts to Furi and the other sectors (and the link to Cervinia) are over 1km away. Staying near the lifts to Furi gives swift access to three of the four sectors. But a more central location is better for the Gornergrat and Sunnegga railways and most of the resort's shops, bars and restaurants.

Some accommodation is up the steep hill across the river in Winkelmatten, which has its own reliable bus service.

SCENERY ★★★★★
On a grand scale

Zermatt's emblematic, unmistakable Matterhorn is not visible from central parts of the village – if you want the famous view from your balcony, stay on the east side of the village, or at the south end – but once you are on the slopes its unique profile dominates the views wherever you go. And the cable car trip up to the Klein Matterhorn opens up vast panoramas, as well as close-up glacier views.

THE MOUNTAINS

Practically all of the slopes are above the treeline – a run served by the Sunnegga funicular is the main exception, and once you pass below the Patrullarve chair this is mainly a path to the village.

A single piste map covers both Cervinia and Zermatt fairly clearly, and lists recommended 'ski safari' routes

of either 10,500m or 12,500m vertical. Runs are numbered on the map and the ground (though only at the start). The map has a key which names runs, but not lifts (though the Cervinia map has a key which names lifts too).

In each sector there are runs, marked in yellow on the resort map and dotted on ours, called 'itinéraires' on the Zermatt map and 'freeride' on the Cervinia one. We'll call them itineraries. These runs aren't patrolled, but this is not explained – a risky state of affairs. Don't ski these alone, particularly late in the day.

On Thursdays, you can get first tracks from Trockener Steg. For 42 francs you can take the lift at 7.40am, about an hour ahead of the herd, ski deserted pistes for a while, then have a buffet breakfast at a restaurant that seems to change each year. We prefer our daily routine of taking the 8am train to Gornergrat, to enjoy deserted pistes before the hordes get up there.

There are monthly moonlight descents from Rothorn with the ski patrol, including a fondue at the restaurant at the top (70.50 francs).

Over recent years, service has improved to a high standard: polite and helpful lift staff; big boards at the bottom of each sector indicating which lifts and pistes are open in all sectors; useful announcements in English on the train and some cable cars; and free tissues at most lift stations.

EXTENT OF THE SLOPES ★★★★☆
Beautiful and varied

There are four main sectors. **Rothorn** is reached by an underground funicular to Sunnegga, starting by the river, not far from the centre of the village. The main nursery area is just below

skitracer*

CHALETS, HOTELS
& APARTMENTS
Call us today
020 8600 1650
skitracer.com

ALPINE ANSWERS
The UK's No.1 Chalet Specialist

For choice and service look no further!

alpineanswers.co.uk
call: 020 7801 1080   ABTA

Sunnegga, reached from there by a miniature funicular. A chondola goes from Sunnegga to Blauherd, where a cable car goes up to Rothorn.

The second main area, **Gornergrat**, is reached from Zermatt by cog railway trains that take 30 or 40 minutes to the top – arrive at the station early to get a seat (best on the right-hand side to enjoy the fabulous views). We love getting the 8am train with the lifties and restaurant staff. It arrives at the top just as they drop the rope to open

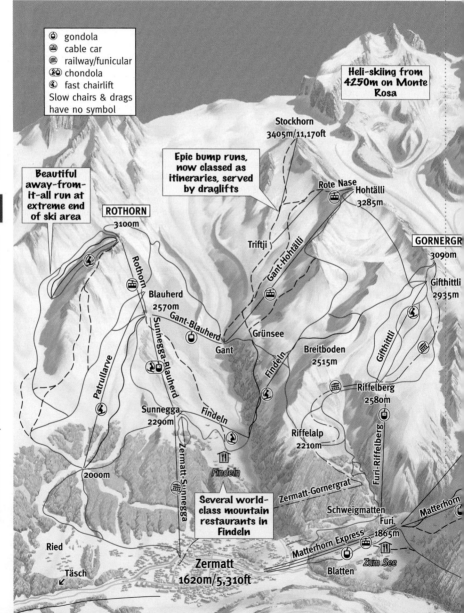

gondola
cable car
railway/funicular
chondola
fast chairlift
Slow chairs & drags
have no symbol

Heli-skiing from 4250m on Monte Rosa

Stockhorn
3405m/11,170ft

Epic bump runs, now classed as itineraries, served by draglifts

Beautiful away-from-it-all run at extreme end of ski area

ROTHORN
3100m

Rote Nase
Hohtälli
3285m

Rothorn

Triftji

Gant-Hohtälli

GORNERGR
3090m

Blauherd
2570m

Gifthittli
2935m

Gant-Blauherd

Sunnegga-Blauherd

Grünsee

Gant

Findeln

Breitboden
2515m

Gifthittli

Patrullarve

Riffelberg
2580m

Sunnegga
2290m

Findeln

Riffelalp
2210m

Furi-Riffelberg

2000m

Zermatt-Sunnegga

Findeln

Several world-class mountain restaurants in Findeln

Zermatt-Gornergrat

Schweigmatten

Matterhorn

Furi
1865m

Ried

Matterhorn Express

Zum See

Täsch

Zermatt
1620m/5,310ft

Blatten

the pistes, and you have the slopes to yourself for an hour or two.

The Rothorn and Gornergrat sectors, separated by the Findel valley, are linked by pistes and itineraries descending to two lift stations.

The Matterhorn Express gondola from the south end of the village goes first to Furi (where you can change to another gondola to go to Riffelberg, for Gornergrat) and on to the small but worthwhile **Schwarzsee** area. The same gondola goes on up to Trockener Steg, focal point of the fourth sector, the super-high **Matterhorn Glacier Paradise**. This can also be reached by a jumbo cable car from Furi – quicker if you time it right, and less affected by wind. Above Trockener Steg another cable car makes a spectacular ascent to Klein Matterhorn. At the top, you walk through a long tunnel to the highest piste in Europe. From the glacier there are two ways to Cervinia (via the cable car to Klein Matterhorn or via two long successive draglifts).

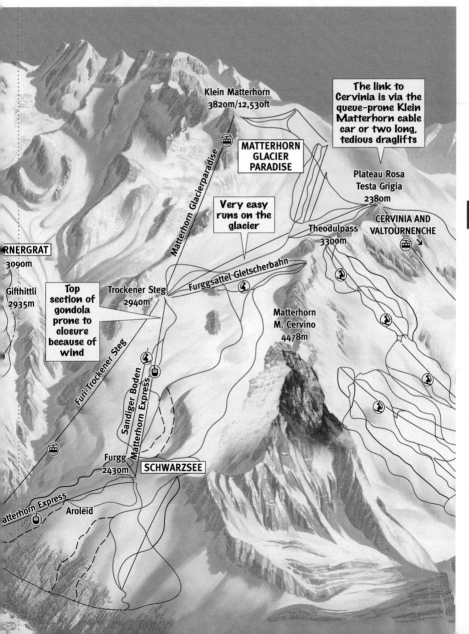

Klein Matterhorn
3820m/12,530ft

MATTERHORN GLACIER PARADISE

The link to Cervinia is via the queue-prone Klein Matterhorn cable car or two long, tedious draglifts

Plateau Rosa
Testa Grigia
2380m

Very easy runs on the glacier

Theodulpass
3300m

CERVINIA AND VALTOURNENCHE

RNERGRAT
3090m

Gifthittli
2935m

Top section of gondola prone to closure because of wind

Trockener Steg
2940m

Furggsattel-Gletscherbahn

Matterhorn
M. Cervino
4478m

Furi-Trockener Steg

Sandiger Boden

Matterhorn Express

Furgg
2430m

SCHWARZSEE

atterhorn Express

Aroleid

Zermatt offers a wide variety of off-piste runs for all abilities, from off-piste beginner to expert. And if the runs reached from the lift system aren't enough, heli-skiing is available (and popular).

Zermatt's 'itineraries' (explained under 'The mountains') open up a lot of terrain to explore without needing guidance. If you love long mogul pitches, those on the Stockhorn are the stuff of dreams. Being north-facing and high, this area keeps good snow long after a new snowfall (but it needs deep snow, and does not normally open until February, or even March). The itineraries carry on down below the Triftji T-bar to Gant, but snow quality can deteriorate on this lower part. There are excellent itineraries in other sectors, too – though again they generally need good snow-cover to be really enjoyable. Our own favourites include the two wonderful runs from Rothorn (16 and 17), with spectacular views. A recent visitor particularly liked 10 from Blauherd to Findeln. The runs in the Schwarzsee sector – 58, 59 and 60 – are steeper, shadier and narrower than most.

Away from the marked runs, there are marvellous off-piste possibilities from the top lifts in each sector, but they are dangerous, because of rocky and glacial terrain; guidance is essential. Stockhorn is a great starting point; descending towards Gant, one special run goes down 'the lost valley'; going in the other direction, there is an excellent descent to the Gornergletscher, ending at Furi. Be warned: getting off the glacier may involve narrow rocky paths above long drops, or side-stepping down steep slopes, depending on snow levels (we've encountered both). In the Schwarzsee sector there are many good slopes, including 'innru waldieni', right under the Matterhorn, reached from the Hörnli T-bar.

Zermatt is the Alps' biggest heli-skiing centre; at times the helipad has choppers taking off every few minutes. There are only a few drop points. The classic run is from over 4250m on Monte Rosa and descends over 2300m vertical through wonderful glacier scenery to Furi; note our warning above.

LIFT PASSES

Zermatt

Prices in francs

Age	1-day	6-day
under 16	38	186
16 to 19	64	315
20 to 64	75	371
65 plus	71	349

Free Under 9

Beginner Wolli Pass covering nursery area at Sunnegga

Notes Covers Swiss side of the border; half-day passes and single-ascent tickets on some lifts

Alternative passes International for Zermatt and Cervinia; International-Aosta for Zermatt and Cervinia plus 2 days in Val d'Aosta; Peak Pass for pedestrians

There are pistes back to the village from all sectors – though some can be closed or tricky due to poor snow conditions (and crowds).

FAST LIFTS ★★★★★
Now top-notch

All Zermatt's four sectors are well connected by fast chairs, gondolas, big cable cars or mountain railways. There are of course slow lifts in places, but most can be avoided. The low speed of the Gornergrat train is something you just have to accept.

QUEUES ★★★☆☆
Still a few bottlenecks

Zermatt has improved its lift system hugely in recent years, eliminating major bottlenecks. This year's reporters are generally positive again, but a few problems remain.

There may be queues to get up to the Matterhorn sector, and the gondola to Trockener Steg is prone to closure in high winds, putting pressure on the alternative cable car. The Klein Matterhorn cable car often has serious queues in good weather (up to an hour mid-morning; quieter in the afternoon).

A real bottleneck is Gant in the Findel valley – notably the old, slow gondola to Blauherd. Half-hour waits are common here in high season. There are plans to construct a piste

from Gant down the valley to the Findeln chairlift so that the gondola can be retired, but nothing had been confirmed when we went to press. There can also be queues for the Hohtälli cable car from Gant. And the top section of piste from Hohtälli can get dangerously busy.

TERRAIN PARKS ★★★☆☆
Summer and winter

Gravity Park, next to the Furggsattel six-seat chair has a variety of jumps, rails, a half-pipe and big rollers. One reporter last year said the park was 'well received, but less funky than Verbier', while another notes: 'It is far away and very cold if the weather is at all bad.' In the summer, the park moves up to Plateau Rosa where a crew of six shape the 600m park daily. A nicely integrated 120m-long super-pipe sits next to an array of kickers, rails, a quarter-pipe, wall ride, mail box and tree jib.

SNOW RELIABILITY ★★★★☆
Generally good

Zermatt has rocky terrain and a relatively dry climate. But it also has some of the highest slopes in Europe. As well as the glacier, two other sectors go over 3000m, and there are loads of runs above 2500m, many of which are north-facing.

On repeated March visits we have

been impressed by the snowmaking, in all four sectors, on pistes from above 3000m down to resort level. Piste grooming is generally excellent.

FOR EXPERTS ★★★★★
Head off-piste
There is some great off-piste when conditions are right, and the off-piste itineraries include some excellent runs – read our feature panel. But Zermatt doesn't get huge snowfall, so you can't always count on good conditions, particularly early in the season. The handful of black runs are not worthy of their classification; the one with the steepest pitches (Blauherd-Patrullarve) is also very wide.

FOR INTERMEDIATES ★★★★★
Mile after mile of beautiful runs
Zermatt is ideal for adventurous intermediates. Many of the blue runs tend to be at the difficult end of their classification. Reds vary unhelpfully: some are quite tough; some ought to be blue. Few are really what you might call 'cruising' runs.

Among our favourites in the Gornergrat sector are the very beautiful reds down lift-free valleys from both Gornergrat (Kelle) and Hohtälli (White Hare) to Breitboden – we love these first thing in the morning, before anyone else is on them. The steepest part of Kelle is classified black, but an easier red variant bypasses it. From Breitboden you can go on down to Gant, or to the mid-station of the Findeln chairlift, or to Riffelalp on a run that includes a narrow wooded path with a sheer cliff and magnificent views to the right.

On the Rothorn sector, the 5km Kumme/Tufternkumme run – from Rothorn itself to the Patrullarve chair – also gets away from the lift system and has an interesting mix of straight-running and mogul pitches (but it gets a lot of sun and lacks snowmaking).

In the Matterhorn Glacier Paradise sector the reds served by the fast quad chair from Furgg are gloriously set at the foot of the Matterhorn. The Furggsattel chair from Trockener Steg serves more pistes with stunning views, notably the Matterhorn piste – blue in gradient for most of its great length, but classified red because of a short, steep pitch near the end that causes problems for many skiers.

For timid intermediates, the best

ZERMATT TOURIST OFFICE
The magnificent Matterhorn dominates the view wherever you are on the slopes
↓

Zermatt

Build your own shortlist: **www.wheretoskiandsnowboard.com**

experience Zermatt with all your senses

Unique
HOTEL ❄ POST
Zermatt

restaurants • bars • clubs

book now and get a free gift

discover more:

www.hotelpost.ch - info@hotelpost.ch

The choice of restaurants is enormous, the standard (and prices) high – with the best serving food worthy of a top London restaurant. We list here only a selection. It is best to book – this is not a resort where it is always easy to just stop for a bite when you are hungry. Restaurants are marked on the piste map, but only a few places are explicitly named. The tourist office restaurant directory has photos, and clues about the style of food, but not prices. Beware: some places don't take cards.

Below Sunnegga, at Findeln, are several attractive, expensive, rustic restaurants sharing a great Matterhorn view. Our favourites are Chez Vrony (967 2552) where service can be stretched but is reliably friendly and the food excellent; and Findlerhof (967 2588) aka Franz and Heide's where we've had delicious lamb. Readers also recommend the nearby Adler (967 1058), with its outdoor BBQ ('delicious food', 'impeccable service'), and Paradies (967 3451).

Further up the Findel valley, in splendid isolation, Fluhalp (967 2597) is another favourite; excellent food and service, often with live music on the huge terrace – enthusiastically endorsed by two readers this year. Up at Blauherd, Blue Lounge is a cool modern bar with lots of sofas and a 'super gas fire', serving simple food such as tapas and 'great burgers' to jazz and other music.

At Riffelalp, Alphitta (967 2114) is 'traditional with friendly service and the least expensive place we found to eat all week', says a 2014 reporter. At Trockener Steg we love the Ice Pizzeria (967 1812) – a smart, modern table-service place with great views; delicious pizzas, as readers agree. The higher Gandegghütte (079 607 8868) has stunning views and good, simple food ('lovely' pasta dishes); but no milk, so no hot choc. Over at Schwarzsee, the Stafelalp (967 3062) remains a reader favourite – glorious position, 'interesting food', 'great service'.

SNOWPIX.COM / CHRIS GILL

At Furi, restaurant Furri (966 2777) offers a really friendly welcome and good simple food, and the 'always welcoming' Simi (967 2695), tucked away a bit lower down, does 'great grills on its open fire'. Just above Furi, Aroleid (967 2658) is recommended for rösti, and hotel Silvana (966 2800) is 'spacious, with good food, decent value'. Below Furi are countless places to pause on the way home. Our favourite is Zum See (967 2045), a charming old hut, and one of the best (and most expensive) restaurants on the mountain. Blatten (967 2096) serves 'one of the best strudels'.

runs are the blues from Blauherd on Rothorn, and above Riffelberg on Gornergrat, and in good weather the super-high runs between Klein Matterhorn and Trockener Steg. Of these, the Riffelberg area often has the best combination of good snow and easy cruising, and is understandably popular with the ski schools.

In the Matterhorn Glacier Paradise sector most of the runs, though marked red on the piste map, are very flat and include the easiest slopes Zermatt has to offer, as well as the best snow. Even an early intermediate can make the trip to Cervinia, via Theodulpass rather than the more challenging run from Plateau Rosa.

Beware the black run from Furgg to Furi at the end of the day. It is not steep, but gets chopped up, moguled in places and very crowded. A much more relaxed alternative is the scenic Weisse Perle run from Schwarzsee (the Stafelalp variant is even more scenic but has a short uphill section). The final red run from Furi to the village gets unpleasantly crowded.

FOR BEGINNERS ★★★★★
Still far from ideal
These days the resort makes an effort to cater for beginners – there are beginner areas dotted around on all four sectors, and a main one has been developed (with three moving carpets and two rope tows) at Leisee, just below Sunnegga, reached from there by a short funicular. There is a half-price pass to get you to and from that area. But some readers judge this small area inadequate. And progression to longer runs is awkward – the slopes as a whole are very challenging for near-beginners, which includes fast learners who are ready to

SCHOOLS

Swiss (Matterhorn)
t 966 2466

Stoked
t 967 7020

Summit
t 967 0001

European Snowsport
t 967 6787

Adventure
t 967 5020

Alpine Swiss
t 967 3170

Prato Borni
t 967 5115

Classes (Swiss prices)
5 days (10am to 3.30 with lunch break)
405 francs
Private lessons
145 francs for 1.5hr

GUIDES

Alpin Center
t 966 2460

CHILDCARE

Kinderparadies
t 967 7252
Ages from 3mnth

Kidactive
t 077 405 3957

Kinderclub Pumuckel
(Hotel Ginabelle)
t 966 5000
Ages from 30mnth

Schwarzsee (Stoked)
t 967 7020
Ages from 30mnth

Nico Kids Club
(Schweizerhof hotel)
t 966 0000
Ages from 2 to 8

Snowli Village (Swiss)
t 966 2466
Ages 4 to 5

Private babysitters
List at tourist office

Ski school
Ages 6 to 14

---

quit the nursery slopes after a couple of days. Of course, you can learn to ski here, but we would go elsewhere.

FOR BOARDERS ★★★★★
Beware the flat spots
The slopes are best for experienced freeriders but there are adequate beginner areas, where we've seen many beginner snowboarders. The main lifts are boarder-friendly: train, funicular, gondolas, cable cars and fast chairs. There are some flat bits, including on runs 27, 44, 52 and 69.

FOR CROSS-COUNTRY ★★★★★
Down the valley
There are 25km of trails from Täsch to Randa (but don't count on good snow at these altitudes).

SCHOOLS AND GUIDES ★★★★★
Competition paying off
The main Swiss school – once a real embarrassment – seems to have improved since competing schools were permitted, and our most recent reports have been positive ('lovely instructor, good sense of humour'). Of the other schools, Summit and European Snowsport are staffed mainly by Brits. Summit was praised this year for its 'good value and excellent' private lessons. Last year we had two reports praising European Snowsport ('professional and accommodating').

FOR FAMILIES ★★★★★
Good hotel nurseries
The prices, the general inconvenience of the place and the challenges facing beginners and near-beginners all work against families. But, as our margin panel shows, there are plenty of facilities for children and we don't doubt that they are thoroughly well run. The tourist office has a list of babysitters. 'Choose your location with care,' advises one reader. Another notes that the number of hotels offering family suites is a plus-point.

STAYING THERE

Chalets Several operators have pulled out of Zermatt this season (see the editorial on p13). But Supertravel has a handful of smart places sharing a pool and sauna. VIP has a couple of places. Independently run chalets include a 6-bedroom one by new operator Matterhorn Chalets; prices include an instructor / mountain guide.

SUPERTRAVEL SKI
020·7204·4691
Book a full chalet and receive a FREE case of 6 bottles of Champagne delivered to your chalet or home when you quote 'ski/snow2015'

Luxury chalet holidays
COURCHEVEL·ST ANTON·ZERMATT ABTA

Hotels There are over 100 hotels, mostly traditional-style 3-stars and 4-stars, but taking in the whole range. What distinguishes Zermatt is the number of 'hip' places, some of which are listed below.

★★★★★Mont Cervin (966 8888) Biggest in town. Pool etc. We enjoyed a stay here in 2013 – it's now a perfect blend of traditional and modern style.

★★★★★Omnia (966 7171) Designer hotel, minimalist, central, reached by a lift in the rock, smart fitness centre.

★★★★Alex (966 7070) Close to train stations. An old favourite, though no recent reports. Large pool, sauna.

★★★★Beau Site (966 6868) Grand place over the river with Matterhorn views.

★★★★Cervo (968 1212) Hip place with rooms, suites, chalets for up to 10. At the end of the piste from Sunnegga.

★★★★Europe (966 2700) Over the river from the church, with fab modern rooms in new extension.

★★★★Matterhorn Focus (966 2424) Super-stylish B&B designed by Heinz Julen, right by the Matterhorn lifts. Indoor pool, outdoor hot tub, sauna.

★★★★Mirabeau (966 2660) Heartily tipped by two reporters – 'outstanding food, friendly staff, excellent spa'.

★★★★Monte Rosa (966 0333) Well-modernized original Zermatt hotel in centre; full of climbing mementos. 'Wonderful,' says a reporter.

★★★★Post (967 1931) All rooms/suites unique and smartly modernized. Sauna, vapour-bath, hot-tub. Central with several restaurants, bars, clubs.

★★★★Sonne (966 2066) In quiet setting and highly praised by a regular: 'Superb' spa, great food, and the staff couldn't do enough for us.'

★★★★Sunstar Style (966 5666) Recent addition to the Sunstar group. Modern decor. Pool, spa.

★★★★Walliserhof (966 6555) Good reports – 'convenient, very friendly, good food, spacious rooms'. Mini-spa.

Build your own shortlist: www.wheretoskiandsnowboard.com

UK PACKAGES

Alpine Answers, Alpine Weekends, Carrier, Crystal, Crystal Finest, Elegant Resorts, Elysian Collection, Erna Low, Flexiski, Inghams, Interactive Resorts, Kaluma, Lagrange, Luxury Chalet Collection, Matterhorn Chalets, Momentum, Mountain Beds, Mountain Exposure, Neilson, Oxford Ski Co, Powder Byrne, PowderBeds, Scott Dunn, Ski Bespoke, Ski Club Freshtracks, Ski Expectations, Ski Independence, Ski Line, Ski Monterosa, Ski Safari, Skitracer, Skiweekends.com, Skiworld, Snow Finders, Snow-wise, STC, Switzerland Travel Centre, Supertravel, Thomson, VIP, White Roc, Zenith

GETTING THERE

Air Geneva 240km/ 150 miles (3hr30); Zürich 250km/ 155 miles (4hr30); Sion 80km/ 50 miles (1hr30)

Rail Station in resort

ACTIVITIES

Indoor Hotel saunas and swimming pools (some open to public), climbing wall, museums, cinema

Outdoor Ice rinks, curling, 70km cleared paths, snowshoeing, tobogganing, helicopter flights, ice climbing, paragliding

***Alpenroyal** (966 6066) Reached by elevator near Sunnegga lift. 'Really super. Clean and tidy with lovely staff – efficient, friendly and funny.'
***Continental** (966 2840) Central and great value; fantastic food and friendly staff – we stayed here in 2013.
***Romantica** (966 2650) Central B&B in old part of town. 'We stayed in one of their "cottages" – very romantic in a converted listed hay shed!'
Atlanta (966 3535) Good past reports, and tipped for 'excellent value, great staff, rooms and food'. Good position, too.
*Bahnhof** (967 2406) Basic place with various forms of accommodation. No meals, but 'very clean, well equipped kitchen for self-catering'.
Apartments There are lots. We have enjoyed staying in the apartments of the hotel Ambassador (966 2611), with free use of pool and sauna. The Alouette apartments are 'relatively reasonably priced'.
At altitude There are several hotels on the hill, and they are not your regular mountain refuges. The pick is the 5-star Riffelalp Resort (966 0555), at the first stop on the Gornergrat railway, with pool, spa and its own evening trains. We fancy staying a couple of nights at the Kulmhotel Gornergrat (966 6400) at the top of the mountain – the highest hotel in Switzerland.

EATING OUT ★★★★★
Huge choice
There are over 100 restaurants to choose from: top-quality haute cuisine, through traditional Swiss food, Chinese, Japanese and Thai, to egg and chips. There is even a McDonald's. The tourist office produces a directory, with photos. One reader reckons that you pay a lot less in restaurants at the south end of the village, well away from the centre.

At the top end of the market, the Heimberg ('continues to be fab'), Ristorante Capri (in the hotel Mont Cervin), and After Seven (part of the Vernissage/Backstage hotel complex) each have a Michelin star. A Zermatt regular who knows his food tips the cool hotel Cervo ('excellent food, very smart, nice small dining rooms, impeccable service'), Omnia ('Bond-like experience – wonderful decor, interesting food and wine') and Chez Gaby ('great grilled food, prawns, etc'). Sonnmatten has 'fantastic food,

atmosphere and service – expensive, but excellent'.

At more modest prices, we've enjoyed the Schwyzer Stübli (local specialities and live Swiss music and dancing), good-value Mexican and Swiss dishes at the Weisshorn and decent Thai food at Rua Thai. Sparky's pub/restaurant has been praised for 'good tasty pub grub at its best', which includes vegetarian options, stews and curries. Grampi's has been tipped repeatedly for 'very good simple food, good service'.

Other reader tips include: Klein Matterhorn for fish/pasta; the Brown Cow in the hotel Post ('the best-value meal we had; great burgers in a relaxed bar environment'); Schäferstube ('the best lamb dishes in the village'); Stockhorn ('generous portions, delicious venison'); and the dear old Whymper-Stube.

APRES-SKI ★★★★★
Something for everybody
There's a good mix of sophisticated and informal fun, though it helps if you have deep pockets. Promenading the main street checking out expensive clothes and watches is a popular early-evening activity.

There are lively places to pause on your final descent. On the way back from Rothorn, Othmar's Skihütte has great views and the afternoon sun, and the funky Cervo where the piste ends has a popular outdoor bar with live music. Caffè Snowboat (near the Sunnegga funicular) is a small, modern place that looks like, er, a boat with a deck and lounge bar. On the way back from Furi there are lots of options, some described under 'Mountain restaurants'. Very near the end of the run, Hennu Stall blasts out loud music and attracts huge crowds – live bands play most days.

For a lively bar through the evening you won't beat the revamped Papperla Pub. The long-established North Wall doesn't get many mentions in reports but still seems to be a seasonaires' favourite. Potters Bar (geddit?) is a relaxed 'perfectly nice' British pub. Gee's pop-up bar was popular last season with locals and visitors alike – here's hoping it returns next year. Elsie's famous wood-panelled bar continues to please our more mature readers ('much enjoyed for its cosy traditional ambience and excellent wine'); it gets seriously busy early and

Phone numbers
From elsewhere in
Switzerland add the
prefix 027; from
abroad use the prefix
+41 27

TOURIST OFFICE
www.zermatt.ch

SNOWPIX.COM / CHRIS GILL

Plateau Rosa is on
the border of Italy (to
the right) and
Switzerland (on the
left). The Swiss slopes
here are very gentle
↓

late. Other reader tips include Brit-run
Sparky's ('best priced beer in town'),
the Little Bar (crowded if there are 10
people in) and the cosy, quirky Hexen.
Of the hotel bars, the Alex has comfy
sofas, good service and a pool table.

Later on, the hotel Post complex
has something for everyone, from a
quiet, comfortable bar (Papa Caesar's)
to a lively disco (Broken), live music
(Pink) and various restaurants. The
T-Bar draws a young crowd for dancing
and bands. At Grampi's ('very lively
later in the evening') there is a disco
below. The Schneewittchen nightclub
(at the Papperla) is very popular.

OFF THE SLOPES ★★★★☆
Considerable attractions
Zermatt is an attractive place to spend
time. As well as expensive jewellery
and clothes shops, there are
interesting places selling food, wine,
books and art. It is easy (but costly)
for pedestrians to get around on the
lifts and meet others for lunch, and
there are some splendid walks (70km)
– a special map is available.

If the weather is good, the Klein
Matterhorn cable car is an experience
not to be missed: there is a small self-
service restaurant at the top as well as
a viewing platform and an ice cave,
with 'incredible carvings'. Be aware
that the air is thin up there, though.

The Matterhorn Museum in the
village is well worth a visit. You can
take a helicopter trip around the
Matterhorn. There is a cinema, and
free village guided tours. For an icy
experience, visit (or stay at) the Igloo
above Riffelberg. It's easy to visit
various Swiss cities by rail.

DOWN-VALLEY VILLAGE – 1450m
TÄSCH

Täsch, where visitors must leave their
cars, is just a 12-minute train ride from
Zermatt, so it makes a viable base.
There are several 3-star hotels
charging half the Zermatt price. The
Täscherhof (966 6262) and Walliserhof
(966 3966) ('nice and friendly, very
good chef') have been recommended
by reporters. Täsch is very quiet in the
evening, but it's no problem to spend
evenings in Zermatt – trains run until
12.30am Monday to Wednesday, and
hourly all night from Thursday to
Sunday. And taxis can operate up to
the edge of Zermatt.

Zermatt

Build your own shortlist: www.wheretoskiandsnowboard.com

hotel garni matterhorn ★★★★ **FOCUS**

Design and Lifestyle

Hotel Matterhorn Focus
Winkelmattenweg 32 • CH-3920 Zermatt
Tel. +41 27 966 24 24 • Fax. +41 27 966 24 25
www.matterhorn-focus.ch

Most people who give it a try find the USA is pretty seductive, despite the relatively small size of its ski areas. What got the USA started in the UK market was its (generally) reliable snow, and that remains a key factor. Other factors are the relatively deserted pistes, the high quality of accommodation, the excellent and varied resort restaurants, the high standards of service and courtesy, and the immaculate piste grooming. Depending on the resort, you may also be struck by the cute Wild West ambience and the superb quality of the snow.

Of course, US skiing does have disadvantages, too. Not the least of these is the cost – long-haul air fares have risen, and the costs of lift passes and instruction are high, despite an improvement in the exchange rate over the last year.

We have organized our US chapters in regional sections – California, Colorado, Utah, Rest of the West (which covers two major resorts in Wyoming and Montana) and New England.

Most American resorts receive serious amounts of snow – typically season totals in the region of 6m to 12m (or 250 to 500 inches, as they measure it there) ; that's around double the 3m to 6m that resorts like Chamonix, St Anton and Val d'Isère in Europe average. The snow tends to arrive in more frequent falls than in Europe, too, so your chances of hitting fresh snow are appreciably higher. And most resorts have serious snowmaking facilities that are used well – laying down a base of snow early in the season rather than patching up shortages later. There are wide differences in quantity and quality of snowfall, both between individual resorts and between regions.

The classification of pistes (or trails, to use the local term) is different from that in Europe. The colours used are combined with shapes. There are no red runs. Green circles correspond fairly closely to greens in France and easy blues in the rest of Europe. American blue squares correspond to blues and easy reds in Europe; the tougher ones are sometimes labelled as double squares, or as blue-black squares. Then there are black-diamond runs, which is

PATROLLED AND AVALANCHE-CONTROLLED OFF-PISTE

One of the great attractions of North American resorts is that they have patrolled and avalanche-controlled ungroomed terrain that in Europe would be classified as ski-at-your-own-risk off-piste. Each resort has a ski area boundary; this may be marked by signs on the trees bordering the trails or there may be a rope; the boundary may be moved, depending on snow conditions. Anywhere within the boundary ('in-bounds') is patrolled and avalanche controlled.

In-bounds terrain includes areas between marked and groomed trails and often big areas of ski-anywhere bowls or steep couloirs (or chutes, to use the local term). In Europe such terrain is normally off-piste, and we recommend you ski it only with a qualified local guide, which is of course expensive.

Terrain outside the ski area boundary ('backcountry') is often accessible through gates placed at various points on the boundary. In some places the official position is that you cannot cross the boundary. Backcountry terrain is not controlled or patrolled and should be treated like European off-piste and skied only with a guide.

SNOWPIX.COM / CHRIS GILL

← Skiing in the USA normally means skiing below the treeline, but often there are lightly wooded areas ('glades') that are much less tricky than most tree skiing in the Alps. This is Aspen where things get interesting. Single diamonds correspond fairly closely to European blacks and really tough reds. But then there are multiple diamonds. Double-diamond runs are seriously steep – usually steeper than the steepest pistes in the Alps. A few resorts have wildly steep 'extreme' double diamonds, or triple diamonds.

The most obvious drawback to the US is that many resorts have slopes that are very modest in extent compared with major Alpine areas. But usually there are other resorts nearby – so if you are prepared to travel a bit, you won't get bored. Roads are good, and car hire is relatively cheap (watch out for extra insurance charges, though). But if snow is expected, you will need a 4WD or snow chains; bizarrely, you have to buy your chains – we've yet to find a US rental company that will provide them. It's also true that in many resorts the mountains are slightly monotonous, with countless similar trails cut through the forest. You don't usually get the spectacular mountain scenery and the distinctive high-mountain runs of the Alps. But the forest runs do offer good visibility in bad weather and, unlike in Europe, it's normal to be able to ski in among the trees themselves; a particular delight is lightly wooded areas they call glades, often manufactured by thinning out the natural forest.

GREAT GROOMING AND DESERTED SLOPES

Piste grooming is taken very seriously – most US resorts set standards that only the best Alpine resorts seem to be able to match. Every morning you can expect to step out on to perfect 'corduroy' pistes. But this doesn't mean that there aren't moguls – far from it. It's just that you get moguls where the resort says you can expect moguls, not everywhere.

The slopes of most US resorts are blissfully free of crowds – a key advantage that becomes more important as the pistes of Europe become ever more congested. If you want to ski quickly and safely with less fear of collisions, head for the States.

Ski schools offer consistently high standards but work in a way that's different from the European pattern – people don't sign up for a week, only for one or two lessons as they feel the need. Most resorts offer free guided tours of the ski area once or twice a day (usually carried out by volunteers); and many have 'mountain hosts' on hand to help you find your way. Piste maps are freely available at lift stations, and signposting is generally exemplary.

Lifts are generally efficient, and queues are orderly and short, partly because spare seats are religiously filled with the aid of cheerful, conscientious attendants. You find Americans on chairlifts expect to chat – weird to Europeans, but we like it. First-time visitors are surprised that some chairlifts in the States do not have safety bars; even on a chair that has a bar, you will find Americans curiously reluctant to use it, and eager to raise it as soon as the top station is in view. They worry about being trapped, not falling off. The lifts close irritatingly early – as early as 3pm in some cases (and some upper lifts might start closing as early as 1.30pm). That may explain another drawback of the USA – the dearth of decent mountain restaurants. The norm is a monster (but crowded) self-service refuelling station – designed to minimize time off the slopes.

US resort towns vary widely in style and convenience, from cute restored mining towns to purpose-built monstrosities. Two important things the resorts have in common are high-quality,

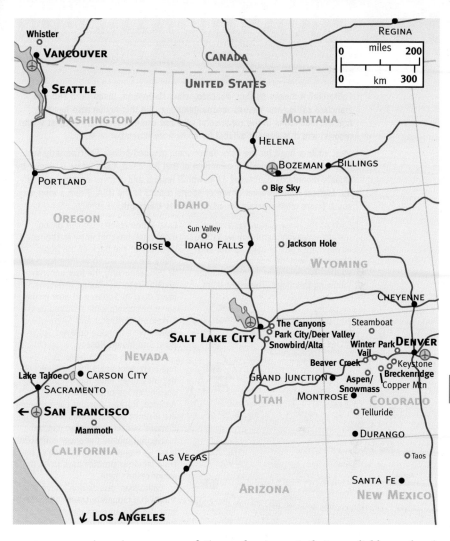

spacious accommodation and restaurants that are reliably good and varied in cuisine. Young people should be aware that the rigorously enforced legal age for drinking alcohol is 21; even if you are older, carry evidence of age, especially if you look younger than you are.

Crossing the pond is no longer cheap and extras such as lift passes, ski hire and ski school are generally much more expensive than in Europe. Take a look at our price panels for each resort for an idea of what to budget for. With lift passes, you can often save huge amounts by buying in advance through tour operators or websites.

Of course, a key factor is the exchange rate. As we go to press in July 2014 the rate is much improved on a year ago – up about 12% to $1.64. But this still means local prices are 22% higher in £££ than they were in the heady days of 2007, when we got $2 to £1.

In the end, your reaction to skiing and snowboarding in the USA may depend on your reaction to the USA. If repeated exhortations to have a nice day wind you up – or if you like to ride chairlifts in silence – you'd better stick to the Alps. We love skiing there.

California/Nevada

California? It means surfing, beaches, wine, Hollywood, Disneyland and San Francisco cable cars. Nevada means gambling. But this region also has the highest mountains in the continental USA and some of America's biggest winter resorts, and it is usually reliable for snow from November to May.

Most visitors head for the Lake Tahoe area, mapped below. Spectacularly set high in the Sierra Nevada 320km east of San Francisco, Lake Tahoe is ringed by skiable mountains containing 14 downhill resorts and 7 cross-country centres – the highest concentration of winter sports resorts in the USA. Then, a long way south (more often reached from LA), there is Mammoth.

Each of the three major 'destination' resorts – Heavenly and Squaw Valley, at opposite ends of Lake Tahoe, and Mammoth, way off our map to the south – is covered in its own chapter following this page. The other main

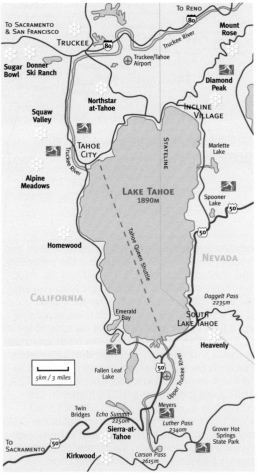

Lake Tahoe resorts (shown on our map) each have an entry in the resort directory at the back of the book. Many are well worth visiting for a day or two, especially the four second-division resorts – Alpine Meadows (next door to Squaw and now in the same ownership with a shared pass), Kirkwood, Northstar and Sierra-at-Tahoe. We have also enjoyed Sugar Bowl and Mount Rose.

Californian resorts have had relatively poor years for snow recently but they often have the deepest accumulations of snow in North America. Rockies powder connoisseurs are inclined to brand it as wet 'Sierra Cement' because the snow can be heavy. But mostly the snow is fine, at least by Alpine standards – we've had truly fabulous powder days in all the major resorts here.

Californian resorts don't have the traditional mountain-town ambience that can add an extra dimension to holidays in other parts of the States, particularly Colorado. The car-free plaza in South Lake Tahoe called Heavenly Village and the pedestrian Village at Mammoth – both linked to the slopes above by gondola – are not at all special. But Squaw Valley and Northstar have both developed more substantial base villages.

You could visit all the Tahoe resorts by car (best to have a 4WD) from a single base; but a two-centre holiday including some time at both ends of the lake would be better. A six-pack of lift tickets covering seven resorts around the lake is available (go to www.skilaketahoe.com).

The drives from major airports are non-trivial. Consider taking onward flights to Reno (for Tahoe) and Mammoth Yosemite.

532

HEAVENLY SKI RESORT / SCOTT MARKEWITZ

Heavenly

Heavenly is unique: one of the USA's biggest mountains, with fabulous lake and 'desert' views, above a tacky casino town

RATINGS

The mountains

Extent	★★★
Fast lifts	★★★★
Queues	★★★★
Terrain p'ks	★★★★★
Snow	★★★★
Expert	★★★
Intermediate	★★★★
Beginner	★★★★
Boarder	★★★★
X-country	★★
Restaurants	★
Schools	★★★★
Families	★★

The resort

Charm	★
Convenience	★
Scenery	★★★★
Eating out	★★★★
Après-ski	★★★
Off-slope	★★★

RPI	150
lift pass	£300
ski hire	£120
lessons	£180
food & drink	£170
total	**£770**

SNOWPIX.COM / CHRIS GILL

The lake views make you sit and stare – and delay tackling the bumpy black below ↓

➕ Spectacular views of Lake Tahoe and the Nevada 'desert' from slopes	➖ Town at base, South Lake Tahoe, is a messy, traffic-ridden place
➕ Fair-sized mountain that offers a sensation of travelling around	➖ No trail back to central SLT
	➖ Lifts vulnerable to wind closure
➕ Large areas of widely spaced trees – fabulous in fresh powder	➖ Pronounced step from easy groomed blues to mogulled blacks
➕ Some serious challenges for experts	➖ If natural snow is poor, most of the challenging terrain may be closed
➕ Other worthwhile resorts reachable	
➕ Good snow and snowmaking	➖ Mountain restaurants dire
➕ Unique nightlife in town at base	➖ Very little traditional après-ski

With a top height of 3060m and vertical of 1060m, Heavenly is the highest and biggest of the resorts around famously deep, pure and beautiful Lake Tahoe. It has the best lake views, too. But anyone drawn by the scenic setting is likely to be dismayed by the barren base town of South Lake Tahoe, straddling busy US Highway 50. You could stay out of town, close to one of the other lift bases.

And the skiing? If your taste is for easy Alpine blacks or tough reds, just be sure you are ready to step up to ungroomed stuff – you'll find the blues tame.

THE RESORT

South Lake Tahoe, on the shore of the lake, is primarily a summer resort. It straddles the California-Nevada border, and its economy is based on gambling, which Nevada permits. The central area is dominated by a handful of high-rise casino hotels on the Nevada side of the border.

These brash but comfortable hotels offer good-value rooms (subsidized by the gambling), swanky restaurants and various entertainments. Picking your way between the slot machines in ski gear, carrying skis or board, is weird.

Near the casino area is the small Heavenly Village, purpose-built around the main lift base. There are other lift base areas (with lodgings) on both the

NEWS

2014/15: Activities at Adventure Peak have been expanded to include two rope courses, a canopy tour and a zipline centre including a 1km-long line.

KEY FACTS

Resort	1900m
	6,230ft
Slopes	2000-3060m
	6,570-10,040ft
Lifts	29
Pistes	4,800 acres
Green	20%
Blue	45%
Black	35%
Snowmaking	73%

California and Nevada sides of the hill.

Other resorts around the lake are easily visited, and lift passes that cover several areas are available. A car is handy to explore them (although buses, some free, are available) and to get to many of the best restaurants, but parking can be expensive.

The obvious gateway airport is San Francisco, but Reno is much closer, and the road up less likely to be affected by snow.

VILLAGE CHARM ★✩✩✩✩
The highway rules
From a distance the casinos look like a classic American downtown area, which you'd expect to be full of shops and bars. But there's hardly any of that – just the seriously busy and pedestrian-hostile Highway 50. The rest of the town spreads for miles along the road – dozens of low-rise hotels and motels (some quite shabby), stores, wedding chapels and so on. The general effect is less dire than it might be, thanks to the camouflage of tall trees. Heavenly Village provides a downtown après-ski focus (basically just one bar), but is otherwise not a great success.

CONVENIENCE ★✩✩✩✩
Gamble on the gondola?
The central area close to Heavenly Village and the gondola looks the obvious place to stay, despite the lack of trails down to it. Some of the casino hotels are within five minutes' walk of the gondola, but others are a hike away. There are lodgings close to the other lift bases – California Lodge, up a heavily wooded slope 2km out of town, and the more remote Nevada bases, Boulder Lodge and Stagecoach Lodge. And there are cheaper places literally miles from a lift, used largely by people with cars. But there are free shuttle-buses. You can ski down to all these other bases.

SCENERY ★★★★✩
Splendid panoramas
The views over Lake Tahoe, ringed by snow-capped mountains, are spectacular. The casinos are a conspicuous part of those views from the lower slopes, though not from above mid-mountain; Ridge Run is good for lake views. In the other direction is arid Nevada – sufficiently arid to be classified as desert, though the Sahara it ain't.

THE MOUNTAINS

Practically all of Heavenly's slopes are cut through forest, but in many areas the forest is not dense and there is excellent tree skiing. The trail map gives a good indication of the density of trees. As elsewhere in the US, this 'off-piste' terrain is 'patrolled', but only by hollering – ineffective if you are unconscious; don't ski the trees alone. Two days a week, am and pm, there are free and 'excellent' mountain tours led by forest rangers.

EXTENT OF THE SLOPES ★★★✩✩
Interestingly complex
The mountain is complicated, and getting from A to B requires more careful navigation than is usual on American mountains. Quite a few of the links between different sectors involve long, flat tracks.

There is a clear division between the California side of the mountain (above South Lake Tahoe) and the Nevada side. If lift closures leave you on the wrong side, it's not a big deal – the bus rides don't take long.

The gondola from South Lake Tahoe goes to one end of the California side. There is no skiing back to the town. At the other end of this side, the steep lower slopes are served by the Aerial Tramway (cable car) and Gunbarrel fast chair from California Lodge. The much more extensive upper slopes are served by four fast chairs, one going up to the Skyline trail to the Nevada side.

The Nevada side is more fragmented, but the central focus is East Peak Lodge. Above it is an excellent intermediate area, served by two fast quad chairs, with a downhill extension served by the Galaxy chair. From the fast Dipper chair back up, you can access the open terrain of Milky Way Bowl, leading to the seriously steep chutes of Mott and Killebrew Canyons, served by the Mott Canyon chair. Below East Peak Lodge are runs down to Nevada's two bases, Stagecoach and Boulder – the latter often quiet because its chairs are slow.

FAST LIFTS ★★★★✩
California does it better
Most people can spend practically all their time on fast chairs. The Mott Canyon chair is slow, but that's a niche market. The main weaknesses are the slow chairs up from Boulder Lodge.

LIFT PASSES

Heavenly

Prices in US$

Age	1-day	6-day
under 13	55	270
13 to 18	87	408
19 to 64	95	498
65 plus	87	408

Free Under 5

Beginner Combined lesson/limited lift pass/equipment deals

Notes These are online prices for early February booked at least 3 days in advance; reduced prices to international visitors who pre-book through a UK tour operator; ticket window prices are much higher; half-day passes available at ticket window

QUEUES ★★★★
Gondola up and down

The gondola can have queues to go up and particularly to go down – and because of this you'll see signs advising you to get back to the gondola ridiculously early. Pay no attention – have a beer or two at the top while waiting for the queue to dissipate. Or forget the gondola and head for one of the other bases, and jump on a shuttle. A couple of recent visitors have found queues for the slow Groove chair and the Sky Express at the end of the day when people are returning to base. Another reported crowds around the lifts from East Peak Lodge on the Nevada side. Some lifts, including the gondola, also seem prone to closure because of wind. Most reporters have had few other problems, often commenting on uncrowded slopes.

TERRAIN PARKS ★★★★★
Splendid for all abilities

Heavenly has something for everyone – all sensibly located on the California slopes. Progression Park, at Adventure Peak near the top of the gondola, is part of the newish kids' adventure zone; it has small rails, gentle jumps and boxes designed to help youngsters explore.

Groove Park, at the top of the lifts up from California Lodge, has beginner/intermediate features such as small jumps and boxes for riders wanting to move to the next level. Ante Up Park under the Tamarack chair is intended for advanced and intermediates. High Roller Park, near the top of the Canyon chair, serves expert riders. There is a large double-jump line – with jumps exceeding 20m in length – as well as large boxes, rails and wall rides. A half-pipe (5.5m high and 152m long) has also been built here in the last couple of seasons.

SNOW RELIABILITY ★★★★
Fewer worries for intermediates

Heavenly averages an impressive 360 inches per year, but the weather here is much less consistent than further inland. When snow is poor and temperatures are cold enough, intermediates can still have a good time thanks to impressive snowmaking and grooming. But much of the challenging ungroomed terrain can be closed when snow is poor. Lake Tahoe TV provides updates on snow conditions each day.

gondola
cable car
fast chairlift
Slow chairs & drags have no symbol

3060m/10,040ft

Milky Way Bowl

2985m

Skiways Glades

Killebrew Canyon

Mott Canyon

Dipper

Comet

Sky

Tamarack

Canyon

Powderbowl

Powderbowl Woods

2545m

East Peak Lodge
2630m/8,630ft

Adventure Peak
2785m/9,140ft

Olympic

Lakeview Lodge
2515m/8,250ft

Gunbarrel

Stagecoach

North Bowl

2410m

Gondola

CALIFORNIA SIDE

California Lodge
2000m/6,570ft

NEVADA SIDE

Heavenly Village

Stagecoach Lodge
2280m/7,480ft

Boulder Lodge
2210m/7,250ft

SOUTH LAKE TAHOE

roped gateways, and are not to be underestimated. The Mott Canyon chair is slow, but you may not mind. Good natural snow is needed for the Canyons to be enjoyable (or open).

FOR INTERMEDIATES ★★★★☆
Lots to do

The California side offers a progression from the relaxed cruising of the long Ridge Run, starting right at the top of the mountain, to more challenging blues dropping off the ridge towards Sky Deck. More confident intermediates will want to spend time on the Nevada side, where there is more variety of terrain, more carving space and some great longer cruises down to the lift bases. But really strong intermediates looking for challenges need to be prepared to step up to the tree runs – maybe starting with Powderbowl Woods or The Pines – or to the blacks, which are often mogulled.

FOR BEGINNERS ★★★★☆
An excellent place to learn

There are excellent beginner areas at the top of the gondola, at California Lodge and at Boulder Lodge. On the California side there are gentle green runs to progress to at the top of the cable car. Package deals of tuition and lift ticket are worth looking into.

↑ Practically all Heavenly's trails are cut through the forest; there's great ungroomed skiing through the glades as well

SNOWPIX.COM / CHRIS GILL

GETTING THERE

Air San Francisco 320km/200 miles (3hr30); Reno 90km/55 miles (1hr15); South Lake Tahoe (15min)

FOR EXPERTS ★★★☆☆
Some specific challenges

The black runs under the California base lifts – including the Face and Gunbarrel (often used for mogul competitions) – are seriously steep. We've seen lots of people struggling on the top-to-bottom icy bumps. Many of the single diamonds higher up are at the easy end of the range. Ellie's, at the top of the mountain, may offer continuous moguls too, but was groomed and a great fast cruise when we last skied it. Skiways Glades and the Pinnacles, to skier's right of that, offer friendly, widely spaced trees. Lower down, a trusted reader raves about Maggie's Canyon.

On the Nevada side there are some excellent single-diamond glade areas too – notably to skier's left of the slow North Bowl chair. And there is some really steep stuff. Milky Way Bowl provides a gentle single-diamond introduction to the double-diamond terrain beyond it: the chutes in the otherwise densely wooded Mott and Killebrew Canyons are seriously steep and narrow. They are accessed through

FOR BOARDERS ★★★★☆
Perfect playground – nearly

Heavenly has several terrain parks, and the resort's naturally varied terrain makes a perfect playground for advanced freeriders. Intermediates will have fun too, especially if there's powder in the trees. And there are good areas for beginners. But beware: there are many flat spots where you'll have to scoot. Boardinghouse at Heavenly Village is the local snowboard-only shop.

FOR CROSS-COUNTRY ★★☆☆☆
A separate world

Heavenly does not provide cross-country skiing. But there is plenty at centres around the lake.

MOUNTAIN RESTAURANTS ★☆☆☆☆
Dire – but improving slowly

The on-mountain catering is grossly inadequate, especially in bad weather. The newish self-service Tamarack Lodge at the top of the gondola has been welcomed by reporters: 'a great

SCHOOLS

Heavenly
t 303 504 5870

Classes
1-day intermediate
lesson $105

Private lessons
From $449 for 3hr for
up to 2 people

CHILDCARE

Day Care Center
t 303 504 5870
Ages 6wk to 6yr

Ski school
Ages 4 to 13
(boarding 5 to 13)

UK PACKAGES

Alpine Answers,
American Ski Classics,
Erna Low, Momentum,
Scott Dunn, Ski
Independence, Ski
Safari, Skitracer,
Skiworld, Supertravel,
Virgin Snow

ACTIVITIES

Indoor Casinos, spas,
galleries, cinema,
museums

Outdoor Lake cruises,
snowmobiling,
snowshoeing,
tobogganing, gondola
rides, helicopter tours,
tubing, ski biking,
sleigh rides, dog
sledding, hot springs,
small ice rink,
ballooning

Phone numbers
Different area codes
are used on the two
sides of the state line;
for this chapter,
therefore, the area
code is included with
each number

From distant parts of
the US, add the prefix
1. From abroad, add
the prefix +1

TOURIST OFFICE

www.skiheavenly.com

improvement', 'fairly standard food but quality fine, and the place is large and comfortable'. The even newer sports bar, Booyah's, in Lakeview Lodge offers table-service, build-you-own burgers and 97 varieties of microbrews. The other options are outdoor decks serving BBQs and pizzas (hugely unenjoyable in a blizzard, as we can testify) and grossly overcrowded cafeterias.

SCHOOLS AND GUIDES ★★★★
No recent reports
Past reports have generally been favourable but we lack recent ones. As usual in the US, groups are generally small.

FOR FAMILIES ★★
Head for Adventure Peak
Heavenly offers various children's programmes and facilities. There's a kids' ski school building and adventure zone at Adventure Peak, which is also home to family activities such as tubing.

STAYING THERE

Accommodation in the South Lake Tahoe area is abundant and ranges from the huge casinos to small motels.
Hotels Of the main casino hotels, Harrah's (775 588 6611) and Harveys (775 588 2411) are the closest to the gondola.
★★★★Embassy Suites (530 544 5400) Luxury suites close to the gondola. Breakfast and après cocktails included.
★★★Aston Lakeland Village (530 544 1685) Wide range of lodgings from studios to five-bedroom condos. Right by the lake. Bus or drive to lifts.
★★★Avalon Lodge (530 544 2285) Award-winning small boutique hotel two blocks from the gondola.
★★★Inn by the Lake (530 542 0330) Less convenient but big rooms, some with good views. Hot tub, pool.
★★★Stardust Lodge (800 262 5077) Rooms and suites over the road from the gondola, tipped by two readers last year – 'lovely apartments, friendly, great hot tub, convenient'.
★★★Station House Inn (530 542 1101) A Best Western near the gondola; approved by past reporters for comfortable rooms and good cooked breakfasts.
★★★3 Peaks Resort (530 544 4131) Convenient, with large rooms. Pool.
Apartments Plenty of choice.

EATING OUT ★★★★
Good value and choice
There's a huge variety, at least if you are prepared to drive (and not drink). The casino hotels' all-you-can-eat buffets offer great value and variety, and there are 'gourmet' choices too – try 19 Kitchen and Bar on the 19th floor at Harveys.

LewMarNel's at the Station House Inn serves good fish, pasta, steak and veal. The Stateline Brewery does pub fare. MacDuff's Public House, near the Inn by the Lake, is billed as a Scottish pub and has a wood-fired pizza oven and pub grub.

Other recent reporter tips include Fresh Ketch at Tahoe Keys Marina, Evan's American Gourmet Cafe and the 'good value' Applebees. Other options include Heidi's for breakfast, Nikki's Chaat Cafe (Indian), the Blue Angel and the Driftwood Cafe.

APRES-SKI ★★★
From bars to baccarat
For years there has been a bit of late-afternoon action to the top of the gondola, to provide an alternative to simply queuing for the lift down. But now there's an organized party: 'Unbuckle at Tamarack runs from 3.30pm to 5.30pm Thursday to Saturday, featuring live DJs, dancing, half-price drinks and the Heavenly Angel dancers,' they say.

Fire+Ice at the foot of the gondola (with an outdoor seating area with open fires and heaters) gets busy. Whiskey Dick's, on the main highway, has regular live music.

Later on, the casinos have shows, occasionally with top-name entertainers, as well as endless opportunities for throwing your money away gambling.

OFF THE SLOPES ★★★
Quite a bit to entertain
If you want to get away from the bright lights, try a boat trip or a hot-air balloon ride. Pedestrians can use the cable car or the gondola to share the lake views. Adventure Peak at the top of the gondola has tubing, snow biking tobogganing and a zipline. There's ice skating and lots of snowshoe trails.

Mammoth Mountain

A big, sprawling mountain above a car-oriented, sprawling but pleasantly woody resort, a five-hour drive from Los Angeles

538

RATINGS

The mountains

Extent	★★★
Fast lifts	★★★★
Queues	★★★★
Terrain p'ks	★★★★★
Snow	★★★★
Expert	★★★★
Intermediate	★★★★
Beginner	★★★★
Boarder	★★★★★
X-country	★★★★
Restaurants	★
Schools	★★★★
Families	★★★★

The resort

Charm	★★
Convenience	★★
Scenery	★★★
Eating out	★★★★★
Après-ski	★★★
Off-slope	★

RPI	150
lift pass	£290
ski hire	£125
lessons	£215
food & drink	£140
total	**£770**

NEWS

2014/15: Rhythm Ridge, a new four-acre area of bowls, berms, banks and bumps for all levels, is due to open.

2013/14: June Mountain, under the same ownership as Mammoth and a scenic 30-minute drive away, reopened after being closed the previous season. It is covered by the Mammoth lift pass.

Beginner terrain park areas were expanded.

+ Slopes to suit all abilities

+ Mix of open Alpine-style bowls and classic American wooded slopes

+ Impressive snowfall record

+ Uncrowded trails most of the time

+ Mightily impressive terrain parks

+ Good views by US standards

– Mammoth Lakes is a rather straggling place with no focus, where life revolves around cars

– Most, though not all, lodgings are miles from the slopes

– Weekend crowds in high season

– Wind can be a problem

Mammoth may not be mammoth in Alpine terms – from end to end, it's less than one-third of the size of Val d'Isère-Tignes, in area more like one-sixth. But in American terms it's a decent size, with enough to keep most visitors happy. These days there is something resembling a village to stay in – The Village, a typically careful Intrawest confection of lodgings, restaurants and shops. But most people stay elsewhere – in hotels, condos and houses spread around the vast wooded area of Mammoth Lakes – and never go near it. Pick your location carefully, and you can walk to a lift; get a car, and you open up lots of options.

THE RESORT

The mountain is set above Mammoth Lakes, a small year-round resort that spreads over a wide area of woodland and is close to Yosemite National Park (local entrance road closed in winter). The drive up from Los Angeles takes around five hours (more in poor conditions). You pass through the Santa Monica mountains close to Beverly Hills, then the San Gabriel mountains and Mojave Desert (with the world's biggest jet-plane parking lot) before reaching the Sierra Nevada.

The place is almost entirely geared to driving, with no discernible centre – hotels, restaurants and little shopping centres are scattered along the four-lane highway called Main Street and Old Mammoth Road, which crosses it.

Two lift bases are both a mile or two from most of the hotels and condos. The major one is Canyon Lodge, with a big day lodge and hotels and condos in the area below it. A green run (very flat in parts) from here goes down to The Village, a car-free approximation to a village with a gondola back up to Canyon Lodge. The minor base is Eagle Lodge (aka Juniper Springs, the adjacent condos).

A road skirts the mountain to two other lift bases: Mill Cafe, and Main Lodge, a mini-resort with a big day lodge. You can stay here, in the Mammoth Mountain Inn.

June Mountain, half an hour away from Mammoth, reopened after a year's closure. The slopes are covered by the lift pass, spectacularly under-used, and well worth a visit when Mammoth's slopes are crowded.

VILLAGE CHARM ★★
Good first impressions
The resort buildings are generally timber-clad in traditional style – even the McDonald's is tastefully designed – and are set among trees. So although it may be short on village ambience, the place has a pleasant enough appearance – particularly when under several feet of snow. The Village is car-free, and neatly designed.

CONVENIENCE ★★
Canyon Lodge is closest
Even ignoring outlying parts, Mammoth Lakes is spread over an area roughly two miles square, so location obviously matters. If you stay at one of the lift bases, you'll have only a short walk to a lift. But out at Main Lodge you'll be four miles from the 50+ restaurants in Mammoth Lakes. With its gondola link to Canyon Lodge, The Village is also a fairly convenient base.

Reliable, frequent and free shuttle-buses run on several colour-coded routes serving the lift bases. Less frequent night buses run until midnight. But a car is useful.

KEY FACTS

Resort	2425m
	7,950ft
Slopes	2425-3370m
	7,950-11,050ft
Lifts	28
Pistes	3,500 acres
Green	25%
Blue	40%
Black	35%
Snowmaking	33%

SCENERY ★★★☆☆
Hint of the Alpine

The resort has a wooded setting below open Alpine-style ridges. From the top there are great views north-east into Nevada, and of the jagged Minarets.

THE MOUNTAINS

The 28 lifts access an impressive area, suitable for all abilities. The high runs are open, the lower ones sheltered by trees; lightly wooded slopes at mid-mountain are great on a stormy day.

Finding your way around is not easy at first. All the chairlifts are numbered (the traditional practice), and many are also named (a relatively new practice), but the trails are rather ill defined, and signposting on the mountain could be better. The resort trail map uses six grades of difficulty instead of the usual four, of which we approve. Free tours on Saturdays and Sundays cover the ski area's environment as well as show you around the trails.

EXTENT OF THE SLOPES ★★★☆☆
Lots for everyone

As you can see from our star ratings, Mammoth is good for every ability of skier and boarder. But it's not huge – it falls right on the borderline between our ★★ and ★★★ extent ratings and we've erred on the generous side.

From **Main Lodge** the two-stage Panorama gondola goes via McCoy

Station right to the top. From here, there are countless ways down the front of the mountain that range from steep to very steep – or vertical if the wind has created a cornice, as it often does. Or you can go off the back of the hill, down to **Outpost 14**, whence Chair 14 or Chair 13 brings you back to lower points on the ridge. The third option is to follow the ridge, which curls around and eventually brings you down to the Main Lodge area – though you might not realize that from the trail map. This route brings you past an easy area served by a double chair, and a very easy area served by the Discovery fast quad.

McCoy Station can also be reached using the Stump Alley fast chair from **Mill Cafe**, on the road up from town. The fast Gold Rush quad, also from Mill Cafe, takes you into the more heavily wooded eastern half of the area. This has long, gentle runs served by lifts up from **Canyon Lodge** and **Eagle Lodge** and seriously steep stuff as well as some intermediate terrain served by lifts 25 and 22 and some excellent tree skiing.

FAST LIFTS ★★★★☆
Where it counts

The main access lifts from every base are fast chairs or gondolas. But there are still several slow old lifts. The Outpost area is the least well served for fast lifts. Usefully, the trail map lists the ride time of every lift.

PEATROSS / MMSA

The mid-mountain area is lightly wooded and great on a snowy day. But we doubt it will stay this untracked for long now that the sun is coming out ↓

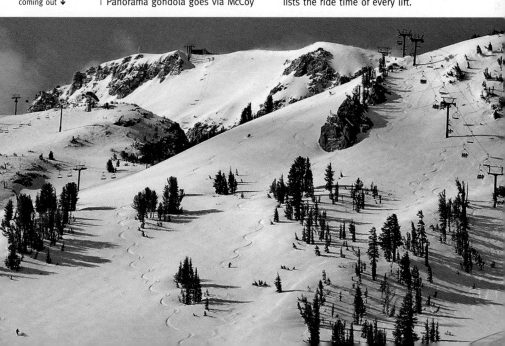

LIFT PASSES

Mammoth Mountain

Prices in US$

Age	1-day	6-day
under 13	35	210
13 to 18	73	370
19 to 64	94	474
65 plus	80	402

Free Under 7, over 80
Beginner Pass for four chairs $57
Notes Prices are for booking online 14 days in advance; ticket window prices are more expensive; afternoon pass available

QUEUES ★★★★
Normally quiet slopes

Mammoth's lifts and slopes are usually very quiet, with few queues: 'Queues? What queues?' says a reporter. But on fine peak-season weekends hordes of people may arrive from Los Angeles, and the lifts can struggle to cope. Which explains why one of the privileges of membership of the exclusive Mammoth Black club is that you get lift priority. If crowds are a problem, just head for June Mountain and ski its delightfully deserted pistes.

TERRAIN PARKS ★★★★★
Difficult to beat

'Absolutely awesome,' is the summary of a recent reporter. Mammoth's world-class Unbound Terrain Parks (several of them) offer a huge variety of challenges from elementary to mind-blowing, all looked after with artistic proficiency. There are over 50 jumps, 100 jibs and two half-pipes in over 100 acres of freestyle territory.

Easiest are the three Unbound Playgrounds at Eagle, Canyon and Main Lodges (with small rails, boxes and jumps). Forest Trail at Main Lodge is one step up. For intermediate to advanced riders South Park and Jibs Galore offer a bewildering choice of rails and kickers. Alternatively, take on the X-Course snowcross run or, new for 2014/15, Rhythm Ridge's four-acre area of berms, banks and bumps.

Main Park, above Main Lodge, is huge; everything here is up to pro standard. Kickers range from 18m to 24m and border the famous super-

duper pipe (150m long, with 7m walls) that looms over the car park and dwarfs the super-pipe beside it; it is cut daily. Main Park is serviced by a fast chairlift, allowing for a full lap time of only eight minutes.

SNOW RELIABILITY ★★★★
A long season

Mammoth has an impressive snow record – an annual average of 400 inches, which puts it ahead of major Colorado resorts. Its slopes are appreciably higher than those of Heavenly and the other Tahoe resorts, and it has an ever-expanding array of snow-guns, so it enjoys a long season – it sometimes has slopes open on 4 July. The mountain faces roughly north-east; the relatively low and slightly sunny slopes down to Eagle Lodge are affected by warm weather before others. Strong winds are not uncommon on the upper mountain, and the snow quality can be affected. But you may find powder is just shifted down the hill. Visitors continue to report 'excellent' grooming.

FOR EXPERTS ★★★★
Some very challenging terrain

The steep double-diamond chutes strung across the width of the mountaintop provide wonderful opportunities for experts. Fortunately for the rest of us, there are three or four broad single-diamond slopes, requiring rather less bottle.

There is lots of challenging terrain lower down, too, much of it lightly wooded and therefore good to ski in

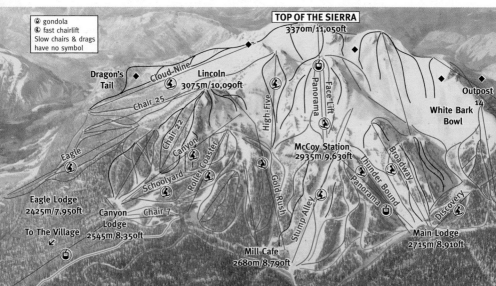

A good view of the mountain, with steep, open slopes at the top and mellow wooded ones lower down. Note the spread-out nature of the town, where car is king →

MAMMOTH MOUNTAIN

bad conditions; Chair 5, Chair 22 (the top of which is higher than the very top of Heavenly) and Broadway are often open in bad weather when the top is firmly shut, and their more sheltered slopes may in any case have the best snow. There are plenty of good slopes over the back, too.

Many of the steeper trails are short by Alpine standards (typically under 400m vertical), but despite this we've had some great powder days here.

FOR INTERMEDIATES ★★★★
Lots of great cruising
Although there are exceptions, most of the lower mountain, below the treeline, is intermediate cruising territory and generally flattering.

Some of the mountain's longest runs – blue-blacks served by the Cloud Nine Express and Chair 25 – are ideal for good intermediates. There are also some excellent, fairly steep woodland trails down to Mill Cafe. Most of the long runs above Eagle Lodge, and some of the shorter ones above Canyon Lodge, are easy cruises. There is a variety of terrain, including lots of gentle stuff, on skier's left of the area.

FOR BEGINNERS ★★★★
Good, gentle slopes
Chair 7 and the Schoolyard Express chair (at the Canyon Lodge base) and Discovery Chair (at Main Lodge) serve quiet, gentle green runs – perfect terrain for novices. These lifts are included in a beginner lift pass. Excellent instruction and top-notch piste maintenance usually make progress speedy, delighting reporters.

FOR BOARDERS ★★★★★
Great parks and terrain
Regularly voted one of the best snowboard resorts in the USA by *Transworld Snowboarding* magazine readers, Mammoth has encouraged snowboarding since its early days: 'We felt like we were being welcomed home here!' said a reporter. A huge amount has been spent on the terrain parks, and this tends to overshadow just how good the mountain's natural terrain really is. Largely serviced by hassle-free fast chairs and gondolas, this is a snowboarder's heaven with terrain to suit every ability level. Lower Road Runner is reportedly the only unbearably flat trail. Specialist shops include Wave Rave and P3.

FOR CROSS-COUNTRY ★★★★
Very popular
The specialist Tamarack Centre has 31km of groomed trails, some going round the pretty Lakes Basin area, and provides lessons and tours. Members of a 2014 reporter's party had 'a wonderful time on excellent tracks'.

MOUNTAIN RESTAURANTS ★
Back to base ...
The already limited lunch options on the hill were narrowed further a couple of years ago. The pleasant table-service Parallax at mid-mountain is now open only to members of the exclusive Mammoth Black club. We cut our rating to ★ as a result.

McCoy Station, the plebs' self-service facility at mid-mountain, offers a wide choice. Top of the Sierra is small and very functional but has

Build your own shortlist: www.wheretoskiandsnowboard.com

Resort news and key links: www.wheretoskiandsnowboard.com

SCHOOLS

Mammoth Mountain
t 1 800 626 6684

Classes
Half-day (2.5hr) $151
Private lessons
From $535 for 3hr

CHILDCARE

Mammoth Child Care
t 1 800 626 6684
Newborn to 6yr

Ski school
Ages 3 to 13

GETTING THERE

Air Los Angeles
515km/320 miles
(5hr); Reno
275km/170 miles
(3hr15)

ACTIVITIES

Indoor Spa, art
gallery, arts centre,
cinema, theatre

Outdoor Ice rink, dog
sledding, tubing,
snowmobiling,
snowshoeing

UK PACKAGES

American Ski Classics,
Momentum, Ski
Independence, Ski
Safari, Skitracer,
Skiworld, Snow Finders,
Supertravel, Virgin
Snow

Phone numbers
From distant parts of
the US, add the prefix
1 760; from abroad,
add the prefix +1 760

TOURIST OFFICE

www.mammoth
mountain.com

---

lovely views. A fair-weather option is the primitive outdoor BBQ at Outpost 14. The Little Mill snowcat drives around the hill selling food.

Mammoth says you can eat your packed lunch in any of its places. Try that in the Parallax.

SCHOOLS AND GUIDES ★★★★☆
More reports needed
We have no recent reports. But adult group lessons have a maximum of four guests and there are three-day 'camps' (eg terrain park, all mountain, moguls).

FOR FAMILIES ★★★★☆
Family favourite
Mammoth is keen to attract families. The focal points are the Mammoth Childcare centres at the Inn and at The Village, with comprehensive facilities for children up to six years old. And there are two non-skiing Play Zones, an Igloo ('great attraction') and a tubing park with its own lift. Kids from age three can have ski lessons, and there are four Kids Adventure zones with fun features for skiers and boarders and two Fun Zones with mellow rollers and small spines as an introduction to a terrain park.

STAYING THERE

There's a good choice of hotels (none very luxurious or pricey) and condos. The condos tend to be out of town, near the lifts or on the road to them.
★★★★Westin Monache Resort (934 0400) Condo hotel near The Village gondola: restaurant, hot tubs, pool.
★★★Alpenhof Lodge (934 6330) Comfortable and central; shuttle-bus stop and plenty of restaurants nearby.
★★★Mammoth Mountain Inn (934 2581) Opposite Main Lodge, so convenient for the slopes but not the town. Outdoor pool and hot tubs.
★★★Sierra Nevada Resort (934 2515) Central; recently renovated. Spa. One reporter was so taken he went back again the next year: 'Nice rooms, really friendly staff, good value.'
Apartments The Village Lodge is close to many restaurants and shops; Juniper Springs Resort is near the Eagle base; both are of high quality. Other comfortable options are the Seasons 4 condos (close to The Village), the 1849 Condos (Canyon Lodge area) and the nearby Mammoth Ski and Racquet Club.

EATING OUT ★★★★★
Outstanding choice
Mammoth has 50+ restaurants offering a wide choice from typical American to Japanese. There's a local menu guide covering many but not all.

The chalet-style Lakefront in the Tamarack Lodge is one of the best and was endorsed by a 2014 reporter ('beautiful views, great dinner and wine plus excellent service'). Rafters and the Red Lantern Chinese in the Sierra Nevada Lodge both have 'excellent cuisine and are good value for money, especially in happy hour', says a recent reporter who also rates the Mogul for 'the best steak in town' and Jimmy's Taverna for 'high-quality Greek food and fish dishes at decent prices'. We've had excellent dinners at Skadi (fine dining). Giovanni's is good for pizza and pasta and does 'very good take-aways'. Slocums is a popular steakhouse. Angels has typical American family food – burgers, steaks, ribs. Chart House is a chain place doing seafood and steaks.

Other possibilities include Shogun for Japanese or Gomez's for Tex-Mex. The Side Door cafe is an appealing eatery in The Village. The Parallax at McCoy Station opens for snowcat dinners up the mountain. For a hearty breakfast, try the Breakfast Club.

APRES-SKI ★★★☆☆
OK if you know where to go
At the close of play, the Yodler at Main Lodge is the liveliest spot – an old chalet (brought from Switzerland, they claim). Tusks, also at Main Lodge, and the Dry Creek bar in the Mammoth Mountain Inn across the road are other choices. Lakanuki in The Village is a 'Hawaiian-style bar that attracts a younger crowd'. Chart House is recommended this year for its 'welcoming fire and happy hour – lasts beyond an hour'. A couple of bars that are said to liven up at weekends are Grumpy's sports bar and Slocums.

OFF THE SLOPES ★☆☆☆☆
Mainly outdoors
Outdoor activities include skating, tubing, snowmobiling, snowshoeing, 'enjoyable' walks in the forest, thermal hot springs and pleasant drives. Mono Lake and the WW2 centre at Manzanar on the road to Los Angeles have been recommended. There is factory shopping nearby, too. But overall, Mammoth isn't great for non-skiers.

SQUAW VALLEY SKI CORP / NATHAN KENDALL

Squaw Valley

The site of the 1960 Olympics has a lot to offer novices and experts, and the little purpose-built village is worth a few days' stay

TOP 10 RATINGS

Extent	★★★
Fast lifts	★★★
Queues	★★★★
Snow	★★★★
Expert	★★★★
Intermediate	★★
Beginner	★★★★
Charm	★★★
Convenience	★★★★
Scenery	★★★

RPI 150

lift pass	£310
ski hire	£110
lessons	£200
food & drink	£150
total	**£770**

KEY FACTS

Resort	1890m
	6,200ft
Slopes	1890-2760m
	6,200-9,050ft
Lifts	30
Pistes	3,600 acres
Green	25%
Blue	45%
Black	30%
Snowmaking	17%

SQUAW VALLEY / TOM DAY

The Village at the foot of the slopes looks bigger here than it feels when you are there. The night skiing happens on 'selected dates' only ↓

- ➕ Lots of challenging terrain
- ➕ Impressive snow record
- ➕ Superb beginner slopes
- ➕ Convenient 'village' at the base
- ➖ Not for mile-hungry intermediates
- ➖ Lifts prone to closure by wind
- ➖ Limited range of village amenities

When Intrawest built a neat little car-free base 'village' a decade or so ago, Squaw became a more attractive place to stay; but the Village remains small. And keen piste-bashers who like cruising groomed runs will find the ski area limited too. But Squaw now shares ownership and its lift pass with Alpine Meadows, a very worthwhile resort only 15 minutes away and linked by free shuttle-buses, which means there is quite a lot to do locally. Even so, we would always combine a stay in Squaw with one in Heavenly.

THE RESORT

Squaw is the major resort at the north end of Lake Tahoe. Staying here has become more attractive since the car-free Village was built; but it is still also popular with day trippers. There are other lodgings around the lake, and at Tahoe City. The lift pass also covers neighbouring Alpine Meadows (a 15-minute ride by half-hourly free shuttle-buses).

Village charm The Village is very small but works well, and older buildings next to it are not unpleasant.

Convenience The Village is at the base of the main lifts. The self-contained, luxurious, conference-oriented Resort at Squaw Creek hotel is well outside the Village, but it is situated right on the slopes.

Scenery There are fabulous views of Lake Tahoe from Squaw Peak.

THE MOUNTAINS

One of the attractions of the area is that the slopes are lightly wooded. Until recently the resort was stupidly unhelpful about navigation. Only from 2011/12 have trails been shown on the mountain map and signposted on the ground.

Slopes From the base, a big cable car rises 600m to High Camp (the biggest of two mid-mountain bases) and a big gondola to Gold Coast (the other mid-mountain base). Above them is a wide area of beginner slopes, and beyond that the three highest peaks of the area, with lifts of modest vertical; much the biggest is Squaw Peak's Headwall six-pack with a vertical of just 535m.

From High Camp you can descend into a steep-sided valley from which the Silverado chair is the return.

Two other peaks are accessed directly from the Village. A fast quad serves steep KT-22; a slow triple goes to rather neglected Snow King.

Squaw's cable car runs late on selected dates to serve floodlit slopes (including a 5km run to the base).

Fast lifts There are fast lifts in each sector, but also slow old chairs.

Queues There are few problems usually, but the weather and weekend invasions are key factors. A lack of snow in January 2014 produced waits of 10 to 15 minutes says a visitor.

Terrain parks The Mainline park has the biggest jumps plus a super-pipe and is aimed at advanced riders. The Gold Coast park has features for all standards from beginner freestyler to expert. The Belmont park offers small

NEWS

2014/15: There are plans to redevelop the base area and build more lodgings, which will include a luxury hotel. And Squaw plans to be the first ski resort to launch an app for Google Glass – initial capabilities will include viewing open and closed lifts and trails.

2013/14: There was further investment in terrain park features, snowmaking and grooming. The Village at Squaw Valley condos have been revamped and there were improvements to the base area.

UK PACKAGES

American Ski Classics, Momentum, Scott Dunn, Ski Bespoke, Ski Independence, Ski Safari, Skitracer, Skiworld, Supertravel, Virgin Snow

Phone numbers
From distant parts of the US, add the prefix 1 530; from abroad, add the prefix +1 530

TOURIST OFFICE

www.squaw.com

to medium features for beginners and intermediates. There are other parks designed for kids and novices. All are dependent on there being enough snow.

Snow reliability An impressive 450 inches on average, plus snowmaking. But the last few years have seen unusually low snowfalls and a January 2014 reporter found many lifts and runs closed because of lack of snow.

Experts The possibilities for experts on KT-22, Squaw Peak, Granite Chief and the Silverado valley are huge, with lots of steep chutes and big mogul fields; many extreme skiing and boarding movies are made here.

Intermediates Blue-run skiers have a choice of some lovely cruises in the Emigrant and Snow King sectors and a 5km run down to the Village. But there is not much more groomed cruising, so keen piste-bashers will find the area limited. There is, however, lots of steep blue and easy black terrain to test your deep-snow or mogul skills.

Beginners The SnoVentures Activities Zone at the base has a gentle slope served by a triple chairlift and three moving carpets. A special beginner package, with lift pass, is planned. There's a superb choice of easy runs to progress to at altitude, notably at High Camp.

Snowboarding This is one of the most snowboarder friendly resorts around. The higher areas are full of steep and deep gullies, cliff drops, kicker building spots and tree runs, and the parks are kept in excellent shape.

Cross-country There are 18km of groomed trails at Squaw Creek.

Mountain restaurants Uninspiring, except in terms of views.

Schools and guides As well as group lessons, the school runs specialist workshops – eg all-mountain excursions, jib and jumps and women-only clinics.

Families Squaw offers slope-side convenience and a children's on-slope play area at the SnoVentures Activities Zone at the base, with tubing and mini-snowmobiles. Squaw Kids takes children from three years.

STAYING THERE

Hotels The PlumpJack Inn (583 1576) is our favourite – comfortable, stylish, central. The Resort at Squaw Creek (583 6300) is set apart but is right on the slopes and offers luxury rooms, an outdoor pool and hot tubs. The Red Wolf Lodge (344 0686) at the base is 'comfortable' says a 2014 reporter.

Apartments The Village has well-appointed ski-in/ski-out condos.

Eating out The PlumpJack Inn has an excellent restaurant. Graham's is worth the 10-minute walk from the Village for its 'great chowder and tarte tatin', says a 2014 visitor. More routine places include the Auld Dubliner pub ('good Guinness stew'), Fireside (pizza/pasta) and Mamasake (sushi).

Après-ski The Olympic House has several venues. In the Village, the places above mostly function as bars, too: Auld Dubliner has live music on a Friday, but can be dead during the week. Uncorked at Squaw Valley is a wine bar with live music and wine tastings. Rocker@Squaw is 'friendly'.

Off the slopes High Camp has an ice rink and other activities. The Trilogy Spa offers a range of treatments.

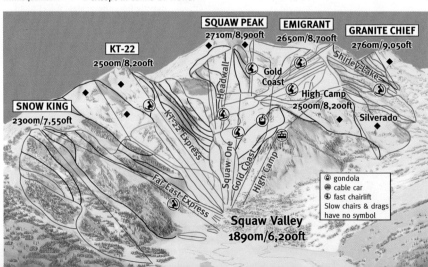

SQUAW PEAK 2710m/8,900ft

EMIGRANT 2650m/8,700ft

GRANITE CHIEF 276om/9,05oft

KT-22 2500m/8,200ft

Shirley Lake

Gold Coast

High Camp 2500m/8,200ft

SNOW KING 2300m/7,55oft

Headwall

KT-22 Express

Silverado

Squaw One

Gold Coast

High Camp

Far East Express

⑨ gondola
⊜ cable car
④ fast chairlift
Slow chairs & drags have no symbol

Squaw Valley 189om/6,200ft

VAIL RESORTS / BOB WINSETT

Colorado

Colorado is the most popular American destination state for UK visitors, and justifiably so: it has the most alluring combination of attractive resorts, slopes to suit all abilities and excellent, reliable snow – dry enough to justify its 'champagne powder' label. It also has direct scheduled BA flights to Denver, an easy drive or shuttle transfer from some of the resorts (less easy if it's snowing). But you may be able to save money by taking an indirect flight – and if you are going to a resort far from Denver, this makes sense because you can fly into a nearer airport.

Resorts such as Breckenridge, Vail and Winter Park are around a two-hour transfer from Denver. But Aspen and Snowmass are around four to five hours, and places such as Crested Butte and Telluride even more. For these more remote places you might want to consider an indirect flight, changing to a plane that lands at a nearby airport: Aspen, for example, has its own airport a few minutes from town. Even for Vail, you may prefer to change planes and fly into Eagle airport, only 45 minutes away.

Colorado has amazingly dry snow. Even when the snow melts and refreezes, the moisture seems to be

magically whisked away, leaving it soft and powdery. Even the artificial snow is of a quality you'll rarely find in Europe. And like most North American rivals, Colorado resorts generally have excellent, steep, ungroomed areas that you can ski safely without a guide.

The resorts vary enormously. If you want cute restored buildings from the mining boom days of the late 19th century, try the dinky old towns of Telluride and Crested Butte or the much bigger Aspen. Other resorts (such as Aspen's modern satellite, Snowmass) major on convenience. Some (such as Vail and Beaver Creek) deliberately pitch themselves upmarket, with lots of glitzy, expensive hotels, while others (such as Breckenridge and Winter Park) are much more down to earth.

You could consider renting a car and touring several resorts – maybe cutting costs by staying in valley towns rather than resorts. One regular reporter recently did a tour staying In Avon, near Beaver Creek and Vail, and then Frisco, near Breckenridge, Keystone, Copper Mountain and Arapahoe Basin.

Six major resorts get write-ups in this section of the book. The others with blue circles on the map have entries in the resort directory at the back of the book – of these, Steamboat, Copper Mountain, Keystone, Crested Butte, Telluride and Durango have proper resort villages; the others cater more for day visitors.

Many Colorado resorts are at an extremely high altitude. As a result, visitors arriving straight from sea level are at risk of altitude sickness, which can spoil your trip. We always try to start in one of the lower resorts – or spend a night or two in Denver to acclimatize.

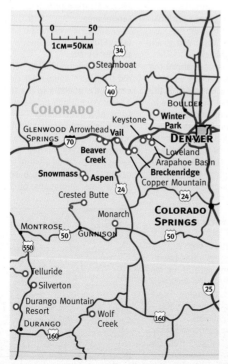

Map:

0 — 50
1CM=50KM

34 Steamboat

40

COLORADO

Keystone • Winter Park

GLENWOOD SPRINGS Arrowhead Vail

70 BOULDER

DENVER

Beaver Creek

Loveland
Arapahoe Basin

Snowmass Aspen Breckenridge
Copper Mountain

Crested Butte 24 24

Monarch COLORADO SPRINGS

MONTROSE 50 GUNNISON 50

550

Telluride

Silverton

25

Durango Mountain Resort

Wolf Creek 160

DURANGO 160

ASPEN / DOUG CHILD

Aspen

Don't be put off by the ritzy image – with a fun, historic town and quiet, extensive slopes, this is the USA's best resort

RATINGS

The mountains

Extent	★★
Fast lifts	★★★★
Queues	★★★★
Terrain p'ks	★★★★★
Snow	★★★★★
Expert	★★★★★
Intermediate	★★★★★
Beginner	★★★★★
Boarder	★★★★
X-country	★★★★
Restaurants	★★★
Schools	★★★★★
Families	★★

The resort

Charm	★★★★
Convenience	★★
Scenery	★★★
Eating out	★★★★★
Après-ski	★★★★
Off-slope	★★★★

Our extent rating excludes Snowmass. Including Snowmass would rate ★★★★

546

RPI	180
lift pass	£360
ski hire	£200
lessons	£215
food & drink	£155
total	**£930**

NEWS

2014/15: The Hideout, a new $10 million children's centre, is being built at the base of Buttermilk. The Aspen Art Museum is being extended with a new building.

2013/14: Two new gladed areas opened at Highland bowl, adding 20 acres of new terrain. Little Nell's pop-up champagne bar is back on Aspen Mountain.

- Notably uncrowded slopes
- Attractive, characterful old town, with good restaurants and shops
- Excellent Aspen Highlands and Snowmass just up the road
- Convenient airport on edge of town
- Extensive slopes of all kinds, but ...

- Slopes split over four separate mountains (including Snowmass), served by efficient, free buses
- Expensive, and tending to become more so as cheap places disappear
- A bit isolated – no other major resorts within easy day-trip distance

Aspen is our favourite American resort. It has everything we look for – well, everything except convenience. Our affection depends heavily on the presence of Aspen Highlands, a little way down the valley, and on Snowmass, much further down the valley (covered in a separate chapter). So most days you have to ride a bus; that doesn't worry us, and doesn't seem to worry readers who report on the place – most people who try it are captivated.

Many rich and some famous guests jet in here, and for connoisseurs of cosmetic surgery the bars of the top hotels can be fascinating places. And the place does seem to be drifting even further upmarket, with ever fewer funky bars and ever more international-brand shops. But, like all other 'glamorous' ski resorts, Aspen is actually filled by ordinary holidaymakers. Don't be put off.

THE RESORT

Aspen was built on silver-mining – in 1892 it had 12,000 inhabitants; it declined until skiing started here in the late 1930s, when there were only 700 inhabitants. The first lift was opened shortly after World War 2, and Aspen hasn't looked back.

Aspen Mountain is right above the town, its access lifts starting yards from the main street. But most of the slopes covered by the ski pass are a bus ride away. Around 3km away are Buttermilk and Aspen Highlands. Buttermilk has the Inn at Aspen hotel at the base. Highlands has a limited amount of lodgings (including the very smart Ritz Carlton Club). Snowmass, 14km away, is a proper resort that gets its own chapter.

VILLAGE CHARM ★★★★
Smart old town
Aspen's historic centre – with a typical American grid of streets – has been preserved to form the core of the most fashionable ski town in the Rockies, and one of the most charming. There's a huge variety of restaurants, bars, swanky shops and galleries.

A mixture of developments spreads out from the centre, ranging from the homes of the super-rich through

surprisingly modest hotels and motels to mobile homes for the workers. Though the town is busy with traffic, it moves slowly, and pedestrians effectively have priority in much of the central area.

CONVENIENCE ★★
Better by bus
Aspen is very unusual in being a cute old town with a major lift close to the centre: the gondola to the top of Aspen Mountain is only yards from some of the top hotels. Downtown Aspen is quite compact by American resort standards, but it spreads far enough to make the free ski-bus a necessity for some visitors staying less centrally. You also need buses to get to the other mountains, of course.

Aspen

KEY FACTS

Resort	2425m
	7,950ft

Aspen Mountain

Slopes	2425-3415m
	7,950-11,210ft
Lifts	8
Pistes	675 acres
Green	0%
Blue	48%
Black	52%
Snowmaking	31%

Aspen Highlands

Slopes	2450-3560m
	8,040-11,680ft
Lifts	5
Pistes	1,040 acres
Green	18%
Blue	30%
Black	52%
Snowmaking	12%

Buttermilk

Slopes	2400-3015m
	7,880-9,900ft
Lifts	8
Pistes	470 acres
Green	35%
Blue	39%
Black	26%
Snowmaking	23%

Total with Snowmass

Slopes	2400-3815m
	7,880-12,510ft
Lifts	42
Pistes	5,517 acres
Green	10%
Blue	45%
Black	45%
Snowmaking	12%

Generally, they work well. But they can get crowded, and you may need to keep an eye on the timetables. You might even decide to stay near the main bus station for the easiest possible access to Snowmass etc.

SCENERY ★★★★★
Beautiful Bells

The views are generally unremarkable, but those from the upper part of Highlands and Buttermilk are notable – they include the distinctive Maroon Bells that appear on many postcards.

THE MOUNTAINS

Most of the slopes are in the trees. At Snowmass, free guided tours run each day at 11am and 1pm. The ratio of acres to visitor beds is high, and the slopes are usually blissfully quiet. Trail classification is generally reliable, and if the blacks on Buttermilk are a bit soft that is forgivable. Signposting could be better where runs merge.

EXTENT OF THE SLOPES ★★★★★
Widely dispersed

Each of the four mountains is worth a visit. Much the most extensive mountain in the area is at Snowmass – see separate chapter. Note that our extent rating excludes Snowmass; including it would give ★★★★.

Once you are up the gondola, a series of chairs serves the ridges of Aspen Mountain. In general, there are long cruising blue runs along the valley floors and short, steep blacks down from the ridges.

Buttermilk is the smallest, lowest and least challenging mountain, accessed by a fast quad from the fairly primitive main base lodge. The runs fan out from the top in three directions – back to the base, down to Tiehack and down to West Buttermilk (with fast quads back from all three).

Aspen Highlands consists essentially of a single ridge served by three fast quad chairs, with easy and intermediate slopes along the ridge itself and steep black runs on the flanks – very steep ones at the top. And beyond the lift network, a free snowcat ride leads to Highland Bowl, of entirely double-black gradient.

FAST LIFTS ★★★★★
Serving bottom to top

Each mountain has a few key fast chairs or a gondola up to the top.

QUEUES ★★★★★
Few problems

Major queues are rare on any of the mountains – you may hit a few during the college spring break in March. At Aspen Mountain, the gondola can still have delays at peak times, and we have one report of epic queues on a January powder day. You can use the slow Shadow Mountain chair, instead,

ASPEN / DAVID PERRY

Highland Bowl is Aspen's signature expert terrain. The higher you hike, the steeper it gets →

SKIWORLD

Catered chalets,
hotels and
self catering
apartments in

**Europe, USA
and Canada**

skiworld.co.uk
08444 930 430

ABTA V2151 ATOL 2036

GET THE BEST OF THE SNOW, ON- AND OFF-PISTE

Aspen offers special experiences for small numbers of skiers or riders.

First Tracks *The first skiers to sign up each day get to ride the gondola up Aspen Mountain at 8am the next day and get first tracks on perfect corduroy or fresh powder. Well worth doing. Free, but numbers are limited. When we did it, we took our time over the descent, to let the start-of-day queue at the bottom dissipate, but we're told you now ski in a guided group at a set pace.*

Powder Tours *Spend the day finding untracked snow in a guided group in 1,500 acres of backcountry beyond Aspen Mountain, with a 12-passenger heated snowcat as your personal lift. You're likely to squeeze in about 10 runs in all. You break for lunch at an old mountain cabin. It costs about $400 per person.*

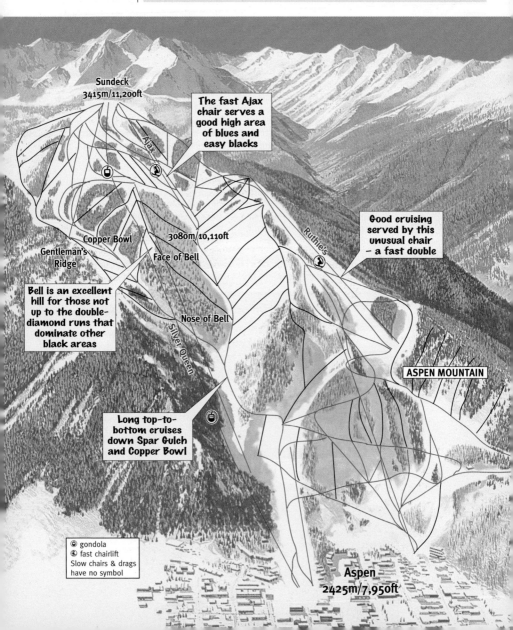

Sundeck
3415m/11,200ft

The fast Ajax chair serves a good high area of blues and easy blacks

Ajax

Good cruising served by this unusual chair – a fast double

Copper Bowl   3080m/10,110ft
Gentleman's Ridge   Face of Bell
Ruthie's

Bell is an excellent hill for those not up to the double-diamond runs that dominate other black areas

Nose of Bell

Silver Queen

ASPEN MOUNTAIN

Long top-to-bottom cruises down Spar Gulch and Copper Bowl

ⓖ gondola
ⓕ fast chairlift
Slow chairs & drags
have no symbol

Aspen
2425m/7,950ft

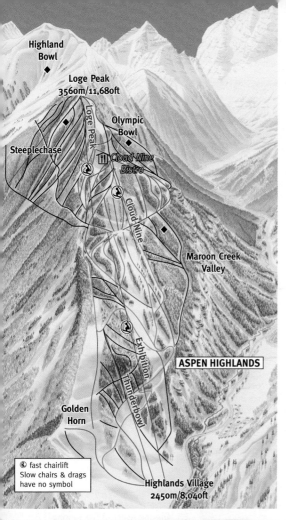

Highland Bowl
Loge Peak
3560m/11,680ft
Olympic Bowl
Steeplechase
Loge Peak
Cloud Nine Bistro
Cloud Nine
Maroon Creek Valley
Exhibition
Thunderbowl
Golden Horn

ASPEN HIGHLANDS

fast chairlift
Slow chairs & drags have no symbol

Highlands Village
2450m/8,040ft

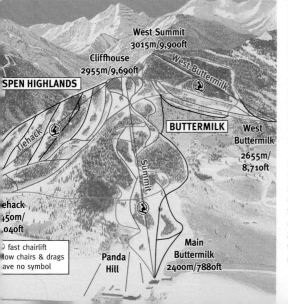

West Summit
3015m/9,900ft
Cliffhouse
2955m/9,690ft
West Buttermilk

SPEN HIGHLANDS

Tiehack

BUTTERMILK
West Buttermilk
2655m/8,710ft

Summit

ehack
450m/
040ft

fast chairlift
low chairs & drags
ave no symbol

Panda Hill

Main Buttermilk
2400m/788oft

with a short uphill walk to reach it. Aspen Highlands is almost always queue-free, even at peak times.

TERRAIN PARKS ★★★★★
X Games standard
Aspen has two pipe and park mountains – Snowmass (see separate chapter) and Buttermilk. Buttermilk Park is famous as the home of the Winter X Games, and stretches over 3km from the top to the bottom of the mountain – it is said to be the longest in the world. It has over 100 features, the X Games slope-style course and a world-class super-pipe that's over 150m long with 6.7m walls.

SNOW RELIABILITY ★★★★★
Rarely a problem
Aspen's mountains get an annual average of 300 inches of snow – not in the front rank, but not far behind. In addition, all areas have substantial snowmaking. Immaculate grooming adds to the quality of the pistes, and the light traffic (particularly on mountains other than Aspen) can only help maintain snow quality.

FOR EXPERTS ★★★★★
Buttermilk is the only soft stuff
There's plenty to choose from – all the mountains except Buttermilk offer lots of challenges, and it is relatively easy to find untouched powder in the many gladed areas.

Aspen Mountain has a formidable array of double-black diamond runs. From the top of the gondola, Walsh's, Hyrup's and Kristi are on a lightly wooded slope and link up with Gentleman's Ridge and Jackpot to form the longest black run on the mountain. A series of steep glades drops down from Gentleman's Ridge. The central Bell ridge has less extreme single diamonds on both its flanks, including some delightful lightly wooded areas. On the opposite side of Spar Gulch is another row of double blacks, collectively called the Dumps, because mining waste was dumped here.

At Highlands there are challenging runs from top to bottom of the mountain. Consider joining a guided group as an introduction to the best of them. Highland Bowl, beyond the top lift, is superb in the right conditions: a big open bowl with access gates reached by hiking (but there are usually free snowcat rides to cut out the first 20-minute walk). The

Aspen

Build your own shortlist: www.wheretoskiandsnowboard.com

LIFT PASSES

Four Mountain Pass

Prices in US$

Age	1-day	6-day
under 13	83	378
13 to 17	110	540
18 to 64	119	594
65 plus	110	540

Free Under 7: $5 for unlimited period

Senior Over 70: $429 for unlimited period

Beginner Included in price of lessons

Notes Includes shuttle-bus between the areas. 6-day prices are online 7 days in advance (window prices are higher). Savings if you purchase in advance through certain UK tour operators and if you purchase in conjunction with lodging

COLORADO

ASPEN / SNOWMASS / DANIEL BAYER

The retail therapy is unmatched, except perhaps by St Moritz in Switzerland ↓

trail map usefully gives key facts for each run – orientation and average and steepest pitch, from a serious 38° to a terrifying 48°.

Left of the bowl, the Steeplechase area consists of a row of natural avalanche chutes, and their elevation means the snow keeps well. The Olympic Bowl area on the opposite flank of the mountain has great views of the Maroon Bells and some serious moguls. The Thunderbowl chair from the base serves a nice varied area that's often underused.

FOR INTERMEDIATES ★★★★★
Grooming to die for
Most intermediate runs on Highlands are concentrated above the mid-mountain Merry-Go-Round restaurant, many served by the Cloud Nine fast quad chair. But there are other good slopes – don't miss the vast, neglected expanses of Golden Horn.

Aspen Mountain has its fair share of intermediate slopes, but they tend to be on the tough side. Copper Bowl and Spar Gulch, running between the ridges, are great cruises but can get crowded. Upper Aspen Mountain, at the top of the gondola, has a dense network of well-groomed blues served by the Ajax fast chair. Ruthie's chair – a fast double, apparently installed to rekindle the romance that quads have destroyed – serves more cruising runs.

Buttermilk offers good, easy slopes to practise on, and can be extraordinarily quiet. For good intermediates it offers easy black runs – and it's a great place for early experiments off-piste.

Read the Snowmass chapter too.

FOR BEGINNERS ★★★★★
Can be a great place to learn
Buttermilk is superb. West Buttermilk has beautifully groomed, gentle, often deserted runs, served by a quad. The easiest slopes of all, though, are at the base of the Main Buttermilk sector – on Panda Hill. Despite its macho image, Highlands boasts the highest concentration of green runs in Aspen.

FOR BOARDERS ★★★★
Loads of scope
There is a huge amount of terrain to explore, which will satisfy all levels of boarder – especially when you include Snowmass (see our separate chapter). The hills are free of draglifts and have few flat sections. Buttermilk is the least testing of the mountains – but also has a huge terrain park.

FOR CROSS-COUNTRY ★★★★
Backcountry bonanza
There are 90km of groomed trails between Aspen and Snowmass in the Roaring Fork valley – the most extensive cross-country network in the US. And the Ashcroft Ski Touring Center maintains around 35km of trails around Ashcroft, a mining ghost town. The Pine Creek Cookhouse (925 1044) does excellent food and is accessible only by ski, snowshoe or horse-drawn sleigh. Aspen is at one end of the 370km Tenth Mountain Division Trail.

MOUNTAIN RESTAURANTS ★★★
Good by American standards
Surprisingly, Highlands and Snowmass (see separate chapter) have good table-service places and Aspen Mountain doesn't.

Editors' choice At Highlands, Cloud Nine bistro (544 3063) is the nearest thing in the States to a cosy Alpine hut, with excellent food – thanks to an Austrian chef. Not wildly expensive, either – $40 for the daily changing set menu of two courses. We had delicious elk stew on our last visit.

SCHOOLS

Aspen
t 923 1227

Classes
Full day (5hr) $149
Private lessons
From $660 for full day
for up to 5 people

CHILDCARE

Childcare
t 923 1227
Ages 8wk to 4yr
**Cubs on Skis, Pandas
and Grizzlies**
t 923 1227
Various different
groups for ages
30mnth to 4yr, 3 to 4
and 5 to 6
Babysitting services
Several

Ski school
Ages 7 to 12

GETTING THERE

Air Aspen 6km/
4 miles (15min); Eagle
110km/70 miles
(1hr30); Denver
360km/225 miles
(4hr)

Rail Glenwood Springs
(65km/40 miles)

UK PACKAGES

Alpine Answers,
American Ski Classics,
Carrier, Crystal, Crystal
Finest, Elegant Resorts,
Erna Low, Flexiski,
Frontier, Interactive
Resorts, Momentum,
Oxford Ski Co,
PowderBeds, Scott
Dunn, Ski Bespoke, Ski
Club Freshtracks, Ski
Expectations, Ski
Independence, Ski
Safari, Ski Weekend,
Skitracer, Skiworld,
Snow Finders,
Supertravel, Thomson,
Virgin Snow

Worth knowing about On Aspen Mountain there's the Sundeck self-service – about as good as an American self-service restaurant gets – light and airy with great views across to Highland Bowl. Bonnie's self-service is another option: 'fantastic white chilli bean soup', 'hearty stews and burgers'. On Highlands, the recently refurbished mid-mountain Merry-Go-Round self-service has 'a comfortable bar area', where one recent reporter enjoyed 'one of the best pastas ever'.

On Buttermilk the mountaintop Cliffhouse specializes in a Mongolian barbecue stir-fry, and Bumps (self-service) offers a 'good range'. You can picnic at The Cafe West, Top of West warming hut, Bottom of Tiehack warming hut and No Problem Cabin.

SCHOOLS AND GUIDES ★★★★★
One of the best?
Aspen's school is highly regarded, and group classes are usually small and of a high standard: 'Maximum of three people in our lessons and the same instructor for the three days,' says a reporter. Another praises the free, full-day 'Inside Tracks' tours run twice a week by the ski school for Limelight hotel guests.

FOR FAMILIES ★★☆☆☆
Choice of nurseries
Aspen caters well for families, with Buttermilk the focus for lessons. Children are bussed to and from the mountain's impressive Fort Frog, and the kids' trail map is a great idea. But Snowmass makes a better base.

STAYING THERE

Hotels There are places for all budgets, including very grand places such as the Hyatt and St Regis on which we never get reports. Most smaller hotels provide a good free après-ski cheese and wine buffet.
*****Jerome (429 5028) Step back a century: Victorian authenticity combined with modern-day luxury, including a spa. Several blocks from the gondola.
*****Little Nell (920 4600) Stylish, modern hotel right by the gondola, with popular bar. Fireplaces in every room, outdoor pool, hot tub, sauna. Smart condos, too.
***Aspen (925 3441) Spacious, basic rooms; pool, hot tub; 10 minutes' walk to gondola. Near bus stop.

***Aspen Mountain Lodge (925 7650) Small, friendly, in a quiet location. 'Very friendly, helpful staff.'
***Limelight (925 3025) Modern style, central. Pool, tubs. Approved 'on just about every count': 'great rooms, good breakfasts, pretty good location'. Owned by the lift company – see 'Schools and guides'. Fleet of shuttles.
***Molly Gibson Lodge (925 3434) Pool, hot tub. Opposite hotel Aspen. Recent reports are in conflict; more reports, please.
***The Sky (925 6760) Hip, swanky New York-style hotel in great location by gondola.
**Mountain Chalet (925 7797) Cosy lodge five minutes from gondola. Pool, sauna, steam and fitness centre.
**St Moritz Lodge (925 3220) Aspen's 'youth hostel', with a heated pool and complimentary après wine! Super-friendly staff and 'mature' guests.
Apartments The standards here are high, even in US terms. Many of the smarter developments have their own free shuttle-buses. The Gant, Aspen Square and Aspen Meadows Resort have been recommended. A 2014 reporter was very happy with the 'well-appointed' Durant, close to the gondola with outdoor hot tubs.

EATING OUT ★★★★★
Dining dilemma
Aspen has plenty of seriously good upmarket places – as our most trusted American reporter puts it this year, dining is 'a real highlight of staying in Aspen – there aren't that many cities in the US with better restaurants'. But there are also plenty of cheaper options, some mentioned below. Some giveaway magazines include menu guides, and there are listings at www.eataspen.com.

Top of the range places include: Syzygy, Piñons and Element 47 ('mountain dishes and international fusion') in the Little Nell hotel – all with innovative American cooking; Matsuhisa (Japanese fusion); and the Rustique Bistro, Brexi Brasserie ('lovely food, but a bit dark') and Cache Cache (all French). Steakhouse 316 is a small steakhouse in 1920s style: 'Pricey, but fantastic steaks! Great service.' The tiny Wild Fig has 'a varied, Mediterranean-influenced menu'. The underground Zocalito offers Latin American cuisine: 'absolutely delicious' was one reporter's view. The main dining room at the Jerome hotel is

Resort news and key links: www.wheretoskiandsnowboard.com

↑ The terrace of the swanky Little Nell hotel, at the base of Aspen mountain, is the obvious spot for those first après beers
ASPEN / JEREMY SWANSON

ACTIVITIES

Indoor Recreation Center (pool, ice rink, climbing wall), Club & Spa (spa, fitness), galleries, cinemas, theatre, museum

Outdoor Snowshoeing, ice skating, snowmobiling, dog sledding, ballooning

Phone numbers
From distant parts of the US, add the prefix 1 970; from abroad, add the prefix +1 970

TOURIST OFFICE
www.aspensnowmass.com

'very good, very glamorous', says a 2013 visitor.

You can eat more cheaply at a lot of the smart places by eating at the bar – basically, you get smaller portions and can't book, which of course may suit you. We did this very happily on our last visit at Jimmy's (American), L'Hostaria and Campo de Fiori (both Italian). Some places include food deals in their happy hours, too – typically 4pm to 6pm.

Mid-market and cheaper choices include: 'spiffy bistro' Mezzaluna (the 'fried calamari was as light as Rocky Mountain powder' says a 2014 visitor), Little Annie's ('massive portions', 'a meat feast'), Asie (Asian fusion – 'astonishingly good' dumplings); Brunelleschi's ('good Italian food', 'excellent service', 'very family friendly'); Cantina ('friendly service and good Tex-Mex'); Su Casa (Mexican – 'central; good value'); Ute City (American-style bistro – 'varied menu, great value'). We're delighted to hear that two unpretentious, lively Aspen institutions live on – the refurbished Red Onion (established 1892, they say) for 'large portions of steak, burgers and salads' and Hickory House, specializing in 'excellent ribs'.

APRES-SKI ★★★★
Lots of options
In the late afternoon, we've known Cloud Nine on Highlands to turn into an Austrian-style après-ski venue – booze-fuelled dancing on the tables in ski boots. We hear that the local police have taken an interest in this very un-American activity, so take care. A few bars at the bases get busy –

notably Out of Bounds at Highlands and Ajax Tavern ('very lively upmarket crowd') in Aspen. The Terrace Bar at the Little Nell is a great place for gazing at facelifts. For a sharp contrast, join the local snow bums at Zane's for its 'great atmosphere' and 'happy hour chicken wings'.

Later on, wine connoisseurs could try Victoria's Espresso & Wine Bar. Many of the restaurants are also bars. The J-bar of the historic Jerome hotel has a great traditional feel. Aspen Billiards adjoining the fashionable Cigar Bar is an upscale venue for playing pool. There is a microbrewery, The Aspen Brewing Company.

For music and dancing, head for Belly Up ('good selection of live music') or the Regal Watering Hole. Or you can get a week's membership of the famous Caribou club.

OFF THE SLOPES ★★★★
Silver service
Aspen has lots to offer, especially if your credit card is in good shape. There are literally dozens of art galleries, with an impressive new building at the Aspen Art Museum opening in summer 2014. As well as the predictable clothes and jewellery shops, here are plenty of shops selling affordable stuff. And 'one of the best bookshops I have ever seen', says a 2013 visitor. Glenwood Springs is worth a visit for its hot-spring outdoor pool. The Aspen Recreation Center at Highlands has a huge swimming complex and an indoor ice rink. Hot-air ballooning is possible. Some mountain restaurants are accessible to pedestrians.

JACK AFFLECK

Beaver Creek

Exclusive and very pricey modern resort with quiet, varied slopes.
Good for an indulgent stay and a required day trip from Vail

TOP 10 RATINGS	
Extent	★★★
Fast lifts	★★★★★
Queues	★★★★★
Snow	★★★★★
Expert	★★★★
Intermediate	★★★★
Beginner	★★★★★
Charm	★★
Convenience	★★★★
Scenery	★★★

RPI	180
lift pass	£340
ski hire	£170
lessons	£240
food & drink	£185
total	**£935**

NEWS

2014/15: The focal Centennial chairlift is being replaced by a hybrid chondola with greatly increased capacity. Along with Vail, Beaver Creek will host the FIS (International Ski Federation) Alpine World Ski Championships in February 2015.

2013/14: The Talons restaurant opened on the lower slopes, housed in the relocated Red Tail Camp building. A new village escalator opened near the ice rink.

➕ Slopes generally quiet on weekdays

➕ Mountain has it all, from superb novice runs to daunting moguls

➕ Fast chairlifts all over the place

➕ Compact, traffic-free village centre

➖ Lacks any Wild West atmosphere

➖ Very expensive

➖ Table-service mountain restaurants are members-only

➖ Not much going on at night

'Not exactly roughing it' is the ironic slogan of Vail's kid sister resort, coyly underlining its status as about the smoothest resort in the US. We don't find the exclusive resort village particularly appealing, but the mountain certainly is. If the budget is tight, consider staying down in the valley, in Avon.

THE RESORT

Beaver Creek, 16km to the west of Vail and developed in the 1980s, is unashamedly exclusive. The lift system spreads across the mountains to Bachelor Gulch, a small collection of relatively new condos and houses and a Ritz Carlton hotel, and then to Arrowhead, another slope-side hamlet. Below Bachelor Gulch is the valley town of Avon, where you can stay much more cheaply than in Beaver Creek or Vail. There are free car parks in Avon for day visitors (parking in the resort itself is expensive and limited); you can take a free shuttle to the resort, or a fast chair up to Bachelor Gulch. A gondola links the Riverfront area of Avon to this chair.

Day trips to Vail, Breckenridge and Keystone (all covered by the lift pass) and Copper Mountain are possible.

Village charm The village centres on a small, smart, modern pedestrian area with upmarket shops, open-air ice rink and heated pavements.

Convenience There are top-quality hotels and condos right by the slopes, and escalators up from the centre.

Scenery The scenery is pleasantly woody rather than dramatic.

THE MOUNTAINS

All the slopes are below the treeline, though there are some more open areas. Free two-hour mountain tours for intermediates/experts run daily at 10am. At the top of most main lifts is a big piste map board (and lights showing which runs have been groomed – a great idea). They take 'slow skiing zones' seriously here too – with big banners across the piste warning that skier speed is monitored.

Slopes The slopes immediately above Beaver Creek divide into two sectors, each accessed by a fast quad chair – one centred on Spruce Saddle, the other on Bachelor Gulch (which links to Arrowhead). Between these are Grouse Mountain and Larkspur Bowl, again with fast quads. Off to the left is another sector, with a fast quad.

553

VAIL RESORTS, INC

There's a good range of trails cut through dense forest, including some genuine double-black diamonds ➔

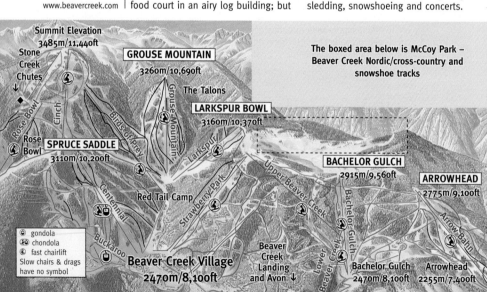

KEY FACTS

Resort	2470m
	8,100ft
Slopes	2255-3485m
	7,400-11,440ft
Lifts	25
Pistes	1,832 acres
Green	19%
Blue	43%
Black	38%
Snowmaking	37%

UK PACKAGES

Alpine Answers, American Ski Classics, Elegant Resorts, Frontier, Momentum, Oxford Ski Co, PowderBeds, Ski Bespoke, Ski Independence, Ski Safari, Skitracer, Skiworld, STC, Supertravel

Central reservations phone number
496 4900

Phone numbers
From distant parts of the US, add the prefix 1 970; from abroad, add the prefix +1 970

TOURIST OFFICE

www.beavercreek.com

Fast lifts Nearly all key lifts are fast chairs; beginners have a gondola.
Queues Not normally a problem.
Terrain parks Park 101 is a small beginners' park, Zoom Room has intermediate-level features, and Rodeo has big hits for advanced riders. There's a 110m-long half-pipe, off Barrel Stave. Parkology is a park and pipe programme for kids.
Snow reliability An impressive snow record (average 325 inches) and snowmaking mean you can relax. But Grouse Mountain can have thin cover (some call it Gravel Mountain).
Experts There is plenty of satisfying steep terrain. In the Birds of Prey and Grouse Mountain areas most runs are long, steep and mogulled, but the downhill race course pistes are groomed periodically, making great fast cruises. Grouse and Stone Creek Chutes have great steep glades.
Intermediates There are marvellous long, quiet, cruising blues everywhere you look, including top-to-bottom runs with a vertical of 1000m.
Beginners There are excellent nursery slopes at resort level – served by a short gondola – and a further large area at altitude. And there are plenty of easy long runs to progress to.
Snowboarding Good riders will love the excellent gladed runs and perfect carving slopes.
Cross-country There's a splendid, mountaintop network of tracks up at McCoy Park (over 32km).
Mountain restaurants Spruce Saddle at mid-mountain is the main place – a food court in an airy log building; but

it can get very busy. Lower down, Talons opened last season and has an appetizing menu. But for table-service you have to head down to the base.
Schools and guides We lack reports, but the school is doubtless excellent.
Families Small World Play School looks after non-skiing kids from two months to five years from 8.30 to 4pm. At the top of the Buckaroo gondola are adventure trails and a tubing hill.

STAYING THERE

Lodgings are pricey and luxurious.
Hotels Lots of upmarket places, such as the Ritz Carlton and Park Hyatt. The Osprey, Charter and Pines Lodge combine hotel facilities with luxury condo convenience.
Apartments Slope-side condos include Elkhorn Lodge, Oxford Court, St James Place, Bear Paw and SaddleRidge.
Eating out SaddleRidge is plush and packed with photos and Wild West artefacts. Toscanini, the Golden Eagle Inn, Dusty Boot (in St James Place), and Beaver Creek Chophouse have been recommended. You can take a sleigh ride to dine at swanky Beano's or Zach's cabins on the slopes. Or try the numerous restaurants in Avon (buses run to and from there until 10pm): the Blue Plate was recommended by a 2013 reporter ('good duck and schnitzel').
Après-ski Try the Coyote Cafe and McCoy's (live bands) and the 8100 Mountainside Bar at Park Hyatt.
Off the slopes Smart shops and galleries, an ice rink, ballooning, dog sledding, snowshoeing and concerts.

VAIL RESORTS INC / BOB WINSETT

Breckenridge

A sprawling resort with a cute 'Wild West' core, beneath a wide,
varied mountain; increasing amounts of slope-side accommodation

RATINGS

The mountains

Extent	★★★
Fast lifts	★★★★
Queues	★★★★
Terrain p'ks	★★★★★
Snow	★★★★★
Expert	★★★★
Intermediate	★★★★
Beginner	★★★★★
Boarder	★★★★★
X-country	★★★★
Restaurants	★★
Schools	★★★★★
Families	★★★★

The resort

Charm	★★★
Convenience	★★★
Scenery	★★★
Eating out	★★★★★
Après-ski	★★★
Off-slope	★★★

RPI 160

lift pass	£320
ski hire	£145
lessons	£215
food & drink	£150
total	**£830**

NEWS

2014/15: The Colorado quad chair on Peak 8 will be replaced by a six-pack, increasing capacity by 30%. The restaurant at Peak 9 is being revamped.

2013/14: The new Peak 6 area opened on Christmas Day 2013, adding 400 acres of lift-served and 143 acres of hike-to terrain (an increase of over 25%) served by a new six-pack.

- Slopes have something for all abilities – good for mixed groups
- Cute Victorian Main Street, with mainly sympathetic new buildings
- Plenty of lively bars and restaurants
- Shared lift pass with four other worthwhile resorts nearby
- Efficient lifts mean few queues
- Some slope-side accommodation
- Short transfer from Denver, but ...

- At 2925m the village poses a risk of altitude sickness if you go there directly from the UK
- Very prone to high winds, affecting mainly the high, advanced slopes
- Groomed trails not very extensive, with few long runs
- Lack of good central hotels
- Main Street is a thoroughfare, and always busy with traffic

Breckenridge has a lot going for it, but it has non-trivial flaws. Main Street is attractive, with a Wild West flavour, and lots of lively places to eat and drink. But the resort's dormitory areas are a lot less appealing. The slopes have something for everyone, provided the ungroomed top slopes are open – sadly, they often are not. There are now five peaks to ski, but they add up to less than you might expect. Those keen on piste mileage and variety should plan to visit other resorts (covered by the lift pass) by car or bus too; they'll find Breck limited for a week's stay.

Heed our warning about altitude sickness. At almost 3000m, this is the highest resort to get a full chapter in this book – and the altitude you sleep at is a key factor. Like many readers, Editor Gill has been affected by altitude sickness here, and now always spends time in a lower resort before hitting Breckenridge; a couple of nights in Denver is an alternative way to cut the risk.

THE RESORT

Breckenridge was founded in 1859 and became a booming gold-mining town. Old clapboard buildings line much of Main Street, and the streets nearby have been well renovated. Small shopping malls and other buildings have been added in similar style. But there are some (rather out-of-place) modern buildings too, especially around the base of Peak 9.

The resort is in the same ownership as Vail, Beaver Creek and Keystone. A multi-day lift ticket covers all these plus Arapahoe Basin. All of them plus Copper Mountain can be reached by bus (free to Keystone and Arapahoe Basin; paid-for the others).

VILLAGE CHARM ★★★
A festive treat
The town centre is lively in the evening – particularly at weekends – with lots of people strolling around the shops on their way to or from the 100-plus restaurants and bars in and around the busy main street.

Christmas lights and decorations remain throughout the season, giving the town a festive air. This is enhanced by festivals such as Ullr Fest – honouring the Norse God of Winter – and snow sculpture championships.

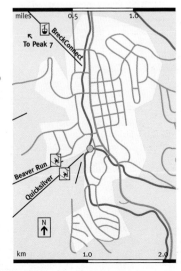

SKIWORLD

Catered chalets, hotels and self catering apartments in

Europe, USA and Canada

skiworld.co.uk
08444 930 430

ABTA V2151 ATOL 2036

KEY FACTS

Resort	2925m
	9,600ft
Slopes	2925-3915m
	9,600-12,840ft
Lifts	34
Pistes	3,308 acres
Green	14%
Blue	31%
Black	55%
Snowmaking	20%

CONVENIENCE ★★★
Slope life or nightlife
There are a lot of slope-side lodgings, including smart recent developments at the bases of Peaks 7 and 8. But there is also some inconveniently distant from both Main Street and the lift base stations. Hotels and condos are spread over a wide area and linked by regular, free shuttle-buses (less frequent in the evening – worth staying centrally if you plan to spend much time in Main Street).

SCENERY ★★★
Peak after peak
This is high country; on a clear day above the treeline there are extensive views of Colorado's highest summits – many of which reach over 4000m.

THE MOUNTAINS

The slopes are mainly cut through the forest, but there is quite a lot of steeper skiing above the treeline, and this is prone to closure by high winds.

The resort used to have some runs classified as blue-black, particularly on Peak 10. These are now straight black runs – a real backward step.

EXTENT OF THE SLOPES ★★★
Growing but fragmented
There are now five sectors, linked by lift and piste. Two fast chairlifts go from one end of the town up to **Peak 9**, one accessing mainly green runs on the lower half of the hill, the other mainly blue runs higher up. From there

you can get to **Peak 10**, with black runs (including former blue-blacks) served by one fast quad.

The **Peak 8** area – tough stuff at the top, easier lower down – can be reached by a fast quad from Peak 9. The base lifts of Peak 8 can also be reached by the slow Snowflake lift from the suburbs, or by gondola from a car park on the fringes of town. The six-pack serving **Peak 7** can be accessed from Peak 8 and from the gondola's mid-station. **Peak 6** opened for 2013/14, with 543 acres of new terrain accessible from the Peak 7 area by two new lifts.

The higher open slopes on Peaks 7 and 8 are accessed by a T-bar – a rarity in these parts – reachable from either base, and by the Imperial fast quad at the top of the Peak 8 lift network. The resort claims a top height of 3960m, but that involves a hike of 45m vertical at the very top.

FAST LIFTS ★★★★
Good coverage
Breckenridge's gondola and many fast chairlifts cover all five sectors and provide good access from either end of town – the slow Snowflake chair to Peak 8 in between is an obvious exception, which will be an irritant if you are based nearby.

QUEUES ★★★★
Peak times possibly
A 2013 reporter encountered 20-minute queues on President's weekend but no queues midweek. Outside peak

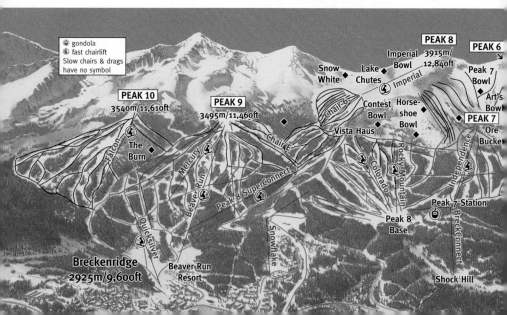

↑ You might guess from this shot that the trails below the treeline are a wee bit samey, with Peak 10 on the left a bit steeper than the rest

BRECKENRIDGE SKI RESORT / JEFF ANDREW

LIFT PASSES

Prices in US$

Age	1-day	6-day
under 13	64	330
13 to 64	105	522
65 plus	95	462

Free Under 5

Beginner Included in price of lessons

Notes 3-day-plus pass covers Breckenridge, Keystone and Arapahoe Basin, plus 3 days (of a 6-day pass) at Vail and Beaver Creek; prices are online rates for early February purchased 14 days in advance of trip; window rates in resort are considerably higher; international visitors will get best prices by pre-booking through a UK tour operator (it is not necessary to buy a complete holiday package to obtain these prices)

periods, reporters confirm there are few problems. There may be queues for the old Chair 6 on a powder day and the slow Snowflake chair that gives access to Peak 8 for thousands of condo-dwellers.

TERRAIN PARKS ★★★★★
Five to choose from
The main focus is Peak 8, with three parks for different ability levels. Freeway is one of the best parks in North America and the largest of Breck's park, featuring a series of big jumps, obstacles and a super-pipe. Next to it, Park Lane offers a variety of challenging features. And Trygves has gentle jumps and rollers for beginner freestylers. On Peak 9 are two more parks: Bonanza is a beginner progression park, and Gold King bridges the gap between Bonanza and Park Lane.

SNOW RELIABILITY ★★★★★
Normally ample quantities
With its high altitude, Breckenridge boasts a good natural snow record – annual average 300 inches. That is supplemented by substantial snowmaking (used mainly early in the season to form a good base). There are a lot of east- and north-east-facing slopes, which hold snow well. But high winds can remove or spoil the snow, notably on exposed upper runs.

FOR EXPERTS ★★★★
Lots of short but tough runs
A remarkable 55% of the runs are classified black – that's a higher proportion than famous 'macho'

resorts such as Jackson Hole, Taos and Snowbird. And a good proportion are classified as 'expert' (double diamond) or 'extreme' terrain. But most runs are short – most of the key lifts offer verticals of around 300m.

Peak 8 is at the core of the tough skiing. The lightly wooded slopes served by Chair 6 are a good place to start – picturesque and not too steep. Below, steeper runs lead further down to the junction with Peak 9. Above, the Imperial quad accesses huge amounts of above-the-treeline terrain and longer runs.

You can hike up to the double-diamond Imperial Bowl, and the 'extreme' Lake Chutes and Snow White areas. Or you can traverse round the back towards Peak 7 and double-diamond runs in the bowl (we had a great time in fresh snow there on our last visit); the T-bar on Peak 8 accesses the lower parts of these runs (single diamonds) and the double-diamond Horseshoe and Contest bowls. On the lower part of Peak 8 is a worthwhile area of single diamonds.

Peak 9's wooded North Slope under Chair E is excellent – shady, sheltered and steep – we've had great runs down Devil's Crotch, Hades and Inferno. Peak 10 has easy black runs (former blue-blacks) down the central ridge, but more challenging stuff on both flanks. To skier's left is a lovely, lightly wooded area called The Burn.

The new Peak 6 area has opened up three new bowls and ten new cut trails. It includes the resort's first above-treeline intermediate terrain as well as an area of hike-to terrain.

ACTIVITIES

Indoor Recreation centre on outskirts (accessible by bus): pool, gym, tennis, climbing wall; spas, ice rink, theatre, cinema, museums, galleries

Outdoor Horse-drawn sleigh rides, dog sledding, snowmobiles, ice rink, snowshoeing, tobogganing, zipline

GETTING THERE

Air Denver 165km/ 105 miles (2hr15)

BRECKENRIDGE SKI RESORT / JEFF ANDREW

The Victorian style is kept up pretty consistently around Main Street, but not elsewhere ↓

FOR INTERMEDIATES ★★★★
Nice cruising, limited extent

Breckenridge has some good blue cruising runs for all intermediates. But dedicated piste-bashers are likely to find the runs short and limited in variety. Peak 9 has the easiest slopes. It is nearly all gentle, wide, blue runs at the top and almost flat, wide, green runs at the bottom.

Peak 10 has a number of easy, normally groomed, black runs that used to be classified blue-black, such as Crystal and Centennial, which make for good fast cruising. Peaks 7 and 8 both have blues on trails cut close together in the trees, which feel very similar and offer little variety. Adventurous intermediates can also try some of the high bowl runs and more gentle gladed runs such as Ore Bucket glades on the fringe of Peak 7 and the runs beneath Chair 6 on Peak 8.

FOR BEGINNERS ★★★★★
Excellent

The bottom of Peak 9 has a big, virtually flat area and some good, gentle nursery slopes. There's then a good choice of green runs to move on to. Beginners can try Peak 8 too, with another selection of green runs and a choice of trails back to town. There is a special beginner package available (see 'Schools and guides').

FOR BOARDERS ★★★★★
One of the best

Breckenridge is pretty much ideal for all standards of boarder and hosts several major US snowboarding events. Beginners have ideal nursery slopes and greens to progress to. Intermediates have good cruising runs, all served by chairs. The powder bowls at the top of Peaks 7 and 8 make great riding and can be accessed via the Imperial quad, so avoiding the awkward T-bar. Boarders of all levels will enjoy the choice of excellent terrain parks.

FOR CROSS-COUNTRY ★★★★
Specialist centre in woods

The Nordic Center is set in the woods between the town and Peak 8 and served by shuttle-bus. It has 32km of trails and 15km of snowshoeing trails.

MOUNTAIN RESTAURANTS ★★
Improved by more base options

Of the self-service places above base level, Ten Mile Station, where Peak 9 meets 10, is the place we gravitate to. Both it and the dreary Vista Haus on Peak 8 are food-court operations and get nightmarishly busy at weekends. Peak 9 restaurant serves 'reasonable' food, says a reporter. Sevens is a table-service restaurant at the Peak 7 base.

SCHOOLS

Breckenridge
t 496 3272

Classes
Day (4.5hr) from $164
Private lessons
$525 for 3hr for up to 6 people

CHILDCARE

Child Care Centers
t +1 888 576 2754
Age 8wk to 3yr
Summit Sitters
t 513 4445
Mountain Sitters
t 512 261 5053

Ski school
Ages 3 to 14

UK PACKAGES

Alpine Answers, American Ski Classics, Crystal, Crystal Finest, Erna Low, Flexiski, Frontier, Inghams, Interactive Resorts, Momentum, Oxford Ski Co, PowderBeds, Ski Bespoke, Ski Expectations, Ski Independence, Ski Safari, Skitracer, Skiworld, Snow Finders, STC, Supertravel, Thomson, Virgin Snow

Phone numbers
From distant parts of the US, add the prefix 1 970; from abroad, add the prefix +1 970

TOURIST OFFICE

www.breckenridge.com

SCHOOLS AND GUIDES ★★★★★
Usual high US standard
We lack recent reports but past ones have been positive. The beginner package includes lessons, equipment rental and lift pass, and the school's special clinics include telemark.

FOR FAMILIES ★★★★★
Excellent facilities
Past reports on the children's school and nursery have been full of praise. The Mountains of Discovery Program aims to combine teaching and fun on the slopes (for kids aged 3 to 13).

STAYING THERE

Chalets Skiworld has a four-bedroom house built in traditional clapboard style near Main Street with an outdoor hot tub. Skiworld and Crystal both feature privately-run Chalet Chloe, a smart six-bedroom log cabin with hot tub in the woods near Peak 8.
Hotels There's a noticeable lack of good places close to Main Street.
★★★★Barn on the River (453 2975) B&B on Main Street. Hot tub.
★★★★DoubleTree by Hilton (547 5550) A short walk to the slopes and a bearable walk to Main Street.
★★★★Lodge & Spa at Breckenridge (453 9300) Stylish luxury spa resort – being renovated during summer 2014 – set out of town among 32 acres, with great views. Private shuttle-bus.
★★★Beaver Run (453 6000) Huge, slope-side resort complex with 515 spacious rooms. Pools, hot tubs.
Apartments There is a huge choice. Mountain Thunder Lodge (near the gondola and the supermarket), Hyatt Main Street Station (near the Quicksilver lift) and One Ski Hill Place at Peak 8 are recommended at the luxury end. A regular visitor tips The Village at Breckenridge and River Mountain Lodge (for quality, value and location), also Trails End, Corral, One Breckenridge Place and Saddlewood Townhomes.

EATING OUT ★★★★★
Over 100 restaurants
There's a wide range, from typical US food to fine dining. At peak times they get busy, and many don't take bookings. The Breckenridge Dining Guide (available online) lists the full menu of most places.
Recent visitors confirmed the attractions of the Hearthstone (modern

---

American cuisine in a beautiful 100-year-old house): 'Excellent food, decor and atmosphere good.' For no-nonsense grills-and-fries in a pub ambience, we've enjoyed both the Brewery (famous for mega 'appetizers', such as buffalo wings, and splendid beers) and the Kenosha steakhouse. Reader tips: Whale's Tail (mainly, but not only, seafood), Mi Casa (Mexican), SouthRidge (predominantly fish), Downstairs at Eric's (burgers and pizzas), Michael's (Italian), Steak & Rib ('bit of an institution; stacks of photos and memorabilia') and Spencer's, at Beaver Run resort (steaks and seafood). The Blue Moose does killer breakfasts.

APRES-SKI ★★★
The best in the area ...
There's not much teatime animation at the lift bases. The Maggie, at the base of Peak 9, 'has music on the terrace but doesn't stay open much beyond 5pm'. Park Avenue Pub, just off Main Street, and the Brewery were lively on our recent visits. Later on we've enjoyed the Gold Pan saloon (reputedly the oldest bar west of the Mississippi); reader tips include the Liquid Lounge and Fatty's. Cecilia's serves good cocktails; Burke and Riley's is an Irish bar; Downstairs at Eric's is a disco sports bar, and Three20South has live bands.

OFF THE SLOPES ★★★
Pleasant enough
Breckenridge is a pleasant place to wander around, with souvenir and gift shops plus a museum. Silverthorne (about 30 minutes away by free bus) has bargain factory outlet stores.

NEARBY TOWN – 2765m

FRISCO

Staying in Frisco makes sense for those touring or on a tight budget. It's a pleasant small town with bars, restaurants and good-value lodgings and linked to resorts by a free bus. A 2013 reporter liked the Baymont Inn & Suites Lake Dillon (668 5094) – pool, hot tub, good breakfasts. Hotel Frisco (668 5009) is on Main Street. Restaurants include Tuscato (Italian), Blue Spruce Inn ('fantastic steaks and ambience'), the Boatyard (pizzas), Food Hedz World Cafe ('good duck and steak') and Ollie's ('Wednesday $2 burger night is great value').

Build your own shortlist: www.wheretoskiandsnowboard.com

ASPEN/SNOWMASS PICTURE LIBRARY

Snowmass

Aspen's modern satellite – with impressively varied and extensive slopes, and a smart new fledgling Base Village

TOP 10 RATINGS

Extent	★★★
Fast lifts	★★★★★
Queues	★★★★
Snow	★★★★★
Expert	★★★★★
Intermediate	★★★★★
Beginner	★★★★★
Charm	★★
Convenience	★★★★★
Scenery	★★★★

Our extent rating is for Snowmass alone. Including the other Aspen mountains would make it ★★★★

RPI	175
lift pass	£360
ski hire	£195
lessons	£200
food & drink	£150
total	£905

560

NEWS

2013/14: The new restaurant at the top of the Elk Camp gondola started to run 'Ullr Nights' each Friday, with sledding, bonfires, snow biking and ice skating.

+ Varied mountain, with the biggest vertical in the US – 1340m

+ Aspen accessible by free bus. Aspen airport only a few minutes away

+ Uncrowded slopes

+ Lots of slope-side lodgings

− Limited dining, shopping and nightlife options

− Diversions of Aspen town are a bus ride away

The slopes of Snowmass are a key part of the attraction of nearby Aspen as a destination. The skiing here is great for all standards. As a base, Snowmass has obvious appeal for families wanting easy cruising on their doorstep; but the resort is still a long way from being an entertaining place to stay.

THE RESORT

Snowmass is a modern, purpose-built resort, with low-rise buildings set next to the gentle home slope. Within these buildings is Snowmass Village Mall. Further down the hill is the recent Base Village development, which has been slowed by the current recession.
Village charm Base Village has added a bit of style to what is a rather plain modern resort.
Convenience Much of the lodging is ski-in/ski-out, and Snowmass Village Mall has a small cluster of shops and restaurants. Efficient free bus services (crowded at times) link Snowmass with Aspen's mountains and town – the one to Aspen runs to 2am.
Scenery The views from the high-points are long but not dramatic.

THE MOUNTAIN

Most of the slopes are in the forest; higher ones are only lightly wooded.
Slopes Snowmass is big by US standards – almost 8km across, with the biggest vertical in the US. Chairlifts and a gondola diverge from the base to go up to two high-points at either end of the ski area – Elk Camp and Sam's Knob. Links higher up go to the two sectors in the middle, High Alpine and Big Burn, where a draglift goes to the high-point on The Cirque. The Two Creeks base is nearer Aspen.
Fast lifts Most key lifts are fast. But there are still a couple of long, slow chairs that can be cold in midwinter.
Queues The home slope gets busy. The locals come out early on big powder days.

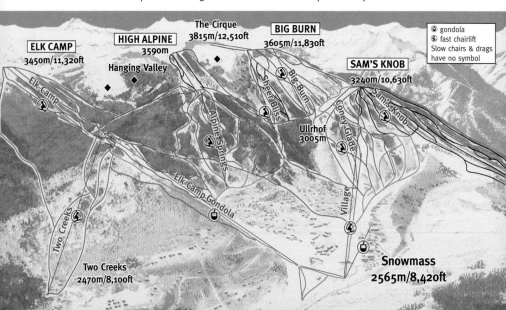

SNOWMASS
VILLAGE

ASPEN / SNOWMASS / JEREMY SWANSON

↑ Base Village and the Village Mall are linked by a short gondola

KEY FACTS

Resort	2565m
	8,420ft

Snowmass only	
Slopes	2470-3815m
	8,100-12,510ft
Lifts	21
Pistes	3,332 acres
Green	6%
Blue	47%
Black	47%
Snowmaking	7%

See Aspen chapter for statistics on other mountains

UK PACKAGES

Alpine Answers, American Ski Classics, Ski Independence, Ski Safari, Supertravel

Phone numbers
From distant parts of the US, add the prefix 1 970; from abroad, add the prefix +1 970

TOURIST OFFICE

www.aspen
snowmass.com

Terrain parks Snowmass has a super-pipe and three parks: Lowdown (beginner) with half-pipe, Little Makaha (intermediate) and Snowmass (expert), with about 90 features including jibs, rails, boxes and jumps.

Snow reliability With 300 inches a year plus snowmaking, it's good.

Experts There's great terrain, although the steep runs tend to be short. Consider joining a guided group as an introduction. Our favourite area is around the Hanging Valley Wall and Glades – beautiful scenery and steep wooded slopes. The other seriously steep area is The Cirque, reached by draglift from Big Burn to the area's highest point. From here, the Headwall is not terrifyingly steep, but there are also narrow, often rocky, chutes – Gowdy's is one of the steepest. Try the new gladed black runs mentioned under 'Intermediates' too.

Intermediates Excellent – this is the best mountain in the Aspen area for intermediates (and by far the biggest). Highlights include: the top slopes on Big Burn – a huge, varied, lightly wooded area, including the Powerline Glades for the adventurous; long, top-to-bottom cruises from Elk Camp and High Alpine; regularly groomed single-black runs from Sam's Knob. Then there are glorious runs set in the forest starting a short hike from the top of Elk Camp: these are around 5km long, end at Two Creeks and include a long-time favourite, the blue Long Shot, and three gladed black runs that were new for last season and classified black only because of a narrow and quite steep traverse out.

Beginners In the heart of the resort is a broad, gentle beginners' run. An even easier slope (and less busy) is Assay Hill, at the bottom of Elk Camp. There's also a beginner area served by three lifts at the top of the Elk Camp gondola. From Sam's Knob there are long, gentle cruises back to the resort.

Snowboarding A great mountain, whatever your boarding style.

Cross-country Excellent trails between here and Aspen – see Aspen chapter.

Mountain restaurants There are three table-service places: long-established Gwyn's High Alpine ('our favourite' says a 2014 visitor – 'good views, good choice, reasonable prices'), Lynn Britt Cabin (cosy old log cabin, elegant table settings) and the newish Sam's Smokehouse (big windows, great views, decent food). Self-service options include the new Elk Camp restaurant and Up 4 Pizza. You can picnic at Wapiti Wildlife Center at Elk Camp and in the warming huts at Sam's Knob, Big Burn and High Alpine.

Schools and guides Reports have been mixed, but predominantly positive.

Families Snowmass is a family-friendly resort. The Treehouse adventure centre at Base Village is a very impressive facility and there are special trails and trail maps for children.

STAYING THERE

Most accommodation is self-catering.
Hotels Several options on or close to the home slope. The focal hotel is the plush Westin (formerly the Silvertree) (923 8200). A 2014 visitor raves about the Stonebridge Inn (923 2420): 'Very convenient and comfortable, great bar with open fire, excellent restaurant.'
Apartments Capitol Peak and Hayden Lodge are luxury condos at Base Village. Tamarack Townhouses and Crestwood Condos are popular. A recent visitor thought Snowmass Villas had a 'great location' with 'convenient bus stop', but were 'a bit run down'.
Eating out Eight K restaurant in the Viceroy hotel is highly recommended, especially the chef's tables where the atmosphere is 'more laid back'. Venga Venga does Mexican with an 'upscale modern feel (heavenly deep-fried Churros)', says a 2014 visitor. Il Poggio is tipped for Italian and Base Camp Bar & Grill is good value.
Après-ski Try Base Camp (live music) or Venga Venga Cantina & Tequila Bar ('excellent cocktails').
Off the slopes Snowshoe trails, snowcat rides, dog sledding plus swimming at the Recreation Center.

Snowmass

561

Build your own shortlist: www.wheretoskiandsnowboard.com

Vail

A vast, swanky resort with some very swanky hotels at the foot of one of the biggest (but also busiest) ski areas in the States

SNOWPIX.COM / CHRIS GILL

RATINGS

The mountains

Extent	★★★★
Fast lifts	★★★★★
Queues	★★
Terrain p'ks	★★★★★
Snow	★★★★★
Expert	★★★★
Intermediate	★★★★★
Beginner	★★★
Boarder	★★★
X-country	★★★
Restaurants	★★
Schools	★★★★
Families	★★★★

The resort

Charm	★★★
Convenience	★★★
Scenery	★★★
Eating out	★★★★★
Après-ski	★★★
Off-slope	★★★

RPI   175

lift pass	£340
ski hire	£165
lessons	£240
food & drink	£170
total	**£915**

KEY FACTS

Resort	2500m
	8,200ft
Slopes	2475-3525m
	8,120-11,570ft
Lifts	31
Pistes	5,289 acres
Green	18%
Blue	29%
Black	53%
Snowmaking	9%

➕ One of the biggest areas in the US – especially great for confident intermediates

➕ The Back Bowls are big areas of treeless terrain – unusual in the US

➕ Fabulous area of ungroomed, wooded slopes at Blue Sky Basin

➕ Largely traffic-free resort centres, very pleasant in parts – but ...

➖ Resort is a vast sprawl

➖ Slopes can be crowded by American standards, with serious lift queues

➖ Inadequate mountain restaurants

➖ Blue Sky Basin and the Back Bowls may not be open in early season; warm weather can close the Bowls

➖ Expensive, with lots of luxury lodgings but few budget options

We always enjoy skiing Vail; it's a big mountain with a decent vertical, and Blue Sky Basin's 'adventure' skiing is a key attraction. But it is far from being our favourite American mountain. In an American resort you expect the runs to be pretty much crowd-free – and in any resort you expect 20-minute lift queues to be a thing of the past. In these respects, Vail disappoints.

When the budget runs to a swanky billet in Vail Village or the new Lionshead area, we're happy enough with the resort, too; it is a pleasant place to wander around. But we're not enthusiastic about Vail Village's pseudo-Tirolean style, and the rest of the huge resort lacks character. In the end, Vail can't compete with more distinctively American resorts based on old mining towns.

THE RESORT

Vail is an enormous resort, stretching almost four miles along the I-70 freeway running west from Denver. Beaver Creek, 16km away, is covered by the lift pass and is easily reached by bus. Breckenridge and Keystone – both owned by Vail Resorts and covered by the lift pass – and Copper Mountain are other possible excursions.

VILLAGE CHARM ★★★☆☆
No real identity
Standing in the centre of Vail Village, surrounded by chalets and bierkellers, you could be forgiven for thinking you were in the Tirol – which is what Vail's founder, Pete Seibert, intended back in the 1950s. 'Beautifully lit in parts at night,' said a 2014 reporter. But this is now just one part of a huge resort, and the rest is mostly in anonymous (although smart) modern style.

CONVENIENCE ★★★☆☆
There's always the bus
The vast village has a free and efficient bus service ('always on time'), – frequent from Lionshead to Golden Peak, less frequent to the outskirts. But the most convenient (and expensive) places to stay are in the mock-Tirolean Vail Village or at Lionshead – an area that has smart lodgings to match Vail Village; both areas have gondolas out. There is a lot of accommodation further out – some on the far side of the I-70.

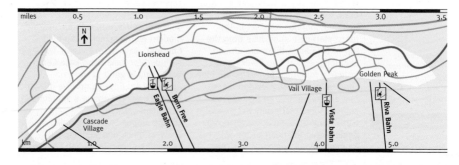

Build your own shortlist: www.wheretoskiandsnowboard.com

↑ Eagle's Nest has lots of amenities, including one of Vail's two table-service mountain restaurants, Bistro Fourteen

VAIL RESORTS, INC / DANN COFFEY

NEWS

2014/15: Along with Beaver Creek, Vail will host the FIS (International Ski Federation) Alpine World Ski Championships in February 2015. The 'historic' Lodge at Vail is to be renovated.

2013/14: A new six-pack replaced the Mountaintop quad at Mid-Vail, increasing capacity by 33%. A double chair on the nursery slopes at Golden Peak was replaced by a triple.

SCENERY ★★★☆☆
Rolling Colorado
Like most Colorado resorts, Vail is set among rather softly contoured mountains with forest reaching to the top of the slopes. From the top you can see for miles.

THE MOUNTAINS
You get a real sense of travelling around Vail's mountains – something missing in many smaller American resorts. Run classification exaggerates the difficulty of some slopes – some of the blacks, in particular. Several runs are partly classified blue, partly black, which means fewer surprises if you study the map. Compared with most American resorts the runs are usually crowded – though nothing like as bad as in Europe. There are free mountain tours at 10.30am, with separate tours of Blue Sky Basin at 11am from Monday to Thursday and full-day tours for skiers aged 50+ each Monday from 9.15am. The slopes have yellow-jacketed patrollers to stop people speeding, but they don't seem to have much effect.

EXTENT OF THE SLOPES ★★★★☆
Something for everyone
Vail's 5,289 acres of lift-linked slopes make it one of the biggest ski areas in the US. The slopes can be accessed via three main lifts. From Vail Village, a gondola goes up to the major mid-mountain focal point, Mid-Vail; from Lionshead, the Eagle Bahn gondola goes up to the Eagle's Nest complex; and from the Golden Peak base area just to the east of Vail Village, the Riva Bahn fast chair goes up towards the Two Elk area.

The front face of the mountain is largely north-facing, with well-groomed trails cut through the trees. At altitude the mountainside divides into three bowls – Mid-Vail in the centre, with Game Creek to the south-west and the area below Two Elk Lodge to the north-east. Lifts reach the ridge at three points, all giving access to the **Back Bowls** (mostly ungroomed and treeless) and through them to **Blue Sky Basin** (mostly ungroomed and wooded, with a 'backcountry' feel).

FAST LIFTS ★★★★★
Plenty of them
There are lots of fast lifts on both sides of the mountain. All three of Blue Sky Basin's lifts are fast chairs.

QUEUES ★★☆☆☆
Can be bad
The front side of Vail has had some of the longest lift lines we've hit in the US, especially at weekends because of the influx from nearby Denver. A 2013 visitor took weekend lessons to jump the queues. And even on a mid-December visit we hit big queues. Mid-Vail is a bottleneck that is difficult to avoid; 20-minute waits are common

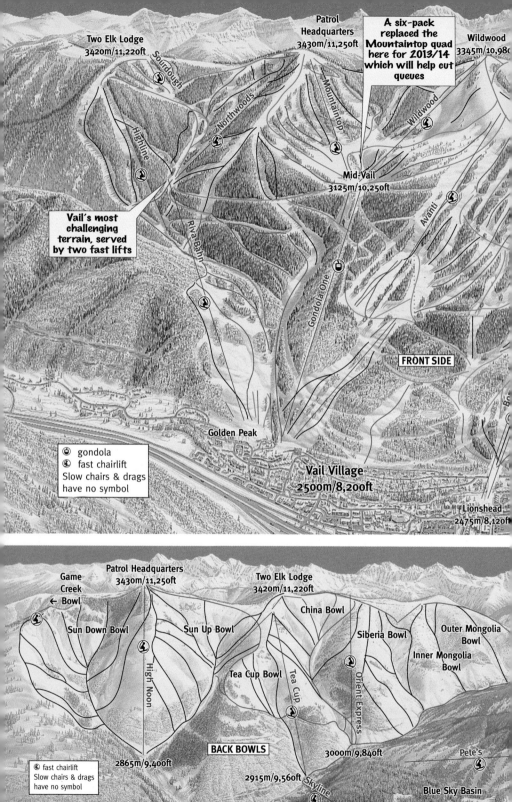

Two Elk Lodge
3420m/11,220ft

Sourdough

Patrol
Headquarters
3430m/11,250ft

Mountaintop

A six-pack
replaced the
Mountaintop quad
here for 2013/14
which will help cut
queues

Wildwood
3345m/10,98(

Wildwood

Northwoods

Highline

Mid-Vail
3125m/10,250ft

Avanti

Vail's most
challenging
terrain, served
by two fast lifts

Riva Bahn

Gondola One

FRONT SIDE

Golden Peak

gondola
fast chairlift
Slow chairs & drags
have no symbol

Vail Village
2500m/8,200ft

Lionshead
2475m/8,120ft

Game
Creek
← Bowl

Patrol Headquarters
3430m/11,250ft

Two Elk Lodge
3420m/11,220ft

China Bowl

Sun Down Bowl

Sun Up Bowl

Siberia Bowl

Outer Mongolia
Bowl

Inner Mongolia
Bowl

High Noon

Tea Cup Bowl

Tea Cup

Orient Express

BACK BOWLS

2865m/9,400ft

2915m/9,560ft

Skyline

3000m/9,840ft

Pete's

fast chairlift
Slow chairs & drags
have no symbol

Blue Sky Basin

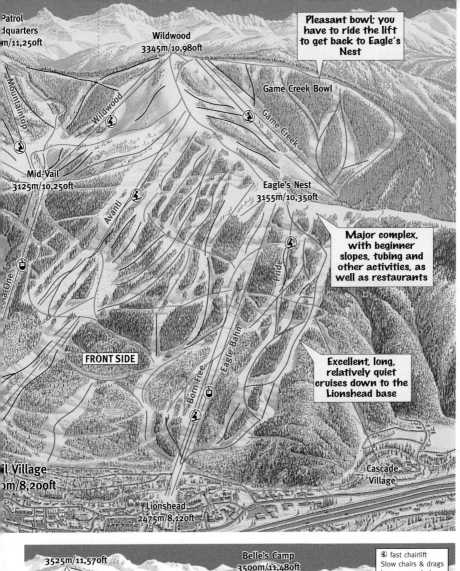

Patrol quarters m/11,25oft

Wildwood 3345m/10,98oft

Pleasant bowl: you have to ride the lift to get back to Eagle's Nest

Game Creek Bowl

Game Creek

Mid-Vail 3125m/10,25oft

Avanti

Eagle's Nest 3155m/10,35oft

Major complex, with beginner slopes, tubing and other activities, as well as restaurants

Pride

FRONT SIDE

Eagle-Bahn

Born Free

Excellent, long, relatively quiet cruises down to the Lionshead base

Village m/8,2ooft

Cascade Village

Lionshead 2475m/8,12oft

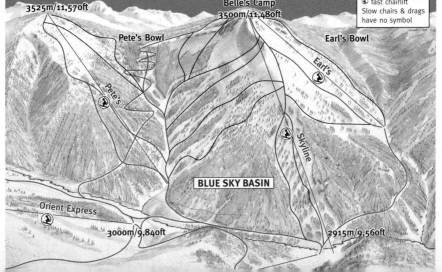

3525m/11,57oft

Belle's Camp 3500m/11,48oft

④ fast chairlift
Slow chairs & drags have no symbol

Pete's Bowl

Earl's Bowl

Earl's

Pete's

Skyline

BLUE SKY BASIN

Orient Express

3000m/9,84oft

2915m/9,56oft

SKIWORLD

Catered chalets, hotels and self catering apartments in

Europe, USA and Canada

skiworld.co.uk

08444 930 430

ABTA V2151 ATOL 2036

www.ski–i.com

ski independence

Call the Tailor-made Ski Specialists

0131 243 8097

LIFT PASSES

Colorado

Prices in US$

Age	1-day	6-day
under 13	79	372
13 to 64	110	564
65 plus	100	504

Free Under 5

Beginner Included in price of lessons

Notes 3+ day passes cover Vail, Beaver Creek, Breckenridge, Keystone and Arapahoe Basin; prices are online rates for early February purchased 14 days in advance of trip; window rates in resort are considerably higher; international visitors will get best prices by pre-booking through a UK tour operator (it is not necessary to buy a complete holiday package to obtain these prices)

UK PACKAGES

Alpine Answers, American Ski Classics, Carrier, Crystal, Crystal Finest, Elegant Resorts, Erna Low, Flexiski, Frontier, Interactive Resorts, Oxford Ski Co, PowderBeds, Scott Dunn, Ski Bespoke, Ski Expectations, Ski Independence, Ski Safari, Ski Weekend, Skitracer, Skiworld, Snow Finders, STC, Supertravel, Thomson, Virgin Snow

(and 45 minutes is not unheard of). The six-pack replacement for the Mountaintop Express may help – reports please. The Northwoods chair and the Eagle Bahn gondola are other hot spots.

TERRAIN PARKS ★★★★★
Three to choose between

There are three parks. Beginner and intermediate freestylers will want to explore the Bwana and Pride parks, located under the Eagle Bahn gondola on Bwana run. Here, a selection of small to medium-sized jumps and boxes gradually become more challenging as you progress through each park.

More advanced riders will be best served at the Golden Peak Terrain Park. Located halfway down the Riva Bahn chairlift, the park is home to various high-profile events and is often in the top ten in terrain park lists and polls. Last season there were nine jumps ranging up to 15m in length, and 30 jibs, boxes and rails. It also has two super-pipes.

SNOW RELIABILITY ★★★★★
Excellent, except in the Bowls

As well as an exceptional natural snow record (average 354 inches), Vail has extensive snowmaking, normally needed only in early season. Grooming is excellent. Both the Back Bowls and Blue Sky Basin usually open later in the season than the front of the mountain. Blue Sky is largely north-facing (and wooded) and keeps its snow well. But the Bowls are sunny, and in warm weather snow can deteriorate to the point where they are closed or only a traverse is kept open to allow access to Blue Sky Basin; for the best snow, head skier's right from the top of the Game Creek chair, where the sun has least effect because the runs are east-facing.

FOR EXPERTS ★★★★★
Lots of variety

Vail's Back Bowls are vast areas, served by four chairlifts and a short draglift. You can go virtually anywhere you like in the half-dozen identifiable bowls, trying the gradient and terrain of your choice. There are interesting, lightly wooded areas, as well as open slopes. The Bowls are largely classified black but are not particularly steep; they disappoint some expert reporters.

Blue Sky Basin has much better snow than the Back Bowls and some great adventure runs in the trees – some widely spaced, some very tight, some on relatively gentle terrain, some quite steep. All the runs funnel into the same run-out so you can't get lost.

On the front face there are some genuinely steep double-black diamond runs, which usually have great snow; they are often mogulled, but they are sometimes groomed to make wonderful fast cruising. The fast Highline lift – on the extreme east of the area – serves three black runs. Prima Cornice, served by the Northwoods Express, is one of the steepest runs on the front of the hill.

If the snow is good, try the backcountry Minturn Mile – you leave the ski area through a gate in the Game Creek area to descend a powder bowl and end up at the atmospheric Saloon. Go with a local guide.

FOR INTERMEDIATES ★★★★★
Ideal territory

The majority of Vail's front face is great intermediate terrain, with easy cruising runs. Above Lionshead, especially, there are excellent, long, relatively quiet blues – Bwana, Born Free and Simba all go from top to bottom. Game Creek Bowl, nearby, is excellent, too. Avanti, underneath the chair of the same name, is a nice cruise.

As well as tackling some of the easier front-face blacks, intermediates will find plenty of interest in the Back Bowls. Some of the runs are groomed and several are blue, including Silk Road, which loops around the eastern edge, with wonderful views. Some of the unpisted slopes are ideal for learning to ski powder. Confident intermediates will also enjoy Blue Sky Basin's clearly marked blue runs and the easier ungroomed runs there (Cloud 9 is a lovely gentle area of groomed glades; In the Wuides is a bit steeper but still lovely).

SCHOOLS

Vail
t 800 475 4543

Classes
Full day from $160
Private lessons
From $595 for 3hr for
up to 6 people

CHILDCARE

Child Care Centers
t 754 3285
Ages 2mnth to 6yr

Ski school
Ages 3 to 12

FOR BEGINNERS ★★★☆☆
Good but can be crowded
There are fine nursery slopes at resort level and at altitude, and easy longer runs to progress to. But they can be rather crowded, with lots of faster skiers passing through.

FOR BOARDERS ★★★☆☆
Big isn't always best
The terrain is about as big as it comes in America. Beginners will enjoy the front side's gentle groomed pistes (but not the crowds), good for honing skills and serviced by fast chairlifts. But beware of flat areas, especially at the top of the Wildwood and Northwoods lifts, and cat tracks. The back bowls will keep most expert and intermediate riders busy for days. Blue Sky Basin offers acres of natural trails, gladed trees and cornices.

FOR CROSS-COUNTRY ★★★☆☆
Go for Golden
Vail's cross-country areas (17km) are at the foot of Golden Peak and at the Nordic Center on the golf course.

MOUNTAIN RESTAURANTS ★★☆☆☆
Surprisingly poor
Vail's mountain restaurants are just inadequate for a major upscale resort. We can't believe Vail doesn't get this.

There are only two table-service places. Bistro Fourteen at Eagle's Nest is an airy room and does decent food. The newer 10th at Mid-Vail is Vail's 'premier' spot and looks good, but we lack reader reports.

The major self-service restaurants can be unpleasantly crowded from 11am to 2pm. The 'flagship' (hah!) Two Elk is huge and airy, and does 'fine cafeteria-style food' according to a 2014 reporter; good luck finding a table. Try Wildwood for BBQs and Buffalo's for soup and sandwiches. You can cook your own food on free BBQs at Belle's Camp at the top of Blue Sky Basin (take your own booze too).

SCHOOLS AND GUIDES ★★★★☆
Generally excellent, but ...
The school has an excellent reputation and reports are usually wholly positive. But a 2013 reporter had a mixed experience: 'Snowboard lesson was fantastic, hiked to get untracked powder. Brill, brill, brill.' But his wife's lesson was 'dreadful – she asked for a change of instructor for day two but was told that wasn't possible', and his nine-year-old was taught by 'an older gentleman with no enthusiasm'. More reports, please.

You can sign up for lessons on the mountain. Full-day Adventure Sessions offer guided instruction for experts and intermediates.

FOR FAMILIES ★★★★☆
Good all round
The main children's centre is at Golden Peak and takes kids aged 3 to 15; the nursery takes kids from two months to six years. There are splendid areas with adventure trails and themed play zones, such as the Magic Forest and Chaos Canyon. There's even a special

VAIL RESORTS, INC / JACK AFFLECK

Some of the runs in the Back Bowls get groomed ... ➔

↑ There's ice skating here at Solaris Plaza in Vail Village, at Vail Square in Lionshead, and indoors at Dobson Ice Arena between the two

VAIL RESORTS, INC / CHRIS MCLENNAN

GETTING THERE

Air Eagle 55km/ 35 miles (45min); Denver 195km/ 120 miles (2hr15)

ACTIVITIES

Indoor Athletics clubs and spas

Outdoor Tubing, ski biking, snowmobiling, snowshoe excursions, bungee trampolining

Central reservations phone number
t 496 4500

Phone numbers
From distant parts of the US, add the prefix 1 970; from abroad, add the prefix +1 970

TOURIST OFFICE

www.vail.com

kids' cafe area at Mid Vail. There are kids' snowmobiles and trampolines at Adventure Ridge.

STAYING THERE

There's a big choice of packages to Vail and it's easy to organize your own visit too, with regular airport shuttle services.

Chalets Skiworld has a couple of smart chalets with outdoor tubs in East Vail.

Hotels Vail's hotels are nearly all upmarket and expensive (becoming even more so with the opening in recent years of the luxurious Ritz Carlton, Four Seasons and Solaris hotels). Other top-rank places include the Vail Cascade (with its own lift into the slopes), the plushly Bavarian Sonnenalp, and the brilliantly convenient Lodge at Vail. Other slightly more affordable places include:

****Manor Vail Resort At Golden Peak. Suites with sitting area, fireplace, kitchen, terrace. Hot tub and pools.

****Marriot Mountain Resort At Golden Peak. Spa, pool, hot tub.

***Evergreen Lodge Between village and Lionshead. More affordable than others. Outdoor pool, sauna and hot tub. Sports bar.

Apartments There's a wide range of condos, from standard to luxury. The Racquet Club at East Vail has lots of amenities. At Vail Village, Mountain Haus is central and high quality. Vail Cascade Resort and Spa is good value, including breakfast and use of the hotel's leisure facilities. And Manor Vail might be a preferred family choice – it's beside the children's ski school. Good value places at Lionshead

include the Lodge at Lionshead, Village Inn Plaza, Vantage Point, the Antlers, Enzian, Westwind and Vail 21.

EATING OUT ★★★★★
Endless choice

Whatever kind of food you want, Vail has it – but most of it is expensive.

Fine-dining options include Elway's (in the Lodge), the Tour (modern French) and Ludwig's (in the Sonnenalp). For Alpine ambience try Pepi's (in the hotel Gramshammer) or the Alpenrose. You can take gondolas up to The 10th at Mid-Vail or to Eagle's Nest and then be driven by snowcat to the Game Creek Club for dinner (it's a private members' club at lunchtimes).

For more moderate prices, we've found Blu's 'contemporary American' food satisfactory; Campo de Fiori is an excellent Italian; and the Chophouse at Lionshead serves seafood and steaks. Reader recommendations include: Pazzo's ('Said to be the best pizza in Vail, and we loved it,' said a 2014 visitor), Sweet Basil (modern American) and Lancelot (steaks), both in Vail Village; May Palace (Chinese) and Nozawa (Asian) in West Vail; also Matsuhisa (Asian, in the Solaris hotel), Montauk (seafood), Los Amigos (Mexican), and Russell's (steak).

APRES-SKI ★★★★★
Fairly lively

Lionshead is quiet in the evenings; but Garfinkel's has a DJ, sun deck and happy hour. The Red Lion in Vail Village has live music, big-screen TVs and huge portions of food. The George models itself on an English-style pub. Pepi's is popular, and Los Amigos is lively at four o'clock. The Tap Room is a relaxed woody bar.

You can have a good night out at Adventure Ridge at the top of the gondola. As well as restaurants and bars, there's lots to do on the snow.

OFF THE SLOPES ★★★★★
A lot to do

Getting around on the free bus is easy, and there are lots of activities. The factory outlets at Silverthorne are a must if you can't resist a bargain. Pedestrians can get to Eagle's Nest or Mid-Vail for lunch by gondola; and we hear the Eagle Bahn is free after 4pm – just in time for G&T at the top. The National Mining Museum in Leadville, a 35-minute drive away, is tipped.

Winter Park

A radical alternative to the run of Colorado resorts, for those more interested in snow and space than in après-ski amusements

WINTER PARK / BYRON HETZLER PHOTOGRAPHY

RATINGS

The mountains

Extent	★★★
Fast lifts	★★★★
Queues	★★★★
Terrain p'ks	★★★★★
Snow	★★★★★
Expert	★★★★
Intermediate	★★★★
Beginner	★★★★★
Boarder	★★★
X-country	★★★★
Restaurants	★★★
Schools	★★★★★
Families	★★★★

The resort

Charm	★★
Convenience	★★★
Scenery	★★★
Eating out	★★
Après-ski	★
Off-slope	★

RPI	135
lift pass	£260
ski hire	£155
lessons	£160
food & drink	£125
total	**£700**

WINTER PARK RESORT

There are open steep slopes at the top, but most of the runs are cut through forest ↓

+ The best snowfall record of Colorado's major resorts

+ Good terrain for all abilities

+ Quiet on weekdays

+ Leading resort for teaching people with disabilities to ski and ride

+ Largely free of ski-resort glitz

- 'Village' at the lift base is still very limited, and dead in the evening

- Town is a bus ride away and has few shops and restaurants

- Trails tend to be either easy cruises or stiff mogul fields

- Some tough terrain is prone to closure by bad weather

Winter Park's ski area – developed for the recreation of the citizens of nearby Denver, and still owned by the city – is world class. When Intrawest (developers of resorts such as Whistler) got involved a few years ago, there was the prospect of a world-class resort being developed at the base, too. But things have stalled, and expansion plans now seem to have been put on hold.

For the present, there's only a small, very quiet 'village' at the base, and most lodging, shops and restaurants are a bus ride away in the rather limited town of Winter Park. But we quite like the low-key, glitz-free ambience.

THE RESORT

Winter Park started life in the 19th century: when the Rio Grande railway was built, workers climbed the slopes to ski down. One of its mountains, Mary Jane, is named after a legendary 'lady of pleasure' who is said to have received the land as payment for her favours. The resort (at 2745m) is one of the highest to get a chapter in this book (only Breckenridge is higher) and there is some risk of altitude sickness if you go straight there from the UK.

The approach road from Denver over the Continental Divide at Berthoud Pass is spectacularly high (3450m) and Alpine in character, with very un-American hairpin bends. Don't plan on driving over in the dark: if you hit a snowstorm, you'll regret it. Having a car permits day trips to resorts such as Copper Mountain, Keystone and Breckenridge (see separate chapter).

You can stay at The Village at the base of the slopes or in the town of Winter Park, linked by shuttle-bus.

2014/15: The Lunch Rock Cafe, at the top of Mary Jane, will be replaced by a new 250-seat restaurant with heated terrace. Yum!

KEY FACTS

Resort	2745m
	9,000ft
Slopes	2745-3675m
	9,000-12,060ft
Lifts	25
Pistes	3,081 acres
Green	8%
Blue	36%
Black	56%
Snowmaking	10%

VILLAGE CHARM ★★☆☆☆
Old or new?

Most lodgings are in spacious condos scattered around either side of US highway 40, the road through the town of Winter Park. At night, the neon lights make it seem like a real ski resort town; in the cold light of day it's different. You have to drive to Fraser to find a proper supermarket.

Stylish lodgings have been built at or near the foot of the slopes, to form a very small car-free mini-resort known as The Village at Winter Park. An area between the mountain and the town is known as Old Town.

CONVENIENCE ★★★☆☆
Walk or ride

If you stay in The Village, you are right by the slopes. Shuttle-buses run between town and the lift base, and hotels and condos also have shuttles.

SCENERY ★★★☆☆
See the Continental Divide

You are almost on the Continental Divide here, with views of the rolling hills in the other direction from the top of Parsenn Bowl.

THE MOUNTAINS

There's a good mix of terrain that suits all abilities – when it's all open; bad weather closures can be an issue There are guided tours twice daily. Route finding can be tricky in places.

EXTENT OF THE SLOPES ★★★☆☆
Interestingly divided

Winter Park's ski area is big by US standards. There are five distinct, but well-linked, sectors. From the main base, a fast quad takes you to the peak of the original **Winter Park** mountain. From there, you can descend in all directions.

Some runs lead back towards the main base and over to the **Vasquez Ridge** area on skier's left, served by the Pioneer fast quad.

Or you can descend to the base of **Mary Jane** mountain, where four chairs up the front face serve tough runs; other chairs serve easier terrain on the flanks. Going down the back of Mary Jane you can head for the **Parsenn Bowl**, riding the Panoramic Express chair for intermediate terrain above and in the trees. From Parsenn,

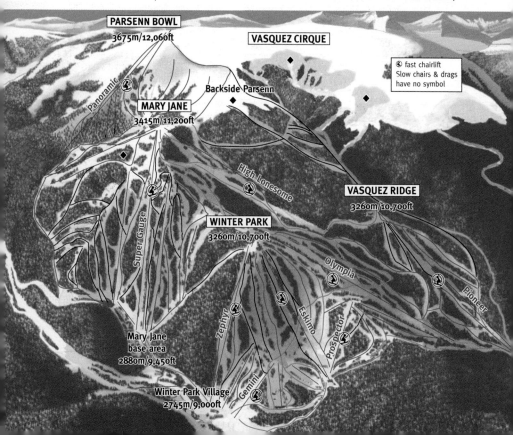

PARSENN BOWL
3675m/12,060ft

VASQUEZ CIRQUE

④ fast chairlift
Slow chairs & drags have no symbol

Panoramic

Backside Parsenn

MARY JANE
3415m/11,200ft

High Lonesome

VASQUEZ RIDGE
3260m/10,700ft

WINTER PARK
3260m/10,700ft

Super Gauge

Olympia

Pioneer

Zephyr

Eskimo

Prospector

Mary Jane
base area
2880m/9,450ft

Gemini

Winter Park Village
2745m/9,000ft

SKIING AND BOARDING FOR THE DISABLED

Winter Park is home to the US National Sports Center for the Disabled (NSCD) – the world's leading centre for teaching skiing and snowboarding to people with disabilities. If you are disabled and want to learn to ski or snowboard, there's no better place to go. It's important to book ahead so that a suitably trained instructor is available. The NSCD can help with travel and accommodation arrangements. See www.nscd.org. In Winter Park itself, you can inquire at the Colorado Ski Authority in the main base station area.

LIFT PASSES

Prices in US$

Age	1-day	6-day
under 13	52	254
13 to 64	90	427
65 to 69	81	384

Free Under 6
Seniors Age 70+, season ticket is $350
Beginner Included in price of lessons
Notes These are 2-days-in-advance-purchase prices; window ticket prices are considerably higher; special deals for disabled skiers

ACTIVITIES

Indoor Fitness clubs, hot tubs (in hotels), museum

Outdoor Ice rink, snowshoeing, ski biking, snowcat tours, tubing, sleigh rides

conditions permitting, you can hike for up to half an hour to access advanced and extreme terrain at **Vasquez Cirque**. You can return to Parsenn Bowl using the Eagle Wind chair, saving a long run-out to the base of the Vasquez Ridge area and the Pioneer lift.

FAST LIFTS ★★★★
Adequately covered
Fast chairs have gradually replaced old lifts, though a few slow ones remain.

QUEUES ★★★★
Quiet during the week
During the week the mountain is generally very quiet; however, the Zephyr Express can get busy at peak times and there are often weekend crowds and queues ('Half an hour for the Zephyr; up to 10 minutes up the mountain,' says a 2013 visitor).

TERRAIN PARKS ★★★★★
Parks for all standards
All six parks were upgraded a few seasons ago. The flagship Rail Yard park – with 30 features including big jumps, jibs, boxes, a host of variously shaped rails and quarter-, half- and super-pipes – is enough to challenge most experts. It runs down much of the front of Winter Park mountain for 1.3km. Halfway down it crosses a bridge to the Village Way green run and you enter Dark Territory (the name is a railroad term, apparently), a park with such huge features it is open only to special pass holders. You have to pay $20, sign a waiver and watch a safety video to get the pass. For those who prefer smaller hits, there are the Re-Railer and Gangway parks for intermediates nearby. There's also the beginner-intermediate Ash Cat on the Jack Kendrick green run, plus the Starter park under Prospector Express and the Bouncer park in The Village – both for beginners. Check them out at www.rlyrd.com.

SNOW RELIABILITY ★★★★★
Among Colorado's best
Winter Park's position, close to the Continental Divide, gives it an average yearly snowfall of 330 inches – higher than most major Colorado resorts. Snowmaking covers a lot of Winter Park mountain's runs.

FOR EXPERTS ★★★★
Some hair-raising challenges
Mary Jane has some of the steepest

mogul fields, chutes and hair-raising challenges in the US. On the front side is a row of long black mogul fields that are quite steep enough for most of us. There are some good genuine blacks on Winter Park mountain, too.

Some of the best terrain is open only when there is good snow and/or weather – so it's especially unreliable early in the season. The fearsome chutes of Mary Jane's back side – all steep, narrow and bordered by rocks – need a lot of snow, are marked as 'Extreme Terrain' on the trail map and are accessed by a control gate. Parsenn Bowl has superb blue/black gladed runs and black diamond gladed runs on the back side down to the Eagle Wind chair. Vasquez Cirque, the least reliably open area, has excellent ungroomed expert terrain but not much vertical before you hit the forest.

FOR INTERMEDIATES ★★★★
Choose your challenge
From pretty much wherever you are on Winter Park mountain and Vasquez Ridge you can choose a run to suit your ability. Most blue runs are well groomed every night, giving you perfect early-morning cruising on the famous Colorado corduroy pistes. Black runs, however, tend not to be groomed, and huge moguls form. If bumps are for you, try Mary Jane's front side. If you're learning to love them, the blue/black Sleeper enables you to dip in and out.

Parsenn Bowl has grand views and several gentle cruising pistes as well as more challenging ungroomed terrain. There are blue and blue-black runs and glades here, offering a nice range of gradients. It's also an ideal place to try powder for the first time. But when it's actually snowing you are better off riding lower lifts, sticking to the powdery edges of treelined runs for better visibility. The blue-black Hughes is a great thrash home at close of play.

FOR BEGINNERS ★★★★★
About the best we've seen
Discovery Park is a 25-acre dedicated area for beginners, reached by a high-speed quad and served by two more chairs. As well as a nursery area and longer green runs, it has an adventure trail through trees. Sorensen Park learning zone at the base area is good too. There are lots of long green runs, but some are perilously close to flat.

SCHOOLS

Winter Park
t 1 800 979 0032
National Sports Center for the Disabled
t 726 1540
Special programme for disabled skiers and snowboarders

Classes
Day (5.5hr) from $99
Private lessons
From $349 for 3hr for 1 to 3 people

CHILDCARE

Wee Willie's
t 1 800 420 8093
Ages 2mnth to 6yr

Ski school
Takes ages 3 to 14

GETTING THERE

Air Denver 150km/ 95 miles (2hr15)
Rail Fraser 19km/ 12 miles

UK PACKAGES

Alpine Answers, American Ski Classics, Crystal, Erna Low, Interactive Resorts, Momentum, Ski Independence, Ski Safari, Skitracer, Skiworld, Snow Finders, Supertravel, Thomson, Virgin Snow

Central reservations
Toll-free number (from within the US)
1 800 979 0332

Phone numbers
From distant parts of the US, add the prefix 1 970; from abroad, add the prefix +1 970

TOURIST OFFICE

www.winterparkresort.com

FOR BOARDERS ★★★
Beware the moguls and flats

There is some great advanced and extreme boarding terrain and a high probability of fresh powder to ride. And the terrain parks are great. The resort is also good for beginners and intermediates, with excellent terrain for learning. But there are quite a few flat spots to beware of, and a lot of the steep runs have huge moguls, which many boarders find tricky. Beginners can meet their instructors and learn about the sport before taking a lesson if they go to the Burton Experience Snowboarding Lounge at Winter Park Resort Rentals.

FOR CROSS-COUNTRY ★★★★
Lots of it nearby

There are several areas nearby (none actually in the resort) with over 200km of groomed trails plus backcountry tours and generally excellent snow.

MOUNTAIN RESTAURANTS ★★★
The news is good

The big news is the replacement for Christmas 2014 of the tiny Lunch Rock Cafe, at the top of Mary Jane, by an entirely new 250-seat restaurant with heated terrace, making the most of the excellent views. The Lodge at Sunspot, at the top of Zephyr, has a welcoming (but busy) bar with a log fire and table- and self-service sections ('good soups'). And there is Snoasis, by the beginner area – 'reasonable prices' but 'overcrowded'. Otherwise, it's down to the bases; the Club Car at the base of Mary Jane offers table-service and a varied menu. You can eat your own packed lunch at Moffat Market (at the base) and Mary Jane Market (at The Village).

SCHOOLS AND GUIDES ★★★★★
No recent reports

We have no reason to doubt the school is up to the usual high US standards. Two variations on standard classes are 3-hour Max Four Lessons (which start at 11.45 and limit group size to four) and Adult Full Day Group Lessons that include lunch.

FOR FAMILIES ★★★★
Some of the best

Wee Willie's Child Care at the base area houses day-care facilities, taking kids from two months to six years, and is the meeting point for children's classes, which have their own areas.

STAYING THERE

Chalets Skiworld has a lovely log-cabin chalet with outdoor hot tub: 'The best we've ever stayed in – very spacious, bus stop outside,' says a visitor.
Hotels There are a couple of hotel/ condo complexes with restaurants and pools near, but not in, The Village.
★★★Iron Horse Resort Outdoor pool and hot tubs, steam room.
★★★Vintage Hotel Linked by the car park bucket lift to The Village. Good value. Outdoor pool and tub.
Apartments The Zephyr Mountain Lodge, Fraser Crossing and Founders Pointe are all in The Village. There are a lot of comfortable condos in or on the way to town. Reader tips: Beaver Village, Sawmill Station, Red Quill, Meadowridge, Crestview Place.

EATING OUT ★★
A real weakness

There isn't the range of places you get in most 'destination' resorts. For fine dining you have to drive 13km to Devil's Thumb Ranch, where there's Heck's Tavern and Ranch House Restaurant. In town, reporters are keen on Deno's (seafood, steaks etc and '600 different wines'), New Hong Kong (Chinese), Gasthaus Eichler (German-influenced food), Carlos and Maria's (Tex-Mex), Fontenot's (seafood and Cajun), Hernando's (pizza/pasta) and Lime ('good Mexican food'). At The Village, Cheeky Monk does pub grub – 'excellent sausage and mash'.

APRES-SKI ★
If you know where to go ...

At close of play, there's action in The Village at the Derailer Bar, Cheeky Monk (pub grub – see above – and a huge selection of Belgian beers) and Doc's Roadhouse ('great atmosphere'); and at the Club Car at the base of Mary Jane. It's very quiet after 8pm; a reader reports that the main hot spots later on are Deno's and the Winter Park Pub in town. Moffat Station microbrewery has good beer.

OFF THE SLOPES ★
Mainly the great outdoors

Past reporters have enjoyed floodlit tubing at Fraser – and there is now a tubing hill at the lift base. There's also ice skating at the base and snowmobiling to the Continental Divide. Outings are possible to Denver, which has an attractive centre.

Utah

'The Greatest Snow on Earth' is Utah's marketing slogan. And usually it's not far from the truth. The last three seasons have been poor for snow by Utah standards but normally the snowiest Utah resorts do get huge amounts of usually light, dry powder. If you like the steep and deep, you should at some point make the pilgrimage here. And if you like an après-ski beer or two, don't be put off by the image of a 'dry' Mormon state – getting a drink is not a problem. But boarders beware: two of its top resorts don't allow snowboarding.

The biggest dumps fall at Alta (which bans boarding) and Snowbird. Their average of 500 inches of snow a year (twice as much as some Colorado resorts) has made them the powder capitals of the world.

Park City, over the hill from Alta but 45 minutes away by road, is the main 'destination' resort of the area and a sensible holiday base; as well as its own slopes it has upmarket Deer Valley (which also bans boarding) right next door, and Canyons only a short drive away. Park City and neighbours get 'only' 300 to 350 inches of snow.

We have separate chapters on these five resorts.

Of course, you're not guaranteed fresh powder. The last three seasons have been disappointing for snow (and as one 2014 reporter said, 'It's a

long way to go for 13 days of sun and blue skies'). But in 2008 we spent a week in Park City when it virtually never stopped snowing. Every day we had fresh, knee-high powder.

Other resorts worth visiting (covered in the resort directory at the end of the book) include **Brighton** and **Solitude**, in the valley that separates Park City from Alta. The snow here is almost a match for Alta/Snowbird in quantity but gets tracked out less quickly because of fewer expert visitors. The main claim to fame of **Sundance** is that it's owned by Robert Redford; it averages 320 inches of snow. **Snowbasin** (400 inches), well to the north, hosted the Olympic downhill events in 2002. **Powder Mountain** (500 inches), a bit further north, is aptly named. As well as lift-served slopes it has 3,000 acres of snowcat skiing.

Until 2009 the sale and consumption of alcohol was tightly controlled in Utah, the Mormon state. Until then, to get a drink in bars and clubs you had to jump through various hoops. These rules have now been scrapped and as long as you are over 21 (and have ID to prove it) you should have no problem getting alcoholic drinks.

You normally fly in to Salt Lake City, which means changing planes somewhere en route – a bit of a drag. But transfers are short – 45 minutes or less for the five resorts we feature.

You could consider staying in Salt Lake City and driving to a different resort each day. Two of our 2014 reporters did that and list the advantages as including: lower prices for lodging and lift passes (you can buy passes at a discount from certain sports shops), lots of choice of restaurants and bars and cultural attractions (eg concerts, the Mormon Temple, heritage sites).

573

TOURIST OFFICE

Ski Utah
www.skiutah.com

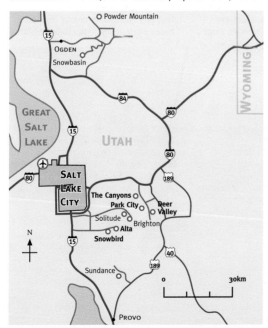

Alta

Cult powder resort linked to Snowbird but with less brutal architecture and a friendlier, old-fashioned feel

TOP 10 RATINGS

Extent	★★★
Fast lifts	★★★★
Queues	★★★
Snow	★★★★★
Expert	★★★★★
Intermediate	★★★
Beginner	★★★
Charm	★★
Convenience	★★★★★
Scenery	★★★

RPI   145

lift pass	£270
ski hire	£185
lessons	£160
food & drink	£145
total	**£760**

NEWS

2014/15: There are plans to remodel some runs above the Wildcat base to improve both an intermediate trail and the run out from an advanced trail.

ALTA SKI AREA

Pray for more snow. It's powder not moguls that you go to Alta for ↓

+ Phenomenal snow and steep terrain mean cult status among experts
+ Linked to Snowbird, making one of the largest ski areas in the US
+ Ski-almost-to-the-door convenience
+ No snowboarding allowed

− 'Resort' is just a scattering of lodges, so not much goes on off the slopes
− Limited groomed runs for intermediates
− No snowboarding allowed

Alta and linked Snowbird are the powder capitals of the world, and add up to a great area for adventurous skiers. Alta has a friendlier, more personal feel than Snowbird, which gets its own chapter a few pages on.

THE RESORT

Alta sits at the craggy head of Little Cottonwood Canyon, 2km beyond Snowbird and less than an hour's drive from downtown Salt Lake City. Both the resort and the approach road are prone to avalanches and closure: visitors can be confined indoors.

Village charm Where once there was a bustling and bawdy mining town, there is now just a dozen lodges plus several parking areas.

Convenience Life revolves around the two lift base areas – Albion and Wildcat – linked by a rope tow along the valley floor. All the lodges are convenient for the lifts.

Scenery Alta is recognized for its impressively rugged scenery and challenging, sparsely wooded ridges.

THE MOUNTAINS

Most of Alta's slopes are lightly wooded. Alta does not differentiate between single- and double-black diamond trails – regrettable, we think.

Slopes The dominant feature of the terrain is the steep end of a ridge that separates the area's two basins. To the left, above Albion Base, the slopes stretch away over easy green terrain towards the blue and black runs from Point Supreme and from the top of the Sugarloaf quad (also the access lift for Snowbird). To the right, above Wildcat Base, is a more concentrated bowl with blue runs down the middle and blacks either side. The two sectors are linked at altitude.

Fast lifts Fast chairs depart from each base; another one links to Snowbird.

KEY FACTS

Resort	2600m
	8,530ft
See Snowbird for Alta/Snowbird area	

Alta only	
Slopes	2600-3215m
	8,530-10,550ft
Lifts	11
Pistes	2,200 acres
Green	25%
Blue	40%
Black	35%
Snowmaking	Some

UK PACKAGES

American Ski Classics, Momentum, Skitracer

Phone numbers
From distant parts of the US, add the prefix 1 801; from abroad, add the prefix +1 801

TOURIST OFFICE

www.alta.com

Queues The slopes are normally uncrowded and queues are rare. But boarding the Collins chair at the mid-station is difficult at times because of the number of people skiing to the base and getting on there.

Terrain parks There isn't one.

Snow reliability The quantity (an average of 500 inches a year) and quality of snow and the northerly orientation put Alta in the top rank. But the last three seasons have seen well below average snowfalls.

Experts Alta has long held cult status among experts. There are dozens of steep slopes and chutes. But finding the best spots is tricky without local guidance and quite a lot of traversing.

Intermediates There isn't a lot of groomed terrain (more in Snowbird). But adventurous intermediates happy to try powder can have a good time.

Beginners Albion has a nursery area and gentle lower slopes, with a beginner lift pass covering three lifts.

Snowboarding Boarding is banned.

Cross-country 3km of groomed track.

Mountain restaurants There's one in each sector. Watson Shelter on the Wildcat side is light and airy with big windows, self- and table-service sections and a small coffee bar; we enjoyed the table-service Collins Grill here. Alf's on the Albion side is a standard self-service.

Schools and guides The ski school specializes in powder lessons – though there are regular classes, too.

Families Day care for children from six weeks to nine years is available at the Children's Center at Albion Base.

STAYING THERE

None of the hotels is luxurious in US terms, but most fill up with repeat visitors and, unusually for the US, offer half-board (ie dinner included).

Hotels We've twice enjoyed staying at the venerable Alta Lodge (742 3500): comfortable rooms, an atmospheric bar, meals served at shared or private tables. Rustler Lodge (742 2200) is more luxurious, with a big outdoor pool, but impersonal. The comfortable, modern Goldminer's Daughter (742 2300), the basic Peruvian Lodge (742 3000) and the canyon's oldest lodge – dating from 1938 but now restored, of course – Snowpine Lodge (742 2000) are cheaper.

Eating out It is possible, but eating in is the normal routine.

Après-ski The Goldminer's Daughter Saloon is the main après-ski bar; the upstairs lounge has sofas, an open fire and huge floor-to-ceiling windows.

Off the slopes There are few options other than snowshoeing, the Cliff Lodge spa down the road at Snowbird, or a sightseeing trip to Salt Lake City.

Alta

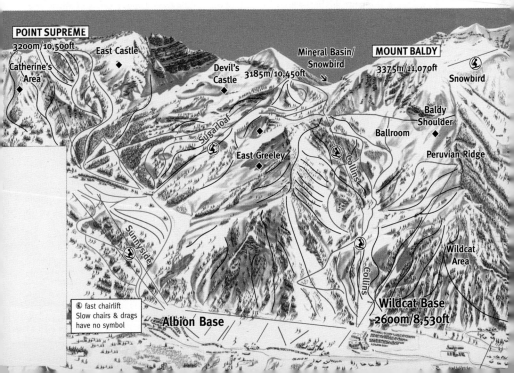

POINT SUPREME
3200m/10,500ft
Catherine's Area
East Castle
Devil's Castle
Mineral Basin/ Snowbird
3185m/10,450ft
MOUNT BALDY
3375m/11,070ft
Snowbird
Baldy Shoulder
Ballroom
Peruvian Ridge
Sugarloaf
East Greeley
Collins
Sunnyside
Collins
Collins
Wildcat Area
fast chairlift
Slow chairs & drags have no symbol
Albion Base
Wildcat Base
2600m/8,530ft

Canyons

One of the five biggest ski areas in the US, with a small purpose-built resort at the base, just outside Park City

TOP 10 RATINGS

Extent	★★★
Fast lifts	★★★
Queues	★★★★
Snow	★★★
Expert	★★★★
Intermediate	★★★★
Beginner	★★
Charm	★★
Convenience	★★★★
Scenery	★★★

RPI 165

lift pass	£310
ski hire	£185
lessons	£200
food & drink	£150
total	**£845**

NEWS

2014/15: Cloud Dine eatery at the top of the Dreamscape lift is due to be renovated with its capacity being doubled.

2013/14: Vail Resorts – operator of Vail, Beaver Creek, Breckenridge and Heavenly among other resorts – took over operation of the resort in 2013. You can now buy the Epic pass which allows skiing at other Vail resorts.

- ✛ Relatively extensive area of slopes
- ✛ Modern lift system with few queues
- ✛ Easy access to Park City and Deer Valley ski areas
- ✛ Can stay at the base, but ...

- ━ Village is very small and limited
- ━ Snow on the many south-facing slopes is affected by sun
- ━ Many runs are short
- ━ Few green runs

We find it difficult to warm to Canyons. The ski area may be bigger than nearby Park City and Deer Valley but it is less interesting, the snow is normally not as good and the 'village' is small and dull. Anyone having a holiday in Park City should plan to visit – there are good bus services. Whether you would want to stay here is another question. Vail Resorts took over running the resort from last season, so things may change. But for now, we'd stay in Park City.

THE RESORT

Canyons has been transformed over the past 20 years or so. The area of the slopes has more than doubled, and a small car-free village has been built at the base. And it has the potential to become the biggest ski area in the US.

Village charm The village has lodgings and a few shops, restaurants and bars. But it doesn't add up to much – you can stroll round it in 10 minutes or so.

Convenience Staying at the base is convenient for the Canyons ski area. There are buses from the base of the access lift direct to Park City and its ski area; Deer Valley requires one change. A 2013 visitor found the bus services quick and convenient.

Scenery A series of broad, long ridges are separated by valleys and most of the area is fairly densely wooded.

THE MOUNTAINS

Canyons claims that its slopes spread over nine mountains. It is certainly a complicated and extensive area.

Free mountain tours start daily at 10.30, and paid-for First Tracks tours run twice a week – former Olympic skiers guide you round the slopes before they officially open.

Slopes Red Pine Lodge, at the heart of the slopes, is reached by an eight-seat gondola from the village. A fast quad reaches a higher point. From the top of both lifts you can move in either direction across a series of ridges and valleys. Runs come off both sides of each ridge and generally face north or south. Most runs are quite short (less than 500m vertical), with some long, quite flat run-outs.

Fast lifts The core of the lift system either side of Red Pine Lodge consists

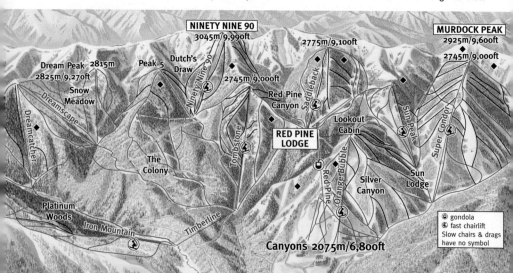

Dream Peak 2815m	NINETY NINE 90	MURDOCK PEAK
2825m/9,270ft	3045m/9,990ft	2925m/9,600ft

2775m/9,100ft

2745m/9,000ft

Peak 5   Dutch's Draw

2745m/9,000ft

Red Pine Canyon

Snow Meadow

Dreamscape

Ninety Nine 90

Saddleback

Sun Peak

Super Condor

Dreamcatcher

Lookout Cabin

RED PINE LODGE

Tombstone

Red Pine

Orange Bubble

Sun Lodge

The Colony

Silver Canyon

Platinum Woods

Iron Mountain

Timberline

Canyons 2075m/6,800ft

- ◉ gondola
- ④ fast chairlift
- Slow chairs & drags have no symbol

↑ The area consists of several linked, lightly wooded canyons. But it lacks variety and we find it difficult to warm to

CANYONS RESORT / ROB BOSSI

KEY FACTS

Resort	2075m
	6,800ft
Slopes	2075-3045m
	6,800-9,990ft
Lifts	19
Pistes	4,000 acres
Green	10%
Blue	44%
Black	46%
Snowmaking	6%

UK PACKAGES

American Ski Classics, Frontier, Scott Dunn, Ski Independence, Ski Safari, Skitracer

Central reservations
Call 1 866 604 4171 (toll-free from within the US)
Phone numbers
From distant parts of the US, add the prefix 1 435; from abroad, add the prefix +1 435

TOURIST OFFICE

www.canyonsresort.
com

of fast quads, but the Dream Peak sector has no fast lifts.

Queues We found no queues, and reporters have no problems either.

Terrain parks Painted Horse is the park to progress in. Transitions has five large jumps, 27 jibs and two wall rides, and Elwoods is a natural zone.

The average snowfall of 350 inches is a match for Park City and more than Deer Valley. But the south-facing slopes suffer from the sun and we've never found them in good condition. Snowmaking is very limited.

Terrain parks There are three parks.

Experts There is steep terrain all over the mountain. We particularly liked the north-facing runs off Ninety Nine 90, with steep double-black diamond runs plunging down through the trees. We had a great time here on our last visit, after fresh snow. A short hike from the top accesses some fine powder runs even days after a snowfall. And there is also lots of double-diamond terrain on Murdock Peak (a 20-minute hike from the Super Condor lift). Runs off the Peak 5 chair are more sheltered. And there's heli-skiing too.

Intermediates There are groomed blue runs for intermediates on all the main sectors except Ninety Nine 90. Some are quite short, but you can switch from valley to valley for added interest. From the Super Condor and Tombstone fast chairs there are excellent double-blue square runs. The Dreamscape area can be quiet, and is great for early experiments in powder.

Beginners There are good areas with moving carpets up at Red Pine Lodge. But the run you progress to is rather short and gets very busy.

Snowboarding Except for the flat run-outs from many runs, it's a great area, with lots of natural hits and half-pipes.
Cross-country None in resort. The Park City golf course has 20km and Soldier Hollow near Homestead Resort 30km.
Mountain restaurants Red Pine Lodge is a large, attractive building with a busy cafeteria and big deck. Reporters have found the Sun Lodge quieter. The smart table-service Lookout Cabin has wonderful views from huge windows, and we had excellent game stew there on our last visit. The Dreamscape and Tombstone Grill snack huts offer simple food outdoors. People can bring their own lunch into any of the self-service places.
Schools and guides As well as the usual classes, there are 'Mountain Experience' groups. Children's classes are for ages 2 to 12, teens from 13 to 17 – 'very good' says a 2014 visitor.
Families There's day care in the Grand Summit Hotel for children from six weeks to six years.

STAYING THERE

Hotels The Waldorf Astoria is the best, set below the village and served (until 5.30pm) by its own gondola. We stayed at the Grand Summit, but were disappointed with our standard King room. Silverado Lodge is the other main hotel. All have pools and tubs.
Apartments The Hyatt Escala Lodge (with pool and hot tubs) and Westgate Resort and Spa are pricey and luxurious. Of the cheaper places Timberwolf condos have been praised; other options include Bear Hollow, Hidden Creek, Red Pine and Sundial.
Eating out We had a great meal (fillet steak and buffalo osso bucco) at The Farm – the best place in town. Red Tail Grill does Tex-Mex, and Bistro offers 'modern American' kosher food. Red Pine Lodge at the top of the gondola does a BBQ on some weekends, with a C&W band and dancing. See the Park City chapter for lots of options there.
Après-ski It's generally pretty quiet. The Umbrella Bar is the main focus as the lifts close.
Off the slopes There's a great zipline tour that we enjoyed (two short training wires followed by a minute-long whizz above a deep canyon), guided snowshoeing, snowmobiling, dog sledding, horse-drawn sleigh rides, a factory outlet mall, and Salt Lake City and Park City nearby.

Build your own shortlist: www.wheretoskiandsnowboard.com

Deer Valley

Top of the Ivy League of US ski resorts: it promises, and delivers, the best ski and gastronomic experience – we love it

TOP 10 RATINGS

Extent	★★
Fast lifts	★★★★
Queues	★★★★
Snow	★★★★
Expert	★★★
Intermediate	★★★★
Beginner	★★★★
Charm	★★★
Convenience	★★★★
Scenery	★★★

RPI 165

lift pass	£310
ski hire	£185
lessons	£210
food & drink	£150
total	**£855**

NEWS

2013/14: A new green run, Gnat's Eye, was opened on Little Baldy Peak to make access from there to the main base easier for beginners.

Snowmaking was improved and three new grooming machines were bought.

KEY FACTS

Resort	2195m
	7,200ft
Slopes	2000-2915m
	6,570-9,570ft
Lifts	21
Pistes	2,026 acres
Green	24%
Blue	43%
Black	33%
Snowmaking	33%

UK PACKAGES

American Ski Classics, Frontier, Momentum, Oxford Ski Co, Scott Dunn, Ski Independence, Ski Safari, Skitracer

578

+ Good snow and varied terrain

+ Brilliant free black diamond tours

+ Many fast lifts and no queues

+ Good restaurants and lodgings

− Expensive, even by US standards

− Mostly short runs

− Quiet at night, though Park City is right next door

Deer Valley prides itself on pampering its guests, with valets to unload your skis, gourmet dining, immaculately groomed slopes, limited numbers on the mountain – and no snowboarding. Park City ski area is right next door – nothing more than a fence separates the two – and any skier visiting the area should try both. For most people, Park City town is the obvious base; but there are some seductive hotels here at mid-mountain Silver Lake.

THE RESORT

Just a mile from the end of Park City's Main Street, Deer Valley is overtly upmarket – famed for the care and attention lavished on the slopes and the guests. But it is unpretentious.

Village charm The resort spreads along a road up the mountain but the Silver Lake area is something of a focus.

Convenience Most lodgings are right on the slopes.

Scenery From Bald Mountain there are extensive views to Park City and the Jordanelle reservoir. And the views of the reservoir on the run down to the Jordanelle gondola are spectacular.

THE MOUNTAINS

The slopes are varied and interesting. Deer Valley's reputation for immaculate grooming is justified, but there is also a lot of exciting tree skiing and some steep bump runs. There are free mountain tours for different standards. We have been on two three-hour black-diamond tours, and they were both brilliant, taking us through fresh powder in the trees that we would never have found on our own.

A 2014 reporter who was involved in two collisions on one day complains of reckless skiing and not enough fences to slow people down, especially in the Silver Lake area.

Slopes Two parallel chairs take you up Bald Eagle Mountain, just beyond which is the mid-mountain focus of Silver Lake Lodge. You can ski from here to the isolated Little Baldy Peak, served by a gondola and a fast quad chairlift, with mainly easy runs to serve property developments there (though a local loves skiing these first

thing because they are immaculately groomed and deserted, with great views). But the main skiing is on three linked peaks beyond Silver Lake Lodge – Bald Mountain, Flagstaff Mountain and Empire Canyon. The top of Empire is just a few metres from the runs of the Park City ski area but crossing the fence that divides the two is banned.

Fast lifts Fast quads rule; the three main peaks have nine.

Queues Waiting in lift lines is not something that Deer Valley wants its guests to experience, so it limits the number of lift tickets sold. But it has built four lifts ending at the same place at the top of Flagstaff – resulting in hordes of people trying to go in different directions (insane – and not what you'd expect in Deer Valley).

Terrain parks There isn't one.

Snow reliability Excellent, and there's plenty of snowmaking too.

Experts Despite the image of luxury there is excellent expert terrain on all three main mountains, including fabulous glades, bumps, chutes and bowls. And the snow doesn't get skied out quickly. The Ski Utah Interconnect Tour to Alta starts here (read about this in the Park City chapter).

Intermediates There are lots of superbly groomed blue runs.

Beginners There are nursery slopes at Silver Lake Lodge as well as at the base, and gentle green runs to progress to.

Snowboarding Boarding is banned.

Cross-country There are 20km of trails on Park City golf course and 30km at Soldier Hollow near Homestead Resort.

Mountain restaurants The best in the local areas, with attractive wood-and-glass self-service places at Silver Lake, Empire Canyon and the base lodge.

A fabulous start to the day: immaculate grooming, deserted trails and views of the Jordanelle reservoir →

DEER VALLEY

You can eat your own packed lunches at all three. For table-service, try the Stein Eriksen Lodge, Goldener Hirsch or Royal Street Cafe at Silver Lake.

Schools and guides The ski school is doubtless excellent; book in advance.

Families The Children's Center accepts children from two months to 12 years.

STAYING THERE

Deer Valley, Park City and Canyons are linked by efficient shuttle-buses. But a car is useful for visiting other nearby Utah resorts (eg Alta, Snowbird).

Hotels The St Regis, Montage Deer Valley, Stein Eriksen Lodge and Goldener Hirsch Inn are some of the plushest hotels in any ski resort.

Apartments There are many luxury places to rent.

Eating out Of the gourmet restaurants, Mariposa is the best. We enjoyed the all-you-can-eat Seafood Buffet (it's not just seafood) and 'Fireside Dining' at Empire Canyon Lodge: four courses, each served at a different fireplace.

Après-ski Edgar's Beers & Spirits Lounge at the base area is the main après-ski venue, with live music at weekends. For more choice, it's not far to Main Street in Park City.

Off the slopes Park City has lots of shops and galleries etc. Salt Lake City has concerts, sights and shopping. Balloon rides, snowmobiling and snowshoeing are popular.

Central reservations
Call 645 6538

Phone numbers
From distant parts of the US, add 1 435; from abroad, add the prefix +1 435

TOURIST OFFICE
www.deervalley.com

Deer Valley

579

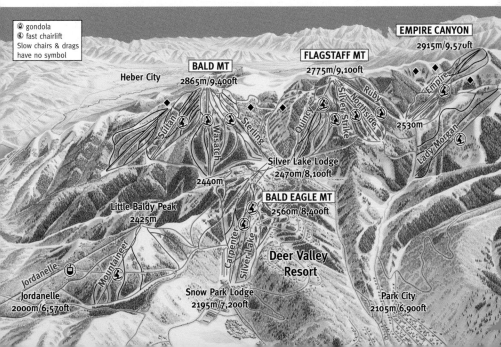

SNOWPIX.COM / CHRIS GILL

Park City

With its cute and lively Main Street, the most attractive base for skiing three very worthwhile areas on one lift pass

RATINGS

The mountains

Extent	★★★
Fast lifts	★★★
Queues	★★★★
Terrain p'ks	★★★★★
Snow	★★★★
Expert	★★★★
Intermediate	★★★★
Beginner	★★★★
Boarder	★★★★
X-country	★★★
Restaurants	★★
Schools	★★★★
Families	★★

The resort

Charm	★★★
Convenience	★★
Scenery	★★★
Eating out	★★★★★
Après-ski	★★★
Off-slope	★★★

RPI	160
lift pass	£310
ski hire	£185
lessons	£180
food & drink	£150
total	**£825**

PARK CITY MOUNTAIN RESORT
The town is very spread out – this pic shows only a tiny fraction of it. Most lodging is in the characterless suburbs ↓

+ Entertaining, historic Main Street

+ Lots of bars and restaurants make nonsense of Utah's Mormon image

+ Easy to ski Deer Valley and Canyons as well as the Park City slopes

– Resort is an enormous, charmless sprawl, with most lodgings a drive from Main Street and the slopes

– Runs tend to be rather short

– Still too many slow chairlifts

Park City is an excellent base for touring all of Utah's main resorts. Staying near Main Street puts you near the historic heart and its lively bars and restaurants.

Park City Mountain Resort (covered in this chapter) is just one of three local ski areas covered by the Three Resort Pass (available through some UK tour operators but not locally – buy before you go) and easily reached by frequent free buses. Deer Valley is separated from the Park City slopes only by a fence between two pistes, and by separate ownership – all very strange, to European eyes. Canyons is a little further away. Then there are the famously powdery resorts of Snowbird and Alta, less than an hour away; you need a separate lift pass for them. These four resorts all have their own chapters.

THE RESORT

Park City is about 45 minutes by road from Salt Lake City. It was a silver-mining boom town, and at the turn of the 19th century it boasted a population of 10,000, a red-light area, a Chinese quarter and 27 saloons.

VILLAGE CHARM ★★★
A colourful past
Careful restoration has left the town with a splendid historic centrepiece in Main Street, now lined by a colourful selection of bars, restaurants, galleries and shops, many quite smart, but there are touristy souvenir places too. New buildings have been tastefully designed to blend in smoothly. But most lodging is in the sprawling and characterless suburbs, a drive or bus ride from Main Street.

CONVENIENCE ★★
Depends on your base
The slow Town chairlift goes up to the slopes from Main Street, but the main lifts are on the fringes at Resort Base; there are lodgings out there but most are a bus ride away.

Deer Valley, Canyons and Park City are linked by efficient free shuttle-buses which run until fairly late – but we've found it a pain to wait for buses in the evenings. A car is useful to avoid this, and for visiting Alta/Snowbird.

If you're not hiring a car, pick a location that's handy for Main Street and the Town chair or the free bus.

SCENERY ★★★
Gently undulating ridges
In contrast to Park City's sprawling mass, the rounded mountain ridges have a modest and gentle presence.

2014/15: When we went to press, Park City Mountain Resort was in a court dispute about the lease for its ski area. But it expected to operate as normal for the 2014/15 season.

THE MOUNTAINS

Park City Mountain Resort consists mostly of blue and black trails cut through the trees, with easier runs running along the ridges and the valleys between. The more interesting terrain is in the lightly wooded bowls and ridges at the top. The trail map marks 13 'Signature Runs' that are groomed every night ('A great blast first thing,' says a reporter) – and five 'Adventure Alley' blue runs among the trees ('great fun').

Reporters have enjoyed the free mountain history tours of the slopes that look at the area's silver-mining heritage and take place twice a day. A long intermediate run, a beginner run and the Three Kings terrain park are floodlit for night skiing till 8pm.

It is much cheaper to buy lift passes in advance than on the spot. Signposting is clear. Grooming reports are available daily.

EXTENT OF THE SLOPES ★★★★★
Bowls above the woods

The ski area is bigger than Deer Valley but smaller than Canyons. Most of the easy and intermediate runs lie between Summit House and the base area, and are spread along the sides of a series of interconnecting ridges. Virtually all the steep terrain is above Summit House in a series of ungroomed bowls, and accessed by the McConkey's six-pack and the old, slow Jupiter double chair.

FAST LIFTS ★★★★★
Not up to usual US standards

Two fast chairlifts whisk you up from Resort Base and others beyond take you to Summit House. But there are still too many slow lifts serving the upper mountain and some of the best steep slopes.

QUEUES ★★★★★
Peak period crowds

It can get pretty crowded (on some trails as well as the lifts) at weekends ('massive, well-managed queues on Saturday') and in high season. You can pay extra for a Fast Tracks pass to jump queues on the six busiest lifts.

TERRAIN PARKS ★★★★★
Among the best in the world

There are three terrain parks here to suit all levels. The vast number of kickers, rails and pipes are maintained daily, and rank among the best in the world. See www.irideparkcity.tv. Neff Land is a great entry-level park, Three Kings is for all abilities and floodlit for night riding till 8pm, and King's Crown is the park for pros, with the biggest jumps and features. The Eagle super-pipe was used for the 2002 Winter Olympics and today is consistently one of the best pipes in the world. Intermediate level kids aged 11 to 15 can join three-day 'I Ride Park City' freestyle camps to learn park and all-mountain skills.

SNOW RELIABILITY ★★★★★
Not quite the greatest on Earth

Utah is famous for the quality and quantity of its snow. Park City's record doesn't match those of Snowbird and Alta, but an annual average of 360 inches is still impressive, and ahead of most Colorado figures. When it falls it is 'well managed'. Snowmaking covers about 15% of the terrain.

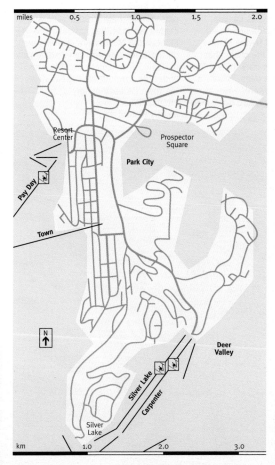

KEY FACTS

Resort	2105m
	6,900ft
Slopes	2105-3050m
	6,900-10,000ft
Lifts	16
Pistes	3,300 acres
Green	17%
Blue	52%
Black	31%
Snowmaking	15%

LIFT PASSES

Prices in US$

Age	1-day	6-day
under 13	69	342
13 to 64	107	570
65 plus	69	342

Free Under 7

Beginner Lower Mtn ticket ($66) covers First Time and 3 Kings lifts only

Note Prices quoted are advance-purchase prices

Alternative pass
Three Resort (Park City, Canyons, Deer Valley) International Pass available only to international visitors and in advance of holiday departure

FOR EXPERTS ★★★★
Lots of variety

There is a lot of excellent steep terrain at the top of the lift system. It is all marked as double diamond on the trail map, but many runs deserve only a single-diamond rating.

McConkey's Bowl is served by a six-pack and offers a range of open pitches and gladed terrain; we've had some great runs here on each of our visits. The slow, old Jupiter lift accesses the highest bowls, which include some serious terrain – with narrow couloirs, cliffs and cornices – as well as easier wide-open slopes. We had some enjoyable runs through fresh snow in lightly wooded terrain by heading to the right at the top of the lift, then skiing down without hiking. But if you are prepared to hike, you can find fresh powder most of the time – turn left for West Face, Pioneer Ridge and Puma Bowl, right for Scott's Bowl and the vast expanse of Pinecone Ridge, stretching for miles down the side of Thaynes Canyon.

Lower down, the side of Summit House ridge, serviced by the slow Thaynes and Motherlode chairs, has some little-used black runs, plus a few satisfying trails in the trees. There's a zone of steep runs towards town from further round the ridge. And don't miss Blueslip Bowl near Summit House – so

called because in the past when it was out of bounds, ski company employees caught skiing it were fired, and given their notice on a blue slip.

Skiers (no snowboarders, due to some long flat run-outs) should consider doing the Ski Utah Interconnect Tour – see the feature panel opposite. Park City Powder Cats offers snowcat skiing, and Wasatch Powderbird Guides offers heli-skiing.

FOR INTERMEDIATES ★★★★
OK for a day or two

There are blue runs served by all the main lifts, apart from Jupiter. The areas around the King Con high-speed quad and Silverlode six-pack have a dense network of great (but fairly short) cruising runs. There are also more difficult trails close by, for those looking for a challenge. The 'Signature Runs' and 'Adventure Alleys' (see the first paragraph under 'The Mountain') are good ideas and worth trying.

But there are few long, fast cruising runs – most trails are 1 to 2km, and many have long, flat run-outs. The Pioneer and McConkey's chairlifts are off the main drag and serve some very pleasant, often quiet runs. The runs under the Town lift have great views of the town. Mileage-hungry intermediates should explore other nearby resorts, too.

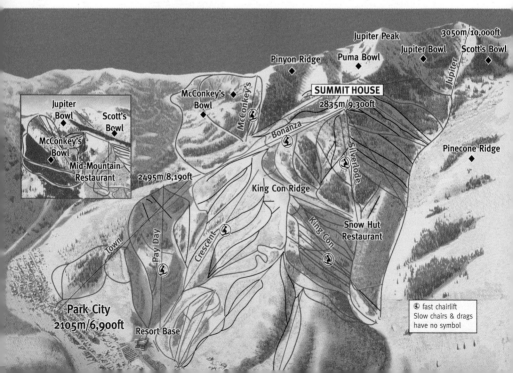

SCHOOLS

Park City
t 1 800 227 2754

Classes
One 3hr lesson $105
Private lessons
From $400 for 3hr

CHILDCARE

Guardian Angel
t 435 640 1229
Babysitting service
Kid's Clubhouse
t 940 1607
Ski Town Sitters
Babysitter finder
service
Signature Programs
(run by ski school)
t 1 800 227 2754
Ages 3½ to 5

Ski school
Ages 6 to 14

UK PACKAGES

Alpine Answers,
American Ski Classics,
Crystal, Crystal Finest,
Frontier, Inghams,
Momentum,
PowderBeds, Scott
Dunn, Ski Club
Freshtracks, Ski
Independence, Ski
Safari, Skitracer,
Skiworld, Thomson,
Virgin Snow

FOR BEGINNERS ★★★★☆
A good chance for fast progress
An excellent area for beginners. The 'Never Ever' deal offers first-timers a half-day taster lesson including a restricted lift pass and equipment rental. In the beginner area, novices start on moving carpets; classes graduate up the hill quite quickly, and there's a good, gentle 'easiest way down' – the three-and-a-half-mile Home Run. It's easy enough for most to manage after only a few lessons. The Town chair can be ridden down.

FOR BOARDERS ★★★★☆
Plenty of scope
It was not until 1996, when Park City won its Olympic bid, that the resort lifted its ban on snowboarding. Since then it has steamrollered ahead to attract boarders by building some of the best terrain parks in the world. And there's some great ungroomed terrain as well: the higher bowls offer treelined powder runs and great kicker-building spots. Beginners will have no trouble on the lower slopes.

FOR CROSS-COUNTRY ★★★☆☆
Some trails; lots of backcountry
There are 20km of prepared trails on the Park City golf course, next to the downhill area, and 30km at Soldier Hollow near Homestead Resort just out of town.

MOUNTAIN RESTAURANTS ★★☆☆☆
Standard self-service stuff
The Mid-Mountain Lodge is a picturesque 19th-century mine building

7 NIGHTS
FROM ONLY
£999

Inghams

PARK CITY
▶ NEW this Winter ▶ Extensive Powder

inghams.co.uk 01483 371 236 ABTA V4871 ATOL 0025

that was heaved up the mountain to its present location near the bottom of Pioneer chair. The food is standard self-service fare. The Summit House has chilli, pizza, soup and good views from a big deck (now with a much-needed glass surround); Snow Hut is a log building that often has an outdoor grill; Viking Yurt is a coffee house in a tent halfway down the Bonanza chairlift; Snowed Inn has 'the cheapest food on the mountain'. There are more options down at Resort Base – the Pig Pen Saloon 'does a very good sandwich and beer'.

SCHOOLS AND GUIDES ★★★★☆
Good past reports
We lack recent reports, but past reviews have been very positive.

FOR FAMILIES ★★☆☆☆
Well organized
There are a number of licensed carers. The ski school takes children from age three and a half. Book in advance.

THE SKI UTAH INTERCONNECT TOUR

Good skiers prepared to do some hiking should consider this excellent guided backcountry tour that runs five days a week from Deer Valley to Snowbird. (Two days a week it runs from Snowbird, but only as far as Solitude.) When we did it (several years back, starting from Park City) we got fresh tracks in knee-deep powder practically all day. After a warm-up run to weed out weak skiers, we went up the top chair, through a 'closed' gate in the area boundary and skied down a deserted, prettily wooded valley to Solitude. After taking the lifts to the top of Solitude we did a short traverse/walk, then down more virgin powder towards Brighton. After more powder runs and lunch back in Solitude, it was up the lifts and a 30-minute hike up the Highway to Heaven to north-facing, treelined slopes and a great little gully down into Alta. How much of Alta and Snowbird you get to ski depends on how much time is left. The price ($295) includes guides, lunch, lift tickets and transport home.

SNOWPIX.COM / CHRIS GILL

Build your own shortlist: www.wheretoskiandsnowboard.com

ACTIVITIES

Indoor Silver Mountain Sports Club and Spa (pools, hot tubs, sauna, steam room, gym); other fitness clubs, spa treatments, bowling, cinema, museum, galleries

Outdoor Ice skating, snowmobiles, sleigh rides, hot-air ballooning, dog sledding, tubing, snowshoeing, winter fly fishing, Alpine Coaster

GETTING THERE

Air Salt Lake City 55km/35 miles (45mins)

Phone numbers
From distant parts of the US, add the prefix 1 435; from abroad, add the prefix +1 435

TOURIST OFFICE

www.parkcitymountain.com
www.visitparkcity.com

STAYING THERE

We prefer to stay near Main Street and its bars and restaurants, but most accommodation is in the sprawling suburbs. These, such as Kimball Junction, are relatively cheap and convenient if you have a car.

Hotels There's a wide variety, from typical chains to individual little B&Bs.
*****Park City (200 2000) Swanky all-suite place on outskirts. Pool, sauna, steam, hot tub.
****Silver King (649 5500) De luxe hotel/condo complex at base of the slopes, with indoor-outdoor pool.
****Washington School House (649 3800) Historic old inn, well renovated, in a great location near Main Street.
***Best Western Landmark Inn (649 7300) At Kimball Junction. Pool.
***Park City Peaks (649 5000) On outskirts, large rooms, indoor-outdoor pool, outdoor hot tub. We stayed here and thought it adequate.
***Yarrow (649 7000) Another adequate base, a 15-minute walk from Main Street. Pool, hot tub.
Apartments There's a big range. The Town Lift condos near Main Street and Park Avenue condos are both modern and comfortable, the latter with a pool and hot tubs. Silver Cliff condos are adjacent to the slopes and have spacious units and two outdoor hot tubs. Other ski-in/ski-out recommendations from reporters are the Lodge at the Mountain Village, Silver Star and Snow Flower. Blue Church Lodge is a well-converted 19th-century Mormon church with luxury condos and rooms.

EATING OUT ★★★★★
Lots of choice

There are over 100 restaurants. Our favourites are Wahso (Asian fusion; excellent food, but slow service on our 2012 visit), 350 Main (new American – 'very good and excellent service') and Riverhorse (in a grand, high-ceilinged first-floor room with live music). Zoom is the old Union Pacific train depot, now a trendy restaurant owned by Robert Redford (past reports have been mixed though).

For more basic food we like the atmospheric No Name Saloon and enjoyed their signature buffalo burgers and draft beers on our last visit. Squatters is a good microbrewery a bit out of town. Other reporter tips include Baja Cantina (Mexican), Legends (American; at the mountain), and Bandit's Grill ('basic but satisfying', 'great cowboy food'). Bear in mind the option of upscale dining at next-door Deer Valley.

APRES-SKI ★★★★★
Plenty around

As the slopes close, Legends is the place to head for at Resort Base. After that, go to Main Street. The Wasatch Brew Pub makes its own ale. O'Shuck's and No Name Saloon are lively, and there's usually live music and dancing at weekends. Or try Cisero's or the Black Diamond Bar at the Jupiter Bowl bowling alley.

OFF THE SLOPES ★★★★★
Some things of interest

At the resort there's a roller coaster style toboggan ride on rails, tubing and a zipline. Backcountry snowmobiling, balloon flights and trips to Nevada for gambling are popular. There is a bowling alley. You can try lots of activities including the Olympic bob track at the Olympic Park down the road. There is a museum on Main Street. Robert Redford's Sundance Film Festival is held each January. There are lots of shops and galleries, plus discount shopping at a factory outlet mall at Kimball Junction. Salt Lake City is easily reached and has some good concerts, shopping and Mormon heritage sites.

Snowbird

A powder-pig paradise linked to neighbouring Alta; with big concrete and glass base buildings that remind us of Flaine

SNOWBIRD / DEREK SMITH

TOP 10 RATINGS	
Extent	★★★
Fast lifts	★★★★★
Queues	★★★
Snow	★★★★★
Expert	★★★★★
Intermediate	★★★
Beginner	★★
Charm	★
Convenience	★★★★★
Scenery	★★★

RPI	150
lift pass	£260
ski hire	£185
lessons	£190
food & drink	£145
total	**£780**

NEWS

2013/14: The Gad 2 double chairlift was replaced by a fast quad.

+ Unrivalled quantity and quality of powder snow, combined with fabulous ungroomed slopes

+ Link to Alta makes it one of the largest ski areas in the US

+ Slopes-at-the-door convenience

− Limited groomed intermediate runs, but more than at Alta

− Tiny, claustrophobic resort 'village'

− Stark concrete architecture

− Very quiet at night

There can be few places where nature has combined the steep with the deep better than at Snowbird and next-door Alta. The resorts' combined area is one of the top powder-pig paradises in the world (at least for skiers – boarders are banned from Alta). So it is a shame that Snowbird's concrete, purpose-built 'base village' is so lacking in ski resort ambience.

THE RESORT

Snowbird lies 40km from Salt Lake City in Little Cottonwood Canyon – just before Alta. Both the resort and (particularly) the approach road are prone to avalanches and closure: visitors are sometimes confined indoors for safety.

Village charm The resort buildings are mainly block-like and lack any semblance of charm.

Convenience The resort area and the slopes are spread along the road on the south side of the narrow canyon. The focal Snowbird Center (lift base/shops/restaurants) is towards the eastern, up-canyon end. All lodgings are within walking distance, and most are ski-in/ski-out. There are free shuttle-buses, and a service to Alta.

Scenery Snowbird's setting is rugged and rather Alpine. Hidden Peak's lofty heights give impressive views.

THE MOUNTAINS

Snowbird's link with Alta (see separate chapter) forms one of the largest ski areas in the US. The stats show Snowbird and Alta's ski areas to be of fairly similar size, but Snowbird's feels much bigger to us. There are free mountain tours at 9.30 and 10.30 each morning. The nursery slopes are floodlit three evenings a week.

Slopes The north-facing slopes rear up from the edge of the resort. Six access lifts are ranged along the valley floor, the main ones being the 125-person cable car (the Aerial Tram) to Hidden Peak, the Peruvian Express quad and the Gadzoom fast quad. To the west, in Gad Valley, there are runs ranging from very tough to very easy. Mineral Basin, behind Hidden Peak and accessed from there or through a tunnel with a moving carpet at the top of the Peruvian Express chair, has 500 acres of terrain for all abilities, but it can be badly affected by sun.

Fast lifts All the key lifts are fast.

Queues The big problem has always been the cable car, with queues of up to an hour at times. But the Peruvian Express chair provides an alternative way to almost the top and to Mineral Basin (from which you can get to the top via the Mineral Basin Express).

Terrain parks There is one aimed at beginners and intermediates with rails and jumps.

Snow reliability Like Alta, Snowbird averages 500 inches of snowfall a year – twice as much as some Colorado resorts and around 50% more than the nearby Park City area. But the snowfall in the last three seasons has been

SNOWBIRD

Snowbird looks much better viewed from a distance at night than it does close up in the cold light of day ↓

KEY FACTS

Resort	2470m
	8,100ft

For Snowbird and Alta combined area

Slopes	2365-3350m
	7,760-11,000ft
Lifts	22
Pistes	4,700 acres
Green	26%
Blue	39%
Black	35%
Snowmaking	12%

Snowbird only

Slopes	2365-3350m
	7,760-11,000ft
Lifts	11
Pistes	2,500 acres
Green	27%
Blue	38%
Black	35%
Snowmaking	21%

UK PACKAGES

Alpine Answers, Momentum, Ski Independence, Ski Safari, Skitracer, Skiworld

Phone numbers
From distant parts of the US, add the prefix 1 801; from abroad, add the prefix +1 801

TOURIST OFFICE

www.snowbird.com

---

well below average. There's snowmaking in busy areas.

Experts The trail map is liberally sprinkled with double-black diamonds, and some of the gullies off the Cirque ridge – Silver Fox and Great Scott, for example – are exceptionally steep and frequently neck-deep in powder. Lower down lurk the bump runs, including Mach Schnell – a great run straight down the fall line through trees. There is wonderful ski-anywhere terrain in the bowl beneath the high Little Cloud chair, and the Gad 2 lift opens up attractive tree runs (and is the best place to be in a white-out). Fantastic go-anywhere terrain under the High Baldy traverse is controlled by gates. Mineral Basin has some expert terrain too. Backcountry tours and heli- and cat-skiing are also offered.

Intermediates The winding Chip's Run provides the only comfortable route from the top back to town. There's good cruising in Mineral Basin – take the narrow Path to Paradise traverse for a wide blue-black and head up the Baldy Express lift for the easiest cruises. For adventurous intermediates wanting to try powder skiing, the bowl below the Little Cloud lift is a must. There are some challenging runs through the trees off the Gad 2 lift. The groomed runs don't add up to a lot but there's more than in Alta.

Beginners There is a nursery slope next to Cliff Lodge, a ski school Mountain Learning area part way up the hill and a special lift pass ($24). But progression to longer runs is not easy. Go and learn elsewhere.

Snowboarding Competent freeriders will have a wild time in Snowbird's powder, though there are some flat spots to beware of. Be aware that Alta bans boarders.

Cross-country No prepared trails (though there are in next-door Alta).

Mountain restaurants It's the Mid-Gad Lodge self-service or back to one of the bases – try the table-service Forklift and Rendezvous.

Schools and guides The school has a good reputation, though we lack recent reports.

Families Camp Snowbird takes children aged 12 and under. The 'kids ski free' programme allows children (six and under) to ski for free with an adult. Baby Thunder is a gentle family area.

STAYING THERE

Hotels There are several lodges and smaller condo blocks. Cliff Lodge, a huge concrete building, and The Lodge at Snowbird are both convenient and have pools and hot tubs, but they lack charm – and we lack recent reports.

Eating out Cliff Lodge and Snowbird Center are the focal points, with various options, including the 'fine dining' Aerie in the Cliff Lodge.

Après-ski Après-ski is a bit muted. The Tram Club and El Chanate Cantina are lively as the slopes close, but don't expect them to be later on.

Off the slopes There's not much to do apart from snowshoeing, snowmobiling and visiting Salt Lake City and the spas in various lodges.

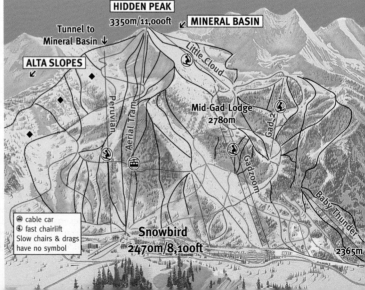

HIDDEN PEAK
3350m/11,000ft
MINERAL BASIN
Tunnel to Mineral Basin ↓
ALTA SLOPES
Little Cloud
Mid-Gad Lodge 2780m
Peruvian
Aerial Tram
Gad 2
Gadzoom
Baby Thunder
Snowbird
2470m/8,100ft
2365m

cable car
fast chairlift
Slow chairs & drags have no symbol

Rest of the West

This section of the book contains detailed chapters on just two resorts – Jackson Hole in Wyoming and Big Sky in Montana. Below are notes on these and various other resorts in different parts of the great chain of mountains that stretches from Washington in the north to New Mexico in the south.

UK PACKAGES
Grand Targhee Ski Safari

TANYA BOOTH

The super-quiet slopes of Big Sky ↓

The resorts of Washington state and Oregon are covered in our resort directory at the end of this book. We visited Oregon a few seasons back, when our exploration was hampered by poor early-season snow. If you want to try somewhere largely undiscovered by fellow Brits, Oregon is worth considering. The major resorts are **Mt Hood** (which has three separate areas of slopes: Mt Hood Meadows, Mt Hood Skibowl and Timberline) and **Mt Bachelor**. These get extended entries in the resort directory.

Sun Valley, Idaho, was the USA's first purpose-built resort, developed in the 1930s by the president of the Union Pacific Railway. It quickly became popular with the Hollywood movie set and has managed to retain its stylish image and ambience; it has one of our favourite luxury hotels. Also in Idaho is the USA's newest purpose-built resort – **Tamarack**, two hours north of Boise. The company developing the resort went bankrupt in 2009, but it has operated four days a week for the past few seasons, and continuously over the Christmas/New Year holiday period.

Jackson Hole in Wyoming is a resort with an impressive snow record and equally impressive steep slopes. Jackson town has a touristy Wild West cowboy atmosphere. Check out the separate chapter. A 90-minute drive from Jackson over the Teton pass (slower if you go by excursion bus) brings you to **Grand Targhee**, which gets even more snow. The slopes are usually blissfully empty, and are much easier than at Jackson. The main Fred's Mountain offers 1,500 acres and 610m vertical accessed from a central fast quad. One-third of smaller Peaked Mountain is accessed by a fast quad, while the rest – around 500 acres – is used for guided snowcat-skiing.

About four hours north of Jackson, just inside Montana, is **Big Sky**, which has now absorbed neighbouring Moonlight Basin and much smaller Spanish Peaks to become the biggest ski resort in the US. When we visited, we were very impressed – particularly by the lack of crowds. Check out the Big Sky chapter. From Big Sky you might also visit **Bridger Bowl**, a 90-minute drive away. It boasts broad, steep, lightly wooded slopes that offer wonderful powder descents after a fresh snowfall.

A long way south of all these resorts, **Taos** in New Mexico is the most southerly major resort in the USA, and because of its isolated location is largely unknown on the international market. There's a small chalet-style base village with a handful of lodges; the adobe town of Taos, home to many famous artists and writers over the years, is 30km down the road. There's some good terrain for all standards, but the ski area is best known for challenging terrain, some of which involves hiking.

BIG SKY RESORT

Big Sky

The USA's biggest ski area, with extraordinarily quiet slopes; unappealing modern resort village, though

RATINGS

The mountains

Extent	★★★★
Fast lifts	★★
Queues	★★★★★
Terrain p'ks	★★★★
Snow	★★★★★
Expert	★★★★
Intermediate	★★★★
Beginner	★★★★★
Boarder	★★★★
X-country	★★★★
Restaurants	★
Schools	★★★★
Families	★★★★

The resort

Charm	★★
Convenience	★★★★
Scenery	★★★
Eating out	★★★
Après-ski	★
Off-slope	★★

RPI 150

lift pass	£350
ski hire	£125
lessons	£170
food & drink	£120
total	**£765**

NEWS

2014/15: Gladed areas are being extended. Pinnacle restaurant at the top of Andesite will reopen after a closure of three or four years.

2013/14: In 2013 the resort acquired the two smaller resorts right next door – Moonlight Basin and Spanish Peaks. Huntley Lodge and Mountain Mall were revamped and new shops opened, including a grocery and deli.

➕ Biggest lift-served ski area in the USA – comfortably bigger than Vail; big vertical by US standards, too

➕ By far the quietest slopes you will find in a major resort, anywhere

➕ Among the cheapest resorts in the US for food and drink

➕ Excellent snow record

➕ Some slope-side lodgings, but ...

➖ Many condos are spread widely away from the lift base

➖ Resort amenities are limited, with little choice of nightlife and no resort-village atmosphere

➖ Tiny top lift accessing the most testing terrain is prone to queues

➖ Getting there from the UK involves at least one plane change

Big Sky is phenomenal. Last year it overtook Vail in the size stakes by acquiring two adjacent mountains – small but interesting Moonlight Basin, with which it shared a lift pass, and tiny (and much less interesting) Spanish Peaks, a private resort. The area now totals 5,750 acres; its lifts can carry 29,000 people an hour. Typically there are only about 3,000 people on the hill – so you get about 2 acres of snow each.

(That's enough statistics – Ed.) The point is, skiing Big Sky is unlike skiing anywhere else. As an experienced reporter put it this year, 'the busiest runs would be considered empty in other resorts'. The resort has other attractions – notably abundant powder, steeps and big vertical. But if you like ambling around in the evening soaking up the mountain village atmosphere, forget it.

THE RESORT

Big Sky is set amid the wide open spaces of Montana, one hour from Bozeman airport. The resort has been purpose-built at the foot of the slopes, and the main focus of development is Mountain Village, at the lift base. Bridger Bowl ski area (75 trails, 8 chairs) is an easy day trip by car.

VILLAGE CHARM ★★
Some way to go
Mountain Village is a hotchpotch of buildings in different styles set vaguely around a traffic-free central plaza and bordered by car parks and unattractive service roads. There are a few hotels, a handful of bars, restaurants and shops, and some slope-side condos. The French-style underground Mountain Mall has further shops and gives access to many of these facilities. There are also cabins and condos around the Moonlight Basin lift base at Moonlight Lodge.

CONVENIENCE ★★★★
Generally fine
There is quite a bit of lodging at or close to the lift base. Some outlying condos and houses are served by lifts

to the slopes, but most rely on the 'comparatively poor' free bus services; a car is a better idea.

SCENERY ★★★
The lone ranger
Lone Mountain is Big Sky's signature peak, its distinctive summit rising over 1000m above the village and Andesite Mountain's wooded slopes. From the top, there are panoramic views of Montana and Yellowstone park.

THE MOUNTAINS

The formula is familiar in America: mainly steep open slopes at the top, and gentler wooded slopes lower down. There are free mountain tours. Recent visitors complain of poor signposting, especially for some black runs and gladed blues, and inconsistent trail classification.

EXTENT OF THE SLOPES ★★★★
Big – the name's right
Yes, it is big – in terms of piste extent, now in the top 10 areas in the world, and over 7km from end to end. **Lone Mountain** provides the resort's poster shot, with some seriously steep, open upper slopes. From Mountain Village a

↑ The tiny Lone Peak Tram drip-feeds skiers on to the steepest runs at the top of the mountain
STUART McWILLIAM

KEY FACTS

Resort	2285m
	7,500ft
Slopes	2070-3405m
	6,800-11,165ft
Lifts	29
Pistes	5,750 acres
Green	16%
Blue	26%
Black	58%
Snowmaking	10%

LIFT PASSES

Prices in US$ inc tax

Age	1-day	6-day
under 11	50	303
11 to 18	81	488
18 to 69	102	575
70 plus	81	488

Free Under 6; also under 11 with lessons
Beginner First half-day lesson includes a base area pass
Notes Prices include 3% tax and are online advance purchase prices. Discounts if purchased with lodging; half-day pass available

fast quad goes to mid-mountain. From there you can get to the Lone Peak triple chair, which takes you up to the Lone Peak Tram – two 15-person gondola cabins, operated as if they were a cable car. This leads to the top and fabulous 360° views. The Dakota triple chairlift serves Lone's south face and its steep bowls and glades. But a couple of reporters have found the area prone to closure due to avalanche risk. Lone Mountain's lower slopes are wooded and varied, as are those of **Andesite Mountain**, which has less vertical but three of the five fast lifts, including one from Mountain Village. At the bottom of Andesite's Southern Comfort chair is one of the two chairs on the very limited slopes of newly acquired **Spirit Mountain**, formerly Spanish Peaks. (On another flank of Andesite is part of the famously exclusive private resort, the Yellowstone Club.) From various points on Lone Mountain you can head down to the **Moonlight Basin** slopes, which start with a slow chair from Moonlight Lodge. Runs from the top of that lead to the Six Shooter fast chair, from the Madison base area, which, together with the slow Lone Tree quad, serves nearly all Moonlight's wooded, largely easy intermediate terrain. The Headwaters double chair at the top serves expert-only runs.

FAST LIFTS ★★☆☆☆
Needs some more
There are five fast quad chairs, but many of the chairs are still old triples and doubles.

QUEUES ★★★★★
Only for the Tram
The tiny Tram naturally builds serious queues on powder days and in peak season; but at least that means you don't get crowds on the top runs. Queues are rare otherwise: 'Even on a Saturday morning powder day, the most we stood in line was two minutes,' says a 2012 visitor. Usually 'no queues at all,' says a March 2014 reporter.

TERRAIN PARKS ★★★★☆
Plenty of choice
Swifty Park on Lone Peak has large jumps, rails and boxes for advanced riders. There is a natural half-pipe near the Lone Peak triple chair and an intermediate park, Swifty 2.0, near the village. There is a beginner park by the Explorer chair. The Moonlight slopes have the Zero Gravity park under the Six Shooter chair, and a beginner park near the base.

SNOW RELIABILITY ★★★★★
No worries here
Snowfall averages 400 inches – more than most resorts in Colorado. Grooming is 'exceptional' too.

FOR EXPERTS ★★★★☆
Enough to keep you amused
All of the terrain accessed from the Tram is single- or double-black diamond. The steepest runs are the Big Couloir on the Big Sky side and the North Summit Snowfield on the Moonlight side. Take local advice on equipment and guidance.

Big Sky

589

Build your own shortlist: www.wheretoskiandsnowboard.com

There are easier ways down, though – Liberty Bowl is easiest. Marx and Lenin are a little steeper. The Dakota Territory has 212 acres of black-diamond glades, chutes and high bowls, to skier's right of Liberty Bowl – served by a triple chairlift. Lower down, the Lone Peak Triple, Challenger and Shedhorn chairs also serve good steep terrain. There are some excellent gladed runs, especially on Andesite (and more are being created). In the Moonlight sector the Headwaters is the biggest challenge – but it gets windblown and you may have to pick your way through rocks at the top. The further you hike to skier's left the steeper the couloirs. There are some good gladed runs lower down.

FOR INTERMEDIATES ★★★★
Great deserted cruising

The bulk of the terrain is of intermediate difficulty (including lots of easy blacks). The main complaint we have is that they don't seem to groom any blacks – with no traffic, they would be fabulous when groomed. But there is lots of excellent cruising on empty blue runs served by fast chairs: Ramcharger, Southern Comfort and Thunder Wolf on Andesite, Swift Current on Lone Mountain, and Six Shooter in the Moonlight sector. Several wide, gentle bowls offer a good introduction to off-piste. And there are some good easy glade runs, such as Singlejack at Moonlight and The Congo on Andesite. In general the groomed blues at

cable car
fast chairlift
Slow chairs & drags have no symbol

Andesite has great cruising runs, although the vertical isn't huge

ANDESITE
2680m/8,800ft

Spirit Mountain lifts and slopes

Southern Comfort

Ramcharger

Thunder Wolf

Mountain Village
2285m/
7,500ft

2070m/6,800ft
Lone Moose Meadows

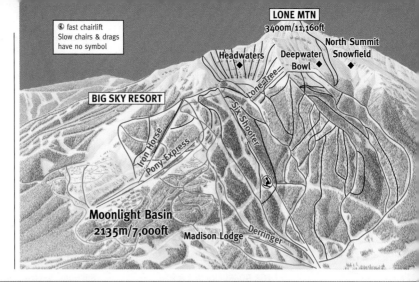

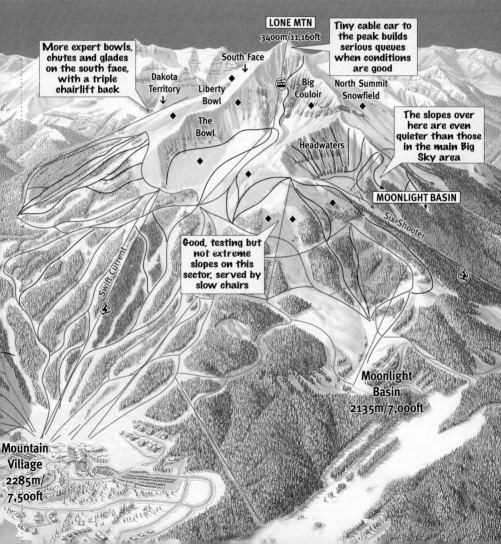

Resort news and key links: www.wheretoskiandsnowboard.com

SCHOOLS

Big Sky
t 995 5743

Classes
Half day (2.5hr) $84
(inc 3% tax)

Private lessons
From $293 for 2hr

CHILDCARE

Lone Peak Playhouse
t 993 2220
Ages 6mnth to 8yr

Ski school
Ages 4 to 14

ACTIVITIES

Indoor Solace Spa
(massage, beauty
treatments), fitness
centres in hotels

Outdoor Snowmobiles,
snowshoeing, sleigh
rides, tubing, climbing
wall, ice climbing,
ziplining, high ropes
course, bungee
trampolining, visiting
Yellowstone National
Park

UK PACKAGES

American Ski Classics,
Ski Bespoke, Ski
Independence, Ski
Safari

GETTING THERE

Air Bozeman 70km/
45 miles (1hr15)

Central reservations
Call 995 5000; toll-
free number (from
within the US)
1 800 548 4486

Phone numbers
From distant parts of
the US, add the prefix
1 406; from abroad,
add the prefix +1 406

TOURIST OFFICE

www.bigskyresort.com

Moonlight are easier than those on Lone, especially the ones served by the Lone Tree chair. Adventurous intermediates could try Liberty Bowl from the top of the Tram; but be prepared for a rocky, windswept traverse between wooden barriers at the top to access the run.

FOR BEGINNERS ★★★★★
Ideal – lots of lovely greens
There's a good, well-developed nursery area at the base of the Explorer chair with a separate Explorer pass. There are long, deserted greens to progress to from the Explorer and Swift Current chairs, and on Andesite. The Berringer quad at the Madison base in the Moonlight sector is good, too.

FOR BOARDERS ★★★★☆
Something for everyone
The terrain has lots of variety, with few flats. Experts will enjoy the steeps and the glades, freestylers the good terrain parks, and novices the easy cruising runs served by chairlifts.

FOR CROSS-COUNTRY ★★★★☆
Head for the Ranch
There are 85km of 'excellent' trails at Lone Mountain Ranch ('helpful staff'), and more at West Yellowstone.

MOUNTAIN RESTAURANTS ★☆☆☆☆
Back to base for lunch?
The main weakness. The re-opening of the Pinnacle is welcome news. Shedhorn Grill is a yurt on the south side of Lone Mountain, doing simple meals – 'great fun, and decent BBQ nosh'. Then there's the Black Kettle on the front of Lone Mountain – soup and snacks – and the Burrito Shack at the top of the Swift Current chairlift.

SCHOOLS AND GUIDES ★★★★☆
Good reputation
The Big Sky school has a good reputation. Visitors have praised the beginner snowboard classes: 'Exceptionally happy with the quality of the instruction.'

FOR FAMILIES ★★★★☆
Usual high US standard
Lone Peak Playhouse in the slope-side Snowcrest Lodge will take kids to and from ski school. Children five years and under ski free with an adult. There's a Kids' Club in the Huntley Lodge – 'very well run' according to a 2014 visitor who put two kids in it.

STAYING THERE

Hotels There's not much choice.
★★★★Summit (548 4486) Central, slope-side, good rooms, outdoor hot pool, good views, and shuttle to other base areas. 'Best property here, breakfast excellent,' says a 2014 visitor.
★★★Huntley Lodge (548 4486) Big Sky's original hotel; central, part of Mountain Mall; outdoor pool, hot tubs, saunas. Our 2014 reporter was happy but beware noisy rooms. 'Phenomenal breakfast buffet.'
★★★The Lodge at Big Sky (995 7858) Five minutes' walk to slopes; a shuttle at peak times. Indoor pool, indoor/outdoor hot tubs. 'Large rooms, friendly staff, but basic food.'
Apartments Reader tips include Stillwater, Village Center, Arrowhead, Snowcrest, Big Horn, Black Eagle and, way out of town, Powder Ridge ('fantastic accommodation', 'beautiful' said two 2013 reporters). Check location carefully.

EATING OUT ★★★☆☆
A fair choice for a small place
One 2014 visitor particularly enjoyed the 'excellent' Peaks restaurant in the Summit hotel – 'delicious pheasant ragout'. The Andiamo Italian Grille is very popular and pleases most reporters. Others tip MR Hummers ('cheerful staff, good atmosphere'; 'good kids' menu, really nice steak'), Whiskey Jack's (burgers, 'fresh and tasty' Tex-Mex, 'huge portions'), the Cabin ('excellent gourmet style food – elk and bison') and Lone Peak Brewery ('excellent eatery').

APRES-SKI ★☆☆☆☆
Limited
Things are generally quiet but there is live music in a couple of spots. Whiskey Jack's is the main après bar – 'good atmosphere'. Scissorbills Saloon is a 'great American bar'.

OFF THE SLOPES ★★☆☆☆
Mainly the great outdoors
There's snowmobiling, snowshoeing, sleigh rides, dog sledding, a floodlit tubing hill, ziplines, snowcat tours, treatments at the Solace Spa; the Huntley Lodge pool and spa are open to all for a fee. You can visit Yellowstone National Park (highly recommended by reporters); a reader also recommends the Grizzly and Wolf Discovery Centre at West Yellowstone.

JACKSON HOLE / JONATHAN SELKOWITZ

Jackson Hole

Touristy 'Wild West' town 12 miles from big, exciting slopes, and a small, modern base village with a famous après-ski saloon

RATINGS

The mountains

Extent	★★★
Fast lifts	★★★★
Queues	★★★
Terrain p'ks	★★★
Snow	★★★★
Expert	★★★★★
Intermediate	★★
Beginner	★★★
Boarder	★★★
X-country	★★★★
Restaurants	★★
Schools	★★★★
Families	★★★★

The resort

Charm	★★★
Convenience	★★★★
Scenery	★★★
Eating out	★★★★★
Après-ski	★★★★
Off-slope	★★★

RPI 145

lift pass	£310
ski hire	£140
lessons	£180
food & drink	£120
total	**£750**

+ Lots of expert-only terrain and one of the USA's biggest verticals

+ Jackson town has an entertaining Wild West ambience

+ Unspoiled, remote location

+ Excellent snow record

+ Some unique off-slope diversions

+ The airport is only minutes away

– The town is 30 minutes by bus from the slopes, though the lift base has attractive places to stay

– Low altitude and sunny orientation mean snow can deteriorate quickly

– Groomed cruising is in relatively short supply

– Getting there from the UK involves at least one plane change

When we first visited Jackson in the early 1990s, you went for its gnarly mountain, shedloads of snow and big vertical – simple as that. It had few facilities at the base or on the mountain, and an antiquated lift system. The place attracted hardcore expert skiers, many of them regulars or locals.

Now there's a modern (though still inadequate) cable car, a gondola, three fast chairs serving easy and intermediate terrain, a bunch of upscale hotels at the base, a table-service restaurant on the mountain – and many more beginners, intermediates and families around as a result. Some old stagers hate the changes; we love them. Now, we get the best of both worlds – superb snowy steeps on the one hand, decent lunches and stylish lodgings on the other.

THE RESORT

The town of Jackson, with its wooden sidewalks, cowboy saloons and pool halls, sits on the edge of Jackson Hole – a high, flat valley surrounded by mountain ranges in Wyoming. Jackson gets many more visitors in summer than in winter, thanks to the nearby national parks. The slopes are a short drive away. At the base is Teton Village, which has developed a lot over the past few years, with an increased choice of bars, restaurants and hotels – some notably upscale.

A popular excursion by car or daily bus is over the Teton pass to the smaller resort of Grand Targhee, which gets even more snow. Read the Rest of the West intro.

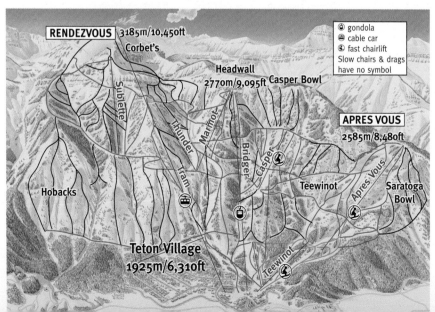

RENDEZVOUS 3185m/10,450ft
Corbet's
Sublette
Headwall
2770m/9,095ft Casper Bowl
Thunder
Marmot
Bridger
Casper
APRES VOUS
2585m/8,480ft
Tram
Tram
Hobacks
Teewinot
Apres Vous
Saratoga Bowl
Teton Village
1925m/6,310ft
Teewinot

gondola
cable car
fast chairlift
Slow chairs & drags have no symbol

Resort news and key links: www.wheretoskiandsnowboard.com

NEWS

2014/15: In the run-up to its 50th season (15/16) Jackson will be announcing some major developments we can expect 'in the coming years'.

KEY FACTS

Resort	1925m
	6,310ft
Slopes	1925-3185m
	6,310-10,450ft
Lifts	13
Pistes	2,500 acres
Green	10%
Blue	40%
Black	50%
Snowmaking	8%

LIFT PASSES

Prices in US$

Age	1-day	6-day
under 15	63	305
15 to 64	101	503
65 plus	82	401

Free Under 6 (Eagle's Rest and Teewinot lifts only)

Beginner Ticket for Eagle's Rest and Teewinot lifts ($29)

Notes Prices are online advance purchase; ticket window prices are higher; afternoon ticket available

Alternative passes Grand Targhee; Snow King Mountain

VILLAGE CHARM ★★★★★
Cowboy or convenient

To amuse summer tourists, Jackson town cultivates a Wild West flavour – saloons with swing doors, country and western music and dancing, cowboys in Stetsons. It has lots of clothing and souvenir shops, plus upmarket galleries aimed at second-home owners. In winter it's all a bit quiet, but still quite amusing and pleasant. The friendly and helpful locals are praised by reporters. For a modern lift base development, Teton Village is quite pleasant.

CONVENIENCE ★★★★★
Stay at the slopes

From Jackson, getting to the slopes means a $3 30-minute bus ride or a slightly quicker drive followed by payment of $15 to park close to the mountain ($5 further away). Our preferred option is to stay at the base and take the bus into town for the occasional night out.

SCENERY ★★★★★
You can see forever

You get great long views across the wide plain of Jackson Hole from the slopes, which rise abruptly from the valley floor.

THE MOUNTAINS

Most of the slopes are below the treeline, but most of the forest is not dense. The trail classification is pretty accurate; but some visitors reckon the toughest single diamonds would be double diamonds elsewhere. There are free mountain tours twice daily.

EXTENT OF THE SLOPES ★★★★★
One big mountain, one small

The main lifts out of Teton Village are the Bridger gondola and the Tram (US-speak for cable car). The Tram takes you up 1260m to the summit of **Rendezvous** mountain – an exceptional vertical for the US. It can be very cold and windy at the top, even when it's warm and calm below. To the right looking up, fast quads access **Apres Vous** mountain, with half the vertical of Rendezvous and mostly much gentler runs. Between these two, the Bridger gondola goes up over a broad mountainside split by gullies, and gives speedy access to the slow Thunder and Sublette chairs – serving some of the steepest terrain on Rendezvous – and the fast Casper chair, from which you can traverse over to the Apres Vous area.

Snow King is a separate ski area right by Jackson town. Locals use it at lunchtime and in the evenings (it's partly floodlit).

FAST LIFTS ★★★★★
Few at mid-mountain

Fast lifts access both mountains; slow chairs rule on the upper part of Rendezvous, but a reader points out that they rise steeply, and permit a lot of vertical in a day.

QUEUES ★★★★★
Only for the Tram

The Tram holds only 100 people, and many locals do laps on it all day long. So it generates queues – we waited 20 minutes on our last visit, and a more recent visitor waited 30 minutes. On powder days, the queue can start at 7.30am, a reporter says. One reader's tip in these circumstances is to head for Apres Vous and 'great first tracks in Saratoga Bowl' (though the Teewinot chair to get there can be busy these days). Queues elsewhere on Rendezvous are rare, unless wind closes the Tram.

TERRAIN PARKS ★★★★★
Six plus a pipe

In addition to two terrain parks on the lower mountain with features from beginner through to advanced, there are four Burton Stash parks featuring wooden and natural obstacles. Plus there's a half-pipe; and Dick's Ditch is a 450m-long natural half-pipe.

SNOW RELIABILITY ★★★★★
Deep snow, strong sun

The claimed average of 460 inches of snow is much more than the average for most Colorado (and some Utah) resorts. But the base elevation is low for the Rockies, and the slopes are fairly sunny – they basically face south-east (Apres Vous more south). The steep lower slopes, such as the Hobacks, may be in poor shape, and on our last visit the higher slopes were frozen solid following a melt. The flanks of some ridges have a more northerly orientation, and a reporter says that Saratoga Bowl keeps its snow well. Locals claim that you can expect powder roughly half the time. Don't assume early-season conditions will be good.

↑ Teton Village at the base has developed hugely in the years we've been visiting
TANYA BOOTH

Build your own shortlist: www.wheretoskiandsnowboard.com

FOR EXPERTS ★★★★★
Best for the brave

For the good skier or boarder who wants challenges without the expense of off-piste guides, Jackson is one of the world's best resorts. Rendezvous mountain offers virtually nothing but black slopes. The routes down the main Rendezvous Bowl are not particularly fearsome; but some of the alternatives are. Go down the East Ridge at least once to stare over the lip of the notorious Corbet's Couloir. It's the jump in that's special; the slope you land on is a mere 50°, people say.

Below Rendezvous Bowl, the wooded flanks of Cheyenne Bowl offer serious challenges, at the steep end of the single-black diamond spectrum. If instead you take the ridge run that skirts this bowl to the right, you get to the Hobacks – a huge area of open and lightly wooded slopes, gentler than those higher up, but still black and usually with big moguls; check snow conditions before embarking on these – there's no turning back.

Corbet's aside, most of the steepest slopes are more easily reached from the slightly lower quad chairs. From the Sublette chair, you have direct access to the short but seriously steep Alta chutes, and to the less severe Laramie Bowl beside them. Or you can track over to Tensleep Bowl – pausing to inspect Corbet's from below – and on to the less extreme (and less chute-like) Expert Chutes, and the single-black Cirque and Headwall areas. Casper Bowl often has good powder, and the Crags is an area of bowls, chutes and glades reached by hiking – both are accessed through gates. Thunder chair serves steep, narrow, fairly shady chutes. Again, the lower part of the mountain here offers lightly wooded single-diamond slopes.

The gondola serves some good, underused expert terrain, particularly to skier's left of the lift, including the glades of Woolsey and Moran Woods. Even Apres Vous has serious, usually quiet, single blacks in Saratoga Bowl.

The gates into the backcountry access over 3,000 acres of amazing terrain, which should be explored only with guidance. You can stay out overnight at a backcountry yurt (tent). There are some helicopter operations.

FOR INTERMEDIATES ★★★★★
Exciting for some

They have tried hard to improve the intermediate terrain, with fast lifts and much more grooming than in the old days. There are good cruising runs on the front face of Apres Vous, from the Casper chair and top-to-bottom quite gentle blues from the gondola. But they don't add up to a great deal of mileage, and you shouldn't consider Jackson unless you want to tackle ungroomed runs. It's then important to get guidance on steepness and snow conditions. A good number of blues are identified on the trail map as more difficult, and many of these are less

SCHOOLS

Jackson Hole
t 739 2779

Classes
Full day $140
Private lessons
Half day (3hr) from $440

CHILDCARE

Kids Ranch
t 739 2788
Ages 6mnth to 6yr

Ski school
Ages 7 to 14

JACKSON HOLE MOUNTAIN RESORT
The 'new' Tram more than doubled the hourly capacity of the old one when built in 2008, but demand still exceeds supply ↓

frequently groomed too – these are the places to get the hang of powder. The steepest single blacks are steep, intimidating when mogulled and fearsome when hard. The daily grooming map is worth consulting, but falling snow will mean moguls form.

FOR BEGINNERS ★★★★★
Fine, up to a point
There are good broad, gentle beginner slopes and a lift pass covering the two chairs that serve them. The progression to the blue Werner run off the Apres Vous chair is gradual enough and the mid-mountain blues from the Casper chair are reached via the chairs from the beginner area. But few other runs will help build confidence.

FOR BOARDERS ★★★★★
Steep and deep thrills
Jackson Hole is a cult resort for expert snowboarders. It's not bad for novices either. But intermediates not wishing to venture off the groomed runs will find the resort limited. Six terrain parks and a half-pipe provide the freestyle thrills. There are some good snowboard shops, including the Hole-in-the-Wall at Teton Village.

FOR CROSS-COUNTRY ★★★★★
Plenty of scenic choices
The Saddlehorn Nordic Center at Teton has 17km of trails and organizes trips into the National Parks.

MOUNTAIN RESTAURANTS ★★★★★
Bridger blossoms
The complex at the top of the Bridger gondola has a coffee shop and fast food pizza area downstairs, and upstairs a light and airy self-service with good views serving fresh stir-fry Asian dishes, as well as standard fare. We enjoyed the Couloir table-service section – sit near the entrance for great views over the valley and town through floor-to-ceiling windows, or further in for views of the Headwall and Corbet's. The food is good but not gourmet – burgers, salads, upmarket sandwiches, pasta. Corbet's Cabin has 'great waffles', and the Casper at the base of the Casper chairlift does a wide range of self-service food. There are simple snack bars at four other points on the mountain. There are some excellent places at the base, notably in various hotels.

SCHOOLS AND GUIDES ★★★★★
Learn to tackle the steeps
The school is highly regarded and has generated favourable reports. As well as the usual lessons, there are also special Camps on certain dates (pre-booking required). An experienced regular visitor reckons this is the best school in the US, and this year recommends particularly the 'fun, great value' Elevate Women's Camp for intermediate/expert skiers.

Rendezvous Backcountry Tours has been recommended for exploring the backcountry from Teton Pass.

FOR FAMILIES ★★★★★
Adventures on the Ranch
We've seen lots of kids around having fun here. The 'Kids' Ranch', near the Bridger gondola, offers childcare and ski/snowboard lessons, as well as pizza parties in the evenings.

STAYING THERE

Teton Village is our preferred base. You can catch the bus to town for a night out – the last one back is around 11pm. Some town hotels are far from central.
Hotels Because winter is low season, town hotel prices are low.
TETON VILLAGE
*****Four Seasons Resort (732 5000) Stylish luxury, with art on the walls, superb skier services, health club, an exceptional outdoor pool; perfect position just above the base.

UK PACKAGES

Alpine Answers,
American Ski Classics,
Elegant Resorts,
Frontier, Inghams,
Momentum, Oxford Ski
Co, Scott Dunn, Ski
Bespoke, Ski
Independence, Ski
Monterosa, Ski Safari,
Skitracer, Skiworld

ACTIVITIES

Indoor Fitness
centres, spas (in
hotels), concerts,
wildlife art and other
museums

Outdoor Snowmobiles,
snowshoeing, sleigh
rides, dog sledding,
paragliding, National
Park tours

Phone numbers
From distant parts of
the US, add the prefix
1 307; from abroad,
add the prefix +1 307

TOURIST OFFICE

www.jacksonhole.com

****Snake River Lodge & Spa** (732
6000) Smartly welcoming and
comfortable, with fine spa facilities.
****Terra** (739 4000) Smart, boutique
'eco' hotel, rooftop 'infinity' hot tub,
pool. Spa. Nice breakfast cafe. No bar.
****Teton Mountain Lodge & Spa**
(855 318 6669) Very comfortable.
Good pool, fitness, hot tub, spa.
***Alpenhof** (733 3242) Tirolean-style,
with varied rooms, but 'friendly, great
value and ultra-convenient', according
to a 2014 visitor. Good food, relaxed
bar. Pool, sauna, hot tub, spa.
*Hostel** (733 3415) Basic, good value
and recommended by a reporter.

JACKSON TOWN
****Rusty Parrot Lodge** (733 2000)
Stylish, small, with a rustic feel. Hot
tub, spa.
****Wort** (733 2190) Central, above
Silver Dollar Bar. Hot tub. Comfortable.
***Lodge at Jackson Hole** (739 9703)
Western-style on outskirts. Big rooms.
Free breakfast. Indoor/outdoor pools,
spa, hot tub. Shuttle to the slopes.
***Parkway Inn** (733 3143) Central.
'Decent-sized rooms. Friendly. Highly
recommended.' Free breakfast. Pool,
sauna, hot tubs. Shuttle to the slopes.
49'er Inn and Suites (733 7550)
Central, good value, free breakfast and
shuttle.
The Lexington (733 2648) Fairly
central. Pool, hot tubs, free breakfast
and shuttle.
BETWEEN THE TWO
*****Amangani Resort** (734 7333)
Hedonistic luxury in isolated position
way above the valley.
****Spring Creek Ranch** (733 8833)
Exclusive retreat; cross-country on
hand. Hot tub, spa, shuttle.
Apartments There is lots of choice at
Teton Village and better-value places a
mile or two away. Surprisingly little in
and around Jackson town. Love Ridge
and Snow King are 'good value'.

EATING OUT ★★★★★
A wide range of options
Jackson offers a range of excellent
dining options. To check out menus,
get hold of the local dining guide.
  At Teton Village, Il Villaggio Osteria
at the hotel Terra has a good choice of
Italian and seafood dishes. The Couloir
at the top of the gondola opens on
Thursday and Friday nights with a
four-course gourmet menu for $95 –
we had great foie gras and bison.
  In Jackson town there is a wide
choice. Our regular Jackson reporter

favours the 'superb' Wild Sage at the
Rusty Parrot Lodge, and also rates the
Gamefish at Snake River Lodge. Not to
be confused with the Snake River
brew-pub – 'great, happy atmosphere'
and good beers – or the more upscale
Snake River Grill. We loved the Asian/
Japanese-fusion dishes to share at The
Kitchen. The Cadillac Grille (steaks,
burgers, seafood) is 'great for families'.
Blue Lion is small and serves seafood
and meat dishes. Other suggestions:
the Merry Piglets (Mexican), Bubba's
BBQ, Thai Me Up and Bon Appe-Thai
('the real thing, with authentic herbs
and flavours').

APRES-SKI ★★★★
Amusing saloons
The renowned Mangy Moose is the
focus of après-ski activity at Teton
Village – a big, happy place, often
with live music – though it closed at
10pm mid-week during our last stay.
Nick Wilson's Cowboy Cafe is a popular
hangout for locals and staff. In town,
the Silver Dollar Bar (with 2,032 silver
dollars inlaid in the counter) was
packed with locals dancing to live
country music at 8pm on the Saturday
night. Round the corner the big Million
Dollar Cowboy Bar, featuring saddles
as bar stools, gets lively later and also
has live music and dancing. The
Rancher is an upstairs bar with pool
and live music and attracts a younger
crowd. Town Square Tavern also has
pool and often live music. Out of
town, the Stagecoach Inn at Wilson is
famously lively on Sunday nights.

OFF THE SLOPES ★★★
'Great' outdoor diversions
Yellowstone National Park is 100km to
the north. You can tour the park by
snowcat or snowmobile with a guide;
numbers are now restricted to reduce
pollution. Some visitors really enjoy
the park; we were underwhelmed –
largely because of the noise and
fumes from the snowmobiles and
driving everywhere in convoy. The
National Elk Refuge, with the largest
elk herd in the US, is next to Jackson
and across the road from the National
Museum of Wildlife Art. Reporters
recommend both – and walks beside
the Snake river, spotting eagles and
moose. In town there are some 40
galleries and museums plus Western
arts and crafts shops. Shopping and
restaurant discounts can be gained by
joining the Jackson Hole Ski Club ($30).

Jackson Hole

Build your own shortlist: **www.wheretoskiandsnowboard.com**

AMERICAN SKIING COMPANY / NATHAN BILOW

New England

You go to Utah for the deepest snow, to Colorado for the lightest powder and swankiest resorts, to California for big mountains and relatively low prices. You go to New England for ... well, for what? Extreme cold? Rock-hard artificial snow? Mountains too limited to be of interest beyond New Jersey? Yes and no: all of these preconceptions have some basis, and in the end the East can't compete with the West. But they don't give the full picture.

PACKAGES

Killington American Ski Classics, Ski Independence, Ski Safari, Skitracer, Skiworld, Virgin Snow
Stowe American Ski Classics, Elegant Resorts, Ski Independence, Ski Safari, Skitracer, Virgin Snow

Yes, it can be cold: one of our reporters recorded –27°C, with wind chill producing a perceived –73°C. Early in the season, people routinely wear face masks to prevent frostbite. It can also be warm – another reporter had a whole week of rain that washed away the early-season snow. The thing about New England's weather is that it varies – rather like old England's. The locals' favourite saying is: 'If you don't like the weather, wait two minutes.'

Many of the resorts get impressive amounts of natural snow over the season – in some years. But New England doesn't usually get much deep powder to play in. And snowmaking plays a big part in the resorts' operations. They have big snow-gun installations, designed to ensure a long season and to help the slopes to recover after a thaw. They were the pioneers of snowmaking technology; and 'farming' snow, as they put it, is something they do superbly well.

The mountains are not huge in terms of trail mileage, although Killington in particular packs in more than you would think – and this year has magically doubled its acreage, by tidying up forest areas to make them skiable. But several have verticals of over 800m (on a par with Colorado resorts such as Keystone), and most have over 600m, and are worth considering for a short stay, or even for a week if you like familiar runs. For more novelty, a road trip is the obvious solution.

Most resorts suit snowboarders well, and many have numerous and serious terrain parks.

You won't lack challenge – most of the double-black diamond runs are seriously steep. And you won't lack space: most Americans visit over weekends, which means deserted slopes on weekdays, mostly.

It also means the resorts are keen to attract long-stay visitors, so UK package prices are low. But the big weekend and day-trip trade also means few New England resorts have developed atmospheric resort villages – just a few condos and a hotel, maybe, with places to stay further out geared to visitors with cars.

New England is easy to get to from Britain – a flight to Boston, then perhaps a three- or four-hour drive to your resort. And there are some pretty towns to visit, with their clapboard houses and big churches. You might also like to consider spending a day or two in Boston – one of America's most charming cities. Or have a shopping spree at the factory outlet stores that abound in New England.

We cover two of the most popular resorts on the UK market, Killington and Stowe, briefly on the opposite page. But there are many other small areas, too, shown on the map and covered in our index/directory.

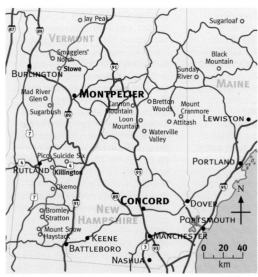

KEY FACTS

Resort	670m
	2,200ft
Slopes	355-1285m
	1,170-4,220ft
Lifts	22
Pistes	1509 acres
Snow-guns	80%

TOURIST OFFICE

www.killington.com

Killington

- New England's biggest ski area
- Excellent nursery slopes
- Lively après-ski and nightlife

- Widely spread lodgings, with no proper resort village
- Terminally tedious for non-skiers

Killington caters mainly for weekend visitors who drive in from the east-coast cities. There is no resort village in the usual sense.

Most of Killington's hotels and restaurants are spread along a five-mile approach road; the car is king. But there's also a free day-time shuttle-bus. The lift pass includes Pico – a separate little mountain next door.

The ski area spreads over a series of wooded peaks, with an impressive number of runs crammed into a small area. Amazingly, the Schrahe report (read our piste extent feature) reveals that they total 124km. Killington Base is the main focus, with chairs radiating to three peaks. Crowds can arrive at weekends. It's a complex mountain, but the map and signing are fine. It has a good snow record (average 250 inches) and lots of snowmaking.

There are no fewer than six terrain parks, including Burton's The Stash, an all-natural park with more than 50 features, as well as two pipes.

There are a handful of genuine double-diamond fall-line runs, many of them gladed. There are also lots of easy cruising blue and green runs all over the slopes. The resort is excellent for complete beginners too: the Snowshed base home slope is really one vast nursery slope. The Snowshed base lodge has several eating options.

Most hotels are a drive or bus ride away, but there is a wide choice of places to stay and dine. The Grand Resort at Snowshed is a swanky 4-star, newly renovated. Try the Santa Fe Steakhouse, or Peppino's for Italian. Killington has a well-earned reputation for a vibrant après-ski scene, led by the famous Wobbly Barn – a bar-club-steakhouse with live music.

Off the slopes? There's a tubing park plus snowmobiling and sleigh rides, but do take a car.

KEY FACTS

Resort	475m
	1,560ft
Slopes	390-1135m
	1,280-3,720ft
Lifts	13
Pistes	485 acres
Snow-guns	80%

TOURIST OFFICE

www.stowe.com

Stowe

- Classic, cute Vermont town
- Queue-free except at weekends
- Great children's facilities

- Slopes a bus ride from town
- Slow chairlifts in main area
- Lacks après-ski animation

Stowe is one of New England's cutest towns, with dinky clapboard shops and restaurants, and a pretty white church. The slopes have something for all.

The small slopes of Mount Mansfield, Vermont's mainly wooded highest peak, are a 15-minute drive away. There's a good, free, day-time shuttle-bus service, but a car is useful.

The slopes span two main sectors, Mansfield and Spruce Peak, linked by the Over Easy gondola at base level. There are few queues during the week. Snowmaking is extensive, with a big investment two seasons ago.

The main slopes are dominated by the famous Front Four – a row of double-black diamond runs, with genuine challenges for experts. But there is plenty of easier stuff, too. The nursery slopes at Spruce Peak are excellent, and there are splendid long green runs to progress to. There are six terrain parks, and the resort is popular with snowboarders. Children's facilities are excellent, too. There are a couple of decent eateries. The table-service Cliff House, at the top of the

gondola, has impressed readers this year and last.

Much of the lodging is along the road between the town and the slopes – though you can now stay at the swanky Stowe Mountain Lodge, right by the lifts. Elsewhere, the Green Mountain Inn is a reader favourite. There are restaurants of every kind in the town; the Spruce Camp Base Lodge, Whip in Green Mountain Inn ('always good'), Frida's ('a lively bar with solid Tex-Mex') and Piecasso pizzeria are reader recommendations. Nightlife is muted, especially later on, but the Matterhorn is 'a Stowe institution not to be missed' and the Den at Mansfield base 'still rocks'.

Stowe is a pleasant place to spend time off the slopes – at least if you like shopping. There is a cinema, and snowmobiling and dog sledding too. Ben & Jerry's ice cream factory is just down the road.

New England

Build your own shortlist: www.wheretoskiandsnowboard.com

Canada

In many ways Canada combines the best that the US has to offer – good service, a warm welcome, relatively quiet slopes, good lift systems with lots of fast lifts, frequent dumps of snow, great grooming and a high standard of accommodation – with more spectacular scenery. It also has the advantage that you can get direct flights to its main airports without having to change planes and go through customs part-way through your journey. But it is no longer cheap – long-haul air fares have risen and local prices are high (all Canadian resorts fall into our red category – the most expensive – for their RPI).

If Canada – well, western Canada at least – has one central attraction, it is snow. In an average year, you can expect frequent and abundant falls to provide the powder you dream of. And, as in the US, there is lots of steep terrain within resort area boundaries, which is avalanche protected and safely skiable without guidance. And there is lots of skiing among the trees – something that is rare in Europe and is great fun, especially in fresh snow. If you really want untracked powder and are feeling flush, there is nothing to beat western Canada's heli-skiing and snowcat-skiing operations.

The east is completely different: expect snow and extremes of weather much like New England's. The main attraction of Québec for us is the French culture and ambience, plus the advantage of a shorter flight time. In both east and west, lifts close much earlier than in Europe – as early as 3pm in some cases (and some upper lifts might start closing as early as 1.30pm).

The Canadian people are another attraction. They share the American service culture but have a sincerity in putting it into practice that we (and our reporters) appreciate. In the west you'll also find spectacular scenery and may see an impressive wildlife, especially in the Rockies and the interior of British Columbia.

The resorts obviously vary. But most have purpose-built villages (much more tastefully done than the French monstrosities of the 1960s and 70s) at the foot of the slopes – Banff and Lake Louise are notable exceptions because they are in a National Park where building is severely restricted. Whistler's village is huge but many of the others are tiny. A couple – notably Revelstoke and Fernie – have small towns nearby with decent restaurants and places to stay.

NOT AS CHEAP AS IT WAS

Canada is not as cheap a ski destination as it was. There used to be cheap charter flights but these have been dramatically reduced. At today's poor exchange rate, local prices for lift passes, ski school and equipment rental are all much more expensive than in Europe. And eating and drinking is no longer the bargain it once was. Take a look at our price panels for each resort for an idea of what to budget for. In many resorts you can save money by buying lift passes in advance through tour operators or websites.

Note that the legal age for buying and consuming alcohol is 18 in Alberta and Québec and 19 in British Columbia. The law is strictly enforced, so carrying your passport as evidence of age is a good idea even if you are well over the required age.

SNOWPIX.COM / CHRIS GILL

← Lake Louise is spectacularly set in Banff National Park

For international visitors to Canada, the main draw is the west. It has fabulous scenery, good snow and a wonderful sense of the great outdoors. The big names of Whistler, Banff and Lake Louise capture most of the British market, but there are lots of good smaller resorts that the more intrepid visitors are now exploring. You can have a great trip by renting a car and combining two or more of these, perhaps with a couple of days on virgin powder served by helicopters or snowcats as well.

The three big resorts mentioned above and six of the smaller ones get their own write-ups in this section.

Whistler is plenty big enough to amuse you for a whole holiday. Most visitors to Banff or Lake Louise, a half-hour drive apart, will spend time at both (and could also fit in day trips to Kicking Horse and Panorama).

But none of the others has enough terrain to keep a keen piste-basher amused for a week or ten days without skiing the same runs a lot. So we'd suggest that if you want variety, you combine two or more on one holiday. Even if you don't want to drive, it is easy to combine, say, Sun Peaks with Whistler, Big White or Silver Star (and the latter two with each other) using regular buses. Places that don't get a full chapter

that you might also consider include Jasper (which you can reach via the spectacular Icefields Parkway drive from Lake Louise), Apex, Red Mountain, Panorama and Kimberley – these all have entries in the resort directory at the back of the book.

We once spent two weeks driving from Whistler to Banff, calling in at lots of smaller resorts on the way. It was a fantastic trip; for eight days in the middle it did not stop snowing, and the variety of slopes and resorts made for great contrasts. In 2013 we combined Fernie, Kicking Horse, Revelstoke and Whistler.

If you fancy a day or two snowcat-skiing, there are lots of possibilities, including great operations near Fernie (see chapter). Revelstoke has both cat- and heli-skiing.

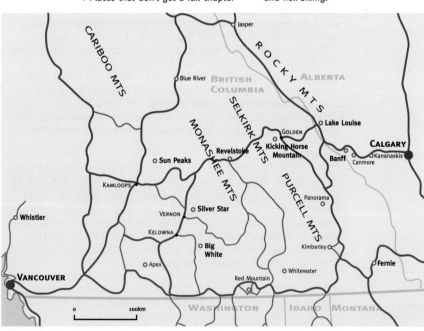

SNOWPIX.COM / CHRIS GILL

Banff

*A major summer resort amid spectacular National Park scenery,
with varied ski areas – including Lake Louise – nearby*

RATINGS

The mountains

Extent	★★★
Fast lifts	★★★★
Queues	★★★★
Terrain p'ks	★★★★
Snow	★★★★
Expert	★★★★
Intermediate	★★★★
Beginner	★★★
Boarder	★★★★
X-country	★★★★
Restaurants	★★★
Schools	★★★★
Families	★★★★

The resort

Charm	★★★
Convenience	★
Scenery	★★★★
Eating out	★★★★★
Après-ski	★★★
Off-slope	★★★★★

RPI	150
lift pass	£290
ski hire	£115
lessons	£190
food & drink	£170
total	**£765**

NEWS

2014/15: At Norquay they're widening several runs, and enlarging the tubing park.

2013/14: Sunshine Introduced guided snow shoe tours with a heritage focus, followed by a typical Canadian fondue.

➕ Spectacular high-mountain scenery – quite unlike the Colorado Rockies

➕ Lots of touristy shops, restaurants and bars

➕ Good-value lodging because winter is the area's low season

➕ Excellent snow at main local area, Sunshine Village, but ...

➖ It's a 20-minute bus ride then a long gondola ride away

➖ You'll probably want to ski Lake Louise too, 45 minutes away

➖ Most lifts/runs are of limited vertical

➖ Can be very cold (–30°C or less)

➖ Banff lacks ski resort atmosphere, though it's not an unattractive town

Banff is nothing like your typical ski resort. We enjoy its restaurants and bars, but not the daily commuting to Sunshine Village or Lake Louise (which gets its own chapter). Even the small local hill, Norquay, is a bus ride out of town.

The alternative is to stay a few nights mid-mountain at Sunshine Village and a few at Lake Louise. Lake Louise also has the advantage of being much closer to Kicking Horse, which makes a great day trip for powderhounds.

THE RESORT

Banff is a big summer tourist town, with two ski areas nearby. Mt Norquay is a tiny area of slopes overlooking the town. Sunshine Village – whose base station is 20 minutes' drive from Banff – is a much bigger mountain; despite the name, it's not a village (it has just one hotel at mid-mountain), nor is it notably sunny (sitting on the Continental Divide, it has an excellent snow record).

Most visitors buy a three-area pass that also covers the resort of Lake Louise, 45 minutes' drive away – dealt with in a separate chapter. Bus excursions are available to the more distant resorts of Panorama and Kicking Horse (the latter especially worthwhile) and the smaller (and closer) resort of Nakiska, and day trips for heli-skiing are offered locally.

VILLAGE CHARM ★★★☆☆
Pleasantly touristy
Banff consists basically of a long main street connecting the 'downtown' area – a small network of side roads built in grid fashion, lined with clothing and souvenir shops aimed at summer visitors – with a large area of hotel and condo lodgings. The buildings are low-rise, and some are wood-clad. The town is pleasant enough, but it's essentially a modern tourist town, without the character of the classic American cowboy or mining towns.

CONVENIENCE ★☆☆☆☆
Sprawling town, outlying slopes
Banff is a sprawling place, and many of the lodgings (even on the main Banff Avenue) can be quite a way from the downtown area. A car can be helpful here, especially in cold weather. But taxis are plentiful.

To get to the slopes, bus services for each mountain (free with the Tri-area lift pass) pick up from many of the main hotels – but getting from your hotel to the lift base can take much longer than by car because of the number of stops, though the buses 'run like clockwork', says a 2013 visitor. At Sunshine when you arrive there is a long access gondola to ride.

SCENERY ★★★★☆
Distinctive and dramatic
Banff National Park offers spectacular scenery – that's what brings the millions of summer visitors – and the town's setting is dramatic. Sunshine's Lookout mountain, right on the Continental Divide, gives panoramic views into British Columbia.

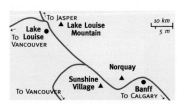

LIFT PASSES

Tri-area lift pass

Prices in C$

Age	1-day	6-day
under 13	33	165
13 to 17	88	446
18 to 64	99	507
65 plus	88	446

Free Under 6

Beginner Lift, lesson and rental package

Notes Covers transport between Banff, Lake Louise, Norquay and Sunshine Village; prices include 5% tax

THE MOUNTAINS

The Sunshine Village slopes are mostly above the treeline, although there is a wooded sector, and some lightly wooded slopes higher up. Mt Norquay is a much smaller area of quiet, wooded slopes. Each area (and Lake Louise) has its own trail map, and there's another that shows all three areas. The signposting at the top of each lift is praised, but at Sunshine subsequent signs are 'small and difficult to spot', says a reporter.

There are good, free mountain tours led by friendly volunteer hosts.

EXTENT OF THE SLOPES ★★★★★
Lots of variety
The main slopes of **Sunshine Village** are not visible from the base station: you ride a gondola to Sunshine Village itself, with a mid-station at the base of Goat's Eye Mountain. Goat's Eye is

served by a fast quad rising 580m – much the most serious lift on the mountain. Although there are some blue runs, this is basically a black mountain, with some genuine double diamonds (including extreme terrain in the Wild West area – see 'For experts').

Further up at Sunshine Village, lifts fan out in all directions, with short runs back from Mount Standish and longer ones from Lookout Mountain. From the top here you can access the more extreme terrain of Delirium Dive – see 'For experts'.

The 2.5km green run to the gondola base is a pretty cruise. Go down while the lifts are still running, and you can take the Jackrabbit chair to cut out a flat section. Delay your descent and you'll avoid the close-of-play crowds. The Canyon trail is a fun alternative for more advanced skiers and riders. The lower part is marked black; it's just a bit narrow and twisty

Goat's Eye has some great steep terrain – single- and double-black diamond runs and an extreme zone. But it's very rocky and windswept and needs a lot of snow to be enjoyable

GOAT'S EYE
2600m/8,530ft

Goat's Eye

Deliri
Div

Wild West

Wolverine

Gond

1660m/5,440ft

2020m/6,630ft

If it's snowing hard, visibility is usually best on the easy runs in the trees around here and on the long run down to the bottom of the gondola

ⓖ gondola
ⓕ fast chairlift
Slow chairs & drags have no symbol

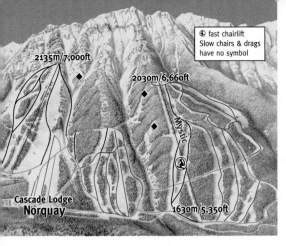

⚃ fast chairlift
Slow chairs & drags
have no symbol

2135m/7,000ft

2030m/6,660ft

Mystic

Cascade Lodge
Norquay

1630m/5,350ft

FAST LIFTS ★★★★

Most sectors well served

At Sunshine, most sectors of the slopes have fast chairs. The main weakness is the Wawa chair, and this has been speeded up a bit by the addition of a moving carpet. Norquay is so small that lift speed is hardly an issue, but it does have one fast chair.

QUEUES ★★★★

Sunshine can get busy

Many visitors are day-trippers from cities such as Calgary – so the slopes are fairly quiet during the week. Public holidays and weekends at Sunshine have provoked past complaints of long queues. But queues generally move quickly, and there are effective singles lines (well managed, as usual) you can use if in a hurry. On busy weekends, we're told the trick is to arrive at the gondola by 9am.

in places. The final option is to ride the gondola down; many people do.

The slopes at **Norquay** are served by a row of five parallel lifts and have floodlit trails twice a week.

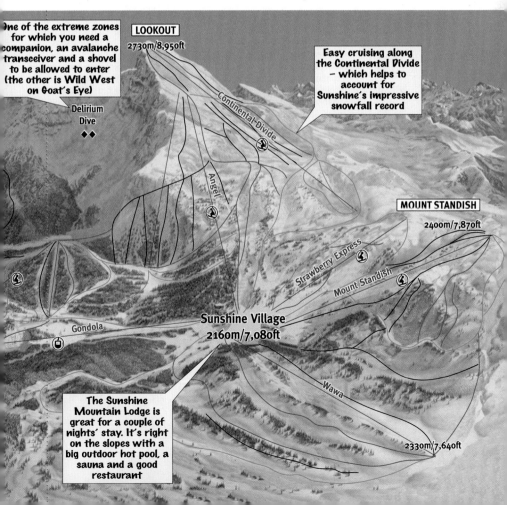

One of the extreme zones for which you need a companion, an avalanche transceiver and a shovel to be allowed to enter (the other is Wild West on Goat's Eye)

LOOKOUT
2730m/8,950ft

Delirium
Dive
◆◆

Continental Divide

Angel

Easy cruising along the Continental Divide – which helps to account for Sunshine's impressive snowfall record

MOUNT STANDISH
2400m/7,870ft

Strawberry Express

Mount Standish

Gondola

Sunshine Village
2160m/7,080ft

Wawa

2330m/7,640ft

The Sunshine Mountain Lodge is great for a couple of nights' stay. It's right on the slopes with a big outdoor hot pool, a sauna and a good restaurant

SKIWORLD

Catered chalets, hotels and self catering apartments in

Europe, USA and Canada

skiworld.co.uk

08444 930 430

ABTA V2151 ATOL 2036

KEY FACTS

Resort	1380m
	4,530ft

Norquay, Sunshine and Lake Louise

Slopes	1630-2730m
	5,350-8,950ft
Lifts	26
Pistes	7,748 acres
Green	23%
Blue	39%
Black	38%
Snowmaking	24%

Norquay only

Slopes	1630-2135m
	5,350-7,000ft
Lifts	6
Pistes	190 acres
Green	20%
Blue	36%
Black	44%
Snowmaking	85%

Sunshine only

Slopes	1660-2730m
	5,440-8,950ft
Lifts	12
Pistes	3,358 acres
Green	20%
Blue	55%
Black	25%
Snowmaking	2 guns
	early season only

TANYA BOOTH

You're looking at the Continental divide: take a wrong turn and you could end up in Vancouver ➔

TERRAIN PARKS ★★★★☆
Fun on both areas

At Sunshine, the terrain park on Lookout Mountain covers an impressive 12 acres in three sections: Rogers has a wide selection of obstacles and jumps from S to XL; Grizzly has L and XL rails, jumps and boxes; and Springhill has S and M features. Experts should not miss the Norquay park, which has an airbag and is littered with gap jumps, tabletops, rails and boxes. The park is floodlit twice a week January to March.

SNOW RELIABILITY ★★★★☆
Excellent

Sunshine Village used to claim '100% natural snow', a neat reversal of the usual snowmaking hype. Now it has two snow-guns, which are used on weak spots, at the beginning of the season. In a poor snow season, some black runs can remain rocky (especially those on Goat's Eye), but the blues are usually fine. 'Three times the snow' is another slogan – a sly comparison between the impressive average snowfall here (360 to 400 inches, depending on the source) and the modest 180 inches at Lake Louise and 120 inches on Norquay. But we're told the Sunshine figures relate to Lookout, and that Goat's Eye gets less. At Norquay there is snowmaking on green and blue pistes. Late-season snow on Sunshine is usually good (we've had great April snow there).

FOR EXPERTS ★★★★☆
Pure pleasure

Sunshine has plenty of open runs of genuine black steepness above the treeline on Lookout, but Goat's Eye is much more compelling. It has a great area of expert double-black diamond trails and chutes, both above and below the treeline. But the slopes are rocky and need good cover, and the top can be windswept. The double-diamond runs at skier's left reportedly hold their snow better than the rest of the mountain.

There are short, not-too-steep black runs on Mount Standish. One more challenging novelty here is a pitch known as the Waterfall run – because you do actually ski down over a snow-covered frozen waterfall. But a lot of snow is needed to cover the waterfall and prevent it reverting to ice. Also try the Shoulder on Lookout Mountain; it is sheltered, tends to accumulate powder and has been deserted whenever we've been there (probably because access to it involves a long traverse that can be tricky and is poorly marked).

A popular backcountry route follows the back of the Wawa ridge, through a river valley ('great fun – tight turns in the trees of the river bed'); a guide is essential, of course.

Real experts will want to get to grips with Delirium Dive on Lookout Mountain's north face and the Wild West area on Goat's Eye (with some

ACTIVITIES

Indoor Film theatre, museums, galleries, swimming pools (one with water slides), gym, squash, weight training, bowling, hot tub, sauna, climbing wall

Outdoor Swimming in hot springs, ice rink, sleigh rides, dog sledding, ice climbing, snowmobiles, ice walks, ice fishing, helicopter tours, snowshoeing, tobogganing, tubing

GETTING THERE

Air Calgary 140km/85 miles (1hr45)

SCHOOLS

Ski Big 3
t 1-877 760 7731

Banff-Norquay
t 762 4421

Sunshine Village
t 1 877 542 2633

Classes (Big 3 prices) 3 days' guided tuition of the three areas C$335 incl. tax

Private lessons Half day (3hr) C$419, incl. tax, for up to 5 people

narrow chutes and rock bands). For both you must have a companion, an avalanche transceiver, probes and a shovel – and a guide is recommended. It is best to book in advance and rent your equipment in Banff (you can't in Sunshine). We tried Delirium in a group with the ski patrol, who provided equipment, and the scariest part was the walk in, along a narrow, icy path with a sheer drop (protected by a flimsy-looking net).

Norquay's two main lifts give only 400m vertical, but both serve black slopes, and the North American chair accesses a couple of serious double-diamond runs.

Heli-skiing is available from bases outside the National Park in British Columbia – roughly two hours' drive.

FOR INTERMEDIATES ★★★★
Ideal runs

Half the runs on Sunshine are classified as intermediate. Wherever you look there are blues and greens – and some of the greens are as enjoyable (and pretty much as steep) as the blues.

We particularly like the World Cup Downhill run, from the top of Lookout to the Village. All three chairs on Mount Standish are excellent for building confidence, provided you choose a sensible route down. The slow Wawa chair gives access to the Wawa Bowl and Tincan Alley ('great first blues'). This area also offers some shelter from bad weather.

There's a delightful wooded area under the second stage of the gondola served by the Jackrabbit and Wolverine chairs. The blue runs down Goat's Eye are good cruises too, some of them with space to indulge in fast carving.

The Mystic Express at Norquay serves a handful of quite challenging treelined blues and a couple of blacks that are sometimes groomed.

FOR BEGINNERS ★★★
Pretty good terrain

Most beginners start with a package that includes a lift pass, equipment hire and tuition. Sunshine has a good nursery area at the Village, served by a moving carpet. And there are great long green runs to progress to, served by the fast Strawberry Express chair.

Norquay has a good small nursery area with a moving carpet and gentle greens to progress to, served by the Cascade chair.

Banff is not the ideal destination for a mixed party of beginners and more experienced friends. The beginners are likely to want familiar surroundings, while the more experienced will want to travel.

FOR BOARDERS ★★★★
A good base

Boarders will feel at home in Banff, and there is some excellent freeriding terrain. Natural features are part of the appeal, with ledges, jumps and tree gaps aplenty. But Sunshine has some flat areas to beware of (such as the green run to the base – see 'Extent of the slopes'), and the blue traverse on Goat's Eye is tedious.

There are specialist snowboard shops in Banff: Rude Boys, Rude Girls and Unlimited Skate & Snow.

FOR CROSS-COUNTRY ★★★★
High in quality and quantity

It's a good area for cross-country. There are trails near Banff, around the Bow River, and on the Banff Springs golf course. But the best area is around Lake Louise. Altogether, there are around 80km of groomed trails within Banff National Park.

MOUNTAIN RESTAURANTS ★★★
Quite good

With a mini-resort at mid-mountain, Sunshine offers better options than usual in North America. Our favourite is the welcoming Chimney Corner Lounge in the Sunshine Mountain Lodge with a big open fire – endorsed by reporters ('Tasty and good value,' said a recent visitor). The Day Lodge offers different styles of catering on three floors – the table-service Lookout Lounge has great views and does a buffet.

At Norquay, the big, stylish, timber-framed Cascade Lodge is excellent – it has table- and self-service restaurants.

SCHOOLS AND GUIDES ★★★★
Some great ideas

Each mountain has its own school. But recognizing that visitors wanting lessons won't want to be confined to just one mountain, the resorts have organized an excellent Club Ski Program – three-day courses starting on Sundays and Thursdays that take you to Sunshine, Norquay and Lake Louise on different days, offering a mixture of guiding and instruction. Reporters are full of praise for these.

Banff

Build your own shortlist: www.wheretoskiandsnowboard.com

CHILDCARE

Tiny Tigers (Sunshine)
t 1-877 542 2633
Ages 19mnth to 6yr

Kid's Place (Norquay)
t 760 7709
Ages 19mnth to 6yr

Childcare Connection
t 760 4443
Childminding in guest
accommodation

Ski school
Ages 6 to 12

UK PACKAGES

Alpine Answers,
American Ski Classics,
Canadian Affair, Crystal,
Crystal Finest, Elegant
Resorts, Flexiski,
Frontier, Inghams,
Momentum, Neilson,
Oxford Ski Co,
PowderBeds, Ski
Bespoke, Ski Club
Freshtracks, Ski
Independence, Ski
Safari, Skitracer,
Skiworld, Snow Finders,
Supertravel, Thomson,
Virgin Snow

Phone numbers
From distant parts of
Canada, add the
prefix 1 403; from
abroad, add the prefix
+1 403

TOURIST OFFICE

www.skibanff.com
www.banffnorquay.
com
www.SkiBig3.com

FOR FAMILIES ★★★★★
Excellent choices

There are various school and activity programmes for all ages. We've had good reports of the schools in the past – new reports please. All three resorts offer childcare. The Tiny Tigers Ski and Play Program at Sunshine introduces youngsters to the slopes.

STAYING THERE

A huge amount of accommodation is on offer, with lots of varied hotels.
Hotels Summer is peak season here, with generally lower prices in winter.
★★★★★Fairmont Banff Springs (762 2211) A late-19th-century, castle-style property outside town (no shuttle-bus – you have to use taxis). It's a town in itself – 2,000 beds, 40 shops, several restaurants and bars, a nightclub and a superb spa (which costs extra).
★★★★Banff Caribou Lodge (762 5887) On the main street, slightly out of town. Wood-clad, individually designed rooms (some small). 'Massive' hot tub; spa. Repeatedly praised by reporters ('fantastic service', 'good food').
★★★★Rimrock (762 3356) Spectacularly set out of town, with great views and a smart health club. Luxurious.
★★★Buffalo Mountain Lodge (762 2400) Slightly out of town but a 'wonderful building' in a 'beautiful location'. 'Excellent food.' Hot tub.
★★★Irwin's Mountain Inn (762 4566) Good value; on Banff Avenue.
★★Homestead Inn (762 4471) Central, with cheap, good-sized rooms.
Apartments The Banff Rocky Mountain Resort is set in the woods on the edge of town, with indoor pool and hot tubs. Douglas Fir resort is a bit out of town but has a free shuttle and is popular with families; lots of facilities such as adults' and kids' swimming pools and a giant indoor playground.
At altitude The Sunshine Mountain Lodge (705 4000) makes a very welcoming, comfortable base at Sunshine Village. Luggage is transported while you ski. Rooms vary in size and include luxury loft rooms. Big outdoor hot pool. Sauna. Good restaurant. Guests can get on the slopes half an hour early.

EATING OUT ★★★★★
Lots of choice

Banff boasts over 100 restaurants, from McDonald's to the fine-dining restaurant in the Banff Springs hotel.

The award-winning Maple Leaf grill offers fine seafood and steak dishes, and over 600 different wines. We've enjoyed the designer-cool Saltlik – good game, steak and fish. A 2013 reporter who got about a bit recommended the Keg Steakhouse in Caribou Lodge ('delicious, large portions'), Cafe de Paris ('massive and tasty wild boar shank') and particularly Buffalo Mountain Lodge a mile out of town ('magnificent meal in wonderful timber building'). Of the dozens of other places that readers recommend, popular spots are Melissa's (central, 'varied menu and good ambience'), Athena ('excellent large pizzas – good value for money'), Giorgio's (beef, fish, Italian) and Magpie & Stump (aka Maggers – Tex-Mex, with Wild West decor). Old Spaghetti Factory is a good family choice. Try Bison for steaks, fish and live music. And for burgers and ribs try Bumper's, Wild Bill's or Tony Roma's.

APRES-SKI ★★★★★
Night on the town is best

There's little teatime après-ski because the town is a drive from the slopes. Mad Trapper's Saloon at the top of the Sunshine gondola is the place to be during the close-of-play happy hour.
In town later, the two main live music venues are the Rose & Crown and Wild Bill's. The Banff Avenue Brewing Company is the local microbrewery. The Elk and Oarsman has a lively sports bar and the St James's Gate is the local Irish pub. There are a couple of good nightclubs.

OFF THE SLOPES ★★★★★
Lots to do

Banff has lots to do off the slopes. Outdoor activities include skating, snowshoeing, dog sledding and snowmobiling. Ice canyon walks are popular – notably Johnson Canyon – and there's wildlife to see.
Shopping and soaking in the spas and hot springs are popular – the Red Earth Spa at the Caribou Lodge has the works. There are sightseeing tours and several museums – a 2013 visitor recommends the Whyte Museum of the Canadian Rockies and the Banff Park Museum. Many reporters have enjoyed evenings in Calgary watching the ice hockey. Banff is quite near one end of the Columbia Icefields Parkway, a three-hour drive to Jasper through spectacular national parks.

BIG WHITE SKI RESORT / KLAUS GRETZMACHER

Big White

It's a big village by Canadian standards and it's certainly white. There are few places to match it for learning to ski powder

TOP 10 RATINGS

Extent	★★★
Fast lifts	★★★★
Queues	★★★★★
Snow	★★★★★
Expert	★★★
Intermediate	★★★★
Beginner	★★★★
Charm	★★
Convenience	★★★★
Scenery	★★★

RPI — 140

lift pass	£280
ski hire	£125
lessons	£145
food & drink	£170
total	**£720**

NEWS

2013/14: Two new restaurants, the Blarney Stone Irish Tavern and The Woods, opened. Cross-country, snowshoe and dog sledding trails and walking paths were upgraded.

+ Great for learning to ski powder

+ Slopes quiet except at weekends

+ Convenient, purpose-built village with high-quality condos and a traffic-free centre; good for families

+ Lots of non-skiing snow-based activities at Happy Valley

– Visibility can be poor, especially on the upper mountain, because of snow, cloud or freezing fog

– Few off-slope diversions, and it's isolated without a car

– Limited après-ski

'It's the snow' says the Big White slogan. And as slogans go, it's spot on. If you want a good chance of skiing powder on reasonably easy slopes, put Big White high on the shortlist. If you want a suntan (or lively après-ski, or extensive steep terrain), look elsewhere; but if you are an intermediate looking to learn to ski powder or try gladed skiing, there can be few better places. Consider combining it with another BC resort such as Silver Star or Whistler for variety.

THE RESORT

Big White is a purpose-built resort that has more visitor beds than any other BC resort except Whistler. It's less than an hour from Kelowna airport.

Village charm The resort is rather spread out but attractively built in wood and stone, with a family-friendly traffic-free centre.

Convenience Much of the place is ski-in/ski-out of smart modern condos.

Scenery Trees fill the views wherever you look; and near the top of the mountain the trees usually stay white all winter and are known as 'snow ghosts'; they make visibility tricky in a white-out but are great fun to ski between on clear days.

THE MOUNTAINS

Much of the terrain is heavily wooded. But the trees thin out towards the summits, leading to almost open slopes in the bowls at the top. There's at least one green option from the top of each lift, but the one from Gem Lake is narrow and can be tricky and busy. In general, the easiest slopes are on the right as you look at the mountain (including some very easy glade skiing) and get steeper the further left you go.

Slopes Chairs run from points below village level to above mid-mountain, serving the main area of wooded beginner and intermediate runs above and beside the village. A T-bar and

gondola
fast chairlift
Slow chairs & drags have no symbol

Sun-Rype Bowl

North-East Peak
2250m

2220m/7,290ft

Big White Peak
2320m/7,610ft

The Cliff

Gem Lake

Snow Ghost

Ridge Rocket

Bullet

Black Forest

Big White Village Centre
1755m/5,760ft

Lara's

Westridge Warming Hut
1510m/4,950ft

Ridge Day Lodge
1650m/5,410ft

Happy Valley Lodge

KEY FACTS

Resort	1755m
	5,760ft
Slopes	1510-2320m
	4,950-7,610ft
Lifts	16
Pistes	2,765 acres
Green	18%
Blue	54%
Black	28%
Snowmaking	
	In terrain park

UK PACKAGES

Alpine Answers, American Ski Classics, Canadian Affair, Frontier, Momentum, Ski Independence, Ski Safari, Skiworld

Central reservations Call 765 8888; toll-free (within Canada) 1 800 663 2772

Phone numbers From distant parts of Canada, add the prefix 1 250; from abroad, add +1 250

TOURIST OFFICE

www.bigwhite.com

four chairs serve the higher slopes. Quite some way across the mountain is the Gem Lake fast chair, serving a range of long top-to-bottom runs; with its 710m vertical, this lift is in a different league from the others.

'Snow hosts' (highly praised by reporters) run free guided ski tours starting at 10.30 every morning. The signposting and piste map and classification are good ('excellent', says a recent visitor). There is night skiing Tuesday to Saturday on three main slopes and the terrain park.

Fast lifts The lifts from the village and the Gem Lake lift are all fast. But the other upper lifts are tediously slow.

Queues Queues are very rare.

Terrain park Served by a double chair and snowmaking, the excellent Telus park includes jumps, rails and hits for all levels, large-diameter tube rails, a half-pipe and a snowcross, and is highly praised by reporters.

Snow reliability Big White has a reputation for great powder; average snowfall is about 300 inches, which is similar to many Colorado resorts. On each of our three visits it snowed practically non-stop, the powder was excellent and we hardly saw the sun.

Experts The Cliff area at the top right of the ski area is of serious double-black diamond pitch; the runs are short, but you can ski them repeatedly using the Cliff chair. Sun-Rype bowl at the opposite edge of the ski area is more forgiving ('Excellent place to ski deep powder,' says a reporter). There are some long blacks off the Gem Lake chair and several shorter ones off the Powder and Falcon chairs. There are plenty of glades to explore – and bump runs too.

Intermediates The resort is excellent for cruisers and families, with long blues and greens all over the hill. Good intermediates will enjoy the easier blacks and some of the gladed runs too. There is marvellous easy skiing among the trees in the Black Forest area (which we loved when it was snowing) and among the snow ghosts (see 'Scenery'), which we loved when it was clear. Some of the blues off the Gem Lake chair are quite steep, narrow and challenging.

Beginners There's a good dedicated beginner learning area at Happy Valley and lots of long easy runs to progress to. Every day three slopes are designated slow zones, gated and patrolled.

Snowboarding There's some excellent beginner and freeriding terrain with boarder-friendly chairlifts and few flat areas to worry about.

Cross-country A reporter enjoyed the 25km of trails. There are free guided tours daily at 10.30am.

Mountain restaurants There aren't any – it's back to the bottom for lunch. You can eat a packed lunch at any of the four day lodges.

School and guides We have received rave reviews from reporters for both skiing and snowboarding lessons for adults and children alike.

Families The excellent day care centre takes children from 18 months to five years; it has a list of babysitters too.

STAYING THERE

A good range of accommodation is featured by specialist tour operators like Frontier Ski and Ski Independence.

Hotels The choices are Chateau Big White, the White Crystal Inn and the Inn at Big White. We would prefer to stay in a smart condo.

Apartments Condo standards are high. Stonebridge and Towering Pines are both central, ski-in/ski-out, with big, well-furnished rooms and private hot tubs on the balconies. Other reporter tips include Black Bear and (a bit less luxurious) Eagles and Whitefoot Lodge.

Eating out The best restaurants here have a great selection of local Okanagan wines (there are over 130 wine producers in the valley). We had a superb meal at the 6 Degrees bistro, sharing delicious dishes (tapas-style); endorsed by a recent reporter; not cheap. We've also had good meals in the Kettle Valley Steakhouse at Happy Valley. Reporters have recommend the upstairs restaurant at Snowshoe Sam's and the 'excellent' Globe ('imaginative food, served tapas-style'). The BullWheel is a family place with handmade burgers. The Blarney Stone Irish Tavern is in the Inn at Big White – it's run by the people who own the Globe. The Woods is in the main square and has a patio with a firepit.

Après-ski In general, it is fairly quiet. But the ground floor of Snowshoe Sam's has a DJ and live entertainment.

Off the slopes Happy Valley is a great area for families, with ice skating, snowmobiling, snow biking, tubing, dog sledding, sleigh rides, 15km of snowshoeing trails and an 18m ice climbing tower. There are two spas and a shopping shuttle to Kelowna.

SNOWPIX.COM / CHRIS GILL

Fernie

Lots of snow and lots of steeps – one of our favourites, with a choice of convenient base lodging or a valley town

RATINGS

The mountains

Extent	★★★
Fast lifts	★★
Queues	★★★★
Terrain p'ks	★★
Snow	★★★★
Expert	★★★★★
Intermediate	★★
Beginner	★★★★
Boarder	★★★
X-country	★★★
Restaurants	★
Schools	★★★★
Families	★★★★

The resort

Charm	★★
Convenience	★★★★
Scenery	★★★
Eating out	★★★
Après-ski	★★★
Off-slope	★★

RPI 145

lift pass	£290
ski hire	£145
lessons	£155
food & drink	£170
total	**£760**

SNOWPIX.COM / CHRIS GILL

Polar Peak is proper black-diamond territory ↓

- ➕ Good snow record, with less chance of rain than at Whistler
- ➕ Blissfully quiet much of the time
- ➕ Great terrain for those who like it steep and deep; good for confident intermediates too
- ➕ Snowcat operations nearby
- ➕ Some good on-slope accommodation available, but ...

- ➖ Mountain resort is very limited
- ➖ Access to many excellent runs is via slow lifts and long traverses
- ➖ Not a huge amount of groomed cruising to do
- ➖ After a dump it can take time to make the bowls safe (and to get the groomed trails groomed again)
- ➖ One basic mountain restaurant

Fernie has long had cult status among the residents of Calgary. Before the recession and exchange rate changes started to bite, we also got a good flow of reports from enthusiastic British visitors impressed by the adventurous skiing – it's mostly ungroomed, and much of it is steep, with a lot of lightly wooded slopes (rare in Europe). It's now quite a good resort for novices, too. The ones who may want to look elsewhere are keen but cautious intermediates.

Us? We're hooked. Despite a distressing absence of proper mountain restaurants, we pretty much always include Fernie in our Canada trips. A regular reporter who went back this year is similarly taken with the place: 'Hard to explain how it gets under your skin,' she says. It is, Tanya, it is.

THE RESORT

Fernie Alpine Resort is set a little way up the mountainside from the flat Elk Valley floor and a couple of miles from the little town of Fernie. Outings to Kimberley are possible; a coach goes weekly, taking about 90 minutes.

VILLAGE CHARM ★★☆☆☆
Unpretentious small town

A slope-side resort has grown from very little in recent years, but there's still not much there except convenient lodging and a few restaurants, bars and sports shops. It is quiet at night. There's much more going on in the

NEWS

2013/14: Signage improvements continued; a firepit was installed on the deck of the Slopeside cafe at the base.

KEY FACTS

Resort	1065m
	3,490ft
Slopes	1065-2135m
	3,490-7,000ft
Lifts	10
Pistes	2,500 acres
Green	30%
Blue	40%
Black	30%
Snowmaking	15%

nearby town, named after the guy who discovered coal here and triggered a boom in the early 1900s. Some 'historic' buildings have survived.

Fernie town is primarily a place for locals, not tourists, but there are some lively bars, decent places to eat and a reasonable range of shops. It is down to earth rather than charming, and reporters' reactions to it vary: some like staying in a 'real' town while others are put off by the highway that runs through it, close to the centre. Most stress the friendly locals.

CONVENIENCE ★★★★☆
Base lodging or bus ride
There is accommodation at the resort and in town. Buses between the two run hourly and cost C$3 one way, stopping at some of the bigger hotels on the way. They run until 2am on Friday and Saturday. A reporter found drivers 'happy to be flagged down'.

SCENERY ★★★☆☆
The rocky ridges are impressive
Fernie's two main peaks, Grizzly and Polar, are part of the steep-sided Lizard Range. They provide an impressively rocky backdrop. There are good views across the Elk Valley too.

THE MOUNTAINS

Fernie's 2,500 acres pack in a lot of variety, from superb green terrain at the bottom to scary chutes, open bowls and huge numbers of steep runs in the trees. Quite a few runs go directly down the fall line.

Over the years we've been visiting,

both the trail map and the signposting have improved, to the point where you can find your way around most of the time with confidence. But we still find it quite easy to be misled by the map in certain areas; you get the best out of the area with some sort of local guidance. Without it, you can end up in tight trees on slopes of double-diamond steepness. The map employs some ludicrously small type.

EXTENT OF THE SLOPES ★★★☆☆
Bowl after bowl
What you see when you arrive at the lift base is a trio of impressive mogul slopes towering above you. These excellent black runs exemplify one of the weaknesses of Fernie's lift system: to get to them you must ride lifts way off to the left or right, and then make long traverses to get to the start of the runs proper – a slow business.

The slow Deer chair serves green runs at the foot of these black slopes, but goes no further.

On the right, riding the slow Elk quad followed by the fast Great Bear quad takes you to the ridge where **Lizard Bowl** meets **Cedar Bowl**. You can traverse across the head of both of these open/lightly wooded bowls and descend pretty much wherever you like, though both have trails marked on the map. At the far side of Cedar Bowl are steeper runs among tighter trees from Snake Ridge. The Haul Back T-bar brings you out of Cedar to ride the Boomerang chair. This serves a mini-bowl between Lizard and Cedar.

Off to the left, the Timber Bowl fast

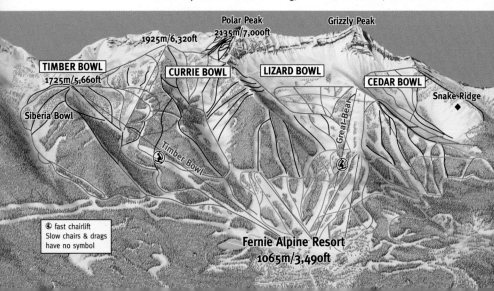

Fernie Alpine Resort
1065m/3,490ft

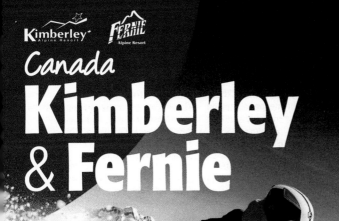

Canada
Kimberley
& Fernie

2-for-1 Lift Passes

2-for-1 Lift Pass Offer
Book by 30 Nov 2014.
Not available in resort.
Terms and conditions
apply to each resort.

SAVE £££s WITH OUR *Inghams PLUS* DEALS

CASH-BACK OFFER! SAVE £50 per couple | **2-FOR-1 TUITION OFFER**
$100 TO SPEND IN MOUNTAIN RESTAURANTS in Fernie | **GREAT VALUE SKI SAVER PACKS**
FREE CONNECTING FLIGHTS TO CRANBROOK AIRPORT FOR SHORTER TRANSFERS
FREE EQUIPMENT AND LIFT PASS for children under 12 | **FREE SKI INSURANCE** for children

Our featured hotel in Fernie is **LIZARD CREEK LODGE & CONDOS**
and in Kimberley it's **TRICKLE CREEK LODGE**. Both offer outstanding value,
a warm welcome and an excellent range of facilities, in perfect locations.

2013 WINNER 2012 WINNER 2011 WINNER 2010 WINNER
British Annual Canada Travel Awards
WINNER - Best Ski Tour Operator to Canada

Award winning
in-resort service from the
best team in the mountains

inghams.co.uk/kimberley   inghams.co.uk/fernie
Call us on **01483 371 235**

100% BONDED SECURITY | **ATOL** 0025 | **IATA** | **ABTA** V4871

Terms and Conditions apply to all offers.

LIFT PASSES

Prices in C$

Age	1-day	6-day
under 13	38	200
13 to 17	71	392
18 to 64	94	497
65 plus	75	395

Free Under 6

Beginner Rental, limited pass and tuition deals

Notes Prices are advance purchase online and include taxes; half-day pass available

GETTING THERE

Air Calgary 305km/ 190 miles (3hr45)

SNOWPIX.COM / CHRIS GILL

There are long views over the resort village and the town of Fernie from the slopes ↓

quad chair gives access to **Siberia Bowl** and the lower part of **Timber Bowl**. But for access to the higher slopes of Timber Bowl and to **Currie Bowl** you must take the slow White Pass quad. A long traverse from the top gets you to the steeper slopes on the far flank of Currie (our favourite area). The traverse takes you past a short, slow triple chair which accesses **Polar Peak**, the high point of the ski area – 210m higher than the White Pass chair; the run from Polar Peak to the base is over 1000m vertical.

Any descent of Currie or Siberia, and some descents in Timber Bowl mean you have to go all the way to the lift base, and it takes quite a while to get back up.

Free mountain tours are available twice a day, but they do no more than scratch the surface.

FAST LIFTS ★★✫✫✫
A poor show
There are only two fast chairs, serving opposite ends of the mountain. Slow chairs and a draglift elsewhere soak up time. Then you spend more time traversing to many of the descents. But keen intermediates can rack up the miles doing laps in Siberia and Timber bowls on the fast Timber Bowl chair and in Lizard on the fast Great Bear quad.

QUEUES ★★★★✫
Not usually a problem
Queues are generally rare unless there are weekend crowds from Calgary or heavy snow keeps part of the mountain closed. The slopes are usually very quiet; in March 2013 we skied lots of runs more or less alone.

TERRAIN PARKS ★★✫✫✫
Just a rail park
There is no proper park, but there is a patrolled rail park beside the Great Bear Express – you'll need a special pass (C$5 per day) and must sign a waiver to use it.

SNOW RELIABILITY ★★★★✫
A key part of the appeal
Fernie has an excellent snow record – with an average of 360 inches per year, it's better than practically anywhere in Colorado, for example. But the altitude is modest: rain is not unknown, and in warm weather the lower slopes can suffer. Too much snow can be a problem, with the high bowls prone to closure; the headwalls hold a lot of snow and require a lot of bombing to be made safe. As a whole, the area faces roughly north-east; but many runs are on the flanks of the ridges, facing south-east, so the sun can affect things in late season.

On our most recent visits we've been impressed by the quality of the groomed runs, despite less than ideal weather; we put it down to the very low levels of traffic. Snowmaking has been increased over recent years and now covers most of the lower runs.

FOR EXPERTS ★★★★★
Wonderful with guidance
The combination of heavy snowfalls and abundant steep terrain with the shelter of trees makes this a superb mountain for good skiers, so long as you know where you are going. If you don't, consider getting guidance.

There are about a dozen identifiable faces offering genuine black or double-black slopes, each of them with several alternative ways down and all worth exploring. Pay attention to the diamonds: the doubles are the genuine article.

The recently opened Polar Peak is of limited vertical but serious double-

SCHOOLS

Fernie Telus
t 423 2406

Classes
C$143 for full day
(incl. taxes)
Private lessons
From C$144 (incl.
taxes) for 1.5hr

CHILDCARE

Resort Kids
t 423 2430
Age 18mnth to 6yr

Ski school
Ages 6 to 12

diamond gradient; there is one single diamond run, but even this can have a tricky entry. You can hike to a steep gated area where transceivers (and great care) are required.

There are a few areas where you can do laps fairly efficiently, but mostly you have to put up with a cycle of long traverse–descent–run-out–lift–lift on each lap (with an extra lift to get to the Polar Peak area).

There are backcountry routes you can take with guidance (some include an overnight camp) and snowcat operations in other nearby mountains – read the feature panel overleaf. A regular reporter enjoyed exploring Fish Bowl, a short hike outside the resort boundary from Cedar Bowl.

FOR INTERMEDIATES ★★★★★
Getting better

In recent years Fernie has made great strides to broaden its appeal. These days, the resort grooms quite a wide range of runs, including some great blue cruisers down all the bowls – but there are also quite a few blacks that get regularly groomed. And the lack of crowds makes fast skiing on these runs a real pleasure. But the groomed stuff doesn't add up to much when you compare it with many other resorts with the same sort of acreage, and after a big dump the grooming takes time. If you are not happy to try some of the easier ungroomed terrain you may find the place a bit limited. For the adventurous willing to give the powder a go, though, Fernie can be fabulous.

FOR BEGINNERS ★★★★★
Surprisingly, pretty good

There's a good nursery area served by two lifts (a moving carpet and a drag), and the lower mountain served by the Deer and Elk chairs has lots of wide, smooth trails to gain confidence on.

FOR BOARDERS ★★★★★
Fine if you're good

Fernie is a fine place for good boarders (and there are a lot of local experts). Lots of natural gullies, hits and endless off-piste opportunities – including some adrenalin-pumping tree runs and knee-deep powder bowls – will keep freeriders of all abilities grinning from ear to ear. But there's a lot of traversing involved to get to many of the best runs – hard work in fresh snow and bumpy later. The main

board shops, Board Stiff and Edge of the World, are in downtown Fernie. It's not a brilliant place for freestylers – there's just a rail park, for which you'll need a special pass.

FOR CROSS-COUNTRY ★★★★★
Some possibilities

There are 10km of trails in the forest adjacent to the resort. In the Fernie area as a whole there are around 50km of tracks.

MOUNTAIN RESTAURANTS ★★★★★
One tiny sit-down hut

Lost Boys Cafe is a tiny self-service place in a fine position with great views at the top of Timber Bowl with a basic, limited menu. It gets busy even when the mountain isn't. Bear's Den at the top of the Elk chair is an open-air fast-food kiosk. Naturally, most people eat at the base area. The ancient no-frills Day Lodge at the Griz Lodge serves soups, burgers and daily specials. Look at 'Eating out' to see other options – we usually head for the Corner Pocket.

SCHOOLS AND GUIDES ★★★★★
Highly praised

Reporters have praised the school, which seems to achieve rapid progress. A recent visitor was very happy with his 'really brilliant' private lessons, but also noted that class sizes are often very small, making group lessons very good value.

There are several programmes to help you get the best out of the mountain. The Steep and Deep camp has had good feedback; it is a two-day programme (C$329) where you get technique tips while exploring steep terrain – a great way to get to know at least some of the mountain. We've had good sessions being guided by some of their instructor-guides. 'First Tracks' (from C$269 for three people) is a two-hour private lesson that gets you up the mountain at 8am, before the lifts are open to others.

FOR FAMILIES ★★★★★
Good day care centre

There's a day care centre in the Cornerstone Lodge. Once a week there's a craft night for children aged 6 to 12. And there's an adventure park with cut-outs of bears and wolves. The ski school offers a 'family' private lesson option for up to two adults and three kids.

Fernie

615

Build your own shortlist: www.wheretoskiandsnowboard.com

RIDE THE SNOWCATS – HELI-SKIING AT AN AFFORDABLE PRICE

Good skiers who relish off-piste should consider treating themselves to some cat-skiing, where you ride snowcats instead of lifts; there are several operations in this area. We've had two or three fabulous days at Island Lake Lodge (423 3700), which does all-inclusive packages in a luxury lodge (spacious rooms, big lounge, hot tubs, bar, excellent food) 10km from Fernie, reached only by snowcat, in 7,000 acres of spectacular bowls and ridges. It has 26 rooms and three cats. In a day you might do 10 to 14 powder runs averaging 500m vertical, taking in all kinds of terrain from gentle open slopes to some very Alpine adventures. You can do single days on a standby basis. Fernie Wilderness Adventures (877 423 6704) has three cats accessing 5,000 acres.

SNOWPIX.COM / CHRIS GILL

WESTERN CANADA

616

Resort news and key links: www.wheretoskiandsnowboard.com

UK PACKAGES

Alpine Answers, American Ski Classics, Canadian Affair, Canadian Powder Tours, Crystal, Crystal Finest, Frontier, Inghams, Momentum, Ski Independence, Ski Safari, Skitracer, Skiworld, Snow Finders, Thomson

ACTIVITIES

Indoor Aquatic Centre (pool, hot tub, steam), fitness centre, climbing wall, spas, cinema, museum, gallery, library, brewery tour

Outdoor Walking, snowmobiling, ice rink, curling, dog sledding, sleigh rides, snowshoe excursions, ziplining

Central reservations phone number Call 1 403 209 3321

Phone numbers From distant parts of Canada, add the prefix 1 250; from abroad, add the prefix +1 250

TOURIST OFFICE

www.skifernie.com

STAYING THERE

Chalets Canadian Powder Tours has one with an outdoor hot tub in town. **Hotels** There's an adequate choice. Lizard Creek and other places can be booked through Inghams, Frontier, Crystal and Ski Independence.

AT THE LIFT BASE
****Lizard Creek Lodge** Best ski-in/ski-out condo hotel, with good rooms and a grand, high-ceilinged lounge; spa, outdoor pool and hot tub. Good food (read 'Eating out'). We've enjoyed staying here a couple of times.
***Alpine Lodge** B&B on edge of resort. 'Homely and welcoming.'
***Cornerstone Lodge** Modern condo hotel with hot tub.
***Griz Inn Sport Hotel** Condo hotel at foot of slopes. Pool.
***Slopeside Lodge** Formerly Wolf's Den. At base of slope. Basic but convenient. Hot tub.

NOT AT THE LIFT BASE
****Best Western Plus Fernie Mountain Lodge** Next to the golf course near town. Pool, hot tub, fitness room.
***Park Place Lodge** Close to centre of town, lively pub; pool in main lobby.
Apartments Snow Creek Lodge is 'ski in and out, well equipped, very comfy, with hot tubs and pool in a lovely slope-side location'. Timberline Lodges are very comfortable condos a shuttle-ride from the lifts.

EATING OUT ★★★☆☆
Better choice in town
At the base, Lizard Creek Lodge offers 'generous portions – lamb shank particularly good'. The Corner Pocket

is an airy modern place at the Griz Inn, simply furnished, with quite a wide-ranging menu, good service and generally excellent food. Yamagoya in the Alpine Lodge does Japanese ('good to eat some lighter food for a change', 'wonderful ice cream'); there's another branch in town. Kelsey's (part of a chain) serves standard and reliable steaks, burgers, pasta and pizza.

In the town of Fernie, there are quite a few options, though some places we have liked in the past have closed. On our last visit we enjoyed an excellent simple dinner at the jolly, busy Brick House (all BC wines though, which means pricey). We've also enjoyed various Asian cuisines at Curry Bowl – and the Indian food at Tandoor & Grill in the out-of-town Stanford hotel is a reader tip.

APRES-SKI ★★★☆☆
Have a beer
When the lifts close, head for the Griz Bar above the Day Lodge. During the week, the resort bars are pretty quiet later on. In town, the bars of the Royal hotel are popular with locals, as is the Park Place Lodge Pub (with pool, table-football and big-screen TVs).

OFF THE SLOPES ★★☆☆☆
Get out and about
The Arts Station has two galleries, a theatre and craft studios, and there is a walking tour of historic Fernie – you buy a C$5 self-guided booklet from the visitor information centre or retailers. Watching the local ice hockey team, the Ghostriders, is 'well worth doing – good fun'. There's a pool at the Aquatic Centre in town.

SNOWPIX.COM / CHRIS GILL

Kicking Horse

One of Canada's newest resorts: only a few lifts, but great powder at the top, and a small village at the base

TOP 10 RATINGS

Extent	★★★
Fast lifts	★★★
Queues	★★★★
Snow	★★★★
Expert	★★★★
Intermediate	★★
Beginner	★★★
Charm	★★
Convenience	★★★★
Scenery	★★★

RPI	160
lift pass	£310
ski hire	£125
lessons	£200
food & drink	£180
total	£815

- ➕ Great terrain for experts and some for adventurous intermediates
- ➕ Big vertical served by a gondola
- ➕ Splendid mountaintop restaurant

- ➖ Resort village still embryonic
- ➖ Gondola needs a mid-station to make the most of the mountain
- ➖ Few groomed intermediate runs

Kicking Horse was developed from a small local hill in 2000, when a long gondola was built accessing two high, powder-filled bowls – previously heli-skiing country. There were great ambitions to turn it into a major resort. But of course things have moved much more slowly than was planned.

In 2011 KH was sold to Resorts of the Canadian Rockies, owner of Fernie, Kimberley and other resorts, but there is no sign of any great transformation. The lift system and the 'village' at the base remain very limited, but the place is worth incorporating in a tour, or visiting for a day from Banff or Lake Louise.

THE RESORT

Eight miles from the logging/railway town of Golden, Kicking Horse still has only two main lifts and a tiny base village. Daily Powder Express buses run from Banff and Lake Louise – the 2013/14 cost was C$89.95, including a lift pass.

Village charm The small resort village at the lift base has several lodges, a few restaurants and bars, a ski shop and a general store. The town of Golden has no real appeal, but there is (slightly) more going on there.
Convenience Fine if you stay at the mountain – and why not?
Scenery The scenery is not without drama – especially from the top.

THE MOUNTAINS

The lower two-thirds of the hill is wooded, with trails cut in the usual style. The upper third is a mix of open and lightly wooded slopes spread over four separate bowls, with scores of ways down for experts through the open terrain, chutes and trees.
Slopes The eight-seat gondola rises 1150m to the peak of Eagle's Eye; it does so in a single stage, which suits summer visitors but not skiers. It serves three bowls and CPR Ridge. To the left as you ride the gondola is Bowl Over. Or take the narrow Milly Goat Traverse along a ridge towards Super Bowl – the last part of this 'traverse' is a hike up to Terminator Peak, but you can opt for an easier walk/skate around the back. To the right of the gondola is Crystal Bowl; you can do laps here on the slow chair to the slightly higher peak of Blue Heaven, which also accesses Feuz Bowl. From Bowl Over, Super Bowl and Feuz Bowl – and if you go below the chair in Crystal Bowl – you have to make the full descent to the base. Two chairlifts near the base serve the lower runs that formed the original ski area

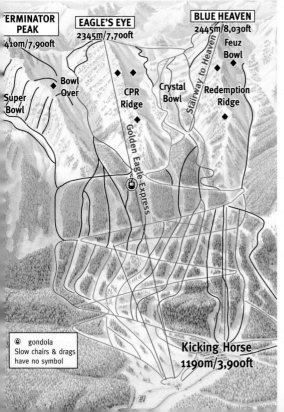

Kicking Horse
1190m/3,900ft

gondola
Slow chairs & drags have no symbol

Snowboarding Freeriders will love this powder paradise.

Cross-country Dawn Mountain has loops of 30km including skating trails.

Mountain restaurants Strangely, for such a limited and unpretentious resort, Eagle's Eye at the top of the gondola is Canada's best mountain restaurant; a 2014 reporter confirms that it offers excellent food and service in stylish log-cabin surroundings, as well as splendid views. The Heaven's Door yurt (tent) in Crystal Bowl serves snacks. Most people lunch at the base; Slopeside Cafe does 'excellent fresh soups, wraps and stews'.

Schools and guides A reporter took a group lesson, which 'was worth every cent – a lot of fun and we learned a lot'; she also enjoyed the free tours.

Families The school teaches children from the age of three.

STAYING THERE

There are smart, quite large condo-style lodges on the slopes. But we'd choose to stay in one of three much more captivating family-run places (each with about 10 rooms and outdoor hot tubs) a short walk away – described below.

Hotels The log-built Vagabond Lodge features a fabulous first-floor living room and comfortable, traditional-style rooms. Copper Horse Lodge has spacious but more austere rooms in modern styles. Winston Lodge (formerly Highland Lodge) has handmade wooden furniture, a welcoming sitting room with a floor-to-ceiling stone fireplace and a cosy, woody saloon. In Golden, a reader has enjoyed staying at the Auberge Kicking Horse B&B.

Apartments The Whispering Pines and the Selkirks townhomes have been recommended.

Eating out Eagle's Eye at the top of the gondola opens on Friday and Saturday evenings. The Saloon in Winston Lodge does burgers, steaks, pizzas etc. Corks in Copper Horse Lodge does much the same. In Golden, Kicking Horse Grill, Eleven22 and the out-of-town Cedar House are rated.

Après-ski Quiet. In Golden, Mad Trapper and Taps are lively bars.

Off the slopes There is snowmobiling, snowshoeing, tubing and an ice rink; plus a wolf centre near Golden.

NEWS

2013/14: A new daycare facility opened at the base, taking kids from 18 months to 6 years old. The Slopeside Cafe opened in the day lodge. Various jobs were undertaken on the mountain, eg glading to open up new descents into Crystal Bowl.

KEY FACTS

Resort	1190m
	3,900ft
Slopes	1190-2445m
	3,900-8,030ft
Lifts	5
Pistes	2,825 acres
Green	20%
Blue	20%
Black	60%
Snowmaking	Some

UK PACKAGES

Alpine Answers, Canadian Affair, Frontier, Momentum, Ski Independence, Ski Safari, Skitracer, Skiworld

Central reservations
Call 439 5425
Phone numbers
From distant parts of Canada, add the prefix 1 250; from abroad, add the prefix +1 250

TOURIST OFFICE

www.kickinghorse
resort.com

here. There are free mountain tours twice a day.

Fast lifts Just the gondola.

Queues We've had reports of serious weekend queues for the gondola. During the week, though, it's quiet.

Terrain park No sign of one yet.

Snow reliability The top slopes average 250 to 300 inches a year (a good but not spectacular record) and usually have light, dry powder. But the lower ones may have crud and thin cover and average only 100 inches a year; and with most of the runs, you have to descend the lower slopes every time – a real drawback.

Experts From the top, you can go right into the gentle Crystal Bowl via an easy piste, or via serious chutes from CPR Ridge; or go left down pleasantly wooded single-diamond slopes into Bowl Over; or head to Super Bowl. The Stairway to Heaven chair serves further single-diamond wooded slopes. Feuz Bowl offers various challenges, not all of genuine double-diamond steepness, and gets tracked out less quickly. The lower half of the mountain has short black runs cut through the woods, some with big moguls. There is heli-skiing nearby.

Intermediates Adventurous types will have a fine time learning to play in the powder from Blue Heaven down to Crystal Bowl. Most of it is open, but you can head off into trees if you want to. The area of groomed cruising is increasing – there's a top-to-bottom 10km winding green run, and long blues down the front, but for now the timid are better off elsewhere.

Beginners The beginner area at the base is fine, with easy slopes (but maybe poor snow) on the lower mountain for progression.

SKI BANFF / LAKE LOUISE / ALEC PYTLOWANY

Lake Louise

Stunning views and the biggest ski area in the Banff region, with some good places to stay but no real village

RATINGS

The mountains

Extent	★★★
Fast lifts	★★★★
Queues	★★★★
Terrain p'ks	★★★★
Snow	★★★
Expert	★★★★
Intermediate	★★★★
Beginner	★★★
Boarder	★★★
X-country	★★★★★
Restaurants	★★
Schools	★★★★
Families	★★★★

The resort

Charm	★★★
Convenience	★
Scenery	★★★★
Eating out	★★
Après-ski	★★
Off-slope	★★★★

RPI 150

lift pass	£290
ski hire	£115
lessons	£190
food & drink	£180
total	£775

NEWS

2014/15: Temple Lodge is being improved. The famous après-ski dinner and torchlit descent is being reinstated at Whitehorn Lodge. There will be further improvements to snowmaking.

2013/14: Whitehorn Lodge at mid-mountain, out of winter action for some years, reopened for bistro meals with fantastic views. The resort hosted the FIS (International Ski Federation) Snowboard Cross World Cup for the first time.

- ➕ Spectacular high-mountain scenery, in a largely unspoiled wilderness
- ➕ Large ski area by local standards
- ➕ Snowy Sunshine Village within reach (read the Banff chapter)
- ➕ Excellent, very scenic cross-country

- ➖ 'Village' is just a few hotels and shops, quiet in the evening
- ➖ Slopes a drive or bus ride away
- ➖ Snowfall record modest
- ➖ Can be very cold, and the chairlifts have no covers

If you care more for scenery than for après-ski action, Lake Louise is worth considering. We've seen a few spectacular mountain views, and we reckon the view from the Fairmont Chateau Lake Louise hotel across frozen Lake Louise to the Victoria Glacier is as spectacular as they come: simply stunning.

Even if you prefer the more animated base of Banff, you'll want to make expeditions to Lake Louise during your holiday. It can't compete with Sunshine Village for quantity of snow, but it's an interesting mountain. And from the slopes you get a distant version of that stunning view.

THE RESORT

Lake Louise is small, but it's a resort of three distinct parts. First, there's the splendid lake itself overlooked by the huge Fairmont Chateau Lake Louise hotel. Then there's Lake Louise 'village' – a spacious collection of hotels, condos, petrol station, liquor store and a few shops a couple of miles away in the valley bottom. Finally, a mile or two across the valley, there's the lift base station.

Sunshine Village and Norquay ski areas (covered in our Banff chapter) are 45 minutes away by road. Buses (covered by the Tri-area lift pass) run only two days a week to each (on the days the ski school Club Ski Program goes there), so having a car helps. Bus trips also run to the more distant resorts of Kicking Horse and Panorama, subject to demand, and there are heli-skiing day trips.

VILLAGE CHARM ★★★
Low key and relaxed
The 'village' has no focus other than a small shopping mall, but it's a quiet and relaxing place, even if the peace is disturbed by the occasional mile-long train. Up at the lake, it's all about the setting: the scenery provides the charm, and somehow the scale of the giant hotel seems appropriate.

CONVENIENCE ★
Lake or village, not slopes
Most lodging is around the 'village'. Buses run every half hour to the ski area. Staying up at the Chateau, or near it, just means a slightly longer bus ride. Taxis are said to be 'ridiculously expensive'.

SCENERY ★★★★
Splendid lakes and mountains
Lake Louise itself is in a spectacular setting beneath the Victoria Glacier. Tom Wilson, who discovered it in 1882, declared: 'As God is my judge, I never in all my exploration have seen such a matchless scene.' Neither have we. It can be appreciated from many of the rooms of the Fairmont Chateau Lake Louise hotel on the lake shore, and there are grand views from the ski area of other peaks and glaciers, including Canada's Matterhorn lookalike, Mount Assiniboine.

THE MOUNTAINS

There's an attractive mixture of high, open slopes, low trails cut through forest and gladed slopes between the two. There are good, free guided tours at 10am and 1.15pm. Louise is known for fiercely low temperatures; we've luckily escaped them on recent visits.

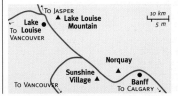

KEY FACTS

Resort	1645m
	5,400ft

Sunshine, Norquay and Lake Louise

Slopes	1630-2730m
	5,350-8,950ft
Lifts	28
Pistes	7,748 acres
Green	23%
Blue	39%
Black	38%
Snowmaking	24%

Lake Louise only

Slopes	1645-2635m
	5,400-8,650ft
Lifts	10
Pistes	4,200 acres
Green	25%
Blue	45%
Black	30%
Snowmaking	40%

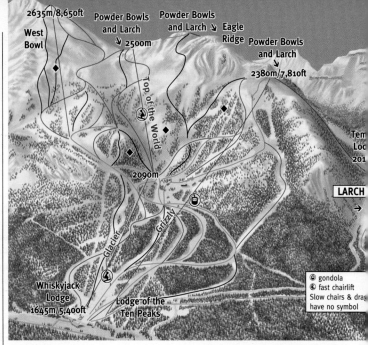

EXTENT OF THE SLOPES ★★★☆☆
A wide variety

The Lake Louise ski area is a fair size by North American standards but is quite modest by Alpine standards; a good intermediate could ski the groomed trails in a day or two.

From the base area you have a choice of a fast quad to mid-mountain, followed by a six-pack to the top centre of the **Front Side** (or South Face), or a gondola direct to a slightly lower point off to the right side. From both, as elsewhere, there's a choice of green, blue or black runs (good for a group of mixed abilities who want to keep meeting up). Or you can stay on the lower part of the mountain using the chairs. From mid-mountain on the left, the long Summit draglift takes you to the high point of the area.

From here or the top chair you can go over the ridge and into the **Powder Bowls** – almost treeless, shady and mainly steep (though there are easy ways round the steep parts). From the top of the gondola, the Ptarmigan area is more wooded.

From below the bowls you can take the Paradise lift back to the top again or go on down to Temple Lodge, base station of the Ptarmigan chair to the main mountain and a fast chair to the separate **Larch** area (just off our map). Its lift-served vertical is a modest 375m, but the sector has pretty wooded runs for all abilities. From Temple Lodge there's a long green path back to the base area. A 2013 visitor found the signposting confusing: 'I'd start on a green but end up on a black diamond.'

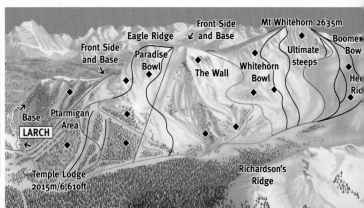

Tri-area lift pass

Prices in C$

Age	1-day	6-day
under 13	33	165
13 to 17	88	446
18 to 64	99	507
65 plus	88	446

Free Under 6

Beginner Lift, lesson and rental package

Notes Covers transport between Banff, Lake Louise, Norquay and Sunshine Village; prices include 5% tax

TANYA BOOTH

From the Larch area you can inspect the good tree skiing served by the Ptarmigan chair; Temple Lodge is at the bottom ↓

FAST LIFTS ★★★★
Beware the cold rides
There is gondola and fast chair access to most of the slopes on the Front Side, and to Larch. The few slow lifts serve steep slopes where your descent may take some time, so the lift ride time is bearable. This is a famously cold resort, and reporters regularly complain of extremely cold rides.

QUEUES ★★★★
Not during the week
Queues are rarely a problem midweek. But half of the area's visitors come for the day from cities such as Calgary, so there can be queues for some lifts at weekends and public holidays ('up to 45 minutes for the gondola on the Saturday'). Busy pistes can be a problem too.

TERRAIN PARKS ★★★★
Better every year
The terrain park improves year on year and, once the snow is in good shape, is found on the lower slopes under the Grizzly Express. Last season it had 32 features set out in clearly defined areas including progression and XL jumps, plus a snowcross and an airbag. The FIS (International Ski Federation) Snowboard Cross World Cup returns in December 2014.

SNOW RELIABILITY ★★★
Usually OK
Lake Louise gets around 180 inches a year on the Front Side, which is not a lot, and nowhere near as much as Sunshine Village down the road (see the Banff chapter). The Front Side faces south-west, which is not good; but the Powder Bowls face north-east, and Larch north. Snowmaking covers 40% of the pistes. Grooming is fine.

FOR EXPERTS ★★★★
Widespread pleasure
There are plenty of steep slopes – but bear in mind that powder is less likely here than in many other Canadian resorts. On the Front Side, as well as a score of marked black-diamond trails in and above the trees, there is the alluring West Bowl, reached from the Summit drag – a wide, open expanse of snow outside the area boundary to be explored with a guide.

Inside the boundary, the Powder Bowls area on the Back Side offers countless black mogul/powder runs, though there is no great variation in character. From the Summit drag, you can drop into The Ultimate Steeps area if it is open, directly behind the peak – a row of exceptional chutes almost 1km long. Starting from the blue Boomerang trail, you can also access much tamer, wide, open slopes in Boomerang Bowl.

The Top of the World six-pack takes you to the very popular Paradise Bowl/ Eagle Ridge area, also served by its own triple chair on the Back Side – there are endless variants here, ranging from comfortably steep single diamonds to very challenging double diamonds. The seriously steep slope served by the Ptarmigan quad chair has great gladed terrain and is a good place to escape the crowds.

The Larch area has some steep double-diamond stuff in the trees. And with good snow-cover, the open snowfields at the top are great for those with the energy to hike up.

Heli-skiing day trips are available to bases outside the National Park.

FOR INTERMEDIATES ★★★★
Some good cruising
Almost half the runs are classified as intermediate. But from the top of the Front Side the blue runs down are little more than paths in places, and there are very few blues or greens in the Powder Bowls. Once you get part-

ACTIVITIES

Indoor Hotel-based pools, saunas and hot tubs

Outdoor Ice skating, walking, swimming in hot springs, sleigh rides, dog sledding, snowshoeing, tubing

GETTING THERE

Air Calgary 200km/ 125 miles (2hr15)

TANYA BOOTH

The base lodge is a good example of its kind, with various eating and drinking options ↓

way down the Front Side the blues are much more interesting. And when groomed, the Men's and Ladies' Downhill black runs are great fast cruises on the lower half of the mountain. Juniper, in the same area, is a varied cruise. Meadowlark is a beautiful treelined single black run to the base area, curling away from the lifts – to find it from the Grizzly Express gondola, first follow the Eagle Meadows green. The Larch area has some short but ideal intermediate runs – and reporters have enjoyed the natural lumps and bumps of the aptly named blue, Rock Garden ('never had so much fun; really away from it all').

The adventurous should try the blue Boomerang run – which starts with a short side-step up from the top of the Summit drag – and also some of the ungroomed terrain in the Powder Bowls reachable from that run.

FOR BEGINNERS ★★★★★
Some long greens

Lake Louise offers first-timers a package that includes a beginner pass with tuition and equipment rental. There is a decent nursery area near the base served by three moving carpets. You progress to the gentle, wide Wiwaxy (a designated 'learning area'), Pinecone Way and the slightly more difficult Deer Run or Eagle Meadows. The greens in the Powder Bowls and in the Larch area are worth trying for the views, though some do contain slightly steep pitches and can get busy ('Our beginner was very nervous trying the Saddleback Bowl,' said one past reporter).

FOR BOARDERS ★★★★★
Something for everyone

Lake Louise is a great mountain for freeriders, with plenty of challenging terrain in the bowls and glades. Beginners will have fun on the Front Side's blue and green runs. But beware of the vicious Summit button lift (top left looking at the trail map). Also avoid the long, very gentle green run through the woods from Larch back to base. This is flat in places and a nightmare for boarders. Freestylers will enjoy the varied terrain park.

FOR CROSS-COUNTRY ★★★★★
High in quality and quantity

It's a very good area for cross-country, with around 80km of groomed trails in the National Park – plenty of scenic stops needed. There are 14km of excellent trails in the local area and at Lake Louise itself. An alternative is the secluded Emerald Lake Lodge, 40km away and with some lovely trails.

MOUNTAIN RESTAURANTS ★★★★★
Good base facilities

Last season Whitehorn Lodge, which in recent years had not been operating in winter, reopened as a 'full-service Alpine-style Bistro'; reports please. Temple Lodge near the bottom of Larch and the Ptarmigan chair is a rustic-style building with 'very good' table-service and 'reasonable' self-service restaurants, let's hope the planned revamp deals with the frequent overcrowding.

Most people eat at the base, where there are big-scale facilities. The Northface Bistro in the Whiskey Jack

SCHOOLS

Ski Big 3
t 1-877 760 7731
Lake Louise
t 522 3555

Classes (Big 3 prices)
3 days guided tuition
of the three areas
C$314 incl. tax
Private lessons
Half day (3hr) C$419,
incl. tax, for up to 5
people

CHILDCARE

Lake Louise Daycare
t 522 3555
Ages 18 days to 6yr

Ski school
Ages 5 to 12

UK PACKAGES

Alpine Answers,
American Ski Classics,
Canadian Affair, Crystal,
Crystal Finest, Elegant
Resorts, Flexiski,
Frontier, Inghams,
Momentum, Neilson,
Oxford Ski Co,
PowderBeds, Ski
Bespoke, Ski
Independence, Ski
Safari, Skitracer,
Skiworld, Snow Finders,
Supertravel, Thomson,
Virgin Snow

Phone numbers
From distant parts of
Canada, add the
prefix 1 403; from
abroad, add the prefix
+1 403

TOURIST OFFICE

www.skilouise.com
www.SkiBig3.com

Lodge offers fixed-price, 'high-quality' buffet lunches and 'good-value' breakfasts. The Lodge of the Ten Peaks is a hugely impressive log-built affair with various 'fairly efficient' eating, drinking and lounging options.

SCHOOLS AND GUIDES ★★★★
All reports positive
All past reports are positive, for both adults' and children's classes and a 2013 visitor was enthusiastic: 'The school is well run and the instructors are extremely professional. Probably the friendliest group of instructors we have ever come across. Excellent.' See the Banff chapter for details of the excellent three-day, three-mountain Club Ski Program. The First Tracks programme gives you exclusive lift access half an hour before the resort opens to the public and includes instruction.

FOR FAMILIES ★★★★
Good facilities
The resort has good school and childcare facilities that have been praised by reporters. Parents are lent free pagers too. The Minute Maid Wilderness Adventure Park is a kids' learning area at the base. The school gets good reviews and offers a fun programme for teenagers.

STAYING THERE
You might like to consider a two-centre holiday, combining Lake Louise with, say, Banff or Kicking Horse.
Hotels Summer is the peak season here. Prices are much lower in winter.
*****Fairmont Chateau Lake Louise (522 3511) Huge old place with 550 rooms, seven restaurants and stunning views over frozen Lake Louise to the glacier beyond; shops, pool, hot tub, spa, steam room.
****Post (522 3989) Small, relaxed Relais & Châteaux place in the village, with excellent restaurant (huge wine list), new Stübli fondue restaurant, Outpost Pub, pool, hot tub, steam room. Avoid rooms on railway side. 'Beautifully furnished; friendly, helpful.'
***Deer Lodge (522 3991) Charming old hotel next to the Chateau. Small rooms, but helpful staff and good food. Roof-top hot tub.
***Lake Louise Inn (522 3791) Cheaper option in the village, with pool, hot tub and steam. One recent reporter has stayed there nine times.

Apartments Some are available but local shopping is limited. The Baker Creek resort (522 3761) is a popular retreat for a traditional 'log cabin, log fire, isolation and wildlife' experience.
At altitude Skoki Lodge (522 1347) is a charming log cabin, 11km on skis from Temple Lodge. Built in the 1930s and still offering a backcountry experience, with no electricity or running water.

EATING OUT ★★
Limited choice
The Post hotel's restaurant has repeatedly impressed us and reporters with its ambitious food and excellent service. We and they have also enjoyed the simpler food and cosy ambience of its Outpost Pub. The Chateau offers five different dining experiences, including the top-notch Fairview Dining Room and the 'really good' Glacier Saloon ('sea chowder and bison pie both excellent'). Readers also like the Timberwolf Cafe (Italian) at the Lake Louise Inn, the Mountain restaurant (pasta, burgers) and Village Grill (Western/Chinese menu) for cheaper options.

APRES-SKI ★★
Lively at teatime, quiet later
We're pleased to hear that après-ski dinners plus torchlit descents are being reinstated at Whitehorn Lodge. At close of play there is some action in the main base lodge, but the hub is the Kokanee Kabin, which has live music most weekends, a terrace and an outdoor fire. Later on, things are fairly quiet. Try the Glacier Saloon, in Chateau Lake Louise, the Explorer's Lounge in the Lake Louise Inn or the Outpost Pub in the Post hotel.

OFF THE SLOPES ★★★★
Beautiful scenery
Lake Louise makes a lovely, peaceful place to stay for someone who enjoys the great outdoors. The lake itself makes a stunning setting for walks, snowshoeing, cross-country skiing and ice skating. Reporters highly recommend the dog sledding and the Wilson Icefield discovery tour – a helicopter flight, snowshoe walk and lunch ('BBQ with superb steaks'). There are lots of attractions around Banff too (read the Banff chapter).
Lake Louise is near one end of the Columbia Icefields Parkway, a three-hour drive to Jasper through spectacular national parks.

Lake Louise

Build your own shortlist: www.wheretoskiandsnowboard.com

Revelstoke

Recently developed resort with a ready-made reputation for steep terrain and deep snow; shame it's so remote and isolated

TOP 10 RATINGS

Extent	★★★
Fast lifts	★★★★★
Queues	★★★★★
Snow	★★★★
Expert	★★★★★
Intermediate	★★
Beginner	★★
Charm	★★
Convenience	★★★
Scenery	★★★★

RPI   145

lift pass	£290
ski hire	£140
lessons	£150
food & drink	£170
total	**£750**

KEY FACTS

Resort	510m
	1,680ft
Slopes	510-2225m
	1,680-7,300ft
Lifts	5
Pistes	3,121 acres
Green	7%
Blue	45%
Black	48%
Snowmaking	at base

➕ Fabulous steep, ungroomed terrain and an impressive snow record

➕ North America's biggest vertical, with some epic black runs going from top to bottom

➕ Great cat- and heli-skiing next door

➕ Fine views over the Columbia valley

➖ Not much intermediate groomed terrain

➖ No snowmaking on main slopes

➖ Very remote location – awkward to get to from the UK

➖ Resort base village still tiny, and Revelstoke town a drive away

Revelstoke has long been known as a heli-skiing base, but it's only in the last few years that it has become a ski resort for the rest of us. A gondola and two fast chairs have transformed its little local ski hill into a serious resort with a vertical of over 1700m – the biggest in North America.

The resort claims over 3,000 acres of terrain – more than many Canadian and American rivals (notably Fernie and Jackson Hole) – but the quantity of defined trails is not huge. More than most places, this is a resort where you need to be happy in the trees to spend a long stay here. You might want to combine it with Kicking Horse and/or Lake Louise, both on the way from Calgary airport.

THE RESORT

Revelstoke is remote. Getting there from the UK involves two flights to get to Kelowna or Kamloops followed by a three-hour drive. Or it's a drive of five hours from Calgary, or six hours from Vancouver – and that's assuming good weather.

There is an embryonic village at the base of the slopes – one smart condo hotel, a restaurant, a coffee shop, a wine bar, a sports shop. Five minutes down the hill, there's a wider choice of lodging and restaurants in Revelstoke itself, a working town between the dammed Columbia river and the Trans-Canada Highway.

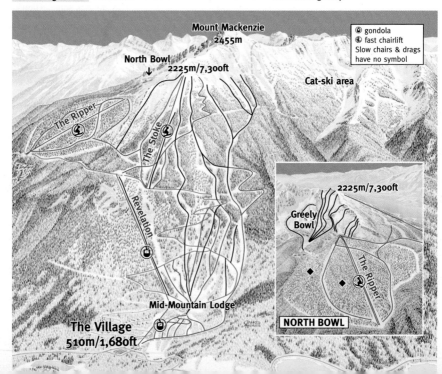

Mount Mackenzie 2455m

North Bowl 2225m/7,300ft

Cat-ski area

ⓖ gondola
④ fast chairlift
Slow chairs & drags have no symbol

The Ripper

The Stoke

Revelation

Greely Bowl

2225m/7,300ft

The Ripper

Mid-Mountain Lodge

The Village 510m/1,680ft

NORTH BOWL

TANYA BOOTH

Temperature inversions and valley fog are common occurrences ↓

Village charm At the lift base, the Village is quite polished, but it is not yet a village. The town developed on the back of forestry, mining and the railroad. There are some 'historic' brick and wooden buildings, but overall it is a rather plain, 'down to earth' place.

Convenience The Village could not be more convenient: the access gondola is mere yards from your door. Town shuttle-buses are regular and reliable, but Village residents going out on the town in the evening are reliant on the hotel shuttle ($20 a trip, regardless of number of people) or taxis.

Scenery There are wide views from the upper slopes over the Columbia valley and snow-capped mountains beyond.

THE MOUNTAINS

A two-stage gondola takes you from the Village to mid-mountain, from which you can reach both fast quad chairs. Be prepared for extreme cold (we once got −41°C with wind chill on a December visit).

Slopes The lift-served terrain puts Revelstoke among the biggest Canadian resorts (leaving massive Whistler aside). As we've said in our introductory summary, the quantity of defined trails is not huge, but there are top-to-bottom runs of exceptional length, three of them classified black. There are 5,000 acres of cat-skiing

next door, and vast amounts of heli-skiing on hand.

Fast lifts All three main lifts are fast.

Queues We have no reports of queues, and both we and readers have often skied trails alone.

Terrain parks There is a small rail park.

Snow reliability They claim 360 to 540 inches a year; an average mid-range figure of 450 is up there with the best. But warm weather is not unknown, and the lower slopes can suffer (and may be closed). There's snowmaking only on the beginner area at the base.

Experts Experts are in their element here. On skier's left, there are exceptionally long top-to-bottom black runs (not exceptionally steep, of course), which are often groomed. On skier's right, reached by traversing and possibly hiking from the top chairlift, is the entirely ungroomed North Bowl. This has excellent steep open slopes at the top giving way to gentler woods at the bottom; for many of us the major challenge, though, is access through the band of cliffs at the top. There are about 10 identified ways in, ranging from merely tricky Meet the Neighbours to much more scary options which are now marked on the trail map as double-diamond runs.

Between the long blacks and North Bowl are several big areas of glades with nicely spaced trees. And there are

↑ There are some good gladed areas, but much of the tree skiing is much tighter than this

DOUG MARSHALL PHOTOS

UK PACKAGES

Canadian Affair, Frontier, Luxury Chalet Collection, Momentum, Oxford Ski Co, Pure Powder, Ski Bespoke, Ski Independence, Ski Safari, Skitracer, Skiworld

Phone numbers
From distant parts of Canada add the prefix 1 250; from abroad use the prefix +1 250

TOURIST OFFICE

www.revelstoke
mountainresort.com

further wide areas of glades served by the Ripper chair, below North Bowl. The ski school runs affordable day and half-day Inside Tracks groups, to show you terrain to suit your ability – exactly what you need on this hill.

Intermediates Most blues are steepish and suit adventurous intermediates best. The Ripper chair accesses the easiest blues. And there's a 15km-long blue/green run from top to bottom. But the intermediate groomed terrain doesn't add up to much (the claimed 45% gives a misleading impression).

Beginners Moving carpets serve small beginner areas at the bottom and at the gondola mid-station. They have widened and realigned long, winding green runs from mid-mountain and the very top, which were already an asset.

Snowboarding There's fabulous freeriding but lots of flats, especially getting to and from North Bowl.

Cross-country 26km of groomed trails.

Mountain restaurants The self-service mid-mountain Revelation Lodge serves 'limited, best of its type' food but gets packed. You can eat your own food here. At the base pick up fresh baked goods and gossip with the ski patrollers at La Baguette; for table-service, it's the smart Rockford restaurant.

Schools and guides The ski school aims to help people progress from groomed runs to the backcountry. Read 'For experts'.

Families This is far from an ideal family resort.

STAYING THERE

Hotels In 2013 we enjoyed Sutton Place (814 5000), at the lift base – perfect location, exceptionally smart and well-equipped rooms, a good pool and hot tubs – endorsed by a reader in 2014. There are various options in and around the town. We've also enjoyed the friendly Courthouse Inn (837 3369) – great breakfast. A reporter this year tips Swiss Chalet motel (837 4650) – 'small but immaculate rooms, excellent value'. Probably the best downtown option is the 'historic' Regent (837 2107). Reporters have also enjoyed the Inn on the River (837 3262), with a panoramic rooftop hot tub; and, slightly out of town, the Hillcrest (837 3322) – Selkirk-Tangiers Heliski base – and the Best Western Plus (837 2043).

Eating out At the Village, the Rockford is a smooth modern place doing grills and wok dishes. In town, 112 at the Regent is polished and intimate, with good gourmet food at tables or at the bar. Woolsey Creek is another gourmet option. In contrast, the Village Idiot is a lively pub-style joint doing good burgers and gigantic pizzas. Kawakubo has a super-high reputation for sushi.

Après-ski The Rockford at the lift base is popular. Good downtown bars are the Village Idiot and the Last Drop (sofas; in Powder Springs Inn) and River City (music, pool; in the Regent).

Off the slopes The Aquatic Centre offers pools, hot tubs, saunas.

Silver Star

Car-free, purpose-built village designed to resemble a Victorian-era mining town, with slopes for all standards

TOP 10 RATINGS

Extent	★★★
Fast lifts	★★★★
Queues	★★★★★
Snow	★★★★
Expert	★★★★
Intermediate	★★★
Beginner	★★★★
Charm	★★★
Convenience	★★★★★
Scenery	★★★

RPI 140

lift pass	£270
ski hire	£125
lessons	£150
food & drink	£170
total	£715

NEWS

2014/15: There are plans to expand the gladed areas on both Vance and Putnam Creeks.

2013/14: 'The Zone' was created at the foot of Vance Creek – with gentle slopes for beginners, an area with small rails for learning terrain park skills and, on Friday and Saturday evenings, an airbag.

KEY FACTS

Resort	1610m
	5,280ft
Slopes	1155-1915m
	3,790-6,280ft
Lifts	12
Pistes	3,065 acres
Green	20%
Blue	50%
Black	30%
Snowmaking	none

➕ Cute, colourful village

➕ Very family-friendly

➕ Some good runs for all abilities

➕ Excellent cross-country skiing

➖ Tiny village; very quiet at night

➖ Limited choice of accommodation (but some high-quality condos)

➖ Ski area not huge

This quiet, family-friendly resort has a tiny traffic-free centre resembling a 19th-century mining town. The ski area has slopes to suit everyone but it is small, so we suggest you combine a stay here with one at another BC resort such as Big White, Sun Peaks, Revelstoke or Whistler.

THE RESORT

Silver Star is a small, purpose-built resort right on the slopes.
Village charm The village has brightly painted Victorian-style buildings with wooden sidewalks and faux gas lights. It's a bit Disneyesque but works well.
Convenience The centre is compact and car-free. Ski-in/ski-out chalets are dotted in the trees too.
Scenery The views from Silver Star's summit are over gently rolling hills.

THE MOUNTAINS

The mountain has trees going right to the top and four main linked sectors.
Slopes The Vance Creek area has mainly easy intermediate runs served by the Comet six-pack, which starts below the village. From there you can ski down to the Silver Woods high-speed quad, which serves an area of mainly intermediate slopes and glades. The top of the Comet chair links to the Attridge area, which has a mix of easy runs and short, steep

blacks served by its own slow chairs too. It also links to the Putnam Creek sector on the back side, which has lots of steep blacks and easier blues, all served by a fast quad. There's night skiing on Friday and Saturday.
Fast lifts There's one for each sector.
Queues 'No queues,' says a recent visitor. We skied here on a busy Saturday and waited a few minutes for the Comet chair at peak times but the trails were still delightfully deserted.
Terrain parks The 16-acre Rockstar park on Vance Creek is excellent for expert, intermediate and beginner freestylers. There's also a snowcross on Putnam Creek.
Snow reliability Silver Star gets an average of 276 inches a year – not in the top flight but not far off.
Experts Putnam Creek has a dense network of single- and double-black diamond runs plunging through the trees, many of them mogul runs. The runs to the left as you ride up the chair are north-facing and keep their snow well. There are some good short

627

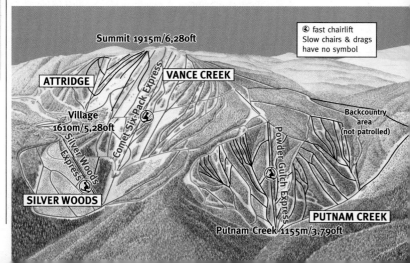

Summit 1915m/6,28oft

ATTRIDGE

VANCE CREEK

Village
1610m/5,28oft

SILVER WOODS

Backcountry area (not patrolled)

PUTNAM CREEK

Putnam Creek 1155m/3,79oft

④ fast chairlift
Slow chairs & drags have no symbol

↑ The views are of rolling hills. But Silver Star's slopes vary from very gentle to super-steep
SILVER STAR MOUNTAIN RESORT

UK PACKAGES

Frontier, Momentum, Ski Independence, Ski Safari, Skitracer, Skiworld

Central reservations Call 558 6083; toll-free (within Canada) 1 800 663 4431

Phone numbers From distant parts of Canada, add the prefix 1 250; from abroad, add +1 250

TOURIST OFFICE

www.skisilverstar.com

blacks in the Attridge area, too. Heli-skiing is available.

Intermediates Vance Creek has mainly easy cruising runs. Silver Woods has lovely, gentle runs cut through the trees and easy blues among the trees themselves. Putnam Creek also has excellent blue cruising. Good intermediates will appreciate the groomed black runs (they groom at least two each night – look on the boards for which ones).

Beginners There's a good nursery slope area (The Zone) by the village with a moving carpet and long easy green runs to move on to.

Snowboarding Intermediates will enjoy the blue runs and glades. But the steep bump runs in Putnam Creek are tough on a snowboard. And there are some flat areas (including the way to Putnam Creek).

Cross-country They claim 'The Best Nordic Skiing in North America' and there's over 100km of trails in the area.

Mountain restaurants The small atmospheric table-service Paradise Camp on Putnam Creek is popular and serves good stews and soups.

Schools and guides A recent visitor's children 'improved by leaps and bounds; the instructors made the lessons fun'; and the two parents were able to 'tidy up our skills. I'd return to Silver Star for the ski school alone.'

Families Star Kids takes children aged 18 months to five years.

STAYING THERE

It is mainly specialist North American operators that come here, such as Frontier Ski and Ski Independence.

Hotels A past reporter liked the Bulldog Hotel but thought the rooms fairly basic. The Vance Creek, Lord Aberdeen and Pinnacles are the other main options. The Samesun Backpackers Hostel has both regular and dorm rooms.

Apartments We stayed in a huge, luxurious condo with private hot tub in the Snowbird Lodge, and loved it – as have reporters. It and Firelight Lodge (ask for a condo overlooking the skating pond and tubing hill) are the best in town – both ski-in/ski-out. Other recommendations include Chilcoot Lodge, Creekside, Grandview and Pinnacles.

Eating out Reporters' favourite is the Bulldog Grand Cafe (Asian-influenced food). Other tips: the Silver Grill Steak & Chop House for fine dining, Long John's Pub with silver-mining theme decor. Isidore's claims to offer 'Swiss with a twist'). Bugaboos Bakery Café is good for breakfast.

Après-ski It's very quiet. But the Saloon, Den and Lord John's Pub may be lively and have live entertainment.

Off the slopes There's a natural ice rink on a lake, tubing, snowshoeing, snowmobiling, bowling and sleigh rides; the first three are free with a lift pass (as is cross-country skiing).

SUN PEAKS RESORT

Sun Peaks

Attractive car-free village at the foot of three linked mountains with varied slopes, including some unusual easy groomed glade runs

TOP 10 RATINGS

Extent	★★★
Fast lifts	★★
Queues	★★★★★
Snow	★★★★
Expert	★★★
Intermediate	★★★★
Beginner	★★★★
Charm	★★★
Convenience	★★★★
Scenery	★★★

RPI   145

lift pass	£290
ski hire	£120
lessons	£170
food & drink	£170
total	**£750**

NEWS

2014/15: New trails are planned for Mt Morrisey and Mt Tod, adding 500 acres and making Sun Peaks the second biggest ski area in Canada.

2013/14: A new glade was created on Sundance. Some double-black diamond runs started to be regularly groomed as well as single blacks.

➕ Great terrain for early intermediates

➕ Excellent glades

➕ Slopes very quiet during the week

➕ Good for families

➖ Village may be too small and quiet for some tastes

➖ Ski area modest by Alpine standards (but big by Canadian ones)

Sun Peaks has a friendly, attractive small village that has been developed since the mid-1990s. And the ski area expansion planned for 2014/15 will mean that Sun Peaks will have the second biggest ski area in Canada – only Whistler is bigger. But that doesn't make it big by Alpine standards. The terrain is nicely varied but a keen skier could cover the groomed trails in a couple of days. We still suggest combining it with a stay at another resort such as Whistler.

THE RESORT

Until 1993 Sun Peaks was Tod Mountain, a local hill for the residents of nearby Kamloops. Since then the ski area has been expanded, and a small, attractive resort village has developed. There are regular transfers to other resorts such as Whistler – making a two-centre trip easy.

Village charm The low-rise pastel-coloured buildings have a vaguely Tirolean feeling to them. It's a pleasant place to stroll around and very family-friendly. The traffic-free main street is lined with lodgings, restaurants and shops, including a smart art gallery.

Convenience Much of the accommodation is ski-in/ski-out.

Scenery The slopes are pleasantly wooded and Mt Tod's modest summit gives views over gently rolling terrain.

THE MOUNTAINS

There are three linked mountains, but the links to and from Mt Morrisey from the other two are roundabout and flattish. Free guided tours are run twice a day (9.15am and 1pm), and you can ski for free with Nancy Greene (former Olympic champion, Canada's Female Athlete of the 20th Century and a Canadian senator) when she's in town. Don't miss it – she's great fun. At the top of each main lift there is a board showing which pistes in that area have been groomed. Each day at least one black piste is groomed.

Slopes With the new trails for 2014/15 Sun Peaks will have 4,200 acres of skiable terrain – in Canada, only Whistler is bigger. But it's not huge by Alpine standards.

One lift goes from the centre of the village to mid-mountain on the resort's original ski hill, Mt Tod. This has mainly black runs, but there are easier blues and greens, too. Many of Mt Tod's steepest runs are served only by the slow Burfield quad, which takes over 20 minutes to get to the top and is frequently the subject of complaint by reporters (there's a mid-station that allows you to ski the top runs only). The Sundance area – also reached from the village centre – has mainly blue and green cruising runs. Mt Morrisey is reached by a long green run from the top of Sundance and has a delightful network of easy blue runs with trees left uncut in the trails, effectively making them groomed glade runs that even early intermediates can try. There are also great gladed areas for good

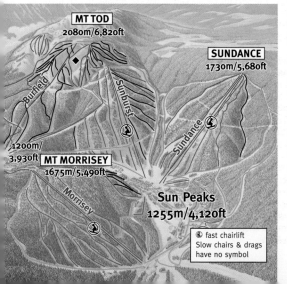

MT TOD
2080m/6,820ft

SUNDANCE
1730m/5,680ft

Burfield

Sunburst

Sundance

1200m/
3,930ft

MT MORRISEY
1675m/5,490ft

Morrisey

Sun Peaks
1255m/4,120ft

🚡 fast chairlift
Slow chairs & drags
have no symbol

↑ Most of the lodging is right by the slopes

SUN PEAKS / ADAM STEIN

KEY FACTS

Resort	1255m
	4,120ft
Slopes	1200-2080m
	3,930-6,820ft
Lifts	11
Pistes	4,200 acres
Green	10%
Blue	58%
Black	32%
Snowmaking	3%

UK PACKAGES

American Ski Classics, Canadian Affair, Erna Low, Frontier, Ski Bespoke, Ski Independence, Ski Safari, Skitracer, Skiworld, Snow Finders, Virgin Snow

Phone numbers
From distant parts of Canada, add the prefix 1 250; from abroad, add the prefix +1 250

TOURIST OFFICE

www.sunpeaksresort.com

intermediates and experts to play in where the trees are tighter (14 of them marked on the trail map – mainly on Mt Tod and Sundance).

Fast lifts The three distinct sectors are each served by a high-speed quad. The other lifts are painfully slow.

Queues Weekdays are usually very quiet; it's only at peak weekends that you might find short queues.

Terrain parks The park has advanced, intermediate and beginner areas, plus snowmaking. But there is no half-pipe.

Snow reliability Sun Peaks gets an average snowfall of 220 inches a year: not in the top league but better than some. The snow can suffer on the lower part of Mt Tod's south-facing slopes, especially later in the season.

Experts Mt Tod has most of the steep terrain, and you can ski some good (but short) steep and gladed runs without descending to the bottom by riding the Burfield quad from its mid-station and the Crystal and Elevation chairs. Some of the blacks on Mt Morrisey (such as Static Cling) have steep mogul sections, too.

Intermediates This is great terrain for early intermediates: there are the easy and charming groomed glades of Mt Morrisey, lovely swooping blues on Sundance and the long 5 Mile run from Mt Tod. More adventurous intermediates can also tackle the easier glades (such as Cahilty) and blacks (such as Peek-A-Boo).

Beginners There are nursery slopes right in the village centre, with long easy greens to progress to.

Snowboarding Boarders can explore the whole mountain. But there are flat greens to and from Mt Morrisey.

Cross-country 30km of groomed trails and 20km of backcountry trails.

Mountain restaurants The Sunburst Lodge is the only option and it gets busy; its cinnamon buns are highly praised. The Umbrella Cafe at the Morrisey base serves hot soup and sandwiches. And it's easy to return to the village for lunch. You can eat your own picnic at Bento's Day Lodge.

Schools and guides Past reports have been good, but we lack recent ones. As well as standard lessons, there are Super Groups (maximum of three people), women-only lessons, race and off-piste camps and freestyle sessions for children and teenagers.

Families The Sundance Kids Centre takes children from 18 months and the ski school children from three years.

STAYING THERE

Hotels Nancy Greene's Cahilty Lodge is a comfortable ski-in/ski-out base, and you get the chance to ski with her and husband Al Raine (former Canadian ski team coach and now mayor of Sun Peaks). The ski-in/ski-out Sun Peaks Grand (was Delta Sun Peaks until 2014; has kept the same management) is in the village centre, has an outdoor pool and hot tub and has regularly been recommended by reporters. We've enjoyed staying at both.

Apartments The Residences at the Sun Peaks Grand are luxurious, ski-in/ski-out and central. Fireside Lodge, Crystal Forest and McGillivray Creek condos have been tipped – some have private hot tubs. Other well-positioned condos include Forest Trails, Snow Creek Village and Timberline Village.

Eating out For a small resort, there's a good choice of restaurants. Reader tips include Powder Hounds, Steakhouse ('top-quality ribs and steaks, but need to book'), Bella Italia, Oya (Japanese) and Mantles in the Sun Peaks Grand. Cahilty Creek Bar and Grill and Voyageur are other options.

Après-ski It's quiet. Bottom's and Masa's are the main après-ski bars. Morrisey's in the Sun Peaks Grand is supposed to be like a British pub. At weekends The Club in the Grand can get lively. The fondue evenings with torchlit descents are 'lots of fun' says a 2014 reporter.

Off the slopes There's skating, tubing, tobogganing, snowmobiling, bungee trampolining, rides on piste bashers, dog sledding, sleigh rides, snowshoeing and swimming.

WHISTLER RESORT ASSOCIATION/
PAUL MORRISON

Whistler

North America's biggest area of slopes, with terrain to suit every standard; plus a big, purpose-built, largely car-free village

RATINGS

The mountains

Extent	★★★★
Fast lifts	★★★★★
Queues	★★
Terrain p'ks	★★★★★
Snow	★★★★
Expert	★★★★★
Intermediate	★★★★★
Beginner	★★★
Boarder	★★★★★
X-country	★★★
Restaurants	★★
Schools	★★★★★
Families	★★★★

The resort

Charm	★★★
Convenience	★★★★
Scenery	★★★
Eating out	★★★★★
Après-ski	★★★★
Off-slope	★★★

RPI   165

lift pass	£360
ski hire	£145
lessons	£180
food & drink	£180
total	**£865**

KEY FACTS

Resort	675m
	2,210ft
Altitude	650-2285m
	2,140-7,490ft
Lifts	37
Pistes	8,171 acres
Green	18%
Blue	55%
Black	27%
Snowmaking	8%

➕ North America's biggest ski area

➕ Excellent combination of high open bowls and woodland trails

➕ Good snow record

➕ Almost Alpine scenery

➕ Attractive modern village, purpose-built with car-free central areas

➕ Good range of village restaurants and lively après-ski

➖ Proximity to Pacific Ocean means a lot of cloudy weather, and rain at resort level is not unusual

➖ Inadequate lift system; queues can be a big problem at peak times

➖ Overcrowded runs also a problem

➖ Mountain restaurants are overcrowded and mostly no more than functional

➖ Resort restaurants over-busy, too

Whistler is unlike any other resort in North America. In some respects – the scale, the high bowls and glaciers, the scenery, the crowds – it is more like an Alpine resort. But like most resorts on the western side of North America, it offers the advantages of excellent snow and a lot of woodland runs as well.

All things considered, the mountain is about the best that North America has to offer, and for us a visit here is always a highlight of the season. But we'll admit that we are generally lucky with the weather, and haven't had to put up with much rain at resort level – a real hazard. And we try to time our visits to avoid peak periods and weekends, and therefore the worst of the crowds.

THE RESORT

Whistler Village sits at the foot of its two mountains, Whistler and Blackcomb, a scenic 135km drive from Vancouver on Canada's west coast.

Whistler started as a locals' ski area in 1966 at Creekside. Whistler Village, a 10-minute bus ride away, was developed in the late 1970s; Upper Village – around the base of Blackcomb Mountain and a 10-minute walk from Whistler Village – was started in the 1980s.

VILLAGE CHARM ★★★
High rise but tasteful
The three main centres are all traffic-free. The architecture is varied and, for a purpose-built resort, quite tasteful – but it is all a bit urban, with lots of blocks approaching 10 storeys high. There are also many chalet-style apartments on the hillsides. Some reporters find the central Village Square area noisy in the early hours.

CONVENIENCE ★★★★
Take your pick
The Peak 2 Peak gondola opened in 2008 and made Whistler Village, Upper Village and Creekside all equally convenient places to stay – from all

you can easily access both mountains by taking a maximum of three lifts.

Whistler Village – by far the biggest and liveliest – has a gondola to each mountain. A pedestrian bridge over an access road links the main centre to newer Whistler Village North (further from the lifts), making a huge car-free area of streets lined with shops, condos, bars and restaurants.

Upper Village is much smaller and quieter. So is Creekside, which was revamped and expanded for the 2010 Winter Olympics.

There is a free bus between central Whistler and Upper Village, but it can be just as quick to walk. Some lodging

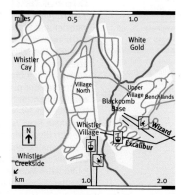

NEWS

2014/15: The 26-year-old Whistler Village gondola is due to be replaced by a new one with eight-seater cabins. It will have 12% more capacity, so waiting times should be reduced. Hands-free lift passes (rare in North America) will be introduced.

2013/14: Whistler got its first six-pack, which replaced the notoriously queue-prone Harmony chair near the top of Whistler mountain, increasing the carrying capacity by 50%. The slow Crystal chair on Blackcomb has been replaced by a fast quad, increasing capacity by 65%. This new chair starts lower down than the old one, making previously little-used runs much more attractive to ski and significantly cutting the long run-out from the Blackcomb Glacier and Spanky's Ladder runs. Snowmaking (15 snow-guns) was added to runs served by the chair too.

LIFT PASSES

Prices in C$

Age	1-day	6-day
under 13	56	312
13 to 18	94	532
19 to 64	111	626
65 plus	94	532

Free Under 7

Beginner Lift and lesson deal

Notes Prices include sales tax and are online advance-purchase price

is a long way from the centre and means taking buses (not free) or taxis. Some hotels have free buses, which will take you to and pick you up from restaurants and nightlife.

SCENERY ★★★★★
Almost Alpine

There are splendid views of the deep Fitzsimmons Creek valley from both mountains, and especially from the Peak 2 Peak gondola, which goes right across it – the views from the two cabins with glass floors are particularly spectacular (these cabins are painted silver rather than red). The upper slopes give good views to coastal sounds, high open bowls, glaciers and ridges.

THE MOUNTAINS

The mountains offer an excellent combination of high, open bowls and sheltered forest runs.

Many reporters enthuse about the mountain host service and the 'go slow' patrol – some find the latter over-zealous, but crowded slopes, especially on the runs home, mean they're often needed; we approve.

Signposting is generally good. But a 2014 reporter had some complaints and every year some reporters complain about inaccuracies on the trail map; most seem to be happy with it though. A separate Wonder Routes map has suggested tours with different themes – such as powder stashes, steeps, families and panoramic views. There's a special kids' trail map too.

One thing that annoys most people is the crazily early closing times of the lifts – 3pm or 3.30pm till late February, with the top lifts closing even earlier.

EXTENT OF THE SLOPES ★★★★★
The biggest in North America

Whistler and Blackcomb together form the biggest area of slopes in North America. They claim almost 8,200 acres (50% more than their nearest rivals, Vail and Big Sky). The Schrahe report (see our piste extent feature near the front of the book) puts Whistler's pistes as 252km (around 10% more than Vail and Big Sky and the fifth biggest in the world, on a par with Alpine ski areas such as Zermatt-Cervinia and the Milky Way).

Whistler Mountain is accessed from Whistler Village by a two-stage

gondola, due to be replaced in 2014/15 by a more comfortable one with a higher capacity, which rises over 1100m to Roundhouse Lodge at mid-mountain. Or you can use two fast quads (which reporters say don't always run).

Runs down through the trees fan out from the gondola: cruises to the Emerald and Big Red chairs and longer runs to the gondola mid-station.

From Roundhouse you can see the jewel in Whistler's crown – magnificent open bowls, served by the fast Peak and Harmony chairs. The bowl beyond Harmony is served by the Symphony fast quad. The bowls are mostly go-anywhere terrain for experts, but there are groomed trails, so anyone can appreciate the views. Roundhouse is the departure point of the Peak 2 Peak gondola to Blackcomb.

A six-seat gondola from Creekside also accesses Whistler Mountain.

Access to **Blackcomb** from Whistler Village is by an eight-seat gondola, followed by a fast quad. From the base of Blackcomb you take two consecutive fast quads up to the main Rendezvous restaurant – departure point of the Peak 2 Peak gondola. From Rendezvous, on skier's right is great cruising terrain and the Glacier Express quad up to the Horstman Glacier area; on skier's left are steeper slopes, the terrain park and the traverse over to the 7th Heaven chair. The 1610m vertical from the top of 7th Heaven to the base is one of the biggest in North America. A T-bar from the Horstman Glacier brings you (with a short hike) to the Blackcomb Glacier in the next valley – away from all lifts.

Fresh Tracks is a deal that allows you to ride up Whistler Mountain (at extra cost) from 7.15am, have a buffet breakfast and get on the slopes early – very popular with many reporters. We prefer to ski first on deserted runs and breakfast later – check what time breakfast ends (9am on our March 2013 visit). Free guided tours of each mountain are offered at 11.15am.

FAST LIFTS ★★★★★
Can't cope with the crowds

While the resort has more fast lifts than any other in North America, the lift system is antiquated compared with those in the Alps and can't handle the crowds (see 'Queues'). Gondolas provide the main access, with lots of fast quads after that – but

↑ The hub of Blackcomb's slopes with the Rendezvous restaurant, trails leading in three different directions and the Peak 2 Peak gondola link to Whistler mountain

TOURISM WHISTLER / MIKE CRANE

only last season was the resort's first six-pack installed and there are no eight-seaters, which are becoming common in Europe.

QUEUES ★★☆☆☆
A big problem
Whistler has become a victim of its own success. At peak holiday periods and weekends when people pour in from Vancouver, queues can be horrendous. There are displays of waiting times at different lifts, which readers generally find useful.

Some reporters have signed up with the ski school just to get lift priority. Others have visited Vancouver at the weekend to avoid the crowds.

The routes out of Whistler Village in the morning can be busy (we had one report of a queue of more than 200 metres for the Blackcomb gondola). We hope the new gondola up Whistler will improve things. Creekside is less of a problem, but gets long queues at weekends. Some of the chairs higher up also produce long queues (even the singles lines took 10 minutes or so on our March 2013 visit); the Emerald and Peak chairs are bottlenecks – one reporter noted a 45-minute wait for the Peak chair on a Sunday in January. The worst queues have been for the Harmony chair but reporters tell us the new six-pack for 2013/14 has reduced problems there. Another issue is that

some of the higher lifts, especially the Peak chair, are prone to open late on powder days while the ski patrol finish their avalanche control. Crowds on the slopes, especially the runs home, can be annoying, too.

TERRAIN PARKS ★★★★★
World class for all abilities
While both mountains have parks, freestylers tend to head to Blackcomb, which is home to the Olympic-standard Nintendo Super Pipe (with walls almost 7m high and shaped daily), the Mini Pipe with 4.5m high walls, a snowcross course ('a good laugh with friends') and three terrain parks. There's a clear rating system in place, based on size (S, M, L, XL). On Blackcomb, novices should begin in the Big Easy Terrain Garden. It features small rails and rollers to help you get a feel for airtime and improve your control. The M-L Choker Park is vast, but is usually the busiest. With many step-up jumps, hips, tabletops, rails and boxes, this park will suit intermediate to advanced riders. Very confident freestylers should hit the XL Highest Level Park. The obstacles are huge and you have to wear a helmet. On Whistler mountain, novices should hit School Yard which has beginner rails and jumps. The Habitat Park by the Emerald chair is a 'belter' and has three lines for different skill levels.

Build your own shortlist: www.wheretoskiandsnowboard.com

SKIWORLD

Catered chalets, hotels and self catering apartments in

Europe, USA and Canada

skiworld.co.uk

08444 930 430

ABTA V2151 ATOL 2036

www.ski-i.com

ski independence

Call the Tailor-made Ski Specialists

0131 243 8097

SNOW RELIABILITY ★★★★
Excellent at altitude

Snow conditions at the top are usually excellent – the snowfall averages over 462 inches a year (that's way more than most Colorado resorts). But last season was a poor one, with a mere 356 inches (still more than average for most Colorado resorts). Because the resort is low and close to the Pacific, the bottom slopes can have poor snow or slush – leading people to 'download' from the mid-stations,

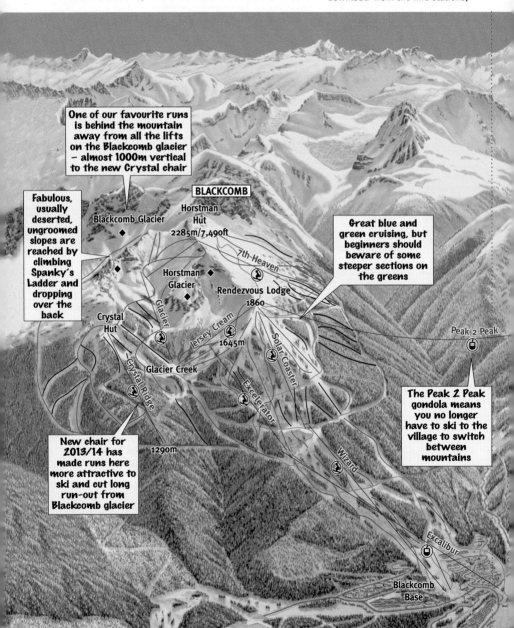

One of our favourite runs is behind the mountain away from all the lifts on the Blackcomb glacier – almost 1000m vertical to the new Crystal chair

Fabulous, usually deserted, ungroomed slopes are reached by climbing Spanky's Ladder and dropping over the back

BLACKCOMB

Horstman Hut
2285m/7,490ft

Blackcomb Glacier ◆

Horstman ◆
Glacier

7th Heaven

Rendezvous Lodge
1860

Great blue and green cruising, but beginners should beware of some steeper sections on the greens

Crystal Hut

Glacier

Jersey Cream
1645m

Solar Coaster

Peak 2 Peak

Glacier Creek

Crystal Ridge

Excelerator

The Peak 2 Peak gondola means you no longer have to ski to the village to switch between mountains

New chair for 2013/14 has made runs here more attractive to ski and cut long run-out from Blackcomb glacier

1290m

Wizard

Excalibur

Blackcomb Base

especially in late season. Reporters generally praise piste maintenance this year. 'Whistler did a great job under difficult conditions,' says one. However another was concerned about 'one or two ungroomed blues with moguls'.

FOR EXPERTS ★★★★★
Few can rival it

Whistler Mountain's bowls are enough to keep experts happy for weeks. Each has endless variations, with chutes and gullies of varied steepness and width. The biggest challenges are around Flute, Glacier, Whistler and West Bowls – you can go anywhere in these high, wide areas.

Blackcomb's steep slopes are not as extensive as Whistler's, but some are more challenging. From the top of the 7th Heaven lift, traverse to Xhiggy's Meadow for sunny bowl runs. If you're feeling brave, go in the opposite direction and drop into the extremely steep chutes down towards Glacier Creek, including the infamous

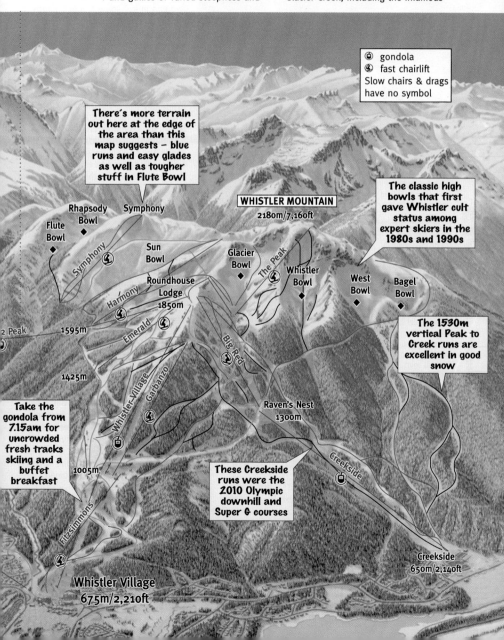

⊚ gondola
⊛ fast chairlift
Slow chairs & drags have no symbol

There's more terrain out here at the edge of the area than this map suggests – blue runs and easy glades as well as tougher stuff in Flute Bowl

The classic high bowls that first gave Whistler cult status among expert skiers in the 1980s and 1990s

WHISTLER MOUNTAIN
2180m/7,16oft

Rhapsody Bowl

Symphony

Flute Bowl

Symphony

Sun Bowl

Glacier Bowl

The Peak

Whistler Bowl

West Bowl

Bagel Bowl

Harmony

Roundhouse Lodge
1850m

2 Peak   1595m

Emerald

Big Red

The 1530m vertical Peak to Creek runs are excellent in good snow

1425m

Whistler-Village

Garbanzo

Raven's Nest
1300m

Creekside

Take the gondola from 7.15am for uncrowded fresh tracks skiing and a buffet breakfast

1005m

Fitzsimmons

These Creekside runs were the 2010 Olympic downhill and Super G courses

Creekside
650m/2,140ft

Whistler Village
675m/2,210ft

↑ Traffic-free Whistler Village is where most of the lodgings are, and there are gondolas up both mountains from here
TOURISM WHISTLER / MIKE CRANE

ACTIVITIES

Indoor Sports arena (ice rink, pool, gym, squash), tennis, spa and health clubs, climbing wall, art galleries, museums, library, cinema

Outdoor Flightseeing, snowshoeing, snowmobiling, walking, tobogganing, snowcat tours, dog sledding, tubing, sleigh rides, ziplining, bobsleigh

Resort news and key links: www.wheretoskiandsnowboard.com

41° Couloir Extreme (which can have massive moguls at the top), Secret Bowl and the very steep Pakalolo couloir. Our favourite runs are the less frequented but also seriously steep bowls reached by a short hike up Spanky's Ladder, after taking the Glacier Express lift. You emerge after the hike at the top of a huge deserted area with several ways down; best to have a guide.

Both mountains have challenging trails through trees. The Peak to Creek area offers 400 acres below Whistler's West Bowl to Creekside.

There's also backcountry guiding, cat-skiing and heli-skiing available by the day. One reporter had 'two incredible days' with Powder Mountain cat-skiing. Other reporters used Coast Range mountain guides ('top-quality guides and superb skiing') and found the heli-skiing 'expensive but a great experience'. We recommend the two-day Extremely Canadian clinic (see 'Schools and guides') for getting the most out of the in-bounds steeps and their one-day Backcountry Adventures.

FOR INTERMEDIATES ★★★★★
Ideal and extensive terrain
Both mountains are an intermediate's paradise. In good weather, good intermediates will enjoy the easier slopes in the high bowls. One of our favourite intermediate runs is down the Blackcomb Glacier, from the top of the mountain to the new Crystal chair almost 1000m below. This 5km run,

away from all lifts, starts with a two-minute walk up from the top of the Showcase T-bar. Don't be put off by the 'Experts only' sign. You drop over the ridge into a wide bowl and traverse the slope to get to gentler gradients – descend too soon and you'll get a shock in the very steep double-diamond Blowhole. The tedious run-out at the end has been made a lot shorter by the new Crystal chair.

The blue runs served by the 7th Heaven chair start above the treeline and end in it – some can get bumpy in parts. Lower down, including from the new Crystal chair, there are lots of perfect cruising runs through the trees – ideal for bad weather days and enjoyed by several reporters this year.

On Whistler Mountain, the ridges and bowls served by the Harmony and Symphony chairs have lots to offer – not only groomers but also excellent terrain for experiments off-piste. Symphony in particular has some very gentle and usually uncrowded terrain and widely spaced trees to play in. The Saddle run from the top of the Harmony Express lift is a favourite with many of our reporters, though it can get busy. The blue Highway 86 path, which skirts West Bowl from the Peak to Creek trail, has beautiful views over a steep valley and across to the rather phallic Black Tusk mountain. The 7km-long Peak to Creek blue run is good too, but it's rarely all groomed – check before setting off. The green Burnt Stew Trail has great views, and accesses lots of easy off-piste terrain.

Lower down the mountain there is a vast choice of groomed blue runs, with a series of fast chairs to bring you back up to the top of the gondola. It's a cruiser's paradise – especially the aptly named Ego Bowl. A great long run is the fabulous Dave Murray Downhill all the way from mid-mountain to the finish at Creekside – used as the 2010 Olympic men's downhill course. Although it is classed black, it's a wonderful fast and varied cruise when it has been groomed.

FOR BEGINNERS ★★★★★
OK if the sun shines
Whistler has excellent nursery slopes by the mid-station of the gondola, as does Blackcomb at the base. Both have facilities higher up too. There is a lift pass, lesson and rental deal on certain dates (see 'Schools and guides'), but no free lifts.

On Whistler, there are some gentle runs from the top of the gondola. Their downside is other people speeding past. On Blackcomb, there are green runs from top to bottom. The top parts are very gentle, with some steeper pitches lower down.

In general, greens can be trickier than in many North American resorts – steeper, busier and, on the lower slopes, in less good condition. Another reservation is the weather. Beginners don't get a lot out of heavy snowfalls, and rain might put them off.

FOR BOARDERS ★★★★★
Epic – winter and summer
Whistler has world-class terrain parks as well as epic terrain for freeriders: bowls with great powder and awesome steeps, steep gullies, tree runs, and shedloads of natural hits, wind lips and cliffs. There are mellow groomed runs ideal for beginners and intermediates, too, and the lifts are generally snowboard-friendly; there are T-bars on the glacier, but they're not vicious. The resort has as high a reputation for summer snowboarding and camps on the glacier as for its winter boarding, and the summer

Camp of Champions is hugely popular. 'Great' specialist snowboard shops include Showcase and The Circle.

FOR CROSS-COUNTRY ★★★☆☆
Picturesque but low
There are over 28km of cross-country tracks around Lost Lake, starting by the river on the path between Whistler and Blackcomb. But it is low altitude, so conditions can be unreliable. One trail is floodlit. A specialist school, Cross-Country Connection (905 0071) offers lessons and rental. Keen cross-country merchants can go to the Whistler Olympic Park and its 90km of trails (around 20 minutes away by car – there's no public bus).

MOUNTAIN RESTAURANTS ★★☆☆☆
Overcrowded
The main restaurants sell decent food but are charmless self-service stops with long queues; most get incredibly crowded. They're huge, but not huge enough. 'Seat-seekers' are employed to find you space, but success is not guaranteed. The piste map advises eating lunch before 11.30 (sorry?) or after 1pm. Blackcomb has the 500-seat Rendezvous and 775-seat Glacier

Whistler

Build your own shortlist: www.wheretoskiandsnowboard.com

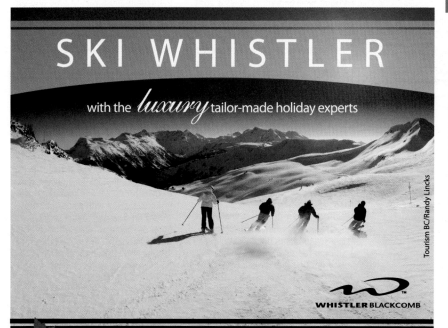

SKI WHISTLER

with the *luxury* tailor-made holiday experts

Tourism BC/Randy Lincks

WHISTLER BLACKCOMB

 FrontierSki
the finest tailor-made ski holidays

 AITO
 ABTA
ABTA No W3207

020 8776 8709
frontier-ski.co.uk/whistler

↑ Open slopes above and wooded ones below, so great whether it's sunny or snowing (just hope it doesn't rain)
WHISTLER BLACKCOMB / PAUL MORRISON

Camp. There's an average of six to a group and the aim is to improve your skiing in all types of terrain. Video analysis, optional race training and après-ski are included.

Extremely Canadian two-day camps run three times a week and are for those who want guiding (with a bit of coaching) in Whistler's steep and deep terrain and are a great way of finding the best steep terrain. We have been with them several times and have been impressed (as have reporters).

Extremely Canadian also runs Backcountry Adventures day trips. Backcountry day trips or overnight touring are also available with Whistler Alpine Guides Bureau.

SCHOOLS

Whistler/Blackcomb
t 967 8950
Extremely Canadian
t 1 800 938 9656

Classes
Full day from C$222
(max 4 in class)
Private lessons
Half day (3hr) C$558
for up to 5 people

GUIDES

Whistler Guides
t 932 7807

Creek. Whistler has the gigantic (2,080-seat) Roundhouse.
Editors' choice Christine's (938 7437) table-service restaurant in the Rendezvous building on Blackcomb is the place to book for a decent lunch. We had a delicious bouillabaisse and 'flight' of four different Okanagan wines with tasting notes there. Endorsed by a 2014 reporter.
Worth knowing about On Whistler, Steep's Grill (905 2379) in the Roundhouse is the table-service place ('Good food and views,' says a 2013 visitor), but we much prefer Christine's for both ambience and food.

There are other smallish (self-service) places, but they get packed, and may be closed in early and late season. On Blackcomb are two tiny huts with great views – Crystal Hut ('great waffles') and Horstman Hut ('excellent goulash and mulled wine'). On Whistler, Raven's Nest is small and friendly, and does soups, sandwiches and BBQs; the Chic Pea ('cinnamon rolls to die for') and Harmony Snack Shack are other options.

You can eat your own picnic at the Roundhouse or Rendezvous.

SCHOOLS AND GUIDES ★★★★★
Very good reputation
The school limits the number in an adult group to a maximum of four. And they run Discover Whistler Days in some periods – you get a discount (30% in 2013/14) off the normal cost of lessons (and rentals and lift pass for beginners). A 2014 reporter who took private lessons says they were 'good quality, well planned and enjoyable'. The school also runs special programmes such as 3- or 4-day coaching sessions called The

FOR FAMILIES ★★★★
Impressive
Blackcomb's base area has the slow-moving Magic chair to get children part-way up the mountain. Whistler's gondola mid-station has a splendid kids-only area. A reporter found the staff 'friendly, instilling confidence'. The school uses the Flaik GPS real-time tracking system so that each child's exact location is known at all times. There's a Magic Castle on Blackcomb and a Family Zone and Tree Fort on Whistler. One reporter enthused about 'climb and dine': kids combine dinner with three hours of climbing at The Core.

STAYING THERE

Whistler has every kind of lodging you might want. Ski Independence and Frontier Ski offer an impressive range of hotels and apartments.
Hotels There is a wide range, including a lot of top-end places.
★★★★★Fairmont Chateau Whistler (938 8000) Well run, luxurious, at the foot of Blackcomb. We and reporters love it. Excellent spa with pools and tubs.
★★★★★Four Seasons (935 3400) Luxury hotel five minutes' walk from Blackcomb base, but with ski valet service at the base. Unremarkable public areas but good service, food and fitness/spa facilities.
★★★★★Westin Resort & Spa (905 5000) Luxury all-suite hotel at the foot of Whistler mountain. We enjoyed our 2013 stay except the pool and hot tubs were always so crowded we didn't use them. Sauna, steam.
★★★★Crystal Lodge (932 2221) In Whistler Village. Pool/sauna/hot tub.

Whistler

Build your own shortlist: www.wheretoskiandsnowboard.com

CHILDCARE

Whistler Kids
t 1 800 766 0449
Ages 18mnth to 4yr

Ski school
Ages 3 to 12

UK PACKAGES

Alpine Answers, American Ski Classics, Canadian Affair, Carrier, Cold Comforts Lodging, Crystal, Crystal Finest, Elegant Resorts, Erna Low, Flexiski, Frontier, Inghams, Interactive Resorts, Kaluma, Momentum, Neilson, Oxford Ski Co, PowderBeds, Scott Dunn, Ski Bespoke, Ski Expectations, Ski Independence, Ski Line, Ski Safari, Skitracer, Skiworld, Snow Finders, STC, Supertravel, Thomson, Virgin Snow

GETTING THERE

Air Vancouver
135km/85 miles
(2hr15)

Phone numbers
From distant parts of
Canada, add the
prefix 1 604; from
abroad, add the prefix
+1 604

TOURIST OFFICE

www.whistler
blackcomb.com
www.tourismwhistler.
com

Discounts in several restaurants and shops in building.
****Glacier Lodge (905 4607) In Upper Village. Large rooms.
****Pan Pacific Mountainside (905 2999) Luxury, all-suite, at Whistler Village base. Pool/steam/hot tub.
****Sundial Boutique (932 2321) In Whistler Village; one- and two-bedroom suites. Rooftop hot tubs.
****Summit Lodge & Spa (932 2778) In Whistler Village. Pool/sauna/hot tub, 'free hot drinks in lobby'.
***Lost Lake Lodge (580 6647) Out by the golf course; studios and suites. Pool/hot tub.
***Tantalus Resort Lodge (932 4146) In Whistler Village; targets families and groups. Hot tub/sauna.
***Whistler Village Inn & Suites (932 4004) Central, side-by-side buildings. Relatively cheap. Pool/hot tub/sauna.
Apartments There are plenty of spacious, comfortable condominiums. Price tends to be dictated by location – ski-in/ski-out condos are pricier than those a shuttle ride from the lifts.

EATING OUT ★★★★★
Good but crowded
Reporters are enthusiastic about the range, quality and value of places to eat, but there aren't enough restaurant seats to meet demand. You have to book well ahead (which may mean months ahead in some cases), or resign yourself to queuing for one of the places that doesn't take bookings.
At the top of the market, the Rimrock Cafe near Whistler Creek specializes in seafood and game and has several different small areas that make it feel more intimate than many Whistler restaurants; we have eaten very well there (most recently in 2013, when we booked three weeks ahead); endorsed by a 2014 reporter who booked a month in advance.
In Whistler Village, we've enjoyed Araxi ('Brilliant, visited three times,' says a 2014 reporter), Il Caminetto di Umberto (a classy Italian, but 'stay away from the piano if you wish to hear speech!') and 21 Steps (mid-market place up, er, 21 steps, where we enjoyed several delicious small plates on our 2013 visit). The pricey Ric's Grill and cheaper Keg are both parts of chains but do good seafood and steak. Mid-market places include: Quattro and Old Spaghetti Factory ('Amazing value, great service,' says a 2014 reporter) for Italian, Bocca

(modern Canadian, heated outdoor terrace), Three Below ('reasonably priced; great banana in puff pastry with caramel'), and Earl's (burgers, ribs, microbeers). Others to try are Sushi Village and Teppan (both Japanese), Mongolie (Asian) and Kypriaki Norte (Greek). In Village North, Hy's Steakhouse ('good food and service, free garlic bread') and the lively Brewhouse are good for steaks and ribs (we enjoyed the Brewhouse in 2013). There are plenty of budget places, including Fat Tony's ('tasty pizzas') and the après-ski bars below. You can also take a snowcat to the Crystal Hut for fondue and music.

APRES-SKI ★★★★☆
Something for most tastes
Whistler is very lively. We get most reviews on the Garibaldi Lift Company, which is still 'buzzing from 4pm onwards, with good live music'. Other tips are the Brewhouse (where a model train runs all the way round the interior), Longhorn (with a terrace), Dubh Linn Gate Irish pub ('fun', 'great live music') and Tapley's. Merlin's is the focus at Blackcomb base, with sports TV, 'great' quiz nights and music. Dusty's at Creekside has good beer and loud music.
Later on, Buffalo Bill's is lively. Tommy Africa's, Maxx Fish, Moe Joe's and Garfinkel's are the main clubs.

OFF THE SLOPES ★★★☆☆
Quite a lot to do
Meadow Park Sports Centre has fitness facilities. There are several luxurious spas and an eight-screen cinema. Reporters recommend walks around the lake and the climbing wall at The Core. Ziptrek Ecotours offers tours on ziplines and suspension bridges through the forest between Whistler and Blackcomb mountains – 'great fun' says a reporter. You can also do all-terrain-vehicle/snowmobile trips and dog sledding. A reporter raves about the bobsleigh run at the Sliding Centre ('for adrenaline junkies'). Another recommends the Whistler Museum. The free Sunday evening Fire & Ice show is popular. Excursions to Squamish (for eagle watching) and to Vancouver are easy. And non-slope users can get around the mountain easily (and take the Peak 2 Peak gondola for great views – especially if you get in one of the cabins with a glass bottom).

Eastern Canada

For us the main attraction of skiing or riding in eastern Canada is the French culture and language that are predominant in the province of Québec. It really feels like a different country from the rest of Canada. And the resorts are only a 6-hour flight from the UK, compared with a 10-hour flight for western Canada.

Be prepared for variable snow conditions, including rock-hard pistes and ice; and be prepared for extreme cold in early and midwinter. But cold weather means the extensive snowmaking systems can be effective for a long season. Don't go expecting light, dry powder – if that's what you want, go west.

UK PACKAGES

Tremblant Alpine Answers, American Ski Classics, Crystal, Crystal Finest, Erna Low, Frontier, Inghams, Neilson, Ski Bespoke, Ski Independence, Ski Safari, Skitracer, Skiworld, STC, Thomson, Virgin Snow

For people heading on holiday for a week or more, eastern Canada really means the province of Québec, its capital, Québec City, and the main destination resort Tremblant (covered below) nearer Montreal. French culture and language dominate the region. Notices, menus, trail maps and so on are usually printed in both French and English. Many ski area workers are bilingual or only French-speaking. And French cuisine abounds.

Slopes in all resorts are small, both in extent and vertical. The weather is very variable, so the snow – though pretty much guaranteed by snowmaking – varies greatly in quality.

Québec City makes a good base for access to several ski areas. Old Québec, at the city's heart, is North America's only walled city and is a World Heritage site. Within the city walls are narrow, winding streets and 17th- and 18th-century houses. It is situated right on the banks of the St Lawrence river. In January/February there is a famous two-week carnival, with an ice castle, snow sculptures, dog-sled and canoe races, parades and balls. But most of the winter is low season, with good-value rooms available in big hotels.

Stoneham is the closest ski area to Québec City, around 20 minutes away. The biggest and most varied resort is Mont-Ste-Anne 30 minutes away. Le Massif is around an hour away – a cult area with locals. These three resorts have extended entries in the resort directory at the back of the book.

KEY FACTS

Resort	265m
	870ft
Slopes	230-875m
	750-2,870ft
Lifts	14
Pistes	654 acres
Snow-guns	71%

TOURIST OFFICE

www.tremblant.ca

Tremblant

- ✚ Charming, purpose-built core village
- ✚ Some good runs for all abilities
- ▬ Very limited in extent
- ▬ Weekend queues and crowds

Tremblant is eastern Canada's leading destination ski resort, about 90 minutes' drive from Montreal.

The core village is purpose-built in the cute style of old Québec, with buildings in vibrant colours and narrow, cobbled, traffic-free streets; it feels very French. There is a regular, free ski-bus and a local town service.

The slopes are pleasantly wooded. A heated gondola from the village takes you to the top of the so-called South Side. From here you can drop over the back on to the North Side. Most lifts are fast chairs. At weekends there can be queues, but they tend to move quickly. Half the runs are blacks; most are at the easier end of their grading, but there are bump runs and glades. There is good intermediate cruising, an excellent nursery area with long, easy greens to progress to and three terrain parks aimed at advanced, intermediate and beginner freestylers; plus a children's adventure area. There's over 80km of cross-country.

Many people return to town for lunch, but the Grand Manitou at the top of the gondola has good views and decent food. The Refuge on the Soleil sector of the South Side is 'more charming but has a very limited menu'. Of the hotels, the Fairmont Tremblant is the most luxurious. There are ample condos. Restaurants and bars are plentiful. Try the Forge Grill or Ya'ooo Pizza Bar. The Shack brews its own beer. Off the slopes there is an 'expensive' pool complex, snowshoeing, skating, tubing and a casino. Visiting Montreal is popular.

Spain

RPI	95
lift pass	£190
ski hire	£130
lessons	£70
food & drink	£105
total	**£495**

UK PACKAGES

Baqueira-Beret Neilson, Scott Dunn, Ski Inspired, Ski Miquel, Skitracer
Formigal Ski Inspired, Skitracer, Zenith
Sierra Nevada Zenith

+ Vibrant Spanish culture gives a different experience from the Alps
+ Low prices for food and drink
+ Few crowds outside peak times

− Access can be difficult, with lengthy drives to reach Pyrenean resorts
− Still lots of old lifts, but improving

Spanish resorts vary enormously, so it's difficult to generalize. Nearly all the main ones, though, are benefiting from recent investment. The three we feature here have respectably sized and varied terrain that compares favourably with many smaller Alpine resorts.

Key parts of the appeal of Spanish skiing are the relatively low cost and the relaxed ambience, with a distinct emphasis on eating, partying and posing. Most resorts are in the Pyrenees. The villages are built more for convenience than charm – but they do offer a wide range of lodging set in some stunning scenery.

There is a group of worthwhile resorts in the west, between Pau and Huesca. Formigal is now the largest, and making a steady comeback on the wider market. Candanchu and Astún nearby are popular on the Spanish market. The downside is access, which can be tricky from France if snowfall closes key mountain passes. There are long drives up from Spanish airports, too, but weekly charter flights to Huesca have cut some transfer times.

The other main group of Pyrenees resorts, just east of Andorra, includes La Molina and Masella (Alp 2500). These have brief descriptions in our resort directory.

In the south of Spain is the high resort of Sierra Nevada – a quite different experience, close to the coast. A two-centre trip is possible.

KEY FACTS

Resort	1500m
	4,920ft
Slopes	1500-2510m
	4,920-8,230ft
Lifts	33
Pistes	120km
Snow-guns	608 guns

TOURIST OFFICE

www.baqueira.es

Baqueira-Beret

+ Compact modern resort
+ Lots of good intermediate slopes

− Main village lacks atmosphere
− Still some old, slow lifts

Baqueira's village is not inspiring, but the resort has a well-linked and developing ski area that appeals to intermediates. Fine for beginners too.

Baqueira celebrates its 50th birthday in December 2014, so look out for celebrations. It has its fair share of drab high-rise blocks in the central area, clustered below the road that runs through to the high pass of Port de la Bonaigua, with the main lift base just above it. The village is small enough for location not to be too much of an issue. And there are big car parks with shuttles to the lift base.

The slopes are split into three distinct but well-connected areas – Baqueira, Beret and Bonaigua – with long, intermediate runs, practically all of them on open, treeless slopes. Most are above 1800m with extensive snowmaking; but afternoon sun is a problem in spring. There are fast chairs dotted around, including a long six-pack.

Experts will find few on-piste challenges, but there is extensive off-piste and five ungroomed itinerary runs (including Escornacrabes, which both our recent reporters said was not for the faint-hearted). There are good nursery slopes with moving carpets at Beret, and at the top of the gondola – the blues there are on the tough side, though. Queues are rarely of major concern. The Brit-run BB Ski School is praised, including for off-piste guiding. The mountain restaurants disappoint and lack variety, but Pla de Beret and Bonaigua ('good pizza') have table-service, and a reporter tips the San Miguel tapas bar at Bonaigua and the small bar at Tanau 1700 for 'hearty mountain soups and stews'.

There are good hotels: the 5-star AC Baqueira (a Marriott) is 'the best'. But the best restaurants and bars are down the valley. Some hotels have pools and spas, but there is little else to amuse non-skiers.

When quality
and value
matter,
do more with

zenith
·holidays·

0203 137 7678
zenithholidays.co.uk
ABTA
ABTA No.Y1542

Formigal

KEY FACTS	
Resort	1550m
	5,090ft
Slopes	1500-2250m
	4,920-7,380ft
Lifts	21
Pistes	137km
Snow-guns	22%

TOURIST OFFICE

www.aramon.co.uk
www.formigal.com

- ➕ Sizeable, varied area for all abilities
- ➕ Linked valleys give sense of travel
- ➖ Traffic congestion in resort
- ➖ Wind-prone slopes, lacking trees

Formigal has the largest ski area in the Spanish Pyrenees, and varied terrain. Recent investment is slowly attracting more British visitors – reports welcome.

The resort is on the Spanish-French border at the Col de Portalet, which can be closed in heavy snowfall, preventing direct access from France.

The village – of purpose-built apartment blocks and smart hotels – is on the east side of the Tena valley. The central street is pleasant enough, with an attractive clock tower and a replica church as its focus, but it is spoiled by heavy traffic.

There are excellent free shuttles to and from the slopes, which span the west side of the valley and spread over four side-valleys. Most slopes are treeless, and prone to wind; they are north- or south-facing. Grooming is good and snowmaking extensive. Queues are rare outside holiday periods. Sextas is the nearest of the four bases to the village, with an eight-seat chair. All four have big car parks and US-style day lodges including big self-service cafeterias. There are fast chairs linking the lower parts of each valley, and runs for all standards from the tops.

Experts have three freeride areas, plus heli-skiing. Many of the black runs could be red, though. The nursery slopes are excellent. There are good intermediate runs; the gentle blue Rio from Cantal to Sextas is ideal for the more timid. The only tree-lined run is a remote lovely cruise, quiet because access is by a long, slow chair.

Confident skiers can ride a snowcat above Portalet, which accesses remote runs and freeride terrain to Anayet. The huge terrain park is one of the best we've seen, and there's a kids' mini park and snowcross. We enjoyed good Italian food at the Cantal Trattoria. The school has a good reputation. They have been focusing on activities for families – well catered for with 'slow ski zones', family zones and an Indian 'village'.

There is a choice of 3- and 4-star hotels (the Aragon Hills and Abba Formigal have pools and spas), lots of apartments and over 30 restaurants, from Spanish to pizzerias. We had good gourmet food at the Vidocq. Après-ski is low-key, but the Marchica bar at Sextas is lively at close of play. Later on, there are two discos: the popular Cueva and the Tralala.

Off-slope activities include dog sledding, floodlit tobogganing and snowmobile outings up to a mountain hut. Thermal baths are nearby.

Sierra Nevada

KEY FACTS	
Resort	2100m
	6,890ft
Slopes	2100-3300
	6,890-10,830ft
Lifts	29
Pistes	105km
Snow-guns	350 guns

TOURIST OFFICE

www.sierranevada.es

- ➕ Reasonably good snow record
- ➕ Fine beginner slopes
- ➖ Exposed, and prone to wind
- ➖ Crowds at weekends

Despite its southerly position near Granada, Sierra Nevada is a high, modern resort with a modest area of slopes. It gets its own weather, of course.

Pradollano is the hub, a stylish modern base with shops, restaurants and bars set around traffic-free open spaces. Most of the accommodation is in older, less smart buildings along a steeply winding road.

From town, two gondolas go up to the mid-station at Borreguiles, and a two-stage fast quad goes up above there. There are four identifiable sectors, well linked, with a good range of intermediate and easy runs but not a lot for experts. There are excellent nursery slopes at mid-mountain (with a moving carpet), and a terrain park with an FIS standard half-pipe. There are also good views from the mountain of the plains and towns – and on a clear day across the Med to Africa. Weekends can be busy, and queues may develop for some of the older lifts, especially the chair up the village slope. The home run can get crowded too. Snow here may be good when it's poor in the Alps, and vice versa. Most slopes face north-west, but some get the afternoon sun. And when the wind blows, as it does, the slopes close; there are no trees.

The Sol y Nieve hotel – with spa and good kids' facilities – was recommended by a recent reporter.

Finland

- Good for families and beginners
- Ideal terrain for cross-country
- Reliable snow well into spring
- Chance of seeing Northern Lights

- Can be bitterly cold (and dark in the early season)
- Small ski areas lacking challenge
- Draglifts are the norm

For skiers with no appetite for the hustle and hassle of Alpine resorts in high season – especially families, perhaps – escaping to the white silence of Lapland can be an attractive alternative. Finland has the lion's share of Lapland, and a few years back we got a healthy flow of reader reports on it – but they've more or less dried up. The resorts are small but rapidly developing.

The Arctic landscape of flat and gently rolling forest, countless lakes and the occasional treeless hill is a paradise for cross-country skiing.

It also offers good beginner and intermediate downhilling, albeit on a small scale. None of the areas has significant vertical by Alpine standards, and in some cases it is seriously limited. The resorts usually open a few runs in late November. For two months in midwinter the sun does not rise – at least, not at sea level. Most areas have floodlit runs. The mountains do not open fully until mid-February, when a normal skiing day is possible and Finnish schools have holidays that usually coincide with ours – making it a busy time. Finland comes into its own at the end of the season, with friendlier temperatures and long daylight hours. Easter is extremely popular, and the slopes are crowded. If you're lucky, you may see the Northern Lights – one March visitor saw them three times ('a great sight').

Conditions are usually hard-packed powder or fresh snow from the start of the season to the end (early May).

The temperature can be extremely variable, yo-yoing between 0°C and −30°C several times in a week. Fine days are the coldest, but the best for skiing: it may be 10 to 15 degrees warmer on the slopes than at valley level. 'Mild' days of cloud and wind are worse, and face masks are sold.

The staple Finnish lift is the T-bar; chairs and gondolas are rare. Pistes are wide and well maintained, as are nursery slopes. The Finns are great boarders, and consider their terrain parks far superior to those in the Alps; super-pipes are increasingly common. There are few mountain restaurants

– but you are never far from the base, with its self-service restaurants. The ski areas also have shelters or 'kotas' – log-built teepees with an open fire and a smoke hole – where you can warm up and cook your own food.

Ski schools are good, with English widely spoken. All ski areas have indoor playrooms for small children, but they may be closed at weekends.

Excursions are common and generally very popular – husky sledding, snowmobile safaris, a reindeer sleigh ride and tea with the Lapp drivers in their tent. Reporters are generally very enthusiastic about these off-slope adventures.

Hotels are self-contained resorts, large and practical rather than stylish, typically with a shop, a cafe, a bar with dance floor, and a pool and sauna with outdoor cooling-off area. Hotel 'dinner' is typically served no later than seven, sometimes followed by a children's disco or dancing to a live band.

Finns usually prefer to stay in cabins, and tour operators offer the compromise of staying in a cabin but taking half-board at a nearby hotel. Cabins vary, but are mostly well equipped, with a sauna and drying cupboard as standard.

The main resorts are Levi and Ylläs, respectively 17km north and 50km west of Kittilä, which has charter flights from Britain. They are described here. Three other resorts worth considering are: Ruka, 80km south of the Arctic Circle, close to Kuusamo airport and the Russian border; Pyhä, 150km north-east of Rovaniemi; and Iso-Syöte, Finland's southernmost fell region. These are covered in our resort directory at the back of the book.

643

UK PACKAGES

Ylläs Inghams, Inntravel, Ski Line
Levi Inghams, Skiworld

Phone numbers
From abroad use the prefix +358 and omit the initial '0' of the phone number

FINLAND

Resort news and key links: www.wheretoskiandsnowboard.com

KEY FACTS

Resort	255m
	840ft
Slopes	255-715m
	840-2,350ft
Lifts	29
Pistes	53km
Snow-guns	40 guns

TOURIST OFFICE

www.yllas.fi

Ylläs

➕ Best for novices and Nordic fans
➕ Few queues and reliable late snow

➖ Slopes a bus ride from the villages
➖ Bars and restaurants not a highlight

Ylläs is Finland's largest resort; it's a quiet family area with an increasing choice of accommodation dotted around its two villages.

Ylläs mountain has lift systems on two sides – Sport Resort Ylläs with most lodging 4km away at Ylläsjärvi, and Ylläs-Ski with lodging similarly distant at Äkäslompolo. Development is taking place at villages, and closer to the slopes too.

This is Finland's largest downhill ski area – but it still has only 53km of pistes that suit novices best. Second- and third-week skiers will rapidly conquer the benign black runs. The maximum vertical is 460m, which is quite respectable. Grooming is 'good'. Past reports of the ski school have been positive. And there's a mountaintop restaurant.

The area has 330km of cross-country trails, 38km of which are floodlit, transforming it from awkward sprawl to doorstep ski resort of limitless scope. There are also 15 cafes along the tracks. From the lift base

trails fan out around the mountain, across the frozen lake and away through the endless forest.

The Äkäs cabins at Äkäslompolo have been recommended, as has the 'comfortable' Saaga Spa hotel at Sport Resort Ylläs, which has 'gym, pool, kids' pool, sauna, steam and hot tub, and a useful drying cabinet in the bedrooms'.

Eating out is slowly improving, with four restaurants at Sport Resort Ylläs opening a few seasons ago. These include a pizzeria. Established favourites in town include more upmarket Poro for traditional fish and meat dishes. Julie's suits families better (pizza and burgers). Tower was new last year at Äkäslompolo.

Off-slope activities include snowmobiling (410km of tracks), dog sledding, reindeer safaris, snowshoeing and ice fishing.

KEY FACTS

Resort	205m
	670ft
Slopes	205-530m
	670-1,740ft
Lifts	26
Pistes	44km
Snow-guns	20%

TOURIST OFFICE

www.levi.fi

Levi

➕ Lodging convenient for slopes
➕ Airport transfer only 15 minutes

➖ Only one challenging piste
➖ Can be very windy

Levi's convenience is its key appeal for visitors. There are good hotels and plentiful off-slope diversions too. Midwinter can be bleak on the hill, though.

Levi is a small, purpose-built village of hotels, apartments and cabins at the foot of its slopes.

The runs are mostly intermediate (only two green runs and one genuine black, plus a couple of fakes). A six-pack takes you up from the village base, but virtually all the lifts are drags. Most rise no more than 200m vertical. The slopes can be bleak and exposed in bad weather, but the area usually has a long season. Many slopes are floodlit. The back side of the hill, which is good for beginners, is getting some investment this year – another six-pack and a revamped base restaurant. The main terrain park, up the hill, is 'large and varied' with 'several jumps and lots of rails'. There is also a super-pipe and snow park on the slopes at the base, with big jumps. Cross-country trails total 230km, with lots floodlit. Vilpuri Kids' Land has lifts and tobogganing areas, plus day care.

Levi's biggest hotel is the Spa Levitunturi (016 646301), with a bowling alley and huge spa facility – including 17 pools and nine saunas. The hotel Levi Panorama (336 3000) is at altitude, reached by gondola. The Sokos hotel (016 3215 500) and the Levilehto apartments are tipped.

There are dozens of places to eat. The Hullu Poro (Crazy Reindeer) complex has several restaurants including the Pihvipirtti steakhouse, which serves 'outstanding rare meats', and the Valkea Vaadin ('near gourmet standard'). At close of play Vinkkari at the base gets 'busy and very loud'. For a quiet drink one reporter favours the 'relaxed' Kota in the Holiday Club hotel. Nightlife is 'very lively', especially at holiday times – there are several nightspots. Off-slope activities include snowmobiling, reindeer and husky safaris, snowshoeing, ice fishing and skating on the frozen lake. You can visit a reindeer park.

+ One of the best places in Europe for serious cross-country skiing
+ The home of telemark – plenty of opportunities to learn and practise
+ Freedom from the glitz and ill-mannered lift queues of the Alps
+ Impressive terrain parks
+ Usually reliable snow conditions throughout a long season

− Very limited downhill areas
− Very basic mountain restaurants
− Booze is prohibitively taxed
− Scenery more Pennine than Alpine
− Après-ski that is either deadly dull or irritatingly rowdy
− Short daylight hours in midwinter
− Highly changeable weather
− Limited off-slope activities

NEWS

2014/15: At Hemsedal a new 4km blue run from the Skisenter down Sentrum is being created. The new Skigaarden development on the slopes – with apartments, shops and restaurants – is to open.

2013/14: A new charter flight service began linking Gatwick to Fagernes Lufthavn, 80km from Hemsedal. The terrain park has been moved and redesigned.

For downhillers who fancy a change from the conspicuous consumption that characterizes Alpine ski resorts, Norway could be just the place. Families with young children, in particular, will have no trouble finding junk food to please the kids – the mountain restaurants serve little else. For us, any one of our first three negatives listed above is reason to pause. Add together all the negatives, and you can count us out. We find Scotland more attractive.

We've recently detected a small surge of interest in Norway in the UK travel trade, with more tour operators entering the fray in several resorts. (Our list over the page is for Hemsedal, but Geilo and Trysil attract more operators.)

There is a traditional friendship between Norway and Britain, and English is widely spoken.

For the Norwegians and Swedes, skiing is a weekend rather than a special holiday activity, and not an occasion for extravagance. So at lunchtime they haul sandwiches out of their backpacks as we might while walking the Pennine Way, and in the evening they cook in their apartments. Don't expect tempting restaurants.

The Norwegians have a problem with alcohol. Walk into an après-ski bar at 5pm on a Saturday and you may find young men already inebriated. And this is despite incredibly high taxes on booze. In restaurants wine prices are ludicrous and the wine quality is poor – though our resident consultant on matters Norwegian says that the state liquor stores offer very good value at the top end. Other prices are generally not high by Alpine standards.

Cross-country skiing comes as naturally to Norwegians as walking; even if you're not very keen, the fact that cross-country is normal, and not a wimp's alternative to 'real' skiing, gives Norway a special appeal. Here, cross-country is both a way of getting about the valleys and a way of exploring the hills. What distinguishes Norway for the keen cross-country skier is the network of long trails across the gentle uplands, with refuges along the way where backpackers can pause for refreshment or stay overnight. More and more Norwegians are taking to telemarking, and snowboarding is very popular – local youths fill the impressive terrain parks at weekends. For downhill skiing, the country isn't nearly so attractive. Despite the fact that it is able to hold downhill races, Norway's Alpine areas are of limited appeal. The most rewarding resort is Hemsedal, covered on the next page.

The other downhill resorts most widely known are Geilo and Voss, on the railway line from Bergen to Oslo. Tryvann is just 20 minutes from the centre of Oslo, on a spur of the underground system, and popular with the locals. Lillehammer is well known too, of course – host of the 1994 Olympics; but it's a lakeside town not a downhill ski resort (the Alpine races were held some distance away). Other main resorts are Trysil, on the border with Sweden, Beitostølen in the Jotunheimen National Park, and Oppdal. All are covered in the directory at the back of the book.

KEY FACTS	
Resort	640m
	2,100ft
Slopes	670-1450m
	2,200-4,760ft
Lifts	24
Pistes	47km
Snow-guns	45%

Hemsedal

- ➕ Convenient slope-side lodging
- ➕ Some quite challenging slopes
- ➕ Excellent children's nursery slopes
- ➖ Not much of a village
- ➖ Weekend queues
- ➖ Exposed upper mountain

Hemsedal is both an unspoiled valley and a village, the latter also referred to as Trøym and Sentrum ('Centre') – but you can also stay at the lift base or higher up in the slopes, a mile or so away.

Hemsedal is a three-hour drive from Oslo and geared mainly to weekenders arriving by car or coach. But there is a ski-bus linking all parts and floodlit paths to/from the centre. The lift pass also covers smaller Solheisen, up the valley. Geilo is an hour away.

Sentrum is a bus ride from the slopes and little more than a small area of low-rise apartments/hotels, shops, a garage, a bank and a couple of cashpoints. There's a developing area of lodgings close to the base. You can also stay further up the hill where there are several areas of more or less ski-in/ski-out lodgings.

Hemsedal's slopes pack a lot of variety into a small space. Fast lifts serve a high proportion of the slopes, though a few awkward drags remain. There can be weekend crowds and queues for the main access lifts. Otherwise it is quiet. There are three terrain parks and a mini park for kids, plus ski cross, speed ski and giant slalom areas. Snowmaking covers 45% of the slopes.

There is quite a bit to amuse experts: several black pistes and wide areas of gentler off-piste terrain served by drags. Mileage-hungry piste-bashers will find Hemsedal's runs very limited. There are quite a few red and blue runs to play on, and splendid long

green runs – but they get a lot of traffic. There is floodlit skiing several nights a week. Beginners have a separate, gentle nursery area. The resort caters well for families, with day care offered for children from six months; the kids' nursery slopes at the lift base are very well developed.

There are 120km of prepared cross-country trails in the valley and forest, and (in late season) 90km at altitude.

The best hotel is the Skogstad (320 55000) in Sentrum – comfortable, with a spa; but its bar and nightclub may be noisy at weekends. The hotel Skarsnuten (320 61700), on the hill, is stylishly modern. But apartments dominate. The chalet-style Alpin Lodge by the nursery slopes includes 30 apartments, restaurants and shops.

The dining choices are OK; the Big Horn at Fjellandsby is a popular steakhouse, and there's the Lodgen bar and restaurant (Mediterranean cuisine) at the Alpin Lodge; plus more places in town.

Après-ski starts at the Skistua (Skisenter), which also has live music at the weekends. The bars and clubs get rowdy at weekends and holidays, but can be very quiet midweek.

Off-slope diversions include bowling, tobogganing, dog sledding, ice climbing and snowmobiling.

UK PACKAGES

Crystal, Crystal Finest, Ski Safari, Thomson

Phone numbers
From abroad use the prefix +47

TOURIST OFFICE

www.hemsedal.com
www.skistar.com/hemsedal

HEMSEDAL.COM / FRANK TOLPINRUD

There are lodgings high up on the mountain ↓

Sweden

- ➕ Snow-sure from December to May
- ➕ Unspoiled, beautiful landscape
- ➕ Uncrowded pistes and lifts
- ➕ Super Nordic and off-slope activities
- ➖ Limited challenging downhill terrain
- ➖ Small areas by Alpine standards
- ➖ Lacks dramatic Alpine scenery
- ➖ Short days during the early season

Sweden appeals most to those who want an all-round winter holiday in a different environment and culture. Standards of accommodation, food and service are good, and the people are welcoming, lively and friendly, but most of the downhill areas are limited in size and challenge.

Holidaying in Sweden is a completely different experience from holidaying in the Alps. Although virtually everyone speaks good English, menus and signs are often written only in Swedish. The food is delightful, especially if you like fish and venison. And resorts are very family-friendly. It is significantly cheaper than neighbouring Norway, but reporters still complain that eating and drinking is very expensive.

Days are very short in early season. But from early February the lifts usually work from 9am to 4.30pm and by March it is light until 8.30pm. Most resorts have some floodlit pistes. On the downside, downhill slopes are limited in both challenge and extent, and the lift systems are dominated by T-bars. There's lots of cross-country and backcountry skiing.

Après-ski is taken very seriously – with live bands from mid- to late afternoon. There is plenty to do off the slopes: snowmobile safaris, ice fishing, dog-sled rides, ice climbing, saunas galore and visiting local Sami villages.

The main resort is Åre, described below. Others include Sälen (big but fragmented) and Vemdalen. These two, plus Riksgränsen, Björkliden (both above the Arctic Circle) and tiny Ramundberget are covered in our directory at the back of the book.

KEY FACTS

Resort	380m
	1,250ft
Slopes	380-1275m
	1,250-4,180ft
Lifts	47
Pistes	100km
Snow-guns	70%

UK PACKAGES
Ski Safari, Skitracer

TOURIST OFFICE
www.skistar.com

Åre

- ➕ Good for intermediates and novices
- ➕ Excellent children's facilities
- ➖ High winds can affect snow and lifts
- ➖ Few expert challenges

Sweden's biggest ski area, with lots to do off the slopes as well as on. Not great for keen skiers but good for families wanting a change from the Alps.

The centre of this small lakeside town has old, pretty, coloured wooden buildings and some larger modern additions. Lodgings are spread out along the valley.

There are two separate areas of slopes linked by a ski-bus. In both areas, the main lifts from the valley are fast. But nearly all other lifts are drags. New investment is promised now that Åre will host the Alpine World Championships in 2019. More snowmaking is planned for the Duved area for 2014/15. Queues are rare.

The slopes offer mainly beginner and intermediate tree-lined terrain, with two windswept bowls above, which are prone to closure. Experts will find the slopes limited, especially if the high bowls are closed. But there is a lot of off-piste. For intermediates there are steep, sometimes icy, black and red runs back to town, and lots of pretty blue runs through the trees. You get a real sense of travelling around on the main area. Beginners have good facilities in both sectors. There are three terrain parks and 58km of groomed cross-country trails. The ski school has a good reputation, and children have special areas. Kids under seven get free lift passes if wearing helmets. Mountain huts are good.

The best central hotel is the charming old Diplomat Åregården. There are ample apartments and cabins and lots of restaurants, from Japanese to pizza – a new Italian will open in 2014/15. Après-ski is lively, with the Tott, Fjällgården and Åregården busy from 3pm. Off-slope diversions are plentiful.

Bulgaria

RPI	60
lift pass	£130
ski hire	£45
lessons	£75
food & drink	£70
total	£320

- ➕ Costs very low by Alpine standards
- ➕ Good ski schools
- ➕ Lively bars and nightlife

- ➖ Poor snow record, though snowmaking has been improved
- ➖ Small ski areas
- ➖ Cheap booze attracts 18–30 crowds

Bulgaria best suits novices and early intermediates looking for a jolly time at bargain-basement prices. Bansko's arrival on the scene ten years ago raised the bar for the country's other main resorts, which are now starting to catch up.

Bulgaria has traditionally been a place for a cheap and cheerful holiday. It is well worth considering if you are a beginner or early intermediate on a budget and want a lively time, fuelled by cheap booze. Don't expect sophistication or big ski areas. A keen piste-basher could ski even the biggest resort in a matter of hours.

But the ski schools have an excellent reputation. And Bansko has some good hotels and a modern lift system. Even Pamporovo now has a six-pack. The scenery and culture provide a very different holiday experience from the Alps.

KEY FACTS

Resort	1300m
	4,270ft
Slopes	1300-2560m
	4,270-8,400ft
Lifts	12
Pistes	58km
Snow-guns	150 guns

TOURIST OFFICE
www.borovets-bg.com

UK PACKAGES
Borovets Balkan Holidays, Crystal, Neilson, Ski Line, Skitracer, Thomson
Bansko Balkan Holidays, Crystal, Crystal Finest, Neilson, Skitracer, Solos, Thomson
Pamporovo Absolutely Snow, Balkan Holidays, Crystal, Skitracer, Thomson

Borovets

- ➕ Lively, convenient village
- ➕ Some good intermediate slopes

- ➖ Not ideal for beginners
- ➖ Nightlife can be tacky

Borovets is a mixture of large, modern hotels and small bars, clubs and restaurants. The slopes suit intermediates best.

Most people come here on packages and stay in big hotels with their own bars, restaurants and shops within them. There is also a large selection of quirkier and lively small bars, shops and eating places lining 'The Strip', as one reporter describes the 300m long street, counting 'at least 26'. He goes on: 'There must be over 40 if you include the back streets. Borovets is now the Benidorm of skiing, with touts outside most bars trying to get you in; it's a shanty-town mix of wooden huts plus big hotels.' Another reporter complained of 'dogs roaming the streets'.

Nevertheless, the resort's beautiful woodland setting gives a degree of Alpine-style charm.

A long, slow gondola rises over 1000m in 25 minutes to reach both the short, easy slopes of Markoudjik and the longer, steepish Yastrebets pistes. The runs are best for good intermediates, and include some longish reds. The resort is not ideal for novices: nursery slopes are crowded, and the step from easy blues to testing reds is a big one. There is night skiing on four runs and 35km of cross-country.

Queues form for the gondola at peak times ('45 minutes', says a recent reporter) and for the nursery draglifts. The gondola is also said to be prone to closure by wind. Grooming is erratic but a new machine for 2014/15 may improve this. Snow-guns are being doubled from 75 to 150 for 2014/15. The ski schools are praised – a reporter says of the school attached to the Samokov Hotel: 'I progressed from complete beginner to red runs in a week; my instructor regularly spent more than the allotted time with the group.'

Most reporters stay at the Samokov or the Rila. Noise can be a problem at the Rila, say reporters; and one found it 'a good basic hotel but a bit tired; the self-service buffet meals were always cold'. Recent visitors found the Lion 'clean, tidy, with friendly staff' and thought the villas at the Iglika Palace were 'basic, but quiet and comfortable'. Food shopping is limited.

The Black Cat restaurant has 'good food, service and a lovely open fire'. There are plenty of lively bars with 'dancing girls and live music'. Buzz is said to be one of the liveliest, and there's a night club in the Rila hotel.

A reporter recommended Katy's Pub 'with a guitarist in the attic' and Mamacita's Mexican restaurant and bar. There are also 'adult' bars, but they are away from the main streets, and advertising is now said to be banned, though there are plenty of touts.

Tour operator reps organize pub crawls, folklore evenings etc. Excursions to the Rila monastery or to Sofia by coach are interesting.

KEY FACTS

Resort	990m
	3,250ft
Slopes	990-2600m
	3,250-8,530ft
Lifts	13
Pistes	70km
Snow-guns	190 guns

TOURIST OFFICE

www.banskoski.com

DAVID MAXWELL-LEES

Borovets and Pamporovo have beautiful wooded settings and runs. Bansko has some more open slopes ↓

Bansko

➕ Lots of fast lifts on the mountain
➕ Atmospheric town centre
➕ Friendly, helpful locals

➖ Long, queue-prone access gondola
➖ Few off-slope diversions
➖ Some unfinished buildings evident

Bansko is an old valley town in the scenic Pirin National Park, catapulted into the 21st century in 2004 by the construction of modern lifts and smart lodgings. Reporters like what they find, and some go back repeatedly.

The area near the base of the access gondola to the slopes has a lot of modern hotels, apartments, bars and restaurants. Some are ski-in, and many others run shuttle-buses to the lift.

The older part of town looks no great beauty on the outskirts, but the central square reveals a quiet and charming heart, and there are few outward signs of commercial tourism.

The slopes are reached by an eight-seat gondola to Bunderishka, for which there are long queues in the morning ('can take hours'). Some people start queuing well before the lift opens. An alternative is to pay for a VIP card, we're told. A planned additional gondola is on hold. Queues further up the hill are rare.

There is an easy blue piste back to the town, with snowmaking and floodlighting. Most lifts are fast chairs, and successive ones take you up mainly north-facing slopes to the high point of the area. You can ski down reds or blues to Shiligarnika, or a red followed by the Tomba black to Bunderishka. Some of these are quite long and challenging. Reporters judge the piste classification accurate.

Bulgaria
Slovenia · Romania
Ski & Board Holidays
from 8 UK Airports

- Just £70pp Deposit
- Free 20kg Luggage
- Non Euro Value
- Free Child Places*
- Free Storage*
- 5% Loyalty Discount

Prices from
£244
per person

Reservations
0845 130 1114

Balkan Holidays

*Conditions apply

www.balkanholidays.co.uk

Bulgaria's huts are not a highlight and food is basic but cheap →

A reporter notes that small variations on the pistes and skiable trees beside them make the area add up to more skiing than you might expect. There is a small terrain park.

The nursery slopes near the top of the gondola are good, with little through-traffic. The main school – Ulen – is 'excellent', says a reporter. There's a snow garden, and the kindergarten takes children from four years.

Reporters find the grooming good, but one complains about lack of piste marker poles. Snow is more reliable than the Bulgarian norm. 30 new snow-guns were installed for 2013/14.

Mountain huts are mostly self-service, and the food 'basic'. A reporter advises: 'The lift company runs all the on-piste places, but a short stroll through the woods will take you to independent hotels with good-value fresh food.'

Hotels near the gondola station (the obvious place to stay) include the swanky Florimont with its own casino; the 5-star Kempinski Grand Arena ('spa to die for') – its Tepanyaki Japanese restaurant is 'a special experience'; and the MPM Sport ('spacious, with a good spa'). The Emerald has 'superb rooms, friendly staff and tasty, hot food'. The Lion has 'spacious, spotlessly clean rooms and a pool, steam and sauna'.

There are some smart bars near the lift. Staying there, you are a short taxi ride from the town and its many mehanas (traditional inns) with roaring fires, real Bulgarian food and good wine. And there are lots of lively bars – readers' tips include Harry's bar behind the Victoria restaurant ('a good buzz'), the Flora in the Emerald hotel ('happy hour from noon till midnight with two-for-one drinks; open till 5am'), Diamonds and Amigos.

Other activities include paragliding, skating, snowmobiling and bowling.

Pamporovo

KEY FACTS

Resort	1650m
	5,410ft
Slopes	1450-1935m
	4,760-6,350ft
Lifts	15
Pistes	37km
Snow-guns	90%

TOURIST OFFICE

www.
pamporovoresort.com

- ➕ Pretty, tree-lined slopes
- ➕ Good, low-cost choice for novices
- ➖ Limited extent and short runs
- ➖ Poor piste maintenance

Pamporovo is a purpose-built village, in a pretty woodland area a short shuttle-bus ride from its easy slopes that suit beginners best.

The resort is strictly for beginners and near-beginners, with mostly easy and short runs. Others will find the limited area rather inadequate. The 37km of slopes are pretty and sheltered, with pistes cutting through pine forest. Some beginners find the runs rather too narrow. There's a half-pipe and a terrain park. Snow reliability is poor, but snowmaking covers 90% of the slopes. There are plenty of mountain huts, though they are not enticing.

Past reports have praised the ski schools but we lack recent reports. There are 25km of cross-country trails.

A reporter recommends the hotel Finlandia ('comfortable; friendly staff; plentiful but plain food').

Romania

RPI	50
lift pass	£110
ski hire	£50
lessons	£45
food & drink	£50
total	£255

UK PACKAGES

Poiana Brasov Balkan Holidays

Phone numbers
From abroad use the prefix +40 and omit the initial '0' of the phone number

TOURIST OFFICE

www.poianabrasov.com

➕ Cheap packages, and very low prices on the spot

➕ Interesting excursions and friendly local people

➕ Good tuition from keen instructors

➖ Primitive facilities, especially mountain restaurants and toilets

➖ Uninspiring food

➖ Very limited slopes

Romania sells mainly on price. On-the-spot prices, in particular, are very low. Provided you don't have unreasonably high expectations, you'll probably come back from Poiana Brasov content. It allows complete beginners to try a ski holiday at the minimum cost, and to have a jolly time in the evenings without adding substantially to that cost.

Romania's main resort – and the only one featuring in any UK package programme – is **Poiana Brasov** (1030m) in the Carpathian mountains. It is a short drive above the city of Brasov, about 120km (on alarmingly rough, slow roads) north-west of the capital and arrival airport, Bucharest.

The resort is purpose-built, and has the air of a spacious, pleasant holiday camp. But it is not designed for the convenience of skiers: some serious-sized hotels are right by the lifts, but most are scattered about a pretty, wooded plateau, served by regular buses and cheap taxis.

The slopes are extremely limited – 24km of pistes in total. They consist of intermediate tree-lined runs with a decent vertical of about 825m, roughly following the line of the main cable car and gondola, plus an open nursery area at the top. A few years ago four new slopes (two blues and two reds) opened, accessed by a quad and a six-pack. There are some nursery lifts at village level, which are used when snow permits. Night skiing is also available. The resort gets weekend crowds from Brasov and Bucharest, and queues can result, but during the week there are few problems.

A key part of the resort's appeal is the friendly and effective teaching from enthusiastic instructors.

Hotel standards are higher than you might expect. The linked 3-star Bradul and 4-star Sport hotels (0268 407330) are handy for the lower nursery slopes and for one of the cable cars. Guests in both have use of the Sport's spa facilities. Après-ski revolves around the hotel bars and nightclubs – plus outings to rustic barns for BBQs with gypsy music and to the bars and restaurants in the nearby town of Brasov. With cheap beer and very cheap spirits on tap, things can be quite lively. Off-slope facilities are limited: there are two good-sized pools (in hotels) and bowling. An excursion to nearby Bran Castle (Count Dracula's lair) is also popular.

POIANA BRASOV TOURIST OFFICE

← Poiana Brasov allows beginners to try a ski holiday at minimum cost

Slovenia

RPI	65
lift pass	£130
ski hire	£60
lessons	£65
food & drink	£90
total	**£345**

UK PACKAGES
Kranjska Gora Balkan Holidays, Crystal, Inghams, Thomson
Bled (for Vogel) Balkan Holidays, Crystal, Crystal Finest, Thomson

TOURIST OFFICES
www.slovenia.info
Bled
www.bled.si

KRANJSKA GORA TOURIST OFFICE
Kranjska Gora is one of the most popular resorts with British visitors and has its own small area of mainly gentle slopes
↓

+ Low prices
+ Beautiful, varied scenery
+ Good beginner slopes and lessons

− Limited, mostly easy slopes
− Still lots of slow, antiquated lifts
− Mountain huts not a highlight

Slovenia offers lower prices and fewer crowds than the Alps, attracting economy minded visitors from neighbouring Italy and Austria as well as Britain and the Netherlands. The ski areas are limited and a bit antiquated; most suit novices well. Some Slovenian resorts are making obvious investments but some are struggling. Sadly, one of the best, Kanin – which has Slovenia's highest terrain and cross-border skiing into Italy – was closed for the 2013/14 season, and we have been told that it will be unlikely to be operational for the 2014/15 season. For information see www.boveckanin.si/en/ski-resort.

Slovenia – which is bordered by Italy, Austria and Croatia – has 30 or so ski areas, the main ones concentrated in the Julian Alps in the west, dominated by its highest mountain, Mt Triglav; all are small and some are tiny. None is likely to keep the adventurous piste-basher amused for a week; but you can have an enjoyable trip touring by car or by combining several resorts from one base. EasyJet (from Stansted) and Adria (from Gatwick) fly to Ljubljana.

The season is shorter than in the Alps and the resorts low. Most slopes are below 2000m.

Prices are low, and there is a positive feel – and a warm and hospitable welcome. Standards of service and accommodation have improved – the hotels may not be particularly attractive, but many are new or modernized, complete with pools, spas and often free Wi-Fi.

Getting around is relatively easy, and most ski areas are within a 40-minute drive of each other on good roads. And the main resorts are within a two-hour bus ride of Ljubljana.

Bled, with its beautiful lake and fairly lively nightlife, is an attractive base and is featured by a few British tour operators. It has just one steepish slope. But other resorts nearby include Kranjska Gora, Krvavec, Kanin, Vogel and Kobla (the only ski area in Slovenia reachable by train).

The other main group of resorts centres on Maribor to the east, a quite different area of low-slung wooded ridges. But it has the biggest ski area in the country at 43km.

The Ski Pass Slovenia covers all resorts in Slovenia.

Most resorts fit best into the intermediate category but differ on their suitability for novices. Experts will find few black runs, but there is good off-piste when conditions permit. Lift systems are improving and queues are rare. Most Slovenians visit at weekends; midweek the slopes can be deserted. A common feature of many areas is an access lift with no runs back to valley level. One drawback for us is the lack of quality lunches: snacks and picnics are the norm, hearty menus and cute huts are rare. Ski schools are of a high quality and cheap, with good spoken English. Other winter activities are big in Slovenia, too, so there is plenty to do off the slopes.

KEY FACTS

Resort	1450m
	4,760ft
Slopes	1450-1970m
	4,760-6,460ft
Lifts	11
Pistes	30km
Snow-guns	95%

TOURIST OFFICE

www.rtc-krvavec.si

Krvavec

🞣 Convenient for short breaks
🞣 Quiet slopes midweek
🞣 Jolly, family atmosphere

🖿 Lacks proper resort base
🖿 Short, mainly south-facing runs
🖿 Not ideal for novices

Krvavec has been voted Slovenia's best ski area and is just 8km from Ljubljana airport. There's no central village, but then most visitors are locals on day trips from the city.

Krvavec has some of the country's steepest slopes, including five black runs. It is a lively place, especially at weekends. Most visitors are families on day trips. Bled is 40 minutes by daily bus (free with the lift pass). There is no resort, but there is one hotel on the slopes and some lodging in nearby Cerklje. The local lift pass also covers Rogla, near Maribor.

A gondola goes up to the slopes, which span three partly wooded hills from a high point of 1970m. The lifts include a six-pack and a quad; queues are rare. The pistes get a lot of sun, though snowmaking is extensive and grooming good. There's a good nursery slope and a children's area with fun park, moving carpet and drag lift; but there are few easy blues to progress to. The mid-mountain Plaza has picnic spots and snack bars. There are huts on the Kriska Planina area. Snowshoeing is popular, and you can try airboarding and tobogganing – floodlit on Friday and Saturday evenings.

KEY FACTS

Resort	810m
	2,660ft
Slopes	810-1295m
	2,660-4,250ft
Lifts	18
Pistes	20km
Snow-guns	Some

TOURIST OFFICE

www.kr-gora.si

Kranjska Gora

🞣 Good for novices and families
🞣 Convenient, good, slope-side hotels

🖿 Slopes limited in extent, variety, length and vertical
🖿 Still some old lifts, and gets busy

Despite limited slopes (most other areas are bigger), Kranjska Gora is offered by a few UK tour operators. It's a good-value, pretty and compact resort that is popular with families. Since the centre is fairly small, most facilities are near the slopes, too.

Kranjska Gora is close to the Austrian and Italian borders. Day trips to ski in resorts over the borders are possible.

The 20km of wide, tree-lined pistes rise to 1295m and best suit very unadventurous intermediates and

Build your own shortlist: **www.wheretoskiandsnowboard.com**

around involves tedious traversing. Queues are rare despite fairly busy slopes here. Snow reliability is poor, but snowmaking covers many pistes, and 10 more snow-guns were installed for 2013/14.

There is a terrain park and a children's area with a moving carpet. Cross-country trails total 40km. It is back to base for lunch and Bedanc is a good self-service beside chair 7.

Hotels are plentiful and of a high standard, most with pools and spas. For slope-side convenience, the Lek, Prisank and Larix are best. The Alpina is popular with families. We liked the Kompas, with good breakfast buffet and pool.

For eating out try the Kotnik and Via Napoli (hotel Prisank) pizzerias, and the Ostarija for finer dining. Ice skating, night tobogganing and snowshoeing are popular.

↑ Huts generally are not a highlight in Slovenia but this one looks nice
MARIBOR POHORJE

novices – though there is a World Cup slalom black run. The slopes above Podkoren are quiet and gentle.

There are four quad chairlifts, but still lots of draglifts. And getting

KEY FACTS	
Resort	570m
	1,870ft
Slopes	1535-1800m
	5,040-5,910ft
Lifts	9
Pistes	22km
Snow-guns	Some

TOURIST OFFICE
www.vogel.si

Vogel

➕ Beautiful lake setting, pretty runs
➕ Good choice of huts

➖ Bus ride from most lodging
➖ Limited in extent and challenge

Vogel overlooks stunning Lake Bohinj, part of the Triglav National Park. It's tiny, but is the main ski area within commuting distance of Bled.

Vogel has the best conditions and prettiest slopes in the area. Buses arrive daily from Bled; but there are small hotels and restaurants near the base and in villages along the lakeside (served by free ski-bus).

The 22km of partly wooded slopes are reached by a cable car up from the valley. A fast quad serves a mid-mountain area, with a single-seat chair to the high point at 1800m (great views). Pistes served by another chair and three drags include a lovely gentle blue. There is a separate nursery slope, with snowmaking and a moving carpet, a children's area and, for

2014/15, a terrain park and a snowcross.

When conditions permit, a long red run returns to the bottom cable car station via a quiet, pretty valley. Several of the huts are nicer than the Slovenian norm.

For a change of scene Kobla, with 24km of wide, wooded runs, is a short bus ride away at Bohinjska Bistrica – the railway terminus. The 5-star Bohinj Park hotel is eco-friendly, with pool, cinema and bowling. Next door is a huge aqua park. Near Vogel, the 3-star Zlatarog is comfortable.

KEY FACTS	
Resort	325m
	1,070ft
Slopes	325-1330m
	1,070-4,360ft
Lifts	21
Pistes	43km
Snow-guns	95%

TOURIST OFFICE
www.maribor-pohorje.si

Maribor-Pohorje

➕ Good access, close to the city
➕ Gentle, sheltered slopes for novices

➖ Mostly short runs
➖ Few challenges except the FIS run

Slovenia's second city, Maribor, is just 6km from its local slopes – where there's also limited lodging. There's some varied terrain but most runs are short and served by drag lifts running along one side of a ridge.

This is the country's biggest ski area, twice the size of better-known Kranjska Gora.

The lifts include a six-pack and a gondola to Pohorje summit. There's night skiing, and snowmaking covers 95% of the area. There are 27km of

cross-country trails. The area lift pass also covers Kranjska Gora. The Pohorje school offers a wide range of classes. There are several atmospheric old inns serving good, Hungarian-influenced food. The 4-star Arena and 3-star Videc hotels are slope-side.

Scotland

- ➕ Easy to get to from northern Britain
- ➕ It is possible to experience perfect snow and very satisfying skiing
- ➕ Decent, cheap accommodation and good-value packages
- ➕ Midweek it's rarely crowded
- ➕ Lots to do off the slopes

- ➖ Weather is extremely changeable and sometimes vicious
- ➖ Snowfall is erratic
- ➖ Slopes limited; runs mainly short
- ➖ Queuing can be a problem
- ➖ Little ski resort ambience and few memorable mountain restaurants

Scottish skiing conditions are unpredictable, to say the least. If you live nearby and can go at short notice when things look good, the several ski areas are a tremendous asset. But booking a holiday here as a replacement for your usual week in the Alps is just too risky.

Most of the slopes in most of the areas suit intermediates best. But all apart from The Lecht also offer one or two tough or very tough slopes.

For novices who are really keen to learn, Scotland could make sense, especially if you live nearby. You can book instruction via one of the excellent outdoor centres, many of which also provide accommodation. The ski schools at the resorts themselves are also very good.

Snowboarding is popular, and all of the resorts have some special terrain features, but maintaining these facilities in good nick is problematic. When the conditions are right, the natural terrain is good for freeriding.

CairnGorm Mountain is the best-known resort, with 11 lifts and 30km of runs. Aviemore is the main base (with a shuttle-bus to the slopes) –

the 'friendly' Dunroamin B&B was recently praised. The slopes are accessed by a funicular from the main car park up to Ptarmigan at 1100m.

Nevis Range is the highest Scottish resort, with 20km of groomed runs on the north-facing slopes of Aonach Mor reaching 1190m. It has 11 lifts plus a long six-seat access gondola. There are many B&Bs and hotels in and around Fort William, 10 minutes away by bus.

Glenshee is the largest ski area, with 40km of runs spread out over three minor parallel valleys served by 22 lifts, including a recent chairlift link to the Cairnwell cafe and the slopes in that area. It has some natural quarter-pipes. Glenshee is primarily a venue for day-trippers, though there are hotels, hostels and B&Bs in the area.

Glencoe's seven lifts and 20km of runs lie east of moody Glen Coe itself. A 2014 visitor was 'surprised at how good the set-up was'. A double chairlift and a drag go up to the main slopes, including the nursery area. There are freeriding opportunities and a challenging descent on black Flypaper, the resort's steepest run. The cafe at the base serves 'traditional hearty fare'. The isolated Kings House Hotel is 2km away.

The Lecht is largely a novices' area, with 13 lifts and 20km of runs on the gentle slopes beside a high pass, with a series of parallel lifts and runs above the car parks. With a maximum vertical of only 200m, runs are short. There's extensive snowmaking, a terrain park, and a day lodge at the base. The village of Tomintoul is 10km away.

FURTHER INFORMATION

The VisitScotland organization runs an excellent website at: ski.visitscotland.com

Japan

- ☐ Reliable deep powder snow in Hokkaido resorts, lift-served
- ☐ Fabulous food
- ☐ Polite and gracious locals
- ☐ Night skiing is the norm, allowing a long ski day if you want one

- ☐ Pricey and lengthy trip; 6,000 miles and 24 hours door to door
- ☐ Lack of off-slope diversions
- ☐ Snowfall can go on for weeks in Hokkaido resorts
- ☐ Main hotels vast, modern, charmless

Although it is roughly the same size as the British Isles, Japan has hundreds of ski resorts. And places on the northern island of Hokkaido have developed something like cult status with keen skiers and riders from Australia. The reason is simple: humongous, frequent and reliable falls of powder snow.

UK PACKAGES
Niseko Crystal, James Orr Heliski, Mountain Tracks, Oxford Ski Co, Ski Independence, Ski Safari, Ski Weekend, Skitracer, Skiworld, Thomson
Rusutsu Crystal, Ski Safari, Skitracer, Thomson
Furano Ski Safari, Skiworld
Hakuba Ski Safari, Skitracer, Skiworld

You fly in to Sapporo (about three hours by bus to the resorts), via Tokyo or Osaka. Ski Independence says a week in Niseko and a two-night stopover in Tokyo on the way home would cost around £2,000.

Few of the locals speak English but we were struck by how friendly, charming, polite and helpful they all were. The food is delicious – and the menus often have photos to help you.

Hokkaido has a well-deserved reputation for powder snow, which usually falls almost constantly from December to the end of February. Skiing waist-deep powder is normally an everyday occurrence. You go for

that, not for the piste skiing. The slopes are not steep and some people are disappointed by that; but there is tremendous skiing among nicely spaced trees. Strangely, off-piste is officially prohibited in many resorts including in Rusutsu and Furano (which has a special zone where it is allowed) and there are prominent signs saying it is not allowed – but nearly everyone ignores the ban and we are told that the authorities turn a blind eye to it. In Niseko, though, off-piste is allowed (except in two dangerous areas marked on the piste map) and there are gates into the backcountry.

On our 2013 visit we were unlucky with the weather – it was warm and either foggy or windy most of the time. That meant avalanche danger was high and so out-of-bounds skiing was out of the question most of the time. But nearly all reporters have been luckier. Getting the most out of the off-piste means hiring a guide. We used Hokkaido Powder Guides one day when we were in Furano – we went to the tiny resort of Kamui and they found us the legendary waist-deep powder at last. And a recent reporter in Niseko was very happy with Black Diamond Tours.

Niseko is made up of three areas of slopes – Grand Hirafu (Hirafu and Hanazono), Annupuri and Niseko Village. All except Hanazono open until 8pm or 8.30 thanks to one of the world's largest – and most heavily

SAPPORO
Furano
Niseko
Sahoro
Rusutsu
HOKKAIDO

NORTH KOREA
SEA OF JAPAN

Yamagata Zao
HONSHU

SOUTH KOREA
Myoko
Naeba/Kagura
Nozawa Onsen
Hakuba
Shiga Kogen
TOKYO

OSAKA

SHIKOKU
KYUSHU

0   200   400
km

← There are lots of resorts on the main island of Honshu – only the better-known ones are shown on our map. But the best snow is on Hokkaido

Nicely spaced trees, not-too-steep slopes, somewhat more powder than this and views of volcanoes are the norm in Japan. This is Niseko →

TANYA BOOTH

KEY FACTS

Niseko		
Slopes	235-1210m	
	770-3,970ft	
Lifts		30
Pistes		48km
Blue		30%
Red		40%
Black		30%

Rusutsu	
Lifts	19
Pistes	42km
Blue	30%
Red	40%
Black	30%

Furano		
Slopes	235-1210m	
	770-3,970ft	
Lifts		10
Pistes		25km
Blue		40%
Red		40%
Black		20%

More information
To really get to grips with the resorts on offer in Japan, spend some time delving into this site:
www.snowjapan.com

TOURIST OFFICES

Niseko
www.nisekotourism.com
www.niseko.ne.jp/en/index.html
Hirafu
www.grand-hirafu.jp/winter/en/
Niseko Village
www.niseko-village.com
Annupuri
www.annupurivillage.com

Rusutsu
www.rusutsu.co.jp
Furano
www.furanotourism.com

used – night skiing operations. The three are linked, but not as efficiently as you might wish. There are some modern lifts, but also lots of old chairs – including three ancient singles.

The biggest and most popular area, Grand Hirafu, has an eight-seat gondola from the base and a smart day lodge and restaurant.

There are modern rather isolated ski-in/ski-out hotels (but little else) at the Annupuri and Niseko Village bases. We (and a reporter) stayed happily at the Green Leaf in Niseko Village in 2013 – lovely onsen (see below), good buffet food, friendly staff. The Hilton Niseko Village has spectacular views from most rooms and its own onsen.

Or you can stay in the little town of Hirafu which has varied architecture – ancient and modern; a bit ramshackle but with a very friendly feel with lots of small bars and restaurants serving excellent traditional Japanese food as well as burgers and the like, many quite lively and busy. We enjoyed the Tamashii bar – full of Australians, with music, dancing, pool and dartboards. There are some good modern apartments alongside traditional pensions and lodges. Beware of the pavements – they were icy and treacherous when we were there and reporters warn of them.

Free shuttle-buses run between the lift bases every 20 minutes, but they were oversubscribed on our visit and they stop at 8.30pm. Taxis from Hirafu to Niseko Village cost 3,000 yen.

Rusutsu is about half an hour from Niseko, and makes a viable day trip. The slopes, over three interlinked mountains, are slightly more limited but have a much better lift system (four gondolas and seven fast chairs). The snow here can be as good as in Niseko (though it doesn't fall in quite the same quantity), and it doesn't get tracked out so quickly. But they blast out pop music from speakers on the lift pylons which spoils the charm of the surroundings. New for 2014/15 is the Side Country Park – wooden obstacles such as log rides, rainbows

and jibs in the trees. The vast Rusutsu Resort Hotel complex is the only place to stay and is quite bizarre to western eyes – with a huge summer roller coaster and big wheel outside. Inside there are surreal touches such as life-size dummies playing jazz and a huge carousel for kids to ride. None of the bars open till 5pm so there is a distinct lack of après-ski. There's a wide choice of restaurants serving good Japanese food. The Pension Clydesdale, a few kilometres away was recommended by a 2014 reporter.

Furano is four to five hours from Niseko and offers a tad more vertical, over two linked sectors. But the ski area is half the size, the slopes are easy and there are a lot of old lifts. You can visit other nearby resorts such as Kamui and also go with a guided group to the lift-served but ungroomed Asahidake mountain (a live volcano, around an hour away). The New Furano Prince is a vast modern, isolated hotel at the foot of the slopes and a 10-minute bus ride from town.

The largest ski area in Japan is on the main island of Honshu: **Shiga Kogen**, comprising 21 interlinked resorts and a huge diversity of terrain. It was the site of several major events in the 1998 Winter Olympics. **Hakuba** is a group of nine resorts accessing more than 200 runs.

THE ONSEN EXPERIENCE

Onsen are complexes of hot baths to soak in, showers and communal volcanic thermal pools; they are a key part of Japanese culture and a major part of après-ski. All onsen are basically set up in the same way: men and women shower and bathe in their separate areas. Then, if they wish, they can congregate to soak and have a drink in a communal thermal pool, which more often than not will be outside and surrounded by snow.

SKI BUSINESSES

This is a list of ski businesses including all the holiday operators and ski travel agents we know about.

360 Sun and Ski
Family holidays in Les Carroz, French Alps
Tel +33 450 903180

Absolute Alps Holidays
Catered chalet in Châtel
Tel 0844 774 0608

Absolutely Snow
Holidays to France, Andorra, Norway and Bulgaria
Tel 01248 712567

Action Outdoor Holidays
All-inclusive holidays in the French Alps
Tel 020 3328 5443

ActivityBreaks.com
Flexible breaks and group specials
Tel 028 9140 4080

Adventure Base Ltd
Accommodation in Morzine, Méribel and Chamonix
Tel 0845 527 5812

Aiglon de Morzine
Apartments in Morzine
Tel +33 450 047738

Alpine Action
Catered chalets in Méribel and La Tania
Tel 01273 466535

Alpine Answers
Ski travel agent + tailor-made holidays
Tel 020 7801 1080

Alpine Club
Chalets in St-Martin-de-Belleville
Tel +33 778 845710

Alpine Elements
Holidays in France and Austria
Tel 020 3642 3431

Alpine Encounters
Chalet hotel in Morzine
Tel +33 450 790842

Alpine Guru
Chalets and hotel agency
Tel 0203 004 8750

Alpine Inspirations
Self-catered chalets in Les Gets
Tel 0845 474 7901

Alpine Life
Catered chalet in Saas-Fee
Tel 07801 982645

Alpine Weekends Ltd
Weekends in the Alps
Tel 020 8944 9762

Alps Accommodation
Accommodation in Samoëns and Morillon
Tel +33 450 985056

Alpsholiday
Farmhouse apartments in Serre-Chevalier
Tel +33 492 204426

Altitude Holidays
Ski travel agent
Tel 020 3290 8671

AmeriCan Ski
North America specialist plus France
Tel 01892 779909

American Ski Classics
Holidays in major North American resorts
Tel 020 8607 9988

Andorra-resorts.com
Andorra holiday specialist

Ardmore Educational Travel
Tel 01628 826699

Avery Crest
Luxury catered chalets in Méribel
Tel 07518 582147

Balkan Holidays
Bulgaria, Slovenia and Romania holidays
Tel 0845 130 1114

BedsnBoard.com
Seasonal accommodation in the Alps
Tel 020 3137 5204

Belvedere Travel
Catered chalets in Méribel and self-catered in Verbier
Tel 01264 738257

Bigfoot Chamonix
Holidays in the Chamonix Valley
Tel 0870 300 5874

Borderline
Apartments, chalets and hotels in Barèges
Tel +33 562 926895

Boutique Chalet Company
Chalets in Morzine
Tel 020 3582 6409

Bramble Ski
Chalets in Switzerland and Austria
Tel 020 7060 0824

Canadian Affair
Flights and holidays to Canada
Tel 020 7616 9184

Canadian Powder Tours Chalet Holidays
Chalet holidays in Western Canada
Tel +1 250 423 3019

Carrier
Upmarket chalets and hotels in the Alps, the USA and Canada
Tel 0161 491 7670

Catered Ski Chalets
Ski travel agent
Tel 020 3080 0202

Chalet Bezière
Chalet in Samoëns
Tel +33 450 905181

ChaletBook Limited
Accommodation agency in the Portes du Soleil
Tel 0845 680 6802

Chalet Chez Bear
Chalet in Serre-Chevalier
Tel +33 614 384794

Chalet Chocolat
Self-catered chalet in Morzine
Tel 01872 580814

Chalet Le Dragon
Chalet in La Chapelle d'Abondance, close to Châtel
Tel +33 450 172913

Chalet Entre Deux Eaux
Chalet in Morzine
Tel +33 450 37 47 55

Chalet Espen
Chalet in Engelberg
Tel +41 41 637 2220

Chaletfinder
Ski travel agent
Tel 0161 408 0441

Chalet la Forêt
Self-catered chalet in Chamonix
Tel 07545 575277

Chalet Kiana
Self-catered chalet in Les Contamines
Tel 07968 123470

Chalet One
Catered chalet in Ste-Foy
Tel 07899 911855

Chamonix.uk.com
Apartment holidays in central Chamonix
Tel 01224 641559

Le Chardon Mountain Lodges Val d'Isère
Luxury chalets in a private hamlet in Val d'Isère
Tel 0131 209 7969

Chez Michelle
Self-catering apartment in Samoëns
Tel 01372 456463

Chez Serre Chevalier
Flexible chalet, apartment and hotel trips to Serre-Chevalier
Tel 020 8144 1351

Chill Chalet
Chalet in Bourg-St-Maurice (Paradiski)
Tel 020 8144 2287

Classic Ski Limited
Holidays for 'mature' skiers/ beginners
Tel 01590 623400

Club Europe Schools Skiing
Tel 0800 496 4996

Club Med
All-inclusive holidays in 'ski villages'
Tel 0845 287 8302

Cold Comforts Lodging
Whistler specialist
Tel 020 7993 8544

Collett's Mountain Holidays
Ski safaris in the Dolomites
Tel 01799 513331

Collineige
Chamonix valley specialist
Tel 01483 579242

Connick Ski
Chalet with in-house ski school in Châtel
Tel +33 450 732212

Consensio Holidays
Luxury chalets in the Three Valleys, Val d'Isère and Les Gets
Tel 020 3393 0833

Contiki Holidays
Holidays for 18-35s
Tel 0845 075 0990

The Corporate Ski Company
Event management company
Tel 020 8542 8100

Cru Chalets Chamonix
Catered and self-catered accommodation in Chamonix
Tel 07920 445826

Crystal Ski
Major mainstream operator
Tel 0871 231 2256

Crystal Finest
Ski holidays to Europe and North America
Tel 0871 971 0364

Delicious Mountain
Catered chalets in Méribel
Tel +33 (0)647 213576

Directski.com
Holidays in Europe
Tel +353 1 254 6300

Elegant Resorts
Luxury ski holidays
Tel 01244 897333

Elevation Holidays
Holidays in the Austrian Alps
Tel 01622 370570

Elysian Collection
Luxury chalets in Zermatt and Klosters
Tel 020 3468 2235

Equity School Travel
Tel 01273 622111

Erna Low
Self-catering apartments in the Alps
Tel 020 7584 2841

Esprit Ski
Families specialist in Europe
Tel 01483 791900

EurekaSki Ltd
Chalet and apartment agent in Serre-Chevalier and La Grave
Tel +33 679 462484

Family Friendly Skiing
Family specialist in La Tania – in-house nannies
Tel +33 450 327121

Family Ski Company
Family skiing holidays in France
Tel 01684 540333

Ferme de Montagne
Chalet hotel in Les Gets
Tel 0844 669 8652

Flexiski
Tailor-made ski holidays to Europe, the USA and Canada, including short breaks and ski weekends
Tel 020 8939 0864

Friendship Travel
Holidays for singles 25 to 60
Tel 0844 800 2770

Frontier Ski
Luxury holidays in Canada and the USA
Tel 020 8776 8709

Go Montgenevre
Holidays in Montgenèvre
Tel +33 688 358473

Green Rides
Chalet holidays in La Rosière and Val d'Isère
Tel 020 3286 2218

Hanski
Weekends and short breaks
Tel 01638 596373

Headwater Holidays
Cross-country skiing holidays
Tel 0845 564 9078

High Mountain Holidays
Holidays in Chamonix
Tel 01993 775540

Holiday in Alps
Self-catered chalets and apartments in St-Gervais and Les Contamines
Tel 01327 828239

Host Savoie
Catered chalets in Morzine
Tel 07714 508395

Hugski Holidays
Catered chalet in Les Gets
Tel 020 3239 4933

Huski
Catered and self-catered chalet holidays in Chamonix
Tel 0800 520 0935

Ice and Fire
Catered chalets in La Plagne (Paradiski)
Tel 07855 717997

Ifyouski.com
Ski travel agent
Tel 020 3384 3300

Iglu.com
Ski travel agent
Tel 020 8542 6658

Igoski
Weekends and short breaks in France and Austria
Tel 020 3627 6433

Independent Ski Links
Ski tour op and travel agent
Tel 01964 533905

I Need Snow
Ski travel agent
Tel 020 8123 7817

Inghams
Major mainstream operator
Tel 01483 791111

Inntravel
Mainly cross-country skiing and snowshoeing trips
Tel 01653 617001

Inspired to Ski
Holidays with tuition in France and Italy
Tel 020 8133 4131

Interactive Resorts
Agent specializing in catered chalets worldwide
Tel 020 3080 0200

Interhome
Self-catered apartment and chalet rentals in Europe
Tel 01483 863500

Interski
Family/group holidays with tuition in the Aosta valley
Tel 01623 456333

Jagged Horizons
Corporate trips to the Alps
Tel 020 8123 7817

James Orr Heliski
Heli-skiing packages in Canada, Alaska, Italy and Japan
Tel 01799 516964

Jeffersons Private Jet Holidays
Luxury holidays by private jet
Tel 020 8746 2496

Just Skiing
Courmayeur specialist plus La Thuile
Tel 01202 479988

Kaluma Ski
Tailor-made corporate and private holidays in the Alps
Tel 01730 260263

Kwik Travel
Ski travel agent
Tel 0800 655 6518

Lagrange
Accommodation only, self-drive and rail packages primarily to France
Tel 020 7371 6111

Le Ski
Chalets in Courchevel, Val d'Isère and La Tania
Tel 01484 548996

Live the Season
Seasonal and long-term holiday accommodation in Europe and Canada
Tel 0203 286 5959

Livigno Snow Holidays
Livigno specialist
Tel +39 340 393 5474

Luxury Chalet Collection
Luxury chalets in the Alps
Tel 01993 899429

Mark Warner
Chalet hotel holidays in big-name resorts
Tel 0844 273 6793

Marmotte Mountain Adventure
Chalets in the Chamonix Valley
Tel +33 682 891523

Matterhorn Chalets
Chalet in Zermatt

Meriski
Chalet specialist in Méribel
Tel 01285 648518

MGS Ski Limited
Hotel and apartments in Val Cenis
Tel 01603 742842

Momentum Ski
Specialist in ski weekends and tailor-made holidays
Tel 020 7371 9111

Mountain Beds
Accommodation agent and Verbier specialist
Tel 01502 471960

Ski businesses

Resort news and key links: www.wheretoskiandsnowboard.com

Mountain Exposure
Chalets and apartments in Saas-Fee and Zermatt
Tel 0845 425 2001

Mountain Heaven
Catered and self-catered accommodation in France and Switzerland
Tel 0151 625 1921

Mountain Lodge
Chalet hotel in Les Crosets, Portes du Soleil
Tel 0845 127 1750

Mountain Lodge Adventures
Chalet in St-Martin-de-Belleville
Tel +33 695 466237

Mountainsun Ltd
Chalets in Europe – short breaks and week-long trips
Tel 01273 257008

Mountain Tracks
Off-piste, hut-to-hut touring and avalanche awareness
Tel 020 8123 2978

Mountain Wave Travel
Ski travel agent
Tel 01964 550741

Neilson
Major mainstream operator
Tel 0844 879 8155

Nick Ski
Catered chalet in La Tania
Tel +33 673 436769

The Oxford Ski Company
Ski travel agency
Tel 01993 899420

Peak Pursuits
Catered chalet in St-Martin-de-Belleville
Tel 01322 866726

Peak Retreats
Holidays to traditional French Alps resorts
Tel 0844 576 0170

Peak Ski
Chalets in Verbier
Tel 01442 832629

PGL Ski
Tel 0844 371 0101

Pierre & Vacances
8,000+ ski apartments in France
Tel 0870 026 7145

Pilaski
Holidays in Pila, Aosta Valley
Tel 01478 613561

PowderBeds
Hotels and apartments in Europe and North America
Tel 0845 180 5000

Powder Byrne
Luxury holidays and weekends in European resorts
Tel 020 8246 5300

Powder N Shine
Luxury chalets in Reberty (Les Menuires)
Tel 0845 163 7596

Powder White
Holidays in big-name resorts
Tel 020 8877 8888

Première Neige
Catered/self-catered holidays in Ste-Foy
Tel 0131 510 2525

PT Ski
Holidays in Klosters
Tel 020 7736 5557

Pure Powder
Powder skiing in Canada, Alaska, Chile and Turkey
Tel 020 7736 8191

Purple Ski
Chalet holidays in Méribel
Tel 01885 488799

Pyrenees Collection
Pyrenees specialist
Tel 0844 576 0176

Ramblers Holidays
Mostly cross-country skiing holidays
Tel 01707 331133

Reach4theAlps
Holidays in the French Alps
Tel 0845 680 1947

Richmond World Holidays
Christian holidays
Tel 020 3004 2661

Ride&Slide
Chalets in Morzine
Tel +33 683 734137

Rocketski.com
Club hotels and chalets in Austria, France and Italy
Tel 01273 810777

Rude Chalets
Holidays in Morzine, Avoriaz and Chamonix
Tel 0870 068 7030

Scott Dunn Ski
Luxury chalet and hotel holidays in the Alps and North America
Tel 020 8682 5050

Select Chalets
Chalets in Hochkönig
Tel 01444 848680

Silver Ski
Chalet holidays in France
Tel 01622 735544

Simon Butler Skiing
Holidays in Megève with ski instruction included
Tel 01483 212726

Simon Swaffer
Apartment in La Plagne
Tel 07919 170227

Simply Alpine
Agent for accommodation in Europe and North America
Tel 023 9279 8901

Simply Val d'Isère
Specialist agent for Val d'Isère
Tel 0845 021 0222

Ski 2
Specialist in Champoluc (Monterosa)
Tel 01962 713330

Ski Addiction
Chalets/hotels in the Portes du Soleil
Tel +33 607 979736

Skialot
Chalet in Châtel
Tel 0780 156 9264

Ski Amis
Catered chalet and self-catered holidays in the French Alps
Tel 020 3411 5439

Ski Basics
Catered chalets in Méribel
Tel 01225 731312

Ski Beat
Catered chalets in the French Alps
Tel 01243 780405

Ski Bespoke
Tailor-made holidays in the Alps and North America
Tel 01243 200202

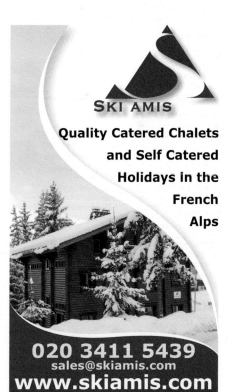

SKI AMIS

Quality Catered Chalets and Self Catered Holidays in the French Alps

020 3411 5439
sales@skiamis.com
www.skiamis.com

Ski businesses

661

Build your own shortlist: www.wheretoskiandsnowboard.com

Ski Blanc
Chalet holidays in Méribel
Tel 020 8502 9082

Ski Bluebird
Chalet holidays in Courchevel
Tel 0808 134 9903

SkiBound
Tel 01273 244570

Skibug
Catered chalets in La Plagne,
Tignes and the Three Valleys
Tel 0845 260 7573

Ski Club Freshtracks
Group holidays for Ski Club
of Great Britain members
Tel 020 8410 2022

Ski Collection
French 3- and 4-star self-
catering apartment specialist
Tel 0844 576 0175

Ski Cuisine
Chalets in Méribel
Tel 01702 589543

Ski Dazzle
Chalet holidays in Les Trois
Vallées
Tel +33 479 001725

Ski Deep
Self-catered chalets in La
Tania and Le Praz
Tel +33 479 081905

Ski Etoile
Hotels and self-catered
chalets and apartments in
Montgenèvre
Tel 01225 290998

Ski Europe
Ski travel agent
Tel 01350 728869

Ski Expectations
Small travel agency
specializing in ski holidays
Tel 01799 531888

Ski Famille
Family properties in the Alps
Tel 0845 644 3764

Ski France
Packaged and tailor-made
holidays in France
Tel 01273 358396

Ski Freedom
Catered and self-catered
chalets in Verbier and
Champéry
Tel +41 277 671505

Ski Hame
Catered chalets in Méribel
and La Tania
Tel 01875 320157

Ski Hiver
Chalets in Paradiski
Tel 020 8144 4160

Ski-in.co.uk
Self-catered apartment in
Serre-Chevalier
Tel 01630 672540

Ski Independence
USA, Canada, Japan, France,
Switzerland and Austria
Tel 0131 516 8110

Skiing Austria
Agent for accommodation in
Austria
Tel 020 8123 7817

Ski Inspired
Holidays in Baqueira-Beret
and Formigal
Tel 01903 233323

Ski La Cote
Self-catered chalet in the
Portes du Soleil
Tel 01482 668357

Ski Line
Ski travel agent; catered ski
chalets, hotels and
apartments in Europe and
North America
Tel 020 8313 3999

Ski Magic
Chalet holidays in La Tania
Tel 0844 993 3686

SkiMcNeill.com
Ski travel agent
Tel 028 9568 0101

Ski Miquel Holidays
Small but eclectic
programme
Tel 01457 821200

Ski Monterosa Ltd
Monterosa (Alagna)
specialist
Tel 020 7361 0086

Ski Morgins Holidays
Self-catered and B&B
holidays in Morgins
Tel +41 79 279 3463

Ski Morzine
Accommodation in Morzine
Tel 0845 370 1104

Skiology.co.uk
Catered chalets in Les Carroz
and Morzine
Tel 020 7183 0688

Ski Olympic
Chalet holidays in France
Tel 01302 328820

Ski Peak
Specialist in Vaujany
Tel 01428 608070

SkiPlan Travel Service
Tel 0871 222 6565

Ski Safari
Multi-resort safaris
Tel 01273 224060

Ski Soleil
Chalet and apartments in
Montchavin (La Plagne)
Tel 020 3239 3454

Ski Solutions
Ski travel agent
Tel 020 7471 7700

Ski Supreme
Holidays to the French Alps
and to Pila (Italy)
Tel 0845 194 7541

Ski Total
Quality chalet holidays in
Europe
Tel 01483 791933

Skitracer
Ski travel agent
Tel 020 8600 1650

Ski Travel Centre
Ski travel agent
Tel 0845 601 8993

Ski-Val
Catered chalets in Val d'Isère
and St Anton
Tel 01822 611200

Ski Verbier
Specialist in Verbier chalets
Tel 020 7401 1101

Ski Weekend
Tailor-made short breaks and
event management,
specializing in corporate and
group packages
Tel 01392 878353

Ski Weekender
Weekends in La Clusaz, Le
Grand Bornand and the
Grand Massif
Tel 0845 557 5983

Skiweekends.com
Weekend, short-break and
full-week trips to the Alps
Tel 023 8020 6971

Skiworld
Catered chalets, hotels and
self-catering apartments in
Europe, USA and Canada
Tel 0844 493 0430

Ski Yogi
Hotels and catered chalets
agent in Italy
Tel 01799 531888

SkiZinal
Catered/self-catering chalets
in Zinal (Val d'Anniviers)
Tel 020 8144 7575

Sno
Ski travel agent
Tel 020 8133 8899

Snowbizz
Family ski specialist in Puy-
St-Vincent
Tel 01778 341455

**Snowcard Insurance Services
Ltd**
Tel 0844 826 2699

Snowchateaux
Catered chalet holidays in
Paradiski and Tignes
Tel 0800 066 4996

The Snowco
Ski travel agent for the Alps
and Canada
Tel 01522 811173

Snowcoach
Holidays to France
Tel 01727 866177

SnowCrazy
Chalets in the French Alps
Tel 0845 260 2910

Snowed Inn Chalets
Catered chalets in Serre-
Chevalier
Tel 020 3514 2394

Snow Finders
Travel agent + tour operator
to Europe and North America
Tel 01858 466888

Snowfocus
Catered chalet with childcare
in Châtel
Tel 01392 479555

Snowhounds
Ski travel agent
Tel 01243 788487

Snowlife
Catered chalet in La Clusaz
Tel 01534 863630

Insure for adventure

The UK's Leading Independent specialist in activity travel insurance

Call: 0844 826 2699

snowcard

www.snowcard.co.uk

Snow Finders

Ski holidays

snowfinders.co.uk
or call 01858 466888

ABTA J5552. ATOL 9279

Snoworks Ski Courses
Performance ski courses and adventure skiing
Tel 0844 543 0503

Snowpod
Hosted apartments with a twist in Tignes
Tel 07881 725062

Snowscape
Weekly and flexible trips to Austria
Tel 01905 731269

Snowslippers
Tel 07837 093989

Snowstar Holidays
Agent for accommodation in Tignes
Tel 020 8133 8411

Snow-wise
Tailor-made hotel holidays to the Alps
Tel 020 3397 8450

Snowy Pockets
Chalet/apartment holidays in France and Switzerland
Tel +41 79 833 3608

Solos
Singles holidays
Tel 0844 815 0005

La Source
Accommodation in Villard-Reculas (Alpe-d'Huez)
Tel 01707 655988

Stanford Skiing
Megève specialist
Tel 01603 477471

Star Ski Chalets
Catered chalets in Morzine
Tel +33 679 181401

STC Ski
Europe and North America, specializing in Austria
Tel 01483 771222

STC Switzerland Travel Centre
Specialist in Swiss resorts
Tel 020 7420 4900

Summit Retreats
Luxury chalet agent
Tel 01178 856966

Supertravel
Upmarket European and North American holidays
Tel 020 7962 9933

Susie Ward Alpine Holidays
Upmarket accommodation in Châtel
Tel +33 450 734087

Ted Bentley Chalet Holidays
Self-catered holidays in Nendaz
Tel 01934 820854

Thomson Ski
Major mainstream operator
Tel 0871 971 0578

Tracks European Adventures
Customized tours in the Alps
Tel +41 24 498 1347

TravelSAC
Ski travel agent
Tel 01323 842599

Val d'Isère A La Carte
Specialist in Val d'Isère hotel/self-catering holidays
Tel +33 629 894457

VIP
Chalets in the Alps
Tel 020 8870 4807

Virgin Snow
Holidays to America and Canada
Tel 0844 557 4321

Wake Up In France
Accommodation in France
Tel +33 251 597800

White Roc
Weekends and tailor-made hotel and self-catering holidays
Tel 020 7792 1188

YSE
Chalet holidays in Val d'Isère
Tel 0845 122 1414

Zenith Holidays
Holidays in Europe with flexible transport arrangements
Tel 0203 137 7678

RESORT DIRECTORY / INDEX

This is an index to the resort chapters in the book; you'll find page references for about 400 resorts that are described in those chapters (note that if the resort you are looking up is covered in a chapter devoted to a bigger resort, the page reference will be to the start of the chapter, not to the exact page on which the minor resort is described). You'll also find here brief descriptions of around 1,000 other resorts, most of them smaller than those we've covered in full.

Key

↥ *Lifts*
↨ *Pistes*
⋈ *UK tour operators*

49 Degrees North   USA
Inland area with best snow in Washington State, including 120-acre bowl reserved for powder weekends.
1195m; slopes 1195–1760m
↥ 5 ↨ 780 acres

Abetone   Italy
Resort in the exposed Apennines, less than two hours from Florence and Pisa.
1400m; slopes 1200–1940m
↥ 25 ↨ 70km

Abtenau   Austria
Sizeable village in Dachstein-West region near Salzburg, on large plain ideal for cross-country.
710m; slopes 710–1190m
↥ 7 ↨ 12km

Achenkirch   Austria
Unspoiled, low-altitude Tirolean village close to Niederau and Alpbach. Beautiful setting overlooking a lake.
930m; slopes 930–1800m
↥ 30 ↨ 50km

Adelboden   451

Les Aillons-Margériaz   France
Traditional village near Chambéry. Nicely sheltered slopes.
1000m; slopes 1000–1900m
↥ 21 ↨ 40km

Alagna   412
Small resort on the east fringe of the Monterosa Ski area.

Alba   Italy
Picturesque Trentino village with a small, quiet area; access to the Sella Ronda at nearby Canazei.
1515m; slopes 1515–2428m
↥ 6 ↨ 15km

Alberschwende   Austria
Village in Bregenzerwald with a small area popular with beginners.Ice rink; 16km of cross-country tracks.
720m
↥ 8 ↨ 18km

Albiez-Montrond   France
Authentic old French village in Maurienne valley with panoramic views. Own easy slopes and close to other ski areas.
1500m; slopes 1500–2200m
↥ 13 ↨ 67 hectares

Alleghe   Italy
Dolomite village near Cortina in a pretty lakeside setting close to numerous areas.
1000m
↥ 24 ↨ 80km

Les Allues   280
Rustic village on the road up to Méribel.

Alpbachtal-Wildschönau – Ski Juwel   Austria
Exceptionally pretty and friendly old village near the head of a valley, looking south across it to the slopes of Wiedersbergerhorn. It is now forms the Ski Juwel area with Wildschonau, best known in Britain as the area that includes the smaller resort of Niederau, although its major resort in skiing terms is Auffach. A two-stage gondola is all it has taken to link Alpbach and Auffach, and the linked area offers an appealing mix of small, friendly villages and fairly extensive intermediate slopes.
1000m; slopes 670–2025m
↥ 46 ↨ 145km
⋈ *Alpine Answers, Crystal, Inghams, Thomson, Zenith*

Alpe-d'Huez   198

Alpe-du-Grand-Serre   France
Small resort close to Grenoble, off road to Alpe-d'Huez and Les Deux-Alpes. 800m vertical, split between a broad open bowl above the treeline and a worthwhile sheltered sector below it. Mainly blue and red slopes served by draglifts.
1370m; slopes 1370–2185m
↥ 14 ↨ 55km

Alpendorf   Austria
Outpost of St Johann im Pongau, at one end of an extensive three-valley lift network linking via Wagrain to Flachau – all part of the Salzburger Sportwelt area. Good intermediate runs.
850m; slopes 800–2185m
↥ 64 ↨ 200km

Alpenglow   USA
Alaskan ski resort.
762m; slopes 2500–3900m
↥ 4 ↨ 320 acres

Alpenregion Bludenz   Austria
Area centred on the medieval town of Bludenz, in the west of Austria, bordering Switzerland. Two main ski areas: Brandnertal to the west and Sonnenkopf in the Klostertal to the east, covered by the Arlberg ski pass.
560m; slopes 940–2320m
↥ 13 ↨ 72km

Alpine Meadows   USA
Squaw Valley's neighbour – and covered on the same lift pass – with similar, lightly wooded terrain, an impressive snow record and runs of all classifications, but a modest total vertical; excellent beginner slopes and mostly uncrowded. The resort boundary is open – expeditions require guidance. There's no resort in the European sense, but there's lots of lodgings close by in lakeside Tahoe City.
2085m; slopes 2085–2635m
↥ 13 ↨ 2400 acres

Alps Resort   South Korea
Korea's most northerly, snow-reliable resort, about five hours from Seoul. ↥ 5

Alta   574

Alta Badia   425
Part of the Sella Ronda circuit.

Radstadt-Altenmarkt   Austria
Unspoiled village, well placed just off the Salzburg-Villach autobahn for numerous resorts including snow-sure Obertauern and those in the Salzburger Sportwelt.
855m; slopes 855–1570m
↥ 8 ↨ 20km

Alto Campoo   Spain
Barren, desolate place near Santander, with undistinguished slopes, but magnificent wilderness views.
1650m; slopes 1650–2130m
↥ 13

Alt St Johann   Switzerland
Old cross-country village with Alpine slopes connecting into Unterwasser area near Liechtenstein.
900m; slopes 900–2260m
↥ 17 ↨ 60km

Alyeska   USA
Alaskan area 60km from Anchorage, with luxury hotel.
75m; slopes 75–1200m
↥ 9 ↨ 785 acres
⋈ *Frontier, Skiworld*

Aminona   459
Purpose-built resort in the Crans-Montana network.

Andalo   Italy
Trentino village not far from Madonna.
1050m; slopes 1035–2125m
↥ 16 ↨ 60km
⋈ *Rocketski*

Andelsbuch   Austria
Village in Bregenzerwald that shares with Bezau the little Niedere area.
615m ↥ 8 ↨ 15km

Andermatt   454

Andorra la Vella   88
Andorra's capital.

Angel Fire   USA
Intermediate area near Taos, New Mexico. Height usually ensures good snow.
2620m; slopes 2620–3255m
↥ 5 ↨ 455 acres

Les Angles   315

Ankogel   Austria
Limited but varied area in the Hohe Tauern region in Carinthia; close to the Mölltal Glacier and Slovenia. Mostly red and black runs; longest is 7km. Lift station a short drive from Mallnitz village.
1300m; slopes 1300–2635m
↥ 7 ↨ 35km

Annaberg-Lungötz   Austria
Peaceful village near Filzmoos in a pretty setting, sharing a sizeable area with Gosau.
775m; slopes 775–1620m
↥ 33 ↨ 65km

Annupuri   656
Interlinked area in Niseko, Japan.

Antagnod Italy
Day-trip area near Champoluc, above Aosta valley. Great views to Monte Rosa. No village, but family oriented with quiet nursery slopes and a handful of runs.
1710m; slopes 1710–2305m
⛷ 4 ⛷ 14km

Anthony Lakes USA
Small area in Oregon with one chair and two beginner lifts.
2165m; slopes 2165–2435m
⛷ 3 ⛷ 21 trails

Anzère Switzerland
Sympathetically designed modern resort on a sunny balcony near Crans-Montana, with uncrowded slopes suited to leisurely intermediates. Lots of old, slow lifts but the area is very much a family resort, with village nursery slopes and spa centre. Little to challenge skiers except the 5km Pas de Maimbre black run, an itinerary and some gentle off-piste. There's a terrain park. For a small place there is a reasonable choice of restaurants and bars. Lots of marked walks and a 3km toboggan run.
1500m; slopes 1500–2420m
⛷ 14 ⛷ 58km
🚡 Mountain Beds

Aosta Italy
Historic valley town with a long gondola ride up to mountain resort of Pila. Aosta is a real working town with people in suits rather than skiwear. It has good-value accommodation, a lot more bars and restaurants than Pila, and a lovely traffic-free centre. Other resorts in the Aosta valley are within day-trip distance and are covered by the lift pass.
1800m; slopes 1550–2750m
⛷ 14 ⛷ 70km

Aosta valley Italy
Region north of Turin with Italy's highest skiing and dominated by Monte Bianco (Mont Blanc). Lots of resorts covered by the Valley pass.

Apex Canada
Small, friendly, rather isolated modern village. Well worth stopping off here for a night or two on a tour of western BC resorts. Varied terrain that suits confident intermediates best, but also excellent beginner slopes.
1575m; slopes 1575–2180m
⛷ 4 ⛷ 1112 acres
🚡 Frontier, Ski Safari

Aprica Italy
Ugly, straggling village between Lake Como and the Brenta Dolomites, with bland slopes and limited facilities.
1180m; slopes 1180–2300m
⛷ 18 ⛷ 50km

Arabba 425

Aragnouet-Piau France
Purpose-built mid-mountain satellite with lifts up from the old valley town too. Best suited to families, beginners and early intermediates.
1850m; slopes 1420–2500m
⛷ 12 ⛷ 65km

Arapahoe Basin USA
Exceptionally high day-skiing area near Keystone. Excellent snowfall record and very long season. Good mix of open and wooded runs of every standard, plus serious steeps.
3285m; slopes 3285–3800m
⛷ 7 ⛷ 900 acres

Araucarias Chile
Exotic area in central Chile, around and below a mildly active volcano in the Conguillío National Park.
1500m ⛷ 4 ⛷ 350 hectares

Arcalis 88
Isolated ski area in Andorra.
1940m; slopes 1940–2625m
⛷ 13 ⛷ 28km

Les Arcs 208

Ardent 218
Quiet hamlet with quick access to Avoriaz.

Åre 647

Arêches-Beaufort France
Secluded little village 25km from Albertville, with mostly intermediate terrain on two areas 3km apart. The slopes of both Les Saisies and Les Contamines are less than 25km away.
1080m; slopes 1080–2300m
⛷ 12 ⛷ 55km

Argentière 225
Village beneath Chamonix's Grands Montets.

Arinsal 90

Arizona Snowbowl USA
Small but interesting area just outside the pleasant town of Flagstaff. Worth a visit if en route to the nearby Grand Canyon. Low snowfall despite the high altitude.
slopes 2690–3290m ⛷ 4

Arnoldstein / Dreiländereck Austria
One of several little areas overlooking Villach.
680m; slopes 680–1455m
⛷ 7 ⛷ 17km

Arolla Switzerland
Tiny village in pretty riverside setting south of Sion in the Val d'Hérens. Main attraction is heli-skiing. Wonderful descents from 3800m.
2000m; slopes 2000–2890m
⛷ 6 ⛷ 47km

Arosa Switzerland
A classic all-round winter resort, near Chur. High and remote, in a sheltered basin at the head of a beautiful wooded valley and lovely train ride up. The centre is not particularly pretty, with block-like buildings, though its lakeside setting adds charm. It is a quiet family place, with a lot of non-skiers. A hill separates this area from the older, prettier chalet-style Inner-Arosa up the valley. Lodging spreads widely, but there is an excellent free shuttle-bus. The local slopes cover two main sectors mostly above the treeline; mainly enjoyable, undemanding cruises. Beginners have easy slopes at mid-mountain, but they can get crowded, though queues are rare. In 2013/14 Arosa's slopes were linked with Lenzerheide's by a new 150-person cable car and two new six-packs to form an area of 225km with slopes to suit all abilities, including excellent off-piste. There are two 5-star hotels: the Tschuggen Grand is ultra-modern with a spectacular award-winning spa and its own private train up the slopes; the Kulm is more conventional, comfortable with a stylish spa.
1740-1830m; slopes 1230–2865m ⛷ 42 ⛷ 225km
🚡 Alpine Answers, Inghams, Momentum, Powder Byrne, PowderBeds, Ski Bespoke, Ski Safari, Ski Weekend, Skitracer, Snow Finders, Snowy Pockets, STC Switzerland Travel Centre, White Roc

Arrowhead 553
Slope-side hamlet next to Beaver Creek.

Artesina Italy
Purpose-built Piedmont resort south of Turin, lacking character and atmosphere. Part of Mondolé ski area with Prato Nevoso.
1300m; slopes 1320–2100m
⛷ 23 ⛷ 130km

Ascutney Mountain USA
Family resort in Vermont 60km from Killington, 200km from Boston.
⛷ 6 ⛷ 200 acres

Asiago Italy
Sizeable resort close to Verona, but at low altitude and with limited vertical.
1000m; slopes 1000–1380m
⛷ 8 ⛷ 12pistes

Aspen 546

Attitash USA
One of the biggest ski areas in eastern US. Uncrowded slopes. Lodging in nearby North Conway, and other New Hampshire areas close by.
slopes 180–715m
⛷ 12 ⛷ 280 acres

Au Austria
Village in Bregenzerwald near Lech that shares with Schoppernau the Diedamskopf intermediate ski area, which boasts Bregenzerwald's highest lift station with fabulous views.
800m; slopes 800–2060m
⛷ 8 ⛷ 44km

Auffach Austria
Small, quiet, attractive old village with the longest, highest, sunniest runs in the Wildschönau part of Ski Juwel.
875m

Auris-en-Oisans 198
Quiet hamlet linked to Alpe-d'Huez.

Auron France
Pleasant, family-oriented resort with varied, sheltered, intermediate slopes; a stark contrast to nearby Isola 2000. Good choice of mountain restaurants.
1600m; slopes 1150–2450m
⛷ 20 ⛷ 135km

Auronzo di Cadore Italy
Sizeable village that's a cheaper base for visiting Cortina. Its own slopes are of negligible interest.
865m; slopes 865–1585m
⛷ 5 ⛷ 7km

Aussois France
Charming rustic working village near Modane in the Maurienne valley. Small but interesting south-facing ski area, good for intermediates and families.
1500m; slopes 1500–2750m
⛷ 10 ⛷ 55km
🚡 Peak Retreats

Autrans France
Major cross-country village, close to Grenoble. Two limited areas of downhill slopes.
1050m; slopes 1050–1650m
⛷ 12 ⛷ 20km

Avon USA
Small town only a couple of miles from Beaver Creek.

Avoriaz 218

Axamer Lizum Austria
Mountain outpost of the Inn-side village of Axams. A simple ski station and nothing more, but it does have some good slopes and reliable snow conditions. Covered by standard Innsbruck pass.
1580m; slopes 830–2340m
🚡 Crystal, Thomson

Axams Austria
Quiet village in Innsbruck area, at the bottom of the Axamer Lizum ski area.
880m 🚡 Inghams

Ax-les-Thermes 315

Bad Gastein 104

Badger Pass USA
Base for 350 miles of superb backcountry touring in Yosemite National Park.
2195m; slopes 2195–2435m
⛷ 5 ⛷ 90 acres

Bad Hofgastein 104
Relaxed and spacious spa resort in the Gastein Valley.

Badia (Pedraces) 425
Roadside village linked via La Villa to the Sella Ronda.

Bad Kleinkirchheim 107

Banff 603

Bansko 648

Baqueira-Beret 641

Barboleuse 510
Quiet base for skiing the Villars slopes.

Bardonecchia Italy
Sizeable railway town set in an attractive valley near the entrance to the Fréjus road tunnel; overlooked until the 2006 Turin Winter Olympics brought investment and raised its profile as a good-value intermediate destination. What it lacks in classic mountain charm, it gains in a fairly extensive area of slopes on two separate mountains linked by free bus. There are plenty of hotels, and the former Olympic village residence has spacious apartment accommodation. The resort's easy road and rail links mean it is popular with weekenders from Turin, but otherwise fairly quiet during the week with plenty of leisurely cruising on uncrowded pistes – worth considering as a base for touring other nearby French and Italian resorts too. Snow reliability isn't particularly great though and, coupled with the large number of awkward draglifts, may deter some visitors.
1310m; slopes 1290–2695m
⛷ 23 ⛷ 100km
🚠 *Alpine Answers, Crystal, Erna Low, Lagrange, Neilson, Thomson*

Barèges 315

Bariloche (Catedral) Argentina
The place to stay when skiing Cerro Catedral, this was once a quaint lakeside town, but is now a substantial resort – including the Llao Llao Resort and Spa. The slopes at Cathedral are 20 minutes by shuttle-bus.
slopes 1030–2180m
⛷ 39 ⛷ 103km

Les Barzettes 459
Smaller base along the road from Crans-Montana.

Bayrischzell Germany
Bavarian resort south of Munich and close to Austrian border.
800m; slopes 1090–1563m
⛷ 25 ⛷ 40km

Bear Mountain USA
Southern California's main area, in the beautiful San Bernardino National Forest region. Full snowmaking.
slopes 2170–2685m
⛷ 12 ⛷ 195 acres

Bears Town South Korea
Modern resort with runs cut out of thick forest. Biggest resort near Seoul (only an hour's drive), so it can get very crowded. ⛷ 9

Bear Valley USA
Resort in northern California, between Lake Tahoe and Yosemite.
2010m; slopes 2010–2590m
⛷ 10 ⛷ 1280 acres

Beaulard Italy
Little place just off the road between Sauze d'Oulx and Bardonecchia.
1215m; slopes 1215–2120m
⛷ 6 ⛷ 20km

Beaver Creek 553

Beaver Mountain USA
Small Utah area north of Salt Lake City, too far from Park City for a day trip.
2195m; slopes 2195–2680m
⛷ 3 ⛷ 525 acres

Beitostølen Norway
Small family resort in southern Norway (east of Bergen), with lots of cross-country in the region.
900m
⛷ 9 ⛷ 25km
🚠 *Crystal, Inntravel, Ski Safari, Thomson*

Belleayre Mountain USA
State-owned resort near Albany, New York State. Cheap but old lifts and short runs.
775m; slopes 775–1015m
⛷ 7 ⛷ 170 acres

Bellwald Switzerland
Traditional Rhône valley resort near Fiesch, Riederalp and Bettmeralp. Part of the Goms Valley region.
1600m; slopes 1600–2560m
⛷ 5 ⛷ 30km

Ben Lomond Australia
Small intermediate/beginner area in Ben Lomond National Park, Tasmania, 260km from Hobart.
1450m; slopes 1460–1570m
⛷ 6 ⛷ 14 hectares

Berchtesgaden Germany
Pleasant old town close to Salzburg, known for its Nordic skiing but with several little Alpine areas nearby.
550m

Bergün Switzerland
Traditional, quiet, unspoiled, virtually traffic-free little family resort on the rail route between Davos and St Moritz. 5km toboggan run.
1375m; slopes 1400–2550m
⛷ 3 ⛷ 23km

Berkshire East USA
Resort in Massachusetts, southern New England, near the Mohawk Trail.
slopes 165–525m
⛷ 5 ⛷ 200 acres

Berwang Austria
Quiet village in a spacious valley close to Lermoos. It claims the most skiing of the region too (36km) – though many runs are short and easy. The Zugspitz Arena lift pass, to which our figures relate, covers these and the other resorts of the valley. The village enjoys a splendid winter-wonderland setting, with lifts rising on two sides. There is a good mix of sunny and shady slopes, shared with Bichlbach; some of these give over 500m vertical to the lift station. There are good cross-country loops at altitude, plenty of huts and a long toboggan run.
1340m; slopes 990–2960m
⛷ 52 ⛷ 147km
🚠 *Ski Bespoke*

Bessans France
Old cross-country village near Modane well placed for touring Maurienne valley resorts.
1710m; slopes 1740–2200m
⛷ 2 ⛷ 3km

Besse France
Charming old village built out of lava, with purpose-built slope-side satellite Super-Besse. Beautiful extinct-volcano scenery.
1050m; slopes 1300–1850m
⛷ 23 ⛷ 43km

Bethel USA
Pleasant, historic town very close to Sunday River, Maine. Attractive alternative to staying in the resort.

Le Bettex 267
Small base above St-Gervais, with links to Megève.

Bettmeralp Switzerland
Central village of the sizeable Aletsch area near Brig, high above the Rhône valley, amid spectacular glacial scenery. Reached by cable cars from the valley.
1950m; slopes 1925–2870m
⛷ 35 ⛷ 100km

Beuil-les-Launes France
Alpes-Maritimes resort closest to Nice. Medieval village which shares area with Valberg.
1460m; slopes 1400–2011m
⛷ 26 ⛷ 90km

Bezau Austria
Virtually no slopes of its own, but the main village lies in low Bregenzerwald region north-west of Lech.
620m
⛷ 8 ⛷ 15km

Biberwier Austria
Village near Lermoos, with mainly shady local slopes more or less split equally into red and blue runs. Makes a quiet base from which to access the rest of the Zugspitz Arena (to which our figures

relate). The main lift from the valley is a six-pack, and there are quiet nursery slopes at the base – with a very long moving carpet. There is a terrain park, half-pipe and boardercross course. There are a couple of pleasant restaurants and bars. Like Lermoos, the village benefits from a tunnel to remove traffic from the centre.
990m; slopes 990–2960m
⛷ 52 ⛷ 147km

Bichlbach Austria
Smallest of the Zugspitz Arena villages, sharing slopes with Berwang. Austria's first chondola lift starts here. An unspoiled base for visiting the rest of the area.
1080m; slopes 990–2960m
⛷ 52 ⛷ 147km

Bielmonte Italy
Popular with day trippers from Milan. Worthwhile on a bad-weather day.
1200m; slopes 1200–1620m
⛷ 9 ⛷ 20km

Big Powderhorn USA
Area with the most 'resort' facilities in south Lake Superior region – and the highest lift capacity too. The area suffers from winds.
370m; slopes 370–560m
⛷ 10 ⛷ 250 acres

Big Sky 588

Big White 609

Bischofshofen Austria
Working town and mountain resort near St Johann im Pongau, with very limited local runs and the main slopes starting nearby at Muhlbach (Hochkönig area).
545m; slopes 545–1000m
⛷ 1 ⛷ 2km

Bivio Switzerland
Quiet village near St Moritz and Savognin, with easy slopes.
1770m; slopes 1780–2560m
⛷ 4 ⛷ 40km

Björkliden Sweden
538m vertical. Feb-to-May Arctic Circle area. Ultra snow-reliable. You can even ski in caves – beautiful ice formations. Magnificent Lapland views.
⛷ 5 ⛷ 15km
🚠 *Ski Safari*

Björnrike Sweden
20 minutes from Vemdalsskalet (same pass). 385m vertical.
⛷ 9 ⛷ 15km

Black Mountain USA
New Hampshire area with lodging in nearby Jackson.
⛷ 4 ⛷ 143 acres

Resort news and key links: www.wheretoskiandsnowboard.com

Blatten Switzerland
Mountainside hamlet above Naters, beside the Rhône near Brig. Small but tall Belalp ski area, with larger Aletsch area nearby.
1320m; slopes 1320–3100m
⛷9 ⛷ 60km

Bled 652
Lakeside base in Slovenia.

Blue Cow Australia
Part of Perisher resort, Australia's highest and expanding ski area. Accessible only by tube train. Nearest town – Jindabyne. Six hours from Sydney.
1890m; slopes 1605–2035m
⛷47 ⛷ 3075 acres

Blue Mountain Canada
Largest area in Ontario, with glorious views of Lake Huron. High-capacity lift system and 100% snowmaking.
230m; slopes 230–450m
⛷15 ⛷ 275 acres

Blue River Canada
Base of world-famous Mike Wiegele heli-ski operation in Cariboo and Monashee mountains.

Bluewood USA
Particularly remote area even by American north-west standards. Worth a visit if you're in Walla Walla.
1355m; slopes 1355–1725m
⛷3 ⛷ 530 acres

Bogus Basin USA
Sizeable area overlooking Idaho's attractive, interesting capital, Boise. Limited accommodation at the base.
1760m; slopes 1760–2310m
⛷8 ⛷ 2600 acres

Bohinj Slovenia
Lakeside village near Bled set in a beautiful valley, with lovely views from its plateau area of short runs high above.
540m; slopes 540–1480m
⛷6 ⛷ 23km
🚌 *Balkan Holidays, Crystal, Thomson*

Bois-d'Amont France
One of five resorts that make up Les Rousses area in Jura region on the Franco-Suisse border.
1050m; slopes 1120–1680m
⛷40 ⛷ 50km

Boi Taull Spain
A typical Pyrenean resort set high above the Boi Valley, close to the stunning Aigues Tortes National Park. Good intermediate terrain.
slopes 2020–2750m
⛷15 ⛷ 44km

Bolognola Italy
Tiny area in Macerata region near the Adriatic Riviera.
1070m; slopes 1070–1845m
⛷5 ⛷ 8km

Bolton Valley USA
Resort near Stowe with mostly intermediate slopes.
465m; slopes 465–960m
⛷6 ⛷ 155 acres

Bonneval-sur-Arc France
Unspoiled, remote old village in the Haute Maurienne valley with many of its slopes at high altitude. Pass to neighbouring Val d'Isère is closed in winter.
1800m; slopes 1800–3000m
⛷11 ⛷ 25km

Bons 250
Rustic, unspoiled old hamlet linked to Les Deux-Alpes.

Boreal USA
Closest area to north Lake Tahoe town, Truckee. Limited slopes, best for novices.
2195m; slopes 2195–2375m
⛷9 ⛷ 380 acres

Bormio Italy
An attractive old spa town, distinctly Italian and within day-trip distance from Livigno and Santa Caterina. The main slopes are a 15-minute walk from the centre, where a gondola goes to the hub at Bormio 2000, with fast lifts to the high point at 3010m. The mountain is confined, long (vertical of 800m) and narrow – mainly suited to intermediates. The men's downhill course is a tough red. The nursery slopes are snow-sure, but there are few progression runs. There's a good terrain park and ample mountain huts. There are more slopes in a separate area, with fast lifts from Le Motte or Isolaccia, on the other side of town. The resort has over 40 hotels, plus a wide choice of restaurants. Après-ski is quite lively.
1225m; slopes 1225–3010m
⛷35 ⛷ 110km
🚌 *Erna Low, Ski Club Freshtracks*

Borovets 648
Bosco Chiesanuova Italy
Weekend day trippers' place near Verona. A long drive from any other resort.
1105m; slopes 1105–1805m
⛷18 ⛷ 20km

Bosco Gurin Switzerland
Highest ski area in Ticino. The only German-speaking village in the Italian canton.
1500m; slopes 1480–2400m
⛷6 ⛷ 30km

Les Bottières France
Hamlet at the edge of the Sybelles area, with limited infrastructure and poor access to the main network – it takes three lifts to reach La Toussuire, before setting off for L'Ouillon.
1300m

La Bourboule France
Spa and cross-country village with the Alpine slopes of Le Mont-Dore nearby. Spectacular extinct-volcano scenery.
850m; slopes 1050–1850m
⛷17 ⛷ 42km
🚌 *Lagrange*

Bourg-d'Oisans France
Pleasant valley town on main Grenoble-Briançon road. Cheap base for visits to Alpe-d'Huez and Les Deux-Alpes.

Bourg-St-Maurice 208
French valley town with a funicular to Les Arcs.

Bovec 652
Town linked to Kanin-Sella Nevea on the Italian border.

Boyne Highlands USA
Area with impressive, high-capacity lift system for weekend Detroit crowds. Fierce winds off Lake Michigan a major drawback.
225m; slopes 225–390m
⛷10 ⛷ 240 acres

Boyne Mountain USA
Popular with weekend Detroit crowds. Not as windy as sister resort Boyne Highlands.
190m; slopes 190–340m
⛷12 ⛷ 115 acres

Bozel France
Small town that, in good snow conditions, you can ski down to off-piste from Courchevel and catch a bus back. Also near access road for Champagny-en-Vanoise (La Plagne ski area).
860m

Bramans France
Old cross-country village near Modane. Well placed for touring numerous nearby resorts such as Val Cenis and Valloire.
1200m
⛷1 ⛷ 3km

Bramberg Austria
Village near Pass Thurn (Kitzbühel area). Shares slopes with Neukirchen.
820m; slopes 820–2150m
⛷15 ⛷ 55km
🚌 *STC*

Brand Austria
Family resort with small, low area. Linked to Bürserberg ski area via a high-altitude cable car across a dividing valley.
1035m; slopes 890–1920m
⛷14 ⛷ 55km
🚌 *STC*

Les Brasses France
Collective name for six traditional hamlets with some of the closest slopes to Geneva, but best known for cross-country.
900m; slopes 900–1600m
⛷14 ⛷ 50km

Braunwald Switzerland
Sunny but limited area near Zürich, a funicular ride above Linthal.
1255m; slopes 1255–1900m
⛷9 ⛷ 32km

Breckenridge 555
Bregenzerwald Austria
Unspoiled area tucked away between Germany and Switzerland at the western end of Austria, in the Vorarlberg.

Brentonico Italy
Little resort just off Verona-Trento motorway, with linked slopes of La Polsa and San Valentino above.
1160m; slopes 1160–1520m
⛷15 ⛷ 35km

Bressanone Italy
Valley town 20 minutes by free ski-bus from the lift base of Plose.
565m

La Bresse France
Largest resort in the northerly Vosges mountains near Strasbourg. Three separate downhill areas (with a lot of snowmaking), but also extensive ski de fond and lots of other activities.
900m; slopes 900–1350m
⛷24 ⛷ 220 hectares
🚌 *Lagrange*

Briançon 325
Part of the Grand Serre Chevalier region.

Brian Head USA
Utah area south of Salt Lake City, too far from Park City for a day trip.
2925m; slopes 2925–3445m
⛷10 ⛷ 500 acres

Brides-les-Bains 280
Quiet spa town in valley below Méribel.

Bridger Bowl 587
Day-trip resort near Big Sky, Montana.
1855m; slopes 1855–2460m
⛷7 ⛷ 1200 acres

Brigels-Andiast Switzerland
In the same valley as Laax/Flims. Access from two sunny villages. Mostly red runs.
1300m; slopes 1100–2420m
⛷7 ⛷ 75km

Brighton USA
Linked with Solitude. Total acreage is half that of Alta/Snowbird (in the next valley), but attracts fewer people so the powder doesn't get tracked out in hours. Four fast chairs, including one serving the resort's maximum vertical of 530m on Clayton Peak. This and the slightly lower Mt Millicent are almost all expert terrain, but other lifts serve a wide spectrum of runs. The resort's boundaries are open, and there are excellent backcountry adventures.

Accommodation is in the slope-side Brighton Lodge and some cabins.
2670m; slopes 2435–3200m
⛷ *13* ⛇ *2250 acres*

Brixen im Thale 172
Grossraum village that shares slopes with Söll and Ellmau.

Bromley USA
New York City weekend retreat, reputedly the warmest place to ski in chilly Vermont.
595m; slopes 595–1000m
⛷ *9* ⛇ *300 acres*

Bromont Canada
Purpose-built resort an hour east of Montreal, with one of the best small areas in eastern Canada, popular for its night skiing.
slopes 405–575m
⛷ *6* ⛇ *135 acres*

Bruck am Grossglockner
Austria
Low beginners' resort, but also a quiet base from which to visit Zell am See.
755m

Brundage Mountain USA
Remote, uncrowded Idaho area with glorious views across the lake towards Hell's Canyon. Mostly intermediate slopes. Also has a snowcat operation.
1760m; slopes 1760–2320m
⛷ *5* ⛇ *1300 acres*

Bruneck Italy
Town with gondola link into the Plan de Corones/Kronplatz area. Italian name is Brunico.

Brunico Italy
Town with gondola link into the Plan de Corones/Kronplatz area. Bruneck in German.

Bruson 499
Relaxing respite from Verbier's crowds.

Brusson Italy
Major cross-country village in the Aosta valley, near Antagnod. Sunny downhill slopes up a side valley at Estoul (Palasinaz ski area).
1330m
⛷ *3* ⛇ *17km*

Les Bugnenets–Savagnieres
Switzerland
Very small area in the Jura mountains, north of Neuchatel. Short runs served by drag lifts. Valid with the Valais Ski Card.
slopes 1090–1440m
⛷ *7* ⛇ *30km*

Bukovel Ukraine
Ukraine's second highest resort.
slopes 900–1370m
⛷ *14* ⛇ *50km*

Burke Mountain USA
Uncrowded, isolated family resort in Vermont with mostly intermediate slopes. Great views from the top.
385m; slopes 385–995m
⛷ *4* ⛇ *130 acres*

Bürserberg Austria
Undistinguished valley town linked to Brand via a high-altitude cable car across a dividing valley.
890m; slopes 890–1920m
⛷ *14* ⛇ *55km*

CairnGorm Mountain 655
Scottish ski resort.
slopes 550–1100m
⛷ *11* ⛇ *37km*

Caldirola Italy
Genoese weekend day-tripper spot in a remote region off the motorway to Turin.
1010m; slopes 1010–1450m
⛷ *3* ⛇ *4km*

Cambre-d'Aze France
Quiet ski area in the Pyrenees with few British visitors. Good beginner and intermediate terrain. Forms part of the Neiges Catalan (10 resorts on one pass).
1640m; slopes 1640–2400m
⛷ *17* ⛇ *35km*

Camigliatello Italy
Tiny area on the foot of the Italian 'boot' near Cosenza. Weekend/day-trip spot.
1270m; slopes 1270–1750m
⛷ *4* ⛇ *6km*

Campitello 425
Village in Val di Fassa.

Campitello Matese Italy
The only slopes near Naples. Surprisingly large area when snow-cover is complete. Weekend crowds.
1440m; slopes 1440–2100m
⛷ *8* ⛇ *40km*

Campo di Giove Italy
Highest slopes in L'Aquila region east of Rome.
1070m; slopes 1145–2350m
⛷ *15* ⛇ *21km*

Campodolcino Italy
Valley town with funicular up to Madesimo's slopes.
1070m; slopes 1545–2880m
⛷ *6* ⛇ *8km*

Campo Felice Italy
Small resort in Abruzzo, east of Rome. Shares a lift pass with equally small Ovindoli, nearby.
1410m; slopes 1400–2065m
⛷ *15* ⛇ *30km*

Campo Imperatore Italy
One of the best of the areas east of Rome in L'Aquila.
1980m
⛷ *8* ⛇ *20km*

Canazei 425
Lively rustic village in the Sella Ronda.

Candanchu / Astún Spain
French border resort on Pau road set in some of the Pyrenees' most stunning scenery. Almost exclusively challenging open slopes.
1450m; slopes 1560–2400m
⛷ *24* ⛇ *80km*

Canillo 92
Small, quiet village linked to Soldeu.

Canmore Canada
Old frontier town on the way to Nakiska/Fortress, well placed for touring the region and an attractive alternative to staying in Banff.

Cannon Mountain USA
One of several small New Hampshire resorts scattered along the Interstate 93 highway; a ski area and nothing more. High, steep mountain by eastern standards.
605m; slopes 605–1260m
⛷ *9* ⛇ *165 acres*

Canyons 576
Cardrona New Zealand
Three large basins with slopes for all standards. Good snow record and childcare facilities. Super views. An hour from Queenstown.
1650m; slopes 1260–1860m
⛷ *8* ⛇ *345 hectares*

Carezza Italy
Dense network of short lifts close to Val di Fassa, also called Passo Costalunga.
⛷ *16* ⛇ *40km*

Les Carroz 223

Caspoggio Italy
Attractive, unspoiled village north-east of Lake Como, with easy slopes (and more at nearby Chiesa).
1100m; slopes 1100–2155m
⛷ *8* ⛇ *22km*

Castelrotto Italy
Picturesque village west of Sella Ronda circuit with small sunny Alpine area and good cross-country trails.
1060m

Castel S Angelo Italy
Tiny area in Macerata region near Adriatic Riviera.
805m
⛷ *4* ⛇ *2km*

Castle Mountain Canada
Remote resort south of Calgary. Good proportion of intermediate and advanced terrain. Area on Haig Ridge provides beginner and intermediate terrain.
1410m; slopes 1410–2270m
⛷ *6* ⛇ *1750 acres*
⛴ *Ski Safari*

Catedral (Bariloche) Argentina
One of South America's most developed resorts, linked with Lado Bueno and 19 km from San Carlos de Bariloche. Sheltered intermediate slopes,

but very crowded in peak season. Slope-side luxury lodgings available.
slopes 1030–2180m
⛷ *39* ⛇ *103km*

Cauterets 315

Cavalese Italy
Unspoiled medieval town in Val di Fiemme with pretty slopes at Alpe Cermis.
1000m; slopes 975–2265m
⛷ *9* ⛇ *70km*

Caviahue Argentina
Mountain village at the foot of the Copahue Volcano, 357km from Neuquén City.
1645m; slopes 1645–2045m
⛷ *8* ⛇ *37km*

The Cedars Lebanon
The largest of Lebanon's ski areas, 130km inland from Beirut. Good, open slopes; a surprisingly long season.
1850m; slopes 2100–2870m ⛷ *6*

Ceillac France
Tight cluster of rustic old buildings near Serre-Chevalier. Not far from the highest village in Europe, St-Veran.
1600m; slopes 1600–2450m
⛷ *7* ⛇ *25km*

Celerina 488
Quiet village with links to St Moritz's slopes.

Cerkno Slovenia
Modern, family resort 50km from Ljubljana. Lifts include three fast chairs.
900m
⛷ *8* ⛇ *18km*

Cerler Spain
Very limited, purpose-built resort with a compact ski area similar to that of nearby Andorra's Arinsal.
1500m; slopes 1500–2630m
⛷ *18* ⛇ *76km*

Le Cernix France
Hamlet near Megève where Les Saisies' slopes link to those of Crest-Voland, part of the Espace Diamant to which our figures relate.
1250m; slopes 1000–2070m
⛷ *84* ⛇ *179km*

Cerrato Lago Italy
Very limited area near the coastal town of La Spezia.
1270m; slopes 1270–1890m
⛷ *5* ⛇ *3km*

Cerro Bayo Argentina
Limited area amid stunning scenery 10km from La Angostura, and 90km from San Carlos de Bariloche.
slopes 1050–1780m
⛷ *12* ⛇ *200 hectares*

Cerro Castor Argentina
The most southern ski runs in the world, on Tierra del Fuego. Lodgings are in Ushuaia, the southernmost city in the world. Also plenty of cross-country skiing on the island.
195m; slopes 195–1057m
⛷ *11* ⛇ *24km*

Build your own shortlist: www.wheretoskiandsnowboard.com

Cerro Mirador   Chile
Chile's most southerly snow-zone, located 8km outside Punta Arenas. Tiny but attractive woodland runs. No base lodging.
600m 🛏 *2*

Cervinia   387

Cesana Torinese   Italy
Little Italian village linking the Sauze d'Oulx, Sestriere and Sansicario side of the Milky Way to the Clavière, Montgenèvre side.
1350m

Le Châble   499
Small village below Verbier.

Chaillol   France
Cross-country base on the edge of the beautiful Ecrins National Park, near Gap. Small Alpine area, lots of snowmakers.
1600m; slopes 1450–2000m
🎿 *10* 🚡 *13km*

Chamois   Italy
Small area above Buisson, a few miles down the road from Valtournenche (near Cervinia) – worth a look on bad-weather days.
1815m; slopes 1815–2270m
🎿 *9* 🚡 *20km*

Chamonix   225

Champagny-en-Vanoise 303
Charming village linking to the La Plagne network.

Champéry   456

Champex-Lac   Switzerland
Lakeside hamlet tucked away in the trees in Ski St-Bernard area near Verbier. A quiet, unspoiled base from which to visit Verbier's area. Small area of slopes due to open again after being closed by a fire.
1480m; slopes 1480–2220m
🎿 *4* 🚡 *15km*

Champfèr   488
Lakeside hamlet between St Moritz and Silvaplana.

Champoluc   412
Unspoiled village at one end of the Monterosa Ski area.

Champorcher   Italy
Small village south of Aosta valley with tall but narrow ski area, mostly red runs on open slopes, with one black through the trees to the lift base at Chardonney.
1430m; slopes 1430–2500m
🎿 *5* 🚡 *21km*

Champoussin   456
Quiet village with links to the rest of the Champéry slopes.

Chamrousse   France
Functional family resort near Grenoble, with good, sheltered slopes. Chairlifts

and a cable car from three bases serve largely beginner and intermediate slopes.
1650m; slopes 1400–2250m
🎿 *19* 🚡 *90km*
🎟 *Crystal, Erna Low, Lagrange, PowderBeds, Ski Independence, Ski Line, Thomson, Zenith*

Chandolin   495
Village in the Val d'Anniviers.

Chantemerle   325
One of the villages making up Serre-Chevalier.

Chapa Verde   Chile
60km north-east of Rancagua and 145km from Santiago.
1200m; slopes 1200–2500m
🎿 *4* 🚡 *1200 hectares*

Chapelco   Argentina
Small ski area with full infrastructure of services 19km from sizeable town of San Martin de Los Andes. Accommodation in hotels 11km from the slopes.
slopes 1250–1980m
🎿 *10* 🚡 *140 hectares*

La Chapelle-d'Abondance 235
Unspoiled village 5km down the valley from Châtel.

Charlotte Pass   Australia
Oldest and most remote resort in NSW, on a charming Alpine pass near Mt Kosciusko. Reached only by snowcat from Perisher. Scenic chalets and five lifts. Nearest town Jindabyne. 6.5 hours from Sydney.
1765m; slopes 1850–2000m
🎿 *5* 🚡 *123 acres*

Chastreix Sancy   France
Small family ski area near Mont Dore and Super-Besse. Limited but varied terrain. All draglifts.
1400m
🚡 *7* 🚡 *16km*

Château d'Oex   Switzerland
Pleasant French-speaking valley town sharing a lift pass with neighbouring, but unconnected, Gstaad. Good rail links to other sectors. Low slopes. Famous for its Alpine Balloon festival.
950m; slopes 890–1630m
🚡 *8* 🚡 *30km*

Châtel   235

Le Chatelard   France
Small resort in remote Parc des Bauges between Lake Annecy and Chambéry.

Le Chazelet   France
Tiny hamlet 5km above La Grave, useful on bad weather days.
1800m; slopes 1800–2300m
🚡 *6km*

Chiesa   Italy
Attractive beginners' resort with a fairly high plateau of easy runs above the resort.
1000m; slopes 1700–2335m
🎿 *16* 🚡 *50km*

Le Chinaillon   France
Chalet-style village at lift base above Le Grand-Bornand.
1300m; slopes 1000–2100m
🎿 *29* 🚡 *90km*
🎟 *PowderBeds*

Chiomonte   Italy
Tiny resort on the main road east of Bardonecchia and Sauze d'Oulx. A good half-day trip from either.
745m; slopes 745–2210m
🎿 *6* 🚡 *10km*

Chsea   Algeria
Largest of Algeria's skiable areas, 135km south-east of coastal town of Alger in the Djur Djur mountains.
1860m; slopes 1860–2510m 🛏 *2*

Chur–Brambruesch
Switzerland
Chur's local ski area, a cable car and gondola ride from the town.
595m; slopes 1170–2200m
🎿 *6* 🚡 *25km*

Churwalden   Switzerland
Hamlet on fringe of Lenzerheide-Valbella area, linked via a slow chair. Four short local runs served by a quad and steep drag.
1230m; slopes 1230–2865m
🎿 *35* 🚡 *155km*

Claviere   289
Village linked to Montgenèvre and the Milky Way ski area.

La Clusaz   France
Genuine mountain village near Geneva that exudes rustic and Gallic charm. Attracts a lot of weekend visitors, so can be crowded. Buses also link with Le Grand Bornand. Together they offer over 200km slopes – covered by the area lift pass. The local slopes sprawl over five attractively wooded and varied sectors. All are below 2500m, so snow conditions are unreliable; but there is a lot of snowmaking. Good steep blacks and bumps on La Balme (the highest sector), as well as decent off-piste when conditions permit. There are challenging but wide blues, as well as gentle cruises and nursery slopes up the mountain. But there are still a lot of old chairs and drags. There's a park and pipe, plentiful rustic huts, and a few lively bars.
1100m; slopes 1100–2600m
🎿 *53* 🚡 *220km*
🎟 *Absolutely Snow, Alpine Answers, Classic Ski, Crystal, Crystal Finest, Erna Low, Flexiski, Lagrange, Peak Retreats, Pierre & Vacances, PowderBeds, Ski Independence, Ski Weekend, Ski Weekender, Skiweekends.com, Snowlife, STC, Thomson, Zenith*

Les Coches   303
Purpose-built village, linked to the La Plagne ski area.

Cogne   Italy
One of Aosta valley's larger villages. Main resort in the Gran Paradiso national park. Worth a visit from nearby Pila. Limited, mostly red slopes. Major cross-country centre, with 70km trails.
1535m; slopes 1530–2250m
🎿 *4* 🚡 *9km*

Colfosco   425
Smaller, quieter satellite of Corvara in the Sella Ronda.

Colle di Tenda   Italy
Dour, modern resort that shares a good area with much nicer Limone. Not far from Nice.
1400m; slopes 1120–2040m
🎿 *33* 🚡 *80km*

Colle Isarco   Italy
Brenner Pass area – and the bargain-shopping town of Vipiteno is nearby.
1095m; slopes 1095–2720m
🎿 *5* 🚡 *15km*

Le Collet-d'Allevard   France
Ski area of sizeable summer spa Allevard-les-Bains in remote region east of Chambéry-Grenoble road.
1450m; slopes 1450–2140m
🎿 *11* 🚡 *35km*

Collio   Italy
Tiny area of short runs in a remote spot between lakes Garda and d'Iseo.
840m; slopes 840–1715m 🎿 *14*

Les Collons   499
Near Thyon 2000 in the Verbier area.

Combloux   267
Quiet, unspoiled alternative to linked Megève.

Les Contamines   France
Largely unspoiled but sprawling chalet resort close to Megève and Chamonix, with a fair-sized intermediate area and a good snow record for its height. The main access lift is a shuttle-bus ride from the centre, with a few lodgings at its base. Most of the slopes are above the treeline and on both sides of the Col du Joly – from where a long red run descends over 1000m vertical. There's a good mix of blue and red runs, and substantial off-piste opportunities. Complete beginners are better off elsewhere though. Reports of the school are mixed too. The village is quiet with few amenities, but there are other sporting activities.
1160m; slopes 1160–2485m
🎿 *24* 🚡 *120km*
🎟 *Action Outdoors, Alpine Answers, Chalet Kiana, Classic Ski, Hanski, Holiday in Alps, Lagrange, Peak Retreats, Ski Expectations*

Copper Mountain   USA
Modern, but pleasant purpose-built village with some of Colorado's best terrain. And good value by regional standards. Worthwhile outing from nearby resorts such as Vail. The Village at Copper is the main base, with smart condo lodging and fast chairs into the slopes. Two other bases are served by free shuttle-buses and with easier terrain above them. The slopes spread across two main peaks, Union and Copper, with an attractive mix of open and wooded areas. There is lots of expert terrain in the upper bowls, some seriously steep. There are top-to-bottom greens and excellent nursery slopes. The terrain park is well regarded. Queues are rarely a problem outside peak weekends. Limited off-slope diversions. Reports of the school are favourable. Nightlife livens up at weekends.
2925m; slopes 2925–3765m
⛷ 23 🚡 2465 acres
✉ *Alpine Answers, American Ski Classics, Erna Low, Momentum, Ski Safari, Skitracer, Skiworld, Supertravel*

Le Corbier   France
A no-compromise functional resort centrally placed in the Sybelles area. The resort is purpose-built and compact, as well as being traffic-free – so it suits families very well. Nearly all of the lodging is in slope-side apartments, some in a traditional style. There are bars and restaurants, but evenings are generally very quiet. Lifts link directly to St-Jean-d'Arves and La Toussuire, as well as a higher level connection to St-Sorlin. But progress can be slow – only seven fast chairs in the whole area. One belongs to Le Corbier and serves local slopes. The gentle terrain is mostly north-east facing and makes ideal cruising, if rather lacking in variety – though there's a black run from the top. Beginners have good slopes at resort level.
1550m
✉ *Erna Low, Lagrange, Pierre & Vacances, Rocketski*

Cordon   France
Traditional little family resort near Megève. 'Ideal for a relaxing ski before catching an early evening flight' says a 2013 visitor.
870m; slopes 1000–1600m
⛷ 6 🚡 11km

Corno alle Scale   Italy
Small resort in the Emilia Romagna region of the Apennines.
1355m; slopes 1355–1945m
⛷ 9 🚡 36km

Coronet Peak   New Zealand
Closest area to Queenstown (20 minutes). Good mix of bowls, chutes, varied level pistes. Biggest vertical is 462m. Relies on large snowmaking facility for good snow-cover. Splendid views.
1230m

Corrençon-en-Vercors   France
Charming, rustic village at foot of Villard-de-Lans ski area. Good cross-country, too.
1160m; slopes 1145–2170m
⛷ 25 🚡 125km

Cortina d'Ampezzo   **393**

Corvara   **425**

Courchevel   **240**

Courmayeur   **398**

Cranmore   USA
Area in New Hampshire with attractive town/resort of North Conway. Easy skiing. Good for families.
150m; slopes 150–515m
⛷ 9 🚡 190 acres

Crans-Montana   **459**

Crested Butte   USA
One of the cutest old Wild West towns in Colorado, and the steep, gnarly terrain enjoys cult status among experts. It's a small area, but it packs in an astonishing mixture of perfect beginner slopes, easy cruising runs and expert terrain. Snowfall is modest by Colorado standards, but for those who like steep, ungroomed terrain, if the snow is good, it's idyllic. You can stay there or at the mountain, a couple of miles away, with its modern resort 'village'.
2860m; slopes 2775–3620m
⛷ 15 🚡 1547 acres
✉ *American Ski Classics, Ski Independence, Ski Safari*

Crest-Voland   France
Attractive, unspoiled traditional village near Megève and Le Grand Bornand with wonderfully uncrowded intermediate slopes linked to Les Saises and beyond to Praz sur Arly, as part of the Espace Diamant region – to which our figures relate.
1035m; slopes 1000–2070m
⛷ 84 🚡 179km

Crissolo   Italy
Small, remote day-tripper area, south-west of Turin. Part of the Monviso ski area.
1320m; slopes 1745–2340m
⛷ 4 🚡 20km

La Croix-Fry   France
On the pass to La Clusaz. Couple of hotels and good gentle slopes.
1480m

Les Crosets   **456**
Micro-resort above Champéry in the Portes du Soleil.

Crystal Mountain   USA
Area in glorious Mt Rainier National Park, near Seattle. Good, varied area given good snow/weather, but it's often wet. Lively at weekends.
1340m; slopes 1340–2135m
⛷ 9 🚡 2300 acres

Cuchara Valley   USA
Quiet little family resort in southern Colorado, some way from any other ski area.
2800m; slopes 2800–3285m
⛷ 4 🚡 250 acres

Cutigliano   Italy
Sizeable village near Abetone in the Apennines. Less than two hours from Florence and Pisa.
1125m; slopes 1125–1850m
⛷ 9 🚡 13km

Cypress Mountain   Canada
Vancouver's most challenging area, 20 minutes from the city and with 40% for experts. Good snowfall record but rain is a problem.
920m; slopes 910–1445m ⛷ 5

Daemyeong Vivaldi Resort   South Korea
One of the less ugly Korean resorts, 75km from Seoul.
⛷ 10

La Daille   **358**
Ugly apartment complex at the entrance to Val d'Isère.

Daisen   Japan
Western Honshu's main area, four hours from Osaka.
800m; slopes 740–1120m ⛷ 21

Damüls   Austria
Scattered but attractive village in Bregenzerwald close to the German and Swiss borders.
1430m; slopes 700–2010m
⛷ 31 🚡 105km
✉ *Ski Club Freshtracks*

Davos   **461**

Deer Mountain   USA
South Dakota area close to 'Old West' town Deadwood and Mount Rushmore.
1825m; slopes 1825–2085m
⛷ 4 🚡 370 acres

Deer Valley   **578**

Les Deux-Alpes   **250**

Les Diablerets   Switzerland
Spacious chalet resort towered over by the Diablerets massif, with two areas of local slopes, plus Glacier 3000. A high-speed quad followed by a slow chair lead up to the red runs of the Meilleret area and the link to Villars. A gondola in the centre of town takes you to

Isenau, a mix of blues and reds served by draglifts. From Isenau there's a red run down to Col du Pillon and the cable car to and from the glacier. On Glacier 3000, you'll find blue runs at over 3000m, stunning views and the long, black Combe d'Audon – a wonderful, usually quiet, run away from all the lifts with sheer cliffs rising up on both sides. Snow reliability away from the glacier is not great – especially on sunny Isenau.
1150m; slopes 1115–3000m
⛷ 44 🚡 130
✉ *Alpine Answers, Lagrange, Momentum, Neilson, PowderBeds, Ski Club Freshtracks, STC Switzerland Travel Centre*

Diamond Peak   USA
Quiet, pleasant, intermediate area on Lake Tahoe, with lodging in Incline Village five minutes' drive away. Its narrow area consists of a long ridge served by one fast chair; there are great lake views from the run along the ridge and from the terrace of Snowflake Lodge. There are black runs off the ridge, but nothing seriously steep.
2040m; slopes 2040–2600m
⛷ 6 🚡 655 acres

Dienten   Austria
Quiet, tiny, picturesque village with a handful of traditional hotels and guest houses east of Saalbach and at the heart of the large, low-altitude Hochkönig area that spreads over a series of gentle peaks linking Maria Alm to Mühlbach.
1070m

Dinner Plain   Australia
Attractive resort best known for cross-country skiing. Shuttle to Mt Hotham for Alpine slopes. Four hours from Melbourne.
1520m; slopes 1490–1520m

Discovery Ski Area   USA
Pleasant area miles from anywhere except Butte, Montana, with largely intermediate slopes but double-black runs on the back of the mountain – and the chance of seriously good snow. Fairmont Hot Springs (two huge thermal pools) nearby.
1975m; slopes 1760–2485m
⛷ 8 🚡 2200 acres

Disentis   Switzerland
Unspoiled old village in a pretty setting on the Glacier Express rail route near Andermatt. Scenic area with long runs.
1125m; slopes 1150–2830m
⛷ 10 🚡 60km

Dobbiaco Italy
One of several little resorts in the South Tyrol near the Austrian border; a feasible day out from the Sella Ronda. Toblach is its German name.
1250m; slopes 1250–1610m
5 15km
Headwater, Ramblers

Dodge Ridge USA
Novice/leisurely intermediate area north of Yosemite. The pass from Reno is closed in winter, preventing crowds.
2010m; slopes 2010–2500m
12 815 acres

Dolonne 398
Quiet suburb of Courmayeur.

Donnersbachwald Austria
Small area in the Dachstein-Tauern region.
950m; slopes 950–1990m
4 25km

Donner Ski Ranch USA
One of California's first ski resorts, still family owned and operated.
2140m; slopes 2140–2370m
6 460 acres

Dorfgastein 104
Quieter, friendlier alternative to Bad Gastein.

Doucy-Combelouvière France
Quiet hamlet tucked away in the trees at the foot of Valmorel's slopes, linked by easy green pistes, a fast chair and draglifts into the main sector.
1250m
Lagrange

Dundret Sweden
Lapland area 100km north of the Arctic Circle with floodlit slopes open through winter when the sun barely rises.
slopes 475–825m
7 15km

Durango Mountain Resort USA
Not a resort to cross the Atlantic to visit – it's a small area even by US standards. Directly above the resort is a steepish slope with a slow double chair off to the right serving gentle green runs. All link to the shady slopes that form the main part of the area, served by a row of three chairs with a vertical of not much over 350m. Snowcat skiing is said to operate from the top. The heart of the resort is Purgatory Village, a modern, purpose-built affair. Evening options in the 'village' are extremely limited. The city of Durango is worth visiting.
2680m; slopes 2680–3300m
11 1200 acres

Eaglecrest USA
Close to Yukon gold rush town Skagway. Family resort famous for its ski school.
365m; slopes 365–790m
3 640 acres

Eben im Pongau Austria
Part of Salzburger Sportwelt Amadé area that includes nearby St Johann, Wagrain, Flachau and Zauchensee.
855m; slopes 855–2185m
100 350km

Egg Austria
Biggest village in Bregenzerwald, with a small ski area at Schetteregg.
565mm; slopes 1100–1400m
6 10km

Ehrwald Austria
Pleasant village with easy access to three small and varied ski areas, notably the Zugspitze glacier. Access to the slopes there is by cable car a couple of miles outside the resort at Obermoos. There are gentle nursery slopes and good open intermediate terrain – including a couple of genuine reds. Most are of limited extent. There's a half-pipe and three restaurants. Après-ski is fairly lively. The Zugspitz Arena lift pass covers all three sectors, plus the other resorts of the valley.
1000m; slopes 990–2960m
52 147km

El Colorado / Farellones Chile
Scattering of accommodation around a base station 40km east of Santiago, sharing Valle Nevado's ski area (to which our figures relate).
slopes 2430–3670m
43 113km

Eldora Mountain USA
Day-visitor resort with varied terrain (including plenty of steep stuff) close to Denver Boulder (45min by regular scheduled bus). All forest trails, but with some good glade areas. Crowded at weekends.
2795m; slopes 2805–3230m
12 680 acres

Elk Meadows USA
Area south of Salt Lake City, more than a day trip from Park City.
2775m; slopes 2745–3170m
6 1400 acres

Ellmau 110

Elm Switzerland
One hour from Zürich, at the head of a quiet, isolated valley. Good choice of runs including a long black to the valley.
1020m; slopes 1000–2105m
6 40km

Encamp Andorra
Traffic-choked town, with a gondola link to the Pas de la Casa slopes. Popular for its nightlife and low prices.
Absolutely Snow

Enego Italy
Limited weekend day-trippers' area near Vicenza and Trento.
1300m; slopes 1300–1445m
7 30km

Engelberg 468

Entrèves 398
Cluster of hotels at the lift up to Courmayeur's slopes.

Escaldes Andorra
Central valley town, effectively part of Andorra la Vella.

Estoul Italy
Village in the Aosta valley up a side valley near Brusson. Sunny, easy red slopes.
1800m; slopes 1800–2235m
2 9km

Etna Italy
Scenic, uncrowded, short-season area on the volcano's flank, 20 minutes from Nickolossi.
1800m; slopes 1800–2350m
5km

Evolène Switzerland
Charming rustic village in the Val d'Hérens. Small ski area in unspoiled, attractive setting south of Sion. Area lift pass gives access to the 4 Valleys.
1370m; slopes 1405–2680m
7 42km

Faak am See Austria
Limited area, one of five overlooking town of Villach.
560m; slopes 560–800m
1 2km

Fai della Paganella Italy
Trentino village near Madonna that shares its slopes with Andalo.
1000m; slopes 1035–2125m
16 60km

Fairmont Hot Springs Canada
Major luxury spa complex ideal for a relaxing holiday with some gentle skiing thrown in.
2 60 acres

Faistenau Austria
Cross-country area close to Salzburg and St Wolfgang. Limited Alpine slopes.
785m; slopes 785–1000m
3 3km

Falcade Italy
Trentino village south of the Sella Ronda with lifts up to slopes at San Pellegrino.
1150m; slopes 1150–2245m
19 75km

Falera 476
Village with access to ski area shared by Flims and Laax.

Le Falgoux France
One of the most beautiful old villages in France, set in the very scenic Volcano National Park. Several ski areas nearby.
930m; slopes 930–1350m

Falkertsee Austria
Base area rather than a village, with bleak, open slopes in contrast to nearby Bad Kleinkirchheim.
1850m; slopes 1690–2310m
5 15km

Falls Creek Australia
Alpine-style modern family resort, 5 hours from Melbourne, near Mt Hotham. Fair-sized area of short intermediate runs. Access by snowcat to Mt McKay's steep slopes. Lavish spa resort nearby.
1600m; slopes 1500–1780m
14 1115 acres

La Feclaz France
One of several little resorts in the remote Parc des Bauges. Popular cross-country ski base.
1165m

Feldberg 378
Small resort in the Black Forest.
31 55

Fernie 611

Fieberbrunn Austria
Atmospheric and friendly Tirolean village, sprawling along the valley road for 2km, but mostly set back from the road and railway. Its small but attractive area of wooded slopes is a bus ride away. One sector consists mainly of blue runs, the other mainly of easy reds, many below the treeline. Across a valley are separate lifts going up to the high point of 2020m on Hochhörndl – gondola down to 1284m accesses some good off-piste here. The resort is boarder-friendly, with a popular terrain park. Accommodation in the village is in hotels, and there is also lodging at the lift station.
800m; slopes 830–2020m
11 43km
Crystal, Snowscape, Thomson

Fiesch Switzerland
Traditional Rhône valley resort near Brig, with a lift up to Fiescheralp (2220m) part of the lovely Aletsch area; includes Bettmeralp to Riederalp.
1050m; slopes 1925–2870m
35 100km

Fiescheralp Switzerland
Mountain outpost of Fiesch, down in the Rhône valley. At one end of the beautiful Aletsch area extending across the mountain via Bettmeralp to Riederalp.
2220m; slopes 1925–2870m
35 100km

Filzmoos Austria
Charming, unspoiled, friendly village with leisurely slopes that are ideal for novices. Good snow record for its height. Quiet pistes, good grooming and decent nursery slopes.
1055m; slopes 1055–1645m
8 32km
Inghams, STC

Finkenberg 113
Village between Mayrhofen and Hintertux.

Fiss Austria
Nicely compact, quiet, traditional village sharing an extensive, sunny area with bigger Serfaus.
1435m; slopes 1200–2750m
⛷ 70 ⛷ 190km
✉ Ski Bespoke

Flachau Austria
Quiet, spacious village in a pretty setting at one end of an extensive three-valley lift network linking via Wagrain to Alpendorf. Central to an impressive lift system. On the Salzburger Sportwelt lift pass.
925m; slopes 800–2185m
⛷ 64 ⛷ 200km
✉ Ski Bespoke, STC

Flachauwinkl Austria
Tiny ski station beside Tauern autobahn. Centre of an extensive three-valley lift network linking Kleinarl to Zauchensee. Near similarly sized Flachau. All these resorts are covered by the Salzburger Sportwelt ski pass.
930m; slopes 800–2185m
⛷ 15 ⛷ 65km

Flaine 256

Flims 476
Long-established resort sharing an area with Laax.

Flumet France
Surprisingly large traditional village, the main place from which to ski the Espace Diamant area, linked through to Les Saisies/ Crest Voland. Near Megève.
1000m; slopes 1000–2070m
⛷ 84 ⛷ 179km
✉ Lagrange

Flumserberg Switzerland
Collective name for the villages sharing a varied area an hour south-east of Zürich. Part of the wide Heidiland region. Mostly red and black runs, served by good network of fast lifts.
425m; slopes 1220–2220m
⛷ 16 ⛷ 65km

Folgaria Italy
Sizeable area east of Trento.
1165m; slopes 1185–2005m
⛷ 22 ⛷ 74km
✉ Solos, STC, Zenith

Folgarida 407
Small Trentino village linked to Madonna di Campiglio.

Foncine-le-Haut France
Major cross-country village in the Jura Mountains with extensive trails.
✉ Lagrange

Fonni Gennaragentu Italy
Sardinia's only 'ski area' – and it's tiny.
⛷ 1 ⛷ 5km

Font-Romeu 315

Foppolo Italy
Relatively unattractive but user-friendly village, a short transfer from Bergamo.
1510m; slopes 1610–2160m

Forca Canapine Italy
Limited area near the Adriatic and Ascoli Piceno. Popular with weekend day-trippers.
1450m; slopes 1450–1690m
⛷ 11 ⛷ 20km

Formazza Italy
Cross-country base with some downhill slopes.
1280m; slopes 1275–1755m
⛷ 8km

Formigal 641

Formigueres France
Small downhill and cross-country area in the Neiges Catalanes. There are 110km cross-country trails.
slopes 1700–2350m
⛷ 8 ⛷ 19km

Le Fornet 358
Rustic old hamlet 3km up the valley from Val d'Isère.

Forstau Austria
Secluded hamlet above Radstadt–Schladming road. Very limited area (Fageralm) with old lifts, but nice and quiet.
930m; slopes 930–1885m
⛷ 7 ⛷ 14km

La Fouly Switzerland
Small area in Ski St-Bernard area near Verbier, with west-facing slopes, 10km of cross-country trails and a floodlit toboggan run. Good base for ski touring. Hotel Edelweiss serves excellent food.
1600m; slopes 1600–2200m
⛷ 3 ⛷ 20km

La Foux-d'Allos France
Purpose-built resort that shares a good intermediate area with Pra-Loup (Val d'Allos ski area).
1800m; slopes 1800–2600m
⛷ 51 ⛷ 180km

Frabosa Soprana Italy
One of numerous little areas south of Turin, well placed for combining winter sports with Riviera sightseeing.
850m; slopes 860–1740m
⛷ 7 ⛷ 40km

Frisco 555
Small town down the valley from Breckenridge.

Frontignano Italy
Best lift system in the Macerata region, near the Adriatic Riviera.
1340m; slopes 1340–2000m
⛷ 8 ⛷ 10km

Fucine Italy
Old Trentino valley village near Marilleva/Folgarida.
980m

Fügen Austria
Unspoiled Zillertal village with road up to satellite Hochfügen – part of fair-sized Ski Optimal area, along with Kaltenbach.
550m
✉ Skiweekends.com, STC

Fulpmes 188
Village in the Stubai valley.

Furano 656
Resort on Hokkaido island, Japan.

Fusch Austria
Cheaper, quiet place to stay when visiting Zell am See. Across a golf course from Kaprun and Schuttdorf.
805m; slopes 805–1050m
⛷ 2 ⛷ 5km

Fuschl am See Austria
Attractive, unspoiled, lakeside village close to St Wolfgang and Salzburg, 30 minutes from its slopes. Best suited to part-time skiers who want to sightsee as well.
670m

Gålå Norway
Base for downhill and cross-country skiing, an hour's drive north of Lillehammer.
930m; slopes 830–1150m
⛷ 7 ⛷ 20km

Gallio Italy
One of several low resorts near Vicenza and Trento. Popular with weekend day-trippers.
1100m; slopes 1100–1550m
⛷ 11 ⛷ 50km

Galtür 118
Charming traditional village near Ischgl.

Gambarie d'Aspromonte Italy
Italy's second most southerly ski area (after Mt Etna). On the 'toe' of the Italian 'boot' near Reggio di Calabria.
1310m; slopes 1310–1650m ⛷ 3

Gantschier Austria
No slopes of its own but particularly well placed for visiting all the Montafon areas.
700m

Gargellen Austria
Quiet, tiny and secluded village tucked up a side valley in the Montafon area, with a small but varied piste network of blues and reds on Schafberg that is blissfully quiet. For experts there is lots of off-piste terrain plus ski routes, and there is a special day tour of Madrisa (Klosters). Snowmaking on the valley pistes is good, and you can ski to the door of some hotels.
1425m

Garmisch-Partenkirchen 380

Gaschurn Austria
A pleasant village in the Montafon area, bypassed by the valley traffic, with a gondola to the Nova area of

slopes – the valley's largest, with 114km of pistes.This is generally the most challenging area in the valley, with many red runs, and blues that are not entirely easy. Most of the slopes are above the treeline, typically offering a very modest 300m vertical. There is lots of off-piste potential, including steep (and quite dangerous) slopes down into the central valley. Snowmaking covers almost half the area, including runs down to the valley. The NovaPark terrain park features a half-pipe and boardercross course. There are lots of mountain restaurants. It also links to the Hochjoch ski area (see St Gallenkirch).
1000m
✉ Ski Bespoke

Gaustablikk Norway
Small snow-sure Alpine area on Mt Gausta in southern Norway with plenty of cross-country. ⛷ 15km

Gavarnie France
Traditional village and fair-sized ski area, with the longest green run in the Pyrenees. Grand views of the Cirque de Gavarnie.
1400m; slopes 1850–2400m
⛷ 11 ⛷ 45km

Gazprom Laura Russia
One of the venues for the Sochi Winter Olympics in 2014.
560m; slopes 940–2320m
⛷ 13 ⛷ 72km

Geilo Norway
Small, quiet, unspoiled community on the railway line from Bergen, on the coast, to Oslo. It provides all the basics of a resort – a handful of cafes and shops around the railway station, a dozen hotels more widely spread around the wide valley, children's facilities and a sports centre. Geilo is a superb cross-country resort. It's very limited for downhillers, and none of the runs is very difficult, but it does claim to have Scandinavia's only super-pipe.
800m; slopes 800–1180m
⛷ 18 ⛷ 39km
✉ Absolutely Snow, Crystal, Crystal Finest, Headwater, Inntravel, Ski Line, Ski Safari, Skitracer, Thomson

Gérardmer France
Sizeable lakeside resort in the northerly Vosges mountains near Strasbourg, with plenty of amenities. Limited downhill slopes nearby include one of almost 4km. Extensive ski de fond trails in the area.
665m; slopes 750–1150m
⛷ 20 ⛷ 40km
✉ Lagrange

Gerlitzen Austria
Carinthia's central ski area. A worthwhile outing from Bad Kleinkirchheim. Gondola ride from the valley near Villach, with good views and varied but short runs.
500m; slopes 1000–1910m
⛷ 15 ⛚ 26km

Gerlos 142
Village in the Zillertal Arena.

Gerlosplatte Austria
Inexpensive but fairly snow-sure area above the village of Krimml, linked to Königsleiten, Gerlos and Zell am Ziller to form a fair-sized intermediate area.

Les Gets 263

La Giettaz 267
Tiny village between La Clusaz and Megève.

Gitschtal / Weissbriach Austria
One of many little areas near Hermagor in eastern Austria, close to Italian border.
690m; slopes 690–1400m
⛷ 4 ⛚ 5km

Glaris Switzerland
Hamlet base station for the uncrowded Rinerhorn section of the Davos slopes.
1460m; slopes 1460–2490m
⛷ 5 ⛚ 30km

Glencoe 655
Scottish ski resort.
305m; slopes 305–1110m
⛷ 7 ⛚ 20km

Glenshee 655
Scottish ski resort.
610m; slopes 610–1070m
⛷ 22 ⛚ 40km

Going 110
Small area near Ellmau, linked to the huge SkiWelt area.

Goldegg Austria
Year-round resort famous for its lakeside castle. Limited slopes but Wagrain (Salzburger Sportwelt) and Grossarl (Gastein valley) are nearby.
825m; slopes 825–1250m
⛷ 4 ⛚ 12km

Golden Canada
Small logging town, the place to stay when visiting Kicking Horse resort 15 minutes away. Also the launch pad for Purcell heli-skiing.

Golte Slovenia
Ski area in the East Karavanke mountains, above Mozirje. Gondola to the slopes from Zekovec village. Mostly advanced runs.
7 ⛚ 18km

Gore Mountain USA
One of the better areas in New York State. Near Lake Placid, sufficiently far north to avoid worst weekend crowds. Intermediate terrain.
455m; slopes 455–1095m
⛷ 9 ⛚ 290 acres

Göriach Austria
Hamlet with trail connecting into one of the longest, most snow-sure cross-country networks in Europe.
1250m

Gornaya Karusel Russia
One of the venues for the Sochi Winter Olympics in 2014.
560m; slopes 940–2320m
⛷ 13 ⛚ 72km

Gortipohl Austria
Traditional village in the pretty Montafon valley.
920m; slopes 900–2395m
⛷ 61 ⛚ 243km

Gosau Austria
Family-friendly resort, with straggling village. Plenty of pretty, if low, runs. Fast lifts mean queues are rare. Snow-sure Obertauern and Schladming are within reach.
755m; slopes 755–1800m
⛷ 37 ⛚ 80km

Göstling Austria
One of Austria's easternmost resorts, between Salzburg and Vienna. A traditional village in wooded setting.
530m; slopes 530–1880m
⛷ 8 ⛚ 18km

Götzens Austria
Valley village base for Axamer Lizum and Mutters, near Innsbruck. Gondola from village to Mutteralm and red run back down.
870m; slopes 830–2100m
⛷ 4 ⛚ 15km
✉ Inghams, Lagrange

Gourette-Eaux-Bonnes France
Most snow-sure resort in the French Pyrenees. Very popular with local families, so best avoided at weekends.
1400m; slopes 1400–2400m
⛷ 14 ⛚ 30km

Grächen Switzerland
Charming chalet-village reached by tricky access road off the approach to Zermatt. A small area of open slopes, mainly above the trees and of red-run difficulty, reached by two gondolas – one to Hannigalp (2115m), the main focus of activity with a very impressive children's nursery area. The village has almost a score of hotels, mostly 3-star; most of the accommodation is in chalets and apartments.
1615m; slopes 1615–2865m
⛷ 9 ⛚ 42km

Le Grand-Bornand France
Covered by the Aravis lift pass, and much smaller and even more charming than La Clusaz. The base can be accessed from either the outskirts of the village or from the satellite village of Le Chinaillon. There are worthwhile shady black runs on Le Lachat, and on the lower peak of La Floria. There

are plenty of good cruising blue and red intermediate runs, and also good beginner slopes. And there are extensive cross-country trails in the Vallée du Bouchet and towards Le Chinaillon.
1000m; slopes 1000–2100m
⛷ 29 ⛚ 90km
✉ Erna Low, Lagrange, Peak Retreats, PowderBeds, Ski Independence, Ski Weekender, Zenith

Grand Targhee 587
Powder skiing paradise an hour from Jackson Hole.
2439m; slopes 2260–3005m
⛷ 5 ⛚ 2100 acres

Les Granges 208
Hamlet at the mid-station of the funicular up from Bourg to Les Arcs.

Grangesises Italy
Small satellite of Sestriere, with lifts up to the main slopes.

Granite Peak USA
One of the oldest areas in the Great Lakes region, and now one of the largest. New base village. Good selection of black runs on the upper mountain.
7 ⛚ 400 acres

Grau Roig 95
Mini-resort between Pas de la Casa and Soldeu.

La Grave 265

Great Divide USA
Area near Helena, Montana, best for experts. Mostly bowls; plus near-extreme Rawhide Gulch.
1765m; slopes 1765–2195m
⛷ 6 ⛚ 720 acres

Gresse-en-Vercors France
Resort south of Grenoble. Sheltered slopes worth noting for bad-weather days.
1250m; slopes 1600–1750m
⛷ 13 ⛚ 18km

Gressoney-la-Trinité 412
Village in Monterosa Ski area.

Gressoney-St-Jean Italy
Larger and lower of the two villages in the central valley of the Monterosa Ski area. Good for cross-country as well as downhill. Varied slopes and well-equipped nursery area.
1390m
✉ Alpine Answers

Grimentz 495
Village in the Val d'Anniviers.

Grindelwald 470

Grossarl 104
Secluded village in the Gastein valley.

Grossglockner area Austria
Two linked areas near Heiligenbluit, above the villages of Kals and Matrei. Remote position west of Bad

Gastein. Uncrowded, fairly extensive slopes. Some long, varied runs.
1000m; slopes 1000–2620m
⛷ 15 ⛚ 110km

Grosskirchheim Austria
Area near Heiligenblut, not linked but access to 55km of slopes.
1025m; slopes 1025–1400m

Grouse Mountain Canada
The Vancouver area with the largest lift capacity. Superb city views from mostly easy slopes; night skiing.
880m; slopes 880–1245m
⛷ 11 ⛚ 120 acres

Grünau Austria
Spacious riverside village in a lovely lake-filled part of eastern Austria. Nicely varied area, but very low.
525m; slopes 620–1600m
⛷ 15 ⛚ 40km

Gryon 510
Village below Villars.

Gstaad Switzerland
Despite its exclusive reputation, an attractive, traditional village where anyone could have a relaxing holiday. Of the four sectors, the largest is above Saanenmöser and Schönried, reached by train. Snow-cover can be unreliable except on the Glacier des Diablerets, 15km away. Few runs challenge experts. Black runs rarely exceed red or even blue difficulty. There is off-piste potential. Given good snow, this is a superb area for intermediates, with long, easy descents in the major area. The nursery slopes at Wispile are adequate, and there are plenty of runs to progress to. Time lost on buses or trains is more of a problem than queues.
1050m; slopes 950–3000m
⛷ 53 ⛚ 220km
✉ Alpine Answers, Bramble Ski, Luxury Chalet Collection, Momentum, Oxford Ski Co, Powder Byrne, PowderBeds, Ski Bespoke, Ski Independence, Ski Weekend, STC, STC Switzerland Travel Centre, STC Switzerland Travel Centre, White Roc

Gunstock USA
One of the New Hampshire resorts closest to Boston, popular with families. Primarily easy slopes. Lovely Lake Winnisquam views.
275m; slopes 275–700m
⛷ 8 ⛚ 220 acres

Guthega Australia
Australia's most challenging and diverse slopes (at Perisher). Comfortable accommodation in the resort's

only commercial lodge. Free
shuttle from Jindabyne. 6.5
hours from Sydney.
1640m; slopes 1605–2035m
🚡 *47* 🎿 *3075 acres*

Guzet   France
Charming cluster of chalets
set in a pine forest at Guzet
1400. Three main sectors offer
slopes for all levels.
1400m; slopes 1100–2100m
🚡 *14* 🎿 *40km*

Hafjell   Norway
Main ski area for Lillehammer.
🚡 *12* 🎿 *33km*

Haider Alm   Italy
Area in the Val Venosta in the
South Tyrol close to Nauders.
Malda Haider is its Italian
name.

Hakuba   656
European-style resort four
hours from Tokyo.

Harper Mountain   Canada
Small, family-friendly resort in
Kamloops, British Colombia.
1100m; slopes 1100–1525m
🚡 *3* 🎿 *400 acres*

Harrachov   Czech Republic
Closest resort to Prague, with
enough terrain to justify a day
trip. No beginner area.
650m; slopes 650–1020m
🚡 *4* 🎿 *8 runs*

Hasliberg   Switzerland
Four rustic hamlets on a
sunny plateau overlooking
Meiringen and Lake Brienz.
Two of them are the bottom
stations of a varied
intermediate area.
1050m

Haus   163
Village next to Schladming.

Haystack   USA
Minor satellite of Mount Snow,
in Vermont, but with a bit
more steep skiing.
580m; slopes 580–1095m
🚡 *26* 🎿 *540 acres*

Heavenly   533

Hebalm   Austria
One of many small areas in
Austria's easternmost ski
region near Slovenian border.
No major resorts in vicinity.
1350m; slopes 1350–1400m
🚡 *6* 🎿 *11km*

Heiligenblut   Austria
Picturesque village in
beautiful surroundings at the
foot of the Grossglockner,
west of Bad Gastein. Quiet,
mainly red runs in two main
areas. Lifts include three
gondolas and a fast chair.
1300m; slopes 1300–2910m
🚡 *12* 🎿 *55km*

Heiterwang   Austria
Small lakeside village with
access to Berwang's slopes in
the Zugspitz Arena. Bus ride

to the lift station. Couple of
local downhill slopes and
popular cross-country venue.
995m
🚡 *2* 🎿 *2km*

Hemlock Resort   Canada
Area 55 miles east of
Vancouver towards Sun Peaks.
Mostly intermediate terrain
and with snowfall of 600
inches a year. Lodging is
available at the base area.
1000m; slopes 1000–1375m
🚡 *4* 🎿 *350 acres*

Hemsedal   645

Heremence   Switzerland
Quiet, traditional village in
unspoiled attractive setting
south of Sion. Verbier's slopes
are accessed a few minutes'
drive away at Les Masses.
1250m

Hermagor   Austria
Main village base for the
Nassfeld ski area in Carinthia.
600m; slopes 610–2000m
🚡 *30* 🎿 *100km*

High 1 Resort   South Korea
Small ski area at the High 1
leisure complex, 250km from
Seoul by train. 🎿 *21km*

Hinterglemm   157
One of the villages making up
Saalbach-Hinterglemm.

Hintermoos   Austria
Tiny village east of Saalbach
and part of the large, low-
altitude Hochkönig area that
spreads impressively over a
series of gentle peaks linking
Maria Alm to Mühlbach.

Hintersee   Austria
Easy slopes very close to
Salzburg. Several long top-to-
bottom runs and lifts, so size
of the ski area is greatly
reduced if the snowline is
high.
745m; slopes 750–1470m
🚡 *9* 🎿 *40km*

Hinterstoder   Austria
A very quiet valley village –
neat but not overtly charming
spread along the road up
the dead-end Stodertal in
Upper Austria. The local Höss
slopes are pleasantly wooded,
less densely at the top, with
splendid views. It's a small
area, but has a worthwhile
vertical of 1250m, and 450m
above mid-mountain. A
gondola from the main street
goes up to the flat-bottomed
bowl of Huttererböden
(1400m), where there are very
gentle but limited nursery
slopes and lifts up to higher
points. Most of the mountain
is of easy red steepness. The
run to the valley is a pleasant
red with one or two tricky bits
where it takes a quick plunge;
it has effective snowmaking.
600m; slopes 600–1860m
🚡 *14* 🎿 *36km*

Hinterthal   Austria
One of five villages in the
varied Hochkönig area that
spreads over a series of
gentle peaks from Maria Alm
to Mühlbach. The village is
small – little more than a few
four-star hotels and chalets,
shops and bars – but it
connects well with the main
area via a newish gondola.
There are good nursery slopes
and some challenging reds.
990m
✉ *Elevation Holidays, STC*

Hintertux / Tux valley   113

Hippach   142
Hamlet near a crowd-free lift
into Mayrhofen's main area.

Grand Hirafu   656
Interlinked area in Niseko,
Japan.

Hittisau   Austria
Village in Bregenzerwald that
shares with Riefensberg the
Hochhäderich ski area, which
has mainly blue and reds but
with a couple of blacks served
by four T-bars and a quad
chair. It has 16km of cross-
country tracks at altitude and
12km of walking paths.
800m; slopes 800–1600m
🚡 *5* 🎿 *9km*

Hochfügen   Austria
High-altitude ski-station
outpost of Fügen, part of Ski
Optimal area linked with
Kaltenbach. Best suited to
intermediates.
1500m; slopes 560–2500m
🚡 *35* 🎿 *155km*

Hochgurgl   148
Quiet village with connection
to Obergurgl's slopes.

Hochkönig   Austria
Varied area that spreads over
four linked mountains from
Maria Alm via Hinterthal and
Dienten to Mühlbach.
800–1070m; slopes 800–1900m
🚡 *33* 🎿 *120km*

Hochpillberg   Austria
Hamlet with fabulous views
towards Innsbruck and an
antique chairlift into varied
terrain above Schwaz with
good vertical of 1000m.
Wonderfully safe for children;
all accommodation within two
minutes of lift.
1300m; slopes 1300–2100m
🚡 *5* 🎿 *10km*

Hochsölden   167
Satellite above Sölden.

Hoch-Ybrig   Switzerland
Purpose-built complex only
64km south-east of Zürich,
with facilities for families.
1050m; slopes 1050–1830m
🚡 *12* 🎿 *50km*

Hochzillertal   Austria
Along with Hochfugen forms
the large Ski Optimal area
above the valley village of
Kaltenbach. Best suited to

intermediates – but there is
plenty of potential for off-
piste too.
1500m; slopes 560–2500m
🚡 *35* 🎿 *155km*

Holiday Valley   USA
Family resort in New York
State, an hour's drive south-
east of Buffalo.
slopes 485–685m
🚡 *12* 🎿 *270 acres*

Hollersbach   Austria
Hamlet near Mittersill, over
Pass Thurn from Kitzbühel,
with a gondola up to the
Resterhöhe above Pass Thurn.
805m; slopes 805–1000m
🚡 *2* 🎿 *5km*

Homewood   USA
Uncrowded area near Tahoe
City with the most sheltered
slopes in the vicinity. Apart
from one fast quad, most
slopes are served by slow
chairlifts, and the views are as
much of an attraction as the
slopes. Set right on the
western shore of the lake, so
access is quick and easy. The
notably quiet slopes include
plenty of short black pitches
as well as cruisers.
1900m; slopes 1900–2400m
🚡 *7* 🎿 *1260 acres*

Hoodoo Ski Bowl   USA
Small area in Oregon with
short runs and limited vertical
of around 300m. Some 65km
from Bend (see Mount
Bachelor).
1420m; slopes 1420–1740m
🚡 *5* 🎿 *800 acres*

Hopfgarten   172
Small chalet village with lift
link into the SkiWelt area.

Horseshoe Resort   Canada
Toronto region resort with
high-capacity lift system and
100% snowmaking. The
second mountain – The
Heights – is open to members
only.
310m; slopes 310–405m
🚡 *7* 🎿 *60 acres*

Les Houches   225
Varied area at the entrance to
the Chamonix valley.

Hovden   Norway
Big, modern luxury lakeside
hotel in wilderness midway
between Oslo and Bergen.
Cross-country venue with
some Alpine slopes.
820m; slopes 820–1175m
🚡 *5* 🎿 *14km*

La Hoya   Argentina
Small uncrowded resort 15km
from the town of Esquel.
slopes 1350–2150m
🚡 *9* 🎿 *22km*

Huez   198
Charming old hamlet on the
road up to Alpe-d'Huez.

Hunter Mountain USA
Popular New Yorkers' area so
it gets very crowded at
weekends.
485m; slopes 485–975m
14 ⛷ 230 acres

Hüttschlag Austria
Hamlet in a dead-end valley
with lifts into the Gastein area
at nearby Grossarl.
1020m; slopes 1020–1220m ⛷ 1

Hyundai Sungwoo Resort
South Korea
Modern high-rise resort,
140km from Seoul. Host to
the 2009 World Snowboard
Championships. ⛷ 9

Idre Fjäll Sweden
Collective name for four areas
490km north-west of
Stockholm.
slopes 590–890m
30 ⛷ 28km

Igls Austria
Almost a suburb of Innsbruck
– the city trams run out to the
village – but it is a small
resort in its own right. Its
famous downhill race course
is an excellent piste.
900m
*Crystal, Lagrange, STC,
Thomson*

Iizuna Japan
Tiny area 2.5 hours from
Tokyo.
slopes 1080–1480m ⛷ 7

Incline Village USA
Large village on northern
edge of Lake Tahoe – it is a
reasonable stop-off if you are
touring.

Indianhead USA
South Lake Superior area with
the most snowfall in the
region. Winds are a problem.
395m; slopes 395–585m
12 ⛷ 195 acres

Inneralpbach Austria
Small satellite of Alpbach,
3km up the valley.
1050m

Inner-Arosa Switzerland
The prettiest part of Arosa,
with lifts into the slopes and
a quiet, 'gentle' children's
area.
1800m

Innichen Italy
Small resort in South Tyrol.
San Candido in Italian.
1175m; slopes 1175–1580m
4 ⛷ 15km

Innsbruck Austria
Lively and interesting former
Olympic city at Alpine
crossroads, surrounded by
small areas, each ideal for a
day trip. Among them is the
Stubai glacier. Area pass
available.
575m; slopes 860–3210m
83 ⛷ 266km
*Ski Safari, Skiweekends.
com*

Interlaken Switzerland
Large lakeside summer resort
at entrance to the valleys
leading to Wengen,
Grindelwald and Mürren.
Neilson

Ischgl 118

**Ishiuchi Maruyama-Gala-
Yuzawa Kogen** Japan
Three resorts with a shared
lift pass 90 minutes from
Tokyo by bullet train and
offering the largest ski area in
the central Honshu region.
255m; slopes 255–920m ⛷ 52

Isola 2000 France
A compact purpose-built
resort 90km from Nice, which
makes it great for short
breaks and very convenient.
The doorstep snow, high
slopes and an improving
range of amenities make it
equally appealing to families
and beginners; there are
some excellent nursery slopes
near the base. But the core of
the resort village isn't pretty:
mostly block-like and tatty
apartment buildings. The
slopes spread across three
main sectors, with varied runs
suiting confident
intermediates best; most are
above the treeline and often
sunny, but the resort's
southerly aspect means that
the area can have masses of
snow when it is in shorter
supply elsewhere in the
French Alps. And most slopes
keep their snow well.
2000m; slopes 1840–2610m
22 ⛷ 120km
*Erna Low, Lagrange, Pierre
& Vacances, PowderBeds, Ski
Collection, Ski France, Zenith*

Iso Syöte Finland
Finland's most southerly fell
region, 150km south of the
Arctic Circle but receiving the
most snow in the country. A
family-friendly resort that suits
beginners and intermediates
best, since there are only two
black runs. But there are two
freeride areas. Most runs are
short, with the longest 1200m
and a maximum vertical of
less than 200m. And all the
lifts are drags. There's a
terrain park, expanded
children's nursery area, tubing,
tobogganing, and igloo hotel.
Cross-country is big here, with
120kms of trails. There's a
choice of hotels and cabins.
430m; slopes 240–430m
9 ⛷ 21km
Crystal, Thomson

Itter 172
Next to Söll.

Jackson USA
Classic New England village,
and a major cross-country
base. A lovely place from
which to ski New Hampshire's
Alpine areas.

Jackson Hole 593

Jasná Slovakia
Largest ski area in Slovakia, in
the Low Tatras mountains. Big
children's area, terrain park,
night skiing. Several tough
'freeride zones'.
slopes 940–2005m
26 ⛷ 36km
Zenith

Jasper Canada
Set in the middle of Jasper
National Park, this low-key,
low-rise little town appeals
more to those keen on
scenery and wildlife (and
cross-country skiing) rather
than piste miles. Could
combine a stay with Whistler,
Banff or Lake Louise. Snowfall
is modest by North American
standards and there is lots of
steep terrain that needs good
snow to be fun. Keen piste-
bashers will cover all the
groomed runs in half a day.
There are excellent nursery
slopes. Visitors have
commented on few crowds
and queues. There are 300km
of cross-country trails. Most
accommodation is out of town
or on the outskirts and the
local slopes are a 30-minute
drive.
1695m; slopes 1695–2610m
8 ⛷ 1675 acres
*American Ski Classics,
Canadian Affair, Crystal, Crystal
Finest, Frontier, Inghams,
Momentum, Ski Independence,
Ski Safari, Skiworld, Thomson,
Virgin Snow*

Jay Peak USA
Vermont resort near Canadian
border with best snowfall
record in the east. Tree-lined
intermediate/advanced slopes
– as many classified black as
blue. Experts also have access
to hike-in/out terrain in West
bowl.
550m; slopes 550–1205m
8 ⛷ 385 acres
*American Ski Classics, Ski
Safari, Virgin Snow*

Jochberg 125
Straggling village, 8km from
Kitzbühel.

La Joue-du-Loup France
Slightly stylish little purpose-
built place a few km north-
west of Gap. Shares a fair-
sized intermediate area with
Superdévoluy. A ski-in/ski-out,
family-oriented resort;
accommodation in good-value
apartments and chalets; good
choice of affordable
restaurants. Easily reached
using budget flights to
Marseille.
1450m; slopes 1450–2450m
22 ⛷ 100km
*Erna Low, Lagrange, Ski
France*

Jouvenceaux 420
Less boisterous base near
Sauze d'Oulx.

Jukkasjärvi Sweden
Centuries-old cross-country
resort with unique ice hotel
rebuilt every December.

June Mountain USA
Small area a half-hour drive
from Mammoth and in same
ownership. Closed during the
2012/13 season but reopened
for 2013/14.
2300m; slopes 2300–3090m
8 ⛷ 500 acres

Juns 113
Small village between
Lanersbach and Hintertux.

Kals am Grossglockner
Austria
Remote valley village north of
Lienz. Now linked to Matrei.
1325m; slopes 975–2620m
15 ⛷ 110km

Kaltenbach Austria
Valley village with one of the
larger, quieter Zillertal areas,
with plenty of high-altitude
slopes, mostly above the
treeline. Ski Optimal is the
name given to the linked area
of slopes of the Hochzillertal-
Hochfügen above the resort.
The pistes suit intermediates
best – but there is plenty of
potential for off-piste, too.
560m; slopes 560–2500m
35 ⛷ 155km

Kamui Ski Links Japan
Small area on Hokkaido with
excellent powder reputation
and access to it allowed more
than in many other resorts.
Easy day trip from Furano.
slopes 510–750m ⛷ 6

Kananaskis Canada
Small area near Calgary, nicely
set in woods, with slopes at
Nakiska.
slopes 1525–2465m
12 ⛷ 605 acres
Frontier

Kandersteg Switzerland
Good cross-country base set
amid beautiful scenery near
Interlaken. Easy, but limited,
slopes. Popular with families.
1175m; slopes 1175–1900m
7 ⛷ 14km
*Headwater, Inntravel,
Neilson, STC Switzerland Travel
Centre*

Kanin Slovenia
Area near Bovec with
uncrowded intermediate
slopes that are Slovenia's
highest, offer the biggest
vertical (1150m) and are
linked to nearby Sella Nevea
in Italy. Sadly it was closed
during the 2013/14 season
and is unlikely to be open for
2014/15.
460m; slopes 1140–2290m
9 ⛷ 30km

Kappl Austria
A 15-minute bus ride down
the valley from Ischgl, and
worth a visit. Both the village
and the slopes are family-
oriented, and delightfully

quiet compared with Ischgl. The village, with a couple of dozen hotels and guest-houses, sits on a shelf 100m above the valley floor. The slopes – served by an access gondola from the roadside and fast quads above it – offer plenty of variety, with several tough reds. Most of the slopes are open, but the run down the gondola offers some shelter for bad-weather days.
1260m ⚏ *Interactive Resorts*

Kaprun 190
Classic Austrian charmer near Zell am See.

Les Karellis France
Resort with slopes that are more scenic, challenging and snow-sure than those of better-known Valloire, nearby.
1600m; slopes 1600–2550m
⛷ *15* ⛡ *60km*

Kastelruth Italy
German name for Castelrotto.

Kasurila Finland
Siilinjarvi ski area popular with boarders. ⛷ *5*

Katschberg Austria
Cute hamlet above the road pass from Styria to Carinthia, by-passed by Tauern motorway. Non-trivial area of high intermediate slopes. Popular with families.
1640m; slopes 1065–2220m
⛷ *16* ⛡ *70km*
⚏ *Neilson*

Keystone USA
Sprawling condo-dominated resort below three varied mountains; the nearest thing to a proper village is a handy development near the gondola. Evenings are quiet, with limited restaurants/bars. The lift pass covers Breckenridge and nearby Arapahoe Basin. Fast lifts link all three mountains, with varied terrain including ungroomed steep bowls, forest glades and cat skiing. There's a beautifully groomed network of tree-lined blues and greens, and good nursery slopes. Reporters praise the school for small classes. There's a huge terrain park and super-pipe, floodlit skiing and tubing. A favourite hut is the table-service Alpenglow Stube.
2830m; slopes 2830–3780m
⛷ *20* ⛡ *3148 acres*
⚏ *Alpine Answers, American Ski Classics, Erna Low, PowderBeds, Ski Safari, Skitracer, Snow Finders*

Kicking Horse 617
Killington 598
Kimberley Canada
Mining town turned twee mock Austro-Bavarian/English Tudor resort scenically set 2 hours from Banff. The terrain

offers a mix of blue and black runs (and occasional green) and a vertical of 750m. The mainly forested runs are spread over two rather bland hills. There are only a few short double diamonds, but classification tends to understate difficulty, and many of the single diamonds are quite challenging. It has a reputation for good powder, although it doesn't get huge amounts by the standards of this region. 'Superb grooming and the off-piste doesn't ski out if you are lucky enough to get a powder day,' says a 2014 visitor.
1230m; slopes 1230–1980m
⛷ *5* ⛡ *1800 acres*
⚏ *Frontier, Inghams, Ski Safari, Skiworld*

Kirchberg 125
Lively town close to Kitzbühel.

Kirchdorf Austria
Attractive village a bus ride from St Johann in Tirol, with good local beginner slopes.
640m
⚏ *Crystal, Ski Line, Thomson*

Kirkwood USA
Renowned for its powder, and has a lot to offer experts and confident intermediates, but it's limited for intermediates who are not happy to tackle black runs. It makes a great outing from South Lake Tahoe, though heavy snowfall may close the high-level passes to get there. Deep snow is part of the attraction, often reportedly better than Heavenly.
2375m; slopes 2375–2985m
⛷ *14* ⛡ *2300 acres*

Kitzbühel 125
Kleinarl Austria
Secluded traditional village up a pretty side valley from Wagrain, part of the three-valley lift network linking Flachauwinkl to Zauchensee – our figures relate to this area.
1015m; slopes 800–2185m
⛷ *15* ⛡ *65km*

Kleinwalsertal 378
Area in the German Alps.

Klippitztörl Austria
One of many little areas in Austria's easternmost ski region near Slovenian border.
1550m; slopes 1460–1820m
⛷ *6* ⛡ *25km*

Klösterle Austria
Valley village at the base of the Sonnenkopf ski area a few km west of the Arlberg pass – and covered by the Arlberg ski pass.
1100m; slopes 1100–2300m
⛷ *10* ⛡ *39km*

Klosters 474
Kobla 652
Slovenian village a bus ride from Vogel.

Kolasin 1450 Montenegro
Small ski area on Bjelasica Mountain above the town of Kolasin, where you stay.
1450m
⛷ *5* ⛡ *20km*

Kolsass-Weer Austria
Pair of Inn-side villages with low, inconvenient and limited slopes.
555m; slopes 555–1010m
⛷ *3* ⛡ *14km*

Königsleiten 142
Quiet resort sharing area with Gerlos in the Zillertal Arena.

Konjiam South Korea
Purpose-built resort 40 minutes north of Seoul. The slopes suit beginners best, and offer the area's longest run at 1.8km. The base village has over 400 condos, a restaurant and spa. Popular with families.
⛷ *3* ⛡ *11 runs*

Kopaonik Serbia
Modern, sympathetically designed family resort in a pretty setting.
1770m; slopes 1110–2015m
⛷ *23* ⛡ *60km*

Koralpe Austria
Largest and steepest of many gentle little areas in Austria's easternmost ski region near the Slovenian border.
1550m; slopes 1550–2050m
⛷ *10* ⛡ *25km*

Korea Condo South Korea
A single condo complex built some way from the three slopes. ⛷ *2*

Kössen Austria
Village near St Johann in Tirol with low, scattered and limited local slopes.
600m; slopes 600–1700m
⛷ *9* ⛡ *25km*

Kötschach-Mauthen Austria
One of many little areas near Hermagor in eastern Austria, close to the Italian border.
710m; slopes 710–1300m
⛷ *4* ⛡ *7km*

Kranjska Gora 652
Krimml Austria
Sunny area, high enough to have good snow usually. Shares regional pass with Wildkogel resorts (Neukirchen).
1075m; slopes 1640–2040m
⛷ *9* ⛡ *33km*

Krippenstein Austria
A mainly freeride resort on Dachstein glacier near Salzburg. Cable car from Obertraun in the valley. 30km off-piste routes and 11km long blue/red run. Shares lift pass with Annaberg-Gosau region.

Krispl-Gaissau Austria
Easy slopes very close to Salzburg. Several long top-to-bottom lifts mean the size of the area is greatly reduced if the snow line is high.
925m; slopes 750–1570m
⛷ *11* ⛡ *40km*

Kronplatz Italy
Distinctive ski area in South Tyrol, with amazingly efficient lifts from Brunico and San Vigilio di Marebbe. Plan de Corones is its Italian name.
1200m; slopes 1200–2275m
⛷ *32* ⛡ *114km*
⚏ *Crystal, Inghams, Mountainsun, Thomson, Zenith*

Krvavec 652
Kühtai Austria
A collection of comfortable hotels beside a high road pass only 25km from Innsbruck – higher than equally snow-sure Obergurgl or Obertauern, but cheaper than either. Covered also by the standard Innsbruck pass. A modern gondola, three fast quads and a handful of drags serve red cruisers of about 500m vertical on either side of the road, plus some token black runs; not ideal for novices – few easy blues to graduate to. Very quiet in the week, but liable to weekend crowds if lower resorts around Innsbruck are short of snow. Limited mountain huts. Quiet in the evening, but for its size a reasonable selection of hotels.
2020m; slopes 800–2620m
⛷ *12* ⛡ *44km*
⚏ *Crystal, Erna Low, Inghams, Ski Line, STC, Thomson*

Kusatsu Kokusai Japan
Attractive spa village with hot springs, three hours from Tokyo.
slopes 1250–2170m ⛷ *13*

Laax 476
Le Lac Blanc France
Mini-resort with six-pack in the northerly Vosges mountains near Strasbourg. Extensive ski de fond trails.
830m; slopes 830–1235m
⛷ *9* ⛡ *14km*

Laces Italy
Village in the Val Venosta in the South Tyrol covered by the Ortler Skiarena pass.

Lachtal Austria
Second largest ski resort in the Styrian region NE of Salzburg.
1600m; slopes 1600–2100m
⛷ *8* ⛡ *29km*

Ladis Austria
Smaller alternative to Serfaus and Fiss, with lifts that connect into the same varied ski area.
1200m; slopes 1200–2750m
⛷ *70* ⛡ *190km*

Build your own shortlist: www.wheretoskiandsnowboard.com

Lagunillas Chile
83km south-east of Santiago.
⏏ 494 acres

Le Laisinant 358
Tiny hamlet down the valley
from Val d'Isère.

Lake Louise 619

Lake Tahoe USA
Collection of 14 ski areas
spectacularly set on California-
Nevada border.

Lamoura France
One of four villages that
makes up the Les Rousses
area in the Jura.
1120m; slopes 1120–1680m
🎿 40 ⏏ 40km

Landeck–Zams Austria
Small ski area in the Tirol
region. 780m; slopes 816–
2210m 🎿 7 ⏏ 22km

Lanersbach 113
Village near Hintertux.

Lans-en-Vercors France
Village close to Villard-de-Lans
and 30km from Grenoble.
Highest slopes in the region;
few snowmakers.
1020m; slopes 1400–1805m
🎿 16 ⏏ 24km

Lanslebourg 355
One of the villages that make
up Val Cenis.

Lanslevillard 355
One of the villages that make
up Val Cenis.

Laterns Austria
Small, low altitude resort in
the Vorarlberg near
Friedrichshafen. Two fast
chairs serve mainly red runs
and some ski routes.
900m; slopes 900–1785m
🎿 6 ⏏ 27km

Lauchernalp-Lötschental
Switzerland
Small but tall and challenging
slopes reached by cable car
from Wiler in the secluded,
picturesque, dead-end
Lötschental, north of Rhône
valley. Glacier runs above
3000m.
1970m; slopes 1420–3110m
🎿 6 ⏏ 33km

Lauterbrunnen 479
Valley town with rail
connection up to Mürren.

Le Lavancher 225
Quiet village between
Chamonix and Argentière.

Lavarone Italy
One of several areas east of
Trento, good for a weekend
day trip.
1195m; slopes 1075–1555m
🎿 13 ⏏ 12km

Leadville USA
Old mining town full of
historic buildings. Own easy
area (Ski Cooper) plus
snowcat operation.
Picturesque inexpensive base
for visiting Copper Mountain,
Vail and Beaver Creek.

Lech 133

The Lecht 655
Scottish ski resort.
640m; slopes 610–825m
🎿 13 ⏏ 20km

Lélex France
Family resort with pretty
wooded slopes between Dijon
and Geneva.
900m; slopes 900–1680m
🎿 29 ⏏ 50km

Las Leñas Argentina
European-style resort, 400km
south of Mendoza, with
varied, beautiful terrain and
extensive off-piste. But it's a
stormy place that can close
the lifts for days. Lodgings at
the foot of the slopes.
2240m; slopes 2240–3430m
🎿 14 ⏏ 64km
📧 Skiworld

Lenggries-Brauneck 378
Bavarian resort south of
Munich.
680m; slopes 700–1710m
🎿 18 ⏏ 34km

Lenk Switzerland
Traditional village sharing a
sizeable area with Adelboden,
and with its own separate
slopes at Betelberg. Buses to
lifts at Rothenbach, or to the
six-pack from Buhlberg.
1070m; slopes 1070–2360m
🎿 56 ⏏ 185km

Lenzerheide Switzerland
Lenzerheide and Valbella lie at
either end of a lake, in a
pretty wooded setting, but
along a busy main road. The
villages are pleasant enough
but rather spoiled by the
traffic – but that won't worry
Roger Federer who has a
chalet on the hillside above.
They share an extensive area
of 155km of local slopes on
both sides of the valley. The
east-facing, morning-sun
slopes are mainly fairly gentle.
The west-facing slopes have
more character, both in skiing
and visual terms, including a
black World Cup downhill
piste and a red run on the
back of the dramatic peak of
the Rothorn which includes a
long tunnel. There is
considerable off-piste
potential. In 2013/14
Lenzerheide's slopes were
linked by two new six-packs
and a 150-person cable car to
those of Arosa, to form an
area of 225km.
Accommodation is mostly in
4-star hotels: the
Schweizerhof and slightly
out-of-town rustic Guarda Val
are excellent. Priva Alpine
Lodge has smart new self-
catering apartments near the
Rothorn gondola.
1470m; slopes 1230–2865m
🎿 42 ⏏ 225km
📧 Alpine Answers, Powder
Byrne, Ski Safari, STC, STC
Switzerland Travel Centre

Leogang 157
Quiet village with link to
Saalbach-Hinterglemm.

Lermoos Austria
Pleasant little village with
30km of shady intermediate
slopes on Grubigstein, and a
access to a variety of other
areas in the locality, including
the Zugspitze, on the border
with Germany. The village is
compact, with good family-
friendly hotels. Fast lifts go
from both ends, serving some
worthwhile descents –
including a fine black run and
an area of ready-made
moguls. The runs below mid-
mountain are worthwhile
blues and reds, with good
nursery slopes at village level.
Lots of cross-country trails
along the flat valley.
1005m; slopes 990–2960m
🎿 52 ⏏ 147km 📧 STC

Lessach Austria
Hamlet with trail connecting
into one of the longest, most
snow-sure cross-country
networks in Europe.
1210m 🎿 1

Leukerbad Switzerland
Major spa resort of Roman
origin, spectacularly set
beneath towering cliffs, which
are scaled by a cable car up
to high-altitude cross-country
trails. The downhill slopes are
on the opposite side of the
valley, mainly above the
treeline and of red gradient.
1410m; slopes 1410–2700m
🎿 10 ⏏ 52km

Leutasch Austria
Traditional cross-country
village with limited slopes but
a pleasant day trip from
nearby Seefeld or Innsbruck.
1130m; slopes 1130–1605m
🎿 3 ⏏ 6km
📧 Headwater, Inntravel

Levi 643

Leysin Switzerland
This is a spread-out village,
climbing up a wooded
hillside. The lifts are to the
east of the village and take
you to a pretty mix of mainly
red and blue runs. Itineraries
from the top of Chaux de
Mont provide the best options
for experts, along with a heli-
operation. There are nursery
slopes at village level. The
revolving Kuklos restaurant at
La Berneuse has stunning
views.
1250m; slopes 1300–2200m
🎿 14 ⏏ 60km
📧 PowderBeds

Lienz Austria
Pleasant town in pretty
surroundings.
675m; slopes 730–2280m
🎿 17 ⏏ 40km

Lillehammer Norway
Cultural fjord-side town, 2 to
3 hours north of Oslo by train/
car, with its two Olympic areas
15 and 35km away, poorly
served by bus.
200m; slopes 200–1030m
🎿 10 ⏏ 25km

Limone Italy
Pleasant old town not far
from Turin, with a pretty area,
but far from snow-sure.
1010m; slopes 1030–2050m
🎿 15 ⏏ 80km

Lincoln USA
Sprawling New Hampshire
town from which to visit Loon
mountain.

Lindvallen-Högfjället Sweden
Two of the mountains that
make up the four unlinked ski
areas of Sälen.
800m; slopes 590–890m
🎿 46 ⏏ 85km

Le Lioran France
Auvergne village near Aurillac
with a purpose-built satellite
above. Spectacular volcanic
scenery.
1160m; slopes 1160–1850m
🎿 24 ⏏ 60km

Livigno 403

Lizzola Italy
Small base development in
remote region north of
Bergamo. Several other little
areas nearby.
1250m; slopes 1250–2070m
🎿 9 ⏏ 30km

Loch Lomond Canada
Steep, narrow, challenging
slopes near Thunder Bay on
the shores of Lake Superior.
Candy Mountain is nearby.
215m; slopes 215–440m
🎿 3 ⏏ 90 acres

Lofer Austria
Quiet, traditional village in a
pretty setting north of
Saalbach with a small area of
its own, and Waidring's
relatively snow-sure
Steinplatte nearby.
640m; slopes 640–1745m
🎿 10 ⏏ 46km
📧 STC

Longchamp France
Dreary purpose-built resort
with little to commend it over
pretty Valmorel, with which it
shares its ski area.
1650m

Loon Mountain USA
Small, smart, modern resort
just outside Lincoln, New
Hampshire. Mostly
intermediate runs.
290m; slopes 290–910m
🎿 10 ⏏ 275 acres
📧 Virgin Snow

Lost Trail USA
Remote Montana area, open
only Thursday to Sunday and
holidays. Mostly intermediate
slopes.
2005m; slopes 2005–2370m
🎿 6 ⏏ 800 acres

Loveland USA
Exceptionally high and snowy slopes right next to highway I70, just east of the Continental Divide, easily reached from other Colorado resorts, especially Keystone.
3230m; slopes 3230–3870m
⛷ 9 ⛰ 1365 acres

Luchon France
Sizeable village with plenty of amenities, with gondola (eight minutes) to its ski area at purpose-built Superbagnères.
630m; slopes 1440–2260m
⛷ 16 ⛰ 35km
🚟 Lagrange

Lurisia Italy
Sizeable spa resort, a good base for visits to surrounding little ski areas and to Nice.
750m; slopes 800–1800m
⛷ 8 ⛰ 35km

Lutsen Mountains USA
In Minnesota, the largest ski area in between Vermont and Colorado, with panoramic views of Lake Superior. Four small linked hills offer surprisingly good and extensive terrain.
80m; slopes 80–335m
⛷ 9 ⛰ 1000 acres

Luz-Ardiden France
Spa village below its ski area. Cauterets and Barèges nearby.
710m; slopes 1730–2450m
⛷ 15 ⛰ 60km

Macugnaga Italy
Two quiet, pretty villages dramatically set at the head of a remote valley, over the mountains from Zermatt and Saas-Fee. Lifts run up to the foot of the Belvedere glacier. A chairlift rises very slowly from the village to Burky, in the middle of the small, woody area of gentle runs. There is an excellent nursery slope beside the village and a two-stage cable car going over sunny slopes to the Swiss border. Good, varied red runs down the 1100m vertical of the top cable car, and considerable off-piste possibilities given good snow.
1325m; slopes 1325–2800m
⛷ 11 ⛰ 35km
🚟 Ski Club Freshtracks

Madesimo Italy
Lots of fast lifts but limited extent of slopes. Not ideal for a week, but the mountain has something for everyone and the system copes well with weekend visitors– it's a couple of hours from Bergamo or Milan. The village spreads along both sides of a river; a random mix of traditional buildings and narrow streets on one side and more modern development on the other, but with a good choice of mid-priced hotels. The slopes have an almost equal share of blue and red runs that make great

intermediate territory, though there are a few notable challenges – including the classic Canalone ski route. For a resort with a respectable altitude and a generally quiet and queue-free mountain, it is worth considering.
1550m; slopes 1550–2945m
⛷ 12 ⛰ 60km
🚟 Momentum

Madonna di Campiglio 407
Mad River Glen USA
Cult resort, co-operatively owned, with some tough ungroomed terrain, a few well-groomed intermediate trails and antique lifts. Snowboarding is banned.
485m; slopes 485–1110m
⛷ 4 ⛰ 115 acres

La Magdelaine Italy
Close to Cervinia, and good on bad-weather days.
1645m; slopes 1645–1870m
⛷ 4 ⛰ 4km

Maishofen Austria
Cheaper place to stay when visiting equidistant Saalbach and Zell am See.
765m

Malbun Liechtenstein
Quaint user-friendly little family resort, 16km from the capital, Vaduz. Limited slopes and short easy runs.
1600m; slopes 1595–2100m
⛷ 6 ⛰ 21km

Malcesine Italy
Large summer resort on Lake Garda with a fair area of slopes, served by a revolving cable car.
1430m; slopes 1430–1830m
⛷ 8 ⛰ 12km

Malga Ciapela Italy
Resort at the foot of the Marmolada glacier massif, with a link into the Sella Ronda. Cortina is nearby.
1445m; slopes 1445–3270m
⛷ 8 ⛰ 18km

Malga Haider Italy
Small area in Val Venosta, close to Austrian border. Haideralm is its German name.
1200m
⛷ 5 ⛰ 20km

Mallnitz Austria
Village in a pretty valley close to Slovenia, with two varied areas providing a fine mix of wooded and open runs. Closest is Ankogel. The snow-sure Molltal Glacier is nearby, above Flattach.
1200m
⛷ 15 ⛰ 88km

Mammoth Mountain 538
Manigod France
Small valley village, sharing quiet, wooded slopes with La Clusaz – over the Col de la Croix-Fry.
1100m ⛰ 132km

Marble Mountain Canada
Tiny area in the Humber Valley on Newfoundland. Good snow record by east coast standards. Splendid base lodge, and some slope-side lodging. Blomidon Cat Skiing operates nearby.
85m; slopes 10–545m
⛷ 5 ⛰ 175 acres
🚟 Frontier

Les Marecottes Switzerland
Small area in Ski St-Bernard area near Verbier and 15 minutes from Martigny. Good views. Popular with families and freeriders.
1100m; slopes 1720–2200m
⛷ 4 ⛰ 25km

Maria Alm Austria
Charming unspoiled village at one end of the varied Hochkönig area that spreads over a series of gentle peaks via Hinterthal and Dienten to Mühlbach. Maria Alm, though small, is one of the two largest villages in the area, and the most animated in the evening; it's a pretty place with a splendid old church boasting the highest spire in Salzburgerland. The Hochkönig area is best for adventurous intermediates, but for beginners there is a good local nursery slope. Experts can explore the ungroomed off-piste and the excellent off-piste. Snowboarders may find there are too many draglifts. Maria Alm also has its own small local area of slopes. There are 40km of cross-country trails in the area.
800m
🚟 Crystal, Interactive Resorts, Rocketski, Select Chalets, Thomson

Mariapfarr Austria
Village at the heart of one of the longest, most snow-reliable cross-country networks in Europe. Sizeable Mauterndorf-St Michael Alpine area and Obertauern area are nearby.
1120m
⛷ 5 ⛰ 30km

Mariazell Austria
Traditional Styria village with an impressive basilica. Limited slopes.
870m; slopes 870–1265m
⛷ 5 ⛰ 11km

Maribor-Pohorje 652
Marilleva 407
Small Trentino resort linked with Madonna di Campiglio.

Le Markstein France
Long-standing small resort in the northerly Vosges region near Strasbourg, which has hosted World Cup slalom races. Extensive Nordic trails.
slopes 770–1270m ⛷ 10

Masella Spain
Friendly Pyrenean village linked with the slopes of La Molina to form the Alp 2500 area. Weekend crowds.
1600m; slopes 1600–2535m
⛷ 31 ⛰ 121km

La Massana Andorra
Pleasant valley town linked by gondola to the Arinsal/Pal slopes and fairly convenient for trips to Arcalis.
slopes 1550–2563m
⛷ 31 ⛰ 63km
🚟 Lagrange

Les Masses 499
A hamlet below Les Collons in the Verbier ski area.

Le Massif Canada
One of several small but developing areas near historic Québec City, dramatically set in a UNESCO World Bio Reserve overlooking the St Lawrence river; the views of the ice floes from the summit lodge are stunning. The varied but limited tree-lined slopes offer Eastern Canada's biggest vertical at 770m – including a couple of steep double-black-diamond runs and some good intermediate cruising.
35m; slopes 35–805m
⛷ 6 ⛰ 406 acres
🚟 Frontier, Ski Safari

Matrei in Osttirol Austria
Large market village south of Felbertauern tunnel. Mostly high slopes, linked to Kals on the other side of the hill.
1000m; slopes 975–2620m
⛷ 15 ⛰ 110km
🚟 Zenith

Maurienne Valley France
A great curving trench with over 20 winter resorts, from pleasant old valley villages to convenience resorts purpose-built in the 1960s.

Mauterndorf Austria
Village near Obertauern with tremendous snow record.
1120m; slopes 1075–2360m
⛷ 10 ⛰ 35km

Maverick Mountain USA
Montana resort with plenty of terrain accessed by few lifts. Cowboy Winter Games venue – rodeo one day, ski races the next.
2155m; slopes 2155–2800m
⛷ 2 ⛰ 500 acres

Mayens de Riddes Switzerland
Hamlet at the base of lifts on the back of Verbier's Savoleyres sector, more often referred to as La Tzoumaz.
1500m

Mayens-de-Sion Switzerland
Tranquil hamlet off the road up to Les Collons – part of the Verbier area.
1470m

Mayrhofen 142

Build your own shortlist: www.wheretoskiandsnowboard.com

Méaudre France
Small resort near Grenoble with good snowmaking to make up for its low altitude.
1000m; slopes 1000–1600m
⛷ 10 ⛷ 18km

Megève 267

Meiringen Switzerland
An old town in the broad Haslital valley, a good outing from the nearby Jungfrau resorts or Interlaken and 90 minutes' drive from Zürich or Bern. High-speed lifts take you into the slopes, which are on a broad, sunny mountainside spread across two main sectors. The area is particularly suitable for beginners and confident intermediates – experts will find little to challenge them and early intermediates will find a lack of blue runs. The area is popular with boarders but there are some flat sections. There's a good choice of mountain restaurants, and the resort is great for families with kids' snow gardens, special restaurants and fun areas. There's a choice of hotels and plenty of apartments; most of the restaurants are hotel-based. Après-ski is lively up the mountain but quiet and relaxed in town later on. There's plenty to do off the slopes – including visiting the Sherlock Holmes museum, of course.
600m; slopes 1060–2435m
⛷ 14 ⛷ 60km

Melchsee-Frutt Switzerland
Limited, but high and snow-sure bowl above a car-free village. Family-friendly.
1920m; slopes 1080–2255m
⛷ 10 ⛷ 32km

Mellau Austria
Quiet and peaceful village that shares with Damüls the biggest area entirely in Bregenzerwald. There are 20km of walking trails and 43km of cross-country tracks too.
700m; slopes 700–2000m
⛷ 31 ⛷ 105km

Les Menuires 274

Merano 2000 Italy
Small ski area just outside Merano, with main lift base at Falzeben above Avelengo/Hafling.
2000m; slopes 2000–2240m
⛷ 7 ⛷ 40km

Méribel 280

Métabief-Mont-d'Or France
Twin villages in the Jura region, not far from Geneva.
900m; slopes 880–1460m
⛷ 22 ⛷ 42km

Methven New Zealand
Nearest town/accommodation to Mt Hutt, and helicopter base for trips to Arrowsmith

range – good for intermediates as well as advanced.

Mieders Austria
An unspoiled village with a small selection of hotels and guest houses at the entrance to the Stubai valley. Its own area of slopes at Serles is tiny, just four runs – two blue, two red. But there are extensive cross-country trails at altitude.
980m

Mijoux France
Pretty wooded slopes between Dijon and Geneva. Lélex nearby.
1000m; slopes 900–1680m
⛷ 29 ⛷ 50km

Mission Ridge USA
Area in dry region with higher-quality snow than other Seattle resorts but less of it. Good intermediate slopes.
1390m; slopes 1390–2065m
⛷ 6 ⛷ 300 acres

Misurina Italy
Tiny village near Cortina. A cheap alternative base.
1755m; slopes 1755–1900m
⛷ 4 ⛷ 13km

Mittenwald 378
Cute town in the Bavarian Alps.
915m

Mittersill Austria
Valley-junction village south of Pass Thurn. A gondola runs from Hollersbach up to the Resterhöhe sector above Pass Thurn.
790m; slopes 1265–1895m
⛷ 15 ⛷ 25km

Moena Italy
Large village between Cavalese and Sella Ronda resorts, ideally located for touring the Dolomites area.
1200m; slopes 1200–2500m
⛷ 8 ⛷ 35km

La Molina Spain
Cheap, basic resort near Andorra, sharing a fair-sized, varied area with Masella to form Alp 2500.
1400m; slopes 1400–2535m
⛷ 31 ⛷ 121km

Mölltal Glacier Austria
Little-known high glacier slopes above Flattach on the other side of the Tauern tunnel from Bad Gastein. Varied runs and fast lifts. Worthwhile excursion when the snowline is high. Summer skiing available.
2570m; slopes 695–3120m
⛷ 8 ⛷ 53km

Molveno Italy
Lakeside village on the edge of the Dolomites, with a couple of lifts – but mostly used as a base to ski nearby Andalo.

Monarch USA
Wonderfully uncrowded area, a day trip from Crested Butte. Great powder. Good for all but experts.
3290m; slopes 3290–3645m
⛷ 5 ⛷ 800 acres

Monesi Italy
Southernmost of the resorts south of Turin. Close to Monaco and Nice.
1310m; slopes 1310–2180m
⛷ 5 ⛷ 38km

Le Monêtier 325
Quiet little village with access to Serre-Chevalier's slopes.

La Mongie 315

Montafon Austria
The 40km-long Montafon valley contains eleven resorts and four main lift systems. The valley is well worth a look. The biggest is the Nova area (linking Gaschurn and St Gallenkirch) and this is now linked to the Hochjoch area and Schruns. Gargellen and Golm are smaller ski areas in the valley.
655–1425m; slopes 655–2395m
⛷ 61 ⛷ 219km
🚠 Crystal, Thomson

Montalbert 303
Traditional village with access to the La Plagne network.

Mont Blanc Canada
Small locals' hill near Tremblant, with only 300m of vertical and no resemblance to the Franco-Italian item.
⛷ 7 ⛷ 36

Montchavin 303
Attractive village on the fringe of La Plagne.

Mont-de-Lans 250
Low village near Les Deux-Alpes.

Le Mont-Dore France
Attractive traditional small town, the largest resort in the stunningly beautiful volcanic Auvergne region near Clermont-Ferrand.
1050m; slopes 1350–1850m
⛷ 17 ⛷ 42km

Monte Bondone Italy
Trento's local hill.
1300m; slopes 1185–2090m
⛷ 5 ⛷ 20km

Monte Campione Italy
Tiny purpose-built resort, spread thinly over four mountainsides; 80% snowmaking helps to offset the low altitude.
1100m; slopes 1200–2010m
⛷ 16 ⛷ 80km

Monte Livata Italy
Closest resort to Rome, popular with weekenders.
1430m; slopes 1430–1750m
⛷ 8 ⛷ 8km

Monte Piselli Italy
Tiny area with the highest slopes of the many little resorts east of Rome.
2100m; slopes 2100–2690m
⛷ 3 ⛷ 5km

Monte Pora Italy
Tiny resort near Lake d'Iseo and Bergamo. Several other little areas nearby.
1350m; slopes 1350–1880m
⛷ 11 ⛷ 30km

Monterosa Ski 412

Mont Gabriel Canada
Montreal area with runs on four sides of the mountain, though the south-facing sides rarely open. Two short but renowned double-black-diamond bump runs. ⛷ 9

Montgenèvre 289

Mont Glen Canada
Least crowded of the Montreal areas, so a good weekend choice.
680m; slopes 680–1035m
⛷ 4 ⛷ 110 acres

Mont Grand Fonds Canada
Small area sufficiently far from Québec not to get overrun at weekends.
400m; slopes 400–735m ⛷ 4

Mont Habitant Canada
Very limited area in the Montreal region but with a good base lodge. ⛷ 3

Mont Olympia Canada
Small, two-mountain area near Montreal, one mostly novice terrain, the other best suited to experts. ⛷ 6

Mont Orford Canada
Cold, windswept lone peak (no resort), worth a trip from nearby Montreal on a fine day.
slopes 305–855m
⛷ 8 ⛷ 180 acres

Mont-Ste-Anne Canada
Quebec City's biggest and most varied local ski area. Wide choice of amenities at the base. The slopes are limited, but the vertical is a decent 625m. A gondola goes to the top, from where slopes span north and south sides of the mountain. The views are spectacular. Over a third of the area is classified black or double-black, so it's a good place for experts. The Beast (double-black diamond) has one of the steepest pitches in the east at 65%. But there are decent intermediate trails too, adequate nursery slopes and an easy top-to-bottom green run. The Dual mountain lift pass is valid at Stoneham.
175m; slopes 175–800m
⛷ 8 ⛷ 530 acres
🚠 Frontier, Ski Safari

Mont-St-Sauveur Canada
Perhaps the prettiest resort in Canada, popular with Montreal (60km) day trippers and luxury condo owners.

Mont Sutton Canada
Varied area with some of the best glade skiing in eastern Canada, including some for novices. Quaint Sutton village nearby.
⛷9 ⛸ 175 acres

Moonlight Basin 588
Quiet area of slopes linked to Big Sky, Montana.

Morgins 456
Resort on the Swiss side of the Portes du Soleil circuit.

Morillon 256
Valley village in the Flaine network.

Morin Heights Canada
Area in the Montreal region with 100% snowmaking. Attractive base lodge. ⛷6

Morzine 294

Les Mosses Switzerland
Peaceful scenic resort and area, best for a day trip from Villars or Les Diablerets. There's a terrain park, a few chalet-style hotel-restaurants, shops and a rather fine church. There are only draglifts to access the mainly red and blue runs. Prides itself on the number of activities on offer – such as ice-diving, a natural ice rink and an international dog-sled track.
1500m; slopes 1500–2200m
⛷14 ⛸ 60km

Mottaret 280
Purpose-built but reasonably attractive part of Méribel.

Mottarone Italy
Closest slopes to Lake Maggiore. No village – just a base area.
1200m; slopes 1200–1490m
⛸ 25km

Les Moulins Switzerland
Village down the road from Château d'Oex with its own low area of slopes, part of the big Gstaad lift-pass area.
890m; slopes 890–3000m
⛷58 ⛸ 250km

Mount Abram USA
Small, pretty, tree-lined area in Maine, renowned for its immaculately groomed easy runs.
295m; slopes 295–610m
⛷5 ⛸ 170 acres

Mountain High USA
Best snowfall record and highest lift capacity in Los Angeles vicinity – plus 95% snowmaking. Mostly intermediate cruising.
2010m; slopes 2010–2500m
⛷12 ⛸ 220 acres

Mount Ashland USA
Arty town in Oregon renowned for Shakespeare performances. Tiny ski area best for experts run by local charity.
1935m; slopes 1935–2285m
⛷4 ⛸ 200 acres

Mount Bachelor USA
Extinct volcano in Oregon with a big ski area and runs on all sides. Higher elevation means better chance of good snow than many other resorts in north-west USA and average annual snowfall of 370 inches is more than any major Colorado resort. Good cruising and beginner terrain lower down and plenty to occupy experts, including tree-lined blacks and steep terrain on the south-facing slopes. No lodging at the base; stay 30 mins away at Sunriver Resort – a big lodge with bar, restaurant, chalet lodging and excellent spa – or in Bend, an attractive small town served by free shuttles.
1920m; slopes 1755–2765m
⛷13 ⛸ 3680 acres
🚠 Ski Safari

Mount Baker USA
Almost on the coast near Seattle, yet one of the top resorts for snow (averages 600 inches a year). Plenty of challenging slopes. Known for spectacular avalanches.
1115m; slopes 1115–1540m
⛷9 ⛸ 1000 acres

Mount Baldy Canada
Tiny area, but a worthwhile excursion from Big White. Gets ultra-light snow – great glades/powder chutes.
slopes 1705–2150m
⛷2 ⛸ 150 acres

Mount Baldy USA
Some of the longest and steepest runs in California. Only an hour's drive from Los Angeles so a day trip is feasible, but 20% snowmaking and antiquated lifts are major drawbacks.
1980m; slopes 1980–2620m
⛷4 ⛸ 400 acres

Mount Baw Baw Australia
Small but entertaining intermediate area in attractive woodland, with great views. Closest area to Melbourne (150km).
1450m; slopes 1450–1560m
⛷7 ⛸ 35 hectares

Mount Buffalo Australia
Site of Australia's first ski lift. Plateau area best suited to beginners. Short season. On-mountain accommodation. four hours from Melbourne.
1400m; slopes 1455–1610m
⛷8 ⛸ 66 acres

Mount Buller Australia
Three hours from Melbourne and Victoria's largest ski area. Proper resort village, with a 360-degree network of short runs on its isolated massif. Luxury hotel and spa.
1600m; slopes 1600–1790m
⛷22 ⛸ 80km

Mount Dobson New Zealand
Mostly intermediate slopes in a wide, treeless basin near Mt Cook, with good snow-cover. Accommodation in Fairlie, 40 minutes away.
1610m; slopes 1610–2010m
⛷3 ⛸ 990 acres

Mount Falakro Greece
Area two hours' drive from Salonica in northern Greece; almost as big as Parnassos, uncrowded and with good views. Has a fast quad.
1720m
⛷8 ⛸ 22km

Mount Hood Meadows USA
The biggest and most varied ski area on Mt Hood in Oregon served by 11 lifts including five fast quads. Good beginner area, intermediate cruising, single-black diamond runs in the centre of the main ski area and a big area of double-black-diamond runs roped off and entered through gates. Up to six terrain parks, depending on snow conditions. No accommodation at the base – stay at Timberline (see separate entry) half an hour away or Government Camp (near Mount Hood Skibowl, which also gets its own entry) 20 minutes away.
1635m; slopes 1375–2225m
⛷11 ⛸ 2150 acres
🚠 Ski Safari

Mount Hood Skibowl USA
Small area of mainly tough gladed runs, offering the steepest and most extreme slopes in the Mount Hood area. Claims to be America's largest night skiing area with a lot of runs open up to 10/11pm nightly. Two floodlit terrain parks, tubing hills, snow bikes and snowmobiles. Just below Timberline ski area; stay there or in Government Camp at the foot of Skibowl's slopes, a sizeable settlement with a choice of lodgings and restaurants. Other local ski area is Mt Hood Meadows.
1075m; slopes 1075–1530m
⛷7 ⛸ 960 acres

Mount Hotham Australia
Australia's highest ski village. Built on a ridge above the slopes. Intermediate and advanced skiing. Good snow record. Nearest town Bright, four hours from Melbourne.
1750m; slopes 1450–1845m
⛷13 ⛸ 30km

Mount Hutt New Zealand
Steepest, most snow-sure area in NZ, with ocean views, but prone to bad weather; 100km from Christchurch, a tricky drive up from Methven.
slopes 1405–2085m
⛷4 ⛸ 365 hectares

Mount Lemmon USA
Southernmost area in North America, close to famous Old West town Tombstone, Arizona. Reasonable snowfall.
2500m; slopes 2500–2790m
⛷3 ⛸ 70 acres

Mount McKay Australia
Australia's steepest skiing accessed from Falls Creek, with genuine black-diamond terrain and snowcats.
1600m

Mount Pilio Greece
Pleasant slopes cut out of dense forest, only 15km from the holiday resort of Portaria above town of Volos.
1500m ⛷3

Mount Rose USA
Much the highest base elevation in the Tahoe area – a good 600m above the lake – and with an annual snowfall average of 400 inches. The Chutes is a shady bowl mainly of serious double-diamond gradient on the front face of the slopes. But there are blue and easy black runs to the base and a wider, gentler, lightly wooded area. The slopes have a lot to offer, especially if staying in Heavenly – where the groomed stuff may be too dull and the ungroomed stuff too challenging.
2520m; slopes 2410–2955m
⛷6 ⛸ 1200 acres

Mount Shasta Ski Park USA
Californian resort 300 miles north of San Francisco.
⛷4 ⛸ 425 acres

Mount Snow USA
A one-peak resort, with a long row of lifts on the front face (two fast quads among them) serving easy and intermediate runs of just over 500m vertical. Separate area of black runs on the north face – including a couple of short but serious double blacks – served by a triple chair and a six-pack. And on the opposite side a small area of intermediate runs above Carinthia base, accessed by a third fast quad. Reputed to have some of the best terrain parks in the east. Lodgings at the base include a Grand Summit hotel.
580m; slopes 580–1095m
⛷19 ⛸ 590 acres
🚠 Ski Safari

Mount Spokane USA
Little intermediate area near Spokane (Washington State).
1160m; slopes 1160–1795m
⛷5 ⛸ 350 acres

Mount St Louis / Moonstone
Canada
Premier area in Toronto region, spread over three peaks. Very high-capacity lift system and 100% snowmaking. ⛷ 13 ⛷ 175

Mount Sunapee   USA
Area in New Hampshire closest to Boston; primarily intermediate terrain.
375m; slopes 375–835m
⛷ 10 ⛷ 230 acres

Mount Vermio   Greece
Oldest ski base in Greece. Two areas in central Macedonia 6okm from Thessaloniki. Barren but interesting slopes.
slopes 1420–2000m ⛷ 7

Mount Washington Resort
                         Canada
Scenic area on Vancouver Island with lodging in the base village. Good snowfall record but rain is a problem.
1110m; slopes 1110–1590m
⛷ 6 ⛷ 970 acres ⛷ Frontier

Mount Washington Resort
                         USA
One of several small resorts in New Hampshire scattered along the Interstate 93 highway. The slopes are on a single mountain face but highly rated, particularly by families, who relish the top-to-bottom easy trails on the main peak, Mt Rosebrook. There is a good mix of terrain, with West Mountain consisting mainly of double-diamond slopes. Snowmaking is comprehensive. There's a terrain park, half-pipe and boardercross. There are a few places to stay near the base, with the grand old Mount Washington hotel five minutes away.
480m; slopes 480–940m
⛷ 8 ⛷ 435 acres

Mount Waterman   USA
Small Los Angeles area where children ski free. The lack of much snowmaking is a drawback.
2135m; slopes 2135–2440m
⛷ 3 ⛷ 210 acres

Mühlbach   Austria
Sprawling village along the main road at one end of the Hochkönig area that spreads over a series of gentle peaks via Dienten to Maria Alm. The Hochkönig area is best for adventurous intermediates, but for beginners there is a good local nursery slope. Experts can explore the ungroomed ski routes and the excellent off-piste. Snowboarders may find there are too many draglifts. There are 4okm of cross-country trails in the area. *855m*

Mühltal   Austria
Small village halfway between Niederau and Auffach in the Wildschönau. No local skiing of its own.
780m; slopes 830–1905m
⛷ 25 ⛷ 70km

Muhr   Austria
Village by Katschberg tunnel well placed for visiting St Michael, Bad Kleinkirchheim, Flachau and Obertauern.
1110m

Muju Resort   South Korea
Largest area in Korea and with a fair amount of lodging. Though it is the furthest resort from Seoul (four hours south) it is still overcrowded.
⛷ 14

Mürren   479
Charming rustic village near Innsbruck, at the foot of long slopes of 900m vertical that extend along the Götzens valley to Axamer Lizum. Good for families and beginners.
830m

Mutters   Austria

Myoko Suginohara Kokusai
                         Japan
A series of small resorts two or three hours from Tokyo, which together make up an area of extensive slopes with longer, wider runs than normal for Japan. ⛷ 15
⛷ Ski Safari

Naeba   Japan
Fashionable resort with lots of accommodation two hours north of Tokyo. Crowded slopes.
900m; slopes 900–1800m ⛷ 30

Nakiska   Canada
Small area of wooded runs between Banff and Calgary, with emphasis on downhill speed. Unreliable snow, but state-of-the-art snowmaking and pancake-flat grooming.
1525m; slopes 1525–2260m
⛷ 5 ⛷ 230 acres

Nasserein   179
Quiet suburb of St Anton.

Nassfeld Ski Arena   Austria
Carinthia's biggest: scenic and sunny area on the Italian border. Good intermediate slopes. Stay in Tröpolach, by the gondola, or larger Hermagor, further east.
1500m; slopes 610–2195m
⛷ 30 ⛷ 110km
⛷ Interactive Resorts, STC

Nauders   Austria
Spacious, traditionally Tirolean village tucked away only 3km from the Swiss border and almost on the Italian one. Its slopes start 2km outside the village (free shuttle-bus) and are mainly high and sunny intermediate runs spread over three areas. Lots of snowmaking. Not ideal for experts, though there is a lot

of off-piste terrain. Not ideal for complete beginners either – the village nursery slopes are some way out. There are five cross-country trails.
1400m; slopes 1400–2850m
⛷ 24 ⛷ 120km
⛷ Crystal, Thomson

Nax   Switzerland
Quiet, sunny village in a balcony setting overlooking the Rhône valley. Own little area and only a short drive from Veysonnaz.
1300m ⛷ 6 ⛷ 35km

Nendaz   499
A sizeable family resort linked in to the Verbier ski area.

Neukirchen   Austria
Quiet, pretty resort sharing slopes with Bramberg. Fairly snow-sure plateau at the top of its mountain.
855m; slopes 855–2150m
⛷ 15 ⛷ 50km

Neustift   188
Village in the Stubai valley.

Nevegal   Italy
Weekend place near Belluno, south of Cortina.
1030m; slopes 1030–1650m
⛷ 14 ⛷ 30km

Nevis Range   655
Scottish ski resort.
90m; slopes 655–1220m
⛷ 11 ⛷ 35km

Niederau   Austria
Chalet-style village, the main resort in the Wildschönau part of Ski Juwel, and a favourite with beginners and early intermediate skiers. Quite spread out, but few hotels are more than five minutes' walk from a main lift.
830m
⛷ Crystal, Inghams, Neilson, Ski Line, Skitracer, Thomson

Niederdorf   Italy
Cross-country village in South Tyrol. Villabassa is its Italian name.

Niseko   656
Resort on Hokkaido island, Japan.

Niseko Village   656
One of Niseko's three interlinked areas.

Nockberge Innerkrems Austria
Area just south of Katschberg tunnel.
1500m; slopes 1500–2020m
⛷ 10 ⛷ 33km

Nordseter   Norway
Cluster of hotels in deep forest north of Lillehammer. Some Alpine facilities but best for cross-country.
850m; slopes 1000–1090m
⛷ 2 ⛷ 2km

Norefjell   Norway
Norway's toughest run, a very steep 600m drop. 120km north-west of Oslo.
185m; slopes 185–1185m
⛷ 10 ⛷ 23km ⛷ Ski Safari

La Norma   France
Traffic-free, purpose-built resort near Modane and Val Cenis.
1350m; slopes 1350–2750m
⛷ 18 ⛷ 65km
⛷ Erna Low, Peak Retreats

Norquay   603
Banff's quiet local hill.

North Conway   USA
Attractive factory-outlet-shopping town in New Hampshire close to Attitash and Cranmore ski areas.
⛷ Virgin Snow

Northstar-at-Tahoe   USA
Classic US-style mountain, with runs cut through dense forest and a pleasant base village that is still growing. The whole area is very sheltered and good for bad-weather days. A gondola and a fast quad go up to a lodge at Big Springs, only 16om above the village. From this point three fast chairs radiate to serve a broad bowl with some short steep pitches at the top, with easier blue runs lower down and around the ridges. From the ridge you can access the Backside, a steeper bowl with a central fast quad chair serving a row of easy black runs. Lookout Mountain has more black runs and a modest vertical of 390m.
1930m; slopes 1930–2625m
⛷ 19 ⛷ 3000 acres
⛷ American Ski Classics, Scott Dunn, Ski Independence, Ski Safari, Skiworld, Supertravel, Virgin Snow

Nôtre-Dame-de-Bellecombe
                         France
Pleasant 'very French' village spoiled by the busy road. Inexpensive base from which to visit Megève, though it has fair slopes of its own. Queues and slow lifts can be a problem now it is linked to Les Saisies. Free bus to/from Crest Voland.
1150m; slopes 1035–2070m
⛷ 84 ⛷ 175km
⛷ Erna Low, Lagrange, Peak Retreats

Nova Levante   Italy
Village close to Bozen/Bolzano with lifts up to small network around Passo di Costalunga.
1200m
⛷ 16 ⛷ 40km

Nozawa Onsen   Japan
Spa village with good hot springs three hours from Tokyo. The runs are cut out of heavy vegetation.
500m; slopes 500–1650m ⛷ 21
⛷ Ski Safari

Nub's Nob   USA
One of the most sheltered Great Lakes ski areas (many suffer fierce winds). 100%

snowmaking; weekend crowds from Detroit. Wooded slopes suitable for all abilities.
275m; slopes 275–405m
⬜8 ⬆ 245 acres

O2Resort　South Korea
Built up the mountain in Gangwon province and with Korea's best snow. Slopes suit all levels and include a 3.2km long run. Facilities include: condos, youth hostel, fitness centre, spa and restaurants.
1420m ⬆ 16 runs

Oberammergau　**378**
Village in the Bavarian Alps.
835m

Oberau　Austria
Pretty village in the Ski Juwel (Alpbachtal-Wildschönau) area – but least convenient for the slopes.
935m 📧 Inghams, Neilson

Obereggen　Italy
Tiny resort close to Bozen/ Bolzano with modest area of slopes also accessible from Predazzo in Val di Fiemme.
1550m; slopes 1550–2200m
⬜6 ⬆ 10km

Obergurgl　**148**

Oberjoch–Hindelang Germany
Small, low-altitude resort, particularly good for beginners.
850m; slopes 1140–1520m
⬜12 ⬆ 32km

Oberlech　**133**
Car- and crowd-free family resort alternative to Lech.

Oberndorf　Austria
Quiet hamlet with beginners' area and a chair connecting it to St Johann's undemanding ski area.
700m

Oberperfuss　Austria
Small village west of Innsbruck, with tall but limited slopes. On the Innsbruck lift pass.
820m 📧 Inghams

Obersaxen-Mundaun-Lumnezia　Switzerland
Several quiet villages above Ilanz, in the Vorderrhein Valley, near Laax. Sizeable area of mainly red and blue runs on four linked mountains. The main lifts are fast chairs.
1300m; slopes 1200–2310m
⬜18 ⬆ 120km

Oberstaufen　Germany
Three small areas: Steibis; Thulkirchdorf and Hochgrat. Within an hour of Friedrichshafen.
600m; slopes 860–1880m
⬜30 ⬆ 45km

Oberstdorf　**378**
Town in the German Alps near the Austrian border.
815m; slopes 800–2220m
⬜31 ⬆ 30km

Obertauern　**154**

Ochapowace　Canada
Main area in Saskatchewan, east of Regina. It doesn't get a huge amount of snow but 75% snowmaking helps.
⬜4 ⬆ 100 acres

Ohau　New Zealand
Some of NZ's steepest slopes, with great views of Lake Ohau 9km away (where you stay). 320km south of Christchurch.
1500m; slopes 1425–1825m
⬜3 ⬆ 310 acres

Okemo　USA
Worthwhile and nicely varied intermediate area above the old Vermont town of Ludlow. Family oriented, with good child care. Comprehensive snowmaking and highly rated grooming.
345m; slopes 345–1020m
⬜18 ⬆ 624 acres
📧 American Ski Classics

Oppdal　Norway
One of the larger Norwegian resorts, but very far north. Many runs are quite short.
715m; slopes 715–1020m
⬜17 ⬆ 60km

Orcières-Merlette　France
High, convenient family resort a few km north-east of Gap, Merlette being the ugly, purpose-built ski station above the village of Orcières (1450m). Snow-sure beginner area. Slopes have a good mix of difficulty spread over several mountain flanks.
1850m; slopes 1850–2725m
⬜28 ⬆ 100km
📧 Erna Low, Lagrange, Ski France

Ordino　Andorra
Rustic valley village near La Massana, on the way up to Andorra's best snow at Arcalis.

Orelle　**368**
Village in the Maurienne with access to Val Thorens.

Oropa　Italy
Little area just off the Aosta–Turin motorway. An easy change of scene from Courmayeur.
1180m; slopes 1200–2390m
⬆ 15km

Les Orres　France
Friendly modern resort with great views and varied intermediate terrain, but the snow is unreliable, and it's a long transfer from Lyon.
1550m; slopes 1550–2720m
⬜23 ⬆ 62km
📧 Crystal, Lagrange, Thomson

Orsières　Switzerland
Traditional winter resort near Martigny. Close to Grand St Bernard resorts, including Champex-Lac. Well-positioned base from which to visit Verbier and the Chamonix valley.
900m

Ortisei　**433**
Market town in Val Gardena.

Oslo　Norway
Capital city with cross-country ski trails in its parks. Alpine slopes and lifts in Nordmarka region, just north of city boundaries.

Otre il Colle　Italy
Smallest of many little resorts near Bergamo.
1100m; slopes 1100–2000m
⬜7 ⬆ 7km

Ötz　Austria
Village at the entrance to the Ötz valley with an easy/ intermediate ski area of its own and access to the Sölden, Kuhtai (sharing a lift pass) and Niederau areas.
820m; slopes 820–2200m
⬜11 ⬆ 34km

Oukaimeden　Morocco
Slopes 75km from Marrakech with a surprisingly long season.
2600m; slopes 2600–3260m
⬜7 ⬆ 15km

Ovindoli　Italy
Small area in Abruzzo, east of Rome, claiming the distinction of Europe's longest magic carpet lift. The town is about 3km from the slopes. Shares a lift pass with equally small Campo Felice, nearby.
1375m; slopes 1470–2055m
⬜11 ⬆ 30km

Ovronnaz　Switzerland
Pretty village set on a sunny shelf above the Rhône valley, with a good pool complex. Limited area but Crans-Montana and Anzère are close.
1350m; slopes 1350–2080m
⬜8 ⬆ 30km

Owl's Head　Canada
Steep mountain rising out of a lake, in a remote spot bordering Vermont, away from weekend crowds.
⬜7 ⬆ 90 acres

Oz-en-Oisans　**198**
Old village with satellite at the lifts into Alpe-d'Huez.

Pajarito Mountain　USA
Los Alamos area laid out by nuclear scientists. Atomic slopes too – mostly ungroomed. Open Fridays, weekends and holidays. Fun day out from Taos.
2685m; slopes 2685–3170m
⬜6 ⬆ 220 acres

Pal　**90**
Prettily wooded mountain linked with slopes of Arinsal.

Palandöken　Turkey
Varied skiing area, transformed by three big hotels, overlooking the Anatolian city of Erzurum.
slopes 2150–3100m ⬜4

Pampeago　Italy
Trentino area convenient for a trip from Milan.

Pamporovo　**648**

Panarotta　Italy
Smallest of the resorts east of Trento. At a higher altitude than nearby Andalo, so worth a day out from there.
1500m; slopes 1500–2000m
⬜6 ⬆ 7km

Panorama　Canada
Home to one of North America's biggest verticals (1220m), with something for everyone on its quiet, wooded mountain. Small, purpose-built place at the foot of the slopes and on two levels. The upper 'village' is centred on a hot-pool complex, while the mostly condo accommodation in the lower area. The slopes rise steeply above the resort, but steepest at the top – with genuine blacks and two expert bowls (Taynton and Extreme Dream). Excellent terrain for adventurous intermediates too. More limited for novices. Heli-ski trips are available. There's a big park, pipe and floodlit mini-park. The school is 'very professional' and facilities for families good.
1160m; slopes 1150–2375m
⬜9 ⬆ 2847 acres
📧 Canadian Affair, Crystal, Frontier, Ski Independence, Ski Safari, Skiworld, Snow Finders, Thomson

Panticosa　Spain
Charming old Pyrenees spa village near Formigal with limited but varied slopes.
1500m; slopes 1500–2220m
⬜16 ⬆ 35km

Paradiski　**301**

Park City　**580**

Parnassos　Greece
Biggest and best-organised area in Greece, 180km from Athens and with surprisingly good slopes and lifts.
slopes 1600–2300m
⬜9 ⬆ 14km

Parpan　Switzerland
Pretty village linked to the large intermediate area of Lenzerheide.
1510m; slopes 1230–2865m
⬜35 ⬆ 155km

Partenen　Austria
Traditional village in a pretty setting at the end of the Montafon valley. The slopes start at Gaschurn, and there are lots more in the vicinity.
1100m

La Parva　Chile
Only 50km east of Santiago and condoville for the capital's elite. A collection of apartments occupied mostly at weekends, linked with Valle Nevado and El Colorado (no area pass).
2750m; slopes 2430–3630m
⬜43 ⬆ 113km

Resort directory / index

Resort news and key links: www.wheretoskiandsnowboard.com

Pas de la Casa 92

Passo Costalunga Italy
Dense network of short lifts either side of the road over a pass, close to Val di Fassa, with links up from Nova Levante.

Passo Lanciano Italy
Closest area to Adriatic. Weekend crowds from nearby Pescara when the snow is good.
1305m; slopes 1305–2000m
⛷ *13*

Passo Rolle Italy
Small group of lifts either side of the road over a high pass just north of San Martino di Castrozza.

Passo San Pellegrino Italy
Smallish ski area south of the Sella Ronda, with lifts each side of the pass road and links with the valley village of Falcade.
1920m; slopes 1150–2245m
⛷ *19* ⛷ *75km*

Passo Tonale 418

Pass Thurn 125
Road-side lift base for one of Kitzbühel's ski areas.

Passy-Plaine-Joux France
Small, quiet village 25km from Chamonix. Draglifts serve woody slopes best suited to novices.
1340m ⛷ *6* ⛷ *12km*

Pebble Creek USA
Small area on Utah-Jackson Hole route. Blend of open and wooded slopes.
1920m; slopes 1920–2530m
⛷ *3* ⛷ *600 acres*

Pec Pod Snezku Czech Republic
Collection of hamlets spread along the valley road leading to the main lifts and the very limited ski area.
770m; slopes 710–1190m
⛷ *10* ⛷ *9km*

Peisey 208
Small village linked to Les Arcs.

Peisey-Vallandry 208
Group of villages linked to Les Arcs and Paradiski area.

Pejo Italy
Trentino spa resort near Madonna. New cable car now serves slopes to 3000m.
1400m; slopes 1400–3000m
⛷ *7* ⛷ *15km*

Penitentes Argentina
180km from Mendoza. Accommodation at the base.
⛷ *10* ⛷ *300 hectares*

Perelik Bulgaria
Development aiming to link Pamporovo with Mechi Chal.

Perisher / Smiggins Australia
Expanding resort with slopes on seven mountains, which between them offer plenty of

short, intermediate runs. 30km from Jindabyne town, six hours from Sydney.
1640m; slopes 1680–2035m
⛷ *47* ⛷ *3075 acres*

Pescasseroli Italy
One of numerous areas east of Rome in L'Aquila region.
1250m; slopes 1250–1945m
⛷ *6* ⛷ *25km*

Pescocostanzo Italy
One of numerous areas east of Rome in L'Aquila region.
1395m; slopes 1395–1900m
⛷ *4* ⛷ *25km*

Pettneu Austria
Snow-sure beginners' resort with an irregular bus link to nearby St Anton.
1250m; slopes 1230–2020m
⛷ *4* ⛷ *15km*

Petzen Austria
One of many little areas in Austria's easternmost ski region near the Slovenian border.
600m; slopes 600–1700m
⛷ *5* ⛷ *16km*

Peyragudes 315

Pfelders Italy
Resort near Merano in the South Tyrol covered by the Ortler Skiarena pass.
⛷ *4* ⛷ *5km*

Pfunds Austria
Picturesque valley village with no slopes but quick access to several resorts in Switzerland and Italy, as well as Austria.
970m

Phoenix Park South Korea
Golf complex with 12 trails in winter. Two hours (140km) from Seoul.
slopes 650–1050m ⛷ *9*

Piancavallo Italy
Uninspiring yet curiously trendy purpose-built village, an easy drive from Venice.
1270m; slopes 1270–1830m
⛷ *17* ⛷ *45km*

Piani delle Betulle Italy
One of several little areas near the east coast of Lake Como.
730m; slopes 730–1850m
⛷ *6* ⛷ *10km*

Piani di Artavaggio Italy
Small base complex rather than a village. One of several little areas near Lake Como.
875m; slopes 875–1875m
⛷ *7* ⛷ *15km*

Piani di Bobbio Italy
Largest of several tiny resorts above Lake Como.
770m; slopes 770–1855m
⛷ *10* ⛷ *20km*

Piani di Erna Italy
Small base development – no village. One of several little areas above Lake Como.
600m; slopes 600–1635m
⛷ *5* ⛷ *9km*

Piau-Engaly France
User-friendly St-Lary satellite in one of the best Pyrenean areas.
1850m; slopes 1420–2530m
⛷ *17* ⛷ *65km* ⛷ *Lagrange*

Piazzatorre Italy
One of many little areas in the Bergamo region.
870m; slopes 870–2000m
⛷ *5* ⛷ *25km*

Pichl 163
Hamlet outside Schladming.

Pico USA
Low-key little family area (no resort village) close to Killington.
605m; slopes 605–1215m
⛷ *9* ⛷ *160 acres*

Piesendorf Austria
Cheaper, quiet place to stay when visiting Zell am See. Tucked behind Kaprun near Niedernsill.
780m
⛷ *3* ⛷ *3km*

Pievepelago Italy
Much the smallest and most limited of the Apennine ski resorts. Less than two hours from Florence and Pisa.
1115m; slopes 1115–1410m
⛷ *7* ⛷ *8km*

Pila Italy
Modern, purpose-built, car-free resort that's popular with families and school groups and is set above the old Roman town of Aosta – a 15-minute gondola ride away or reached by a 30-minute drive on a winding road. Chairlifts (some fast, most slow) and a cable car fan out to serve a fair-sized and interesting mix of well-groomed, snow-sure slopes. The treeline is high, at about 2300m, and most runs are below it, making this an excellent bad-weather resort. From the top heights there are grand views to Mont Blanc in the west and the Matterhorn in the east. There are runs for all standards, but mostly they are reds. The few blacks, above the treeline at the top of the area, don't amount to much, but there is quite a bit of off-piste. There are two short beginner lifts, but progression to longer runs means using a central run, which when the resort is busy is unpleasant. Like so many other Aosta Valley resorts, Pila is pretty quiet during the week but can be hectic at weekends – and it does attract lots of British school groups. 'A good day trip,' says a 2014 visitor.
1800m; slopes 1800–2750m
⛷ *12* ⛷ *70km*
⛷ *Crystal, Erna Low, Interski, Pilaski, Ski Line, Ski Supreme, Ski Yogi, STC, Thomson*

Pinzolo 407
Trentino resort near Madonna.

Pitztal Austria
Long valley with good glacier area at its head, accessed by underground funicular.
1680m; slopes 880–3440m
⛷ *12* ⛷ *68km*
⛷ *Zenith*

Pla-d'Adet France
Limited purpose-built complex at the foot of the St-Lary ski area (the original village is further down the mountain).
1680m; slopes 1420–2450m
⛷ *32* ⛷ *80km*
⛷ *Lagrange*

La Plagne 303

Plan de Corones Italy
Distinctive ski area in South Tyrol, with amazingly efficient lifts from Brunico and San Vigilio di Marebbe. Better known by its German name, Kronplatz.
1200m; slopes 1200–2275m
⛷ *32* ⛷ *103km*
⛷ *Luxury Chalet Collection*

Plan-Peisey 208
Small development with link to Les Arcs.

Plose Italy
Varied area close to Bressanone, with the longest run in the South Tyrol.
560m; slopes 1065–2500m
⛷ *11* ⛷ *40km*

Poiana Brasov 651
Cheap, informal resort in Romania.
1020m; slopes 1020–1775m
⛷ *10* ⛷ *24km*

Pomerelle USA
Small area in Idaho on the Utah–Sun Valley route.
2430m; slopes 2430–2735m
⛷ *3* ⛷ *300 acres*

Pontechianale Italy
Highest, largest area in a remote region south-west of Turin. Day-tripper place.
1600m; slopes 1600–2760m
⛷ *8* ⛷ *30km*

Ponte di Legno 418
Attractive sheltered alternative to Passo Tonale.

Pontresina Switzerland
Small, sedate, sunny village with one main street, rather spoiled by the sanatorium-style architecture. All downhill skiing involves travel by car or bus, except the single long piste on Pontresina's own hill, Languard. It's cheaper to stay here than in St Moritz.
1805m; slopes 1730–3305m
⛷ *54* ⛷ *350km*

Port-Ainé Spain
Small but high intermediate area in the Spanish Pyrenees near Andorra. Lifts include a six-pack; eponymous 3-star hotel at base.
1975m; slopes 1650–2440m
⛷ *8* ⛷ *44km*

Port del Comte Spain
High resort in the forested region of Lleida, north-west of Barcelona. The slopes spread across three linked sectors.
slopes 1700–2400m
⛷ 15 🚡 40km

Porté Puymorens France
Little-known Pyrenean area close to Pas de la Casa in Andorra.
slopes 1600–2470m
⛷ 12 🚡 45km

Porter Heights New Zealand
Closest skiing to Christchurch (one hour). Open, sunny bowl offering mostly intermediate skiing – with back bowls for powder.
1340m; slopes 1340–1950m
⛷ 5 🚡 200 acres

Portes du Soleil 314

Portillo Chile
Luxury hotel 150km north-east of Santiago. Quiet snow-sure slopes used for training by US national ski team. Suits experts best.
2880m; slopes 2450–3310m
⛷ 14 🚡 1235 acres
✉ Momentum, Scott Dunn, Skiworld

Powderhorn USA
Area in west Colorado perched on the world's highest flat-top mountain, Grand Mesa. Sensational views. Day trip from Aspen.
2490m; slopes 2490–2975m
⛷ 4 🚡 300 acres

Powder King Canada
Remote resort in British Columbia, between Prince George and Dawson City. As its name suggests, it has great powder. Plenty of lodging.
880m; slopes 880–1520m
⛷ 3 🚡 160 acres

Powder Mountain USA
Massive Utah area sprawled over six slopes, an hour and a quarter's drive from Salt Lake City. An ample 2,800 acres of its terrain is lift served, a mix of mainly north-facing slopes with enough green, blue and black runs to satisfy all abilities. You access the rest by snowcat or snowmobile tow, buses and hiking. It is the abundance of intermediate freeride terrain that makes it special. You can also stay in Ogden, 32km away.
2100m; slopes 2100–2740m
⛷ 7 🚡 2800 acres

Pozza di Fassa Italy
Pretty Dolomite village with its own slopes, three other small areas close by, and access to the Sella Ronda at Campitello.
1320m; slopes 1320–2428m
⛷ 7 🚡 16km
✉ Crystal, Thomson

Pragelato Italy
Inexpensive base, linked by cable car to Sestriere. Its own area is worth a try for half a day.
1535m; slopes 1535–2700m
⛷ 6 🚡 50km
✉ Erna Low, Ski Line

Prägraten am Grossvenediger Austria
Traditional mountaineering/ski touring village in lovely setting south of Felbertauern tunnel. The Alpine ski slopes of Matrei are nearby.
1310m; slopes 1310–1490m
⛷ 2 🚡 30km

Prali Italy
Tiny resort east of Sestriere – a worthwhile half-day trip.
1450m; slopes 1450–2500m
⛷ 7 🚡 25km

Pralognan-la-Vanoise France
Unspoiled traditional village overlooked by spectacular peaks. Champagny (La Plagne) and Courchevel are close by.
1410m; slopes 1410–2355m
⛷ 14 🚡 30km
✉ Erna Low, Lagrange

LAGRANGE
Prestige

High-standard
Self-catering
Apartments

020 7371 6111
lagrange-holidays.co.uk

Pra-Loup France
Convenient, purpose-built family resort with an extensive, varied intermediate area linked to La Foux-d'Allos (Val d'Allos region).
1500m; slopes 1500–2600m
⛷ 51 🚡 180km
✉ Lagrange

Prati di Tivo Italy
Weekend day-trip place east of Rome and near the town of Teramo. A sizeable resort by southern Italy standards.
1450m; slopes 1450–1800m
⛷ 6 🚡 16km

Prato Nevoso Italy
Purpose-built resort with rather bland slopes. Part of Mondolé ski area with Artesina.
1500m; slopes 1500–1950m
⛷ 25 🚡 90km

Prato Selva Italy
Tiny base development (no village) east of Rome near Teramo. Weekend day-trip place.
1370m; slopes 1370–1800m
⛷ 4 🚡 10km

Le Praz 240
Lowest of the Courchevel resorts.

Les Praz 225
Quiet hamlet near Chamonix.

Praz-de-Lys France
Small family resort close to Geneva with slopes fanning out in all directions. Short runs and old lifts, but nicely varied skiing, and its snow-pocket location means it can have better conditions than neighbouring resorts such as La Clusaz. A good day out.
1450m; slopes 1240–1965m
⛷ 23 🚡 60km

Praz-sur-Arly France
Traditional village in a pretty, wooded setting just down the road from Megève ('but without the price tag!' says a 2014 visitor). Shares slopes with Notre Dame de Bellecombe and beyond to Crest Voland / Les Saises, to form the Espace Diamant.
1035m; slopes 1035–2070m
⛷ 84 🚡 175km

Predazzo Italy
Small, quiet place between Cavalese and the Sella Ronda resorts, with lift into modest area of slopes above Obereggen.
1015m; slopes 995–2205m
⛷ 8 🚡 17km

Premanon France
One of four resorts that make up Les Rousses area in Jura region.
1050m; slopes 1120–1680m ⛷ 40
✉ Lagrange

La Presolana Italy
Large summer resort near Bergamo. Several other little areas nearby.
1250m; slopes 1250–1650m
⛷ 6 🚡 15km

Les Prodains 218
Village at the foot of the cliffs on which Avoriaz sits.

Pucón Chile
Ski area on the side of the active Villarrica volcano in southern Chile, 800km south of Santiago. Lodgings are at Pucón village, 30 minutes away from the slopes.
1200m; slopes 1200–2440m
⛷ 9 🚡 20 runs

Puigmal France
Resort in the French Pyrenees with accommodation in nearby villages.
1830m; slopes 1830–2700m
⛷ 12 🚡 34km

Puy-St-Vincent France
Modern apartment complex above an old village south of Briançon; convenient access to an area of slopes that are limited in extent but offer a decent vertical and a lot of variety, including a bit of steep stuff. Most accommodation is in self-catering apartments at the foot of the slopes. It is relatively inexpensive and makes an attractive choice for a family not hungry for piste miles.
1400-1600m; slopes 1250–2700m
⛷ 12 🚡 75km
✉ Erna Low, Lagrange, Snowbizz, Zenith

Pyhä Finland
Expanding resort 150km north-east of Rovaniemi. Much of the area is in a National Park, with the 14 slopes on two sides of a part-wooded hill. Vertical is only 280m and there's no steep terrain but good off-piste. The best powder runs are on both sides of a long T-bar on the north side. Most pistes open for floodlit skiing. There's a well-developed terrain park, hosting regular competitions.
220m ⛷ 8
✉ Inghams

The Pyrenees 315

Pyrenees 2000 France
Tiny resort built in a pleasing manner. Shares a pretty area of short runs with Font-Romeu. Impressive snowmaking.
2000m; slopes 1750–2250m
⛷ 32 🚡 52km

Québec City Canada
French-speaking capital and old city with a number of ski areas a short drive away.

Queenstown New Zealand
South Island's outdoor adventure capital, in a stunning lakeside setting. Two local resorts: the Remarkables and Coronet Peak. Treble Cone and Cardrona are easily reached by car. Typically commercialized but lively and relaxed, and where most people stay. The slopes are a 30-40 minute drive away. The Remarkables appeals mainly to families and beginners, while Coronet Peak is more satisfying to intermediates. Both resorts have challenges for experts too.
310m; slopes 1170–1650m
⛷ 8 🚡 280 hectares
✉ Contiki

Radium Hot Springs Canada
Summer resort offering an alternative to the purpose-built slope-side resort of Panorama.
slopes 975–2155m
⛷ 8 🚡 300 acres

Radstadt Austria
Unspoiled medieval town near Schladming, with its own small area and the Salzburger Sportwelt slopes accessed from nearby Zauchensee or Flachau.
855m; slopes 855–2185m
⛷ 100 🚡 350km

Ragged Mountain   USA
Family-owned ski area in New Hampshire.
⛷9 ↑ 200 acres

Rainbow   New Zealand
Northernmost ski area on South Island. Wide, treeless area, best for beginners and intermediates. Accommodation at St Arnaud.
1440m; slopes 1440–1760m
⛷5 ↑ 865 acres

Ramsau am Dachstein Austria
Charming village overlooked by the Dachstein glacier. Renowned for cross-country, it also has Alpine slopes locally, on the glacier and at Schladming.
1200m; slopes 1100–2700m
⛷18 ↑ 30km

Ramundberget   Sweden
Small, quiet, ski-in/ski-out family resort with very limited pistes but lots of cross-country. ↑ 22km

Rasos de Peguera   Spain
The only resort in the Barcelona province. 14km from Berga. Ten pistes, mostly red classified.

Rauris   Austria
Small village in a quiet, dead-end valley south-east of Zell, about 25km by road. Across the valley road from the village are nursery draglifts and a gondola accessing intermediate slopes with a vertical of 1250m. Good for an all-round winter holiday as there are lots of activities to try, all set within the beautiful Hohe Tauern National Park.
950m; slopes 950–2175m
⛷10 ↑ 30km
◪ Crystal, Crystal Finest, Thomson

Ravascletto   Italy
Resort in a pretty wooded setting near Austrian border, with most of its terrain high above on an open plateau.
920m; slopes 920–1735m
⛷12 ↑ 40km

Reallon   France
Traditional-style village, with splendid views from above Lac de Serre-Ponçon.
1560m; slopes 1560–2115m
⛷6 ↑ 20km

Red Lodge   USA
Picturesque Old West Montana town. Ideal for a combined trip with Big Sky or Jackson Hole.
1800m; slopes 2155–2860m
⛷8 ↑ 1600 acres

Red Mountain Resort Canada
Up there with the likes of Fernie as a cult resort for expert skiers who can handle its steep terrain, wide glades and powder-filled bowls. While not big in European terms, it packs a lot of tough stuff into its mountains. For the 2013/14 season the ski

area was hugely expanded by a new quad chair up Grey Mountain, adding some more intermediate runs to its existing mainly gnarly black runs through the trees. But it's still the black and double-black stuff that is the real attraction; it's marked on the map, but not on the mountain. There is good cat-skiing here too – and another 200 acres are being added for 2014/15. Accommodation has recently been built at the base, but otherwise you stay at the small old mining town of Rossland just 4km away.
1185m; slopes 1185–2075m
⛷7 ↑ 2680 acres
◪ Frontier, Ski Safari

Red River   USA
New Mexico western town – complete with stetsons and saloons – with intermediate slopes above.
2665m; slopes 2665–3155m
⛷7 ↑ 290 acres

Reichenfels   Austria
One of many small areas in Austria's easternmost ski region near Slovenia.
810m; slopes 810–1400m

Reinwald   Italy
Resort near Merano in the South Tyrol covered by the Ortler Skiarena pass.

Reit im Winkl   Germany
Southern Bavarian resort, straddling the German–Austrian border. Winklmoos ski area is best suited to intermediates.
750m; slopes 750–1800m
⛷7 ↑ 40km

The Remarkables
   New Zealand
Three bleak basins with great views of 'remarkable' jagged alps, 45 minutes from Queenstown. Popular with families and beginners, but some tougher terrain too. Big terrain park.
1580m; slopes 1580–1945m
⛷6 ↑ 545 acres

Rencurel-les-Coulumes
   France
One of seven little resorts just west of Grenoble. Unspoiled, inexpensive place to tour. Villard-de-Lans is the main resort.

Reschenpass   Austria
Area in the Tirol right on the Swiss border; includes Schöneben and Haider Alm in Italy. Nauders is the main resort. 1520m

Rettenberg   Germany
Small resort near Austrian border.
750m; slopes 820–1650m
⛷15 ↑ 40km

Reutte   Austria
500-year-old market town with many traditional hotels, and rail links to nearby Lermoos.
855m; slopes 855–1900m
⛷9 ↑ 19km

Revelstoke   **624**

Rhêmes Notre Dame   Italy
Unspoiled village in the beautiful Rhêmes valley, south of Aosta. Handful of hotels and tiny amount of downhill – including two black runs.
1725m; slopes 1625–3605m
⛷4 ↑ 5km

Riederalp   Switzerland
Pretty, car-free village high above the Rhône valley near Brig; part of the Aletsch Arena. Cable car or gondola from the valley village of Mörel. Quiet, friendly, uncrowded slopes.
1925m; slopes 1050–2870m
⛷35 ↑ 100km

Riefensberg   Austria
Village in Bregenzerwald that shares with Hittisau the Hochhäderich ski area, which has mainly blue and reds but with a couple of blacks served by four T-bars and a quad chair. It has 16km of cross-country tracks at altitude and 12km of walking paths.
780m ↑ 14km

Rigi-Kaltbad   Switzerland
Resort on a mountain rising out of Lake Lucerne, with superb all-round views, accessed by the world's first mountain railroad.
1440m; slopes 1195–1795m
⛷4 ↑ 9km

Riihivuori   Finland
Small area with 'base' at the top of the mountain. 20km south of the city of Jyväskylä.
⛷5

Riksgränsen   Sweden
Unique Arctic Circle Alpine area not open until late February. You can use the slopes under the midnight sun (lift-served) from mid-May to June. 20 hours by train from Stockholm.
600m; slopes 600–910m
⛷6 ↑ 21km
◪ Ski Safari

Riscone   Italy
Dolomite village sharing a pretty area with San Vigilio. Good snowmaking. Short easy runs.
1200m; slopes 1200–2275m
⛷35 ↑ 40km

Risoul   **375**
Small, convenient family resort linked with Vars to form a sizeable skiing area.

Rittner Horn   Italy
Resort near Merano in the South Tyrol covered by the Ortler Skiarena pass.
⛷3 ↑ 15km

Rivisondoli   Italy
Sizeable mountain retreat east of Rome, with one of the better lift systems in the area.
1350m; slopes 1350–2050m
⛷7 ↑ 16km

Roccaraso   Italy
Clearly largest of the resorts in Abruzzo, east of Rome, with lodgings in the town of Roccaraso and at three lift bases on the mountain.
1280m; slopes 1325–2140m
⛷24 ↑ 110km

Rohrmoos   **163**
Suburb of Schladming, with vast area of nursery slopes.

Rosa Khutor   Russia
One of the venues for the 2014 Sochi Winter Olympics.
560m; slopes 940–2320m
⛷13 ↑ 72km

La Rosière   **319**

Rossland   Canada
Remote little town 5km from Red Mountain.

Rougemont   Switzerland
Cute rustic hamlet just over the French/German language border near Gstaad, with local slopes and links to Gstaad's Eggli sector.
990m; slopes 950–3000m
⛷58 ↑ 250km

Les Rousses   France
Group of four villages – Les Rousses, Premanon, Lamoura and Bois d'Amont – in the Jura mountains, 50km from Geneva airport.
1120m; slopes 1120–1680m
⛷40 ↑ 40km ◪ Lagrange

Ruka   Finland
80km south of the Arctic Circle, close to Kuusamo airport and the Russian border, in a region known for abundant and enduring snow. Lively, upbeat resort with a newly developed pedestrian village. Good but widely spread cabin lodging served by the ski bus. Slopes on two sides of a single low hill, with a mix of open and forest terrain, most floodlit and with snowmaking. None is particularly steep and the vertical very modest. There's a terrain park and boardercross course. The cross-country scope is vast: 500km, of which 40km are floodlit.
200m ⛷20 ↑ 20km
◪ Crystal, Crystal Finest, Thomson

Russbach   Austria
Secluded village tucked up a side valley and linked into the Gosau-Annaberg-Lungotz area. The slopes are spread over a wide area.
815m; slopes 780–1620m
⛷33 ↑ 65km

Rusutsu   **656**
Resort on Hokkaido, Japan.

Saalbach-Hinterglemm   **157**

Saalfelden Austria
Town ideally placed for touring eastern Tirol. Lift networks of Maria-Alm and Saalbach are nearby.
745m; slopes 745–1550m
⛷ 3 �› 3km

Saanen Switzerland
Cheaper and more convenient alternative to Gstaad – but much less going on.
slopes 950–3000m
⛷ 58 �› 250km

Saanenmöser Switzerland
Small village with rail/road links to Gstaad. Scenic and quiet local slopes, with good mountain restaurants.
1270m; slopes 950–3000m
⛷ 58 �› 250km

Saas-Almagell Switzerland
Compact village up the valley from Saas-Grund, with good cross-country trails and walks, and a limited Alpine area.
1670m; slopes 1670–2400m
⛷ 7 �› 12km

Saas-Fee 483

Saas-Grund Switzerland
Sprawling valley village below Saas-Fee, with a separate small but high Alpine area.
1560m; slopes 1560–3200m
⛷ 8 �› 35km

Saddleback USA
Small area between Maine's premier resorts. High slopes by local standards.
695m; slopes 695–1255m
⛷ 5 �› 100 acres

Sahoro Japan
Ugly, purpose-built complex on snowy northern Hokkaido island, with a limited area.
610m; slopes 610–1030m
⛷ 8 �› 15km
🛏 Club Med

Les Saisies France
Traditional-style cross-country venue, surrounded by varied four-mountain Alpine slopes. Now part of Espace Diamant. Easy runs, but some lift queues at peak times.
1650m; slopes 1035–2070m
⛷ 84 �› 175km
🛏 Classic Ski, Erna Low, Lagrange, Peak Retreats, PowderBeds, Ski Independence

LAGRANGE
Prestige

High-standard
Self-catering
Apartments

020 7371 6111
lagrange-holidays.co.uk

Sälen Sweden
Well-developed family resort with extensive lift system, and some good off-piste for experts.
550m; slopes 550–950m
⛷ 101 �› 144km

Salt Lake City USA
Underrated base from which to ski Utah. Cheaper and livelier than the resorts.

Salzburg-Stadt Austria
A single, long challenging run off the back of Salzburg's local mountain, accessed by a spectacular lift-ride from a suburb of Grodig.
425m

Samedan Switzerland
Valley town, just down the road from St Moritz. A run heads back to base from Corviglia-Marguns.
1720m

Samnaun 118
Shares large ski area with Ischgl.

Samoëns 323

San Bernardino Switzerland
Pretty resort south of the road tunnel, close to Madesimo.
1625m; slopes 1600–2525m
⛷ 8 �› 35km

San Candido Italy
Resort on the border with Austria on the road to Lienz. Innichen is its German name.
1175m; slopes 1175–1580m
⛷ 4 �› 15km
🛏 Neilson

San Carlos de Bariloche Argentina
Year-round resort, with five areas nearby and the place to stay when skiing Cerro Catedral – 20 minutes away by bus. Once a quaint lakeside town, but now a substantial resort.
slopes 1030–2180m
⛷ 39 �› 103km

San Cassiano 425
Quiet village linked via the Alta Badia to the Sella Ronda circuit.

Sandia Peak USA
The world's longest lift ride ascends from Albuquerque. Mostly gentle slopes; children ski free.
slopes 2645–3165m
⛷ 7 �› 100 acres

San Grée di Viola Italy
Easternmost of resorts south of Turin, surprisingly close to the Italian Riviera.
1100m; slopes 1100–1800m ⛷ 30km

San Martin de los Andes Argentina
Sizeable town with accommodation, 19 km from the Chapelco ski area.

San Martino di Castrozza Italy
Trentino village south of Val di Fassa.
1465m; slopes 1465–2610m
⛷ 20 �› 50km

Sansicario 420
Small, stylish resort in the Milky Way near Sauze d'Oulx.

San Simone Italy
Tiny development north of Bergamo, close to unappealing Foppolo area.
2000m; slopes 1105–2300m
⛷ 9 �› 45km

Santa Caterina Italy
Pretty, user-friendly village near Bormio, with a snow-sure novice and intermediate area.
1740m; slopes 1740–2725m
⛷ 8 ⛷ 25km 🛏 Solos

Santa Cristina 433
Quiet village in Val Gardena.

Santa Fe USA
Interesting area only 15 miles from beautiful Santa Fe town. A tree-filled bowl with a good variety of terrain crammed into its small area. Ideal stopover en route from Albuquerque airport to Taos.
3145m; slopes 3155–3680m
⛷ 7 ⛷ 550 acres

Santa Maria Maggiore Italy
Resort south of the Simplon Pass from the Rhône valley, and near Lake Maggiore.
820m; slopes 820–1890m
⛷ 5 ⛷ 10km

San Vigilio di Marebbe / Kronplatz Italy
Pretty village in South Tyrol with lifts on two mountains, one being the quite impressive Plan de Corones / Kronplatz.
1200m; slopes 1200–2275m
⛷ 31 ⛷ 116km

San Vito di Cadore Italy
Sizeable, alternative place to stay to Cortina. Negligible local slopes, though.
1010m; slopes 1010–1380m
⛷ 9 ⛷ 12km

Sappada Italy
Isolated resort close to the Austrian border below Lienz.
1215m; slopes 1215–2050m
⛷ 17 ⛷ 21km

Sappee Finland
Resort within easy reach of Helsinki, popular with boarders and telemarkers. Lake views. ⛷ 7

Sarnano Italy
Main resort in the Macerata region near Adriatic Riviera. Valley village with ski slopes accessed by lift.
540m ⛷ 9 ⛷ 11km

Le Sauze France
Fine area near Barcelonnette, sadly remote from airports.
1400m; slopes 1400–2440m
⛷ 23 ⛷ 65km

Sauze d'Oulx 420

Savognin Switzerland
Pretty village with a good mid-sized area; a good base for St Moritz, Davos/Klosters and Laax.
1200m; slopes 1200–2715m
⛷ 10 ⛷ 80km
🛏 Ski Club Freshtracks

Scheffau 110
Rustic village near Söll.

Schia Italy
Very limited area of short runs – the only ski area near Parma. No village.
1245m; slopes 1245–1415m
⛷ 7 ⛷ 15km

Schilpario Italy
One of many little areas near Bergamo.
1125m; slopes 1125–1635m
⛷ 5 ⛷ 15km

Schladming 163

Schnalstal Italy
Valley and high ski area, in the Dolomites near Merano. Val Senales is its Italian name.
3210m; slopes 2110–3210m
⛷ 12 ⛷ 35km

Schöneben Italy
Area in the Val Venosta in the South Tyrol, close to Austrian border and Nauders.
1520m

Schönried Switzerland
A cheaper and quieter resort alternative to Gstaad.
1230m; slopes 950–3000m
⛷ 58 ⛷ 250km

Schoppernau Austria
Village near Lech that shares with Au the Diedamskopf intermediate ski area, which boasts Bregenzerwald's highest lift station for fabulous views.
860m; slopes 860–2060m
⛷ 8 ⛷ 44km

Schröcken Austria
Small pretty village that shares its slopes with Warth, which is linked to Lech – see Lech chapter.
1260m; slopes 1260–2100m
⛷ 15 ⛷ 66km 🛏 Snow-wise

Schruns Austria
Pleasant little working valley town with a car-free centre at the heart of the Montafon region, with access to both the Hochjoch area (see St Gallenkirch) from a cable car near the centre of town and the Golm ski area (a few km away). At Golm four chairs and a drag serve easy blue and red slopes above the trees. A six-pack goes to the top of the area, linked via a ski tunnel to slopes on the back of the hill, including the Diabolo black run (the steepest in the valley). Snowmaking covers many of the upper slopes and the run to the valley. Ernest Hemingway ensconced himself in Schruns in 1925/26, and his favourite drinking table in the hotel Taube can be admired. Après-ski is not the big deal it is in many Austrian resorts, but a few places get quite lively. There's a big sports centre. *700m*

Schüttdorf 190
Ordinary dormitory satellite of Zell am See, with easy access to the shared ski area. Kids' area and nursery slopes at the base.

Schwarzach im Pongau
Austria
Riverside village with rail links. There are limited slopes at Goldegg; Wagrain (Salzburger Sportwelt) and Grossarl (Gastein valley) are also nearby.
600m ⛷ *4* 🚡 *12km*

Schwarzenberg Austria
Village in Bregenzerwald with 24km of runs (mainly easy blues and reds) served by nine lifts (nearly all draglifts). There are also 10km of cross-country tracks and 35km of walking trails.
700m; slopes 1145–1465m
⛷ *9* 🚡 *24km*

Schwaz Austria
Valley town beside the Inn with a lift into varied terrain shared with the village of Pill and its mountain outpost, Hochpillberg.
540m; slopes 540–2030m
⛷ *6* 🚡 *10km*

Schweitzer USA
Family-friendly resort in northern Idaho, 85 miles from Spokane (Washington state) and 45 miles from Canada. 'Excellent childcare,' says a 2014 visitor.
1220m; slopes 1229–1950m
⛷ *10* 🚡 *2900 acres*

Schwemmalm Italy
Resort near Merano in the South Tyrol covered by the Ortler Skiarena pass.
⛷ *5* 🚡 *18km*

Scopello Italy
Low area close to the Aosta valley, worth considering for a day trip in bad weather.
slopes 690–1700m
⛷ *6* 🚡 *35km*

Scuol Switzerland
Year-round spa resort close to Austria and Italy, with an impressive range of terrain.
1225m; slopes 1225–2780m
⛷ *15* 🚡 *80km*

Searchmont Resort Canada
Ontario area with modern lift system and 95% snowmaking. Fine Lake Superior views.
275m; slopes 275–485m
⛷ *4* 🚡 *65 acres*

Sedrun Switzerland
Sizeable roadside village east of the Oberalp Pass, and covered along with Andermatt by the Gotthard Oberalp lift pass. The most extensive piste skiing in the area. There's a good choice of red runs, a rewarding black and a 'freeride' route, plus plenty of scope for off-piste. At Milez

there's a terrain park and family restaurant area. Spa centre.
1450m; slopes 1450–2350m
⛷ *10* 🚡 *50km*

Seefeld Austria
Classic winter holiday resort, well designed in traditional Tirolean style, with a large pedestrian-only centre and lots of upmarket hotels (including three 5-stars). Lots of people come here to enjoy the superb cross-country trails and off-slope activities rather than the downhill skiing, but there are two main downhill sectors on the outskirts – Gschwandtkopf and Rosshütte – the latter served mostly by fast lifts. Both areas have intermediate runs of decent vertical; Rosshütte is more extensive, with a cable car across to the separate peak of Härmelekopf, and some worthwhile challenges for experts. There's a good long red run back to village level and a gentle nursery area too. But overall the terrain is far too limited to keep most folk entertained for a week's stay. You can always make excursions to Innsbruck, not far away and easily reached by train, or to the Stubai and Zugspitze glaciers.
1200m; slopes 1200–2065m
⛷ *30* 🚡 *48km*
🚠 *Crystal, Crystal Finest, Erna Low, Headwater, Inghams, Momentum, STC, Thomson*

See im Paznaun Austria
Small family-friendly area in the Paznaun Valley, near Ischgl, with rustic old village set quietly 100m above the valley floor and main road.
1050m

Le Seignus-d'Allos France
Close to La Foux-d'Allos (which shares large area with Pra-Loup) and has own little area, too.
1400m; slopes 1400–2425m
⛷ *13* 🚡 *47km*

Seis Italy
German name for Siusi.

Sella Nevea Italy
Limited but developing resort in a beautiful setting on the Slovenian border, and now linked to Bovec-Kanin. Summer glacier nearby.
1140m; slopes 1190–2300m
⛷ *12* 🚡 *30km*

Sella Ronda 425

Selva / Val Gardena 433

Selvino Italy
Closest resort to Bergamo.
960m; slopes 960–1400m
⛷ *9* 🚡 *20km*

Selwyn Snowfields Australia
Popular with beginners and families. 6 hours from Sydney. Good lift system and cheaper passes than the major Oz resorts.
1520m; slopes 1490–1615m
⛷ *10* 🚡 *111 acres*

Semmering Austria
Long-established winter sports resort set in pretty scenery, 100km from Vienna, towards Graz. Mostly intermediate terrain.
1000m; slopes 1000–1340m
⛷ *5* 🚡 *14km*

Semnoz France
Small, family and beginner focused resort above Lake Annecy with views of the lake and Mont Blanc.
1705m
⛷ *11* 🚡 *18*

Les Sept-Laux France
Improving family resort near Grenoble. Modern lift system – 90% of lifts having been replaced in recent years. Pretty slopes.
1350m; slopes 1350–2400m
⛷ *21* 🚡 *120km*
🚠 *Zenith*

Serfaus Austria
Virtually unknown in the UK, but it is a charming village of chalet-style buildings set on a sunny shelf and kept largely traffic-free by an underground railway to the lifts. Most of the accommodation is in hotels, frequented by well-heeled German families. It shares with Fiss and Ladis a broad area of high slopes, with long runs spanning several ridges – well-suited to mixed-ability parties and especially good for families. The vast kids' facilities at mid-mountain level and ample nursery slopes are key attraction. A lack of English speakers may be a drawback though.
1430m; slopes 1200–2830m
⛷ *67* 🚡 *212km*
🚠 *Ski Bespoke, Ski Club Freshtracks, STC*

Serrada Italy
Very limited area near Trento.
slopes 1250–1605m ⛷ *5*

Serre-Chevalier 325

Sesto Italy
Dolomite village off the Alta Val Pusteria, surrounded by pretty little areas. Sexten is its German name.
1310m; slopes 1130–2200m
⛷ *31* 🚡 *50km*

Sestola Italy
Apennine village a short drive from Pisa and Florence with its pistes, some way above, almost completely equipped with snowmakers.
900m; slopes 1280–1975m
⛷ *23* 🚡 *50km*

Sestriere 440

Seven Springs Mountain USA
Pennsylvania's largest resort.
slopes 220–2995m
⛷ *18* 🚡 *494 acres*

Sexten Italy
Dolomite village off the Hochpustertal, surrounded by pretty little areas. Sesto is its Italian name.
1310m; slopes 1130–2200m
⛷ *31* 🚡 *50km*

Shames Mountain Canada
Remote spot inland from coastal town of Prince Rupert and with impressive snowfall record. Deep powder.
670m; slopes 670–1195m
⛷ *3* 🚡 *183 acres*

Shawnee Peak USA
Small area near Bethel and Sunday River renowned for its night skiing. Spectacular views. Mostly groomed cruising.
185m; slopes 185–580m
⛷ *5* 🚡 *225 acres*

Shemshak Iran
Most popular of the three mountain resorts within easy reach of Tehran (60km).
3600m; slopes 2550–3050m 🚡 *7*

Shiga Kogen 656
Largest area in Japan.

Showdown USA
Intermediate area in Montana forest north of Bozeman. 50km to the nearest hotel.
2065m; slopes 2065–2490m
⛷ *4* 🚡 *640 acres*

Sierra-at-Tahoe USA
A Colorado-style resort, with runs cut on densely wooded slopes. It claims an impressive average of 420 inches of snow. The slopes are spread over two flanks of Huckleberry Mountain. The fronts of both offer good intermediate cruising plus some genuine single-diamond blacks. The backside of Huckleberry has easier blue and green slopes. This is a natural day trip for those staying in South Lake Tahoe.
2210m; slopes 2025–2700m
⛷ *14* 🚡 *2000 acres*

Sierra Nevada 641

Sierra Summit USA
Sierra Nevada area accessible only from the west. 100% snowmaking.
2160m; slopes 2160–2645m
⛷ *8* 🚡 *250 acres*

Silbertal Austria
Low secluded village in the Montafon valley, linked to Schruns. A good base for touring numerous areas.
890m

Sillian Austria
A gondola and two fast quads serve this varied area in Austria's Hochpustertal region.
1100m ⛷ *6* 🚡 *45km*

Sils Maria 488
Lakeside village linked to the St Moritz Corvatsch slopes.

Silvaplana 488
Pretty village near St Moritz.

Silver Mountain USA
Northern Idaho area near delightful resort town of Coeur d'Alene. Best for experts, but plenty for intermediates too.
1215m; slopes 1215–1915m
⛷ 6 ✠ 1500 acres

Silver Star 627

Silverthorne USA
Factory outlet town on main road close to Keystone and Breckenridge. Good budget base for skiing those resorts plus Vail and Beaver Creek.

Silverton USA
Expert-only area in southern Colorado that used to be heli-ski country. Served by one lift. Avalanche transceiver, shovel and probe compulsory.
3170m; slopes 3170–3750m ⛷ 1

Sinaia Romania
Dreary main-road town with a modest, open area of slopes. Recent investment in new lifts, included a gondola.
795m; slopes 795–2030m
⛷ 10 ✠ 20km

Sipapu USA
Great little New Mexico area, with mostly treelined runs. Snow unreliable, but 70% snowmaking. Nice day out from Taos when conditions are good.
slopes 2500–2765m
⛷ 4 ✠ 70 acres

Siusi 433
Village west of the Sella Ronda circuit; Seis in German.

Siviez 499
A quieter, cheaper base for Verbier's Four Valleys circuit.

Sixt-Fer-a-Cheval 256
Village near Samoëns.

Sjusjøen Norway
Cluster of hotels in deep forest close to Lillehammer. Some Alpine facilities but better for cross-country.
885m; slopes 1000–1090m
⛷ 2 ✠ 2km
⛵ Inntravel

Ski Apache USA
Apache-owned area south of Albuquerque noted for groomed steeps. Panoramic views. Nearest lodging in charming Ruidoso.
2925m; slopes 2925–3505m
⛷ 11 ✠ 750 acres

Ski Cooper USA
Small area close to historic Old West town of Leadville. Good ski/sightseeing day out from nearby Vail, Beaver Creek and Copper Mountain.
slopes 3200–3565m ⛷ 4

Ski Windham USA
Two hours from New York City and second only to Hunter for weekend crowds. Decent slopes by eastern standards.
485m; slopes 485–940m
⛷ 7 ✠ 230 acres

Smugglers' Notch USA
French-style purpose-built family resort with sympathetic instructors, comprehensive childcare, child-friendly layout and long, quiet, easy runs. There are varied and satisfying slopes, spread over three hills, with a worthwhile vertical of 800m. It's a great area for beginners, but mileage-hungry intermediates should go elsewhere. Snowboarding is encouraged, and there are three impressive terrain parks and an Olympic-size super-pipe.
315m; slopes 315–1110m
⛷ 8 ✠ 1000 acres

Snowbasin USA
Underrated hill, usually with very good snow. No base village, but a worthwhile day out from Park City. The crowd-free slopes cover a lot of pleasantly varied terrain. This is a great mountain for experts – the Grizzly Downhill course drops 885m and is already claimed to be a modern classic. Between the race course and the area boundary is a splendid area of off-piste wooded glades and gullies. Middle Bowl is great terrain for the adventurous, with a complex network of blues and blacks. You have to stay in the town of Ogden on the Salt Lake plain in the backwater of Huntsville. 'Well worth the drive to visit for a day – fabulous views and exceptional lodges,' says a 2014 visitor.
1965m; slopes 1965–2850m
⛷ 11 ✠ 3000 acres

Snowbird 585

Snowbowl (Arizona) USA
One of America's oldest areas, near Flagstaff, Arizona, atop an extinct volcano and with stunning desert views. Good snowfall record.
2805m; slopes 2805–3505m
⛷ 5 ✠ 135 acres

Snowbowl (Montana) USA
Montana area renowned for powder, outside lively town of Missoula. Intermediate pistes plus 700 acres of extreme slopes. Grizzly Chute is the ultimate challenge.
1520m; slopes 1520–2315m
⛷ 4 ✠ 1400 acres

Snowmass 560

Snow Park New Zealand
Dedicated terrain park across the valley from Cardrona. Features galore, including new 7m pipes. Budget lodging at the base.
1530m ⛷ 1

Snow Summit USA
San Bernardino National Forest ski area near Palm Springs. Lovely lake views. 100% snowmaking. High-capacity lift system for weekend crowds.
2135m; slopes 2135–2500m
⛷ 12 ✠ 230 acres

Snow Valley USA
Area quite near Palm Springs. Fine desert views. High-capacity lift system copes with weekend crowds better than nearby Big Bear.
2040m; slopes 2040–2390m
⛷ 11 ✠ 230 acres

Sochi Russia
Host of the 2014 Winter Olympic Games. Three developing areas: Gasprom, Rosa Khutor and Mountain Carousel.
520m
⛷ 19 ✠ 100km
⛵ Crystal, Thomson

Solda Italy
The other side of the Stelvio Pass from Bormio. Very long airport transfers. Sulden is German name.
1905m; slopes 1905–2625m
⛷ 10 ✠ 40km

Sölden 167

Soldeu 92

Soldier Mountain USA
Family resort in Central Idaho; backcountry snowcat tours.
slopes 1770–2195m
⛷ 4 ✠ 670 acres

Solitude USA
Smart, car-free mini-village linked with Brighton in the valley next to Alta and Snowbird. Most (not all) of the slopes are easy or intermediate, including a wide area served by the one fast quad. When open, the top lift accesses lots of steeps in Honeycomb Canyon, on the back of the hill, with a short quad to bring you back to the front face. Headwall Forest and Eagle Ridge also have good blacks. The resorts' boundaries are open, and there are good backcountry adventures to be had. 'An appropriately named resort as it was all but empty on our visit,' says a 2014 visitor.
2490m; slopes 2435–3200m
⛷ 13 ✠ 250 acres
⛵ American Ski Classics, Ski Safari

Söll 172

Solvista USA
Child-oriented resort close to Winter Park. Low snowfall record for Colorado.
2490m; slopes 2490–2795m
⛷ 5 ✠ 250 acres

Sommand France
Purpose-built base that shares area with Praz-de-Lys.
1420m; slopes 1200–1800m
⛷ 22 ✠ 50km

Sonnenkopf Austria
Ski area above Klösterle a few km west of the Arlberg pass – and covered by the Arlberg ski pass. 'Good range of runs for a small area,' says a reporter.
slopes 1100–2300m
⛷ 9 ✠ 30km

Sorenberg Switzerland
Popular weekend retreat between Berne and Lucerne, with a high proportion of steep, low runs.
1165m; slopes 1165–2280m
⛷ 16 ✠ 50km

South Lake Tahoe USA
Tacky base for skiing Heavenly, with cheap lodging, traffic and gambling.

Spindleruv Mlyn Czech Republic
Largest Giant Mountains region resort but with few facilities serving several little low areas.
715m; slopes 750–1310m
⛷ 16 ✠ 25km

Spital am Pyhrn Austria
Small village near Hinterstoder in Upper Austria, a bus ride from its limited intermediate slopes at Wurzeralm.
650m; slopes 810–1870m
⛷ 8 ✠ 20km

Spittal an der Drau Austria
Historic Carinthian town with a limited area at Goldeck starting a lift-ride above it. A good day trip from Bad Kleinkirchheim or from Slovenia.
555m; slopes 1650–2140m
⛷ 8 ✠ 30km

Spitzingsee Germany
Beautiful small lake (and village) an hour from Munich.
⛷ 18 ✠ 25km

Splugen Reinwald Switzerland
Small intermediate area south of Chur.
1485m; slopes 1455–2215m
⛷ 6 ✠ 30km

Sportgastein 104
Remote, high ski area at the top of the Badgastein valley.

Squaw Valley 543

Stafal 412
Isolated village with access to the Monterosa Ski area.

St Andra Austria
Valley-junction village ideally placed for one of the longest, most snow-sure cross-country networks in Europe. Close to the Tauern pass and to St Michael.
1045m

St Anton 179

Starhill Resort South Korea
Purpose-built resort formerly called Cheonmasan, 30km north-east of Seoul. ⛷ 8

Stari Vrh Slovenia
About 30 minutes from Ljubljana airport. Runs include a never-groomed black, three interesting reds and a winding blue virtually from top to bottom.
slopes 580–1200m
⛷ 5 ⛷ 12km

Stary Smokovec Slovakia
Spa town in the High Tatras mountains, with three small areas – Tatransky Lomica is the biggest. Funicular railway and snowmaking facilities.
1480m; slopes 1000–1500m
⛷ 8 ⛷ 4km

St Cergue Switzerland
Limited resort in the Jura mountains, less than an hour from Geneva and good for families with young children.
1045m; slopes 1045–1680m
⛷ 16 ⛷ 21km

St Christoph 179
Small village on Arlberg pass above St Anton.

St-Colomban-des-Villards France
Small resort in next side valley to La Toussuire. Series of drags link to the rest of the area, with a pretty run to return.
1100m

Steamboat USA
A few miles from the old cattle town of Steamboat Springs, and famed for its powder snow. Huge investment continues to equip the slope-side base with modern lodging, shops and restaurants. The slopes are compact but varied, with pretty treelined runs rising to 3220m; many of them are ideal for novices. Fast chairs serve each area. The main attraction for experts is the glades, but also the steep chutes and bowls on the backside of the area. Much of the mountain is ideal cruising terrain, although there is limited vertical to be achieved. The nursery slopes at the base are excellent, revamped recently. And family facilities are splendid.

Steamboat town has countless hotels, condos and restaurants.
2105m; slopes 2105–3220m
⛷ 18 ⛷ 2965 acres
📖 *Alpine Answers, American Ski Classics, Crystal, Crystal Finest, Momentum, Ski Independence, Ski Safari, Skitracer, Skiworld, Supertravel, Thomson*

Ste-Foy-Tarentaise 334

Steinach Austria
Pleasant market town with small area of slopes in picturesque surroundings, just off the autobahn up to the Brenner Pass, south of Innsbruck.
1050m; slopes 1050–2200m
⛷ 6 ⛷ 25km

Stevens Pass USA
A day trip from Seattle, and accommodation 60km away in Bavarian-style town Leavenworth. Mostly intermediate slopes, with long expert runs on backside. Busy at weekends Jan to March.
1235m; slopes 1235–1785m
⛷ 14 ⛷ 1125 acres

St-François-Longchamp France
Sunny, gentle slopes, with a couple of harder runs. Linked to Valmorel.
1400m
📖 *Erna Low, Lagrange, Peak Retreats*

St Gallenkirch Austria
Village in the Montafon strung along the main road and spoiled by traffic. A gondola goes up to Valisera on the west ridge of the Nova ski area (see Gaschurn) and a blue run comes back down to the gondola base. From the 2011/12 season a new gondola from the same area as the old one goes up the opposite side of the valley to Grasjoch on the Hochjoch ski area – but there is no piste back. Hochjoch is a fair-sized area of easy blue runs, with occasional red alternatives. Apart from the new gondola and one eight-pack, the lifts are slow chairs and drags. The blue/red run from Kreuzjoch down to Schruns is a notable 12km long and 1700m vertical (and includes a section through the longest ski tunnel in the world – 473m). Snowmaking covers almost half the runs.
900m

St-Gervais 267
Small town sharing its ski area with Megève.

St Jakob am Arlberg Austria
Quiet St Anton village, beyond Nasserein. Depends on shuttle-bus to the slopes.
1295m

St Jakob in Defereggen Austria
Unspoiled traditional village in a pretty, sunny valley close to Lienz and Heiligenblut, and with a good proportion of high-altitude slopes.
1400m; slopes 1400–2525m
⛷ 7 ⛷ 52km

St Jakob in Haus Austria
Snowy village with its own slopes (Buchensteinwand). Fieberbrunn, Waidring, St Johann are nearby.
855m; slopes 855–1500m
⛷ 8 ⛷ 19km
📖 *Inntravel*

St-Jean-d'Arves France
Small, scattered community with 'friendly locals', set in the Sybelles area. The original old village, with the usual ancient church, is set across the valley from the slopes, which are at the mid-mountain hamlet of La Chal. Here, where a tasteful development of chalet-style buildings has been expanding, there are nursery slopes and the lift link to and piste back from Le Corbier. Not the best base to exploit the whole area, given the slow chair to Le Corbier, but a bus goes to St-Sorlin-d'Arves.
1550m
📖 *Erna Low, Peak Retreats, Ski France*

St Jean d'Aulps France
Small village in Portes du Soleil area, not part of main circuit but with its own interesting slopes consisting of two small areas – Domaine Chèvrerie and Domaine Grande Terche. 'A little gem,' says a 2014 visitor.

St-Jean-de-Sixt France
Traditional hamlet, a cheap base for La Clusaz and Le Grand-Bornand (3km to both).
960m

St-Jean-Montclar France
Small village at the foot of thickly forested slopes. Good day out from nearby Pra-Loup.
1300m; slopes 1300–2500m
⛷ 18 ⛷ 50km
📖 *Zenith*

St Johann im Pongau Austria
Bustling, lively working town with its own small area. An extensive three-valley lift network starts 4km away at Alpendorf, linking via Wagrain to Flachau – all part of the Salzburger Sportwelt ski pass area.
650m; slopes 800–2185m
⛷ 64 ⛷ 200km

St Johann in Tirol Austria
Friendly valley town, an attractive place for beginners and leisurely part-timers – keen piste-bashers will ski all the local slopes in a day and need to go on to explore nearby resorts covered by the Kitzbüheler Alpenskipass as well. There is nothing here to challenge an expert. The main access lift is a 10-minute walk from the centre. It gets more snow than neighbouring Kitzbühel and the SkiWelt, and also has substantial snowmaking. Given good snow, St Johann is one of the best cross-country resorts in Austria – trails total 275km. 'Some horrid slow lifts, but great for a day out from Kitzbuhel – and it's included in the All Star pass,' says a 2014 visitor.
650m; slopes 660–1605m
⛷ 17 ⛷ 43km
📖 *Crystal, Crystal Finest, Inghams, Snowscape, STC, Thomson*

St Lary Espiaube 315
Satellite of St-Lary-Soulan in the Pyrenees.

St-Lary-Soulan 315

St Leonhard in Pitztal Austria
Village beneath a fine glacier in the Oetz area, accessed by underground funicular.
1250m; slopes 880–3440m
⛷ 12 ⛷ 68km

St Luc 495
Village in the Val d'Anniviers.

St Margarethen Austria
Valley village near Styria/Carinthia border, sharing slopes with higher Katschberg.
1065m; slopes 1065–2210m
⛷ 16 ⛷ 70km

St Martin bei Lofer Austria
Traditional cross-country village in a lovely setting beneath the impressive Loferer Steinberge massif. Alpine slopes at Lofer.
635m; slopes 640–1745m
⛷ 10 ⛷ 46km

St-Martin-de-Belleville 337

St Martin in Tennengebirge Austria
Highest village in the Dachstein-West region near Salzburg. It has limited slopes of its own but nearby Annaberg has an interesting area.
1000m; slopes 1000–1350m
⛷ 4 ⛷ 5km

St-Maurice-sur-Moselle France
One of several areas near Strasbourg. No snowmakers.
550m; slopes 900–1250m
⛷ 8 ⛷ 24km

St Michael im Lungau Austria
Quiet, unspoiled village in the Tauern pass snowpocket with an uncrowded but disjointed intermediate area. Close to Obertauern and Wagrain.
1075m; slopes 1065–2220m
⛷ 16 ⛷ 70km

St Moritz 488

St-Nicolas-de-Véroce 267
Small hamlet in the Megève network.

St-Nicolas-la-Chapelle France
Small village close to larger Flumet, in the Val d'Arly.
1000m; slopes 1000–1600m
⬒ 10 ⟟ 40km

St-Nizier-du-Moucherotte France
Unspoiled, inexpensive resort just west of Grenoble with no lifts of its own. Villard-de-Lans is the main resort.

Stoneham Canada
The closest resort to Québec City, around 20 minutes away. It also has its own small base 'village', with condo accommodation and an impressive lodge that has its own lively après-ski bar, restaurant and spas. But night owls should probably head for the city as the evenings are generally quiet in resort. Like most resorts in this region, the ski area is small. The slopes spread across three linked peaks, with mainly sheltered intermediate and beginner pistes. It suits families well and has a special nursery area equipped with a moving carpet. A key attraction is the resort's four terrain parks and half-pipe, regularly revamped and chosen to host the 2013 Snowboard World Championships.
210m; slopes 210–630m
⬒ 7 ⟟ 333 acres
⬛ Frontier, Ski Safari

Stoos Switzerland
Small, unspoiled village an hour from Zürich. Weekend crowds. Splendid views of Lake Lucerne.
1300m; slopes 500–1935m
⬒ 7 ⟟ 35km

Storlien Sweden
Small family resort amid magnificent wilderness scenery, one hour from Trondheim, 30 minutes from Åre.
600m; slopes 600–790m
⬒ 7 ⟟ 16km

Stowe 598

St-Pierre-de-Chartreuse France
Locals' weekend place near Grenoble. Unreliable snow.
900m; slopes 900–1800m
⬒ 14 ⟟ 35km

Stratton USA
Something like the classic Alpine arrangement of a village at the foot of the lifts: a smart, modern development with a car-free shopping street. The slopes are mostly easy and intermediate, with some blacks and some short double-black pitches, spread widely around the flanks of a single peak, served by modern lifts. Stratton calls

itself the 'snowboarding capital of the east', with no fewer than five terrain parks. The Suntanner Park has a super-pipe.
570m; slopes 570–1180m
⬒ 14 ⟟ 660 acres

Strobl Austria
Close to St Wolfgang in a beautiful lakeside setting. There are slopes at nearby St Gilgen and Postalm.
545m; slopes 545–1510m
⬒ 7 ⟟ 12km

St-Sorlin-d'Arves France
A refreshing contrast to the stark, functional resorts of Le Corbier and La Toussuire, with which it shares the extensive Les Sybelles ski area. And the resort accesses some of the most interesting slopes. The village is a picturesque collection of traditional buildings, alongside a more modern development that spreads out along the main road and has attracted some major tour operators. The local slopes form the biggest single sector of the linked network, with lifts serving two distinct mountains. Some of the most varied slopes in the whole area are here, and reached by fast quads to Les Perrons – which also has some of the best off-piste opportunities. There are leisurely cruising runs on La Balme. *1600m*
⬛ Erna Low, Lagrange, Peak Retreats, Ski Club Freshtracks, Ski France

St Stephan Switzerland
Unspoiled old farming village at the foot of the largest sector of slopes in the area around Gstaad.
1000m; slopes 950–3000m
⬒ 58 ⟟ 250km

Stubai valley 188

Stuben 179
Small, unspoiled village linked to St Anton.

St Veit im Pongau Austria
Spa resort with limited slopes at Goldegg; Wagrain (Salzburger Sportwelt) and Grossarl (Gastein valley) are nearby.
765m ⬒ 4 ⟟ 12km

St-Veran France
Said to be the highest 'real' village in Europe, and full of charm. Close to Serre-Chevalier and the Milky Way. Snow-reliable cross-country skiing.
2040m; slopes 2040–2800m
⬒ 15 ⟟ 30km

St Wolfgang Austria
Charming lakeside resort near Salzburg, some way from any slopes, best for a relaxing winter holiday with one or two days on the slopes.
540m; slopes 665–1350m
⬒ 9 ⟟ 17km
⬛ Crystal, Crystal Finest, STC, Thomson

Sugar Bowl USA
Exposed area north of Lake Tahoe with highest snowfall in California, best for experts. Lodging in Truckee but Squaw Valley nearby.
2100m; slopes 2100–2555m
⬒ 8 ⟟ 1500 acres

Sugarbush USA
Dynamic resort in upper Vermont, with two mountains linked by fast chair, and something resembling a village at the foot of one of them. Good range of runs, including some real challenges.
480m; slopes 450–1245m
⬒ 16 ⟟ 508 acres
⬛ Ski Safari

Sugarloaf USA
Developing Maine resort, 5 hours from Boston, with the Eastern US's best open terrain.
430m; slopes 405–1290m
⬒ 15 ⟟ 1410 acres
⬛ American Ski Classics, Ski Safari

Sulden Italy
The other side of the Stelvio Pass from Bormio. Very long airport transfers. Solda is its Italian name.
1905m; slopes 1905–2625m
⬒ 10 ⟟ 40km

Summit at Snoqualmie USA
Four areas – Summit East, Summit Central, Summit West and Alpental – with interlinked lifts. Damp weather and wet snow are major drawbacks.
slopes 915–1645m
⬒ 24 ⟟ 2000 acres

Sun Alpina Japan
Collective name for three ski areas four hours away from Tokyo. ⬒ 21

Sundance USA
Robert Redford-owned, tastefully designed family resort set amid trees in snow-sure Utah. It's a small, narrow mountain but the vertical is respectable, the setting is spectacular and there is terrain to suit all abilities. The lower mountain is easy-intermediate, the upper part steeper. There are 17km of cross-country trails, of varying difficulty.
1860m; slopes 1860–2515m
⬒ 4 ⟟ 450 acres

Sunday River USA
One of the more attractive resorts in the East, four hours from Boston, best for

intermediate cruisers. The slopes spread across eight peaks, but it's a small area. Only four of the chairs are fast quads but queues are not a problem – midweek, the resort is very quiet. Cross-country is big around here.
245m; slopes 245–955m
⬒ 16 ⟟ 820 acres
⬛ American Ski Classics, Ski Independence, Ski Safari

Sunlight Mountain Resort USA
Quiet, small area 10 miles south of Glenwood Springs. Varied terrain with some serious glades.
2405m; slopes 2405–3015m
⬒ 3 ⟟ 470 acres

Sun Peaks 629

Sunrise Park USA
Arizona's largest area, operated by Apaches. Slopes are spread over three mountains; best for novices and leisurely intermediates.
2805m; slopes 2805–3500m
⬒ 12 ⟟ 800 acres

Sunshine Village 603
One-hotel mountain station in Banff's ski area.

Sun Valley 587
Purpose-built resort in Idaho.
1750m; slopes 1750–2790m
⬒ 17 ⟟ 2054 acres

Suomu Finland
A lodge (no village) right on the Arctic Circle with a few slopes but mostly a ski-touring place.
140m; slopes 140–410m ⬒ 3

Superbagnères France
Little more than a particularly French-dominated Club Med; best for a low-cost, low-effort family trip to the Pyrenees. Said to have good off-piste if the snow is good.
1880m; slopes 1440–2260m
⬒ 16 ⟟ 35km
⬛ Lagrange

Super-Besse France
Purpose-built resort amid spectacular extinct-volcano scenery. Shares area with the spa town of Mont-Dore. Limited village.
1350m; slopes 1300–1850m
⬒ 22 ⟟ 43km
⬛ Lagrange

Superdévoluy France
Purpose-built but friendly family resort in a remote spot near Gap, with huge apartment blocks plus traditional chalets. Sizeable intermediate area shared with more appealing La Joue-du-Loup.
1450m; slopes 1450–2450m
⬒ 22 ⟟ 100km
⬛ Erna Low, Ski France

Build your own shortlist: www.wheretoskiandsnowboard.com

Super Espot Spain
Small area on the eastern
edge of the Aigues Tortes
National Park, close to the
valley town of Sort.
slopes 1500–2500m
⛷ 8 ⛷ 28km

Supermolina Spain
Dreary, purpose-built satellite
of Pyrenean resort of La
Molina, with a reasonable
sized area of its own and
linked to the slopes of
Masella to form an area called
Alp 2500.
1700m; slopes 1600–2535m
⛷ 31 ⛷ 121km

Les Sybelles France
A group of linked ski resorts
in the Maurienne massif,
forming an impressively large
network.
slopes 1100–2620m
⛷ 72 ⛷ 310km

Tahko Finland
Largest resort in southern
Finland. Plenty of intermediate
slopes in an attractive,
wooded, frozen-lake setting.
⛷ 9

Tahoe City USA
Small lakeside
accommodation base for
visiting nearby Alpine
Meadows and Squaw Valley.

Talisman Mountain Resort
Canada
One of the best areas in the
Toronto region, but with a
relatively low lift capacity.
100% snowmaking.
235m; slopes 235–420m ⛷ 8

Tamsweg Austria
Large cross-country village
with rail links in snowy region
close to Tauern Pass and St
Michael. *1025m*

La Tania 340

Taos 587
Isolated resort in New Mexico.
2805m; slopes 2805–3600m
⛷ 14 ⛷ 1294 acres

Tärnaby-Hemavan Sweden
Twin resorts in north Sweden,
offering downhill, cross-
country and heliskiing. Own
airport.
slopes 465–1135m
⛷ 13 ⛷ 44km

El Tarter 92
Relatively quiet, convenient
alternative to Soldeu.

Tarvisio Italy
Interesting, animated old
town bordering Austria and
Slovenia. A major cross-
country base with fairly
limited Alpine slopes.
750m; slopes 750–1860m
⛷ 12 ⛷ 15km

Täsch 518
The final road base on the
way to car-free Zermatt.

Tatranská Lomnica Slovakia
Second largest resort in
Slovakia, set in the High
Tatras mountains.
890m; slopes 890–2635m
⛷ 7 ⛷ 11km

Tauplitz Austria
Traditional village at the foot
of an interestingly varied area
north of Schladming. Few
queues and decent lift
system, including some fast
chairs.
900m; slopes 900–2000m
⛷ 18 ⛷ 40km

Telluride USA
An isolated resort in south-
west Colorado, but a
beautifully renovated old
mining town with great Wild
West charm and fairly
dramatic mountain scenery.
It's a friendly, small-scale
resort, with a smartly
developing slope-side base
above it. Both have lifts into
the ski area. Mountain Village
has new luxury hotels and spa
facilities. The slopes are
limited in overall extent, but
quite varied and with recently
expanded expert terrain. Most
runs are below the treeline,
but the top lifts and bowls
give great views. Queues are
rarely a problem. Experts have
some truly challenging terrain
to play such as the Gold Hill
Chutes, while there are
splendid blue and greens runs
for intermediates and
beginners too – but it's not a
resort for keen piste bashers.
There are three terrain parks.
Nightlife revolves around the
bars.
2665m; slopes 2660–3830m
⛷ 18 ⛷ 2000 acres
📧 *Alpine Answers, American
Ski Classics, Elegant Resorts,
Momentum, Ski Safari, Skiworld*

Temù Italy
Sheltered hamlet near Passo
Tonale. Worth a visit in bad
weather.
1155m; slopes 1155–1955m
⛷ 4 ⛷ 5km

Tengendai Japan
Tiny area three hours by train
and bus from Tokyo. One of
Japan's best snow records,
including occasional powder.
920m; slopes 920–1820m ⛷ 4

Termas de Chillán Chile
Ski and spa resort 400km
south of Santiago. Base
village has lodgings or you
can stay at Las Trancas a few
minutes' drive away.
1650m; slopes 1600–2700m
⛷ 9 ⛷ 35km
📧 *Momentum*

Termignon 355
Rustic village 6km from
Lanslebourg and the linked
slopes of Val Cenis.

Terminillo Italy
Purpose-built resort 100km
from Rome with a worthwhile
area when its lower runs have
snow-cover.
1500m; slopes 1500–2210m
⛷ 15 ⛷ 40km

Teton Village 593

Thollon-les-Mémises France
Attractive base for a relaxed
holiday. Own little area and
close to Portes du Soleil.
1000m; slopes 1600–2000m
⛷ 19 ⛷ 50km

Thredbo Australia
Oz's best, 6 hours from
Sydney; has
uncharacteristically long (and,
in places, testing) runs,
snowmaking, lots of
accommodation and active
nightlife.
1365m; slopes 1365–2035m
⛷ 14 ⛷ 480 acres

Three Valleys 344

La Thuile 442

Thyon 2000 499
Mid-mountain resort above
Veysonnaz in the Verbier area.

Tignes 346

**Timberline (Palmer
Snowfield)** USA
Fair-sized area of largely
intermediate slopes served by
six lifts including four fast
quads on Mt Hood in Oregon.
1800m; slopes 1510–2600m
⛷ 6 ⛷ 1430 acres

Toblach Italy
Small resort in South Tyrol.
Dobbiaco is its Italian name.
1250m; slopes 1250–1610m
⛷ 5 ⛷ 15km

Togari Japan
One of several areas close to
the 1998 Olympic site.
Nagano, 2hr30 from Tokyo.
slopes 400–1050m ⛷ 9

Torgnon Italy
Small village off the road up
to Cervinia, good for bad-
weather days. Some good
cross-country loops.
1500m; slopes 1500–1965m
⛷ 7 ⛷ 6km

Torgon Switzerland
Old village in a pretty wooded
setting, with a connection to
the Portes du Soleil. Still
some steep draglifts.
1150m; slopes 950–2300m
⛷ 197 ⛷ 650km

Le Tour 225
Charming hamlet at the head
of the Chamonix valley.

La Toussuire France
Highest and most central of
the Sybelles resorts, and
convenient base for exploring
the whole area. The centre
has fairly dreary buildings, of
apartments and hotels
spreading widely into the car-
free centre. But the local
slopes have three of the
seven fast chairs in the area,

so access to Pte de L'Ouillon
and the rest of the linked
network is fairly quick. Two
drags were installed in 2009
to reduce queues here too.
Above the resort is a wide
bowl with drags and chairs all
around. Locally, the pistes are
short cruisers with few
challenges – but judged by a
reporter as the most varied
and snow-sure in the area. A
splendid longer run goes to
Les Bottières. There are gentle
nursery slopes and good,
easy progression runs. Eating
out is relatively inexpensive
for France, but nightlife is
dull. *1700m*
📧 *Erna Low, Lagrange, Peak
Retreats, PowderBeds, STC*

LAGRANGE
Prestige

High-standard
Self-catering
Apartments

020 7371 6111
lagrange-holidays.co.uk

Trafoi Italy
Quiet, traditional village in the
Val Venosta in the South Tyrol
covered by the Ortler Skiarena
pass.
1570m; slopes 1570–2550m
⛷ 4 ⛷ 10km

Treble Cone New Zealand
Plenty of good skiing opened
up by two main lifts. Varied
open terrain suitable for all
levels. Great powder bowls.
Nearly 2 hours from
Queenstown.
1260m; slopes 1260–1960m
⛷ 4 ⛷ 550 hectares

Tremblant 640

Trentino Italy
Fabulously scenic area of the
Dolomites, with a great many
small ski areas that you won't
have heard of, as well as a
few large ones that are better
known – Madonna di
Campiglio chief among them.

Troodos Cyprus
Ski area on Mt Olympus, a
70-minute drive from Nicosia.
Pretty, wooded slopes and
fine views.
slopes 1730–1950m
⛷ 4 ⛷ 5km

Tröpolach Austria
Small village at base of access
gondola for Nassfeld ski area.
610m; slopes 610–2195m
⛷ 30 ⛷ 110km

Trysil Norway
Extensive area, some distance
from the town, spread around
the conical Trysilfjellet, with

some good, long runs of up to 4km. On the border with Sweden.
350m; slopes 350–1100m ▣ 24
▣ Absolutely Snow, Ski Safari, Zenith

Tryvann Norway
Small area close to Oslo and popular with ocals. Vertical of 380m – are served by two drags and two chairs, one of them fast. ▣ 6

Tschagguns Austria
Village the Montafon valley – effectively a suburb of Schruns.
700m; slopes 700–2100m
▣ 13 ⟡ 32km

Tsugaike Kogen Japan
Sizeable resort four hours from Tokyo, three hours from Osaka. Helicopter service to the top station.
800m; slopes 800–1700m ▣ 26

Tulfes Austria
Hamlet on mountain shelf close to Innsbruck, with small main area above the trees and long runs back to base.
920m; slopes 920–2305m
▣ 7 ⟡ 22km

Turoa New Zealand
On the south-western slopes of Mt Ruapeha, with NZ's biggest vertical. Shares lift pass with Whakapapa. Mix of open, gentle and steeper runs. Good scope for off-piste.
slopes 1600–2320m
▣ 23 ⟡ 2590 acres

Turracherhöhe Austria
Tiny, unspoiled resort on a mountain shelf, with varied intermediate slopes above and below it. A good outing from Bad Kleinkirchheim.
1765m; slopes 1400–2205m
▣ 14 ⟡ 38km

Tyax Mountain Ski Resort Canada
Heli-skiing operation in the Chilcotin mountains – transfers from Whistler or Vancouver.

La Tzoumaz 499
Hamlet in Verbier's ski area.

Uludag Turkey
Surprisingly suave, laid-back, well-equipped, purpose-built resort near Bursa, south of Istanbul.
1750m; slopes 1750–2322m
▣ 14 ⟡ 15km

Unken Austria
Traditional village hidden in a side valley. Closest slopes to Salzburg.
565m; slopes 1000–1500m
▣ 4 ⟡ 8km

Untergurgl 148
Valley-floor alternative to staying in Obergurgl.

Unternberg Austria
Riverside village with trail connecting into one of the longest, most snow-sure

cross-country networks in Europe. St Margarethen slopes close by.
1030m

Unterwasser-Toggenburg Switzerland
Old but not especially attractive resort 90 minutes from Zürich. Fabulous lake and mountain views. The more challenging half of the Toggenburg area shared with Wildhaus.
910m; slopes 900–2260m
▣ 17 ⟡ 60km

Uttendorf-Weiss-See Austria
Astute alternative to crowded Kaprun when the snowline is high.
805m; slopes 1485–2600m
▣ 8 ⟡ 23km

Vail 562
Convenient but ordinary village sharing large intermediate Lenzerheide area.
1540m; slopes 1230–2865m
▣ 35 ⟡ 155km

Valberg France
Large Alpes-Maritimes resort (bigger than better-known Isola 2000) close to Nice.
1650m; slopes 1430–2100m
▣ 26 ⟡ 90km

Val Cenis Vanoise 355

Val d'Anniviers 495

Val di Fassa 425
Valley area of Campitello and Canazei – part of the Sella Ronda circuit.

Val d'Illiez 456
Peaceful, unspoiled village near Champéry.

Val d'Isère 358

Val Ferret Switzerland
Old climbing village near Martigny, with spectacular views. Own tiny area.
1600m
▣ 3 ⟡ 20km

Valfréjus France
Small and unusual modern resort on a narrow, shady shelf in the Maurienne valley – built in the woods, with the slopes higher up above the treeline. The focus is Plateau d'Arrondaz, a steep, open slopes above, offering genuine bumpy blacks with excellent snow (snowmaking on the lower runs is urgently required, though). There's a natural terrain park, and good off-piste is available above the main plateau. The nursery slopes are at mid-mountain and village levels. Recent investment in new lifts.
1550m; slopes 1550–2740m
▣ 9 ⟡ 65km
▣ Erna Low, Lagrange, PowderBeds

Val Gardena 433
Valley area of Selva, Ortisei and Santa Cristina.

Valgrisenche Italy
Small, peaceful village on the southern side of the Aosta valley. Established heli-ski centre – about 20 drop points on the local peaks. A couple of intermediate runs, nursery area and a few cross-country loops.
1665m
▣ 4 ⟡ 12km

Vallandry 208
Satellite of Les Arcs.

Valle Nevado Chile
Developing purpose-built resort 46km east of Santiago. Varied, intermediate terrain.
3025m; slopes 2860–3670m
▣ 14 ⟡ 2225 acres
▣ Momentum

Valloire France
A compelling combination of an old mountain village with extensive slopes, branded as Galibier Thabor, and shared with the more modern two-part resort of Valmeinier. The village is the best known of the Maurienne valley resorts and retains a quiet, rustic charm of narrow streets, shops and restaurants set around a lively market square. The slopes spread widely across three sunny sectors, served by two gondolas out of the village, and are particularly good for intermediates wanting lots of gentle cruising and a sense of travel. Experts will find the challenges limited, although there is some decent off-piste opportunity towards Valmeinier.
1430m; slopes 1430–2600m
▣ 31 ⟡ 150km
▣ Crystal, Erna Low, Lagrange, Peak Retreats, Pierre & Vacances, PowderBeds, Ski France, Thomson, Zenith

Vallorcine 225
Backwater on road between Chamonix and Switzerland.

Vallter 2000 Spain
Small resort on the far eastern fringes of the Pyrenees, close to the Costa Brava.
slopes 1960–2535m
▣ 10 ⟡ 420 acres

Valmeinier France
Quiet, old mountain village with a modern purpose-built satellite where most people stay. Shares with Valloire most extensive slopes in the Maurienne region, spreading widely over three mostly sunny sectors.
1500-1800m; slopes 1430–2600m
▣ 31 ⟡ 150km
▣ Erna Low, Lagrange, Pierre & Vacances, PowderBeds, Ski France, Snowcoach

Valmorel France
The main resort in the Grand Domaine ski area, sharing slopes with St-François and Longchamp. The purpose-built village is prettily designed with a traffic-free centre, though lodging is broadly scattered among six 'hamlets' – mainly of simple hotels or apartments. The slopes offer a fair-sized area of varied skiing, with runs criss-crossing a number of minor valleys. Most are blue runs. Fast chairs serve the key links, but there are lots of slow drags. So, queues can be evident at peak times. The area appeals mainly to intermediates, and beginners. Few slopes are challenging, and there are good gentle greens for progression. Children are well catered for too. Nightlife is generally quiet and there is little off-slope diversion, although the slope-side cafe-bars are 'jolly'. 'Very friendly and I liked the short transfer time,' says a 2014 visitor.
1400m; slopes 1250–2550m
▣ 50 ⟡ 165km
▣ Alpine Answers, Club Med, Crystal, Erna Low, Inghams, Interactive Resorts, Lagrange, Peak Retreats, Pierre & Vacances, PowderBeds, Ski Line, Ski Supreme, Skitracer, Thomson, Zenith

Val Senales Italy
Top-of-the-mountain hotel, the highest in the Alps, in the Dolomites near Merano.
3210m; slopes 2110–3210m
▣ 12 ⟡ 35km

Val Thorens 368

Valtournenche 387
Cheaper alternative to Cervinia.

Vandans Austria
Sizeable working village well placed for visiting all the Montafon areas. A gondola goes up directly from here into the Golm area.
655m

Vars / Risoul 375

Vasilitsa Greece
Resort in northern Greece, in the Pindos range, offering intermediate skiing.
1780m ▣ 8

Vaujany 198
Tiny village in the heart of Alpe-d'Huez ski area.

Las Vegas Ski Resort USA
Tiny area formerly known as Lee Canyon, cut from forest 50 minutes' drive north-west of Las Vegas.
2595m; slopes 2595–2855m
▣ 4 ⟡ 200 acres

Velka–Raca Slovakia
Small resort near Oscadnica, with a modern lift system, including a 'chondola'.
630m; slopes 630–1050m
🚟 6 🚠 14km

Vemdalen Sweden
Twin areas of Björnrike and Vemdalsskalet (same pass) 20 minutes apart. 385m vertical.
🚟 18 🚠 28km

Vemdalsskalet Sweden
20 minutes from Björnrike (same pass). 385m vertical. Said to have hottest après-ski in Sweden.
🚟 18 🚠 28km

Venosc France
Captivating tiny village of cobbled streets, ancient church and craft shops with fast gondola to Les Deux-Alpes.
▨ *Peak Retreats*

Vent Austria
High, remote Oztal village known mainly as a touring base, with just enough lift-served skiing to warrant a day trip from nearby Obergurgl.
1900m; slopes 1900–2680m
🚟 4 🚠 15km

Ventron France
Small village near La Bresse in the northerly Vosges mountains near Strasbourg, with more ski de fond than downhill terrain.
630m; slopes 900–1110m
🚟 8 🚠 15km

Verbier 499

Vercorin 495
Cluster of chalets in the Val d'Anniviers.

Verditz Austria
One of several small, mostly mountain-top areas overlooking the town of Villach.
675m; slopes 675–2165m
🚟 5 🚠 15km

Vex Switzerland
Major village in unspoiled, attractive setting south of Sion. Verbier slopes accessed nearby at Mayens-de-l'Ours.
900m

Veysonnaz 499
Little old village within Verbier's Four Valleys network.

Vichères–Liddes Switzerland
Small area in Ski St-Bernard area near Verbier that is popular with families. Good off-piste down to near La Fouly to be explored with a guide.
1350m; slopes 1600–2270m
🚟 4 🚠 15km

Vic-sur-Cère France
Charming village with fine architecture, beneath Super-Lioran ski area. Beautiful extinct-volcano scenery.
680m; slopes 1250–1850m
🚟 24 🚠 60km ▨ *Lagrange*

Viehhofen Austria
Cheaper place to stay when visiting Saalbach. 3km from the Schönleiten gondola, there's a run back to the village from the Asitz section.
860m 🚟 1

Vigla-Pisoderi Greece
The longest run in Greece (over 2km), in an unspoiled setting 18km from the town of Florina in the north.
1600m 🚟 5

Vigo di Fassa Italy
Best base for the Fassa valley, with Sella Ronda access via nearby Campitello.
1390m; slopes 1390–2060m
🚟 6 🚠 16km

La Villa 425
Quiet Sella Ronda village.

Villabassa Italy
Cross-country village in South Tyrol. Niederdorf is its German name.

Villach-Dobratsch Austria
One of several small, mostly mountain-top areas overlooking the town of Villach.
900m; slopes 980–2165m
🚟 8 🚠 15km

Villar-d'Arêne France
Tiny area on main road between La Grave and Serre-Chevalier. Empty, immaculately groomed, short easy runs, plus a couple of hotels.
1650m

Villard-de-Lans France
Unspoiled, lively, traditional village west of Grenoble. Snow-sure, thanks to snowmaking.
1050m; slopes 1145–2170m
🚟 25 🚠 125km

Villard-Reculas 198
Rustic village on periphery of Alpe-d'Huez ski area.

Villaroger 208
Rustic hamlet with direct links up to Arc 2000.

Villars 510

Villeneuve 325
One of the villages making up the resort of Serre-Chevalier.

Vipiteno Italy
Bargain-shopping town close to Brenner Pass.
960m; slopes 960–2100m
🚟 12 🚠 25km

Virgen Austria
Traditional village in a beautiful valley south of the Felbertauern tunnel. Slopes at Matrei.
1200m; slopes 975–2620m
🚟 15 🚠 110km

Vitosha Bulgaria
Limited area of slopes and a few widely scattered hotels, 22km from Sofia, leading to

crowds at weekends. The slopes are north-facing and have a decent snow record.
1810m; slopes 1515–2290m
🚟 12 🚠 29km

Vogel 652

Vorderlanersbach 113
Village with access to Mayrhofen's ski area.

Voss Norway
Well-equipped winter sports resort attractively set on a lake, with relatively limited Alpine slopes.
60m; slopes 150–945m
🚟 10 🚠 40km ▨ *Ski Safari*

Vuokatti Finland
Small mountain in a remarkable setting, surrounded on three sides by lots of little lakes. Good activity base. 🚟 8

Wagrain Austria
A towny little resort at the centre of a lift system that is typical of many in Salzburgerland – spreading widely across several low, partly wooded ridges. Flachau and Alpendorf/St Johann are at its extremities, and all these resorts are covered by Salzburger Sportwelt lift pass that our figures relate to. It's pleasant without being notably charming, and though it's a compact place the main lift bases are still a good walk apart. The slopes – wooded at the bottom, open higher up – are practically all easy/intermediate stuff, but cover a huge area almost 15km across. The lift system is impressive, with a lot of fast chairs and gondolas. Despite the altitude, most of the upper slopes are fairly open. Some get too much sun for comfort, and snow reliability is not a strong point.
850m; slopes 850–2000m
🚟 18 🚠 160 hectares ▨ *STC*

Waidring Austria
Quiet valley village north of Kitzbühel. Mainly gentle open and north-facing slopes, also accessible from Germany. Impressive lift system, but still prone to weekend queues.
780m; slopes 1230–1860m
🚟 10 🚠 35km

Waiorau Snow Farm New Zealand
Specialist cross-country base just over an hour from Queenstown. Spectacular views. Overnight huts.
1500m

Wald im Pinzgau Austria
Cross-country village surrounded by Alpine areas – Gerlos, Krimml and Neukirchen – and with Pass Thurn also nearby.
885m
🚟 50 🚠 160km

Wanaka New Zealand
Quiet, diffuse village in beautiful lakeside mountain setting close to four ski areas; the nearest is Treble Cone.

Warth 133
Bregenzerwald village near Lech.

Waterville Valley USA
Compact New Hampshire area with runs dropping either side of a broad, gentle ridge rising 615m above the lift base. A couple of short but genuine double-black-diamond mogul fields, but most of the slopes are intermediate. The village is a Disneyesque affair a couple of miles away down on the flat valley bottom.
600m; slopes 600–1215m
🚟 12 🚠 255 acres

Watles Italy
Village in the Val Venosta in the South Tyrol covered by the Ortler Skiarena pass.
🚟 3 🚠 18km

Weinebene Austria
One of many gentle little areas in Austria's easternmost ski region near the Slovenian border. No major resorts in the vicinity.
1580m; slopes 1560–1835m
🚟 7 🚠 22km

Weissbach bei Lofer Austria
Traditional resort between Lofer and Saalfelden. No slopes of its own, but it's well placed for touring the Tirol. Kitzbühel, Saalbach, St Johann and Zell am See are nearby.
665m

Weissensee Naggeralm Austria
Little area in eastern Austria and the location of Europe's largest frozen lake, which is used for all kinds of ice sports, including ice-golf.
930m; slopes 930–1400m
🚟 5 🚠 6km

Weisspriach Austria
Hamlet on snowy pass near Obertauern that shares its area with Mauterndorf and St Michael.
1115m; slopes 1115–2050m
🚟 13 🚠 47km

Wengen 513

Wentworth Canada
Long-established Nova Scotia area with largest accessible acreage in the Maritime Provinces. Harsh climate ensures good snow-cover despite low altitude.
55m; slopes 55–300m
🚟 6 🚠 150 acres

Werfen Austria
Traditional village spoiled by the Tauern autobahn, which runs between it and the slopes. Good touring to the Dachstein West region. *620m*

Werfenweng Austria
Hamlet with the advantage over the main village of Werfen of being away from the autobahn and close to the slopes. Best for novices.
1000m; slopes 1000–1835m
♦ 9 ↑ 25km
🚠 *Crystal, Thomson*

Westendorf 172
Friendly family resort with modest area of gentle skiing; part of the SkiWelt.

Whakapapa/Turoa
New Zealand
NZ's largest area, on a volcano close to Turoa with similarly superb views and shared pass. The Grand Chateau is a lovely old hotel in the tiny village 6km away.
1630m; slopes 1630–2320m
♦ 23 ↑ 2590 acres

Whistler 631

Whitecap Mountains Resort
USA
Largest, snowiest area in Wisconsin, close enough to Lake Superior and Minneapolis to ensure winds and weekend crowds.
435m; slopes 435–555m
♦ 7 ↑ 500 acres

Whiteface Mountain USA
Varied area in New York State 15km from attractive lakeside resort of Lake Placid. 93% snowmaking ensures good snow-cover. Plenty to do off the slopes.
365m; slopes 365–1345m
♦ 10 ↑ 211 acres

Whitefish Mountain Resort
USA
Resort set close to the Canadian border and to Montana's Glacier National Park, this place has revamped its image in recent years. Lots of redevelopment has taken place, both on and off the slopes. Its 3,000 acres embrace a wide range of slopes that are not only impressively snowy but also blissfully devoid of people. There's easy cruising in dense forest around the base area, and steeper stuff higher up on 'gladed' slopes. There are two good terrain parks. There's lodging at the base and you can stay in the small town of Whitefish, a few miles away.
1360m; slopes 1360–2135m
♦ 13 ↑ 3000 acres
🚠 *Ski Safari*

White Pass Village USA
Closest area to Mt St Helens. Remote and uncrowded during the week, with a good snowfall record. Some genuinely steep, expert terrain, as well as intermediate cruising.
1370m; slopes 1370–1825m
♦ 5 ↑ 635 acres

Whitewater Canada
Renowned for powder (40% off-piste), food and weekend party atmosphere. Accommodation in the historic town of Nelson or a great day out from nearby Red Mountain.
1640m; slopes 1640–2040m ♦ 3
🚠 *Frontier*

Wildcat Mountain USA
New Hampshire area infamous for bad weather, but one of the best areas on a nice day. Lodging in nearby Jackson and North Conway.
slopes 600–1250m
♦ 4 ↑ 225 acres

Wildhaus Switzerland
Undeveloped farming community in stunning scenery near Liechtenstein; popular with families and serious snowboarders. Shares its slopes with Unterwasser.
1050m; slopes 900–2260m
♦ 17 ↑ 60km

Wildschönau Austria
Dramatic-sounding name adopted by a group of small resorts in the Tirol – Niederau, Oberau and Auffach. It is now forms the Ski Juwel area with Alpbach – a two-stage gondola is all it has taken to link Alpbach and Auffach, and the linked area offers an appealing mix of small, friendly villages and fairly extensive intermediate slopes.
830m

Willamette Pass USA
Set in national forest near beautiful Crater Lake, Oregon. Small area of varied slopes. An average of 430 inches of snow a year – that's up there with Utah.
1560m; slopes 1560–2035m
♦ 6 ↑ 550 acres

Williams USA
Tiny area above the main place to stay for the Grand Canyon.
slopes 2010–2270m
♦ 2 ↑ 50 acres

Willingen Germany
Resort in Sauerland, east of Düsseldorf. ♦ 8

Windham Mountain USA
Boutique resort in the Catskill Mountains 2.5 hours from New York.
455m; slopes 455–945m
♦ 10 ↑ 269 acres

Windischgarsten Austria
Large working village in Upper Austria with cross-country trails around and downhill slopes at nearby Hinterstoder and Spital am Pyrhn.
600m

Winterberg Germany
Resort in Sauerland, east of Düsseldorf. ♦ 24

Winter Park 569

Wolf Creek USA
Remote area on a pass of the same name, with 'the most snow in Colorado' – 465 inches a year. One-third of the terrain is standard American trails through the trees; two-thirds is 'wilderness', served by a single lift. Great stop en route between Taos and Telluride. Stay in Pagosa Springs to the west, or South Fork to the east.
3140m; slopes 3140–3630m
♦ 6 ↑ 1600 acres

Wolf Mountain USA
Utah area close to Salt Lake City, due to be expanded and renamed Skyline Mountain Base for 2014/15 for 2014/15.
♦ 3 ↑ 100 acres

Xonrupt France
Cross-country venue only 3km from nearest Alpine slopes at Gérardmer.
715m
🚠 *Lagrange*

Yangji Pine Resort
South Korea
Modern resort an hour (60km) south of Seoul, with runs cut out of dense forest. Gets very crowded. ♦ 6

Ylläs 643

Yong Pyong Resort
South Korea
200km east of Seoul, close to the east coast, also known as Dragon Valley. The self-contained purpose-built resort village is centred on 200-room Dragon Valley Hotel. Modern lifts serve a small, mainly wooded slope area, with snowmaking on all its runs.
750m; slopes 750–1460m
♦ 15 ↑ 20km

Zakopane Poland
An interesting old town 100km south of Kraków on the Slovakian border. Mostly intermediate slopes, branded as 14 small and fragmented sectors. Reported to have renovated its 70-year-old cable car.
830m; slopes 1000–1960m
♦ 60 ↑ 60km

Zao Japan
Big area with unpredictable weather, four hours from Tokyo by train. Known for 'chouoh' – pines frozen into weird shapes. Hot springs.
780m; slopes 780–1660m ♦ 42

Zauchensee Austria
Purpose-built resort part of big three-valley lift network linking it via Flachauwinkl to Kleinarl – which our figures relate too. Also on the Salzburger Sportwelt ski pass. 'Attractive, compact village,

shops limited to ski kit, no nightlife, dining only in hotels, relatively easy family-friendly skiing'.
855m; slopes 800–2185m
♦ 15 ↑ 88km

Zell am See 190

Zell im Zillertal 142
Sprawling valley town with slopes on two mountains.

Zermatt 518

Zillertal Austria
Valley of ten ski resorts, of which the most well known is Mayrhofen.

Zinal 495
Village in the Val d'Anniviers.

Zug 133
Tiny village with Lech's toughest skiing.

Zugspitz Arena Austria
The name of Germany's highest mountain, and part of Austria's Zugspitz Arena over the border – a collection of small, gentle but low ski areas, with pretty villages.
990–1340m; slopes 990–2960m
♦ 55 ↑ 148km

Zuoz Switzerland
An unspoiled village in a sunny setting just down the valley from St Moritz, with gentle slopes at village level and some more challenging runs higher up.
1715m; slopes 1720–2465m
♦ 5 ↑ 15km 🚠 *Inntravel*

Zürs 133
High village on road to Lech.

Zweisimmen Switzerland
Limited but inexpensive base for slopes around Gstaad, with its own delightful little easy area too.
965m; slopes 950–3000m
♦ 58 ↑ 250km

A FREE LUNCH DOES EXIST!

Alpine Answers, the UK's leading specialist ski travel agency, are giving our readers an exclusive offer

Simply book your next ski holiday through Alpine Answers and get a 5% discount. That should be enough to finance a FREE blow-out mountain lunch?

ALPINE ANSWERS use over twenty years of ski holiday planning to offer the ultimate chalet & hotel collection across the world's best ski resorts.

To find out more and register for the discount simply go to our online form at: www.bit.ly/wtss-aa

Call: **020 7801 1080**
www.alpineanswers.co.uk

 ATOL NO. 4791   ABTA NO. D4050